The Linguistic Atlas of the Upper Midwest

THE LINGUISTIC ATLAS
OF THE
UPPER MIDWEST
In Two Volumes

by

HAROLD B. ALLEN

Volume 1 • University of Minnesota Press 1973

Library of Congress Catalog Card Number: 72-96716

ISBN 0-8166-0686-2

Preface

Here in the preface the editor may drop the austere mantel of detached objectivity and use the first person. It is not hard to do this, because of all the branches of linguistic research none, save perhaps the study of child language, so involves the researcher with people on a personal basis.

The historical linguist must find his evidence in the written word and can only imaginatively reconstruct the actual speech of the long-dead writers. The theoretical linguist, though he deals with the rules and relationships underlying the living language, can effectively conduct his research with little or no attention to the variations of language among a variety of speakers.

Not so the dialectologist. Even if, besides his primary interest in language variation, he is also concerned with the rules that generate the forms and relationships of the language, he begins with his observed evidence as the point of departure. That evidence he finds in the recorded speech of his informants. Whether his primary interest focuses upon social variation or regional variation, he cannot, even if he would, escape from the people whose language he studies. Later analysis of the written transcription or taped recording will occur in the academic office, but the interview itself takes place where the informant lives or works, where he feels at home and can talk freely and naturally.

True, at the opening of an interview an informant may well be somewhat self-conscious and on his guard, if for no other reason than that he is talking to a stranger identified as someone from a university, but the experienced interviewer soon takes advantage of the familiar setting to help the informant revert to his usual way of speaking. The several sessions of an interview become increasingly friendly as a genuine rapport develops between the fieldworker and the informant. Such interviews in particular are likely to live long in the memory as pleasant human experiences. For me they are among the richest fringe benefits of dialect research.

Most of the interviews in the Upper Midwest took place in the living room of the informant's home, but I recall vividly other scenes as well: a housewife ironing in her kitchen while I wrote at the kitchen table, a railroad crossing watchman in his shanty keeping a wary eye out for the inspector who might catch him breaking the strict rule against visiting, a farmer sitting in the hot sun on his tractor in a partly plowed field while I wrote on the fender, a barber alternating his replies to me with snips at a customer's hair, a woman in a hospital bed recovering from an operation and answering questions whenever the suspicious nurse would allow me to remain for a few minutes, an 82-year-old county welfare director still, as he colorfully insisted, so "full of piss and vinegar" that he was too busy for several interviews and insisted upon one unbroken and exhausting six-hour session during which I managed to eat the egg sandwich he made for me in his bachelor's kitchen.

Most fieldworkers, I suspect, can recall experiences like some of the others I also remember: selling a pair of shoes for an old shoe clerk who, oddly enough, did not know how to fit a little girl's foot, being "stood up" by a retired farmer who that morning decided that he'd rather go fishing for a weekend than answer any more "fool questions," being taken, once, as a Communist agent because I was asking "suspicious" questions, and, several times, as an encyclopedia salesman trying out a new gimmick to get my foot inside the door, following a knowledgeable informant in western Nebraska as he hiked around a butte to show me the traces of the Oregon Trail, sampling with pleasure an informant's buf-

faloberry jelly in the South Dakota Badlands and, with less pleasure, another
informant's home-made dandelion wine in
North Dakota, and finding to my dismay
that the different voltage of a small
Nebraska cowtown's local electric plant
had successfully put my tape recorder
out of commission for the rest of that
trip. I have had one kind of experience
that recent technology prevents current
fieldworkers from enjoying, that of
spending frustrating hours in a desolate
small town hotel trying to unravel beneath its single unshaded overhead electric light the hopeless tangle of fine
wire that had malevolently sprung from
its spool on the wire recorder and that
somehow had to be straightened out because it contained within its mysterious-
ly rearranged ions the words spoken that
day by my informant.

Most informants, within my own experience, are notably generous with their
time and cooperative in the interview.
Often I have been asked--but only once
by an informant--whether informants are
paid. I reply that an unwritten rule in
dialect research is that the interview
is a voluntary contribution on the part
of the informant, not a business trans-
action. Once, back in Michigan many
years ago, a spry 93-year-old informant
became so dry after dancing a jig for
me that he claimed to be unable to finish
the interview unless I took him to town
for a stiff shot of whiskey. He got his
whiskey, and I completed the interview!
No Upper Midwest informants apparently
became that thirsty, but I do admit
taking a box of chocolates to more than
one elderly housewife during the final
interview. But these are exceptions. My
gratitude to the 208 patient and helpful residents of the Upper Midwest who
gave me of their time and often took me
into their confidence must take the form
of verbal appreciation. The debt is un-
derstandably immense, for without their
contribution there would be no Atlas of
the Upper Midwest. Yet it would be less
significant without the additional information provided by the hundreds of
mail respondents who, usually without
the stimulus of personal contact, nevertheless filled out and returned the mail
checklists. To them, too, I am very
grateful.

But appreciation is deserved by many
others as well. Into the analysis of the
field data and the preparation of these
volumes has gone the work of a number of
persons whose contribution is gratefully
acknowledged.

Between 1949 and 1962 the following
helped in various clerical and pre-edi-

torial capacities for varying periods:
Artis Bernard, Maja Burić, Nancy Czatt,
Keith Fountain, Lois Hood, Paul Kirchner,
Phyllis Myers, Elvera Porter, Florence
O'Rourke, Rose Marie Service, Helen
Stenberg, and Nancy Jean Walsh. Of these
Mrs. Myers served longest, from 1952 to
June, 1956. I am particularly grateful
for her assuming the responsibility of
the office during my absence in Egypt
in 1954-55, the year during which she
made the statistical analysis of the
137,000 checked items on replies from
mail correspondents.

In 1956 and 1957 Barbara F. Lukerman
prepared an annotated bibliography of
the population history of the Upper Midwest together with detailed bibliographies of the settlement history of
the several communities investigated
for the Atlas. In 1958 Ira E. Robinson
gathered material and prepared a rough
draft of the chapter on the settlement
history of the region.

Initial editing began in 1967 with
the help of Gary N. Underwood, research
fellow, who continued for three years,
the last of which as assistant editor.
He was responsible for the basic analyses
of the lexical items and most of the morphological items. Michael Linn, in 1970-
71, and Gregory Iverson, in 1971-72,
served as graduate research assistants
with special concern for tabulating and
analyzing the phonological data.

Because of the arrangement with the
University of Minnesota Press the preparation of the manuscript has called
for unusual care and competence, not
only because of the difficult typing
but also because of the need to prepare
pages in final form for photo offset.
For their great help in this critical
part of the work I am especially grateful to Patricia Huss, who served in 1970-
71, and to Joy Simpkins, who served in
1971-72.

Although the original base map for the
Upper Midwest Atlas was made by Edgar J.
Shaw in 1958, all subsequent maps as published in these volumes were put into
their final form through the sympathetic
and professional ministrations of Patricia
Burwell, senior cartographer and director
of the cartography laboratory in the department of geography at the University
of Minnesota.

Equally sympathetic with the sometimes
unusual problems of manuscript preparation
for the Atlas project and always helpful
with competent advice, Anne Jirasek of
the University of Minnesota Press has
followed the progress of the manuscript
as the editor assigned to proofread the
rough copy and to counsel upon the many

questions of form and arrangement. If any matters of editorial form in the printed books are subject to adverse criticism, it is certainly because her good advice has been cavalierly ignored.

No American dialectologist is free of a deep obligation to the pioneer linguistic geographer in this country, Hans Kurath, and I gladly acknowledge that obligation on my own part. I also am grateful to Albert H. Marckwardt, who provided the opportunity for my first field experiences, and to Raven I. McDavid, Jr., whose richer experience over the years has enabled him to give me much valuable advice and counsel.

Yet there is a nonprofessional appreciation more deeply felt than any gratitude expressed above, an appreciation of the uncomplaining understanding of my wife, Elizabeth, and my daughters, Marjorie and Susan, during the weeks and summers when I--with the family car-- was away on field trips and during the many other periods when I couldn't take time for this and couldn't take time for that because I had to "work on the Atlas."

H. B. A.

vii

CONTENTS

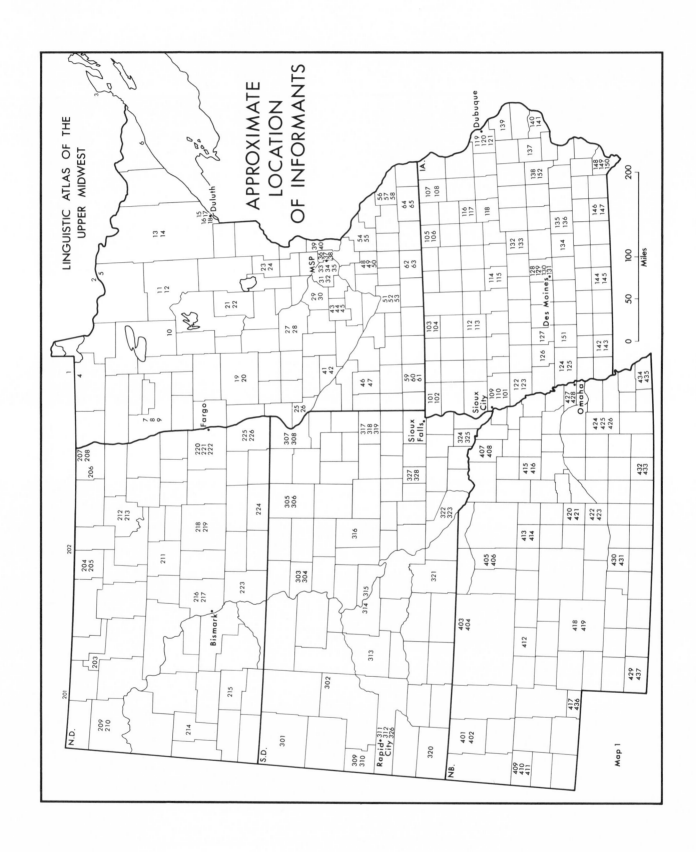

LINGUISTIC ATLAS OF THE
UPPER MIDWEST

APPROXIMATE
LOCATION
OF INFORMANTS

Map 1

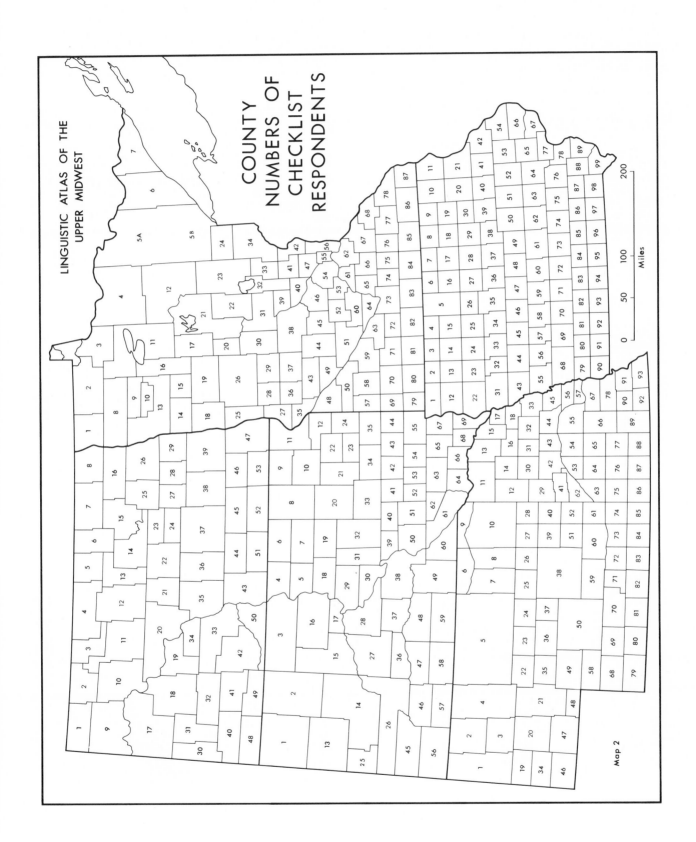

LINGUISTIC ATLAS OF THE
UPPER MIDWEST

COUNTY
NUMBERS OF
CHECKLIST RESPONDENTS

Map 2

COUNTY NUMBERS AND NAMES

MINNESOTA

1 Kittson	23 Aitkin	45 Meeker	67 Goodhue
2 Roseau	24 Carlton	46 Wright	68 Wabasha
3 Lake of the Woods	25 Wilkin	47 Anoka	69 Pipestone
4 Koochiching	26 Otter Tail	48 Lac Qui Parle	70 Murray
5A,B St. Louis	27 Traverse	49 Chippewa	71 Cottonwood
6 Lake	28 Grant	50 Yellow Medicine	72 Watonwan
7 Cook	29 Douglas	51 Renville	73 Blue Earth
8 Marshall	30 Todd	52 McLeod	74 Waseca
9 Pennington	31 Morrison	53 Carver	75 Steele
10 Red Lake	32 Mille Lacs	54 Hennepin	76 Dodge
11 Beltrami	33 Kanabec	55 Ramsey	77 Olmsted
12 Itasca	34 Pine	56 Washington	78 Winona
13 Polk	35 Big Stone	57 Lincoln	79 Rock
14 Norman	36 Stevens	58 Lyon	80 Nobles
15 Mahnomen	37 Pope	59 Redwood	81 Jackson
16 Clearwater	38 Stearns	60 Sibley	82 Martin
17 Hubbard	39 Benton	61 Scott	83 Faribault
18 Clay	40 Sherburne	62 Dakota	84 Freeborn
19 Becker	41 Isanti	63 Brown	85 Mower
20 Wadena	42 Chisago	64 Nicollet	86 Fillmore
21 Cass	43 Swift	65 Le Sueur	87 Houston
22 Crow Wing	44 Kandiyohi	66 Rice	

IOWA

1 Lyon	26 Humboldt	51 Benton	76 Washington
2 Osceola	27 Wright	52 Linn	77 Muscatine
3 Dickinson	28 Franklin	53 Jones	78 Louisa
4 Emmet	29 Butler	54 Jackson	79 Mills
5 Kossuth	30 Bremer	55 Harrison	80 Montgomery
6 Winnebago	31 Woodbury	56 Shelby	81 Adams
7 Worth	32 Ida	57 Audubon	82 Union
8 Mitchell	33 Sac	58 Guthrie	83 Clarke
9 Howard	34 Calhoun	59 Dallas	84 Lucas
10 Winneshiek	35 Webster	60 Polk	85 Monroe
11 Allamakee	36 Hamilton	61 Jasper	86 Wapello
12 Sioux	37 Hardin	62 Poweshiek	87 Jefferson
13 O'Brien	38 Grundy	63 Iowa	88 Henry
14 Clay	39 Black Hawk	64 Johnson	89 Des Moines
15 Palo Alto	40 Buchanan	65 Cedar	90 Fremont
16 Hancock	41 Delaware	66 Clinton	91 Page
17 Cerro Gordo	42 Dubuque	67 Scott	92 Taylor
18 Floyd	43 Monona	68 Pottawattamie	93 Ringgold
19 Chickasaw	44 Crawford	69 Cass	94 Decatur
20 Fayette	45 Carroll	70 Adair	95 Wayne
21 Clayton	46 Greene	71 Madison	96 Appanoose
22 Plymouth	47 Boone	72 Warren	97 Davis
23 Cherokee	48 Story	73 Marion	98 Van Buren
24 Buena Vista	49 Marshall	74 Mahaska	99 Lee
25 Pocahontas	50 Tama	75 Keokuk	

NORTH DAKOTA

1 Divide	7 Cavalier	13 Pierce	19 Mercer
2 Burke	8 Pembina	14 Benson	20 McLean
3 Renville	9 Williams	15 Ramsey	21 Sheridan
4 Bottineau	10 Mountrail	16 Walsh	22 Wells
5 Rolette	11 Ward	17 McKenzie	23 Eddy
6 Towner	12 McHenry	18 Dunn	24 Foster

25 Nelson
26 Grand Forks
27 Griggs
28 Steele
29 Traill
30 Golden Valley
31 Billings
32 Stark

33 Morton
34 Oliver
35 Burleigh
36 Kidder
37 Stutsman
38 Barnes
39 Cass
40 Slope

41 Hettinger
42 Grant
43 Emmons
44 Logan
45 La Moure
46 Ransom
47 Richland
48 Bowman

49 Adams
50 Sioux
51 McIntosh
52 Dickey
53 Sargent

SOUTH DAKOTA

1 Harding
2 Perkins
3 Corson
4 Campbell
5 Walworth
6 McPherson
7 Edmunds
8 Brown
9 Marshall
10 Day
11 Roberts
12 Grant
13 Butte
14 Meade
15 Ziebach
16 Dewey
17 Armstrong
18 Potter

19 Faulk
20 Spink
21 Clark
22 Codington
23 Hamlin
24 Deuel
25 Lawrence
26 Pennington
27 Haakon
28 Stanley
29 Sully
30 Hughes
31 Hyde
32 Hand
33 Beadle
34 Kingsbury
35 Brookings
36 Jackson

37 Jones
38 Lyman
39 Buffalo
40 Jerauld
41 Sanborn
42 Miner
43 Lake
44 Moody
45 Custer
46 Washington
47 Washabaugh
48 Mellette
49 Tripp
50 Brule
51 Aurora
52 Davison
53 Hanson
54 McCook

55 Minnehaha
56 Fall River
57 Shannon
58 Bennett
59 Todd
60 Gregory
61 Charles Mix
62 Douglas
63 Hutchinson
64 Bon Homme
65 Turner
66 Yankton
67 Lincoln
68 Clay
69 Union

NEBRASKA

1 Sioux
2 Dawes
3 Box Butte
4 Sheridan
5 Cherry
6 Keya Paha
7 Brown
8 Rock
9 Boyd
10 Holt
11 Knox
12 Antelope
13 Cedar
14 Pierce
15 Dixon
16 Wayne
17 Dakota
18 Thurston
19 Scotts Bluff
20 Morrill
21 Garden
22 Grant
23 Hooker
24 Thomas

25 Blaine
26 Loup
27 Garfield
28 Wheeler
29 Boone
30 Madison
31 Stanton
32 Cuming
33 Burt
34 Banner
35 Arthur
36 McPherson
37 Logan
38 Custer
39 Valley
40 Greeley
41 Nance
42 Platte
43 Colfax
44 Dodge
45 Washington
46 Kimball
47 Cheyenne
48 Deuel

49 Keith
50 Lincoln
51 Sherman
52 Howard
53 Polk
54 Butler
55 Saunders
56 Douglas
57 Sarpy
58 Perkins
59 Dawson
60 Buffalo
61 Hall
62 Merrick
63 Hamilton
64 York
65 Seward
66 Lancaster
67 Cass
68 Chase
69 Hayes
70 Frontier
71 Gosper
72 Phelps

73 Kearney
74 Adams
75 Clay
76 Fillmore
77 Saline
78 Otoe
79 Dundy
80 Hitchcock
81 Red Willow
82 Furnas
83 Harlan
84 Franklin
85 Webster
86 Nuckolls
87 Thayer
88 Jefferson
89 Gage
90 Johnson
91 Nemaha
92 Pawnee
93 Richardson

PART A

The Upper Midwest Project

CHAPTER 1

The History of the Project

The Linguistic Atlas of the Upper Midwest began in 1947 as a study of Minnesota folk speech. The director intended then that it ultimately would be incorporated in the Linguistic Atlas of the North Central States, a survey for which earlier he had done fieldwork under the direction of Albert H. Marckwardt. At this point, however, Marckwardt generously advised the expansion of the Minnesota survey as an independent study that would include also the Dakotas, Iowa, and Nebraska. Dean Theodore H. Blegen of the University of Minnesota Graduate School approved this suggestion.

At an informal conference in New York, in December, 1948, an understanding among the dialectologists present recognized the Linguistic Atlas of the Upper Midwest as a separate research survey within the broad outlines of what had once been envisaged as the monolithic Linguistic Atlas of the United States and Canada. Present at the conference were the following: Hans Kurath of the University of Michigan, who had directed the New England survey; Albert H. Marckwardt of the University of Michigan, who headed the North Central project; Frederick G. Cassidy of the University of Wisconsin, who had done the fieldwork in that state; Alva L. Davis of Western Reserve University; Raven I. McDavid, Jr., fieldworker for the South Atlantic survey; and the Upper Midwest director.

By 1947 the original pilot study had been completed under Kurath's direction and its findings published as *The Linguistic Atlas of New England*, in the form of a *Handbook* and three large folio volumes of hand-prepared maps. Fieldwork was also nearly completed for its associated projects, the atlases of the Middle and South Atlantic states, which soon were to be drawn upon for three important publications: Kurath's *A Word Geography of the Eastern United States* (1949), E. Bagby Atwood's *A Survey of Verb Forms in the Eastern United States* (1953), and Kurath and McDavid's *The Pronunciation of English in the Atlantic States* (1961).

But even before the appearance of *The Linguistic Atlas of New England* it had become evident that financial support would not be found for the extension of that enterprise as a nucleus of a single international, or even national, investigation. Regrettably, the magnificent dream of a single linguistic atlas for both the United States and Canada had to be replaced by the viable hope that independent and independently supported projects could be established to yield information that presumably would be comparable with that from New England and the Atlantic states and hence in effect would provide the data that had been expected from a unified international survey.

Such a project was that begun by Marckwardt in 1938 for the North Central area comprising Michigan, Ohio, Indiana, Kentucky, Illinois, Wisconsin, and southern Ontario. The time was thus propitious for the Upper Midwest project, with its study of the speech of that region into which people had moved west from the east coast and from the North Central states.

Funds to support the initial fieldwork in Minnesota came from the Graduate School of the University of Minnesota, whose Dean Blegen, a Minnesota historian, gave strong encouragement and was helpful in the awarding of annual grants for fieldwork and data analysis over the next dozen years.

During the first year of the investigation two decisions led to innovations in American dialectology. One was the decision to supplement as many field interviews as possible with voice recordings. Originally it was hoped that entire interviews could be recorded; unfortunately, lack of funds limited the voice transcriptions to brief conversations that took place after the formal interviews. More than half of the field informants were thus recorded. The other innovation was the supplementing of the wide-meshed field interviews by mail questionnaires, an innovation suggested by the doctoral study of Alva Davis based upon data obtained in this way.

In 1949 a request to the University of Iowa for assistance in conducting the Iowa component of the fieldwork brought a warm response from Professor Erich Funke of the department of German and Professor John McGalliard of the department of English. They revealed the coincidence that Mrs. Rachel Kilpatrick, a former fieldworker for the New England survey, was then living in Iowa City. Through their efforts she was given a temporary appointment to teach a course in field methods in linguistic geography for students interested in doing fieldwork in the state. As the assistant director for Iowa, Mrs. Kilpatrick subsequently directed the work of the two students chosen to receive summer fellowhips granted by the University of Iowa as a means of supporting their travel and interviewing. That university, then, bore the expense both of training the fieldworkers and of the actual fieldwork, including the cost of recording equipment.

In the summer of 1950 fieldwork in North Dakota was undertaken and completed. Four of the interviews there were paid for through the assistance of Dean G. E. Giesecke of the North Dakota Agricultural College (now North Dakota State University), who obtained a contribution from the North Dakota Institute of Regional Studies, of which he was executive secretary.

Most of the fieldwork in South Dakota occurred in the summers of 1951 and 1952. The cost of two of the records there was supported through the generosity of the department of English at South Dakota State College, whose chairman, Joseph Giddings, arranged for a lecture by the Atlas director with the understanding that the fee was to be used for field expenses.

Attempts to obtain any local financial aid for the fieldwork in Nebraska in 1952 and 1953 were unsuccessful. In that state the entire cost was borne by grants from the research funds of the University of Minnesota Graduate School.

During the decade after the completion of fieldwork several circumstances combined to thwart the desired progress in pre-editing the field records. In 1954-1955 and in 1958-1959 the director was in Egypt upon Fulbright and Smith-Mundt missions. A great deal of the director's time was demanded by his involvement with a national organization and his responsibility as director or co-director of three successive U.S. Office of Education research projects. But most important of the adverse circumstances was the continuing difficulty in obtaining funds to support necessary clerical and editorial staff.

In 1966, however, a change in fortune came with a grant from the new National Endowment for the Humanities. This grant, renewed in 1968 for one more year, allowed for hiring some clerical help and a research assistant and gave the director one-third released time from teaching. Subsequently, from National Defense Act funds allocated to the Graduate School, money was provided for continuing the employment of a research assistant, and the department of English generously provided continued released time for the director.

In anticipation of the problems of pre-editing and editing, a detailed questionnaire was sent to American dialectologists in January, 1958, asking for their advice and suggestions with respect to the tentative plans for preparing the Upper Midwest Atlas. The following replied with perceptive and useful counsel: E. Bagby Atwood, Walter Avis, Sumner Ives, Marjorie Kimmerle, Albert H. Marckwardt, Raven I. McDavid, Jr., Carroll Reed, and David W. Reed.

The basic proposal presented to the dialectologists called for a two-volume format, essentially that of the present publication. A base map would bear informant numbers indicating the location of their communities, but there would be no series of large-scale maps bearing phonetically-transcribed responses. The earlier New York conference had recognized the extraordinary cost of preparing such maps as well as the difficulty the non-specialist found in using them. Instead of such maps it was proposed that the Upper Midwest Atlas follow the practice of certain European atlases by listing the serial numbers of all informants using a given form or pronunciation.

Although three of the dialectologists strongly regretted the proposed absence of a full phonetic representation of all the responses, the consensus favored most of the various aspects of the tentative plan, now realized in the present publication.

The lack of a complete phonetic transcription of all the responses for each item, what is technically known as a list manuscript, is due primarily to the inability to obtain funds permitting the publication of the nearly 150,000 such responses. Although unique support has been found for the printing of the list manuscripts of the Middle and South Atlantic materials at the University of Chicago, no such support has been available for the Upper Midwest Atlas. An additional reason appears in the uneven quality of the phonetic transcription. An editorial comparative analysis has been found necessary, for example, to equate the practice of the Iowa fieldworkers with that of the others. Without such editorial emendation the field records are liable to a certain measure of misunderstanding. Any such editorial interpretation is indicated specifically at the relevant points in the second volume.

The forced decision not to attempt to provide list manuscripts led to the proposal realized in the present two volumes. With few exceptions each lexical or grammatical item in the first and second volumes appears in normal spelling, followed by the serial numbers of the informants using it. The dialectally significant feature of a phonetic item in Volume II appears likewise with the serial numbers of the informants having it, but the entire response is not reproduced.

Because the Upper Midwest Atlas is intended for students as well as for specialists, its practice follows the examples of the *Word Geography* and *The Pronunciation of English in the Eastern States* in providing descriptive analyses. If an analysis describes the distribution of a form as markedly regional, then that distribution is made graphic through the use of symbols or graphs on an accompanying small-scale map.

A further reliance upon the model of *The Pronunciation of English in the Eastern States* appears in the use of detailed charts revealing the basic vowel patterns of informants. There, however, only the Type III informants are thus represented; here, all 208 informants.

As the editorial work progressed in

preparing the materials as sketched above, the problem of future publication became increasingly severe because of the mounting cost of printing. The problem was happily solved in 1969 when the University of Minnesota Press agreed to publish by photo-offset instead of by more expensive letterpress, much of which would have required hand composition.

This difference in format and the other differences described above should not, however, obscure the fact that the present study directly inherits the tradition of American dialect research initiated by Hans Kurath, both in purpose and in scope. Its basic purpose is to ascertain and make known the regional patterns of variations in American English through the study of the distribution of folk speech forms as found in the speech of selected informants. Its scope is the chronological and social spread between the oldest and uneducated informants and the younger and educated informants.

As in Kurath's New England survey, the lexical portion of the present study is deliberately oriented toward the folk speech of rural and small-town life. The population trend from country to city is recognized in the use of some informants in the major cities, but neither in the vocabulary studied nor in the small proportion of urban informants does the Linguistic Atlas of the Upper Midwest purport to investigate the contemporary city speech of the younger generation.[1] Other research is needed for that purpose, just as further research is needed to study in depth the speech of numerous distinctive homogeneous communities in the five-state area.

A further limitation has been imposed by the unanticipated duration of the project, so that in effect these volumes are almost historical documents. They portray not a contemporary speech situation but rather that of the mid-century and, even then, not that of the younger generation. In some ways this fact heightens, rather than diminishes, the importance of the findings, for here is a record of a period already past, and otherwise lost--a time when an Iowa farmer sitting on his tractor could recall that not long before he

---

1. Failure to appreciate this planned restriction led some years ago to an attack upon American dialect studies. See Glenna R. Pickford, "American linguistic geography: a sociological appraisal," *Word*, 12.211-233 (1956).

had plowed with horses, and a Minnesota farmwife could still use such a term as "baker's bread" because "bread" for her named simply what she baked at home every week.

Although some inferences about language change can be drawn from contrasts between the speech patterns of the oldest and those of the youngest informants interviewed, a broader basis of judgment must be sought in a comparison of the findings of this survey and those that can be provided by subsequent studies of the speech of younger informants, both in local communities as in-depth research and throughout the entire region as wide-meshed surveys. Likewise, some inferences about social variation can be drawn from the contrasts between the speech of educated informants and the speech of the uneducated. But the recent concern with social variation, particularly with reference to the language characteristics of ethnic groups, calls for much more intensive future research both in urban and in certain rural areas. These two volumes, then, must be considered as offering only the first chapter in a continuing history of language investigation in the Upper Midwest.

CHAPTER 2

The Land and the People

The five states composing the Upper Midwest are Minnesota, Iowa, Nebraska, South Dakota, and North Dakota. These states occupy an area lying between 40° and 49°23' north latitude and between 89°34' and 104°3' west longitude. They are bordered on the east by Wisconsin and Illinois, on the south by Missouri, Kansas, and Colorado, on the west by Wyoming and Montana, and on the north by the Canadian provinces of Ontario, Manitoba, and Saskatchewan. Two important geographic centers lie in the Upper Midwest. The geographic center of the United States is in Butte County in western South Dakota, and the geographic center of North America is at Rugby in Pierce County in north-central North Dakota.

Although the person whose familiarity with the Upper Midwest is limited to Rolvaag's Giants in the Earth or Lewis's Main Street might think that the Upper Midwest is a vast, level prairie, the topography is actually rather varied. The lowest elevation in the Upper Midwest is at Keokuk, Iowa, in the Central Lowlands, which is only 477 feet above sea level. The Central Lowlands then rise in a northwestern direction by gentle swells to an elevation of about 2,000 feet, and the elevation of the Missouri Plateau varies between 2,000 and 3,000 feet, with an average of 2,800 feet. The highest elevation in the five states, that of Harney Peak in the Black Hills of South Dakota, is 7,242 feet. Several other mountains in the Black Hills are over 7,000 feet.

The Upper Midwest is drained by the four major watersheds of the Great Lakes, the Mississippi River, the Red River of the North, and the Missouri River. The Great Lakes system drains northeast Minnesota. The Pigeon, St. Louis, and numerous shorter, rapid-flowing rivers flow in a generally eastern direction into Lake Superior. The Mississippi River, with its source at Lake Itasca, flows through Minnesota and along the eastern borders of southern Minnesota and Iowa. Fed by its tributaries the Minnesota, St. Croix, Wapsipinicon, Iowa, Skunk, and Des Moines rivers, the Mississippi drains the southern two-thirds of Iowa. The third watershed is that of the Red River of the North, which forms the boundary between Minnesota and North Dakota. Although not fed by any large rivers, the Red River drains the wide Red River valley, flows northward into Canada, and empties into Lake Winnipeg. The largest watershed in the Upper Midwest is by far that of the Missouri River. The Missouri River enters the region in Western North Dakota, arcs through the state, bisects South Dakota, and serves as a section of the Nebraska-Iowa state line. With its northern tributaries the Little Missouri, Grand, Moreau, Cheyenne, White, James, Vermillion, and Big Sioux rivers, it drains virtually all of North and South Dakota. Its Nebraska tributaries the Niobrara River, the Platte River System-- the Platte, North Platte, South Platte, Loup, and Elkhorn rivers--and the Republican River drain all of Nebraska. Its tributaries the Little Sioux, Boyer, and Nishnabotna rivers drain the western one-third of Iowa.

The Upper Midwest has four major geographic subdivisions: the Superior Uplands, the Central Lowlands, the Great Plains, and the Black Hills. The Central Lowlands can be further divided into three distinguishable areas: the Wisconsin Driftless area, Young Drift Plains, and Dissected Till Plains. The Great Plains can also be divided into six distinguishable regions: the High Plains, the Plains Border, the Sand Hills, the glaciated Missouri Plateau, the unglaciated Missouri Plateau, and the Badlands. Although these divisions are made on the basis of rather complex geological phe-

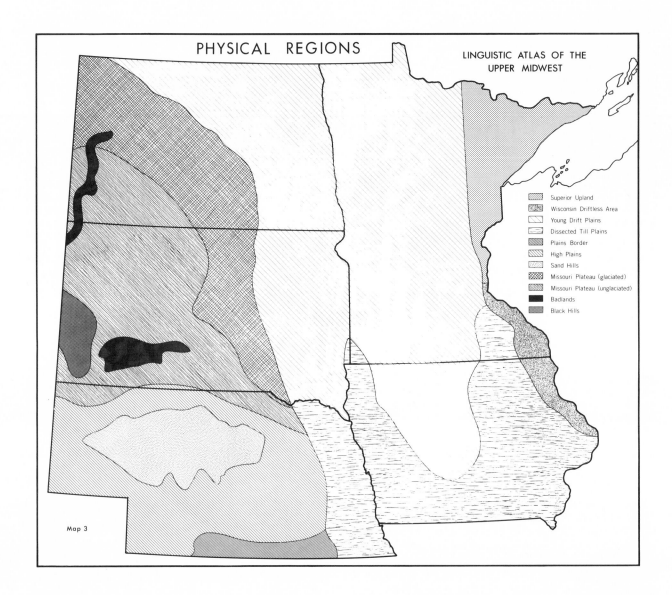

PHYSICAL REGIONS

Superior Upland
Wisconsin Driftless Area
Young Drift Plains
Dissected Till Plains
Plains Border
High Plains
Sand Hills
Missouri Plateau (glaciated)
Missouri Plateau (unglaciated)
Badlands
Black Hills

Map 3

nomena and the boundaries are often obscure, each region has its characteristic features that the layman can distinguish. Needless to say, the geography
has significantly affected the settlement of the area.

The westernmost part of the Superior
Upland extends into the upper Midwest in
northeastern Minnesota. It stretches over
the "Arrowhead" country north of Lake
Superior and along the west bank of
the St. Croix River to just above the
confluence of the St. Croix and Mississippi Rivers. The Superior Upland, a
crust of ancient Precambrian rocks, is
characterized by great expanses of exposed granite, altered sediments, and

lava flows. The country is heavily forested with pine and spruce and dotted
with numerous small lakes. In its northern regions lie the Vermilion and Mesabi iron ranges.

The Wisconsin Driftless Area, extending
along the Mississippi River in southeast Minnesota and northeast Iowa, is a
portion of the Central Lowlands not covered by the first glacial movement. The
ice is believed to have been too thin to
rise over the highlands. Because the ice
split and moved around the area, the present-day terrain differs from the plains
to the west. It is characterized by heavily wooded rolling hills and valleys and
vertical cliffs towering 300-400 feet

above the Mississippi River.

The Dissected Till Plains cover eastern, south-central, and western Iowa, small corners of southeastern and southwestern Minnesota, and eastern Nebraska. This is a region of rolling, relatively smooth, plains with a gentle southeast slope. Covered by the second glacial advance in the Pleistocene Ice Age, which smoothed the hills and valleys and deposited drift or till (a mixture of boulders and clays), the area is characterized by a well-developed drainage system. It lacks the swamps and irregular lakes of the Young Till Plains and the angular bluffs of the Great Plains.

The Young Drift Plains cover almost all of Minnesota, north-central Iowa, the eastern third of south Dakota, and eastern and north-central North Dakota. Since this area was more recently glaciated than was the Dissected Till area, it has not yet become smooth and regular from extended erosion. Unlike the Dissected Till Plains to the south, the land is marked by moraines (low ridges of sand and stone) and thousands of lakes and swamps in low areas of poor drainage. In northern Minnesota it is also heavily forested. The Mississippi and Minnesota rivers have cut deep river valleys with 300- to 500-foot bluffs, and in the central portion are the wide, flat valleys of the James and Red rivers, which are the floor of ancient Lake Agassiz. The plains are covered with a heavy mantle of glacial drift, a rich black loam.

The line that separates the Great Plains from the Central Lowlands is obscured by a thick mantle of loess that covers both. Often the glaciated portion of the Great Plains is hard to distinguish from the Central Lowlands, but they are separated in places by a distinct band of hummocky hills about 15 to 20 miles wide called the Missouri Coteau. To the north this line is marked by an east-facing 300- to 400-foot escarpment, but the differences in elevation are less distinct to the south. In general, though, the two areas are distinguished by the higher elevations and semiarid climate of the Great Plains.

The portion of the Great Plains known as the High Plains covers most of Nebraska from about 75 miles west of the Missouri River westward. This is a flat, elevated prairie with few streams and few valleys. The High Plains are covered by a heavy mantle (100 to 400 feet thick) of silt, sand, and gravel, so porous that it quickly absorbs rainfall. A southern strip of Nebraska is covered by the northern extension of the Plains Border. This region is much like the High Plains except that it is not so flat; it has more varied relief and prominent uplands features.

The Sand Hills cover about 24,000 square miles of northwest Nebraska. In this region hundreds of sand dunes about 100 feet high and several miles long stretch in an east-west direction. These dunes are generally covered with a thin growth of grass and herbs, but some of them are still bare, and the sand continues to shift. The area is also characterized by occasional meadows and lakes.

The Missouri Plateau is separated from the High Plains by the Pine Ridge Escarpment, a north-facing line of cliffs of varying height, up to 1,000 feet in northwest Nebraska. The glaciated portion of the Missouri Plateau is generally east of the Missouri River in North and South Dakota. Its till soil is generally undistinguishable from that of the Central Lowlands, but the two areas are separated by the Missouri Coteau. The glaciated portion of the Missouri Plateau is rolling upland country, and it is marked by areas of buttes and canyons.

The most spectacular relief in the Missouri Plateau is the Badland country. There are two prominent Badlands areas, one in southwest South Dakota along the White River and the other in southwest North Dakota along the Little Missouri River. The Badlands are highly eroded river valleys where the rather light rainfall has eroded the soft shales and limestones--and some semiarid vegetation grows with difficulty. The badlands are not like canyons, which extend along the main channel of a river; they extend back along every little stream bed, and where these eroded areas fuse, they produce vast expanses of cliffs, canyons, and gullies of exposed multicolored layers of greys, browns, yellows, whites, and reds.

The Black Hills are actually a mountain range related to the Rocky Mountains, 120 miles farther west. These rugged granite mountains rise about 4,000 feet above the Missouri Plateau, and numerous peaks are over 7,000 feet high. In these mountains are rich mineral deposits, especially of gold.

The climate of the Upper Midwest is almost as extreme in variation as the physiography. The annual mean temperature varies from 49.3°F in Nebraska to 39.4° in North Dakota. The annual summer mean temperature varies from 72.7° in Nebraska to 66° in North Dakota and the winter mean from 25.3° in Nebraska to a mere 9.5° in North Dakota. The record high temperature for the area is 121°, and the record low is -60°, both recorded in North Dakota. The entire area receives heavy annual snowfall, from 29.9 inches in Iowa to 39.9 inches in Minnesota. Annual precipitation varies from 30-50 inches in eastern Iowa, southeastern Minnesota, and southeast Nebraska to only 10-20 inches in almost all of North and South Dakota. The growing season varies from 160-180 days in south Iowa and southeast Nebraska to only 80-100 days in extreme North Dakota and Minnesota.

THE SETTLEMENT

The Upper Midwest was an important area in the fur trade of the late seventeenth and early eighteenth centuries, when the British and the French established posts on many rivers. There were also a few small agricultural settlements such as the Scottish community in North Dakota just across the border from Canada at what is now Pembina. However, these early intruders left little impact on the eventual character of the region. Although the Upper Midwest became United States territory as part of the Louisiana Purchase of 1803, it was not until 1833 that the government opened any part of the Upper Midwest for legal settlement. Lasting settlement began only after that.

The first territory opened in the Upper Midwest was southeast Iowa, which had no more than 50 white inhabitants before 1832. At the end of the Black Hawk War in 1832 the Indians ceded to the U.S. six million acres of land on the west side of the Mississippi River, extending from the northern border of Missouri to the mouth of the Upper Iowa River, a strip of land about 50 miles wide. This area, known as the Black Hawk Purchase, was opened to settlement in 1833. Soon extensive packet service carried passengers and freight from Pittsburgh and other points on the Ohio River to Keokuk. Settlers from Kentucky and Tennessee, as well as those from Pennsylvania, Ohio, and even Virginia, entered Iowa from the south by way of the Ohio and Mississippi rivers, landing at Keokuk, Ft. Madison, and Burlington. Others came overland from Illinois and Indiana and crossed the Mississippi River by ferry at those same river towns and farther to the north at Dubuque. These early settlers took up land near the Mississippi, but by 1836 settlements were as far west as Jefferson County in the southeast and the Iowa River valley to the north. During this year the Sac,

Fox, and Sioux Indians ceded an additional 1,250,000 acres west of and adjacent to the Black Hawk Purchase. By 1837 counties were organized all along the river from Clayton County to the Missouri border and as far west as Linn and Benton counties on the Cedar River. Within two more years Iowa City was laid out.

In 1837 a second enclave was established in the Upper Midwest with the opening of a small triangle of land between the Mississippi and St. Croix rivers, extending north to the Crow Wing River. This was an area valued for its forests, hardwood in the south and coniferous to the north. When rights to this land were obtained from the Dakota and Chippewa Indians, lumbermen moved into the land and began cutting trees and building mills. These men came mostly from Vermont and Maine, some directly and others by way of lumbering sites in Michigan and Wisconsin. Further movement into Minnesota was slow for two reasons. First, the fur traders and lumbermen did not welcome permanent settlers; more important, the area was isolated from settlements in Wisconsin, Illinois, and Iowa by over 100 miles of wilderness unpenetrated by either road or railroad.

Iowa, then the most accessible portion of the Upper Midwest, continued to attract settlers during the 1840's as the Indians surrendered more and more land. In 1843 the Sacs and Foxes vacated the remainder of their lands, and the Iowa territory was open for settlement as far west as a north-south line through Marion county. Settlers from Illinois, Indiana, Kentucky, Missouri, and to a lesser extent from Wisconsin, Virginia, and Pennsylvania camped on the edge of this land, and when the territory was opened with the firing of a gun at midnight on April 30, 1843, they surged across the line, staked out thousands of farms, and established a half-dozen towns before sundown of May 1. The frontier was pushed westward with settlement extending from the northeast corner to the southwest corner of the state when it was admitted to the union in 1845. In 1846 the Pottawattamie Indians relinquished their lands in southwest Iowa, and in 1848 the Winnebagos moved from their lands in northeast Iowa into Minnesota Territory; thus when the Sioux agreed to vacate their land in northern Iowa in 1851, all of the state was open for settlement. As the settlers moved westward they tended to ignore the open prairies. As late as 1850 there were still large areas of uninhabited land in the eastern counties. While people were pushing the frontier westward across Iowa, settlement in Minnesota was still confined to the "St. Croix Triangle." During the 1840's the population in Minnesota grew slowly as towns grew up around mills built on the St. Croix and Mississippi rivers. The first land sale in the area in 1848 attracted settlers from New York, Pennsylvania, and New England, especially to the new towns of St. Paul and St. Anthony. When the area became a territory in 1849 the white population had increased to 2,879. By 1850 lumber mills had been established at St. Croix Falls, Marine Mills, Lakeland, and Arcola on the St. Croix River and at St. Anthony Falls on the Mississippi River. The 1850 census showed that 488 of the residents were from New York and 655 from New England, 365 of the latter being from Maine. The New England influence was strong in Minnesota, since many of the settlers born in New York, Pennsylvania, and Illinois were of New England parentage. One-third of the population was foreign-born, but most of these were Canadian. In the rural areas were also Irish, German, English, Scottish, French, Dutch, Swiss, Norwegians, and Swedes.

The decade of the 1850's was a period of heavy migration into the Upper Midwest because of a drought in Ohio, cholera epidemics in the Middle Atlantic states, the completion of the railroad to the Mississippi River, and vigorous campaigns for settlers. Great numbers from New England, New York, and the trans-Allegheny states came by wagon train or railroad and crossed into Iowa at Prairie du Chien, Dubuque, Burlington, Davenport, and Keokuk. It is estimated that at the peak of the migration as many as 7,000 people crossed on the ferry at Burlington in a single day, and the population of Iowa increased from 192,000 to 675,000 in this decade.

At the same time Minnesota began to grow more rapidly as more land became available and as the territory became more accessible. Before 1850 people coming to Minnesota either came by overland routes through the Wisconsin wilderness or, after traveling overland from Chicago to Galena, Illinois, took a steamboat up the Mississippi. The difficulty of these routes contributed to the isolation of Minnesota, but in 1850 the railroad was completed to Rock Island, Illinois, and migrants could reach the Minnesota-bound steamboats with less difficulty. Settlement was still confined to the St. Croix Triangle, however, as long as the Sioux and Mendota Indians owned all the land west of the Mississippi River in Minnesota.

That condition changed, however, in 1851 with the two treaties, the Traverse des Sioux and the Mendota. The Sioux gave up their claims to much of the land in southern Minnesota, a strip of northern Iowa, and the eastern part of the Dakotas, and they agreed to move into a tract reserved for them along the upper Minnesota River. All together, the Indians ceded 28 million acres. After the proclamation of the Sioux treaties in 1853, migrants rushed into southern Minnesota, but movement into the Dakota portion was slow because of the lack of protection from Indians until after the Civil War. From Ft. Snelling they moved up the Minnesota River valley and into the "Big Woods," a belt of hardwood along and to the north of the Minnesota River. By 1854 people had settled Minneapolis and as far west as Lake Minnetonka. In the Minnesota valley they had built the towns of Shakopee, Le Sueur, Traverse des Sioux, Kakota, Mankato, Henderson, and New Ulm, and they had bought 5 million acres of the land gained through the Sioux treaties. In the southeastern part of the territory they moved up the valleys of the Root, Zumbro, and Cannon rivers. This part was a center for Norwegians, who founded some of the earliest settlements in the area of Spring Grove in Houston County, Root Prairie in Fillmore County, Six Mile Grove in Mower County, and Jackson Lake in Faribault County, all established before 1856. During the 1850's settlers also pushed up the Mississippi River to Stearns County. At Sauk Rapids the settlers tended to remain in the hardwood forests rather than to move upriver into the pine woods, but in the later '50's settlers moved westward from St. Cloud along the Sauk valley to the Red River; and Sauk Center, Alexandria, Brandon, and Elbow Lake developed into towns. From 1855 to 1858 a total of 700 new towns, with 300,000 lots, were platted in the state. Although in the fifties such immigrants came as the Norwegians in the southeast and the Germans in Stearns and Brown counties, the character of the population continued to be "Yankee," since the largest numbers of the new arrivals to Minnesota were from New York, New England, Pennsylvania, Ohio, and Wisconsin.

Two events in 1855 stimulated expansion on widely separated frontiers. One was the opening of the Sault Ste. Marie Canal between upper Michigan and Ontario; the other was the organization of Nebraska Territory. The canal opening encouraged the growth of Minnesota at the head of Lake Superior. A trading post and mission had been at Fond du Lac since

POPULATION DENSITY, 1850

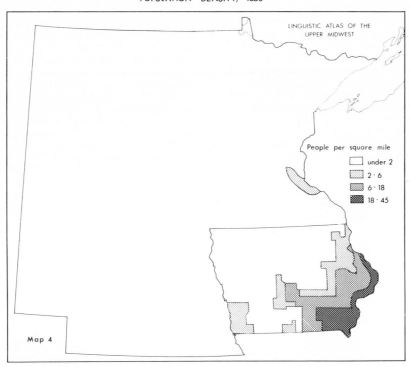

People per square mile

under 2
2 - 6
6 - 18
18 - 45

Map 4

POPULATION DENSITY, 1870

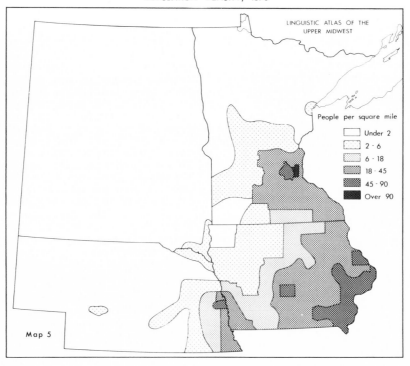

People per square mile

Under 2
2 - 6
6 - 18
18 - 45
45 - 90
Over 90

Map 5

10

1832, and in 1853 a road was built from Lake Superior to the lumber camps on the St. Croix River, but the canal established the importance of the Great Lakes water route. Also in 1854 and 1855 the Chippewa Indians gave up their lands north of Lake Superior and in the north-central part of the state. Duluth was laid out in 1856, and soon roads were built from Lake Superior to St. Paul, St. Cloud, and Little Falls as settlers moved into the central part of the state.

Meanwhile, the organization of Nebraska Territory stimulated expansion not only into Nebraska, but also into neighboring South Dakota (then a part of Minnesota Territory). Although Ft. Atkinson was established in 1819 on the Missouri River about sixteen miles north of present-day Omaha, there were no permanent settlements along the west bank of the Missouri River until the territory was organized in 1855. After the passage of the Kansas-Nebraska Act and the creation of Nebraska Territory, settlers arrived from Ohio, New York, Pennsylvania, Indiana, Illinois, Iowa, and Missouri. Some came overland from Iowa; others came by steamboat up the Missouri River from St. Louis; almost all of them entered Nebraska at Omaha and Brownsville and settled in the southeast corner of the territory. Although a few went up the Elkhorn River valley in the 1850's, most confined themselves to the Platte and Nemaha River valleys, going about as far west as Lincoln and south to the Kansas border. Within five years (1855-1860) the population of Nebraska Territory increased from 4,480 to 28,826.

The first newcomers moved into what is now South Dakota in 1856 and settled in the Big Sioux valley. In the following year settlements were made farther west near Yankton on the James River. In 1858 the Sioux, according to the terms of the Yankton Treaty, gave up most of their lands in the southern part of South Dakota between the Big Sioux and Missouri rivers, relinquishing a total of 14,000,000 acres and retaining only the Yankton reservation in Charles Mix County. When the Indians were removed in 1858, settlers crossed from Nebraska into Bon Homme, Yankton, Clay, and Union counties, laid out the towns of Yankton, Meckling, Vermillion, and Bon Homme, and took up farms all along the Missouri River from Sioux City, Iowa, to Bon Homme. Most people in the earliest parties were from Iowa and Minnesota, but many of those who settled near Vermillion were Norwegians.

The panic of 1857 slowed much of the land speculation in the Upper Midwest, and the Civil War retarded the westward migration of U.S. citizens and halted the European immigration. But Minnesota and the newly created (1861) Dakota Territory were further affected by the Sioux uprising of 1862, when the entire nation of 7,000 Sioux united against the settlers, and about 1,500 braves went on the warpath, killing over 400 whites in a few days. New Ulm, defended by about 1,500 residents and refugees, was almost annihilated by the Sioux, and for a time after the battle it was abandoned. In Dakota Territory the Big Sioux valley was virtually deserted; the settlers left Sioux Falls, which was later burned by Indians, and many of them retreated to Yankton. Bon Homme was also deserted from 1862 to 1868. The fear created by the uprising made people reluctant to move into Minnesota and Dakota, but in the long run it resulted in further white settlement in Minnesota. Compensation to settlers was paid out of Sioux trust funds, and the Sioux title to reservation lands was wiped out.

Between the end of the Civil War and the panic of 1873, migrants surged into the Upper Midwest. During the 1860's approximately 58,000 New Yorkers migrated, followed by large numbers of people from Illinois, Ohio, Wisconsin, Pennsylvania, and New England. Essentially, the new migration was due to two causes: the Homestead Act of 1862 and railroad construction. Although Iowans began to leave their farms to homestead land farther west under the provisions of the Homestead Act, migrants, largely from Illinois (58,000 from Illinois alone), Ohio, Wisconsin, New York, and Pennsylvania, and immigrants from Germany, Scandinavia, Britain, and Bohemia took over abandoned farms and settled in the land passed over by earlier settlers, resulting in a net population increase in Iowa.

At the close of the Civil War Minnesota was the closest state offering a large area of unsettled land under the provisions of the Homestead Act. Most of the new settlers in Minnesota then came from New York, Wisconsin, Illinois, Ohio, and New England: 27,000 moved from New York and 18,000 from Wisconsin, more than from all other states combined. The bulk of these new settlers remained in the older section of the state, east of New Ulm and south of St. Cloud; settlement of the prairie frontier to the west and northwest did not get under way until the '70's and '80's after construction of railroads.

Nebraska illustrates the influence of the railroad on the settlement of the Upper Midwest. During the first years of settlement of Nebraska Territory, settlers remained along the Missouri River or slow-

POPULATION DENSITY, 1890

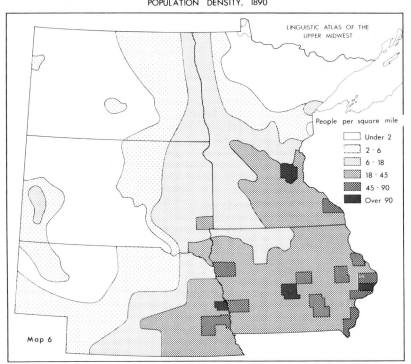

LINGUISTIC ATLAS OF THE
UPPER MIDWEST

People per square mile

Under 2
2 - 6
6 - 18
18 - 45
45 - 90
Over 90

Map 6

POPULATION DENSITY, 1910

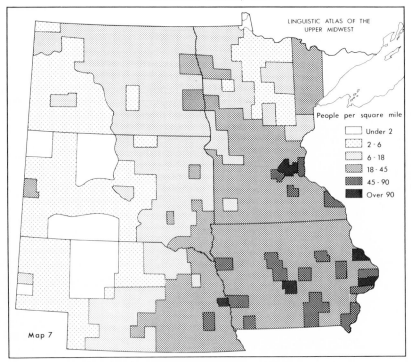

LINGUISTIC ATLAS OF THE
UPPER MIDWEST

People per square mile

Under 2
2 - 6
6 - 18
18 - 45
45 - 90
Over 90

Map 7

ly moved up the Platte and Elkhorn valleys. The Union Pacific, the most important contribution to the development of Nebraska, began construction in Omaha in 1863 but had laid only about 40 miles of track by 1865. Anticipating the railroad, some settlers moved into the Platte River valley, following the routes established earlier by the migrants to California, Oregon, and Utah in the '40's and '50's. By 1866 the railroad reached Kearney, the company had established towns such as Fremont and Kearney, and the trains were carrying passengers as far as the end of the line. In two more years the railroad reached Cheyenne, and North Platte and Sidney were built in the process. The railroad encouraged the settlement of immigrants along the railroad line: for example, in 1873 the Union Pacific settled 2,000 families, most of them Scandinavians, as far west as Buffalo County. But most of the new arrivals were from Illinois, New York, Ohio, Pennsylvania, and Indiana. Between 1870 and 1874 the area south of the Platte was solidly organized through Frontier County and north of the Platte into Cheyenne County in the southern part of the Nebraska panhandle.

Between 1868 and 1873 southern Dakota Territory experienced a period of rapid settlement. The Homestead Act of 1862 had little effect until the Civil War was over; after the war, however, the law attracted homesteaders from New England, Pennsylvania, Ohio, Illinois, Wisconsin, Minnesota, and Iowa as well as foreigners arriving in the postwar wave of immigration to the United States. Tensions were eased in 1868 with the conclusion of the Red Cloud War, and the Sioux were given nearly all of Dakota west of the Missouri River for a reservation. In 1868 the railroad was completed to Sioux City, Iowa, making southeast Dakota more accessible to migrants. One significant group consisted of 500 Bohemian families, about 1,200 people, who came from Chicago and settled northwest of Yankton in Yankton and Bon Homme counties. Also into the Yankton vicinity came large numbers of Norwegians, Swedes, and Russo-Germans, and by 1870 almost all of the land in the counties bordering the Missouri River-- Union, Clay, Yankton, and Bon Homme--was occupied. A series of good crops from 1868 to 1873 continued to draw more settlers. In 1873 about 100 families of Russo-Germans came to southern Dakota and settled in the James River valley, pushing up the river into Hutchinson and Turner counties; in the following year another 600 families arrived. They were joined by another large colony of Germans from Ohio. About the time when the

Germans and Russo-Germans were pushing up the James River valley, Norwegians, most of them from older Norwegian communities in Houston County, Minnesota, and Allamakee and Winneshiek counties, Iowa, moved into the Big Sioux valley in Brookings County.

The northern part of Dakota Territory, now North Dakota, was opened for settlement in 1863, but, unlike the southern part, the northern portion did not attract many settlers until 1870. Before 1870 there was only one settlement in North Dakota, the Selkirk colony at Pembina on the Red River. Although this colony had been in existence since 1811, when Pembina County was organized as the first county in North Dakota, it had an estimated white population of only 500. Settlement was discouraged by the Civil War, Indian troubles, the reputation of the area as a land of blizzards and grasshoppers, and the inaccessibility of the country. The nearest land office where homesteaders could file their claims was for a time in Vermillion, 400 miles to the south. Lack of accessible and attractive river valleys meant that settlement of the territory depended very heavily upon the construction of railroads across the prairie. The settlement of all of North Dakota, like the settlement of the Minnesota prairie, the area west of the James River in South Dakota, and the Platte valley in Nebraska, was closely tied to the expansion of the railroad.

The Northern Pacific Railway, built west from Duluth in 1870, reached Moorhead, Minnesota, on the east side of the Red River on December 31, 1871, and hastened the settlement of the prairie country of northwestern Minnesota and northern Dakota. In March 1872, the railroad crossed the river to Fargo (on the bridge constructed by the father of Informant 220), and by the end of the summer it was extended westward to Jamestown on the James River. Despite the panic of 1873, the railroad reached the Missouri at Bismarck in that year. Settlers moved into homesteads near the line and the towns of Jamestown and Bismarck grew up rather quickly. After the panic of 1873 the Northern Pacific encouraged settlement by Europeans, and its efforts resulted in large numbers of Russo-Germans coming to North Dakota. Also influential was a bureau of immigration, set up in 1875, which attracted many Norwegians. Most of the Norwegians who arrived in the 1870's, however, came from Minnesota, Iowa, and southern Wisconsin. During this decade the counties along the west bank of the Red River were settled and organized, as well as those westward along the route

POPULATION DENSITY, 1930

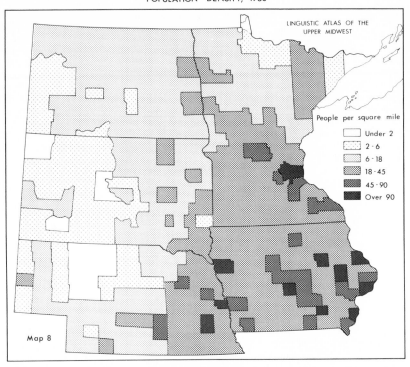

Map 8

POPULATION DENSITY, 1950

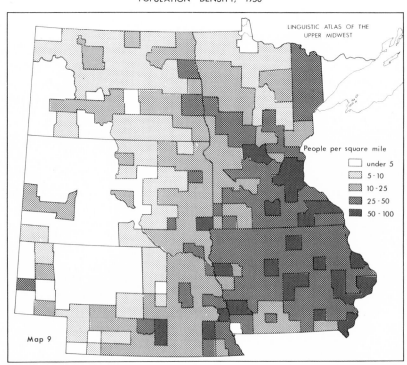

Map 9

to Bismarck.

Although the panic of 1873 temporarily slowed growth in southern Dakota, the discovery of gold in the Black Hills in 1874 began the Dakota boom period. Many native Americans were lured to the gold fields; others stopped in eastern Dakota. During the early 1870's they continued to move into the Big Sioux and James River valleys. By 1879 there was no more desirable land in the Big Sioux valley, and people began to move west along the railroad lines. By 1880 the Western Railroad had reached the Missouri River at Pierre, and the Milwaukee had reached it farther south at Chamberlain. With the exception of the Black Hills region, the land west of the Missouri River belonged to the Sioux Indians, and neither railroad nor settlers could cross the river. However, people continued to pour into the eastern part of the territory, and within five years Mitchell, Madison, Brookings, Watertown, Huron, Redfield, Aberdeen, Webster, Milbank, and Pierre were all important towns. During the boom between 1878 and 1885, the population in southern Dakota jumped from 50,000 to 400,000. The boom slowed in the later 1880's because of a severe drought in 1886 and 1887 and because by this time most of the free land east of the Missouri River was taken.

To the north the boom was tied not only to the progress of the railroads but also to the success of what was known as "bonanza farming." During the 1880's, while the Northern Pacific was reaching westward from Bismarck into Montana, construction was begun on the Great Northern Railway. Unlike many of the other railroads, the Great Northern progressed slowly, built numerous feeder lines, and brought in large groups of settlers who supported its construction. Extending from Duluth, where it connected with the shipping routes of the Great Lakes, to Grand Forks, the Great Northern route was built west to Devil's Lake, then to Minot in 1887, and across the western portion of the territory to Montana in 1888. In addition to the railroads, the success of bonanza farming in northern Dakota attracted many to the area in the 1880's. By 1885 Oliver Dalrymple was operating a 34,000 acre wheat farm in Cass County, and there were similar farms in Cass, Traill, and Barnes counties. The success of the farms attracted widespread publicity in the east, where many workers were recruited. Hundreds of men would be employed during harvest and planting time; often they returned to the east in the winter with fantastic tales which prompted settlers to move to North Dakota to farm. They

came from all over the United States, especially from Minnesota, Wisconsin, New York, Iowa, Michigan, Illinois, New England, Ohio, and Pennsylvania, and from Europe in such numbers that between 1880 and 1890 the population jumped from 36,909 to 190,983, an increase of 500 percent. Newcomers continued to arrive after the boom decade of the 1880's, but they did not begin to homestead the country west of the Little Missouri until after 1902.

After North and South Dakota became separate states in 1889, settlement west of the Missouri was possible. The Sioux had occupied the Great Sioux reservation, which included all of the land in the Dakotas west of the Missouri except for the Black Hills, but in 1889 they ceded about eleven million acres of land and agreed to live on five separate reservations west of the river. This ceded land was opened for homesteading in 1890. The new land and a series of wet years attracted settlers from eastern South Dakota as well as from other states and foreign countries. Many came to this area from the south--Nebraska, Kansas, and Texas-- as well as from the Middle Atlantic States.

The Upper Midwest early became a melting pot of nationalities, for its residents can trace their ancestry to many countries. Instead of a few nationalities dominating the population, no fewer than twelve important sources of national origin are represented in significant numbers. They are, in order of their proportions: Germany, Sweden, Norway, Denmark, Russia, Canada, Czechoslovakia, the Netherlands, England, Ireland, Finland, and Poland.

Although the Scandinavians collectively constitute the largest element of the population of the Upper Midwest, the largest single nationality group is German. Germans, the major nationality group in Iowa, Minnesota, and Nebraska, first came to the Upper Midwest around 1848 and settled along the Mississippi River in Iowa; in the 1850's they arrived in large numbers and settled in the southern part of the state and along the Mississippi River. Today there remain well-defined German communities (Guttenberg, Luxemburg, and Holy Cross, for example) in Clinton County on the Mississippi River, in Bremer County on the Cedar River, in the river cities of Davenport and Dubuque, and in the Iowa River valley where the Amana Colonies were established in 1855. In Minnesota the Germans were among the earliest settlers, arriving in the 1850's in St. Paul and New Ulm. They also founded many farm colonies: Stearns and

Brown counties were almost entirely German for years. Today they are throughout Minnesota, but the heaviest concentrations remain in the southeast, particularly in Brown, McLeod, Carver, Stearns, Ramsey, and Winona counties. The Germans were also the first immigrants to arrive in significant numbers in Nebraska; in the 1850's they established German communities on the Platte River at Columbus and later in 1857 at Grand Island. Today Germans constitute 35 percent of Nebraska's foreign stock. In the 1860's many Germans came to South Dakota directly from Germany as well as from German communities in Illinois and Wisconsin. During the Dakota boom the Frieslanders came to Lincoln County and later to Turner County; the Germans from Wisconsin and other eastern states came to Codington and Brown counties. Today Germans represent the second largest nationality group in South Dakota. In North Dakota, where the Germans are the third largest group, the most prominent German communities are in the southeastern counties, in Ward County in the northwest, and in several counties in the Missouri slope region: Stark, Grant, Mercer, Morton, and Hettinger counties.

Swedish immigration to the Upper Midwest began in 1846 when Peter Cassel brought a group of twenty-one people to Iowa. Today people of Swedish extraction live throughout Iowa and constitute the second largest nationality group in that state. They were also among the first to settle in Minnesota, arriving in the 1850's and settling throughout the state and later moving into the cities of Minneapolis, St. Paul, and Duluth in large numbers. Although Swedes are found everywhere in Minnesota, their main stronghold is still where they first came, in the counties of east-central Minnesota, particularly Isanti, Chisago, Washington, Ramsey, and Hennepin. Swedes first arrived in Nebraska in 1860, and came in large numbers after the Civil War. The first wave settled in Kearney in 1865, the Union Pacific being responsible for numerous Swedish settlements near the railroad. About the same time the Swedes reached southeast South Dakota, and their immigration continued until 1920, when they were moving into Dewey, Harding, Stanley, and Lawrence counties west of the Missouri River. Although they are the fourth largest nationality group in South Dakota, there are not many compact settlements of Swedes in the state. North Dakota has the smallest proportion of Swedes. They are found primarily in Cass County in the east part of the state and in Burleigh and McLean coun-

ties on the east side of the Missouri River.

The Norwegians are most heavily concentrated in the northern portion of the Upper Midwest. The region's first Norwegian colony on Sugar Creek in Lee County in southeast Iowa failed because the settlers could not endure the warm climate, but Norwegians took root in the 1850's with the settlement at Decorah in Winneshiek County, and from this parent colony they have moved throughout the state and into the other Upper Midwest states. Next, the Norwegians came to southeast Minnesota, and there are still heavy Norwegian concentrations in Fillmore, Freeborn, and Goodhue counties. They also came to the North Woods as lumberjacks, and many moved westward to farm in the Red River valley. Today Norwegians are fairly evenly spread throughout the south and west portions of the state, exceeded only by the Germans and Swedes. In contrast to the large numbers of Norwegians in the rest of the Upper Midwest, there are few Norwegians in Nebraska, where the Scandinavian element is predominantly Swedish and Danish. On the other hand, Norwegians make up the largest nationality group in both North and South Dakota. Among the earliest foreigners to arrive in South Dakota, they did not settle in compact areas; instead they spread throughout the state into almost every township. They first came in 1859 into Clay, Hutchinson, and Turner counties. After the Civil War they came primarily to the Big Sioux valley (where they are still most thickly located), many coming from Winneshiek County, Iowa, and Fillmore County, Minnesota; later in the 1880's and '90's Aberdeen was the center for Norwegian migration. Norwegians are likewise spread throughout eastern North Dakota. As late as 1940 30 percent of the population were of Norwegian stock and 29 percent of the foreign-born were Norwegians.

In contrast to the Norwegians, the Danes are located most thickly in the more southern states of Iowa and Nebraska. The third largest nationality group in Iowa, the Danes first settled near Luzerne in Benton County in 1854; now they live throughout the state. After the Civil War thousands of Danes came to southeast Minnesota and then later to the north. The Danish population is still heaviest in Freeborn County in the southeast and Lincoln County in the southwest on the South Dakota state line, although they are now widely distributed throughout the state. Danish immigration to Nebraska began in the 1860's, and reached its peak in the 1880's. The earliest colonies were Davey in Lancaster County and Dannebrog and Dannevirke in Howard County. In South Dakota the Danes often did not settle thickly in communities, but their concentration is largely in Yankton, Clay, and Turner counties in the southeast. In North Dakota the Danes make up a rather small nationality group; they are found mostly in the southeastern counties of Cass, Barnes, and Stutsman along the Northern Pacific Railway and in Pembina and Cavalier counties in the northeast.

The Russo-Germans were relative latecomers, and perhaps for that reason they are found in more significant numbers in the Dakotas. There are few in Iowa and Minnesota, and in Nebraska they are still largely concentrated in Lancaster County, where they first settled. In North and South Dakota, where the Russo-Germans are respectively the second and third largest nationality group, they are concentrated in a broad band of counties along the James River from Yankton County, South Dakota, to Dickey County, North Dakota, and westward into Emonds, McPherson, Campbell, Walworth, Dewey, Corson counties, South Dakota, and neighboring McIntosh, Logan, and Emmons counties in North Dakota, and farther west on the Missouri Slope.

The Czechs first settled in the Upper Midwest in 1853 at St. Ansgar in Mitchell County, Iowa, and in the following year at Spillville in Winneshiek County and in Linn and Johnson counties. They also established New Prague and settled Le Sueur and Scott counties, Minnesota, and remain concentrated in that portion of southeastern Minnesota. The Czechs constitute relatively small portions of the population in all of the states except Nebraska, where they are the second largest nationality group, with the largest numbers living in Douglas County. In the Dakotas, where they constitute a small proportion of the population, they are concentrated around Tabor, in Bon Homme County, where they first settled, in the neighboring counties of Douglas, Charles Mix, and Brule on the east side of the Missouri River, and in counties to the west which were settled in 1904 when the Rosebud reservation was opened: Gregory, Gripp, Todd, Mellette, and Bennett--all in South Dakota. In North Dakota they are largely found in Richland and Walsh counties in the Red River valley and Stark County in the Missouri Slope area.

The Dutch were among the earliest foreigners to arrive in the Upper Midwest, when in 1847 a group came up the Mississippi River from St. Louis and established the village of Pella, in Marion County, Iowa. From this community they have spread throughout the state and have migrated into Nebraska, Minnesota, and the Dakotas. In addition to the Dutch who came to South Dakota from Iowa, others came from Wisconsin and directly from Europe; they are largely found in twelve counties in the east part of the state from Grant County south and to the east of Charles Mix County.

Except in North Dakota, the English and Irish are widely spread throughout the Upper Midwest. In 1850 about one-half of the foreign population of Iowa was English-born, and English immigrants continued to arrive in groups in Iowa until the 1870's, when the last large group arrived to establish farming communities at Le Mars in Plymouth County and Eden and Center townships in Clinton County. Today, however, people of English stock are found mostly in the larger cities: Des Moines, Dubuque, Sioux City, Council Bluffs, Davenport, Clinton, Cedar Rapids, and Burlington. The Irish are also found in largest numbers in the Iowa cities, but when they first came in the 1850's they settled on farms; by 1880 the Irish were living in every township of the state. Both the Irish and the English continue to be most heavily concentrated in the southeast and central parts of Minnesota, where they originally settled. The largest numbers are found today in the Twin Cities, St. Paul being more heavily Irish. In Nebraska and South Dakota the English and Irish are spread throughout the states without any particular concentrations, but there are no significant numbers of either in North Dakota.

Finns are found in Minnesota and the Dakotas. They came rather late, in the 1890's, primarily to work in the iron mines in northeast Minnesota. They are still most numerous in St. Louis and Carlton counties in northeast Minnesota, but they are also found farther to the west in Itaska, Aitkin, and Crow Wing counties in central Minnesota, Becker, Otter Tail, and Wadena counties in west Minnesota, and Wright and Meeker counties in south-central Minnesota. In South Dakota there are two principal concentrations, Hamlin and Brown counties in the northeast and Lawrence, Butte, and Harding in the west. In North Dakota they are spread throughout the southern and western portions of the state.

There are three concentrated settlements of Poles in the Upper Midwest. Two are in Minnesota, in Duluth and St. Louis County in the northeast and in St. Paul. The other one is Day County, South Dakota. Poles are not found in Iowa in significant numbers, but they are sprinkled across the rest of the Upper Midwest.

Prior to the urban influx from the South in the 1960's the Negro population of the Upper Midwest had been extremely small, constituting only .89 percent of the total in 1960. Before the Civil War only a few Blacks were in the area, some of them coming by way of the underground railroad stations in places such as Clinton, Iowa, and Nebraska City, Nebraska. A few Blacks came to Iowa after the Civil War, but most of them have come in the twentieth century to work in the coal and manufacturing industries in the larger cities. The 1960 census reported less than one percent of the Iowa population as Black (25,354), about one-third of them living in Des Moines. In 1850 there were only 39 Blacks in Minnesota; in 1960 there were about 22,263, .65 percent of the total, and almost all of them live in the Twin Cities. Nebraska has the largest Black population in the Upper Midwest. In 1880 there were 2,395 Blacks in the state; in 1960 there were 29,262, slightly more than 2 percent of the state total. Most of the Blacks in Nebraska live in the Omaha area, where they were drawn by job opportunities with the railroads. The Black population in North and South Dakota is even smaller than that of the other three states. In 1960 there were 1,114 Blacks in South Dakota and 777 in North Dakota, about one-tenth of one percent of the population of each state.

Although the Upper Midwest constitutes about 10.1 percent of the area of the United States, the region contains only 4.95 percent of the national population. The national population has a density of 49.6 people per square mile, but the Upper Midwest has a density of only 24.4 people per square mile. Iowa is the most densely settled of the five states with a density almost the same as that of the nation, 49.2. Minnesota has a density of 40.6, Nebraska 18.4, South Dakota 9.46, and North Dakota 9.14. The unevenness of the population distribution is further shown by the population density of individual counties. Three counties have densities of over 1,000 people per square mile: Hennepin County (1,491.8) and Ramsey County (2,640.8), Minnesota, and Douglas County (1,031.5), Nebraska. At the other extreme, seventeen counties have densities of fewer than 2 people per square mile: Arthur, Banner, Blaine, Cherry, Grant, Hooker, Logan, Loup, McPherson, Sioux, and Thomas counties in Nebraska; Haakon, Harding, Washabaugh, and Zieback counties in South Dakota; and Billings and Slope counties in North Dakota. The difference between the population distribution of the Upper Midwest and the nation as a whole is also revealed in the differences in rural-urban distribution. The U.S. population is 70 percent urban, whereas that of the Upper Midwest is only 54 percent urban. Three states in 1960 were more urban than rural, Minnesota (62.2 percent), Nebraska (54.3 percent), and Iowa (53 percent); the other two are slightly more rural: South Dakota (39.3 percent urban) and North Dakota (35.2 percent urban).

18

THE UPPER MIDWEST

A. General History and Population Movement

Billington, Ray A. *Westward Expansion, A History of the American Frontier*. New York, 1950.

Briggs, Harold E. *Frontiers of the Northwest; A History of the Upper Missouri Valley*. New York, 1940.

Brown, Ralph H. *Historical Geography of the United States*. New York, 1958.

Clark, Dan E. *The West in American History*. New York, 1937.

----------. "The westward movement in the Upper Mississippi Valley during the fifties," *Mississippi Valley Historical Association Proceedings*, 7.212-219 (1914).

Dale, Edward E. *The Range Cattle Industry*. Norman, Okla., 1960.

Dick, Everett N. *The Sod-House Frontier, 1854-1890; A Social History of the Northern Plains from the Creation of Kansas and Nebraska to the Admission of the Dakotas*. New York, 1937.

----------. *Vanguards of the Frontier: A Social History of the Northern Plains and Rocky Mountains from the Earliest White Contacts to the Coming of the Homemaker*. New York, 1947.

Fenneman, Nevin M. *Physiography of Western United States*. New York, 1931.

Goodrich, Carter L. *Migration and Economic Opportunity*. Philadelphia, 1936.

Goodwin, Cardinal. *The Trans-Mississippi West (1803-1853), A History of Its Acquisition and Settlement*. New York, 1922.

Hafen, LeRoy R., and C. C. Rister. *Western America; The Exploration, Settlement and Development of the Region beyond the Mississippi*. New York, 1941.

Kuznet, Simon Smith. *Popular Redistribution and Economic Growth*. Philadelphia, 1957.

Osgood, Ernest S. *The Day of the Cattleman*. Minneapolis, 1929.

Paullin, C. O., and John K. Wright. *Atlas of Historical Geography of the United States*. Washington and New York, 1932.

Paxon, Frederick L. *The Last American Frontier*. New York, 1937.

Peterson, William J. "Population advance to the Upper Mississippi Valley," *Iowa Journal of History*, 32.312-353 (1934).

Schmidt, Louis B. "The westward movement of the wheat growing industry in the United States," *Iowa Journal of History and Politics*, 18.396-413 (1920).

Shannon, Fred A. *The Farmers' Last Frontier*. New York and Toronto, 1945.

Thornthwaite, Charles W., and Helen I. Slentz. *Internal Migration in the United States*. Philadelphia, 1934.

Turner, F. J. *The Frontier in American History*. New York, 1920.

----------. *Rise of the New West*. New York, 1906.

Webb, Walter P. *The Great Plains*. Boston, 1931.

B. Ethnic Groups

Blegen, Theodore C. *Norwegian Migration to America, 1825-1860*. Northfield, Mn., 1931.

Herigstad, Omon B. "Norwegian Immigration," *North Dakota Historical Society Collection*, 2.186-201 (1908).

Johnson, Hildegard B. "The location of German immigrants in the Middle West," *Annals of the Association of American Geographers*, 41.1-42 (1951).

Kildahl, J. N. "The Scandinavian influence in the development of the Northwest," *University of North Dakota Quarterly Journal*, 1.52-56 (1911).

Nelson, Helge. *The Swedes and Swedish Settlements in North America*. New York, 1943.

Qualey, Carlton C. *Norwegian Settlement in the United States*. Northfield, Mn., 1938.

IOWA

A. Settlement History

Allen, Arthur F. *Northwestern Iowa; Its History and Traditions, 1804-1926*. Chicago, 1927.

Andreas, A. T. *Illustrated Historical Atlas of the State of Iowa, 1875.* Chicago, 1875.

Bergmann, Leola N. "The Negro in Iowa, 1833-1947," *Iowa Journal of History and Politics*, 46.3-90 (1948).

Cole, Cyrenus. *A History of the People of Iowa.* Cedar Rapids, 1921.

Gallaher, Ruth A. "The first hundred years, a brief history of Iowa," *Iowa Journal of History and Politics*, 31.531-576 (1933).

Goodwin, Cardinal. "The American occupation of Iowa, 1833-1860," *Iowa Journal of Histroy and Politics*, 17.83-103 (1919).

Gue, B. F. *History of Iowa from the Earliest Times.* New York, 1903.

Harter, William, and R. E. Stewart. *The Population of Iowa: Its Composition and Changes.* Ames, 1930.

Peterson, William J. *The Story of Iowa.* New York, 1952.

Trachsel, Herman H. "The hairy nation," *Palimpsest*, 8.393-407 (1927).

B. Ethnic Groups

Christensen, Thomas P. History of the Danes in Iowa. University of Iowa Studies. *Abstracts in History from Ph.D. theses 1922-1930*, pp. 105-119.

Flom, George T. Chapter on Scandinavian immigration to Iowa. Repr. in *Iowa Journal of History and Politics*, 3.57-91, 347-383, 583-615; 4.220-244, 267-285 (1905-06).

Gallaher, Ruth A. "The English community in Iowa," *Palimpsest*, 2.80-94 (1921).

Griffith, Martha E. "Czechs in Cedar Rapids," *Iowa Journal of History and Politics*, 42.114-162, 266-316 (1944).

Horn, H. H. *English Colony in Iowa.* Boston, 1931.

Van der Zee, Jacob. *The British in Iowa.* Iowa City, 1922.

----------. *The Hollanders of Iowa.* Iowa City, 1912.

MINNESOTA

A. Settlement History

Andreas, A. T. *Illustrated Historical Atlas of the State of Minnesota.* Chicago, 1874.

Blegen, Theodore C. *Minnesota, Its History and Its People.* Minneapolis, 1937.

Burnquist, J. A. A. (ed.). *Minnesota and Its People.* Chicago, 1924.

Folwell, William W. *A History of Minnesota.* St. Paul, 1921-30.

Goodwin, Cardinal. "The movement of American settlers into Wisconsin and Minnesota," *Iowa Journal of History and Politics*, 17.406-428 (1919).

Jenks, Albert E. *The People of Minnesota.* Minnesota Academy of Social Science, 2.198-213 (1909).

Jerabek, Esther. "The expansion of Minnesota's population," *Minnesota Alumni Weekly*, 33.43-44 (1933).

Larsen, Arthur J. "Roads and the Settlement of Minnesota," *Minnesota History*, 21.225-244 (1940).

Murchie, R. W., and M. E. Jarchow. *Population Trends in Minnesota.* University of Minnesota Agricultural Experiment Station Bulletin 327, 1936.

Qualey, Carlton C. "Some national groups in Minnesota," *Minnesota History*, 31.18-32 (1950).

Robinson, Edward Van Dyke. *Early Economic Conditions and Agriculture in Minnesota.* University of Minnesota Studies in the Social Sciences, No. 3, 1915.

Upham, Warren. "The settlement and development of the Red River Valley," *Minnesota Historical Society Collections*, 8.11-24 (1898).

Wilson, Leonard S. "Some notes on the growth of population in Minnesota," *Geographical Review*, 30.660-664 (1940).

Wirth, Fremont P. *The Discovery and Exploitation of the Minnesota Iron Lands.* Cedar Rapids, 1937.

B. Ethnic Groups

Christensen, Thomas P. "Danish settlement in Minnesota," *Minnesota History*, 8.363-385 (1927).

Egan, Howard E. "Irish immigration to Minnesota, 1865-1890," *Mid-America*, 12 (n.s. 1).133-136 (1929).

Heilbron, Bertha L. "Swiss settlement in Minnesota," *Minnesota History*, 8.174-175 (1927).

Johnson, Hildegard B. "The distribution of the German pioneer population in Minnesota," *Rural Sociology*, 6.16-34 (1941).

Van Cleef, Eugene. *The Finn in America.* Duluth, 1918.

NEBRASKA

A. Settlement History

Anderson, David. "The early settlements of the Platte Valley," *Nebraska Historical Society Collections*, 3rd ser., 16.193-205 (1911).

Barton, T. F. "Settlement of Nebraska interfluves as exemplified by the Hastings interfluve," *Nebraska History*, 16.115-125 (1935).

Johnson, Harrison. *History of Nebraska*. Omaha, 1880.

Olson, James C. *History of Nebraska*. Lincoln, 1955.

Overton, Richard C. *Burlington West: A Colonization History of the Burlington Railroad*. Cambridge, Mass., 1941.

Sheldon, Addison E. *Nebraska, the Land and the People*. Chicago, 1931.

Shumway, Grant L. *History of Western Nebraska and Its People*. Lincoln, 1921.

Wenstrand, John F. "A history of population trends in Nebraska as shown by the U.S. Decennial Census, 1860-1940," M.S. thesis, University of Nebraska, 1945.

B. Ethnic Groups

Alexis, Joseph. "Swedes in Nebraska," *Nebraska Historical Society Publications*, 19.78-85 (1919).

Martin, M. A. "Early Catholic colonization in Nebraska," *Mid-America*, 15.229-237 (1933).

NORTH DAKOTA

A. Settlement History

Andreas, A. T. *Historical Atlas of Dakota*. Chicago, 1884.

Briggs, Harold. "The great Dakota boom,"1879-1886," *North Dakota Historical Quarterly*, 4.78-108 (1930).

----------. "The Settlement and development of the Territory of Dakota, 1860-1870," *North Dakota Historical Quarterly*, 7.114-150 (1933).

Kazeck, Melvin E. *North Dakota, A Human and Economic Geography*. Fargo, 1956.

Loundsberry, Clement A. *Early History of North Dakota*. Washington, D.C., 1919.

----------. *North Dakota History and People*. Chicago, 1917.

McCulloch, Hazel. *A Survey of Settlement in North Dakota in 1890*. M.A. thesis, University of Minnesota, 1935.

Tanner, Jesse. "Foreign immigration into North Dakota," *North Dakota Historical Society Collections*, 1 (1906).

B. Ethnic Groups

Beck, Richard. "The founding of the Icelandic settlement in Pembina County," *North Dakota Historical Quarterly*, 6.150-164 (1932).

Bemis, Myrtle. "History of the settlement of Swedes in North Dakota," *North Dakota Historical Society Collections*, 3.247-309 (1910).

Harlich, Wasyl. "Ukrainians in North Dakota," *North Dakota Historical Quarterly*, 18.219-233 (1951-52).

Loynes, Hazel J. "Mennonite settlements in North Dakota," *North Dakota Historical Society Collections*, 3.324-336 (1910).

Qualey, Carlton C. "Pioneer Norwegian settlement in North Dakota," *North Dakota Historical Quarterly*, 5.14-37 (1930).

SOUTH DAKOTA

A. Settlement History

Batchelder, G. A. *Sketch of the History and Resources of Dakota Territory*. Yankton, 1870.

Briggs, Harold E. "The development and decline of open range ranching in the Northwest," *Mississippi Valley Historical Review*, 20.521-536 (1934).

Foster, James S. *Outline of the Territory of Dakota and Emigrants' Guide*. Yankton, 1870.

Green, Charles L. "The administration of the public domain in South Dakota," *South Dakota Historical Collections*, 20.7-280 (1940).

Kingsbury, George W. *History of Dakota Territory*. Chicago, 1915.

Peterson, Frank E. *Atlas of South Dakota*. Chicago, 1904.

Robinson, Doane. *Encyclopedia of South Dakota*. Pierre, 1925.

Sampson, York (ed.). *South Dakota: Fifty Years of Progress, 1889-1939*. Sioux Falls, 1939.

Schell, Herbert S. *Dakota Territory During the 1860's*. Vermillion, 1954.

21

Visher, Stephen S. *The Geography of South Dakota*. South Dakota State Geological Survey Bulletin 8, 1918.

B. Ethnic Groups

Johansen, John P. *Immigrant Settlements and Social Organization in South Dakota*. Brookings, 1937.

Ravndal, G. Bie. "The Scandinavian pioneer of South Dakota," *South Dakota Historical Society Collections*, 12.301-309 (1924).

Young, Gertrude S. "Mennonites in South Dakota," *South Dakota Historical Society Collections*, 10.470-507 (1920).

CENSUS REPORTS

U.S. Bureau of the Census. 7th Census, 1850. Washington, D.C.

---------. 8th Census, 1860, Vol. 1, Pt. I, pp. 10-589, Table 5. Washington, D.C.

---------. 9th Census, 1870, Vol. 1, Pt. I, pp. 327-335. Washington, D.C.

---------. 10th Census, 1880, Vol. 1, Pt. I, pp. 480-491. Washington, D.C.

---------. 11th Census, 1890, Vol. 1, Pt. I, pp. 560-567, 576-579. Washington, D.C.

---------. 12th Census, 1900, Vol. 1, Pt. I, pp. 686-693, 702-705. Washington, D.C.

---------. 13th Census, 1910, Vol. 1, Pt. I, pp. 730-744. Washington, D.C.

---------. 14th Census, 1920, Vol. 2, Pt. I, Ch. 5, pp. 626-630, Table 17, Washington, D.C.

---------. 15th Census, 1930, Vol. 2, Ch. 4, pp. 153-157, Table 21. Washington, D.C.

---------. 16th Census, 1940, pp. 15-19, Table 20, State Birth of the Native Population. Washington, D.C.

---------. 17th Census, 1950. Washington, D.C.

---------. 18th Census, 1960. Washington, D.C.

---------. Historical Statistics of the United States, 1789-1945. U.S. Department of Commerce, 1949.

---------. Population and Social Characteristics of the United States in 1870. Washington, D.C., 1872.

---------. Statistics of the Population of the U.S. at the Tenth Census, Vol. 1. Washington, D.C., 1882.

CHAPTER 3

Methodology

THE SELECTION OF COMMUNITIES

In the Upper Midwest the choice of communities was determined in terms sometimes of a single urban center, such as Minneapolis; sometimes of a population enclave, such as that of the French-Canadian settlers east of Crookston, Minnesota; and sometimes of an entire sparsely inhabited county, such as Harding County in South Dakota. The essential determinant in the selection was the need to obtain, within the framework of a fairly wide-meshed survey, a representative sample of the varied population.

Preceding the actual fieldwork in each state, the settlement history was carefully studied in order to provide for an equitably distributed selection of communities, as well as of informants, with respect to population density and major immigration patterns.

An initially prepared rough grid of possible sites for field studies offered a base for subsequent modification that recognized the greater density of population in Iowa, southeastern Minnesota, and the eastern portions of the Dakotas and Nebraska. Communities are more closely spaced in those areas, less closely spaced in the north and west. Indeed, the recency of settlement in some sparsely settled areas restricted informant selection as well, since at the time of the fieldwork there were literally no local informants who were more than sixty years old and who had been born in the community. No community existed there sixty years earlier.

A further criterion of selection of communities derives from the fact that most Upper Midwest residents have ancestral origins in non-English-speaking countries. Although the various Atlas projects in the United States are essentially designed to study the speech of native speakers of English, the distribution of the heterogeneous elements in the Upper Midwest population base makes it undesirable, if not impossible, to adhere to the New England Atlas policy of choosing only communities and informants that represent the original English-speaking stock. One reason is that the original European population in some fairly large rural areas was almost exclusively non-English-speaking. Another reason is that in some other areas the original homesteaders, of east coast English-speaking stock, moved on after selling their land to immigrants from non-English-speaking countries, so that at the time of the field study the residents were second- or third-generation descendants of those immigrants.

The diversity of origin of the immigrant groups, however, prevented representation of more than those elements that were either most numerous or that had preserved fairly cohesive communities. Thus, either by choice or by necessity the German and Scandinavian majority in the Upper Midwest is represented by widely scattered informants. Then, for example, Green Leafton in Minnesota and Westfield in South Dakota were chosen because of their Dutch population; Minneota in Minnesota and Akra in North Dakota because of their Icelandic population; Ellendale in North Dakota because of the German Russian base; and Winona, Minnesota, in part because of the strong Polish element in the city.

An additional factor in the selection of communities is like that which led to the use of New Brunswick informants in the New England Atlas survey and to the use of southern Ontario informants in the North Central Atlas investigation. It was well known that the Canadian middle border constituted only a minimal barrier to travel for the purpose of shopping and recreation, and that many Canadians had settled south of the border just as American citizens had moved north of it. Accordingly, it seemed desirable to include a few communities in the neighboring Canadian provinces of Ontario, Manitoba, and Saskatchewan. A preliminary report of language relationships based upon the interviews in the five Canadian communities is Harold B. Allen, "Canadian-American speech differences along the middle border," *Journal of the Canadian Linguistic Association*, 5.17-25 (1959).

The ratio of informants to population that had been accepted in New England suggested the need for approximately 200 informants in the Upper Midwest. Ultimately, with the inclusion of the five in Canada, the total reached 208. They are distributed in 97 loosely defined communities as follows: Minnesota, 65 informants in 26 communities; Iowa, 52 in 23; North Dakota, 26 in 14; South Dakota, 28 in 16; and Nebraska, 37 in 18. Because the nature of a community varies widely from a metropolitan unit such as Minneapolis to a rural county, with two unlike and separated informants, the community can not be treated as having a significance quite like that in New England. Accordingly, the numbering system applies to informants and not to communities, and the informants are grouped by counties in Chapter 5 as well as in the arrangement of phonetic synopses in Volume II.

THE SELECTION OF INFORMANTS

Although choice of communities was ordinarily determined by the director, the selection of informants necessarily was the responsibility of the fieldworker once he had arrived in a community. Again in conformity with the eastern Atlas studies the informants were to be sought within three general categories identified as Types I, II, and III, as follows:

I. Particularly important, in view of the objective of ascertaining the basic speech patterns of the region, was the selection of informants in this category. Such an informant was characterized as an elderly locally-born lifelong resident with little education. Typically he had been born about 1880 (although the oldest informant interviewed was born in 1859) and had obtained no more than eighth grade schooling.

II. The second type included informants perhaps a generation younger, born about 1895 or 1900, with a high school education or its equivalent. They also were to be locally-born lifelong residents.

III. Informants in this type were likewise locally-born and lifelong residents, between 40 and 50 years of age, with a college or university education attained at an institution within the region. Such informants, sought on the assumption that they would help to identify the general features of standard speech in the region, constitute only 13 percent of the total. All except one are residents of large or small urban centers having a college or university; the exception is a stock-raiser living only a few miles from such a city.

In practice it was not always possible to adhere strictly to the limitations imposed by the description of a given type. Because of the age of the community itself, the fieldworker sometimes had to settle for a Type I informant who was brought there as an infant. Sometimes an informant had to be used who had lived elsewhere for a few years. Oftener than had been expected, the fieldworker had to rely upon an informant whose family background included non-English-speaking grandparents or even parents. An intuitive acceptance of this circumstance resulted from the fact that the informants had to learn their English in the community and conceivably had little opportunity to acquire regional forms other than those found locally. This inference was later supported by a comparative study that justified the use of these informants in a study of the geographical variations of English in the region. See Harold B. Allen, "The use of Atlas informants of foreign parentage," in the Festschrift for Hans Kurath, due for publication by the University of Alabama Press in 1973.

Particularly in the first communities studied in Iowa, informants were inadequately contrasted between Types I and II. These circumstances, in addition to the fact that the Upper Midwest is less marked by sharp social contrast than is New England, has made it unfeasible to break down the various types into the New England Atlas subdivisions A and B to indicate greater or less measure of cultural sophistication. In general the Upper Midwest Type I informant may be taken as not only older and old-fashioned but also uneducated; a Type II informant may be taken as not only middle-aged but also as having a fair amount of schooling; and a Type III informant may be considered well-educated. This dual set of characteristics for each type makes possible some inference as to whether a language form is obsolescent or new as well as whether it is typically non-standard or standard.

Infrequently an auxiliary informant is used, but is identified only with an asterisk, not a separate serial number. Such an informant is nearly always a sibling or spouse of the regular inform-ant, with a similar background and similar characteristics. Auxiliary responses are recorded when they provide information not known to the regular inform-ant, as when a man is unfamiliar with certain household terms or a woman is unfamiliar with farm terms or boys' words.

INFORMANTS BY TYPE

Minnesota

I	II	III	I	II	III
1					34
	2		35		
3			36		
4				37	
5					38
6			39		
7				40	
	8		41		
		9		42	
10				43	
11			44		
	12		45		
13			46		
	14			47	
15			48		
16				49	
	17				50
		18	51		
19			52		
	20			53	
21				54	
	22		55		
23			56		
	24			57	
25					58
	26		59		
27				60	
	28			61	
29			62		
	30			63	
31				64	
32			65		
	33				

Iowa

I	II	III	I	II	III
101			127		
	102			128	

I	II	III	I	II	III
103			129		
104				130	
	105				131
	106		132		
107			133		
	108			134	
109			135		
		110		136	
	111		137		
112				138	
113			139		
114			140		
	115		141		
116			142		
117			143		
118				144	
	119			145	
	120		146		
	121			147	
		122	148		
123				149	
124					150
	125		151		
126				152	

North Dakota

I	II	III	I	II	III
201			214		
	202			215	
	203		216		
204				217	
	205		218		
206				219	
207			220		
	208				221
209					222
	210		223		
	211		224		
212			225		
	213			226	

South Dakota

I	II	III	I	II	III
301				315	
	302		316		
303			317		
	304			318	
305					319
306			320		
307				321	
	308		322		
309				323	
	310		324		
311				325	
	312				326
	313		327		
314				328	

Nebraska

I	II	III	I	II	III
401				420	

I	II	III	I	II	III
	402			421	
403					
	404				422
405					
	406				423
407					424
	408			425	
409					426
	410			427	
		411		428	
	412			429	
413				430	
	414			431	
415				432	
	416			433	
417				434	
418				435	
	419			436	
				437	

Total I, 103; II, 89; III, 16.

PREPARATION OF THE FIELDWORKER

The records constituting the raw materials of the Linguistic Atlas of the Upper Midwest were made by seven regular fieldworkers. In addition, two Iowa records (118, 151) made several years earlier by the late Guy Loman, east coast fieldworker, were given to the project by Hans Kurath; and two more (150, 152) resulted from interviews taped by Mrs. Kilpatrick, the assistant director for Iowa, and later transcribed by Allen.

Not all the fieldworkers had identical preparation for interviewing, although ultimately preparation of each was based upon the training program devised in 1930 and 1931 for the fieldworkers for the New England Atlas.

Both Allen and McDavid were trained by Kurath and Bloch in a special program during the Linguistic Institute at the University of Michigan in 1937. Subsequently Allen had done the preliminary fieldwork in Michigan and in Illinois for the North Central Atlas; McDavid had served as fulltime fieldworker for the Atlas project in the Middle and South Atlantic States.

Glenn and Weber were trained by Allen, and Glenn received further preparation at the University of Michigan in the summer of 1947.

Wilson was trained by Marckwardt and Kurath at the University of Michigan and subsequently did fieldwork in Nova Scotia.

Hanlin and Peterson were trained by Kilpatrick at the University of Iowa.

Kilpatrick and Loman underwent training in the original intensive course during the Linguistic Institute at Yale University in the summer of 1931. Subsequently both served as fieldworkers for the New England survey.

THE INTERVIEW

In their training, all fieldworkers became familiar with the instructions for conducting an interview as detailed in *The Handbook of the Linguistic Geography of New England*, pp. 45-50.

Although it seems unnecessary to repeat those detailed instructions here, a summary will indicate how the field investigator is expected to interview an informant.

For each interview the fieldworker is equipped with a bound copy of the worksheets and a bound book with pages that are blank except for the left-hand marginal numbers 1-8 to correspond with the item numbers within a numbered section of the worksheets. Each page is recorded in duplicate through the use of a sheet of carbon paper.

Although the items in the worksheets are arranged so as to make possible a semi-conversational approach, a fieldworker has latitude in determining the order in which he asks the questions. Sometimes it is expedient to begin with simple counting so that the numerals, always lexically the same for all informants, can provide a basis for a tentative analysis of the informant's phonemic system and allophonic features. In general, however, questioning begins with items 4 or 5 in section 3.

The fieldworker also has latitude in determining how he elicits the response. One questioning technique, that employed in the Survey of English Dialects but not ordinarily in American fieldwork, seeks to control the interview by the requiring of the fieldworker to read verbatim the question as printed in his workbook. This technique has the advantage of reducing, if not eliminating, the danger that different fieldworkers will ask questions so differently that they will not collect comparable responses. In American fieldwork, however, this is discounted in favor of a freedom that allows a trained fieldworker to exercise his own discretion and ingenuity in seeking a response in different ways best suited to the occasion and the informant, and hence often to obtain relevant information that rigidly controlled questions would not elicit.

In both techniques, however, different kinds of items call for different approaches. The simplest approach is that of pointing to an object within sight of the informant or to a picture and asking, "What do you call that?" Almost as simple is such a question as, "What kinds of vegetables might be grown in a garden?" More difficult to formulate and to use successfully is a question that asks the informant to name what the interviewer describes. A similar question is one that seeks to discover the terms the informant has for various abstract relationships, emotions, and attitudes. Sometimes such a response can best be obtained through use of the unfilled blank, as: "Suppose you have attended the funeral of someone you know and afterward you are asked whether you know the cause of his death. You might say something like this, 'No, I don't know what he ____.'" The informant presumably will complete the sentence with "died of," "died with," or "died from." The success of this device depends in part upon the interviewer's producing an intonation pattern that demands fulfillment and also upon the informant's alertness.

Two kinds of information should never be sought directly. The interviewer should not ask the informant how, for example, he pronounces deaf, for obviously the fieldworker's own pronunciation is likely to have an effect upon the response. Ordinarily matters of pronunciation are sought as if the fieldworker were interested in ascertaining the name for something and not in how the word sounds. In extreme cases a fieldworker may resort to spelling a term and asking how the informant pronounces it. The very act of spelling, however, is likely to put some informants on guard so that if they know two pronunciations they may choose the one they consider more prestigious regardless of their normal practice. A second kind of information not to be sought directly is grammatical. No useful response will be made to such a question as: "Do you ever say 'ain't'?" Very few persons can be objective in reporting their own usage. If a question is needed, the interviewer may either use the completion device or set up a dramatic situation in which the informant presumably will be led to use his particular variant of the desired form without being aware of what the fieldworker actually is seeking.

But the most useful phonological and grammatical information is that provided unconsciously by the informant during free conversation and recorded then or as soon as possible by the fieldworker. The interviewer is expected to draw as much from free conversation as he can, not only for pronunciation and grammar but also for the informant's everyday use of terms which, in reply to a direct question, he might replace with words he considers more formal or proper.

A basic caution the fieldworker is expected to observe is to avoid any manifestation of his personal reaction to any word or pronunciation used by the informant.

Except for incidental information, the responses of the informants are transcribed in a finely discriminating phonetic alphabet. This alphabet, a version of the International Phonetic Alphabet as slightly modified for American use, is described in Volume 2 but the symbols appear in this volume with the abbreviations at the beginning of Part B. A detailed treatment of the alphabet and its use appears in *The Handbook of the Linguistic Geography of New England*.

Whenever appropriate, the interviewer is expected to supplement the actual response by marginal comments, either his own or the informant's, that provide relevant interpretation or significant information.

Additional information about the situation or the informant's response often may be added to the field record through the use of abbreviations and arbitrary symbols. The list is given at the beginning of Part B, The Lexicon, and also in Volume 2. These abbreviations indicate a variety of reactions and attitudes on the part of the informant, such as reluctance, amusement, hesitation, desire to correct a previously given form, belief that the form is archaic or innovative, willingness to respond to a suggestion, and uncertainty or doubt. An asterisk denotes a response provided by the auxiliary informant.

After the formal interview, which may require three or even four sessions, the fieldworker needs to be sure that his file is complete with data about the informant himself and the family background, the community and its characteristics, and the pronunciation of the names of the town and the county. The pronunciation is shown in Volume 2.

In the Upper Midwest about one-half of the interviews were supplemented by a voice recording of spontaneous speech.

The content varies from anecdotes to family and community history, with some occasional philosophizing. Most informants were thus recorded for seven or eight minutes each, but several Type I informants with unusual historical backgrounds were recorded for twenty or thirty minutes.

During the first two years of fieldwork only the Webster wire recorder was available. Subsequently tape recorders of various makes were used, and the original wire recordings were transferred to tape as well. These voice recordings serve primarily as a check upon the transcription practice of the field interviewer, but they have also a value as a source of additional conversational items, both lexical and grammatical.

Glenn, McDavid, and Wilson did not follow their interviews with voice recordings. The voices of their informants were subsequently recorded by Allen.

Unfortunately, the Iowa wire spools and also the later transcribed disks were lost at the time when the assistant director for Iowa left the state. In December, 1968, one-half of the disks, however, were found in the University of Iowa library, and tape recordings were made from them. In October, 1969, Gary Underwood, then assistant editor of the Atlas, made partial interviews, using the worksheet questions, of two Iowa informants still available, one who had originally been interviewed by Hanlin and the other by Peterson. These added recordings, despite the time lapse, were valuable in checking the phonetic transcription of the Iowa fieldworkers.

All the tapes are in the collection in the Atlas headquarters.

FIELDWORKERS' VARIATIONS

In any kind of field investigation that requires subjective judgment of even highly trained and competent interviewers, their individual differences are bound to have some effect upon their work. In dialect research the personal element must be minimized as much as possible, but some variations in the practice of the Upper Midwest fieldworkers should be noted here. Individual differences in phonetic recording will be considered in Volume 2.

Only three of the six regular fieldworkers had had previous experience: McDavid had made 369 interviews; Allen,

'18; and Wilson, 6. The following table shows the sequence of interviews by years.

FW	Year	Serial sequence		Total
Allen	1947	19 --	21	3
	1948	22 --	31	10
	1949	32 --	50	19
	1950	51 --	75	25*
	1951	76 --	84	9
	1952	85 --	98	14
	1953	99 --	116	18
	1954	117 --	119	3
	1956	120 --	121	2
	1957	122 --	123	2
Glenn	1947	1 --	4	4
	1948	5 --	20	16
Hanlin	1950	1 --	24	24
McDavid	1949	370 --	375	6
Peterson	1950	1 --	24	24
Weber	1952	1 --	7	7
	1953	8 --	19	12
Wilson	1951	6 --	13	8

* This figure includes two interviews recorded on wire by Kilpatrick and later transcribed by Allen.

Fieldworkers interviewed specific informants as follows:

Allen: 1-12, 19-31, 33-38, 41-42, 49-50, 54-55, 64-65; 201-26; 301-4, 309-15, 320-28; 401-12, 417-19, 429, 436-37.
McDavid: 13-18.
Glenn: 32, 39-40, 43-48, 51-53, 56-63.
Hanlin: 101-16, 119-21, 137-39.
Lowman: 118, 151.
Peterson: 117, 122-36, 140-49.
Kilpatrick/Allen: 150, 152.
Weber: 413-16, 420-38, 430-35.
Wilson: 305-8, 316-19.

Although some informants, either hurried or taciturn, offer few opportunities for valuable conversational items, fieldworkers also differ widely in their concern for recording them. G was most conscientious and observant in noting spontaneously produced language forms; she averaged 84 per field record. Other interviewers have the following averages for conversational items per field record: M 73, A 56, Wr 54, H 21, Wn 20, and P 11.

Of the fieldworkers, M was least inclined to explore the informant's vocabulary by jogging his memory with a suggested word. Only 3.5 suggested words per interview appear in his records. For the others the average per inter-

For the others the average per interview is: Wn 5.5, P 6.9, A 10.5, H 11.1, G 12.8, Wr 18.3.

Fieldworkers varied considerably in manifesting curiosity about the use of terms by others in the community as a way to supplement the information from the informant. For A, the average per interview of forms marked ⌐ is 15.3; for the others it is as follows: G 14.9, Wr 13.6, P 5.4, Wn 5, H 3.7, and M 2.2.

Great variation appeared also in the fieldworkers' interest in ascertaining older usage and recording old-fashioned terms once used by the informant. G and A have 13.8 and 13.7 respectively, as the average number of terms in each interview marked with the obelisk †. The others average as follows per interview: P 4.5, Wr 3.2, H 2.4, Wn 2.3, and M 0.5.

Although the nature of the vocabulary range exploited by the worksheets almost excludes concern with modern technology and other sources of new words, social change sometimes affects names for familiar things, making some archaic and replacing them with innovations. The process is only weakly represented in the fieldworkers' questions, however, if the incidence of the innovation symbol → is an indication. The average number of occurrences per interview is as follows for each fieldworker: A 3.1, M 2.5, G 1.4, P 0.8, Wn 0.5, H 0.25, and Wr 0.

More than the others, A, M, and G offer detailed marginalia with definitions, descriptions, comments about usage, and the like. P has the fewest marginal notes.

THE SUPPLEMENTARY MAIL STUDY

At the time when the Upper Midwest Atlas project was instituted, Alva L. Davis was using a mailed questionnaire to check the validity of the field responses in the North Central Atlas investigation. His University of Michigan dissertation in 1949, A Word Atlas of the Great Lakes Region, so effectively demonstrated the supplementary and corroboratory value of lexical data obtained by mail that a similar ancillary study was begun in the Upper Midwest.

With Davis's permission, his checklist, slightly modified so as to yield a total of 136 items, was employed in a wide direct-by-mail collection of vocabulary choices.

The checklist component of the Upper

Midwest study is distinctly supplementary and not additive. Although the general picture revealed by fieldwork may be compared with that based upon checklist returns, the precise data from the two separate studies can not be added together. In the second part of this volume the information summarized from one set of data is always kept sharply distinct from that summarized from the other set.

The reason for the lack of congruity between the two sets of data lies primarily in the contrast between the two sets of people supplying the data. As has been described, field informants could be carefully selected by the fieldworker so as to meet the requirements of type and residence. In practice, however, it turned out to be impossible to be that restrictive with respect to mail respondents. Hence they constitute a somewhat amorphous group of Upper Midwest citizens characterized generally as being middle-aged or elderly at the time of the study and also as being lifelong residents of their communities. More than half had received no more than eighth grade schooling; the remainder had some high school education or had gone on to graduate. Only a bare handful had gone to college.

Respondents were reached in a number of ways. Names of likely persons came from students at the University of Minnesota, the University of Iowa, Iowa State Teachers College (now Northern Iowa University), North Dakota State University, the University of South Dakota, and the state teachers colleges at Wayne and Chadron, Nebraska. About sixty county superintendents of schools also contributed names of possible respondents, and others came from a variety of miscellaneous sources. Some were obtained by direct request of a fieldworker who, driving through a community, would stop long enough to locate one or two respondents and leave checklists with them to be filled out later and returned by mail.

The mail survey was carried on during 1951, 1952, and 1953, with some subsequent additional searching in order to fill in lacunae. Exactly two-thirds of the persons invited to participate actually responded with validly filled out checklists. The ultimate total is 1,064 checklists for the five states, so widely distributed that the projected goal of at least two for each of the 401 Upper Midwest counties was almost attained. Only two sparsely inhabited counties in South Dakota and Nebraska lack representation. The total is distributed as follows: Minnesota, 267; Iowa, 256; North Dakota, 135; South Dakota, 178; Nebraska, 228.

Although the checklist returns usually exhibit rather remarkable correspondence with the findings of the field investigations, the contradictory data for a few items raise again the unanswered questions always associated with the use of a questionnaire to be filled out by mail. Is the respondent influenced by the order of the possible terms, so that he is inclined to circle the first or, perhaps, the last in the series? Is he likely to circle a term that is familiar to him through reading or otherwise but that is not actually in his own productive vocabulary? Is he likely to misunderstand the meaning of a term because of the lack of a full description? Such questions do point to an inherent weakness in a mail questionnaire, the weakness due to the absence of the field-worker with his ability to explain what is wanted without suggesting possible answers. The care with which the checklists were prepared and the rejection of those returned lists that obviously failed to meet the requirements (e.g., several respondents circled all the terms in all items) have materially reduced, however, the likelihood that the checklists have only an insignificant value. As a whole, .they proved to be extremely important.

An unforeseen benefit yielded from the checklist returns is that found in the terms voluntarily added by respondents who felt that the suggested words did not include one representing their own usage. These "write-ins" have high validity. They are indicated in the specific lexical treatments in Part B.

CHAPTER 4

The Investigative Instruments

A. THE WORKSHEETS

The key language items used during the fieldwork for the Linguistic Atlas of the Upper Midwest appear below in the same order and form found in the revised edition of the Upper Midwest worksheets, a bound copy of which provided the guidelines for the fieldworker during each interview.

Page numbers of the worksheets are underlined. Item numbers on a page are in plain roman type. For each item the clue word is given -- in italics if sought specifically for its pronunciation, and in roman if sought primarily as a possible lexical or grammatical variant. Suggested context is enclosed with parentheses, and definitions or guiding comments to the fieldworker are enclosed within square brackets.

To make the interview less artificial, the lexical and phonetic items are arranged in conversationally directed topical groups, as in the worksheets of the Linguistic Atlas of New England. Most of the grammatical items are scattered, to be sought directly only as a last resort if they do not occur incidentally during the interview. With very few exceptions the various items are categorized sequentially as follows:

1.1 --	2.5	numerals
3.1 --	5.2	expressions of time
5.3 --	6.5	the weather
6.6 --	10.3	the dwelling
10.4 --	13.6	the farm (with some *verb forms* 10.6 -- 11.2)
13.7 --	15.6	the kitchen; utensils, etc.
15.7 --	20.5	the farm; implements, etc.
20.6 --	21.6	*verb forms*
21.7 --	23.7	clothing and bedding
23.8 --	25.5	typography, roads, etc.
25.6 --	26.2	*prepositions*
26.3 --	32.8	domestic animals and calls to animals
33.1 --	33.4	*adverbial expressions*
33.5 --	34.6	the farm; crops, etc.

34.7 --	35.4	*pronouns*
35.5 --	40.7	food, cooking, mealtime
41.1 --	41.7	*miscellaneous non-vocabulary*
42.1 --	44.9	fruits, vegetables
45.1 --	45.6	*miscellaneous non-vocabulary*
45.7 --	48.8	fauna and flora
49.1 --	53.7	the family; names and nicknames
54.1 --	54.5	*miscellaneous non-vocabulary*
54.6 --	56.3	the human body
56.4 --	57.7	personal characteristics; emotions
58.1 --	61.1	illness; death
61.2 --	61.4	*verb forms*
61.5 --	64.4	social life and institutions
64.5 --	65.4	states and cities
65.5 --	65.7	*miscellaneous non-vocabulary*
66.1 --	67.2	religion; superstition
67.3 --	68.3	*miscellaneous non-vocabulary; greetings*
68.4 --	76.4	*miscellaneous non-vocabulary; activities*

The Upper Midwest worksheets are ultimately derived from those prepared in 1931 for the survey in New England and from the later ones modified for use in the Middle and South Atlantic states. These two sets constituted the corpus from which, in 1937, Hans Kurath constructed a smaller questionnaire used by the fieldworkers directed by Albert H. Marckwardt in beginning the research in the North Central states in 1938. The North Central worksheets, slightly modified by the addition of western terms, next provided the basic questionnaire for the initial field investigation in the Upper Midwest. At that time the "first edition" of the Upper Midwest worksheets contained 584 words and phrases grouped in 529 numbered items on 27 pages. Additions the following year led to a 1950 edition with 659 words and phrases grouped in 576 numbered items. For the western cattle country two more lexical items were added in 1951, making a final total of 661 words and phrases in 578 numbered items. In the following reproduction of the worksheets the date for the addition of any later item is given in brackets.

1. 1 *one; two.* 2 *three; four.* 3 *five; six.* 4 *seven; eight.* 5 *nine; ten.* 6 *eleven; twelve.* 7 *thirteen; fourteen.*

2. 1 *twenty; twenty-seven.* 2 *thirty; forty.* 3 *seventy; hundred.* 4 the *first* (man); the *second* (man). 5 the *fifth* (man); the *sixth* (man). 6 all at *once* to ~. 7 *twice* (as good).

3. 1 *January; February; April.* 2 *Tuesday; Wednesday.* 3 *Thursday; Saturday;* Sabbath. 4 good *morning!* [until what time?]. 5 *afternoon* [the part of the day before supper], evening. 6 evening [the part of the day after supper], night. 7 (We start to work before), night. 7 (We start to work before) sunrise [referring to time of day], sunup. 8 [1949] fortnight.

4. 1 (the sun) rose (at six) [when did the sun rise?], riz, raised, came up. 2 (we work until) sunset [referring to time of day], sundown. 3 *yesterday.* 4 tomorrow. 5 (a gold) *watch.* 6 *half* past seven, ~ after ~. 7 *quarter* of eleven, 10:45, ~ to ~, ~ till ~.

5. 1 *this year.* 2 *a year ago.* 3 (it's) clearing up, clearing, fairing up, fairing off. 4 thunder storm, thunder shower, tempest, storm, electric(al) storm. 5 (the wind) blew (hard), blowed. 6 *fog.* 7 *foggy.*

6. 1 *drought* [get terms for short and long periods], drouth, dry spell. 2 (the wind is) picking up, breezing on, breezing up fresh, getting stronger, rising, raising, coming up, blowing higher, gusting. 3 (it's) letting up, laying, going down, dying down, easing up. 4 (we had a) frost, freeze. 5a (the lake) froze over (last night), friz, skimmed over, scaled over. 5b scum, shale ice, anchor ice, mush ice [first thin coating of ice]. 6a sitting room [where guests are entertained], parlor, front room, living room, best room, big house. 6b [get a list of other rooms in the house]. 7 *chimney.* 8 [1949] kitchen matches [that will strike anywhere], parlor ~, farm(ers') ~.

7. 1 *hearth* [of fireplace or of stove?]. 2 andirons, dogirons, firedogs. 3 mantel shelf, mantelpiece, mantel, tussock,

clock shelf, fire board. 4 back log. 5 *soot.* 6 *white ashes* or *ash.* Ashes is white, ~ are ~. It burns to white ash(es). 7 *chair.* 8 [1949] *furniture.*

8. 1 *sofa* [describe], lounge, couch, davenport, chesterfield. 2 *bedroom,* chamber. 3 window shades [roller shades], blinds, curtains. 4a *clothes closet* [built in], clothes press, closet, press. 4b attic, garret, sky parlor, cock-loft. 6 *kitchen* [describe], porch, cook room, kitchen house, cook house, summer kitchen. 7 pantry, buttery. 8 [1947] storeroom, junk ~, lumber ~. 9 [1949] *bureau,* dresser, chest of drawers.

9. 1 she cleans up (every morning), tidies ~, redds ~, rids ~. 2 *broom.* 3 (the broom is) behind (the door), in back of, tohind, hindside. 4a [1947] file cloth [damp cloth for wiping floor]. 4b [1947] file (the floor) [wipe with a damp cloth]. 5 (who does the) laundry? wash, washing and ironing. 6 *porch* [at front door, at back door; describe construction], gallery, veranda, piazza, balcony, stoop, breezeway. 7 *shut the door,* close ~ ~. 8 (I) drove (in a nail), druv, driv. 9 [1949] weatherboards [define], clapboards.

10. 1 (I have) driven (many a nail), druv. 2 *roof.* 3 eave(s) troughs [built in or suspended?], gutters, spouts. 4 shed [for wood, tools, etc.; separate or built on?], ell, lean-to. 5 [1947] privy [outdoors], backhouse, johnny, biffy, closet, outhouse. 6 I have *heard* it (lots of times) [unstressed have]. 7 (I) haven't (done it) [both stressed and unstressed], ain't. 8 (He) does [stressed], do.

11. 1 he doesn't *care,* don't ~. 2 I have been thinking (about it). 3 *house, houses* [record singular and plural]. 4 *barn* [what is it used for?]. 5 *corn crib* [building for storing corn], corn barn, ~ house, crib. 6 granary [building, or part of a building, for storing grain]. 7 loft [upper part of barn; describe or make sketch], barn chamber, mow, scaffold.

12. 1 [place(s) for hay in the barn; describe], loft, bay, mow, ground mow. 2 hay stack [observe shape and size; outdoors or in barn?], rick, mow, Dutch cap, barrack. 3 haycock [in the field], cock, tumble, doodle, coil, pile, heap. 4 cowbarn [shelter for cows; describe], barn, stable, tie-up, lean-to. 5 hogpen [shelter and enclosure for hogs and pigs; describe] hogrun, hogcrawl, sty, hogboist, hoghouse, pen. 6 dairy. 7 barnyard [where stock is kept or fed], stable lot, cow ~, horse ~. 8 farm, ranch.

13. 1 *pasture* [where cows, sheep, etc., graze], lot, range. 2 picket fence, paling ~, pale ~, slat ~, garden ~, shingle garden. 3 barbedwire fence, bobwire ~. 4 rail fence [describe construction], worm ~, herring bone ~, snake ~, stake and rider ~, straight rail ~. 5 post(e)s [the plural form]. 6 stone wall [of loose stones], rock fence, rock wall. 7 *china* [record also *china egg*], Delf(-ware).

14. 1 bucket [wooden vessel; shape and use], pail. 2 pail [large open metal vessel for water, milk], bucket. 3 garbage pail [describe shape and use], garbage can, swill bucket, ort pail, slop bucket, slop pail. 4 frying pan [flat or round bottom? iron or sheet metal or aluminum? legs?], skillet, spider, creeper, fry pan, fryer. 5 kettle [heavy iron vessel with large opening; shape], pot, caldron. 6 spoon. 7 vase, flower pot.

15. 1 (I must) *wash* the dishes. 2 (she) *rinses* (the dishes). 3a dish rag [for washing dishes]. 3b dish towel [for wiping dishes], dish wiper, tea towel, dry rag. 4 bath *towel*, Turkish ~. 5a faucet [on water pipe at kitchen sink), tap, cock, spigot, spicket. 5b spigot [on barrel], tap, cock, spicket. 6 funnel, tunnel. 7 *whip* [for driving horses? oxen?], hickory, gad, goad, goard. 8a [1949] mouth organ [blown], French harp, juice ~, jew's ~, harmonica. 8b [1949] jew's harp [plucked], juice ~, French ~, breath ~.

16. 1 *bag* [made of paper; size; record paper ~, burlap ~]. 2 *sack* [made of cloth; size], bag, poke. 3 burlap sack, ~ bag, ~ poke, gunny sack, potato ~, grain ~. 4 *barrel* [for flour, meal], gum. 5a turn (of corn, wood, etc.), armful, armload. 5b [1949] jag [partial load on wagon]. 6 clothes *basket*. 7 *keg*.

17. 1 *hoops*. 2 cork [for bottle], ~ stopple, stopple, stopper. 3 *hammer*. 4 tongue [of a wagon], neap, pole, spear. 5 shafts [of a buggy], shavs, thills, fills, drafts. 6 whiffletree [behind one horse], whippletree, swingletree, single-tree. 7 evener [behind two horses], doubletree, spreader, double singletree.

18. 1 (he was) hauling (wood in his wagon), drawing, carting, teaming. 2 *plow*. 3 *harrow* [describe], drag. 4 stone boat [for taking stones from fields], drag, mud boat. 5 sled [for boys; describe types used], bobsled, bob, cutter, double-cutter, double-runner, double-ripper, roller-coaster, pung. 6a sawbuck [for firewood], rack, jack, wood buck, saw-horse, horse. 6b [1949] sawhorse [used by carpenters], horse, rack, trestle, saw-

buck, jack. 7 *brush* [the noun].

19. 1 strop [for sharpening razor], strap, strope. 2 *cartridge*. 3a seesaw, teeter-totter, dandle, tilt(s), tilting board. 3b [1949] flying jenny [home-made merry-go-round], whirligig, flying Dutchman, ricky horse. 3c [1949] juggling board. 4 coal hod, scuttle, coal pail, coal bucket. 5 [1947] (burn coal) in (the stove), into. 6 *wheelbarrow*, trucks. 7 *whetstone* [for sharpening scythe], whet-rock, rifle, rubstone. 8 *grindstone*.

20. 1 grease (the car) [verb]. 2 *greasy*. 3a *oil*. 3b [1949] kerosene, coal oil, lamp oil. 4 (inner) *tube*. 5 (they are going to) *launch* the boat. 6 I am going (today) [is the auxiliary verb omitted?]; we ~ ~; they ~ ~. 7 Am I going (to get some)? ~ they ~ ~?

21. 1 here are (your clothes!) [mother to child], here's. 2 I am not (going to hurt him); ain't; he ~, they ~. 3 (I'm right), am I not? ain't I? 4 we were (going to do it anyway), ~ was, you ~; they ~. 5 no, it *wasn't* me. 6 be you going? [Enter any phrases with *be* as finite verb form]. 7 *apron*. 8 [1949] (the apron) shrank [preterit], shrunk, srunk.

22. 1 *coat*. 2 vest. 3 trousers, pants, breeches, jeans. 4 (I have) brought (your coat), brung, fetched. 5 (his coat) fitted (me), fit. 6 *new suit*. 7 (the pockets) *bulge*. 8 [1947] (the coat has buttons) on (it), onto.

23. 1 *purse* [for coins]. 2 *bracelet*. 3 put it *on* [of a bracelet, piece of clothing, etc.; stressed *on*]. 4 (an old) *umbrella*. 5 bedspread, coverlet, cover-lid, counterpane. 6a quilt [quilted], comforter, comfort. 6b [1949] comforter [tied; filled with ?], comfortable, quilt, puff, hap. 7 pallet [bed on floor], shakedown. 8 [1949] (it goes) clear *across*, clean ~, plumb ~, jam ~.

24. 1 *loam* [rich black soil] loom. 2a *meadow* [low-lying grassland], swale, bayou, bottom land. 2b [1949] (to) meadow (cows) [to put cows to pasture], pasture [get verb]. 3 swamp [define], slough, marsh, bog, gall, pot-hole. 4 [1947] coulee [small depression with usually dry watercourse], draw, seep, swale. 5 creek [small freshwater stream; arrange by size], stream, brook, run, branch, fork, prong, rivulet, riverlet, gutter. 6 [names of streams in the neighborhood]. 7 *mountain*. 8 [1949] butte [define].

25. 1 *wharf* [for passengers and freight; any size distinction?], landing, dock,

pier. 2a cement *road*, concrete ~, hard ~, surface ~, pavement, slab, pike. 2b [1949] [bituminous], tarvia road, tarvy ~, oiled ~, pavement. 3 byway, neighborhood road, back~, side~, lane. 4 (he) threw (a stone at the dog), throwed, chucked, chunked, flung, pitched. 5 (he threw a) *stone* (at the dog), rock, dornick, donnick, doney, canorry, hooney. 6 (he isn't) to *home*, at ~. 7a *without milk* [get pronunciation of both words]. 7b *with* milk [*with* followed by voiced consonant]. 8 [1949] *toward(s)*.

26. 1 (I) ran across (him) [met him], met, ran into, ~ on, ~ afoul of. 2 (We named the child) for him, after ~. 3 *dog*. 4 [call of dog to attack another dog, e.g. *sic 'im*]. 5 [call to summon dog, e.g. *Here, Jack!*]. 6 mongrel, cur, ~ dog, scrub, fice. 7 (he was) bitten (by a dog), bit.

27. 1 bull, animal, beast, male, top-cow, cow-brute, toro, cow-critter [special words used by farmers? special words used by women or in the presence of women, as *gentleman cow*?]. 2 *cow*. 3 (two) yoke(s) (of oxen), pair. 4 *calf* [terms for female? for male?]. 5 (the cow is going to) calve, find a calf, freshen, come fresh, come in, drop a calf, spring. 6 *horse*. 7 (I have never) ridden (a horse), rode. 8 [1949] stallion, stud horse.

28. 1a (he fell) off (the horse) [prep., not the adverb], off of, offen. 1b spook [to shy, of a horse], shy. 2 horseshoes. 3 horseshoe [the game], horseshoes, quoits, quates, quakes. 4 hoofs, hooves. 5 ram, buck sheep, buck, male sheep [special words used by farmers? special words used by women or in the presence of women?]. 6a *ewe*. 6b [1949] bell wether. 7 *wool*.

29. 1 boar, ~hog, male hog, hog, seed-~, breeding ~. [special words used among farmers? special words used for or by women?]. 2 *hogs* [male and female? old and young?]. 3 tusks, tushes. 4 *bristles*. 5 *trough*, troughs. 6 castrate [horses, bull-calves, boars, cats], alter, change, slice, trim, cut, dress, nut. 7 bawl [of calf being weaned], blare, cry, blat, blart, bell.

30. 1a low [during feeding time], moo. 1b [1949] [loud and soft noises of calf]. 2 whinny [during feeding time], whinner, nicker, whicker, neigh. 3 a settinghen, cluck, cluckhen, hatchinghen, brooder. 4 chickencoop [describe], chicken house, hen house. 5 wish-bone, lucky~, pully~, pulling ~. 6 harslet [comprehensive term for edible insides of a pig or calf; distinguish meanings if different], has-

let, chittlins, pluck, skwin, liver and lights. 7 feeding time, fodder ~, chore ~, time to feed, milking time.

31. 1 [calls to cows mark stress and intonation in all calls. Note repetition], co, boss! saw, saw, boss! saw (madam)! 2 [calls to cows from a pasture] co, boss! come, boss! sook! 3 [calls to cows to quiet during milking] saw, boss! so, boss! hoist! 4 [calls to calves] sook, calf! sook, sook! 5 [calls to draft-oxen to direct right or left], gee! haw! 6 [calls to horses from pasture] ku-jack! co-jack! kope! kwope! kwoby! kwowa! curph! (or whistling). 7 [calls to horses to urge them on] get up! gee up! come up! (clucking).

32. 1 [calls to horses to stop them] ho! whoa! back up! 2 [calls to pigs at feeding time] chook, chook! poke! sooie! sook, sook! sookie! nerky! poo-ie! su-boy! kong, kong, kong! 3 [calls to sheep from pasture] co-sheep! co-nan(nie)! kudack! 4 [calls to chickens at feeding] chickie! chick, chick! 5 (I want to) harness (the horses), tackle up, rig up, gear up. 6 *stirrups*. 7 the nigh horse [horse on the left], near ~, lead ~, leader, wheel horse, saddle ~, line ~. 8 [1949] lines [for guiding horses], reins.

33. 1 a little way (down the road), ~ ~ ways, ~ ~ piece, ~ ~ distance. 2 a long way (to go), ~ ~ ways, ~ ~ distance. 3 (you can find that), anywheres, any-where. 4 (we'll not see any more trouble) e'er a bit, nary, at all [any use of *nary*?]. 5 *furrows* [trenches cut by plow]. 6 (we raised a big) *crop of wheat*. 7 (we) cleared (the land), cleared up, swamped out, shrubbed, grubbed out. 8 [1949] bar-row pit [ditch by side of upgraded road], bar ditch, bar pit, borrow pit, grader ditch.

34. 1 second cutting (of clover, al-falfa, etc.), ~ crop, aftermath, rowen. 2 a sheaf (of wheat), a bind, a bundle. 3 (forty) bushel (to the acre), bushels. 4 a shock (of corn, wheat, etc.) [how many bundles?], stook. 5 oats is thrashed, ~ are ~. 6 (two miles is) the farthest (he can go), all the farther, ~ ~ further. 7 (it's) yours, yourn; ours, ourn.

35. 1 (it's) theirs, theirn; his, hisn; hers, hern. 2 (when are) you (coming again), yous, you'ns, you-all [get sing. and pl.]; you-all's [genitive]. 3 who-all (was there?) who-all's [Is it used in any context?]. 5 [usual type of home-made bread; ingredients, shape, size?]. 6 wheat *bread* [in loaves], white ~, light ~, ~. 7 [other kinds of bread made

34

of flour; preparation, shape?], rim, waspnest, riz bread, yeast ~, whole-wheat ~, potato ~, rye, limpa, biscuits, hot rolls, bannocks, poverty cakes, parker house rolls, cloverleaf ~.

36. 1a corn bread [in large cakes], johnnycake, corn pone, pone. 1b [1949] [other types of corn bread], corn sticks, muffins. 2 (home-made bread and) bought-(en) bread, baker's ~, store ~, bakery ~, town ~. 3a doughnut [made with cake dough], friedcake, cruller, fatcake. 3b [1949] raised doughnut [raised], dough-nut, cake ~. 4 griddle cakes [of wheat], pancakes, batter cakes, hot ~, flannel ~, flapjacks, slapjacks, fritters, flit-ters, wheat cakes. 5 (two) pounds (of flour), pound. 6a (a cake of) yeast, east, dry yeast, soft yeast, potato yeast. 6b [1947] spookyeast [define]. 7 *yolk*, yelk, yellow.

37. 1 (the yoke is) *yellow* [name of the color]. 2 *boiled eggs*. 3 poached eggs [how are they prepared?], dropped ~. 4a *sausage*. 4b [1949] dried beef, chipped ~, jerked ~, jerky. 5 *butcher*. 6a (the meat is) *spoiled*. 6b [1949] (the butter is) rancid. 7 headcheese, souse [get liv-er sausage, blood sausage, scrapple]. 8 [1949] salt pork, side of bacon, flitch, sowbelly, bacon [not smoked, but salted; get other bacon terms]. 9 [1949] rind, skin.

38. 1 curdled milk, bonny-clabber, lob-bered milk, clabber, thick milk. 2 cot-tage cheese, pot ~, Dutch ~, smear ~, smear case, clabber ~, sour milk ~, curd. 3 sauce [sweet liquid served over pud-ding], dip, dope. 4 a bite [food eaten between meals], snack, piece, lunch. 5 (we) ate (at six o'clock) [when did you eat?], et, eat. 6 (how often have you) eaten (today?), et, eat, ate. 7 (I'm going to) make (some coffee), cook, boil. 8 [1949] deep (apple) pie, cobbler, deep dish pie, family pie.

39. 1 a *glass of water*. 2 I drank (a lot of it), drunk. 3 (how much have you) drunk? drank, drunken. 4 sit down! [in-vitation to sit down at table; dis-tinguish terms used in addressing rela-tives or friends and those addressed to strangers], draw up, set by. 5 (I) sat down, set. 6 *help* yourself (to potatoes!), take out, take. 7 I don't care for any [when declining food], ~ ~ choose.

40. 1 warmed over [of food], ~ up, het over, ~ up. 2 *chew*. 3 mush, hasty pudding; grits; lye hominy. 4 *vegetables* [home-grown], sass, garden ~. 5 vegetable *garden* [for home use], garden, kitchen ~. 6 *genuine* maple *syrup* [or for *genuine* try

genuine leather], real ~ ~. 7 *jelly*.

41. 1 give me *a(n) apple*. 2 them there boys, them ~, those ~. 3 (it's) over yonder, over there, back yonder, back there. 4 (do it) *this-a-way*. 5 what's that? [when failing to hear an utterance], how's that? how? 6 (he's the man) who owns (the orchard), owns, as owns, that owns. [nominative relative pronoun omit-ted?] 7 (he's a boy) whose father (has a lot of money), that the ~, that his ~.

42. 1 seed [of a cherry], stone, pit. 2 stone [of a peach], seed, pit, kernel. 3 clingstone peach, cling, clinger, plum peach, press ~. 4 freestone peach, clear-seed ~, soft ~, open ~, cleavestone. 5a *core* [of an apple]. 5b [1949] snits [pieces of dried apple]. 6 shell [hard cover of walnut or hickory nut], hull, shuck, husk. 7 hull [green outer cover of walnut or hickory nut], shuck, husk, shell. 8 [1949] peanuts, pinders, goobers.

43. 1 the *oranges* are all gone, the oranges are all. 2 *radishes*. 3 *tomatoes*. 4 *onion*. 5 spring onions, young ~, green ~, shallot, scallion, rareripe. 6 (to) shell (beans), hull, shuck, pod. 7 butter beans [large, yellowish flat seeds, not pods; distinct varieties?] lima ~, sivvy ~, broad ~. 8 [1949] string beans, snap ~, sallet ~, green ~. 9 [1949] greens [edible tops of turnips, beets, etc.], sallad, sallet.

44. 1 husks [on ear of corn], shucks, cap. 2 sweet *corn* [served on cob], sugar ~, mutton ~, green ~. 3 tassel [top of corn stalk], tossel, spindle, top-gallant. 4 *silk* [on ear of corn]. 5 muskmelon, mushmelon, canteloupe. 6 *mushroom*, mush-roon, mushyroon. 7 toadstool, frogstool. 8 [1948] stem rust [on wheat; describe varieties], black rust, red rust. 9 [1949] *squash*, simlin [Does expression *simlin head* occur as epithet?].

45. 1 (he couldn't) *swallow* it. 2 (she was) singing and laughing [enter instances of -n for -ng and instances with the a-prefix], a-singin' and a-laughin'. 3 I *can't* [stressed]. 4 I done worked (all day) [only emphatic]. 5 (he) hadn't ought to [negative of *he ought to*], oughtn't to've. 6 (I) *won't* do it. 7 screech owl, squeech owl, hooowl, hootowl [get local varieties]. 8 [1949] dragon fly, darning needle, devil's darning needle, sewing needle, mosquito hawk, snake feeder. 9 [1949] crawfish, crayfish, crawdad.

46. 1a varmints [define]. 1b [1949] skunk, polecat. 2 ground squirrel [not pocket gopher], gopher, chipmunk, picket pin, quack. 3 woodpecker [get varieties].

4 bullfrog, ~-paddock, ~-paddy, bloody noun. 5 spring frog, spring peeper. 6 toad, toad-frog, hoptoad, warty-toad. 7a earthworm, angleworm, bait, mudworm, red-worm, fishworm, fishing worm. 7b [1949] night crawler [the large variety]. 8 [1947] prairie rattler, mossauger, mas-sauga. 9a [1949] turtle, cooter. 9b [1949] terrapin.

47. 1 *moth, moths* [record both singular and plural]. 2 firefly, lightning bug, fire bug, candlefly, june bug. 3 *wasp* [size, shape, color; nest; sting], yel-lowjacket, dirt-dauber. 4 hornet [size, shape, color; nest; sting]. 5 minnows [a bait], minnies, shiners. 6a spider web [in the house], dust web, cobweb, spider's web. 6b spider web [outdoors], cobweb, spider's web, dew-web, spidernest. 7 roots. 8 [1949] clump [group of trees on the prairie], grove, motte.

48. 1 sycamore, button wood, plane tree, button ball [ignore this item in regions where sycamore is not an in-digenous tree]. 2 *cherry* tree. 3 *poison* ivy, poison oak, poison vine, mercury. 4 *sumach*. 5 *strawberries*. 6 *raspberries*. 7 (some berries are) poisonous, poison. 8a [1947] sugar maple, ~ tree, hard maple, rock ~. 8b [1947] maple grove, sugar bush, sugar orchard, sap bush.

49. 1 (I must ask) my husband, my man, the mister. 2 (I must ask) my wife, my woman, the old woman, the wife, the mis-sis. 3 *widow*, widow-(w)oman. 4 *father*. 5 [What do you call your father? usual term and terms of affection?], ma, maw, mama, mom, mommer, mommy, mother. 7 *parents*.

50. 1 grandfather [usual term and terms of affection?], grandpa, grandpap, grampy, granther, granddad. 2 grandmother [usual term and terms of affection?], grandma, granny. 3 *daughter*. 4 *girl*. 5 baby carriage, ~ buggy, ~ coach, ~ cab. 6 midwife. 7 (the boy) resembles (his father), takes after, favors, features, looks like, is the spittin' image of.

51. 1 (she has) reared (three children), raised, brought up. 2 (Bob) grew (a lot last year), growed. 3 (you've) grown (a lot since I last saw you), growed. 4 bastard [an illegitimate child], woods-colt, catch-colt. 5 nephew. 6 *guardian* [note stress]. 7 *orphan(t)*.

52. 1 (her) relatives, people, folks, kinfolks, home-folks, kinnery. 2 *Mary; Martha*. 3 *Nelly; Billy*. 4 *Matthew*. 5 *Mrs. Cooper* [slow and fast forms of *Mrs*]. 6 *your aunt*. 7 *General* (MacArthur). 8 [1949] jackleg preacher [itinerant min-ister], yard axe.

53. 1 *Judge* (of a court). 2 *student*. 3 *secretary*. 4 postman, mailman. 5 *an American*. 6 *negro* [neutral and derogatory terms], darky, colored man, nigger, coon, shine, smoke, monkey. 7 a rustic [neutral and derogatory terms], mountain boomer, yahoo, hillbilly, cracker, countryman, backwoodsman, jackpine savage, hick, rube, hay-shaker, mossback, clodhopper, hayseed, farmer, country bumpkin.

54. 1 *just* a *minute!* 2 how *far* (is it to...) [*far* followed by a vowel. 3 *look here!* [exclamation; serious or jesting?]. 4 how *often* (do you go to town?). 5 (I'm not going to do it!) Nor I (n)either. 6 *forehead*. 7 (the) *right ear*.

55. 1 *beard*. 2 *mouth*. 3 *tooth; teeth*. hayseed, farmer, country bumpkin.

4 *gums*. 5 *palm* (of the hand). 6 *fists*. 7 *joint*.

56. 1 *chest*. 2 *shoulders*. 3 strong, stout, husky, powerful. 4 (she's) quite lively [of young people? of old people? of both?], right peart, spry, brash, peppy, active. 5 (I'm) afraid, scared, scary, afeared. 6 (she) didn't use to (be afraid) [negative of *used to be*], usen't to be. 7 *careless*. 8 [1949] stingy, tight, chinchy, chintzy.

57. 1 *queer* [what does it mean?]. 2 (don't be so) obstinate, set, sot, pig-headed, bull-headed, stubborn. 3 touchy [easily offended], ficety, testy, touch-ous, fretful, otsny. 4 (he got awfully) angry, mad, het up, ashy, ugly, vigorous, owly, shirty. 5 keep calm, keep quiet, keep cool. 6 tired, exhausted [normal and strong terms], fagged out, perished, beat out, tuckered (out), used up, done up, done out, done in, petered out, killed, whipped, pooped. 7 (he is) worn out, wore out.

58. 1 (she) got sick, took ~, was taken ~. 2 (he) caught a cold, caught ~, took ~. 3 I'm *hoarse*. 4 (he has a) *cough*. 5a (haven't you) taken (your medicine yet?), took. 5b [1949] (I never) took (medicine until last year), taken. 6 *deaf*. 7 he sweat (hard), sweated.

59. 1 *boil* [discharging], cattair. 2 pus, matter, corruption. 3 *wound* [noun]. 4 proud flesh [stress]. 5 (I don't know what) he died of, ~ with, ~ from. 6 cemetery, graveyard, burying ground, burial ground. 7 casket, coffin.

60. 1 (they are in) *mourning*. 2 *don't worry*. 3 rheumatism is (painful), rheumatiz are, rheumatics is/are, etc.

4 *diphtheria*. 5 *jaundice*, yellow ~, janders, yellow ~. 6 *appendicitis*, inflammation of the bowels. 7 vomit [neutral, crude and jocular terms], purge, puke, skin a goat, vomick, upswallow, heave, toss (one's) cookies.

61. 1 (he is sick) at his *stomach*, to ~ ~, on ~ ~, in ~ ~. 2 (he came over) for to tell (me about it), to tell, for tell. 3 I shall be (going next Saturday), I will. 4 we shall be (glad to see you), we will. 4 (he is) courting (her), going with, walking out with, sitting up to, a-talking to, keeping company with, sparking. 6 (she) turned him down [serious and jocular terms], gave him the sack, gave him the gate, gave him the mitten, threw him over, jilted him, kicked him, give him the air. 7 chivaree [noisy, burlesque serenade after wedding; describe local characteristics], serenade, belling, dish-;anning, skimmelton, callathump. 8 [1947] (I'll) go and spank (you), take and spank, spank. 9a [1949] best man, waiter. 9b [1949] bridesmaid, waiter.

62. 1 *married*. 2 the whole crowd [depreciative terms], bilin', kittle and bilin', kit and bilin', kaboodle, kit and kaboodle, gang, mob, lay-out. 3 a *dance*, ball, hoe-down, a German, breakdown, frolic, shindig. 4 (he) skipped class, played hookey, bolted, skipped school, cooked Jack. 5 education. 6 *first class*. 7 *college*. 8 [1947] kaffeeklatch [women's informal afternoon party, usually with coffee], kaffee kalas, coffee party.

63. 1 *library*. 2 *post office*. 3 railroad station, railway station, *depot*. 4 *hotel*. 5 *theater*. 6 *hospital*. 7 nurse. 8a [1947] boulevard [grass strip between sidewalk and street], grass strip, berm, parkway, parking, parking strip. 8b [1949] sidewalk, pavement. 9 [1949] county seat, county site, county town.

64. 1 (on the) streetcar, trolley car, trolley, surface car, tram car, tram. 2 (I) want to get off (at the next stop), want off. 3 Civil *War*, the Rebellion, the War between the States. 4 *law and oder*. 5 *Michigan; Illinois*. 6 *Ohio; Dakota*. 7 *New York* state, York state; *Pennsylvania*. 8 [1947] *Iowa; Minnesota*.

65. 1 [1949] *Wisconsin*; [1949] *Canada*; *Nebraska; Missouri*. 2 *Chicago*; [1949] *St. Paul; Des Moines*. 3 *Detroit*; [1949] *Duluth; Omaha*. 4 *Minneapolis; Washington* [the city]. 5 (it seems) like (he'll never pull through), as if, as though. 6 (I won't go) without (he goes), 'thouten, 'douten, unless, 'lessen. 7 (I like him) 'count of (he's so friendly), because.

66. 1 (they) *joined* (the church). 2 *God* [as pronounced in church]. 3 my *god*! [an oath]. 4 *sermon*. 5 *beautiful*. 6 *music*. 7 *devil* [also veiled and jocular terms], bad man, boogy man, bugger man, black man, old harry, old nick, old scratch.

67. 1 spook, ghost, spirit, haunt, fraid, poky spot. 2 a *haunted* house. 3 (it's) *rather* (cold), kind o', sort o', middling. 4 I'd rather (not go). 5 certainly! [strong affirmation], sure! you bet! of course! surely! 6 yes, sir *or* yes, ma'am [record intonation and stress, both normal and emphatic], yes, yeah, ya. 7 how are you? [to an intimate friend; intonation].

68. 1 how do you do? [to a stranger; intonation]. 2 come again! [to a visitor], come back. 3a [1949] *Merry Christmas*! Christmas gift! 3b Happy New Year! 4 (it) costs (too much), costes. 5 (money is) *scarce*, tight. 6 (the bill is) *due*. 7 (pay) the *dues*.

69. 1 *borrow*. 2 coast lying down, bellybunt, ~-flop, bumps, ~-gut, ~-kachug. 3 somersault, somerset. 4 I swam (across), swum. 5 (he) dived (in), dove, div. 6 (he was) drowned, drownded. 7 (he) clumbed (up the tree), clum, clomb, clim.

70. 1 (I have often) climbed (up), clum, clomb, clim. 2 (she) kneeled (down), knelt. 3 (I'm going to) lie down, lay down. 4 (he) lay (in bed all day), laid. 5 (I) dreamed (all night), dreamt, dremp. 6 I woke up (early), wakened, waked up, roused. 7 stamp (the floor), stomp. 8 [1949] (the baby) creeps, crawls.

71. 1 (may I) take you home? see ~ ~, carry ~ ~, bring ~ ~. 2 *pull*. 3 *push*. 4 I lugged (that heavy suitcase down to the station), packed, toted, hiked, sacked [try to get *tote* in any use, as in *tote-road*]. 5 don't you *touch* it! 6 go bring (me a knife), fetch, get. 7 goal [in children's games]. 8 [1949] hurry up! hurry on!

72. 1 *catch* (the ball!). 2 (who) *caught* (it?), ketched, kotch. 3 (I'll wait) for you (at the corner), on you. 4 *give me another chance*! 5 (in good) *humor*. 6 (I want to) get rid of him, get shet of him. 7 (I have) written (to him), wrote. 8 [1947] rubber band, ~ binder, binder. 9 [1949] (to) address (a letter), back.

73. 1 (I expect an) *answer*. 2 (who) *taught* (you that?), teached, learned. 3 [children's nicknames for one who 'tattles']. 4 pick (flowers), pull, pluck. 5 (that's the one you) gave (me), give. 6 (he) began (to talk), begun, commended, started. 7 (he) ran (away), run. 8 [1949]

fought, fout, fit.

74. 1 (he) came (over to see me), come. 2 (he) saw (me go in), see, seen. 3a (the road was all) torn up, tore up. 3b [1949] (the road was) slippery, slick. 4 (he) done (it last night) [preterit], did. 5 *nothing*. 6 *something*. 7 (it's) *such a* (good one). 8 [1949] might could (do it), might be able to.

75. 1 *always*. 2 *since*. 3 (he did it) on purpose, a-purpose. 4 [affirmation; get intonation], ʔmˋmm, ʔəˋhə. 5 [negation; get intonation], ʔəʔə, ˋʔmʔm. 6 [1949] fought, fit. 7 [1949] might, mought.

76. 1 [1949] chuck hole [depression in road], chug ~, pot ~, hole. 2a [1949] cattywampus, antigodlin, antigoglin, everywhich way, this-a-way and that-a-way, antisigoglin. 2b [1949] sashaying, antigodlin, antigoglin, slabbing, going cattywampus. 3a [1949] marbles, migs, mibs, miggles, mibbies. 3b [1949] starting line [in marbles], taw, ~ line, lag ~, lagging ~. 4 [1949] duck bumps, goose ~, goose pimples, ~ flesh. 5 [1951] cowboy, ~-hand, ~poke, ~puncher, haywaddy. 6 [1951] catch rope, throw ~, lariat, lasso.

B. THE CHECKLIST

When a prospective mail informant was asked to cooperate, he typically replied by a return postcard. He then was sent the checklist, which consisted of one page for personal information and instructions and six pages that contained the items to be checked. These pages are reprinted here.

LINGUISTIC ATLAS OF THE UPPER MIDWEST

State_____ County_____ Town_____

Name_____ Age_____

Highest grade finished in school_____

Birthplace_____ Length of residence
in county_____ Previous places of
residence, with dates_____

Birthplace of father___, father's grand-
father___, father's grandmother___,
mother___, mother's grandfather___,
mother's grandmother___

Have you traveled much outside the
state?____ Where?_____

Occupation(s)_____

Do you speak any other language than
English?___ If so, what is it?_____

For many ordinary things around the house and the farm and in daily living, people in various parts of the country use different words. As people came west from New England, New York, Pennsylvania, and Virginia, they brought with them the words used in their home states. We are trying to find out something about how these different words are used in this part of the country. On the following pages are some of the differences known to occur. Will you help us by recording your own usage?

Directions:
1. Put a circle around that word in each group which you yourself ordinarily use.
2. If you ordinarily use more than one word in a group, then put a circle around each of the words you use.
3. Don't put a circle around any word you do not use, even though it is familiar.
4. If the word you ordinarily use is not listed in the group, then please write it in the space below the item.
5. The words printed in capital letters are there just for explanation.
   Example: TOWN OFFICERS: selectmen, trustees, councilmen, supervisors, commissioners

1. THE PART OF THE DAY BEFORE SUPPER: afternoon, evening
2. sunrise, sun-up
3. sunset, sun-down
4. thunderstorm, thunder shower, tempest, storm, electric storm
5. andirons, dog-irons, fire irons, fire-dogs
6. SHELF OVER FIREPLACE: mantelpiece, mantle, tussock, clock-shelf, fireboard shelf
7. window shades, roller shades, blinds, curtains, shades (ON ROLLERS)
8. UNFINISHED ROOM AT TOP OF HOUSE: garret, attic, loft, cock-loft, sky-parlor
9. close, shut (THE DOOR)
10. LARGE PORCH WITH ROOF: porch, veranda, stoop, portico
11. SMALL PORCH WITH NO ROOF: porch, veranda, stoop, portico
12. CHANNEL FOR RAINWATER AT EDGE OF ROOF: gutters, eavestroughs, eavetroughs
13. SHED FOR WOOD, ETC. -- A SEPARATE BUILDING: wood shed, wood house, tool shed, tool house
14. SHED BUILT ONTO THE HOUSE: wood shed, wood house, tool house, lean-

to, back shed

15. UPPER PART OF BARN USED FOR STORING HAY: loft, mow, scaffold, barn chamber, hay-mow
16. SHELTER AND YARD FOR HOGS: hog house, pig pen, hog run, hog crawl, sty, hog boist
17. YARD ADJOINING BARN: barnlot, feed-lot, barnyard
18. IRON UTENSIL WITH LARGE OPEN TOP FOR BOILING POTATOES, MEAT, ETC.: pot, kettle
19. IRON UTENSIL FOR FRYING: skillet, spider, frying pan
20. LARGE, OPEN TIN VESSEL FOR WATER, MILK, ETC.: pail, bucket
21. WOODEN VESSEL: bucket, pail
22. swill bucket, swill pail, ort pail, slop bucket, slop pail
23. paper sack, paper bag, poke, sack, bag (MADE OF PAPER)
24. burlap sack, burlap bag, gunny sack (MADE OF BURLAP)
25. cork, stopper, stopple, cork-stopple (MADE OF CORK)
26. cork, stopper, stopple (MADE OF GLASS)
27. coal hod, coal scuttle, coal bucket, coal pail
28. FUEL FOR LAMPS: kerosene, oil, coal oil, lamp oil
29. bedspread, coverlet, coverlid, counterpane
30. comforter, puff, comfortable, comfort, tied quilt (TIED, NOT QUILTED)
31. johnnycake, cornbread, cornpone
32. warm over, warm up, heat up (FOOD)
33. WHEAT BREAD IN LOAVES: white bread, light bread, bread, yeast bread, wheat bread
34. doughnut, cruller, fried-cake, fat-cake, raised doughnut (ROUND, FLAT, WITH HOLE IN CENTER, AND MADE WITH BAKING POWDER)
35. doughnut, cruller, fried-cake, fat-cake, raised doughnut (ROUND, FLAT, WITH HOLE IN CENTER, AND MADE WITH YEAST)
36. SWEET LIQUID SERVED WITH PUDDING: sauce, dip, dope, dressing
37. FOOD TAKEN BETWEEN MEALS: a bite, a snack, a piece, lunch
38. headcheese, souse, headsouse, head-meat, panihoss, scrapple, hog-head cheese
39. dutch cheese, smearcase, clabber cheese, clobber cheese, crud, cottage cheese
40. SOUR MILK: clabber, thick milk, curdled milk, clabbered milk, clobbered milk, bonny clabber, blinky milk, sour milk, cruddled milk, cruddy milk
41. TO) shell, hull, pod, shuck (BEANS

42. lima beans, butter beans (LARGE, FLAT, YELLOWISH; NOT PODS)
43. faucet, tap, spigot (OVER A SINK)
44. clean up, redd up, rid up, do up, straighten up, tidy up (A ROOM)
45. seed, stone, pit (OF A CHERRY)
46. seed, stone, pit (OF A PEACH)
47. cling-stone, cling-peach, plum-peach, press-peach
48. GREEN OUTER COVER OF A WALNUT: shuck, husk, shell, hull
49. HARD INNER COVER OF A WALNUT: shell, shuck, husk, hull
50. spring onions, young onions, green onions, shallot, scallion, rare-ripes, multipliers, live-forevers, potato onions
51. vegetable garden, kitchen garden, garden patch, garden
52. GREEN LEAFY COVER OF EAR OF CORN: shuck, husk
53. CORN EATEN ON COB: green corn, sweet corn, roasting-ear, sugar corn, mutton corn
54. wish-bone, pulley-bone, lucky-bone, break-bone
55. PART OF BUGGY: shafts, fills, thills
56. whippletree, whiffletree, singletree, swingletree (FOR ONE HORSE)
57. doubletree, evener, spreader, double singletree, double evener (FOR TWO HORSES)
58. TERM FOR TRANSPORTING WOOD IN WAGON: hauling, carting, drawing, teaming
59. SMALL PILE OF HAY IN THE FIELD: hay-cock, hay doodle, tumble, shock, cock
60. a sheaf, a bind, a bundle (OF WHEAT) PILE OF BUNDLES: shock, stook
61. feeding time, fodder time, chore time, time to feed
62. second crop, second cutting, rowen, aftermath, lattermath, seed crop (OF HAY OR OF CLOVER)
63. THE HORSE ON THE LEFT SIDE: nigh horse, near horse, lead horse
64. DEVICE FOR BREAKING CLODS AFTER PLOWING: harrow, drag
65. DEVICE TO HOLD WOOD FOR SAWING: rack, jack, sawbuck, sawhorse (FOR CORD WOOD)
66. DEVICE TO HOLD WOOD FOR SAWING: trestle, sawhorse (FLAT ON TOP, USED BY CARPENTERS)
67. mongrel, cur, cur dog, common dog, scrub, fice, fiste, no-count
68. NAME FOR SOUND MADE BY COW DURING FEEDING TIME: low, moo, bellow, blat
69. NAME FOR SOUND MADE BY CALF AT FEEDING TIME: blat, blare, bellow, bawl
70. CALL TO COWS: co, boss; saw, saw, boss; saw, madam; sook
71. CALL TO COWS TO MAKE THEM STAND STILL: so, boss; so, wench; here; stand still; histe; hey, there

72. TO CALVE: freshen, come fresh; be fresh, come in
73. CALL TO CALVES: sook, calf; sook, sook; come, calfy; come, boss no special call
74. CALL TO HORSES TO URGE THEM ON: get up, gee up, come up, giddap, giddy up whistle, clucking
75. CALL TO HORSES TO BRING THEM IN FROM PASTURE: co-jack; kwope; kope; come up; call by name, whistle
76. CALL TO PIGS AT FEEDING TIME: chook, chook; poke; suwee; poo-wee; kong, kong, kong; pig, pig; piggy, piggy
77. CALL TO SHEEP TO BRING THEM IN FROM PASTURE: coo-sheep; coo-nannie; coo-nan; kudack; kuday; sheepie
78. CALL TO CHICKENS AT FEEDING TIME: chickie-chickie; chick, chick; chuck-chuck; cut, cut; kip; kit
79. NAME FOR SOUND MADE BY HORSE AT FEEDING TIME: whinny, nicker, neigh, whicker, whinner
80. toadstool, frogstool
81. toad, toad-frog, hop-toad, warty-toad
82. fishworm, angleworm, fishingworm, earthworm, dew-worm, mudworm, redworm
83. lightning bug, firefly, firebug, candlefly
84. WEB OUTDOORS: spider web, spider's web, cobweb, spidernest, dew-web
85. WEB INDOORS: spider web, spider's web, cobweb, spidernest, dust web
86. poison ivy, poison vine
87. sugar maple, sugar tree, hard maple, rock maple
88. PLACE WHERE SAP IS GATHERED: maple grove, sugar bush, sap bush, sugar orchard, sugar maple grove, sugar camp, sugar grove
89. ROAD PAVED WITH CONCRETE: cement road, hard road, surface road, slab, pike, pavement
90. ROAD WITH BITUMINOUS SURFACE: pavement, oiled road, blacktop, tarvia road
91. A SHORT DISTANCE: a little way, a little piece, a little ways
92. FAMILIAR TERM FOR FATHER: pa, paw, pop, popper, papa, pappy, pap, dad, daddy
93. FAMILIAR TERM FOR MOTHER: ma, maw, mom, mama, mammer, mammy
94. widow, widow lady, widow woman
95. raised, brought up, reared, fetched up (OF CHILDREN)
96. relatives, people, folks, kin, kinfolks, home-folks, relation, family, relations
97. country jake, hayseed, country gentleman, mossback, yahoo, mountain-boomer, clodhopper, countryman, backwoodsman, hick, pumpkinhusker, railsplitter, jackpine savage
98. resembles, takes after, favors, features, looks like (HIS FATHER)
99. teeter-board, teeter, dandle, teeter-totter, tinter-board, tilt(s), teetering board, teetering horse, see-saw
100. quoits, quates, horseshoes (THE GAME)
101. HE THREW a stone, a rock, a dornick, a donnick, canorry (AT THE DOG)
102. mid-wife, granny-woman, godmother
103. NOISY CELEBRATION AFTER A WEDDING: belling (bee), horning (bee), chivaree, serenade, skimmiton
104. LIVELY (APPLIED TO OLD PEOPLE): active, quick, brash, peart, spry, quick stepper, sassy, peppy
105. LIVELY (APPLIED TO YOUNG PEOPLE): active, quick, brash, peart, quick stepper, sassy, peppy
106. OBSTINATE: set, sot, pig-headed, bull-headed, headstrong, ornery, contrary, stubborn, owly, otsny
107. mad, het up, ashy, ugly, hot, riled, roiled, wrathy, owly
108. fagged out, all in, played out, perished, beat out, tuckered
109. used up, done up, done out, petered out, killed, give out
110. TO: get sick, take sick, be taken sick
111. TO: take cold, catch a cold, catch cold, get a cold
112. TO: court, go with, walk out with, sit up to, talk to, keep company with, spark with
113. TO: turn him down, give him the mitten, throw him over, jilt him, kick him, give him the bounce, give him the air, give him the cold shoulder
114. TO: skip class, skip school, play hookey, play truant, run out of school, slip off from school, cook Jack, bolt
115. bad man, bugger man, boogey man, black man, old nick, old harry, old scratch
116. TO COAST LYING DOWN: belly-bunt, belly-bust, belly-bump, belly-gut, belly-flop, belly-down, belly-grinder, belly-kachug
117. TO CARRY: lug, pack, tote, hike (A HEAVY SUITCASE)
118. rubber binder, rubber band
119. GRASS STRIP BETWEEN SIDEWALK AND STREET: boulevard, boulevard strip, parkway, parking, sidewalk plot, parking strip, berm
120. baby buggy, baby carriage, baby coach, baby wagon, baby cab
121. sitting room, big house, parlor, front room, living room, best room
122. griddle cakes, pancakes, batter cakes, hot cakes, flannel cakes,

flapjacks, slapjacks, fritters,
flitters
123. INSTRUMENT TO BE BLOWN: french
harp, breath harp, mouth harp,
mouth organ, harp, harmonica, juice
harp, hew's harp
124. INSTRUMENT HELD BETWEEN THE TEETH
AND PLUCKED: french harp, breath
harp, juice harp, jew's harp, mouth
harp, harp
125. THE ROAD IS: slippery, slick
126. yeast, everlasting yeast, liquid
yeast, holy water, dry yeast, soft
yeast, spook yeast, potato yeast
127. dried beef, chipped beef, jerked
beef, jerky
128. DITCH BY THE SIDE OF A GRADED ROAD:
bar pit, barrow pit, borrow pit,
bar ditch, barrow ditch, borrow
ditch, grader ditch, ditch, gutter
129. SLIGHT DEPRESSION, SOMETIMES WITH
LITTLE STREAM: draw, seep, swale,
coulee
130. SWAMPY GROUND WITH SMALL STREAM
RUNNING THROUGH IT: slough, swale,
draw, seep, marsh, swamp
131. MEAT FROM SIDES OF HOG, SALTED BUT
NOT SMOKED: salt pork, side pork,
flitch, bacon, sowbelly, side meat,
middlin meat, middlin
132. FIRST THIN COATING OF ICE ON LAKE
OR POND: scum, anchor ice, mush ice,
shale
133. HOLES IN ROADS: chuck holes, chug
holes, pot holes, holes
134. GOING FROM SIDE TO SIDE: sashaying,
antigodling, antigogling, slabbing,
going cattywampus
135. duck bumps, goose bumps, goose
pimples, goose flesh
136. IN MARBLES: starting line, taw,
taw line, lag line, lagging line

CHAPTER 5

Communities, Informants, and Respondents

COMMUNITIES AND FIELD INFORMANTS

INTRODUCTORY COMMENT

Interpretation of the data of linguistic geography is facilitated by some knowledge of the history and character of the communities investigated and of the ancestry, education, life, and personality of the informants. This information is present here in condensed and abbreviated descriptions.

Communities are not numbered; informants are numbered as follows: Minnesota, 1-65; Iowa, 101-149; North Dakota, 201-226; South Dakota, 301-328; and Nebraska, 401-435. Numbering for each state begins in the northwestern corner and moves serially from west to east in successive rows. Exceptions (151, 152, 326, 327, 328, 436, and 437) are due to the making of some field records after the initial survey. The five Canadian informants are included in the North Dakota and Minnesota series. The location of each informant is indicated by the place of his serial number on the base map, Page x.

Information about the communities appears as follows:

1. The county name, in capital letters; the town or city name, underscored; and the number(s), in parentheses, assigned to the informant(s) from that county. For the informant's pronunciation of his community and the county see Volume 2.
2. The date(s) of settlement, organization, or incorporation.
3. Provenience of the settlers.
4. Description of the community at the time of the interview, including notes on its economy and characteristics of the population. This information is based largely upon the fieldworker's notes made when he was in the community.
5. Population figures. These are given for the first census that includes that community, the census of 1950, and the selected intervening censuses that best indicate rate of growth.
6. Bibliographical notes on community history. These are not exhaustive. Some

items, such as pamphlets, newspapers, and locally published books, may be unavailable except in the community library.

The community sketch is followed by the *vita* of each informant interviewed there. The number of each *vita* is that assigned to the informant on the maps of the Atlas. When two or more informants are listed for that same community the number of the informant who is the most old-fashioned and, usually, the oldest is entered first. The most modern and, usually, the youngest is entered last.

The *vita* for each informant contains the following information, so far as it is available in the record submitted by the fieldworker:

1. The occupation of the informant.
2. The informant's date of birth.
3. Birthplace. If none is listed, the informant may be presumed to have been born in the community.
4. Any residence outside the community, and its duration.
5. Birthplace of parents (F = father; M = mother).
6. Birthplace of immediate ancestors (PFG = paternal grandfather; PGM = paternal grandmother; PGP = paternal grandparents; MGF = maternal grandfather; etc.).
7. Education. Occasionally, significant informal educational influence is noted.
8. Social contacts; church affiliation and club membership; community involvement.
9. Personality as seen by the fieldworker; temperament, interests, habits.
10. Speech and paralinguistic features; awareness of regional differences; attitude toward language usage.
11. Voice recording. Wire and tape recordings were made of the free conversation with selected informants; this fact is noted for each by the symbol VR-Wr (i.e., voice recording made by Weber), etc. Scholars may consult these record-

ings in the Atlas office.

12. Identification of the fieldworker making the interview, the serial number of the record, and the date of the interview. Fieldworkers are denoted by initials: A = Allen, G = Glenn, H = Hanlin, L = Lowman, M = McDavid, P = Peterson, Wr = Weber, Wn = Wilson. The serial number locates the particular record in the sequence of all field interviews made by the interviewer in this atlas project or any other; it thus enables the reader to distinguish between early and late records made by the interviewer. For example,

A 39 (1949) means that the interview was the thirty-ninth ever conducted by Allen and that he made it in 1949.

An occasional *vita* contains information about an auxiliary informant whose contributory responses were recorded and are included in the tabulation, where they are always marked by *. Auxiliary informants are not separately numbered. Such an informant is usually a relative living in the same house and having characteristics and background comparable with those of the principal informant.

MINNESOTA (WITH CANADA)

(1) PROVENCHER ELECTORAL DISTRICT, MANITOBA, CANADA

Sprague. Originally (1901) RR shipping point for lumber. With gradual deforestation settlers, chiefly Swedish and Norwegian, moved in from neighboring Roseau Co., Mn.--Present farm community includes 6 twps. Sprague itself consists of one store, a filling station, a cafe (owned by inf. and run by daughter), and a 3-teacher HS.--Pop. '21, 1036; '49, c600.

1. Retired RR agent and telegraph operator; farmed 2 yrs.--B. 1886 Emerson, 62 m. w.; lived in Duluth, Mn. 1 yr. as child; to Sprague, 1901.--F b. Bedfordshire, Eng.; to Ont. 1867; to Man. 1870. M b. Sarnia, Ont. MGP b. Eng.--Rural sch.; reading limited to newspapers and a few periodicals.--As station agent met a variety of people who would come to a pioneer lumbering community; ill health limits social contacts, but still active on community council; United Ch. of Can. --Mentally alert; discusses current issues clearly; open-minded, friendly, cooperative.--Enunciation weak, especially of both initial and terminal consonants, perhaps because of partial deafness. Wide allophonic range of /ɑʊ/ before voiceless consonants. Untroubled by notions about 'correct' grammar, but has many standard forms.--A 39 (1949).

(2) RAINY RIVER COUNTY, ONTARIO, CANADA Became Judicial Dist., 1914.--Lumbering, fishing, some farming, iron mining. Many game reserves.--Sparse pop.

Fort Francis. Inc. 1903.--Settled c1870; originally a fur-trading post and military post, first permanently settled by English and Scottish.--Although some farming remains, chief industries are lumbering and wood-pulp mfg.; some mining

and cement and building-stone works; current mixed pop. includes Ukrainians and other s.e. Europeans brought as mill workers after WWI. Many American summer tourists.--Pop.: '01, 697; '11, 1981; '21, 2290; '31, 5470; '50, 5897.

2. Housewife.--B. 1889.--F b. Hamilton, Ont. PGF b. Cornwall of Scottish ancestry; PGM b. Eng. M b. Birmingham, Eng.-- HS 3 yrs.--Active in women's work of Anglican Ch.; OES.--Pleasant, quiet, eventempered, somewhat reticent, with gentle sense of humor; volunteered no information and declined voice recording. Speech slow, even, clearly enunciated, with weak offglides and rather advanced low back vowel. Grammar tends to be formally 'correct'.--A 41 (1949).

(3) THUNDER BAY COUNTY, ONTARIO, CANADA Became Territorial Dist. 1871.--Fishing, hunting, mining. Small area given to agriculture; dairying near the cities.

Fort William (Paipoonge Township). Established as trading post 1678. Settled from e. Can., Eng., and Scot. Modern development began with arrival of RR in 1885. Became center for grain trade as head of Canadian navigation on Great Lakes and RR center.--Flour mills, fishnet factories, brickyards, pulp and paper mills. Surrounding area rich in minerals. Collegiate Institute.--Pop.: '81, 690; '01, 3633; '21, 20,541; '31, 26,277; '50, 30,585.

3. Farmwife.--B. 1874 Leicestershire, Eng.; to Prince Arthur's Landing, now Port Arthur (Fort William's twin city), 1883; to Fort William, 1909.--F b. Aberdeen, Scot.; to Can., 1883. PGP b. Scot. M b. Eng.--Equivalent of 8th gr. Fairly well read; husband left her an extensive personal library.--Active in Presbyterian Ladies' Aid and local hist. soc.;

knows most older residents. Hospitable and responsive, though not loquacious. Memory of dates and names erratic but otherwise in full mental vigor. Much interested in interview.--Rate of speech variable; distinct. Canadian features are [ɐʊ] before voiceless consonants, /raðər/ /ɑnt ɑɪ/, and some lexical items. Inconsistent weak retroflexion with /ər/. Nonstandard grammatical forms usually paralleled by standard forms.--VR-A--A 50 (1949).

(4) ROSEAU COUNTY
Org. 1894.--Forested area with no urban center. Small communities and farms; lumbering, fishing, and trapping. Many farmers cut lumber or trap furs during the winter. Pop. mainly Norwegians, with some Swedes, Slavs, and Germans.--Pop.: '00, 6694; '20, 13,305; '50, 14,505.--Chapin, E. B., "The Early History of the Roseau Valley," *Mn. Hist.* 24.318-27 (1943). Durham, J. W., *Minnesota's Last Frontier*, Minneapolis, 1925. Eschambault, A., *Discovery of Lake of the Woods*, Roseau, 1937.

Roseau. Settled 1890's by Scandinavians. Some German settlers and a few from e. US arrived later.--Trading center for a diversified farming area. Largely Protestant with 13 chs. Co. seat.--Pop.: '00, 301; '20, 1012; '50, 2231.

4. Housewife and pastry cook.--B. 1892 Sweden; to Roseau, 1893.--F and M b. Sweden.--4th gr.--President of Ladies' Aid of Lutheran Ch., but limited social contacts.--Pleasant, hard-working, ambitious for children, who are HS graduates. --Helpful in interview, but had difficulty with 'completion' questions--Speech distinct, with weak offglides; traces of parents' Swedish in pitch and stress, unguarded pronunciation of early-learned words, and syntax, e.g. "He called him for a fool." Grammatical forms close to standard, perhaps through influence of children. Though not an observer of differences, she remembered forms now out of date.--VR-A--A 40 (1949).

(5) KOOCHICHING COUNTY
Org. 1906.--Forested area mostly taken up by game preserves and an Indian reservation. Little agriculture, because of the problem of drainage and clearing. Farmers cut lumber and trap furs in the winter. Lumber and tourists are chief sources of income. Large foreign-born pop. is mainly Swedish, Norwegian, and German. Sparse pop. concentrated along the Rainy R.--Pop.: '10, 6431; '20, 13,520, '50, 16,910.

International Falls. Inc. 1909.--Settled late 1880's and early 90's by English and Canadian homesteaders. Early community contacts were with Kenora and then Fort Frances, Ont. In early 1900's and after WWI, newcomers from Poland, the Ukraine, and Scandinavia came to work in the paper mill, the city's major industry.--Summer tourist trade important. Co. seat.--Pop.: '10, 1487; '20, 3488; '50, 6269.--*International Falls Echo*, Anniversary no., Jan. 5, 1956.

5. Housewife, former bookkeeper.--B. 1898.-- F b. Scotland; came here in 1881. M b. Scotland of Scottish and Irish ancestry; came c. 1890.--4th gr.--Little social life; always at home to care for aged father, one of the community's first settlers; older sister was first white child born here. Roman Catholic.--Bouncy, genial, cooperative; slow to answer 'completion' questions.--Speech distinct; diffident with interviewer. Volunteered local forms different from her own. Proud of command of standard grammar and avoidance of ain't.--VR-A--Aux. inf.: Husband, c. 55.--B. N.D. of Danish parentage. Farmed in N.D. until 1925, when he came to International Falls to work in the paper mill. Supplied farm terms unknown to his wife.--A 42 (1949).

(6) COOK COUNTY
Org. 1883.--Co. almost entirely wooded wilderness, mostly 2nd-growth timber, from Lake Superior to Canadian border. Except for logging camps and, in summer, resorts and hunting lodges, pop. is concentrated along shore of Lake Superior, where fishing has been an important industry. Large percentage of the pop. Norwegian.--Pop.: '80, 65; '90, 98; '20, 1841; '50, 2900.

Grand Marais. Town founded by PGF and uncle of inf. Once a thriving lumber port with current revival through pulpwood shipping. Other income from commercial fishing and summer tourists. Largest community in Co. and Co. seat.--Pop.: '10, 355; '20, 443; '50, 1078.

6. Co. official; former lake steamer purser, guide, cook, and customs officer. --B. 1879.--F b. Pa. of colonial ancestry; to Mi.; to Nb.; to Mn. M b. De. of English stock; to Mi.; to Mn.--HS less than 1 yr. Assiduous newspaper reader.-- As 1st white child b. in Co. he played only with Chippewa children. Later unusu-

al variety of social contacts, but not in organizations. Alert, dynamic, rugged. Friendly and cooperative despite thinking interview silly. Keen sense of humor; judicious observer of people.--Speech distinct and free from peculiarities. Moderate tempo. Aspiration weak, even with initial voiceless stops. Marked retroflexion, affecting preceding vowel. Aware of, but not attentive to, regional differences. Not concerned about 'correctness.'--A 19 (1947).

(7,8,9) POLK COUNTY
Org. 1872.--Part of the Co., in the Red River Valley, is well known for its hardy spring wheat; now farming is more diversified. In 1890 almost half the pop. was foreign-born, mostly Norwegian. Later immigration added Swedes and Germans.--Pop.: '60, 240, '80, 11,433; '90, 30,192; '20, 37,090; '50, 35,900.--Holcombe, R. I., *Compendium of History and Biography of Polk Co.*, Minneapolis, 1916. *History of the Red River Valley Past and Present*, Grand Forks, N.D., 1909. McLellan, H. D., *The History of Polk County*, M.A. thesis, Northwestern Univ., 1928.

Gentilly. Settled c1880 by 2 French families from Que. Prov. Can.; descendants maintain French dialect differences between Montreal and Quebec city patois.-- Declining village, the center of a French Catholic parish 10 m. e. of Crookston at e. edge of Red River Valley. Cohesive community, with almost no 'outsiders.' Crops: Hay, wheat, barley.--Pop.: '90, 514 (twp.), '20, 502; '50, 421.

7. Hay-farmer; rural teacher 3 yrs.; carpenter, rural mail carrier 20 yrs.-- F and M b. near Montreal, Can., of French ancestry; to Gentilly, 1881.--Rural sch.; business sch., Crookston, 3 winters; reads daily paper, religious journal, Life.--A bachelor; social contacts very limited. Roman Catholic.--Uneducated, but alert and open-minded. Diffident, modest, friendly.--Speech clear, slow, and retaining some French influence in pronunciation and stress. Offglides often imperceptible. Tries to observe some remembered grammar shibboleths.--VR -A--A 37 (1949).

Fisher. Homesteaded late 1870's. Village 10 m. w. of Crookston; predominantly Scandinavian and German, but inf. lives in nearby farming area settled by Presbyterian Scottish Canadians; strong local pride in "Scottishness."--Pop.: '80, 583; '90, 385; '20, 654; '50, 302.

8. Farmer.--B. 1889.--F and M b. Ont.,

Can., of Scottish ancestry; to Fisher, 1889.--Rural sch.; Northwestern Sch. of Agriculture, Crookston, 3 yrs.--Presbyterian. Member Farm Bureau; Mason; pres. of Robert Burns Soc.--Affable and cooperative.--Speech clear and unaffected, with very weak offglides and sharply articulated final consonants. Occ. offered a conventional grammatical form and then used another in conversation, as in 70.3 and 73.7. Also: "If he'd a' broke it."-- VR-A--Aux. inf.: Wife, of similar age, stock, and background.--A 36 (1949).

Crookston. Inc. 1879.--Some of early settlers from e. US, but bulk were French Canadians, with later influx of Scandinavians and some Germans and others from central US. French descendants acutely proud of their ancestry.--Prosperous commercial and shipping center for diversified farming area in the Red River Valley. Co. seat. Northwestern Sch. of Agriculture.--Pop.: '80, 1227; '90, 3457; '20, 6825; '50, 7352.--Crookston Diamond Jubilee Committee, *Crookston's 75 Yrs. 1879-1954*, Crookston, 1954. Seixas, F. L., "Crookston, the Queen City of the Red River Valley," *Northwest Mag.* 19. no. 9 10-15 (1901). Smalley, E., "A Visit to the 'Queen City' of the Red River Valley," *Northwest Mag.* 7. no. 12. 18-22 (1889).

9. Physician.--B. 1903.--F b. near Montreal, Que., of French ancestry; to Gentilly, 1878. M b. near Montreal, Que., of French ancestry; to New York City; to St. Paul; to Crookston about age 16.-- M.D., Univ. of Mn. Medical Sch. Well informed; widely read.--BPOE; Roman Catholic. Social and civic contacts with whole range of the pop.--Highly socialized; gregarious; genial and uninhibited. Intensely interested in the investigation. --Speech clear and distinct; moderate tempo. Weak offglides and strong retroflexion. Grammar generally standard, though he remarked that his bilingual background sometimes put him at a disadvantage. Once or twice knew only the French term. Familiar with local speech differences; careful to distinguish between own usage and that heard from others.--VR-A--Aux. inf.: Wife, of similar age and stock; to Crookston c1920 from Upper Peninsula of Mi.--A 38 (1949).

(10) BELTRAMI COUNTY
Org. 1871-97.--Much of Co. consists of game reserves and an Indian reservation. Lumbering, tourist trade, and dairy farming are important. Most of the pop. of Scandinavian or German ancestry.--Pop.: '70, 80; '90, 312; '20, 27,079; '50, 24,962.

Bemidji. Lumbering town in late 1890's and 1900's with a varied foreign and native pop.--Some of the lumbermen remained as settlers, but pop. now mainly Scandinavian and German. Trade center for farming, dairying, and summer recreation district. Co. seat. State college. --Pop.: '00, 2183; '20, 7086; '50, 10,001.--Geil, E., H. Carlson, & C. Warner, *Round Table Discussion of Early Bemidji*, Bemidji, 1952. Hagg, H. T., "Bemidji. A Pioneer Community of the 1890's," *Mn. Hist.* 23.24-34 (1942). Solis, R. F., "Town Building in Minnesota," *Northwest Mag.* 17.20-22 (1899).

10. Housewife; postal clerk 18 yrs.--B. 1889 Willmar; to Bemidji, 1899.--F b. Il.; to In.; to Mn., 1877. PGP b. Pa. M b. St. Cloud; to Bemidji, 1889. MGF b. Ire.; PGM b. Can.--8th gr.--Active in women's work of Catholic Ch. and as Scout mother and Forester.--Sociable, kind, intelligent, with ready responses. --Speech clear and forceful, with rather deliberate articulation of single words. Grammatical forms mostly standard. Aware of regional and local variants.--VR-A--A 43 (1949).

(11,12) ITASCA COUNTY
Org. 1887.--Forested area with a game refuge and an active tourist trade. Some farming and also pulp cutting of 2nd-growth timber. Many Finns and Swedes.--Pop.: '60, 97 (incl. Beltrami Co.); '70, 96; '90, 743; '20, 23,876; '50, 33,321.

Grand Rapids. Only a lumbering community in 1870's, with Swedes, French Canadians, Germans, and Irish predominating, but with some 'Yankees' from Mi. lumber camps.--Pop. now has large number of Finns. Market center, paper mfg., and summer tourist recreation.--Pop.: '90, 2914 (twp.); '20, 2914; '50, 6019.-- Rossman, L. A., *Fifty Years: A Church and a Community*, 1940. Smalley, E. V., "Grand Rapids, Minnesota, Rail, and Water Transportation, Timber, Iron, Waterpower and Agricultural Lands," *Northwest Mag.* 11.18-24 (1893). Writers' Program, *Logging Town: the Story of Grand Rapids, Minnesota*, 1941.

11. Housewife; former hotel operator.-- B. 1873; to Aitkin, 1879; to Minneapolis, 1909; to Grand Rapids, 1919.--F b. Me.; to Mn., 1865; built stopover loghouse on site of Grand Rapids for travelers to lumber camps. PGP b. Me. M b. White Oak Point of Chippewa Indian ancestry.--HS 3 yrs. Recently visited Calif.--Very active socially, especially in Catholic women's circle.--Extraordinarily dynam-

ic, forthright, outspoken, well known and liked in community. Thought interview silly but cooperated alertly.-- Speech strong and forceful; moderately rapid but with good control of rate variation. Frequently weak retroflexion; said her Me. father talked that way.-- VR-A--A 48 (1949).

12. Co. official; former police officer. --B. 1892 Mi.; to Grand Rapids at 5 mos. --F and M b. Mi. of Irish ancestry.--HS; US Army in France, WWI.--Occupation has led to many social contacts; well known in community. American Legion, VFW, KC, Roman Catholic.--Sanguine, friendly, helpful. Few conversational items, since lack of time hurried the interview.-- Speech distinct, with exaggerated slowness in single-word responses. Offglides weak or, after checked stressed vowels, missing altogether. Some nonstandard grammar; hardly speech-conscious, though he responded with /t/ in often but never used it in conversation.--VR-A--A 49 (1949).

(13,14,15,16,17,18) ST. LOUIS COUNTY
Org. 1856.--Forested area which became important for iron mining in the '80's, With opening of mines, large numbers of Finns and Slavs moved into the area. In 1890 more than half the pop. was foreign-born; even now a large percentage is foreign-born.--Some farming, lumbering, and a large tourist trade. Large part of co. is in national forests and game preserves.--Pop.: '60, 406; '70, 4561; '90, 44,862; '20, 206,391; '50, 206,062.--Carey, J. R., "History of Duluth and of St. Louis County to the Year 1870," *Mn. Hist. Soc. Coll.* 9.241-78 (1901). Culkin, W. E., *St. Louis County, Minnesota Chronology from the Earliest Times to, and Including the Year, 1900*, Duluth, 1924. Van Brunt, W., ed., *Duluth and St. Louis County, Minnesota. Their Story and People*, Chicago & New York, 1921. Woodbridge, D. E., *History of Duluth and St. Louis County*, Chicago, 1910.

Virginia. Inc. 1894.--Platted 1892 at the height of the Mesabi Iron Range boom; original dominant lumbering and sawmill industry was replaced gradually by iron mining with workers chiefly of Scandinavian and Finnish origin, secondary from s.e. Europe.--Pop.: '00, 2692; '20, 14,022; '50, 12,486.--Fawcett, G., *Queen City of the Iron Range*, Virginia (series of radio talks, no. 9), Duluth. Hannaford, W. E., *Iron Ranges of Minnesota*, historical souvenir of *The Vir-*

ginia Enterprise, 1909. *Mountain Iron Golden Jubilee*, 1890-1940, Virginia, 1940. Landis, P. H., *Cultural Change in the Mining Towns. A Sociological Study of Three Mesabi Iron Range Towns, Eveleth, Hibbing, and Virginia*, Minneapolis, 1935. Sirjamaki, J., "The People of the Mesabi Range," *Mn. Hist.* 27.203-15 (1946). Skaurud, M., "A History of Virginia, Minnesota," M.A. thesis, Univ. of Mn., 1941. *The Virginia Story, Historical Souvenir Booklet of the Virginia Centennial Celebration*, July 14-17, 1949. Webb, J. W., "An Urban Geography of the Minnesota Iron Ranges," Ph.D. thesis, Univ. of Mn., 1958.

<u>13</u>. Co. official.--B. 1893 Ely, 44 m. nw.--F b. Croatia; to Mn., 1886. M b. Hungary of German descent; to Mn., 1888. --HS.--Many social contacts; LOOM, Swedish Lutheran Ch.--Affable; talkative and anecdotal. Cooperated to the extent of postponing a fishing trip to finish interview.--Speech rapid, with nasality and unexpected variations in voicing and unvoicing of consonants. Many nonstandard forms.--VR-A--M 374 (1949).

<u>14</u>. Insurance counselor (woman).--B. 1902.--F and M b. Finland; M to Virginia on 2nd train to reach community.--HS; business college.--Many business contacts. Active Lutheran.--Warm and friendly; proud of Finnish heritage, but is no not 'professional' Finn (perhaps because of marriage to a Scandinavian-American). --Speech slightly nasal. Little evidence of foreign language background except that voiceless consonants are often lenis where normally greater fortisness is expected, and normally voiced lenis sounds are often voiceless throughout.--VR-A--M 375 (1949).

<u>Duluth</u>. Inc. 1887.--Originally (1753-1847) a French fur-trading post. Settled c1854 by miners and prospectors from n. Mi. and s. Mn. After being nearly deserted, suddenly expanded in 1866 with discovery of gold-bearing quartz at Lake Vermilion and news that terminus of new RR from St. Paul was to be located there. Pop. included lumbermen from Me., settlers from the central US, and later many immigrants, from Finland, Scandinavia, and central Europe.--Dynamic, major port for the Midwest; shipping point for iron ore. Some local industry. Co. seat. Branch of Univ. of Mn.--Pop.: '60, 71; '70, 3131; '90, 33,115; '20, 98,917; '50, 104,511.--Carey, J., *History of Duluth and Northern Minnesota*, Duluth, 1898. "Duluth Centennial 1856-1956," Duluth News Tribune, Souvenir Ed., June 29,

1956. "Fifty Years of Progress, 1883-1933" *Duluth Herald*, April 10, 1933. Leggett, W. F., *Duluth and Environs*, Duluth, 1895. Macdonald, D. M., *This Is Duluth*, Duluth, 1950. Phelps, W. F., "The Rise and Progress of a Great Trade Center--Duluth," *Mag. of Western Hist.*, 9.148-62 (1888-89).

<u>15</u>. Marine engineer.--B. 1871; lived in Portland, Or., 1910-15.--F and M b. Eng. --7th gr.--Little social life; no lodge membership. Episcopal Ch.--Rugged, hardworking veteran of yrs. of Lake Superior and Duluth harbor navigation; still on night shift as tugboat engineer. Sure of position in community; no pretensions. Cooperative and friendly. Deafness retarded pace of interview, although inf. talked freely about many topics.--Speech high-pitched, clearly enunciated. Post-vocalic retroflexion varies from strong to zero. Fairly strong stress. No /o/-/ɔ/ contrast before /r/. Despite family's amusement was unabashed in use of archaic folk forms.--VR-A--M 372 (1949).

<u>16</u>. Widow.--B. 1872; lived a few yrs. in Ely and Winton.--F b. Belgium (Flanders); to Duluth, 1855. M b. Germany; to Ontonagon, Mi.; to Duluth.--Parochial sch.; convent sch., Minneapolis, 1 yr.--Social contacts very limited; has led quite restricted life. Roman Catholic (uncle and brother are priests).--Taciturn and timid, but could be induced to tell anecdotes about early days.--Soft-spoken, with little nasality and variable tempo. Daughter, present during interview, sometimes aided by directing questions to inf.'s own experiences.--VR-A--M 373 (1949).

<u>17</u>. Building superintendent.--B. 1893 Superior, Wi.; lived in Mattawa, 30 mi. n., 1912-15.--F b. Sweden; to Duluth, 1891. M b. Wi. of Norwegian ancestry.-- 8th gr.--Normal social contacts, no lodge membership. Former Lutheran; now Presbyterian.--Good humored and easygoing, but careful in statements. Well liked among associates.--Speech has some Swedish intonation. Knows differences between his speech and that of library staff where he works but makes no effort to 'correct' his speech.--VR-A--M 370 (1949).

<u>18</u>. Librarian (man).--B. 1907; lived 7 yrs. in Milwaukee, Wi.--F and M b. Sweden.--B.S. in library science, Univ. of Mn.--Active in education and church groups; choir; Lutheran.--Self-contained, efficient, somewhat conservative; fair sense of humor.--Speech rather rapid and

nervous, with muffled articulation. Sure of his responses; careful to abide by 'correct' grammar.--VR-A--M 371 (1949).

(19,20) OTTER TAIL COUNTY
Org. 1858-68.--Rich dairy and farming area with an active tourist trade. Most of pop. is of Scandinavian or German descent.--Pop.: '60, 240; '70, 1968; '90, 34,232; '20, 50,818; '50, 51,320.--Mason, J. W., ed. *History of Otter Tail County, Minnesota*, Minneapolis, 1916.

Fergus Falls. Inc. 1872.--Platted 1870 by a group from e. US.--Pop. now chiefly of Scandinavian or German origin; originally Protestant but with recent Catholic growth. Center of rich dairy and farming area, with large co. creamery; on edge of popular summer resort district.--Pop.: '80, 1635; '90, 3772; '20, 7581; '50, 12,917.--"Fergus Falls Golden Jubilee, 1882-1932," *Fergus Falls Daily Journal*, 1932. *Golden Jubilee Homecoming Souvenir Program*, Fergus Falls, 1932. Leonard, H. C., "Fergus Falls, Manufacturing City of Northern Minnesota," *Northwest Mag.* 4.14-19 (1886). Ohles, J. F., *A Short History of Fergus Falls, Minnesota*, pub. by the author, 1950. "The Pride of the Park Region," *Fergus Falls Daily Journal*, 1886.

19. Farmer.--B. 1874 Goodhue Co.; to farm 2 mi. n. of Fergus Falls, 1875.--F b. Norway; to Mn., 1868. M b. Norway; to Mn., c1871.--Rural sch.--As director of state association of local creameries meets prominent farmers throughout state; active Lutheran.--Sturdy, independent, thrifty, pious, and firm-minded. Completed interview with obvious reluctance. Tactiturn except when stirred by memory of distant experience; found suppletion questions difficult.--Speech distinct and rather slow. Norwegian spoken in home when he was a child; traces appear sporadically, as in devoicing of final voiced consonants, in /j/ for /ǰ/ and /w/ for /v/, and in "We had a name on it" for "We had a name for it." Grammar often nonstandard, but inconsistently.--VR-A--A 44 (1949).

20. Housewife.--B. 1895 Grant Co., 29 m. s.--F and M b. Norway; to Mn., c1885.--HS; Moorhead Teachers College 1 yr.--Fairly active social life, especially in Ladies' Aid of Evangelical Lutheran Ch.--Pleasant, intelligent, thoughtful. Responded easily and fully.--Speech clear and distinct, of moderate tempo. Grammar largely standard (says it was due to her 6th-gr. teacher). Only trace of Norwegian influence is the occ. devoicing of

a final voiced spirant after a voiced consonant.--VR-A--A (1949).

(21,22) CROW WING COUNTY
Org. 1870.--Part of the cutover region where farming and dairying are now main industries. Game reserves attract summer tourists. Pop. is Scandinavian, German, and Finnish. About half of pop. is centered in Brainerd.--Pop.: '60, 269; '70, 200; '90, 8852; '20, 24,566; '50, 30,875.

Brainerd. Inc. 1881.--Established 1870 as division point on new NPR; RR shops still located here. For yrs. a lumbering town with mixed pop., now mainly Scandinavian and German. Trade center for dairying and farming area; much of city's prosperity depends upon summer resort business. Co. seat.--Pop.: '80, 1865; '90, 5703; '20, 9591; '50, 12,637.--Dillan, I., *Brainerd's Half Century*, Minneapolis, 1923. "Brainerd, Minnesota, 65th Anniversary from 1872-1937," *The Brainerd Tribune*, Sept. 9, 1937. "Brainerd, the City of the Pines," *Northwest Mag.* 3.2-5 (1885). Zapffe, C., *Brainerd, Minnesota, 1871-1946, 75th Anniversary*, Minneapolis, 1946.

21. Retired RR blacksmith.--B. 1873.--F and M b. Wales; to Brainerd, 1873. 8th gr.--Highly social. One of best-known 'old-timers' in community. Former KP; Congregationalist.--Cheerful, co-operative, garrulous. Slightly deaf.--Speech firm and clear. Naive about own speech forms, but humorously observant of others' regional variants. "Maine people say 'fit'; we say 'fought'." "My mother always said, 'Side the table' when she meant 'Clear it'."--VR-A--Aux. inf.: Wife. Same age. B. Norway; to US as a child.--A 46 (1949).

Bay Lake Township (PO Deerwood)
Farming and summer lake resort area, with strong Scandinavian farm group.--Pop.: '00, 255; '20, 238; '50, 454.--Zapffe, C., *It Happened Here*, Brainerd, 1948.

22. Farmwife; department manager in Woolworth's in Brainerd 5 yrs.--B. 1895; lived in Brainerd from age 3 to 37.--F b. Germany; to Cincinnati, Oh., 1871; to Brainerd, c1890. M b. Brooklyn, N.Y. MGP b. Germany.--HS.--Active in Ladies' Aid of Lutheran Ch. (treasurer); once member of local sch. board. Meets variety of people to whom she and her husband rent resort cabins during the summer.--Plain and unpretentious, industrious, generous, friendly, talkative, with firm

48

ethical views. Curious about interview; asked about backgrounds and meanings of words.--Speech rapid but distinct. At first sought to provide 'correct' forms until she realized that interviewer did not consider her usual forms 'wrong.'--VR-A--Aux. inf.: Husband, slightly older; of Swedish parentage.--A 47 (1949).

(23,24) KANABEC COUNTY
Org. 1881.--Settled 1870's.--In a cutover region now taken over by sheep-grazing and dairy farms. Many Swedes; also Germans and Norwegians. Co. is well populated.--Pop.: '60, 30; '70, 93; '90, 1574; '20, 9086; '50, 9192.

Mora. Platted 1882 just before advent of RR from St. Cloud. First a logging center with 'Yankee' workers and, after large-scale coming of Swedish immigrants, a growing trade center for farming.--Area now chiefly devoted to sheep raising and dairy farming, with oats and corn as forage crops. Progressive and dynamic community; co. creamery, gristmill, mfg. of buttermilk driers. Co. seat.--Pop.: '00, 785; '20, 1006; '50, 2018.

23. Retired accountant; Co. auditor, 1894-1904; newspaper publisher, '04-47; state legislature 4 terms (speaker of the house 1 term); state treasurer, '17-25; member important state commissions. --B. 1872 Sweden; to Mora as infant.--F b. Sweden; died in Mora when informant was 1 yr. old. Step-F b. Me.; to Mn. before 1861. M b. Sweden.--"5th reader" in sch.; widely read and self-educated. --Many diverse social contacts through politics and publishing; social life still continues.--Outstanding personality; genial, tolerant, humorous, wise, and alert, highly respected. Still writes weekly historical article for his old newspaper; enjoys reminiscing.-- Speech clear and forceful, with no pronounced idiosyncrasies. Grammar usually standard, though with lapses into popular English.--VR-A--A 26 (1948).

24. Retired hardware merchant.--B. 1893 Dodge Center; to Mora, 1894; worked in Ia. 2 yrs., c1910.--F b. Ont.; to Mi.; to Mn. PGP b. Ulster, Ire. M b. Oh.; to Mi.; to Mn.; MGP b. Mi.--HS 1 yr.; business sch., Ia., 1 yr.; WWI in France.--Serious-minded, reserved, public-spirited. Wealthy; accepts obligation to serve community; hence acts as head of hospital board, village president, and chief volunteer fire dept.--Speech clear and decisive, with minimum of diphthongization. Rate moderate. When not in wife's

presence prefers to use nonstandard morphology to conform with community practice.--VR-A--A 27 (1948).

(25,26) BIG STONE COUNTY
Org. 1881.--Agricultural area; well settled but with no urban center. Quarrying is important source of income, and also canning. Pop. has large number of Germans and Scandinavians.--Pop.: '70, 24; '90, 5722; '20, 9086; '50, 9607.

Graceville. Countryside settled 1870's by group of Irish colonists financed through efforts of late Archbishop Ireland of St. Paul, with later influx of Polish immigrants and some Belgians and Scandinavians.--Trade center for diversified farming area; wheat, flax, barley, and oats. Little cultural life.--Pop.: '80, 40; '90, 508; '20, 1022; '50, 962. --A Transcript's Story of a Year. A Sketch of Graceville, Minnesota., 1887.

25. Retired state highway employee; garage mechanic 4 yrs.; farmer 7 yrs.; with state 25 yrs.--B. 1881, lived 17 yrs. on farm 6 m. w.--F and M b. Ire.; to Graceville, early 1870's.--8th gr.-- Social life restricted to a few friends, fellow employees, and ch. KC; Roman Catholic.--Pleasant and friendly. Lacks usual store of general information, but generous with anecdotal material from his youth.--Speech not always articulate; strong retroflexion, tense words, especially back ones, tend to be centered. [θ] often becomes strongly aspirated stop [tʰ]. Grammar almost entirely nonstandard; syntax, too, has nonstandard features.--VR-A--A 32 (1949).

26. Housewife; store clerk until 5 yrs. ago.--B. 1901; lived on farm 5 m. w. until age 28.--F b. Wi.; to Graceville, c1890. PGP b. Poland. M b. St. Paul; to Graceville, c1886. MGP b. Poland.--Local Catholic academy graduate is HS.-- Usual social life of small town, especially in Catholic Ch.; widely known through previous employment in local store.--Alert, cheerful, pleasant, intelligent inf. Answered questions readily but without elaboration or voluntary material; hence few conversational items. --Speech distinct; tense vowels often pure monophthongs; /aʊ/ and /aɪ/ diphthongs have noticeably different beginnings. Not speech conscious.--VR-A--Aux. inf.: Husband, c. same age; Mn.-born of German ancestry; to Graceville 5 yrs. ago as painter and decorator. He supplied a few terms unknown to her.--A 33 (1949).

(27,28) STEARNS COUNTY
Org. 1855.--Originally settled almost
entirely by Germans, still has large German pop.--Much of the pop. is centered
in St. Cloud and surburban area. Diversified farming.--Pop.: '60, 450; '70,
14,206; '00, 34,844; '20, 55,741; '50,
70,681.--Sister Ardis Hartman, "The First
German Migration into Stearns Co.," *Acta
et Dicta*, 7, no. 2, 1936. Mitchell, W.
B., *History of Stearns County, Minnesota*,
Chicago, 1915.

Sauk Centre. Inc. 1876.--Settled 1860's
by 'Yankee' stock, with later influx of
Scandinavians and Germans.--Fairly progressive. Shopping and shipping center
for diversified agricultural region in
w. end of Stearns Co. and s. part of
Todd Co. Sinclair Lewis, Main Street.--
Pop.: '70, 1155; '90, 1695; '20, 2699;
'50, 3140.--*A Historical Sketch of Sauk
Centre Commemorating the Completed Mod-
ernization of the Building and Equipment of the First State Bank of Sauk
Centre*, 1954.

27. Bricklayer.--B. 1869 on farm 3 m.
s., lived 2 yrs. in St. Paul during
1900's; in Chicago, '25-30.--F and M b.
N.Y. PGP and MGP b. New England.--6th
gr. rural sch.--Extremely restricted social contacts, mostly card-playing at
local tavern. Once member AOUW; past
sporadic attendance at various Protestant chs., but never a member.--Mild-
mannered, unimaginative, slow-thinking.
Frequently responded, "That's too deep
for me." Not unfriendly, but attitude
throughout interview was one of passive
resignation.--Speech slow, answers
usually monolexical. Articulation usually weak; offglides weak. Grammatical
forms frequently, but inconsistently,
nonstandard.--Aux. inf.: Wife, in 70's,
b. Prince Edward Island, Can.--A 30
(1948).

28. Housewife.--B. 1889.--F b. Prince
Edward Island, Can.; to Sauk Centre,
c1875. PGP b. Ire.; M b. New York City;
to Il.; to Sauk Centre. MGP b. Ire.--
HS; Minneapolis School of Music 1 yr.--
Active socially, but not civically. Roman Catholic.--Genial, responsive; interested in interview.--Speech fairly
rapid; offglides weak. Has /ju/ diphthong after non-labials. Conscious of
'correct' forms and disturbed by fieldworker's interest in forms she considered wrong.--VR-A--Aux. inf.: Husband,
retired dentist, lifelong resident of
German descent. Answered a few questions
with amused skepticism.--A 29 (1948).

(29,30) WRIGHT COUNTY
Org. 1855. Agricultural co. with no ur-
ban center. Summer tourist trade is an
important source of income. Pop. mainly
of German, Swedish, and Finnish descent.
--Pop.: '60, 3729; '70, 9457; '90,
24,164; '20, 28,865; '50, 27,716.--
Curtiss-Wedge, F., *History of Wright
County, Minnesota*, Chicago, 1915. French,
C. A., & F. B. Lamson, comp., *Condensed
History of Wright County, 1851-1935*,
Delano, Mn., 1935.

Clearwater. Clearwater twp. first settled by 'Yankee' farmers 1853, with
Clearwater village as its focus. Some
descendants remain, but Irish in '70's
and then Scandinavians diversified the
pop.--General farming area. Until recently community was isolated and self-
contained.--Pop.: '60, 240; '70, 552;
'90, 658; '20, 331; '50, 224.

29. Retired farmer.--B. 1882.--F b.
Wayne Co., N.Y.; to Clearwater, 1856.
PGP b. N.Y. of New England ancestry
("Mayflower tradition" in family). M b.
Brooklyn, N.Y.; to Clearwater, 1858.
MGP b. N.Y. (probably).--"Didn't finish
8th gr."--Active for yrs. in community;
secretary of sch. board. 35 yrs. Methodist.--Affable, deliberate, magnani-
mous. Conservative in viewpoint but able
to discuss with open mind. Enjoys reminiscing, takes pride in family and community history.--Speech of moderate tempo, with unusually distinct articulation
of emphasized words. No special peculiarities.--VR-A--A 115 (1953).

30. Farmer.--B. 1904.--F b. on same
farm where inf. lives. PGF b. De.; PGM
b. Oh. M b. Clearwater twp. MGP b. Germany.--HS--Social life limited to immediate relatives and neighbors. Farm Bureau. Methodist.--Friendly, deliberate,
even-tempered.--Slow and carefully articulated speech. Slips into nonstandard
grammar in conversation.--VR-A--A 116
(1953).

(31,32,33,34,35) HENNEPIN COUNTY
Org. 1852.--Originally diversified farming outside the villages of Minneapolis
and St. Anthony.--Now a densely populated industrial area, with 92 per cent
of the pop. centered in Minneapolis and
suburbs. Many people of German and Swedish descent, but many other ethnic
elements in the pop.--Pop.: '70, 31,566;
'90, 185,294; '20, 415,419; '50, 676,597.
--Mitchell, W. H., *Geographical and Statistical Sketch of the County of Hennepin*, Minneapolis, 1868. Neill, E. D., &

J. F. Williams, *History of Hennepin County and the City of Minneapolis*, Minneapolis, 1881. Warner, G., & C. Foote, *History of Hennepin County and the City of Minneapolis*, Minneapolis, 1881.

Minneapolis. Inc. 1872.--Formed 1872 by the union of the earlier St. Anthony on the e. bank and Minneapolis on the w. bank of the Mississippi R. at the present head of navigation, St. Anthony Falls. St. Anthony, the older, had an initial pop. in the late 1840's of French Canadian fur traders and settlers from e. US. Lumbering and milling aided in its growth to become the largest city in the Upper Midwest, with greatly diversified industry and a stable economy.--Native pop. derived chiefly from Wi., N.Y., and Mi.; with a larger influx of Swedish and other n. Europeans. Co. seat. Univ. of Mn. Numerous important cultural activities.--Pop.: '60, 538 (St. Anthony); '70, 18,081 (Minneapolis & St. Anthony); '90, 164,738; '20, 380,582; '50, 521,718. --Atwater, I., *History of Minneapolis*, New York & Chicago, 1896. Garber, A. E., *Early Days in Minneapolis*, 1955. Hasbrouck, S., *A History of the Minneapolis Lower Loop*, Minneapolis, 1956. Hudson, H. B., ed., *A Half Century of Minneapolis*, 1908. Leonard, E. W., "Early Days in Minneapolis," *Mn. Hist. Soc. Coll.*, 15.497-514 (1915). Parsons, E. D., *Making Minneapolis*, Minneapolis, 1926. Shutter, M. D., *History of Minneapolis, Gateway to the Northwest*, Chicago, 1932. Walker, C. R., *American City: A Rank and File History*, New York, 1937. Writers' Program, *Minneapolis--the Story of a City*, Minneapolis, 1940.

31. Housewife.--B. 1874 on farm now part of the city.--F b. R.I.; to Mn. after Civil War. PGF b. R.I.; PGM b. Netherlands. M b. Ire.; to Minneapolis 1865. MGM b. Ire.;--Rural sch. (First teacher was Harriet Godfrey, member of one of families founding Minneapolis.); traveled to Pacific Northwest several times. --Has had active social life; Royal Neighbors (held various offices), OES, Episcopal Ch.--Genial, cooperative, fairly alert, loquacious with good sense of humor and a fund of uninhibited anecdotes.--Speech ready, clear, well-articulated. Regularly uses /n/ for /ŋ/ in -ing suffix. Some nasality. Believes in 'correct' English, but her speech has many nonstandard forms.--A 113 (1953).

32. Widow.--B. 1863.--F and M b. Vt.; to Minneapolis, 1861.--Grammar sch.--Has had normal social contacts, but not in organizations.--A cooperative inf., but

with some tendency to make a reply she thought was wanted rather than her natural form. Not loquacious, hence few spontaneous items. Some traces of senility. Nearly blind.--Speech distinct; normal tempo sometimes unnaturally retarded in responses, a factor perhaps producing [t] where [ṭ] or [ɾ] might be expected. Considerable unrounding and fronting of back vowels.--G 7 (1948).

33. Housewife; taught sch. 3 yrs.--B. 1888.--F b. near Portland, Me.; to Wi.; to Mn. M b. Janesville, Wi.; to Mn. at age 18. MGF b. Pa. MGM b. Pa.?--HS; Univ. of Mn. 1 yr.--Social contacts through husband's profession, engineering, and through her college-bred children.--Genteel, intelligent. Good inf.--Without conspicuous idiosyncrasies, her speech is soft-spoken, somewhat precise and deliberate; adheres closely to norm of standard English. Training and background made her a devotee of formal sch. grammar. Has acquired /ɑ/ in /rɑðər/. --VR-A--A 34 (1949).

34. Physician.--B. 1907 in house where now residing, in older and deteriorating section.--F b. Germany. M b. Plato of German ancestry.--M.D., Univ. of Mn. Medical Sch.--Social contacts largely those with professional groups.; infrequent attendant of Lutheran Ch. where he is a member.--Cheerful, easygoing family practitioner, with lower-middle-class clientele. Conversation personal and anecdotal rather than intellectual; not a wide range of interests. Very cooperative as inf.--Speech clearly enunciated with moderate tempo; pronounced retroflexion, even of pre-/r/ vowels. Cheerfully objective about his occasional nonstandard usages.--A 35 (1949).

35. Retired store maintenance worker; pullman dining car employee, 1892-1921. B. 1876.--F b. Al. of African ancestry; to Mn., 1862? M b. Cincinnati, Oh., of ancestry part African and part Cherokee Indian; to Mn. c1860.--3rd gr.--Active in Negro fraternal orders and Methodist ch.; a widower, he still "gets around a lot."--Friendly, affable, and cooperative. Enjoys reminiscing; takes pride in health and continued activity. Well known and respected among his neighbors. --Often has heightened intonation contrasts. Lengthened initial element of /ɑʊ/ and /ɑɪ/; /ər/ only weakly retroflex. Rate moderate; enunciation fairly distinct. A 117 (1954).

(36,37,38) RAMSEY COUNTY
Org. 1849.--Pop. centered in St. Paul

and the surrounding suburbs, but some farms in the n. half of the Co. Large numbers of Germans and Swedes, and many other ethnic groups represented. Very densely populated industrial area.--Pop.: '50, 2227 (incl. Hennepin Co.); '70, 23,085; '90, 139,796; '20, 244,554; '50, 355,332.--Neill, E. D., *History of Ramsey County and the City of St. Paul*, Minneapolis, 1881. Warner, G. E., & C. M. Foote, *History of Ramsey County and the City of St. Paul*, Minneapolis, 1881. Williams, J. F., "A History of the City of St. Paul and of the County of Ramsey, Minnesota," *Minn. Hist. Soc. Coll.* 4 (1876).

Little Canada (New Canada Township).
Farming community settled 1850's by French Canadians.--Still retains high degree of homogeneity despite increasing encroachment of St. Paul suburban pop. and urban employment of some of the residents. French still spoken by oldest generation. Pop.: '50, 194 (twp.); '70, 798 (twp.); '90, 1276 (twp.); '20, 1729 (twp.); '50, 9286 (twp.).

36. Widow; lives with married daughter.
--B. St. Paul, 1873.--F b. Quebec, Can., of French ancestry. M b. Rivière du Loup, Que., of French ancestry.--4th gr. Schooling was in English but initial language experience was French.--Social life limited to immediate environment, principally that of the Catholic parish constituted almost entirely of persons of similar background. Never joined clubs; never traveled. Husband was carpenter and odd-jobs man until death in 1951.--Friendly, cheerful, with keen sense of humor. Intelligent, but not alert (perhaps because of age); memory beginning to fail, and she had trouble with completion questions. Health good. --Speech slow, with imperfect articulation only in part owing to dentures. French substratum persists in some nonusual intonation contours and in tenseness of /ɪ/ and /ɛ/. In general, the consonant articulation is less firm than the transcription would indicate. Morphology has two standards: her normal one, and that acquired from her HS graduate daughter, e.g., the clum-climbed contrast.--VR-A--A 120 (1956).

St. Paul. Inc. 1849.--Small group of French Canadians and Canadians from Pembina settlement preceded the coming of 'Yankees' in the flood of migration in the 1850's. Huge influx of Irish and Germans after the Civil War, with later Scandinavian addition. City then the focal point for regional settlement since it was first the Mississippi R. terminus

and later a RR center.--Today it is a major shipping point and home of diversified industry. State capital; Co. seat. 6 colleges.--Pop.: '50, 1112; '70, 20,030; '90, 133,156; '20, 234,698; '50, 311,349. Andrews, C.C., *History of St. Paul, Minnesota*, Syracuse, 1890. Babcock, W. M., *Father Galtier and the Beginnings of St. Paul*, St. Paul, 1893. Bliss, F. C., *The Past and the Present of the Twin Cities*, St. Paul, 1888. Castle, H. A., *History of St. Paul and Vicinity*, Chicago & New York, 1912. Flandrau, G., "St. Paul: The Personality of a City," *Mn. Hist.* 22.1-12 (1941). Hennessey, W. B., *Past and Present of St. Paul, Minnesota*, Chicago, 1906. *St. Paul History and Progress*, St. Paul, 1897. Schmid, C. F., *Social Saga of Two Cities*, Minneapolis, 1937.

37. Food processor.--B. 1894; lived in Bemidji briefly as a young man.--F b. Mn. of Irish ancestry. M b. St. Paul of Irish ancestry.--Graduate of local Catholic academy.--Active in association of manufacturers' representatives and other business organizations; occupation provides numerous business and social contacts, and family is socially active; 2 daughters are students at Univ. of Mn. Former KC.--Well-to-do, poised and sure of himself; genial, friendly, most cooperative as inf.--Speech unmarked by idiosyncrasies; clear, moderate in tempo, and usually with standard grammar. Aware of social differences, but sufficiently cognizant of purpose of interview not to depart from usual practices.--VR-A--A 51 (1950).

38. Banker (municipal bond specialist).
--B. 1909.--F b. St. Paul. PGP b. Germany. M b. St. Paul. MGF b. France; MGM b. St. Cloud.--B.A. in business administration, Univ. of Mn.--Active in business association and in Catholic Ch. Eldest child is univ. student.--Conservative; chiefly concerned with family and business; little intellectual curiosity; surprisingly uninformed about public affairs. So resentful of interview questions which he could not answer that interviewer subsequently ignored most of the rural items. Though well-to-do, thought he should be paid for thus wasting his time.--Speech without special features except for concern for 'correct' English and an occasional revelation of his own nonstandard substratum, e.g., ain't.--A 21 (1956).

(39,40) WASHINGTON COUNTY
Org. 1859.--Part of the cutover region. Early pop. was varied, made up of lumbermen from New England, many other

parts of the US, and many countries.--
Present pop. has a New England background, with many people of German, Swedish, and British descent. Some farming,
but most important source of income is
summer tourist trade.--Pop.: '50, 1056;
'70, 11,809; '90, 25,942; '20, 23,761;
'50, 34, 544.--Neill, E. D., *History of
Washington County and the St. Croix Valley*, Minneapolis, 1881. Easton, A. E.,
History of the St. Croix Valley, Chicago,
1909.

Marine on St. Croix. Inc. 1875.--2nd-
oldest settlement in the state; settled
1838 by 2 Il. lumberman. Pop. came from
Me. and Vt., many of them Irish; but with
them was a mixture from other states and
countries. Lumbering was main industry
until '80's, when sawmills stopped operating and pop. dwindled.--Today known as
a summer resort and for its 'writer's
colony.' Older pop.: 'Americans' (from
e. US), Swedes, and a very few s. Europeans. Mostly Protestant. Natives call
town 'Marine'; summer residents have
gotten it officially changed to 'Marine
on St. Croix.'--Pop.: '50, 114; '70;
1698; '90, 674; '20, 361; '50, 334.

39. Housewife.--B. 1864.--F b. Pa. M b.
Eng.--Grammar sch.--When younger, active
in clubs, lodges, and church activities.
Now lives part of yr. in Minneapolis and
part in Marine where she has usual social contacts for her age.--Willing, affable inf. Intelligent, uneducated,
highly respected.--Speech of normal tempo, fairly distinct; retroflexion occasionally weak; little nasalization. Few
opinions of 'correctness' or usage.--
Aux. inf.: Daughter. Has lived entire
life in Marine and Minneapolis, her present home.--G 6 (1948).

Stillwater. Inc. 1854.--Founded 1839.
Once center for the logging industry in
St. Croix Valley, with a varied pop. As
timber disappeared, town declined.--Now
a small port, with a few grain elevators
and no major industries. Pop. largely n.
European and Protestant. Townspeople
proud of early hist. Co. seat.--Pop.:
'50, 621, '70, 4124; '90, 11,260; '20,
7735; '50, 7674.--Glaser, E., "How
Stillwater Came to Be," *Mn. Hist.* 24.195-
206 (1943). Larson, A. G., "When Logs and
Lumber Ruled Stillwater," *Stillwater
Daily Gazette*, World's Fair Special Ed.,
Aug. 22, 1904. Stillwater Trades Review,
The City of Stillwater, Minnesota, Stillwater, 1898.

40. Housewife.--B. 1888 2 mi. from Stillwater; lived in Duluth a few yrs., c1910.

--F b. Me.; to Mn., c1870. M b. Grant, 2
m. from Stillwater. MGP b. Jackson, Mi.
--Some HS; nurses' training course.--
Normal social contacts. After death of
1st husband, worked as a nurse. Now re-
married.--Interested in the investigation because of her descent from early
settlers. Very alert; often volunteered
information.--Speech fairly rapid, but
distinct; little nasalization. Quick to
censor 'improper' forms, but used run as
preterit.--G 5 (1948).

(41,42) CHIPPEWA COUNTY
Org. 1868.--Agricultural area with no
large urban center. Large Norwegian and
German elements in the pop.--Pop.: '80,
1467; '90, 8555; '20, 15,720; '50,
16,739.--Moyer, L. R., & O. G. Dale, *History of Chippewa and Lac qui Parle Counties, Minnesota*, Indianapolis, 1916.

Montevideo. Inc. 1879.--Original settlers (1868) were 'Yankees.' Norwegians
soon followed, and later large numbers
of Swedes and Germans.--Business center
for a prosperous and diversified farming
region. Town has strong civic organizations and chs. Co. seat.--Pop.: '00,
2146; '20, 4419; '50, 5459.

41. Farmer.--B. 1877.--F b. Norway; to
St. Paul, 1868; to Montevideo, 1869. M
b. Norway; to Mn., c1871.--Rural sch.;
state agricultural sch., St. Paul, 1 winter; business sch. 1 short session in
bookkeeping.--Active farm leader, treasurer of Lutheran Ch., member of various
boards in the community (sch. board, REA
board, etc.), active in Farmers' Union.
--Genial and pleasant. Retired, but
still lives in farm home and keeps busy
with his chickens and his civic jobs.
Mentally alert, keeps up with day's news;
conservative in general viewpoint. Very
cooperative in the interview. Confined
himself to direct answers, offering little spontaneous material.--Although Norwegian was spoken in his home, only 2
obvious traces persist in his speech; a
tendency to bilabialize /v/ to [w] or
[β] and a habit of unvoicing final /z/,
to either [z̥] or [s]. Moderate tempo,
without nasål quality; very little diphthongization. Offglides weak and brief
when present. Somewhat concerned with
'correctness,' but did not hesitate to
acknowledge own nonstandard forms.--VR-
A--Aux. inf.: Wife. B. 1878 Wadena; to
Montevideo at age 1. Pleasant, more
loquacious than her husband. Volunteered
answers before he could think of a reply.
Taught rural sch. 2 yrs. Strong sense of
'correctness.'--A 28 (1948).

42. Housewife.--B. 1884.--F b. N.Y. of Ct. parents. M b. N.Y.; to Mn. before marriage. MGP b. New Eng. and Holland.-- HS 3 yrs.; Windom Institute 2 yrs.; some work in music at Oberlin College.--A widow, with children grown and living elsewhere; devotes her time to community affairs. Active in ch., hospital auxiliary, OES, Co. Hist. Soc., Woman's Relief Corps, and GAR aux.; has held offices in all these organizations.--Dynamic, explosive, sanguinary, with a sense of humor. Civic-minded, alert, very positive about what she knows. Well-informed, partly because a son has been employed in Singapore for many yrs. Extreme loquaciousness provided unusually large number of spontaneous items.--Speech rapid in conversation, often abrupt, even staccato, and almost free from pronounced diphthongal offglides. 'Correctness-conscious' but revealed some lapses into the vulgar.--A 31 (1948).

(43,44,45) MCLEOD COUNTY
Org. 1856.--Agricultural area with dairy and fur farms. Largest pop. element is German; also Czechs, Danes, Austrians, Scandinavians, and a few British. The American pop. came mainly from the nearby states: Ia, In., Mi., and Wi.--Pop.: '50, 1285; '70, 5643; '90, 17,026; '20, 20,444; '50, 22,198.--Curtiss-Wedge, F., ed., *History of McLeod County, Minnesota*, Chicago & Winona, 1919.

Hutchinson. Inc. 1881--Settled 1858 by members of the famous 'singing Hutchinson' family. Populated first by English, later by Irish, Germans, and Czechs.-- At present, English and Czechs predominate. Many Protestant chs., one Catholic. Mainly a farming town, but also Kraft cheese factory, grain elevators, and large lumber mills. Seminary.--Pop.: '50, 94; '70, 440; '90, 1414; '20, 3379; '50, 4690.--McPherson, G., *A Souvenir, Hutchinson, Minnesota*, Red Wing, 1900. Pendergast, W. W., "Sketches of the History of Hutchinson," *Minn. Hist. Soc. Coll.* 10.69-89 (1905).

43. Farmer.--B. 1899.--F b. Czechoslovakia; to Hutchinson, c1865. M b. near Racine, Wi., of Czech parents.--Rural sch. 8th gr.--Limited social contacts, except in own social and ethnic group. Active in Farm Bureau.--Fairly cooperative, but bored. Sometimes refused to reply. Often thought of answer in Czech, then translated it.--Weak, high-pitched, but pleasant voice. Little nasalization, average tempo. When inf. was tired, /d/ and /t/ were often substituted for /ð/

and /θ/, probably a reflection of Czech background. Habitually answered own question, e.g., "It is sour milk? Yes."--G 18 (1948).

44. Retired farmer and storekeeper.--B. 1866 Norfolk, Eng.; to Hutchinson, 1872. --F b. Eng.; to Hutchinson, '70. M b. Stow, Eng.; to Hutchinson, '72.--Rural sch.--As storekeeper in country town for 40 yrs., came to know everyone in the community. Active in Baptist Ch. in the days of the famous Hutchinsons.--Affable and talkative. Found the study interesting. Alert for his age and prided himself on his vigor. Excellent sense of humor, delighted in telling anecdotes and reminiscing.--Spoke quickly and distinctly. Little nasalization. Traces of British home, e.g., /ɑ/ in half, but /bɪn/ for been. Postvocalic [r] characteristic of American English. Intonation sometimes British.--G 16 (1948).

45. Retired painter, paperhanger, and taxidermist.--B. 1872; lived in Glencoe 5 yrs.--F b. 6 m. s.e. of Hutchinson. PGP b. N.Y. and Pa. M b. Oh.; to Hutchinson at age 12.--Grammar sch.; HS 2 yrs. --Active social life. Secretary local hist. soc. Known and respected by community. Taught district sch. 2 yrs. Proud of descent from Gov. Bradford of Ma.-- Co-operative. Regarded survey as cross between hist. research and quiz show. Interested in recalling older names in community. Very alert.--Speech slow when giving responses, almost deliberate. Spontaneous conversation sometimes very rapid. The /ɑʊ/ and /ɑɪ/ phonemes varied between a fairly front beginning [a] and a retracted one [ɑˑ]. Retroflexion varied, sometimes almost entirely missing in post-vocalic position in conversation; in answers to questions, usually present. --G 17 (1948).

(46,47) LYON COUNTY
Org. 1869.--Prosperous agricultural area; largest town is Marshall. Largest ethnic element is Norwegian.--Pop.: '80, 6257; '90, 9501; '20, 18,837; '50, 22,253.-- Heilbron, B. L., "The Icelandic and Belgian Settlements in Lyon County," *Mn. Hist.* 8.280-81 (1927). Rose, A.P., *An Illustrated History of Lyon County, Minnesota*, Marshall, 1912.

Marshall. Inc. 1876.--Settled 1872 on RR. Many of early settlers were Civil War veterans, some coming from Ia.; also Belgians, Icelanders, Germans, Norwegians, and Swedes.--Half Protestant, half Catholic. Center of prosperous farming area. Some industry connected with

54

agriculture: roller mill, hatcheries, creamery, wholesale fruit company, produce plant. Co. seat.--Pop.: '80, 961; '90, 1203; '20, 3092; '50, 5923.

46. Housewife.--B. 1860 Clayton Co., Ia.; to near Marshall, 1870.--F b. Montreal, Can., of Scottish parents; to Ia., 1837. M b. Berrien Co., Mi., of English and French parents; to Ia., 1837.--8th Gr.-- Began teaching at 16, taught for 3 yrs. until marriage. Active in ch. groups, OES, other soical groups.--Affable, cooperative; enjoyed the questioning. Occ. forgetful, generally alert. Speech fairly close to standard English. Average tempo, occ. slow in answering. Little nasalization. Occ. weak retroflexion of post-vocalic /r/; pre-vocalic /r/ also had a tendency to be weak. /ɑu/ and /ɑɪ/ diphthongs alternated in beginning from [a] to [ɑ]. /s/ often [sˀ] or [s].--VR- A--Aux. inf.: Daughter. B. 1890. HS. Always lived near Marshall and recently in Otter Co.--G 19 (1948).

Minneota. Settled 1878 when RR chose it as a site for a water tower.--Ethnic mixture: Swedes, Norwegians, Icelanders, Germans, Belgians, and Irish. Half Catholic, half Protestant. Grain elevators. --Pop.: '80, 113; '90, 325; '20, 894; '50, 1274.

47. Retired storekeeper.--B. 1890.--F b. Iceland; to Minneota, 1879. M b. Iceland; to Minneota, 1878.--HS; reads widely.--As owner of general store knows everyone in town, has met all kinds of people. Now active in ch. and civic work. --Cooperative, although she found many of the questions silly.--Average to quick tempo; very distinct; little nasalization. /u/ often fronted to [uˑ] or [ʉ], sometimes diphthongal, e.g., [jʉ] after /t/ and /d/. Strong theories of 'correctness.'--VR-A--Aux. inf.: Friend. B. 1890; parents Icelandic. HS. Answered a few of the questions.--G 20 (1948).

(48, 49, 50) RICE COUNTY
Org. 1855.--Rich agricultural area, mostly dairy farms. Large number of Germans and many New Englanders. Part of a large Norwegian settlement in Goodhue Co. extends into Rice Co. Almost half the pop. is centered in Faribault.--Pop.: '50, 7543; '70, 16,083; '90, 23,968; '20, 28,307; '50, 36,235.--Curtiss-Wedge, F., *History of Rice and Steele Counties*, Chicago, 1910. Neill, E. D., *History of Rice County, Including: Explorers and Pioneers of Minnesota, and Outline History of the State of Minnesota*, Minneapolis, 1882.

Faribault. Inc. 1872.--Settled 1827 by French Canadians and New Englanders. In 1850's outnumbered by Germans, Irish, Scottish, English, and Scandinavian.-- Still remains New Eng. character. Diversified industry; lies in center of rich agricultural area. Co. seat. 3 preparatory schs.; state schs. for blind and deaf.--Pop.: '50, 1508; '70, 3045; '90, 6520; '20, 11,089; '50, 16,028.--Citizens Committee, *Description of Faribault and Vicinity*, Faribault, 1884. Frink, F. W., *A Short History of Faribault and Some of Its People*, Faribault, 1901.

48. Retired farmer and merchant.--B. 1872.--F and M b. Duchy of Hess, Germany; to Mn., 1866.--Rural sch. few yrs.; German sch. in summer from age 8 to 14. --Active social life. As merchant knew everyone in town. Enjoys talking, and regularly walks to town to talk with friends.--Cooperative, although he could see no purpose in the questioning.--Speech slow and distinct. Some pronunciation and grammar archaic. Did not volunteer many items, but admitted older usages when suggested. Uses double negative and ain't freely. German characteristics: /w/ for /v/, /t/ for /θ/, /d/ for /ð/.--Aux. inf.: 2nd wife. Both parents from Germany about same time as inf.'s.--G 4 (1947).

49. Housewife: previously office worker, assistant city recorder, city treasurer, manager of summer resort. Husband is city engineer.--B. 1890 near Faribault. --F b. Waddington, N.Y.; to Faribault, 1853 or '54. M b. Shutesbury, Ma.; to Faribault, 1853.--HS.--Active and varied social life. Charter member BPW, past state president; League of Women Voters, past treasurer; past matron OES, and many others.--Dynamic, cheerful, competent, fine sense of humor. Unusually favorable impression. Wide acquaintance and knowledge of people. Community leader. Very cooperative. Interview necessarily conducted in 2 intense sessions; hence the paucity of conversational items.--Speaks clearly in a pleasant voice, free from unusual traits. Aware of sch. grammar, reinforced by mother's sister, so she actually says, "It's I." Grammar and syntax unusually close to standard.--A 24 (1948).

50. Farmer and stockman.--B. 1906 in house where he lives.--F b. New Brunswick, Can., of English parents; to Faribault, 1876. M b. Warsaw (near Faribault) of Canadian parents.--HS; Creighton Univ., Omaha. Outstanding athlete.--Rural leader. President of Rice Co. Farm

Bureau Federation; active in Cannon City Farm Bureau. Member of Elks; Episcopal Ch. Once ran for state representative.--Quiet-spoken, deliberate, mild-mannered, friendly, cooperative. Not loquacious, but volunteered information and anecdotes. Competent, prosperous, assured, and secure without being pompous or dictatorial.--Speech deliberate, even-toned, with heavy contrasts; occ. lack of force required repetition for clarity. Enunciation is fairly distinct. Morphological patterns represent system of nonstandard English of folk speech. Only rarely indicated awareness of 'correctness.' Sometimes has 2 alternate forms, used apparently interchangeably, as done and did for preterits.--VR-A--Aux. inf.: Wife. B. 1912 near Omaha, Nb.; to Mn., 1932. HS; some nurse's training.-- A 25 (1948).

(51,52,53) BLUE EARTH COUNTY
Org. 1853.--Rich agricultural region; quarrying is also an important industry. Many people of German, Scandinavian, and British descent. About half the pop. is centered in Mankato.--Pop.: '50, 4803; '70, 17,302; '90, 29,210; '20, 31,477; '50, 38,327.--Chapman, C. A., *Mankato and Blue Earth County, Minnesota*, Mankato, 1878. Clark, E. M., *Mankato and Blue Earth County*, 1872.

Mankato. Inc. 1858.--Settled 1852 by a small group from St. Paul when Minnesota River Valley was rapidly being occupied.--Now leading city in s.w. Mn. Trading center of s.w. Mn., s. S.D., and n. Ia. Limestone quarries and many varied industries. Largest pop. group is German, but many Scandinavians. Co. seat. State College; Bethany Lutheran College. --Pop.: '55, 1558; '70, 3482; '90, 8838; '20, 12,469; '50, 18,809.--"History and Fiftieth Anniversary of Mankato," *Daily Free Press* (Mankato), June 30, 1902. *Mankato, Its First Fifty Years, 1852-1901*, Mankato, 1903. *Mankato Centennial Souvenir Program, Century of Progress*, Mankato, 1952.

51. Retired painter and carpenter; now curator of a museum.--B. 1870.--F b. Prussia; to New Ulm; to Mankato, 1867. M b. Bohemia; to Mankato, 1868.--Grammar sch. run by Notre Dame Sisters few yrs. until age 13; widely read.--Claims to know everyone in town and most of the people in the Co. His jobs have given him wide social contacts.--Willing inf. though doubtful of use of questions. Talkative; sometimes difficult to interrupt him. Well informed; conscious of lack of education.--Fairly distinct

articulation. Average to rapid tempo; no nasalization. Reading has not influenced his usage. Good ear for local dialect; claimed to be something of an authority on the speech of lower classes in Mankato.--G 13 (1948).

52. Retired farmer.--B. 1867 6 m. from Mankato.--F b. Wales; to N.Y.; to Wi.; to Mankato, 1866. M b. Wales; to Wi.; to Mankato, 1866.--A little grammar sch.-- Fairly active in ch., but social life centered about his family; other contacts are few.--Delighted to act as inf. Regarded proceeding as harmless idiocy. Not talkative, still alert, but memory sometimes failed him; response often had to be wrung from him.--Fairly slow speech, distinct. Voice very soft, little nasalization. Speech perfectly natural and unselfconscious. Little feeling for local dialect. No knowledge of grammatical 'correctness.'--G 14 (1948).

Mapleton. Older village org. 1861; superseded by RR village platted 1871.-- Small country town. Predominantly Scottish. Inhabitants closely connected with farm life. Main shopping center is Mankato, 20 m. n.--Pop.: '50, 315; '70, 583; '90, 607; '20, 857; '50, 1083.

53. Garage proprietor; mayor.--B. 1904 near Mapleton.--F b. Wi. of Scottish parents; to Mapleton, 1875. M b. Blue Earth Co. of Scottish parents.--Grammar sch., a little HS.--Wide social contacts with all members of community.--Affable and cooperative, but not talkative.--Very distinct articulation; generally rapid tempo. Little nasalization. No ideas of 'correctness.' Not conscious of differences in older persons, but could remember older expressions if asked.--G 15 (1948).

(54,55) GOODHUE COUNTY
Org. 1854.--Early center for Norwegian settlement; many Norwegians went from here to S.D. and N.D.--Agricultural area of dairy and grain farms. Many people of German and Scandinavian descent. Large urban pop. in Red Wing.--Pop.: '50, 8977; '70, 22,618; '90, 28,806; '20, 30,799; '50, 32,118.--Curtiss-Wedge, F., *History of Dakota and Goodhue Counties*, Chicago, 1910. *History of Goodhue County Including a Sketch of the Territory and State of Minnesota*, Red Wing, 1878. Mitchell, W. H., *Geographical and Statistical Sketch of Goodhue County*, Minneapolis, 1869. Rasmussen, C. A., *A History of Goodhue County, Minnesota*, Red Wing, 1935.

Featherstone Township. Org. 1858.--Set-

tled 1855.--Nearest community is Red
Wing. Nearby farmers are mainly relatives
of inf. German and New Eng. elements are
the strongest.

54. Farmer.--B. 1888 in house where he
now lives.--F b. Ont., Can.; to Red Wing,
1858. PGF b. Eng.; to Que.; to Oh.; to
Ont. M b. Ont., Can.; to Red Wing, 1860.
MGF b. Eng.; to Can.--Rural sch.; HS.
Likes to listen to univ. radio station
and especially enjoys convocation talks.
--Social life limited to his family (c50
relatives in the vicinity), his ch., his
wife's ch., and the Farmer's Club.--Well-
to-do, self-contained assurance resulting from competence and security. Pleasant, unassuming, modest,friendly. Alert;
interested in public affairs. In 2nd and
3rd interviews became talkative, volunteered spontaneous forms.--Deliberate
speech. Some nasality. Tendency to
lengthen initial element of falling diphthongs. /aʊ/ is inconsistent in pronunciation, sometimes quite fronted [æʊ]
and sometimes backed to [ɑʊ]. Cooperative; was aware that usual forms and not
book forms were wanted. Tries to abide by
what he remembers of sch. grammar, but
is also disdainful of it. Admits to
cheerful uncertainty about spelling.--
VR-A--A 22 (1948).

Red Wing. Inc. 1857.--Established 1836
as Swiss Protestant missionary post.--
Present pop. largely of German and New
England background. Chief industry is
mfg. of pottery and clay pipe. Several
other industries: shoes, plate glass,
etc. Co. seat. Mn. Training Sch.--Pop.:
'50, 1150; '70, 4260; '90, 6294; '20,
8637; '50, 10,645.--"County History for
100 Years, Saga of Progress," *Daily Republican Eagle* (Red Wing), Goodhue Co.
Centennial Ed., July 7, 1954. Irvine, S.
T., *History of Red Wing to 1942*, Red
Wing, 1943. Rasmussen, C. A., *A History
of the City of Red Wing, Minnesota*, Red
Wing, 1933.

55. Retired manager of photography studio; previously worked in bookstore and
furniture factory, and helped father on
milk route.--B. 1868.--F b. Germany; to
New Orleans; to St. Louis; to Red Wing,
1859. M b. Germany; to Buffalo; to St.
Louis; to Red Wing, 1859.--7th gr.--Ac-
tive Methodist. 12 yrs. on sch. board.
Knows many people and is known throughout community. Many diversified and
broadening contacts.--Genial and cooperative. Substitution items hard to
elicit; usually supplied equivalent terms.
Alert, but somewhat forgetful, liked to
reminisce.--Speech clear and vigorous,

though he is hard of hearing. Contacts
have made him speech-conscious; apparently he has eliminated nonstandard
forms, such as ain't and double negatives.
Mother never spoke English, but seems to
be no trace of that fact in his speech.
-- A 23 (1948).

(56,57,58) WINONA COUNTY
Org. 1854.--Rich farming area with a
large urban pop. in Winona. Limestone
quarrying is also an important industry.
Large German pop.--Pop.: '50, 9208; '70,
22,319; '90, 33,797; '20, 33,653; '50,
39,841. Curtiss-Wedge, F., *History of
Winona County*, Chicago, 1913. *History of
Winona, Olmstead and Dodge Counties*, Chicago, 1884. *History of Winona and Waba-
sha Counties*, Chicago, 1884.

Winona. Inc. 1857.--Settled by 'Yankees'
1852; later joined by large groups of
Germans. An important lumbering and
shipping city for many yrs.--Now has
many varied industries, the largest being
the Watkins Co. Poles and New Englanders
are largest pop. elements, but there are
many Germans and Irish. Children often
sent e. to sch. Shopping center for an
agricultural area on both sides of the
Mississippi. Co. seat. State Teachers
College, College of St. Teresa.--Pop.:
'50, 2462; '70, 7192; '90, 18,208; '20,
19,143; '50, 25,031.--Bunnell, L. H.,
*Winona and Its Environs an the Mississip-
pi in Ancient and Modern Days*, Winona,
1897. Evans, W., *Winona, Minnesota*, Winona, 1890. "Pioneers for 100 Years 1855-
1955," *Winona Daily News*, Centennial Ed.
Nov. 19, 1955. Sinclair, D., *City of
Winona and Southern Minnesota, a Sketch
of their Growth and Prospects*, Winona,
1858. Smalley, E. V., "Winona: the Prosperous 'Gate City' of Southern Minnesota," *Northwest Mag.* 3.2-8 (1885). "Winona 75th Anniversary Edition, 1855-
1930," *Winona Republican Herald*, Nov. 20,
1930.

56. Retired farmer.--B. 1859 Rushford;
to Can.; to Winona.--F b. Tyrol; to Il.;
to Mn., 1855. M b. Czechoslovakia; to
Il.; to Mn., 1855.--8th gr.--Little social contact. Previously took part in
usual social activities of farmers, but
not since retirement.--Alert, cooperative, not talkative. Too ready to comply
with suggested forms. Insisted on knowing what interview was for.--Speech slow,
enunciation weak. Vocabulary and pronunciation definitely of his generation;
little influence from younger people.
No attempts at 'correctness.'--VR-A--G 1
(1947).

57. Manager of Winona Athletic Club; fireman on CB & Q RR 2 yrs.--B. 1895.--F b. Rochester of Irish parents. M b. Wi. of Irish parents.--HS; widely read. --Social contacts mainly through his work, includes all groups in the community. 2 yrs. in Army in WWI.--Ideal inf. Excellent sense of humor; acute observer. --Speech extremely rapid, but clear. No attempt at 'correctness.' Pronunciation and vocabulary 'up-to-date'. Interested in etymology, and in the study. Many conversational items. Aware of linguistic differences in community and discussed them.--VR-A--G 2 (1947).

58. Attorney.--B. 1905.--F b. Poland; to Winona, 1873. M b. Poland.--LL.B., Univ. of Mn.; George Washington Univ., 1 yr.--Active social life. Contacts with most of the community. Head of Winona Co. Welfare Board for yrs.--Cooperative because of public spirit. Thought questions silly. Not loquacious.--Speech clear, tempo moderate. Avoided colloquialisms; conscious of 'correct' grammar. --VR-A--G 3 (1947).

(59,60,61) NOBLES COUNTY
Org. 1872-74.--Rich agricultural area of dairy farms and orchards. Only urban center is Worthington, which is not large. Large German pop.; some Scandinavians and Irish.--Pop.: '50, 35; '70, 117; '90, 7958; '20, 17,917; '50, 22,435.--Rose, A. C., *An Illustrated History of Nobles County*, Worthington, 1908.

Worthington. Inc. 1873.--Established 1871 as prohibition colony.--Pop. mainly n. European; many English, German, and Scandinavian. 17 Protestant chs., 1 Catholic. Market and shopping center for surrounding agricultural region. Chiefly poultry and dairy products. Also shopping center for nearby Ia. and S.D. towns. Co. seat.--Pop.: '00, 2386; '20, 3481; '50, 7923.--Moore, C. F., "Sketch of the 'National Colony' at Worthington, Minnesota, in the Early Seventies," typed MS. in Minn. Hist. Soc. Library, St. Paul.

59. Carpenter; formerly a farmer.--B. 1864 near Rochester; to Worthington at age 8.--F b. Oh. M b. Oh. of N.Y. parents.--Some grammar sch. A graduate of Oberlin College and a United Brethren minister.--Social contacts mainly with farmers who are his customers. Devout Presbyterian.--Quiet, dignified, pleasant. Had to be persuaded to finish the record at end of each interview, although he came to enjoy it. Memory some-

what slow, responses hard to get.-- Voice high-pitched, weak, with tendency to become weaker with talking. Normal tempo. Not much nasalization.--VR-A--G 8 (1948).

60. Office worker in lumberyard.--B. 1898 near Worthington.--F b. Il. of German parents; to Worthington, 1888. M b. Il. of German parents; to Worthington, 1896.--Grammar sch.; HS 2 yrs.--Fairly wide social contacts.--Affable but not talkative.--Rapid tempo, distinct articulation, little nasalization, fairly short vowels. In grammatical questions tended to give 'correct' answers rather than natural ones. Genuine local speech --VR-A--Aux. inf.: Sister. Housewife, always lived in or near Worthington. Although she has had some HS, speech is that of an uneducated person. Quite concerned with 'correctness."--G 9 (1948).

61. Retired owner of nursery.--B. 1888 near Worthington.--F b. N.J. of English parents; to Mn., 1871; to Worthington, 1875. M b. N.Y.; to Wi.; to Worthington, 1875.--Univ. of Mn. experimental station, Minneapolis, 3 yrs.--Wide social contacts. Kiwanis Club. Knows everyone and is respected throughout the town.--Cooperative, liked to reminisce and tell jokes. Quick, keen mind.--Average tempo and distinctness. More than usual nasalization. Honest about his speech; unconcerned with 'correctness.'--VR-A--G 10 (1948).

(62,63) FREEBORN COUNTY
Org. 1857.--Agricultural area of diversified farming. Large number of Norwegians, Danes, and Germans. About half the pop. is centered in Albert Lea.--Pop.: '50, 3367; '70, 10,578; '90, 17,962; '20, 24,692; '50, 34,517.--Curtiss-Wedge, F., *History of Freeborn County*, Chicago, 1911. *History of Freeborn County, Minnesota*, Minneapolis, 1882.

Albert Lea. Inc. 1878.--Pop. is largely of Scandinavian descent. Chs. are mostly Protestant. Prosperous town with meat-packing plant, gas and stove factory, and co. dairy and oil business. Shopping center for a large agricultural area. Co. seat.--Pop.: '50, 262; '70, 1167; '90, 3305; '20, 8056; '50, 13,545. --"Historical Edition of Albert Lea and Freeborn County," *The Evening Tribune* (Albert Lea), Commemorative Issue, May 27, 1940.

62. Retired bank official.--B. 1871; lived 5 yrs. at Owatonna.--F and M b. N.Y. to Albert Lea, 1865.--Rural sch.; some HS.--Work resulted in a variety of

social contacts. Active in community until he became ill.--Cooperative; his
enforced inactivity made him enjoy the
chance to talk.--Speech indistinct, sometimes unintelligible when he was smoking
a cigar. Little nasalization. Average
tempo. No views on 'correctness.'--VR-A
--Aux. inf.: Wife. B. Albert Lea.
Attended college.--G 11 (1948).

Clark's Grove. Org. 1890.--Oldest Danish settlement in Mn. Small rural town.
Social life centers about large Danish
Baptist Ch. Albert Lea, 9 m.s., is main
shopping center for the town. Important
in the dairy co. movement.--Pop.: '30,
150; '50, 254.
63. Housewife.--B. 1888 near Clark's
Grove.--F b. Denmark; to Wi.; to Clark's
Grove, c'63. M b. Denmark; to Clark's
Grove, c'65.--Rural sch.; HS 1 yr.--So-
cial contacts limited to people in the
community and nearby. Ch. clerk.--Co-
operative, felt it her 'duty.' Said at
end that she didn't understand why material couldn't have been gotten from a
dictionary.--Speech distinct; average
tempo. Tendency to whisper parts of
words. Final /z/ and /d/ were often un-
voiced, even inaudible.--G 12 (1948).

(64,65) FILLMORE COUNTY
Org. 1853.--Agricultural area of dairy
farms and sheep-grazing. No urban center. Many people of Norwegian and German
ancestry, but also many from New England.
--Pop.: '50, 13,543; '70, 24,887; '90,
25,966; '20, 25,330; '50, 24,465.--Bish-
op, J. W., *History of Fillmore County*,
Chatfield, Mn., 1858. Curtiss-Wedge, F.,
History of Fillmore County, Chicago,
1912. Neill, D. D., *History of Fillmore
County*, Minneapolis, 1882. Nelson, T. O.,
Atlas of Fillmore County, Fergus Falls,
1956.

Green Leafton. Founded 1856 by Dutch
settlers from Ia. and Wi.; 1st Dutch settlement in Mn. Later new immigrants came
directly from The Netherlands. Settlers
in the adjoining areas chiefly from New
Eng. and N.Y., with a few Irish.--Small,
isolated rural community. Surrounding
area has several hundred people with sim-

ilar backgrounds and interests. Community is centered about the Dutch Reformed
Ch.--Pop.: c50; York Twp.: '50, c743.

64. Housewife; taught rural sch. before
marriage.--B. 1889.--F and M b. Netherlands; to Green Leafton, 1881.--HS; county normal institute 1 summer.--Active in
ch., which is main social, integrating
force in the community. Has been out of
the community for some distance only once
to the Canadian Rockies.--Pleasant,
firm personality. Reluctant to be an inf.
but cooperative. Not loquacious, but
provided a few spontaneous items. Local
in outlook.--Speech firm and distinct.
Uses nonstandard forms, but sometimes
reveals awareness of 'correctness.' A-
mused to learn that other terms for certain objects exist elsewhere; in general,
linguistically naive.--VR-A--Aux. inf.:
Husband. Farmer; parents from Holland.
HS 1 yr. Contributed 6 or 8 terms unfamiliar to his wife.--A 20 (1947).

Spring Valley. Inc. 1872--Settled 1850's
by New Englanders and New Yorkers. Many
people later from Wi.--Present pop. includes a few Germans and Scandinavians;
pipeline terminal operations have brought
in a mixed group of newcomers. Shopping
and shipping center for a rich agricultural area. No mfg.--Pop.: '50, 723; '70,
1279; '90, 1381; '20, 1871; '50, 2467.

65. Housewife; now has a housekeeper;
once taught grammar sch.--B. 1859 Wi.;
to Spring Valley at age 7; lived on a
farm at Cherry Grove near Spring Valley.
20 yrs.--F b. N.Y. of New Eng. parents;
to Wi.; to Mn. M b. Oh. of New Eng. parents; to Wi.; to Mn.--8th gr.; normal
sch. 2 terms. F a teacher. Self-educated
through reading and alert observation.--
Until recently led an active social life;
leader in the community and the Congregational Ch. Founding member of local
women's organization.--Good spirits, excellent health; an optimist. Good inf.;
cooperative, offered much spontaneous
material.--Speech slow, enunciation
fairly precise. Awareness of 'correctness' made her avoid common usage of the
community.--VR-A--A 21 (1947).

IOWA

(101,102) LYON COUNTY.
Org. 1871.--Earliest settlers from Ma.,
Mn., and Wi. A large colony of Norwe-
gians from Clayton and Fayette Cos. in
Ia.--Prosperous farming area, stock-rais-

ing and dairying.--Pop.: '70, 221; '80,
8680; '20, 15,431; '50, 14,697.--*Compendium of History, Reminiscence and Biography of Lyon County, Iowa*, Chicago,
Geo. A. Ogle & Co., 1904-5. Monlux, G.,

Early History of Lyon County, Rock Rapids, pub. by author, 1909.

Rock Rapids. Settled in the 1870's from Webster Co., Ia. Pop. now largely of mixed foreign elements with Scandinavian, Dutch, and Irish predominating.--Library, fine school, many churches. Librarian states there is an unusually high proportion of college graduates, even among the older people. Co. seat.--Pop.: '90, 1394; '20, 2172; '50, 2640.--McMillan, H. G., "Reminiscences of Rock Rapids," *Rock Rapids Review*, April 28, 1921.

101. Policeman (past 28 yrs.), locomotive fireman, U.S. army, raised on farm. --B. 1882 near Rock Rapids.--F b. Pa.; to Mn.; to Ia. PGM b. Vt. M b. Wi.; to Mn.; to Ia.--9th gr.--Not a member of any clubs, but has had wide social contacts. Traveled a good deal as a young man.--Average intelligence, alert. Cooperative and interested in the interview. Answers natural and prompt; little conversation. Friendly despite gruff manner. Great vitality.--Speech is clear, well enunciated. Moderate tempo, except in conversation when he hurries over some words.--VR-H--H 21 (1950).

102. Housewife.--B. 1896 near Rock Rapids; spent 2 yrs. in Luverne, Mn. as a child.--F b. Ia.; 2 yrs. in Mn. M b. Clayton Co., Ia.; to S.D. for a few yrs. as young woman; to Mn. for 2 yrs.--10th gr.--Navy Mother's Club. Prefers social visits in her home and visiting others. Recently traveled to Europe with son and daughter who work in Arabia.--Jolly, seldom worries; neat and friendly. Cooperative.--Speech rapid. Many modern expressions and slang.--H 20 (1950).

(103,104) EMMET COUNTY
Org. 1859.--First settlers from N.Y., Me., and Winneshiek Co., Ia.; pop. now includes many Scandinavians. Good farming area: hogs, corn, beef cattle, dairying. Estherville only large pop. center. --Pop.: '60, 105; '70, 1392; '90, 4274; '20, 12,627; '50, 14,102.--*History of Emmet County and Dickinson County, Iowa*, Chicago, Pioneer Pub. Co., 1917. "Early Settlers of Emmet County," *Estherville News*, Oct. 16, 1931.

Estherville. Settled in 1857 from Maine and N.Y. Shipping and trading town for surrounding agricultural area. Packing plant employs about 100 people.--Pop.: '70, 168; '90, 1475; '20, 4699; '50, 6719.--Jarvis, C. W., "Pioneer Days in Estherville," *Estherville Republican*, Nov. 23, 1921. Lee, N. J., "An Historical Sketch of Estherville," *Estherville News*, April 30, 1936.

103. Housewife.--B. 1872.--F b. Me.; to Ia. age 9. M b. Me.; to Ia. age 22.--2nd yr. HS--Wide circle of friends, member of several women's organizations. Church member. Reads a great deal; modern outlook.--Active and healthy. Outspoken and frank, cooperative, but saw no sense in the survey. Proud of the pioneering spirit of her family, who were first settlers in area. Answers prompt and to the point, sometimes changed to a shorter answer. Firm opinions, subtle sense of humor. GF whaling captain in Me.--Speech clear and precise, with many modern expressions.--VR-H--H 16 (1950).

Armstrong. Owes existence to construction of the Albert-Estherville branch of the CRI & P RR. Settled late because the surrounding area had sloughs and swamps not drained until recently. Many Scandinavians in the community, though fewer than in nearby towns.--Pop.: '70, 45; '90, 293; '20, 818; '50, 943. Burt, Peter H., "Early History of Armstrong Grove," *Armstrong Journal*, July 26, 1929.

104. Housewife.--B. 1890 near Armstrong. --F b. Il.; to Emmet Co. as young man. PGF b. Oh.; PGM b. Pa. M b. Black Hawk Co., Ia. MGF b. N.Y.; MGM b. Can.--8th gr.--Member Royal Neighbor Lodge; Presbyterian. Social life centered around family and neighbors.--Shy at first, later friendly and cooperative. Answers brief with little additional comment.--Small, round mouth gave effect of overrounding vowels from /o/ upward but did not seem to affect /ɔ/, which was usually lowered and perhaps slightly centered. Usual midwestern vowel /ɑ/ in /fɑðər/ was almost always fronted to [ɑ˂] or [a˃].--VR-H--Aux. inf.: Husband. Danish parentage. About 60 yrs. of age.--H 17 (1950).

(105,106) MITCHELL COUNTY.
Org. 1851. Settled by Norwegians from Wi. in 1853. Number of Irish came later, and a few settlers from e. US. Named for Irish patriot.--Agricultural area, chiefly potatoes and onions.--Pop.: '60, 3409; '70, 9582; '90, 13,299; '20, 13,921; '50, 13,945.--Clyde, J. F. & H. A. Dwelle, eds., *History of Mitchell and Worth Counties, Iowa*, Chicago, S. J. Clarke Pub. Co., 1918. *History of Mitchell and Worth Counties, Iowa*, Springfield, Il., Union Pub. Co., 1884.

St. Ansgar. Settled in 1853 by Czechoslovakians. Town is now predominantly

Norwegian with minor German and Czech elements.--Market center for potatoes and onions. Norwegian Lutheran Seminary once located here.--Pop.: '70, 360; '90, 609; '20, 844; '50, 981.--Bohach, Leona J., "Settlement of St. Ansgar--Miniature Melting Pot," *Iowa Journal*, 46.296-315 (July 1948).

105. Farmer. B. 1879 near St. Ansgar.--F b. Wi. of N.Y. parents; to Ca. for 3 yrs. as young man; to Ia., 1877.--M b. Pa.; to Wi.; to Ia.--2nd yr. HS--Methodist. Former member Lions Club. Neighborhood parties when younger. Secretary of Dist. Sch. Traveled a little.--Friendly and jovial. Enjoyed the interviews, volunteered many anecdotes.--Speech natural, not influenced by sense of 'correctness.' Spoke rapidly, in short phrases.
  Although his mailing address is Mitchell, all his social and business affairs are centered in St. Ansgar.--VR-H--H 7 (1950).

106. Housewife. B. 1891 near St. Ansgar. --F and M b. Norway; to Wi.; to Ia.--8th gr., Lutheran seminary 2 yrs.--Active member of Lutheran Ch. and church-sponsored women's groups. Often used to go to dances. Now social life centered in family and associates of husband (the postmaster).--Good sense of humor and ready laugh. Proud of Norwegian ancestry. --Learned Norwegian before English, but carry-over into English was not great. Uses different speech when speaking to local friends (heard in telephone conversation): vowels are more central; final /z/ becomes [s] or [ẓ], rarely [s]; and the accentual patterns are more like those of Norwegian. The /ɑ/ vowel is not consistent, often being raised to [ɑ^] in repeated pronunciation of the same word. The offglide of /ɑʊ/ and /oᵁ/ is often rounder than is normally heard, hence is transcribed [uᵛ].--H 8 (1950).

(107,108) WINNESHIEK COUNTY. Org. 1851. Settled in 1848 from Va., Oh., Pa., Vt.; later Norwegians from Wi. and Il.--Agricultural area, mainly hay, corn, and flax. No urban centers.--Pop.: '50, 546; '70, 23,570; '90, 22,528; '20, 22,091; '50, 21,639.--Alexander, W. E., *History of Winneshiek and Allamakee Counties, Iowa*, Sioux City, Western Pub. Co., 1882. Bailey, Edwin C., *Winneshiek County, Iowa, Past and Present*, Chicago, S. J. Clarke Pub. Co., 1914.

Decorah. Settled by easterners from Va., Oh., and Pa., and by English and Norwegians. Became a center for Norwegians w. of the Mississippi. Market center for surrounding area. Norwegian Luther College and Decorah College for Women. Co. seat.--Pop.: '60, 1920; '70, 2110; '90, 2801; '20, 4039; '50, 6060.--Horn, H. H., *English Colony in Iowa*, Boston, Christopher Pub. House, 1931.

107. Farmer. B. 1863 near Decorah.--F b. e. Can. of English and Irish parents. M b. Pa., probably of Pa. German parents. --8th gr.--Belongs to no clubs or organizations. Well known in Decorah, but little contact beyond the county. Plays cards with friends. Traveled little.-- Carefree and talkative. Enjoys telling jokes and reciting poems learned as a boy. Partial deafness made the interview difficult and lengthy.--Speech clear and well enunciated, sometimes quite rapid and loud. Answers often long and elaborate.--VR-H--H 6 (1950).

108. Farmer, automobile dealer, machinist, rooming-house proprietor. B. 1894; 1 yr. on w. coast.--F b. Il.; to Wi.; to Decorah, 1893. PGF b. Scot.; PGM b. N.Y. M b. Wi.; to Decorah, 1893. MGM and MGF b. Eng.--1 yr. HS--Member BPOE, American Legion. Goes to parties and plays cards occ.--Quiet and easy to get along with. Offered no information unless asked a question.--Speech sometimes rapid. Single-word answers. /æ/ vowel usually far front.--H 5 (1950).

(109,110,111) WOODBURY COUNTY. Org. 1853. Settled from N.Y., Vt., Pa., Oh., and Il. Foreign pop. mainly German, but there is also a British element.-- Agricultural area, livestock raising, but also many industries.--Pop.: '60, 1119; '70, 6172; '90, 55,632; '20, 92,171; '50, 103,917.--Garver, Frank H., "The Settlement of Woodbury County, Iowa," *Ia. J. of Hist. & Pol.*, 9.359-384 (1911). *History of the Counties of Woodbury and Plymouth, Iowa*, Chicago, A. Warner & Co., 1890-1891. Marks, Constant R., ed., *Past and Present of Sioux City and Woodbury County, Iowa*, Chicago, S. J. Clarke Pub. Co., 1904.

Sioux City. Inc. 1857. In its early days was an important shipping point and supply base. Little shipping on the rivers now, but still an important center for distribution of wholesale groceries. Trading area draws people from Ia., Nb., and S.D. Fifth largest stockyard in the country, and numerous meat-packing plants. Many of the original settlers were from N.H., although it now has a pop. of mixed ethnic groups from many of areas of the US. Co. seat. Catholic College for Women, Methodist coeducation sch. Hdqr. of Roman Catholic diocese.--

Pop.: '70, 3401; '90, 37,806; '20, 71,227; '50, 83,991.--*History of Sioux City, Iowa, from Earliest Settlement to January, 1892.* O'Connor, R. A., *Sioux City, a True Story of How it Grew*, Sioux City Public Library, 1932.

109. Farmer. B. 1877 near Sioux City; 1 1/2 yrs. in S.D. as young man.--F b. Pa.; to Il.; to Ia. M b. Il.--7th gr. 1 yr. business sch.--Social contacts limited. Lives with daughter on farm in isolated district on outskirts. Goes into the city occ.--Likes to tell anecdotes and reminisce; old-fashioned in outlook, cooperative.--Speech slow and deliberate. Vocabulary limited and old-fashioned. No concern with 'correctness.'--H 22 (1950).

110. Housewife; former teacher. B. 1903. Also lived in Minneapolis and Des Moines. --F b. Ia.; to Tx. 5 yrs. as young man. PGF b. In.; PGM b. Pa.; M b. Ia. MGF b. Pa.; MGM b. Me.--Graduate of Northwestern Univ. Reads current books and magazines. --Member several local and national clubs; Congregationalist. Wealthy and prominent; social contacts are extensive, among the most prominent families and some rural people. Traveled widely in US and Europe.--Gracious and down-to-earth. Cooperative and eager to help, interested in the survey.--Speech rapid and low. Voice often trailed off. Does not use an extensive vocabulary.--H 24 (1950).

111. Retired accountant. B. 1895. F b. Oh.; to Il.; to Ia. PGP b. Pa. M b. Il. --HS, night course in commerce at Morningside College.--Congregationalist.-- American Legion, dinner clubs. Attends concerts; travels a lot. Worked in a bank before retirement.--Alert, well-read, cooperative. Interested in the survey.--Tempo moderate. Rather large vocabulary.--H 23 (1950).

(112,113) POCAHONTAS COUNTY.
Org. 1858. First settled in the s.e. by a large Irish colony from Pa.; later in the n.e. by Scotch from Can. and New Eng. --Pop. largely foreign-born or of foreign-born parentage: Czech and Swedish, some Irish and German.--Prosperous farming area: dairying, beef cattle, corn, and hay.--Pop.: '60, 103; '70, 1446; '90, 9553; '20, 15,602; '50, 15,496.--Berry, William J., "The Influence of Natural Environment in North-Central Iowa," *Ia. J. of Hist. & Pol.*, 25.277-298 (1927). "How Pocahontas County Impressed Early Settlers," *Pocahontas Record*, Jan. 17, 1929.

Havelock. Pop.: 1900, 1012; '20, 381; '50, 307.

112. Retired farmer. B. 1897 in Pocahontas Co.--F b. Chicago of Czech parents; to Ia., age 6. M b. Ia. of Czech parents--8th gr. country sch.--Serious, but jovial. Cooperative, enjoyed the interview. Served in both wars, enlisted in the navy in WWII. Independent.--Speech slow, often ponderous, but intense. Concerned about 'correct usage' but used 'clumb' and 'run' as preterits. Avoided contractions when answering questions, but used them in conversation.--VR-H--H 18 (1950).

Fonda. Settled in the late 1860's. Rural community with a predominantly Irish pop. and many Germans and Swedes. Four churches, largest Catholic; public sch. and Catholic sch. Small library. Market and shopping town for a large area.--Pop.: '80, 168; '90, 625; '20, 1665; '50, 1120. --Petersen, William J., "When Fonda Was Young," *Palimpsest*, 40.105-112 (1959).

113. Retired farmer. B. 1870.--F b. Il.; to Ia. age 18. PGF and PGM b. Me. M b. Il.; to Ia. age 17.--Country sch. until c19.--Member, infrequent attendant Presbyterian Ch.; member IOOF. Traveled little, few contacts outside the country.-- Happy, likes to tell stories about 'old times.' Alert, answered questions promptly. Most cooperative; enjoyed the interview.--Speech rapid, voice high-pitched. --VR-H--H 19 (1950).

(114,115) HAMILTON COUNTY
Org. 1857. In the n. part of the Co. pop. is from the e. and middle states, in the s.e. from Norway and Sweden.--Prosperous farming area, dairying and beef cattle, and some crops. Several small industries make food products and machinery.--Pop.: '60, 1699; '70, 6055; '90, 15,319; '20, 19,531; '50, 19,660. Lee, J. W. ed., *History of Hamilton County, Iowa*, Chicago, S. J. Clarke Pub. Co., 1912.

Blairsburg. Pop.: '70, 310; '90, 530; '20, 272; '50, 257.

114. Farmer. B. 1872 near Blairsburg.-- F b. Il.; to Ia. age 27. PGF German descent. M b. N.Y. of Scottish parents; to Ia. as girl.--8th gr.--Member Congregational Ch. Member local schoolboard 26 yrs., president most of the time. Member Modern Woodmen of America. Travels to Chicago or Omaha to sell stock. Lives with middle-aged daughter.--'Old-fashioned,' but tireless worker for progress and improvement of the sch. Willing to be interviewed, but showed no interest in the survey. Often did not understand the questions. Never spoke unless addressed; then replied in short staccato

phrases; tempo moderate. Frequent pronounced nasality in vowels preceding /n/
plus consonant, often with omission of
the [n].--H 12 (1950).

Jewell. Platted in 1880.--Pop.: '90,
414; '20, 1090; '50, 973.--"Pioneer Days
in Jewell," *Jewell Record*, March 5, 1931.

115. Housekeeper, practical nurse. B.
1889.--F b. N.Y.; to Wi. age 5; to Ia.
age 14. PGF b. N.Y. of German parents.
PGM b. N.Y. of Scottish parents. M b.
Dubuque Co., Ia.; to Decatur Co. age 17;
to Hamilton Co. age 27. MGF b. Oh. of
English parents. MGM b. Oh.--10th gr.
Reads fiction, history.--Known in town
and Co. as local historian. Occ. writes
articles for Webster City newspaper. Has
not traveled extensively.--Talkative,
very interested and cooperative.--Speech
rapid, high-pitched, sharp. Answers
on grammatical items usually natural,
but occ. guarded.--VR-H--H 13 (1950).

(116,117) BREMER COUNTY.
Org. 1847. Pop. about equally German and
American, the latter coming from New Eng.,
N.Y., Pa., Oh., and In., and the former
from n. Germany.--Pop.: '60, 4915; '70,
12,528; '90, 14,630; '20, 16,728; '50,
18,884.--*History of Butler and Bremer
Counties, Iowa*, Springfield, Il., Union
Pub. Co. 1883.

Janesville. Settled c1849 by Germans,
Irish, and native Americans. After this
initial growth, the town received few
new immigrants; most of the present residents are descended from early settlers.
--Pop.: 1900, 311; '20, 261; '50, 445.--
"Founding of Janesville," *Waverly Democrat*, Sept. 2, 1932. McCaffree, Ruth,
"Beginnings of Janesville," *Waverly in-
dependent-Republican*, Feb. 7, 1934.

116. Housewife. B. 1868 in Bremer Co.;
as adult spent 7 yrs. in Butler Co.,
1 1/2 yrs. in Wy.--F and M b. N.Y.; 12
yrs. in Wi.--8th gr. country sch.; 1 yr.
HS; taught country sch. 2 yrs.--Method-
ist.--American Legion Aux. Social contacts mostly with local residents and
rural people. Lived on a farm until recently.--Charming, good sense of social
responsibility. Well known and respected
in the community. Many visitors during
the interview. Cooperative and eager to
help.--Speech slow and well articulated.
Some concern for 'correctness.'--VR-H--
Aux. inf.: Husband. B. in Marshall Co.,
Ia., 1865. Came to Bremer Co. c1874; 1
lived in Butler Co. 7 yrs. as adult; in
Wy. for 1 1/2 yrs.--F b. Pa.; M b. N.Y.;
to Ia. as young girl.--H 9 (1950).

117. Farmer, shop foreman of manufacturing co. B. 1902.--F b. Il.; to Bremer
Co. age 9. M birthplace unknown; to Bremer Co., 1900. MGF and MGM b. Ct. and Ire.
--8th gr.--Social contact mostly with
fellow-workers, none outside of town.--
High-strung. Recently had a nervous
breakdown, but has learned to relax,
and now appears at ease. Unaffected; cooperated generously.--Speech easy and
relaxed. Final /ŋ/ is usually /n/; the
second element of some final diphthongs
is dropped.--VR-H--Aux. inf.: Wife, 19-
yr.-old daughter, and 9-yr.-old son.
Daughter had completed 2 yrs. of college.
Unless otherwise indicated, answers
given by the aux. inf. were given by the
wife.--P 7 (1950).

(118) BLACK HAWK COUNTY.
Org. 1853. Earliest settlers from Mi. and
Johnson Co., Ia. Later settlers from N.Y.,
Pa., Oh., and the New Eng. states: now
many of German and British descent.
--Several industries; a rich agricultural
region.--Pop.: '50, 135; '70, 21,706;
'90, 24,219; '20, 56,570; '50, 100,448.
--Hartman, John C., ed., *History of
Black Hawk County, Iowa, and Its People*,
Chicago, S. J. Clarke Pub. Co., 1915.
The History of Black Hawk County, Iowa,
Chicago, Western Historical Co., 1878.

Cedar Falls. Inc. 1853. First settled
1845. Was early shipping point for surrounding area and chief milling town.
Now several manufacturers of farm equipment, and a woolen mill. State Teachers
College.--Pop.: '70, 3070; '90, 3459;
'20, 6316; '50, 14,334. Pop. history is
similar to that of the Co., including
in the 1880's a few Southerners, some
Danes and Irish. Leavitt, Roger, *When
Cedar Falls Was Young*, Cedar Falls, Record Press, 1929.

118. Housewife. B. Ackley, Ia. (Age not
recorded.)--F b. N.Y.; to Detroit as infant; to Kalamazoo Co.; to Ia. age 28.
PGP b. N.Y. M b. Yadkin Co., N.C.; age
13. MGP b. Yadkin Co., N.C.--Has had
some schooling.--Christian Scientist.--
No distinction between vowels in 'hole'
and 'whole.'--L (1938).

(119,120,121) DUBUQUE COUNTY.
Org. 1836. One of first areas settled
because of lead mines near Dubuque. From
beginning its pop. has been cosmopolitan.
Rich agricultural area, many industries.
Lumbering important in the 1890's.--Pop.:
'40, 3059; '50, 10,841; '70, 38,969; '90,
49,848; '20, 58,262; '50, 71,337.--Good-
speed, W. A., *History of Dubuque County*,

Dubuque, pub. by author, n.d. *History of Dubuque County, Iowa*, Chicago, Western Historical Co., 1880.

Epworth. Settled in the 1840's. Small, rural community. Onetime seat of a Methodist preparatory sch., which has since become a Catholic Mission House. Mainly Catholic.--Pop.: '90, 348; '20, 468; '50, 536.

119. Hardware and coal retailer, farmhand, railroad engineer, rural schoolteacher. B. 1874 in Dyersville; spent some time in Waterloo and East St. Louis, Il.--F and M b. Pa.--HS or prep sch.--Member, irregular attendant, Methodist Ch. Many friends among all classes. Entertains often, frequently has 'open house.'--Dry sense of humor, shrewd, economical in speech and movement. Well read, intelligent, not ostentatious. Speaks intelligently on current affairs. Firm opinions.--Speech slow and deliberate, but with assurance and little hesitation. Large vocabulary; offered excellent definitions of terms used. Diction precise.--H 4 (1950).

Dubuque. First settled 1788, then abandoned. Founded 1833. Inc. 1841. Oldest town in Ia.; settled early because of lead mines nearby. Served as gateway for settlers entering Ia., and received pop. from many states and countries. In the 1890;s lumbering was the most important industry, but woodworking has taken its place. Important shipping and manufacturing city. In heart of wealthy agricultural and dairy area, providing it with a profitable market. Co. seat. Residence of Catholic archbishop. Two Catholic colleges, Lutheran theological seminary, and a Presbyterian college and theological seminary.--Pop.: '50, 3108; '70, 18,434; '90, 30,311; '20, 39,141; '50, 49,671.--Hoffman, Mathias M., *Antique Dubuque, 1673-1833*, Dubuque Telegraph-Herald Press, 1930. Langworthy, Lucius H., *Dubuque: Its History, Mines, Indian Legends, etc.*, Dubuque Institute, 1855.

120. Member of investment firm, public utilities. B. 1879; spent some time in Evanston, Il.--F b. Ma.; to Milwaukee; to Dubuque, 1858. PGP b. Eng. M b. Wi. of English parents.--2 1/2 yrs. HS, Business college.--Family well-do-do and somewhat aristocratic. Social contact with the most important people in town. Well read and well informed. Member Episcopal Ch., Masonic Lodge, BPOE, several philatelic clubs, state hist. soc., president of Dubuque hist. soc.--Impulsive, somewhat nervous. Called interview 'damn

foolishness' and bragged about being hard to get along with, but later became interested. Often spelled words rather than pronouncing them. Frequently sought references in books for word usage or items of historical interest. Active, blunt, but friendly.--Speech precise, occ. clipped, sometimes rapid. Careful about 'correctness' and improper expressions. Would never say, "The dog wants out."--Aux. inf.: Wife. B. Il. of English parents. Now 62 yrs. old. HS, wide reader, student of history and current affairs. Several social organizations. Pleasant and attractive.--H 2 (1950).

121. Housewife; Dubuque packing plant during WWII. B. 1896; spent 4 yrs. in Davenport as adult.--F b. Wi.; lived in Ca. short time as young woman; English ancestry. M b. Il. of French ancestors. --3 1/2 yrs. HS--Member and previous officer of Ladies Aux. of AFL and of the Truck Drivers' Union. Weekly poker and rummy parties with other couples, occ. parties at a club where husband is bartender.--Seems carefree and happy. Works hard for her family. Very hospitable. Older sister and one daughter with her husband and child live with them.-- Speech rapid; vocabulary not extensive, but colorful. Voice of medium high pitch, somewhat loud, usually pleasant. Her /æ/ vowels are often quite far front, and the /ɑʊ/ diphthong often has the final element as an unrounded offglide.--H 3 (1950).

(122,123) MONONA COUNTY
Org. 1854. First settled by Mormons, later by settlers from Oh., Ill., e. Ia., and the e. states and from the Scandinavian countries. Agricultural area with little industry: cattle-breeding, hogs, and corn. Pop.: '60, 832; '70, 3654; '90, 14,515; '20, 17,125; '50, 16,303. *History of Monona County, Iowa*, Chicago, National Pub. Co., 1890.

Onawa. Platted 1857. First settlers from the e. states, but an influx of Scandinavians (mostly Swedes) soon outnumbered them.--Shopping and market center for the surrounding area. Co. seat. Flour mills, 2 RR.--Pop.: '80, 882; '90, 1358; '20, 2256; '50, 3498. "Founding of Onawa," *Onawa Democrat*, June 30, 1932.

122. Retired lawyer. B. 1871.--F b. N.Y.; to Sioux City age 13; to Onawa age 25. PGP b. Pa. M b. Ma.; to Onawa age 20. MGP b. Ire.--HS; law school in Iowa City 1891-96.--Social contact through his business. Most of his clients are farmers. Social life centered around his relatives in the outlying farms.--Shy, in-

troverted, suspicious. Moderately cooperative, but enjoyed interview thoroughly.
--VR-P--Aux. inf.: Wife. B. Shelby Co.,
parents from N.Y. Grandparents from N.Y.
and Vt.--Town librarian until a few yrs.
ago.--Alert, chipper, interested in many
things.--P 20 (1950).

123. Beauty operator, housewife. B.
1897 in Monona Co.--F and M b. in Monona
Co. PGF b. N.Y.; PGM b. Pa. MGP b. Pa.--
Present contacts are merchants in town.
Grew up on farm.--Vivacious, high-spirit-
ed. Active in public affairs. Member DAR.
Quick wit and penetrating sense of humor.
Mother a teacher, made her conscious of
grammar.--Speech rapid and animated.
Vowels crisp and distinct.--Aux. inf.:
Husband. B. in Monona; jobs during vaca-
tion in the west. College at Ames.--F b.
Wi., of English parents.--P 18 (1950).

(124,125) POTTAWATTAMIE COUNTY.
Org. 1848. First settled by Mormons; later by easterners and Scandinavians.--Ag-
ricultural area of stock farms and pumpkin growing. Some industry, mostly connected with canning and meat packing.
Pop.: '50, 7,828; '70, 16,893; '90,
47,430; '20, 61,550; '50, 69,682. Baskin,
O. L., ed., *History of Pottawattamie
County*, Chicago, O. L. Baskin & Co.,
1883. Field, Homer H. & Joseph R., *History of Pottawattamie County*, Chicago,
S. J. Clarke Pub. Co., 1907.

Crescent. Laid out in 1856 by Mormons.
Once had good business prospects, but
is now a static, rural community. Pop.
has changed little since first settlement.--Pop.: '60, 535; '70, 1117; '90,
500; '20, 752; '50, 636.

124. Retired farmer. B. 1879 near Logan,
Ia.; spent 1 yr. in Harrison Co., Nb.--
F b. Mi.; to Harrison Co. age 9. PGP
from New Eng.; ancestors believed to
have come on the Mayflower. M b. In.;
to Mo.; to Harrison Co.--8th gr.--Pa-
tient, slow-thinking. Spends his time
now with woodcraft.--F 10 (1950).

125. Cafe and motel owner, tavern operator, farmer. B. 1895.--F b. Ga.; to
Crescent age 17. PGP b. N.Y. and Ire. M
b. Ky.; to Crescent, 1892. MGP b. Ire.--
HS--Early social contacts among his rural neighbors, now mainly with townspeople and customers.--Genial and cooperative.--P 16 (1950).

(126) SHELBY COUNTY.
Org. 1853. Agricultural area. Almost no
industry. Area first settled by Mormons
and others from e. Ia., Il., In., Oh.,

and Pa. Later many Germans and Danes arrived; they now make up the majority of
the pop.--Pop.: '60, 818; '70, 2540; '90,
17,611; '20, 16,065; '50, 15,942.--Louis,
John J., "Shelby County--A Sociological
Study," *Ia. J. of Hist. & Pol.*, 2.81-101,
218-255 (1904). White, Edward S., *Past
and Present of Shelby County*, Indianapolis, B. F. Bowen & Co., 1915.

Elk Horn. Settled 1854 by Danes, most
of them coming directly from Denmark in
the last quarter of the 19th century.
Still predominantly Danish. Rural shopping community. Small but prosperous.
No industry.--Pop.: '60, 818; '70, 2540;
'90, 17,611; '20, 16,065; '50, 15,942.--
Esbeck, M., "Hardships and Trials of
Early Days," *Elk Horn Review*, Oct. 21,
1926.

126. Farmer; taught sch. 4 yrs. B. 1878
in Shelby Co.--F and M b. Denmark; to
Ia. as young adults.--9 yrs. country sch.,
1 1/2 yr. normal sch.--Social contacts
limited to his family. 3 children have
been in college.--Optimist; loves a good
joke and is fond of telling stories.
Reads a great deal. Conscious of 'correctness.'--Influence of radio perhaps
revealed in glides: new, Tuesday, few.
--P 11 (1950).

(127) AUDUBON COUNTY.
Org. 1855. Settled 1851. Large Danish
pop. Agricultural area, canneries, sor-
ghum. Little industry.--Pop.: '60, 454;
'70, 1212; '90, 12,412; '20, 12,520; '50,
11,579.--Andrews, H. F., ed., *History of
Audubon County, Iowa*, Indianapolis, B.
F. Bowen & Co., 1915.

Audubon. Platted in 1878 by CRI & P RR.
Large Danish pop. Canning factory. Market town. Co. seat.--Pop.: '70, 381; '90,
1310; '20, 2108; '50, 2808.

127. Housewife. B. 1900 in Audubon Co.
--F b. Mahaska Co. PGP b. Pa. and Va. M
b. Mahaska Co.--8th gr.--Social contacts
with neighbors and family.--Pleasant,
amiable, responsive wit. Death of son
in WWII reduced her interest in life.
Interview and questions seemed pointless
to her.--Low mid-back vowel frequently
raised, but fronted only in 'county.'
This may be typical of Audubon.--P 9
(1950).

(128,129,130,131) POLK COUNTY.
Org. 1846. Rich agricultural area, with
many industries. Earliest settlers from
In. and the e. settlements in Ia. Varied
pop., but many Scandinavians.--Pop.: '50,
4513; '70, 27,857; '90, 65,410; '20,

154,029; '50, 226,010.--Brigham, Johnson, *Des Moines Together with the History of Polk County, Iowa*, Chicago, S. J. Clarke Pub. Co., 1911. *The History of Polk County, Iowa*, Des Moines, Union Historical Co., 1880. Porter, William, *Annals of Polk County, Iowa*, Des Moines, George A. Miller Printing Co., 1898.

Des Moines. Inc. 1857. State capital, Co. seat. On a main trail to the Ca. gold fields; many prospectors remained in Des Moines. Diverse pop.: many Italians, Swedes, Negroes, Germans, and Dutch. Insurance and publishing center, important commercial and marketing center. Sch. for handicapped children. Drake Univ.--Pop.: '50, 502; '70, 12,035; '90, 50,093; '20, 126,468; '50, 177,965. --Brigham, Johnson, *Des Moines, The Pioneer of Municipal Progress*, Chicago, S. J. Clarke Pub. Co., 1911. Turrill, H. B., *Historical Reminiscences of the City of Des Moines*, Des Moines, Redhead & Dawson, 1857.

128. Farmer, golf course owner, road repairer. B. 1890 in Polk Co.--F b. Boone Co. of Swedish parents. M b. Sweden; to Hamilton Co. age 13; to Polk Co. age 17.--HS--Social contacts previously were farmers. Made his farm into a golf course and now social contacts are with business and professional men from Des Moines.--Modest, retiring, intelligent, independent, self-confident. Inventive, has a few patents. Interest in politics, scientific farming.--Speech clipped and precise.--F 17 (1950).

129. Blacksmith. B. 1869 in Polk Co.--F b. Germany; to America, 1845. M b. Germany; to America, 1840's.--8th gr.--Social contacts with neighbors and people he works with.--Genial, friendly, great deal of self-respect. Spends evenings in the public library. No amusements except reading.--Heavy aspiration of /b/ and /p/. High front vowels are raised.--VR-P--P 23 (1950).

130. Laborer. B. 1890 in Polk Co.--F b. Va.; to Des Moines, 1875. M b. Mo.; to Des Moines as a child.--HS--Social contacts with neighbors and other laborers. Is Negro; contacts mainly with Negroes.--Quick mind; demonstrated a shrewd intelligence. Annoyed at implication that Negroes might speak differently.--Middle front vowels lowered. Occ. does not form final stops: [bɑɚnjɚ].--VR-P--Aux. inf.: Sister. First Negro woman graduate of State Univ. of Iowa.--P 24 (1950).

131. Teacher, secretary, housewife. B. 1899; spent 5 yrs. in Audubon Co.--F b.

Jefferson Co.; to Polk Co. age 20. PGP b. Jefferson Co. and Pa. M b. Czechoslovakia; to America age 4.--2 yrs. college in Des Moines.--Social contacts with professional people in Des Moines. Acquainted with lawyers, doctors, professors. Takes part in such activities as the Chicago Great Books Course.--Modest, slightly retiring, but of boundless interests. Alert.--Partial conversion in the use of the glide found in new. Occ. it is [ʉᵘ] and sometimes it is [ɪ̞ᵘ] or [ɪᵘ]. This represented to the interviewer the glide used by many radio speakers in such words as few, Tuesday, suit. Speech nasal throughout.--VR-P--Aux. inf.: Teenage son contributed a few words.--P 16 (1950).

(132,133) MARSHALL COUNTY. Org. 1849. Agricultural area, mostly corn. Canning is an important industry. in the Co., also quarrying. One large urban center.--Pop.: '50, 338; '70, 17,576; '90, 25,842; '20, 32,630; '50, 35,611.--Battin, William, & F. A. Moscrip, *Past and Present of Marshall County*, Indianapolis, B. F. Bowen & Co., 1912. *History of Marshall County, Iowa*, Chicago, Western Historical Co., 1878.

Laurel. Settled in 1850's from Ky. and N.C. Small, rural community. No industry. Pop.: '10, 179; '20, 195; '50, 257.

132. Farmer. B. 1866.--F b. Ky.; to Ia. as young man. M b. Il.; to Ia. as young woman. MGF b. N.C. of Pa.-German descent. --8th gr. country sch.--Social contacts limited to neighbors. Has traveled in Midwest.--Happy, enjoys conversation. Arthritis forces him to use a cane. Enjoyed the interview, very cooperative. --Speech shows many South Midland characteristics. Low-central vowels consistently fronted. High variety of rounded low-back vowels approaches the central-back position. Offglide in [dɔɔˣg] is longer than usual. Conversation contains colorful expressions.--VR-H--H 10 (1950).

133. Housekeeper. B. 1890 near Laurel; lived on same farm all her life.--F b. near Laurel. PGM b. In.; PGF b. Pa. (Pa.-German). M b. Marshall Co., Ia. MGM b. In. MGF b. Ky. (Scotch-Irish).--Country sch. until 17.--Methodist.--Women's soc. of ch. Occ. social gatherings with neighbors. Traveled little.--Pleasant and cooperative, but not very alert.--Many South Midland characteristics. Speech natural. Interviewer had the good fortune to stay in her home for several days getting many of the items through conversation. Average tempo, rather sharp voice.--VR-H--H 11 (1950).

(134) MARION COUNTY
Org. 1845. Large Dutch pop., a few Quaker communities, and many people of Welsh descent. Agricultural area, with several coal mines, and some manufacturing.--Pop.: '50, 5482; '70, 24,436; '90, 23,058; '20, 24,957; '50, 25,930.--Wright, John W., *The History of Marion County, Iowa, and Its People*, Chicago, S. J. Clarke Pub. Co., 1915. *The History of Marion County, Iowa*, Des Moines, Union Historical Co., 1881.

Pella. Inc. 1855. Settled by Dutch in 1847. Pop. still mainly Dutch; language and customs have been preserved. Dutch is spoken, mixed with English, in everyday intercourse. Market center for a rich agricultural area. Central College. --Pop.: '80, 2430; '90, 2408; '20, 3338; '50, 4427.--Cole, Cyrenus, "A Bit of Holland in America," *Annals of Iowa*, 3rd series, 3.241-270 (1897-99). *A Souvenir History of Pella*, Pella, 1922.

134. Housewife. B. 1900 in Mahaska Co.; to Marion Co., 1912.--F b. Holland; to Ia. M b. Mahaska Co. of Dutch parents.--Fifth gr.--Social contacts with faculty of Central College. Two of her daughters are college students.--High-spirited, quick sense of humor. Very cooperative. Devoted to her family. Active in ch. affairs. Aux. inf.: Husband. B. in Mahaska Co. of Dutch parents.--P 14 (1950).

(135,136) MAHASKA COUNTY.
Org. 1844. Rich agricultural area, raising of pure-bred cattle and hogs, some manufacturing; at one time an important coal mining area attracting many Welsh immigrants. Although the mines have closed, most of the Welsh people have remained to take up farms. Also a large Dutch pop. First settlers were from the s., e., and middle states, many of whom settled first in Il.--Pop.: '50, 5989; '70, 22,503; '90, 28,805; '20, 26,270 '50, 24,672. Hedge, Manoah, *Past and Present of Mahaska County*, Chicago, S. J. Clarke Pub. Co., 1906. *History of Mahaska County, Iowa*, Des Moines, Union Historical Co., 1881.

Oskaloosa. Inc. 1855. Settled in 1843 by a group of Quakers. Still a Quaker community, with a large number of Welshmen. Marketing center with industries connected with dairy and poultry farms in the surrounding area. Co. seat. John Fletcher College, William Penn College. --Pop.: '50, 625; '70, 3204; '90, 6558; '20, 9427; '50, 11,124.--Barnhart, Cornelia M., "Osceola and Oskaloosa," *Pal-*

impsest, 28.300-309 (Oct. 1947). "The Story of Oskaloosa," *Oskaloosa Herald*, May 13, 1924.

135. Retired farmer. B. 1862 in Mahaska Co.--F b. Tn.; to Ia., 1847. M b. Ky.; to Ia., 1848.--Country sch.--Social contacts with other retired farmers in the area. Genial, friendly, calm disposition, easygoing. Enjoyed the interview.--An occasional intrusive /r/. Unaccented initial elements are generally light, occ. omitted. Pronounces 1 in palm and calm. --P 15 (1950).

136. Housewife, teacher. B. 1892 in Mahaska Co.--F b. Oh.; to Ia. age 21. PGF b. Va. M b. In.; to Ia. age 18. MGP b. N.C.--HS, 1 yr. college in Oskaloosa.--Social contacts with neighboring farmers and members of the local Friends Ch. of which she is a member.--Genial, ready laughter. Enjoys children. Taught Sunday sch. for many yrs.--Inconsistently deliberate. Weariness throughout the interview may have made pronunciation less deliberate and careful.--P 13 (1950).

(137) CEDAR COUNTY.
Org. 1836. Agricultural area of dairy farms and pure-bred stock-raising. Some Quaker settlements.--Pop.: '40, 1253; '50, 3941; '70, 19,731; '90, 18,253; '20, 17,560; '50, 16,910.--Aurner, Clarence R., ed., *A Topical History of Cedar County, Iowa*, Chicago, S. J. Clarke Pub. Co., 1910. *The History of Cedar County, Iowa*, Chicago, Western Historical Co., 1878. *The History of Cedar County with a History of Iowa*, Cedar Rapids & Chicago, Historical Pub. Co., 1910.

West Branch. Small farming center.--Pop.: '80, 501; '90, 474; '20, 688; '50, 769.--Jackson, Albert W., "West Branch in the Early Seventies," *West Branch Times*, Oct. 7, 1926.

137. Housewife, practical nurse. B. 1873 in Johnson Co., Ia.; to Cedar Co., 1907.--F b. N.C.; to Ma. age 4. PGP b. N.C. M b. Pa.; to Ia. age 6. MGP b. Pa. (Pa.-German).--Country sch., 8th gr. Well read.--Member DAR, Daughters of Union Veterans, WCTU, Methodist Ch., several women's social and study groups. Traveled throughout US and Can.--Capable, efficient, very energetic. Intelligent, enjoys reading. Answers prompt and precise; clearly formed definitions. Very cooperative.--Speech slow and clear. Definite South Midland characteristics. --H 14 (1950).

(138,152) JOHNSON COUNTY.
Org. 1838. Earliest settlers were from

n. In. Rich agricultural region of dairying and beef cattle. A few small industries: food products and publishing.--
Pop.: '40, 1491; '50, 4472; '70, 24,998
'90, 23,082; '20, 26,462; '50, 45,756.
--*History of Johnson County, Iowa*, Iowa
City, 1883. Irish, Capt. F. M., "History
of Johnson County, Iowa, Iowa City, 1883.
1st series, 6.23-31 (1868).

Solon. Pop.: '80, 383; '90, 353; '20,
471; '50, 527.

138. Farmer. B. 1896.--F and M b. Solon.
PGM b. Ma.; PGF b. Oh. MGF b. Germany;
MGM b. Oh.--8th gr. country sch.--Prom-
inent farmer, director REA; often attends
meetings as far away as Des Moines. Traveled through s. US during recent yrs.
Served in WWI.--Easy to talk with, very
cooperative. Up-to-date on farming methods. Added comments only when he thought
they would be of interest.--Spoke in
short, clipped phrases. Tempo varied from
slow to rapid.--H 15 (1950).

Iowa City. Inc. 1853. Laid out in 1839
as site for state capital. When capital
was moved later, Iowa City was given the
state univ. Primarily a college town
with a few industries and businesses associated with farming. Medical and shopping center for the area.--Pop.: '50,
1250; '70, 5914; '90, 7016; '20, 11,267;
'50, 27,212.--Hoover, John F., et al.,
Souvenir and Annual for 1881-82, Iowa
City, 1882. Shambaugh, B. F., *Iowa City,
a Contribution to the Early History of
Iowa*, State Hist. Soc., Iowa City, 1893.
Shambaugh, B. F., *The Old Stone Capital
Remembers*, Iowa City, State Hist. Soc.,
1939.

152. Housewife. B. 1868.--F b. Oh. of
Scottish parents. M b. Oh. of Irish and
English parents.--HS, 1 yr. State Univ.
--A 119 (1950).

(139) JACKSON COUNTY.
Org. 1838. Agricultural area of dairy
farms. Some industry. The first settlers
mainly from New Eng., some from N.Y., Pa.,
and Oh., a few Southerners, and a few
from the closer states. Many Germans
arrived later.--Pop.: '40, 1411; '50,
7210; '70, 22,619; '90, 22,771; '20,
19,931; '50, 18,622.--Ellis, James B.,
History of Jackson County, Iowa, Chicago,
S. J. Clarke Pub. Co., 1910. *The History
of Jackson Co., Iowa*, Chicago, Western
Historical Co., 1879.

Maquoketa. Inc. 1857. Pop. history is
similar to that of the Co. Co. seat.
Trading town for surrounding area.--Pop.:
'50, 168; '70, 1756; '90, 3077; '20,

3626; '50, 4307.--Jewett, W. H., "A Typical Iowa Town: The City of Maquoketa,"
Midland Monthly, 6.1-18 (Sept. 1896).

139. Housewife. B. 1866 in Emeline, Ia.
--F b. Oh. of German parents; to Ia.; to
Nb.; to Ia. M b. Va.; to Ia. age 9; to
Bb.; to Ia. MGF b. Ire.; MGM b. Germany
--Country sch. until 16, 3 mos. in Dubuque sch.--Presbyterian. Few social
contacts, mainly with neighbors in surrounding area. Traveled little. Lives
in rooming house with people of her age
and background.--Pleasant, easy to talk
with. Tried hard to please and give additional information. Remembered some
items only when they were suggested.--
Speech clear and moderately well articulated. Often had a lowered [æ] vowel and
unusual mid-central vowel before /ʃ/ as
[mɝˢʃ] [brɝˇʃ]. Vocabulary not extensive. Used [tʃɪlbleˡˆmz] for chilblains
and [kʌntrɪdʒɪˆg] for country-jake. Aux.
inf.: Cousin. B. in Jackson Co., 1869.
Country sch. until 16. Often gave wrong
answer in jest.--H 1 (1950).

(140,141) SCOTT COUNTY.
Org. 1837. First settled after Blackhawk
Purchase in 1833 by people from the e.
and s. states, most of whom had settled
previously in Il. They came mainly from
Oh., N.Y., Pa., and New Eng. states, and
Va. Now a large German pop. Rich agricultural area with some limestone quarrying.
--Pop.: '40, 2140; '50, 5986; '70,
38,599; '90, 43,164; '20, 73,952; '50,
100,698.--Downer, Harry E., *History of
Davenport and Scott Counties, Iowa*, Chicago, S. J. Clarke Pub. Co., 1915. *History of Scott County, Iowa*, Chicago,
Interstate Pub. Co., 1882.

Walcott. Established in 1853 by Scotch
Irish, now predominantly German. Rural
village.--Pop.: 1900, 362; '20, 384; '50,
480.--Doyle, Darrell E., "Locating at
Walcott," *Davenport Democrat and Leader*,
Dec. 8, 1929. Richter, August P., "The
Settlement of Walcott," *Davenport Times*,
May 24, 1924.

140. Machinist, farm laborer. B. 1879
near Walcott.--F b. St. Louis of German
parents; to Scott Co. age 3. M b. Davenport of French and German parents.--Sch.
until 15.--For some yrs. was itinerant
farmer and laborer, working where he
could find employment; spent some time
in Wy. and Mt. Social contact with people he meets in his jobs.--Individualist,
eccentric. Loves music, has large as-
sortment of violins, harmonicas, banjos,
and guitars.--Speech slow, not deliberate. Vowels all of extra length.--P 1
(1950).

Princeton. Inc. 1857. Small river town with no industries. At one time a thriving trading center, but the growth of Davenport reduced its importance. Earliest settlers came from the midland states, Ky., W.V., Il., In., Oh., N.Y., and Pa. Most of them had settled previously in Il.--Pop.: '60, 468; '70, 498; '90, 398; '20, 414; '50, 495.--Underwood, Martha, "Old Times in Princeton," *Clinton Herald*, May 29, 1931.

141. Retired RR employee. B. 1874; lived in Bettendorf, Ia.; worked 1 yr. in Ca. --F b. Princeton. PGP b. Vt. and In. M b. Ia. MGP b. Boston and N.H.--Grammar sch.--Social contacts with neighbors in Princeton and men he worked with on the R.R.--Cooperative. Tried to recall old words. Wished to know full purpose of study before agreeing to be an inf.-- Speech slow, but not careful. No peculiarities except in closet [klʌzət] and coffee klatch [...klʌtʃ] both of which he was aware of.--Aux. inf.: Wife. B. in Ia. F b. in Il.--P 2 (1950).

(142,143) PAGE COUNTY.
Org. 1851. First settled from Jackson Co., Mo. Agricultural area with a small coal mine.--Pop.: '50, 551; '70, 9975; '90, 21,341; '20, 24,137; '50, 23,921.--*History of Page County, Iowa*, Des Moines, Iowa Historical Co., 1880. Kershaw, W. L., *History of Page County, Iowa*, Chicago, S. J. Clarke Pub. Co., 1909. Milmer, E., *History of Page County, Iowa, from the Earliest Settlement in 1843 to the 1st Centennial of American Independence, July 4, 1876*, Clarinda, Ia., pub. by author, 1876.

Clarinda. Once a stopping point on the underground railway. Still has a sizable Negro pop. State Institute for the Insane. Co. seat.--Pop.: '80, 2011; '90, 3262; '20, 4511; '50, 5086.--Beam E. Belle, "Early Days in Clarinda," *Clarinda Herald Journal*, Dec. 30, 1935.

142. Farmer. B. 1869 in Page Co.--F and M b. In.; to Page Co., 1856.--Country sch.--Social contacts with neighbors.-- Somewhat intolerant and restricted in viewpoint. Formerly active in the Farm Bureau.--Lives just outside of town.-- P 21 (1950).

143. Retired farmer. B. 1894 in Page Co. --F b. Page Co., spent 6 yrs. in Co. PGP b. In. and Jackson Co.--8th gr.--Social contacts with other farmers, not with town neighbors.--Industrious, completely without pretense.--Unpredictable array of mid-back and low-mid vowels.--P 22 (1950).

(144,145) DECATUR COUNTY.
Org. 1850. Early settlers from Oh., In., and Germany. Also a Hungarian colony which eventually scattered to other parts of the country. Many people from Mo. mistook it for part of Mo. and settled here. Prosperous agricultural area.-- Pop.: '50, 965; '70, 12,018; '90, 16,566; '50, 12,601.--*Biographical and Historical Record of Ringgold and Decatur Counties, Iowa*, Chicago, Lewis Pub. Co., 1887. Howell, J. M. & H. C. Smith, eds., *History of Decatur County, Iowa, and Its People*, Chicago, S. J. Clarke Pub. Co., 1915.

Lamoni. Platted 1879 as colony for members of the Reorganized Ch. of Jesus Christ of Latter Day Saints. Graceland College.--Pop.: '80, 869; '90, 1215; '20, 1787; '50, 2996. "Fiftieth Anniversary of the Founding of Lamoni," *Leon Journal*, Aug. 29, 1929.

144. Woman, never employed or married; always remained at home. B. 1879 in Decatur Co.--F b. In. or Ky.; to Il., then Ia. M b. N.Y.; to Mn., then Ia.--HS-- Little social contact. Lives with sister, who has a M.A. and has just retired from college teaching.--Shy and independent. Considered some questions silly. Interview impeded by workmen repairing the furnace.--Unstressed [ɨ] perhaps should be recorded as [ɩ˃]. /ɔ/ often raised.-- P 8 (1950).

Garden Grove. Established by Mormons in 1838. Small, in-bred community, quite isolated.--Pop.: '60, 536; '70, 859; '90, 554; '20, 666; '50, 417.

145. Housewife. B. 1897 in Decatur Co. --F and M b. Decatur Co.--HS--Social contacts with other farming families in the area.--Responded with fair rapidity, but would occ. let 'correctness' affect her answers. Aux. inf.: Mother. B. Clark Co. F b. Decatur. PGP b. Il.--P 12 (1950).

(146,147) DAVIS COUNTY.
Org. 1844. Agricultural area, mainly sheep-raising. About half the pop. is of s. ancestry. Earliest settlers from Mo., Ky., In., and s. Il.--Pop.: '50, 7264; '70, 15,565; '90, 16,498; '20, 12,574; '50, 9959.--*History of Davis County, Iowa*, Des Moines, State Historical Co., 1882.

Bloomfield. Co. seat. Important livestock and distributing center. Teachers college.--Pop.: '50, 287; '70, 1553; '90, 1913; '20, 2064; '50, 2688.

146. Retired farmer; drove oil truck for 6 yrs. B. 1872 near Stiles, Ia.;

lived in Nb. 3 yrs.--F b. Il., to Davis Co. age 30. M b. In.; to Ia. age 5. MGP b. De. and Md.--Country sch., 1 yr. college in Bloomfield.--Contacts mostly with farmer neighbors in the country. Son has Ph.D. in history.--Shy, reluctant to commit himself. Difficult to interview; often refused to consider what his word would be.--P 6 (1950).

147. Farmer. B. 1883 in Davis Co.--F and M b. Davis Co.; M lived 10 yrs. in Ks. and s. Mo. PGF b. In.; PGM b. Va.--Country sch. 11 yrs.--Social contacts with neighboring farmers and people he meets through his hobby, raising and training bird dogs.--Easygoing, patient. Often hard to maintain his interest.--Speaks slowly, with minimum of effort. Hollow = [hɑlɚ].--P 5 (1950).

(148,149,150) LEE COUNTY.
Org. 1836. Site of half-breed tract, first area open to white settlement. Varied pop. from the beginning, with the majority being of South Midland ancestry. Norwegian colony from Shelby Co., Mo.--Rich farming area with many industries. --Pop.: '40, 6093; '50, 18,861; '70, 37,210; '90, 37,715; '20, 39,676; '50, 43,102.--*History of Lee County, Iowa*, Chicago, Western Historical Co., 1878. Roberts, N. C., & S. W. Moorhead, eds., *Story of Lee County, Iowa*, Chicago, S. J. Clarke Pub. Co., 1914.

West Point. Small rural community which has declined for many yrs. Originally settled by southerners, but Germans, arriving in the 1870's, almost replaced them.--Pop.: '50, 546; '70, 794; '90, 498; '20, 591; '50, 662.--Gingerich, Melvin, "Mennonites: In Lee and Henry Counties," *Palimpsest*, 40.187-193.

148. Rural mail carrier, retired farmer, harness shop proprietor. B. 1885.--F b. Oh.; to Lee Co. age 7. M b. Pa., to Lee Co. c. age 4.--2 yrs. HS--Social contacts with the local farmers and tradesmen.--Suspicious, somewhat bigoted and pompous. Hard to get him to agree to be interviewed.--Speech slow and careless. Successive pronunciation often varied. He used [ən] for final [əŋ] in conversation more often than the record indicates.--Aux. inf.: Friend. Age 71. Has been over most of US and Can. doing odd jobs.--P 3 (1950).

Donnellson. Surveyed 1881. Market center for surrounding area. People are

mainly Mennonite of German stock.--Pop.: '00, 270; '20, 456; '50, 589. Gingerich, Melvin, "Mennonites: In Lee and Henry Counties," *Palimpsest*, 40.187-193 (1959).

149. Farmer. B. 1885 in Lee Co.--F b. Ohio of German parents; to Lee Co. age 8. M b. Lee Co. of Virginian parents.--Sch. until 19.--Social contacts with local people. President Farm Bureau, chairman sch. board, President Mennonite Ch. congregation for 15 yrs.--Alert, intelligent. Lively sense of humor. Answers careful and considered. Keen and accurate observer.--Speech influenced by German; [vɛl] sometimes for 'well':[dʒ] compromised with [tʃ].--P 4 (1950).

Keokuk. Platted in 1837. Inc. 1847. In 1840's was gate city to the west. Has a diverse pop. Marketing center for rich agricultural area. Also some manufacturing and fishing.--Pop.: '50, 2478; '70, 12,766; '90, 19,645; '20, 19,421; '50, 18,532.--Petersen, William J., "Crossroads of Empire," *Palimpsest*, 32.377-379 (Oct. 1951). Smith, Frederic C., "The Gate City of Iowa," *Palimpsest*, 32.380-408 (Oct. 1951).

150. Secretary. B. 1903; lived in Iowa City 2 yrs.--F b. Keokuk. PGF b. Alsace-Lorraine; PGM b. Oh. M b. Keokuk of Irish parents.--Iowa State Teachers College, Cedar Falls.--Traveled in US, Can., and Mexico.--A 118 (1950).

(151) CASS COUNTY.
Org. 1851. First settlers were Mormons; followed by settlers from N.Y., Il., and Oh. Stock-raising area, also pumpkins. Several canning and meat-packing plants.--Pop.: '50, 1612; '70, 5464; '90, 19,645; '20, 19,421; '50, 18,532.--*History of Cass County, Iowa*, Springfield, Il., Journal Co., 1884. Young, Lafe, *History of Cass County, Iowa, together with Brief Mention of Old Settlers*, Atlanta, Ia. pub. by author, 1877 (pamphlet).

Griswold. Rural community. Early settlers from Il., In., Oh., Pa., and N.Y.; also many Swedes and some German and Irish.--Pop.: '80, 350; '90, 752; '20, 1264; '50, 1149.

151. Housewife. Age 73, b. Mason Co., Il.; to Cass Co. age 13.--F b. Il., PGP b. Va. and Ky. M b. Va.; MGP b. Va.--Limited education.--Limited social contacts.--L (1938).

(152. Follows 138.)

(201) SASKATCHEWAN, CANADA.

Estevan. Inc. 1899. Settled in the 1800's from e. Can., Eng., Man., and, later, N.D.--Oil and trading center for the great Saskatchewan wheat-growing area. Large lignite mine. Brick and tile plants.--Pop.: '01, 141; '21, 2290; '50, 3120.--*Estevan*, Board of Trade, Estevan, 1908.

201. Housewife. B. 1890 in Alameda, Sask., 30 m. e. of Estevan; to farm 8 m. from Estevan; to town.--F b. lower Ont. of Scottish parents; to Sask. c1882. M b. Ont. of German and English parents; to Sask. c1882.--Equivalent of 8th gr.-- Member aux. of Canadian fraternal organization; ladies' circle of Presbyterian Ch. Much social experience and travel as wife of long-time and present mayor.-- Friendly, pleasant, cooperative. Very interested in, and proud of, her family. Often sluggish in responding, expecially to completion questions. Health poor.-- Speech has mixture of older Canadian characteristics [ʧɟ] vs. [tɩ], [ɒ] vs. [ɑ], and newer ones, and such inconsistencies as [ant] as a nominal vs. [ænt] as attributive. Occ. trilled r suggest Scottish mother. Grammar fairly close to standard.--VR-A--A 63 (1950).

(202) MANITOBA, CANADA.

Killarney. First settled in 1882 from e. Can. and Eng., by English, Irish, and Scottish stock. Known as an 'English' town, because there are no non-English immigrants. Popular tourist resort. Several small industries. Prosperous farming community. Leading churches are Protestant.--Pop.: '91, 501; '21, 871; '50, 1091.--*Killarney*, Women's Institute, Killarney, 1933. Monteith, G. B., *History of Killarney*, 1950.

202. Retired farmer. B. 1887 in Ont., to Killarney as infant.--PGF b. Pa. M b. Ont. of Irish parents; to Man., 1882.-- Equivalent of 8th gr.--1/2 yr. collegiate institute, 1/2 yr. business sch.--Once member KP. Member Chamber of Commerce, mayor, once chairman of Provincial Assoc. Active as citizen, chiefly responsible for getting local hospital built. Self-possessed, reserved, but easily becomes talkative. Influential in the community, public-spirited, high-principled. Though having little formal education, he is well-informed and has read widely. Has traveled considerably with his wife, visiting most of the US. Cooperative.-- Speech somewhat tight-lipped, but with quite distinct articulation. Phonetically distinctive chiefly because of the [ɜʊ] before voiceless sounds. Diphthongization not marked. Aware of regional differences in vocabulary and pronunciation because of winter trips to the deep south. Some grammatical forms were more 'correct' than those observed as conversational items.--VR-A--Aux. inf.: Wife. B. Ont. Speech is like husband's in most respects, with a hint of Irish brogue from her parents. Somewhat more speech-conscious, with strong notions of 'correctness.'--VR-A--A 59 (1950).

(203) WARD COUNTY.
Org. 1885. Opened to homesteaders 1896. First settled by Norwegians from Racine, Wi., later by Norwegians and Swedes from Mn. Large German pop. in n.w. Wheat region. A few small industries. One of largest lignite strip mines in the country. About half the pop. is centered in Minot, an important medical and wholesale trade center, and site of Minot State Teachers' College.--Pop.: '90, 1681; '20, 28,811; '50, 34,782.

Kenmare. Inc. 1903. First opened in 1896 and settled by a group of Danish families. Later settlers from Canada and e. states, and some Swedes, Norwegians, and Germans. Large percentage HS and college graduates in community. HS is progressive and influential. Shopping center. Lignite mining.--Pop.: '10, 1437; '20, 1446; '50, 1712.

203. Housewife (former farmwife). B. 1897 in Osakis, Mn.; to Kenmare as infant. F and M b. Denmark; to Mn.; to N.D.--HS-- Former member Women's Federation; member Ladies' Aid of Lutheran Ch. Red Cross leader during WWII. Socially active in community. Recently traveled to the W. Coast and South.--Intelligent and cooperative, good house manager and mother. Friendly, openhearted, hospitable.-- Speech has occ. only a hint of Danish accent, although she still speaks Danish. One translation term 'cut it over' (cut it in two) was noticed. In first part of interview used 'correct' forms, but

as stiffness decreased, her speech became more natural. Diphthongization noticeably weak. The [e^{e}ˆ], [o^{o}ˆ], [i˘i], transcriptions really represent the presence of only a very weak offglide. Rate moderate and articulation distinct.--VR-A--Aux. inf.: Husband. Several yrs. older. Came from Glencoe, Mn.; also of Danish extraction.--A 62 (1950).

(204,205) ROLETTE COUNTY.
Org. 1873. First settled by e. Canadians; later groups from the Scandinavian countries and the e. states. Pop. still has many Canadians. Also a large Indian pop., with nearby Turtle Mountain reservation. Wheat region, cattle, hogs. No mfg. Rolla largest city in Co. Part of Co. is timberland in the Turtle Mts.--Pop.: '90, 2427; '20, 10,061; '50, 11,102.--Law, Laura, *History of Rolette County, North Dakota*, Minneapolis, Lund Press, 1953.

Rolla. Inc. 1891. Settled in 1888 by Canadians. Pop. now diverse with Americans from the e. states, Norwegians, Finns, and Canadians from Man. Shopping center of wheat-growing area. Industrial jewel plant employing Chippewa Indians. E. gateway to Turtle Mts. Office Secretary International Peace Garden. Co. seat.--Pop.: '90, 255; '20, 675; '50, 1176.

204. Retired farmer. B. 1871 near London, Ont., Can.; to N.D. 1884.--F b. Eng. PGF b. France; PGM b. England. M b. Eng. --Rural sch.--Member Workmen of the World, IOOF, FOE. Former member twp. board; former twp. assessor; twice independent candidate for sheriff. Wide acquaintance in community; liked and respected.--Independent, outspoken, rugged, honest, sanguine. Interesting and excellent inf. Provided much conversational material. Knows the community and its members well.--VR-A--Aux. inf.: Wife. French Canadian background. Grew up in Ma. Strong e. accent; still speaks French. Exuberant and jolly.--A 61 (1950).

205. Farm housewife. B. 1905 2 m. from present home.--F b. Ingersoll, Ont., Can.; to Duluth; to S.D.; to N.D. c1891. PGP Scottish. M b. Guelph, Ont., Can.; to N.D. c1891. MGP Scottish.--HS--Member OES, Presbyterian Women's Guild, and Homemakers' Club.--Friendly, cooperative, but somewhat shy and reserved. Occupied with her home and family. Little time for reading. Willing inf. Never volunteered information or reminiscence.-- Distinct enunciation generally, perhaps noticeable because of conscious effort. Little tendency to offglides. Grammar

reflects puristic training of the HS, when she recalls it.--A 60 (1950).

(206,208) PEMBINA COUNTY.
Org. 1867. First settled in the early 1800's from Lord Selkirk's settlement near Winnipeg (Irish, Scottish, French, and Swiss). Later Germans from Mo., originally from Pa. With more active settlement: Canadians, French, Icelanders, and Danes. Largest Icelandic settlement in US. In fertile Red River Valley, general farming region, sugar beets and potatoes. Largest town is about 1500.--Pop.: '70, 1213; '90, 14,334; '20, 15,117; '50, 13,990. Arnold, H. V., *History of Old Pembina, 1780-1872*, Larimore, N.D., 1917. Lee, Charles H., *The Long Ago*, Walkall, N.D., Semi-weekly Mountaineer Print, 1898.

Akra. Uninc. Founded 1878 by Icelandic settlers. Pop. still mainly Icelandic. On fringe of large Icelandic settlement where Icelandic customs tend to be preserved. Very small, consisting of a store and village hall.--Pop.: '90, twp.838; '20, twp.457; '50,twp.259.

206. Farmer. B. 1881 in Elk Rapids, Mi., while parents were en route to N.D.--F and M b. Iceland; to Nova Scotia c1875; to N.D., 1881.--Rural sch.--Member Modern Woodmen of America; Lutheran. Once twp. supervisor and once member sch. board. Social life limited to local community, but has one son at Univ. of N.D. --Reserved, almost taciturn, but not unfriendly. Fairly cooperative. Unwilling to grant final interview, so that some gaps occur in the record.--/z/ generally [$\underset{\checkmark}{z}$] when medial and terminal. Both an occasional staccato effect and the Iceland stress pattern sometimes occurred. Speech soft, without force, usually deliberate.--Aux. inf.: Wife. Also of Icelandic background, with social life and education similar to husband's.--A 54 (1950).

Pembina. Inc. 1885. Settled 1797-98 by Scotch, Irish, French, and Swiss from Selkirk colony. Original pop. has disappeared, and town has diminished in size and importance. Pop. now mixed, including some French halfbreeds, some Germans, and a few Ukrainians. Trading center for part of the Red River Valley, but not a shipping point. Unprogressive, showing little community spirit.--Pop.: '80, 287; '90, 670; '20, 802; '50, 640. --Belleau, J. M., *Brief History of Old Pembina, 1818-1932*, n.p., 1933. *Pembina, Dakota, the Pioneer City of the Red River Valley and Her Industries*, Chicago,

Il., Steen & Boyce, 1882. Steffen, Bernard R., *Penbina, North Dakota's Oldest Settlement*, Pembina Community Club, 1957.

207. Farmer, 1895-1903; deputy sheriff in Steele 1904-5, in Pembina c1912-14; clerk. Now does hauling and draying, has contract to bring mail to the PO from Emerson and Noyes RR stations. B. 1872 in Winnipeg, Can. (as US citizen); to Pembina, 1879; spent 3 yrs. in w. N.D., 1904-7.--F and M b. Germany; to St. Paul, 1850; to Winnipeg, 1869; to N.D., 1879. --8th gr., 2 yrs. business sch. at St. John's Univ. and in St. Paul, 1889.00 No fraternal or church affiliation. Once belonged to now defunct Presbyterian Ch. in Pembina. Little social life, but work gives him wide acquaintance with the community.--Genial, loquacious, and industrious. Cooperative; his work made it hard to find time for interviews. Not widely read, fairly intelligent, but slow-thinking. Good sense of humor, cheerful disposition.--Speech affected by loss of teeth; /f/ usually a distinct [Φ] and /v/ a distinct [β]. The [f] and [v] which are transcribed are so chiefly by reason of acoustic effect, since they could not be labio-dentals. Grammar in single responses more standard than in conversation, where numerous nonstandard forms appeared. Speech fairly rapid; not always distinct, yet generally quite vigorous.--VR-A--Aux. inf.: Wife. B. in Minneapolis of German parents. To N.D. in 1917.--A 56 (1950).

208. Farmer. B. 1902 in Pembina twp. F b. Ma.; to N.D., 1875. M b. Bathgate, Pembina Co. PGP b. Que.--HS, 1/2 yr. normal sch., 1/2 yr. Jamestown College.-- Director of Farmers' Union Oil Co., and prominent in the local of the Farmers' Union. At present is twp. treasurer, was once twp. clerk. Fairly prominent and active in the community. Catholic.--Modest, friendly, quiet, and cooperative. Alert and progressive. Remarked that he had actually enjoyed the interview.-- 'Correct forms' often appeared in single answers, but popular forms in conversation. Speaks at a normal rate with moderate distinctness.--VR-A--Aux. inf.: Wife.--A 55 (1950).

(209,210) WILLIAMS COUNTY. Org. 1873. Settled by Canadians, Germans, Norwegians, and Irish. Williston Basin oil fields. Wheat region with much of the land under irrigation. About a third of the pop. is centered in Williston.-- Pop.: '80, 14; '90, 109; '20, 980; '50, 16,442.

Williston. Inc. 1894. First settled in 1890 by easterners, but main settlement in early 1900's and 1910, from Mn. and Ia., later from Syria, Germany, and Norway. Pop. now diverse. Important as center of Williston Basin oil fields; oil companies have built office buildings and brought large numbers of employees into the city. Also important as trade center for large agricultural area; turkey market; RR stockyards; division headquarters of GNR. Co. seat. Growing rapidly.--Pop.: 1900, 763; '10, 3124; '20, 4178; '50, 7378.

209. Woman. Does housework in various local homes; helped at home until age 33. B. 1894.--F b. Saxony, Germany; spent short time in several states, including Tx.; to N.D. 1893. M b. Bohemia; to Mn., age 18; to N.D., age 33 (1893).--5th gr. --Once attended Congregational Ch., but recently joined Lutheran Ch. Restricted social life. Except for relatives, she seems to live in isolation.--Pleasant but not very alert. Made a trip some yrs. ago to Mn., no other traveling. Information limited to her immediate environment. Interview mystified her, but she was willing to finish even though she considered it silly. Quiet, but not taciturn. Became more open as interview progressed.--Speech rate moderate or faster, with fairly clear articulation and not much pitch range. Most interesting feature was consistent use of nonstandard morphology; the double negative, for instance, was quite frequent, as was [wʌz] for were. Only rarely, as with driven, did she offer a standard form which was at variance with her conversational form. One or two unusual variants, such as for orphan, ivy (q.v.), appeared. --VR-A--Aux. inf.: Brother. Uneducated, background similar to his sister's.--A 68 (1950).

210. Housewife; saleslady and buyer in ladies' ready-to-wear department of local department store for 28 yrs. B. 1888 in Marinette, Wi.; to Fargo, N.D. 1889; to Williston, 1891; for c. 10 yrs. lived on homestead 30 m. s. in McKenzie Co.-- F b. Schleswig-Holstein; to Chicago c1880; to Wi.; to N.D., 1889; PGF b. Denmark and Germany (considered himself Danish). M b. Denmark; to Chicago c1880; to Wi.; to N.D., 1889.--HS--Congregationalist, OES, Pioneer Daughters, Old Settlers Soc. Held numerous offices in these. For yrs. was on district sch. board and was president in McKenzie Co. Socially prominent. Has often been in Minneapolis and Chicago, and in Ca. for the winter.--Intelligent and friendly; is at home in the community and is modestly self-confident. Sympathetic with

the purpose of the interview and cooperated readily. Unwilling to interrupt questioning; thus almost no conversational material was obtained. Dentures gave all [s] sounds a lisping hiss not indicated in the transcription. Speech is typical local cultivated speech, generally free from nonstandard forms. Sufficiently speech-conscious so that she often volunteered other terms or forms used locally or elsewhere.--A 69 (1950).

(211) WELLS COUNTY.
Org. 1873. Early settled by English gentlemen. Large groups came to area around Sykeston, but did not stay permanently. Also small early settlements from Mo., Mi., Norway, and Wales. Pop. now mainly of Russian-German and Norwegian background. Wheat region in fertile valleys of James R. and Sheyenne R. Largest town is Harvey.--Pop.: '90, 1212; '20, 12,957; '50, 10,417. Spokesfield, Walter E., *The History of Wells County, North Dakota, and Its Pioneers*, Valley City, N.D., 1929.

Harvey. Settled after the arrival of RR in 1894. Pop. heterogeneous. Large settlement of Russian-Germans w. of town; in town many Scandinavians and people from Wi. and Mn. Market and shipping town; conservative and unprogressive. Pop. shift made it hard to find a reasonably suitable inf., since most of the first generation have moved away or gone to college.--Pop.: '10, 1443; '20, 1950; '50, 2337.

211. Housewife (widow); taught rural and grade sch. before marriage. B. 1892 in Traverse Co., Mn.; to Velva, N.D., 1902; to Manfred, N.D., 1915; to Harvey, 1923.--F and M b. Sweden; to Mn. 1867; to N.D., 1902.--HS; summer at Minot Normal Sch.--Member Federated Women's Club, PTA, OES, American Legion Aux. Lutheran Ch. Ladies Aid. Active in social life until lately, now devotes time to her grandchildren.--Widow 17 yrs., managed farm and brought up 4 children. Strong, pleasant; ordinary intelligence, with some business ability. Not well read. Not talkative, providing only a few conversational items.--Speech moderate in tempo; fairly distinct enunciation. No marked nasalization, although occ. (and mild) before stressed n (e.g. [kænt]). Most noticeable is frequent, but not consistent, devoicing of final [z], a trait probably due to Swedish background. Can still speak Swedish. Morphology unusually regular (because of teaching background), but there are lapses. Strong notions of 'correctness.'--A 65 (1950).

(212,213) RAMSEY COUNTY.
Org. 1873. Early settlement of Norwegians from Northfield, Mn.; pop. includes Swedes and Canadians. Wheat is main crop. Nearly half of pop. is centered in Devils Lake.--Pop.: '80, 281; '90, 4418; '20, 15,427; '50, 14,373.--Millar, W. D., *Ramsey County, North Dakota, Its Resources*, Devils Lake, N.D., Inter-Ocean Steam Print, 1894. *Ramsey County Pioneer Association; Constitution, Officers, List of Residents in Ramsey County in 1857*, St. Paul, Mn., D. Ramaley & Son, Printers, 1886.

Devils Lake. Inc. 1884. First settled in 1880's by mixed pop. Present pop. contains French Canadians, Norwegians, Germans, and Russians, as well as many from S.D., Mn., and some e. states. Once important as head of navigation on Devils Lake. Shopping center. 2 RR, main shop of GNR. A few small industries make good products. Center for duck and goose hunting. Prosperous and progressive; good HS and library. Co. seat. State Sch. for Deaf and Dumb.--Pop.: '90, 846; '20, 5140; '50, 6427.--Arnold, H. V., *Early History of Devils Lake Country*, Larimore, N.D., pub. by author, 1920. *Devils Lake's Seventy-Five Years*, Devils Lake Diamond Jubilee Assoc., 1957.

212. Housewife (widow). B. 1876 in Ft. Sisseton, S.D.; to Ft. Totten (20 m. s. of Devils Lake), 1878; to farm w. of Devils Lake after marriage.--F b. Ont., Can., of Irish parents; to Albany, N.Y.; to US army in Civil War; sent to S.D., then N.D., M b. Ks.; to S.D.; to N.D. (cook at Ft. Totten). MGP b. Mo.(?) of African descent.--Some rural sch.--Member Catholic Daughters of America, Lady Foresters, St. Joseph's Altar Soc. A mulatto, she is accepted in community and leads a very active social life. Knows local history well and is often referred to for information regarding early days.--Despite age and some infirmities, is dynamic, ebullient, gregarious, and loquacious. Great fund of optimism and good cheer. Uneducated, but not unintelligent; still quite alert.-- Speech forceful and clear in spite of dentures. Rate moderate. Grammar and syntax consistently of 'vulgar' English, with an occ. anomaly like "Am I not?" Diphthongization is weak.--VR-A--A 58 (1950).

213. Housewife, office manager for trucking business operated by husband. B. 1886 10 m. w. of Devils Lake; lived in Id., 1913-24.--F b. Ont. of English parents; to St. Louis, Mo.; to N.D.,

1881. M b. Oh. of Irish parents; to Mo.;
to N.D., 1883.--HS--Member American Legion Aux., Catholic Daughters of America, PTA, Pioneer Daughters (secretary).
Wide acquaintance, fairly active social
life. Has civic consciousness, strong
and active interest in local history.--
Intelligent and alert; ready and receptive inf. Interview was rushed because
of her schedule, and few conversational
items were obtained.--Speech clear and
distinct; moderate in tempo; unmarked
by any unusual features. Grammar generally that of standard English.--VR-A--A
57 (1950).

(214) BILLINGS COUNTY.
Org. 1878. Wheat and cattle region in
the Badlands. Sparsely populated with
very few stores. Part of Co. in Roosevelt National Park, which attracts many
tourists. Pop. is Irish, Canadian, and
Austrian, with a few Hungarians and
Ukrainians.--Pop.: '80, 1323, '90, 170;
'20, 3126; '50, 1777.

Medora. Founded 1883 by Marquis de Mores
in midst of the cattle ranch country,
near site of Theodore Roosevelt's ranch.
Mixed pop. Still a 'cowtown' serving as
a shopping place. Co. seat. Tourist
attraction because of history and
scenery.--Pop.: '10, twp. 136; '20, twp.
260; '50, twp. 241.

214. Housewife (lives alone as widow).
B. 1880 in Rush City, Mn.; to Medora,
1883; lived for some yrs. on Custer
Trail Ranch near Medora, and for 3 yrs.
in Sidney, Mt.--F b. Cayuga Co., Oh.;
volunteered for army in 1861 from Ill.;
discharged in 1865, went to Mn.; to N.D.,
1883; one trip to Ca. M b. N.Y.; to Chicago, to Mn.; to N.D., 1883. MGP b. New
Eng.--8th gr.--No organizations; dis-
believes in churches; calls herself a
'pagan.' Social contacts limited, has
lived either on a ranch or in Medora;
has never traveled. As a child witnessed
the early cattle days; sang songs for
Roosevelt, for whom her father was a
guide. Husband, a contractor, spent 3
yrs. in Sidney, Mt., on a RR construction job. Daughter, graduate of St. Cath-
erine's College, now in Arabia.--Inde-
pendent and freethinking; friendly and
cooperative. Often forgetful, sometimes
slow in filling in suppletion questions.
--Tempo moderate; articulation good, except that unstressed words and syllables
sometimes were slurred and mumbled. Morphology close to standard, perhaps because of influence of daughter or of
brother, a graduate of Univ. of N.D.--
VR-A--A 70 (1950).

(215) HETTINGER COUNTY.
Org. 1883. Sparsely settled wheat and
cattle area. Pheasant hunting attracts
many visitors in the fall. Many Germans
and Scandinavians, also a few Hungarians.
--Pop.: '90, 81; '20, 7685; '50, 7100.
*Thirtieth Anniversary Booklet in Commem-
oration of the Founding of Hettinger and
Adams County, 1907-1937*, Adams County
Record, 1937.

Havelok. Settled c1885 by New Englanders, most of them coming directly from
Vt., but some from the Vt. settlement
(Loyalton) in S.D. Many of these people
and their descendants later moved and
their place was taken by Scandinavians,
mostly Norwegians. Inf. is one of the
few descendants left. Congregational Ch.
still survives. Shopping town.--Pop.:
'90, 101; '20, twp. 213; '50, 129.

215. Farm housewife; village correspondent for Co. weekly paper; as young woman
taught rural sch. 3 mos., and private
sch. for ranch children 2 terms. B. 1884
in Tx.; to Vt.; to S.D., 1885; to N.D.,
1889.--F b. Orwell, Vt., of English parents; to Tx.; to Vt.; to S.D.; to N.D.
M b. Pittsburgh, Vt. of Scotch-Irish parents; to Tx.; to Vt.; to S.D.; to N.D.--
2 yrs. HS--Member, Havelok Homemakers
Club, American Legion Aux. of New Eng.
(N.D.); Congregationalist. Once president Ladies' Aid of her ch.; Sunday sch.
superintendent for 12 yrs.--Friendly,
open-minded, intelligent, cooperative.
Interviews were carried on in a hospital
in Dickinson, where she was recuperating
from a surgical operation. Plain, sturdy,
honest, good-humored; a fine inf.--
Speech distinct and firm, though voice
became weaker as interviewing progressed.
Speech reveals influence of sch. grammar
but several unguarded uses of nonstandard variants occurred.--A 74 (1950).

(216,217) BURLEIGH COUNTY.
Org. 1873. Part of the great spring
wheat area, with several coal mines.
More than half of pop. centered in Bis-
marck. Several settlements of Finns,
German-Russians, and Scandinavians.--
Pop.: '80, 3246; '90, 4247; '20, 15,578;
'50, 25,673.--*A Brief History of Burleigh
County*, Bismarck, 1938.

Bismarck. Inc. 1875. Settled 1871 by
squatters anticipating course of NPR.
Originally important as head of navigation on Missouri R. In the city there
are large German, Norwegian, and Canadian elements in the pop., with Germans
and Russian-Germans in the surrounding
area. In 1903 several thousand farmers

of German descent migrated from Wi. to area near Bismarck. State capital and Co. seat. Largest source of income is the state government. Shopping center for s.w. prairie area; processing of grain, livestock, and dairy products. Ft. Lincoln (US military post). State penitentiary. Business college.--Pop.: '80, 1758; '90, 2186; '20, 7122; '50, 18,640. Slaughter, L. W., *The New Northwest*, Burleigh County Pioneers Assoc., Bismarck, 1874.

216. Retired farmer, now sells real estate. B. 1883 near Red Wing, Mn.; to N.D., 1887.--F b. Norway; to Sweden; to Norway; to Mn., 1872. M b. Norway; to Mn., 1872.--HS--Member BPOE, FOE, Sons of Norway. N.D. state representative from Burleigh Co., 1921-23; sch. clerk for 12 yrs.; twp. assessor 17 yrs.; rent inspector for FPA, 1945-46; member Co. welfare board; active in Farmers' union, now secretary of its grain elevator organization. Lutheran.--Amiable and cooperative. Rather slow in understanding abstractions or relationships.--Rate moderate, at times slower. Although he has attended HS, has consistent nonstandard morphological patterns. Traces of Scandinavian background (Norwegian spoken in childhood home) appear occ. in intonation, in [jɑᵉ] as alternate with [jæˆᵋs], and in [jɑndɨˤs] for "jaundice" (which he probably learned orally from his parents). Wife speaks with distinct Scandinavian accent.--VR-A--A 72 (1950).

217. Farm housewife; bookkeeper in Bismarck for 2 yrs. B. 1882; moved to farm when she married in 1906.--F b. Brookfield Junction, Ct.; to N.D., 1876. PGP b. New Eng. and Eng. M b. St. Charles, Mn.; to N.D., 1877. MGP b. Ire., to Pa.; to N.D.--HS--Active in Presbyterian Ch. and its Ladies' Aid; member Pioneer Daughters and Homemakers Club. Treasurer sch. board for yrs. Husband well-to-do. --Friendly, generous. Lively curiosity about people and the purpose of the interview. Answers quick and intelligent, but not much conversational material obtained. Reads Life, Newsweek, and Colliers. Rich sense of humor.--Speech quick, with correspondingly weak offglides and slurring of unaccented syllables. Grammar largely standard.--VR-A--A 71 (1950).

(218,219) STUTSMAN COUNTY.
Org. 1873. Wheat region. Earliest settlers French and French Canadians and, temporarily, a few English gentlemen. Now many Germans in the w. and s.w., Norwegians in the central and e., and a number of Danes and Russian-Germans. Almost

a third of the pop. is centered in Jamestown.--Pop.: '80, 1007; '90, 5266; '20, 24,575; '50, 24,158.

Jamestown. First settlers from states to the e.: Mi., Wi., and Mn., the last mostly of Scandinavian background. Pop. now diverse, containing also Canadians, Russians, and Germans. Settled in 1871 by NPR engineers; division hdqr. and repair shop. Important supply center for early settlers, and center of Norwegian settlement in the Co. Trading center for center of state. Large wholesale trade and several mfrs. of food products. Lively and progressive. Co. seat. Jamestown College.--Pop.: '80, 383; '90, 2296; '20, 6627; '50, 10,697.--Stine, Thomas, *Jamestown, a Short History of the Early Days in Jamestown, North Dakota*, Jamestown, Morris Printing Co., 1933.

218. Farmer, recently retired because of ill health. B. 1882 in Homer twp., Stutsman Co.; spent part of a recent winter in Ca.--F and M b. Nunda, N.Y.; to Eaton Rapids, Mi., as children; to N.D., 1881 and 1882. PGP b. New Eng. MGP b. New Eng. and Pa. (Dutch, Scotch, and English).--8th gr.--Methodist, Mason, BPOE, AOUW, Kiwanis. Served as twp. supervisor for 27 yrs., as deputy sheriff 1913-14, and as Republican representative in the state legislature during the 1933-34 session. Member rent control board.--Genial and responsive, good sense of humor. Good talker, but not tedious or longwinded.--Speech generally distinct, but some phrases are mumbled, perhaps because of dentures. Several indications of Mi. or N.Y. influence: /fɑg/ and /hɑg/ and "curtains". Tempo moderate, morphology frequently nonstandard, both in concord and strong verbs.--VR-A-Aux. inf.: Wife. Approximately same age; b. in Bismarck, moved to Stutsman Co. c. age 15. HS graduate.--A 66 (1950).

219. Housewife; secretary and bookkeeper with Midland Continental RR 9 yrs. B. 1894; 7 yrs. as child in Mandan and 3 yrs. as adult in Spokane.--F b. Eng.; to N.D., 1881. M b. Wi.; to N.D., 1881. MGM b. Can. of Scotch-Irish parents. MGF part American Indian.--HS--Member Country Club, PTA, Pioneer Daughters, OES; Methodist. Very active until recent ill health. Well known locally and in this district of the State Federation of Women's Clubs.--Amiable, intelligent, and cooperative.--Speech distinct and regular, with no unusual features. Standard morphology; diphthongization weak.--VR-A--Aux. inf.: Husband. Norwegian parentage; to Jamestown from Mn. in 1919. Busi-

nessman, no HS education.--A 67 (1950).

(220,222) CASS COUNTY.
Org. 1873. General farming. Early settlements of Danes and Norwegians from Houston, Fillmore, and Goodhue Cos. in Mn., and Rock Prairie, Wi. Site of many famous Red River Valley bonanza farms. Pop. now includes Canadians, Germans, and many Swedes. More than half the pop. lives in Fargo.--Pop.: '80, 8998; '90, 19,613; '20, 41,477; '50, 58,877.--Fargo, N.D. Board of Trade, *Green Pastures and Vast Wheat Fields*, Fargo, Republican Steam Printing House, 1888.

Fargo. Settled in 1870 mainly by Norwegians and Swedes. Almost half the pop. now is of Norwegian descent. Pop. also includes Canadians and Russian-Germans. Famous as supply center for Red River Valley in bonanza farming days. Now largest city in state; trade center for large area including parts of Mn., N.D., and S.D. Large wholesale and retail establishments, and a diversified industry including food products, machinery, and concrete products. Transportation facilities of N.D. converge here. N.D. State Univ. 2 business colleges. Co. seat.--Pop.: '80, 2693; '90, 5664; '20, 21,961; '50, 38,256.--*Fargo Diamond Jubilee Celebration*, June 5, 1950, and Souvenir ed., Jan. 18, 1927, of *Fargo Forum*, Fargo. Hunt, W. H., & Randell Hunt, *City of Fargo, Its History and Census*, St. Paul, Mn., 1879.

220. General contractor 40 yrs., now retired. B. 1868 in internationally disputed strip near present Portage la Prairie, Man.; to Moorhead, Mn. age 2; to Fargo, 1880.--F b. Nashville, Tn.; army officer in Mexican War, Civil War, Oregon Indian War; to Dakota Territory; to Mn. as homesteader. M b. Scot.; to Man., Can.; to Moorhead, Mn.--HS in St. Cloud and Moorhead; brief time in veterinary medicine sch. in Minneapolis.--Once active in AOUW and BPOE, now keeps up contacts only in his neighborhood. Presbyterian, but not active. Strong Republican; once ran for city council; now precinct committeeman. Traveled in the n.w. and s.--Independent, kind, and generous. Despite age and recent ill health, is mentally alert, enjoys reminiscing. Interested in the interview and cooperative.--Speech clear and distinct. No attempt to offer 'correct' forms or any other than his natural one. Moderate tempo, occ. nasality before a nasal. Offglides weak. Some awareness of regional differences appeared in his comments upon speech he had heard in Ar. Frequent

nonstandard forms.--VR-A--A 52 (1950).

221. Manager of mortgage loans for insurance company; work has generally been in real estate, once Co. agent, once land development agent for NPR in Mt.--B. 1902 in Leonard, Cass Co.; spent 5 yrs. as adult in Mt.--F b. Luxembourg; to Ia.; to Mn. (iron range and logging); to N.D., 1899. M b. Norway; to N.D., age 3.--Fargo HS; graduate N.D. Agricultural College (now N.D. State Univ.)--Mason (Shriner), BPOE, Kiwanis, Methodist. Active and prominent in town and state. Member advisory committee for the NDAC and member state defense council. Traveled widely in the state and knows it well. Daughter attended NDAC; son at Hamline Univ.--Intelligent, well-informed, responsive, and cooperative. Not very discursive until the interview was finished, therefore few conversational items in the record.--Speech representative of cultured N.D. Speech clear, tempo moderate, no nasalization, only very weak diphthongization of stressed vowels except when prolonged for emphasis. Morphology standard during the interview.--Aux. inf.: Wife. B. 1907 in Madison, S.D.; to N.D. age 3. Graduate of NDAC.--A 65 (1950).

222. Wholesale and retail petroleum dealer, manager city bus system for Northern States Power Company. B. 1893; service abroad in WWI.--F b. N.Y.; to N.D., 1870. PGF b. Scot. M b. Norway; to Wi., 1865; to N.D.--HS; Cornell Univ. (Civil Engineering).--Member Lutheran Ch., Rotary Club. Many business contacts; wife socially active.--Prominent, conservative business man. Affable and willing to cooperate despite some personal inconvenience.--Speech clear, tempo moderate; some nasality occ. before [n]. Single-word responses enunciated with unusual distinctness. Aware of speech differences and commented occ. about Southern terms. Grammar generally standard.--VR-A--A 53 (1950).

(223). EMMONS COUNTY.
Org. 1879. Wheat-growing region. Pop. includes Russian-Germans, Norwegians, and Hollanders.--Pop.: '80, 38; '90, 1971; '20, 11,288; '50, 9715.

Westfield. Founded in 1885-87 by settlers of Holland-Dutch background, some coming directly from Holland, others from Mi., Mn., and Ia. There are several other similar communities in the s. part of the state. Town consists of one store, filling station, and PO. Life centers around the Dutch Reformed Ch. and its

dominie. People are conservative, uneducated, pious, and in-centered.

223. Farmwife (husband now retired). B.
1886 in S.D. as parents were en route to
Westfield.--F and M b. Netherlands; to
Wi. (F, 1857; M, 1859); to Green Leafton,
Mn., 1867; to N.D.--4th reader in country sch.--Member Ladies' Missionary Aid
Soc. of Hope (Dutch) Reformed Ch.--Re-
served, but not unfriendly. Willing to
cooperate but not to have her voice recorded. Conservative, devoutly religious,
not open-minded nor well informed. Not
unintelligent; quick to respond to all
types of questions.--Speech distinct,
moderate to fast tempo, weak diphthongization, no trace of foreign influence
except the /jɑ/ [jɒ] for yes instead of
[jɛə] or [jɛɑ]. Grammar has many standard forms, perhaps because of her educated sons.--Aux. inf.: Husband. Also
Dutch, b. in Green Leafton, Mn. Answered
one question.--A 73 (1950).

(224) DICKEY COUNTY.
Org. 1881. Early settlers from Pa., Mo.,
and N.Y., and Norwegians from Wi. Pop.
now mainly Norwegians and Russian-German.
Wheat and diversified farming, with a
few small industries making food products.--Pop.: '90, 5573; '20, 10,499; '50,
9121.--Black, R. M., A History of Dickey
County, North Dakota, Ellendale, Dickey
Co. Hist. Soc., 1930.

Ellendale. Inc. 1883. First settlers
were Norwegians from Wi. Pop. now mainly
Norwegian and Russian-German. Early distributing point for settlers' supplies.
Now a market town. Co. seat. State Normal and Industrial Sch.--Pop.: '90, 761;
'20, 1334; '50, 1759.

224. Retired farmer. B. 1885 in Ukraine,
Russia; to N.D., 1887; to Ia. for 1 1/2
yrs.; to Il. for 3 yrs.; to Dickey Co.,
1905 (9 m. n.e. of Ellendale); to Ellendale, 1948.--F b. Ukraine of German ancestry; to N.D., 1887. M b. Ukraine (ancestors from Bremen, Germany); to N.D.,
1887.--4th gr., rural sch.--Methodist,
Farmers' Union, Homemakers Club. Twp.
assessor 18 yrs.; twp. sch. board treasurer 21 yrs. Normal social contacts of
farm life.--Intelligent and friendly,
willing to cooperate. Prosperous through
hard work. Great integrity, imagination,
and sense of humor.--Speaks with considerable force, in a big voice and with
fairly distinct articulation. Morphology
nonstandard for many items, but syntax
revealed no trace of German despite its
use in his childhood home.--A 75 (1950).

(225,226) RICHLAND COUNTY.

Org. 1873. Diversified farming area in
fertile Red River Valley. Early settlers
from Mi., Wi., Ia., and Mn. Among these
were a Bohemian colony from Ia. and Wi.,
and many Scandinavians and Germans. Site
of some of the famous bonanza farms.--
Pop.: '80, 3597; '90, 10,751; '20,
20,887; '50, 19,865.--Callan, F. G., A
History of Richland County, North Dakota, Wahpeton, Globe-Gazeteer Printing
Co., 1937. Crandall, Horace B., A History of Richland County, Colfax, N.D.,
1886. Elznic, W. H., "Bohemians in Richland County," N.D. State Hist. Soc. Coll.,
4.62-80. Old Settlers' Association of
Richland County, North Dakota, Wahpeton,
Globe-Gazette Printing Co, n.d.

Fairmount. Founded c1884 by homesteaders
from Mi. Pop. now largely of German and
Scandinavian background. Rural trading
town, suffers from competition with
Wahpeton. Only industry is a packing
plant reportedly about to close. US Fish
and Wildlife Service Bird Banding Station.--Pop.: '90, 91; '20, 706; '50, 660.
--Pinkney, Charles R., Early History of
Fairmount, Fairmount Pub. Co., 1937.

225. Retired farmer (50 yrs.) and rural
mail carrier (30 yrs.). B. 1879 in Wau-
toma, Wi.; to Fairmount, 1884.--F b. Man-
chester, Eng.; to Ripon, Wi., 1852; to
N.D., 1882. M b. N.Y. of Scottish parents; to Wi.; to N.D.--8th gr.--Mason
(past secretary), Methodist; once secretary former volunteer fire company. Well
known, once active, but recent stroke
keeps him home. Has traveled to Mexico,
Ca., and Tx. Belongs to oldest family in
the community.--Friendly, cooperative,
mildly loquacious.--Rate moderate, enunciation sometimes poor. Stroke has not
affected articulation, but has affected
his memory. Often familiar words could
not be remembered. Grammar old-fashioned
(/klɪm/) and often nonstandard ("I
done"), though standard forms occasionally appeared in direct response.--Aux.
inf.: Wife. c8-10 yrs. younger. B. in
Co. of Czech parents. No HS education.
--A 85 (1952).

Wahpeton. Settled in 1869 from the e.
states, and later by many Germans and
Scandinavians, especially Norwegians.
Pop. now diverse. Trading center for sur-
rounding area; commercial development of
clay desposits; several other industries.
Alert and lively town. Co. seat. State
Sch. of Science; Conservatory of Music;
Lutheran Bible Sch.; Government Indian
Sch.--Pop.: '80, 400; '90, 1510; '20,
3069; '50, 5125.

226. Housewife; taught sch. in Cavalier

Co. for c. 3 yrs. (1915-17). B. 1896 in
Fairmount; to Wahpeton when married in
1917.--F b. Jackson, Mi.; to N.D. c1887.
PGP b. N.Y. M b. Hartford, Mi.; to N.D.
c1887. MGP b. Pa. (Pa.-German).--Fair-
mount HS; 1 yr. Valley City Normal Sch.
--Active in civic affairs. Member American Legion Aux. (former local president
and former district president), Red Cross,

Congregational Ladies' Aid.--Intelligent,
cooperative, open-minded. Because of busy
schedule she refrained from conversation.
Strong personality, responsible and ca-
pable.--Rate moderate; articulation generally clear and natural. Grammar and
syntax generally standard. Strong feel-
ings about 'correctness,' but admits her
nonstandard forms.--VR-A--A 86 (1952).

SOUTH DAKOTA

(301) HARDING COUNTY.
Org. 1909. In 1880's part of cattlemen's
empire. Opened to settlement 1910; earliest permanent settlers from other parts
of S.D., Tx., Ia., Ks., and Mo., and
Norway and Sweden. Several colonies of
Finns established farming settlements
after leaving gold mines in the Black
Hills. Sparsely settled; cattle and
sheep ranching; very few stores. National Forests cover part of Co.--Pop.: '90,
167; '20, 3953; '50, 2289.--Hanson, M.
G., "A History of Harding County, South
Dakota, to 1925," *S.D. Hist. Soc. Coll.*,
2.515-567 (1946).

Buffalo. Inc. 1943. Laid out in 1909 in
geographical center of Co. as Co. seat.
Pop. history is like that of the Co.
Shopping center for large ranching area;
quiet prairie town.--Pop.: '20, twp. 236;
'50, 380.

301. Retired cattle rancher. B. 1880 in
Mankato, Mn.; to w. S.D. near Belle
Fourche, 1884; to Buffalo, 1897.--F b.
Oh.; to Mo.; to Ok.; to Mn. PGF b. Ct.
M b. Green Bay, Wi.; to Mankato, Mn.;
to S.D. MGF b. Ct.; MGM b. Ma.--2 yrs.
HS in Aberdeen.--One of the early cattle
ranchers; quite prosperous; has traveled
to W. Coast, Minneapolis, and Chicago;
met variety of people. Mason; well
thought of in community. Alert, well informed on current topics.--Friendly,
forthright, cooperative. Responded readily, with some difficulty on the morphological constructs.--Speaks clearly in
spite of dentures. Rate moderate. Aware
of regional differences, but not of own
nonstandard deviations.--A 83 (1951).

(302) MEADE COUNTY.
Org. 1889. Once part of cattlemen's empire. Settled c1908-10 by miscellaneous
pop.: Nb., Ia., Mo., Il., Oh., Germany
and Scandinavia. Cattle and sheep ranching; sparsely settled. About a third of
the pop. centered in Sturgis.--Pop.: '90,

4640; '20, 9367; '50, 11,516.

Faith. Settled c1908-10 with a miscellaneous pop. similar to that of Co. No
one group dominates. Western town; shopping center for large ranching area.
Important stock-shipping point; at end
of MRR branch line. Little cultural life,
some civic consciousness: new airport,
and campaign for a municipal hospital.
--Pop.: '20, 575; '50, 599.

302. Barber. B. 1898 near Lindsey, S.D.,
on Indian reservation; to area near Ft.
Pierre as a child; to n. of Dupree; to
Faith, 1910.--F b. Nb.; to S.D. PGP probably French. M b. near Pierre. MGF
French Canadian. MGM Sioux Indian.--2
yrs. HS; 2 yrs. Conception College in
Mo.; barber sch.--Active member Alcohol-
ics Anonymous; nominal Catholic. In occupation meets about half the male pop.
of community. Little travel except to
the Twin Cities a few times.--Friendly
and cooperative. Interview conducted in
barbershop while he worked. Intelligent
and receptive to ideas. Not talkative.--
Speaks clearly, no peculiarities. Influenced by nonstandard language he hears
daily. Aware of this and regrets it. Ear
for regional differences; volunteered
remarks about speech of the southern cowhands who come to his shop.--A 82 (1951).

(303,304) WALWORTH COUNTY.
Org. 1883. Settled in 1880's from the n.
central states; many from Walworth Co.,
Wi. Later Germans and some Russian-Germans and Norwegians. Cattle and sheep
ranching with some diversified farming.
About half the pop. lives in Mobridge.--
Pop.: '80, 46; '90, 2153; '20, 8447;
'50, 7648.

Selby. Founded 1899 when buildings from
old town of Bangor were moved to main
line of MRR. Pop. mixture similar to
that of Co. Trade center. Lively community with energetic and public-spirited

citizens. Large number of college graduates. Co. seat.--Pop.: '10, 558; '20, 564; '50, 706.

303. Crossing flagman for MRR; formerly a farmer and a drayer. B. 1887 on farm near Selby.--F b. Henry Co., Oh.; to Walworth Co., 1884. MGP b. Holland.--4th gr. in sch. with 3-mo. term.--Social contacts limited. Member Woodmen of America, Methodist, and former member volunteer fire dept.--Slow, unimaginative, and uninformed. Willing to be interviewed, but thought it foolish. Slow in responding; did not volunteer conversation.--In spite of dentures speaks distinctly but deliberately. Grammar nonstandard, but he seems unaware of this.--A 81 (1951).

304. Deputy Co. auditor; worked in auditor's office since 1919. B. 1899 in Bangor (4 m. s. of Selby).--F b. Oh.; to Wi.; to Walworth Co., 1887. M b. Austin, Mn.; to Walworth Co., 1885. MGP b. Germany.--HS--Active in community; member Selby Women's Club, American Legion Aux., Methodist.--Affable, cooperative, alert, intelligent. Rarely volunteered material.--Speaks clearly and distinctly. Rate moderate. Occ. deviation in grammar. /əkrɔst/ appeared in conversation; /əkrɔs/ in a response.--VR-A--A 80 (1951).

(305, 306) BROWN COUNTY.
Org. 1881. First settlers from Il. and Wi., later many from Finland and Russia (Russian-Germans). Prosperous and progressive area; large, diversified farms, spring wheat. Co. contains a wildlife refuge, popular pheasant hunting area, attracting many hunters. More than half the pop. lives in Aberdeen.--Pop.: '80, 353; '90, 16,855; '20, 29,509; '50, 32,617.--Cleworth, Marc H., "Twenty Years of Brown County Agricultural History," *S.D. Hist. Soc. Coll.*, 23.1-184 (1947).

Aberdeen. Inc. 1882. Earliest settlers from E. and central states, Wi., Mi., Il., Mn., and Ia. contributing the majority. Later influx of Russian-Germans and Norwegians. Important distributing center in prosperous James R. valley. MRR stockfeeding yards; International Harvester depot; Northern State Teachers' College; Presentation Junior College; pheasant hunting center. Co. seat. Several industries.--Pop.: '90, 3182; '20, 14,537; '50, 21,051.

Warner. Inf.'s home until 4 yrs. ago was in a crossroads village 10 m. s. of Aberdeen. PO, general store, filling station, Farmers Union Store. Family's farm is 3 m. s. of Warner.

305. Housewife; farm housewife until 4 yrs. ago. B. 1880 in Lautenburg, Prussia, Germany; to Millbank age 2; to Brown Co. --F and M b. Germany; to Westphalia; to Prussia; to US.--4th gr. country sch.-- Member Zion Lutheran Ch. (Aberdeen, previously in Warner), Extension Club in Warner for 25 yrs. Once named "Outstanding Farm Homemaker" by Extension.--Modest, energetic, soft-spoken. Followed questioning alertly and willingly.--No trace of German accent or idiom except in west (22.2) and boulevard (63.8), where confusion may be laid to bilingual background.--VR-A--Wn 8 (1951).

Westport. Social contacts of inf. and family are mainly in Aberdeen, where all their business is done. Farm is 10 m. n. of Aberdeen.--Pop.: '90, twp. 424; '20, twp. 504; '50, twp. 293.

306. Farmer. B. 1902.--F b. Susquehana Co., Pa.; to s.e. Mn., 1869, age 7; to Brown Co., 1884. M b. Welland, Ont., Can.; to Brown Co., 1883, age 7. PGF b. N.Y.--8th gr., twp. sch.--Member West End Methodist Ch. (Aberdeen), 4H assistant leader. Normal rural social contacts. Daughter and son active in 4H.--Friendly and cooperative. Strong family and regional pride.--Speaks clearly and unaffectedly.--Aux. inf.: Wife and 2 children contributed many answers. Wife raised on a farm near Sisseton; moved to Brown Co. when she married. Few yrs. younger than husband.--Wn 9 (1951).

(307, 308) ROBERTS COUNTY.
Org. 1883. In e. part pop. mainly Swedish, Norwegian, Polish, and German; in w. part, Finnish and Russian-German. Rich farming area; stock-raising, grain and dairying. Sisseton Indian Reservation takes part of Co. Region around lakes is developing into resort area.-- Pop.: '90, 1997; '20, 16,514; '50, 14,929.

Sisseton. First settled 1892; most of pop. Scandinavian background, especially Norwegian. Area previously a Sioux Reservation; many Sioux remained as farmers and laborers. Distribution and trading center. Administration Center for the Dept. of Indian Affairs; Indian Hospital. Co. seat. Pop.: 1900, 928; '20, 1431; '50, 2871.--Hummel, E. A., "The Story of Fort Sisseton," *S.D. Hist. Rev.*, 2.126-144 (1937). Morris, H. S., "Historical Stories," *Sisseton Courier*, 1939.

307. Farmer. B. 1892 in St. Paul, Mn.; to Roberts Co. age 1 mo.--F b. County

Wexford, Ire.; to Mn. as adult; to Roberts Co. M b. County Cork, Ire.; to St. Paul; to Roberts Co.--8th gr., twp. sch. --Member Ch. of the Sacred Heart (Effington), Koda Rod and Gun Club (Sisseton), active in ch. affairs and community events.--Amiable, slow-thinking. Bachelor, admirably good housekeeper. Cooperative. Some gaps in the record result from seeking a harder answer to the question. Many gaps filled later with the remark, "Who'd have thought you wanted to know that!"--Clear, unaffected speech. --Wn 7 (1951).

308. RR agent and telegrapher (also owns a farm). B. 1890 in Britton, S.D.; to Andover, S.D., 1895; to Sisseton, 1897.--F b. s. Wi.; to n.e. S.D., age 16. PGP and MGP b. e. US of English stock. M b. Minnesota Falls, Mn.; to Montevideo, Mn.; to Britton, S.D.--1 yr. HS--Mason, member sch. board. Normal social contacts; well known because of occupation. --Friendly, humorous, slow-spoken.--Anxious that the interviewer understand him, making speech more deliberate than usual. No evidence, however, that responses were over-meticulous. Stress patterns in phrases may have been affected.--VR-A-- Wn 6 (1951).

(309,310). LAWRENCE COUNTY.
Org. 1877. Settlement began with discovery of gold in 1875, attracting a diverse pop. from many countries and states. Chief mining area of Black Hills; most of working pop. engaged in mining. Small amount of agriculture is mainly livestock raising, some small, irrigated fruit and vegetable farms in n. Important tourist and skiing area.--Pop.: '80, 13,248; '90, 11,673; '20, 13,029; '50, 16,648.

Lead. Inc. 1890. Diverse, but stable, pop., including a number of foreign-born, mainly from Eng., Italy, and Scandinavia. Homestake gold mine, largest in country. Most of land in town owned by Homestake and most of the pop. employed by it. Winter sports center of Black Hills; popular tourist spot in summer.--Pop.: '80, 1437; '90, 2581; '20, 5013; '50, 6422.

309. Retired machinist. B. 1881; spent 11 yrs. in Butte, Mt., Los Angeles, and other cities on the Pacific Coast.--F b. Co. Lowth, Ire.; to St. Louis, 1848; to Lead, 1878. M b. Dunkirk, N.Y.; to Denver; to Lead c1876. MGP of English background.--8th gr.--Catholic; inactive charter member local KC. Once an Elk. Ran for register of deeds. Bachelor,

with none of the usual adult family contacts. Traveled in w., but never e. of Mississippi.--Friendly and cooperative. Cheerful and genial disposition, good sense of humor. Respected in community. Well read, has contacts with people of better education.--VR-A--A 90 (1952).

310. Housewife; before marriage was partner in local credit bureau, and did office and secretarial work. B. 1904 in Terraville (a few m. w. of Lead).--F b. Henry Co., Il.; to Mn.; to Lead, 1878. PGP b. Ulster Co., Ire. (all were Scotch-Irish). M b. Littleton, Ma.; to Lead in late 1880's. MGM b. Ma.; MGF b. Ire.-- HS; several mos. business sch. in Butte, Mt.--Traveled to Fl. and the W. Coast. Business experience has given her wide acquaintance in area.--Friendly, helpful; alert but not well informed. Proud of pioneer ancestry; but not curious about their history. Offered little conversational material.--Influenced by idea of 'correct' grammar and lexical propriety. Aware of speech variations and often volunteered forms used by others. Answers carefully distinct. Tense vowel offglides weak or missing.--VR-A --A 91 (1952).

(311,312,326) PENNINGTON COUNTY.
Org. 1877. Received varied pop. because of place in gold mining area and cattlemen's empire. Now smaller ranches and small fruit and vegetable farms. Mining of feldspar and other minerals. Much of Co. is in Black Hills National Forest, which attracts a large tourist trade. More than half of pop. is centered in Rapid City.--Pop.: '80, 2244; '90, 6540; '20, 12,720; '50, 34,053.

Rockerville. In 1880's a placer-mining boom town with a pop. of 2000. Now name for an area with filling station at its center.--Pop. from the e. states. Main income from ranching.

311. Rancher; lumber mill owner and operator for 30 yrs.; cowpuncher and gold miner as young man. B. 1876 in Mt. Vernon, Ia.; to Cedar Rapids, Ia., 1882. PGP and MGP b. Eng. M b. Allentown (?), Pa.; to Ia.--3rd reader in district sch. --Mason, BPOE. County commissioner, 1926-34. Once ran for state senate. Widely known as an 'old-timer.' Goes to cattle sales in Rapid City to talk with other ranchers. Little travel, except for trip to San Diego.--Genial, cooperative and individualistic. Cheerfully contemptuous of book-education; thought interview silly, but enjoyed chance to tell stories and talk. Proud of status as an 'old-

timer.' Active and energetic, playing an important part in community affairs.--Nonstandard English, forcefully spoken and clearly enunciated. Offglides weak; rate moderate. Aware of lexical variations and several times mentioned other forms he had heard.--VR-A--Aux. inf.: Wife, c60. B. few m. away; country sch. education.--A 94 (1952).

Rapid City. Settled in 1876 as supply town for mining towns in the Hills; attracted a varied pop. Now metropolis of the Black Hills, with several industries, a large wholesale trade, and a large tourist trade. S.D. state cement plant; state fish hatchery; Air Force Base; S.D. Sch. of Mines. Co. seat. Pop.: '80, 292; '90, 2128; '20, 5777; '50, 25,310.--*Holiday Greeting from Rapid City*, Rapid City Journal, 1915.

312. Hotel owner; with predecessor of FBI in WWI; ranch hand as young man. B. 1892 near Sturgis, S.D.--F b. Adams Co., Il.; to Union Army; to Tx.; to Nb.; to Il.; to S.D., 1878. PGF b. Me.; PGM b. Ky. M b. Virginia City, Mt.; to Ut.; to Co.; to S.D., 1877. MGF b. Germany; MGM b. Wi. (her parents from Me.).--1 yr. HS--Widely known through hotel, which has been hdqr. for ranchers for many years. Traveled to both E. and W. coasts. Belongs to no church or organizations.--Friendly, cooperative. Educated himself through reading. Interested in local history; published one book and several historical articles.--Sch. grammar and own writing have built inconsistent language prejudices. Good ear for language differences; supplied community variants. Speech clear, tempo moderate. Offglides very weak, or even nonexistent.--VR-A--A 92 (1952).

(313) HAAKON COUNTY.
Org. 1915. Part of early cattlemen's empire. Extension of the RR in 1906-7 brought settlers from e. S.D., other states to the e., and many Norwegians. Drought in 1911 drove most of the American settlers back, but the Norwegians stayed. Semiarid region of cattle ranching. Sparsely populated.--Pop.: '20, 4596; '50, 3167.

Philip. Grew up in 1900's with progress of RR. w. Pop. mostly Norwegian and Danish with a few Swedes. Shopping and shipping center for a large area. Co. seat.--Pop.: '10, 578; '20, 647; '50, 810.

313. Housewife; rural sch. teacher for 6 yrs. B. 1894 6 m. n.w. of Philip;

lived in county w. of town until 1927; then to Philip.--F and M b. Denmark; to S.D., 1883.--3 yrs. HS; 1 yr. Spearfish Normal Sch.--Active socially. Secretary Women's Missionary Federation of the Evangelical Lutheran Ch.; past president American Legion Aux.; past matron OES. Traveled several times to the W. Coast. --Intelligent, friendly, sanguine. Good sense of humor. Enjoyed the interview, which was conducted while she did housework. Strong and pleasant personality.--Clear notion of 'correctness' which she adheres to, even "Am I not?" Speaks clearly and with vigor.--A 84 (1951).

(314) STANLEY COUNTY.
Org. 1890. Sparsely settled cattle ranching area. Some farming on tableland and along river bottoms.--Pop.: '80, 793; '90, 1028; '50, 2055.--*History of Central South Dakota*, Ft. Pierre Times Printing Co., 1950.

Ft. Pierre. Site of early military fort on Missouri R. Once trading center for a large area, attracting a diverse pop. Growth of Pierre on e. bank has reduced its importance. Many ranchers on w. bank still do their business in Ft. Pierre. Cultural life centers in Pierre; night life in Ft. Pierre. Co. seat.--Pop.: '80, 287; '90, 360; '20, 805; '50, 951.--Wilson, F. T., "Old Fort Pierre and Its Neighbors," *S.D. Hist. Soc. Coll.*, 1. 263-379 (1902).

314. Now retired; has been cowpuncher, printer, jewelry salesman, jewelry store owner, pool hall owner, off-sale liquor dealer, postmaster in Ft. Pierre, 1898-1906. B. 1867 in St. Joseph, Mo.; to Ft. Pierre, 1883.--F b. n.w. In. or Mi.; to Mo., 1848; to Ft. Pierre, 1882. PGF b. Hillsdale, Mi.; PGF b. R.I. M b. Clay Co., Mo.; to Ft. Pierre, 1883. MGP b. Louisville, Ky.; to Mo., 1848.--8th gr.--Active Mason, once member of Woodmen of America and KP. Widely known in area. Traveled in most of US and in Can.--Unusual mental alertness; self-educated through extensive reading. Marked integrity and moderation in habits; sociable, genial, gifted teller of anecdotes. Unusually good health.--Excellent vocabulary, but general nonstandard grammar and idioms. Speaks with distinctness and vigor.--VR-A--A 87 (1952).

(315) HUGHES COUNTY.
Org. 1880. Coming of RR in 1880 started influx of settlers. On edge of e. farming area; livestock and diversified farming.--Pop.: '80, 268; '90, 5044; '20, 5711; '50, 8111.--Hall, B. L., *Hughes*

315. Assistant postmaster since 1936. B. 1907; spent 1929-32 in Wa. and Or.; 1944-45 in the army; 1950 in the navy.--F b. Pa.; to Ree Heights, S.D., c1890; to Pierre, 1907. PGM Pa.-German; PGF Irish and Welsh. M b. Pierre. MGF b. Sweden; MGM b. in Germany or Wi.--HS--Member VFW, American Legion, Mason, Izaak Walton League, Pierre Country Club, inactive Lutheran. Once precinct committeeman in East Pierre.--Open, friendly, not loquacious. Had trouble with completion questions.--Tempo moderate, no peculiarities. Speaks clearly and distinctly. Grammar standard with some deviations; preterit [kʌm] is his normal form.--A 88 (1952).

(316) HAND COUNTY.
Org. 1882. Early settlers from Ia., In., Il., and other middle states: Oh., Mi., Wi. Later Germans and a Hutterite Colony. Livestock; production of blue grass seed and small grain. Sparsely settled.--Pop.: '80, 153; '90, 6546; '20, 8878; '50, 7149.--Lansing, L. W., "Hand County in the 1880's," *S.D. Hist. Soc. Coll.*, 23. 351-363 (1947).

Miller. Settled c1880 from Ia., In., Il. Pop. now mixed, n. European and central and e. US. Shipping center for grain and cattle; shopping center for a large area. Co. seat.--Pop.: '90, 536; '20, 1478; '50, 1916.--Cotton, M. (ed.), *They Pioneered for US*, Huron, S.D., 1956.

316. Retired storekeeper; onetime farmer and sheriff. B. 1882 in Cary, Il.; to Hand Co., 1886; to Il., 1910-12; to Wa., 1942-44; to Miller.--F and M b. Il.; to Hand Co. PGP b. N.Y. and Can. MGP b. Buffalo, N.Y.--9 yrs. twp. sch.--Member Masons, IOOF. Normal social contacts for the community.--Active and interested. Identifies closely with the community; two long trips away were for business and wife's health.--Speech clear.--Aux. inf.: Wife. B. 1885 in St. Lawrence, Hand Co. F b. Ma.; M b. N.Y. Articulation impeded by loss of teeth. Alert and helpful.--Wn 10 (1951).

(317,318,319) BROOKINGS COUNTY.
Org. 1871. Settled in 1870's from Mn.; Ia., and e. states; between 1873 and 1885 a great influx of Norwegians. Largest pop. group of Norwegian descent. Rich farming area; diversified crops, livestock, potatoes.--Pop.: '70, 173; '90, 10,132; '20, 16,119; '50, 17,851. --*History of Southeastern Dakota, Its Settlement and Growth*, Western Pub. Co., Sioux City, 1881. Sandro, Gustav O., *History of Brookings County*, Brookings, n.d.

Brookings. Settled in 1870's from e. US, also by Norwegians. Chief trading and distributing center for s.e. S.D. Several industries; seed house; hdqr. of Cooperative Wool Growers' Association; S.D. State College (now S.D. State Univ.); Co. seat.--Pop.: '90, 1518; '20, 3924; '50, 7764.

317. Retired farmwife (now lives in town). B. 1870 in Prairie du Sac, Wi.; to Brookings Co., age 3; to Brookings, 10 yrs. ago.--F b. Vt.; to Wi. as youth; to Brookings Co. after Civil War. M b. Boston; to Wi. as child.--7th gr. country sch.--Member Royal Neighbors for 50 yrs. Active and normal social life. Has found many friends in town since retirement.--Sprightly and humorous. Considered interview 'foolishness' but admitted at end she enjoyed it. Likes to talk, often anticipated questions and supplied responses spontaneously. Slightly hard of hearing.--Although toothless, has little trouble with articulation, except for occasional initial lisp (ignored in transcription). Voice strong and clear.--VR-A--Wn 12 (1951).

318. Farmwife (farm is c6 m. s. of Brookings). B. 1911 in Storm Lake, Ia.; to Brookings Co. c. age 2; 3 yrs. in Sioux Falls.--F b. Schaller, Ia., to Sac and Buena Vista Cos., Ia.; to Brookings Co. PGP b. Il. M b. near Hannibal, Mo.; to Schaller, Ia.; to Brookings Co. MGP b. Hamburg, Germany.--HS; 1 yr. commercial college in Sioux Falls.--Member Home Economics Farm Bureau, Methodist Ch., Community Club, Extension Club; leader girls' 4H.--Earnest, hard-working, intelligent. Chief interests are her children (4, ages 5-18), and 4H.--Speech clear with no marked peculiarities.--Aux. inf.: Husband, c. 9 yrs. older, with similar background. 1 yr. HS. 4 yrs. in Mt. as a young man. Parents from Cedar Co., Ia.--Wn 13 (1951).

319. Home economics teacher in junior and senior HS. B. 1903 in Volga, S.D. (7 m. w. of Brookings); to Brookings, age 10; has also worked and lived in Moody, Cook, Walworth, and Minnehaha Cos., and in Pipestone, Mn.--F b. Ettrick, Wi. of Norwegian parents; to Volga. M b. Haland, Norway, to Lincoln Co., age 9. 16; to Volga; to Brookings.--4th gr. in Volga; HS in Brookings; graduate S.D. State College, Brookings.--Member AAUW, churches, and clubs in various towns where she has taught.--Conscientious, somewhat shy. Careful to give variant terms and pronunciations she had heard. --Considered it her duty to help, but seemed to enjoy interviews as they prog-

ressed. Speech clear, without affectation. Conscious of 'correctness' but frank in her responses, giving her form first and the correct one afterward if she thought hers was at variance.--VR-A--Wn 11 (1951).

(320) FALL RIVER COUNTY.
Org. 1883. Once part of cattlemen's empire, still some large ranches, but mostly small, irrigated fruit and vegetable farms and submarginal grazing. Sandstone quarrying. National Forest takes up part of Co. Half the pop. centered in Hot Springs; rest of Co. sparsely settled.--Pop.: '90, 4478; '20, 6985; '50, 10,439.

Hot Springs. First settled in 1879. Warm mineral springs have made it a tourist area and health resort: National Sanitarium, State Soldiers Home, Crippled Children's Polio Center. Quarrying is main industry. Shopping center. Co. seat.--Pop.: '90, 1423; '20, 2141; '50, 5030.--Case, Francis, et al., *Black Hills Engineer, Hot Springs Number*, Rapid City, S.D. State Sch. of Mines, 1928. Clark, Badger, *When Hot Springs Was a Pup*, Hot Springs, Kiwanis Club, 1927.

320. Retired rancher (now has small place 4 m. s. of Hot Springs). B. 1887; as young man spent some time in Wy. as assistant to owner of cattle ranch.--F b. Md.; to Ks. c1868; to S.D., 1879.PGP b. Switzerland. M b. Sidney, Nb.; to Centennial Prairie, S.D., 1876; to Hot Springs, 1878. MGM b. Cork, Ire.; to Can. MGF French Canadian.--8th gr.--Member BPOE, Mason, Christian Ch. In Wy. associated with Eastern dudes, and learned much from them. Known and respected in the community.--Friendly, straightforward, aboveboard. Except for a few non-standard forms, gives the impression of being a man of some education.--Speech distinct, with moderate tempo. /aɪ/ diphthong variable; sometimes has a backed beginning, and before /n/ so strong an [ɨ] offglide as to suggest an extra syllable. Offglides of tense vowels very weak.--VR-A--A 95 (1952).

(321) TRIPP COUNTY.
Org. 1909. First settlers from Nb. and e. S.D., later many Czechs in the s. A few Scandinavians, Germans, and Russian-Germans. Co. formerly part of the Rosebud Indian Reservation and many Sioux have remained. Stock raising and diversified farming. A third of the pop. lives in Winner.--Pop.: '10, 8323; '20, 11,970; '50, 9139.

Winner. Grew up in 1908 with a rush of settlers from e. S.D. and Nb. Present pop. mixed: e. S.D., Nb., Ia., and the e. states; a few Czechs, Scandinavians, Germans, and Russian-Germans. The number of Sioux in the pop. is increasing. Trading and shopping center for a large area. Shipping point for turkeys and other poultry. Pheasant hunting center. Several small industries. Co. seat.--Pop.: '20, 2000; '50, 3252.

321. Co. treasurer; deputy Co. treasurer, 1947-1950; grocery clerk. B. 1910 in Colome, Tripp Co.; to Winner.--F and M b. Norway; to Ia. c1902; to Tn.; to Ia.; to Gregory Co., S.D.; to Tripp Co., 1910.--HS--Social contacts chiefly through her work. Member Women's Club and BPW. Never traveled.--Fairly intelligent, but somewhat slow; background limited. Difficulty with 'fill-in' questions. Cooperative, but amazingly laconic. Answers were single words, and no extra information or anecdotes were supplied.--Tempo fairly fast; single-word answers almost ejaculated. Grammar standard. Very little spontaneous conversation.--A 89 (1952).

(322,323) CHARLES MIX COUNTY.
Org. 1879. W. end of Co. settled in 1880's from states to the e. S. and e. parts, opened later, received a large Bohemian pop. Hollanders settled in n., also a number of Germans. Rich agricultural area with corn as dominant crop; livestock feeding; dairying.--Pop.: '70, 152; '90, 4178; '20, 16,256; '50, 15,558.

Geddes. Founded in 1910. Small town but an important business center for the surrounding farming area.--Pop.: '10, 710; '20, 695; '50, 502.

322. Farmer; once local agent for agricultural implement house in Minneapolis. B. 1885.--F b. R.I.; to Wyoming Co., Pa.; to Bloomington, Il., 1854.; to Union Army; to Ks.; to S.D., 1882. M b. Il. of Irish parents; to Ks.; to S.D.--3rd gr.--Narrow social life. Once member IOOF, former Catholic, now Congregationalist. Known locally as an old-fashioned 'old-timer'.--Friendly and cooperative, but difficult to interview because of garrulity and inability to complete unfinished statements with the implied responses. Thinks slowly and without imagination.--Nonstandard, old-fashioned, pioneer speech. Speaks somewhat slowly, with only fair distinctness (has no teeth).--VR-A--A 79 (1951).

Lake Andes. Shopping and shipping center

for mid-county area. Became important with building of nearby Fort Randall Dam and Reservoir Project. Co. seat.--Pop.: '10, 920; '20, 867; '50, 1851.

323. Deputy Co. treasurer; two terms as Co. auditor; painter and carpenter. B. 1895 near Tyndall, Bon Homme Co.; to Charles Mix Co. as infant; with AEF in France, 1918.--F b. Bohemia; to Cleveland, 1868; to S.D., 1870. M b. Bohemia; to US, 1867.--HS--Founding member American Legion Post, member VFW and Bohemian Fraternal Organization, former Catholic. Well known and respected. Quiet, rather stolid, but friendly and cooperative. Sense of humor. Interested in people; observant of differences in customs and language. Strong sense of civic duty.-- Speaks distinctly at a moderate rate. Only traces of Czech are a rare and slight staccato effect and an occ. non-English intonation pattern. Occ. nonstandard morphological forms, those which are typical in community use.--VR -A--Aux. inf.: Wife. Also Czech and a native of S.D. Supplied one item.--A 78 (1951).

(324,325) CLAY COUNTY.
Org. 1862. Early settlers from states to the e., expecially Wi. and Oh. In 1864 part of a N.Y. colony took claims, later many from Ia. and a large group of Norwegians from Nb. Now pop. is about one-third Anglo-American, one-third Scandinavian, one-sixth Irish, and one-sixth German and French-American. French located e. of Vermillion, Norwegians w. and Swedes n. Prosperous diversified farming area.--Pop.: '70, 2621; '90, 7509; '20, 9654; '50, 10,993.--Briggs, Harold, "Early History of Clay Co.," *S.D. Hist. Soc. Coll.*, 13.69 (1926).

Vermillion. First settled as fur-trading post in 1835. Permanent pop. mainly from n. central states, with some addition of French, Norwegians, and Swedes. State Univ. is chief enterprise in the town. Trading center. Co. seat.--Pop.: '80, 714; '90, 1496; '20, 2590; '50, 5337.

324. Housewife. B. 1881.--F b. Oh.; to S.D. in 1870's. PGP English, M b. Il.; to S.D. in 1870's. MGP Dutch, German, and Irish.--8th gr.--Member Rebekkahs (past officer), Women's Relief Corps, local music club. Once active Congregationalist. Fairly active social life.-- Quiet, pleasant, rather slow-thinking. Not widely read; has limited outlook. Speaks slowly and distinctly, no unusual characteristics. Grammar surprisingly standard, though some nonstandard forms

appeared in conversation.--VR-A--Aux. inf.: Husband. B. 1875 in Ia., to Vermillion, 1881. Speech almost entirely nonstandard, of which he is unaware.--A 76 (1951).

325. Housewife; she and husband own a small trailer camp. B. 1887 in Nb.; to S.D. c. age 2.--F b. In.; to Nb.; to S.D. PGM b. S.C. M b. Nb.; to S.D. MGP b. In.--HS--Member Rebekkahs (since 1923), VFW aux. Former Congregationalist, nominal Catholic since marriage. Social life largely within family circle; 6 children and several grandchildren.--Not talkative, but cooperated readily and pleasantly.--Speaks evenly and slowly, with good articulation. Aware of standard usage, though some nonstandard forms [e.g. "run" as preterit] appeared in conversation.--VR-A--Aux. inf.: Husband. Somewhat older; b. in Nb. Typical nonstandard forms throughout.--A 77 (1951).

(326) PENNINGTON COUNTY. Rapid City.
(See 311-312)

326. Housewife and HS teacher. B. 1901. --F b. Homer, N.Y. in 1870; to Nb., 1880; to Rapid City c1895. M b. Yankton, S.D.; to Rapid City. MGM b. Dubuque, Ia.; MGF b. Watertown, N.Y.--HS; graduate Yankton College; 1 summer Univ. of Mt.-- Leader in YWCA, local Women's Club, PEO, and women's club of Congregational Ch. Active in college social life through husband's connection with S.D. State Sch. of Mines. Held in high esteem in community.--Friendly, genial, sincere, alert, cooperative. Unusual interest in the interview. Excellent example of regional cultivated speaker.--Tempo moderate, speech markedly distinct. Tense vowels have only weak diphthongization. Strong, but not unreasonable, feeling for correctness. Resists husband's effort to make her say /ˈsɛmətrɪ/ instead of /ˌseməˈtɛri/. To be helpful she refrained from comments, so conversational material is sparse.--A 93 (1952).

(327,328) HANSON COUNTY.
Org. 1871. Settlement began in late 1870's from Wi. and Ia. Later large numbers of Norwegians, Germans, and Russian-Germans. Hutterite colony at Rockport. Smallest Co. in state. Diversified farming and livestock raising; purebred cattle center.--Pop.: '80, 1301; '90, 4267; '20, 6202; '50, 4896.

Alexandria. Pop. history similar to that of Co. Market town for a rich farming area. Co. seat.--Pop.: '90, twp. 806; '20, 965; '50, 714.

327. Housewife (widow); taught rural sch. before marriage. B. 1873 in Milwaukee, Wi.; to Alexandria, 1884, age 10; spent 1 yr. in Platte, S.D.--F b. Scot.; to Wi.; to S.D. M b. N.Y.; to Wi.; to S.D. MGP b. Isle of Man.--8th gr. rural sch.--Once active in community life; Epworth League, Methodist Ladies' Aid Soc., 4H. Held in high esteem. Husband, dead 8 yrs., was mayor for 8 yrs.--Very alert. Natural and cooperative. Rather knowledgeable in many ways.--Speaks clearly with excellent articulation. Good English, except for a few nonstandard terms. Rate moderate to fast, with occ. lengthening of tense vowels.--VR-A--A 123 (1957).

328. Housewife; taught sch. 2 yrs. as young woman. B. 1899; spent 2 yrs. in Kadoka, S.D.--F b. Wi.; to Ia.; to S.D., 1891. PGM b. Pa. PGF b. N.Y. M b. Ia.; to S.D. MGF b. Pa. (Pa.-German).--HS-- Active social life: Methodist women's soc., district chairman Co. extension club, OES (past worthy matron), independent missionary society. Knows many farm people from childhood on farm. One son graduated from Univ. of Mn.--Friendly, pleasant, cooperative. Mentally alert and responsive, well informed. Excellent inf. Because of lack of time, didn't volunteer much conversational material.--Speech well articulated, rate moderate.--Aux. inf.: Husband, c60; b. here and lived here all his life except for college yrs. at Univ. of Ia. Dentist. Pleasant and friendly.--A 122 (1957).

NEBRASKA

(401,402) DAWES COUNTY.
Org. 1885. Settled from Oh., Ks., Il., Ia., and Mo. A few Tx. cattlemen remained permanently.--Prosperous ranching and wheat area. Half the pop. in Chadron; rest of Co. sparsely settled. Part of Co. lies in Chadron State Park. --Pop.: '90, 9722; '20, 10,160; '50, 9708.--Rhoads, Minnie A., *A Stream Called Deadhorse*, Chadron Printing Co., 1957. Ricker, L. D., "Early Days in Dawes County," *Nb. Hist.*, vol. 13, no. 3 (1932).

Chadron. Settled 1884. Pop. similar to that of Co. Trading center; several food mfrs. and oil refinery. State college. Co. seat. Division hdqr. CNWRR.--Pop.: '90, 1867; '20, 4412; '50, 4687.--Lutz, Gertrude, *Sketches of Some Pioneers*, Chadron Printing Co., 1953.

401. Housewife; farmwife (12 m. from town) until 7 yrs. ago when she and husband moved to town. B. 1884 in North Loup, Nb.; to Chadron age 6 wks., 1884. --F b. Mn.; to Oh.; to Mn.; to Nb.; at some time joined Confederate Army. M b. Mansfield, Oh.; to Mn.; to Nb.; MGP b. Oh.--Rural sch.--Member Lutheran Ch., Ladies' Aid Soc.; War Dads' Aux.; VFW Aux.; Co. social club.--Open-hearted, strong-minded, pioneer woman. Strong sense of humor. Interested in interview. --Vigorous, fairly rapid speech. Grammar characterized by standard forms recently superimposed upon nonstandard.--VR-A--A 99 (1953).

402. Housewife (husband RR engineer); taught rural sch. for 2 terms at age 18. B. 1900 in Grand Forks, N.D.; to Chadron age 6 wks.--F b. Ks.; to Nb. M b. Ok.; to Nb.; to N.D.; to Nb. MGP b. Belgium; to Ks. or Ok.--HS--Methodist, women's soc.; once belonged to various clubs. Wide number of friends. Daughter college graduate, now in Germany with army husband.--Genial, affable, cooperative. Sense of humor. Puzzled by interview, but interested.--Speech moderate in speed, sometimes deliberate, with careful articulation (probably because husband is quite deaf). Aware of 'correctness'; often commented that her form was not correct. [aʊ] diphthong less fronted than that of 401.--VR-A--A 100 (1953).

(403,404) CHERRY COUNTY.
Org. 1883. Originally part of the cattlemen's empire; homesteaders arriving in 1882-1884 from Ia., Mo., and Il. pushed the cattlemen w. Pop. now varied. E. part of Co. farming and cattle raising. W. part, where the sandhills begin, only cattle ranches. Very sparsely settled. --Pop.: '90, 6428; '20, 11,753; '50, 8397.--Farris, James Robert, "My Recollections of Pioneering in Cherry County," *Nb. Hist.*, 19.3-27 (1938). Reece, Charles Simone, *A History of Cherry County, Nebraska*, Simeon, Nb., 1945.

Valentine. Inc. 1910. Pop. similar to that of Co. Trading center for cattle country. Largest town in Cherry Co. Co. seat.--Pop.: '90, twp. 1177; '20, 1596; '50, 2700.

403. Housewife; taught rural sch. 3 terms at ages 16, 19, and 20. B. 1871 in Boone, Ia.; to Knox Co., Nb., 1873; to Cherry Co., 1881 (20 m. s. of Valentine); to Valentine c1932.--F b. Tn.; to Il. (near Springfield); to Ia.; to Nb. M b. In. (near Indianapolis); to Ia.; to Nb. MGF Pa.-German.--Private teacher, 3 winters in sch. in Valentine, probably equiv. to 8th gr.--Childhood spent in isolated pioneer community; married life, on a farm 10 m. s. of Valentine. Social life enlarged since move to Valentine at husband's death 20 yrs. ago. Presbyterian, OES, only remaining member of Co. Hist. Soc. Traveled to Ca. in 1930.--Intelligent, alert, but occ. could not remember ordinary terms. Wholesome, genial outlook, good sense of humor. Enjoyed interview without fully understanding it.--Tempo moderate; /ɑʊ/ diphthong usually fronted; articulation quite clear; no nasality. Grammar often nonstandard. Aware of regional differences in terms of Mo. and N.Y. speech heard in childhood.--VR-A--A 97 (1952).

404. Police chief; electrician by trade. B. 1905, 8 m. from Valentine; lived in Wy. 1930-31, and Wa. 1942-47.--F b. central Il.; to Ia.; to Wy.; to Ia.; to Nb. M b. Sheridan, Wy.; to Nb. MGP b. Denmark.--HS--Belongs to no ch. or clubs, but knows everyone in town. Became police chief a yr. and a half ago.--Easy going, but a hard-working, forward-looking police official.--Speech slow; offglides not pronounced. /ɑɪ/ diphthong has wide variation: [aɪ] to [e>ɨ]. Grammar often nonstandard, as he ruefully admits. Unusually interested in speech variants. Reported spontaneously on other forms used locally.--VR-A--A 96 (1952).

(405,406) ROCK COUNTY.
Org. 1888. Settled from states to the e. and by Germans and Scandinavians.--Poor farming soil; mixed cattle and hog raising. Very sparsely settled.--Pop.: '90, 3083; '20, 3703; '50, 3026.

Bassett. Settled in early 1880's by people of mixed backgrounds from the states to the e. Later many from Germany and Scandinavia. Enterprising community; HS occ. brings musicians and lecturers for public programs. Trading center for area. Largest town in Rock Co. Co. seat. --Pop.: 1900, 270; '20, 664; '50, 1066.

405. Retired farmer, now does odd jobs. B. 1883 in Evansville, Wi.; to Nb., 1884. --F b. Pa.; to Wi.; to Nb. M b. Ft. Wayne, In.; to Wi.; to Nb.--Country sch. --Belongs to no clubs; social life quite limited. Contacts almost entirely with people of own age.--Steady, conservative; limited education and outlook. Sense of humor. Cooperative. Became talkative after first interview.--VR-A--A 109 (1953).

406. Housewife. B. 1906.--F b. Oh.; to Atkinson, Nb., as small boy. M b. Pa.; to Nb. (near Newport, Rock Co.).--HS-- Once active in ch., women's club, and bridge club. Well known and well-to-do; informal contacts with the higher society of the community. Husband is brand inspector at local cattle yard.--Pleasant, gracious, cooperative. Intelligent, alert, but provided no conversational material.--Strong feeling for 'correct' grammar. Voice pleasant, rate moderate, no unusual characteristics.--VR-A--A 110 (1953).

(407,408) CEDAR COUNTY.
Org. 1857. First settled from Harrison Co., Ia., other parts of Ia., and St. Louis. Germans from Mo. settled in the n. part of the Co. at the time of the Civil War. General settlement was accelerated in the 1880's at coming of the RR, when Scandinavians and Americans from the states to the e. arrived. Pop. now varied. Prosperous, diversified farming. Well settled.--Pop.: '60, 246; '70, 1032; '90, 7028; '20, 16,225; '50, Jones, L. E., *History of Cedar County*, St. Helena, Nb., 1876. McCoy, J. M., *History of Cedar County, Nebraska*, privately printed, Hartington, 1937.

Hartington. Founded by RR in 1884. Settled first by Norwegians, but other groups, especially from states to the e., came later. Trading center for surrounding area. Co. seat.--Pop.: 1900, 471; '20, 1467; '50, 1660.

407. Farmer (30 yrs.); blacksmith, 3 yrs.; implement dealer; well-driller and windmill installer for 30 yrs. B. 1874 6 m. n.w. of town.--F b. Sweden; to US, 1873. M b. Norway; to US.--4th reader, country sch.--Member IOOF; sch. board in rural district for many yrs. Social contacts normal for the community. One trip to Ca. Widower, has lived alone past 28 yrs.--Kindly, friendly, cooperative. Puzzled by questions requiring suppletion.--In some ways, speech reflects Swedish spoken in his childhood home. Gives heavier stress to unstressed syllables; [t] or [tθ] for [θ] in conversation, but not in single responses; final [z] is often [z̦]; and [ʌ] is sometimes lowered to [eᵛ]. In general, speech was deliberate and marked consistently by many nonstandard verb forms.--VR-A-- A 12 (1953).

408. Postal employee (mostly as rural carrier) for 24 yrs.; once RR clerk and a painter; US Army in 1917 (not overseas). B. 1895.--F b. Sweden; to Cedar Co. c1880. M b. Sweden; to Ia., age 15; to Cedar Co. (worked as hired girl for English-speaking family).--HS--Member IOOF, American Legion, Lutheran Ch. Well known and liked in community.--Quiet, friendly, cooperative. Steady, conservative, reasonably alert.--Tempo moderate, no unusual characteristics or traces of Swedish ancestry.--Aux. inf.: Wife, also of Swedish ancestry.--A 111 (1953).

(409,410,411) SCOTTS BLUFF COUNTY. Org. 1888. Settled from e. Nb. and states to the e. Originally part of cattle empire; now irrigation has made farming possible.--Pop.: '90, 1888; '20, 20,710; '50, 33,939.--Brand, Donald D., *History of Scotts Bluff, Nebraska*, Berkeley, Ca., U.S. National Park Service, Field Division of Education, 1934. Green, Thomas L., *Scotts Bluff and the North Platte Valley*, Scotts Bluff Star-Herald Printing Co., 1950. Shumway, G. L., "First Settlement of the Scotts Bluff Country," *Pub. Neb. State Hist. Soc.*, 4th series, 19.103-114 (1919).

Scottsbluff. Settled in 1886. Pop. similar to that of Co. Located where the Oregon and Overland trails converged; lively and important town. Now chief city in w. Nb. Prosperous because of irrigated farming in area.--Pop.: '10, 1746; '20, 6912; '50, 12,858.

409. Sign painter and artist; as youth was bookkeeper, surveyor's assistant. B. 1887 in Scotts Bluff Co.; has spent summers working in Mt., Wy., and N.D. with RR construction crews and on wheat farms.--F b. N. Tonawanda, N.Y.; to e. Nb., 1881; to Scottsbluff, 1887. PGP b. R.I. PGM b. Eng. M b. Solsville, N.Y.; to Nb. PGM b. N.Y. of New Eng. background.--8th gr., a few wks. at Chicago Art Institute.--Member BPOE, once a Mason, Lions Club (past president), Junior Chamber of Commerce, but calls himself a lone wolf. One of the best known and best liked men in the city; very sociable. Both parents are Colgate alumni; brothers and sisters are college graduates. A brother is chief justice of the state supreme court.--Well known in Nb. as painter of western landscapes and authority on local Oregon Trail history. Wide interests, self-educated and self-trained. Affable, generous, high-principled. Excellent conversationalist.--Speech distinct, tempo moderate. Vocabulary and grammar generally standard with

occ. deviations. No pronounced speech mannerisms.--VR-A--A 104 (1953).

410. Housewife. B. 1902 in Mitchell, Nb.--F b. Kilbourn, Wi.; to Nb. (near Bridgeport) age 18. PGF b. Switzerland; to N.Y.; to w. Nb. PGP b. Oh.; to Ka.--HS--Active in Council of Ch. Women. Ch. organist.; close relationships with other local music people. Daughter is college student. Placid, friendly, cooperative. Much interested in interview. --Tempo deliberate; tendency to prolong stressed vowel in a word at end of a phrase. Articulation distinct.--VR-A--A 103 (1953).

411. HS principal; grade school teacher; US Army 3 1/2 yrs. during WWII. B. 1912 in Dawes Co., Nb.; to Scottsbluff, 1936. --F b. Dawes Co., Nb. PGF b. W.V. PGM b. In. M b. Dawes Co., Nb. MGF b. Wi. MGM b. Oh.; to Ia.--Chadron HS, Chadron State College, MA, Northwestern Univ., 1938. --Member Kiwanis, Methodist, Platte Valley Forum. Usual contacts of a small town HS principal. Seems respected and liked in community.--Intelligent, fairly alert, willing to help at some trouble to himself. Interested in people and things, though without wide knowledge. Brother-in-law of Inf. 410. Wife is daughter of local newspaper publisher. --Speaks with care and distinctness. Tried to give his normal form, not the 'correct' one although he has a strong feeling for 'correctness.'--A 101 (1953).

(412) HOOKER COUNTY. Org. 1889. Settled by e. farmers, some from Va. Many left later; some remained to become cattle ranchers. Basic pop. native American. Prosperous; cattle ranching. Sparsely populated. In sandhills region.--Pop.: '90, 426; '20, 1378; '50, 1061.

Mullen. Settled in early 1880's. Pop. similar to that of Co. Shopping center for large, sparsely populated area. Co. seat.--Pop.: '90, twp. 295; '20, 499; '50, 652.

412. Postmaster for 29 yrs.; Navy in 1917. B. 1893 in Cherry Co., 9 m. n. of Mullen.--F b. Il.; to Ia.; to Nb.,1888. PGF b. Ire.; to Il. PGM b. Scot.; to Il. M b. Il.; to Nb.--HS--Job brings him in contact with everyone in community. Well liked. Episcopalian.--Quiet, affable, cooperative, somewhat shy, but eventually opened up and became excellent inf.--Speech well articulated, tempo moderate; generally used standard idioms and morphology. No unusual characteristics.--Aux. inf.: Wife. b. Oh.; to Nb.

Lively, uninhibited.--A 108 (1953).

(413,414) GARFIELD COUNTY. Org. 1881.
Earliest settlers from Mi., Wi., Scot.,
and Eng., but pop. is now varied. On e.
edge of sandhills. Derives most of live-
lihood from horses and cattle. Very
sparsely settled; only one PO in Co.--
Pop.: '90, 1659; '20, 3496; '50, 2912.--
Foght, Harold W., *Trail of the Loup*,
Ord, Nb., 1906.

Burwell. Platted 1883. Varied pop., the
largest number coming from N.Y. and Ia.
Small cowtown with stable pop.; shopping
center for the area. Only PO in the Co.
Co. seat.--Pop.: '90, 378; '20, 1214;
'50, 1413.

413. Farm woman (unmarried, lives in
old family home, manages farm). B. 1871
near Sioux City, Ia.; to farm near Burwell, 1873.--F b. Warren Co., N.Y.; to
Maquoketa, Ia., age 4; to Otoe, Ia.; to
Garfield Co. PGF b. Warren Co., N.Y. or
English stock. PGM b. Vt. of English
stock. M b. Warren Co., N.Y. MGF b. N.Y.
or Vt. or N.H. MGM (sister of PGF) b.
Vt.--Through 5th reader.--Has complete
management of her farms; contacts are
mostly with farmers and tradesmen in the
community. Active Congregationalist; in
civic and social organizations in the
co. Reads several newspapers and magazines; enjoys Civil War novels.--Inter-
ested in local history. Generous, hospitable, cooperative, but shrewd and
'close with a nickel.' Conservative, but
not reactionary or backward. Willing to
be helpful but impatient to be finished.
--Speech slow, subdued, with a hesitant,
uncertain intonation; nasal, with little
pitch variation. Two lower front teeth
missing.--VR-Wr--Wr 15 (1953).

414. Housewife; once ran small feed
store. B. 1893 15 m. n. of Taylor, Loup
Co.; to Burwell, age 2; to Sargent,
1913; to Burwell, 1916.--F b. Butler Co.,
Pa.; to Butler Co., Nb.; to Loup Co.;
to Burwell. PGF b. Pa. of German stock.
PGM b. Pa. of English and German stock.
M b. Allegheny Co., Pa. MGF Irish.--10th
gr.--Active in extension work; has traveled for the extension club in the
state. Does needlework and often spends
time with other women sewing and chat-
ting. Reads several household and farm
magazines.--Good-natured, high-spirited,
fun-loving. Energetic and prodded by a
strong curiosity. Flattered and curious
about the interview; constantly asked
how she compared with others and soon
had a good idea of the purpose of the
interview.--Speech somewhat rapid; some
nasality, but clear and distinct; arti-

ulation good. Wide range of pitch. VR
has a slight simper, absent from most of
her conversation. Somewhat inhibited by
the microphone and was on her good behavior.--VR-Wr--Wr 16 (1953).

(415,416) MADISON COUNTY.
Org. 1867. First settled from Il., later
Germans from Madison Co., Wi., and Germany. Best farming region in Nb.--Pop.:
'70, 1133; '90, 13,669; '20, 22,511; '50,
24,338.--Halderson, Helmer, *Tri-County
Pioneers*, Newman Grove, Nb., 1948. Land-
graf, Edward A., *Early History of Norfolk, Nebraska, and Madison County*, Norfolk, n.d., reprinted from the *Norfolk
Daily News*. Scoville, C. H., *History of
the Elkhorn Valley, Nebraska*, Omaha, Chicago, National Pub. Co., 1892.

Norfolk /nɔrfɔrk/, so-called from its
location on the north fork of the Elkhorn river. Inc. 1881. Settled 1869 by
Germans from Madison Co., Wi. Largest
town in the Co., and largest in n.e.
quarter of Nb. Trading center for a
large, prosperous area. Important center of livestock sales and distribution.
Several mfrs. Large jobbing and wholesale business.--Pop.: '70, 593; '90,
3038; '20, 8634; '50, 11,335.--Hess,
Harry E., *Methodism in Norfolk*, Norfolk,
1947.

415. Retired housewife (lives with her
daughter). B. 1870.--F and M b. Germany;
to Exonia, Wi.; to Norfolk.--8th gr.--
Member of St. Paul's Lutheran Ch., Ladies' Aid Soc. Many elderly friends call
on her, but she rarely leaves the house.
Reads the Bible, Lutheran handbooks, and
an Omaha newspaper.--Agreeable, cooperative, natural. Strong-minded, religious,
conservative, a strict self-disciplinar-
ian. Likes to keep up on political activities of the men in the family.--Speech
slow and deliberate, quite distinct and
unaffected. Often will let an utterance
fade out or stand unfinished. Speaks
German, and her English has a strong German cast in sounds, rhythm, word order,
and occ. in vocabulary. Tone slightly
nasal,with a little of the querulousness
of age.--VR-Wr--Wr 10 (1953).

416. Postal clerk in registry and bonds.
B. 1898; lived briefly in Atkinson and
Creighton, Nb.--F b. Chicago; to West
Point, Nb. after Civil War; to Long Pine,
Nb.; to Norfolk, 1891. PGP Dutch. M b.
Sweden, near Stockholm; to West Point,
Nb., age 13.--11th gr.--Gregarious, po-
litically active, now trying for post-
mastership. Reads little except Omaha
and Norfolk newspapers and some maga-
zines.--Genial, hearty, and ambitous.

Cooperative, giving time at some inconvenience to himself. Responses spontaneous, casual, full, and occ. bawdy. Gained some understanding of the interview and enjoyed it.--Speech quite ordinary for the area. Little labialization, often slurred syllables and function words. Interview interrupted for several weeks.--VR-Wr--Wr 9 (1953).

(417). DEUEL COUNTY.
Org. 1889. Settled from Ia. and e. Nb.; many of Swedish stock. Diversified farming and cattle raising. Rather sparsely settled.--Pop.: '90, 2893; '20, 3282; '50, 3330.

Chappell. Settled in early 1880's. Pop. similar to that of Co. Shopping center. Co. seat.--Pop.: '90, twp. 521; '20, 1131; '50, 1297.

417. Housewife. B. 1883 in Odebolt, Ia.; to Nb., 1885.--F and M b. Sweden; to Ia.; to Nb.--Rural sch.--Always lived on a farm, with little time or opportunity for social activities. Member Lutheran ch., Ladies' Guild, and American Legion Aux. Once belonged to Farmers' Union.--Patient, resigned, hard-working. Average intelligence, slow with many responses. Pleasant and cooperative, enjoyed the interview.--Very slight traces of Swedish background appear in overstressing of unstressed syllables, in final [z̧], and in the [j] of 'jaundice.' Speech somewhat deliberate and clear. --VR-A--Aux. inf.: Husband. c70, also of Swedish background. Came as child from e. Nb.--A 102 (1953).

(418,419) LINCOLN COUNTY.
Org. 1860. Settled in early 1880's from Ia., Il., and e. Nb.; some Swedes and Germans. Cattle raising and farming. Rather sparsely settled except for a concentration of pop. in North Platte.-- Pop.: '70, 17; '90, 10,441; '20, 23,420, '50, 27,380.--Bare, I.L., & W. H. McDonald, *History of Lincoln County*, Chicago, American Hist. Soc., 1920. Breternitz, L., "Settlement and Economic Development of Lincoln County," Univ. of Colorado M.A. thesis, 1931.

North Platte. Inc. 1871. Laid out by UPRR in 1866. Pop. similar to that of Co. Principal RR town and trading center for a large area. Lively and progressive. Has flourishing summer tourist trade as a main overnight stop on US highway 30. Co. seat. Several industries. RR repair shops, sheep-feeding yards, flour mill. --Pop.: '80, 363; '90, 3055; '20, 10,466; '50, 15,433.--Adamson, Archibald R.,

North Platte and Its Associations, North Platte, 1910.

418. Retired farmer; taught rural sch. for 3 yrs. 50 yrs. ago. B. 1878 in Cottonwood Springs (28 m. s.e. of North Platte).--F and M b. Sweden; to St. Louis; to Nebraska City; to Lincoln Co.-- 8th gr., 1 yr. HS in North Platte.--Most of life spent on ranch or farm. Remarked that he had never had a chance to do much talking to people and hence lacked practice. Once member IOOF, Lutheran Ch. Now Presbyterian.--Cooperative, friendly, not very alert. Puzzled by interview; had difficulty with completion questions and in recalling items. Because he tried to cooperate by answering in monosyllables, there are few conversational items. Conservative and sturdy.--Deliberate speech, offglides occ. rather long. Feeling of 'correctness' in some items, but not in others. Lower denture was loose, so that sibilants ([s] and [z], esp.) varied; these variations are ignored in the transcription.--VR-A--A 106 (1953).

419. Retired businessman; once owned leading clothing store in the city. B. 1894.--F b. Germany; to Wi., 1879; to Nb. c1885 (where he worked for Buffalo Bill). M b. Germany; to North Platte, age 12, c1881.--HS, one yr. Midland College.--Lutheran, BPOE, Mason, American Legion. A leading citizen, highly respected and well liked. Widely traveled, often to e. and midwestern cities.--Dynamic, mentally alert, curious, strong feeling of social responsibility. Wide reader, lover of music (wife is a musician; they often go to Lincoln or St. Louis for concerts). Culturally would rank with usual college graduate. Pleasant, genial, without affectation, strong sense of humor. Very cooperative.--Grammar standard with some few exceptions ('come' as preterit). Syntactic patterns and vocabulary are those of a person with formal education and wide reading. Speaks easily and clearly, with no noticeable idiosyncrasies.--A 107 (1953).

(420,421) HOWARD COUNTY.
Org. 1871. First settled by Danes from Wi. and Mo. and by Americans from Wi., Ia., and Mo., and Humboldt, Nb.; N.Y. in n.e. corner. There are now many people of Danish, Swedish, and Canadian descent. Livestock raising. No pop. centers, but the Co. is well settled.-- Pop.: '80, 4391; '90, 9430; '20, 10,739; '50, 7226.--Historical Records Survey, Nb., *Inventory of County Archives, Howard County*, Lincoln, 1941 (hist. sketch, pp. 1-18).

Dannebrog. First settled 1871 by Danish colony from Milwaukee, Wi. Pop. still mainly Danish. Because of proximity to larger cities, it is little more than a corner grocery for the area.--Pop.: '80, 53; '90, 280; '20, 436; '50, 318.

420. House painter and carpenter; once farmer and stockman. B. 1876 in Genoa, Wi.; to Howard Co., c. age 3.--F spent most of life in N.Y. before moving to Wi., then to Nb. PGP probably Scotch. M lived in N.Y.; to Wi.--8th gr. rural sch.--Knows everyone in community, well liked. Member of local groups and lodges and the Evangelical Lutheran Ch. Traveled in central US on vacations and visits with his children. Reads newspapers and the common popular magazines. --Reserved and cautious, but cooperative and agreeable. Interested in politics and sports. Readily understood the nature and purpose of the interview.--Tempo moderate to slow, with distinct nasal 'whine' and a slight sing-song intonation. Voice distinct, soft, and pleasant.--Wr 11 (1953).

St. Paul. Settled in 1871 by Danes from Wi. Still many people of Danish descent. Local trading center and shipping point. Co. seat.--Pop.: '80, 482; '90, 1263; '20, 1615; '50, 1676.

421. Co. assessor. B. 1891 on farm near Cushing, Nb.; to St. Paul, 1942.--F b. Schleswig, Germany; to Fremont, 1886; to Howard Co., 1888. M b. near Copenhagen, Denmark; to Fremont 1886; to Howard Co.--8th gr., c. 1 yr. at local college.--He and his wife come from large families, and have close associations with relatives. Work brings him in contact with everyone in community. Relatives and close friends are farmers with backgrounds similar to his. Member of ch., but not active. Reads newspapers and magazines about business and politics. --Mild, meek, unimaginative, secure in his job and friends. Cooperative, but talked little and volunteered almost no information. Felt moral obligation to cooperate although unaware of the purpose of the project.--Speech average to slow. Slight nasality; intonation occ. sought verification or approval. No trace of foreign background.--VR-Wr-Wr 14 (1953).

(422,423) HALL COUNTY.
Org. 1859. Settled in 1857 from Davenport, Ia.; many settlers were Germans. At present: Low German settlement diagonally across the Co., an Irish settlement in the s.e. corner; and a High German settlement in the n.e. corner with Americans in the n.w. and s.e. corners. Agricultural area, irrigated from the Platte R. Large pop. center in Grand Island.--Pop.: '60, 116; '70, 1057; '90, 16,513; '20, 23,720; '50, 32,186.--Bentley, Arthur F., *The Condition of the Western Farmer as Illustrated by the Eccnomic History of a Nebraska Township*, Baltimore, John Hopkins Press, 1893 (Johns Hppkins Studies in History of Political Science, 11th ser., VII-VIII). *Biographical and Historical Memoirs of Adams, Clay, Hall and Hamilton Counties, Nebraska*, Chicago, Goodspeed Pub. Co., 1890. Buechler, A. F., & R. J. Barr, eds., *History of Hall County, Nebraska: a Narrative of the Past*, Lincoln, Western Pub. & Engraving Co., 1920. Stolley, W. L., *History of the First Settlement of Hall County, Nebraska*, Nb. State Hist. Soc., 1946.

Grand Island. Inc. 1873. Large German settlement in 1857 from Schleswig-Holstein through Davenport, Ia. Present pop. partly transient; basically German. Important trade, industrial, and transportation center. Co. seat. Ordnance depot nearby. Expanded greatly in WWII.--Pop.: '80, 2963; '90, 7536; '20, 13,947; '50, 22,682.--Bienhoff, Esther, "Original German Settlement at Grand Island, 1857-1866," M.A. thesis, Univ. of Mb., 1929.

422. Farmer and livestock dealer. B. 1873.--F b. Alsace-Lorraine; to Baltimore; to Grand Island c. age 25. M b. New Franklin, Oh.; to Merrick Co., Nb., age 12; to Grand Island, age 18, 1866. MGF b. Lancaster Co., Pa. MBM b. Londonberry, Ire.--2nd grammar, c. 8th gr.-- Directs farm, but devotes much of time to horses and local history. Many acquaintances connected with these activities. Reads little, belongs only to organizations related to his activities. Widely known and well liked.--Strong-willed, opinionated, enjoys being considered by many as 'quite a character.' Generous and helpful; a square-shooter and sharp business dealer. Has a large obscene vocabulary, which he uses with freedom and facility.--'Lecture' speech is slow, pontifical, and very distinct (has done a lot of informal public speaking). Conversational speech is slightly more rapid, and less precise. Lecture style has more standard grammar. Doesn't like to wear his false teeth (did not in tape recording); thus his sibilants are often emphasized.--VR-Wr-- Wr 13 (1953).

Doniphan. Surveyed in 1879. Settled from the states to the e. Small country town, shopping center for a small area. Only 10 m. from Grand Island.--Pop.: '80, 85; '90, 437; '20, 482; '50, 412.

423. Housewife. B. 1898 in Omaha (1918-21); to Doniphan; to Lincoln (1950-53); to Doniphan.--F b. Pennsville, Oh.; to Viroqua, Wi., age 15; to Doniphan, 1873. PGP Dutch. M b. Zanesville, Oh.; to Lodi, Ca., age 6; to Doniphan, age 8, 1873. MGP b. Oh. of Scotch-Irish stock.--HS, nurses' training in Omaha, 1918-21.-- Congregationalist, OES, Royal Neighbors, Liederkranz, BPOE, American Legion Aux. Reads common popular magazines and pulp fiction. Traveled over most of US. Knows almost everyone in town.--Drowsy during interview, but willing to be interviewed. Gregarious, dislikes living in a small town.--Speech is slow with a slighter pitch range than usual; nasal, often with a whiny intonation. Articulation is careless; sounds are constantly slurred or omitted. Completely natural in the VR.--VR-Wr--Wr 17 (1953).

(424,425,426) LANCASTER COUNTY. Org. 1855. Settled from the e. states and those between, especially Il. and Ia. At present there is a Danish colony in the n., a Russian-German colony in the center, and a large Swedish pop. Diversified farming, livestock-raising. Extensive deposits of clay and shale used for brick and tile. Well-populated, with a concentration in Lincoln.--Pop.: '60, 153; '70, 7074; '90, 76,395; '20, 85,902; '50, 119,742.--Bade, Gustav A., "History of the Dutch Settlement in Lancaster County, Nebraska," M.A. thesis, Univ. of Nb., 1938. Cox, William W., "The Beginning of Lincoln and Lancaster County," *Trans. & Rep. Nb. State Hist. Soc.*, 3.85-100 (1892). Cox, William W., *History of Seward County, Nebraska, together with a Chapter of Reminiscenses of the Early Settlement of Lancaster County*, Lincoln, State Journal Co., 1888; rev. 1905. Gregory, John S., "Early Days at the Salt Basin," *Proc. & Coll. Nb. State Hist. Soc.*, 15.102-108 (1907) (also vol. 2 in 2nd series, and vol. 15 of *Publications* series). Mason, Oliver P., "Papers Read on the Laying of the Corner Stone of the Lancaster County Court House," *Trans. & Rep. Nb. State Hist. Soc.*, 4.199-203 (1892). *Portrait and Biographical Album of Lancaster County, Nebraska*, Chicago, Chapman Brothers, 1888. Sawyer, Andrew, *Lincoln the Capital City and Lancaster County, Nebraska*, Chicago, S. J. Clarke Pub. Co., 1916.

Lincoln. Established in 1867. Pop. now 2/3 Russian-German, the remainder being

British, Swedish, and Danish. Business is mainly distribution and services; some industries. State capital, Co. seat, state penitentiary, asylum and reformatory, State Univ., 2 demoninational colleges, several business schools. Most of the pop. is employed by these institutions. Conservative; large proportion of older people; no great wealth or great poverty.--Pop.: '70, 2441; '90, 55,154; '20, 54,948; '50, 98,884.--Ames, John H., *Lincoln, the Capital of Nebraska*, Lincoln, State Journal Tower Press, 1870. Brown, Edward P., *The Prairie Capital* Lincoln, Miller & Paine, 1930 (reprinted in *75 Years in the Prairie Capital*, see below). Dick, Everett N., "Problems of the Post Frontier Prairie City as Portrayed by Lincoln, Nebraska, 1880-1890," *Nb. Hist.*, 28.132-143 (1947). Federal Writers' Project, Nb., *Lincoln City Guide*, Lincoln, Woodruff Printing Co., 1937 (American Guide Series). Hayes, A. B., & Sam D. Cox, *History of the City of Lincoln, Nebraska*, Lincoln, State Journal Co., 1889. Lincoln Chamber of Commerce, *Lincoln, Nebraska's Capital City, 1866-1923*, Lincoln, Woodruff Printing Co., 1923. *75 Years in the Prairie Capital*, Lincoln, Miller & Paine Pub. Co., 1955 (contains E. P. Brown pamphlet). William, Hattie P., "A Social Study of the Russian German," Ph.D. thesis, Univ. of Nb., 1916.

424. Housewife. B. 1866 near Roca, Lancaster Co.; to Saline Co. age 5; to Lincoln, 1891.--F b. Wittenberg, Germany; to Milwaukee age 15; to Chicago and Peoria, Il.; to Roca, Nb. M b. Morgantown, W. Va.; to Peoria; to Roca, Nb.-- MGF French. MGM German.--8th gr. in Centerville, 1 m. from Roca.--Used to know many townspeople and farmers, but now contacts are few. Popular with the neighborhood women, but most present activities are with large and devoted family: 28 great grandchildren and 1 great-great grandchild. All her children have HS education. Reads Readers' Digest and political articles. Methodist; no longer active.--Spry and alert, but eyesight and memory are fading. Shy at first, but extremely cooperative. Suggested items brought quick and definite acceptance or rejection. Seldom elaborated or volunteered information.--Tone slightly nasal; rate average to slow. Speaks quietly, tendency to 'swallow' some utterances. Intonation usually slightly questioning, as if seeking confirmation or approval. Wears dentures.--VR-Wr--Wr 3 (1952).

425. Postal transportation clerk. B. 1901 in Balzer, Russia; to Lincoln age 2; to Council Bluffs, Ia., as adult for 3

425. Postal transportation clerk. B. 1901 in Balzer, Russia; to Lincoln age 2; to Council Bluffs, Ia., as adult for 3 yrs.; US Army 10 mo.--F and M b. Balzer, Russia; to Lincoln.--Lutheran parochial elementary sch., 2 yrs. HS.--Congregationalist. Social contacts with ch. and professional friends and many relatives in Lincoln. Bachelor, ardent flower-gardener. Reads National Geographic and common popular and religious magazines. Because of job has traveled between Lincoln, Fremont, Hastings, Superior, Kansas City, and St. Joseph for last 12 yrs. --Agreeable and cooperative, but reserved. Occ. puzzled by the interview, but he eventually understood it and became very interested. Rarely volunteered information except on German migrations or Russian life in Lincoln. Responses certain and unselfconscious.--VR-Wr--Wr 1 (1952).

426. Housewife, widow; has developed profitable real estate business. B. 1894 in Warsaw, In.; to Tilden, Nb., age 6 mo.; to Lincoln, age 2 yrs.--F b. Warsaw, In.; to S.D. for 2 yrs.; to Tilden, Nb. for 1 1/2 yrs.; to Lincoln. PGF b. Can., near Niagara Falls, of Scottish stock; to In. as boy. PGM b. In. of English stock. M b. near Black River, N.Y.; to S.D. with N.Y. colony, 1880. MGF b. Black River, N.Y. MGM b. Hamilton, N.Y.--Private HS; A.B. Univ. of Nb. --Member PEO, Delta Delta Delta sorority, Presbyterian, and several study clubs (civic, travel, hobbies). Active in alumni activities of Univ. and sorority. Widow of M.D. No longer sees medical friends, but has many professional and business contacts. Traveled to 44 states. Ak., Can. Sophisticated, reads a great deal.--Understood nature of interview and was sympathetic and cooperative. Often mentioned other terms, distinguishing between those which were local and those which she had come across in reading. Very talkative. Aware of 'correctness' but often thought a 'wrong' term was 'correct'. Very positive in her responses.--Rate rapid, slightly nasal, tendency to slur unstressed syllables. Changes in pitch, rate, and emphasis exaggerated. Often overarticulated, even in conversation; she says her father and several friends are hard-of-hearing.-- VR-Wr--Wr 2 (1952).

(427,428) DOUGLAS COUNTY. Org. 1854. First attempt at permanent settlement by Mormons. Later, Germans, Bohemians, Americans, and Swedes. Prosperous farming area, mainly livestock. Heavily settled, even outside Omaha.-- Pop.: '60, 4328; '70, 19,982; '90,

158,008; '20, 204,525; '50, 281,020.-- Wakely, Arthur C. (ed): *Omaha, the Gate City, and Douglas County, Nebraska, a Record of Settlement, Organization, Progress, and Achievement*, Chicago, S. J. Clarke Pub. Co., 1917.

Valley. Settled in 1867. Service community in prosperous farming region. 18 m. from Omaha. Pop.: '80, 42; '90, 378; '20, 764; '50, 1113.

427. Farmer (on farm 6 m. from Valley). B. 1877 in Mt. Pleasant, Ia.; to Valley c. age 3.--F b. Butler Co., Oh., to Mt. Pleasant c. age 1 yr.--PGP b. near Dublin, Ire. M b. central In.; to Mt. Pleasant, c. age 10. MGP b. In.--6th reader; 3 mo. business course, age 25, at Fremont, Nb.; 3 mo. agriculture course at Univ. of Nb. in 1900.--Active in Methodist and Presbyterian chs. and their social activities. Widely acquainted; has long served on the rural district sch. board. Member for 35 yrs. in large pinochle club. Reads few books, but many farm journals and popular magazines.-- Curious, garrulous, natural in speech and actions. Not completely at ease during interview, but highly cooperative. --Tempo quite rapid; voice slightly high pitched, but range of pitch about ordinary. Speech distinct. Intonation often questioning. Interview interrupted because of scheduling difficulties.--VR-Wr --Wr 8 (1953).

Omaha. Inc. 1857. Founded in 1854, an early outfitting point for settlers and gold seekers. Has a varied cosmopolitan pop. with neighborhoods of Czechs, Italians, Germans, Swedes, Irish, Danes, Poles, and Russians. Largest foreign-born pop. in the state. Largest city; trading center for large part of e. Nb. and w. Ia. Widely varied industry; meat packing. Transportation center; on Missouri R. where several RR's cross. Co. seat. Medical sch. of Univ. of Nb., 2 colleges (municipal; Catholic), Nb. Sch. for the Deaf.--Pop.: '60, 1861; '70, 16,083; '90, 140,452; '20, 191,601; '50, 251,117. Leighton, George R., "Omaha, Nebraska," *Harpers Magazine*, 177.113-130, 309-328 (July-Aug 1938). Savage, J. W., & J. T. Bell, *History of the City of Omaha*, New York, Munsell & Co., 1894. Sorenson, Alfred R., *History of Omaha from the Pioneer Days to the Present Time*, Omaha, National Printing Co., 3rd. ed., 1923. Byron Reed Co., *The Story of Omaha*, Omaha, 1953.

428. Housewife. B. 1896 in St. Joseph Mo.; to Omaha, 1900.--F and M b. near Madison, Wi.; to Elwood, Ks.; to St.

Joseph, Mo. PGP b. s. Germany. MGM b. Bavaria. MGF b. Ire.--Public sch. and private tutoring through 10th gr.--Active until last yr. when hampered by ill health. Baptist, book study club, Co. extension club (president). Reads few magazines, but once read books such as Dickens novels, Ben Hur, Gone with the Wind. She and husband belong to pitch and poker clubs.--Intelligent, chatty, perceptive. Cooperative, enjoyed chance to occupy her time. Aware of dialect variation and offered Mo. and Tx. variations she had noticed.--Speech rapid and somewhat nasal. Ordinarily quite distinct, but occasionally she 'swallows' whole phrases. Tendency to leave off initial unstressed sounds. On VR speech is completely natural.--VR-Wr--Wr 12 (1953).

(429,437) DUNDY COUNTY.
Org. 1873. A few squatters and cattlemen before 1881, but major influx of settlers came in 1885 from e. Nb. and states to the e. Cattle raising and farming. Sparsely settled.--Pop.: '80, 37; '90, 4012; '20, 4869; '50, 4354.

Benkelman. Settled 1880. Pop. similar to that of Co. Trading center for the area. Small, conservative town with limited cultural opportunities. Co. seat.--Pop.: '90, 357; '20, 1009; '50, 1512.

429. Semiretired (because of health), but serves as lay preacher at Ch. of Christ; formerly rancher-farmer, telephone lineman, construction worker, sheriff, deputy marshal, and marshal at Wauneta. B. 1878 in Nemaha Co., Nb.; to Dundy Co., 1881; spent 1927-44 in Id., and a few yrs. in Wauneta, 35 m. n.--F b. Ky.; to Peoria, Il.; to Omaha; to Nemaha Co.; to Dundy Co., 1881. M b. Monroe Co., Ia.; to Nemaha Co., Nb.; to Dundy Co., 1881. MGP ultimately English he thinks.--Country sch.--Well known, but social life is largely within his ch. and family. Lives alone as widower.--Independent, pious, of great integrity. Avid reader and Bible student. Very cooperative, enjoyed talking about early days.--Tempo deliberate, with good articulation. Reading has given him a good vocabulary; pronunciation sometimes nonstandard and old-fashioned. Grammatical forms generally nonstandard.--VR-A--A 105 (1953).

(430,431) PHELPS COUNTY.
Org. 1873. Early settlers Swedes from Il. Pop. mostly Swedish, remainder German. Farming area, irrigated from Platte R.--Pop.: '80, 2447; '90, 9869; '20, 9900;

'50, 9048.--Arnold's Complete Directory of Phelps County, 1909 (contains brief hist. sketch). Biographical Souvenir of the Counties of Buffalo, Kearney, and Phelps, Chicago, F. A. Battey & Co., 1890. Mitchell, Joseph Clark, "Early History of Phelps County, Nebraska," M.A. thesis, Univ. of Nb., 1927. Young, Raymond, "Early History of Phelps County," MS. in Nb. State Hist. Soc., n.d.

Holdredge. Established 1883 just after arrival of the RR. Most of pop. is of Swedish descent. Shopping center. Staid and conservative; no bars and dances, one small movie house. Co. seat.--Pop.: '90, 2601; '20, 3108; '50, 4381.

430. Farmer. B. 1876 at Elkhart, In.; to Phelps Co., age 2 mo.--F b. Sweden; to Elkhart, In., 1866; to Phelps Co., 1876. M b. Sweden; to Chicago; to Elkhart, In.; to Phelps Co.--Through 5th reader.--Lutheran (Bethel) Ch. Wide variety of friends, mostly farmers, but likes to keep to himself. Reads farm papers and magazines, few books. Enjoys company of large family. Traveled a little: Minneapolis, Yellowstone Park, Tx., on group excursions.--Conservative, hard-working, reserved. Didn't understand purpose of interview but was cooperative. Serious and successful farmer, won Master Farmer Award few yrs. ago. Lives frugally but comfortably.--Speech is more rigid than average. Distinct except when he is unsure of himself. Unstressed syllables slighted and occasionally left out. Pitch range is narrow. Many lenis consonants. Sibilants peculiar, possibly because of false teeth, or characteristically post-alveolar. Swedish pitch and stress pattern.--VR-Wr --Wr 18 (1953).

431. Housewife and Christian Science reader. B. 1895 in Phelps Co.; to Arlington, Nb., 1901; to Holdredge, 1904; to St. Joseph, Mo., 1914; to Holdredge, 1916.--F b. Rochester, N.Y.; to Tucson, Az. 2 yrs. as child; to Il. briefly in early teens; to Ca., 2 yrs.; to Bradshaw, Nb., 4 yrs.; to Phelps Co.--PGP b. Germany. M b. Galesburg, Il.; to Holdredge as infant; to Denver, Co., 2 yrs. in late teens; to Holdredge. MGP b. Galesburg, Il. of Swedish stock.--HS in Arlington and Holdredge.--Member Federated Women's Club, Federated Garden Club, American Legion Aux., local card, dancing, and social clubs. Once active Methodist, now Christian Scientist. Friends include town's business and professional people. Sews much, reads some magazines in addition to heavy religious reading

and studies.--Cooperative, but anxious to finish the interview. Takes herself quite seriously as a cultural guardian in the community. Has a constant attitude of primness and niceness in her speech, as do many of her friends.-- Stresses are exaggerated, unaccented syllables lengthened. Pitch range wider than ordinary. Rate rather fast.--VR-Wr-- Wr 19 (1953).

(432,433) THAYER COUNTY.
Org. 1871. Settled from Ia., Mn., and Oh. Many Germans in n. part. Farming area, but crops undependable because of hot, dry summers. Extensive deposits of clay and shale used for brick and tile. --Pop.: '80, 6113; '90, 12,738; '20, 13,976; '50, 10,563.--Correll, Erasmus M., *Thayer County, Nebraska*, Hebron, Journal Print, 1885. Flicker, Irene, *History of Thayer County*, Bruning, Nb., 192?

Hubbell. Pop.: '90, 330; '20, 231; '50, 199.

432. Housewife. B. 1878, 1 1/2 m. w.; always lived within 10 m. of Hubbell.-- F b. O'Leary, Oh.; to Hubbell. PGP German. M b. Ire.; to O'Leary, Oh., age 16; to Hubbell.--8th gr. in Hubbell and Lowlands, Ks. (just across the line).--Social contacts with farm families in area and with tradesmen and retired farmers in town. She and husband belong to no organized social groups, but are sociable and popular; much more active when younger. Good neighbors and progressive farmers.--Chatty and wiry, interested mainly in her family, farm, and neighbors. Couldn't understand interest in what she does say rather than what she should say. Often gave so many terms that her husband would say, "Which one do you use most?" Occasionally couldn't answer a direct question and would appeal to her husband, who would prod the answer from her. Later repetition of some questions seemed to verify these responses.--Dentures affect sibilants. Articulation a little mushy, voice querulous. Tendency to prolong vowels. Removal of a goiter may have given her voice its peculiar quality.--VR-Wr--Aux. inf.: Husband. B. 1878 in Barrington, Ill.; to Hebron, 1882.--10th gr.--Farmed in vicinity all his life. F b. in N.Y. of Dutch and French stock; M b. in Il. of Irish stock.--Wr 4 (1952).

Hebron. Settled in 1869 by group identified with Disciples of Christ. Settlers mainly from Ia., Mn., and Oh.--Shopping center. Good crops in recent yrs. have made community prosperous, but not rich. Co. seat.--Pop.: '10, 466; '90, 1502; '20, 1513; '50, 2000.

433. Assistant postmaster. B. 1895.--F b. near Joliet, Il.; to St. Louis briefly; to Corning, Ia.; to Hebron. PGP b. near Frankfort, Germany. M b. Dayton, Oh.; to Cincinnati; to Hebron c. age 30. MGP b. Alsace-Lorraine.--HS--Knows most of the local people through his work, but has few close friends. Closest relationships are with members of his family. Presbyterian, but not active; Lions Club. Traveled widely. Takes part in amateur theatricals. Reads hist. novels and popular magazines.--Bachelor, well-groomed. Enjoys talking about the community, his family, travels, job, and childhood. Apparently lonely and welcomed the interview. Answers verbose but natural and spontaneous.--Slightly rapid tempo. Pitch a little high, and sentence intonation somewhat exaggerated. Articulation clear. Grammar usually standard.-- Wr 5 (1952).

(434,435) RICHARDSON COUNTY.
Org. 1855. In the w. are many people of Czech and Swiss descent.--Prosperous farming area. One of the original 8 Co.'s.--Pop.: '60, 2385; '70, 9780; '90, 17,574; '20, 18,968; '50, 16,886.--Edwards, L. C., *History of Richardson County*, Indianapolis, B. F. Bowen & Co., 1917. Larimore, Elma H., *Folklore of A Pennsylvania Colony in Nebraska*, Dawson, Nb., Ross Printing Office, 1956. Weber, Daniel H., *Brief History of Richardson County*, Falls City, Nb., 1949 (?). Wilhite, Sarah E., "Earliest Settlers in Richardson County," *Pub. Neb. State Hist. Soc.*, 19.126-129 (1919).

Humboldt. Settled 1857 by Czechs. Pop. mainly Czech; also many Swiss.--Trading center for w. half of Co. Manufacturing of brick and hollow tile.--Pop.: '70, 605; '90, 1114; '20, 1277; '50, 1404.

434. Farmer. B. 1871, near Salem, Nb.-- F b. near Trenton, Can.; across river to N.Y.; to Milwaukee; to n.e. Ia.; to Brownsville, Nb., 1869. PGF b. Scot. PGM b. Can. in French-Canadian section. M b. Utica, N.Y.; to Ogdensburg, N.Y.; to Milwaukee; to n.e. Ia.; to Brownsville, Nb. MGF b. Holland.--4th reader.--Belongs to no ch. or clubs. Reads much: Bible, 3 newspapers, history, several magazines. Well known, respected, well-to-do, old-fashioned, rugged individualist.--Lonely widower, has refused to move to town. Enjoyed the interview and

the chance to have company. Proud to have his speech recorded. Responses natural, easy, and well directed, especially on farm and old terms.--Speech forceful, but quiet. Often spoke in 'overlapping' fragments. Has none of his own teeth and wears only upper plate, but pronunciation apparently unaffected.-- Vr-Wr--Wr 7 (1952).

435. Assistant bank cashier; taught country sch. 1 yr., age 18. B. 1865; 1 1/2 yr. in artillery in WWI. 1 yr in France.--F b. Cedar Rapids, Ia.; to Humboldt. PGP b. Bohemia. M b. near Prague, Czechoslovakia; to Humboldt.--HS--Member Chamber of Commerce, American Legion, OES, York Masons, Lincoln Shrine, Methodist Ch. (no longer active). Formerly conducted local orchestra. Widely acquainted, socially active. Traveled widely in US on vacations.--Quiet, reserved; placidly cooperative despite feeling that the interview was silly. Seldom volunteered information, but would elaborate willingly if requested. Responses natural, succinct.--Little jaw movement. Speed and intonation ordinary. Grammar usually 'correct'. Seemed to plan whole utterance before speaking, even in casual conversation.--VR-Wr--Wr 6 (1952).

(436) DEUEL COUNTY. Chappell. (See 417.)

436. Rancher, stock buyer. B. 1906 in Deuel Co.--F b. Sweden; to US age 3; to e. Nb.; to Deuel Co., 1880's. M b. Sweden; to Moline, Il.; to Ia.; to Deuel Co., 1880's.--HS--Member Lutheran Ch., Mason. Once member of city board. Prosperous, well known in community. Now resides in town. Daughter college student. --Amiable, cooperative. Offered little conversational material. Tempo moderate. Speech clear, without marked idiosyncrasies.--A 98 (1952).

(437) DUNDY COUNTY. Benkelman. (See 429.)

437. Cattlebuyer, has ranch for livestock and farming; formerly in clothing business, grain, and automobiles. B. 1899.--F b. Geneseo, Ill; to Benkelman, 1884. PGP probably Scotch. M b. Il.; to Benkelman, 1885.--HS--Well known through his job. Once member KP, Lions Club. Methodist. City councilman 12 yrs. Wife teaches English in HS in neighboring town. One daughter in HS, another at Colorado A. and M.--Sturdy, conservative, respected, well-to-do. Willing to cooperate, but not greatly interested.-- Speaks with force and clarity. Admitted that wife's presence part of the time inhibited use of certain grammatical forms. Usage reported appears more standard than it would ordinarily be.--A 114 (1953).

RESPONDENTS

Although lack of space prevents the detailed presentation of the data taken from the mail checklists, reference to the replies of individual respondents occurs often enough, and the varied background they have is of sufficient interest, to justify the listing and summary description of the 1064 persons who returned valid checklists.

Responents are alsways identified by the post office code symbol for the state and by a split numeral, e.g., Mn 17.3. That designates the respondent as number 3 (a purely arbitrary assignment) in county 17 in Minnesota. Reference to the map on page xi will locate the county geographically in the left to right sequence beginning at the northern boundary of the state. If the name of the county is desired, further reference to the accompanying table on page xii will reveal it to be Hubbard County.

In the following list some of the abbreviations and contractions are rather unorthodox because of the demands of space, which, for example, compel "Welsh" to appear in the four-letter limit as "Wels." Most of the shortenings are self-explanatory, however, except possibly "Ys" for "Yugoslavia" and "Phill" for "Phillipines." The symbol for a state of retirement is simply "r." A respondent's overt indication of an absence, as of knowledge of a foreign language, is represented by zero (0). The dash (--), on the other hand, indicates that the respondent left the space blank.

No.	Sex	Age	Sch	Bpl	Yrs Res	Else-where	F	PGF	PGM	M	MGF	MGM	Travel	Occupation	For. Lang
1.1	M	53	10	Norw	47	Norw	Norw	Norw	Norw	Norw	Norw	Norw	0	Hdwe merch	Norw
1.2	M	40	12	ND	30	ND 10y	Ia	Ma	Il	Ia	NY	Can	US, Can	Farmer	0
1.3	F	63	7	Mn	53	Mn 10y	Swed	Swed	Swed	Swed	Swed	Swed	0	Housewife	--
1.4	M	57	8	Mn	57	0	Ct	Irel	Irel	Swed	Swed	Swed	25 States	Hwy dept emp	Swed
2.1	F	65	Bu	Mn	44	Mn 21y	Norw	Norw	Norw	Swed	Swed	Swed	Ca, Wa	Housewife	Norw
2.2	M	67	8	Mn	47	Mn 20y	Norw	Norw	Norw	Norw	Norw	Norw	Or, Ca	Farmer	--
2.3	M	61	8	ND	53	ND 8y	Norw	Norw	Norw	Icel	Icel	Icel	0	Laborer	--
3.1	M	57	8	Mn	38	Mn 19y	Swed	Swed	Swed	Swed	Swed	Swed	EuropeWWI	Storekeeper	Swed
3.2	F	45	12	Mn	25	Mn 20y	Can	--	--	Can	--	--	0	Hswf,asst PM	0
3.3	M	73	8	Engl	52	Ont 83-9	Engl	Engl	Engl	Engl	Engl	Engl	Mi, Wi	Farmer	0
4.1	M	60	3	Lux	37	Mn	Lux	Lux	Lux	Lux	Lux	Lux	Can, West	Operat eng'r	--
4.2	M	74	8	Ia	51	Il 92-98	Oh	--	--	Pa	--	--	NW, S, E	r.Title exam	--
4.3	M	85	8	Mn	50	Mn	Germ	Germ	Germ	Il	Germ	Germ	West	Farmer	Germ
5a.1	F	35	12	Mn	35	0	Ys	Ys	Ys	Ys	Ys	Ys	0	Steam pressr	--
5a.2	F	32	12	Mn	32	0	Pol	Pol	Pol	Pol	Pol	Pol	Mi, Can	Housewife	--
5a.3	M	51	8	Mn	47	Mn 4y	Swed	--	--	Swed	--	--	E&W coast, Hi, Phill	Ex-hotel own, millworker	--
5a.4	M	58	HS	Mn	23	Mn 35y	Swed	--	--	Swed	--	--	0	Chf ore grdr	--
5a.5	M	45	12	Mn	45	0	Ys	Ys	Ys	USA	Ys	Ys	0	Banker	0
5a.6	M	46	12	Mn	46	0	Swed	Swed	Swed	Swed	Swed	Swed	0	Acct clerk	Swed
5a.7	M	50	10	Mn	44	Mn 6y	Mn	Norw	--	Finl	Finl	Finl	Ma, Mi	Mechanic	Finn
5a.8	F	53	12	Mn	49	Fl 3y	Finl	Finl	Finl	Mi	Finl	Finl	0	Bookkeeper	Finn
5a.9	M	47	4	Mn	47	0	Engl	Engl	Engl	Can	Can	Can	0	Mechanic	0
5a.10	M	59	8	Mn	57	Army 2y	Ital	Ital	Ital	Ital	Ital	Ital	Ca, Engl	Laborer	Ital
5a.11	M	41	12	Mn	41	0	Norw	Norw	Norw	Mi	Swed	Swed	0	Locom engr	0
5a.12	M	46	12	Oh	41	Mn 7y, Oh 3y	Ys	Ys	Ys	Ys	Ys	Ys	La, Il	Squatter agent	Croa
5b.1	F	58	8	Mn	48	Mn 10y	Norw	Norw	Norw	Norw	Norw	Norw	0	Housewife	Norw
5b.2	M	58	8	Mn	58	0	Swed	--	--	Swed	--	--	Il, NY	P.O. clerk	--
5b.3	F	61	8	Mn	68	0	Norw	Norw	Norw	Norw	Norw	Norw	E, Can	Housewife	Norw
5b.4	M	67	Bu	Ont	51	Ont 16y	Ont	Ont	Ont	Ont	Ont	Ont	Buffalo, W coast	Insur agent	0
6.1	M	27	12	Mn	27	0	Swed	Swed	Swed	Swed	Swed	Swed	Swed	Farmer, r.r. worker	Swed
6.2	M	45	8	Finl	43	Finl 2y	Finl	Finl	Finl	Finl	Finl	Finl	0	Logger	Finn
7.1	M	59	4	Mn	24	Mn 35y	Norw	Norw	Norw	Norw	Norw	Norw	Norw, W coast	Manager teleph co	Norw
7.2	M	50	8	Mn	40	Mn 4y, Wi 4y, Mt 5y	Mi	Can	Can	Mi	Can	Can	US	Oil co emp	Fren
8.1	F	62	5	Mn	62	0	Germ	--	--	USA	--	--	Ca 3x	Housewife	--
8.2	M	60	12	Mn	36	--	Wi	--	--	Ia	--	--	MW,Fl,Can	Farmer	0
9.1	M	53	HS	Mn	48	Mn 5y	Norw	Norw	Norw	Norw	Norw	Norw	S, E	P.O. clerk	Norw
9.2	M	48	8	Mn	48	0	Norw	Norw	Norw	Norw	Norw	Norw	0	Farmer	Norw
9.3	M	54	8	Swed	34	Swed 19y	Swed	Swed	Swed	Swed	Swed	Swed	Europe	Lumbrmn,farmr	Swed
10.1	M	59	8	SD	51	SD 2y, Mn 8y	Wi	Germ	Germ	Germ	Germ	Germ	MW	Farmer	0
10.2	M	64	6	Mn	64	0	Aust	Aust	Aust	Mn	Germ	Germ	West US	Farmer	Germ
11.1	M	67	8	Swed	48	Swed 19y	Norw	--	--	Swed	--	--	0	Farmer	--
11.2	F	68	2	Ia	32	Mn 25y	Germ	--	--	Germ	--	--		Watchman	--
11.3	F	47	13	Mn	47	Tx, Ca	Ia	--	--	Ia	--	--	Tx, Ca	Housewife	--
11.4	F	65	8	Mn	32	Mn	Engl	--	--	Can	--	--	0	Housewife	--
12.1	F	60	10	Mn	33	Mn 27y	Mn	--	--	Germ	--	--	Ia, Ca	Seamstress	--
12.2	M	45	8	Ia	33	Ia 4y, Mo 9y	Ia	Oh	Oh	Mo	Pa	Pa	West US	Forest serv towerman	0
12.3	M	46	8	Mi	35	Mi 8y, Ok 5y, Tx 5y	Mi	Mi	NY	Mi	In	Mi	SW	Farmer, truck driver	0
12.4	M	43	9	Mn	43	0	Finl	Finl	Finl	Finl	Finl	Finl	0	Merchant	0

No.	Sex	Age	Sch	Bpl	Yrs Res	Else-where	F	PGF	PGM	,	MGF	MGM	Travel	Occupation	For. Lang
13.1	M	67	GS	Mn	67	0	Norw	--	--	Norw	--	--	Fl, Can	r. Mail carr	--
13.2	M	62	14	Mn	59	Mt 3y	Engl	--	--	Engl	--	--	US,Europe	Farmer	--
13.3	F	59	HS	Mn	48	Mn 9y, Man 2y	Me	--	--	Tx	--	--	NY,Ca,Man	Clinic mgr	--
13.4	M	69	10	ND	46	ND 83-06	Icel	Icel	Icel	Icel	Icel	Icel	0	Insur agent	Icel
13.5	M	80	HS	Vt	71	Vt 9y	Vt	Scot	Scot	--	Vt	Vt	NE, W, S	Banker	0
13.6	M	67	7	Mn	67	0	Norw	Norw	Norw	Ia	Norw	Norw	Can,Wi,Ia	Farmer	Norw
14.1	M	64	14	Mn	64	0	Norw	Norw	Norw	Norw	Norw	Norw	0	Farmer	Norw
14.2	F	51	HS	Il	36	Il 15y	Germ	Germ	Germ	Germ	Germ	Germ	0	Housewife	Germ
14.3	F	49	?13	Mn	49	0	Norw	Norw	Norw	Norw	Norw	Norw	ND	Tchr, hsewfe	Norw
14.4	M	71	Co	Mn	71	0	Norw	Norw	Norw	Norw	Norw	Norw	UM	Farmer	Norw
15.1	M	69	4	Norw	50	Norw 6m, Mn 19y	Norw	Norw	Norw	Norw	Norw	Norw	W	Cnty surveyr	Norw
15.2	M	74	6	Ia	36	SD 81-15	A-H	A-H	A-H	A-H	A-H	A-H	A-H	Farmer	Cz
15.3	F	45	8	Ia	35	Mn 8y	Neth	Neth	Neth	Neth	Neth	Neth	Neth	Hsewfe,clerk	Du
16.1	M	46	9	Mn	38	Mn	Wi	Germ	Germ	Mn	Germ	Germ	W, DC	Farmer	0
16.2	M	61	8	Mn	55	Mn 6y	Swed	Swed	Swed	Swed	Swed	Swed	0	Farmer	Swed
17.1	F	64	13	Mn	49	Mn, NY	Pa	--	--	Scot	--	--	US	Piano teachr	--
17.2	F	68	12	Pa	67	Pa 1y	NY	--	--	Pa	--	--	E&W coast	r. Druggist	--
17.3	M	60	3	Mn	52	ND 3y	--	--	--	Mn	--	--	0	Farmhand	--
17.4	F	59	9	Oh	30	Oh 7y, Md 2y, ND 11y	Oh	--	--	Irel	--	--	E,MW,Can	Housewife	--
18.1	F	51	11	Wi	41	Mt 1y, Wi 10y	Me	--	--	Que	--	--	W coast, Can	Housewife	--
18.2	M	81	3	Ont	58	--	Ont	Irel	Irel	Ont	Irel	Irel	Mt, Man	Farmr,butchr	0
19.1	M	54	9	Mn	54	0	Norw	Norw	Norw	Ia	Norw	Norw	0	Farmer	Norw
19.2	M	62	14	Mn	62	0	Mn	Ia	Ia	Wi	Wi	Wi	NW	Probate jdge	Germ Chip Swed Finn
20.1	M	55	8	Mn	55	0	Ia	--	--	Ia	--	--	W, S	Farmer	0
20.2	F	61	9	Ia	49	--	Wi	Germ	Me	Ia	Germ	Germ	Ia, Mt	Housewife	0
20.3	F	52	HS	Mn	48	Pa 12-13	Swed	Swed	Swed	Swed	Swed	Swed	0	Secretary	Swed
21.1	M	54	12	Mn	48	Mn 4y	Mn	Irel	Irel	Ks	Engl	Engl	NY,Fl,Can	Farmer	0
21.2	M	58	15	Nb	40	Ia 92-10	Wi	Irel	Irel	Il	Irel	Irel	W coast	Agric teachr	0
22.1	M	64	8	Mn	64	0	Irel	Irel	--	Irel	Irel	--	E&W coast	Police chief	--
22.2	M	48	8	Mn	32	Mn 02-18	Vt	Vt	Vt	Ia	--	--	0	Farmer	0
22.3	M	57	7	Ia	42	Ia 95-11	Czs	Czs	Czs	Czs	Czs	Czs	EuropeWWI	Farmer	Cz
23.1	M	63	7	Ia	48	Ia 88-01, Mn 01-50	Swed	Swed	Swed	Swed	Swed	Swed	E&W coast	Dairy farmer	Swed
23.2	M	40	8	Mn	40	0	Pa	--	--	Swed	Swed	Swed	0	Farmer	0
23.3	M	64	10	Mn	52	Wi	Wi	Germ	Germ	Wi	NY	NY	S, W	Teachr, r.r. postal clerk	Germ
23.4	M	68	Co	Mn	32	Mn	Germ	Germ	Germ	Mn	Germ	Germ	0	Farmer	Germ
24.1	F	69	8	Mn	50	Mn	Germ	--	--	Mn	--	--	Fl,Ca,W	Housewife	--
24.2	F	54	16	Wi	46	Wi 99-07, Mn 07-13	Norw	Norw	Norw	Norw	Norw	Norw	US, Can	Hsewfe, r. teacher	Norw
24.3	F	57	16	Mn	30	Mn	Denm	Denm	Denm	Ia	Norw	Norw	US, Can, Mex	Hsewfe,store clerk	0
25.1	M	51	7	Mn	51	0	Norw	Norw	Norw	Wi	Norw	Norw	W	Farmer	Norw
25.2	M	69	7	Ia	44	Ia 81-06	Wi	WV	Oh	Wi	WV	Oh	MW	Farmer	0
26.1	M	58	7	Mn	43	ND 08-17	Mn	--	--	Can	--	--	EuropeWWI	Farmer	--
26.2	M	70	5	Mn	70	0	Germ	Germ	Germ	Germ	Germ	Germ	0	r. Farmer	Germ
26.3	M	52	12	Mn	52	0	Norw	Norw	Norw	Norw	Norw	Norw	W, Can	Banker	Norw
26.4	M	66	8	Mn	66	0	--	Norw	Norw	--	Norw	Norw	0	Farmer	Norw
27.1	M	53	8	Mn	52	Can 1y	Swed	--	--	Swed	--	--	E&W coast	Merchant	--
27.2	F	52	8	Mn	52	0	Germ	--	--	Germ	--	--	ND,SD,Can	Housewife	--
27.3	M	53	12	Mn	53	0	Wi	Ma	Ma	Il	Il	Il	EuropeWWI	Merchant	0
28.1	M	34	13	Mn	25	Mn	Ia	Ia	--	Mn	Me	Swed	Can,La,Ca	Grain grader, farm manager	0

No.	Sex	Age	Sch	Bpl	Yrs Res	Else-where	F	PGF	PGM	M	MGF	MGM	Travel	Occupation	For. Lang
28.2	M	30	12	Mn	30	0	Mn	Ia	Wi	ND	Norw	Mn	SD,ND,Wi	Implmnt dlr	Norw
28.3	M	51	Co	Mn	51	0	Norw	Norw	Norw	Swed	Swed	Swed	W, S	Lumber&hdwe dealer	0
29.1	F	64	8	Mn	30	--	Swed	Swed	Swed	Swed	Swed	Swed	Wi	Housewife	Swed
29.2	M	65	8	Mn	65	0	Norw	--	--	Wi	--	--	0	r. Mail carr	--
30.1	M	68	13	Pol	42	--	Pol	--	--	Pol	--	--	W coast, Mo	Banker	--
30.2	M	67	--	Mn	63	Mn 85-89	Mn	Germ	Germ	Mn	Germ	Germ	Nb, Can	Hdwe merch	Germ
30.3	M	58	12	Mn	53	Mn 94-99	Wi	NY	NY	Ia	Oh	Oh	US, Can	Teachr,farmr	0
31.1	M	62	3	Norw	60	--	Swed	Swed	Swed	Norw	Norw	Norw	Can, Ak, Engl,Fran, Norw	Farmer	Norw
31.2	M	59	9	Ia	46	Ia 91-04	Wi	--	--	Wi	--	--	0	Farmer	0
32.1	M	62	10	Ia	38	Nb 90-97, Ia 97-12	Ia	Oh	WV	Ia	Scot	Engl	0	Farmer	0
32.2	M	60	10	Mn	60	0	Swed	Swed	Swed	Swed	Swed	Swed	0	Farmer	Swed
32.3	M	64	13	Mn	60	Il 21-36	Pa	Pa	Pa	Swed	Swed	Swed	Nova Scot	Ice man	0
33.1	M	66	10	Ia	35	Ia 84-89, Nb 89-97	Ia	Oh	Ia	Pa	Pa	Pa	MW	Farmer	0
33.2	F	--	10	Mn	--	--	NY	NY	?NY	Mn	Irel	?NE	Can, Tx	r. Farmer	0
34.1	M	45	12	Il	37	Il 05-13	Swed	Swed	Swed	Swed	Swed	Swed	0	Farmer	0
34.2	F	45	8	Mn	45	0	Germ	Germ	Germ	Mn	Czs	Czs	Wi	Farmer	Germ
34.3	M	43	8	Mn	43	0	Mi	Pol	Pol	NJ	Pol	Pol	Or, Il	Farmer	Pol
34.4	F	48	8	Mn	48	0	Czs	Czs	Czs	Czs	Czs	Czs	0	Farmer	Cz
35.1	M	63	--	Mn	63	0	Wi	--	--	Mn	--	--	ND,SD,Oh	Housewife	--
35.2	M	56	--	Mn	56	0	Ma	Irel	Irel	Ia	Irel	Irel	MW, S	Stockbreeder	0
36.1	M	63	9	Mn	58	Can, Id	NY	--	--	NY	--	---	0	Plumber	--
36.2	M	80	8	Il	70	Il 70-80	Pa	--	--	Il	--	--	0	City mgr, farmr, real estate agent	--
37.1	F	69	8	Ks	69	0	Mo	Mo	Oh	Wi	Irel	Irel	Mi, Or	Postmaster	0
37.2	M	66	8	Mn	66	0	Czs	Czs	Czs	Wi	Czs	Czs	0	Farmer	Cz
38.1	F	60	8	Mn	60	0	Aust	--	--	Mn	--	--	Oh, Or	Housewife	0
38.2	F	60	Co	Mn	40	Mn 11y, Can 11y	Swed	Swed	Swed	Swed	Swed	Swed	US, Can	Bank cashier	?Swe
38.3	F	54	8	Mn	54	0	Mn	--	--	Mn	--	--	0	Housewife	Germ
38.4	F	56	12	Mn	56	0	Germ	Germ	Germ	Germ	Germ	Germ	0	Housewife	Germ
39.1	F	45	14	Mn	36	Mn 9y	Mn	Fran	Fran	Mn	Pol	Germ	E&W coast, MW	Cnty treas	0
39.2	M	45	8	Mn	15	--	Ia	Can	Can	Mn	Irel	Irel	0	Farmer	0
39.3	F	61	6	Mn	61	0	Germ	Germ	Germ	Germ	Germ	Germ	Fl	Housewife	Germ
40.1	F	67	17	Mn	41	Mn	Scot	Scot	Scot	Can	Engl	Irel	E,MW,GB, Fran,Neth	Sch librarn	Germ
40.2	M	83	9	Mn	83	0	NH	Engl	Engl	NH	Engl	Engl	Ca, Mex	r.Farmer, land apprsr	?Chip
41.1	M	52	8	Mn	52	0	Swed	Swed	Swed	Swed	Swed	Swed	Can, W coast	Farmer	Swed
41.2	F	48	8	Mn	48	0	Germ	Germ	Germ	Germ	Germ	Germ	0	Housewife	Germ
41.3	M	54	8	Mn	54	0	Swed	Swed	Swed	Swed	Swed	Swed	W coast	Farmer	Swed
42.1	M	58	8	Mn	58	0	Swed	Swed	Swed	Mn	Swed	Swed	E, EurWWI	Farmer	Swed
42.2	M	74	LLB	Mn	19	Mn	Swed	Swed	Swed	Swed	Swed	Swed	E&W coast	r.Dist jdge	Swed
43.1	M	82	8	Norw	77	Norw 1y, Mn 5y	Norw	--	--	Norw	--	--	0	Banker	--
43.2	M	81	8	Swed	74	Swed 3y, Mn 3y	Swed	--	--	Swed	--	--	E, W, N	Hdwe merch	--
44.1	F	69	8	Mn	48	Mn 80-01	Swed	--	--	Swed	--	--	--	Pract nurse	--
44.2	F	60	8	Mn	30	Mn 30y	Germ	--	--	Germ	--	--	MW, Can	Housewife	--
44.3	M	65	8	Norw	64	ND 06-13	Norw	Norw	Norw	Norw	Norw	Norw	0	r.Grain buyr	Norw
45.1	M	50	8	Mn	30	Mn	Mn	Germ	Germ	Mn	Germ	Germ	0	Farmer	Germ
45.2	F	51	8	Mn	51	0	Norw	Norw	Norw	Mn	Norw	Norw	0	Housewife	Norw
46.1	F	43	12	Mn	30	Mn 15y	Swed	--	--	Swed	--	--	0	Housewife	--

100

No.	Sex	Age	Sch	Bpl	Yrs Res	Else-where	F	PGF	PGM	M	MGF	MGM	Travel	Occupation	For. Lang
46.2	F	24	12	Mn	17	Mn 26-33	Mn	--	--	Mn	--	--	N, W	Housewife	--
46.3	F	59	13	Mn	55	Mn 4y	Ia	Ia	Ia	Mn	Irel	NH	Mo	Housewife	0
47.1	M	40	12	Mn	40	0	Mn	Oh	Pa	Mn	Engl	Engl	NY	Farmer	0
47.2	M	45	12	Mn	44	--	Nb	Vt	Il	Ia	Pa	--	W, S	Frmr, trckr	0
48.1	M	74	4	Norw	64	Norw -86	Norw	Norw	Norw	Norw	Norw	Norw	NY, Wa	Farmer	Norw
48.2	F	45	8	Mn	45	0	Germ	Germ	Germ	Germ	Germ	Germ	0	Housewife	Germ
49.1	M	72	8	Denm	30	Ia 10-20	Denm	Denm	Denm	Denm	Denm	Denm	W, Scand	r.Lettr carr	Dan
49.2	M	74	8	Mn	74	SD 09-13	Norw	Norw	Norw	Norw	Norw	Norw	NW	Carpenter	Norw
50.1	F	58	9	Il	36	Il,Pa,Ia	Czs	Czs	Czs	Czs	Czs	Czs	NW	Housewife	Cz
50.2	M	41	12	Mn	41	0	Mn	Norw	Norw	Mn	Norw	Norw	SD, Can	Farmer	Norw
50.3	M	86	4	Norw	70	Wi 69-81	Norw	Norw	Norw	Norw	Norw	Norw	E&W coast	Insur broker	Norw
50.4	F	75	--	Mn	75	0	Ma	Ma	Ma	Vt	Vt	Vt	0	Teacher	0
50.5	M	76	8	Mn	76	0	Wi	Norw	Norw	Wi	Norw	Norw	S, W	r. Farmer	Norw
51.1	M	50	--	Mn	25	--	--	--	--	--	--	--	--	Farmer	--
51.2	M	53	12	Mn	53	0	Norw	--	--	Norw	--	--	MW	Farmer	--
52.1	M	78	--	Mn	60	Mn	NH	--	--	Ma	--	--	US	Phone co mgr	--
52.2	F	75	16	Mn	62	Ma 06-09, Ok 09-17	NH	--	--	Ma	--	--	US,Eur,SA	r. Teacher	--
53.1	M	54	8	Mn	54	0	In	Swit	Swit	Germ	Germ	Germ	S, MW	Mechanic	Germ
53.2	M	34	13	Mn	29	Mn	Mn	Germ	Germ	Mn	Germ	Germ	E,W Eur WWII	Auctioneer	Germ
54.1	F	63	7	Mn	15	Mn 45y	Germ	--	--	Germ	--	--	0	Houseworker, wash-woman	--
54.2	M	42	7	SD	36	SD 6y	Tn	Il	Il	--	Engl	Engl	MW	Mineralogist	0
54.3	F	64	12	Mn	64	0	Germ	Germ	Germ	Oh	Germ	Germ	0	Rstrnt mgr	Germ
54.4	F	49	12	Mn	49	0	Mn	Irel	Irel	Belg	--	--	0	Housewife	0
54.5	M	27	16	Mn	25	Ca 2y	Mn	Mn	Mn	Mn	Irel	Irel	W coast, Hi, Phill	--	0
55.1	M	51	8	Mn	48	E coast	Swed	--	--	Swed	--	--	US,Europe	Retail merch	--
55.2	F	52	Bu	Germ	20	Wi	Germ	--	--	Germ	--	--	W coast	Housewife	--
55.3	M	49	8	Mn	28	Mn	Swed	--	--	Swed	--	--	W coast	Stcar mtrman	--
55.4	F	45	16	Mn	45	0	Germ	Germ	Germ	Germ	Germ	Germ	E&W coast	Librarian	0
55.5	F	54	8	Mn	54	0	Irel	--	--	Can	Irel	Can	0	Housewife	0
55.6	M	58	8	Il	57	Il 1y	Irel	Irel	Irel	Mo	?Mo	?Mo	Il	Railwy clerk	0
55.7	F	57	14	Mn	57	0	Pa	Pa	Pa	Md	Irel	Irel	W	Housewife	0
55.8	F	69	8	Mn	69	0	Germ	Germ	Germ	Germ	Germ	Germ	0	Housewife	Germ
55.9	M	52	8	Mn	52	0	Mn	Mo	--	Mn	Germ	--	0	Compositor	0
55.10	F	58	11	Mn	58	0	?Ire	?Ire	?Ire	Engl	?Ire	?Ire	0	Housewife	0
55.11	M	64	9	Mn	64	0	Mn	Me	Me	Mn	Irel	Irel	0	Rate clerk	0
55.12	F	40	9	Mn	40	0	Ia	Il	Ia	Ia	Ia	Ia	MW	Housewife	0
56.1	F	44	14	Mn	22	Mn	Mn	Norw	Norw	Mn	Norw	Norw	0	Housewife	Swed
56.2	M	79	--	Mn	79	0	Germ	Germ	Germ	Mo	Germ	Germ	MW, Can	Farmer	Germ
57.1	M	65	12	SD	65	In 1y	Norw	Norw	Norw	Norw	Norw	Norw	0	Postmaster	Norw
57.2	M	82	6	Mn	51	Mn	Germ	Germ	Germ	Lux	Lux	Lux	20 states	r.	Germ
57.3	M	68	--	Ia	60	SD 1y	Denm	Denm	Denm	Denm	Denm	Denm	E&W coast	Store mgr	Norw
57.4	M	58	6	Ia	56	Ca 1y	Denm	Denm	Denm	Denm	Denm	Denm	US	Mgr, retail lumber yard	Dan
58.1	M	81	12	NY	66	Mt 15-21	NY	--	--	NY	--	--	Mt	"Ranch life"	--
58.2	M	63	12	Mn	63	0	In	--	--	Mn	--	--	0	Dist ct clrk	--
58.3	F	69	13	Mn		Mn 19-46	NY	--	--	Ia	--	--	Ca, Can	Housewife	--
58.4	M	57	8	Mn	53	Mn 4y	Ont	Can	Can	Mn	NY	NY	Oh	Merchant	0
58.5	M	54	8	Ia	44	--	In	Engl	Engl	Ia	--	--	W, S	Rur mail car	0
59.1	M	66	8	Mn	60	Mn 6y	Wi	Germ	Germ	Wi	Germ	Germ	US	Frmr,legisltr	Germ
59.2	M	87	4	Mn	60	Mn	Germ	Germ	Germ	Germ	Germ	Germ	W coast, Mex	Grocer	Germ
60.1	M	53	10	Mn	53	0	Wi	Germ	--	Mn	Germ	--	NW, Can	Merchant	Germ Swed
60.2	M	53	9	Mn	53	0	Wi	Germ	Germ	Wi	Germ	Germ	Id,Co,DC	Farmer	Germ
60.3	M	68	GS	Mn	68	0	Irel	Irel	Irel	--	Irel	Irel	0	Farmer	0
60.4	M	54	12	Mn	54	0	Swed	Swed	Swed	Swed	Swed	Swed	0	Farmer	Swed
61.1	F	92	8	Mn	72	Mn	Vt	--	--	Vt	--	--	Sask, Ca	r.Tchr,frmwfe	--

No.	Sex	Age	Sch	Bpl	Yrs Res	Else- where	F	PGF	PGM	M	MGF	MGM	Travel	Occupation	For. Lang
62.1	M	62	8	Mn	62	0	Germ	--	--	Germ	--	--	W coast	Florist	--
62.2	M	67	2	Swed	7	Mn 41y	Swed	Swed	Swed	Swed	Swed	Swed	E, W, N	Farmer	Swed
63.1	M	64	8	Mn	64	0	Denm	Denm	Denm	Denm	Denm	Denm	UMW	Mail carrier	Dan
63.2	F	78	4	Germ	68	Wi 8y	Germ	--	--	Germ	--	--	0	Housewife	--
63.3	M	61	8	Wi	59	Wi 2y	Germ	--	--	Wi	--	--	DC,SD,Tx	Farmer, real estate & in- sur agent	--
63.4	M	57	6	Mn	57	0	Mn	--	--	Mn	--	--	0	r. Farmer	--
64.1	M	86	8	Mn	86	0	Germ	--	--	Germ	--	--	0	r. Farmer	--
64.2	M	55	Bu	Mn	55	0	Mn	Germ	Germ	Mn	Germ	Germ	FranWWI	Farmer	?Ger
65.1	M	56	8	Mn	13	Mn	Czs	--	--	Czs	--	--	EurWWI, W, MW	Police chief	--
65.2	F	57	8	Mn	39	Mn	Mo	--	--	Mn	--	--	0	Housewife	--
66.1	M	77	8	Mn	77	0	Germ	--	--	Germ	--	--	Wi	Farmer	--
66.2	M	52	8	Mn	52	0	Mn	Germ	Germ	Mn	Germ	Germ	DC, Fl	Farmer	0
67.1	F	78	6	Mn	78	0	Germ	--	--	Germ	--	--	Tx	Housewife	--
67.2	M	70	11	Mn	70	0	Me	--	--	Me	--	--	Ca	Farmer	--
67.3	M	57	8	Mn	50	Or 3y	Mn	Irel	Irel	Mn	Norw	Norw	0	Tavern oprtr	0
68.1	M	87	?6	NY	61	NY -89	NY	Engl	Engl	NY	Engl	Engl	30 states	Oil dealer	0
68.2	F	52	13	Wi	29	Wi 03-23	Wi	USA	USA	Wi	USA	USA	E, W, Can	Housewife	0
68.3	F	34	12	Mn	34	0	Mn	Germ	Germ	Mn	Germ	Germ	0	Housewife	0
69.1	M	57	4	Il	27	Mn 18-21	Denm	Denm	Denm	Denm	Denm	Denm	0	Farmer	Dan
69.2	M	51	8	Ia	42	Ia 9y	Norw	Norw	Norw	Norw	Norw	Norw	E&W coast	Farm eqp dlr	Norw
69.3	M	60	8	Mn	24	Wa,Mt,Ia	Wi	--	--	Oh	--	--	EuropeWWI	Granite cutt	Germ
70.1	M	58	8	Mn	58	0	Il	Can	Can	Can	Can	Can	W	Farmer	Fren
70.2	M	58	9	Mn	58	0	Germ	--	--	Germ	--	--	Ca, Fl	Farmer	Germ
71.1	F	46	12	Mn	16	Mn 05-33, Wa 42-45	Ia	Norw	Norw	Wi	Norw	Norw	Wa	Hsewfe, cook	0
71.2	M	55	8	Mn	55	0	Russ	Russ	Russ	Russ	Russ	Russ	0	Inter decrtr	Germ
71.3	M	50	8	Mn	50	0	Russ	Russ	Russ	USA	Russ	Russ	Pol,Denm, 20 states	Farmer, mach operatr	Germ
71.4	M	88	8	Wi	82	Wi 64-70	NY	--	--	NY	--	--	0	Music dealer	0
72.1	M	49	8	Ia	47	Ia 2y	Germ	Germ	Germ	Il	Germ	Germ	0	Farmer	Germ
72.2	M	51	14	Mn	51	0	Ia	Il	Il	Mn	Mn	Mn	US,Eur, Mex,Cuba	Auto dealer	0
73.1	M	75	5	Mn	75	0	Germ	--	--	Germ	--	--	Ca, Can	Farmer	0
73.2	M	68	5	Mn	68	0	NY	--	--	Mn	--	--	UMW	Insur claim auditor	--
73.3	M	56	HS	Mn	43	ND 10-18	Wale	--	--	NY	--	--	E&W coast	Cashier	--
73.4	M	57	8	Mn	57	0	Norw	Norw	Norw	USA	Norw	Norw	S, W	Farmer	Norw
73.5	M	67	11	Mn	67	0	Wale	Wale	Wale	Wale	Wale	Wale	E	Farmer	Wels
73.6	M	58	8	Mn	58	0	Wi	Germ	Germ	Mn	Germ	Germ	28 states	r.P.O. clerk	Germ
74.1	F	55	12	Mn	55	0	Mn	NY	NY	Mn	Germ	Germ	Tx,Can,SD	Housewife	0
74.2	M	62	8	Mn	62	0	Wi	Norw	Norw	Mn	Norw	Norw	0	Farmer	Norw
75.1	M	56	8	Mn	55	Mn 1y	Denm	Denm	Denm	Denm	Denm	Denm	Wi, Mt	Farmer	Dan
75.2	M	84	8	Czs	78	Czs 7y	Czs	Czs	Czs	Czs	Czs	Czs	0	Hdwe merch	Cz Germ
76.1	M	71	8	Mn	71	0	--	--	--	--	--	--	0	Farmer	Germ
76.2	F	--	Bu	Mn	40	Mn 30-36	Mn	Germ	Germ	Mn	Swit	Swit	0	Housewife	0
76.3	M	64	11	Mn	64	0	Mn	--	--	Mn	--	--	0	Depty auditr	0
77.1	M	69	8	Mn	69	0	Germ	Germ	Germ	Germ	Germ	Germ	0	Farmer	0
77.2	F	82	?HS	Mn	82	0	Oh	NY	Oh	Il	NY	Md	NY,Co,Wy	Housekeeper, notary pub, ex-teacher	0
77.3	M	55	--	Nb	30	Nb	Il	Il	Il	Il	Il	Il	US	Secretary	0
78.1	M	55	8	Wi	41	Wi 96-09	Germ	Germ	Germ	Wi	Germ	Germ	0	Farmer	Germ
78.2	M	73	11	Mn	63	Mt	Ct	Germ	Germ	Pa	--	--	E, W	--	0
79.1	M	62	HS	Mn	62	0	Wi	NY	NYC	--	Me	NY	US	Farmr, grain buyr,ins agt	0
79.2	F	42	Bu	Mn	40	Mn 2y	Mn	NY	NY	Mn	Norw	Norw	0	Housewife	0
79.3	M	50	12	Mn	50	0	Mn	Irel	Irel	Mn	Irel	Irel	Half US	Farmer	0

No.	Sex	Age	Sch	Bpl	Yrs Res	Else-where	F	PGF	PGM	M	MGF	MGM	Travel	Occupation	For. Lang
80.1	M	58	8	Ia	35	--	Ia	--	--	Ia	--	--	S,W,Can	Farmer	--
80.2	M	74	GS	Mn	74	0	Swed	Swed	Swed	Swed	Swed	Swed	US	Farmer	Swed
80.3	M	64	10	Ia	57	Ia -96	Germ	--	--	Germ	--	--	0	Mechanic	Germ Du
80.4	M	64	8	Mn	63	--	Irel	Irel	Irel	Irel	Irel	Irel	Ca .	Salesman	0
81.1	M	83	HS	Swed	?65	Swed	Swed	Swed	Swed	Swed	Swed	Swed	US	Farmer, orchardman	Swed
81.2	M	59	9	Il	57	Il 2y	Germ	Germ	Germ	Germ	Germ	Germ	Germ	Frmr,ins agt	Germ
81.3	M	52	8	Ia	49	Ia 98-01	Germ	Germ	Germ	Ia	Germ	Ia	MW	Farmer	Germ
82.1	M	70	8	Wi	70	--	NY	--	--	Oh	--	--	0	r.	0
82.2	M	45	12	Mn	45	0	Il	Germ	Germ	Il	Germ	Germ	W	Hdwe merch	Germ
83.1	M	55	10	Mn	55	0	Mn	Ct	?Ky	Mn	Scot	Scot	0	Farmer	--
83.2	M	44	8	Mn	44	--	Mn	Norw	Mn	Mn	Norw	Norw	0	Farmer	Norw
83.3	M	54	9	Mn	54	0	Pa	Irel	Irel	Wi	Neth	Neth	--	Farmer	0
84.1	M	68	--	Mn	66	Mn 2y	Denm	Denm	Denm	Denm	Denm	Denm	W coast	r. Banker	Dan
84.2	M	83	?8	Mn	83	0	Can	Fran	Fran	Can	Fran	Fran	S, W	Farmer	0
85.1	M	57	8	Mn	57		Il	Germ	Germ	Mn	Germ	Germ	Il,DC,NY, EuropeWWI	Sch janitor	Germ
85.2	M	75	10	Mn	34	Mn	Can	--	--	Me	--	--	MW, NW	Real est & insur agent	--
86.1	F	84	8	Mn	84	0	NY	NY	NY	Pa	RI	RI	0	Housewife	0
86.2	F	61	14	Mn	61	ND 1y, Czs 18-9	Wi	Engl	Engl	Mn	Wale	Wi	US,Eur, Can,Czs	Hsewfe(widow)	0
87.1	M	73	7	Mn	73	NS 8m	Norw	Norw	Norw	Norw	Norw	Norw	Mt, Pa	Merchant	Norw
87.2	M	52	11	Mn	52	0	Mn	RI	Ma	Mn	NY	NY	W coast, Mex, Can	Farmer	0
87.3	M	71	8	Mn	71	0	Ia	Germ	Il	Il	Germ	Germ	MW	Farmer	Germ

IOWA

No.	Sex	Age	Sch	Bpl	Yrs Res	Else-where	F	PGF	PGM	M	MGF	MGM	Travel	Occupation	For. Lang
1.1	M	68	10	Ia	63	Co 06, Phill 06-09, NY 10	Pa	Pa	Vt	Wi	NY	NY	40 states	Policeman	Tagalog
1.2	M	67	12	Ia	67	Ia 03	Il	Il	Can	Oh	Md	Vt	W	Title abst'r	0
2.1	F	67	10	Ia	57	Ia 10y	Oh	Oh	Oh	Pa	Pa	Pa	Ca, Mt	Housewife	0
2.3	F	67	13	Ia	60	Mn 04-11	NY	Engl	Engl	Ct	Ct	Ct	E&W coast	Housewife	0
3.1	M	79	--	Ia	79	0	NY	Fran	Fran	Pa	Pa	Pa	Fl	r. Farmer	0
3.2	M	75	11	Ia	50	Ia 25y	Oh	Engl	Engl	Il	Vt	Vt	E,W,S	Ins agt,bankr	0
4.1	F	70	9	Ia	70	0	Ia	--	--	Ia	Me	Me	0	Hsewfe,printr	0
4.2	M	42	12	Ia	36	Il	Il	--	--	Il	--	--	US	Farmer	0
5.1	M	74	--	Ia	--	Ia	Swed	Swed	Swed	Swed	Swed	Swed	Swed	"Jack-of-all-trades"	Swed
5.2	F	70	10	Ia	42	Ia 15-45	Swed	Swed	Swed	Swed	Swed	Swed	Mn, Co	Housewife	Swed
6.1	F	69	7	Norw	67	--	Norw	--	--	Norw	--	--	E	Housekeeper	Norw
6.2	F	70	10	Ia	70	0	NY	Germ	Germ	Germ	Germ	Germ	MW, Pa	Housewife	0
6.3	F	73	14	Ia	73		Mi	Irel	Irel	In	Oh	In	E&W coast, Can, Mex	r. Teacher, dishwasher	0
6.4	F	42	11	Ia	--	Ia	Mn	Norw	Norw	--	Norw	Norw	0	Housewife	0
6.5	M	80	8	Mn	75	Mn ?5y	Norw	Norw	Norw	Norw	Norw	Norw	Norw	Farmer	Norw
7.1	F	58	--	Ia	39	Ia	Norw	--	--	Wi	--	--	MW,Co,NM	Housewife	Norw
7.2	M	64	--	Ia	64	0	Germ	Germ	Germ	Germ	Germ	Germ	US	Farmer	Germ
8.1	M	81	8	Ia	81	0	NY	--	--	Il	Il	Ky	All W sta	Farmer	0
8.2	F	42	HS	Ia	42	0	Germ	Germ	Germ	Ia	Germ	Ia	Can,Mt,Il	Housewife	Germ
8.3	F	70	NS	Wi	26	Wi,Ia,Mn	NY	Engl	Engl	Wi	Scot	Scot	Dak,Nb,Mn	Hsewfe, tchr	0
8.4	F	78	HS	Ia	74	Il 4y	Il	--	--	Ma	--	NY	Ca	Hsewfe, tchr	0
9.1	F	76	5	Ia	29	Ia 04-21	Germ	Germ	Germ	Germ	Eur	Eur	Can,Mo,Mn	Housewife	Germ
9.2	M	73	16	Ia	73	0	In	In	In	Ma	Ma	Ma	US, Can	Lawyer	0
10.1	F	76	8	Ia	76	0	Pa	NE	NE	Oh	Germ	Germ	Can,La,Ut	Housewife	0
10.2	M	50	8	Ia	50	0	Ia	Irel	Ia	Ia	Irel	Oh	0	Farmer	0
11.1	F	81	8	Ia	?51	Wi 30y	--	Germ	Germ	--	Germ	Germ	0	Housewife	Germ

No.	Sex	Age	Sch	Bpl	Yrs Res	Else-where	F	PGF	PGM	M	MGF	MGM	Travel	Occupation	For. Lang
11.2	F	72	8	Ia	72	0	Pa	Pa	Pa	Ia	Va	Pa	Il	Housewife	0
12.1	F	73	10	Ia	73	0	Neth	Neth	Neth	Neth	Neth	Neth	NY,W coas	Housewife	Du
12.2	F	59	15	Ia	59	0	Neth	Neth	Neth	Neth	Neth	Neth	UMW,W coa	Depty recordr	Du
13.1	M	68	8	Ia	68	0	Pa	USA	USA	Il	USA	USA	0	Farmer	0
13.2	M	65	8	Ia	65	0	Il	USA	USA	Il	USA	USA	0	Farmer	0
14.1	M	83	--	NY	80	NY ?3y	NY	NY	NY	Germ	Germ	Germ	NY, Can	Farmer	0
14.2	M	79	--	Ia	79	0	Pa	Pa	Pa	--	Pa	Pa	--	--	0
15.1	F	79	8	Ia	79	0	Wi	--	Pa	NY	NY	NY	Ca,Can,NY	Housewife	0
15.2	M	72	8	Ia	72	0	Engl	Engl	Engl	Wi	NY	Wi	Ca,Mex,Can	Dist ct clrk	0
16.1	F	84	5	Ia	5	Ia	Me	USA	USA	NY	USA	USA	Fl,Can,Ca	Housewife	0
16.2	F	63	6	Ia	63	0	Germ	Germ	Germ	Germ	Germ	Germ	MW	Housewife	Germ
16.3	M	53	12	Il	51	Il ?2y	Pol	Pol	Pol	Pol	Pol	Pol	US,Mex,Can	Cnty assessr	Germ
17.1	M	51	8	Ia	51	0	Germ	Germ	Germ	Ia	Germ	Fran	US,Mex,Can	Farmer	0
17.2	M	49	16	Ia	18	Ia	Il	Oh	Oh	Il	Il	Il	W, S, MW	Farmer	0
17.3	M	47	12	Ia	44	Mn 20-23	--	Irel	Irel	Irel	Irel	Irel	Mn, Wi	Farmer	0
18.1	M	56	11	Ia	56	0	Ia	Me	NY	Ia	Can	Can	MW	Farmer	0
18.2	F	55	14	Ia	30	NY -35	Ia	Il	Il	Ia	Il	Il	US,Europe	Postmaster	Fren
18.3	F	60	17	Ia	60	0	NY	NY	NY	NY	Vt	NY	E, W, S	retired	--
18.4	M	87	9	Ia	82	Ia,Il 3y	Oh	Neth	Neth	Ct	USA	USA	Il,Mo,Mn	Trainman	0
19.1	F	75	--	Ia	51	--	Irel	Irel	Irel	Il	Irel	Irel	MW	Housewife	0
19.2	F	62	6	Ia	19	Ia	Czs	Czs	Czs	Czs	Czs	Czs	--	Housewife	Cz
20.1	F	79	8	Ia	79	0	Scot	Scot	Scot	Il	Can	Scot	DC, MW	Housewife	0
20.2	M	81	8	Ia	81	0	NY	NY	NY	Pa	Pa	Pa	0	Farmer	0
21.1	F	66	8	Ia	54	--	Germ	Germ	Germ	Germ	Germ	GErm	0	Housewife	Germ
21.2	F	78	8	Ia	39	--	Pa	Pa	Pa	Mi	Mi	Mi	0	Housekeeper	0
22.1	F	60	8	Ia	60	0	Il	Pa	Pa	Il	Pa	Pa	--	Housewife	0
22.2	F	58	8	Ia	58	0	Engl	Engl	Engl	Il	Il	Il	MW, W	Depty sherff	0
23.1	M	70	8	Ia	70	0	Wi	Engl	Engl	NY	NY	NY	0	Greenskeeper	0
23.2	F	73	6	Ia	73	Dak	Engl	Engl	Engl	Il	--	--	0	Housewife, domestic	0
24.1	M	83	--	Wi	79	Ia 71-91	Oh	--	--	Can	Engl	Engl	E&W coast	retired	0
24.2	M	49	10	Ia	44	Ia 03-08	Il	Oh	Oh	Il	--	--	0	Farmer	0
24.3	M	71	HS	Ia	71	0	NY	Germ	Germ	Pa	Pa	Pa	0	Farmer	0
25.1	M	63	12	Ia	59	Ia 4y	Oh	Oh	Oh	Wi	Wi	Wi	Co, NY	Farmer	0
25.2	F	67	--	Mi	39	Il 94-09, Ks 09-12	Engl	Engl	Engl	Braz	Engl	Engl	W, MW	Restaurateur	0
25.3	M	80	GS	Ar	60	--	Ar	Scot	Germ	Ar	--	--	SW, Can	Hdwe&imp dlr	0
25.4	M	64	9	Ia	--	--	Il	NC	Pa	Ia	Oh	Oh	W, SW	Farmer	0
26.1	M	74	8	Ia	74	0	NY	Engl	Engl	Wi	--	--	0	retired	0
26.2	M	67	16	Ia	50	Ia 83-90, 17-21	Norw	Norw	--	Norw	--	--	0	Salesman	Norw
26.3	F	66	8	Ia	66	0	Wi	--	--	Ia	--	--	0	Housewife	0
27.1	M	78	5	Ia	78	0	Oh	Engl	Neth	Ky	--	--	W coast	Mason	0
27.2	F	77	13	Ia	77	0	In	NY	Pa	Swed	Swed	Swed	MW	Housewife	0
28.1	M	70	10	Ia	63	--	NY	NY	NY	NY	NY	NY	0	Farmer	0
28.2	M	--	--	Ia	55		Pa	Pa	Pa	Ia	Pa	Pa	NY, Ca	Farmer	0
28.3	F	55	7	Ia	55	0	Germ	Germ	Germ	Il	Germ	Germ	MW	Farmer	0
29.1	F	69	12	Ia	69	0	Nova	Nova	Nova	NH	NH	NH	NE, Can	Housewife	0
29.2	M	66	8	Ia	60	Ia 5y	NY	NY	NY	Engl	Engl	Engl	Mt, De	Dist ct clrk	0
30.1	M	78	8	Ia	78	0	Germ	Germ	Germ	Germ	Germ	Germ	S, E&W coasts	r. Grocer	Germ
30.2	F	68	?8	Ia	50	Ia 18y	Pa	Pa	Irel	Ia	Irel	Irel	0	Housewife	0
30.2	F	50+	13	Ia	50+	0	Swed	Swed	Swed	Swed	Swed	Swed	E, W	Housewife	Swed
31.1	F	64	12	Ia	62	Ia 2y	In	--	--	Il	--	--	W	Hsewfe,librn	0
31.2	F	62	6	Ia	62	0	Germ	Germ	Germ	Germ	Germ	Germ	--	--	--
32.1	F	71	11	Ia	71	0	Pa	Pa	Pa	Il	Oh	Il	Pa, Ca	Housewife	0
33.1	F	53	16	Ia	48	Ia 5y	Denm	Denm	Denm	Denm	Denm	Denm	Sev states	Housewife	Dan
33.2	F	44	12	Ia	44	0	Ia	Germ	Germ	Ia	Germ	Germ	MW	Farm wife, secretary	Germ
34.1	F	67	8	Ia	67	0	NY	--	--	NY	--	--	Mn,Wy,Il	Farm wife, housekeeper	0

No.	Sex	Age	Sch	Bp1	Yrs Res	Else-where	F	PGF	PGM	M	MGF	MGM	Travel	Occupation	For. Lang
34.2	M	75	8	Ia	75	0	Germ	Germ	Germ	Germ	Germ	Germ	0	r. Farmer	Germ
35.1	M	66	--	Il	64	0	Can	Engl	Engl	Can	Scot	Scot	--	Accountant	0
35.2	M	77	12	Ia	77	0	Ia	NY	NY	Oh	Ma	--	US,Can,Mex	Insur agt	0
36.1	F	68	11	Ia	68	0	Oh	--	Oh	Il	?Va	Va	Ca, Fl	r.Phone oper	0
36.2	M	43	8	Ia	43	0	Scot	Scot	Scot	Scot	Scot	Scot	0	Farmer	0
37.1	M	--	8	Mt	40	--	Ia	Germ	Germ	Ia	Germ	Ia	S, W	Farmer, seed grower	0
37.2	M	39	Co	Ia	12	Wi 18-22, DC 38-48	Il	Il	Il	Ia	Pa	Ia	E	Editor	0
37.3	M	63	--	Ia	53	Hi 14-16	Germ	Germ	Germ	Germ	Germ	Germ	Hi	r. Farmer, YMCA sec'y	Germ
38.1	F	62	12	Ia	62	0	Il	Irel	Irel	Il	Irel	Irel	0	Magazine agt	0
38.2	M	51	13	Ia	51	0	USA	USA	USA	USA	USA	USA	N,E,W cst	Farmer	0
38.3	F	44	12	Ia	44	0	Ia	Germ	Germ	Il	Germ	Germ	NY	Farm wife	Germ
39.1	F	69	12	Ia	49	Ia	Va	--	--	Va	--	--	Pa,Ca,MW	Housewife	0
39.2	M	66	8	Ia	25	Ia 84-25	Can	Tn	Irel	Ia	Pa	Pa	0	Farmer	0
39.3	F	67	8	Ia	25	Ia 83-25	Ia	Ky	Ky	Ia	Scot	Irel	0	Housewife	0
40.1	M	--	--	Ia	78	--	Engl	--	--	Engl	--	--	0	r.	0
40.2	M	36	10	Ia	36	0	Ia	Ia	Engl	Ia	Ia	Ia	20 states	Grain & machine dlr	0
40.3	F	63	12	Ia	56	Ia 7y	Ia	NJ	Ia	Ia	NY	NY	NW,NE,MW	Dist court depty clerk	0
41.1	M	68	8	Ia	68	0	Irel	Irel	Irel	Irel	Irel	Irel	--	Truckr,farmr	0
41.2	M	46	14	Ia	46	0	Ia	Oh	Pa	Ia	Swit	Swit	30 states	Farmr,teachr	0
41.3	M	--	10	Ia	61	--	Ia	--	In	Ia	In	NY	40 states	r. Farmer	0
42.1	M	69	7	Ia	55	SD 84-93, Nb 93-98	Ia	Irel	Irel	Ia	Irel	Irel	0	Bf catl frmr	0
42.2	F	80	12	Ia	31	Va,Ky,Tn 04-19	Germ	Germ	Germ	Engl	Engl	Engl	SD	Housewife, music teachr	0
42.3	M	58	10	Ia	58	0	Pa	--	--	Oh	Germ	--	Irel USNav	Yardman	0
43.1	M	78	--	Ia	78	0	Vt	Vt	--	Me	--	Me	UMW	r. Painter	0
43.2	M	59	?14	Ia	39	Ia 20y	Ia	Va	--	Ia	Irel	Pa	Il, Or	Farmer	0
43.3	F	65	12	Ia	65	0	Il	Il	Il	In	Oh	NW	0	Teachr,grocr	0
44.1	F	69	12	Ia	49	Ia -01	Oh	--	--	Ia	--	--	MW	Farm wife	0
44.2	F	53	8	Ia	53	0	Germ	Germ	Germ	Ia	Germ	Germ	SD	Housekeeper	Germ
45.1	M	68	10	Ia	43	Mn & Wi 10-35	Oh	NY	Oh	In	Pa	In	E, W, N	Upholsterer	0
45.2	M	--	10	Ia	60	Mn 4y	Germ	Germ	Germ	Germ	Germ	Germ	"Various"	Title abst'r	Germ
46.1	M	70	12	Il	70	0	Pa	Pa	Pa	Pa	Pa	Pa	--	Stock farmer	0
46.2	M	--	--	Ia	69	--	Vt	NY	Vt	Pa	Pa	Pa	US, Can	Farmer	0
47.1	M	77	--	Ia	65	Il 98-10	Swed	Swed	Swed	Swed	Swed	Swed	All US	Artist, pict framer	Swed Esp
47.2	M	82	10	Ia	82	0	NY	--	--	Mi	--	--	Tn, W cst	r.Lettr carr	0
48.1	M	57	11	Ia	57	0	Ia	Vt	--	Pa	Pa	Pa	US, Mex	Farmer	0
48.2	F	37	11	Ia	37	0	Ia	Norw	Norw	Ia	Norw	Norw	Co, Ok	Housewife	0
49.1	F	69	9	Ia	69	0	Pa	--	--	Oh	--	--	0	Housewife	0
49.2	M	60	8	Ia	16	Ia	Il	Engl	?Eng	Ia	USA	USA	Il, Mt	Farmer	0
49.3	M	50	12	Ia	50	0	Il	Md	Il	Pa	Pa	Pa	0	City fireman	0
49.4	M	61	10	NC	50	NC -92	NC	--	--	NC	--	Va	0	Farmer	0
50.1	F	80	8	Ia	80	0	Pa	Pa	Pa	In	--	--	45 states	Housewife	0
50.2	M	62	9	Ia	33	Ia	--	--	--	--	Germ	Germ	0	Painter	0
50.3	F	--	--	Ia	51	0	Il	Germ	Germ	Il	Germ	Germ	0	Teacher	0
50.4	M	68	8	Ia	31	Ia	NY	Irel	Engl	Irel	Irel	Irel	MW	Grocer,baker	0
51.1	M	84	9	Ia	51	Ia	NY	Germ	--	Oh	--	--	0	Painter	0
51.2	F	78	8	Nb	--	Ia	In	Scot	Scot	In	Scot	Scot	0	Housewife	--
52.1	F	89	14	Ia	62	Ia 82-85	Pa	Pa	Pa	Can	Irel	Irel	Ca,NY,Mo	Housewife	0
52.2	M	67	7	Ia	11	Ia	Swit	Swit	Swit	Swit	Swit	Swit	0	Farmer	?Ger
52.3	F	61	9	Ia	60	Fl 07	Pa	Germ	USA	Czs	Czs	Czs	Il, Fl	Housewife	Cz
53.1	M	40	--	Ia	40	0	Ia	Germ	Germ	Ia	Germ	Germ	UMW	Farmer	Germ
53.2	M	42	16	Ia	19	Ia 17-30	Ia	Oh	Oh	Ia	Germ	Germ	0	Banker	Germ
54.1	F	86	8	Ia	--	--	Oh	Oh	Oh	Oh	Oh	Oh	Ok, Wi	Housewife	0

No.	Sex	Age	Sch	Bpl	Yrs Res	Else-where	F	PGF	PGM	M	MGF	MGM	Travel	Occupation	For. Lang
54.2	F	73	9	Ia	73	0	WV	--	--	Ill	--	--	--	Housewife	0
54.3	M	65	10	Ia	65	0	Pa	Irel	Scot	--	--	--	W coast	Depty Sherff	0
55.1	F	62	8	Ia	62	0	Oh	Oh	--	In	In	In	0	Housewife	0
55.2	F	--	14	Ia	57	Or 02-03	Oh	Oh	Oh	Ia	Oh	Oh	48 states, Can	Teacher	0
55.3	F	76	8	Ia	76	0	In	In	In	Oh	--	---	16 MW sta	Farm wife	0
56.1	M	71	10	Ia	71	0	Denm	Denm	Denm	Denm	Denm	Denm	E&W coast	Farmer	Dan
56.2	M	63	12	Ia	63	0	USA	Denm	Denm	USA	Denm	Denm	Ca	Mechanic	Dan
56.3	M	62	8	Ia	62	Ia	Ia	Germ	Germ	Ia	Germ	Germ	Co	Dist ct clrk	Germ
57.1	M	75	?10	Ia	62	Ia 74-88	Ky	Ky	Ky	In	Pa	In	MW, W	Insur agent	0
57.2	M	67	19	Ia	--	0	Il	Il	Can	Engl	Engl	Engl	0	r. Farmer	0
57.3	M	70	8	Ia	68	Ia 27-28	Ia	Germ	Germ	Ia	Pa	Pa	0	Farmer	0
58.1	M	69	8	Ia	47	SD 08-12, Co 01	Mo	Oh	Va	Ia	Oh	Oh	W	Blacksmith	0
58.2	-	61	8	Ia	--	--	Ia	In	In	Ia	Il	Il	0	Janitor	0
59.1	F	83	12	Ia	83	0	Mi	--	--	Ia	--	--	0	X-ray tech	0
59.2	M	60	11	Ia	60	0	Wi	Wi	--	Ia	Wi	Wi	E&W coast, Can, Fl, Mex	Real es brkr	0
60.1	M	72	16	Ia	25	0	Irel	Irel	Irel	Oh	Irel	Oh	48 states	Lawyer	0
60.2	M	75	8	Ia	72	Mo 05	Engl	Engl	Engl	NC	NC	NC	38 states	Printer	0
61.1	M	82	8	Ia	82	0	Oh	--	--	In	--	--	W	Farmer	0
61.2	M	90	--	Ia	83	Ia 7y	In	--	--	Oh	--	--	Ca, Pa	Farmer	0
61.3	F	48	12	Ia	25	Ia 04-24	WV	WV	WV	Ia	Ia	Oh	US	Housewife, factry workr	0
62.1	M	76	?5	Ia	75	Mo 98-99	Oh	Oh	Oh	Oh	Oh	Oh	0	Farmer	0
62.2	M	60	13	Ia	59	Ia 18	Pa	Pa	Pa	Va	Va	Va	30 states	Auctioneer, real est agt	0
63.1	M	38	14	Ia	15	0	Ia	Oh	Oh	Ia	Pa	In	0	Factory mgr	0
63.2	M	23	14	Ia	23	0	Ia	Ia	Ia	Ia	Germ	Ia	NE, US, EurWWII	Student	Germ
63.3	F	50	12	Ia	50	0	Ia	Pa	Pa	Ia	Engl	Oh	48 states, Can, Hi	Housewife	0
63.4	F	37	12	Ia	35	--	Ia	Pa	Pa	Ia	Germ	Pa	MW, Tn, Ky	Farm wife	0
64.1	M	90	6	Ia	22	Mn	Wale	Wale	Wale	In	Va	In	MW	r. Farmer	0
64.2	M	60	8	Ia	60	0	In	In	In	Ia	Pa	Pa	E&W coast, Can, Mex	r. Farmer	0
64.3	M	47	15	Ia	35	Ia	Ia	Ks	Pa	Ia	Pa	Pa	MW, S; SW PacifcUSN	Sign paintr, artist	Germ
65.1	M	65	12	Ia	65	0	Ia	Germ	--	Ia	Ia	Ia	US, Can	r. Farmer	0
65.2	F	83	11	Ia	83	Ca 3w	In	WV	--	Oh	Oh	Oh	Ca	0	0
65.3	F	69	--	Ia	69	Nb 04	Germ	Germ	Germ	Ia	Irel	Irel	Can	Farm wife	0
66.1	F	87	8	Germ	84	0	Germ	Germ	Germ	Germ	Germ	Germ	MW	Housewife	Germ
66.2	F	88	8	Ia	88	0	Denm	Denm	Denm	Irel	Irel	Irel	0	Housewife	0
66.3	M	69	10	Ia	11	Ia	Ia	Ia	Ia	Can	Irel	Irel	0	Janitor	0
67.1	M	68	7	Ia	68	0	Germ	Germ	Germ	Germ	Germ	Germ	MW, Ar, Mo	Janitor	Germ
67.2	M	65	12	Ia	65	--	Hung	Hung	Hung	Ct	Ct	Ct	20 states, Europe	Lumber dealr	0
67.3	F	63	8	Ia	20	Ia	Germ	Germ	Germ	Ia	Germ	Germ	0	Farmer	Germ
68.1	M	84	8	Ia	84	0	Scot	Scot	Scot	Scot	Scot	Scot	0	Farmer	0
68.2	M	72	8	Ia	72	0	Germ	Germ	Germ	Germ	Germ	Germ	W coast	--	Germ
68.3	M	55	12	Ia	55	0	Mn	Germ	NE	Ia	Wale	Wale	0	Ofc mgr, frmr	0
69.1	F	60	10	Ia	60	0	Il	Oh	Can	Engl	Engl	Engl	W cst, Co	Farm wife	0
69.2	M	58	12	Ia	52	0	Pa	Pa	Pa	Ia	--	--	E, S, W	Farmer	0
70.1	F	72	6	Ia	68	--	Oh	In	Oh	Ct	Ct	Ct	W	Housewife	0
70.2	M	62	11	Ia	31	Ia	Il	--	--	Ia	--	--	W, NW	Banker	0
70.3	F	60	10	Ia	60	0	Ia	In	In	Ia	Ia	Ia	W	Bookkeeper	0
71.1	M	67	8	Ia	28	Ia 07-22	Il	Va	Va	Ia	Ia	Ia	W coast	Janitor, justice of p	0
72.2	M	68	9	Ia	41	SD, ND, Mt, Mi 04-31	Ia	Ky	Oh	Il	Va	Ky	N, W	Farmer	0
73.1	F	60	13	Ia	60	0	Ia	Oh	Oh	Ia	Irel	Oh	In, Ca, Fl	Librarian	0

No.	Sex	Age	Sch	Bp1	Yrs Res	Else-where	F	PGF	PGM	M	MGF	MGM	Travel	Occupation	For. Lang
73.2	M	60	Bu	Ia	48	Sask 14-24; NY 24,26	Oh	Pa	Pa	Ky	Irel	Can	US	Banker	0
73.3	F	69	8	Ia	64	In	In	In	Ia	Ia	Oh	In	E cst, La	Store clerk, housewife	0
74.1	M	50	Bu	Ia	50	0	Ia	Oh	Oh	Ia	Oh	Oh	Il,In,Mo, Va	Farmer	0
74.2	F	43	13	Ia	43	0	Ia	Ia	Ia	Ia	Ia	Ia	E&W coast	Teacher	0
74.3	M	34	8	Ia	34	0	Neth	Neth	Neth	Neth	Neth	Neth	Co,Fl,NY	Farmer	Du
74.4	M	35	16	Ia	35	0	Ia	Md	Ia	Ia	Scot	Oh	W	Farmer	0
75.1	F	82	12	Ia	82	0	Ia	In	In	In	In	In	W cst, Co	Hsewfe, tchr	0
75.2	F	--	8	Ia	69	0	Can	Engl	Engl	Oh	Va	Va	Ca, MW	Housewife	0
76.1	F	81	--	Ia	59	0	Md	--	--	Md	--	--	0	Housewife	0
76.2	F	81	8	Ia	81	0	WV	Germ	Germ	Oh	Oh	Oh	Pa,Ca,Ar, ND,Can	Housewife	Germ
76.3	F	74	15	Ia	74	Ia	Pa	Pa	NE	Pa	Pa	Pa	19 states	Farm wife	0
76.4	F	51	12	Ia	51	0	Ia	Germ	Ia	Ia	Pa	Md	NW	Housewife	0
76.5	F	37	14	Ia	37	--	Ia	Ia	Ia	Mo	Mo	Mo	0	Housewife	0
77.1	M	46	JD	Ia	46	--	Ia	Ia	Ia	Ia	Pa	Oh	0	Attorney	0
77.2	M	40	Law	Ia	40	0	Mo	Germ	Germ	Ca	Wale	Wale	0	Attorney	0
77.3	M	58	LLB	Ia	58	0	Ia	Oh	In	Ia	Oh	Oh	Bermuda,	Attorney	0
78.1	F	64	8	Ia	60	Ia	Pa	Pa	Pa	Oh	Oh	--	--	Housewife	0
78.2	F	--	8	Ia	76	0	Ky	Ky	Ky	Ky	Ky	Ky	Va,Ca,Co	Housewife	0
78.3	M	63	16	Ia	63	--	Ia	Germ	Germ	Swit	Swit	Swit	E, W	Farmer	Germ
79.1	M	73	11	Ia	73	--	Pa	--	--	Pa	--	--	0	Farmer	0
79.2	F	60	12	Ia	50	--	NJ	Engl	NJ	Oh	--	--	0	Office workr	0
80.1	M	60	10	Ia	59	Tx 29-30	Can	Can	Engl	Ia	Engl	Engl	NY, Mex, Engl	Motel opertr	0
80.2	M	60	8	Ia	60	0	Wale	Wale	Wale	Wale	Wale	Wale	0	Farmer	Wels
81.1	F	64	12	Ia	--	Ia	Il	Il	Il	.Ia	NY	Pa	US	Housewife	0
81.2	F	61	12	Ia	61	0	Il	Fran	Germ	Germ	Irel	Irel	NY,Mt,Id, Al,Ms	Farmer	0
82.1	F	79	--	Ia	79	0	Oh	Pa	Pa	Il	?Pa	NY	E&W coast	Housewife	0
82.2	M	65	7	Ia	65	0	NY	?NY	?NY	Oh	Oh	Oh	Ca	Farmer	0
83.1	M	72	8	Ia	72	0	Oh	--	Irel	Pa	--	--	0	Farmer	0
83.2	F	72	11	Ia	70	Or 49-50	NC	Engl	NC	In	In	In	W	Housekeeper	0
84.1	M	52	12	Ia	52	0	Ia	Oh	Oh	Ia	Va	Va	MW	Hsewfe, tchr	0
84.2	M	47	7	Ia	47	0	Ia	Oh	Oh	Ia	Ia	Ia	SD, Wy	Farmer	0
84.3	F	37	14	Ia	33	Pa 39-40, Mi 41-42	Ia	Irel	Irel	Ia	In	Oh	E, W	Hsewfe, tchr	0
84.4	F	48	12	Ia	45	Ks 29-31, Mn 28	Ia.	--	--	Ia	Swed	Swed	--	Farmer	0
85.1	M	72	10	Ia	70	Ia 81-82	Ia	In	Ia	Va	Va	Va	0	Janitor	0
85.2	F	61	12	Ia	52	Ia 37-45, Ca 45-46	Pa	Pa	--	Oh	Oh	Oh	Ca, S	Bookkpr,typst	0
86.1	M	81	14	Ia	80		Swed	Swed	Swed	Swed	Swed	Swed	MW	r.Hdwe merch	Swed
86.2	F	73	?HS	Ia	73	0	Swed	Swed	Swed	Swed	Swed	Swed	W cst, MW	Teacher	Swed
86.3	M	53	8	Ia	51	Ia 26-27	Ia	Oh	Mo	Ia	Ia	Ia	Mo,Il,Can	Farmer	0
87.1	M	77	17	Ia	77	0	Me	Me	Me	Me	Me	Me	E	Lawyer	0
87.2	F	61	8	Ia	--	--	In	In	In	Ia	In	In	0	Housewife	0
87.3	M	63	16	Ia	63	0	Ks	Germ	Germ	Ia	Germ	Germ	US, Can	Lawyer	0
88.1	M	101	16	Ia	73	Il 65-73	In	--	--	Engl	Engl	Scot	Ca, Fl	Farmer, business man	0
88.2	F	79	--	Ia	64	Ca,Or 2y	In	Oh	Oh	Oh	Oh	Oh	0	Housewife	0
89.1	M	78	8	Ia	78	--	Ia	Pa	Pa	Ia	Va	Va	NW, SW	Clerk	0
89.2	F	59	9	Ia	59	0	Ia	Swit	Swit	Germ	Germ	Germ	S, W	Housewife	--
90.1	F	72	--	Ia	68	Wy, Mt	--	--	--	--	--	--	NW	Housewife	0
90.2	F	70	HS	Ia	70	0	Il	NY	Il	Mi	Que	Engl	40 states	Tchr, hsewfe	0
90.3	F	57	13	Ia	52	Ia 97-02	Il	In	Pa	Il	Oh	NB	0	r. Farmer	0
90.4	F	40	12	Ia	40	Ia 13-54	Ky	Pa	Il	Ia	Irel	Mo	Oh, Ca	Clerk-county enginr's offc	0

No.	Sex	Age	Sch	Bpl	Yrs Res	Else-where	F	PGF	PGM	M	MGF	MGM	Travel	Occupation	For. Lang
91.1	F	70	12	Ia	70	--	Il	Swed	--	Il	--	Swed	0	Housewife	Swed
92.1	M	70	16	Ia	70	0	Pa	Pa	In	In	In	In	DC,Fl,Co	Attorney	--
92.2	M	70	11	Ia	70	0	NY	--	--	Pa	--	--	0	Court clerk	0
92.3	F	67	8	Ia	28	Ia	Engl	Engl	Engl	Engl	Engl	Engl	W, Can	Housewife	0
93.1	F	71	10	Ia	64	Ia 6y	Ia	--	--	Ia	--	--	Nb,Mi,Can	Housewife	0
93.2	F	67	16	Ia	67	0	In	Oh	Va	NY	--	Ct	Ct,others	Librarian	0
94.1	M	70	8	Ia	70	0	In	NY	NY	Oh	Va	Va	0	Farmer	0
94.2	M	63	8	Ia	45	Ia 41-46	Ia	Ky	In	Oh	Oh	Oh	MW	Depty sherff	0
95.1	F	70	12	Ia	70	0	Pa	--	--	NJ	--	--	Wy, Wi	Housewife	0
95.2	M	76	?9	Ia	70	NM 05-10	Vt	Vt	Vt	Il	Ma	Ma	Pa,NM,Wa, Sask	Civil enginr	0
96.1	F	80	8	Ia	68	In 12y	Il	--	--	Il	--	--	0	Housewife	0
96.2	M	74	4	Ia	74	0	Ia	--	--	Oh	--	--	0	Carpenter	0
97.1	F	72	--	Ia	72	0	Ia	De	In	Ia	Oh	Oh	--	Hsewfe,nurse	--
97.2	M	66	--	Ia	66	0	In	Ky	In	Ia	De	Md	0	Farmer, county offcl	0
97.3	F	52	--	Ia	--	--	Ia	Pa	Oh	Ia	Il	Oh	0	Teacher	0
98.1	M	69	8	Ia	64	Ok 00-02, NM 07-08	Oh	Va	Va	Md	Scot	Scot	0	Bank manager	0
98.2	M	52	12	Ia	30	Ia 98-19	Ia	Oh	Oh	Il	Engl	Il	Tx, Wi	Merchant	0
99.1	M	65	9	Ia	65	0	Germ	Germ	Germ	Ia	USA	USA	Mo,Il,Mn	Depty county recorder	0
99.2	F	60	12	Ia	60	0	Germ	Germ	Germ	USA	Neth	Neth	E, S	Housewife	0
99.3	M	85	10	Ia	--	--	Fran	Fran	Fran	Oh	Germ	Germ	0	Blacksmith	0

NORTH DAKOTA

No.	Sex	Age	Sch	Bpl	Yrs Res	Else-where	F	PGF	PGM	M	MGF	MGM	Travel	Occupation	For. Lang
1.1	M	--	8	Ia	46	Ia	Norw	--	--	Norw	--	--	MW,NW,Can	Farmer	--
1.2	M	48	13	Norw	47	ND	Norw	--	--	Norw	--	--	NW,E,Can	Farmer	--
2.1	M	75	8	Norw	50	Mn	Norw	--	--	Norw	--	--	--	r.RR sta agt	--
2.2	F	78	5	Mn	51	Mn	Germ	--	--	Germ	--	--	Mn, Can	Housewife	--
3.1	F	36	12	ND	36	0	Norw	Norw	Norw	Mn	--	--	0	Housewife	0
3.2	M	48	12	ND	48	0	Wi	Il	USA	NY	USA	USA	MW, NW, W	Salesman	0
3.3	F	47	Bu	ND	47	ND 34-42	Wi	Norw	Norw	Norw	Norw	Norw	E, NW, MW	--	Norw
4.1	F	63	--	ND	25	Can 10-28	Norw	Norw	Norw	Norw	Swed	Norw	USA, Can	Rural teachr	Norw
4.2	F	54	8	Mi	45	Mt	Ont	--	--	Ont	--	--	S, M	Housewife	Fren
5.1	M	56	15	ND	--	ND -32	Norw	Norw	Norw	Norw	Norw	Norw	W, S	Restaurateur	Norw
5.2	M	72	9	Norw	53	Mn 83-96	Norw	--	--	Norw	--	--	MW, Can	Farmer	Norw
6.1	F	57	8	Mn	55	Mn	Norw	Norw	Norw	Norw	Norw	Norw	NY	Farm wife	Norw
6.2	M	43	12	ND	43	0	Ia	Denm	Denm	Ia	Germ	Germ	0	Farmer	0
6.3	F	53	10	ND	53	--	Pa	Pa	Pa	In	Oh	In	NW, MW	Farmer	0
6.4	M	44	8	ND	44	--	Finl	Finl	Finl	USA	Finl	Finl	W	Farmer	Finn
6.5	F	37	14	ND	37	--	Can	Irel	Irel	Pa	Engl	Engl	Can, Mex	Tchr,frm wfe	0
7.1	M	68	8	ND	68	--	Norw	--	--	Norw	--	--	Can	Serv stat op	Norw
7.2	M	61	8	ND	61	--	Can	Can	Can	Can	Can	Can	WWI	Postmaster	Fren
8.1	F	48	8	ND	25	ND -25	Ct	--	--	Ct	--	--	0	Farm wife	Fren
8.2	M	60	8	ND	60	ND	Can	Can	Can	Can	Can	Can	Mi, Can	Mail carrier	0
9.1	M	36	8	ND	36	--	Norw	Norw	Norw	Norw	Norw	Norw	--	Bar owner	Norw
9.2	M	58	8	Leb	34	ND 06-16	Leb	Leb	Leb	Leb	Leb	Leb	--	RR employee	Arab
9.3	M	72	12	Norw	40	Ma 04-12	Norw	Norw	Norw	Norw	Norw	Norw	E&W coast	Farmer	Norw
9.4	M	42	6	ND	25	ND 15-42, Ca 42-45	Mn	Norw	Norw	Norw	Norw	Norw	--	Merchant	Norw
10.1	M	61	5	ND	36	ND 88-13	Irel	--	--	Il	--	--	E&W coast	Implemnt dlr	--
10.2	F	30	14	ND	30	ND,Or,Ca, Ar	Mn	Norw	Norw	Mn	Norw	Norw	E&W coast, Mex, Can	Housewife	Norw
11.1	M	54	Co	ND	54	0	Germ	Germ	Germ	Mn	Czs	Czs	W	Booking agt	0
11.2	F	55	Co	ND	55	0	Mn	Norw	Norw	Wi	Norw	Norw	W,S,MW,Can	Housewife	Norw
11.3	M	58	--	ND	58	ND	Denm	Denm	--	NY	Engl	Engl	US	Farmer	0
12.1	M	55	8	ND	52	--	Norw	Norw	Norw	Norw	Norw	Norw	0	Frmr,lumbrmn	Norw

No.	Sex	Age	Sch	Bpl	Yrs Res	Else-where	F	PGF	PGM	M	MGF	MGM	Travel	Occupation	For. Lang
12.2	M	40	12	ND	40	--	Mi	Swit	Germ	Mn	Germ	Germ	MW, Can	Farmer	?Ger
13.1	M	49	8	Ia	47	Wa 2y	Ia	--	--	Irel	Irel	Irel	MW, W	Truck driver	0
13.3	M	80	14	Va	54	Va -81, Nb -97	Va	Va	Va	Va	Va	Va	E&W coast	Teachr,farmr	0
14.1	M	47	12	ND	47	0	Norw	Norw	Norw	Norw	Norw	Norw	MW	Hdwe merch	Norw
14.2	M	51	12	ND	51	0	Swed	Swed	Swed	Swed	Swed	Swed	MW	Farmer	0
15.1	M	77	8	Mn	50	Mn	Me	--	--	Mn	Can	--	0	r. Merchant	0
15.2	F	50	12	ND	50	--	Can	Can	Can	Can	Can	Can	NE, NW	Housekeeper	0
15.3	M	60	7	ND	60	--	Lux	Fran	Fran	Germ	Swit	Swit	S	Farmer	Germ
15.4	M	41	13	ND	41	Mn -42	Norw	Norw	Norw	Mn	Norw	Norw	NE,MW,NW, Can	Farmer	Norw
16.1	M	59	10	ND	59	--	Norw	Norw	Norw	Norw	Norw	Norw	0	Auditor	Norw
16.2	M	52	6	ND	52	--	Norw	Norw	Norw	Norw	Norw	Norw	0	Farmer	Norw
16.3	M	57	12	ND	57	--	Norw	Norw	Norw	Norw	Norw	Norw	MW	Farmer	Norw
17.1	M	49	12	Mn		ND 01-18	Swed	Swed	Swed	Swed	Swed	Swed	--	Farmer	Swed
17.2	M	59	12	Mn		Mn 98-99, Wi 00-10	Wi	Norw	Norw	Wi	Norw	Norw	0	Farmer	0
18.1	F	50	Co	Mn		ND 18-39	Mn	Norw	Norw	Mn	Norw	Norw	SW, W	Housewife	0
18.2	M	51	14	ND		ND 17-29	Mn	Norw	Norw	Ia	Norw	Norw	MW	County offcl	Norw
19.1	M	70	--	Germ	52	Germ1900	Germ	Germ	Germ	Germ	Germ	Germ	W	County judge	Germ ?Fre
19.2	M	68	10	Mn	40	ND	Germ	Germ	Germ	Belg	Fran	Fran	E, W, S	Dpty cnty aud	Germ
20.1	F	44	12	ND	10	ND 34y	Denm	Denm	Denm	Denm	Denm	Denm	W, MW	Farm wife	0
20.2	F	53	12	Mn	32	Mn 97-18	Can	Can	Can	Swed	Swed	Swed	0	Farm wife	0
21.1	M	67	5	Denm	42	Il 03-08	Denm	Denm	Denm	Denm	Denm	Denm	0	r. Farmer	Dan
21.2	M	53	8	Russ	48	Mn 20-25	Russ	Russ	Russ	Russ	Russ	Russ	MW,W,Can	County jdge, deeds regist	Germ
22.1	M	50	8	ND	50	Can	Swed	Swed	Swed	Norw	Norw	Norw	0	Motel opertr	Norw ?Swe
22.2	M	36	14	ND	36	--	Germ	Germ	Germ	SD	Germ	Germ	MW, Can	Nwspapr edtr	?Ger
23.1	M	39	12	ND	--	Mn 14-25	Engl	Irel	Irel	Mo	Mo	?Mo	US, SA	Police offcr, farmr,truckr	0
23.2	F	33	8	Mn	28	Mn 5y	Nb	Ia	Ia	Ia	Il	Ia	28 states	Phone opertr	0
23.3	F	30	12	ND	23	ND 32-39	--	--	--	--	--	--	0	Clerk-typist	0
24.1	M	42	13	ND	33	ND 6y	In	--	--	Mn	--	NY	US Army	Farmer	0
24.2	M	57	8	Mn	50	Ia	Il	NY	--	Ia	Pa	--	0	Farmer	0
24.3	F	40	12	ND	20	ND	Russ	Russ	Russ	Russ	Russ	Russ	0	Farm wife	Germ
25.1	M	61	7	Wi	52	--	Norw	Norw	Norw	Norw	Norw	Norw	0	--	Norw
25.2	M	58	Bu	ND	58	Wa 10m	Norw	--	--	Wi	--	--	E&W coast, Can,EurWWI	County judge	Norw
25.3	M	63	16	ND	63	Mn 05-11	Norw	Norw	Norw	Norw	Norw	Norw	UMW	Insur agent	Norw
25.4	M	56	6	ND	56	0	Norw	Norw	Norw	Norw	Norw	Norw	14 states	Merchant	Norw
26.1	M	81	10	Ont	67	--	Scot	Scot	Scot	Scot	Scot	Scot	E	Farmer	Gael
26.2	F	50	Co	Norw	26	Norw 02-04, ND 04-26	Norw	Norw	Norw	Norw	Norw	Norw	E, MW	Housewife, ex-teacher	Norw Swed
26.3	M	51	Bu	ND	51		Norw	Norw	Norw	Norw	Norw	Norw	E, W, S	Banker	Norw
27.1	M	55	13	ND	55	0	Il	Norw	Norw	Mn	Norw	Wi	UMW	Merchant	Norw
27.2	F	62	9	ND	62	0	Ia	Norw	Norw	Mn	Norw	Wi	0	Houseworker	0
28.1	M	--	HS	Denm	40	Denm	Denm	Denm	Denm	Denm	Denm	Denm	US	Lumbrmn,frmr	Dan
28.2	M	72	HS	Mn	71	0	Norw	Norw	Norw	Norw	Norw	Norw	0	Farmer	Norw
28.3	M	43	8	ND	43	0	Russ	Russ	Russ	Russ	Russ	Russ	0	Farmer	0
28.4	M	62	6	ND	20	ND	Mn	Norw	Norw	Norw	Norw	Norw	Can	Farmer	Norw
29.1	M	80	HS	Ia	61	ND 19y	Norw	Norw	Norw	Norw	Norw	Norw	W cst,Can	Insur agent	Norw
29.2	M	43	Co	Mn	38	Mn ?5y	Mn	Pa	Pa	Mn	Denm	Swed	US	Nwspapr pub	0
30.1	F	48	14	ND	48	0	Norw	Norw	Norw	Norw	Norw	Norw	MW, NW	Farmer	0
30.2	F	45	10	ND	45	0	Swed	Swed	Swed	Swed	Swed	Swed	In, Wa	Housewife	0
31.1	M	59	10	Mn	59	0	Mn	Engl	Engl	Ia	Wale	Irel	UMW	Custodian	0
31.2	M	43	12	ND	43	0	Il	Norw	Norw	Il	Norw	Norw	W coast	Farmr,ranchr	0
32.1	F	43	13	ND	25	ND 07-25	NY	NY	NY	Ia	Ia	Ia	UMW, Can	Housewife	0
32.2	M	43	9	ND	43		Aust	Aust	Aust	Aust	Aust	Aust	0	Farmer	--

No.	Sex	Age	Sch	Bpl	Yrs Res	Else-where	F	PGF	PGM	M	MGF	MGM	Travel	Occupation	For. Lang
32.3	M	31	8	Il	20	Il -34	--	--	--	--	--	--	0	Farmer	0
33.1	M	80	--	Ont	12	Oh 7y, ND 67y	Germ	Germ	Germ	Pol	Pol	Pol	Europe	Police magis	Germ
33.2	M	76	16	Oh		ND 7y,Ia 5y,ND 7y	Irel	Irel	Irel	In	In	In	UMW, Pa, Can	Salesman	Germ
34.1	F	73	15	Mn		Or 00-05	Il	Ky	Va	Vt	--	?E	W, MW	Housewife	Swed Germ
34.2	M	71	GS	Mn	3	Mn, ND	Il	Germ	Germ	Germ	Germ	Germ	0	County offcl	Germ
35.1	F	74	12	WV	66	ND 85-51	WV	Pa	Pa	Ma	WV	Ma	S,W,E,Can	--	0
35.2	M	52	12	ND	39	ND 00-52	Can	Scot	Scot	Can	Can	Can	Centrl US	Hist Soc Spt	0
35.3	M	75	12	NY	67	--	NY	NY	--	Pa	--	--	E&W coast, Jap, Hi	r. Rancher	0
36.1	M	63	12	Russ	28	SD 01-03, Sask 11-15,ND 03-11	Russ	Russ	Russ	Russ	Russ	Russ	W, Can	County audtr	Germ Russ Rom
36.2	M	75	8	Mn	52	Mn, ND	Oh	Oh	Oh	Can	Can	Can	S, W	Farmer	0
37.1	F	46	8	Pol	46	--	Pol	Pol	Pol	Pol	Pol	Pol	Nb,Wi,Mn	Farm wife	--
37.2	M	62	4	Russ	47	--	Russ	Russ	Russ	Russ	Russ	Russ	W, Can	Grain buyer	?Rus
37.3	M	67	8	Wi	65	0	Belg	Belg	Belg	Belg	Belg	Belg	0	Carpenter	0
37.4	M	65	8	Mn	47	0	Mn	Pa	Can	Mn	NC	In	0	Farmer	0
37.5	M	75	8	Wi	71	ND	Can	Can	Can	Wi	Wi	Wi	0	Farmer	0
38.1	F	65	6	ND	65	Mn 10-12	Denm	Denm	Denm	Norw	Norw	Norw	Wi, Mn	Piano teachr	Norw
38.2	F	56	7	ND	12	ND 36-39	Mn	--	--	Mn	--	--	Or, Ca	Housewife	0
38.3	F	51	4	ND	51	0	Norw	Norw	Norw	Norw	Norw	Norw	0	Billing clrk	?Nor
39.1	M	57	12	ND	57	--	Oh	NY	NY	Germ	Germ	Germ	E, W, S	Locksmith	0
39.2	F	67	12	ND	67	--	Germ	Germ	Germ	Germ	Germ	Germ	E, W	Farm wife	0
39.3	F	51	8	Ia	48	--	Il	--	--	Il	--	--	W	Housewife	0
40.1	F	69	8	Swed	42	NY 96-08	Swed	Swed	Swed	Swed	Swed	Swed	E,W,Swed	Farm wife	Swed
40.2	M	64	8	Norw	40	Mn 7y	Norw	Norw	Norw	Norw	Norw	Norw	US, Can, Norw	Farmer	Norw
41.1	F	57	12	ND	44	--	Wi	Wi	Wi	Mn	Norw	Norw	MW, W	Farm wife	0
41.2	M	48	10	Mn	48	--	Norw	Norw	Norw	Mn	Norw	Norw	0	Auto dealer	Norw Germ
42.1	M	65	8	Can	57	ND	Can	Engl	Engl	Can	Scot	Scot	US, Can	Stock raiser	0
42.2	F	40	13	ND	7	ND 10-43	Wi	Norw	Norw	SD	Norw	Norw	US	Housewife	0
42.3	F	37	12	ND	37	--	Russ	Russ	Russ	Russ	Russ	Russ	W	Housewife	Germ
43.1	M	70	---	Russ	21	--	Russ	Russ	Russ	Russ	Russ	Russ	--	--	Russ
43.2	M	52	8	ND	--	--	Il	Irel	Pa	In	In	In	MW	Ranchr,bankr	0
43.3	M	44	Co	Fran	43	0	Russ	Russ	Russ	Russ	Russ	Russ	US, Can	Teachr,farmr	Germ
44.1	M	47	8	Mi	1	ND 04-51	Finl	Finl	Finl	Finl	Finl	Finl	MW	Farmer	Finn
44.2	M	44	Co	ND	37	ND 41-47	Russ	Russ	Russ	Russ	Russ	Russ	0	Insur agent	Germ
45.1	M	41	8	ND	41	--	Germ	--	--	Russ	--	--	0	Frmr,carpntr	--
45.2	M	45	8	ND	45	--	Norw	--	--	Mn	--	--	0	REA employee	--
46.1	M	--	14	Swed	64	Swed 3y	Swed	Swed	Swed	Swed	Swed	Swed	N, Can, Swed	Carpenter	Swed
46.2	F	54	12	ND	54	--	Il	Ma	NY	Il	Oh	Oh	MW, W	Secty,hsewfe	0
47.1	M	69	8	ND	65	SD 4y	NY	NY	NY	In	NY	NY	0	Farmer, grain buyer	0
47.2	F	71	14	ND	--	ND 07-10	Vt	Vt	--	Pa	Pa	Pa	W	r. Statn agt	0
48.1	F	60	14	Ia	45	ND 04-08	In	Engl	Wale	Wa	Ma	Mo	W, S	r.Cnty treasr	0
48.2	M	71	8	Wi	45	Wi 12y, Ar 2y	Mi	Vt	Vt	Engl	Engl	Engl	W, E	Farmr,ranchr	0
49.1	F	73	12	Mn	43	Mn	Swed	Swed	Swed	Swed	Swed	Swed	US	r. Teacher	Swed
49.2	M	--	16	Norw	--	--	--	--	--	--	--	--	W, M	r. Clerk	--
50.1	M	66	9	SD	60	--	Md	--	--	Pa	--	--	SE, NY	Photographer	--
50.2	M	47	14	Russ	38	Russ, ND 10-12	Russ	Russ	Russ	Russ	Russ	Russ	SD	Cnty sch spt lumbr deal'r	Germ
50.3	F	47	14	Mn	25	Mn 21y	Mn	Norw	Norw	Norw	Norw	Norw	Mi, Or	Tchr,cnty spt	Norw
51.1	M	37	5	ND	5	ND	Russ	Germ	--	Russ	--	--	E, S	Bank fieldmn	Germ
51.2	M	54	4	ND	54	--	Russ	Russ	Russ	Russ	Russ	Russ	W, E	Farmer	Germ
52.1	M	71	8	Wi	--	--	Norw	--	--	Norw	--	--	0	r.	Norw

No.	Sex	Age	Sch	Bpl	Yrs Res	Else-where	F	PGF	PGM	M	MGF	MGM	Travel	Occupation	For. Lang
52.2	M	50	16	ND	50	Mn 18-22	Pa	Pa	Pa	Mn	Scot	Scot	E, S	Druggist	0
53.1	F	50	12	ND	50	Or 44-45, ND -48	Mi	Germ	Germ	Mi	Germ	Germ	Wa,Mn,SD, Or	r.Phone op, Cnty ct clrk	0
53.2	M	41	Co	ND	30	Ca 20-33	Norw	Norw	Norw	Norw	Norw	Norw	W	Farmr, cashr	0
53.3	F	52	14	ND	52	---	Mn	Scot	Germ	Mi	Mi	Mi	MW, Can	Teacher	--

SOUTH DAKOTA

No.	Sex	Age	Sch	Bpl	Yrs Res	Else-where	F	PGF	PGM	M	MGF	MGM	Travel	Occupation	For. Lang
1.1	F	74	12	Pa	52	Can 79-86,SD, Oh,Vt	Engl	Engl	Scot	Can	Engl	Can	Oh,Pa,Ca	Housewife	0
1.2	F	69	12	SD	47	SD 83-09	Can	Can	Irel	Engl	Irel	Irel	US,Can, Mex	Clerk	0
1.3	F	64	12	Ks	51	Ks 1y, Nb 12y	Oh	Oh	Oh	Ky	Oh	Oh	MW	Ranch wife	0
1.4	M	60	7	Mt	59	SD 93-09	Wi	--	--	--	--	--	Ca	0	0
2.1	F	36	12	SD	30	ND 29-34	In	--	--	Wi	Mn	Mn	E	Housewife	0
2.2	M	85	8	Il	51	Ia 72-92, Nb 92-96	Germ	Germ	Germ	Irel	Irel	Irel	MW	Museum curtr	0
2.3	F	35	9	SD	35	--	Russ	Russ	Russ	ND	--	--	Can,Ak,W	Hsewfe,merch, Germ postmaster	
2.4	F	39	12	SD	38	Co 42-43	Tn	Irel	Engl	Wi	Germ	Oh	0	Housewife	0
2.5	F	42	10	ND	42	--	ND	Norw	Norw	SD	Norw	Norw	W, MW	Hsewfe, tchr	0
2.6	M	54	8	SD	45	--	Ia	--	--	Ia	--	--	0	Rancher	0
3.1	M	73	8	Ia	32	Nb 79-10, ND 10-18	Il	Scot	Engl	Wi	Engl	Neth	0	r.	0
3.2	M	60	10	Nb	33	0	Swed	Swed	Swed	Denm	Denm	Denm	0	Farmr,ranchr	0
4.1	M	66	0	Russ	54	--	Russ	Russ	Russ	Russ	Russ	Russ	0	r. Farmer	Germ
4.2	F	54	6	SD	54	--	Russ	Russ	Russ	Russ	Germ	Germ	ND, Can	Farm wife	Germ
5.1	F	65	8	Wi	42	SD	Wi	Germ	Germ	Germ	Germ	Germ	Wi	Deeds regist	?Ger
5.2	F	63	17	SD	33	SD 89-19	Ia	Irel	Irel	Ia	Irel	Irel	W	Nurse	0
6.1	M	62	8	SD	62	0	Russ	Germ	Germ	Russ	Germ	Germ	US, Can	Implemnt dlr	Germ
7.1	F	55	8	SD	55	--	Swed	Swed	Swed	Swed	Swed	Swed	M, MW	Housewife	?Swe
7.2	M	56	8	SD	56	Fran 2y	Engl	--	--	Pa	--	--	USA	Farmer	0
8.1	F	47	8	Wi	47	--	Wi	Wi	Wi	Wi	Wi	Wi	MW	Farm wife	Germ
8.2	F	47	8	SD	46	--	Swed	Swed	Swed	Swed	Swed	Swed	MW	Housewife	Swed
9.1	F	60	14	SD	--	0	Norw	Norw	Norw	Norw	Norw	Norw	US	Cnty sch spt	Norw
9.2	F	--	12	Mn	17	Mn 13-16, ND 16-36, SD	Mn	Norw	Norw	Mn	Norw	Swed	Can,E,W	Farm wife	0
10.1	F	56	12	SD	56	--	Swed	Swed	Swed	Swed	Swed	Swed	MW, E	Hsewfe,clerk	Swed
10.2	F	67	8	Wi	67	SD	Germ	Germ	Germ	Wi	Germ	Germ	W	Farm wife	Germ
11.1	F	43	12	SD	43	--	Russ	Russ	Russ	Russ	Russ	Russ	0	Farm wife	Germ
11.2	M	69	11	SD	69	--	Engl	Engl	Engl	Engl	Engl	Engl	0	Farmer	0
11.3	F	33	12	SD	5	Mi 1y	Norw	Norw	Norw	Norw	Norw	Norw	US	Hsewfe, secy	?Nor
11.4	F	38	13	SD	15	SD	Mn	Pa	USA	SD	Swed	Swed	E&W coast	Farm wife	0
12.1	F	14	9	SD	14	--	SD	NY	NY	Ia	Ia	Ia	MW	School girl	0
12.2	M	62	Co	Mn	30	Mn 17-22, Or, Wa	Mn	Can	Can	Can	Can	Can	W, E, S	Wholesaler	Fren
12.3	M	53	8	Il	9	SD 14-53, Ia 11-14	Il	Norw	Norw	Il	Norw	Norw	Ca, MW	Farmer	0
13.1	M	70	11	Ia	43	Ia 80-08	NY	NY	NY	In	In	In	W	r.Implem dlr	0
13.2	F	63	Co	Germ	31	NY 87-19	Germ	Germ	Germ	Germ	Germ	Germ	US, Can	Hsewf,ad agt	--
14.1	F	25	16	SD	25	--	Ms	Ms	Oh	SD	Pa	Can	0	Teacher	0
14.2	M	50	8	SD	50	--	Mo	Ky	Ky	Engl	Engl	Engl	W, M	Farmer	0
14.3	F	43	13	SD	43	--	SD	Engl	Engl	SD	--	--	0	Teacher	0
14.4	M	45	8	SD	45	--	SD	Norw	Norw	SD	Can	Can	0	Rancher	0
15.1	F	39	12	SD	30	--	Norw	Norw	Norw	Pa	Pa	Pa	0	Hsewfe,clerk	0
15.2	F	41	12	SD	20	ND 13-33	Il	Denm	Denm	Il	--	--	0	Housewife	0
16.1	M	71	8	Pol	42	SD	Pol	Germ	Germ	Pol	Germ	Germ	Ca, Can,	Insur agent	Germ

No.	Sex	Age	Sch	Bpl	Yrs Res	Else-where	F	PGF	PGM	M	MGF	MGM	Travel	Occupation	For. Lang
16.2	F	57	9	Ia	41	Ia 96-12	Ks	?Ks	?Ks	Germ	Germ	Germ	Ar	Housewife	0
16.3	M	39	HS	SD	39	0	Il	Il	Il	Il	Ma	Il	0	Farmr,ranchr	0
18.1	F	48	8	SD	48	0	Germ	Germ	Germ	Neth	Neth	Neth	0	Housewife	Germ
18.2	M	55	7	SD	55	0	Russ	Russ	Russ	Russ	Russ	Russ	Ca, Mi	Farmr,ranchr	Germ
19.1	M	49	8	SD	49	0	Germ	Germ	Germ	Germ	Germ	Germ	0	Farmer	Germ
19.2	M	52	13	Ks	52	0	Il	--	--	Ks	--	--	Can,Ca,Il	Mechanic	0
19.3	M	61	GS	SD	61	0	Germ	--	--	Germ	--	--	20 states	Farmer	Germ
20.1	M	58	5	SD	58	FranWWII	Ia	Swit	Va	Oh	Oh	Oh	WWII	Welder	?Fre
20.2	M	63	7	SD	63	Oh 2y	Norw	Norw	Norw	Norw	Norw	Norw	S, W	Custodian	Norw
20.3	M	57	8	SD	57	--	Germ	Germ	Germ	Germ	Germ	Germ	Mi, Can	Farmer	Germ
20.4	M	51	8	SD	51	--	Swed	Swed	Swed	Denm	Denm	Denm	W, E, Can	Farmer	?Swe ?Dan
21.1	M	68	8	Norw	62	Norw	Swed	Swed	Swed	Swed	Swed	Swed	S, W	Frmr,auto dlr	Norw
21.2	M	85	8	Norw		Mn 68-83, SD	Norw	Norw	Norw	Norw	Norw	Norw	0	r. Farmer	Norw
22.1	F	62	7	Il		-- --	Il	Engl	Engl	Il	Engl	Engl	S, E	Farm wife	0
22.2	M	71	4	SD	53	SD 18y	Germ	Germ	Germ	Germ	Germ	Germ	Can	Salesman	Germ
22.3	F	69	4	SD	--	SD	Lux	Lux	Lux	Germ	Germ	Germ	MW	Merchant	Germ
23.1	M	66	8	SD	66	0	Finl	Finl	Finl	Finl	Finl	Finl	W, E	--	Finn
23.2	M	55	9	SD	55	0	Wi	--	--	Mn	NY	--	MW	Farmer	0
24.1	M	60	8	SD	42	ND,Mn,Co	NY	Irel	Scot	Wi	Oh	Il	US, Can, Mex	Mail carrier	0
24.2	F	57	12	Mn	35	--	Oh	Pa	Oh	Me	Me	Me	W	Farm wife	0
25.1	M	49	8	SD	49	--	Can	--	--	USA	--	--	0	Farmer	0
25.2	M	29	Co	SD	29	0	Denm	Denm	Denm	SD	Denm	Denm	MW, W	Farmr,ranchr	0
25.3	M	63	10	SD	53	Wy 22-32	Scot	Scot	Scot	Scot	Scot	Scot	Can, Eur	r. Mine supt	
26.1	M	37	8	SD	37	0	Russ	Russ	Russ	Russ	Russ	Russ	0	Farmer	Germ
26.2	M	68	8	SD	45	0	Germ	Germ	Germ	Germ	Germ	Germ	0	Farmer	Germ
26.3	M	40	11	SD	40	--	Lux	--	--	Ia	--	--	Ca, Or	Farmer	0
27.1	F	15	9	SD	15	0	Ks	--	--	Pa	Pa	Pa	MW	Student	0
27.2	M	44	9	Il	42	SD 07-08	Germ	Germ	Germ	Germ	Germ	Germ	Co,Wy,Mn	Farmer	0
28.1	M	--	8	SD	43	SD	Nb	Germ	Germ	SD	Engl	Engl	US	Implemnt dlr	0
29.1	F	72	8	Ky	54	SD	Ky	USA	USA	Ky	USA	USA	E, W	Cnty ct clrk	0
29.2	F	61	6	SD	56	Wi 04-09	Swed	Swed	Swed	Swed	Swed	Swed	Europe	Housewife	Swed
29.3	M	52	12	SD	52	0	Il	Oh	Oh	Can	Engl	Engl	0	Farmer	0
30.1	F	69	9	SD	49	SD	Il	Ct	Pa	Il	Oh	Oh	Ca	Housewife	0
30.2	F	59	---	SD	59	SD	Germ	Germ	Germ	Germ	Germ	Germ	MW, Can	Housewife	0
30.3	F	70	8	Il	--	SD	Il	Ct	Pa	Il	Oh	Oh	E, Ca	Housewife	0
30.4	F	76	8	Ia	72	Il 79-83, SD	NY	NY	NY	Il	Engl	Engl	MW	Housewife	0
31.1	M	61	8	SD	61	--	Czs	Czs	Czs	Czs	Czs	Czs	MW	Farmer	Cz
31.2	M	57	10	SD	50	SD 21-28	Ia	NY	NY	Ia	Scot	Scot	E&W coast	Estate mgr	0
31.3	F	73	12	Il	--	Il 79-83, SD	Oh	Oh	Pa	In	Engl	Ky	MW	Tchr,bookkpr	0
32.1	F	49	12	SD	43	SD 02-07, Or 36-38	Ky	Engl	--	Mn	Germ	Germ	0	Farm wife, writer	0
32.2	F	42	12	NY	35	SD	--	--	--	--	--	--	MW	Ranch wife	0
33.1	F	71	7	Mn	37	SD	Denm	Denm	Denm	Wi	Wi	Wi	E&W coast	Housewife	0
33.2	F	52	13	Ia	44	Ia 8y	Pa	Engl	Engl	Wi	--	Fran	Can,MW,E	Housewife	0
33.3	F	79	8	Il	63	Il 72-82, SD	Irel	Irel	Irel	NY	Irel	Irel	MW	Teacher	0
33.4	M	72	10	Swed	35	--	Swed	Swed	Swed	Swed	Swed	Swed	--	Farmer	--
33.5	F	82	Co	Ia	70	Ia 80-82	Ky	Pa	Ky	Engl	Engl	Engl	MW, E	Tchr,librarn	0
33.6	F	74	12	Il	67	SD	NY	--	--	Il	--	--	MW, Ca	Teacher	0
34.1	M	72	7	SD	45	SD	Norw	Norw	Norw	Norw	Norw	Norw	MW, Ca	r.Well drill	Norw
35.1	M	87	8	Wi	75	Wi 11y, SD	NY	NY	NY	NY	Irel	Irel	0	Banker	0
35.2	F	47	8	SD	47	--	Germ	Germ	Germ	Germ	Germ	Germ	US	Housewife	Germ
35.3	M	22	12	SD	20	Co, Ks	SD	Norw	Norw	SD	Norw	Norw	W	Student	--
36.1	M	44	12	Ia	44	Mn 13-18	Wi	Wi	SD	SD	Norw	Norw	--	Implemnt dlr	0
36.2	F	42	12	SD	22	SD	Mn	Denm	USA	Ia	USA	Germ	W	Housewife	0

112

No.	Sex	Age	Sch	Bpl	Yrs Res	Else-where	F	PGF	PGM	M	MGF	MGM	Travel	Occupation	For. Lang
36.3	M	41	8	SD	41	--	--	--	--	--	--	--	0	Farmer	Cz
37.1	F	36	9	SD	10	SD	In	--	--	SD	Swed	Swed	MW	Teachr,clerk	0
37.2	F	56	12	Ia	44	Nb 99-06	Ia	Wi	Germ	Ia	Germ	Germ	US	Farmer	Sp
38.1	M	63	12	Ia	57	--	Pa	--	--	Wi	--	--	0	Oil co agent	0
38.2	M	49	--	Mn	6	SD	Il	Germ	--	Il	NY	Pa	NW	Publr,printr	0
38.3	M	75	--	Ia	50	Ia	NY	Irel	Irel	Il	Irel	Irel	--	Grocer	0
38.4	M	--	8	Ia	40	Ia 43y	Oh	--	--	Mi	--	--	NE, W	r. Farmer	0
39.1	M	51	12	Il	2	Il 01-18	Germ	Germ	Germ	Germ	Germ	Germ	MW	Teachr,farmr	?Ger
39.2	F	--	12	SD	26	SD	Oh	Oh	Oh	Mo	Il	Il	0	Ranch wife	0
39.3	F	52	9	SD	41	SD	Mn	--	Mn	Norw	Norw	Norw	W, Can	Teacher	0
40.1	M	60	8	SD	60	0	Oh	Germ	Germ	Mo	--	--	E	Farmer	0
40.2	F	64	12	Mn	27	Mn 18y, SD 6y	Oh	--	--	Mn	--	--	MW, S, E	Tchr,cnty spt	0
41.1	M	60	--	SD	50	SD	Engl	Engl	Engl	Wi	Pa	Pa	E	Teachr,farmr	Germ
41.2	M	58	12	SD	58	--	Il	--	--	Il	--	--	0	Farmer	0
41.3	M	34	14	SD	26	Ca, WWII 3y	SD	Oh	Oh	SD	--	--	WWII	Stock raiser	0
42.1	M	61	10	SD	61	--	Engl	Engl	Engl	Wi	Engl	Engl	W	Farmer	Wels
42.2	M	42	12	Mn	40	--	Mn	--	--	Ia	--	--	E&W coast	Grocer	0
42.3	M	47	12	Il	--	--	Il	--	--	Il	--	--	MW, Can	Merchant	0
43.1	M	77	8	Ia	70	--	NH	NH	NH	NH	NH	NH	E, S	Farmer	0
43.2	F	52	13	SD	52	--	Germ	Germ	Germ	Pol	--	--	E	r.Cnty offcl	Germ
44.1	M	74	12	SD	74	--	Engl	Engl	Engl	Wi	Engl	Engl	MW	Frmr,cnty off	0
44.2	F	58	12	SD	58	--	Oh	Irel	Irel	Mn	Irel	Irel	US, Can	Housewife	0
45.1	F	65	12	SD	65	SD	Il	Can	Vt	Ia	Ma	Pa	MW	Housewife	0
45.2	M	71	12	Ia	67	Ia 4y	--	--	--	Irel	--	--	S, W	Farmer	0
45.3	M	68	8	SD	45	SD	RI	RI	Ma	Nb	--	Nb	W, Can	Rancher	?Ind
47.1	M	40	9	Nb	27	SD	In	In	In	Nb	Nb	Nb	US	Farmer	0
47.2	F	53	9	SD	25	SD	Pol	Pol	Pol	SD	Germ	SD	0	Postmaster	Germ
48.1	F	38	8	SD	25	Nb, Oh	Nb	Swed	Swed	Nb	Swed	Swed	E&W coast	Hsewfe,bkkpr	0
48.2	F	38	12	SD	38	Il 2y, Ca 1y	Ky	Ky	Ks	Nb	In	Ms	W	Hsewfe,bkkpr	0
48.3	F	40	12	SD	40	--	Nb	Czs	Czs	Ks	Czs	Ia	MW,S,Can	Tchr,PO clrk	0
48.4	F	37	8	ND	34	--	In	Swed	Germ	ND	Holl	--	W	Ranch wife	0
49.1	M	64	9	SD	41	SD	Ks	Irel	Irel	Wi	NY	Irel	E, S	Rancher	0
49.2	M	--	8	SD	29	--	Ia	Ia	Ia	Ia	Wi	Ia	E&W coast, Can	Farmer	0
49.3	M	48	12	Nb	30	Nb	Pa	--	--	Oh	--	--	MW	Asst PM	0
49.4	F	60	11	SD	41	SD	Can	Can	Can	SD	Germ	Germ	--	Farm wife	?Ger
50.1	F	62	11	SD	62	0	Germ	Germ	Germ	Mo	Pa	Mo	MW,E,Mex	Farm wife	Germ
50.2	F	64	12	SD	59	SD	Aust	Aust	Aust	Czs	Czs	Czs	MW, Ca	Housewife	Cz
51.1	M	65	14	SD	31	SD	Il	Germ	Il	Pa	Pa	Irel	0	Banker	0
51.2	M	45	7	Ia	18	Ca 32-33, Ia 05-18	Ia	Ia	Ia	Ia	Ia	Neth	W	Farmer	0
51.3	M	51	8	SD	37	SD	Germ	Germ	Germ	Ia	--	--	Ca, Il	Farmer	0
51.4	F	45	12	SD	45	--	Wi	NY	Scot	SD	--	--	W, MW	Lumber dealr	0
52.1	M	67	7	SD	67	SD	Germ	Germ	Germ	Germ	Germ	Germ	0	Farmer	Germ
52.2	M	74	6	Ia	47	Ia 79-06	Md	USA	USA	Oh	USA	USA	0	Farmer	0
53.1	M	--	8	SD	59	SD	NY	NY	NY	Engl	Engl	Engl	MW, Ks	Farmer	0
54.1	F	49	8	SD	49	--	Engl	Engl	Engl	Engl	Engl	Engl	MW	County offcl	Germ
54.2	F	56	9	SD	6	SD	Neth	Neth	Neth	Neth	Neth	Neth	0	Housewife	0
55.1	F	44	10	SD	44	SD	SD	Norw	Norw	Norw	Norw	Norw	MW	Housewife	?Nor
55.2	M	76	4	SD	76	0	Norw	Norw	Norw	Norw	Norw	Norw	US	Farmer	Norw
55.3	M	60	9	Ia	40	Ia 11y	Wi	Norw	Norw	Ia	Norw	Norw	MW	Farmer	0
56.1	M	63	12	SD	63	0	NJ	NJ	NJ	Co	Tx	Mo	0	County offcl	0
56.2	F	57	15	SD	45	Il 4y, Ca 3y	Va	WV	WV	Ia	Ia	Ia	US	Nurse	0
56.3	F	62	12	SD	62	--	Can	Engl	Engl	Wi	Can	Wi	Ca,Ia,NM	County audtr	0
56.4	F	--	9	SD	50	--	NY	Engl	Engl	Denm	Denm	Denm	E&W coast	Teacher	0
57.1	M	64	10	Ma	44	Ma 88-08, SD	Ma	Irel	Irel	Ma	Ma	Ma	E, MW, S	Merch,stockmn	Siou

No.	Sex	Age	Sch	Bpl	Yrs Res	Else-where	F	PGF	PGM	M	MGF	MGM	Travel	Occupation	For. Lang
57.2	M	59	9	Nb	40	Nb	Ia	Pa	Pa	Nb	Pa	Pa	0	Farmer,merch	Siou
58.1	F	60	10	Ia	39	SD	Ia	USA	USA	Ia	USA	Pa	MW	County offcl	0
58.2	M	49	14	SD	30	Ok 23-29, Ca 37-47	Ks	Can	Fran	Ia	--	SD	US	County judge	0
58.3	M	75	8	Nb	50	SD	Mn	--	Mn	Nb	Oh	Nb	US, Can	Clerical wkr	Siou
59.1	F	63	12	SD	63	SD	Mi	Pa	Pa	SD	Oh	SD	US	Housewife	Siou
59.2	F	66	10	SD	66	0	In	In	In	SD	Fran	SD	Wa,Or,Mn	Housekeeper	Siou
60.1	F	41	--	0	41	0	Russ	--	--	Russ	--	--	0	Housewife	Germ
60.2	F	40	8	SD	35	0	Nb	Germ	Germ	SD	Germ	Germ	0	Housewife	Germ
61.1	M	19	14	SD	19	0	Ia	Germ	Ia	SD	Pa	SD	MW	Frmr,student	0
61.2	M	53	10	Nb	45	Nb 8y	Wi	A-H	A-H	Czs	A-H	A-H	MW	Farmer	Cz
62.1	F	65	16	Ks	14	Ks 4y, Ia 2y	Ia	Germ	Oh	Ia	--	--	MW,Can,S	r.Tchr,hsewf	Germ
62.2	M	38	8	SD	38	0	Neth	Neth	Neth	Neth	Neth	Neth	WWII, Australia	Farmer	Du
62.3	F	64	9	Ia	41	0	Germ	Germ	Germ	Wi	Pol	Germ	E&W coast	Farm wife	Germ
62.4	M	--	6	Ia	--	--	Germ	--	--	Germ	--	--	MW, Ca	Farmer	Germ
63.1	M	64	8	Russ	53	Russ 87-98	Russ	Russ	Russ	Russ	Russ	Russ	US	Farmer	Germ
63.2	M	54	14	SD	54	SD	Russ	Russ	Russ	Russ	Russ	Russ	Il, DC	Farmer	Germ
63.3	M	37	8	SD	7	SD	SD	Germ	Germ	SD	Germ	Germ	US, WWII	--	Germ
64.1	F	77	5	SD	77	--	Germ	Germ	Germ	Germ	Germ	Germ	Ky, Tx	Housewife	0
64.2	F	81	10	SD	80	Il 1y	NY	NY	NY	Mi	NH	RI	MW,NW,SW	Housewife	0
65.1	F	66	10	Ia	43	SD	In	--	--	Il	Il	Il	SD	Housewife	0
65.2	M	61	8	SD	--	--	Germ	Germ	Germ	Germ	Germ	Germ	W	r. Farmer	Germ
65.3	M	74	8	SD	74	--	Denm	Denm	Denm	Denm	Denm	Denm	US	Farmer	Dan
66.1	M	42	12	SD	42	--	SD	Norw	Norw	Norw	Norw	Norw	MW	Farmer	0
66.2	M	66	12	SD	66	--	Norw	Norw	Norw	Norw	Norw	Norw	0	r.	0
67.1	M	68	8	SD	63	--	Germ	--	--	Germ	--	--	US, Can	r. Farmer	Germ
67.2	F	58	8	Ia	22	SD	Ia	Germ	Germ	Ia	Germ	Germ	SE	Farm wife	0
68.1	M	46	14	SD	31	Ia 31-46	Ia	Irel	Irel	Can	Can	Can	US	Sheriff, implemnt dlr	0
68.2	F	71	12	Ia	48	Ia, SD	Denm	Denm	Denm	Denm	Denm	Denm	E&W coast	Teacher	Dan
69.1	F	36	16	SD	11	SD	Mn	Can	Can	SD	Wi	Wi	MW	Teacher	0
69.2	M	41	14	Ia	35	Ia 6y	Germ	Germ	Germ	Lux	Lux	Lux	US	Mail carrier	Germ

NEBRASKA

No.	Sex	Age	Sch	Bpl	Yrs Res	Else-where	F	PGF	PGM	M	MGF	MGM	Travel	Occupation	For. Lang
1.1	M	53	13	Nb	--	--	NC	NC	NC	Va	Va	Pa	US,Can,Mex	Rancher	0
1.2	F	60	14	Nb	50	Nb	Wi	Me	Pa	Mn	NY	NY	US	Housewife	0
1.3	F	54	12	Ia	43	Ia 11y	Ia	Irel	Can	Ia	Irel	Irel	Or,Co,Wy	County offcl	?Ger
1.4	F	60	12	Nb	45	Nb	Pa	--	--	Ia	Ks	--	MW, E	Bank cashier	0
1.5	M	55	8	Mo	45	Mo 4y,Tx 2y,Wy 4y	Mo	--	--	Mo	Ky	--	Can,MW,S	Rancher	0
2.1	M	61	14	Nb	61	0	NY	NY	NY	NY	NY	NY	E&W coast	Merchant	0
2.2	M	--	6	Mo	34	Mo, Nb	In	In	In	In	In	In	MW, W	r. Rancher	0
3.1	M	90	--	Ia	52	Ia, Nb	Ia	Irel	Irel	Oh	Pa	Pa	Can, W	Farmer	0
3.2	F	59	10	Nb	49	Id 1y, SD 2y	NH	--	--	NY	Germ	Germ	W	Teacher, housewife	0
3.3	F	63	10	Nb	61	Nb	Nb	Pa	--	Nb	--	--	SW	Farm wife	0
4.1	M	58	10	Nb	56	Nb	NY	NY	--	Oh	Oh	Oh	0	Farmer	0
4.2	M	61	12	Nb	44	--	Il	Pa	Pa	Nb	Va	Va	US	Stock raiser	0
5.1	M	64	11	Nb	64	--	In	Irel	Irel	Pa	Pa	Pa	Can, Mex	Lumber dealr	Siou
5.2	M	58	11	Nb	58	0	Ia	Engl	Engl	In	Scot	Engl	W	Bankr,ranchr	0
5.3	F	49	9	Ks	24	Nb	Ks	USA	USA	Ia	USA	USA	Or, Tx	Tchr,ranchwf	0
6.1	M	41	12	Nb	41	--	NJ	--	--	Ia	--	--	--	Rancher	0
6.2	M	63	9	SD	50	--	Mo	--	--	Ia	--	--	W, S	Banker	0
6.3	M	45	12	Co	43	--	Nb	Me	Oh	Nb	Wi	Il	0	Farmer	0
7.1	M	45	12	Nb	45	Fl 8m	Il	Il	Il	Ia	Germ	Ia	US	Postal clerk	0
7.2	M	--	--	Nb	20	Nb	Il	--	--	In	--	--	--	Bankr,minstr	0

No.	Sex	Age	Sch	Bpl	Yrs Res	Else-where	F	PGF	PGM	M	MGF	MGM	Travel	Occupation	For. Lang
8.1	M	--	4	Il	69	Il	Germ	Germ	Germ	Germ	Germ	Germ	E, W	Rancher	Germ
8.2	M	70	12	Nb	70	--	Nova	Nova	Nova	In	Mi	Va	MW, S	r. Farmer	0
9.1	F	41	12	Nb	50	Nb	Irel	Irel	Irel	Scot	Scot	Scot	MW, S	Housewife	0
10.1	F	59	12	Ks	37	Ks	Mi	Mi	--	Il	Il	Il	Ca,Ks,Mi, Pa	Housewife	0
10.2	M	75	--	Germ	--	Germ 6y, Nb 69y	Germ	Germ	Germ	Germ	Germ	Germ	0	Farmer	Germ
11.1	M	64	12	Nb	60	Nb	Czs	Czs	Czs	Il	Czs	Spai	C	County offcl	Cz ?Ger
11.2	M	69	10	In	25	Nb	Swed	Swed	Swed	Swed	Swed	Swed	W, Ca	Farmer	Swed
11.3	F	78	10	Vt	59	NY 92-93	Vt	Vt	Vt	Vt	Vt	Vt	SW	Farm wife	0
12.1	F	88	--	Denm	25	Nb	Denm	Denm	Denm	Denm	Denm	Denm	0	--	Dan
12.2	M	50	7	Nb	50	--	Ia	Germ	Neth	Il	--	--	0	Farmer	0
12.3	F	70	--	Nb	57	SD 92-10	Il	Vt	Vt	Il	Germ	Germ	MW	r. Teacher	0
13.1	M	75	10	Nb	75	0	Swed	Swed	Swed	Norw	Norw	Norw	W. E	Weed eradctr	Norw Swed
13.2	F	50	--	Nb	--	0	--	--	--	Pa	--	--	0	--	Germ
14.1	M	70	--	Nb	--	Nb	--	--	Germ	Germ	Germ	Germ	SW	r.	Germ
14.2	M	55	12	Nb	55	Nb	Czs	Czs	Czs	Czs	Czs	Czs	0	Farmer	Cz
14.3	F	58	10	Nb	38	Nb	Mi	Neth	Engl	Mi	Engl	Engl	MW,W,Can	Tchr,ofc clk	0
15.1	F	63	8	Nb	50	Nb	Engl	Engl	Engl	Engl	Engl	Engl	MW, W	Farm wife	0
15.2	F	73	8	Nb	30	Wi 02-03, Nb	Engl	Engl	Engl	Engl	Engl	Engl	Ca	r.Tchr,hsewf	0
15.3	F	74	7	Nb	64	Nb	Germ	Germ	Germ	Germ	Germ	Germ	Ca,Tx,Mex	Housewife	0
16.1	M	63	8	Ia	39	Ia 16y	Swed	Swed	Swed	Swed	Swed	Swed	C	Farmer	Swed
16.2	M	55	10	Engl	30	Co 17-25	Engl	Wale	Wale	Wale	Engl	Engl	US	Court officl	Wels
17.1	F	63	12	Nb	63	0	Irel	Irel	Irel	Can	Can	Can	0	Housewife	0
17.2	F	--	5	Nb	79	--	Germ	Germ	Germ	Germ	Germ	Germ	W	Housewife	Germ
18.1	M	70	10	Ia	51	Nb	NY	NY	Germ	NH	NH	NH	W	r. Merchant	0
18.2	M	72	11	Il	56	Nb	Il	--	--	Il	--	--	US	r.Hdwe dealr	0
18.3	F	46	15	Nb	13	Nb	Czs	Czs	Czs	Nb	Czs	Czs	E, W, Can	PO clk,hsewf	?Cz
19.1	M	61	12	Ia	46	--	Wi	Engl	Wi	Pa	Pa	Pa	W	PO clerk	?Ger
19.2	M	42	16	Nb	42	--	Ia	Ia	Oh	Mo	Pa	Oh	US	Publisher	0
19.3	M	41	9	Nb	39	Co 33-35	Russ	Germ	Germ	Russ	--	--	W	Shoe reprman	Germ
20.1	F	41	13	Nb	--	Nb	Nb	Oh	Oh	Nb	Ia	Mn	0	Housewife	0
20.2	F	53	12	Nb	45	Co 23-25, Nb	Irel	Irel	Il	Il	Me		Can,MW,W	Teachr,book- keepr,hsewfe	0
21.1	M	79	6	In	--	Ks 2y,Nb	In	--	--	Ky	--	--	0	r.	0
21.2	M	47	12	Nb	47	0	Ks	--	--	Wi	--	--	0	County ofcr, farmer	0
22.1	M	52	12	Nb	41	Co 09-20	Il	NY	NY	Il	NY	NY	MW,W,Can	Rancher	0
22.2	M	55	12	Nb	55	0	--	In	In	--	Irel	--	E&W coast	Rancher	0
22.3	F	50	13	Nb	50	--	Irel	Irel	Irel	Irel	Irel	Irel	US	Ranch wife	0
23.1	M	73	11	Va	66	Va 1883, Nb	--	--	--	Va	--	--	E&W coast	Rancher	0
23.2	F	36	9	Nb	33	Nb	Va	Va	Va	Va	Va	Va	Or,Ca,Wi	Nurse	0
23.3	F	50	AM	Nb	38	Co 21-25, Hi 28-32	Ia	Wale	NY	Ia	Irel	Irel	US, Can	Teacher	0
24.1	M	36	--	Nb	36	--	--	--	--	Nb	Oh	Oh	0	Merchant	0
24.2	M	45	13	Nb	--	--	Nb	Nb	Nb	Can	Can	Can	US, WWII	Rancher	0
25.1	M	56	12	Nb	56	0	Oh	--	--	Oh	--	--	W	--	0
25.2	M	54	9	Nb	54	0	Oh	Oh	Oh	Pa	Pa	Pa	W, E, S	Rancher	0
25.3	M	50	8	Nb	45	--	Denm	Denm	Denm	Denm	Denm	Denm	N	Rancher	Dan
26.1	F	69	8	Nb	69	--	Nb	--	--	Nb	--	Engl	0	Farm wife	0
26.2	M	73	8	Nb	71	--	Pa	Germ	Germ	WV	--	--	US	r. Farmer	0
26.3	M	41	8	Nb	41	--	Il	--	--	Ia	--	--	0	Farmer	0
27.1	M	79	10	Ia	68	Ia 11y	NY	Ma	Ma	Engl	Engl	Engl	Ca, W	Lumber dealr	0
28.1	M	63	8	Nb	35	Nb	Oh	--	--	Oh	--	--	0	Rancher	0
28.2	M	51	12	Mn	38	Ia 13y	Ia	Norw	Norw	Ia	Norw	Norw	0	Lawyer	0
29.1	F	45	12	Nb	45	--	Ia	Il	Il	Swed	Swed	Swed	0	Bookkeeper	0
29.2	M	--	16	Nb	25	Nb	Il	--	--	Md	--	--	MW, W	County offcl	0

No.	Sex	Age	Sch	Bpl	Yrs Res	Else-where	F	PGF	PGM	M	MGF	MGM	Travel	Occupation	For. Lang
29.3	F	45	12	Nb	31	Nb	Nb	--	--	Il	--	--	Il, Ia	Housewife	0
30.1	M	46	8	Nb	30	Nb	Ia	Swed	Swed	Nb	USA	USA	MW, E	Farmer	0
30.2	F	61	8	Nb	61	--	Germ	Germ	Germ	Germ	Germ	Germ	MW	Housewife	Germ
31.1	F	44	16	Nb	18	Nb	Germ	Germ	Germ	Wi	Germ	Germ	0	Housewife	0
31.2	F	47	--	Nb	41	Nb	Swed	Swed	Swed	Swed	Swed	Swed	0	County supt	0
32.1	M	48	10	Nb	12	Nb	--	--	--	--	--	--	0	Salesman	0
32.2	F	52	12	Nb	52	--	Germ	Germ	Germ	Germ	Germ	Germ	US	Tchr,phone op	Germ
32.3	F	61	10	Nb	61	--	Pa	Pa	Pa	Nb	Germ	Germ	Mo, Co	Teacher	0
33.1	F	54	12	Nb	30	Ks 2y,Nb	Oh	Va	Oh	Mn	Vt	Me	MW, W	Housewife	Germ
33.2	M	61	12	Nb	61	--	Ia	Scot	Pa	Nb	Ia	Va	US	Farmer	0
34.1	F	48	13	Mo	24	Ks, Co 16-27	Mo	Va	Mo	Il	Pa	Ky	E, MW, W, Can	r. PO clerk, teacher	0
34.2	F	45	12	Nb	45	--	Ks	Pa	Pa	Ks	--	--	US	Farm wife	0
35.1	F	57	8	Oh	39	Il 13y	Oh	--	--	Oh	--	--	Oh,Mi,Il, Co	Ranch wife	0
35.2	M	44	10	Nb	43	--	Nb	Denm	Denm	Ks	Mo	Mo	--	Rancher	0
35.3	F	--	8	Ia	46	--	Germ	Germ	Germ	Ia	Germ	Germ	0	Housewife	Germ
36.1	M	46	9	Nb	46	--	Il	--	--	--	--	--	0	Merchant	0
36.2	M	66	8	Nb	65	--	Oh	Engl	Ia	Ia	Ia	Ia	S	Rancher	0
36.3	F	41	13	Nb	41	0	Il	Va	Scot	Oh	Pa	Pa	C	Ranch wife	0
37.1	M	35	12	Nb	32	Nb	Nb	Nb	Nb	Nb	Nb	Nb	S	Banker, r. rancher	0
37.2	M	47	10	Nb	47	--	Wi	Germ	Germ	Il	Germ	Germ	0	Farmer	0
38.1	F	31	12	Nb	31	--	Nb	USA	Ia	Nb	Swed	Mo	W	Housewife	0
38.2	M	42	11	Nb	42	0	Ks	Irel	Irel	Nb	Il	Il	0	Rancher	0
39.1	M	62	8	Nb	31	Nb	Oh	--	--	Il	--	--	Can	Farmer	0
39.2	M	51	10	Nb	51	0	Germ	--	--	Germ	--	--	E, W	Farmer	Germ
39.3	F	80	8	Ia	78	--	NY	Vt	Vt	NY	NY	NY	SE	Farm wife	0
40.1	F	67	9	Nb	60	Nb	Can	Irel	Irel	Mi	NY	NY	Or, Mi	Farm wife	0
40.2[1]	-	--	--	--	--	--	--	--	--	--	--	--	--	--	--
40.3	F	50	12	Nb	50	0	Il	Engl	Engl	Irel	Irel	Irel	0	Teacher	0
41.1	F	--	14	Nb	21	Nb	Denm	Denm	Denm	Denm	Denm	Denm	W, S, Can	Farm wife	Dan
41.2	F	39	13	Nb	39	--	In	Oh	Pa	Nb	--	--	0	Farm wife	0
42.1	F	40	12	Nb	40	0	Nb	Germ	Nb	Germ	Germ	Germ	0	Farm wife	Germ
42.2	F	50	12	Nb	10	Nb	Nb	Czs	Czs	Czs	Czs	Czs	US	Credit mgr	Cz
42.3	F	54	12	Nb	54	--	Il	Il	Il	Nb	Oh	Nb	Ca, U	Teacher	0
43.1	M	62	18	Nb	62	0	Czs	Czs	Czs	Czs	Czs	Czs	W, Can	Attorney	Cz Germ
43.2	M	75	12	Nb	68	Nb	Germ	Germ	Germ	Germ	Germ	Germ	0	Grain & lumbr dealr	0
43.3	M	70	12	Czs	52	Nb	Czs	Czs	Czs	Czs	Czs	Czs	W, NW	Village mgr	Cz
44.1	M	68	9	Mn	53	Mn 84-92, Nb	Ks	Germ	Germ	In	Germ	Germ	--	Mail carrier	Germ
44.2	M	30	12	Nb	30	--	In	Germ	In	Nb	Germ	Germ	E&W coast, Can	Real est & insur agent	0
45.1	M	48	13	Nb	0	Germ	Germ	Germ	Nb	Germ	Germ	Germ	MW	Farmer	Germ
45.2	M	53	12	Nb	53	--	Oh	Oh	Mi	Nb	Fran	Fran	US	Farmer	0
46.1	M	80	8	Swed	67	Il 1y,Nb	Swed	Swed	Swed	Swed	Swed	Swed	C	Cattl raisr, ex-sheriff	Swed
46.2	M	31	12	Nb	31	0	Russ	Germ	Germ	Russ	Germ	Germ	0	Farmer	Germ
47.1	M	62	9	Oh	60	0	--	Engl	Neth	Engl	Engl	Engl	US	Farmer	0
47.2	M	63	12	SD	47	SD -07	Irel	Irel	Irel	Il	Pa	Pa	W, S, N	Farmer	0
47.3	F	58	12	Nb	58	0	Oh	Il	--	Il	--	--	C	r.tchr,bkkpr	?Ger
47.4	M	54	8	Nb	54	0	Irel	Irel	Irel	Irel	Irel	Irel	0	Farmer	0
48.1	M	38	8	Nb	23	Nb	Nb	Il	Germ	Nb	Germ	Germ	M, W	Farmer	Germ
48.2	F	45	12	Nb	28	Nb	Nb	Germ	Germ	Germ	Germ	Germ	W	Housewife	--
48.3	M	43	13	Nb	43	--	Swed	Swed	Swed	Swed	Swed	Swed	W	Farmr, bankr	?Swe
49.1	M	57	8	Nb	57	--	Germ	Germ	Germ	Germ	Germ	Germ	0	Farmer	?Ger
49.2	M	67	9	Nb	22	Nb	NJ	NJ	NJ	Ia	Pa	Pa	W	Farmer	0

1. Known to be one of four acceptable middle-aged lifelong residents.

No.	Sex	Age	Sch	Bpl	Yrs Res	Else-where	F	PGF	PGM	M	MGF	MGM	Travel	Occupation	For. Lang
50.1	M	91	Co	Nb	91	Nb	East	Pa	Tn	NY	--	--	US, Can, Mex	Banker	Siou
50.2	M	73	12	In	68	Nb	In	In	In	In	In	Pa	MW	Farmr,ranchr	0
51.1	F	57	14	Nb	36	Nb	Il	Oh	Va	In	In	In	MW, W, S	Farm wife	0
51.2	F	47	12	Co	28	Co 2y,Nb	Ia	Oh	Ia	Ia	Pa	Il	W	News corresp	0
51.3	F	64	MA	Nb	33	--	Il	Il	Germ	Il	Il	Il	US, Can	Teacher	Germ
52.1	M	76	16	In	45	Ks 11y, Nb	In	NY	NY	Ky	Ky	Ky	W, E	r.	0
52.2	F	65	8	Nb	65	--	Scot	Scot	Scot	Scot	Scot	Scot	MW	Housewife	0
53.1	M	70	--	Nb	70	--	Swed	Swed	Swed	Ia	Swed	Swed	US	r. Farmer	Swed
53.2	F	58	12	Nb	58	--	Swed	Swed	Swed	Swed	Swed	Swed	MW, Can	Farm wife	Swed
54.1	M	51	9	Nb	51	--	Ia	Pa	Pa	Ia	Ia	Ia	W, MW	Printr,sales	0
54.2	M	67	12	Pa	66	--	Pa	Pa	Pa	Pa	Pa	Pa	E&W coast	Postmaster	0
55.1	M	--	12	Ia	60	--	Swed	Swed	Swed	Ia	Swed	Swed	W, NE	Druggist	?Swe
55.2	M	76	8	Germ	62	--	Germ	Germ	Germ	Germ	Germ	Germ	0	Farmer	Germ
56.1	F	51	16	Nb	24	Nb	Il	Il	Il	Il	Il	Il	MW	Farm wife	0
56.2	M	50	12	Nb	46	Ca 25-29	Nb	Denm	Denm	Denm	Denm	Denm	Ca, Mn	Farmr, sales	0
56.3	M	63	9	Nb	63	--	Germ	Denm	Denm	Germ	Denm	Denm	US	Farmer	Germ
56.4	F	54	8	Nb	26	Nb	Germ	Germ	Germ	Il	Germ	Germ	US	Housewife	Germ
56.5	M	57	16	Nb	57	--	NY	NY	NJ	Tn	Vt	NH	W, S, N	Farmer	0
57.1	M	58	12	Nb	58	0	Nb	Oh	Oh	Nb	NY	NY	MW,S,Can	Farmr,meatpkr	0
57.2	M	74	9	Pa	67	Pa,Nb 87	Pa	--	--	Pa	--	--	0	Carpenter	0
57.3	M	63	7	Ia	58	Ia 5y	Ia	--	--	Ia	--	--	E, S, WWI	r. Painter	0
57.4	M	75	14	Nb	75	0	--	--	--	--	--	--	MW, S	Farmer	0
58.1	M	47	14	Nb	47	0	Ia	USA	USA	Swed	Swed	Swed	US	Office clerk	0
58.2	F	37	12	Nb	34	Nb	Nb	Pa	Ia	Nb	Oh	Oh	W, MW, S, Can	Housewife, r. teacher	0
59.1	F	36	12	Nb	36	0	Nb	--	--	Nb	Germ	--	Ca	Housewife	0
59.2	M	50	9	Nb	50	--	Germ	Germ	Germ	Germ	Germ	Germ	W, MW, S	Farmer	Germ
60.1	F	59	16	Nb	59	--	Nb	Denm	Denm	Mo	Mo	Mo	E, W, Can	Housewife, r. teacher	0
60.2	F	60	--	Nb	5	Nb	Mo	Irel	Irel	Il	Irel	Irel	E&W coast	Pharmacist	0
60.3	F	60	16	Nb	52	Id 13-18, Nb	Il	Pa	Pa	Nb	Engl	Nb	World tour	Teacher	0
61.1	M	85	0	Nb	70	Tx 85-99, In, Nb	Germ	Germ	Germ	Germ	Germ	Germ	US, Can	Farmer	Germ
61.2	F	45	13	Nb	24	Nb	Germ	Germ	Germ	Nb	Can	Can	W, MW	Teacher	0
61.3	M	46	8	Nb	46	--	Wi	Germ	Germ	Il	Germ	Germ	0	County offcl	Germ
62.1	M	80	8	Nb	80	0	Can	Can	Can	NY	NY	NY	E&W coast	r.	0
62.2	M	59	12	Ks	56	--	In	--	--	In	--	--	W, Il	County judge	0
63.1	M	58	8	Germ	41	--	Germ	Germ	Germ	Denm	Denm	Denm	S	Farmer	Germ Dan
63.2	F	51	9	Nb	51	--	Denm	Denm	Denm	Denm	Denm	Denm	MW,E,Can	Housewife	Dan
64.1	M	74	14	Wi	73	--	Swit	Swit	Swit	Swit	Swit	Swit	US	Merchant	Swis
65.1	M	39	12	Nb	39	--	Germ	Germ	Germ	Germ	Germ	Germ	Ca,Il,Mo, Oh	Farmer	?Ger
65.2	M	--	10	Nb	68	Nb	Il	NH	NY	Wi	--	--	C	Farmer	0
66.1	F	67	12	Nb	20	Nb	Swed	Swed	Swed	Swed	Swed	Swed	Mn, DC	Housewife	0
67.1	M	85	20	Nb	80	Il	Pa	Pa	Pa	Oh	Oh	Oh	WWI	r. Physician	0
67.2	F	48	16	Nb	48	--	Denm	Denm	Denm	Denm	Denm	Denm	Ia, SD	Farm wife	Dan
67.3	F	73	8	Nb	36	--	WV	--	--	In	--	--	Co, W	Housewife	0
68.1	M	66	12	Nb	12	Nb	Oh	--	--	Il	Il	Il	Mo,Il,Co	r. County clerk,farmer	Germ
68.2	M	--	14	In	33	Nb	In	Scot	In	In	Va	In	US, Can	Farmer	0
68.3	F	55	14	Nb	25	Nb	Mi	NY	Mi	Nb	NY	Pa	E, W, Can	Ranch wife, librarian	0
69.1	M	72	10	In	--	Nb	In	--	--	Mi	--	--	0	r. Ofc clerk	0
69.2	M	91	10	Oh	--	Oh, Ia, Nb 1884	NY	NY	NY	Oh	Ct	--	Ca	Farmer	0
70.1	M	48	14	Nb	--	Il	Il	Pa	Pa	Mo	Scot	Mo	US	Postmaster	0
70.2	F	50	12	Ks	45	Co 5y	Ia	Ia	Ia	Ks	Ks	Ks	Co, Ks	Hsewfe,bkkpr	0

117

No.	Sex	Age	Sch	Bp1	Yrs Res	Else-where	F	PGF	PGM	M	MGF	MGM	Travel	Occupation	For. Lang
71.1	M	64	8	Nb	64	0	Germ	Germ	Germ	Germ	Germ	Germ	E&W coast	Farmer	Germ
71.2	M	74	13	NY	69	Nb	Vt	Vt	Vt	Engl	Engl	Engl	E	Teacher	0
73.1	F	69	9	Nb	69	--	In	Ky	Ky	In	--	--	US	r. Farm wife	0
73.2	M	60	--	Nb	60	--	Denm	Denm	Denm	Denm	Denm	Denm	C, MW	Farmer	?Dan
74.1	M	59	10	Nb	59	0	Il	Il	Il	Il	Il	Il	US, Mex	Farmer	0
74.2	M	60	7	Nb	60	--	Germ	Germ	Germ	Nb	Germ	Germ	0	Farmer	Germ
75.1	M	70	12	Il	44	Co 86-90	In	Va	Va	In	Va	Va	US	r. Salesman	0
75.2	F	64	9	Nb	64	0	Germ	Germ	Germ	Wi	Germ	Germ	MW, C	Insur agent	?Ger
76.1	M	45	12	Nb	45	--	Il	Il	Germ	Il	Il	Il	Il,Ia,Ca, Ok	Farmer	0
76.2	M	--	10	Il	51	0	Swed	Swed	Swed	Il	Swed	Swed	US, WWI	Farmer	0
77.1	M	46	8	Nb	--	--	Eur	Eur	Eur	Nb	Eur	Eur	0	Farmer	Cz
77.2	M	50	10	Nb	20	0	Il	Pa	Pa	Il	Swit	Il	US, Can, Mex	Farmer	0
77.3	F	36	13	Nb	36	--	Nb	Wi	Nb	Nb	Czs	Nb	0	Housewife	Cz
78.1	F	79	--	Nb	42	Ca 06-09, Nb	Il	Irel	Scot	Il	Irel	Irel	SE,SW,Wa	Farm wife	0
78.2	M	60	9	Nb	60	--	Nb	Germ	Germ	Nb	--	--	0	Farmer	0
78.3	M	59	12	Nb	59	0	Pa	Pa	Pa	Nb	Pa	Pa	E&W coast	Farmer	Germ
79.1	M	54	9	Nb	32	Ks 13-19, Nb	Il	Pa	Ky	Ia	In	In	S, E, Can	Farmer	0
79.2	F	46	16	Nb	23	Nb	Nb	Oh	Oh	Nb	Oh	Oh	MW	Farm wife	0
79.3	F	66	--	Nb	66	0	Mi	Can	Can	Can	Can	Can	Mi, W	Housewife	0
80.1	M	51	--	Nb	51	--	Ia	--	--	Ia	--	--	0	Police offcr	0
80.2	F	59	9	Ks	36	--	Il	Il	Il	Pa	Pa	Pa	Il,Co,Mo	Farm wife	0
80.3	M	64	9	Nb	64	--	Irel	--	--	Scot	--	--	Ca,Mo,Il, Ky	Fireman	0
81.1	M	37	11	Nb	37	--	Ia	Nb	Ia	Nb	Oh	Oh	WWII	Parts foremn	0
81.2	M	33	8	Nb	33	0	Nb	Nb	Nb	Ia	Oh	Oh	US	Farmer	0
82.1	M	68	12	Ia	8	Ia 10y, Nb	Il	Il	Il	Il	Il	Il	SW	Farmer	0
82.2	M	64	8	Nb	64	--	Ia	USA	USA	Ia	USA	USA	Co	Farmer	0
83.1	M	59	12	Nb	43	Co 4y,Nb	Oh	Irel	Irel	Mo	--	--	E&W coast	Banker	0
83.2	F	57	12	Nb	50	Nb	Ia	Nova	Wi	Wi	Pa	Wi	Mi, Wi	Real est & insur agent	0
84.1	F	55	13	Nb	53	Nb	Ia	Ky	Ky	In	Pa	Va	0	Housewife	0
84.2	F	52	12	Nb	52	--	Ia	Ia	Ia	Il	Oh	Oh	US	Office clerk	0
85.1	M	75	12	Nb	75	--	Il	Il	Il	Pa	Pa	Pa	MW,E,Can	Merchant	0
85.2	M	99	--	Oh	74	Oh, Nb	Ma	Ma	Ma	Ma	Ma	Ma	Il,Mi,Or	r. Farmer	0
85.3	F	60	12	Nb	48	Tx 4y,Nb	Pa	Pa	Pa	Oh	Oh	Oh	US, Can, Mex	r. Merchant	0
86.1	F	52	8	Nb	40	Nb	In	--	--	Nb	--	--	0	Housewife	0
86.2	M	53	12	Nb	53	0	Mi	Scot	Scot	Il	Can	Mi	US	Banker	0
86.3	F	57	13	Nb	51	--	Wi	Germ	Germ	Ia	Swit	Germ	MW, E, W	Farm wife	0
87.1	M	68	10	Mo	65	--	Il	Va	Il	In	--	--	E	Farmer	0
87.2	M	61	12	Nb	61	0	NY	NY	NY	Pa	Pa	Germ	US, Can, Mex	Banker, insur agent	?Ger
87.3	M	47	14	Nb	37	--	Germ	Germ	Germ	Germ	Germ	Germ	Ca, Il	Farmer	Germ
88.1	M	47	12	Nb	47	--	Germ	Germ	Germ	USA	Germ	Germ	US	Farmer	Germ
88.2	M	64	12	Nb	64	0	Ia	Ia	Ia	Pa	Pa	Pa	US, Can, Mex	Lawyer	0
88.3	F	48	12	Nb	48	--	Ks	Oh	Oh	Nb	Irel	Il	US	Merchant	0
89.1	F	70	13	Ks	60	Ks -92, Nb	Il	Oh	Can	Il	Oh	Pa	Il,Tx,Ca	r. Teacher, farm wife	0
89.2	F	73	10	Ia	50	Co 3y,Wy 1y,Nb	Germ	Germ	Germ	Germ	Germ	Germ	E&W coast	Housewife	?Ger
90.1	M	60	MA	Nb	60	--	Il	NY	NY	Il	Il	Il	US	Sch official	Germ
90.2	F	21	12	Nb	21	--	In	Germ	Germ	Nb	Il	Pol	S, E, MW	Office clerk	0
90.3	F	70	14	Nb	70	Nb	Il	Ky	Irel	Wi	Irel	Wi	E&W coast	r. Teacher, county officl	0

118

No.	Sex	Age	Sch	Bpl	Yrs Res	Else-where	F	PGF	PGM	M	MGF	MGM	Travel	Occupation	For. Lang
91.1	M	41	12	Nb	41	0	Nb	Swit	Lux	Oh	Swit	--	WWII	Bankr, real est agent	0
91.2	M	53	12	Nb	51	Nb	Nb	Ky	Il	Nb	Ky	Il	US	Farmer	0
92.1	F	35	12	Nb	14	Nb	Nb	Germ	Nb	Nb	Germ	Il	0	Housewife	?Ger
93.1	M	61	10	Nb	61	--	Pa	Pa	Pa	Pa	Pa	Pa	C, MW	Farmer	0
93.2	M	66	12	Nb	66	--	Mo	Fran	Fran	Fran	Fran	Fran	US, Can, Mex	Farmer	Fren
93.3	M	43	12	Nb	19	Nb	Nb	USA	USA	Germ	Germ	Germ	Il,Co,Ga	Farmer	?Ger

ABBREVIATIONS

A--Allen (fieldworker)
AAUW--American Association of University Women
AEF--American Expeditionary Force (WWI)
AFL--American Federation of Labor
Ak.--Alaska
Al.--Alabama
AOUW--Ancient Order of United Workmen
Ar.--Arkansas
assoc.--association
aux.--auxiliary
Az.--Arizona
B., b.--born
BPOE--Benevolent and Protective Order of Elks
BPW--Business and Professional Women
c.--circum (about), regarding time and distance
C.--created
Ca.--California
Can.--Canada
CB&QRR--Chicago, Burlington and Quincy Railroad
ch.--church
CNWRR--Chicago and Northwestern Railroad
co.--co-operative
Co.--Colorado; county; company
comp.--compilers
CRI&PRR--Chicago, Rock Island and Pacific Railroad
Ct.--Connecticut
DAm--Dictionary of Americanisms
DAR--Daughters of the American Revolution
D.C.--District of Columbia
De.--Delaware
dept.--department
dist.--district
e.--east(ern)
ed.--editor, edition
Eng.--England
F--father
FOE--Fraternal Order of Eagles
4H--4-H Club
Fl.--Florida
fw.--fieldworker
G--Glenn (fieldworker)
Ga.--Georgia
GAR--Grand Army of the Republic
GNR--Great Northern Railway

gp.; gps.--grandparent; grandparents
gr.--grade in school
H--Hanlin (fieldworker)
hdqr.--headquarters
hist.--history, historical
HS--high school
Ia.--Iowa
Ia. J. of Hist. & Pol.--Iowa Journal of History and Politics
Id.--Idaho
Il.--Illinois
In.--Indiana
inc.--incorporated
incl.--including
inf.--informant
IOOF--Independent Order of Odd Fellows
Ire.--Ireland
KC--Knights of Columbus
KP--Knights of Pythias
Ks.--Kansas
Ky.--Kentucky
L--Lowman (fieldworker)
La.--Louisiana
LOOM--Loyal Order of Moose
m.--mile(s)
M--mother; McDavid (fieldworker)
Ma.--Massachusetts
Mag. of Western Hist.--Magazine of Western History
Man.--Manitoba
Md.--Maryland
Me.--Maine
mfg.--manufacturing
mfr.--manufacturer
MGF--maternal grandfather
MGM--maternal grandmother
MGP--maternal grandparents
Mi.--Michigan
Mn.--Minnesota
Mn. Hist.--Minnesota History
Mn. Hist. Soc. Coll.--Minnesota Historical Society Collections
Mo.--Missouri
MRR--Chicago, Milwaukee, St. Paul and Pacific Railroad
Ms.--Mississippi
MS.--manuscript
Mt.--Montana
mts.--mountains

n.--north(ern)
Nb.--Nebraska
Nb. Hist.--Nebraska History
Nb. Hist. Mag.--Nebraska History Magazine
N.C.--North Carolina
n.d.--no date
N.D.--North Dakota
N.D. State Hist. Soc. Coll.--North Dakota
  State Historical Society Collections
New Eng.--New England
N.H.--New Hampshire
N.J.--New Jersey
N.M.--New Mexico
Northwest Mag.--Northwest Magazine
n.p.--no pagination
NPR--Northern Pacific Railway
Nv.--Nevada
N.Y.--New York
occ.--occasional(ly)
OES--Order of the Eastern Star
Oh.--Ohio
Ok.--Oklahoma
Ont.--Ontario
Or.--Oregon
org.--organized
P--Peterson (fieldworker)
Pa.--Pennsylvania
PGF--paternal grandfather
PGM--paternal grandmother
PGP--paternal grandparents
PO--post office
pop.--population
Proc. & Coll. Nb. State Hist. Soc.--Pro-
  ceedings and Collections of the Nebras-
  ka State Historical Society
prov.--province
PTA--Parent-Teacher Association
pub.--publishing, published
Pub. Nb. State Hist. Soc.--Publications
  of the Nebraska State Historical
  Society
Que.--Quebec

R.--river
r.--retired
REA--Rural Electrification Administration
R.I.--Rhode Island
RR--railroad
s.--south(ern)
Sask.--Saskatchewan
S.C.--South Carolina
sch.--school
Scot.--Scotland
S.D.--South Dakota
S.D. Hist. Rev.--South Dakota Historical
  Review
S.D. Hist. Soc. Coll.--South Dakota His-
  torical Society Collections
soc.--society
Tn.--Tennessee
Trans. & Rep. Nb. State Hist. Soc.--
  Transactions and Reports of the Ne-
  braska State Historical Society
twp.--township
Tx.--Texas
UPRR--Union Pacific Railroad
US--United States
univ.--university
unpub.--unpublished
Ut.--Utah
Va.--Virginia
VFW--Veterans of Foreign Wars
VR--voice recording
Vt.--Vermont
w.--west(ern)
Wa.--Washington
WCTU--Women's Christian Temperance Union
Wi.--Wisconsin
Wn--Wilson (fieldworker)
Wr--Weber (fieldworker)
W.V.--West Virginia
WWI--World War I
WWII--World War II
Wy.--Wyoming
yr.--year

CHAPTER 6

Regional Speech Distribution

PHONETIC REPRESENTATION

In the assignment of content for these two volumes the pronunciation of English in the Upper Midwest was allocated to Volume 2. Although a more detailed description of sounds and symbols will appear there, a minimal use of phonetic transcription in this volume, both in Chapter 6 and in Part B, requires that the convenience of the reader be suited by including the following synoptic chart of the symbols used in this volume.

The symbols are essentially those of the International Alphabet as modified in 1930 by Hans Kurath and Bernard Bloch for use in American fieldwork. (See the full description in *Handbook of the Linguistic Geography of New England*, Chapter 4.) Two differences here result from the need to use type characters available at the time when the manuscript was being typed. Thus IPA /ı/ replaces American /ɪ/ and /ɨ/ replaces /ɨ/. Also used here is the American symbol for the low back unround vowel, /ɒ/, which, though not used in the original New England fieldwork, has been used in subsequent American research.

Vowel symbols used in this volume are shown below in the accepted vowel quadrilateral.

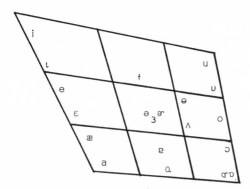

The IPA consonant symbols used are those found in the field records, even

to the use of the affricate digraphs /tʃ/ and /dʒ/ instead of the now more desirable /č/ and /ǰ/ and to the use of /j/ instead of the /y/ which is more suitable for English.

stops	p t		tʃ	k	
	b d		dʒ	g	ʔ
fricatives	f θ s	ʃ			h
	v ð z	ʒ			
sonorants	m n l r			ŋ	
semivowels	w		j		

In this volume only a few diacritics occur. Vowel tongue position slightly different from that customarily indicated by the symbol is shown by directional arrows: ˇ ˆ ˂ ˃. Since usually only a vowel class needs to be indicated, the phonemic virgules / / are used more commonly than the specific phonetic brackets [ ]. Others are:

˛	dentalization	˳	voicelessness
ʰ	aspiration	˵	rounding
ʲ	palatalization	ˈ	primary stress
˜	nasalization	ˌ	secondary stress

INTRODUCTORY COMMENT

The patterns of settlement described in Chapter 2 of this part have produced the patterns of regional variation in Upper Midwest English that are described in this chapter.

In 1949 Kurath effectively demonstrated the existence of distinct Northern and Midland dialects in the eastern

United States.[1] In 1954 Marckwardt drew upon a preliminary analysis of the data from the Linguistic Atlas of the North Central States to demonstrate that the two population groups speaking Northern and Midland varieties of English maintained their separate identities so sturdily during the westward migration that their speech likewise retained the contrast between Northern and Midland.[2]

People moving west from western New England and New York state carried their speechways into the Western Reserve of Ohio, Michigan, a narrow segment of Indiana, and the northern third of Illinois. These people constituted a speech community; they had their own distinctive ways of responding in their language to a situation calling for communication with others. Their dialect is Northern.

Settlers moving west over the Old National Trail from the Mid-Atlantic states carried their speechways into central and southern Ohio, a narrow central belt in Indiana, and the central third of Illinois. They, too, constituted a speech community; they had their own distinctive ways of responding in their language to the need to communicate with others. Their dialect is Midland.

The map-lines, or isoglosses, setting off significant Northern features from Midland features were drawn even more decisively in 1962 by Roger W. Shuy,[3] who found that the main bundle of isoglosses, or dialect boundary, after entering Illinois from Indiana about one hundred miles south of Chicago, gradually bends northward and then turns due west to reach the Mississippi River at Rock Island. A secondary boundary runs somewhat south of that one in the western part of the state, reaching the Mississippi across from Davenport, Iowa.

A contributing population stream constituting a somewhat different speech community moved west through the Cumberland Gap from western Virginia and West Virginia into Kentucky, the southern half of Indiana, and the southern third of Illinois. The speech of these people Kurath has termed "South Midland." Whether a more accurate designation might be "Midland Southern," as Charles-James Bailey has proposed,[4] is here irrelevant to the fact of its existence as identified by the presence of a unique combination of Midland features, Southern features, and other features characteristic of the southern Appalachian regions.

As has been described in Chapter 2, the settlement of the Upper Midwest is essentially a continuation of the western migration that first populated the North Central states. In the Upper Midwest, however, several factors, principally the ready availability of the Mississippi River as a new avenue for northward movement, considerably reduced the fairly sharp dialect contrasts revealed in the North Central survey.

Although this reduction is not so great as to justify concluding that Northern and Midland dialects have merged in the Upper Midwest, it must be recognized that the settlement of some Midland speakers in northern Iowa and southern Minnesota did yield a certain infusion of the prevailing Northern speech by some Midland forms. The first sampling of the Iowa field data revealed a curious and apparently inconsistent distribution of Midland and Northern terms in the speech of more than one informant. Inevitably, the second generation in each speech community would tend to modify its pure dialect by borrowing terms from the other dialect. Thus a given speaker of Northern background might easily use some Midland words acquired from his neighbors; likewise a Midland speaker would acquire some Northern forms. The speech of any one person in such an area, his idiolect, would thus in some measure become a mixture, a hybrid. But the element of chance in such borrowing is large. In northern Iowa and southern Minnesota, for instance, one Midland speaker might shift from *wait on* to *wait for*, but another one might not. There would be no general borrowing of a Northern term by Midland speakers or of a Midland term by Northern speakers.

A striking confirmation of the individual dialect diversity revealed by

1. Hans Kurath, *A Word Geography of the Eastern United States*. Ann Arbor, 1949.
2. Albert H. Marckwardt, "Principal and subsidiary dialect areas in the North Central States," *Publication of the American Dialect Society*, 27.31-15 (1957).
3. Roger W. Shuy, *The Boundary between the Northern and Midland Dialects in Illinois*. Western Reserve University Ph.D. dissertation, 1962.
4. In a paper presented at the summer meeting of the Linguistic Society of America, Urbana, Illinois, July 27, 1968.

the field records appeared later in the study of Iowa checklists by Charles Houck.[5] He subjected to computerized statistical analysis the lexical data taken from 220 of the 256 checklists obtained in that state to supplement the basic fieldwork. No respondent was found to have a completely Northern or a completely Midland dialect profile. Houck concluded, therefore, not only that a Northern-Midland boundary cannot be established in Iowa but also that his statistical method quite discredits the traditional method of analysis. Both conclusions are open to question. The so-called traditional method rests its conclusions upon the distribution of language features per se irrespective of their relative frequency in the speech of a given informant. When a number of language features have a similar distribution, as is shown graphically by the bundling of isoglosses on a map, the dialectologist assumes the existence of at least a minor dialect boundary. The fact that on both sides of such a boundary there are persons whose own idiolects manifest dialect mixture does not render invalid the inference that the boundary exists. At the most, it raises the possibility of another definition of dialect, one based on the distribution of individuals rather than on the distribution of language features.

As Houck has shown, such a way of organizing the field data of language variation is certainly possible. This kind of analysis may well yield new and significant insights when applied to the speech of informants representing an area where population mixture has occurred. Future dialect research in such areas probably should accept a research design calling for a comparison of the distribution of language features as such and the distribution of selected informants classified according to their dialect profiles. Such a study of the Upper Midwest data could be effected through the analysis of the individual informant's complete list of responses. These individual records are available in the Atlas files, where they are accessible to interested scholars. The The basis of the present publication, however, is essentially traditional in that it accepts the long-standing practice of ascertaining dialect divisions in terms of the incidence of specific

language features without regard to the varying characteristics of the idiolects of the informants.

SPEECH EXPANSION AREAS

To provide a rule-of-thumb basis for a regional classification of the Upper Midwest language features a preliminary study of the vocabulary returns made possible a breakdown into what are here termed "speech expansion areas." These areas, first characterized by the presence or absence of certain critical Northern and Midland words, subsequently were found to be significant as well for a few phonological features. The areas correspond roughly to phases in the westward population movement.

Area 1 is that in which occurred the first western settlement of immigrants from New England, New York, Ohio, and Wisconsin, along with others from Indiana, Illinois, and Pennsylvania who came up the Mississippi and then moved west up its tributary streams.

Area 2 is a diversified forest and plains region in which settlement took place a generation later, with two focal centers in addition to the slow northward growth. One center was that of the Minnesota iron ranges, first the Cuyuna and then the Mesabi and Vermilion; the other was the Red River Valley, home of the first bonanza wheat farms.

Area 3 is essentially that of the western extension of wheat farming in central North Dakota, with population settlement determined by the location of the Northern Pacific and Great Northern railroads bringing settlers from the east as well as foreign immigrants.

Area 4 is primarily cattle country, with an eastern population core but with some traces of population that moved north from southern cattle territory.

Area 5 is the territory opened in eastern South Dakota by Indian treaty, with subsequent immigration from Michigan, Wisconsin, and Minnesota as well as from eastern states.

Area 6 comprises the southern two-thirds of Iowa, the first settled part of the Upper Midwest. Initially, immigrants moved into the southeast corner from Indiana, Kentucky, Tennessee, and

5. Charles L. Houck, *A Statistical and Computerized Methodology for Analyzing Dialect Materials*. University of Iowa Ph.D. dissertation, 1969.

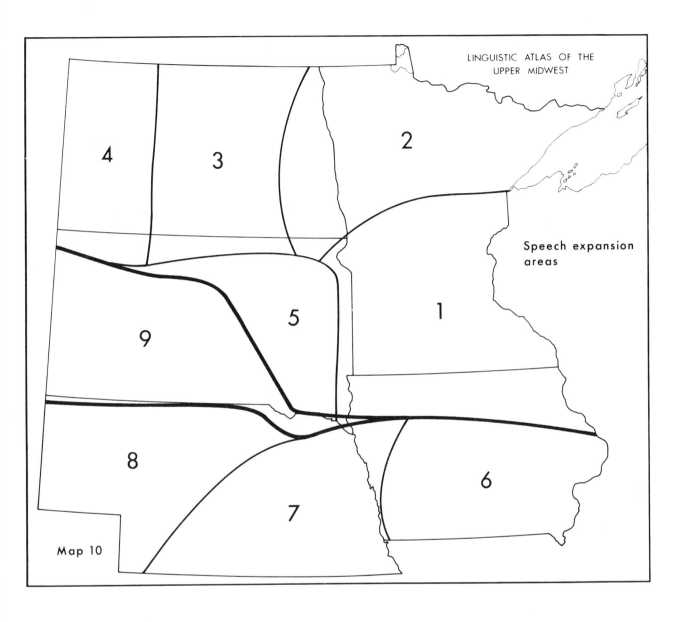

even Virginia; but subsequent settlement was largely by homesteaders from Pennsylvania, Ohio, Indiana, and Illinois as the land rapidly filled up as far west as the Missouri River.

Area 7, eastern Nebraska, comprises the eastern Platte River valley and the prairie area west of the Missouri River. Most of the English-speaking settlers constituted an extension of the Iowa migration except for a number of New York and Ohio groups that homesteaded in the Platte River valley and also except for some Missourians and Kentuckians who followed the Missouri River upstream.

Area 8, northwestern Nebraska, is largely cattle country, with a mixed population, the English-speaking original portion of which had a strong Ohio, Illinois, and Iowa component. In the southern counties there was some influx from Kansas and Missouri.

Area 9, South Dakota west of the Missouri River, is primarily a cattle-raising region except for the Black Hills, where the typical western stream of migration became a whirlpool of eastern and midwestern mixture at the time of the gold rush. It is now a summer tourist area. Along the southern border are two large Sioux Indian reservations, Rosebud and Pine Ridge.

As has been indicated, the principal language variations in the Upper Midwest are found in the contrasts between Northern and Midland dialects.

But the varying rate of western migration and the accompanying intermixture, in varying degrees in different places, of settlers of northeastern and middle Atlantic origins, has led to curious modifications in the expected distribution arrangement. The descriptions that follow are based upon the data from the field records. As is made clear in the item treatments in Part B, supplementary data from the checklists would sometimes alter the specifics with respect to distribution frequency.

The basic pattern is clear in Iowa, where the northern third has critical Northern language features and the southern two-thirds has correspondingly critical Midland language features. This may be termed Pattern A. But west of the Missouri the dialect boundary divides, so that one secondary boundary includes South Dakota in Northern speech territory and another includes most of it in Midland speech territory.

Further modification of the basic pattern appears in the spread of some Northern forms into Midland territory and, conversely, of some Midland forms into Northern territory. Contributing to such modification is the obsolescence of some features, or their inappropriateness to the region, so that some Northern forms and some Midland forms can best be described as recessive, since their distribution may not even extend to the Wyoming borders.

Upper Midwest dialect patterns are described below, with simplified maps and tables that indicate the relative frequency of key features. The degrees of frequency, which are interpreted impressionistically here rather than with statistical precision, are shown as follows: x = common, - = fairly frequent, and . = sporadic.

Pattern A1

Pattern A1 is marked by the expansion of Midland speech features throughout Nebraska and into South Dakota west of the Missouri River as far as Wyoming.

A conspicuous contrast is that between Northern *bellyflop* (69.2) and Midland *bellybuster* (69.2), the latter of which spread even into the flat regions of South Dakota where inhabitants complained

	1	2	3	4	5	6	7	8	9
boulevard	x	x	-	.	-				
bellyflop	x	x	x	.	.				
come in (fresh)	x	.	.	.	.				
/hj/ *in* humor	x	x	-	-	x	.	-	-	-
/sp/ *in* raspberry	.	.	.	.	.				
light bread						-	.	.	.
shucks					.	-	x	x	.
roasting ears					.	x	x	x	.
snake feeder,~ doctor					.	x	x	x	-
ground squirrel						x	x	x	x
parking						x	-	.	x
bellybuster						x	x	x	x
slick					.	x	x	x	-
caterwampus						x	x	x	-
(peach)seed						.	-	.	.
(arm)load					.	x	x	x	x
bottomland					.	x	.	.	.
draw					.	x	x	x	x
haydoodle						.	.		.
/ɔ́n/						-	x	x	x	-
/ð/ *pl.* trough, moth						-	x	-	.	.

that there are no hills to slide on.

Equally conspicuous, though without confirmation from eastern records, is the contrast between two more recent terms, Northern *boulevard* (63.8) and Midland *parking* (63.8) which, though it competes with a number of equivalents in Iowa, still is confined sharply to the Midland speech territory.

Another Northern-Midland contrast not found in the eastern states is that between the eastern *ground squirrel* (46.2a), which has been carried into the Upper Midwest Midland territory, and *gopher* (46.2a), found chiefly in Northern speech territory in Pattern A2.

In the A1 pattern other Midland features pushing through South Dakota include the following: *light bread* (35.5,6), *shucks* (44.1), *roasting ears* (44.2), *snake feeder/snake doctor* (45.8), *slick* (74.3b), *caterwampus* (76.2a), *(peach)seed* (42.2), *(arm)load* (16.5a), *bottomland* (24.2a), *draw* (24.4), *haydoodle* (12.3), stressed /ɔ́n/, and the voiced /ð/ in the plural of *trough* /trɔðz/ and *moth* /mɔðz/.

In this pattern the Northern areas also reveal a much higher incidence of the aspirated beginning /hj/ of *humor* and the presence of voiceless /sp/ in *raspberry*, but the latter feature may be suspect as a possible result of fieldworker variation.

Pattern A2

Pattern 2 is defined primarily by the

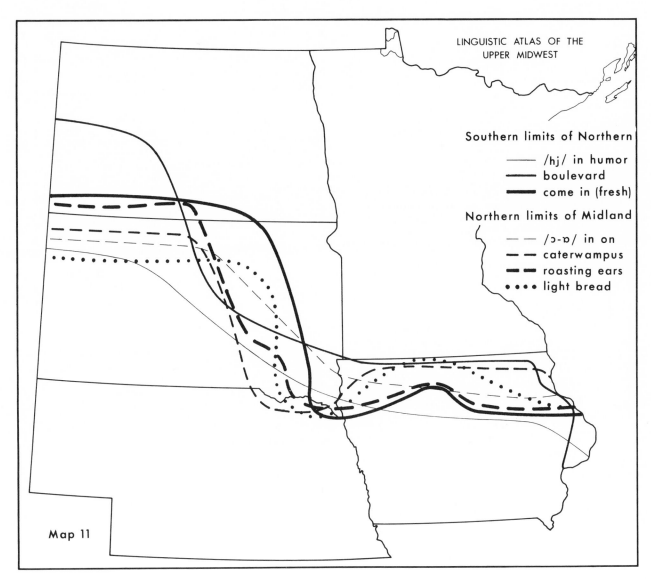

Southern limits of Northern

——	/hj/ in humor
——	boulevard
——	come in (fresh)

Northern limits of Midland

— —	/ɔ-ɒ/ in on
– –	caterwampus
= =	roasting ears
• • • •	light bread

Map 11

PATTERN A1

Pattern A2

	1	2	3	4	5	6	7	8	9
stone boat	x	-	x	.	x			.	.
gopher	x	x	x	x	-				.
dutch cheese	-		.	.	.				.
/u/ *in* loam	x	-	-		.				.
hull						x	x	-	
fish(ing) worm						x	x	x	
nicker						x	x	x	
quarter till						x	.	.	
butter beans						.	x	x	.
crawdad(dy)						.	x	x	x
/ʌɫ/ *in* mush,brush						x	x	-	
/ɔ/, /ɒ/ *in* grandma						x	x	x	
/ɪə/, /ɪɫ/ *in* crib,whip						-	-	-	

distribution of Midland features that did not survive the population movement into South Dakota but also by the expansion of some Northern features throughout South Dakota and even southward across the Nebraska border.

As the map suggests, some of the terms have an uneven distribution in Iowa as well, a fact consistent again with the original finding of population mixture. Midland *quarter till* (4.7), for example, is not as frequent in central Iowa as its eastern frequency would have predicted. *Crawdad* (45.9), on the other hand, is found in the northern tiers of counties, where Northern features predominate.

127

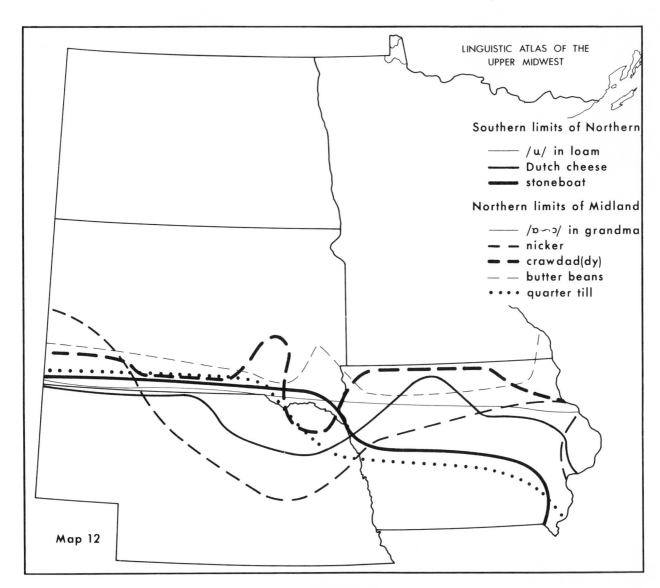

LINGUISTIC ATLAS OF THE
UPPER MIDWEST

Southern limits of Northern

—— /u/ in loam
—— Dutch cheese
━━ stoneboat

Northern limits of Midland

—— /ɒ⌢ɔ/ in grandma
— — nicker
━ ━ crawdad(dy)
– – butter beans
· · · · quarter till

Map 12

PATTERN A2

Among other features Pattern A2 marks the southern range of Northern *stone boat* (18.4), *gopher* (46.2a), *dutch cheese* (38.2), and /u/ in *loam*. It marks the northern range of Midland *hull* (42.6, 7), *fish(ing) worm* (46.7a), *nicker* (30.2), *quarter till* (4.7), *butter beans* (43.7,8), *crawdad(dy)* (45.9), /ʌɨ/ in *mush* and *brush*, /ɔ/ or /ɒ/ in *grandma*, /ɪə/ or /ɪɨ/ in *crib* and *whip*.

Pattern B

Pattern B is essentially defined by the distribution of Midland forms that for one reason or another did not move westward from eastern Nebraska.

B1

Pattern B1 is that of those features that exhibit rather widely separated isoglosses in Iowa but are alike in extending into Nebraska across the wheatlands to the beef cattle country of the western third.

Ecological reasons account for the distribution of some terms. The various *lot* expressions were not carried west where the corral replaced the barnyard. The western area not only is bare of stake-and-rider fences but has few informants who have heard of them. *Sook, boss!* (31.1,2) is limited to rural areas where some dairy cattle are raised.

Obsolescence of the referent itself accounts for the limited spread of (*glass*) *stopper* (17.2d).

Strong competition from other Midland forms or Northern forms probably accounts for the decline of *dip* (38.3), *garret* (8.5), *junk room* (8.8), *comfort* (23.6a,b), *plumb across* (23.8), and *spouting* (15.5b).

The same constricted range exists for the colloquial *looky-here!* (54.3), the expression *I want off* (54.3), the morphological forms *swum* (69.4) as a preterit and *learnt* (73.2) as either a preterit or a participle, and the following phonetic features: /θ/ in *without* and *with* before a voiced consonant, /z/ in *greased* and *greasy*, /e/ in the second syllable of *sumac*, /ɛ/ in *rinse*, /æ/ in *keg*, /υ/ in *Cooper*, and either /o/ or /ɔ/ in *sure*.

Pattern B1

	1	2	3	4	5	6	7	8	9
barnlot, *etc.*						x	x		
dip						x	.		
garret						-	.		
junk room						-	-		
stake-'n'-rider fence						-	.		
(glass) stopper						-	.		
comfort						x	x		
plumb across						-	-		
soo(k), boss!						x	.		
spouting						-	.		
looky-here!						.	.		
I want off						-	-		
swum, *pret.*						.	.		
learnt						-	.		
/θ/ *in* with, without						-	-		
/z/ *in* greasy						-	.		
/e/ *in* sumac						.	.		
/ɛ/ *in* rinse						x	-		
/æ/ *in* keg						x	.		
/υ/ *in* Cooper						x	x		
/o/ *or* /ɔ/ *in* sure						x	-		

B2

Two groups of features have the restricted distribution characteristic of Pattern B2, that is, in southern Iowa and, rarely, the extreme southern strip along the Nebraska-Kansas border. Some features, like *smearcase* (38.2) and *corn pone* (36.1a), are receding Midland terms that apparently became obsolescent as the population spread extended into Nebraska and South Dakota. Others, like *fire dogs* and *dog irons* (7.2), *French harp* (15.8a,b), and the initial /s/ in *shrank* and *shrunk*, are South Midland features brought into southern Iowa by the settlers from Kentucky, Virginia,

Pattern B2

	1	2	3	4	5	6	7	8	9
fire dogs/dog irons						.			
hayrick						-			
ficet (feist)						-			
ficety (feisty)						-			
corn pone						.			
hillbilly						x			
baby cab						.			
take 'im!						.			
French harp						-	.		
mud dauber						-	.		
tushes						x			
/s/ *in* shrank/shrunk						.			
/tʃ/ *in* rinse						x			
/υ/ *in* bulge						x			
/υ/ *in* gums						.			
/ɔ/ *in* barn						.			

Indiana, and Tennessee. So are *poison vine* (48.3), *woods colt* (51.4), *pullybone* (30.5), and the grammatical form *dogbit*, all too rare to be tallied above.

Pattern C

Pattern C is essentially defined by the recorded distribution of Northern forms that for one reason or another did not move westward across North Dakota as far as Montana. Actually, like some of the South Midland features limited in the Upper Midwest to southern Iowa, a few of these forms appear in the Pacific Coast investigations of David Reed and Carroll Reed, e.g., *darning needle*, *mosquito hawk*, and *johnny cake*.

C1

Except for *mosquito hawk* (45.8), the range of which excludes the southern fringe and the northeast triangle but

Pattern C1

	1	2	3	4	5	6	7	8	9
(buggy) pole	-	-	-						
whiffletree	x	x	.			.			
darning needle	-	-				.	.		
pig *terms*	-	-	-						
cluck (hen)	x	-	-						
cook coffee	-	-	.						
green corn	-	.	.			.			
mosquito hawk	x	x							
crab	x	x	.						
drag	x	x	x		-				
skip school	x	x	-		x				
fried cake	x	.	.		-				
farmer's matches	-	x	.		x	.			
swill pail	-	-							
two pound	.	.							
/a/ *or* /ɑ/ *in* aunt	-	-							

129

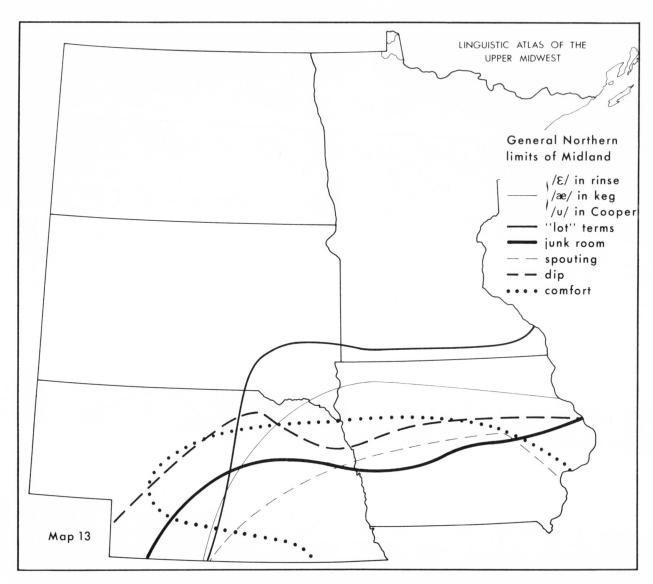

LINGUISTIC ATLAS OF THE
UPPER MIDWEST

General Northern
limits of Midland

⎰ /ɛ/ in rinse	
⎱ /æ/ in keg	
⎰ /u/ in Cooper	
▬▬ "lot" terms	
▬▬ junk room	
– – – spouting	
— — dip	
• • • • comfort	

Map 13

PATTERN B1

does reach into North Dakota, the isoglosses constituting Pattern C1 characteristically coincide in Iowa with those
of Pattern A, but then bend sharply
northward so as to mark off the eastern
quarter of each of the two Dakotas.

No single reason is apparent for the
absence of these terms in the records
from the western Dakotas, especially as
the migration moved steadily straight
westward with the extension of the two
principal railroads, the Great Northern
and the Northern Pacific (now merged as
the Burlington Northern), in North Dakota, and the Chicago, Milwaukee, and
St. Paul (now The Milwaukee Road) in
South Dakota. Some inferences are drawn
in the specific lexical treatments in

Part B. Probably one important factor
is the ecological shift west of the Missouri River, where semi-arid conditions
prevent the kind of farming found in
Iowa and Minnesota and also make scarce
such referents as those for *mosquito
hawk* and *crab* (45.9).

Other representative features whose
distribution is that of Pattern C1 are:
(*buggy*) *pole* (17.4), *whiffletree* (17.6),
(*devil's*) *darning needle* (45.8), *pig*
terms (29.2,2b,c), *cluck* (*hen*) (30.3),
cook coffee (38.7), *green corn* (44.2),
drag (18.3), *skip school* (62.4), *fried
cake* (36.3a), *farmer's matches* (6.8),
swill pail (14.3), *two pound*, and /a/
or /ɑ/ in *aunt*.

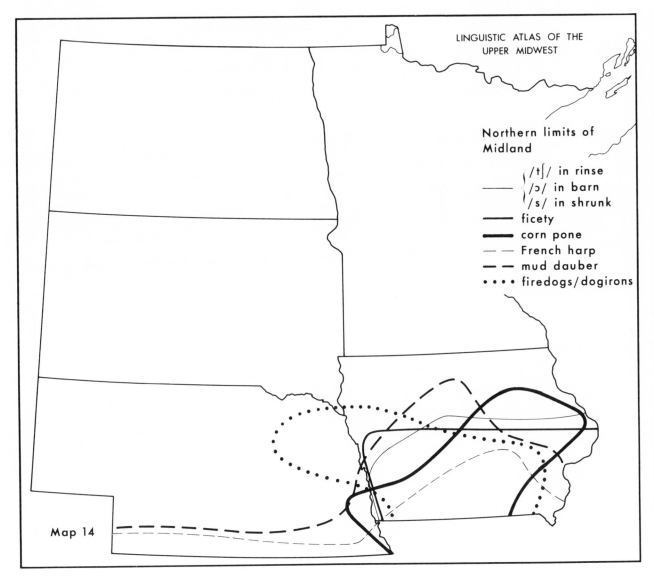

Northern limits of
Midland

/tʃ/ in rinse
/ɔ/ in barn
/s/ in shrunk
——— ficety
━━━ corn pone
– – – French harp
— — mud dauber
• • • • firedogs/dogirons

Map 14

PATTERN B2

C2

Some Northern features seem not to have persisted past the first wave of settlement in southern Minnesota and northern Iowa, or to have survived so barely that they easily succumbed to competition of Midland or other Northern forms.

Brook (24.5), for example, has given way to *creek* except as the designation of a trout stream and as a component in a few place names. *Tap* (15.5a,b) has almost entirely yielded to expanding *faucet*. *Eavespouts* (10.3) first faced competition from Northern *eavestrough* and then became clearly recessive through the dominating use of *gutters* as the

Pattern C2

	1	2	3	4	5	6	7	8	9
eave(s)spouts	-								
tap	•								
spider	-								
fills/thills	-								
brook	-								
sugar bush	x								
clim, *pret.*	•	•							
/ɑ/ *in* fog	x	•			•				
/ʌ/, /θ/ *in* won't	x								
/ʊ/ *in* broom	-	•							
/θ/ *in* trough	-	•	•		•				

commercial designation. The *fills/thills* pair (17.5) were already retreating before advancing Midland *shafts* when the

131

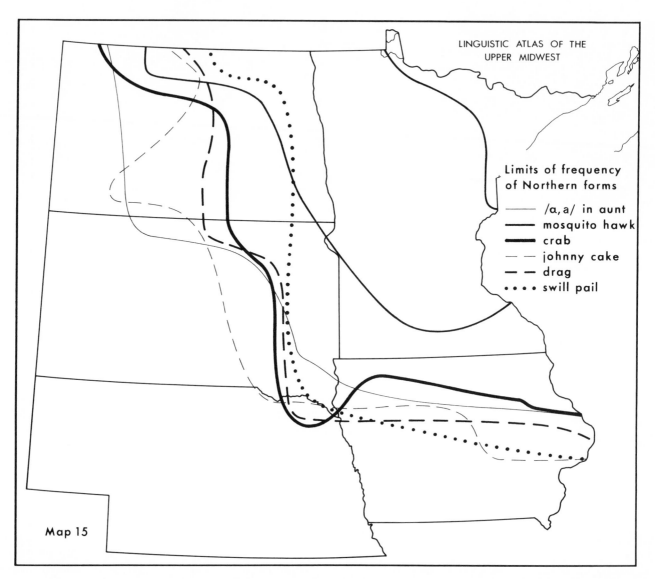

LINGUISTIC ATLAS OF THE
UPPER MIDWEST

Limits of frequency
of Northern forms

——— /ɑ,a/ in aunt
━━━ mosquito hawk
━━ crab
– – – johnny cake
— — — drag
· · · · swill pail

Map 15

PATTERN C1

end of the buggy era made both terms
archaic. *Spider* (14.4) likewise was already giving way to the generic *frying
pan* before more recent *fry pan* and com-
mercialized Midland *skillet* began their
present dominance.

Only one of the listed terms is limited by an ecological factor. Although *sugar bush* (48.8) has recently enjoyed a
recrudescence because of the renewal of
maple sugar production, its range--ex-
cept perhaps as a book term--is necessarily limited to the hard maple regions.

The preterit *clim* and the interdental
/θ/ for /f/ in *trough* are nonstandard
features whose decline may be attributed
to the normalizing influence of schooling. The reasons for the recessiveness

of /ɑ/ in *fog*, /ʌ/ in *won't*, and /ʊ/ in
broom call for further investigation but
may well be found simply in the leveling
tendency that operates upon a mixture
of competing forms.

Pattern D

Pattern D comprises two minor distri-
butions, D1 and D2, characterized by
words or meanings peculiar to the western portion of the Upper Midwest and
not carried there by the western migration.

D1

All the distinguishing Pattern D1
features except *honyocker* (53.7) occur

132

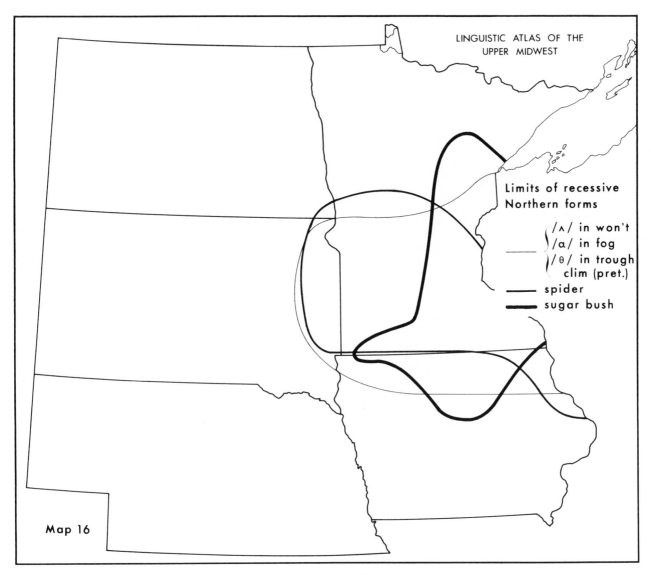

LINGUISTIC ATLAS OF THE
UPPER MIDWEST

Limits of recessive
Northern forms

$/ \wedge /$ in won't
$/ \alpha /$ in fog
$/ \theta /$ in trough
clim (pret.)
spider
sugar bush

Map 16

PATTERN C2

in the western half of North and South Dakota and Nebraska; their isoglosses extend from the Canadian border to the Nebraska border. (Although two inform-ants were queried just north of the Canadian border, it would be presump-tuous to extend the isoglosses into Manitoba and Saskatchewan without in-formation from further dialect research in those provinces.) In the western sense, a homesteader, *honyocker* is not found in Nebraska.

As is detailed in the individual word treatments of Part B, each of the Pat-tern D terms is, not unexpectedly, di-rectly related to the ecology of the western plains, specifically to its chief industry, the raising of beef cat-tle. Man's relation to the land appears in *range* (13.1) for the open country of early cattle days and in the generic *grazing land* (13.1) for both the range and later fenced-in property, as well as in *trail* (25.3), *corral* (12.7), and *ranch* (12.8). Occupational regionalisms are *cowhand* and *cowpoke* (76.5), *throw rope* and *catch rope* (76.6), and the now disappearing *soogan* (23.6), the cow-hand's name for his saddle-roll wool-filled comforter. The related work of hayfarming is represented by *hayflats* (24.2a) and *(hay)bunch* (12.3). The yielding of cattlemen to the fencing homesteader appears in the pejorative *honyocker* (53.7) in the Dakotas.

Since all the preceding terms are

133

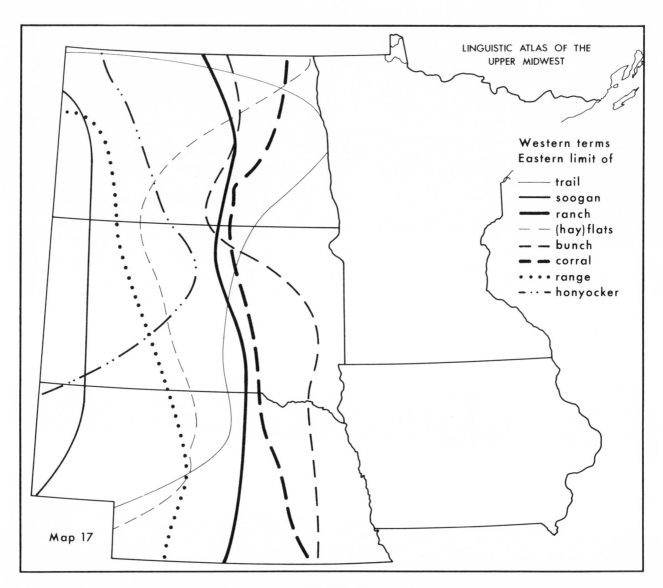

LINGUISTIC ATLAS OF THE
UPPER MIDWEST

Western terms
Eastern limit of

——————— trail
————————— soogan
━━━━━━ ranch
– – – – – (hay) flats
— — — — bunch
━ ━ ━ ━ corral
• • • • range
—··—··— honyocker

Map 17

PATTERN D1

regionally related, their incidence
does not correspond to the distribution
of recognized Northern and Midland expressions.

D2

The western terms in Pattern D2 are
restricted to South Dakota and Nebraska,
that is, to the southwestern quadrant
of the Upper Midwest. Representative
terms follow.

Natural features appear in *gulch* and
canyon (24.4) and in the use of *thicket*
(47.8) as the designation for a small
clump of trees. Fauna appear in the
Great Plains name of the burrowing owl,
prairie (dog) owl (45.7), and in the

southwestern borrowing *civet cat* (46.1b).
Hayfarming terms are *(hay)sled* (18.4)
and *haywaddy* (76.5). Residents of the
Nebraska sandhills region are known as
sandhillers and *Kincaiders* (53.7). Two
roadbuilding terms are *borrow pit* or
bar pit (33.8) and *(oil) mat* (25.2b),
the latter of which seems limited to the
eastern half of Nebraska.

Pattern E

Pattern E comprises a few words found
in the northeastern sector of the Upper
Midwest and, at least according to the
Wisconsin field records of the Linguistic
Atlas of the North Central States, in a
distribution that does not extend into

134

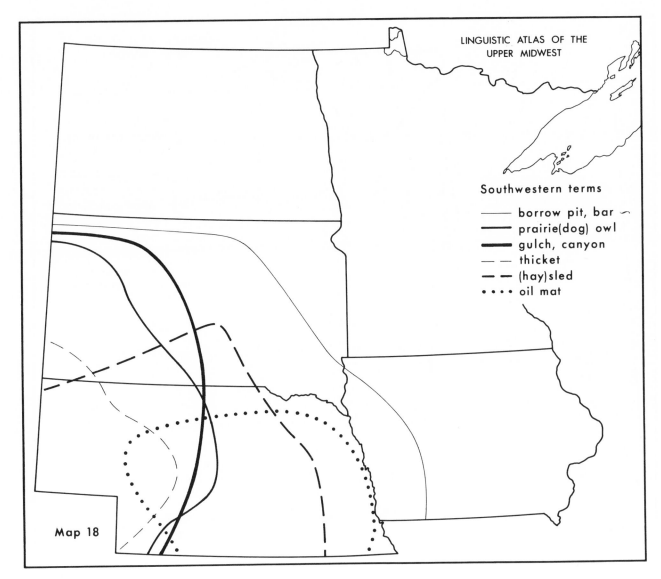

LINGUISTIC ATLAS OF THE
UPPER MIDWEST

Southwestern terms

——— borrow pit, bar ⌐
━━━ prairie(dog) owl
━━━ gulch, canyon
– – – thicket
— — (hay)sled
• • • • oil mat

Map 18

PATTERN D2

Wisconsin. (The much more detailed data collected for the forthcoming *Dictionary of American Regional English* may necessitate a revision of this statement. Its editor, Frederick G. Cassidy, has reported orally that one of the features, *rubber binder*, has turned up in western Wisconsin.)

Northeastern Minnesota still knows several expressions with the form *tote* as peculiar to logging operations in timber country, such as *tote wagon* (18.1) and *tote road* (25.3). *Go-devil* (18.4) has a sense found in logging as well; and *jackpine savage* and *cedar savage* (53.7) are pejorative names applied to less affluent residents of the area where jackpines flourish after the first timber cutting has occurred.

Tarvia and its familiar form *tarvy* (25.2b) are found in Minnesota and the eastern Dakotas as designations of a macadamized road.

A striking northeastern regionalism is *rubber binder* (72.8), which, even if it also appears in western Wisconsin, clearly has the Twin Cities as its focal point.

Also striking is the more localized word *berm* (63.8), with a range almost exclusively in northeastern North Dakota, apparently with the city of Grand Forks as the center.

Pattern F

This minor pattern is distinguished by a few terms having the unusual dis-

135

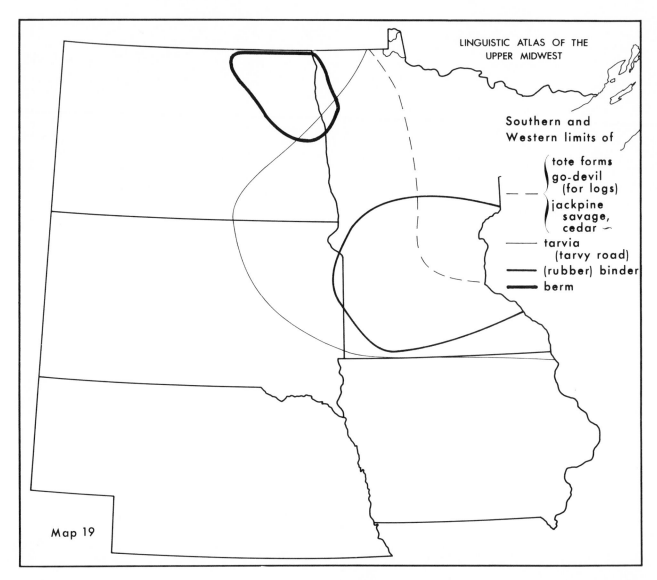

LINGUISTIC ATLAS OF THE
UPPER MIDWEST

Southern and
Western limits of

tote forms
go-devil
(for logs)
jackpine
savage,
cedar –
tarvia
(tarvy road)
(rubber) binder
berm

Map 19

PATTERN E

tribution of occurrence within a vertical
mid-region of the Upper Midwest but in
neither the eastern nor the western
thirds.

Except for *ground owl* (45.7), the Pattern E words seem to be the products of
man's relation to the environment. The
first settlers to break through the
tough prairie grass were known as *sod-
busters* or, sometimes, as *soddies* (53.7),
words which in the cattle country became pejorative.

Because of the need for trees, special
legislation awarded additional land to
homesteaders who agreed to plant trees
on their claims, which then became known
as *tree claims* (47.8), a term persisting
in the eastern Dakotas to designate

woodlots. Haying methods peculiar to the
prairie land gave rise to *handstack*
(12.3).

Because the higher rainfall in this
mid-region offered better pasturage and
a better opportunity for additional
feeding, western range-fed cattle are
often shipped here to be fattened up before being sent to the stockyards. Hence
arose the designations *feedyard* and
feedlot (12.5,7).

NEBRASKA NORTHERNISMS

Deserving of attention but not numer-

136

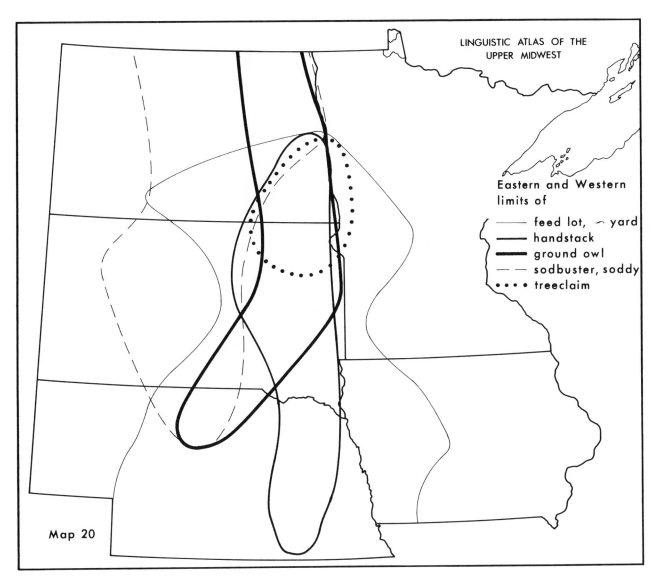

Map 20

LINGUISTIC ATLAS OF THE
UPPER MIDWEST

Eastern and Western
limits of

(—— feed lot, ⌐ yard
—— handstack
━━━ ground owl
– – – sodbuster, soddy
• • • treeclaim

PATTERN F

ous enough to constitute a pattern or to form a "speech island," a number of Northern terms occur in eastern Nebraska because of the influx of New York State and Ohio homesteaders in the lower Platte River valley. Of the nine informants in this sector offering several Northern words each, six have New York or Ohio parentage; three have foreign-born parents.

Among the Northern expressions that remain in Nebraska are the following:

teeter	19.3a	shuck, *n.*	42.7
eavespouts	10.3	darning needle	45.8
fills	17.5	johnny cake	36.1a
whippletree	17.6	fire bug	47.2a
drag	18.3	parlor match	6.8

stone boat	18.4	kudack!	32.3
brook	24.5	fried cake	36.3a
come in	27.5		

Besides these lexical features there are three occurrences of Northern /ɑ/ in *fog*.

CANADIANISMS

A preliminary statement about language features exclusively or dominantly Canadian has already been made.[6] It was based upon a comparison of the field records of the five Canadian informants

137

and the field records of fourteen informants and seventy supplementary checklist respondents living in northern Minnesota and northern North Dakota.

Some modification of that statement may be required after the completion of the current questionnaire survey of Canadian English and still more once a full-scale dialect atlas of the prairie provinces is undertaken, but in the meantime it must suffice to review the analysis offered in the earlier article.

The main English-speaking stock in the Canadian area along the Minnesota-North Dakota border emigrated there from eastern Canada, principally that part of Ontario north of Lake Huron and Lake Erie, with a secondary group coming directly from the United Kingdom. More than ten percent of the Saskatchewan population emigrated from the United States.

Of the more than 800 items in the field worksheets, seventeen elicited from the Canadian informants words not found in the American data. Responses to twenty more items contain terms found only once or twice south of the border but apparently existing with some frequency in Canada. Thirteen phonetic features also appear to be characteristic of the speech of the Canadians interviewed, nine of them actually found only in Canada.

Uniquely and indisputably Canadian is *bluff* (47.8) with the meaning "a clump of trees on the open prairie," a sense that developed in the prairie provinces.

Several of the revealed terms are characteristically rural: *haycoil* (12.3), *sheaf* (34.2), and *stook* (34.4); *hatching hen* or *hatcher* (30.3) and *piggery* or *pigstable* (12.5); *corn rick* (11.5); *feather* (44.4) to designate cornsilk; and to *draw* or *cart* a load of hay (71.4).

A few are household words: *chesterfield* as a designation of a sofa or davenport (81.1), *counterpane* (23.5), *porridge* (40.3), *tidy up* (9.1), and possibly *blinds* (8.3). These last two terms suggest what further research may more clearly demonstrate, the frequency in Canadian English of a number of lexical items that are found also in American Midland but not in American Northern.

Among the others are the following miscellaneous terms: *perambulator* or *pram* (50.5), *quoits* (28.3) for the game

of horseshoe, *elastic band* (72.8), the negative expression *usen't to*, and the interrogation *eh?* (41.5).

Particularly characteristic are these phonetic features: /u/ in *drouth*, [əu] in *south*, /tʃ/ as the initial sound in *Tuesday* and *tube*, and the aspirated [tʰ] medially in *water* and *daughter*. Rarer but also distinctive are /ɪ/ as the stressed vowel in *appendicitis* and the pronunciation /vɑz/ for *vase*.

FOREIGN LANGUAGE INFLUENCES

As was implied in the description of Upper Midwest settlement history, the distribution of large groups of immigrants from European countries was such that in order to effect reasonable geographical coverage some informants had to be chosen neither of whose parents were native English speakers. Of the full total of 208 field informants, as many as 45 had both parents of non-English-speaking background. They are distributed as follows: Iowa 3, Minnesota 18, Nebraska 10, North Dakota 10, and South Dakota 4.

A study to determine the validity of data collected from these informants indicated that their lexical responses are quite representative; they are typically consistent with the responses of native stock informants in the same general region.[7] Their morphology likewise exhibits the same standard and nonstandard characteristics found in the speech of informants from the eastern population base.

Phonologically, however, 17 of the 45 informants do manifest some traces of their parents' speech. This persistence is characteristic of older and uneducated informants; 13 of the 17 are in Type I, only 4 in Type II, and none in Type III.

Nine of the 17 are of Scandinavian background--3 Norwegian, 4 Swedish, 1 Icelandic, and 1 with both Norwegian and Swedish parents. These 9 evince an occasional but inconsistent use of /j/ for /dʒ/ as in /jɛnrəlɪ/ for *generally*, and /jæg/ for *jag*; a similar use of /w/ for /v/ as in /kʌltɪwetɪd/, /wɛdʒtəbel/,

6. Harold B. Allen, "Canadian-American speech differences along the middle border," *Journal of the Canadian Linguistic Association* 5.1.17-24 (Spring, 1959).

7. Harold B. Allen, "The use of Atlas informants of foreign parentage," in the forthcoming Festschrift honoring Hans Kurath; University of Alabama Press.

and /wɑmɨt/; the devoicing of a final voiced fricative as in [hɪʐ], [hɚʐ], and [ɑksɨnʐ]; an infrequent substitution of a dental stop for an interdental fricative as in [ṯuṯʰ] for *tooth*, and [ḏɛr] for *there*; and an occasional inclusion of /g/ after /ŋ/, as in /sɪŋgɨŋ/. Several also reveal, particularly in free conversation, the persistence of a slight foreign intonation pattern; this seems more likely to be true of the Swedish informants.

The five informants of German extraction sometimes replace initial /v/ by /w/, and two of them in conversation with the fieldworker did replace the interdental /θ/ by /t/ as in /trɪ/ and /tæŋks/ for *three* and *thanks*. A fieldworker comments that one of the five has a German intonation.

Intonation difference is also the distinction found in the speech of a northern Minnesotan of French Canadian background and in the speech of a Nebraskan of Czech ancestry. Another northern Minnesotan, a woman with Finnish-speaking parents, reveals that fact only in her characteristic use of lenis rather than fortis voiceless stop consonants.

Vocabulary influence from the various foreign languages in the informants' family backgrounds appears not infrequently in the names of foods for which no suitable English terms exist, such as *kolachy* and *silta*, and occasionally in other lexical sets, e.g., *deichsel* and *schwein*. The French Canadian effect occurs, for example, in the persistence, in an English context, of the familiar kinship expressions *pepére*, *bon papa*, and *bon mama*, and of the greetings *bon jour* and *bonne année*. A Czech informant similarly used *tata* and *maminka* for "father" and "mother" when he was a boy. A Nebraska informant (404), living just south of the Pine Ridge Sioux Indian reservation, says that he and his fellow townsmen regularly use a number of Sioux terms in English context. He cited /ˈoʃɪni/ "cold", /ˈhɑntɑ/ "Get out!", /ˈkɑtɑ/ "hot", /ɪˈtomɑni/ "intoxicated", and /iˈnɑkoni/ "Hurry up!". Another Sioux term /ˈtɑdo/ is used by a South Dakota informant (323) as the synonym for *jerky*. See also the comment on *kapanola* in 12.3, as a borrowing from Finnish.

An occasional idiomatic carry-over from a foreign language turns up in translation phrases and expressions. An informant of Czech background (43) asks, "That is right? Yes?" or "It's this? No?", and says that his wife "cooks" the clothes when washing them. A descendant of Danes (211) says he "cut it over"

when he means that he cut something in half. A Swedish descendant (203) says "My grandchildren call their mother for mama," to mean that they call their mother "mama." Another Swedish descendant (407) reports that a boy "reads for the preacher" when he indicates that the boy is studying with the pastor prior to confirmation. A North Dakota informant (209) says that Norwegians "pick eggs" instead of "gather them," and a South Dakota informant (310) reports that Finns in the Black Hills say, "I had the headache" and I had the sore throat," and that the Cornish people "put down" fruit instead of "canning" it.

RELICS

Even within a century the various forces of language change have operated conspicuously in modifying the vocabulary of the English-speaking population that settled in the Upper Midwest. Inevitably, vocabulary changes with changes in the physical characteristics of daily life--in domestic architecture, in mechanization, in urbanization, for example. It is affected by social change, as by the decline of the custom of shivareeing a newly married couple. It is affected by new technical knowledge, as in the trend toward replacement of folk terms such as *inflammation of the bowels* and *rheumatism* by *appendicitis* and *arthritis*. It is affected by commercialization, as in the decline of *dutch cheese* in the face of the commercial use of *cottage cheese*. It is affected by wellnigh unaccountable fashion, as in the shift from *trousers* to *pants* and now to *slacks*. And it is affected by the need to communicate easily among people with differing dialect backgrounds.

These and other forces were strong enough to prevent the survival of many eastern terms, some vivid and colorful, in the speech of present descendants of the eastern stock. But others have weakly survived, sometimes only as remembered terms in the speech of the older informants. A close study of the single item treatments in Part B will reveal numerous terms that appear only a few times in the Upper Midwest but that were much more frequent in New England or the Mid-Atlantic states. Some of these relics may be mentioned here.

Modern houses with built-in clothes closets have made *clothes press* (8.4a) obsolete along with the movable wardrobe. Nor does a modern house customarily have a separate pantry, so the older terms *butler's pantry* and *buttry* (8.7) barely survive, with four examples of the former and five of the latter, although *pantry* itself still exists because the referent is found in older houses.

Social fashion has moved from *burying ground* (59.6) to *cemetery* and more recently to *memorial park*, but *burying ground* and the equivalent *burial ground* are recalled by several Minnesotans and a few Iowans as the terms they once used. Two or three acknowledge them as their normal usage.

Among the many weakly surviving forms are these additional examples: *coverlet* (23.5,6) with four occurrences in Iowa; Midland *baby cab* (50.5) with scattered instances in Iowa, Nebraska, and South Dakota; *serenade* (61.7) recorded three times in Minnesota; *bell ringing* and *belling* (61.7) once each in eastern Iowa; *belly-bumper* (69.2) in eastern Iowa and eastern Minnesota; *branch* (24.5) in southern and northeastern Iowa; *low* and *mew* (30.1a) with half a dozen occurrences each, one of the latter being in Manitoba; and Midland *flannel cake* (36.4) once each in Minnesota and Iowa and twice in Nebraska.

Relic grammatical forms sometimes survive the onslaught of school normalization. The preterit *rised* appears three times in Minnesota and once in South Dakota; *sot* as a preterit is a single example in Iowa; and Midland *hisn* occurs once or twice in all the states but South Dakota. Other morphological relics are treated in Part A of Volume 2.

Relic pronunciations have also resisted school influence. One southeastern Minnesotan retains the older /dɪf/ for *deaf*. Three informants have /æ/ in *faucet*. Among the other old-fashioned but still surviving pronunciations treated in Part B of Volume 2 are: /e/ in *sumac*, /u/ in *butcher*, /ʊ/ in *won't* and *gums*, and /æ/ in *jaundice*.

BIBLIOGRAPHY

In 1939 *The Handbook of the Linguistic Geography of New England* included a comprehensive bibliography of linguistic geography. It is not necessary to repeat such a general bibliography here in view of the reference sources now available. The subject is represented in the succeeding UNESCO bibliographies prepared by the Permanent International Committee on Linguistics, beginning in 1939, and it is now fully treated in the annual linguistics bibliography of the Modern Language Association. American dialect geography is the exclusive subject of the bibliography found in Harold B. Allen and Gary N. Underwood, *Readings in American Dialectology*, New York: Appleton-Century-Crofts, 1971; and another special bibliography is in preparation at the Center for Applied Linguistics, Washington, D.C. Selected dissertation abstracts in the field appear in Juanita V. Williamson and Virginia M. Burke, *A Various Language*, New York: Holt, Rinehart and Winston, 1971.

Specific attention, however, may be directed to the following books, all of which are relevant to the contents of this study and would be useful library reference resources for anyone concerned with further use of the study:

Atwood, E. Bagby. *The Regional Vocabulary of Texas*. Austin: University of Texas Press, 1962.
----------. *A Survey of Verb Forms in the Eastern United States*. Ann Arbor: University of Michigan Press, 1953.
Davis, Alva L., Raven I. McDavid, Jr., and Virginia McDavid, eds. *A Compilation of the Work Sheets of the Linguistic Atlas of the United States and Canada and Associated Projects*, 2nd ed. Chicago: University of Chicago Press, 1970.
Kurath, Hans. *Handbook of the Linguistic Geography of New England*, 2nd ed., with index prepared by Audrey Duckert. New York: AMS Press, 1972.
----------, et al., director and editor. *The Linguistic Atlas of New England*. 6 vols. in 3. Providence, R.I.: Brown University Press, 1939-1943. Reprinted New York: AMS Press, 1972.
----------. *A Word Geography of the Eastern United States*. Ann Arbor: University of Michigan Press, 1949.
----------, and Raven I. McDavid, Jr. *The Pronunciation of English in the Atlantic States*. Ann Arbor: University of Michigan Press, 1961.
Tarpley, Fred. *From Blinky to Blue-John: A Word Atlas of Northeast Texas*. Wolfe City, Texas: The University Press, 1970.
Wetmore, Thomas H. *The Low-Central and Low-Back Vowels in the English of the Eastern United States*. Publication of the American Dialect Society, No. 32 (1959).
Wood, Gordon R. *Vocabulary Change: A Study of Variation in Regional Words in Eight of the Southern States*. Carbondale, Ill.: Southern Illinois University Press, 1971.

UPPER MIDWEST ENGLISH

(The abbreviation *AS* refers to *American Speech*, a quarterly published by the Columbia University Press and now an official journal of the American Dialect Society.)

Ackerman, Louise M. "Cattle country use of 'spread' for 'ranch,'" *AS*, 38. 302-303 (1963).
----------. "'Generate' and 'generation' among Nebraska farmers," *AS*, 32. 154 (1957).
Aldrich, Ruth. "'Annexation' words from the Midwest," *AS*, 29.79-82 (1954).
Allen, Harold B. "Aspects of the linguistic geography of the Upper Midwest," in Albert H. Marckwardt, ed., *Studies in Languages and Linguistics in Honor*

of *Charles C. Fries*. Ann Arbor: University of Michigan Press, 1964, pp. 303-314. Also as "The primary dialect areas of the Upper Midwest" in Harold B. Allen, ed., *Readings in Applied Linguistics*, 2nd ed. New York: Appleton-Century-Crofts, 1964, pp. 231-241.

----------. "Canadian-American speech differences along the middle border," *Journal of the Canadian Linguistic Association*, 5.17-24 (Spring, 1959).

----------. "Curds and checklists in the Upper Midwest," in Lawrence M. Davis, ed., *Studies in Linguistics in Honor of Raven I. McDavid, Jr.* University, Ala.: University of Alabama Press, 1972, pp. 3-7.

----------. "Distribution patterns of place-name pronunciations," *Names*, 6.74-79 (1958).

----------. "'Haycock' and its synonyms," *AS*, 34.144-145 (1959). [See also Ernest J. Moyne, "The problem of 'kapenola' ('kapanala') solved," *AS*, 35.76-77 (1960).]

----------. "The linguistic atlases: our new resource," *English Journal*, 45.188-194 (1956).

----------. "The Linguistic Atlas of the Upper Midwest of the United States," *Orbis*, 1.89.94 (1952).

----------. "Minor dialect areas of the Upper Midwest," *Publication of the American Dialect Society*, No. 30, pp. 3-16 (1958).

----------. "No epitaphs for 'depot,'" *AS*, 34.233-234 (1959).

----------. "On accepting participial 'drank,'" *College English*, 18.263-265 (1957).

----------. "Pejorative terms for Midwest farmers," *AS*, 33.260-265 (1958).

----------. "Semantic confusion: a report from the Atlas files," *Publication of the American Dialect Society*, No. 33, pp. 3-13 (1960).

----------. "The use of Atlas informants of foreign parentage," in *Studies in Areal Linguistics*, a Festschrift for Hans Kurath. University of Alabama Press. [In press.]

----------. "You and your dialect," in *Many-Sided Language*. University of Minnesota Graduate Research Center, 1964, pp. 35-46.

Birnbaumer, Louise Ackerman. "Dry-land dialect," *AS*, 40.234 (1965).

Brook, Richard. Computer Reduction and Retrieval of Dialect Data: A Methodology for Cartographic and Tabular Display of Lexical and Sociolinguistic Variation. University of Iowa Ph.D. dissertation, 1970.

Buxton, Katherine. "Some Iowa locu-

tions," *AS*, 4.302-304 (1929).

Frink, Maurice. "Hoosier on the high plains," *Nebraska History*, 38.277-284 (December, 1957).

Houck, Charles L. A Statistical and Computerized Methodology for Analyzing Dialect Materials. University of Iowa Ph.D. dissertation, 1969.

Hultin, Neil C. "Dakota speech in 1894," *AS*, 41.65-67 (1966).

Klaeber, Friedrich. "A word-list from Minnesota," *Dialect Notes*, 4.1.9 (1913).

McDavid, Raven I., Jr., and Virginia McDavid. "Plurals of nouns of measure in the United States," in Albert H. Marckwardt, ed., *Studies in Languages and Linguistics in Honor of Charles C. Fries*. Ann Arbor: University of Michigan, 1964, pp. 271-301.

McDavid, Virginia. "'To' as a preposition of location in Linguistic Atlas materials," *Publication of the American Dialect Society*, No. 40, pp. 12-19 (1963).

----------. Verb Forms of the North Central States and Upper Midwest. University of Minnesota Ph.D. dissertation, 1956.

Malmstrom, Jean. A Study of the Validity of Textbook Statements about Certain Controversial Grammatical Items in the Light of Evidence from the Linguistic Atlases. University of Minnesota Ph.D. dissertation, 1958.

Martin, Dick. "Studying Iowa's speech habits," *The Iowan*, 12.16-18 (Fall, 1963).

Meredith, Mamie J. "Charivaria: belling bridal couples in pioneer days," *AS*, 8.22-24 (1933).

----------. "'Choppies' in the Nebraska sandhills," *AS*, 33.79-80 (1958).

----------. "'Clothing refresher' and other terms of pioneer Americans," *AS*, 21.227-228 (1946).

----------. "Squaw patch, squaw corn, calico corn, Yankee corn, tea wheat, sandy wheat," *AS*, 7.420-421 (1932).

Mott, Frank Luther. "A word-list from pioneer Iowa and an inquiry into Iowa dialect word origins," *Philological Quarterly*, 1.202-221 (1922).

----------. "An additional word-list from pioneer Iowa," *Philological Quarterly*, 1.304-310 (1922).

Palmer, Francis W. "Iowa words in *A Word-list from Virginia and North Carolina* (PADS 6)," *Publication of the American Dialect Society*, No. 8, pp. 18-21 (1947).

Pound, Louise. "Dialect speech in Nebraska," *Dialect Notes*, 3.55-67 (1905).

----------. *Nebraska Folklore*. Lincoln: University of Nebraska Press, 1959.

Randel, William. "Minnesota localisms," *AS*, 20.153-154 (1945).

Rush, Laura Belle. A Lexical Survey of Twelve Selected Terms in Iowa. State University of Iowa M.A. thesis, 1951. In typescript.

"Some Nebraskana," *AS*, 26.204 (1951).

Underwood, Gary N. "'Cobweb' and 'spider web,'" *Word Watching*, 45.4.4-6 (1970).

----------. The Dialect of the Mesabi Iron Range in its Historical and Social Context. University of Minnesota Ph.D. dissertation, 1970. (To be printed in *Publication of the American Dialect Society*.)

----------. "Midwestern terms for the ground squirrel," *Western Folklore*, 29.167-174 (1970).

----------. "Semantic confusion: evidence from the Linguistic Atlas of the Upper Midwest," *Journal of English Linguistics*, 2.86-95 (1968).

----------. "'Slop pail'; an example of dialect blending," *AS*. [To appear.]

----------. "Vocabulary change in the Upper Midwest," *Publication of the American Dialect Society*, No. 49, pp. 8-28 (1968).

Van Den Bark, Melvin. "Nebraska cow talk," *AS*, 5.52-76 (1929).

----------. "Nebraska pioneer English," *AS*, 6.237-252 (1931); 7.1-17 (1931).

----------. "Nebraska sandhill talk," *AS*, 4.125-133 (1928).

Weber, Robert H. A Comparative Study of Regional Terms Common to the Twin Cities and the Eastern United States. University of Minnesota Ph.D. dissertation, 1964.

THE ATLAS PROJECT

During the investigation for the Linguistic Atlas of the Upper Midwest a number of descriptive journalistic articles about it appeared, chiefly in Upper Midwest newspapers. Although unscholarly and ephemeral, they are chronologically listed here because they are relevant to the history of the project and also to popular notions about dialect study.

1947

"Midwest dialects' 'invasion' debated," *Minneapolis Tribune*, May 13.

Crane, Ed. "One word's enough for speech detective," *Minneapolis Sunday Tribune*, Dec. 7.

1948

"Common speech OK -- Allen," *Minnesota Daily*, Mar. 4.

Crane, Ed. "'U' professor tracks down odd dialects," *Minneapolis Sunday Tribune*, Dec. 5.

1949

"U. professor here to study speech," *Crookston Times*, July 12.

"U. language specialist to study word habits of border citizens," *International Falls Daily Journal*, July 18.

"Specialist will make study of language here," *Bemidji Pioneer*, July 20.

"U. professor tells findings after word-use study here," *International Falls Daily Journal*, July 21.

"New dialect in sight, language expert says," *University of Michigan Daily*, Aug. 18.

"Professor traces state's speech habits," *St. Paul Pioneer Press*, Aug. 18.

"So close, but so different," *Fort Williams Times-Journal* [Ontario], Aug. 18.

"University checking expressions used by Brainerd people," *Brainerd Daily Dispatch*, Aug. 13.

"Minnesota professor here on Atlas work," *Fort Williams Times-Journal*, Sept. 12.

1950

Strawhecker, Paula. "Expert speaks on Minnesota speech," *Indiana Student* [Indiana University], July 29.

"Study of population drift under way in N.D.," *The Fargo Forum*, Aug. 13.

"Professor starts study of speech habits in region," *Devils Lake Journal*, Aug. 17.

"Studies county language habits," *Turtle Mountain Star* [Rolla, N.D.], Aug. 24.

"Speech study now under way in this county," *Cavalier Chronicle*, Aug. 24.

"Professor studies state folk speech in Jamestown," *Jamestown Sun*, Sept. 7.

"Speech studies made here by Minn. U. prof.," *Williston Herald*, Sept. 11.

"Minnesota U. professor conducts study here," *Bismarck Tribune*, Sept. 19.

"If you call a skillet a frying pan, this dude'll know where you came from," *Dickinson Press*, Sept. 22.

"Institute for Regional Study sponsors Linguistic Atlas of Midwestern States," *The Spectrum* [North Dakota Agricultural College], Oct. 27.

1951

"Harold Allen takes your word for it," *The Minnesotan*, Jan., p. 7.

Deck, Jack. "Teachers urged to interest pupils in region's English," *Louisville*

Courier-Journal [Kentucky], April 12.
"Word detectives trace fourth major dialect," *Los Angeles Times*, July 2.

1952

"Scholar comes to county to learn horse designation," *Falls City Journal* [Nb.], July (date unknown).

1953

Cruse, Martin. "Nebraska natives to talk, help make 'Speech Map' of Midwest," *Sunday Journal and Star* [Lincoln, Nb.], July 26.
Morton, Herbert C. "U. prof bares Midwest speech variations," *St. Paul Dispatch*, Aug. 3.
Porter, Marilyn. "How we talk in the Upper Midwest," *The Ivory Tower* [University of Minnesota], Jan. 4.
Gledhill, Cameron. "Some words stop at Marietta, Ohio," *Collier's*, June 25,

pp. 78-80.

1960

"You may not mean what you say," *Kansas City Star*, April 30.

1962

"Say crick if you want," *Midland Cooperator* [Minneapolis], May 21.

1964

Beck, Fred. "Exploring NWB land with a linguistic geographer," *Northwestern Bell Magazine*, 45.16-18 (Jan.-Feb.).
Eisele, Albert. "U. of M. word sleuth discovers it pays to watch language," *St. Paul Sunday Pioneer Press*, Oct. 25.

1968

Underwood, Gary N. "The Iron Range word survey," *Nashwauk Eastern Itascan*, July 15.

PART B

The Lexicon

Introductory Comment

For ease of reference the descriptive analysis of the vocabulary investigated in the UM is arranged simply in order of the items of the worksheets as given in Part A, Chapter 4, with the same identifying numbers. Thus, 9.3 refers to the third item of Section 9. When two distinct, though perhaps semantically related, terms appear with the same item number, they are identified, for example, as 15.8a and 15.8b. Occasionally, as with 8.1, the situation is so semantically complex that clarity demands subdivisions, hence 8.1(1), 8.1(2), etc.

The maximum treatment of a lexical entry typically has the following material, in this sequence:

1. The key word or meaning for which the informant is queried.

2. Cross reference to the number of the map for the corresponding lexical set in NE, *The Linguistic Atlas of New England*. Elsewhere this atlas is identified as LANE.

3. Cross reference to the page(s) for the corresponding lexical set, though not necessarily the same word, in the *Word Geography of the Eastern United States*, followed by cross-reference to a relevant map, e.g., F64 (Figure 64) in the same work.

4. The descriptive statement summarizing and interpreting the data and often relating them to the known distribution of the lexical variants in the eastern states. In this description the accepted frame of reference limits the meaning of "Northern" to the Northern dialect and the meaning of "Midland" to the Midland dialect, unless the context specifically shows otherwise. "Canada" means only that narrow border region in which informants were interviewed for the UM Atlas.

Forms are given in the usual spelling except when, rarely, an unusual situation makes a phonetic representation de-sirable.

The use of capital letters for a lexical item distinguishes it as a semantic unit from a morphological form. Thus, in item 4.1 ROSE is a morpheme, a blanket designation that includes occurrences of rose, raised, and riz, which in turn are treated as distinct grammatical forms in Volume 2. Here they are considered together as a unit contrasting with the similar grammatically complex unit CAME UP, which in Volume 2 is analyzed as composed of come up and came up as preterits. This use of capitals appears also in the section described in Section 8 below.

5. A map revealing graphically one or more of the regional variations disclosed by the data. Although two or three maps make use of isoglosses, they typically show the distribution of selected variants by distinctive symbols. These symbols do not indicate terms only heard in the community, and only when there is special significance, as with soogan, 23.6b, are obsolescent and archaic forms included. In such a case the symbol ꝉ for "old-fashioned" is on the map. Because the Midland thrust into Northern territory has reduced the clear geographical contrast, the distribution is sometimes more effectively shown by bar graphs or pie graphs. In the second portion of Part B this practice has been replaced by the use of a simple percentage chart.

6. The percentage chart. This statistical table shows the proportionate distribution, by states, of the principal variants. It should be carefully noted that in dialect research percentages are not to be taken as absolutes. They rather simply suggest relative proportions. (This observation would be especially true of returns for Type III informants, if they were given, since the number of informants is too small for percentages to be taken very seriously.) The scholar seeking further

analysis of the data will bypass the quick percentage review and go directly to the data. Such a study is called for with respect to the percentages for Iowa, which includes contrasting Northern and Midland areas. For a given item the analysis desirably would provide percentages for the Northern and Midland speech territories rather than for the state as a whole.

7. CL -- the comparable data from the checklist study, with both a descriptive statement and a table. Here the percentages for northern Iowa and for southern Iowa are sometimes listed separately when marked significance appears in the contrast. Reference to a checklist respondent is to his arbitrary numerical sequence in a numbered county in one of the five states. (See Part A, Chapter 5, and the county base map, p. xi.)

8. The actual listing of the specific variants and of the informants who use them. For a given variant the informants using it are identified by their serial numbers, separated by commas except when a semicolon indicates a state division.

One or several of the following symbols, nearly all of them identical with those used in the *Linguistic Atlas of New England* and described in the *Handbook of the Linguistic Geography of New England*, may precede an informant's number, with meaning as indicated below. A

symbol preceding a series, e.g., †135-139, is relevant to all the numbers in the series, 135, 136, 137, 138, and 139.

c	spoken during conversation
cr	correction by informant
f	response forced by fieldworker
s	suggested by fieldworker
sn	suggested and normal for informant
:	hesitation on part of informant
!	amusement shown by informant
?	uncertainty on part of informant
ɪ	heard in the community
†	archaic; old-fashioned
→	recently introduced; innovation
*	auxiliary informant
~	unchanged portion of repeated term

9. This section includes the material written in the margins of the workbook by the fieldworker. Double quotation marks enclose a direct comment of the informant. Single quotation marks typically indicate a non-linguistic referent considered with respect to its name; they may be interpreted thus "(something) called a (name)." Sometimes an informant's comment is summarized the fieldworker offers his own opinion. "Used by" may refer to the term itself or to the referent. The context indicates which. "Usual term" indicates which of two or three terms used by an informant is his customary one. The = sign means "synonymous with."

The Vocabulary

3.4 <u>Good</u> <u>morning</u>. NE 77.

bonjour 6-7.
good morning 1-7, 9, c10, 11-13, c14, 15, c16, 17, 19-23, !25, 26-35, :36, 37-41, c42, 43-45, c46, 47-54, c55, 56, 58-60, 63-65; 101-17, 119-50, 152; 201-6, c207, 208-20, 222-26; 301-10, c311, 313, c314, 315-22, c323, 324-28; 401-16, 418, c419, 420-35. morning 8, c15-16, 18, 24, 57, c59; c105-6, c147; c314; c404, 436.
hello 6, 39; 307.
hi 8, 17, 24, →46, 49, 62; 208-9; 429.
how are you 437.
no response 61; 118, 151; 221; 312; 417.

Comment:

bonjour: Said to Chippewas and other whites during his youth--6. good morning: Until 8--129. Until 8; after that 'hi' or 'hello'--6. Until 8 or 9; after that 'good day'--307. Until 9--54; 101, 115, 135, 138; 423. Until 9 or 10--63; 407. Until 9:30--112, 126. Until 10--110; 316. Until 10; after that 'hi'--209. Until 10, but greeted interviewer with the expression at noon--108. Until 10 or 11--1, 56; 427. Until 10:30--49; 132. Inf. wouldn't say 'good morning,' but if he did it would be before 10:30--62. Until 11--55, 65; 106-7, 139; 223; 324; 406, 416. Until 11:30--414. Until 11:30 or 12--435. Until 12--7-8, 19, 21, 32, 34-35, 39-41, 43-48, 50-53, 58-60; 102-4, 109, 111, 113-14, 116, 120, 122-25, 128, 130, 133-34, 136-37, 140-46, 150, 152; 210-11, 214, 217-18, 224; 305, 308, 317-19, 325; 401, 405, 408-9, 412, 420-22, 424-26, 428-34. Until midmorning--16. "Most of the forenoon"--64. "Anytime before dinner"--127. Until after lunch--23. Occasionally--208. "Good morning to you"--31. hi: Usual expression --49. To youngsters--429. morning: Until 10; after that 'hi'--24. Until 12--57.

3.5 The part of the day before supper.

NE 75.

For the part of the day before the evening meal <u>afternoon</u> is general except for an instance of <u>evening</u> in Minnesota, another in South Dakota, and 7 in Nebraska. Type I speakers provide 8 of these 9 instances.
CL: The mail replies have a slightly higher proportion of <u>evening</u>, but without marked regional differentiation.

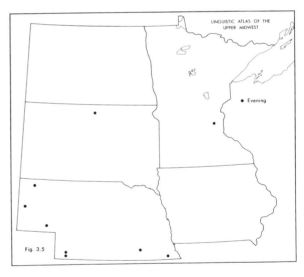

Fig. 3.5

afternoon 1, c2, 3-14, c15, 16-35, 37-43, c44, 45-47, c48, 49-60, 62-65; 101-17, 119-50, 152; 201-16, c217, 218-26; 301-2, 304-28; 402-8, c409, 410-15, c416, 418-22, c423, 424-28, c429, 430-32, 432, 433, 435-36.
evening 36; 303; 401, 409, 417, c429, 432, 434, 437.
midday 44.
no response 61; 118, 151.

Comment:

Length of afternoon indicated by inf.:
Until 4--1, 12, 50; 135; 320; 402. Un-

149

til 4:30 or 5--150. Until 5--6, 11, 40; 128, 137; 205, 209; 302; 432, 435. From 2 until 5--219. Until 5 or 6--9, 56, 65; 215. Until 6--2-5, 7-8, 14, 21-22, 26, 38; 122, 127, 136, 141-43, 145; 204, 207-8, 210-12, 217, 220, 222, 226; 305, 308-11, 315, 321, 323, 325, 327-28; 403-6, 408, 410-11, 419, 428, 436. Until 6 or 7--30. Until the evening meal--17, 31, 64; 116, 125, 134, 152; 203, 206, 208, 214, 221, 223; 306, 316, 326; 424, 426, 433. Until sunset, twilight, or dusk--29, 37; 124, 126, 130-31; 218; 313-14; 412. Until dark--55; 123, 129, 146-47; 322.

Length of evening indicated by inf.:
From 4 until 9--36. From 4 until bedtime--429. From 5 onward; perhaps earlier in winter--401. From 5 until 6 or 7--432. From 5 until 9--437. From 5 until 10--418. From 6 until supper at 7 or 8--434. "Well towards suppertime"--409. Until dark--417. Until 10--303.

3.6 The part of the day after supper. NE 76.

For the part of the day after the evening meal the general term is evening, but with little agreement as to when evening ends. Some infs. define it as ending with dusk and hence hardly existing at all in the winter. Others extend it to specific times or to bedtime. The diversity seems to bear little relation to geography, except for a possible difference between the usage in rural and urban areas.
See Gary N. Underwood, "Semantic confusion: evidence from the Linguistic Atlas of the Upper Midwest," Journal of English Linguistics, 2.86-95 (1968).

evening 1-10, c11, 12, c13, 14, c15-16, 17-29, c30, 31-36, c37, 38-58, c59, 60, 62-65; 101-17, 119-50, 152; 201-13, c214, 215-24, c225, 226; 301-10, c311, 312-19, c320, 321, 323-28; 402-6, c407, 408, c409, 410-13, c414, 415-16, 418-28, c429, 430-31, 433, 435-36. late evening 401.
night c16, 53, 57; 109, 141, 146-47, 149; 306, 322, 401, 410, 417, 428, 432, 434, 437.
no response 61; 118, 151.

Comment:

evening: Begins as early as 4 or 5--1, 36; 125, 135, 137, 140, 149; 205, 209, 219; 320; 402, 418, 429. Ends at sunset or dark--5, 24, 29, 57; 101-3, 111, 116, *117, 122, *123, 124-25, 129-31, 135, 144, 146; 202-3, 207, 209, 222; 302, 304, 306, 308-9, 313; 403-4, 409-10, 416, 419, 423, 426-27, 431. Ends at 8--110, 114-15; 205,

219; 304, 320-21; 402, 407-8, 416. Ends at 9 or 10--3, 7, 9-10, 20-22, 26, 30-31, 36, 53, 56; 104, 109, 112, 121, 126, 132, 137, 141-42; 201, 203, 206, 208, 210, 212, 215-16, 220-21, 225-26; 301, 303, 310, 323, 325-26, 328; 406, 411-13, 418, 420-23. Ends at 11 or 12--11, 19, 28, 35; 113, 123, 127, 133-34, 138, 140, 147-48; 211, 213, 224; 305, 311, 315-16, 324. Ends at bedtime--34; 126, 136-37, 145, 149; 204, 214-15, 217, 223; 410, 414, 424, 429, 436. Shorter in the winter--24; 207, 209; 310; 414. No evening in the winter--122; 222; 309, 323. Longer in winter "because of activities"--413. Ends at 8 or 9 in the country; at 10 or 11 in town--427. "There's a gap between afternoon and evening"--216. Same as dusk or twilight--419. Same as night--428. night: Begins at 7 or 8--53; 432. After 9 or 10 --109. After dark--57; 141, 146-47, 149; 401, 417. After bedtime--133; 306; 410.

3.7 We start to work before sunrise. NE 73.

The usual responses are sunrise and sunup, the distribution of the latter indicating a Midland correlation. No significant contrasts appear among the three types of infs.
CL 2: Checklist responses confirm the field records. Sun-up has a 49% frequency in southern Iowa but only 31% in northern Iowa, with 58% in Nebraska and 38% in South Dakota, but only 8% in Minnesota and 17% in North Dakota.

break of day 37.
crack of dawn 11.
dawn 8, 18, 33; 150; 225-26; 425. ~ of day 7.
daybreak 2, 5, 8, 55; 203; 303.

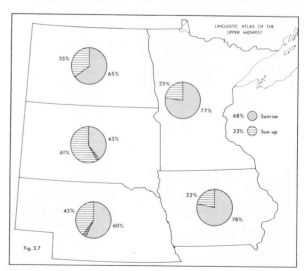

Fig. 3.7

daylight 4, 12, 36, 42; 219, 226; 309.
the sun c56.
sunrise 1-6, s7, 8-10, 13-25, 27, 29-32, 35, 37-40, 42-44, !45, 46-49, 51-53, 56-57, 59-60, 64-65; 101-12, 114-15, 119-23, 126-27, 129-31, 133-41, 143-44, 148-49, :150, 152; 202, ˡ204, 205-8, 210-13, ˡ215, 216-19, 221, 223, 225-26; 303, 305, 307-11, 314, 317, 319, 326-27; 401, 404, 406-7, 410-11, 413, c414, s415, 416, 418-21, 424-28, 431-33, 435.
sunup 7, :11, 12, ˡ20, ˡ23, 26, 28, 34, 41, 46-47, 50, 54, †55, 58, !60, 62-63; 113, 116-17, 124-25, 128, 132, *139, 142, ˡ144, 145-47; 201, 203-4, 209, 214-15, c220, 222, 224; 301-2, 304, 306, 312-13, cvr314, 315-16, 318, 320-25, 328; 402-3, 405, 408-9, 412, 414, 416-17, 422-23, 427, 429-30, f434, 436-37.
no response 61; 118, 151.

Comment:

dawn: Usu.--226. daylight: Usu.--219, 226. sunrise: Inf. recognizes sunrise but says it is not common in his community--58. More usu. in town--60. Used mostly during hunting season--219. Not usu. term--226. "You don't hear much about sunrise here"--309. In conversation with reference to Easter sunrise services--414. sunup: Uses this term sometimes--7. "Farmers say 'sunup'; we'd say 'sunrise'"--20. Not inf.'s usual way of speech--34. "I've heard my forebears use it, too"--54. "Used by people brought up about 1850"--55. "I've heard the phrase 'from sunup to sundown' a thousand times"--62. 'Sunrise' refers to the moment of rising --427.

3.8 fortnight (the period from, for example, one Saturday to the second succeeding Saturday).

This item was added to the worksheets after the interviewing in Minnesota. Only 8.3% of the infs. in the other states offered the specific term fortnight, and more than half of those were in Iowa. Several considered the word old-fashioned or literary.

couple of weeks 106; 317.
fortnight †103, s†116, 117, 122-23, sˡ124, 126, 130-31, 134, 136, 144, 146, 150; 201-2, 221; 318-19; ˡ420, 431.
half a month 145.
two weeks 101-2, 104-5, 107-15, 127, 133, 135, 137-38, 147-49; 324.
no response or no special term 118-21, 125, 128-29, 132, 139-43, 151-52; 203-20, 222-26; 301-16, 320-23, 325-28; 401-19, 421-30, 432-37.

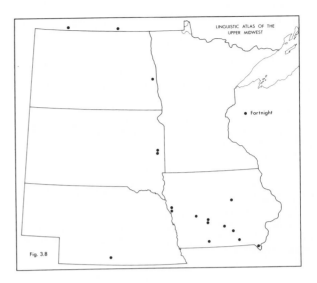

Fig. 3.8

Comment:

fortnight: Used as a girl.--103. Knows term--111. Used to hear when a girl--116. Never heard 'fortnight'--139. "heard it used right smart. . . not as much lately as I used to"--146. "Has used" it, but now "very unusual"--150. Common in the community--201. Not in colloquial English --221. "English," doesn't use it very often--319. Not common here--420.

4.1 The sun rose at six. NE 657.

The two principal responses reveal a Northern/Midland distribution without isoglossic contrast. CAME up is clearly Midland, with its greatest frequency in Minnesota and North Dakota. ROSE, however, dominates the entire UM. Type III speakers favor it by 100%; Type II, by 83%; Type I, by 70%. Raised, the third response, with two occurrences each in Minnesota, Iowa, and eastern South Dakota, is a relic form reported by Type I speakers only.

CAME up 13, c15, 16, 39, 51, 59; 108, 113, 115-16, 119, 128, 134, 139-40, 145-46; 202, 215, 223; 309, 311-12, 321-23, 326, c327; 403, ˡ404, 405-6, c408, 409-10, 413, 417, 419-21, 423-24, 429, 434.
raised c6, 25; c132, 142; 306-7.
ROSE 1-4, 5-12, 14-15, 17-24, 26-31, c32, 33-35, :36, 37-38, 40-47, s48, 49-58, 60, 62-65; 101-12, 114, 117, 119-27, 129-31, 133, 135-38, 140-41, 143-44, 147-50, 152; 201, 203-6, :207, 208-14, 216-22, f223, 224-26; 301-5, 308, 310, 312-20, 324-28; 401-2, 404, 407, 411-16, 418, 420, 422, c423, 425-28, 430-33, 435-37.
no response 61; 118, 151.

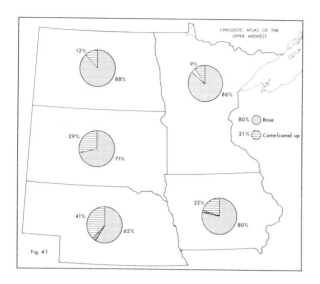

Fig. 4.1

Comment:

came up: More usual expression--51.
raises: Present ts. form--6. rose: Refused to say 'rise'--202.

4.2 We work until sunset. NE 74.

Sunset and sundown are equally common,
with 54% and 53% frequency respectively,
but sunset is firmly established only in
the older areas. Sundown dominates northern Minnesota and, except for a pocket in
Black Hills, the western third of the UM.
No significant difference occurs among
Type I and Type II speakers; Type III
speakers favor sunset by 10 to 7.

CL 3: Mail responses are confirmatory,
with 59% for sunset and 46% for sundown,
which has a more pronounced Midland orientation with 48% for Iowa and 73% for Nebraska in contrast with 23% for Minnesota.

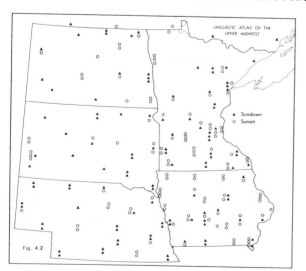

Fig. 4.2

sundown 2-3, 6, 10-13, 15-17, 19, ¹20,
21, 23-24, 26, 28, 30, 33-36, c41, 46-47,
49-50, 54-55, 58, !60, 62, c63, c65; 107,
c113, 116, 117, 124-25, 127-28, 130-32,
138, 141-42, 144-45, 148, s149, 150; 201,
203-4, c205, 206, c207, 209, 214-15, c218,
c220-21, 222-23; 301-5, 307, 312, c313,
315, 318, 320-25, 327-28; 401-3, c404,
405, 408-10, 412, ¹413, 416-17, 420-25,
427-31, 434-37.
sunset 1, 4-5, 7-9, c13-14, 15, 18,
20, 22, 25, 27, 29, 31-32, 37-40, !42,
43-47, !48, 51-53, c55, 56-57, 59-60, 64-
65; 101-6, 108-12, 114-17, 119-23, 125-27,
129-30, 133-37, 139-40, 143, 146-50, 152;
202, 208, 210-13, 216-17, 219, 224-26;
308-12, 314, *316, 317, 319, 326; 406-7,
411, 413-16, 418-19, 426, 432-33.
no response 61; 118, 151; 306.

Comment:

sundown: "A farmer would be apt to say
'sundown'"--20. "We don't use this expression much"--34. Doesn't hear 'sundown'
much here--45. Used with reference to the
time of day--55. Just as common here as
'sunset'--149. Probably more usu.--150.
sunset: Used with reference to the spec-
tacle or scenic effect--15, 55. Heard
about equally--47. Recognizes but says
not common here--58. Emphatic--308.

5.3 It's clearing up. NE 89.

The two common East Coast terms for the
ending of a storm, clearing and breaking,
retain their popularity in the UM; the
third term, fairing, found principally
in Maine and New Hampshire, survives in
the speech of one Minnesota Type I inf.
(42) whose parents were born in New York
state. No pronounced regional pattern appears with clearing; breaking is very
slightly more frequent in the Northern
speech area, and the infrequent variant,
letting up, occurs only there. No marked
variation occurs within the three types
of speakers.

breaking 8, 14, 20; 120; 225; 302-3,
309, 320; 409-10. ~ away 107-8; c220;
311-12; 436. ~ up 13, 50; 133; 202, 221,
224; c307; 404. beginning to break 3.
brightening up 7, 9.
changing 318.
clearing 5, 12, 18-19, :27, 30, 33,
40, 42, c62, 63; 103-4, 106, 109-13, 126,
128-29, 131, 133, 137, 142, 147-48, 150;
201, 211, 219, 221-22; 301, 314, 326;
401, 414, 416, 419, 425-26, 431-33. ~
away 144; c207. ~ off 21, ¹28, 36, 41,
!46; 105, 107, 122, 127, 132, 146; 207,
212, 218; 324-25; 402-3, 411, 413, 417,
c427, 434-35. ~ up 1-2, 4, 6-7, 9-10,
sn11, 15-17, :22, 23-25, :26, 28, c29,

152

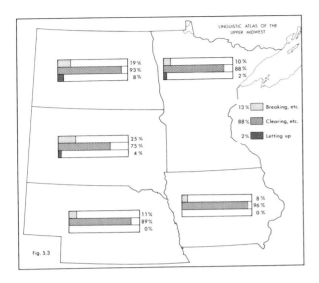

Fig. 5.3

30-32, 34, 37-39, 43-45, 47-48, :49, 51-
60, 62, sn64, 65; 101-2, 105, 107, s108,
114-17, 119, 121, 123-25, 130, 134-36,
138-41, 143, 145, 149, 152; 202-6, 208-
10, 213-17, 223, 225; 304-8, 310, 312,
c313, 315, *316, 317, 321-23, 325, 327-
28; 403, 405-8, 411-12, 415, :418, 420-
21, c422, 423-24, 427-30, 437.
    cracking up 404.
    fairing 42.
    getting better 11; 318.
    improving 316, 319.
    letting up 20; 201, 226; 319.
    passing 115.
    no response 35, 61; 118, 151.
Comment:
    breaking away: Pret. form--220. After
a long storm--312. clearing: More normal
to him than 'clearing up'--62. Pret. form
--432. clearing off: Pret. form--402.
clearing up: Pret. form--56-57, 59. Tail
end of the storm--108. cracking up: Common here--404.

5.4 thunderstorm. NE 94.

    For a rainstorm accompanied by wind,
lightning, and thunder, two principal
terms appear: thunderstorm and elec-
tric(al) storm. No pronounced regional
pattern emerges, although the slightly
greater percentage of replies for the
two electric variants in Iowa and Nebraska suggests slight Midland orientation,
and a similar weighting of thunderstorm
in Minnesota and South Dakota--though
not in North Dakota--suggests a slight
Northern orientation. Both expressions
occur widely in New England.

    CL 4: In the checklist responses thun-
derstorm reveals no regional variation,

but it does have a higher overall frequency, 77%, than electrical storm, with
29%. The latter dominates Nebraska (43%).

    electric shower 42; 109.
    electric storm 4, ¹7, 19, 22-23, 25-
26, 50, 64-65; 105, 107, 113-14, 124-25,
132, 135, 139, 143, 147, 150; 202, 211,
207-9, 216; 301-3, 314, 317, 319, 327;
401, 403, 405, 414, ¹420, 427, 430, 432.
    electrical storm 2, 8, *9, 10, 12-14,
20, 28, 32, 34, *37, 40-41, ¹44, 47, 57,
60, 62; 102, 104, 106, 108-10, 112, 117,
121-23, 128, 133, 136, 138, 141, 144-45,
148-49, 152; 205, 212-13, 215, 220, c222,
224, 226; ¹304, 310, 318, 321, 326; 404,
406, 410, 416, 418, 421, 424-26, 428, 431,
433-35.
    flash storm 409.
    lightning storm 6, 13-14; 140.
    shower 18, 31; 432.
    squall 15-16.
    storm c16, 17, 44, c62; 434.
    thundershower 2, 4, cr29, 30, 52; 103,
s106, →116; ¹211, 223; →411, 437.
    thunderstorm c1, 3, 5, 7, :9, 11, 13-
14, 21, 24, 27, ?29, 31, 33, 36-39, 43-
45, r46, 47-49, 51, 53-56, 58-59, 62-63;
101, 104-5, 107-8, 110-11, 113, 115-17,
119-21, 126-31, 133-34, 137, 142, 146,
149; 201, 203-4, 206, 210, ¹211, 214,
217-18, 221, 225; 302, 304-9, 311-13,
315-16, 319-20, 324-25, 328; 402, 406,
:407, 408, †411, 412-13, 415, 417, 419-
20, 422-23, 429, 436. thunder and lightning storm 15-16; †215, 219; 307, 317-18,
322. thunder and rain storm :323.
    no response 35, 61; 118, 151.

Comment:
    electric storm: = thundershower--4.
"It's always been that, I guess"--65.
electrical storm: More violent than thun-
dershower--2. = shower; they pass over
quickly--32. More lightning than thunder
--110. More severe than 'thunderstorm'--
406. Squall: On water--16. Choice between
'windstorm' and 'electrical storm' depends on dominating element--433. thunder-
shower: Light storm with thunder--106.
Heard recently on radio--116. May have
heard from weather report on new radio
station--411. thunderstorm: = thunder-
shower--29. More thunder than lightning--
110.

6.1 drought. NE 97.

    Three principal responses came in reply
to a question about a rainless period:
drought, drouth, and dry spell. Although
the first two are historically similar,
they have been treated as lexically distinct because they now differ both in

spelling and in pronunciation. <u>Drought</u> is less common, but the two are semantically equivalent. They jointly contrast in meaning with <u>dry spell</u>, which, with only three exceptions, refers to a period shorter than one indicated by <u>drought</u>. For most infs. the question evoked vivid memories of the dust bowl days of the 1930's, but their replies evinced no significant geographical patterning except that the <u>drought</u> cognate is rare in South Dakota and Nebraska.

See Gary N. Underwood, "Semantic confusion: evidence from the Linguistic Atlas of the Upper Midwest," <u>Journal of English Linguistics</u> 2.86-95 (1968).

drought [1], 4, 9, 19-20, c37, 45, r48, [1]51, 55; 103, 106, 113, 120, 126, 152; 206, 209, *218, 226; 304; 401. dry ~ cr4.

drouth 2, s3, s6, 7-8, 10-12, s13, 14-18, 22-30, 33-34, 36-38, s39, 40-43, 46-48, 50, 54, [1]57, 58-60, 62-63, 65; 101-2,

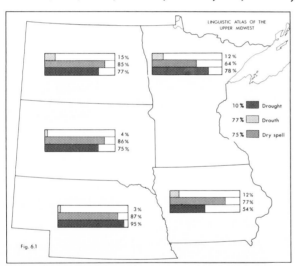

15%
85%
77%

12%
64%
78%

10% ■ Drought

77% ▨ Drouth

75% □ Dry spell

4%
86%
75%

3%
87%
95%

12%
77%
54%

LINGUISTIC ATLAS OF THE
UPPER MIDWEST

Fig. 6.1

104-5, 107-12, 114-18, 122-24, [1]125, 127-33, 135-37, 139, *139, cr140, 141-50; c201, 202-5, 207-8, 210-22, 224-25; 301-3, 305-6, 309-21, 323-28; 402-8, 410-14, c415, 416, 418-27, c428, 429-31, s433, 434-37. ~ weather :35.

dry period 12; 201, 204, 208, 221; 314. ~ season 11, 32, 42; 103, 106, 114; 207, 219; 327; 417, 432.

dry spell 1, 3, 5, s6, 7-10, 13-14, 17-19, :20, 21-24, 26, 28-33, s34, 36-39, 41-45, *46, 47-51, 53-58, c59, 60, 62-64; 101-2, 104-12, 115-16, 118-20, 122, 125, 128, 130, 132-34, 137, 142, 145, 150-51; 202-3, 205-6, 209-16, !217, 218-19, 221-24, s225, 226; 301-4, 306-11, 313, 315, 317, *318, 320-22, 324-26, 328; 401-15, †416, 417-34, s435, 436-37.

dry summer 6. ~ weather 16, 25, 27,

35, 52; 121, 138-39, 152; 323. ~ year 308.
  a hot dry one 409.
  no response 61.

Comment:

drought: Heard, but not so common as 'dry spell'--1. Unguarded form--37. Rare --45. "A fancy word"--119.

drouth: No drouth occurs here, so the word is not used--5. Only in newspapers --13. "A drouth year"--29. Inf. says rare in his community--43-44, 57-58; 433. "Awful dry"--415. No difference between 'drouth' and 'dry season'--11; 114; 327. No difference between 'drouth' and 'dry spell'--14, 18, 36, 43-45, 57-59; 108, 118, 120, 125, 130, 132, 137, 142, 145; 202, 210, 216, 220; 302, 317; 406, 430. No difference between 'drouth' and 'dry weather'--16, 27. Longer and more severe than a dry period--12; 201, 204, 208, 314. Longer and more severe than a dry season --106; 207. Longer and more severe than a dry spell--3, 7-10, 19-20, 22-24, 26, 28-30, 33-34, 37-40, 46, 48, 50-51, 55, 60, *62, 63; 101, 104-5, 107, 109-12, 115, 122, 128, 133, 150; 203, 206, 209, 211-13, 215, 217-18, 222, 224-26; 303-4, 309-11, 313, 315, 320-21, 324-26, 328; 401-5, 407-8, 410-12, 414-16, 418-19, 421-23, 427, 429, 436-37; over 1 week-- 435; over 2 weeks--425; over 2 or 3 weeks --17; 420; over 1 month--424; over 6 weeks--102; over 2 or 3 months--116; a season--301, 306, 318; all summer--211, 214; a year--426. Longer than a dry spell or season--42; 219, 221. Longer than dry weather--323. Damages or kills crops--47, 50; 414, 416, 420, 422-23, 427-28. "When things begin to burn up"--434. No rain at all for a season; a dry spell is a season of inadequate rain--62; 413. No moisture and permanent damage; a dry spell is a shorter and less serious period of inadequate rain--431.

dry period: equivalent to a dry spell; less severe than a drouth--42; 221.

dry season: Longer than a dry spell-- 32; 417. Longer than a dry spell, over several weeks--106. Longer than a dry spell and shorter than a drouth--219. No different from a dry spell--432. More common term--327.

dry spell: Long or short--31. Long and serious--49. Longer and more serious than a drouth--54. Extended period; same as 'drouth'--108. Extended period; same as 'dry year'--308. Shorter than both a drouth and a dry season--219. More common term--6, 8.

dry weather: Shorter period than a drouth--25; 139, 152.

6.2 The wind is <u>rising</u>. NE 91. WG 51; F45.

Six expressions compete with the term <u>rising</u>. <u>Rising</u> is a fairly consistent minority form throughout the UM, though slightly more frequent in Midland territory. <u>Coming up</u>, however, statistically the most common, owes its dominance to its popularity in the three western states (Mn. 17%, Ia. 21%, N.D. 61%, S.D. 43%, Nb. 41%). Four eastern terms have not generally been carried west of the Coteau du Prairie--<u>getting stronger</u> (etc.), <u>raising</u>, <u>picking up</u>, and <u>increasing</u>. <u>Increasing</u>, indeed, is limited to Minnesota and the eastern edge of South Dakota. The decline of <u>raising</u> may be partly due to school influence, since the extent of formal education correlates with its frequency range: I 24%, II 15%, and III 6%.

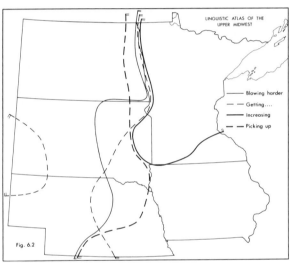

Fig. 6.2

beginning to blow 4; 205; 304, 321; 429.
~ harder 32.
blowing 16. ~ harder 7, 16, 19, :27, 38, 43, 51, 58-59, 63-64; 108, 136, 150; 210; 306, 316, 323; 425, 430, 434.
breezing up 29; 406.
coming in gusts 308.
coming up 2, 5, 14, 20-21, 23-24, 38, 49, 54, 62; 110-11, 115-16, 120, 122-23, 133, 143, 145, 148; 201-3, 206-7, 209, 211, 213, 215, 217-18, c219, 220-21, 224, 226; 302, 304, 307, 309-10, 312-13, 315, 322, 325, :326, 328; 403-4, 409-10, :411, c412, *417, 419, 421-22, 428-29, 431, 435-36.
developing 18.
freshening up 113.
(We're) getting a little breeze 409.
(It's) getting fierce 320. ~ harder 16.
~ higher 130, 135, 139. ~ rougher 427.

~ stronger 8-9, 17-18, 26, 31, 39, 50, 52; 119, 121, 127, 132, 134, 139-41, 147; 320, 323; 413-15, 421, 427. ~ up 53. ~ windy c56. ~ worse 402.
growing faster 319. ~ in strength 317. ~ stronger 40, 42; 126.
gusty 402.
heavy 6.
increasing 7, 9, 14-17, 19, 44, 59; 319.
picking up 6, 39, 44, 57; 109, 124, 128-29, 131, 140; 222; 308, 318; 426, 430.
raising 13, 15, 22, 25, 35, 41, 45, 48, 60, 62; 103, 112, 114, 117, 122, 125, 138, 142, 146, 149; c206, 210, 216, 225; 305, c306, 311, 321, 324; 405, 407-8, cr418, 420-21, 423, 431, 437.
rising 1, 10-11, ¹13, 28, 30, 33-34, 37, 46-47, 56, *62, 65; 101-2, 104-7, 116, 118, 123, 137, 144, :150, 151-52; 202, 204, 212, 214, 223; 301, 303, 314, 327; 401, 404, 406, 412, 416, ?418, 424, 432-33, 435.
starting to blow 3, 12, 55; 208-9; 417, 436.
no response 36, 61.

Comment:

<u>coming up</u>: More natural term--435.
<u>getting stronger</u>: "A fresh wind"--119.
<u>heavy</u>: Used in sailing--6. <u>raising</u>: Usu. --418, 421.

6.3 The wind is <u>letting up</u>. NE 92.

Although more than one-half of the infs., evenly distributed in the UM, use the dominant <u>going down</u>, the remainder offer a surprising number of variants. The two most frequent ones, <u>dying (down)</u> and <u>calming (down, etc.)</u>, occur principally in the eastern half, except for some instances in Nebraska and in the Black Hills. <u>Lulling down</u>, recorded in Maine by New England Atlas fieldworkers, survives in the speech of a Brookings, South Dakota informant of New England ancestry.

abating 7, 39; 201; 314.
blowing out 15.
calmer 402. calming 14, 34; 147; calming down 4, 6, ¹10, 13-14, 17, cr19, 21, 47; 103, 114, 131; 204, :206; 305; 421. getting calm 142. growing calmer 319.
coming down ?19.
decreasing 58; 123.
diminishing 7; 101, 126, 132, 144.
dropping 202, ¹215.
dying 33, 45; 111, 123. ~ down 2-3, 8, 15, 20, 22, 28, 37-39, 41, !46, 49, 51, 54, s55, sn58; 102, 108-10, 112, 126-27, 129, 134, 139, 141, s147, sn150; 222, 225; 310-13, 323, 326; 407, 414, 419-20, 424-25, c428, 435.

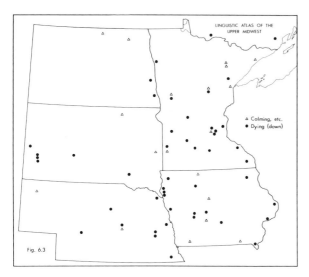

easing down 432. ~ up 35, 37, 48, s58.
fading out 31.
falling 137.
getting lower 135; 413. ~ milder 119.
going 60; 122. ~ down 1, 5, 7, 10, 12,
16, 24-25, sn26, 27, 29-30, 32-33, 36,
40, 45, c50, 52-54, 56, 59-60, 62-65;
102, 104-7, 112-13, 115-18, 120, 124, 128,
132-33, 136, 138, 143, 145-46, 148-49,
151-52; c201, 203, c206, 207, 210-11, 213-
21, 223-24, 226; 301-14, 307, 309, 315,
*318, ?320, 321-22, c324, 325, 327-28;
401, 403-6, 408-12, 416-18, 421, c422,
426-27, 429-31, 433-34, 436.
laying 130; 209; 437.
lessening 42.
letting down 9. ~ up sn11, 14-15, 23,
s39, 40, sn65; sn150; 205, sn208, 212;
*306, 308, cr320; 415.
lowering :150.
lulling down 317.
moderating 316.
quiet 402. quieting down *43; 125, 140;
423.
receding 204, 210; 318.
settling 1. ~ down 140.
slackening 19. ~ up →57.
slowing down 44; 319.
subduing 18.
subsiding 26, 34, 62; 121; ?320.
no response 61.

Comment:

calming down: Frequent here--10. diminishing: Picked this word up through
listening to weather reports--126. dying:
Sailing expression--35. dying down: Usu.
--58. going down: Usu.--26; 320. quieting
down: Says he always uses this--*43.
slackening up: River term--57. subsiding:
Formal--62.

6.4 We had a frost. NE 98.

To denote such a nocturnal freezing
drop in temperature as occurs during the
fall the common term is simply frost, with
sporadic occurrence of specifying variants, black frost, hoarfrost, and white
frost. The East Coast freeze survives in
isolated instances, east of the Coteau
du Prairie except for a pocket in southeastern Nebraska. Its variant, freeze-up,
was not reported at all in the UM, although it was observed as a conversational response once during the Wisconsin
study.

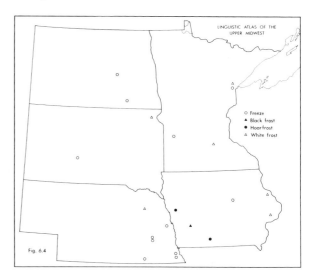

freeze 15, 42; 118; *218, 224; c313;
425-26, c428, 433-35.
frost 1-14, c15, 16-20, c21, 22-45,
c46, 47, 49-55, r56, 57-60, 62-65; 101-
39, 141-43, 145-52; 201-18, c219, 220-26;
301-28; 404-14, 416-24, s425, 426-37.
black ~ 151. hoar~ 122, 144. white ~ 15,
48; 121, 140; 308; 415.
no response 61.

Comment:

freeze: A heavy frost--17; 118; 425,
435. frost: More common term--224. Light,
but affects tender plants--426. Does not
freeze water; a 'freeze' produces ice--
426, 433-34. hoarfrost: A light frost--
122. white frost: More severe than either
frost or freeze--15.

6.5a The lake froze over last night.
NE 648.

FROZE (over), with a total 94% response,
dominates the UM. The few variants appear
almost exclusively in eastern Nebraska
and western Iowa. Within the dominant

form, however, a perhaps significant variation appears. Simple FROZE, without over, may have a Northern orientation. Its frequency drops from 36% in Minnesota to 31% in Iowa, and from 58% in North Dakota and 54% in South Dakota to only 42% in Nebraska.

formed ice 224.
FROZE 1, 3, 5, 8, 11-12, 17, 21-24, 26, 28, 33-36, 41, 45, 50, c54, 62, 65; 104-9, 111, 115, 121, 123-24, 127, 143, 145, 149, 152; 203-5, 208, 210-13, 215-17, 219, 221-22, 225; 301-2, c303, 309-10, 312-14, 316-18, 321, 324-25, 328; 403, 405-7, 409-12, 418, 421, 425, 427, 432, c435, 436-37. ~ over 2, 6, 9-10, 13-20, 25, 27, 29-32, 37-40, 42-49, c51, 52-53, 55, 57-60, *62, 64; 102-3, 110, 112-14, 116-20, 125-41, 146, 148, 150-51; 201-2, 206, 209, 218, 220, 223, c224, 226; 304-8, 311, 315, 319, 322, 326-27; 401-2, 404, 414, 416, 420, 422-23, 426, 428, 430-31, 433-34. ~ up 7, 56; 101; 323; 424.
froze ice 4; 147, 149; 207; 417, 419, 429. ~ a little ice 408, 415. ~ a scale of ice 214. ~ a scum of ice 320.
iced down 432.
scummed over †31; 420.
skimmed over 122, 142; 225; 413.
started to freeze 307.
white frosted 415.
no response 61; 144.

Comment:
scummed over: Her mother's term--31.

6.5b   scum (first thin coating of ice).

The eliciting question was usually "What do you call the ice that forms on a pond the first cold night?" This item, not in the eastern worksheets, was added only after most of the interviewing in Minnesota had been completed. Scum, the most frequent form, has fairly even distribution. Skim, the next most frequent form, has a strong Midland orientation.

CL 132: Mail responses generally confirm the field data, with scum having 44%. As a volunteered write-in response skim had a 14% frequency with Midland emphasis, from 7% in Minnesota to 24% in Nebraska. Shale had 5% frequency and anchor ice 2%. Rubber ice was most common in Minnesota, where it dominated with 32%.

coat of ice 125; 224; 306, 325. light coating 122.
film 107.
flake ice 35.
hickory ice 152.
layer of ice 318.
rubber ice 144, 148, 150, 152; 208; 319;

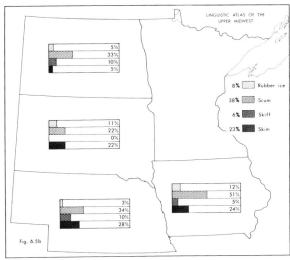

Fig. 6.5b

416. rubbery ice 125; 315.
scale of ice 113; 214.
scum ice 202. ~ of ice 30, s31, 32; 103-5, 108, 116, 119, 121-22, 124, 129, ¹131, 132-33, 138, 141-43, 145-49, s152; c201, c204, 207, 212, s¹213, :216, 217, 220, ¹224; ¹302, 303, 314, 318, 320; 401, 404-6, 408, c409, ¹410, *417, 418, 420, 427, s434.
sheet ice 111. ~ of ice 102, 112; 222; 309, 312; 423.
shell ice 14; 117.
skiff of ice 117, s140; 215, 218; :?411, 422, 429, 437.
skiffling of ice 109.
skim of ice 14-15, 29-30; 101, 120-21, 124, c130, 135, 137-38, s139, 140, 150; 225; c301, 311, 313, 322; c403, ¹†404, 407, 412-13, 421, ¹425, c428, 431, 436.
thin ice 36; 205, 209, 211; 312; :323; 417.
no response 1-14, 16-28, 33-34, 37-65; 106, 110, 114-15, 118, 123, 126-28, 134, 136, 151; 206, 210-11, 219, 226; 302, 304-5, 307-8, 316, 321, 326-28; 402, 415, 419, 424, 426, 430, 432-33.

Comment:

bum ice: Ice refrozen after a thaw--223. hickory ice: Same as rubber ice--152. mush ice: Ice with a melting surface--309. Soft ice after a thaw--324; 435. rubber ice: "Caused by a quick freeze; the ice seems to stretch"--125. Would support a child, but gives under weight--144. "Just about holds weight; the kind kids like to break through"--319. Gives under a skater--416. Not first ice, but still not thick--203. Found in spring, not fall, when ice is melting--205. scum of ice: "Thick as a windowpane"--145. skiff of ice: "Not apt to use this"--411. Do not say 'skiff of ice,' but say 'skiff of snow'--117, 124;

312, 326, 328. skim of ice: Same as rubber ice--150. Used only to refer to ice
on a road--310. "Oldtimers say 'skim of
ice'"--404. "That little crackle on the
top"--426.

6.6a sitting room (where guests are entertained). NE 323. WG 37, 47, 51; F28,
F46, F47.

Two generations ago many houses of the
moderately well-to-do had not only a room
where the family might sit in the evening
but also a room used only on special occasions such as weddings or formal visits.
This latter was commonly known as the parlor or front room, the former as the sitting room or living room. If there was
only one all-purpose room for family and
for entertaining, it generally was called

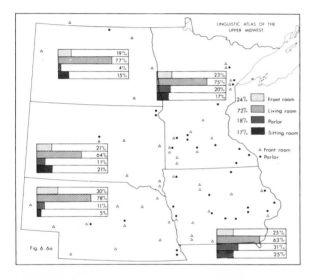

Fig. 6.6a

the sitting room or living room, rarely
the front room (in contrast with the parlor).

The decline of parlor began just when
population pushed into the western UM
states, which consequently have only scattered occurrences (1 in ND, 3 in SD, and
4 in Nb.) in contrast to 20% in Minnesota and 31% in Iowa. Front room fared
little better, reaching farther west
chiefly in Nebraska and pushing only
slightly into the eastern counties in the
Dakotas. Both the repeated designation
"old-fashioned" and the frequency decline
by age groups attest the obsolescence of
these forms. Parlor drops from Type I's
20% to Type II's 18%; front room drops
similarly from 31 to 20%. Neither is used
by Type III infs.
Except in Nebraska, sitting room is

fairly evenly distributed throughout the
region, but also is declining in use. With
Type I speakers its frequency was 26%;
with Type II it was 10%. No Type III
speaker uses it.
Living room, on the contrary, which also is uniformly distributed in the UM,
increases in frequency from 58% in Type
I, through 82% in Type II, to 100% in
Type III. It often is called recent.

CL 121: Mail returns coincide very
closely with the general averages of the
field data: front room, 30%; living room,
71%; parlor, 16%; sitting room, 16%.
Three respondents in Minnesota and Iowa,
of Ohio and Connecticut background, reported the use of best room, a minor variant in New England.

ben ⊥†46.
drawing room ⊥3.
front room ⊥5, †12, 13-17, †26, 29, 35,
†36, 42-43, 46-47, 52, 56, c59, c61, †62;
102, †103, 112-13, †115, 117, c119, †121,
125, 129-30, †131, †134, 141-43, 145,
151; 201, †203, c206, †207, 209, †210-
11, †213-14, 220, 224; 315, *316, *318,
†321, 323-25; †402, †405, 407, 409, †411-
12, 413, 415, 417-18, 421, 425, 427, 429-
30.
library †28; †326.
living room 2-4, 9-12, 14, →16, 17-22,
24-25, →26, 27-31, r32, 33-34, 36-38,
→39, 40, cr41, 45, →46, 47-51, 53-55, 57-
58, 60, c61, 62-63, 65; 101, 103, →104,
→106, 108-11, ⊥112, 115-17, →118, 120-28,
131, 133, 136-37, 141, 143, 145, 147-50,
152; 202-3, 205-8, 210-16, 218-19, 221-23,
225-26; 301-2, c303, 304-6, →309, 310,
312-13, 316, 318-19, †320, 321, →325, 326,
c327, 328; 401-2, 404, →405, 406, 408,
410-13, cvr414, 416, 419-28, 431-37.
front living room *r56.
other room !†53.
parlor !†1, †2-3, ⊥7, !†10, c†11, †12,
14-16, ⊥†19, †20-21, 23, !†27-28, !†30-
31, †33-34, †36-37, †39-40, 42, 44, *45,
46, 48, *48, †49-50, c51, †54, 55, 57,
†60-62, ⊥†63, 65; †101, 102, †103-4, 105,
†106, ⊥†107, †111, 114, ⊥†116, †118, c119,
†120, †122, 123-24, †126, 130, †133,
→134, 135, †136, 137-40, 144-45, 147,
†148; †201-3, 204, †205, †207-10, ⊥†211,
†212-13, †215-19, !⊥220, †221-24, ⊥†226;
*†301, †302, †305, 307-8, †311-13, 314,
⊥319-20, †326, †328; !†401, †404, †406,
⊥†411, ⊥413, ⊥415, 418, †419, 420, †422-
24, †427-28, ⊥431, †?433, 434-35, †436,
†437. back ~ †2, †21, †33, †49; †219.
front ~ †2, †21, †33, †49.
pleasure room *†139.
reception room 317.
sitting room 1, †2, !†4, 5-8, c13, †20-
22, ⊥23, 25, c†31, †33, †34, †37-38, 39,

158

?41, †42, 45, 48, †54, †60, †62, 65; †101, 102-3, 105, †106, 107, 111, 114, †115-16, †118, 119, †131, 132, 137-39, 145-46, †151; 201, †202, 204, †205, ¹212, †213, †215, 217, †221, sn†222, †223, 224; *†301, 303, 307, ¹308, †309, 311, †313, 317, ¹319, 320, 322, †326, †328; 403, †404, †408, 418, †422, ¹†423, ¹430, †437.
    sunken room 308.

Comment:

    ben: Scottish name used by inf.'s grand-mother--46. drawing room: Still heard here--3. front room: = parlor; uses occa-sionally--29. = parlor, once used both terms--36. = parlor--207; 418. = parlor; kept for company--103. = parlor; only in "better houses"--206. Separate room from the parlor--12; 210. Separate from parlor; = sitting room--102. Room closed off--134. Used in youth--47; 121. library: Once = sitting room--28. Term gave way to living room--326. living room: The regular sit-ting room--29. Only in newer, smaller houses--51. = parlor--208. Used in youth --320. The "modern" term--26; 118. other room: Used in youth--53. parlor: Not al-ways the same room as the sitting room --31. A second 'sitting room'--42. Used only when there were two rooms, the par-lor and sitting room--202; *301, 328; 437. The formal room; the sitting room infor-mal--37; 212-13, 215, 217. Separate from the sitting room: only for special occa-sions--102, 137-39, 204; 311. Separate from the living room--55. When the parlor was divided by a partition, the front part was called the 'front room' and the back part the 'sitting room'--62. Only for spe-cial occasions--65; 105-6, 119, 122, 137, 147, 149; 424, 436. "Parlors were just used for weddings and deaths"--148. For persons "of consequence"--422. "A little better room than the rest of the house"--114. "In grandmother's house"--123. Didn't have a parlor in their log house--214. A formal room--218. "That's an extra good living room"--318. Same as sitting room --205. "Some people call their [front rooms] 'parlors'"--415. = living room--419. "Others say 'parlor,' especially the French"--7. "Used by 'city slickers'"--220. "A few probably still call it 'par-lor'"--433. Used by inf.'s parents--50, 60; 226. Used long ago (c. 1900); "first and second parlors"--427. Used in youth--10, 54; 120; 428, 436. Uses occasionally --307. May be a jest--139. double parlor: A parlor plus a sitting room--2. front parlor: For company; also a 'back parlor' --21. Formal room; the back parlor the 'sitting room'--33. reception room: In inf.'s boarding house--317. sitting room: The back parlor in a 'double parlor'--2.

Room used more often than the 'parlor'--119. Used when there are two rooms, the parlor and a sitting room--202, 221-23. Separate from the parlor; used at night--418. = library--326. For guests--25. Children weren't usually allowed in it--22. "Where you didn't go when you came in from outdoors"--404. Used by inf.'s par-ents--38, 60. Term used by inf. in youth --34, 54. Uses term occasionally--201. Usu.--317. sunken room: Special feature of inf.'s house--308.

6.7 chimney. NE 322, 334.

    For the passageway by which smoke is vented from the house the common term is chimney (Mn. 97%, Ia. 85%, N.D. 81%, S.D. 93%, Nb. 100%). A nonstandard variant chim(b)ley was reported in all states but Nebraska, though with distribution large-ly eastern except for northern North Da-kota. By types its frequency is I 12%, II 2.1%, III 0. Flue, only in Iowa and once in Nebraska, appears Midland orient-ed. Stovepipe, always described as no longer used, seems usually to have been applied to the sheetiron pipe conveying smoke directly from a stove and emerging through the room, as in a sod house or other primitive dwelling.

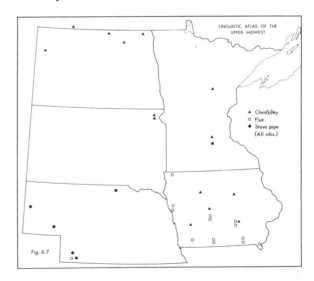

LINGUISTIC ATLAS OF THE UPPER MIDWEST

▲ Chim(b)ley
○ Flue
● Stove pipe
   (All obs.)

Fig. 6.7

    chimbley c35, ¹40, ¹42; !†222. chimley ?3, c21, ¹40, !¹47; 113, c*117, 128, 135, 151; 201, 204, †205, 207, 209, 212; 307, c308.
    chimney 1-2, cr3, 4-20, 22-26, c27, 28-30, !31, 32-34, 37-50, !51, 52-62, !63, 64-65; 101-12, 114-16, c117, 118-22, 124-27, 129-34, 136-41, ¹142, 143, 145-46, 148-50, 152; 202-3, 205-6, 208, 210-11, 213-16, c217, 218-26; 301-16, 309-10,

!c311, 312-25, !326, 327-28; 401-18, c419, 420-33, c434, 435-37.
 draft ¹317.
 flue 101, ¹117, 122-23, 130-31, →135, 136, ¹137, 142, 144, *145, sn146, 147, 149; ¹305; ¹424, 437. smoke ~ ¹21.
 stovepipe †48; †405, †409, †417, †429, †437.
 no response 36.

Comment:

 chimbley: "Improper"--40. Inf. heard a fire chief in the community use this term --42. Says he used to say this--222. chimley: "Most improper"; both chimbley and chimley used by "people who ought to know better"--40. Common in community--47. flue: Partition within the chimney--122. Partition within the chimney taking smoke from one particular fireplace--131. As common as chimney--146. Believes that this is new and in current usage--149. For the external structure, too--437. stove pipe: On sod houses--405. "A man with a brick chimney, we addressed him as 'mister'"--409.

6.8 kitchen matches (that will strike anywhere).

Because this item was added to the UM worksheets no comparison with eastern findings is possible. In the UM more than 40% of the infs. have no special term, using only the generic matches, sometimes in contrast with book matches and safety matches for other kinds. But more than one-half use a wide variety of terms, ranging in frequency from 28% for farm(er('s) matches to numerous colorful single responses. No consistent patterns of distribution by type emerged, but there is some regional variation. Wood(en) matches is concentrated in the Northern speech area; so is farm(er('s) matches, but with a heavier return in the Dakotas. Kitchen matches is most frequent in Minnesota and the North Platte valley in Nebraska, with a scattering in Northern Iowa. Sulfur matches, referring ordinarily to an older type of match no longer made, occurred principally in western South Dakota. All infs. considered it old-fashioned except one in Fort William, Ontario, who offered it as her only term.

 big matches 17; 128; 407.
 brimstone matches 132; †225.
 common matches 139; 209, 224; 419, 429.
 cordwood matches 14; 214.
 country matches 404.
 crack matches 149. cracker matches 42. cracking matches 225.
 diamond matches 29; 432.

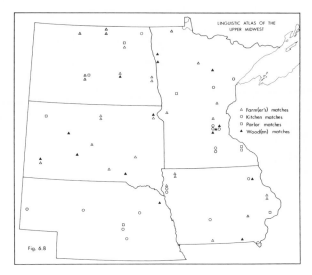

Fig. 6.8

LINGUISTIC ATLAS OF THE UPPER MIDWEST

△ Farm(er's) matches
○ Kitchen matches
□ Parlor matches
▲ Wood(en) matches

 farm matches 203, 213; 308. farmer ~ 101-2, 120-21; ¹302, 303-4, 321, 326, !328. farmer's ~ !4, ¹8-9, !10, 24-25, 31, s¹*43; 109, ¹117, 138, 145; !204, 205, *216, 217, !218, !221, *222; 315.
 firesticks ¹†7; ¹220. sulfur sticks †122.
 good matches 302.
 hard matches 310.
 house matches c25; 132; 207. household ~ 111, 152.
 instant matches 42.
 kitchen matches sn→c15, *21, 33-34, 37, ¹47, 49-50; 108, ¹109, 110-11, ¹125, 131, :sn150; :208; 410, *412, 416, 421-22, ¹437.
 lucifer matches †45. lucifers 309.
 matches 1, 8, 11, 13-16, 18, 21-22, 27, 28-30, 38, 41, 43, c44, 45-47, 54, 59-60; 103-7, 113-17, 119, 122-24, 126-27, 129-30, 133, 136, 142-44, 146, 149; 201-2, 210-11, 215, 220, 223, 226; 305-7, 316-19, 322, 327; 402-3, 405-7, 409, 411-13, 415, 418-19, 423-25, 427-30, 433-36.
 old-style matches *28.
 parlor matches :s2, 19, †23, 54-55; †109, 140; 212, 216, s¹225; 301, †311, †314, ¹322, s†324; c420.
 popping matches 214.
 redheads 309.
 safety matches 414, 431.
 sandrock matches †320.
 scratching matches 112.
 seven-day matches †120; †301.
 stick matches 311, 320.
 striking matches 137.
 sulfur matches 3, †35, 37, †106, †120, †149, †152, 222, c†225; †301, †309, †312, †314, *†316; !†401, ¹420.
 timber matches →426.
 up-north matches 37.
 wood matches 34, 36; 147; 307. wooden

~ 7, :9, :12, 35; 108; 219; 302, 312-13,
323; 408.
  no response or no special term 5-6, 20,
26, 32, 39-40, 48, 51-53, 56-58, 61-65;
118, 134-35, 141, 148, 151; !:206; 325;
417.

Comment:

  brimstone matches: Used in youth--225.
cracker matches: Because they crackle--
42. farmer's matches: Term used by inf.'s
son--8. firesticks: Inf. says Indians
use this term--220. hard matches: Inf.
says common here; contrasts with paper
matches--310. redheads: Early wooden
matches, but inf. still uses the term--
309. sandrock matches: Old matches need-
ing sandrock to scratch on; inf. says cowpunchers used sandpaper under front of
the saddle--320. seven-day matches: Old-
fashioned sulfur matches--120. sulfur
sticks: Old slow-starting matches--122.
up-north matches: Family term; inf.'s
wife thinks it Scandinavian--37.

7.1 hearth (of fireplace or of stove).
NE 329.
  Although most UM infs. accepted hearth
as the name for the floor of a fireplace,
more than one-fourth considered it primarily or exclusively as the designation
of a projecting shelf on either a kitchen
stove or a base-burner. For many infs.,
unfamiliar with actual fireplaces, hearth
is only a bookword. A few, with a fireplace in a recently constructed house,
had no word for the hearth in their own
fireplace. Both meanings are found
throughout the UM; no responses occurred
in southern Iowa, however, where the
fieldworker treated the item only for its
pronunciation.

  apron 419.
  base step 12.
  hearth (of a fireplace) 8, 11, 14, 20,
24-25, 28, 35, 39, 58-59, 62; :122; 202-
5, :210, :212, 214, 217-18; 314, 319,
321-25, 327; 409-10, 414, 423-25, 427-28,
432.
  ~ (of a stove) 11-12, 29-30, c35, 39,
42, 54, 59, 65; 102-4, 109, 113, 115-16;
204, 207-8, :210, :†212, 213-15, :216,
218, 223, 225, †226; 301, ¹†302, 303,
s307, †309-10, 313-14, *316, 322, 324-25,
328; 401, 403, 405, 407, 409, 412-14,
418, 420, 424, 427-28, c429, 432, 434.
  ~ (of either) 11, 35, 39, 59; 204, 210,
212, 214, 218; 314, 322, 324-25; 409,
414, 424, 427-28, 432.
  ~ (function not specified) 1-3, ¹5, 6-
7, 9-10, 13, 16-18, 21-23, 25-27, :s31,
32-34, :36, 37-38, ?43, c44, c45, :46,
c*46, 47, s†48, 49, s50, 51, f52, 53, 55,

s¹56, 57, 60-61, 63-64; 105-6, 108, 110-
11, s112, 114, 117-21, 123-33, :134, 135,
s136, 137, 139, 141-45, *145, 146-51,
:152; 201, 211, 218, *c218, 220-22; 304,
308, c311, 316, 320, 326; 402, ¹404, 411,
s¹421-22, 426, 431, 435.
  plate :404.
  stovehearth 432.
  tile 51. tiling 52, *56.
  no response 4, 15, 19, 41; 101, 107,
138, 140; 206, ?209, 224; 305-6, 312, 315,
317-18; 406, 408, 415-17, 430, 433, 436-
37.

Comment:

  Knows 'hearth,' never uses--9. Fireplaces not in older houses here--7, 25.
Few fireplaces in this area--23, 64; 225.
Never lived in a house with a fireplace;
items are unfamiliar--43, 50; 149. Not
familiar--57. Known through reading only
--304, 319. Not familiar with fireplaces;
hearth is almost synonymous with fire-
place--319. Spelled but did not pronounce
hearth--149, 152. Shelf on front of a
kitchen stove--11; 213. Projecting part
on a kitchen stove--12, 29. On old-fashioned kitchen stove where ashes accumulat-
ed; extended about 1' in front of stove
through the stove under the grate--113.
On a kitchen stove--115; 225; 401. On a
kitchen stove with an elevated oven;
about 1 1/2' from the floor--116. On a
base burner--208. The base where a base
burner sits--328. A platform on a kitchen
stove; obsolete--212. The ash-draft door
on a kitchen stove--413. Below the side
drafts on a kitchen stove; used to remove
ashes--420. On a heating stove--109. A
metal piece extending in front of a heating stove--102. Metal rim on two sides of
a heating stove, about 1' from the floor
--104. A footrest on any stove--207. A
shelf on a stove--213, 214, 226; 309,
313; 403, 407, 418, 429. Front of a stove
where ashes are removed--103.

7.2 andirons. WG 47, 51; F48.

  Unfamiliarity with fireplaces prevented
nearly one-half of the UM infs. from responding to the question, "What do you
call the metal supports for logs in a
fireplace?" Consistently throughout the
UM about three-fourths of those responding used andirons, but a few, used to
burning coal, responded with grates. Related Midland and South Midland variants,
dogs, fire dogs, and dog irons, appeared
mostly in the speech of Type I infs. in
southern Iowa. One instance of fire dog
was recorded in Minnesota from an inf.
whose mother was born in New York city.

161

CL 5: Checklist returns generally cor- roborated the field data except for the greater frequency of fire irons (21%) and for the appearance of handirons, 4 in- stances in Nebraska and 1 each in Minne- sota and North Dakota.

andirons 2, 6, 9-11, 14, 17-18, 20-21, 26, :27, 28-29, :31, s?32, 33-34, 37-40, 42, 44-47, 49, 51, 53-55, s*56, 57-58, 61-62, :s¹63, 65; 105, 110-11, 116-17,

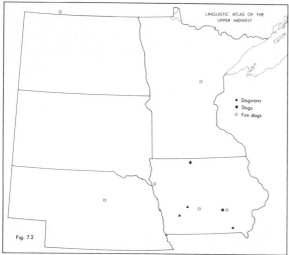

Fig. 7.2

119-24, 128-31, 134, 137, 144, *145, 150, 152; 205, sn210, 211, 213-15, 217-18, 221-23, 226; 308-9, :¹310, 312, 314, 319- 20, 324-26; 401-2, 404, 406, 408-9, 412, s416, 419, 422, 424-26, 428, 431, 433.
    dog irons †118, 127, 146, s148, 151.
    dogs ¹†45; 103, 135. fire ~ ¹3, 22; 111, 131, 135; :201; ¹†314; 413.
    fire irons †306; 429.
    grates 15-16, 48, 52, *56; 305, 316-18.
    irons 3; 108; 414.
    standards 12.
    no response 1, 4-5, 7-8, 13, 19, 23-25, 30, :?35,:?36, 41, 43, 50, 59-60, 64; 101-2, 104, 106-7, 109, 112-15, 125-26, 132-33, 136, 138-43, 147, 149; ?202, 203- 4, 206-8, ?209, 212, 216, ?219, 220, 224- 25; 301-4, 307, ?311, 313, 315, 321-23, 327-28; 403, ?405, 407, 410-11, 415, 417- 18, 420-21, 423, 427, 430, 432, 434-37.

Comment:

    andirons: Known through reading only-- 213. dog irons: Used by inf.'s mother-- 118. fire dogs: A grate for wood; upright pieces are 'andirons'--131. irons: For kettles; no name for andirons--414.

7.3 mantel shelf. NE 328. WG 51; F27.

    For the shelf above the fireplace more

than 80% of the UM infs. regularly use the simple mantel. Variants were reported almost exclusively in Minnesota and Iowa, and, except for two Minnesota college graduates, entirely from Type I and Type II speakers, with the bulk from Type I.
    Clock shelf, infrequently found in New England and then only to name a shelf not over a fireplace, was not recorded in Wisconsin but turns up in the UM for the shelf over the fireplace, with three Min- nesota instances.

CL 6: Mailed replies provide an even distribution of a 61% return for mantel and of a 28% distribution for mantelpiece. Clock shelf has greater frequency than in the fieldwork, with 10 instances in Minnesota, 34 in Iowa, 17 in the Dakotas, and 16 in Nebraska, for a total of 9%. Single instances of these appeared: fire- board and fire ledge in Minnesota, and fire shelf, a rare New Hampshire term, in northwestern Iowa.

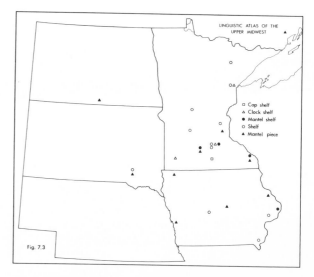

Fig. 7.3

    ledge :63.
    mantel 1-2, 5-6, 8-11, c12, 14-15, 17- 18, 20-24, 26, 28-34, !35, 37, 39-40, 42, 44-47, 51, 53-55, *56, 57, s58, 60-61, *62, 64-65; 102-6, 108-18, c119, 121-24, 126-28, 130-31, 133-38, 141-44, *145, 146-47, *148, 150-52; 201, 203-4, 208-15, 217-22, 226; ¹302, 304, 306, 308-12, 314- 15, *316, 318-21, 324-26, 328; c401, 402, 404, 406, 408-10, ?411, 412-14, 416-17, 419-20, 422-28, 431, 433, 436.
    mantelpiece 3, 38, 52, sn58; 101, 120, 125, 132; †222, 223; 323.
    shelf 13, 16, 27, 36, !43, 48-49; 129, 140, 149; 322. cap ~ 62. clock ~ 16, 48, 59. mantel ~ 48, 51, *r56, s63; 139.
    top 50.
    no response 4, 7, 19, 25, 41; 107; ?202,

:205, 206-7, 216, 224, ?225; 301, 303, 305, 307, 313, 317, 327; 403, ?405, 407, 415, 418, 421, 429-30, 432, 434-35, 437.

Comment:

mantel: The entire top--51. shelf: Rare --13. cap shelf: "The cap of the fire-place"--62. clock shelf: Inf. never had a fireplace--59. mantel shelf: The very top where clocks might be put--51.

7.4 back log.

For the larger piece of wood at the rear of a hearth many infs., unfamiliar with fireplaces, have no designation. The common response of the others is back log, the distribution of which largely coin-cides with the earlier areas of settle-ment. The variant fire log appeared twice in north central Nebraska, and all night chunk, possibly idiosyncratic, occurred once in Iowa.

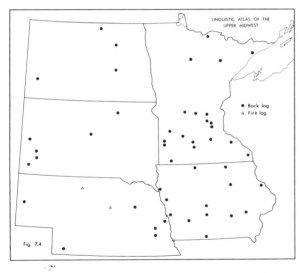

Fig. 7.4

all night chunk 125.
back log 5-6, 10, 14, 23, 28-29, 31, 33, 37, :38, s?†39, s?†40, 42, 45, !46, 47, sn48, 49, 51, 53, s54, 55, 58, 61; 103, 105, 111, 116, †118, 119, 122, 124, 128, 131, 135, 137, *145, 151, s152; 204, 213-14, 218; 306, 309, ¹310, 311, s312, 314, 320, 326; 409, 416, 424, 426, 428-29.
fire log 404, 414.
log 3, c13, c15, c16, 17-18, 32, 35-36, 44, c45, c52, 62; 150, :152; 202, 211, 220-22, c223, 225; 304-5, 325, 327-28; 402, 405-8, 411-12, 417-19, 436.
no response 1-2, 4, 7-9, 11-12, 19-22, 24-26, ?27, 30, 34, 41, 43, 50, 56-67, 59-60, 63-65; 101-2, 104-10, 112-15, 117,

120-21, 123, 126-27, 129-30, 132-34, 136, 138-44, 146-49; 201, 203, 205-8, ?209, 210, ?212, 215-17, ?219, 224, 226; 301-3, 307-8, 313, 315-19, 321-24; 401, 403, 410, 413, 415, 420-23, 425, 427, 430-35, 437.

Comment:

back log: Used by inf.'s mother (from N.C.)--118. Learned from reading--137; 213.

8.1(1) sofa (the long piece of furniture to sit or stretch out on). NE 326.

Although there are certain recognizable types of this "long piece of furniture," changes in furniture design and style have sometimes obscured the differences between one type and another. This fact, coupled with age and dialect mixture, has led to such semantic and lexical com-plexity that a multiple representation seems requisite. In this section all lex-ical responses are listed without regard to semantic distinctions. The following sections, 2 through 6, represent the principal semantic classes corresponding to different physical characteristics of the piece of furniture. In these sections the lexical variants have a common refer-ent. Analysis would reveal considerable overlapping, for it is not unusual that an inf. has two or even three customary designations for the same piece of furni-ture, the choice depending upon the occa-sion or the audience or sheer whim. The description of the term as old-fashioned or new-fangled is sometimes a clue to the basis for choice in a given situation.

In the late 1960's sofa rather swiftly became the generic used in UM furniture advertising and hence gained currency in general speech. A St. Paul newspaper in January, 1968, for example, carried an advertisement announcing a special price for upholstering "ANY SOFA, Including any Hideabed, Loveseat, studio or daven-port, regardless of age, make, size, con-dition or style." During the period of the field investigation, however, the general term was clearly davenport. Its frequency of 75% was nearly uniform throughout the UM. By age-groups davenport even seemed to be gaining in favor at that time, since the percentages rise from 59% for older Type I speakers to 88% for Type II and 100% for Type III. Of the 88 re-sponses of sofa (42% of the total), 29 were actually then described by the inf. as old-fashioned or obsolescent.

No pronounced geographical patterns ap-pear with any of the American variants, although sofa is rare in more recently settled northern Minnesota and South Da-kota, and in North Dakota occurs only along the main line of the Northern Pacific railroad, the earliest homesteaded area. Settee seems similarly influenced. With the historic meaning of a small seat for two persons settee occurs almost exclusively in the two older states of Minnesota and Iowa. It is true that the term turns up with the same frequency in Nebraska, but apparently by the time of the settlement of that state the term had lost its specificity, for there it became a generic often loosely equated with davenport. Lounge, with highest frequency in Iowa and Nebraska (46% and 38%), has Midland orientation. Its frequency elsewhere is: Minnesota, 29%; North Dakota, 27%; and South Dakota, 21%. Divan, not reported at all in Minnesota and infrequent elsewhere, may also exhibit a slight Midland orientation.

In the midcontinent one term, chesterfield, is uniquely Canadian, although it has found American lodging in the San Francisco Bay region in California. It is familiar to residents of the UM communities along the Canadian border, but they have not adopted it.

See Gary N. Underwood, "Semantic confusion: evidence from the Upper Midwest," Journal of English Linguistics 2.86-95 (1968).

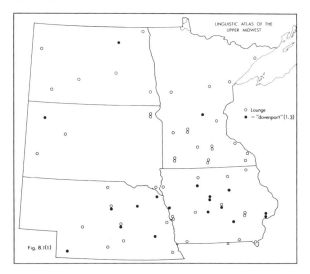

bench 45; 307. love ~ 117.
chesterfield 1-3, ¹47; 201-2.
couch 1-3, s5, ¹7, s8, 10-11, 13, →15, 19, 21, †22, 23-27, c†28, 29, 31, 33, †37, 38, †41, 43, 45, 47-48, 55, 59, †61, 64-65; 102, 107-10, 113, 115, 117, 120-23, 126, 128-30, †131, 134, 137, 140, 144-45, 148-50; 201, †203, 204, †205, c207, †208, 209, †211, 214, c219, 220, 222, †226; 302-4, 307, 309, 316-18, 320, 322, †323, 325-26; 401, 403, †404, 405, →406, †409,
†410-12, 416, †419, 422, 424, 426, cvr427, 428, 431-33, s434, 435.
davenport 2, 4-5, 7-13, 17-20, 22, 24, 26, 28, ¹30, 31-32, 34, 36-43, c44, 46-47, 49-51, 53, 57-58, 60, c61, 62-65; 101-4, 106, 108, 110-12, 115-16, c117, s119, 121-28, 130-39, 141-44, *145, 146-50, 152; c203, 204-18, 221-24, 226; 302-6, 308, →309, 310, 313, 315-19, 321, 323-24, 326-28; 402, 404-6, 408-13, c414, 415, c416, 417, →419, 420-23, 425-28, 430, c431, 433, s434, 435-37.
day bed 2, 58; 305, 308, 318. ~ couch 220.
divan ¹22, †38, s¹58; 117, 144, *145, 150; 212; 319; 431. divano 313; 424.
duofold 414, †421.
lounge ¹1, 6, 16, 19, 21, 29, †30, 36, 42-44, †46, 49-50, 52, 54, 56, 58-60, 62-63; 104, 106-7, 109, 112, 114-16, 123-26, 129, †131, 132-33, 135, 137-38, 140-41, 143, 147, †148, 149; 207, 209, 212, †213, 215, 217-18, †221, †223, 225; 301-2, *†306, 307-8, †310, 311, †324, 325; 405, 407, 413-15, 418, 420-21, †422, 423, 425, 428-30, 434, s¹435, †436. chaise ~ [sic] *62; 150.
love seat 20, 42, 58; 116, 122, 127; 218; 308, *316; 428, 431.
settee 4, 8, 11, 14, 21, 23-24, †37, 39-40, 45-46, 49, 51-53, c57, 59-62, 65; 101, 103, 111, 113-14, 117, 128, 130, 136, 138-39, 142; 205, †208, †213, 221-22; 304, 308, 312, 314, 320, †323, †327; 402, 404, 408, 414, 416, 420, 423, 425, 428, 431, 434. settle 103.
sofa 2, †3, 4-5, ¹7, 8, †9-10, ¹†11, †12, 14-15, 17, 19, s20, †22, s24, 25, †26, s¹†28, ¹29, †30, 32, †33, 34-35, †36, 40-41, *41, 44, †46, 47-48, s49, 50-51, 54-56, 58, 63, s64, s65; 101-2, 105-6, 108, 112, 116, 118-22, 124-25, ¹126, 129, 131, 133, 136-37, 139-41, 145-48, †149, 151-52; 202-3, *204, sn205, †206, 210, †211, 212, 214-15, †216, 217-18, *219, :sn220, 222, †223, 224-25; 301, †302, s303, *306, †309-10, †313, 315, ¹†323-24, 326, †328; !†401, †402, 403, 406-9, 412, 415, 417-18, †419, 420-22, 424-25, c429, 430-31, s¹435, †437.
studio couch 58; 305, 317, 319; 404, †411, 417, 433. studio 127.

Comment:

chesterfield: Canadian name--47. couch: Inf. thinks term general here--7. = davenport; unspecified--427. = davenport and settee; unspecified--130. = davenport, lounge, and settee; unspecified--57. Refers to a folding sanitary cot--409. davenport: Usu.--38. divan: Not a native term--58. lounge: Generic term--6. Refers to a folding sanitary cot--142. Can also be a bed--307. love bench: A window seat

--117. sofa: Inf. couldn't describe it--
49. Generic term--50. "In the parlor in
the old days"--65. "An old horsehair sofa"--202.

(2) couch (a long piece of furniture
with a headrest at one end but without
arms and usually without a back).

couch 1-2, s8, 10-11, †22, 23-24, 26,
c†28, 29, 31, †37, 47, †61, 64-65; 102,
107-8, 110, 115, 117, 123, 126, 128-29,
†131, 134, 137, 140, 144-45, 149-50; 201,
†203, †205, c207, †208, 214, 219-20, 222,
†226; 302, 309, 318, 320, 322, †323, 326;
†404, †410, 416, †419, 422, 426, 428,
431, 435.
    lounge ¹1, 16, 21, 36, 42-44, †46, 49-
50, 52, 54, 56, 58-60, 63; 104, 106-7,
109, 114, 124-26, †131, 132, 137-38, 143,
†148, 149; 207, 209, †213, 217-18, †221,
†223, 225; 301-2, †306, 310-11, †324,
325; 405, 414, 418, 420, 423, 425, 430,
s¹435, †436.
    settee †37, 52; 103.

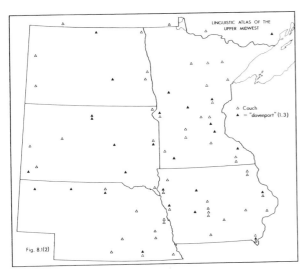

Fig. 8.1(2)

    sofa 2, 4-5, 8, †10, †11-12, 15, 17,
s20, †22, s24, s¹†28, ¹†29, †30, 32, †36,
40, *41, 51, 55-56, 58, 63, s64; 101-2,
105, 108, 112, 118, 122, 124, 133, 136,
139-40, 145, 148, 152; *204, †206, 210,
†211, 212, 215, †216, *219, 224-25; 301,
†313, 315, †324, 326, †328; 403, 406-8,
†417, 418, 420, 424-25, s¹435, †437.

Comment:

    couch: With back--31, 61; 107; 207;
410. With or without back--102; 201.
lounge: With back--207, 225. With or without back--42, 56. Term used by inf.'s
grandfather--306. settee: With one-half
a back--37. With or without back--52.

sofa: With one-half back or without back
--2. With or without back--36, 51, 56;
102, 139; 212, 215-16; 313. With back--
28, 30, 46, 55; 210, 225; 417. With arm
at end opposite from headrest--140.

(3) davenport (a long piece of upholstered furniture having arms and seating
three or more persons).

    chesterfield 1-3; 201-2.
    couch 3, ¹?7, 19, 23, 25, 27, 33, 38,
55, 59; 109, 113, 120, 122, 126, 149;
204, †211, c219; 303-4, 316, 318, 320,
322,; 401, 403, →406, †412, 432.
    davenport 2, 4-5, 7-13, 17-20, 22, 24,
26, 28, ¹30, 31-32, 34, 36-43, c44, 46-
47, 49-50, 53, 57-58, 60, c61, 62-65;
101-2, 104, 106, 110-12, c117, s119, 122-

Fig. 8.1(3a)

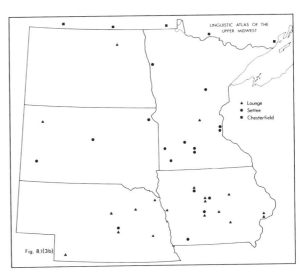

Fig. 8.1(3b)

28, 131-39, 141-44, *145, 146-47, 149-50, 152; c203, 204-18, 221-24, 226; 302-6, 308, →309, 310, 313, 315-19, 321, 323-24, 326-28; 402, 404-6, 408-13, c414, 415, c416, 417, →419, 420-23, 425-26, 428, 430, c431, 433, 435-37.
  day bed 318.
  divan 144, *145; 212; 319; 431. divano 313.
  duofold 414.
  lounge 29; 112, 114-16, 123, 129, 133, 135, 140-41; 212; 301; 407, 414-15, 421, †422, 425, 429.
  settee 8, 21, 39-40, 45-46, 51-52, 59; 113-14, 128, 142; †213; 308, 312, 314; †402, 420.
  sofa †3, ¹?7, †9, †11, 19, 34-35, 44-45, †46, 48, 54; 119, 125, 129, 131, 141, 147, 149; ¹210, 214, 217-18, *219, 222, †223; †302, *306, †309-10; 409, 412, 415, 421-22, 424, c429, 430-31.

Comment:

  couch: Opens as a bed--126; 204; 303, 320; 412. Does not open as a bed--33; 149; 316. davenport: Opens as a bed--8, 44; 112, 146, 149; 309, 316, 409. Does not open as a bed--126, 152; 313. May or may not open as a bed--317. day bed: Opens as a bed--318. divano: Opens as a bed--313. duofold: Opens as a bed--414. lounge: Opens as a bed--115, 141. Does not open as a bed--301. With spindle back instead of upholstered back--116. settee: Does not open as a bed--8. Like a davenport, but not upholstered--308. May or may not be upholstered--312, 314. sofa: Does not open as a bed--149; 409. Used by inf. in youth--9.

(4) studio couch (a couch with removable pillows for a back).
  couch 2, 21, 43, 45, 48; 209; 325; †404, 433.
  day bed 58; 305, 308. ~ couch 220.
  lounge †30, 42, 58, 62; 115; 215; 413, 429.
  settee 62; 111, 142; 314.
  sofa 120, 137; ¹429.
  studio couch 305, 317, 319; 433. studio 127.

(5) settee (a small sofa suitable for two persons).
  couch 405.
  divan 117.
  duofold 421.
  love seat 20, 42, 58; 116, 127; 218; 308, 316, 428, 431.
  settee 11, 23-24, 49, 57, 60-61, 65; 101, 117, 136, 138; †208, 221-22; 304, 320, †323, †327; 408, 414, 416, 423, 425,

431.
  sofa 25, 47; 106, 122, 137, 146; 203.
Comment:

  duofold: Seats only two, but opens as a bed--421. settee: Wooden back and arms --101, 138; 408.

(6) sofa (an old-fashioned seat for two or three people which has arms and an ornamented back raised in the center).
  couch †323.
  settee 205.
  sofa †26, †33, 50; 116; *204, sn205, :sn220; s303; :†401, †402.

8.2 bedroom. NE 337. WG 46; F47.

For the room where one sleeps the usual term throughout the UM is bedroom. (Bed) chamber, typically with the meaning of a large bedroom on the first floor, survives in the eastern half of the region, although even as a survival it is often characterized as old-fashioned or obsolescent. Sleeping room, a minor variant, occurs in the same area. An inf. in Marshall, Minnesota, offered bedsink, a New York state word for a small alcove off a kitchen where older people could sleep warmly in winter.
  bedchamber s†40, †51, 58; cr220; †311. c25, 26, c27, 28, c29, 30-41, c42, c43, 44-51, c52, 53-54, c55, 56-58, c59, 60, c61, 62, c63, 64-65; 101-7, 109-21, 123-52; 201-7, 209-17, c218, 219, ?220, c221, 222-24, c225, 226; 301-28; 401-11, c412, 413-15, cvr416, 417-37.
  bedsink 46.
  chamber ¹1, ¹†2, ¹†21, s†23, †31, 32, †39, †45, st†48, ¹53, s¹†54, s†58, *62; c†103, †118, s¹145; ¹†204, †215, s220; ¹†327; 420.
  guest room 50; 413.
  sleeping room 7, 62-63; c116, 140; ¹305.
  spare room 23, 28; 106-7; †413.
  no response 108, 122; 208.
Comment:
  bedchamber: Inf.'s usual term for his own room--220. chamber: Used by English people--1, 2. Used by inf.'s parent(s)--23; 118; 215. Used by inf.'s grandparent --103. Used by inf.'s parents for room on first floor--204. Heard it as a boy, but rarely; in his family it meant the 'vessel'--54. Any upstairs room--420. guest room: Formerly 'spare room'--413. sleeping room: Translation from Danish--63. spare room: Guest room--23. Extra bedroom--107.

8.3 (window) shade. NE 327. WG 28, 51; F16.

Of the three names for the opaque window-covering attached to a roller, (window) shade is used by four out of five
infs. of all types throughout the UM. The
Midland blind, which two generations ago
was making inroads upon Northern territory in Minnesota and North Dakota--al-
though not in South Dakota--apparently is
declining in the face of the growing popularity of the slatted window-covering and
its designation Venetian blind(s), often
ambiguously shortened to blind(s). Only
one-fifth of the infs. respond with blind,
and then often only as an older or second
term. It remains the normal form in the
Canadian communities, however. Curtain,
an old Northern form, likewise is declining, perhaps in part because of confusion
with the same designation for a hanging
of lace or other cloth. Its frequency is:
Type I 31%, II 22%, III 20%. Consistently,
its distribution is dominantly Northern.

CL 7: Checklist replies (988) confirm
results of the fieldwork, with 94% for
shade, 20% for blind, and 13% for curtain.

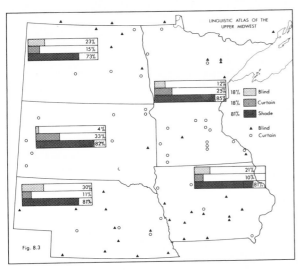

LINGUISTIC ATLAS OF THE
UPPER MIDWEST

☐ Blind
▨ Curtain
■ Shade

▲ Blind
○ Curtain

Fig. 8.3

blind c1, ¹2, †3, 11, 13-15, ¹†26, ¹†28,
†44, 57; ¹109, 118, 122, 127, 130, 135-37,
143, 151; 201-2, 204, †205, 206, ¹209,
213, c220, ¹224; ¹304, ¹313, 319; †401,
406, 410, †411, 412, 414, 421, 423-24,
431, !437. window ~ c3, *45; 125, 145;
†208; 433-34.
    curtain 7, 12, †13, †23, ?27, 30, 32,
34, †36, 38, 41, †42, †45, c46, ¹†47, 48-
50, †51, ?53-54, !¹55, 56, 59, †60, c61,
†62, s†63; 101, ?102, *110, ?111-12, 129,
148, †149; 207, c218, 222; 301, *306, 307-
9, 311, †312, 316, 320; †418, 419, 425,
427, ¹435. draw ~ 421. roll ~ †203. roller
~ 4; 216; ¹308, 322. spring ~ †29. window
~ 32, s†40, c46; †117.

roller ¹58.
    shade 5-6, 8-10, 14-23, 25, ?26, 29-31,
→32, 33-35, →36, 39, ¹41, 43-44, 46-47,
49, 51-52, cr53, 54, 57-58, ¹59, 60-63,
65; 101, cr102, 105-8, 110, ?113, 114-21,
123-24, 128, 130-31, 133-34, 136, 138-44,
149-50; →203, 208-16, c217, 219-21, 224-
25; 304-7, 310, →312, 313-14, 316-19,
323-27; 401-9, 411, ¹412, 414-17, *418,
420, 425-26, 428, 430, ¹431, 432-33, 435-
36. pull ~ ¹308. window ~ 2-3, ¹7, 11,
24, cr26-27, 28, 37, 40, c42, 45, 48, 55,
64-65; 103-4, 109, cr111, cr113, 126, 132,
146, c147, 150, 152; 205, 223-24, 226;
303, 308, 310, 315, 319, 321, 328; 413,
415-16, 421-22, 427, 429, 433-34.
    no response 302.

Comment:
    blind: Used by inf.'s mother--28. Occa-
sional--319. Used in a store--414. window
curtain: Used by inf. in youth--208. curtain: Usu.--30. Older term than 'shade'--
54. Occasional--306. Cloth curtain is a
'lace curtain'--50; 309. "Not the proper
name"--51. "Some people call them 'curtains,' but it isn't right"--55. "A New
England Yankee name"--62. "Real ancient
people would say 'curtains'"--63. "Many
call 'em 'curtains'"--435. shade: Newer
term--34. Usu.--406, 414, 433. window
shade: Other kind is a 'glass curtain'--
152. Change from 'blinds' to 'window
shades' due to store vocabulary--205.
More natural term--416, 421.

8.4a clothes closet (built in). WG 338.

For a small room, usually just large
enough to walk into, designed to contain
articles of clothing, 7 out of 10 UM infs.
have the term closet, a form with Midland
weighting. Most of the rest have the specified variant, clothes closet, which has
Northern weighting. No significant difference in frequency is found among the
three types, a fact suggesting that no
change is occurring.

    chamber †302.
    closet 4, 6-10, 12, 16-20, 23-24, 26-
28, 30-34, c35, 36, 38-39, 41-42, c44,
45-50, 52-56, 58-65; 101, 103-8, 110-15,
c116, 117-20, 122-30, 132-33, 135-39,
141-47, 149-52; 206, 211, 213, 216-17,
220, 222, c225, 226; 301, 303, 305-6,
*306, 307, c308, 312, c314, 316-20, 322,
?323, 324-25, 327-28; 401-9, 411-15, 418,
421-26, 428, 431-37.
    clothes closet 1-3, 5, 10-11, 13-15,
21-22, 25, 29, 37, 40, 43, 51, 55, 57;
102, 109, 121, 131, 134, 140, 148, 150,
152; 201-5, 207-10, 212, 214-15, 218,
c219, 223-24; →302, c303, 304-5, 308-11,
313, 315, 321, cr323, 326; 410, 416-17,

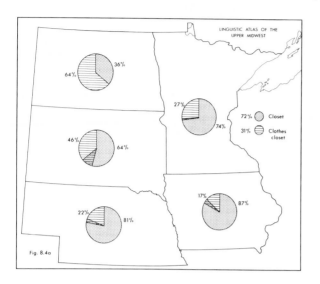

Fig. 8.4a

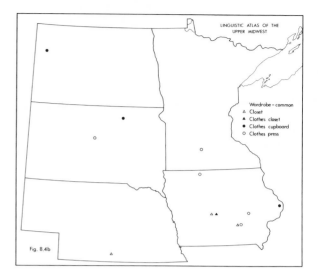

Fig. 8.4b

419-20, 425, 427, 429.
    clothes room 139.
    press 135. clothes ~ †40, ¹42.
    wardrobe 33, 44, †62; 146; 414. ~ clos-
et 423.
    no response 221; 430.

Comment:

    closet: "Proper name would be 'clothes
closet'"--55. clothes closet: Used to be
a 'clothes press'--40. clothes room: Older
term than 'closet'--139. wardrobe: Narrow
enough for one row of clothes, but not
big enough to walk into--33. Either port-
able or built-in--146. wardrobe closet:
Built-in with doors--423.

8.4b clothes closet (movable). WG 338.

    Most UM infs. use wardrobe to designate
a movable piece of furniture in which to
hang clothing, although a few, mostly in
Iowa, retain the expression clothes closet. Inadequate information is available
for Minnesota, because the item was added
to the worksheets after most of the fieldwork there had been completed. Since this
article of furniture is less common in
modern houses, a number of infs. admitted
unfamiliarity with it and said they only
remembered the name from their childhood.
A hybrid variant, clothes cupboard, occurred once each in three Midland speech
states, Iowa, South Dakota, and Nebraska.

    bureau 51.
    chifforobe 134.
    closet 129, 135; 431.
    clothes cabinet †437. ~ closet 129. ~
cupboard 139; 209; 306. ~ hamper †218;
?421. ~ hanger 202. ~ press 51; 103, 135,
137, 144; 314. ~ rack 318.
    commode 320, 322.

wardrobe 29-31, 35-36, 59-60; 101-2,
104, 106-7, 109-13, s114, 115-28, 130-33,
→134, 136, 138-40, 142-43, 145-49, :sn150,
151-52; 201, 203-5, ?206, :207, sn208,
210-15, :216, 217, *218, 219-24, :225,
226; 301-2, 304, sn305, 308-10, s¹311,
312-13, 315, *316, 317, 319, sn320, 321,
s322, :s324, 325-28; 402-14, †416, 417-
18, sn419, 420, 422-26, c427, 428-30,
¹431, 432-33, 435-36, s†437.
    no response 1-28, 32-34, 37, ?38, 39-50,
53-58, 61-65; 105, 108, 141; :?303, 307;
401, 415, 434.

Comment:

    bureau: = clothes press--51. clothes
cupboard: Older than 'wardrobe'--139.
clothes hamper: Inf. positive of this
term and aware of present meaning, too--
218. commode: = wardrobe--320. wardrobe:
Inf. has heard the word, but doesn't know
its meaning--311. Inf. says not common
here--431.

8.5 attic. NE 345.

    For an unfinished upper part of a house
the common term in the UM is attic, with
a 96% frequency quite evenly distributed
throughout the five states. The minor contrasting variant is garret, with a frequency of 8.3% largely based upon the
higher frequency of 19% in Iowa and 11%
in Nebraska. An initial inference that
garret exhibits Midland correlation is
dispelled by several circumstances. Garret is frequent in New England; it has a
34% frequency in the Wisconsin field data;
in the UM its frequency is 11% among Type
I infs.; 6.7% among Type II, and zero a-
mong Type III. These, in addition to the
priority of settlement in Iowa, suggest
rather that garret is simply a disappear-

ing term. Loft, another eastern variant, barely survives in the UM.

CL 8: Replies from 1047 mail respondents are remarkably corroboratory, with a 98% frequency for attic and 6% for garret. Loft was checked 12 times, 9 of which were in Iowa and Nebraska, for a total of nearly 1% and the old name cock-loft was recalled by a southern Minnesotan both of whose parents came from Canada.

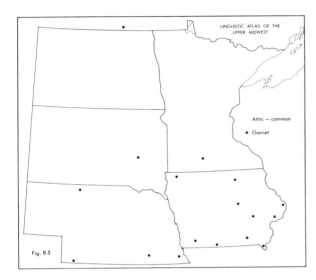

LINGUISTIC ATLAS OF THE UPPER MIDWEST

Attic — common
• Garret

Fig. 8.5

attic 1-14, c15, 16-23, c24, †25, 26-51, c52, 53-61, c62, 63-65; 102-38, sn139, 141, 143-45, 147-52; 201-20, c221, 222-24, 226; 301-6, 308-18, 320-28; 401-2, 404-13, c414, 415-26, c427, 428, !429, 430-31, 433, 435-36.
    garret †36-37, s†39, s†c40, †46-47, s†48, s¹50, 53, †54, †62, ¹64, s¹65; 101, 106, †117, 118, 137, 139-40, 142, 145-46, 149, †151; 202; †305, 327; 403, 432, 434, 437.
    hole !*46.
    loft cvr3, ¹8, ¹47; 129; ¹†310; ¹403.
    upstairs 43.
    no response 225; 307, 319.

Comment:

    attic: "Occasionally used for storing small stuff"--13. Inaccessible part of the house--16. Stairs leading to it--106. Attic smaller than a garret; inf. doesn't use the word often--139. garret: Inf. used both 'attic' and 'garret' in youth, but now only 'attic'--47. "Old people" call it this--48. "Common here"--50. Older than 'attic'--53. Older term than 'attic,' not used in inf.'s family--54. Entered through a trap door--106. Space used for storage--202. "'Garret' is just a common word"--327. loft: Used by inf.'s mother--310.

8.6 Room used as kitchen in summer. NE 343.

When coal- or wood-burning stoves were used for cooking, summer heat made the kitchen so uncomfortable that, particularly on the farm, cooking was frequently done in temporary quarters elsewhere. Although many infs. are unfamiliar with such a place and have no word for it, most of those who do use summer kitchen. As is sometimes indicated, this may be only a porch, enclosed or screened or open, or occasionally, it may be on a western farm or ranch a disused vehicle once serving threshing crews or a round-up crew. A number of equivalents also occur, mostly only once or twice.

    back porch 25, 30; 225; 410, †411. porch 208.
    back room †29.
    built-on kitchen 424.
    caboose 208.
    cook car ¹47. ~ wagon ¹47. ~house 201; 404, s416, 437. ~shack ?¹47; 404.
    lean-to 424. ~ kitchen 214.
    outside kitchen 12; ¹413.
    shanty 29; 102; 203. cook ~ 4, 41, 45; 302.
    shed 11, back ~ 3. cook ~ 302. wood ~ 202.
    smokehouse 403.
    summer house 150; 324.
    summer kitchen 1-5, ¹7, 8, †10, 20-22, 26, †28, †31, †33, 34, †36, 41, 43-47, 51, 53, 55, 60-63; 102-3, 105-6, 112, 115, 117, 120-21, 137-40, 152; 202, †204, 205-7, s¹208, 209-10, ¹211, 212, ¹213, 215-16, cvr218, 220, ¹222, 223-25, †226; *301, 303-4, ¹†310, 312, †313, †323, c324, ¹326, †328; 405-6, *408, 409, 414, 416, s¹†417, 419-22, s¹423, 424-25, ¹426, 428, ¹429, 430, ¹434, s¹435, †436.
    washhouse 325; 418, 430-31.
    no response or no special term 6, 9, 14-19, 23-24, 27, 32, 35, 37-38, 40, 42, 48-50, 52, 54, 56-59, 64-65; 101, 104, 107-11, 113-14, 116, 118-19, 122-36, 141-49, 151; 217, 219, 221; 305-9, 311, 314-22, 327; 401-2, 407, 412, 415, 427, 432-33.

Comment:

    back room: On inf.'s old log house up to 1890--29. caboose: A 'chow wagon' on wheels formerly used for threshing crews --208. cookhouse: Separate from house-- 201; 404, 416, 437. On ranches used for ranch hands--404, 416, 437. cookshack: Dakota name for portable wagon which followed threshing crews--47. = cookhouse-- 404. lean-to: -= summer kitchen--424. outside kitchen: Separate from house and screened--12. "A rare thing here"--413.

shanty: A lean-to--39; 203. cook shanty: Inf.'s usual term; a separate building-- 4. = summer kitchen--41, 45. shed: At- tached to house--11. summer house: = sum- mer kitchen; separate from house and movable--324. summer kitchen: Either at- tached to house or separate--1-3, 5, 10, 43, 60; 213, 215-16, 223; 414, 425, 430. Built on or "just a step off the porch"-- 424. Attached--426. An attached lean-to-- 21, 34, 36, 46, 51, 53; 204, 207, 209; *301, 312, 328; 421. An attached room--7- 8, 26, 28, 33, 62; 103, 117; 202, 225. An attached porch--5, 61; 205; 405-6. En- closed porch--106; 313; 417. A screened- in porch--21. An open porch--226. An at- tached shed--10, 31; 205, 212-13; 309. "A wing of the house"--20. Usually or often separate--22; 224; 434. A separate house or room--41, 44-45, 47, 63; 112, 115, 138, 140, 152; 206, 210; 303-4, 323; 408-9, 416, 419-20, 422, 429. "We didn't call it that until we started to get fancy"--202. Once common among German Russians--304. Inf. heard term in Ohio, but not locally --222.

8.7 pantry. NE 344.

For a small room adjacent to a kitchen and used for dishes and kitchen supplies, the general term in the UM is pantry, al- though a number of infs. admit it as a remembered term appropriate to earlier houses. Only in the first-settled south- eastern quadrant of the UM can be found the two older terms, butler's pantry and buttry, both of which occurred with greater frequency in New England. The four instances of the former were report- ed by infs. who did not have butlers but who still used the term as a specific. The 5 active users of buttry in Iowa and the one in Minnesota are complemented by a larger number in a more extended area who remember the term but consider it old- fashioned and out-of-date. Both terms are clearly on the verge of obsoletion. The single occurrence of cupboard as a syno- nym of pantry, a meaning also found in New England, was that of a western Minne- sota inf., both of whose parents came from Ireland. The same inf. also volun- teered the equivalent china closet.

butler's pantry 58; 111, 130; 317.
buttry ¹†7, †10, †37, †39, s†40, †44, †46, c51, s†65; 103, †105, †109, †111, sn113, †114-116, †118, ¹119, †126, †133, 137, †138, ¹139, †144, 145, 151, †152; ¹211, †214; †327; !†401, ¹413, †420.
closet 15. china ~ 25.
cupboard 25.
pantry 1-6, 8-10, :s11, 12-19, c20, 21- 24, 26-28, c29, 30-50, 52-56, s¹57, 58,

LINGUISTIC ATLAS OF THE UPPER MIDWEST

Pantry – common
△ Butler's pantry
● Buttry

Fig. 8.7

c59, 60-65; 101-9, 111-13, s114, 115-31, s132, 133-44, *145, 146-52; †201, 202-4, †205, 206-16, †217, 218-24, :c225, 226; 301-6, 308-11, 313, c314, 315, 320-21, *322, 323-26, c327, 328; 401-6, :c407, 408-12, ¹413, 414-29, 431-37.
no response 110; 307, 312, 316-19; 430.

Comment:

butler's pantry: Connected to both liv- ing room and dining room--58. "A sort of kitchen"--317. buttry: Heard used by a French Canadian with a good knowledge of English--7. Used by inf.'s grandmother in St. Cloud--10. "Always the older per- son's term"--39. More common than 'pantry' in inf.'s youth--40. Little heard here now--44. Used in youth--46, 65. Used by inf.'s father--65; 118, 152. Used by inf.'s mother--105, 111, 116. Used by older people in the community--119. Used by inf.'s grandparents--133. Inf. says that many in the community, all Scandi- navians, still use the term--211. Used by inf.'s mother-in-law--327. Heard in the community, but rare--413.

8.8 storeroom. NE 344.

When asked, "What do you call the room or space where you keep old furniture and other things not in regular use?" three-fourths (76.5%) of the responding informants answered with storeroom and another 10% with storage room, both of which have fairly even distribution throughout the UM. The minor variant junk room, however, reported by nearly 9% of the infs., may have Midland orientation, but the evidence is not conclusive. (Mn. 6.6%, Ia. 10%, N.D. 4.2%, S.D. 0%, Nb. 16%). A variety of other terms occur, some perhaps as nonce-equivalents.

Fig. 8.8

attic 15.

catchall 21; 122.

closet 429. broom ~ 8. horror ~ 33.

clothes room 139. extra ~ 53. scrap ~ 19. spare ~ 47, 55; 125, 135. trunk ~ 3, 12, 33. utility ~ →8; 122; *316.

fruit cellar 14. root ~ 16.

junk hole *39. ~ room 5, 7, cr26, !43; 188, 121, ¹130, 141, 145, 151; ¹208, !217; 414, 418, 420-21, 423, 429.

storage chamber 51. ~ room 18, 21, 34, 38, 44; 110-11, 119, :130, 149, 151; 207, 215, 219, 224, 226; 314; 422, 425, 431.

storehouse 53; 214.

storeroom 1-2, 4, s8, 9, 11, 17, 20, 22-25, ?26, 27-32, :35-37, 39-40, 42-43, 45-46, c47, 48-49, !50, c52-54, c56, 57, s?58, 59-65; 101-9, 112-17, 120, 123-29, 131-34, 136-38, 142-46, 148, 150, 152; 201-5, 209-13, 216-18, 220, c221, 223, c225; 301-2, 304-5, *306, 307-9, 312-13, c315, 317-18; 401-13, 415-17, 419, !423, 424, 426, c427, 428-29, !430, 432-37.

no response 6, 10, 13, 41; 140, 147; 206, 222; 303, 310-11, 319.

Comment:

catchall: "A smaller space, like one underneath a stairway"--21. clothes room: Used for storing clothes, bedding, unused articles.--139. spare room: Not for guests; filled with junk--135. storeroom: Like a pantry--57. "Before we had attics, we had 'storerooms'"--65. Said of a room in the post office--315. = garret--327.

8.9(1) bureau. NE 339.

The variety of shapes, styles, and purposes of a piece of bedroom furniture that has drawers is partly matched by the variety of terms for it. To provide some clarification the lexical responses are first provided in entirety and then divided into two groups according to whether they designate such an object with a mirror or one without a mirror. Some infs., however, did not indicate a distinction.

Because this item was added to the worksheets after most of the Minnesota records had been obtained, a total picture for the UM is not available. It appears, though, that for the object with a mirror the two common words are bureau and dresser. For some infs. the former designates a tall object with five or six drawers surmounted by a small mirror and the latter a low object with two or three drawers and a large mirror. Many others, however, use the term interchangeably, but with recognition that bureau is older and even old-fashioned, whereas dresser has characteristics of an innovation. Bureau is common in the UM and is almost the only form in North Dakota. Dresser is frequent in Iowa, Nebraska, and South Dakota, but turns up only once in North Dakota. The minor variant, chiffonier, seems to exhibit Midland correlation, with responses in Iowa and Nebraska. For some speakers commode is ambiguous, as they use it also in its more common meaning, that of an object with a mirror and space for a washbowl and a chamberpot.

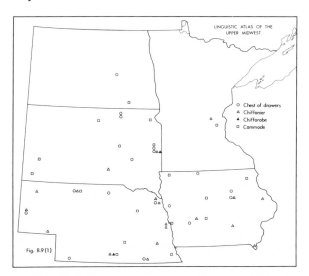

Fig. 8.9(1)

○ Chest of drawers
△ Chiffonier
▲ Chifforobe
□ Commode

bureau 29-31, 35-36; 101, †102, 103-7, †109, ¹110, 111-14, †115, 116, †117-19, 120, †121-22, 123-24, †125-26, 127-29, †130, ¹131, 132-33, 135, c†136, 137-45, s146, 147, 149, 151, †152; 201, †202, 203-8, !209, 210-25, †226; s†302, ¹†304, 306, 308-11, †312-13, 314-15, *316, 319-20, *322, 323-25, †326, 327, †328; ¹403, :sn404, 405, ¹406, s407, 408-10, 412,

171

¹413, 414-16, c417, 418-22, s423, 424-26, c427, 428, sn429, †430, ¹431-32, ¹432, 433, 435-37.

   chest of drawers →103, 116, 118, 122, 151; 218; 305-6, 318-19, 328; 404, †406, †408, 410, 433, †437.

   chiffonier 31; †117, 118, 121, 127, 136, 149; 319, 321, †326; 402, 404, :407, 408-9, †410, 426-28, ¹430, 431, 433, 436.

   chifforobe ¹127; 319; 431.

   commode 36; 101, 108, 114, 119, 125, 130; 224, 304, 308, *311, 316-17, 320; 404, 416, ¹422, 423, 431, 434.

   dresser 31, 38; 101-2, 104-12, 115-19, 121, →124, 125-27, 130-31, 133, →134, 136-39, →140, 141, 144, 146-47, 149-51, →152; 213, 301-14, →306, 307, →312-13, 317-19, 321, 325-28; 402, 405-6, 410, 413, cvr414, s415, 416, 418, 420-22, 424-25, 427-35.

   dressing table 123, 142; 425.

   highboy 121; 308, †310; 409, 431.

   lowboy 431.

   mister and missus →416.

   set of drawers 101.

   vanity 134; →323; 431.

   wardrobe 123.

   no response 1-28, 32-34, 37, 39-65; 148; 401, 411.

   (2) bureau (with a mirror).

   bureau 30, 35-36; 101, †102, 104, 111, 113-14, †118, 124, †125, 137, 142, 144, 149; 201, 203-5, 208, !209, 210-14, 217, 219, 223, †226; 306, 308-11, †312-13, 314, 319-20, 323, 325, †326; ¹403, 405, ¹406, s407, 408-10, 412, 415, c417, 419, 426, 428, s429, 430, 436.

   chest of drawers 319.

   chiffonier 149; 319, †326; 402, 408-9, 427-28, 433, 436.

   chifforobe 319.

   commode 101, 114.

   dresser 31, 38; 101-12, 104, 109-11, 118, →124, 125, 137, 144, 146, 150, →152; 213; 301, →306, 307, →312-13, 317-19, 321, 325-28; 402, 405-6, 410, 413, cvr414, s415, 416, 420-22, 427-31, 433.

   dressing table 142; 425.

   vanity 323; 431.

   wardrobe 123.

Comment:

   bureau: Still used by inf.'s mother--125. Marble topped--320. Larger and heavier than a dresser--410. Tall, with a small mirror--417. chiffonier: Taller than a dresser or bureau with a small mirror --326; 402, 408-9, 427, 433, 436. dresser: Less drawer space than a bureau--325. dressing table: Mirror to be used sitting down--142. vanity: Supplanting 'bureau'--323. A dressing table with a large mirror flanked by small drawers--431.

   (3) bureau (without a mirror).

   bureau 31; 105, 114, †115, 116, 127, 151, †152; †202, 203-4, †205, 206-7, 216, 218-19, 223-25; 306, †312, *316, 325, 327, †328; s407, 415-16, 418, 420-22, s423, 425, c427, 437.

   chest of drawers 116, 118, 151; 218; 306, 318, 328; →406, 433, →437.

   chiffonier 31; 118; 321; :407, 431.

   chifforobe 431.

   commode 36; 114, 125; 224; *311, 316; 423, 434.

   dresser 116; →306; s415, 418, 425.

   highboy †310; 409, 431.

   mister and missus →416.

   set of drawers 101.

Comment:

   bureau: Older than 'chest of drawers'--103; 306. Inf. rare here--202. Taller than a chest of drawers--151. Tall chest of drawers--204-5, 224. Larger than a commode--316; 423. chiffonier: Taller than a bureau or chest of drawers--31, 118. commode: A tall chest of drawers--224. highboy: A tall chest of drawers--409. set of drawers: Family antique--101.

9.1 She cleans up (the room) every morning. NE 336.

The two most common terms for a housewife's morning cleaning activity are clean up and straighten up. Both occur throughout the UM, but straighten up has a stronger Northern correlation, for it is found only twice in the southern half of Iowa and its frequency increases on the range from southern Nebraska to North Dakota. Clean up, on the contrary, dominates southern Iowa. Both forms appear to be gaining ground at the expense of two old terms tidy up and redd up. Tidy up, much more frequent in Minnesota than in Iowa, is characterized several times as old-fashioned, although in Canada it is the only term reported. Redd up, etymologically related to ready, is usually described as an old term now disused. Its variant rid up, perhaps confused with rid, is equally obsolescent. Pick up, a uniformly distributed minor form, is used both as a generic expression and also, by some housewives, to denote a less thorough operation than cleaning up. They might pick up a room each day and clean it up on Saturday. Dust up is limited to Nebraska and immediately adjacent areas.

CL 44: The 1058 responses by mail indicate a uniform distribution of both clean up (81%) and straighten up (33%), with the Iowa division present but less decisive. Redd up and rid up are rare (2%) but clearly Midland since nearly all

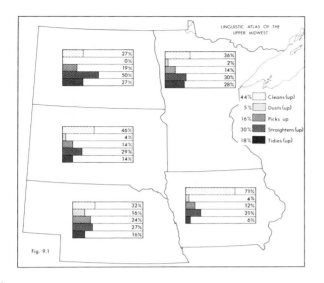

LINGUISTIC ATLAS OF THE
UPPER MIDWEST

27%
0%
19%
50%
27%

36%
2%
14%
30%
28%

46%
4%
14%
29%
14%

71%
4%
12%
21%
6%

32%
16%
24%
27%
16%

44% Cleans (up)
5% Dusts (up)
16% Picks up
30% Straightens (up)
18% Tidies (up)

Fig. 9.1

occurrences are in Iowa. Tidy up is affirmed as Northern with nearly twice as
much frequency in Minnesota and North
Dakota as in Iowa and Nebraska.

brushes up 423.
cleans 14, 18, 24, !52; 104, 113, 117,
126-27, 129, 142, 149; 301, 304, *306,
311, 319; 401, 405, 411. ~ up 9, 13, 16-
17, 20, 23, 25, 27-28, 36, 38, 40, :!42,
45, 50-51, 54, 56, 61; 101, 103, 105,
107, 109, 112, 114-16, 118, 121-23, 125,
128, 130, 132-33, 135, 137-38, 140-41,
143-48; 210, 212, 216, 218, 220-21, 225;
303, 307, 309, 313-14, 318, 322-23; 404,
407-8, 416, 419, 422, 434, 436-37.
does the housecleaning 48. ~ the housework 58; 308. ~ the morning work 64.
dusts 128; 320; 414, 415, 420-21, 425,
434. ~ up 61; s431.
fusses around !62.
gives (it) a smattering 431.
goes over (the room) 209; 415.
housecleans (it) 316.
picks up 12, 22, 28, 31, 33-34, *37,
47, 53; 106-7, 110, 119, 125, 131; 203,
210, 219, *222, *225; *301, 304, 312,
sn326; 406, 409-10, *412, 414, 416, 426-
28.
polices †31.
readies up 119. redds up 8, †45-46,
s†59, †61-62; ¹109, ¹115; ¹212, ¹†214,
!217; †427. rids ¹123. rids up †116;
¹†327; ¹413.
slicks (things) up !59; 108; !426.
straightens 11, 46; 222; 410. ~ out
(the furniture) 221. ~ up 4-5, 10, 12,
29-32, 34, 37, 39, *41, *43, 46, 49, 55,
c59, 62; 102, 110-11, 119-20, 133-34, 136,
139, 150, !152; 203, 205, sn*206, *207,
208-9, 211, 214, 223-24, 226; 305, 310,
321, 324-28; 402-3, 406, 413, 417-18,
429, 432, 435.

sweeps 306. ~ and dusts 151.
tidies 1-3, ¹5, 18, 44; 151; †222. ~
up 6, 15, 19, 21, 26, 33, s35, *37, 39,
†40, !44, †*45, †47, s†48, 57, 60, 63,
65; 124, ¹127, 130; c201, 202, 204,
sn*206, sn212, 213, 215, s¹220, †225;
*301, 302, 317, 319, ¹323; *405, 412,
424, 430, 433, 435.
touches up 315.
no response 7.

Comment:

cleans: "I'd say 'She done the cleaning'"--117. goes over: "I'd go clear over
it"--415. picks up: Used by inf.'s wife
--125. "Things was picked up"--225. polices: Used by inf.'s mother--31. redds
up: Used by inf.'s parents--59. Used occasionally by inf.'s father--61. "A New
England expression"--62. Inf. says heard
locally--212. rids up: Used by inf.'s
mother-in-law from Pa.--327. Used by
inf.'s neighbors from Mo.--413. slicks
up: "From Mother"--426. straightens up:
"Newer expression than 'redds up'--46.
More common than 'tidies up'--435. tidies:
Not heard here--222. tidies up: Usu.--39.
Aux. inf. says old-timers say this--*45.
Used by inf.'s mother--47.

9.4a file cloth (damp cloth for wiping
floor).

This item was added to the UM worksheets to ascertain whether this Pennsylvania term had been carried west by the
mid-19th-century migration. Not one instance was found in the UM, and questioning elicited only a haphazard variety of
responses exhibiting no correlation with
informant type or region, all of them except rag, mop rag, and scrub rag occurring no more than two or three times
each. Because the item was unproductive
it was dropped from the interviews in
South Dakota and Nebraska.

9.4b file the floor (wipe with a damp
cloth).

This item asking about the verb proved
to be similarly unproductive except that
a secondary informant in Graceville, Minnesota, reported hearing the term in the
speech of a Low German family in the community. This use, however, is more likely
to be immediately dependent upon German
feilen, to polish, than upon the Pennsylvania influence. Other responses were
simply of the generics clean, dust, scrub,
wash, and wipe. The item was dropped in
South Dakota and Nebraska.

9.5 Who does the laundry? NE 359.

Even before the advent of the "laundromat," commercial laundries were beginning to influence the designation of the housewife's chore on Monday. The evenly distributed term in the UM, washing, and its variants wash and washing and ironing were at the time of the field investigation sometimes labeled old-fashioned and the term laundry indicated as the accepted replacement. Wash, however, was not reported in South Dakota or Nebraska. The term washing and ironing had its most frequent use in Nebraska, where laundry is barely recorded.

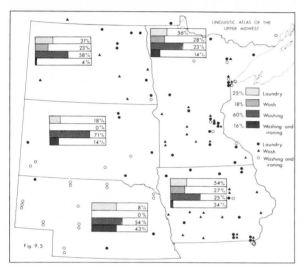

Fig. 9.5

laundry 1, 5-6, 13, 17-18, 20, 22, ¹26, 28, c31, 32, c35, 37, →39, →¹40, ¹42, 49, 55, 59, 65; 102-3, 106-8, 111, 118, 130, 133, 146-52; 204, 206, 208, ¹211, 212-13, →219, 222, *225; 305, *306, 309, →¹316, 319, →323; →401, 425, 431.

wash 13, 15, 17, 26-27, 31, 36, c40, c43, 45, c46, 47-48, *48, ¹49, c51, 58; 116-17, 121, 124, ¹126, 127, 130-31, 135, 141-42, 145, c146, 147-48, c149; 201, †208, c211, †212, 214, 219-20, c224; ¹304.

washing 2, 4, ¹5, c6, 7-9, 11-12, c13, 19, 21, †22, 23-25, ¹28, c29, 30, †32, 34, †37, 38-39, 41-44, 46, 48, 51-53, †55, 57, 59-61, c62, 63-65; 101, 103-16, 119-20, 122-23, 125-26, 128-29, 132-34, 136, 138-40, 151-52; 202-3, †204, 205, †206, 207, 209-11, 213, 215-18, 221, †222, 223-24, s225; 301-4, ¹*306, 307-8, 310-15, *316, 317-18, 322-25, 327; 401, c402, c404, c413, 414, c415, 416, 420-24, 426-28, 430, ¹431, 432-35.

washing and ironing 3, 10, 14, 16-18, 33, 35, 54; 118, 150; 226; 320-21, 326, 328; 403-12, 417, c418, 419, 429, 436-37.

no response 50; 137, 143-44.

Comment:

'Laundry' is sent out; 'washing' is done at home--133. washing: Usu.--6. Inf. says he would have said this some years ago--22. "Years ago they just called it 'washing'"--32. "In olden days; nowadays it's 'laundry'"--55. Older term than 'laundry' --65.

9.6 porch. NE 351. WG 52; F7, F43.

For the open or partly enclosed structure attached to a house the generic throughout the UM is porch, 99% of the informants knowing and using the term. Some informants also use synonyms or partial synonyms. The most common is stoop, a Hudson Valley word that has gained widespread use with the special meaning of a small porch without a roof. This semantic distinction is not rigidly maintained, however, as it is used by other informants, mostly in Iowa, to denote a roofed structure. This development has occurred chiefly in a Midland speech area to which the term has been introduced. Eastern veranda survives chiefly in southern Minnesota and eastern Nebraska, and it is the usual term for some Canadian speakers. Eastern and Southern piazza has nearly disappeared, partly because the long, narrow porch it designated did not become common in the UM. The term appears in eastern Nebraska and is recalled by other speakers as old-fashioned. Southern gallery appears only once. Step(s) has become popular as an equivalent for stoop, meaning a small roofless platform. The overall frequency in the UM for stoop is 26%, for step(s) 20%. Veranda is reported by 12% of the informants.

See Gary N. Underwood, "Semantic confusion from the Linguistic Atlas of the Upper Midwest," *Journal of English Linguistics*, 2.86-95 (1968).

CL 10, 11: For the roofed structure 1,038 respondents report 96% porch and 6% veranda; for the roofless structure 1,090 report 59% porch, 29% stoop, and 22% step(s). No clear geographical pattern emerges.

canopy →117.
entrance 11, 22; 105-6, 108, 132; 433. ~ way 433.
entry 223. ~way 120.
gallery 426.
hokje 223.
landing 51, 53.
patio 426.
piazza †11, †31; c¹†212; !¹311; 414, 428.
platform 34; 151; 302.
porch 1-2, 4, 6-15, c16, 17-18, c19, 20-23, c24, 25-29, c30, 31-36, c37, 38-44, c45, 46-53, c54, 55-56, c57, 58-65;

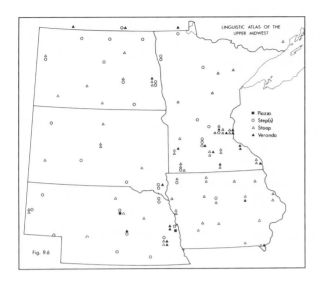

Fig. 9.6

101-3, 105, 107-9, 111, 113-38, 140-46,
*146, 147-52; 202-11, c212, 213-24, c225,
226; 301-3, 305-10, c311, 313-18, 320,
c321, 322, ¹324, 325-27; 401, 403-6,
c407, 408, 410-35. back ~ 2-3, 5, 10, 20,
23, 26, 31, 33-34, 36-37, 49; 104, 107-8,
112, 117, 119, 121-23, 125-26, 128-30,
133-36, 139, 142, 145; 202-3, 208-11,
c213, 214-15, 218-19, 221-22, 224; 304,
309-10, 312-13; 315, 318, 323, c324, 326,
c328; 402, c409, 411, 417-18, 429, 437.
bay ~ 137. circle ~ 52. front ~ 5, 10,
15, 29, 33, 36-37, 41; 106, 112, 121,
133, 139; 203, 208-11, 214-15, 218-19,
224; 304, 312, 315, 318, 323, 326, 328;
402, 409, 429, 436-37. open ~ 44; 323.
outside ~ 104. ~way 25.

portico :152.

step 7-8, 30; 114; 203, 205, 210, 219;
¹*302, 313, 324-25; 408-9, 421, 423, 430.
back ~ 202, ¹219; 323. door~ 10; 427,
432. front ~ 102; 301.

steps 4, 43-45, 61; c211, 222, 224;
407, c413. back ~ 28; 419. door~ 206.
front ~ 33; 221; 402, 419, 425, 436.

stoop 3, 12, 20-21, †29, 31, 33, ¹34,
36-37, 39-40, 42, 46, c47, 48-49, 51,
!52, 57-61, †62, 63; 101, 103-4, 106, 108,
111, 113, 115-16, †118, 119, ¹120, 121,
sn122, 123, 125, 127, 131, 137, !†144,
*147, c150, 151; 209, 213, 215, 217-18,
221-23; ¹*302, 304, 311, 314, ¹†320, 328;
¹402, 406, ¹408, 409-10, c414, 416, 425-
26. back ~ 14, ¹54; 315; ¹435. front ~
150.

terrace 10; ¹213. closed ~ →221.

veranda 1, †3, ¹5, †12, †23, 32, 37,
39-40, †42, 45-46, 51, †53, 54-55, sn58,
†61, *62, ¹65; 118, 150; c201, 202, 206,
220; 324; ¹404, 420, sn425, 426-28, ¹431,
¹435.

no response 319.

Comment:

canopy: Roofed--117. entrance: Roofed--
132. gallery: Inf. says it is an Eastern
term--426. hokje: Used in English context
in this originally Dutch settlement. patio: Roofless--426. piazza: Term used by
inf.'s father (from Me.)--11. "I ain't
heard that for years"--212. Older term
than 'porch'--428. "High class people call
it a 'piazza'"--311. "A fancy, ginger-
bready" porch--414. platform: Roofless--
34; 151. porch: Roofed--4, 7, 11, 19-21,
26, 28-29, 31, 33-34, 37, 40, 43-47, 49,
59-61, 63; 101, 104, 108, 110-16, 123,
125, 133, 137-39, 144, 152; 204, 206, 208,
214, 216-18, 220, 223; 301, 304, 308, 313,
324; 401, 403-8, 410, 417-19, 422, 425,
427, 431, 436-37. "If you can sit on it,
it's a 'porch;' otherwise it's only an
'entrance' or 'entrance way'--433. circle porch: Goes half way around the
house--52. porchway: Roofless--25. portico: Roofless--152. step: Roofed--102.
Roofless--7-8, 10, 30; 114; 202-3, 205,
210, 219; 313, 324-25; 408-9, 421, 423,
427, 430. steps: Roofed--45. Roofless--
4, 28, 33; 206, 221-22, 224; 407, 419,
436. stoop: Roofed--3, 42, 58; 101, 106,
108, 113, 115-16, 121, 123, 125, *147;
315, 328. Roofless--12, 20, 29, 31, 33,
¹34, 36-37, 39-40, 46-47, 49, 51-52, 60-
61, 63; 104, 111, 122, 131, 137, 144,
150-51; 209, 213, 215, 217-18, 221-23;
304, 311, 314, 320; 405, 409-10. Used by
inf.'s father (from N.Y.)--29. 'Porch'
more elegant than 'stoop'; "I haven't
heard that for years"--62. Older term than
'porch'--103. Inf. says it is Eastern--
426. "Not quite big enough for a chair"--
416. veranda: Used by inf.'s mother (from
N.Y.)--61. Formerly used by inf.--12, 23,
42. Inf.'s usual term--37. Inf. says it is
Southern--426. A second-floor porch--206.
Larger than a porch--3, 5, 32, *58, 61,
*62; 202; 427. A big porch "among higher
class of people"--51. Extends on two sides
or more of the house--54; 420, 425, 431,
435. "A porch going clear around a house"
--150. More decorative than a porch--39;
427.

9.7 shut the door. NE 437.

The contrast between the two requests,
"Shut the door" and "Close the door" is
social and perhaps partly chronological,
but not geographical. The balanced and
uniform distribution of both responses
over the UM is in contrast with the variation by types: shut--Type I 62%, II
52%, III 37.5%; close--I 51%, II 67% III
81%. Although a few informants characterize shut as older and close as newer, the
correlation more frequently appears to be

with the degree of civility and politeness, a measure not necessarily but at least sometimes associated with social and educational class. Many consider shut as abrupt and rude, close as more courteous. The frequently associated comment volunteered by a number of infs., "Were (was) you raised in a barn?" occurred twice as often after shut as after close.

CL 9: Checklist returns confirm the conclusion that no regional pattern exists for this item.

close 1-3, 5, 7, 10-12, 14, 17-19, 23-24, !25, 27, 30, 32-33, 36-40, !42, 43, !44, →45, 49-51, !53, 57-58, c59, 60-61, 63-65; 101-2, 104-6, 109-12, ¹117, 118-22, 124, 127-29, 131-34, 137-39, 141, 144, 146-50, 152; c201, 203, !207, 208, 211, 213-14, 216, 219-22, 224-26; 305, *306, 307-8, 313-19, !323, !324, 325-26; →401, 403-4, 406, !410, 412, 414-16, 419-21, 423, 425-26, 430, 434-37.

shut 4, 6, ¹7, 8-9, 12, 15, c16, 20-24, 26, 28-29, 31, 34-37, s38, †40, 41, !†45, 46, !47, 48, 51, !52, 54-56, ¹58, !59, !62, 63, s¹64, 65; 103, 105, 107, 113-18, c119, 122-28, 130, 135-36, 140, 142-45, *146, 148-49, 151; 202, 204-6, 209-12, 215, 217, 222-23, 225; 301-4, 306, *306, 309-13, *316, ¹319, !320, 321, c322, 323, 325-27, !328; †401, 402, 404-5, 407-9, 411, 413-14, c416, 417-18, 422-24, 427, c428, 429, 431-33.

no response 13; 108; 218.

Comment:

close: More polite--23, 36-37, 51; 148-49. More formal--414. "If it was a lady, we'd have to say, 'Close the door'"--24. To an adult, "Close the door, please"--404. shut: More abrupt--38. More emphatic --124; 211. More familiar--323; 414. "When you say 'shut,' you don't add no 'please' to it"--65. Used if annoyed--128. "If I was mad, I'd say, 'Shut the door!'"--225. Said to her husband--328. To his son, "Shut the door, son"--404.

9.9 weatherboards. NE 350.

Although technically weatherboards, clapboards, siding, drop siding, lap siding, and shiplap have referents differing in width, length, and the manner by which a board is joined with or lapped over another, all these designations for some kind of external wooden covering on the side of a frame house are subject to confusion on the popular level. The confusion is compounded for some speakers by the apparent regional frequency higher in the Northern area for the siding terms and higher in the Midland area for weatherboards and weatherboarding. Both weather-

boards and the common eastern clapboards seem to be declining in favor of the generic siding as well as both lap siding and drop siding when the informant does not differentiate the siding variants. A definitive statement cannot be made, since this item was added to the worksheets only after most of Minnesota had been covered. Previously unrecorded, clearboards appears in both Iowa and Nebraska and chipboard and lapboard in Iowa. The kind of semantic split characteristic of overlapping dialect areas occurs with those speakers who, also familiar with weatherboards, identify siding as the boards under the weatherboarding and with those other speakers who identify weatherboarding as the boards under the siding.

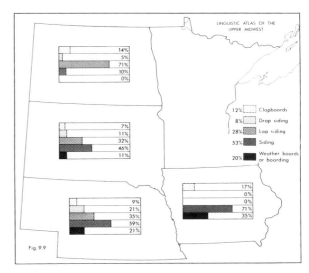

Fig. 9.9

beaverboards ¹†404.
chipboards 121.
clapboards :†31, †36; 101, 103, 112, s113, 118, 120, 131, 146, 149, 152; 215, 219, 222; 315; 413, 426, ¹433.
clapboard siding 310; 402.
clearboards †105; 420.
drop-leaf siding 202. drop ~ 225; 311, 317, 320, 404, 416, 420-21, 427-28, 436.
groove siding 430.
house siding 138.
lap siding c29, 30, :s31, 35; 201, 203, 206-7, 210, ¹211, 214, 216, 218, *219, 220-24, 226; 301-2, 306, :s309, 311, 313-14, 316, 320, 323; 403-6, s407, 408, 412, 416, *417, 418, 429-30, f431, 437.
lapboards 150.
shiplap †209; 431. ~ siding 208.
siding 31, 36, 38; 101-8, 110-13, c114, 115-19, 122-28, 133-34, 137, 139-41, 143-45, 147, 149, 151; 208-9, 211, 221; 304-5, 307-8, 312, 315, 317-19, :321, 324-28; 401-2, 407, 410-11, 413, 417, 420-27, 430-35.

weatherboarding 109, 115, 132, 136, 141-42, 147; 312, 322; 418, 427. ~boards s¹101, 103, s104, 110, 112, s113, s114, 117, 121, 129-30, 135, s137, 138, 146, 148; :303; 404, sn407, :¹419, 420, 424, 428. ~ siding 109.
no response 1-28, 32-34, 37, 39-65; 204-5, 212-13, 217; 409, 414-15.

Comment:

beaverboards: Heard years ago from two old local carpenters--404. clapboards: = siding and weatherboards; rough boards--101. Do not lap--103. Wider than siding--112. The boards under the siding--113. Boards with grooves that fit together--118. Formerly used to make roofs--146. Boards of uniform thickness--149. 8"-9" wide--149. A "New England" term--426. drop siding: Does not overlap like lap siding--311. = lap siding--404. Boards with grooves that fit together--416. Boards on a barn--420-22, 427. About 9" wide--428. groove siding: Boards on a barn--430. house siding: About 6" wide--138. lap siding: Inf. says more common here than 'clapboards'--222. shiplap: Narrow boards--110. 4"-5" wide--112. Outside boards--111. Boards under the weatherboarding--115. Boards thicker on one edge than the other--149. weatherboarding: 6" boards--132. More specific term than 'siding'--312. weatherboards: Boards between the foundation and the siding--103. = siding--104, 112. Overlapping boards--109, 115. Boards under the siding--117. Vertical boards--137. About 12" wide--138. Thicker on one edge than the other--146. Horizontal boards under eaves--404. Rough boards--424.

10.3 eave(s) troughs. NE 349; WG 15, 19, 25, 29, 40, 49, 53; F53, F54.

For the channel at the edge of a roof to catch rainwater the variety of words found on the Atlantic coast is matched by a similar range in the UM. Western New England and New York state eave(s) troughs or eavestroths dominates the UM, although with lower frequency in the Midland areas of southern Iowa and Nebraska. Eastern New England, New Jersey, and South Atlantic Coast gutters is the second most common term, though it is little used in the Dakotas. Eaves spouts, the regional designation in northern New England and northern Pennsylvania, is centered in southern Minnesota and northern Iowa. Spouting and rainspouts, common in Pennsylvania, Maryland, and upper West Virginia, consistently turned up in the Midland speech area, southern Iowa, with a few isolated instances elsewhere.

Although a few responses distinguish between gutter for the channel built into the edge of the roof and eaves trough for the separate channel suspended from the eaves, most infs. seem to have only one term for both kinds. Gutters apparently is the only term in commercial use by carpenters and roofers.

CL 12: The 1,038 responding checklists indicate an 80% for eaves trough and a 25% for gutters, both fairly evenly distributed except that gutters has a 13% return in North Dakota and a 12% return in South Dakota. These figures closely correspond with those from the field investigation. Other terms were reported by mail with less than 1% each.

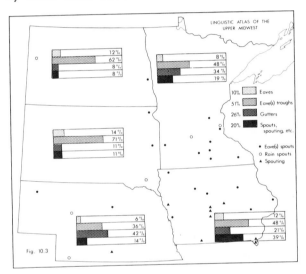

Fig. 10.3

conductors 59.
downspouts *46; 122-23, 129, 143, 146.
drains 9, 14; 418.
drainpipes *145; 213; 303. ~ spouts 48, 57. ~ troughs 429.
eaves 9, 49, 57-58, 63; 102, 110, 128, 136, 141, 144; 201, 209, ¹212, 217; ¹304, 305, 307-8, 319; 432-33. ~ catchers †215. ~ drains 14. eave(s) drops ?43; :?135; 203.
eave(s) spouts 31, 40, 46, 48, 50, 53, ¹54, 62, 64; 101, 113-14, 116, 124, 138-39; 221; 307, 318; 402, 413.
eave(s) troughs 1-2, 5, 7-8, 10, 15-17, 19, 21-23, !24, 25-27, c29, 30-31, ¹40, 42, c44, 45, 47, 51-52, 55, 60-61, c62, 65; 102-9, 112, 115, 117-20, 123, 125-27, 133, 137, 139, 145-46, 150, 152; 202, 204-8, 211, 214, 216, 218, *cr219, 222-23, c224, 225-26; 301-2, s¹303, 304, c306, 308, 310-11, cr312, 313-14, 316-17, 319-20, :321, 323, 325-26, :327, 328; 401, :403, 404-7, ¹413, 420, ¹421, 423, c427, cr428, 434-36. eave troughing 3.

177

gutter troughs ?312.
  gutters ¹1, 2, 6, ¹7-8, s¹11, 12, 15,
17, cr18, 20, s24, 27-28, 33-35, 37-38,
†40, 41-43, 46, 48, 51, 54, 56; 108, 111,
→117, 118, 120, s121, 134, 140, 142-43,
149, 151; 220, →¹221, 226; :!309, ¹315,
322, ¹324, →326; 408-9, 412, 414-16, 421-
22, 424-26, ?428, 431, 435. inset ~ 35.
rain ~ 419. roof ~ 434.
  lead troughs 147, 151.
  rain pipes 209, 212, 215. ~spouts ¹†20,
39, 44; 210, ?219; 324; 412, 437. ~
spouting 430. ~ troughs ?18, 34; 121, 139;
:315, ¹323, 327; 401, 411, 417, 429.
  roof drains ¹221. ~ spouts 138.
  spouting 122, 128-29, 131-32, :145,
148-49.
  troughs 11, 13, ?18; 121, 130, 135.
  water eaves 4. ~spouts ¹10, 36. ~
troughs 13, †42, 43; †129.
  no response 32; 410.

Comment:

  drains: Both horizontal and vertical
channels--9. Suspended--418. eaves: Inf.
admits that he doesn't use this frequent-
ly--9. Inf. insists that this is the
word--49; 201. Either built in or suspend-
ded--58. Suspended--63; 102, 110. Built
in--432-3. eave(s) spouts: = eaves troughs
--31. Suspended--40; 101; 221; 413. Both
horizontal and vertical channels--307,
318; 413. eave(s) troughs: More common
term than 'gutters'--17. "Wisible or not
wisible"--19. Inf. says common here--303.
More usual than 'rain troughs'--327. Inf.
first said 'rainspouts,' but her husband
reminded her that this refers to the
downpipes--219. Suspended--1, 24, 27, 42,
45, 51-52; 102-5, 108-9, 115, 137, 150,
152; 316, 326; 420, 423, 427-28, 434-36.
Built in--306. gutters: Carpenter's term
--11, 51. = eaves troughs--32; 326. More
common than 'eaves troughs'--120. = rain
troughs or troughs--121. Between two
roofs--151. Built in--1, 7-8, 24, 34, 42;
108; 221. Suspended 2, 35, 38, 41, 43;
111, 121; 326; 412, 415, 422, 435. Suspended or built in--28; 220; 416, 428.
Both horizontal and vertical channels--
435. inset gutters: Built in; 'gutters'
are suspended--35. rain gutters: Suspended
--419. rain pipes: Attached--215. rainspouts: Not inf.'s usual term--44. Inf.'s
husband reminded her that these are the
downpipes--219. = gutter--412. Suspended
--34; 121. roof gutters: Built in--434.
spouting: Used more often than 'gutters';
both horizontal and vertical channels--
149. troughs: Suspended--121. water
spouts: Made of wood--36. water troughs:
Used by inf.'s parents--42. Made of wood
--129.

10.4 shed (for wood, tools, etc.).
NE 353.

  Responses to this item are so diverse
that they are conveniently presented in
tabular form to illustrate the relations
of names and structure. Diversification
appears also in the regional distribution.
In the western prairie states scarcity
of wood led to the replacement of wood
house and woodshed by coal house and coal
shed. The various combinations with house
are conspicuously with Midland orientation. Cob house and cob shed occur as minor variants where corncobs were burned
as fuel. On some farms one such small
structure might be used for coal and another for tools, so that more than one
term was reported.

CL 13: For the separate building 1,043
respondents check woodshed as the most
common name (89%), tool shed as the runner-up (14%), and wood house as third
(7%) with its occurrences almost entirely
in Iowa. New terms in this material are
fuel house (once in S.D.) and chunk house
(once in Mn.). Regional distribution is
fairly even for the common forms except
for wood house.

CL 14: For the attached structure lean-
to is the most used term (55%) with fairly
even distribution, a fact that makes suspect the Minnesota orientation in the
field records. Back shed, again in contrast with the field returns, has a 22%
over-all average, with an obvious weighting in favor of Northern correlation (Mn.
24%, Ia. 13%, N.D. 47%, S.D. 29%, Nb. 6%).
  no response 37.

Term	Attached	Unattached	Either	Unspecified
back shed	5; 209,c213.			3; c218; 314.
coal house. . . .	→122.	303,322; 404, 407,422,437.	414.	127; 403,405, 437.
coal shed	218.	216,217,223; 301,303,c†312- 13,322; 404, 417.	c206.	203,207,216, 219,224; 310, 317,320,325.
cob house	115.		421,436.	423.
cob shed	318.			324.
ell	151.			
fuel shed			436.	
junk house. . . .				147.
lean-to	6,c21,27,c34, 39-40,43,47- 50,c51-52, c55,57-59,61- 63,c65; 125; 205,212; 309.			
machine shed. . .	c305.	8; 321.	201; 431.	43,45-46,48, 51,56-58,60, 62-63.
milk house. . . .		114.		
oil shed		204.		205.
outhouse				135.
out shed		207.		
pump shed				205.
root house. . . .				44.
shanty	47; 327.			45; 128.
shed	s65; 139; 215, 222.	5-6,10,12,20, 23,c34,38; 109-11; 205; 311,314,326; 406,409,412, 415,426.	1,4,8,21,30, 35-36,56; 120; 202,216; 302,309,327.	'7,11,13,15,18- 19,25,32,40, c45-46,c51-52, c59; 111,116, 121; 209,226; 410.
shop		149; 223.		126; †208; 306; 418.
storehouse. . . .		311.		403.
storm porch . . .	60.			
storm shed. . . .	45; c212.			
tool house. . . .	119.	10,27-28,65; 65; 220,225; 422.	22; 140,152; 201; 413-14, 427.	39,61; 107, 117,122-23, 128,136,139, 142-46; 320, 324.
tool shed	219; 428.	10,23; 104; 204, 217-18; 313,315, 318,324; 408, 419-21,425,433.	125; 221; 416, 418.	9,c18,24,44; 124,126,†127, 129-31,148, 150; 203,208; 308,316,319, 321,323,325; 401,411,434.
tool shop		134.		147.
washhouse		407.		

Term	Attached	Unattached	Either	Unspecified
wood house. . . .		104,137-39; 225; 420,429.	431.	?24; 117-18, 123,127-28, ?131,132,135, 141-45,147; 432.
woodshed	108,133; 214, 218; 428.	cr7,28,33,41, 64; 101-3,106-7,112-14,134, 148-49; 204, 207; 301,†312, 313,315,320-23, 328; 402,411, 416,418,422, 424,426,430.	2,11,19,25-26, 29,†31,42,49-50,54-55; 105, 119,125-26,140, 150,152; 206, 208,210-11,221-22,224; 302, 325; 401,413-14,421,427. 201.	3,†12,14-17, cr24,!43,46-47,53,56; 118, †122,124,129-30,135-36, *145,146;¹212, 216,219-20; 310,317,319, 405,429,434.
wood shed				
workshop		217.		212; 307.

10.5 privy. NE 354.

Although the outdoor toilet is no longer a familiar feature of the farmstead, its varied nomenclature persists in the memory of the middle and older generations. This variety is widespread, without sharp regional patterns. Much of the variety is occasioned by the desire for a suitable euphemism, a desire often accompanied with the somewhat embarrassed jocularity characteristic of popular allusions to various body functions and their locale. Many infs. admit using more than one term, selecting one in accord with the audience and the situation. Four terms have the same general over-all frequency, each with about one-third of the responses: backhouse, outhouse, privy, and (outdoor) toilet. These four vary, however, in the frequency revealed among the three types of informants. Backhouse decreases from 100% for Type I to 87% for II, and only 16% for III. So does privy, from 46% for Type I to 39% for II and only 19% for III. Outhouse, however, perhaps thus exhibiting a somewhat more genteel acceptance, rises slightly in frequency of occurrence from 29% for Type I to 40% for II and 44% for III. Toilet and its compounds, apparently still more acceptable as a euphemism, ranges from 32% for Type I to 43% for II and 50% for III.

The most vulgar designation, shit house, was recorded from only 7.4% of the infs., but this proportion would probably have been much higher had interviewing conditions always been more favorable. Men were reluctant to say this term to the one female fieldworker, and women, even though they knew the term, were unwilling to provide it at all. Quite likely a comparable situation existed with the slang equivalents can and crap-

per and the compounds involving them, crapper can and crapping can, none of which was recorded in New England.

Another term, originally also a euphemism, may have regional variation. Closet and watercloset have a 13% and 12% frequency in Minnesota and North Dakota respectively, but only 4.2% in Iowa, with 7% in South Dakota and 8% in Nebraska.

Two recent euphemisms are john or johnny and biffy or biff. Both seem to have been transferred from reference to the indoor toilet, and at least the second seems more likely to be used by girls or women.

Peck house, spoken by a Nebraskan of Czech parentage, is almost certainly a phonetic deviation from backhouse. Some other sporadic terms are more or less whimsical. Chic Sale is the name of the fictitious carpenter who gained wealth through mass production of these necessary structures, as described in a best-seller of the early 1920's. Eleanor and and Roosevelt have political overtones, and both probably reflect Republican reaction to the project that also gave rise to the synonyms WPA and WPA project. During the second administration of Franklin D. Roosevelt, the Works Progress Administration sought to alleviate unemployment by the mass production of sturdy cement-based outdoor toilets. White House and Parliament Building could occur only in the countries of their origin, the United States and Canada. Telephone booth and ~ office derive from the shape of the structure; the two examples are confined to Nebraska. References to Mrs. Jones and Mrs. Murphy have a long history in American English; it may be only coincidence that these expressions were reported only from Midland speech territory. Dooley, its origin unknown, seems to be a Canadianism.

A supplementary study by a graduate student reveals that 31% out of 37 interviewed residents of Stillwater, Minnesota, are familiar also with the term donnicker, which apparently has escaped its earlier context of carnival and underworld slang.

backhouse s¹1, ¹2, 3, :4, s!6, ¹†7, †8-9, ¹10, !11, 12, 18, †19, !¹†20, !23, 24, 28, †29-30, 31, 37, :39, s†41, 43, !44, 45, !†46, ¹47, †49, !51, !53, 54, 56, :62, 64; 101, !102, ¹103, 104-7, 112-13, 116, 120, 122, 126, 129, 132-33, 135, 142-43, 149; 202, †203, 204, †205, †208, 209, ¹210, 211, ¹†212, ¹†213-15, !218, 222; 301, 303, †304, 306-7, 309, ¹310, 313, !315, 317, ¹†321, !328; †401, ¹†402, !403, 405, †407, 408, 410, †411, ¹†412, ¹413, 415-16, 419-20, 422, !423, 424, 427, †428, †429, 430, 436, sn437.

biff 9; 121. biffy →12, ¹*26, ¹30, →33; →214; s¹310, !318.

can 1, 12, !21, *26, 30, c35; 102, 108, →117, 128, 132-33; 208, !221; 301, s¹302, 303, ¹†311, ¹314, 320, ¹321, 323; 404, →405, →412, †416, →419, 423, sn437.

Chic Sale 101, †150; †409, 410, 416, 428.

closet 1, 3, †22, 26, 50, 53; 123; 201, †208, 215, †219; 302, 306; 406, 420, 431. water ~ 42, 47, !61; ¹103, 152; 210; ¹433.

coffee house !52.

crapper 314; 409. ~ can 34; 216; †407. crapping can !†8; ¹124; 207, 224; s!309, †315, 322.

dooley !2.

Eleanor →122.

john →150; 307, →¹310, →¹312; →¹411. johnny →33.

library !58; !410. little house 115, 119, 138; 319.

Mrs. Jones 101, 104, 115, 119, 128; !†310, !327, sn328; 427. Mrs. Jones's house 137. Mother Jones 116. outdoors Jones *417.

Mrs. Murphy 119.

office 128.

one-holer 409. two-holer 409. three-holer 125.

outbuilding 435. outdoor plumbing ¹131.

outhouse ¹1-2, 7, ¹†9, 13-14, 17, †19, 20, 24-26, †27, *28, 30, 32-34, !35, †36-37, 38, *41, s42, !51-52, 53-55, 58-59, 64; ¹103-4, 109-12, s113, 115, 117, 119, 121, 131, 134-35, 142, 147, 149-50, 152; 201, 204, 209, ¹213, †214, ¹†215, 217, †*219, 220, ¹222, sn¹†223, 224, ¹225, 226; 301-2, 308-10, ¹311, !313, 314, ¹†315, 317, †318, 320, ¹†326, 328; †401-2, ¹404, 405, 408, ¹409, 410, 412, s415, 419, 421, 424, 426-29, s431, 433, 435, 437.

Parliament building !†202.

peck house 323.

privy 1, 6, †8, !11, :12, ¹20, !21, ¹22, s¹26, †27, †29-31, †35, 36-37, 39-41, †42, 44, !46, ¹47, 48-49, !50-51, !53, 54-55, :62, :!63, 65; 101-5, s106, 108, !111, 112, 114-17, 119-21, 124-27, 129-32, 136-41, 145-47, !152; †210-12, ¹†213, †215-16, ¹217, 218, 220-21, †223, 224-25, ¹†226; s†301, †302, 305, †309, s¹310, 311, →312, ¹†313, 314, 320, 322, !†324, †325, ¹327, !328; †401, ¹403, 404-5, !407, †409, 412, ¹413-14, s415, 416, !417, †418, 419-21, ¹422, s¹†423, 424-25, 427, †428, 430, sn433, 434. outside ~ 14.

Roosevelt 216.

shanty !38; 133.

shit house 29; 107, 113, 140; :207, 216, 218, 224; !¹302, 303, 309, ¹†312, 314-15; 407, 409, 411.

telephone booth 428. ~ office *417.

toilet 2, 4-5, !10, 12, c15, 16, 19, 27, 29, →30, 31, 43, 47, :60, !61, :63, 104, 106, 113, :122, 124, 149-50; 202, →203, →205, 206-9, →210-11, →212, 213-14, 219-20, →221, →!223; 303-4, s305, 307-8, 316, 318-19, 321, →323-24, 325, 327; →401, 404, →406, →410, !411, 413-14, →418, 421-23, 431-33, →437. out ~ 147.

outdoor ~ 8, †20, 22, 38, 50; cr207. outside ~ 101, 114; 220; 326; 409, 436.

vault 121. privy ~ †34.

wee house 3.

White House †203; 306.

WPA 313, *316. ~ project 217.

no response 57; 118, 144, 148, 151.

Comment:

men's terms: backhouse--3, 12, 24, 37; 211; 309-11, 315, 321; 402, 429. can--21; 208; 314, 321; 404, crapper--314; 409. crapper can--34. crapping can--207; 322. outhouse--225. privy--404. shit house--207, 314-15; 407.

women's terms: biffy--12, 30; 310. closet--25. john--310, 312. outhouse--37; 315; 412. privy--320. toilet--303.

boy's terms: backhouse--120. crapper can--34. crapping can--315.

vulgar terms: backhouse--1, *43; 103-4; 408, 419. can--419. outhouse--1; 103. privy--104, 111; 419. shit house--216, 218; 309, 312; 409.

polite terms, family terms, or terms used in mixed company: Mrs. Jones--128. outhouse--*28; 111. privy--31; 112; 224; 409. toilet--10, 31; 416. outdoor toilet--50. water closet--103. wee house--3. White House--203.

backhouse: "That's the real old-time term"--6. Usu. in inf.'s youth--9. Used by inf.'s parents--54. Inf. says older than outhouse--64. The modern term--51. Joking term--132. Inf.'s mother objected to their using it--210. Inf. wouldn't let her children use this--215. biffy: Used by both younger men and women--*26. Inf. thinks it common among Irish--26. Used by college girls--310. can: Inf. thinks it is a railroading term--1. Introduced in the '30's--33. Joking term --132. Becoming more popular--301. Common term--302. Inf. thinks women might use this more than men, but his wife wouldn't--412. Kid's term--416. closet: Used by old Irish people--25. crapper can: Still heard here--407. crapping can: Very common--124. dooley: Inf. doesn't think that this is a family term--2. Eleanor: A GI privy--122. john: Used by college girls--310. library: "Sears-Roebuck library"--58. Mrs. Jones: "Go see Mrs. Jones"--104. "Out to see Mrs. Jones or Mrs. Murphy"--119. Mother Jones: "Going to see Mother Jones"--116. outdoor plumbing--Heard in Colorado--131. outhouse: Used by inf.'s mother--37. Used by inf.'s father--42. Older term than 'privy'--55. More polite than 'privy'-- 111. Was common in the past--223. peck house: Inf. says that this is common among older people of Bohemian background, but he does not think 'peck' is from Czech for 'back'--323. privy: Used 50 years ago--29. Old name--51. More recent term than 'backhouse' or 'outhouse'--37. Usu.--54; 220; 310. "I wouldn't have known what to say to a woman"--312. privy vault: Inf.'s father, a carpenter, first met the word here--34. Roosevelt: Inf. says that this term is common here because of a WPA project--220. shit house: Inf. wouldn't say the word; he said, "It starts with s"-- 29. WPA--Came into use during the depression--313. no response: "Same terms as in the city"; inf. embarrassed--57.

11.4 barn. NE 101.

In response to the question, "What do you call the other principal building on a farm besides the house?" nearly all infs. offered the term barn, although sometimes with a limiting word describing its function. The infrequently used stable and twice used shed represent special purposes by added descriptive modifiers, although stable, as a generic, is also reported but mainly as obsolescent. With the advent of the machine age on the farm the old general purpose structure in which cattle, horses, hay, and some machinery could be kept is no longer needed. The responses to this item clearly reflect the end of an agricultural era in the UM.

barn c1, 2-14, c15, 16-24, c25, 26-28, c29, 30-31, r32, r33, 34-39, c40, 41-42, c43, c44, 45-46, c47, 48-51, c52, 53-54, *54, c55, 56-58, c59, 60-65; 101-18, c119, 120-28, c129, 130-32, c133, 134-43, c144, 145-52; c201, 202-26; 301-21, c322-26, c327; 401-8, c409, 410, c411, 412-21, c422, 423-28, c429, cvr430, 431-35, c436, 437. cattle ~ 4, c25, c34; 118, †149; †208, 209, †221; 325; †429. stock ~ 208. cattle shed 221. implement ~ 221. stable 101, †151; †403, ⊥†405, †418. cow ~ 54. horse ~ 54; c417. livery ~ 214.

Identified uses of a barn:

a. For housing:
animals 61; 424.
cats 110.
cattle 1-6, 8-10, 12, 22, 28, 31, 34, 37, 41, 47, 50, 55, 64; 101-2, 104-20, 126, 132-33, 136, 139-40, 144, 148, 150; 201, 203, 210-11, 213-15, 217, 221, 223-24, †225, 226; 301-4, 306-11, 313-15, 318, 321-22, 324-25, 328; 401-3, 406-8, 410, 414-16, 418, 421, 423, 425-28, 430-32, 434-37.
chickens 204.
hogs 132, 136, 144; 318; 418.
horses 1-2, 4-5, 8-10, 21-22, 28-29, 31, 33-34, 37, 41-42, 50; 101-9, 111-20, 126, 132-33, 136, 139, 144, 148; 203, 210-11, 213-14, †217, 221, 224, †225; 301, †302, 303-4, 309, 311-13, 315, 320-21, †322-25, 328; 401-2, 405, †406, 407-8, 410-12, 415-16, 418-19, 421-23, 425, 427-28, 430-37.
mules 312.
pony 110.
sheep 34; 115; 303.
stock 7, 11, 19-21, 23-25, 27, 30, 47, 49, 54; 106, 114, 124, 132, 137, 147, 152; 201-2, 204, 206-7, 212, 216, 218-22; 305, 314-16; 409, 413, 420, 427-28.

b. For storing feed and grain:
feed 8, 25, 27, 30-31, 41, 49, 54-55; 113, 119; 202, 213, 223; 307-8, 316; 413-16, 419, 427, 431.
fodder 19; 139.
grain 7, 54; 101-2, 104-5, 109, 112, 116, 124, 132, 137, 144, 147; 215, 224; 301, 311, 321; 401-2, 407-8, 410, 413, 422-24, 427, 430, 434, 436-37.
hay 1, 3-12, 19, 21-24, 27-29, 31, 34, 37, 41-42, 47, 49-50, 61, 64; 101-9, 111-15, 120, 124, 126, 132-33, 139-40, 144, 147-50, 152; 201-3, 206-7, 212-13, 215-20, 222-24, †225, 226; 302, 305, 307-11, 313-16, 320-22, 328; 401-3, 406-8, 410-14, 419-28, 430, 432-37.
straw 105.

c. For storing equipment:
automobile 110.
equipment 49.
harnesses 49.
machinery 103; 204, 225; 301; 404, 420, 431.

Comment:

barn: "If the house is bigger than the barn, it shows who wears the pants in the family"--46. cow barn: "We had two barns, a 'cattle barn' and a 'horse barn.' Then we started milking a lot, and the 'cattle barn' became a 'cow barn'"--149. horse barn: This and 'cow barn' were usual when horses were used and there were two buildings--208. cattle shed: Enclosed or open--221. stable: On inf.'s girlhood farm a one-story log building for horses--403. Usually one-story buildings in the early days--405, 418, 429. 'cow stable' and 'horse stable': Terms used in inf.'s family--54. livery stable: Inf. says this is where they kept horses and a 'milk cow'--219.

11.5 corn crib. NE 106. WG 19, 41, 49, 54; F2, F31, F32, F57.

In corn-raising areas corn may be stored in a round or rectangular building with separated slats or wire on the sides in order to provide ventilation. Of the various east coast designations only one has survived in the UM, crib, with the modified form corn crib. (Corn) bin and (corn) rick appear three times each, with no noticeable regional clustering. In the northern fringe of the UM and in Canada infs. usually offered no response, since no corn is grown there.

bin 411. corn ~ ¹132; 313.
crib 1, 3, 11, 30, 35; 122-25, 128-30, 139, 143, 149; 218, 224-25; 308-9; 403, 406. corn ~ 5-8, 10, 12, 18-29, 31-34, 36-45, c46, 47-50, c51, 52-65; 101-2, 104-21, 126-27, 131-38, 140-42, 144-48, 150-52; 204, 206, 208, 210, 212, 214-17, 219-23, 226; 301-7, 310-12, ¹313, 314-19, 321-28; 401-2, 404-5, 407, c409, :410, 411, 413-37.
rick ¹10. corn ~ 202; 436.
elevator 308.
no response 2, 4, 9, 13-17; 103; 201, 203, 205, 207, 209, 211, 213; 320; 408, 412.

Comment:

bin: A temporary small place outdoors--411. corn crib: Not found or rare in this region because of scarcity of corn--5, 6; 206, 214; 321. Inf. says that the modern method is to have the corn crib and granary combined--53. May be a part of the granary--60. A building with sides open for ventilation--6; 144; 220; 308; 424. Sides made of slats or wire--416. Closed or open; roofed or not--315. Slanting sides--37; 220-2; 424. A driveway between the two halves--152. crib: Either a sep-

arate building or built on a barn--139. Inf.'s is temporary, narrow and long; some are round--224. elevator: On a big plant--308.

11.6 granary. NE 105.

UM farmers commonly use granary to refer to a building or part of a building used for storing grain. A few, mostly in Iowa, respond with bin, but this term may also be used to designate a section or division of a granary. House occurs three times in compounds, and grain crib is the term of an old-fashioned Type I farmer whose father came from Kentucky to settle in Iowa.

bin 107-8, 113, 120, 125, 129, 132; 424. grain ~ 131; 217; 321. oats ~ 115, 139.
elevator c305.
feed house :?32; 412. grain ~ →¹218.
grain crib 132.
granary 1-31, s?32, 33-47, c48, 49, c50, 51-59, c60, 61, c62, 63-65; 101-23, *123, 124-31, 133-35, :136, 137-52; 201-2, c203, 204, c205, 206-26; 301-3, c304, 305-16, c317, 318-21, c322, 323-28; 401-7, 409-11, †412, c413, c414, 415, c416, 417-21, c422, 423-24, s→426, 427, c428, 429, c430, 431-37.
no response 408, 425.

Comment:

bin: Oats are stored in a bin in the hay barn--107. Separate section of the granary--108, 120; 424. Upper part of the corn crib; for storing oats--113. Part of the barn--132. Modern circular metal building--125. feed house: Inf. has never heard a special name--32. grain bin: Separate building--217. Modern circular metal building--321. grain crib: Separate building--132. granary: Usually separate, but occasionally attached to a barn or storage room--12, 20, 22, 26, 34, 43, 51; 125; 204, 209, 216; 317. Separate building--25, 40, 45-46, 52-53, 60, 63; 104, 113-14, 117, 133, 144; 214, 217, 223-24; 306-7, 320; 424, 432. Part of a corn crib or barn--138; 323. oats bin: Part of a granary--115. Smaller than a granary, about 10' square--139.

12.1 Place for hay in the barn. NE 102. WG 23, 37, 47, 53, 54; F39, F56.

Because in the UM the place for hay in the barn is typically a second story, responses for 11.7 and 12.1 overlapped in the field records and are here combined. The two common designations for the second story area are (hay)loft and (hay)mow. Their distribution weight reflects the dominance of loft in New England and the dominance of mow in the North Midland, although both terms are so common in the UM that only percentages are indicative. Both terms occasionally name a second floor with a large open space reaching from the ground floor to the roof and rarely name only such an open space. Such a space is the usual designation of infrequent (hay)bay, a New England term found mostly in northern Iowa. The same meaning is represented by bent, used by a North Dakota farmer of New York background; but hay bent, reported in northern Iowa, refers to an unpartitioned division made by vertical studdings. Although unrecorded in the east, hay bent was also recorded in Kenosha, Wisconsin, with this sense.

See Gary N. Underwood, "Semantic confusion: evidence from the Linguistic Atlas of the Upper Midwest," *Journal of English Linguistics*, 2.86-95 (1968).

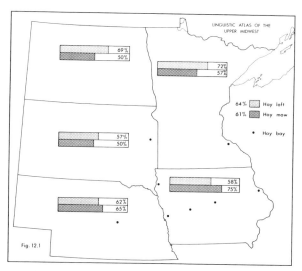

bay †54.
bent 218.
hay bay 109, 119, 124, 126, 132; 317; 420. ~ bent 117. ~ bin 407.
hayloft 2, 4-5, 7-9, 11, 14-16, 18, 20, c21, 22, 24, 26-27, ¹30, 31-32, 34, 36-37, 39, 43-47, 50, c52, 53, 56-57, 59-61, 64-65; 103-4, 106-9, c111, 112-14, 116, 119-21, 123, 126, 133-35, 139, *139, 145, 148, c150, 151; 201-2, →203, 204-5, 207-10, 212-15, 219, 222, 224; 303-5, 307, 310, ¹311, *316, 318, 322, 326, 328; c401, 402-3, 406-7, 410, 413, *417, 418-21, 424, 426-28, 430-31, 433-35.
hay mound ?22, 25.
haymow 6, 8, 10, 12-13, 16-17, 19, 21, cr22, 23, 26, 28-30, 33, c37, 39-40, c41, 46-49, c51, 52-56, 58, 62-64; 101-2, 104-5, c107, 108-10, c111, 112, 114-16, 118,

120-21, 123, ¹125, 127, 130-32, 134, 137-38, 140, 142-46, 149, 152; 202, 206, ¹208, 211-13, 216, 218, 220-21, 223-24, c226; 301-2, 306, 308-9, 311, 314, 317, ¹318, 319, 323-25; ¹401, 404-7, ¹408, 411-12, ¹413, 414, sn415, c416, 417-23, 425, 427-29, 432, ¹433, 434, 436, c437.
hay room 430. ~ run 312. ~ shed 17-18. ~ stairs 223.
loft 1, 3, c6, 21, 23, 25, 32-33, 35, 38-40, 44-45, *45, s48, ¹49, 57-58, 61; ¹117, 122, 125, 127, 129, *130, 133, 137, 139; 215, c217, 221-22; 312-15, 321, 327; 408, c409, 410, 427-28, 431.
mow 15, 34, 39-42, s¹57, s65; 117, :122, 124, 128, 136, 141, 147; 225; 312, 320.
upstairs †203; 321.

Comment:

bay: Used by inf.'s father--54. bent: Extends from ground floor to roof--218. hay bay: Extends from ground floor to roof; a mow covers only the second floor --109, 119, 126; 317; 420. The second floor with a large center section open from ground floor to the roof--132. hay bent: An unpartitioned division made by supports; the only separations are beams and rafters; usually three hay bents to a barn--117. hay bin: Ground to roof--407. hayloft: In some barns it extends from ground floor to roof--61; 418. Second floor with a large center section open from ground floor to the roof--103, 114, 133. Term used when it is empty--212. haymow: Name for loft when full--6. = hayloft--413. One end of the barn--56. In some barns it extends from ground floor to roof--53; 125, 149. The second floor with a large center section open from ground floor to roof--132; 432. From ground floor to roof--114; 408, 418, 428. hay room: The second floor with a large center section open from ground floor to roof; a loft or mow covers only the second floor--312. hay shed: On one end of the barn--17. hay stairs: Local term for the second floor--223. loft: Term used when empty; called a 'mow' when full--39. Used when empty--49. Not for hay; a section of the barn under the roof where inf. stores tools and makes repairs --137. Inf. says rare in the community-- 321. From ground floor to roof--133. The second floor with a large center section open from ground floor to roof--327. mow: In some barns it extends from ground floor to roof--147. upstairs: "I suppose it'd be the 'hayloft' now"--203.

12.2 haystack. NE 104. WG 24, 34, 54; F13, F60.

For a large pile of hay outdoors the universal term in the UM is (hay)stack, with an over-all frequency of 99%. Virginia and Maryland (hay)rick occurs chiefly in southern Iowa, with scattered instances in southern Minnesota and Nebraska. It is used by 11% of Type I infs., 2.3% of Type II, and none of Type I. Both stack and rick denote a variety of shapes, although rick is favored to signify a square or rectangular pile. New York state barrack appears once in the speech of a Duluth woman of European parentage, who identifies its meaning as a haypile surmounted by a protective sliding roof supported on four poles.

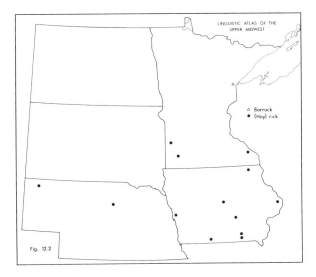

barrack 16.
haymow 39.
  rick c46, 56, c59; s105, c107, 124, s125, †127, 132, 135, sˡ142, c146, 147; c401. hay~ 46; s†137, 139, *145; 413.
  round stack 132.
  stack 1, sn6, 12-14, 17, 22-23, 32, 49-50, r56; 117, 122, 124-25, 128-29, 136, 141, 146-49; 206, 219, 221, 225; 301, 303, s305, 306-7, 309, 312, 316-18, 320-21, 324, 327; 401, 403-4, 406, 409, 412, 415, 433, 436-37. hay~ 2-5, 7-11, 13, 15, 17-21, 24, c25, 26-30, c31, 32-34, :35, 36-48, 51-55, 57-65; 101-6, c107, 108-9, 111-16, 118-20, 123, 126-27, 130-31, 133-35, 137-40, 142-45, 150-52; 201-5, 207-18, 220, 222-24, 226; 302, 304, 307-8, 310-11, 313-15, 319, 322-23, 325-26, 328; 402, 405, 407-8, 410-11, 413-14, c415, 416-28, cvr429, 430-35.
  no response 110, 121.

Comment:

  barrack: With a long sliding roof--16. rick: Long--46, 56; 132, 135, 146-47; 401. Rectangular--132. A small haystack-- 59. Inf. heard mother say, "They ricked up the hay"--127. Inf. says older than

'haystack'--139. hayrick: Long--137; 413. stack: Square--412. Long--17; 219, 225; 305, 317, 320; 409. Round--146-47; 406. Either round or long--306. Common term-- 6. haystack: Square or rectangular--7, 58; 105; 221, †224; 324; 408, 413. Long-- 17, 26-28, 42, 49, 54; 103, 106, 114-16; 205, 207, 209-10, 213, 217, 220, 222; 319, 322; 410, 424-25, 428. Round--36, 46; 108, 135, 150; 224; 401, 405. Either long or round--8, 19, 21, 25, 31, 34, 41, 56, 65; 117, 126; 303, 323; 402-3, 414- 16, 420-21, 423, 426-27, 431, 434-35. Oval--104, 107, 137. Rounded top--7-8, 21, 27-28, 34, 58; 103, 106, 115-16, 126; 205, 207, 210, 213, 217, 220, 222, 224- 25; 319, 322-24; 408, 413, 415, 423-25. Peaked top--34, 36; 105, 150; 209; 426.

12.3 haycock (in the field). NE 104. WG 47, 54; F58, F59.

For a small pile of hay in the field the two principal UM terms, (hay)cock and (hay)shock, are regionally distributed in correlation with the eastern pattern of haycock in the North and North Midland and hayshock in the South Midland and South Atlantic Coast, although shock, perhaps in euphemistic reaction to another meaning of cock, has spread somewhat into Minnesota and North Dakota. The West Midland euphemism, doodle, weakly survives in southwestern UM. Eastern Pennsylvania pile appears only in the western half. Bunch, a minority form in New England, retains vitality in western UM. Sweep bunch and haybuck probably reflect the large-scale hayfarming operations of the western prairies, where it is not uncommon for huge rakes or sweeps to bunch hay into large piles, each of which is large enough to be a buck or load on a haywagon. Coil, the Canadian term, is reported also by a northwest Minnesota farmer whose parents were born in Canada. Stook, another Canadianism, apparently has been transferred by this inf. from its ordinary meaning, "a shock of grain". Tumble, found in western Connecticut, appears as a lone relic in Duluth, used by a Type I inf. whose mother was born in Wisconsin. The originally puzzling kapanola, said by its user in Virginia, Minnesota, to be of Finnish origin, has now been plausibly explained. An inquiring note in *American Speech* was answered by Ernest J. Moyne (*American Speech* 35.76-77 (1960)) with the explanation that it is derived from an old Finnish farming term meaning a patch of land requiring about half of peck of rye in the sowing. Kappa is "half a peck"; ala means "area." Such an area is the equivalent of one square pole or about 30 square yards. It is suggested

that the term came to have the meaning
"the amount of hay grown on one square
pole of ground."

CL 59: The 1,018 checklist infs. confirm the fieldwork data with 51% for haycock and 29% for hayshock. The Iowa distribution is striking, with 69% haycock
in the northern half and 23% in the
southern; hayshock has 17% in the northern half and 65% in the southern. Supplementing the fieldwork lexical items are
hayhop, reported from Mower County, Minnesota; the Pennsylvania handstack, reported five times in South Dakota, twice
in Iowa, and once each in North Dakota
and Nebraska; doodlebug, once in North
Dakota from a farmer born in Minnesota;
buckpile, three times, and rakepile once,
in South Dakota; and sweepload, once in
Nebraska.

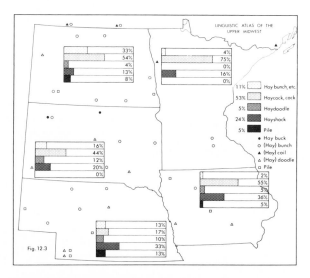

Fig. 12.3

bunch 35; 112; 201-2, 205, 215, sn221,
224; 301, *316, 317, 321; 405, ¹*408,
412. hay ~ 48; 203, 223; 417. sweep ~
404.

bunched hay 404.

cock 1, 7, 12-13, 50, cr56, 59; 148-49;
220-21; 307-9, 323, 327. hay~ 4, *5, 8,
11, 15-16, 18-19, s20, 21-24, 27, 29-30,
33, 39-44, r45, 46-47, †49, c51, 52-55,
59-64, s65; 101-5, 107-9, 113-14, s115,
116-17, 119, ¹124, 126, 137-41, 144, 151-
52; ¹203, 205, 207-8, ¹210, 211-14, 216-
17, 221-22, 224; ¹301, ¹302, 303-5, 311,
¹312, ¹314, ¹316, 318, ¹325, 328; ?409,
413, 419-21, 427, s428.

coil 3; 201-2. hay ~ 8.

doodle 125; 210; 322; 413, ¹414, 429,
sn437. hay ~ 135; 314, 320.

hay buck 301, :303.

hay dump 217.

heap 134.

kapanola 14.

mound 219; 310; 436. hay ~ 2, 58.

pile 102, 128; 215, 225; 411, :419,
429, 437.

rick 148; ¹218; 309; ¹423, ¹431. hay~
44; 422.

shock 17, ¹30, 31, 34, ?56, 59, c65;
118, 122, *123, 124-25, 132-33, 136, 142-
43, 145-47, 149; 218; 302, 313, 324-25;
401, 403-4, 407-8, 418, 428, 436. hay ~
10, 17, *28, 43, :60; 106, 135, 209, 216;
312; 429-30.

stack 433. hay~ 425, 432-34. small ~
:315.

stook 204.

tumble 17.

no response 6, 9, 25-26, 32, 36-37, ?38,
57; 110-11, 121, 127, 129-31, 150; 206,
226; 319, 326; 402, 406, 410, 415, 424,
426, 435.

Comment:

bunch: Used as a verb--107, 112, 114-
15, *116; 307, 317. Raked into a heap--
202, 205; 310; 405, 412. sweep bunch:
Piled by a sweep--404. cock: Used as a
verb--107; 420. Came into use with alfal-
fa--221. haycock: Made with a rake--8.
Made with a fork--224. About 4' high--19;
113; 224. About 2' high--421. Hasn't
heard the term in years--49. Isn't too
common here--65. Heard infrequently--203;
301. The local term, though inf. and her
husband do not use it--210. Not used lo-
cally--409. Derived from reading--419.
coil: = bunch--201. Made with a fork--202.
hay coil: Made with a fork--8. hay doodle: A little round stack--320. hay buck:
Larger than a bunch--301. A buck, or
load, in each pile--303. kapanola: Inf.
says that this is a Finnish word [see
Moyne, Ernest J. "The problem of 'kapanola' ('kapanala') solved," *AS* 35.76-77
(1960)]--14. mound: Made by a sweep--436.
pile: Larger than a 'shock'; piled by a
hay buck--429. rick: "A little stack"--
309. A long low pile made when raking--
431. shock: Inf. says 'haycock' is used
around Centerville (a neighboring community)--335. Smaller than a 'mound'--436. hay
shock: Inf. thinks term incorrect--60.
Larger than a 'hay doodle'--135.

12.4 Shelter for cows. NE 108. WG 21,
41; F31.

Although the subvarieties of the responses to this item reflect different
purposes and physical features, the three
basic terms are distributed in typical
Midland-Northern contrast. The forms including barn show strong Northern correlation; those with shed a Midland orientation; and those with stable, though
apparently UM relics, a Northern orienta-

tion. Dairy barn and milk barn, peculiar
to farms with milch cows, seem more likely to occur where such farms are less
common, as in beef cattle-raising areas.
Massachusetts lean-to survives weakly in
Iowa.

barn 6, 13-14, 18, 20, 32, 38, 43-46,
53, 59-60, c61; 115, 136, 151; 306, 316,
319; 432. basement ~ 48. cattle ~ 9-10,
23, 33, 60; 141; 212, 222, 225; 323;

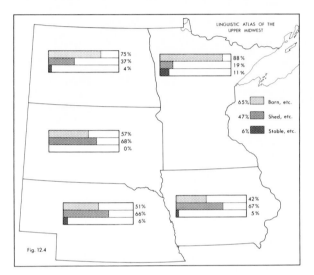

LINGUISTIC ATLAS OF THE
UPPER MIDWEST

75%
37%
4%

88%
19%
11%

65% Barn, etc.

47% Shed, etc.

6% Stable, etc.

57%
68%
0%

51%
66%
6%

42%
67%
5%

Fig. 12.4

408. cow ~ 1, c4, 7-8, 10-12, 17, 19,
21-26, ↑28, 29-31, 33-37, 39-40, c42, 47-
49, 52, 55-59, c61, 62-63, s↑65; 101,
118, 120, 129, 134, 139-40, 147-51; 201-
3, 205-7, 209, 211, 213-15, 219-20, 222,
224-26; 303, 307, 309-10, 315, 317-18,
c320, 322-23, 325-27; c401, 407, 410,
c414, 415, c423, 425, 427, 429, c430,
431, 433-34. dairy ~ *5, 44; :130, 146,
152; 319; 408, 420, 425, c427, 428. feed
~ 225. milk ~ 51; 437. stock ~ 65; 222.
lean 305. cattle ~ 48. lean-to c107,
s↑123, 143.
shed 107-8, 118, 128, 132, 135, 145;
*316. calving ~ 404. cattle ~ 2, 41, 60,
64; 104-7, 109, 112, 115-17, 122, 126,
138, 142; c210, 216, 218, 224; 301, 303-
4, c312, 313, 321, c325, c↑328; 404, 406,
408, 416, 436. cow ~ 8, 21, 27, :28, 29-
30, 46, ↑62; 101, 119-20, 124-25, 133,
135, 137, 146-47, 150; 201, c204, 205,
217, 223; 302, 308, 310-11, 314-15, 320,
322-24, 328; c403, 404-5, 407, 409, 412-
13, 416, 420-22, 424, 426, 428-32, 435.
milk ~ 437. stock ~ 50; c218. straw ~
117, 133; 416.
stable 14-16, 18; 103; 419. cow ~ 3,
15, :45, 54; 137; ↑202, 224; c417, ↑418.
windbreak 406; 437.
no response 102, 110-11, 113-14, 121,
127, ?131, 144; 208, 221; 402, 411.

Comment:

cattle barn: Either a separate building
or a section in the larger barn--60. cow
barn: Enclosed--8; 226; 310, 323. Open
on one side--431. Either open or enclosed
--49; 101; 215; 315, 320; 407, 423, 430.
More substantial than a 'cow shed'--21.
Separate but sometimes with a section for
horses--26, 58. Used if whole building is
for cows--59; 303. Used if there are two
buildings, one for cows and one for horses
--213. Either separate or built on a barn
--62. 'Cow barn' and 'horse barn' are
separate sides of the same building--19.
Section within the barn where cows are
kept--40, 52, 57, 63; 318; 434. In older
buildings a lean-to--61. Inf. says dair-
ies have 'cow barns,' but most farmers do
not call them such--148. = cow shed--150;
322. For milch cows--222; 429. = dairy
barn--225. dairy barn: The regular barn--
146. For milch cows--408. feed barn: =
cattle barn; not necessarily for milch
cows--225. milk barn: A section within a
barn--51. shed: Open on one side--107-18,
128, 145. Built on a barn and open--118.
calving shed: Open on one side; used just
for calving in the spring; now supplanted
by 'hospital' on the modern range--404.
cattle shed: Enclosed--41. Open on one
side--104, 106, 109, 112, 115, 117, 122,
126; 303, 312-13, 321, 328; 404, 408.
Open or enclosed--301; 406, 436. Attached
to barn--138. An open lean-to--224. Either
attached or separate--210. cow shed: Open
on one side--8, 30; 124, 135, 137, 146;
201; 302, 311, 314, 320, 323, 328; 404-5,
407-8, 412, 420, 422, 424, 426, 429, 431,
435. Open or enclosed--29; 125, 137; 409.
Separate; "Old-timers call it 'cow shed'"
--62. Attached to barn--101, 133. Attached
or separate--119; 413, 416, 421. Inf.'s
usual term; an enclosed reserve barn--315.
= cow barn--150; 322. For stock cattle--
429. stock shed: An enclosed building--
50. straw shed: Open on one side and covered with straw--117, 133. A lean-to--
416. cow stable: A section within a barn
--45; 137. An enclosed building; a family
term--54. A solid building with a loft--
224. windbreak: For range cattle; open
on one side--437.

12.5(1) Shelter and enclosure for hogs
and pigs. NE 110. WG 20, 21, 27.

The basic included terms in most of the
responses, pig and hog, reveal a clear
though not sharp Northern-Midland contrast, pig being favored in Northern
speech territory and hog in Midland. Pig-
sty is dominantly Northern in its distribution, with a 34% frequency in Minnesota contrasting with only 2% in Iowa;

but its use was not carried westward into the Dakotas to any extent. Piggery, though found in New England, has survived only with Canadian speakers except for the one response by an aux. mid-Minnesota inf. who was born in Norway.

What complicates the situation is semantic variation and the nature of the physical referent. Many infs. use a term indiscriminately for the shelter or the enclosure or a combination of both, so that only the situational context identifies the specific meaning of a remark, "He's in the pigpen." Others have one term for the shelter and another for the enclosure. The shelter itself varies in size from a small low structure not more than four or five feet high with, often, a slanting roof, to a building large enough for a man to stand in, and with a slanting or A-roof. No one term is regularly applied to any one type of shelter to distinguish it from another. The barn terms appear to have Northern orientation (Mn. 12.5%, Ia. 0, N.D. 0, S.D. 11%, Nb. 5.6%). Those with house may have a slight Midland weighting (Mn. 44%, Ia. 59%, N.D. 50%, S.D. 59%, Nb. 67%). So with pen (Mn. 67%, Ia. 78%, N.D. 58%, S.D. 67%, Nb. 86%). Shed forms are strongly Midland (Mn. 6.3%, Ia. 25%, N.D. 3.8%, S.D. 15%, Nb. 41%).

CL 16: The Northern correlation of the pig forms is substantiated by the 1,050 checklist responses for this item, which shows consistently higher frequency in Minnesota and North Dakota (60% and 64% respectively) than in Iowa (38%). The hog forms have 90% frequency in Iowa and 62% in Minnesota. But the picture is less than clear-cut in the field records.

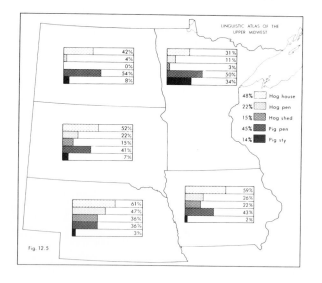

Fig. 12.5

corral 420.
farrowing pen 149. ~ shed 149.
feeding floor 107. ~ pen 25; 407. ~ yard 64.
feed lot 142.
hog barn 8, 26, *28, 30, 41, 59, c60, c*60; ¹226; 305, 319; 413, 415. ~ house 4, 7, 10, 19-20, 25, 28, 34, 41, ¹48, 50, 52-54, 56, 58, 60-62, 64, c65; 101-2, 104-8, 113-15, 117, 119, 122-24, 126, 128, 131-32, c136, 140, 142-43, c144, 145, 147-49, 151-52; 203, 206, c209, 210-11, ¹212, 216-18, 221, 223-24; 302-4, 306-7, c312, 313-14, 318, c322-23, 324-25, c328; →403, 404, 406-9, 412-14, 416, 418-23, 427, c430-31, 432-33, 436. ~ lot ¹8; 114, ?131, 138, 145, 151; c224; 413, 432, 434. ~ pasture 24; 143; c405, 429. ~ pen 19, 34, 40, c49, 53, c59, 64; 101, 105-6, 109, 112, 115, 127, 129-30, 132-33, 139, 146; 222; 302, 313, 315, 321-22, 325; →401, 406, 408, 410, 414, 417-18, 420-21, 424, 428-31, 435-37. ~ run ¹1; 135; 323. ~ shed 24, 26; 101, 109, 112, 115, c125, 133-35, 138, 140, 149; 316, 321, 323, 327; 404-5, 413, 417-18, 421, c422, 428-29, 431, 434-35, 437. ~ stable ¹106. ~ wallow 33. ~ yard c30, 56, 65; 206; 315; *417, 418, 421.
litter pen 111.
lot c405.
pen 40, 43, sn65; 122, 124, 136; 317.
piggery 1-2, *21; 202.
pig barn 305. ~ house 12, 15, 17, 22, 42-43, 48, 63; 207, c209; 301, 317; c417. ~ lot 135; 204. ~ pasture 205, 209, 223. ~pen 2, 4-5, ¹7, 8-9, 11, 16, 18, 20-23, 26-27, 29-32, 35-37, 43, !45, 46-48, 57-59, 62-63; 102-6, 108, 113, 115-16, 118-21, 123, 127-28, 137, 139, 141, c144, 150, 152; 201, 205, c208, 210, 212-15, 219, 221-23, 225-26; 301-4, 308, †309, 311, 314, 316, 319, 324-25, ¹326; 403, 408-9, 411, 414, 416, 420, 422-23, 426-28, 433. ~ run 201. ~ shed 13; 147; 208; :?311; †403, 414, 431. ~ stable ¹119; 202. ~sty 1-3, 10, :11, 12, 14, 21, 23, 33, 37-39, !44, →45, 46-47, 51, ¹54, 55, 57-58, 61; 111; 204, 220; 201, 310, ¹326; †401, 402. ~ wallow 402. ~ yard 15, ¹22; 207, 220, 223.
runway 135.
shelter 225.
stall 7.
straw shed 7.
sty ¹7; 146, 152; 308, →309; 410.
yard 16.
no response 6; 110; 320; 425.

Comment:
hog barn: = hog shed--26. Usu.--60. hog house: Most common here--58. Newer than 'pig pen'--62. hog pen: = hog house--64. hog wallow: Inf. not sure where she ac-

quired this--33. pig pen: Usu.--308. pig-sty: Just dirtier than a pig pen--37. "To be proper now, it's called 'pigsty'"--45. Less common than 'pig pen'--46-47. "Never used on this farm"--54. Rare--61. sty: Learned from working puzzles--410.

(2) Enclosure only.

feeding pen 407. ~ yard 64.
hog house 117. ~ lot 114, 138, 145, 151; 413, 432. ~ pasture 405. ~ pen 101, 106, 112, 132-33; 322; 408, 424, 430-31, 435. ~ run 135. ~ yard 65; 315; 418.
pen 124, 136.
pig lot 134. ~ pasture 205, 209, 223; 429. ~pen 1, 7-8, 11, 20-21, 48, 58; 102, 104, 106, 108, 113, 123, 144, 152; 208, 215, 223, 226; 303, 311, 319; 408-9, 411, 429, 433. ~ run 201. ~sty 58. ~ wallow 402. ~ yard 207, 223.
stall 7.
sty 7; 309.

(3) Shelter or building only.

hog barn 8, 26, 30; 319; 413, 415. ~ house 7, 19-20, 25, 28, 34, 53, 62, 65; 101-2, 104, 106-8, 113-14, 116, 124, 126, 132, 136, 145, 147-48, 151-52; 209-11, 218, 221; 302-3, 312, 322-24, 328; 406-9, 413-14, 416, 418, 420-21, 423, 427, 430, 432-33. ~ pen 129; 315; 418. ~ shed 101, 109, 112, 132, 135, 138, 149; 321, 323, 327; 413, 418, 429, 431, 434-35, 437.
pen 65.
piggery *21.
pig house 22, 42, 62; 207, 209; 301, 317. ~pen 5; 116, 141; 201, 205. ~ shed 147; 208; 403, 414, 431. ~sty 1-3, 11; 111; 204, 220; 301.
shelter 225.
sty 152.

Comment:

hog shed: More temporary than a 'hog house'--101. pen: Section within a 'pig house'--42; 317. pig pen: Section within the building--63.

12.7 barnyard (where stock is kept or fed). NE 113. WG 40, 55; F62.

For the area near or around the barn where stock may be kept or fed, the New England and North Midland term barnyard is common in the eastern half of the UM, although some distinctions of meaning appear. The Southern and South Midland lot, with such combinations as cow lot, feed lot, feeding lot, and cattle lot occur chiefly in the southeastern quadrant of the UM, with the basic barnlot almost limited to the South Midland speech area

of southern Iowa. In the western half of the UM the term corral, designating a small lot fenced with wood or wire and used for horses, suggests the regional dominance of the cattle-raising industry. An intermediate area between west and east is outlined by the distribution of the feed terms, which usually refer to an enclosure for further feeding of cattle shipped in from points west to be fattened before being sent to the packing-houses of Sioux City, Omaha, and South St. Paul. Characteristic of a transition zone, a split in meaning between barnyard and barn lot sometimes appears, with barnyard then referring to open area surrounding a barn and barn lot to a fenced-in enclosure, or with the two terms referring simply to different parts of the land near a barn. Some infs. also distinguish between barnyard and feed yard, the latter being used only for feeding cattle.

CL 17: Responses on 1,059 checklists are confirmatory, with the lot forms strongest in southern Iowa (37%) and Nebraska (32%) and weakest in Minnesota (7%).

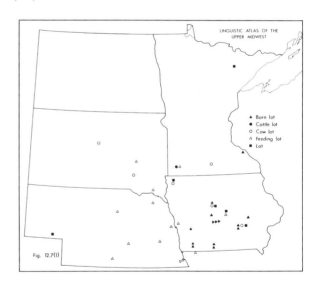

Fig. 12.7(1)

barn lot 54; 114, 128, 135-37, 142-45, 147-49, c150, 151. ~yard ¹1, 3, :4, s6, 7-9, :10, 13-14, 18, ?:s20, 21, :s22, 23, :sn24, 26-28, 30-34, :35, 36-38, 40, 42-43, c44, 45-47, s48, s49, c50, 51-52, 54, 57-58, 61, 63-65; 102, ¹104, 105-8, 112-13, 116-18, s119, 120-27, s128, 129-31, 134, 136, 139-41, *145, 146, 148, 150, 152; 207, 210, 221, 225-26; 305, 307-9, 316-18, 321-22, ¹323, 325, 328; 426.
calf pen 414.
cattle lot 60. ~ pen 211. ~ yard 41,

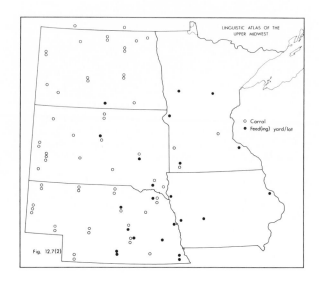

Fig. 12.7(2)

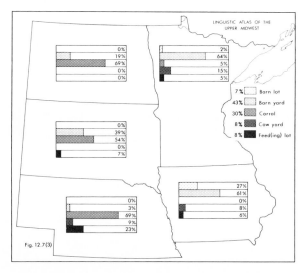

7% Barn lot
43% Barn yard
30% Corral
8% Cow yard
8% Feed(ing) lot

Fig. 12.7(3)

59; 111; 323; 414.
  corral ¹†7, ¹12, 34, c†46, *46, ¹49,
¹†50, 61; 201-2, c203, 204-6, 208-10,
†211, 212-13, c214, 215-19, 224; 301,
c302, 303-4, 309-14, ¹315, c320, 321,
324, 326-27; 401-10, c411, 412, c414,
c416, 417, c418, 419-20, c422, 423, 429,
432, 436-37.
  cow lot 62; 102, 115, 135; 314, 322.
~ pen 47-48. ~ yard 15, 29, 35, 43, c44,
45-46, 48, 53; 104, 109, 117, 138; 403,
†*408, c424, 428.
  farmyard 103; 319.
  feeding ground 12. ~ lot 133. ~ pen
*5. ~ yard 19, c21; 421.
  feed lot ¹1, 25, 55, 60; 124, 127; 325,
328; 407, 413, 422, 425, 427, 431, 434-
35. ~ yard 111, 119; ¹216, 223; 325; 430.
  lot 13; 101, 115, 132, 135; 436.

pen :211; 404.
  stockyard 56; 152; 220; ¹323; 414.
  yard 17, 41, 56, 61; 132, 142, 149;
222; 306-7; 403-4.
  no response 2, ?11, 16, 39; 110; 415,
433.

Comment:

  barn lot: Fenced-in grassy area in
front of the barn; a 'barnyard' is a bare
area behind the barn--54. Various enclo-
sures within the barn lot are the horse
lot, cow lot, and hog lot--135. barnyard:
Not known here; local farms do not have
such things--6. Larger than a cow yard--
44. Area around the barn; not necessarily
the same as the 'cow yard' or 'corral'--
46. Different from feed yard; cattle are
not fed in the barnyard--119. corral:
Inf. says used by early French settlers--
7. Early name--46. Inf. heard "oldtimers"
use this--50. Inf.'s father used this
word, but she doesn't now--211. A fenced-
in lot with an incline for loading cat-
tle--34. Rare, western term--61. May also be away from the barn--210. Usually
for working stock--312. Inf. says usu.
west of the Missouri River--314. Used on
ranches--315. For horses--211; 403. Not
for feeding; for catching and handling--
422. cow pen: Common here; = barnyard--
47. cow yard: The fenced-in area; the
'barnyard' is a larger area all around
the barn--45. feed lot: Fenced-in area
near the barn where stock are fed; the
'barnyard' is the area around a barn that
is not enclosed--124. Larger than a 'barnyard'--325. = barnyard--328. Inf. says
that cattle are bought, fattened in a
'feed lot', and sold--425. feeding yard:
"To fatten 'em up"--21. feed yard: Larger than a 'barnyard'--325. stockyard: =
barnyard--152. Heard infrequently--323.
yard: = cattle yard--41. 'Yard' for older animals; 'pen' for the young--414.

12.8 farm.

  This item was added late in the fieldwork in order to ascertain the eastern
limits of ranch. An original distinction
between farm and ranch became blurred
when ranch came to be applied to a huge
fenceless tract for wheat-growing. Today,
a large tract used for both cattle and
grain production is likely to be termed
ranch rather than farm because the former
tends to bear a prestige value, just as
rancher does in contrast with farmer. In
general, ranch is limited to cattle-raising areas west of the Missouri river.
Spread, synonymous with ranch as a cat-
tle-raiser's term, is attested as a Nebraska term by Louise Ackerman (American

Speech 38.302-3 (1963), but it was not reported by any field inf.

a. For crops:
farm 309, 313, c314, 320-21; 401-2, 405-6, 409-11, 413, c414, 416-23, 425-26, 428-29, cvr430, 431, 433, 436-37.
ranch ¹401, ¹409.

b. For cattle raising:
ranch 301-2, 304, 309-13, c314, c315, c320, 321, 326, †327, c328; †401, 402-5, cvr406, 408-13, cvr414, 416-23, 425-27, cvr429, 430-31, 433, 436-37.

c. For both:
farm 310, 312, 315, 326; 403, c404, 415, 427.
ranch 311; 415, 424, 428.

Comment:

farm: "There ain't no such thing as a farm in western South Dakota. Every damn place in western South Dakota is a ranch" --310. Inf. says that earlier settlers had a combination farm-ranch; terms are sometimes interchangeable now--429. ranch: Originally for cattle only, but now used for farms where soil is tilled; inf. thinks this usage wrong--401. Inf. says some farmers like to call their farms ranches; "a little ego sticking out," "sounds bigger--a little more doggy"--409. There are no ranches here--327; 408, 433. Only difference is size; a 'ranch' is larger--415, 435. Larger than 640 acres; for wheat or cattle--428. "I don't know as there's any difference"--432. Difference is a matter of geography--434. Local prestige term--437.

13.1 pasture (where cows, sheep, etc., graze). NE 114.

Most infs., 99%, respond with pasture as their word for the grazing area, but in the western sector memories of the open cattle country of two and three generations ago persist in the occurrence of range and grazing land even with recognition that today such land, extensive as it might be, ultimately is bound by fences. Commons, labeled obsolete in this sense in the *Dictionary of Americanisms*, is the usual term of a Black Hills rancher.

commons 311.
field 6.
grazing land ?58; 214, 224; 321; 401-2, *412.
hayfield 108.
meadow 6; 430.
pasture c1, 2-3, s4, 5, c7, 8-9, c10, 11-21, c22, 23, c24, 25-28, c29, 30-33, c34, :c35, :36, 37-43, c44, 45-46, c47,

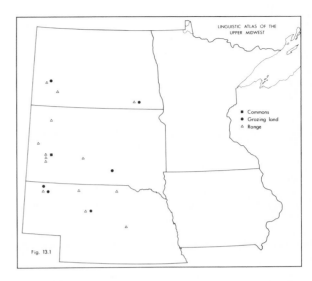

Fig. 13.1

48, c49, 50, c51, 52-54, c55, c56, 57-58, c59, 60-61, c62, 63-65; c101, c102, 103-49, c150, 151, c152; 201-12, c213, 214-25, c226; 301-5, c306, 307-13, c314-15, 316-28; 401, 403-12, c413, 414-20, c421, 422-26, cvr427, 428-33, c434, 435-37. cow ~ 16.
range †109; 215, 224; 301, 309, 311-13, †320, 326; 402, 404-5, ¹406, 412, 420, s426, †429, ¹436. cattle ~ 214. stock ~ 214. summer ~ 301. winter ~ 301. ~ land 404.

Comment:

commons: Government forest reserve leased to inf.--311. grazing land: Term not used locally; inf. says it is for extensive land west of Minnesota and the Dakotas--58. Large unfenced area--214, 224; 321. Larger than a 'pasture'--401. hayfield: Cattle allowed to graze here after the hay has been cut--108. meadow: For occasional grazing; a pasture is for constant grazing--430. pasture: Fenced area--215, 224; 312, 326. Term rarely used by inf.--311. "Might be 7 or 8 sections"--320. Inf. says 'pasture,' 'range land,' 'range' are "same thing"; a pasture may be 15 sections or more--404. "A few acres"--426. Also used here on ranches; range is in Wyoming--436. range: Used by inf. in youth when there were few fences --109. Large unfenced area--215, 224; 309, 313; 402, 420. A large pasture, or total amount of one's pasture land--301. Once open and publicly owned--326. Inf. says a 'range' is 4 or 5 sections--405. Less common than 'pasture' now--406. More usual here than 'pasture'--412. "Many, many square miles"--426. "Open, unfenced land in 1884; only some leased range left here now"--429. cattle range: Large unfenced

area--214. stock range: Large unfenced
area--214.

13.2 picket fence. NE 115; WG 15, 47,
48, 55; F41, F63.

For a fence composed of upright stakes
or pales the wellnigh universal term in
the UM is the Northern picket fence. The
Midland paling fence is reported only
twice, once in Minnesota and once in
North Dakota, by infs. of British and
Ohio ancestry. No trace of it remains in
the Midland speech area of Iowa.

lath fence 13.
lattice fence [1]220; 431.
paling fence 44; 214.
picket fence 1-5, 7-18, s19, 20-24, 26-
33, c34, 35, 37-38, c39, 40-43, 45, c46,
47-61, c62, 63-65; 101-52; 201-2, 204-13,
215-26; 301, 304, 309-14, 320-28; 401-9,
:410, 411-29, s431-432, 433-34, 436-37.
slat fence [1]48; 109; 422, 427.
stake fence 315.
woven willow fence 414.
yard fence 124; 434.
no response 6, ?25, 36; 203; 302-3, 305-
8, 316-19; 430, 435.

Comment:

picket fence: Inf. says that they are
rare here--7. Inf. says that there are
none here; not enough wood--202. slat
fence: Made with horizontal wires and
vertical laths or slats--109; 422. =
picket fence, but perhaps less ornamental
--427. woven willow fence: Made with willow branches woven as uprights with wire
--414. yard fence: Generic term for either wire or wooden fence around a yard
--124.

13.3 barbed wire fence. NE 116.

Although originally a phonetic variant
or folk-etymologized form of barbed wire,
the expression bobbed wire (bob wire) is
lexically differentiated from it by a number of infs. Of all UM infs., with no appreciable contrast among types, 14% use
bob(bed) wire; 89% barb(ed) wire. A few
admit using both. The bob forms occur in
an unusual distribution pattern, since
they are absent from northern Iowa and
the western sectors of South Dakota and,
with one exception, of Nebraska. Aside
from the frequency in southern Iowa, they
thus conform to the typical Northern
speech zone. Their absence in northern
Iowa is possibly a function of the fieldworker who investigated that area, since
he reported only one bob and otherwise
consistently recorded barb.

Fig. 13.3

barb wire fence 1-3, 5, c6, 7.-8, c12,
17-21, 24-26, 29-30, :31, 32, 37, 40-41,
43-48, 50, 52-58, c59, 60-61, c62, 63-65;
101, 104-10, 112-13, 115, 117, 119-20,
122-27, 129-34, 136-39, 142, 145-47, 149-
50, 152; 202, 204-6, 208, 210, 212, 214-
16, 218, *219, 220-21, 223, 225; 301-4,
307, 309, 311-14, 317, 319-22, 324-27;
401, 408-9, 412, 414-22, c424, 429-30,
c434, 435-37.
barbed wire fence 9-10, c12, 13-14, 16,
23, 27, 33-34, 38-39, 42, 51, 57; 102-3,
111, 114, 116, 118, 141, 151; 201, 207,
219, 222, 226; 306, 308, 310, 315-16,
328; 403-6, 410, →411, 413, 423, 425-29,
431, 433.
bob wire fence 4, 11, 15, 28, 35-36,
c58; 121, 128, 135, 140, 143-44, 148;
203, 209, 211, 213, 217, 224; 305, 318-
19, 323; [1]401, 402, 407, †411.
bobbed wire fence 22, [1]42, 49; 308;
432.
wire fence 13-14; 122; 432-33.

Comment:

barbed wire fence: More common than
'wire fence'--433. bob wire fence: Used
by inf.'s husband--401.

13.4 rail fence. NE 117. WG 31, 55; F64.

Northern rail fence dominates the southeastern quadrant of the UM, although Midland worm fence competes weakly with it
in the same area, as does stake and rider
fence. All three refer generally to a
zigzag type of fence (Type A below) composed of split logs or rails laid horizontally upon one another. The stake and
rider fence is a subvariety characterized
by X-shaped supports at the rail ends and
by an extra rail, or rider, laid in the

crotch of the X to provide additional strength. The synonymous snake fence, reported sporadically in southeastern Pennsylvania and New England, occurs in Iowa and Fort William, Ontario, along with a curious fused term, snake and rider, admitted by a southern Minnesota inf.

Pole fence, denominating a structure (Type B below) composed of vertical posts supporting horizontal poles either inserted into holes in the posts or otherwise attached, appears on two sides of the southeastern quadrant, in northern Minnesota and the eastern margin of North Dakota, and in western Nebraska and western North Dakota. Its western distribution overlaps that of the special term for the kind of pole fence or plank fence surrounding a small enclosure for horses known as a corral. Corral is used by some to denote both the enclosure and the fence itself.

A simpler kind, Type C, apparently bears no special name. Its feature is that it has X-supports carrying only a single rail, usually sufficient to confine horses or cattle or to mark a boundary.

The frequency of the common rail fence is: Mn. 80%, Ia. 84%, N.D. 40%, S.D. 33%, Nb. 39%.

See also Mamie Meredith, "The nomenclature of American pioneer fences," *Southern Folklore Quarterly* 16.109-51 (June, 1951).

corral 214-17. ~ fence 216; 312-13, 406, 412-13.

log fence 16, 23, 32, 39-40; †407, 430, †435.

pole corral 301, 312; 405, 412. ~ fence 1, 10, 12, 15, 22; ¹203, †204, 206-7, 221; 311, 313, 320; c418, 436.

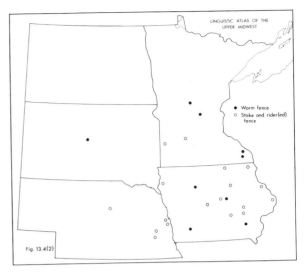

Fig. 13.4(2)

post fence 203. three-~ fence 132.
rail fence 2-5, 7, 10, 13-15, 17-19, 21, c23, 24, 28, 30, †31, 34, 38, *39, 40-41, c42, 43, 45-48, :49, 50-53, ¹54, 55, 57-58, c59, 60-65; 101-3, 105-8, 111-12, 114-17, 119-20, *122, 123-27, 129-31, 133-49; 206, 208-9, †212, 218, 220, 222; 308-9, 324; 406, 413-14, 416, 420-21, s¹422, 423, 425-28, 430, 432, ¹433, s435.
slab fence 427.
snake fence 3; ¹120, 121, :130.
snake and rider fence 53.
split rail fence 37.
stake and rider fence 45-46; 105, 107, 109, 116, 119, 122, 128, 132, 135, 137, 139, 152; 414, 424, 426-28. stake and ridered fence 151; †204.
wood fence 207.
worm fence 27, †29, 56, 58; 113, 118, 137, 151; c314.
zigzag fence 15, 44, 51.
no response 6, 8-9, 11, 20, 25-26, ?33, 35, ?36; 104, 110, 150; 201, ?202, 205, 210-11, 213, ?219, 223-6; 302-7, 310, 315-19, 321-23, 325, ?326, 327-28; 401-4, 408-11, 415, 417, 419, 429-30, 434, 437.

Comment:

rail fence: Not found locally--18, 54, 61, 64-65; 112; 308, 324; 413, 433. Not found locally; seen in Kentucky--49. Seen in Michigan--218. Inf. not very familiar with them--28. Inf. never saw one, but his father told him that there were some here--50. Made of poles stuck in the ground at angles to form X's--212. split rail fence: Seen in Indiana--37. stake and rider fence: Inf. not sure of construction--45.

Type A:

log fence 40; 430.

Fig. 13.4(1)

193

pole fence 1.
rail fence 2, 5, 10, 15, 24, 40, c42,
43, 45-48, 51-52, 55, 57, 60, 62-63; 101-
2, 107-8, 114, 117, 123-27, 129-30, 133-
36, 138, 143, 145-46, 148-49; 206; 309;
416, 420, 426-27, †428, 430.
snake fence 3.
stake and rider fence 109, 116, 132,
137, 152; 424, 427-28. stake and ridered
fence 51; †204.
worm fence 27, †29, 30, 56, 58; 137.
zigzag fence 15, 44, 51.

Comment:

log fence: None found locally--40. rail
fence: None found locally--42, 55; 101-2.
Seen in southern Iowa--102. Some found
in community in earlier days--62; 206;
309. Inf. says it had barbed wire along
the top; called a 'rider'--138. "If you
stake-and-ridered them, you had a good
stiff fence"--149. stake and rider fence:
Inf. has seen them, but not locally--109.
Rare here because of the scarcity of wood
--424. worm fence: Very rare here--58.
None here; seen in southern Iowa--113.

Type B:
corral 214-17. ~ fence 312-13; 406,
412-13.
log fence 16; †407.
pole corral 301, 312-13; 405, 412. ~
fence 10, 12, 22; ┴203, †204, 206-7; 311,
320; c418, 436.
post fence 203. ~'n rail fence 51.
three-~ fence 132.
rail fence 4-5, 17, 19, 21, c23, 24,
40-41, 48, 51-52; 103, 109, 117; 208-9,
220; 406, 414, 426, †428.
snake and rider fence 53.
stake and rider fence ?414.
wood fence 207.

Comment:
log fence: Poles are nailed to posts--
16. Poles pass through holes in posts--
407. pole fence: Poles tied to posts--10.
Tamarack or balsam poles nailed to posts
--12. Poles nailed to posts--22. Poles
pass through holes in posts--22; 207.
Post'n rail fence: Post with holes in it
--51. rail fence: Rails tied with red
willows to posts--4. Rails nailed to
posts--17, 21, 40, 48, 52. Rails nailed
to posts, but criss-crossed instead of
horizontal--111. Rails stuck in holes in
posts--19, 48, 51; 428. Rails stuck in
notched posts--220. Inf. says that rail
is borrowed from Swedish--4. Inf. says
that some were made by early French settlers in the community--7. No longer
found here--30. snake and rider fence:
Rails stuck in holes in posts--53. stake
and rider fence: Inf. thinks this is
right, but is not sure--414. wood fence:

= pole fence--207.
Type C:

pole fence 12.
rail fence 34, 51, 58-59.

Comment:

pole fence: Peeled cedar or spruce
poles--12. rail fence: Inf. has seen only
one fence like this--34. "Stake 'n ridered"--51. Rare here--58. Rails nailed
to supports--59.

13.6 stone wall (made of loose stones).
NE 119. WG 14, 31, 40, 46, 47, 55. F39,
F65.

Much of the UM is unglaciated and hence
without loose stones in fields. Even in
the glaciated area farmers generally preferred to pile up the stones rather than
to undergo the labor of using them for
fences. The eastern terms persist as remembered designations in much of the region outside those sections where such
fences are reported as existing. North
Midland stone fence dominates with Northern stone wall reported as referring to
actual fences in northern Iowa and as a
remembered term in southern Minnesota,
and, three times, in Nebraska. Southern
rock fence is a directly correlated term
in eastern Iowa and a remembered term
three times in Minnesota and once each
in the other states. Rock wall, a rare
South Midland and Southern variant, has
four widely scattered occurrences. Niggerhead fence, a term derived from an old
name for small round boulders, is the usage of two Type I infs. in Minnesota and
North Dakota.

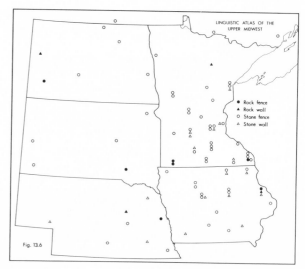

Fig. 13.6

niggerhead fence c47; 220.
   rock fence ?51, 58, 60-61; 119; 214;
322; 427.
   rock wall 11; 121; 210; 414.
   stone fence 2-3, 7, s13, 16-17, 19-21,
c23, 27, *28, c29, 31, 33, 38-39, 42-43,
?46, 48-50, ?51, 53-54, 56-59, :?60, 62-
63, 65; 101, 105, 107, ¹109, ?111, 112-17,
129, 132, 135, 139; 202, c204, 212, 216,
221; 307, 309, 316, c320; 420, 430, 434.
   stone hedge 112.
   stone wall 18, 37, 39, ?40, 44-45, :52,
64; 106, 108, 115, 118, 120, 137, 151;
c408, ¹413, 417, s424, cr426.
   no response 1, 4-6, 8-10, 12, 14-15,
22, 24-26, 30, 32, 34-36, 41, 47, 55;
102-4, 110, 122-28, 130-31, 133-34, 136,
138, 140-50, 152; 201, 203, 205-9, 211,
213, 215, 217, ?218-19, 222-26; 301-6,
308, 310-15, 317-19, 321, 323-28; 401-7,
409-12, 415-16, 418-19, 421-23, 425, 428-
29, 431-33, 435-37.
Comment:

   niggerhead fence: Inf. says farmers
used to make them here--220. rock fence:
Rare here--51; 119. Not found locally--
58, 60-61; 322. Seen by inf. in Pa.--322.
rock wall: Not found locally--11; 414.
Seen by inf. in Pa.--11. stone fence: Not
found locally--2, 7, 16, 23, 31, 34, 39,
42-43, 46, 53-54, 57-60, 62-63; 101, 109,
112-13; 202, 204; 420, 427, 430, 434.
Inf. says they were made by his ancestors
in Canada--7. Seen by inf. in Ill.--57.
Inf. says this is the Ct. name--62. Seen
by inf. in New York and the Dakotas--101.
"Had 'em back in Iowa"--427. "They have
a lot of stone fences back East"--434.
Rare here--17, 27, 48-51, 56; 221. "I've
seen stone fences, but it's too much work
nowadays"--19. Only one stone fence in
the community, a new one at a golf course
--20. Inf. remembers seeing one such
fence--56. Only one fence in community--
212; 320. Inf. says that there are many
in this area around Dubuque--120. stone
hedge: Not found locally--112. stone wall:
Not found locally--39-40, 52, 64; 408,
413, 424, 426. Rare here--45; 417. "I
guess you would call it a 'stone wall'"--
40. Inf. has only the Welsh name for it
--52. "Seen lots back East"--426. no response: Such fences not found locally--
4, 6, 8-10, 12, 24-26, 33, 41, 55; 225;
311, 323, 325; 412.

13.7a china. NE 136.

   The response to the query, "What is
your general term for the objects you set
the table with?" is almost uniformly china throughout the UM. In each state a few
infs. answer with chinaware. One Nebraska

inf. of New York and Indiana ancestry
uses delft; one Minnesotan uses porcelain,
another Haviland china, and two iron
range Minnesotans frankly say that their
word is crockery.

   china 1-5, *9, 10-11, 14, 16-20, :21,
22-23, 25-26, *27, 28, c29, 30-34, c35,
36, 38, 40, *41, 42-45, r46, 47, 49-54,
c55, r56, 57-58, c59, 60-65; s101, 102-
11, 113-23, 126-52; 201-5, sn!206, 207-8,
210-15, :216, 217-19, 221-22, 225-26;
301-2, ¹304, 305, *306, 309-15, 317-19,
321, *322, 323-28; 402-10, ¹411, 412-13,
cvr414, 416-23, 425-30, cvr431, 432-37.
~ dishes 15, 48; 401, 431. ~ware 6-8, 12,
24, 37, 39; 112; 209, 220, 223-24; 303,
c307, 308, 316, 320; 415, 424-25.
   crockery 13-14.
   delft 426.
   Haviland 32. ~ china 32.
   porcelain 14.
   pottery 305, *306.
   no response 124-25.

13.7b china egg.

   Although intended to elicit only a
phonological item, the question about an
artificial egg put into a nest to induce
a hen to lay yielded several lexical variants. No clear regional pattern appears.
Only a few responses represent Minnesota,
as this item was added after fieldwork
had begun.

   china egg 30-31, 35; 101-2, s104, 105-
6, 108-9, 112, s113, 114-17, 124-25, 133,
137-38, 148-50, 152; 215, 225-26; 302,
308-12, 314-15, 320, 325-26; 401, c403,
405-8, f409, 410, s411, 413-14, 416-20,
¹421, 422-24, 426-29, s430, 432, 434-35,
!437.
   china nest egg 316.
   glass egg 104, 127; 305, c*306, 319,
321; 404, 425.
   nest egg 36; 103, 107, 116, 126, 137-
38, 145, 148-49; 305-7, 317-18; 402, 404,
409, 413-14, 430-31, †433.

Comment:

   nest egg: Used by inf.'s mother--433.

14.1 bucket (wooden vessel). NE 129.
WG 12, 13, 47, 48, 56; F42, F86.

   Treated as a single item in the eastern
atlas studies, the question about the
term for a vessel used in carrying milk
or water was divided in the North Central
and UM investigations in order to clari-
fy the designations for the wooden vessel
and those for the metal one. For the former bucket is slightly favored in the UM,
with some evidence of Midland orientation,

especially in western Nebraska and western South Dakota. The vessel is sometimes described as straight-sided or slightly convex, for use in a well; but more generally the vessel is considered as having slightly flaring sides and a bail, with diverse uses. Some Northern speakers identify the term only with the object celebrated in Samuel Woodworth's poem; for them a bucket is always "oaken." These speakers and others in Minnesota distinguish the vessel with flaring sides as a wooden pail.

See Gary N. Underwood, "Semantic confusion: evidence from the Linguistic Atlas of the Upper Midwest," *Journal of English Linguistics*, 2.86-95 (1968).

CL 14.1: The 1,008 respondents checking this item are divided almost precisely like the field infs., 62% with bucket and 44% with pail, the Iowa pattern strongly indicating a Midland orientation; northern Iowa 46% for bucket and 57% for pail; southern Iowa 84% for bucket and only 20% for pail.

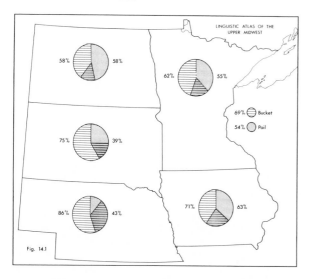

bucket 1, 5, c6, ⊥7, 9, 11, 14, 17-18, 20-22, †24, *26, cr28, c29, 30-34, 37, 39-40, ⊥41-42, *43, c†44, †45, c46, c48, 49, 52, c53, !54, 55, s⊥!56, 57, c60, 62, †63, 64, ⊥65; 101, 105, 108, 111, 113-18, cr119, †120, 121, 124-25, s†126, 127-28, 130, 132-33, 136-38, s⊥139, 140-41, 144-50, †151, 152; 203, 205-7, ?208, 210, 212, †213, 215, 218-19, →221, †223, 224, ⊥225, 226; †301, †303, cr304, 305-6, 308-13, c314, 315-20, c322, †323, 325; 403-6, 409-10, 412, 415-16, 418-20, c421, 422-28, 430-35, 437. candy ~ †301. milk ~ 20; *122, 129, 134-35; 409. oak ~ 47. water ~ 20; 134; 408-9. well ~ †301. wood ~

432, 434. wooden ~ 2, 8, cr15, c31, c35, 52, 58; 204, 212, *216, 222; 302, 321-22, 328; 402, 418, 429.

butter tub 34.

pail 2, 7, 13, 16, 18, 24, ?28, *32, 34, 36, 38-39, 41-42, 44-45, †48, 55, 59; 103-4, 106, 109, 113, 115, 117, ?119, 120, 123, 125-26, 128, 131, 133, 139, 141, †144, 145, 148-50, →151; 201, 206, 216, 221; 305, 307-8, 316, 319, 324, 327; 406-7, 411, 413, 415, →423, 425, c428, 430, c431. candy ~ †21; 323; 404. milk ~ 122, 136, 142-43, 146; 318. scrub ~ 308. water ~ 61; 118, 124, 140; 408. wood ~ ?15; 107. wooden ~ 3-4, 10, 12, ?15, 19, 21, 23, 25, 27, 43, 47, 50-51, 54, 56-57, 59, 63, 65; 102, 112; 202, 209, 211, 214, 217-18, 220, 222, †223, 224-25; 302, ?304, 326; 401, 417, 424. wooden candy ~ c203. wooden water ~ 13.

no response 110; 414, 436.

Comment:

bucket: "Some call it 'bucket,' but I think 'pail' is easier. But the one in the well was the 'bucket'"--7. Inf. says they are rare here--24, 64. "I've never seen many of them"; knows term from "Old Oaken Bucket"--33. Inf. has never seen one--53. Heard, probably from the poem; not a local term--65. Inf. knows 'bucket,' but not what it is--217. Used by inf. when younger--120, 151. Not seen here any more--325. "In Indiana they'd call it a 'bucket'"--42. "Hoosiers call 'em 'buckets'"--225. Inf. thinks this an urban term--221. For candy--421. For milk--127, 140, 146. For water--40, 46, 52-53, 62-63; 108, 132, 140, 150; 421. Used in a well--7, 24, 30, 55; 111; 203, 206, 218-19, 224; 305-6, 312, 318. For slop--421. oak bucket: Used in a well; when there is no well, 'bucket' is not often used--47. water bucket: Inf. says that since 'bucket' is Dutch, "We don't use 'pail'"--134. Inf. more likely to use 'water bucket' than 'water pail'--408. wooden bucket: Larger than a 'pail'--2. For milking in old days--15. For water--58. pail: Sometimes used by inf., but 'bucket' is the normal term--34. = bucket, but 'pail' is more "fancy"--39. = bucket; either wooden or metal--113, 115, 117, 120, 124-26, 128, 133, 136, 139-41, 144-45, 148-49; 308, 316; 406, 415, 425, 430-31. 'Pail' more common than 'bucket' --125, 128. "'Bucket' is more common than 'pail,' but there is no difference"--149. Inf. says most people have changed from 'pail' to 'bucket'--144. 'Pail' used only rarely--148. Used occasionally for the wooden vessel--305. More natural for inf. than 'bucket'--415. Inf. thinks a pail is perhaps smaller than a bucket--430.

Inf. makes no distinction between 'bucket' and 'pail' except in stock phrases: "a bucket of water" but "a pail of milk"-- 431. For milk--123; 307. For water--13, 58; 307. milk pail: = bucket; either wooden or metal--146; 318. water pail: Rarely used by inf.--51. wooden pail: "All we had when I was a boy"--21. Inf. says they are rare here--202. For water-- 43, 51, 58, 63.

14.2 pail (the metal vessel). NE 129. WG 12, 13, 47, 48, 56; F5a, F42, F68.

The two terms, pail and bucket, for a metal vessel for water or milk exhibit a rather sharp Northern-Midland contrast. The frequency for pail is: Mn. 98%, Ia. 79%, N.D. 96%, S.D. 96%, Nb. 76%; for bucket: Mn. 8%, Ia. 54%, N.D. 12%, S.D. 26%, Nb. 59%. The bucket responses in Iowa, furthermore, occur in the southern two-thirds of the state. Distribution by types is consistent, with no indication of marked social or chronological variation.

CL 20: Responses from 1,055 persons conform to the field data, with an 85% dominance of pail and only 26% for bucket, the latter reported chiefly in southern Iowa and Nebraska.

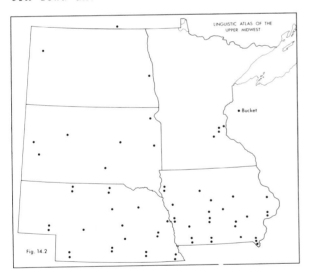

Fig. 14.2

bucket 37-39; 109-10, 113, 115, 117, †120, 121-22, 124-25, s†126, 128, 130-31, 133, 136, 138, s†139, 140-41, 144-46, 148-49, c150, 151; 202, †212, 221; 302, 308-9, 311, †313, 316, 318, 321; 403-6, 415, *417, 418, 420, 422, 424-25, 427, 429-37. aluminum ~ c35. dinner ~ 47. milk ~ 129, 135; 209. water ~ †123, 142-43; 414.

pail 1-10, c11, 12-14, c15, 17, 19-31, c32, 33-34, c35, 36-37, 39-44, 46, 48-50, 52, 54-57, c58, 60-62, 64-65; 101-8, 110-17, 119-20, 124-25, 127-28, 130, 132-34, †135, 137, 139, 141, †144, 145, 147-50; 201-8, 210-20, 222-26; 301, 303-10, *311, 312-16, 320, 322-28; 401-4, 406-13, c414, 415-16, c417, c421, 423, 425-26, 428, 430, c431, 433. lard ~ 13. metal ~ 15. milk ~ 47, 53, 56, 59; 121, 126, 136, 146-47, 152; 317-18, 321; 418-19, 425, 436. milking ~ 18. scrub ~ 318. tin ~ 16, 45, 50-51, 54, 63; 302, 311; 417, 424. water ~ 118, 140; 209; 414.

no response 319.

Comment:

bucket: More usual for inf. than 'pail' --37; 110, 148-49; 309; 404. Used synonymously with 'pail' when younger, but no longer used--120. Inf. says most people in the community have changed from 'pail' to 'bucket'--144. Inf. calls it a 'bucket' if it has a wooden handle; otherwise 'pail'--202. dinner bucket: "A 'pail' when used for carrying lunch"--47. pail: "You never hear a pail called a 'bucket'" --1. 'Bucket' and 'pail' are synonymous; either wooden or metal--39; 110, 113, 115, 117, 120, 124-26, 128, 133, 136, 139-41, 144-45, 148-49; 308, 316; 406, 415, 425, 430-31. Inf. says 'pail' is a more "fancy" word than 'bucket'--39. More usual for inf. than 'bucket'--125, 128; 316; 415. Smaller than a 'bucket'--430, 433. milk pail: = bucket; either wood or metal--146; 318.

14.3 garbage pail. NE 135. WG 12, 13, 23, 56; F67.

To the question requesting the name of a container of food scraps and refuse, especially one that might be used in feeding pigs, the collected responses are complicated by two factors. One is that in urban communities the question is more likely construed without reference to such rural use as pigfeeding; the other is the shift in dialect consistency of the term slop.
The general urban term includes the defining garbage as the first element. Garbage pail is most common in the Northern speech zone, particularly in southern Minnesota. Garbage can has fairly general distribution elsewhere. Neither was recorded in much of the Dakotas, partly because of the fieldworker's directing the question usually at rural use. Some rural dwellers replied, however, with one such term for a container for scraps from the kitchen and another for one used to "swill" pigs.
In light of their East Coast distribution the expected Northern UM designation would be swill pail and the Midland des-

ignation would be the Midland and Southern slop bucket. This pattern is in part reflected in the UM, as swill pail is more frequent in Minnesota, northern Iowa, Nebraska, and South Dakota. But the actually dominant form in the UM is a combination of the Midland slop and the Northern pail. This expansion of slop into Northern territory in the UM compares with a similar situation in Wisconsin. Its 52% frequency in Minnesota is matched by a 64% frequency in that state. The converse combination, of Northern swill and Midland bucket, is rare. Two infs. volunteered the information that slop pail refers also to a container for toilet refuse, sometimes identified as slop jar.

Another referent also appears in the designations slop barrel, slop cart, and swill barrel for a barrel mounted on wheels for taking liquid scraps to pigs.

CL 22: From 1,036 respondents the replies sharply confirm the field data. Slop terms occur with 89% frequency; swill terms with 26% frequency, with marked contrast between northern and southern Iowa. Pail terms have 82% occurrence (cf. 92% in northern Iowa and 31% in southern); bucket terms have 34% frequency (23% in northern Iowa and 79% in southern). One Minnesota respondent, of Scottish and Canadian parentage, checked ort pail, which in the eastern atlas study appeared only in Essex county, Massachusetts.

bucket 35; !¹324.

garbage bucket 437. ~ can 2, 5, →6, 11-12, →25, 28, 31, 33-35, 37-39, c40, →42, 43-45, →46-47, 48-53, 55, 57-62, →64-65; 106-8, 110, 117, 120-22, →134, →136, 149-50, 152; 220-22; 305, 307, →326; 405,

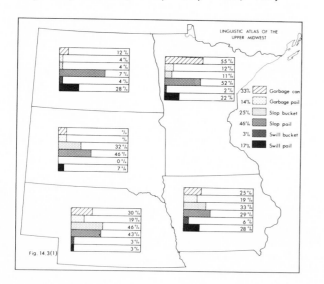

Fig. 14.3(1)

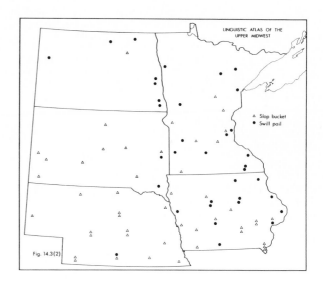

Fig. 14.3(2)

407-8, 410, 417, 425, !426, 430, 435-36. ~ container 44. ~ pail 10, 12-14, 18, c27, 37, ¹62, 63; 103, 111, 118-19, 121, 126, 130, 141, 150-51; 226; 308, 317, 319; →401, 402, →406, 409, 411, 416, 419, ¹437.

   hog pail 318.
   pig pail 15, 36; 202.
   scrap bucket 422. ~ pail 427.
   slop barrel 55; 101, 114. ~ bucket 22, 24, *26, :35, 37, †40, !44, !61; 109, 113, 125, 129, 132, †134, 135-36, 138, 140, 143, 145-46, 148-52; →¹212, 213; ¹302, 304, !310, 311, ¹312, 313, 315-16, 318, 320, ¹321, 322; 404-5, 408, 410, 413-14, 418, !419, 420-21, 425, c429, 431-32, 434, s435, 436-37. ~ can 102; 405, 412. ~ cart 133. ~ jar 9. ~ pail 1, 3-4, !†6, !7, *9, !¹10, 15, 17, 19, 21, 23-24, !¹25, 26-32, :¹33, 34, 39, !†41, 43, 45-47, !48, 49, †50, !52, !†53, 56-59, !60, 62-63; 104, c106, 107, 112, 118, 124-25, 127-28, 130, :¹31, 133, 137, 147, 151; 201, 203-4, 207-10, !211, 214-19, 221-23, ¹226; 301-3, 306, 309, 312, 314, 319, 321, 323, 325, †326, 327-28; 401-4, †406, 407, 409, 411-12, 415-16, !417, 418, †423, !424, 427-28, 433.
   swill barrel 103, 114, 118, 133, ¹149. ~ bucket :2; 123, 142, sn148, ¹149; 224; 422, ¹430. ~ pail 8, 12, sn13, 16, 20, *36, 39, 42, c46, 49, !51, †54, 55, 64-65; 105, 107, 114-17, 119, 122, ¹124, †127, 130, s¹135, 139, 141, 144, s¹145; 205-6, 209, †212, 220, *222, 224-25; 318, 324; c430, ¹431, s435.

Comment:

   bucket: Inf. has heard her grandson from Rapid City say this; she thinks 'bucket' is funny--324. garbage can: Urban term--2, 5, 12, 34-35, 37, 55, 62; 152;

220-21; 407-8, 410, 435-36. A container used in the kitchen--40, 44, 52, 61. A container used outside the house--106, 108, 110. garbage pail: Urban term--226; 409, 411, 419. A container used at camp --37. Used for feeding pigs--12. slop barrel: On wheels to take to pigs--55. slop bucket: Farm term--61; 150, 152; 419, 436. Ranch term--437. Used by inf.'s mother--40. More usual for inf. than 'swill bucket'--148. Used for feeding pigs--24, 37, 40, 44, 61; 149; 413-14. Metal container--22, 26; 213. Wooden container--113, 152; 320; 421. slop can: A 10-gal. can--102. slop cart: = swill barrel--133. slop pail: Farm term--5, 10, 28, 31, 34, 49; 319; 417. "I guess that's what farmers would say"; inf. doesn't think it "nice"--226. Inf.'s usual term in youth--6. Inf. says he has not used the term since c. 1938--50. "A word that I just hate"--319. "I think 'slop' is an awful word"--401. = garbage can--46. Used for feeding pigs--28, 34, 37, 45, 47, 60, 63; 104, 106, 137; 221; 309. Either a wood or metal container--133. Usually a wood container--312. swill barrel: On wheels for taking to pigs--113. swill pail: Farm term--49, 65. Inf.'s normal term--12. Used by inf.'s mother--127. Used for feeding pigs--12, 42, 46, 64; 115, 122.

14.4 frying pan. NE 132. WG 16, 29, 45, 49; F6, F43, F68.

The question eliciting this term usually was "What do you call the kitchen utensil you might use in frying eggs?" It is not, as in the eastern dialect research, directed only to an object made of cast iron, since other materials are now more common.

On the Atlantic Coast a sharp cleavage appeared between Northern spider and Midland skillet, with frying pan naming the sheet iron utensil but also, especially in urban areas, occurring as a generic.

In the UM spider is a relic preserved or remembered by the oldest generation (Type I 18%, II 11%, III 0%) in only the first settled Northern speech communities of southern Minnesota and northeastern Iowa. It normally denotes the cast iron utensil. Skillet, on the other hand, more often is a generic or denotes a utensil made of other metal. In thus extending its semantic range it has also extended its regional range, for it has moved widely into the Northern speech areas of Minnesota and the Dakotas to the point of almost exceeding the frequency of the generic frying pan. One reason for this spread is the commercial use of skillet, which at the time of the field-

work often appeared in newspaper and radio advertising. But while it was gaining acceptance in Minnesota it was yielding to frying pan in Midland speech territory, for a number of infs. there considered it old-fashioned.

Fry pan, apparently an innovation, is scattered, but since the survey seems to have grown in popularity.

The metathesized variant skittle occurs twice; and skewer, reported once, probably is an error.

See also Harold B. Allen, "Semantic confusion: a report from Atlas files," *Publication of the American Dialect Society*, No. 33 (April 1960), pp. 3-13.

CL 20: Data from 1,039 respondents confirm the field records, with spider limited almost entirely to northern Iowa and southern Minnesota, and with skillet dominating southern Iowa and Nebraska. Overall percentages are: frying pan 62%, skillet 45%, spider 10%.

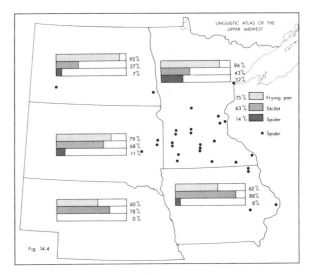

Fig. 14.4

frier 204; 404, 426.
fry pan 11; 106, 116; 328; 404.
frying pan 1-10, 12-19, ↓20, 21-26, ↓27, *27, 28-31, 33-34, →35, c36, 39-40, ↓*41, 42-50, 54, ↓55, 56-61, c62, 63, 65; 101-2, 104-5, s→↓107, 108-9, 112, 117-23, 125-31, 135-37, 139-40, 142, 144-47, 150; 201-17, †218, 219, c220, 221-24, 226; 301-2, 304-8, 310-20, 322-23, ↓324, 325-26; 401, 403, 409-10, !411, 413, 415-22, ↓424, 425, 427-31, ↓433, 434, ↓435, 436.
griddle 58; 121; 217; 316.
pan 18.
Scotch bowl 42.
skewer ?†101.
skillet !↓1, ↓2-3, c6, c7, ↓8, ↓10,

†12, 14, sn15, ¹18, 20, †¹22, 24, !†¹25, ¹*26, sn28, 30-31, →32, 34, †35, 39, →40, 42, 45, →46, 47-48, †49, 54-55, s¹56, 57-58, c59, 60, †61, 62-63, c64; 101-6, 109-17, †118, 119, †120, :122, 123-39, †140, 141-52; sn†201, 204, *206, ¹207, ¹209, †210, ¹211-212, †213, 214, 216, 218, ¹219, 221, *221, †*222, 223; 301-5, †*306, 307, †308, 309-10, *311, ¹312, 313-14, *316, 317, †318, ¹319, 320-22, *323, 324, †325, 328; 401-6, !407, 408-10, 412, ¹413, 414, 417-18, ¹419, 420-26, †427, 428-29, 431-33, ¹434, 435-37.

   skittle †23; ¹209.

   spider ¹3, 16, ¹21, †¹22, s†26, 27, 31, †32-33, c36, 39, †40, ?41, *41, 42, *43, 44, †45, 46-48, †50, 51-53, †54, 57, c59, †¹60, 61, 63, 65; †¹102, †103, †106, 107-8, †113, ¹114, †116, s¹118, †122, s¹123, ¹124, †126, ¹133, 137, 139, †144, ¹*145, †148; †205, 215, †223, 225, †226; ¹305, †¹309, †316, 317, *318, ¹319, †326, 327; ¹414, †¹420, †426.

   no response 37, ?38.

Comment:

   frier: Usu.--204. Used by inf.'s wife --404. Used by "young kids"--426. fry pan: Aluminum--328. Stainless steel--404. frying pan: "Called it that when we was kids"--218. Usu.--304. Generic--2, 8-9, 25, 34, 42, 50, 56; 108; 202, 208, 215-16, 220-21, 224, 226; 310, 312, 315, 317, 324-26; 411, 415-16, 419, 421, 427, 431, 434. Aluminum--7, 19, 28, 49; 120-21, 137, 150; 326; 401. Copper--28. Granite-ware--54. Cast iron--3, †7, †19, 26, 29-30, †31, †49; 101, 104, 106, 121; 430. Sheet iron--3, 6, 65; 214; 314; 401, 403, 409, 430. Stainless steel--29; 120, 137; 220; 320; 422. Lighter than a skillet--24, 46, 57; 109, 112, 119, 127, 139, 142, 145; 410, 412, 428. Heavier than a skil-let--48; 101; 418. Smaller than a skillet --136; 420. griddle: Generic term--217. Cast iron--121. Deeper than a frying pan --58. Scotch bowl: Round bottom; used by inf. for frying doughnuts--42. skewer: Inf. has heard gps. use the term; perhaps deeper than a skillet--101. skillet: For-merly used by inf.--12; 308. Older than 'frying pan'--*26. Used by inf.'s wife; once strange to him, but now his regular term--54. Used by inf.'s mother--118; 201, 213; 318, 325. Generic--55; 102, 106, 138, 152; 216, 223; 309, 321; 405, 407-8, 412, 414, 419, 421, 423, 431-33, 436-37. Aluminum--20, 64; 110-11; 206; 426. Cast iron--6, 20, 24, 28, 64-65; 101, 104-6, 109-15, 127, 132-33, 137, 139, 141, 150; 214, 221-22; 310, 314, 320, 328; 401, 403-4, 409, 413, 417, 422, 424, 426, 428, 435. Sheet iron--30; 404, 435. Stainless steel--113. = frying pan

--25, 40, 59-62; 102, 104, 106; 204, 221; 305, 307; 419, 421, 425, 431, 435. Small-er than a frying pan--206, 212. Deeper than a frying pan--42. Shorter handle than a frying pan--311. = spider--46. Lighter than a spider; longer handle--103. With legs--†45. Flat, a kind of griddle --34. skittle: Inf. says that formerly this was common here--23. spider: Almost unknown now--*43, 44, 63. Used by inf. in youth--103. Used by inf.'s mother--26; 106, 140; 205, 226; 426. Used by inf.'s mother and gm., but never by inf. because she dislikes spiders--33. Term used by inf.'s gm.--50. Generic term--108; 215, 225; *318. Cast iron--46; 107, 137; 223. Steel, with long handle--116. Light or heavy--41. = frying pan--42. Larger than a frying pan--44. = griddle--139. = skil-let--32, 40; 114; 317. Larger than a skillet--113. No legs--39-40, 48, 51-53. With legs--137.

14.5 _kettle_. NE 131.

   For a large metal vessel used outdoors for such purposes as rendering lard, cooking fodder, or making soap the com-mon UM term is kettle, sometimes in com-pounds indicating specific uses such as butchering kettle, hog kettle, and soap kettle. Less frequent is pot, which does not occur at all in Nebraska; and only occasionally occurring is the older cal-dron. A somewhat different utensil is the large Dutch oven, reported principally in South Dakota and Nebraska, where it was a familiar utensil for bread and bis-cuit baking as well as for making stews, often during roundups. One such shown to the fieldworker in western South Dakota was made of cast iron, straight-sided and flat-bottomed with ears and a bail and three short legs, the whole having a diameter of 15 inches and a depth of 8 inches, and weighing 30 pounds. On the bottom was the imprint, "Made in Batavia, Illinois." This Dutch oven was described as having been used by "a cow outfit" in Colorado in the 1880's.

   CL 18: The mail responses overwhelming-ly indicate kettle as the common term. Ten volunteered write-in responses for caldron attest its use, though rare.

   caldron 7; 101; 204-5; 402.
   cooker c16. feed ~ 1.
   cooler 8.
   dutch oven 123; 301, 311-12, 314, 320; †401, 404, 409, †418, 422-23, †429.
   kettle 1, 4, c5, 6, ¹7, s8, 9, 11, 14-15, 17-24, c25, 26, 28, c29, 30, c31, 32-34, c35, 37, cr39, 40, *41, 43-46, c47, 49-50, c51, !52, 53-55, c56, c57, c59,

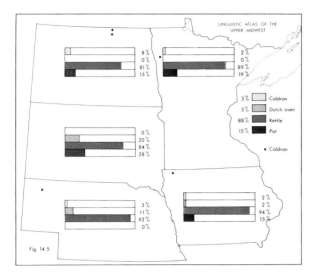

Fig. 14.5

418. "Every chuckwagon had one"--409.
kettle: = pot--6; 134, 144. Larger than
a pot--15. 50 gal.--133. 20 gal.--416.
Over 10 gal.--429. Aluminum--110; 308.
Brass or copper--416. Copper--4. Cast
iron--19, 33, 36; 103, 105-6, 109, 111-12,
116, 132, 138, 146, 148-49; 203; 307,
322; 413, 433, 435. Cast iron, granite-
ware, or aluminum--426. Cast iron, aluminum, or enamelware--431. Bail--19, 21-22,
30, 37, 54; 105, 107-8, 117, 127-28, 145-
46, 149; 203, 206, 208, 212, 214, 216-17,
*219, 225; 311-13, 322, 324-26; 401, 403-
8, 414, 418, 421, 423, 429-31, 437. No
bail--11; 432. With or without bail--30;
409. Flat bottom--103; 415, 425. Round
bottom--11, 19, 21-22, 37, 46, 54; 102,
104, 106-14, 127-29, 132, 138, 145; 203,
206, 208, 214, 216-17, *219, 225-26; 301,
311-14, 322, 324-26; 403-9, 413-14, 418,
421, 423-24, 428-29, 432-33, 435, 437.
Round or flat bottom--116, 133, 149; 416,
422, 426, 430-31, 434. With legs--1, 31;
106-7, 113; 413, 421, 428, 432-33. With
three legs--19, 21-22, 30, 36-37, 45-46,
54; 102, 104, 111-12, 118, 127-29, 138,
145; 203, 214, 216-17, *219, 225-26; 301,
311-14, 322, 324-26; 403-4, 406-7, 414,
423, 429-30, 437. With three or four legs
--109, 114. With four legs--211-12; 401,
405, 408, 418. Without legs--11; 117;
206, 208; 425, 435. With or without legs
--30; 116, 133; 431, 434. With ears--11,
22; 203, 206, 208, 212, 214, 217, *219,
225-26; 311-13, 326; 403, 405, 407, 409,
418, 421, 429, 437. Without ears--19, 37,
54; 117, 127-29, 145; 216; 301, 314, 322,
324-25; 404, 406, *408, 414, 423, 430,
432. With or without ears--30. Used for
cooking fodder--20. For cooking squash,
potatoes, etc.--21. For boiling food--
132. For cooking pork and beans--148.
For making soap--31; 107, 133. Used in
butchering--225; 312. For scalding hogs
and rendering lard--429. cast kettle:
Cast iron; round bottom; legs; bail--427.
hog kettle: Flat bottom; no legs or bail
--25. With or without legs--218. pig kettle: Used to heat water for butchering--
50. soap kettle: Round bottom; legs; c.
3' diameter--58. Round bottom; three
legs; bail--323. pot: More usual for inf.
than kettle--152. 3 gal.--12. Cast iron
--3, 12; 103, 120, 132, 147. Bail--3, 5,
10, 13; 134, 144, 147; 201, 213, 223;
309-10. No bail--6. Flat bottom--132;
310. Round bottom--3, 6, 10, 13; 103,
134, 144; 201, 213, 223; 309. With legs
--103. With three legs--5, 13; 134, 144;
201, 213, 223; 309-10. Without legs--3,
10. With or without legs--6. With ears--
10; 201, 213, 223; 309. Without ears--
134, 144. For boiling--309. For frying--
132. Covered, for roasting--305. Used

60-65; 102-3, c104, 105-8, c109, 110-12,
c113, 114-15, c116, †117, 118-19, 121-27,
129-32, c133, 135, 137, c138, 139-44,
146, 148-52; c202, 203, 206, c209, 210-
12, 214-17, 219, *219, 220-21, :222, 224-
26; 301, 303, 305-6, c307, 308, 312, 314,
317, 320, c322, 324-26, 328; †401, 403-7,
†*408, 409-11, :412, 413-14, c415, 416-
26, 428-35, :†437. butchering ~ 48. cast
~ c427. hog ~ ¹5; 218. iron ~ 15-16, 31,
36, 42; †117, 134, 136, 145; *306, c311,
313, 318-19; 402. lard ~ :436. outdoor ~
128. pig ~ 50; *204. scalding ~ 208.
soap ~ 323; 402. soup ~ 48, 57-58. stew
~ 101; 316.
   pot 2-3, 5-6, 10, 13, 35, 44, c47; 103,
†120, 132, 144, 147, 152; 207, 213; 302,
305, 309-10, ¹313, 327. bean ~ 316.
black ~ 12. iron ~ 15, 46; 133-34; 201,
223; 308. stew ~ 120.
   no response 27, 38; 304, 315, ?321.

Comment:

   caldron: Flat or round bottom; larger
than a stew kettle; used outside in
butchering and soap making--101. Round
bottom; three legs; bail--211. cooker:
For cooking swill or syrup--16. feed
cooker: With or without legs--1. cooler:
Round bottom; no legs or bail; used to
heat water for pigs or making soap, etc.
--8. dutch oven: Cast iron--123; 423.
Bail--311-12, 320; 409, 418, 429. Flat
bottom--301, 311-12, 314, 320; 401, 409,
418, 422, 429. Round bottom--404. With
legs--422-3. With three legs--301, 314,
320. With four legs--311-12; 404, 429.
No legs--409, 418. Used in cow camps or
on roundups--301; 401. Used over an open
fire--312, 314; 418. Placed in fire and
covered with coals--311, 320; 422. For
making bread or biscuits--314; 401, 404,

over open fire--310. stew pot: Aluminum--
120.

14.7 vase.

Although this item, denoting a container for cut flowers, is primarily included for pronunciation, a few lexical variants appeared. No significant correlations are obvious.
flower bowl 57. ~ jar 432. ~ pot 48.
~ urn 135.
  fruit jar 13.
  glass 16.
  urn ¹7; 130; 220.
  tumbler 59.
  vase 1-15, 17-34, c35, 36-41, !42, 43-
58, :59, 60, !61, 62-65; 101-34, 136-52;
201-19, 221-26; 301-10, :311, 312-28;
401-10, 412-25, !426, 427-31, s432, 433-
37.
  no response 411.

Comment:

flower pot: "I didn't dare to say it,
hardly"--48. tumbler: Used if there
aren't many flowers--59. urn: Learned
through crossword puzzles--7.

15.1 I must wash (the) dishes. NE 137.

The competing variant of the widespread
wash in wash (the) dishes is do in do
(the) dishes or, once only, do up the
dishes. The do expressions are most frequent in Minnesota, South Dakota, and
Nebraska. Midland redd up appears in the
conversation of a Manitoban inf. Wash up
the dishes is reported only by the two
informants in Ontario.

dishwashing 48.
do dishes 47; c327; 428.
do the dishes 2, ¹7, 9, 14, 33, 49, 62;
101, 103, *130; 222, 226; 302, 305, 310,
315-16, 322-23, 325; 406, 425, 429, 432-
33.
do up the dishes *306.
redd up the dishes c202.
wash (them) 56-57; 103, 117, 120, 122-
23, 127-28, 130-31, 139-40, 143, 146-47;
315; 407, c413, c429.
wash dishes 1, 4, 11, 18, 29, 32, 34-
35, 38, 41, !46, 47, 61; 107, 115, 119,
138; 214-15, !218, 223; 323, 325; 401,
405, 412, cvr416, 417, ᵗ428, 432.
wash the dishes 5, c6, 7-8, c10, 12-13,
15-17, 19-26, !27, 28, 30-31, 33, 36-37,
39-40, 42-43, !44, 45, 49-55, 58-60, ¹62,
63-65; 101-2, 104-6, 108-14, 116, 118,
121, 124-26, 129, 132-37, 141-42, 144-45,
148-52; !201, 202-6, !207, 208-9, !210-
12, 213, 216, !217, 219-21, 224-25; 301-
4, 307-12, c313, 314, 317-21, !324, 326,
328; 402, c403, 404, 408-11, 413-16, 418-

27, 430-31, 434-37.
wash up the dishes ¹2, 3.
wash them off 13.

Comment:

do the dishes: "The women say 'do the
dishes'"--7. Used by inf.'s wife--323.
Usual expression--33; 432. wash dishes:
Ppl. form--35; 119. Expression formerly
used by inf.--428. wash the dishes: Inf.
also says 'rid up the table'--409. wash
them: Ppl. form--315.

15.2 She rinses the dishes. NE 138.

Primarily a pronunciation item, rinses
is, however, also parallelled by the lexical variant scalds. Some infs. consider
the two terms as synonyms; others use
scald to denote a rinsing operation with
extremely hot water. Neither variant has
any noticeable correlation with either
the type of speaker or geographical area.
The overall frequency is 19% for scalds
and 93% for RINSES, with the overlap
caused by those infs. who use both terms
with differentiated meaning. One inf. in
Fargo, a Type I, responded with drench,
a use perhaps reflecting a confusion with
the phonological variant rench.

drenches 220.
RINSES 1-4, 6-13, c14, c15, 16-18, c19,
20-25, 27-31, r32, 33-34, 37-43, c44, 45-
47, !48, 49-59, ¹60, 61-63; 101-15, c116,
117-19, *120, 121-45, *145, 146-52; 201-
8, 210-19, 221-26; 301-5, *306, 307-11,
*311, 312-21, 323, 325-28; 402-3, 406-12,
c413, r414, 415-31, c432, c433, 434-37.
  scalds 5-6, 14, 22, 26, 35-36, ¹42, 47,
56, s58, 60, 63-65; 105, 109, 113, 116,
120, 128, 133, 144-45; 204-5, 209, 214;
305, *311, 318, *322, 324; 401-2, 404-5,
410, 416, 418, 424, 433.

Comment:

rinses: With cold water--144-45. With
hot water--410. Before washing with soap
--424. scalds: Inf.'s usual term--6, 22,
56. = rinses--47; 204. With hot water--
144-45. With hotter water than for rins-
ing--205; *311. With boiling water--410,
418. After washing with soap--424.

15.3a dishrag (for washing dishes).
NE 139.

Two chief lexical variants compete as
terms for a cloth used in dish-washing.
Dishcloth, with its domination of Minnesota and North Dakota, seems to have
Northern orientation. It is sometimes
identified as a newer form in contrast
with dishrag, which predominates in Iowa,
South Dakota, and Nebraska, but which

three infs. consider old-fashioned. Dish-rag is also slightly favored by older and less educated speakers (Type I 57%, II 56%, III 50%) and dishcloth less favored (Type I 41%, II 41%, III 58%). Washcloth appears in North Dakota and Nebraska, and washrag once each in both Dakotas. Of the four infs. who use dish mop one reports that it refers to a different object, a small mop with a handle.

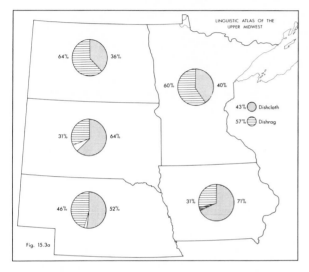

Fig. 15.3a

dishcloth 14-15, 17, 29-31, 38-39, 57; 102, 106, 110-11, 115, 119-20, 123, 125, 133-34, 136-37, 139, 141, 152; 201, →203, 204-7, 213-14, →216, 217, 219-21, 223, 225-26; 303, 305, 307, 309-11, 319, 326, !327; 402-6, 409, →411, 413-14, 421, 424, cr426, 427-29, 432, 434.

dish mop 130; 317; 424, 428.

dishrag 2, 13, 16, 18, cr35, 36; 101, 103-5, 107-9, 112-14, 116-18, ¹120, 121-22, 124, 126-32, 134-35, 138, 140, 142-51; ¹201, †203, 210-12, 215-16, 218, 222, c224, 225, ¹226; 301-2, 304, 306, 308, 312-13, 315-18, ¹319, 320-22, !323, 324-25, ¹326, 328; 401, 403, ¹404, 407-8, †409, 410, †411, 412, 416-18, 420, 423, 425, cr426, 430-31, 433, 435-37.

washcloth 202, 209; 415, 419, 422, ?426. washrag ?35; 209; 314.

no response 1, 3-12, 19-28, 32-34, 37, 40-65; 208.

Comment:

dish mop: Has a handle--424. dishrag: Inf. considers it uncultured--120. "I'm afraid I say 'dishrag'"--131. Usu.--225.

15.3b dish towel (for drying dishes). NE 140.

Besides the older wiping cloth, wiping towel, and wiping rag, two terms usually designate the cloth used to dry dishes. The wiping forms, found almost exclusively in the Northern speech zone, are distinctly old-fashioned, 76% of the occurrences being reported by Type I speakers. The common term, dish towel, with an overall percentage of 73, is uniformly distributed in the UM except in Iowa, where the frequency is only 58%. A newer expression, tea towel, has strong Midland orientation with its weight mostly in southern Iowa and Nebraska, but as a term with increasing social prestige it is moving into Minnesota. It is found also in Canada.

cup towel →151.

dishcloth 2, 12, c13, 35, 44, 58-59; 108-9, 124, ?150; 222; 314, 323; †410, 422, ¹433. ~rag †50, 58. ~ towel 1, ¹3, 4-13, 15-24, 26-27, †28, 29-34, 36-39, †40, 41-43, 45-46, →47, 48-58, 60-64, cr?65; 102-4, 110-12, 114-18, 120-21, 123, 125-28, 130, 132, 134, 136, 138-39, 142, 144-45, 148-49, cr150; †201, 202-3, 205-6, 208-14, 216, ¹217, 218-19, 221, *222, 223-24, 226; 301-2, :¹303, 304-5, 307-10, 312-13, 315-21, 324-28; 401-2, ¹403, 405, *405, 406-9, 411, 413-21, 424-26, 428-31, 436, †437. ~ wiper *9, ¹20, 48, 57; 129, ¹152.

drying cloth 207, 225; 314; 434. ~ rag 135, 147. ~ towel 143, 151; 434.

glass towel ¹33.

tea cloth 434. ~ towel 3, ¹10, ¹22, 28, ¹33, 40, !→42, †47, →¹49, 60; 102, 105-6, 111, 119, 131, 133, 136-37, 141, 152; 201, *202, →¹205, →¹211-12, !→¹214; *306, *311, 319, →325, 326; !¹402, 404, 410, 413, 423-24, 426-27, 431-33, 435, →437.

towel 14; 140, 146.

wiper 122; 204.

wiping cloth 27, 59; 65; 217, 225; 311; 403. ~ rag 311. ~ towel 25, 61; 101, 105, 107, 113; 215, 220, 223; 305, 322.

Comment:

dishcloth: Usu.--59. dishrag: Used by inf.'s mother--50. dish towel: Usu.--58. Inf. first offered 'wiping cloth,' but in next interview wanted it changed to 'dish towel,' as "more proper." But she confessed to 'wiping cloth' as her usual term--65. Inf. says it is older than 'tea towel,' but still used--325. glass towel: A small one for glassware--33. tea cloth: "Most women call them 'tea cloths'"--434. tea towel: Also used by inf.'s mother--3. "Fancy" term--33; 136; 413. Inf. considers this an affected term--211. Used by inf.'s mother--47. Smaller than a dish towel--111. Inf. says this is used less frequently than 'dish towel,' perhaps more by younger girls; also 'tea towels' are

fancier than "plain old flour sacks"--
426.

15.4 <u>bath towel</u>. NE 142.

For the large towel used after bathing
most infs. in all five states (87.5%)
use simply <u>bath towel</u>. More than 13%,
chiefly Type II and III speakers, use
<u>turkish towel</u>, three considering it old-
fashioned and three others calling it
new. Iowa speakers using only <u>towel</u> may
have been inadequately reported by the
fieldworker.

bath towel 1-14, s15, 17-32, 34-42, 44-
48, 50-60, 62-65; 101-2, 104-12, 114-17,
120-21, 123, 127-29, 131-33, cr134, 135-
36, 138-41, 144, 146, *147, 148-52; 201-
19, 221-26; 301-2, 304-5, *306, 308-15,
317-22, 324-28; 402-7, !408, 409-12, 414,
416-19, 421-25, 427-29, 432-37.
towel 13; 103, 108, 113, 122, 124-26,
130, 142-43, 145, 147-48; 307, 316, 318.
turk 309.
turkish bath towel →51; 118, 137; 433.
~ towel c13, 14-16, 28, ¹37, 38, →40,
→¹42, 43, †46, 49, →58, 60-61; 119, †120,
144; 220; ¹302, †309, 316, 323; 404, 413-
15, 420, 426, 430-31, 433.
no response 33; :?303; 401.

Comment:

towel: "A regular towel"--13. turkish
towel: Inf. learned the term through ad-
vertisements--58. Used when younger--120.

15.5a <u>faucet</u> (as on a water pipe at the
kitchen sink). NE 143. WG 15, 47, 56;
F52, F69.

Although 15.5a and 15.5b constitute only a single item in the eastern atlases,
division has taken place here in order to
show the fortunes of <u>spigot</u> in its two
senses. In the eastern states a sharp
distinction appears between Northern <u>fau-
cet</u> and Midland and Southern <u>spigot/spick-
et</u>. But <u>faucet</u> has almost completely replaced <u>spigot</u> everywhere. Even in Iowa
the three speakers who use the latter also use <u>faucet</u>. Actually more frequent
than <u>spigot</u> (2.9%) is the variant <u>tap</u>
(12%), which occurs principally in southern Minnesota and in Canada as a large
reflection of its sporadic and rare appearance in New England and southern New
Brunswick. Some infs. who use <u>faucet</u> will
speak, however, of "tap water."

CL 43: Data from 1,107 checklists tend
to corroborate those from the field records, with an over-all 94% for <u>faucet</u>
and 1.6% for <u>spigot</u>, although <u>tap</u> has only
3.7% and is fairly evenly distributed in
the UM.

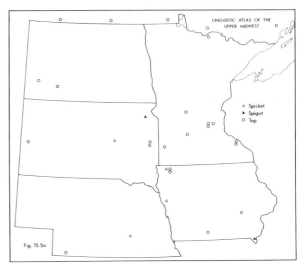

LINGUISTIC ATLAS OF THE
UPPER MIDWEST

△ Spicket
▲ Spigot
○ Tap

Fig. 15.5a

faucet ¹3, 4, 6-24, c25, 26-34, *34,
35-37, :38, 39-51, r52, 53-65; 101-46,
c147, 148-52; 203-13, 216-26; 301-17,
319-28; 401-36.
hydrant 120; 402.
spicket ¹61; 101, ¹105, 122, ¹137;
*316; 422.
spigot s†119, 150; 308, ¹323.
tap 1-3, 5, †11, ¹26, 28, 33-34, 37,
¹42, 45, 47, 54-55, ¹61; 101-2, 144, 152;
201-2, 214-15; 309, 318-19; ¹401, 437.
valve ¹21.

Comment:

faucet: Inf. says this is the "proper"
name--21. Usu.--45. hydrant: An outside
'faucet'--120. Inf.'s usual term--402.
spicket: An outside 'faucet'--422. Usu.--
122. spigot: "Used 50 years ago"--119.
Sometimes used by inf.--150. tap: Used
by inf.'s father (from Me.)--11. Inf.
sometimes uses this, but calls it old-
fashioned--37. Inf. says more common than
'faucet'--47. Inf.'s more usual term was
'faucet' until recently; now it is 'tap'
--54. Used at the university in laborato-
ries; also common in 'tap water'--34. Used
in science laboratories--319.

15.5b <u>spigot</u> (on a barrel).

Although <u>faucet</u> is making some inroads
upon the dominance of the <u>spigot/spicket</u>
forms to designate the device on a barrel, the latter are not in a minority in
any state. The variant <u>spicket</u> has a
marked Midland orientation, <u>spigot</u> having
a 42% frequency in Minnesota and only 21%
in Iowa, whereas <u>spicket</u> has 8% in Minnesota and 25% in Iowa. Tap has a Northern
orientation (Mn. 17%, Ia. 10%, N.D. 25%,
S.D. 4%, Nb. 3%). Two variants with intrusive /r/ appear: <u>sprigot</u> and <u>sprocket</u>,

both of which were insisted upon by the infs. Sprocket, however, and also trap may be simply mistakes due to lexical replacement by similar forms.

    barrel faucet c147.
    beer tap c209.
    bung ?115.
    drain cock 29.
    faucet 13, 16-17, 29; 104, 107, c108, 113-14, 117, 119, 121-22, 126, 130, :?133, 134-36, 142-43, 145, 147, 149; 203, 218-19, 223-24; 305-7, 318; 420-21, 430, 432.
    spicket 35; 101, 105, 111-12, 122, 124-26, 128, 130, cr133, 138, *139, 140, ¹143, 144, *145, 148, s149; 220-21, 224; 316-17, 320; 405, 408, ¹414, †421, 422, 427, *¹432, 436-37.
    spigot 18, s29, 30-31, 38, †46, *46; 102-3, 109-10, 116, *123, 127, 131, 150, 152; 208, 210, 212, 214, 217, *219, 222, 225, :226; 301-2, 304, †306, 308-9, 311, cr312, 313-14, 322, 324-28; 401-2, :403, 404, 406, 409-10, 412-13, s416, *417, 418-20, s¹423, 424-26, 428, 431, 433-35.
    spout 202; 310; 411.
    sprigot 132; ¹218.
    sprocket r215.
    tap 14-15; 106, 119, 124, 137, 150; 201, 204-5, ?216, 209, 213, :216; ?312, 321; 407, ¹430.
    trap 113.
    wood faucet 207. ~en faucet 129; 206; 303.
    no response 1-12, 19-28, 32-34, ?36, 37, 39-45, 47-65; 120, 141, 146, 151; 211, 220; 315, 319, 323; 415, :429.
Comment:

    faucet: Pronounced with [æ]; inf. insists that he contrasts this form with that having [ɔ], which he uses for the device on a waterpipe. spicket: More normal for inf. than 'faucet'--122. spigot: Inf. says it is put into "the bung hole" of a barrel--46. sprocket: Repeated carefully--215.

15.6 funnel. NE 154. WG 16.

For the hollow utensil used in pouring liquids into a container the common UM term is funnel. The similar but etymologically distinct tunnel, carried west from New England, survives as a remembered relic in southern Minnesota. Only one speaker, a Type I inf. born in 1859 of New York and Ohio parentage, still has it as the normal form. The seven instances in Minnesota are matched by eight occurrences in southern Wisconsin, where it also is identified as obsolescent.

    funnel 1-25, :26, 27-41, :42, 43, !44-45, 46-65; 101-8, 110-52; 201-17, 219, 221-26; 301-14, :315, 316-23, s324, 325-

28; 401-9, :s410, 411-18, !419, 420-37.
    tunnel †23, s†40, s†48, †54, †62, sn65; s¹†309.
    no response 109; 218, 220.
Comment:

    tunnel: Used by inf.'s parents--40. "My older folks used it"--54. Used by inf.'s grandmother--62. "We used to call it 'tunnel' in the old days"--23. Inf. says this is still common here; her normal term--65.

15.7 whip. NE 179.

For use in driving horses or oxen two kinds of inciting devices are reported, a prod and a whip.

Typically for oxen the device is a sharp-pointed stick or pole usually called goad or gad. Also for oxen is a blacksnake (whip) or bullwhip, consisting of a handle from two to five feet long, with a generally braided leather lash of varying length. Such a whip with a handle filled with buckshot to provide weight is a shot whip.

For horses the whip consists usually of a long light pole with a short lash at one end.

With the disappearance of oxen as draft animals the various relevant terms became obsolete and are reported by older infs. only as relics. Goad, gad, and the phonetic variants with /r/ seem to have a distinct Northern orientation in contrast with the apparent Midland distribution of the minor variants prod and prodding pole. Except for two occurrences in southern Minnesota bullwhip is limited to the western fringe of the UM.

Whip is common in the UM, though for most infs. it is a term remembered from earlier years when horses were used for both farm implements and vehicles. The device used on one kind of vehicle is sometimes specified as a buggy whip.

In this sense the use of brad, Johnson bar, and shillelagh is atypical and unexplained.

For inf. responses see adjoining table.

Comment:

    binder pole: A long bamboo pole--25. blacksnake: For mules--6. brad: A stick with a nail in the end--113. bullwhip: Also for mules--214. A 'goad' with a long lash--202. A 2' handle with a long lash--309. A 5' stick with a 6' thong--409. gad: Term used by inf.'s father (from Que.)--8. Term used by inf.'s father (from Can.)--54. A lash--48. goad: A sharp stick with a nail in the end--113. Term used by inf. as a boy--55. gore stick: An 8'

Term	For Horses	For Oxen	Undesignated or for both
binder pole. . . .		25.	
blacksnake	48.	6,51; 119,139; 203, 212; 318; cvr413.	4.
blacksnake whip. .		60-61.	
brad		113.	45.
buggy whip	5; 150; 210,214, 224; 303,322-23; 406,410-11,417,429.		
bullwhip		?53,62; 202,212,214; 301,309,320; †404.	409.
coaxer			52.
gad		40,c†54; 201.	†8,s¹48; 118; s¹†302.
gad stick		:44.	
goad		30,39,42,!59; 101, 103,122; 202,214, 223;327; 413.	¹†31,45,!46,*47, s¹48,†55; 424.
goad stick		23; 204.	3,11.
goard stick. . . .		3,c12,21.	:sn224; 306.
gore stick		7.	15.
harvester whip . .			19.
horse whip			16.
Johnson bar. . . .			†202.
lash		427.	*145.
ox gad		c65.	
ox goad		126.	
ox gore		220.	
ox whip		19; 119,135.	
persuader	!¹†303.		*145; 316.
prick		143.	
prod	430.	215; 303; 420.	?¹†302.
prodding pole. . .		427.	
shillelagh			138.
shot whip		320; c405.	
stick		13.	
switch			4-5,c16.
whip	17,19,26,32,39,43, 45,56-57,59-61,64-65; 101,103,109-10, 113,116-17,120,122, 137,139,142-43,149; 205,209,211-12,217, 219,222,226; 304-5, 307,310-11,314,317-18,321,324,326-27; 407,416,420,428,433.	56.	1-3,6-15,18,20-25,27-31,33-34,c35,36-38,40-42,c44,46-50,c51,52-55, 58,62-65; 102,104-8, 111-12,114-15,118-19, 121,123-36,138,141,144-48,150-52; 201-3,c204, 206-8,213,215-16,220-21,223,225; 301-2,306, 308-9,312-13,315-16, 319-20,325,328; 401-5, 408-9,412-13,c414,415, 418-19,421-27,c430,431-32,434-37.

stick--7. "A pricker on it"--15. harvester whip: Extra long; 7'--19. Johnson bar: Heavier than a "whip," with a lash on the end--202. ox gore: Inf. volunteered spelling--220. ox whip: A 3' stick with a 3' leather lash--19. persuader: For mules-- *147. shillelagh: Jocular--138. whip: A pole whip--48. "To spruce 'em along"--112.

15.8a mouth organ. NE 413.

For the small wind instrument the literary and commercial term, harmonica, has a quite uniform distribution throughout the UM. For several speakers it is an innovation, replacing one of the older folk names. Most common of these is mouth organ, which dominates the Northern speech zone. (Data from Minnesota are incomplete, since this item was added after the first year's fieldwork.) Mouth harp, on the contrary, dominates the Midland speech area except for the extreme southeastern sector, where South Midland speech is typical and where the accepted form is French harp. Two uncertain responses of juice harp come from Nebraska infs., and a secondary inf. in South Dakota uses the variant harmonia.

	Mn.	Ia.	N.D.	S.D.	Nb.	Ave.
harmonica	25%	29%	20%	25%	40%	41%
mouth organ	100%	61%	92%	86%	35%	67%
mouth harp	0%	27%	4%	11%	60%	26%

CL 123: The checklist returns from 912 respondents strongly confirm the fieldwork distribution data even to the two extensions of the mouth organ range into southern Iowa. The mailed information also adds 82 instances (9%) of jew's harp and one instance of breath harp, reported by a northern Iowan of Swedish parentage.

	Mn.	Ia.	N.D.	S.D.	Nb.	Tot.
harmonica	37%	30%	50%	50%	40%	41%
mouth organ	87%	57%	83%	72%	32%	63%
mouth harp	1%	15%	3%	15%	57%	21%

Notable is the fact that in the southern two-thirds of Iowa, Midland territory, the frequency of mouth organ is only 23% and that of mouth harp is 26%.

French harp 127, 132, 135-36, 142, *†145, 146-49; 429-30.
harmonia *316.
harmonica ¹†30, →31, →35, 38; 101-2, 110-12, 116-18, 121, 126, 129-30, 141, 144, 150; →204, →206, →¹208, →209, →¹212, →214, 220; 305-6, 308, →¹309, 316, 319-19, 323; →401, 402, 406, →¹411, 412, ¹413, c414, 415, 421, 423-26, 428, 435.
harp 134.
juice harp ?427, ?432.
mouth harp †35; 122, 125-27, 129-31,

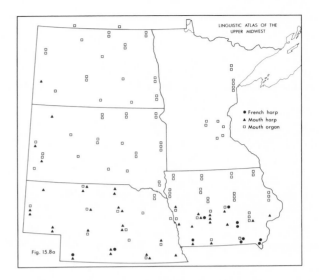

Fig. 15.8a

133-34, ¹137, 140, 143, 145, 151-52; 214; 301, 310, ¹313, 326; †401, 402, →403, 404-6, 410-11, sn412, 413-14, 417, →418, 420-21, 425, 430-31, cr432, 433-34, 436-37.

mouth organ 13-15, c16-17, 18, 29-30, !31, 35-36, 38; 101-15, *116, 117-21, 123-24, ¹126, 127-28, 132, 137-38, 144, 146, 152; !201, 202-5, †206, 207-14, !215, 216-17, 219, !221, 222-26; 302-6, *306, 307-9, 311-19, !320, 321-22, 324-25, 327-28; 403, 407-9, →412, ¹†413, 414, 416, †418, 419, 421-22, 426-27, †428, 433.

no response 1-12, 19-28, 32-34, 37, 39-65; 139; 218.

Comment:

French harp: Inf. says it is different in key from a mouth harp or mouth organ, both of which are in key of C--127. "It should be called a 'french harp'"--132. harmonica: Inf. says it is an "aristocratic word"--35. "The proper name"--319. juice harp: See inf.'s response and comment for 15.8b--427. mouth harp: = mouth organ--152. Used by inf.'s father (from Al.)--35. Inf.'s usual term--402, 433. Inf.'s more usual term until recent use of 'harmonica'--412. mouth organ: Inf.'s common term--112. Inf. says this term was used c1900.

15.8b jew's harp.

The small musical instrument played by being plucked while held against the teeth is called a jew's harp by two-thirds of the UM infs. and juice harp by the remaining third. No geographical pattern emerges. Juice harp, however, clearly correlates with informant types, as its highest frequency (40%) is with Type

I speakers. Only 18% of the Type II speakers use it, and 13% of the college graduates.

CL 124: Among the 828 checklist respondents the proportion of jew's harp is slightly higher (74%) and that of juice harp slightly lower (15%) than in the field responses; 7% reply with mouth harp and 3% with French harp.

Autoharp †223.
French harp ?427.
jew harp 112; !409.
jewish harp 13.
jew's harp 14-15, 29, !30, 36; 101-4, 106, 108-11, 114-17, 120, 123-24, 126, 128-30, :131, 133, 137-38, cr141, 143, 146-47, *148, 152; 202, *203, 204, 207, 210, 213-15, *219, 221-23, 225, :226; :301, →302, ˡ†304, c309, 312-16, 318-19, 321, 323, 325, 327-28; 401-2, 404, :405, 406, 408, 410-14, 416, :417, 419-23, 425, s426, 428, 430, 433-35, :436.
juice harp c16, 31, c35; 105, 107, 113, 119, 122, 125, 127, 132, 135, 140, ?141, 142, 145, 148-49; 201, 205-6, 208, 212, 216, !217, 220, 224; †302, 307-8, 310-11, 317, 320, 322, 324; 403, 418, 429, 432, :437.
mouth harp 407.
zither !431.
no response 1-12, 17-28, 32-34, 37-65; 118, 121, 134, 136, 139, 144, 150-51; ?209, 211, 218; ?303, 305-6, ?326; 415, 425.

Comment:

French harp: "If I remember right" (See inf.'s responses to 15.8a)--427. Jew's harp: "It's not a 'juice harp'"-- 225. Inf. has only a faint memory of this --226. Inf. has never seen one--410. juice harp: Inf. volunteered spelling-- 107. mouth harp: "It has a spring on it" --407.

16.1 bag (made of paper). NE 149. WG 30, 156; F17, F70.

For the variously sized container made of paper two terms are common in the UM, bag and sack. Although some infs. distinguish the terms according to the size of the container, and without any consistent agreement, many use the words interchangeably. An appreciable Northern orientation appears in the distribution of bag and a corresponding Midland orientation is true of sack. West Midland poke survives feebly as a relic recalled by two speakers; a third, in southern Iowa, still uses paper poke. Demands of modern shopping have created the compound shopping bag, but the possible shopping sack is not reported.

CL 23: Returns from 1,058 mail respondents confirm the field data both with respect to the orientation of bag toward Northern and of sack toward Midland speech zones and also with respect to the greater total frequency of sack (74%) than of bag (46%):

	Mn.	Ia.	N.D.	S.D.	Nb.	Ave.
(paper) sack	55%	84%	58%	81%	92%	75%
(paper) bag	65%	25%	69%	45%	33%	46%

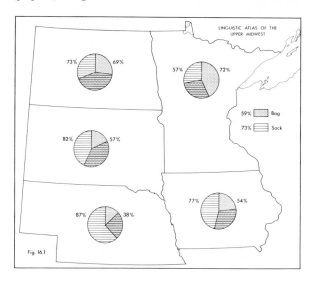

Fig. 16.1

bag 1-9, 11, 14, 17-18, 20, 22-23, 25-26, 28, 30-31, 33, 35-36, 38, 41, 43, 45, ˡ47, 49, 54-55, 64; ˡ116, 149, †151; →203, 216, 219, 225, ˡ226; 302, *306, 308, c312, 316, 319, ˡ323; 404, 412, 417-18, 421-22, 425, ˡ426, 427, s428, 430-31, 437.
candy bag 134; 309. ~ sack 134, 136.
cornucopia !51.
paper bag 10, 12, 14-15, 17, 19, 21, 26, 29, 31-32, 37, 39-40, 43, 46, 48, 50, 56, 58; 101-2, ?103, 104-5, 107-8, 111, 119-21, 124-26, 131, ˡ133, 134-41, 144-49; 201-2, 204-7, →209, 211-12, 214, 218-19, 221-23; 303-5, 310, →312, 314, 317, ?321, 322, 324; 401, 406, 424.
paper sack 2, ˡ6, 10, 13, 15-16, 18, 29, c35, 37, c44, ˡ45, *46, 50, 52-53, 57, sˡ58, 59-63, 65; 102, :?cr103, 104, 106, 109, cr111, 113-14, 116-19, 122-25, 127-33, 135, 138, 142, 144-45, 148, 150-51; 201, 205, 207-11, 213, 215, c216, 217-18, 220-22, ˡ223, 224, *225; 301-2, 304-5, 309, 313, 315, 320, cr321, 322, 328; c401, 405-8, 423, 429, 4·32.
poke †*145; †311. paper ~ 147.
sack 2, 8-9, 11, ˡ21, 24, 26-28, 30, 34, 38, 42, c44, 47-49, 51, 53-54, ˡ55, 57, 65; 110, ?111, 112, 115, 126, 136, 140-41, 143, 152; †203, *219, 226; 306-8, 310, c311, †312, *316, 318-19, 323, 325-

27; 402-4, 409-16, 419-22, 425-26, 428, 431-37.
   shopping bag 208; 305, 318; 423.

Comment:

   bag: "If you was ordering them, you'd say 'bag'"--6. Usu.--11. Inf. says this is rare here--47. Not often used by inf. --*306. Used by inf. in youth--151. Inf. says it is a 'bag' when full and a 'sack' when empty--9. Inf.'s more likely term for a small one--30. Smaller than a 'sack'--54; 422. Larger than a 'sack'-- 38. Larger and heavier than a 'sack'--319; 431. "The 'bag' they [grocers] put the 'sacks' in"--425. cornucopia: A twisted newspaper--51. paper bag: Inf.'s usual term--26; 205; 304, 310. Inf. says not used as much as formerly--135. Has ends folded and sealed, as for sugar--138. Smaller than a 'sack'; holds 20 lbs. or less--140. All sizes up to 100 lbs.--146. paper sack: Inf. thinks 'bag' is "right" but also uses 'sack'--10. Inf. thinks this is more common than 'paper bag'--*46; 222. Inf. thinks this her usual term--321. Inf. not sure whether it is 'bag' or 'sack'--103. Any size up to 100 lbs.--148. Larger than a 'paper bag'--29. Smaller than a 'paper bag'--50; 145; 218, 221. Smaller and lighter than a 'paper bag'-- 131. Smaller than a 'shopping bag'--208. poke: "Used to get a 'poke' of candy"-- 145. sack: Inf. thinks this is more common than 'bag'--8. Inf.'s usual term--412, 437. Smaller than a 'paper bag'--136.

16.2 sack (made of cloth).

   In slight contrast to the distribution of sack and bag when referring to a paper receptacle, the frequency pattern when these terms refer to a cloth container in- dicates a somewhat stronger Northern ori- entation for sack than for bag. Although used interchangeably by many speakers, the semantic distinction others make is, then, likely to exhibit a regional rela- tionship. Sack dominates the UM, both as a single entry and also in the descrip- tive compounds cloth sack, flour sack, and sugar sack. The bag compounds are recorded chiefly in Iowa.

   bag 2-3, 8-9, 11, 16, 18, ¹23, ¹24, 28, 30-31, 37, ?38, 43, 48-49, c53, 55, 60, 64, s65; 110, 112, 122, 130, 132, 137-38, 145, 148, 150; 205-6, 216, 219, 222, 225; 302, 308, 316, 320, 325-26, 328; 401, 404, 409-10, 416, 422-25, 431, 437.
   cloth bag 102, 104, 111, 121, 146. ~ sack 15; 107, 114, 119, 129, 133, 142; 323.
   cotton sack 29; 315.
   flour bag 14, 47, ?51. ~ sack 12, 16,

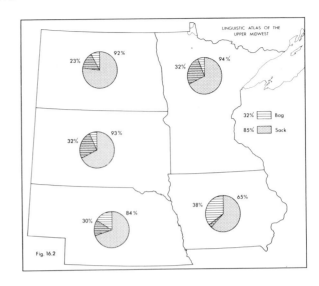

Fig. 16.2

28, 31, !33, :36, 39, 45, 47, c51, ¹*51, 52, 57, 61; 117, 123, 134, 136, 144; 205, 213, 216-17, 220, 225; 302, 311, c312, 315, 321, 324, 326; 424, 437.
   gunny sack 58.
   laundry bag 127.
   poke 147.
   print bag 136.
   sack 1-7, 9-14, 17, †18, 19-28, 30, 32- 34, :35, c36, 37-38, c40, 41-43, *c43, c44, 48-50, 54, c55, c59, 63, 65; 101, 103, 105-6, 108-9, 113, 115-16, 118, 120, 131, 139-41, 143, 149, 152; 202-4, 206- 12, 214-15, 218, *†219, 221, 223-24, 226; 301, 303-4, 306-10, 312-14, *316, 317-19, 321-22, 324-25, 327; 401-3, 405-8, 411- 15, 417-22, 426-36.
   salt sack 205; 324; 408.
   sugar bag 47; 305, 311. ~ sack 26, 29, 31, 46, c47, 53, 58, 61-62; 201, 213, 220; 305, 315.
   wheat bag 56. ~ sack 56.
   no response 124-26, 128, 135, 147, 151.

Comment:

   bag: Usu.--49; 316. Inf. thinks of a 'bag' as full and a 'sack' as empty, but would ask for a 'sack' of flour--9. flour bag: In conversation inf. used 'sack' of- ten but never 'bag'--51. flour sack: "Made in a 'bag' factory"--33. Inf. con- siders 'sack' a farm term and 'bag' a city term--47. Inf. calls them 'bags' when full and 'flour sacks' when empty-- 424. gunny sack: Inf. says a 'flour sack' is called a 'gunny sack' if used outdoors, e.g., for carrying fish or nuts--58. sack: "The more older expression"--48. Used more frequently by inf. than 'bag'--11; 225; 325. "Hardly ever called 'sacks'"-- 206. sugar sack: Cf. "The sugar came in 'bags'"--53.

16.3 <u>burlap</u> <u>sack</u>. NE 150. WG47, 56;
F71.

A large, loosely-woven coarse sack used
mostly for shipping potatoes and other
farm products is commonly known by <u>gunny</u>
<u>sack</u>, <u>burlap</u> <u>sack</u>, or <u>burlap</u> <u>bag</u>. <u>Sack</u>
<u>forms</u> <u>predominate</u>. <u>Gunny</u> <u>sack</u> prevails
throughout the UM; <u>burlap</u> <u>sack</u> occurs
principally in Minnesota and the eastern
sections of the Dakotas and Nebraska;
<u>burlap</u> <u>bag</u> dominates Iowa and the western
third of the region.

The specific <u>potato</u> <u>sack</u> (or <u>bag</u>) is
found as a minor form in all states ex-
cept South Dakota. North Carolina <u>tow</u>
<u>sack</u> is reported three times in South Da-
kota and Nebraska. The mother of the
South Dakota inf. was born in Maryland,
where <u>tow</u> <u>sack</u> is an infrequent variant.

Large sacks of different material and
with other purposes were also identified
by infs. in response to this item. Heavier and more closely woven containers
are the bean bag, bran bag, cake sack for
cotton seed cake for cattle, grain bag,
and wheat sack. <u>Bemis</u> <u>sack</u> and <u>bag</u> are so
called from the name of the manufacturer.

CL 24: The 1,039 checklist respondents
on this item confirm the field data with
an over-all percentage of 45 for <u>burlap</u>
<u>sack</u> and <u>bag</u> and 65 for <u>gunny</u> <u>sack</u>.

bag 105, ?133, 143; †306, *316.
bean bag 12; 416.
Bemis bag 8. ~ sack *203.
bran bag 3, 15.
burlap ¹30, 31, 62; 435. ~ bag 4-5, 8-
9, s10, 11, :32, 33, 38, 44, :52, 61-65;
101, 106, 131, 138, 145, 148-49; 204,
206, 215-16, 219, →221, 223, 225; 308-9,
316, 327; 401, →404, 406, 408-9, 412,
414, 421-22, 425, 432, 435, 437. ~ sack
6-7, 13, 19-22, 27-28, 35, 41, 46, 51,
57-58, 60-61, ¹62; 110, 113, 124, 140,
149; 201-4, 207, →208, †209, 220, c224;
c306, 308, 316, 318, ?322; ¹405, 407,
413, 420, 424, 427, 429, 431-32.
cake sack 301; →412.
canvas sack 48.
corn sack 16.
feed sack 22, 36; 112; c222.
grain bag 33, 37; 119, 128; †420. ~ sack
1, 4, 7-8, 10, 15, 19-21, 24, 26-27, 29,
41, 64; 103, 117, 119, 125-26, 129, 135,
147, 152; 203, 205, c206, 207, 211; 304,
325; 423.
gunny 30. ~ bag 47; 214. ~ sack 1, 4-5,
10-12, 14-19, c20, 22-26, s27, 28-29, 31,
s32, 33-34, snc35, 36-37, 39-40, s¹41,
42-43, 45-50, 53, c54, 55, s¹57, s¹58,
59, *63, 64; s101, 102, sn103, 104, s105,
s¹106, 107-9, 111-12, s113, 114-16, 118-
23, 125-30, 132, cr133, 134-38, s139,

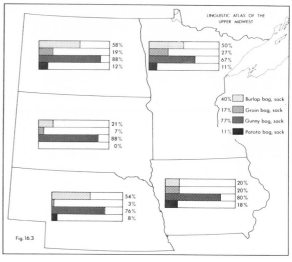

Fig. 16.3

140, s141, 142-44, *145, 146-48, 150-52;
c201, 202-5, †208, 209-13, 215-18, *219,
220-24, sn225, 226; 301-7, 309-15, 317,
319, 321, cr322, 323-28; 401-3, †404,
405-12, 415-16, 418-23, 426, s427, 428-
30, s431, 433-35, :436, 437.
jute bag 141.
knit bag 136. knitted bag 125.
mesh bag 127, 130; 432. ~ sack 145.
potato bag 2; 123-24; 210; 425, 428.
~ sack 2, 7-8, 13, 21, 24, 26; 117, 124-
25, 127, 134, 140, 142, 147; 208, *219;
414, 425.
sack 131; 316.
seamless sack 22.
tow sack 320; ¹401, *417.
twine sack 20, 41.
wheat sack 25.
no response 56, 146, 149.

Comment:

bag: Used by inf.'s father (from Pa.)--
306. Bemis sack: Supplied by inf.'s son--
*203. burlap: Inf. says infrequent here--
30. Inf.'s name for the material but not
for a sack--428, 433. burlap bag: Inf.
says it doesn't sound right; for her 'burlap' is only a pred. adjective--10. Inf.
isn't sure whether she says 'sack' or
'bag'--32. More tightly woven than a 'gunny sack'--215; 408. burlap sack: More
usual for inf. than 'burlap bag'--61.
Still uses the term occasionally--†209.
Inf. would use this term in a store, but
on the farm would say 'gunny sack'--224.
Coarser than a 'gunny sack'--407. cake
sack: So-called because "cotton seed cake
for cattle comes in them"--301. grain
bag: a 'bag' is generally more tightly
woven than a 'sack'--128. grain sack:
Heavier than burlap--19. gunny bag: Inf.
also remembers Gunny Bag Bill, a local

cowboy--214. gunny sack: Usual term--203, 209, 225; 309; 401, 429. Inf. says not common here--202. Inf. says more common than 'burlap bag'--437. Inf. says that this is an older term than 'burlap sack' --22. When full called a 'burlap bag'; when empty called a 'gunny sack'--138. potato sack: When full; called 'burlap bag' when empty--414. wheat sack: Stronger than a 'gunny sack'--25.

16.4 barrel (for flour, meal).

The large cylindrical wooden vessel with slightly bulging sides composed of staves is everywhere identified as a barrel. The South Midland gum for a vessel made of a hollowed section of a log apparently persists in the term gum barrel used earlier by one speaker in southern Minnesota. Cask, hogshead, and tun, offered by a few infs., are, however, associated with similar containers for liquids.

barrel 1-5, c6, 7, c8, 9-17, c18, 19-22, c23, 24, c25, 26, c27, 28, c29, 30, c31, 32-34, c35-37, 38, c39, 40-42, *43, c44, 45-47, 49-50, c51, 52-58, c59, 60-62, c63, 64, c65; 101-8, c109, 110-51, c152; 201, c202, 203, c204-5, 206, c207, 208-18, c219-20, 221-23, c224, 225-26; 301-2, c303, 304-7, c308-9, 310, c311-12, 313-15, *316, c317, 318-21, c322, 323-28; c401, 402, c403, 404-14, 416-27, 429-37.
cask 120.
flour barrel 48; 428.
gum barrel s†48.
hogshead 39; 119, ?145; 316. ~ barrel c220.
tun 7.

Comment:

cask: For liquids--120. hogshead: For molasses and vinegar--39. Larger than a 'barrel'--119. tun: For liquor; larger than a 'barrel'--7.

16.5a turn (of corn, wood, etc.).

Included in order to elicit the term for the quantity of grain or wood that might be carried in a wagon on one trip or the amount of grain that could be carried on horseback on one trip from a mill, this item became productive only when redirected toward the quantity (as of firewood) that one person can carry in his extended arms. The original item yielded only one example of rick and one of turn. As redirected it yielded the variants armful and armload, which have regional variation. Although armful prevails in all five states, it is distinctly Northern in its orientation; and armload, which appears once in Minnesota and once

in Manitoba but not at all in North Dakota, is clearly linked to the Midland distribution pattern.

armful 1-5, 7-13, 15-30, !31, 32-42, 44-47, 49-55, 57-61; 101-9, 112-14, 116-21, 123-24, 126-27, 129-30, !133, 134, 138-41, 143, 149-50, c152; 201, 203-15, 217-26; 301-4, 307-9, 311-12, 314, 316-19, 321-23, !324, 325, 327-28; 404-5, !406, 407, 409, 413, 415-16, 418-21, 423-24, 426, 429-32, 436.
armload 14; 110-11, 114-15, :122, 125,

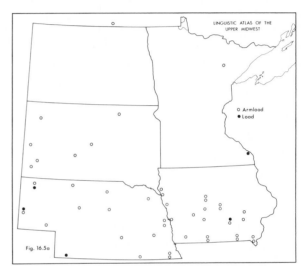

LINGUISTIC ATLAS OF THE UPPER MIDWEST

○ Armload
● Load

Fig. 16.5a

127-28, 131-33, 136-37, 142, 144-48, 150; 202; 301, !302, 306, 310, 313, 315, 320, 326; 401, 403, 406, 408, 411-12, 414, 417, 422, 425, 427-28, 433-35.
double armful 312.
load !54, 56; 135; 402, 410, 437.
rick !204.
turn 48.
no response 6, 43, 62-65; 151; 216; 305.

16.5b jag (partial load on a wagon).

Only one term is common in this sense. Except that it is unknown to a number of infs., it has no appreciable distribution pattern. Some speakers indicated knowledge of the word only in a slang sense referring to intoxication.

dab 311.
dump 46.
half a load 13, 16, 43; 318. halfload :310.
jag 1, sn3, :!4, *5, 7-8, !10, 12, 15, sn19, 21-22, !23, 24-30, sn31, 34, :!†!35, 37, *41, 42, !43, !45, s!46, s48, 50-54, s†55, 59, :!60, 61-65; 101-9, 112-19, 122-30, s132, 133-49, s50, 151-52; !201-2, 203-11, sn212, 213-14, !215, 217-18,

*219, 220-25; 301-4, 306-8, s¹309, 312, s313, 314, 316, !317, 320-21, :322, 323, :324, 325, 327; 401, sn402, 403-6, !407, 408-9, 412-13, ¹414, 415-16, *417, 418, 420-23, s427, 428-30, ¹431-34, 435-17.

litter full 57.
load 17-18, 48.
part load 19. ~ of a load 15; 212.
small load 120.

no response 2, 6, 9, 11, 14, 20, 32-33, ?36, ?38, 39-40, 44, 47, 49, 56, 58; 110-11, 121, 131; 216, :?219, ?226; 305, 315, 319, 326, 328; 410-11, 419, 424-26.

Comment:

jag: Inf. says common here--3; 414, 433. Inf. says not common here--23. Usu.--43. Used with reference to hay only--25. Used with reference to wood only--309.

17.1 hoops. NE 147.

The bands--originally of wood and later of metal--encircling a barrel are generally termed hoops. Bands is an infrequent variant in Minnesota and Nebraska, with one example in North Dakota.

Staves is probably an error, but two examples pronounced without /v/ may be instances of stays with transferred meaning. Infs. 203 and 433 so pronounced it.

bands cr4, 5, 19, 38; 408, s415, 427, ¹431, 437.
barrel bands 19. ~ hoops 13; 104.
hoops 1-3, :?4, 6, c7, 8-12, 14-20, c21, c23, 24-28, c29, c30, 31-32, c33, 34, c35, 36-37, 39-44, r45, 46-50, c51, c52, 53-54, c55, 56-58, c59, 60-65; 101, s102, 103, 105-9, 111-52; 201, c203, 204-8, cr209, 210-11, c212, 213-15, c216, 217-18, c219, 220, c221, 222-26; 301-4, 306-11, :312, 313, c314, 315, *316, 317, 320-28; 401, :402, :403, 404-5, c406, 407, 409-10, :411, c412, c413, 414, 416, c417, 418-25, c426, 427-28, c429, 430, c431, 434-36.
iron bands 16; c203.
loops 305.
staves 203; 319; 431, 433.
no response 22; 110.

17.2 cork (for bottle). NE 144.

For an object to be inserted into the neck of a jug or bottle to prevent spilling of the contents the situation is complicated by variables of nomenclature and material. If made of cork, the object is typically called a cork; if made of glass, a stopper. Ambiguity arose with the advent of such an object made of rubber, which is designated with both terms, even interchangeably by some speakers but with cork slightly dominating on the whole and particularly in Minnesota, South Dakota, and Nebraska.

The use of stopper to refer to the device made of cork is peculiar to the first settled part of the Midland speech territory. Conversely, the use of cork to refer to the device made of glass seems to have a Northern orientation except for its occurrence along the Missouri River in southern Iowa and Nebraska.

Some infs. solve the naming problem by descriptive compounds such as glass cork and rubber cork, and glass stopper and rubber stopper.

No significant variation by type appear except that cork and glass cork referring to the glass object are declining in frequency (Type I 32%, Type II 10%) and stopper and glass stopper show a corresponding increase (Type I 65%, Type II 83%).

CL 25, 26: Replies from 1,030 respondents confirm the field records. The glass object is called cork by 15% and stopper by 83%. The Northern orientation of cork in this sense and the Midland orientation of stopper are attested by the figures:

	Mn.	Ia.	N.D.	S.D.	Nb.	Ave.
cork	17%	10%	22%	19%	12%	15%
stopper	79%	89%	77%	80%	90%	83%

a. as generic or uncategorized
cork 3-7, 10, 12-13, 15-18, 26-27, c35, 36-37, 56, 58, 63-65; 102, 109, 112-13, 138, 140-41, 143; 203, 209, 222; 302, 305-7, 317-19, 322; 405, 408, 411, 417, 426-27, 434, 436.
cork plug 13.
stopper 14, 32, 58; 130, 146, 149; 408, 436.
no response 22.

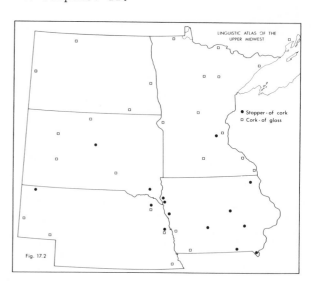

Fig. 17.2

b. made of cork
  cork 1-6, 8-12, 19-21, 23-31, 33-34, c35, 36-45, c46, 47-57, 59-62; 101, 103-38, 110-11, 114, c115, 116-22, 126-27, 130-34, 136-37, 142-44, 147-48, 150-52; 201-16, c217, 218-26; 301-3, 308-16, 320-28; 401-36. ~ stopper 62.
  stopper †11, 32; 107, 110-11, 118, 122, 130, 137, 146, 149; 314, 324; 401, 408, 427.

Comment:

  stopper: Used by inf.'s father (from Me.)--11. "Made from cork, as a rule"--149.

c. made of any material other than cork
  stopper 9, 21, 38, 48, 58; 110-11, 119, 121, 130, 137; 202, 204-6, 211-13, 215, 226; 315, 321, 328; 409-10, 419, 425-26, 430-31.
  stop 225.
  top 437.

Comment:

  stop: spelled out by inf.--225.

d. made of glass
  cork 3-6, 10, 12, 26-27, 36, 50, 55-56; 122, 143; 203, 209, 222, 224; 302-3, 313, 322; 408, 411, 417, 427, 434.
  glass cork 19, 25, 41; 116, 132, :144; 207; 407, 432. ~ stopper 21, 23, 40, 42, 62; 120, 127, 136, 147; 201, 221; 429.
  stop 225.
  stopper 1-3, 8-11, :20, 24, 27-30, ?31, 32-34, 38-40, 43, c44, 45-47, 49-54, 57-60, c61; 101, 103-4, 106-8, 110-11, 114, 116-19, 121, 126, 130-31, 133-34, 137, 142, 146, 148, 150, sn151, 152; 202, 204-6, 208, 210-13, 215-16, 218-19, 223, ¹224, 226; *301, 303, 309-12, ¹313, 314-15, 320-21, 323, 325-28; 401-4, 406, 408-14, 416, *417, 418-27, 430-31, 433, 435.
  stopple †103, 105; 214.
  top 437.

Comment:

  cork: Can also be plastic--3. stopper: Can also be plastic--38. stopple: Term used by inf. years ago--103.

e. made of rubber
  cork 1-2, 4-6, 10, 12, 23-24, 26-27, 30, 33, 37, 41-42, 49-50, 54-56; 122, 142-43; 203, 205, 209, 214, 218-19, 222, 224; 301-3, 311-13, 320, 322, 326; 403, 407-8, 411-14, 416-17, 422-23, 427, 432-34.
  rubber cork 19-20, 25, 35; 207-8, 220; 309-10, 325; 405-6, 415, 421.
  rubber stopper 21; 201; 328; 433.
  stop 225.
  stopper 8-9, 28, 34, 38, 54, 58; 107, 110-11, 119, 121, 130, 137; 202, 204-6, 210-13, 215-16, 221, 223, ¹224, 226; 303,

311-12, 314-15, 321; 404, 408-10, 418-19, 426-28, 430-31, 435.
  top 437.

f. made of wood
  cork 2, 4, 6, 11, 24, 42, 50, 55-56; 143; 203, 209, 214, 217, 222, 224; 302-3, 313, 322; 408, 411, 415, 417, 421, 427; 434.
  plug 210, 223; 414, 416.
  stop 225.
  stopper 33, c44; 107, 110-11, 118-19, 121, 130-31, 137; 202, 204-6, 208, 211-13, 215-16, 221, ¹224, 226; 314-15; 406, 408-10, 419, 422, 425, 427-28, 430-31, 435.
  top 437.
  wood cork 415. ~ stopper 17; 429.

g. made from a corncob
  cork 217; 322; 421, 428.
  plug *412, 423.

17.4 tongue (of a wagon). NE 170. WG 57; F74.

For the shaft extending from a wagon between the two horses of a team the common term is tongue, ranging from 78% in Minnesota to 100% in Iowa and South Dakota. Competing with it is pole, which reveals its New England and Hudson Valley provenience by a strong Northern speech zone correlation. Rare variants are handle, stinger, and deichsel, the last a German word used by an inf. of German parentage.

  buggy pole 223; 320.
  deichsel 415.
  handle 56; ¹404.
  pole 4, ¹*5, 7-8, 12, c13, 25, ¹†29, 30, 36; :37, 39, 43-45, *46, ¹47, 50-51, 53-54; ¹105, †135; 202, 204, ¹205, 206, 208,

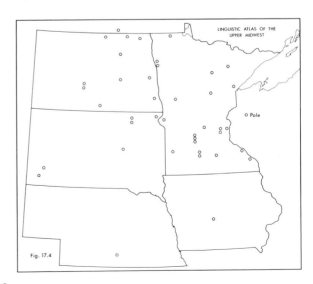

Fig. 17.4

213, ¹†214, 217, ¹221, 225; s305, 306-7, 312; ¹404, ¹413, 430.

stinger *5.

tongue 1-3, 5-6, ¹8, 9-11, 13-17, 20, 23-24, 26-35, 38-42, r43, 44-50, ¹51, 52-53, †54, 55, 57, c59, 60-65; 101-9, 111-52; 201-3, ¹204, 205-7, 209-14, ¹218, 219, 221-23, ¹225, 226; 301-9, 311-21, c322, 323-24, :326, 327-28; 401-2, 404-13, c414, 416-23, 425-35, 437.

tree 58.

wagon pole 18-19, 21, 56; 129; 216, 218, 220, ¹224; 316. ~ tongue 16; 118; †208, 215, †216, 224; 310, 325; 403, 424-25, 436.

no response 22; 110.

Comment:

handle: For oxen--56. Inf. heard this used by residents who came from Missouri --404. pole: Usu.--30. Inf. says this is the more common term here--43, 45; 221. Used by inf.'s in-laws--54. "Yankees called them 'tongues', and the Irish called them 'poles'"--135. Heard only occasionally here--47. The term found in catalogs--413. Used with reference to a buggy--44; 202; 312. Used with reference to equipment other than a wagon--*46. Used with reference to a lighter vehicle --213. stinger: A pole with a hook for another pole in front for a second team, as in logging--*5. tongue: Inf.'s more common term--39; 430. "The proper name, but never used"--51. Inf.'s term for 'traces'--57-58. On a wagon only--44; 202, 223; 320.

17.5   shafts (of a buggy). NE 171. WG17; F75.

For the two poles between which a single horse is hitched in front of a buggy the UM generally uses shafts or the variant shavs /ʃævz/ with an 85% frequency, with competition from thills and its lisped variant fills, the two of which account for 21% of the responses. Both pairs reveal regional correlation. Shafts has Northern orientation at least in the eastern half of the UM (Mn. 48%, Ia. 25%) and shavs has Midland correlation (Mn. 27%, Ia. 65%). The thills and fills reveal their New England and Hudson Valley origin by occurring chiefly in southern Minnesota and northern Iowa, with an extension of the less conservative fills into North Dakota.

CL 55: The 1,020 checklist respondents noting this item confirm the field results, with 88% using shafts or shavs and 16% using thills or fills. They also confirm the regional pattern of the latter pair with 21% for Minnesota, 9% for north-

ern Iowa, and only 2% for southern Iowa.

bars 58.

fills 16, 23, 27, 39-40, :41, ¹42, ¹45, 48, 50, 54, 56, ¹60, 61, 63-65; 103, 105-7, ¹109, 116-17, s¹118, 139, s¹151; 204, 210, 216, †*219, 223, ¹224, 225; 307, 317; 420.

forks *26.

shafts 1-4, *5, 6-7, 11, 14-15, 17-20, 24, :s?26, 28-29, 32, 34, 37, 39-40, 45-46, ?47, 51, 53, 57-58, *60, 62; 108,

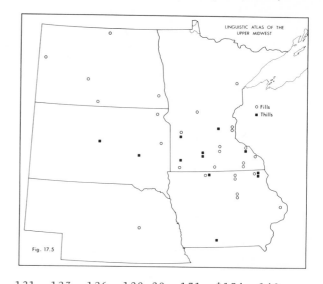

Fig. 17.5

121, 123, 126, 128-29, 131, *134, 140, ?141, c144, 149, sn150, 151; 201-3, 206, 217, :219, 220-22, cr224; 308-9, :sn310, 311-13, 316, 321, 323-25, sn326; 402, :403, 407-10, 412-13, c414, s?415, 417, 422, 424-26, 431-32.

shavs 8, 10, 12-13, 21, 25, 30, :31, 35-36, :43, 44, 49, 54, 57, 60-61; 101-2, 104, 109, 111-15, 117-20, 122, 124-25, 127, 130, 132-33, 135-39, c141, 142-43, 145-48, 152; ¹204, 205, 207-9, 211-15, 218; 301-3, 306, 315-16, 318, 320, 322; 401, 404-5, 411, 416, 418-21, 423, 427-30, 433-37.

thills ¹29, :33, 42, ¹51, 52-53, 55, c59; :103, 107-8, ?116, :144; 314, 327; s424.

no response 9, 22, ?38; 110; 226; 304-5, 319, 328; 406.

Comment:

fills: Pronounced as if 'filts'--41. Inf. ridicules this form--42. Also used by inf.'s father (from Can.)--54. forks: Used in inf.'s family--*26. shafts: Inf. says this is "more proper" than 'fills' --45. Inf. responded with this form but used 'shavs' in conversation--141. shavs: Inf. says this is more common here--54. Inf. also gave [ʃæft] as the singular--

60. Pronounced as if 'shaves'--436.
thills: Inf. says this is common here--
29. "The right name, but never used"--51.
Pronounced as if 'thrills'--108. Inf.'s
husband says 'fills'; she thinks 'thills'
might be "right"--116.

17.6 whiffletree (behind one horse).
NE 172. WG 12, 13, 47, 48, 58; F5a, F5b,
F41, F77.

Words for the bar to which the traces
of a single horse are fastened exhibit a
sharp regional distinction between Northern and Midland in the eastern United
States but in the UM reveal a strong
northward push of the Midland term.
Midland singletree, which began invad-
ing Northern speech territory in Michigan
and in Wisconsin (36% frequency), has so
far extended its range that it dominates
all UM states except Minnesota, where,
however, 41% of the infs. report it. Frequencies in the other states are: Ia.
78%, N.D. 73%, S.D. 68%, Nb. 91%, or an
average of 67% for the entire UM. The older variant swingletree appears once in
southern Iowa.
Northern whiffletree and whippletree
were clearly retreating even before farm
mechanization. They dominate only Minnesota and occur elsewhere only in conservative Northern speech areas except for
five instances in southern Iowa and Nebraska, all of which are reported by infs.
with at least one parent born in New York,
Michigan, Ohio, or Illinois. The whippletree variant is largely restricted to an
inner core of the whiffletree region, specifically southern and eastern Minnesota
and Iowa.
The relic swiveltree appears only once,
in northwestern Nebraska.

CL 56: Of 1,029 responding by mail, 87%
favor singletree. Swingletree is checked
8 times in Minnesota, and is scattered
elsewhere, for a total of 13 instances.

evener ¹21, 52, 57; 132; 305.
singletree 1, 4, *5, 6, 10, 15, 19, 21,
24-25, *26, 29-30, 40-41, c44, 45, 48,
50-51, 53, 56, c58, 60-61, 63; 103-4,
s105, 106-7, 109, 111-14, 116-17, s¹118,
119-23, 125-27, 129-30, ?131, 132-33,
*134, 135-41, 143, 145-52; ¹201, 202,
206-7, c208, 209-10, 212-20, 223-25,
sn226; 301-3, 306-7, 309, 311-13, 315-16,
318, 320-22, 324-25; 401, c403, 404-9,
411-14, 417-22, 424-30, 432-37.
swingletree 142.
swiveltree 402.
whiffle 128.
whiffletree 13, 16-17, 23, 31, 33, c37,

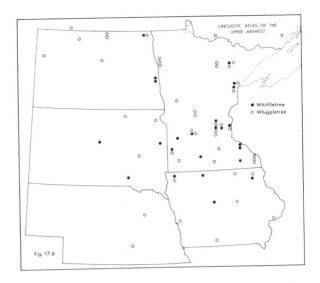

Fig. 17.6

39, 42-43, *46, 53-55, 64; 101, 103, 108,
115, 141; 208, 221-22; ¹313, 314, 317,
323; ¹†413, ¹429.
whippletree 2-3, ¹*5, 7-9, 11-14, 16,
c18, c20, s?24, 27-28, 32, 34-36, 40,
¹42, c*43, 44, †46, 47, c49, c56, 57-59,
62, ?65; 102, 105, 107, 118, 124, c144;
201, :203, 204-5, 208-9, 211, †222; :?304,
305, 308, ¹316, 327, c?328; ¹404, 416,
423.
no response 22, 38; 110; 310, 319, 326;
410, 415, 431.

Comment:

singletree: "More correct" than 'whiffletree'--53. Heard occasionally--201.
Inf. knows only the word, not the refer-
ent--406. whiffletree: "Proper" term--*46.
whippletree: Heard in North Dakota--*5.
Inf. ridicules this term as "wrong"--42.
Used by inf. in youth--46. Inf. so pronounced it but spelled it 'whifeltree'--
105. Inf. says this is the most common
term here, but he generally uses 'whiffletree'--208. Inf. does not remember whether it is for one horse or a team--65. Inf.
not sure of the referent--328.

17.7 evener (for two or more horses).
NE 173.

The device by which two--or more--hors-
es are hitched to a buggy or wagon produces some semantic confusion. For a team
this device consists of three bars, one
each for the two horses and a third to
the ends of which the center of each of
the other bars is attached. Some infs.
have a term for the whole set and another
term for the third bar; others use one
term interchangeably for both the set and
the third bar. Several use evener for the

third or equalizing bar and the plural
eveners for the entire set.

Evener competes with doubletree(s), with
the latter slightly more frequent (82% to
54%). Doubletree seems to be more congen-
ial with Midland speakers. No contrast by
speaker type appears. Double whiffletree/
whippletree is a minority form characteristic of Northern speech territory.

CL 57: Doubletree is also favored by
82% of the 1,015 respondents, evener by
31%. Spreader, rare in the field records,
is reported in 15 checklists, 12 of
which are from Minnesota.

17.7a evener (usually behind two horses;
the entire set).
  doubletree 2, :3, 4, *5, 6, s?9, ?¹10,
14-15, 19, 21, 23-24, *28, ¹30, :35, s36,
39-41, 45-47, 56, 58, 60-61, *64; 101-3,
*104, 107-9, 111-16, 119-22, 124-30,
?131, 132-33, *134, 135-36, 138-44, 146-
52; 201-2, :203, 210, 212, 216-17, 219-
21, ʳ222, 224-25; c301, 302-3, st304,
311, 313-15, 318, 320, 322-23, ?324-25;
401, c405, 407, 409, 411-14, 416, 418-22,
s423, c424, 425, 427-30, 432-37. ~s 117;
204, 208-9, 211, 213-14, 218; 312, 321.
  double whiffletree 42.
  double whippletree 13.
  equalizer 129; ¹202.
  evener 17, ¹21, 26, *28, 30, s?†31, 43,
c44, *46, †49, 53, 58, c59, s64; sn65;
105, s114, 115, †119, 122, *123, s¹124,
125, 127-28, s129, 137-38, s140, 142,
sn146, 147-49; 202, ¹208, 225; 307, ¹311,
s316, 320; 401, 409, 414, 416, 418, s420,
421-22, 424, 427-29, 436-37. ~s 8; 117;
¹208, 222, 224; 413.
  four-horse evener 405.
  hitch 119; 413, 430.
  mapletree ?¹18.
  pair of eveners 216. ~ doubletrees 429.
~ whippletrees 25.
  rigging 6.
  set of eveners 8. ~ doubletrees 54; 207;
404.
  spreader :35.
  three-horse evener c220; *325; 407-8,
*417.
  thribletree 320.
  tripletree *28.
  whiffletree 16; †119, 135; †427. ~s
317.
  whippletree 7, 10, 16, 18, 45, 48, 50,
?65; 104, 106, 114, 140; 212, 216. ~s
118; 206.
  no response 1, ?11, 12, 20, 22, 27, 29,
32-34, 37-38, 51-52, 55, 62-63; 110, 145;
205, 215, 223, ?226; 305-6, 308-10, 319,
326, ?327, 328; 402-3, 406, 408, 410,
415, 426, 431.
Comment:

doubletree: Inf. knows the term but not
its exact meaning--131. Lighter than
'eveners'--224. evener: Inf. remembers the
term, but is not sure of meaning--31.
Used by inf.'s father (from N.Y.)--49.
Term formerly used by inf.--119. Used on
a heavier wagon than a 'doubletree'--58.
Used on a buggy; a 'doubletree' is used
on a wagon--225. For more than two horses
--115, 125, 137, 146; 202; 401, 409, 416,
422, 427, 429, 436-37. For four horses--
142; 311, 320; 428. "For a five-horse
rig"--149. eveners: For more than two
horses--117, 145. For three horses--413.
For five horses--208. equalizer: For more
than two horses--202. singletree: Inf.
corrected by her husband--64. spreader:
For three horses--35. whiffletrees: Pronounced [hwɪvltri·z]--317.

b. evener (behind two horses) the long
bar.
  center stick 311.
  doubletree 1, *5, 24, 26-27, *28, 51,
54-55, 62; 137, 145; 202, 204, 206-8,
223; 306, 309; 403, 407-8, 412, 417.
  evener 6-8, 12, c13, 16, snt20, 23, 25,
*28, 29, 40-41, :sn42, 45, 48, 50, 56,
61, *64; 101, *104, 106-7, 109, 112-13,
116, 126, 134, 145; 205-6, s¹208, 209-10,
213-18, 220-21, 223-24; ¹306, 321.
  three-horse evener 56, *64.
  two-horse evener 19.
  whiffletree 51-52.
  whippletree 63.
  no response 2-4, 9-11, 14-15, 17-18,
22, 30-39, 43-44, 46-47, 49, 53, 55, 57-
60, 65; 102-3, 105, 108, 110-11, 114-15,
117-25, 127-35, 135-36, 138-44, 146-52;
201, 203, 211-12, 219, 225-26; 301-5,
307-8, 310, 312-20; 401-2, 404-6, 408-11,
413-16, 418-37.

Comment:

evener: "I haven't heard that for years"
--20. For more than two horses--145.

c. singletree (behind each horse in a two-
horse rig if response is different from
that for 17.6).
  doubletree 19; 404.
  evener *26, 60.
  singletree 7, 23, 54-55, *64; 108; 221.
  whippletree 25; 215.

18.1 He was hauling wood in his wagon.
NE 180. WG 12, 23, 57-58; F76.

Hauling, the dominant form in the eastern states, has increased its dominance
in the UM. Northern drawing survives only
as a relic with five speakers, one of them
in Manitoba. Carting, found on the Atlantic coast, appears only four times, one
of them in Ontario and one, in the Black

Hills, from an inf. whose father was born in New Jersey.

Characteristic of timbered and formerly timbered areas, tote is used to designate the transporting of supplies to a logging camp, usually in a "tote-wagon" on a "tote-road." Its use extends into the northern prairies of North Dakota as well. The term, however, was not reported in the forest areas of Wisconsin.

See also chart 71.4.

CL 58: Hauling likewise dominates the checklist returns. Toting occurs once as a write-in in northern Minnesota, carting five times in Minnesota and the Dakotas, besides two instances of New England coastal teaming from a Minnesota informant of English and Canadian parents and from an eastern Nebraska informant of New York and New Hampshire ancestry.

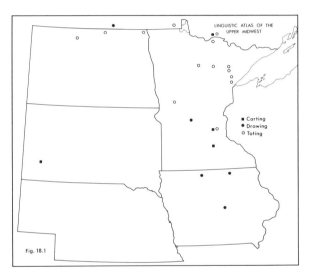

carting 2, 33, 48; 311.
delivering 32.
drawing 28; c103, c105, s¹118, c132; 202.
fetching 114.
hauling 1, 3-8, c9, 10-15, c16, f17, 18-20, c21, 22-24, c25, 26-27, c29, 30, :sn31, 32, sn34, :35, :36, 37, :sn38, 39-41, c42, 43-48, :sn49, 50-60, c61, 62-65; 101-4, 106-18, c119, s120, 121-35, c136, 137-52; 201, c203, 204-7, c208-9, 210-21, c222, 223, c224, 225, :s226; 301-10, c312, 313-21, c322, 323, c324, 325-28; 401-4, c405, 406-8, c409, :s410, 411-12, cvr413, 414-15, cvr416, :c417, 418, 420-21, c422, 423-34, c435, 436, c437.
taking 419.
toting 1-2, 5, ¹†7, sn†8, 10-11, 13-14, c15, 16, 20, ¹†21, †29, †31, 33; sn203, c204, 207, †220.

Comment:

delivering: Pret.--32. drawing: Infin. --103. hauling: More common for inf. than 'carting'--48. toting: Used in context of bringing supplies to a lumber camp over a 'tote-road'--5, 7, 11. "An old lumberjack term"--29. Also 'tote-teams'--†8, c13, 15; †220. Also 'tote-wagon' and 'tote-sled'--¹†21. With reference to a car--20. With reference to a truck--204. Used by inf.'s father (from R.I.)--31.

18.3 harrow. NE 167.

For breaking up clods of earth after plowing three different types of implements are typically employed. The oldest, once made entirely of wood, consists of pegs or spikes set in horizontal bars. A second has teeth of spring steel instead of spikes. A third has rotary disks mounted on an axle. The first is generally known as a drag, although outside the Northern speech zone it is more likely to be called a harrow. The second is commonly known as a harrow. To avoid ambiguity descriptive epithets are often used with each term. The third type of implement is always simply a disk or, rarely, a disk harrow.

CL 64: The 1,043 checklist respondents strongly confirmed the distribution of the terms drag and harrow, without distinction of reference. With a total contrast in the UM of 64% for harrow and 50% for drag, the analysis by states for drag is: Mn. 69%, northern Ia. 67%, southern Ia. 4%, N.D. 71%, S.D. 63%, Nb. 19%; and for harrow it is Mn. 47%, northern Ia. 50%, southern Ia. 98%, N.D. 47%, S.D. 54%, and Nb. 93%.

a. harrow (all lexical responses)
disk 3, 7, 9-10, 12, →15, 18-20, 25,

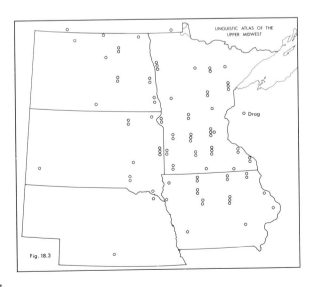

28, 33-34, 42, 44, 48-51, 57-61, 63; 119,
150; †204, 215, 217; 301-3, 306-8, →311,
313, 316, 318, 324-25; 404, →406.
  drag 1, ¹2, 7, :9, 10-13, 15-17, 19,
24-28, ¹†29-30, 31, 34-35, s†36, 37, 41-
51, ¹52, c53, 54-55, 57-58, ¹59, 60-61,
63-65; 102-8, 111-19, 139, 151-52; 201,
203-4, ¹205, ¹207, 208, †210, 211-12,
→213, †214, ¹217, 218-19, 221-22, !223,
225-26; †302-3, 305-7, 312, 317-19, †321,
322-23, 325, 327-28; †404, cvr407, ¹413-
14, 430. ~ plow c35. flexible ~ 7. pounder ~ 117. spiketooth ~ †7, 12, 21, s¹22.
springtooth ~ 1, 10, 12, 21-22, 25. steel
~ 117. straight-tooth ~ 22. tumble ~ 8.
wooden ~ 303.
  harrow 1-3, 5-6, 8, 14-15, 17-20, 22-
23, 26-27, *28, 29, c30, s32, 33, c35,
36-37, 39-40, 42-45, ¹47, 48, s49, 50,
52, 54-56, c†57, 58-59, *60, 61-62, 65;
101, 104-5, 109, 112, 114-17, s118, 119-
34, 136-38, c140, 141-49, s150, 151-52;
202, 204-9, 211, c¹212, †213, 214-15,
217-18, *219, 220-22, →223; 301, ¹302,
304-6, 308-9, 311, 313-15, 317-18, c320,
321, 323, 326, 328; 401-5, 408-29, cvr430,
431-35, c436, 437. "A" ~ 135. boss ~ 7-8;
224; 306. disk ~ 24, 53-54; 308, 320.
field ~ 19. flexible ~ 224. pegtooth ~
24; 206. plow ~ 20. Scotch ~ 216. spiketooth ~ 19; 206, 212. springtooth ~ 3,
10, 19, 24, 41, 58; 216, 220; 306; 437.
  pegtooth 4.
  pulverizer 316.
  spiketooth sn2; 301.
  springtooth 4, *26, *28; 208, 221-22,
225; 301, 306-7.
  no response ?38; 110; 310.

Comment:

  drag: Inf. considers it obsolete, but
says her son-in-law uses the term now--
36. More usual here than 'harrow'--43,
47. Older term than 'harrow'; synonyms--
48.

b. With spiketeeth
  drag :9, 11, 13, 15-17, 19, 24-28, 31,
35, 37, 41-48, 50-51, ¹52, c53, 54-55,
58, 60-61, 63; 103, 106-8, 113, 116, 118;
203-4, ¹205, 208, †210, 212, †214, ¹217,
218-19, 221-22, !223, 225-26; †303, 306,
312, 318, †321, 322-24, 327; 407, ¹413-14.
~ plow c35. pounder ~ 117. spiketooth ~
†7, 12, 21, s¹22. steel ~ 117. straight-
tooth ~ 22. wooden ~ 303.
  harrow †1, 2-3, 18, 20, 23, 26-27, 29,
c30, c35, 36, 40, 44-45, 50, 52, 54, 59,
*60, 61-62; 116, †122, 126, 133, 152;
204-5, 208-9, 211, †213, 214-15, 217,
220-21; 306, †309, 311, 313-15, 317-18,
c320, 321, 323; 402-3, 408-10, 413-14,
421-22, 427-29, cvr430, 431, 433-35. "A"
~ 135. boss ~ 7-8; 224; 306. field ~ 19.
pegtooth ~ 24. spiketooth ~ 19; 206, 212.

pegtooth 4; 206.
spiketooth sn2; 301.

Comment:

  drag: Inf. says this is colloquial for
'pegtooth harrow'--24. Inf.'s usual term
--44. Inf. says this is the most common
term here--43, 45, 47. harrow: Either
homemade or "boughten"--315. spiketooth
drag: Inf. says 'harrows' are bought and
'drags' are homemade--7.

c. With springteeth
  drag 1, 27-28, 49, 54; 115; 203; 407.
flexible ~ 7. springtooth ~ 1, 10, 12, 21-
22, 25. tumble ~ 8.
  harrow 2, 17, 23, 27, *28, 42, s49, 54-
55, 58; 115; 122; ¹212, 218, 222; 323;
408. flexible ~ 224. plow ~ 20. spring ~
15; 305, 323. springtooth ~ 3, 10, 19,
24, 41; 216, 220; 436.
  springtooth 4, *26, *28, 50; 208, 212,
221-22, 225; 301, 306-7.

18.4 stone boat. NE 168. WG 17, 18, 20,
58; F5b, F7, F78.

  Stone boat, the western New England
term for a wheelless vehicle used chiefly
for moving stones off a field, is common
in the UM except in strongly Midland-oriented territory, Nebraska, where Midland
sled dominates. No term is reported by
many speakers in unglaciated southern Iowa. Go-devil, found in former timber country of northern Minnesota, usually refers
to a forked tree trunk upon which the end
of a log rests when it is being dragged
from the woods. One inf. describes a go-
devil as having wheels; another, in Nebraska, describes a large low vehicle with
small wheels, used in transporting hay-
stacks, called a haysled.

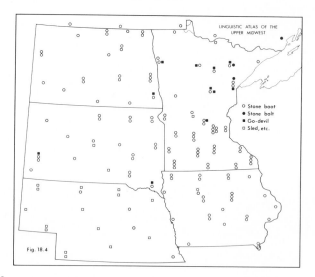

LINGUISTIC ATLAS OF THE
UPPER MIDWEST

○ Stone boat
● Stone bolt
■ Go-devil
□ Sled, etc.

Fig. 18.4

dead man 309.
drag 28, 44; ¹414, 431.
dray 15.
flat boat ?42.
go-devil 7, 10, s11, 12, →13, sn!15,
¹18, 21-23, 30; 225; 311, ?¹312, 324.
  jigger 51.
  jumper 14.
  lizard 132; 314.
  sled *28; 315, 321; 401-3, 405, s406,
408, †409, 410, ?411, 412, c417, 418,
¹423, 429-30, 437. corn ~ †437. hay ~ 406.
stone ~ 425. water ~ †409, 429, 436.
  sledge ¹435.
  sleigh 407.
  slip ¹408.
  stone boat 1, !2, 4-8, 10, 12-13, 17-
19, 21, 23-24, c25, 26-27, c29, 30-31,
33-34, 36-37, 39-64, snc65; 101-6, 108-9,
112-18, s119, 120, 124-25, :¹126, 128-29,
132, s133, 134, 137-39, c141, 143, 148-
49; 201-2, c203, 204-9, !210, 211-18,
*219, 220-22, !223, 224, c225, :s226;
301-6, c307, 308, 311-14, :s315, c316,
317-18, 320, ¹321, 322-23, 325, 327-28;
404, 413, 420, ¹421, ¹†422, ¹†*432, 434.
  stone bolt 3, 13, 15.
  water sleigh 407.
  no response 9, 16, 18, 32, 35, ?38;
107, 110-11, 121-23, 127, 130-31, 135-36,
140, 142, 144-47, 150-52; 310, 319; 415-
16, 419, 424, 426-28, 433.

Comment:

  drag: Usu.--44. Inf. says the object
isn't used here--431. go-devil: Usu.--12.
Name is familiar, but object is not known
--11. Often made of oak fork--21. Homemade with two or four wheels, often of
wood--225. "Used for skidding logs"--311.
For hauling water--324. Inf. says that a
'go-devil' is a child's tricycle--¹†309.
Inf. says a 'go-devil' is a haybuck--323.
Inf. says a 'go-devil' is a disk-like
cultivator for corn--*325; 412. Inf. says
a 'go-devil' is a ditcher--409. jigger:
On four wheels, but set close to the
ground--51. lizard: Made of a tree fork--
132. Mormon: Inf. says it was a horse-
drawn scraper used by Mormons--†409. sled:
For hay--408. corn sled: Used when cutting corn--437. hay sled: On wheels--406.
stone sled: Inf. suggests that he has acquired the term through reading, but
thinks the sleds are used in nearby quar-
ries--425. slip: Heard locally and in
western Colorado--408. stone boat: Usu.--
42. = lizard--132. Heard in Wyoming--422.
Inf. says not common here--421. Inf. says
not used here--434. Also for logs--23. For
dirt--54. For dirt and barrels--55. For
barrels or tanks of water--64; 301, 315,
328. For stones and water--65. Not used
for stones--101, 109. Seldom used for

stones; used for moving any heavy objects
--109. stone bolt: Inf. says she would
spell it 'b-o-l-t'--3.

18.5 sled. NE 573-74. WG 59.

  a. Terms for a vehicle for traveling
over snow exhibit great variety but no
distinctive regional pattern. (The cur-
rently popular motor-driven vehicle, however, is already known by two regional
variants, snowmobile south of the Canadian border and snow toboggan north of
it.) In this part the entire variety is
exhibited; not all these terms appear in
the defined categories in the later sections, since the field records sometimes
fail to indicate the type of vehicle denoted by a given term.

  barrel stave 202.
  bob 118, 120-21, 151; 221; 309. ~sled
3, 6, 9-10, 17-18, 20-21, 23-25, 29-30,
32, 35, c36, 39, s41, 42, 45-54, 56-58,
60-65; 101-4, 106, 108, 111-13, 116-17,
119, 121-31, 133, 135-37, 139-50, 152;
222; 301, *306, 307-9, 314, 316-20, 322-
24; 404-5, *412, sn413, 414-16, 420-23,
sn424, 425-26, 428, 430, 432-35. ~ sleigh
1, 4, 51, 59, c65; 105, 107, 109, 118;
209.
  bobs 55; 141. pair of ~ 118.
  coaster ¹124, 125, 137; 307. ~ sled
34; 308.
  cutter c36, 43-46, 48, 52-53, 59-61,
63; 109, 116, 118, 121, 151; ¹413, 414,
sn415, †421, 422, 426, 428, 430, 433-34.
  double sled 137.
  flat sled 220.
  flier 13; 150.
  ground sled 62.
  hand sled 15, 27, c29, 41; 107, 118-19,
139, 142, 148; 218; 311, *316, 322; 405.
~ sleigh 201-2, 209.
  jumper 109,
  long sled 41.
  mud sled 62.
  pung 103, 116; 426.
  scoop shovel 211, ¹†214, 218.
  scoot 23.
  shay 45.
  shin breaker †120.
  sled 1-2, 4-8, 10-19, 21-26, 28, 30-36,
38-40, 42-47, c49, 50-56, !57, 58-65;
101-6, 108-34, 136-38, 141, 143-47, 149-
52; 203-8, 210-11, c212-13, 214-27, 219,
221-26; 301-2, 304-8, c309, 310, 312-13,
c314, 315-21, 323-28; 401-6, 408-16, 418-
26, 428-37.
  sleigh 3, 13, 34, 45-48, 51-52, c56,
57-58, 60-61; 104, 106, 121, 135; 220;
407, 424, 426, 428, 431, 433.
  sliding sled 41.
  spring-runner sled 35.
  tandem sled 138.

team sled 424.
three-kneed sleigh 225.
toboggan 2-5, 8, 10, 17-18, 28, 32-33, 40, 50, 54, 56; 102-3, 105, 110, 114, 117, 132, 136, 139; c211, 218, 220; 307, 316, 318-19; 413, ⱡ414, 416, 425, 428.
winter sled 62.
no response 37; 303; 417, 427.

Comment:

bobsled: Bought--9. Homemade--21. Larger than a 'sled'--425. bob sleigh: Bought --209. Homemade--11; 404. coaster sled: "Boughten"--34. sled: Bought--33, 38; 210, 219, 222; 304, 326, 328. "Boughten" --34; 141; 321, 309-10, 321; 402, 408. Homemade--ⱡ1, 11; ⱡ401. Object is used in the city rather than the country--17. "Ought to be 'sleigh'"--401. sleigh: Either bought or homemade--2, 34. For hauling--13. no response: No hills here and no sleds; inf. never even saw a sled as a boy--303. Inf. never had one--417.

b. Sled is the common term for the single vehicle with two runners used chiefly by children in sliding downhill. Older informants frequently described the homemade variety, usually with metal-clad wooden runners, that preceded the commercial type with all-metal runners identified by younger informants.
coaster sled 308.
flier 13; 150.
hand sled 15, 27, c29, 41; 107, 118-19, 139, 142, 148; 218; 311, *316, 322; 405.
~ sleigh 201, ⱡ202, 209.
shin breaker ⱡ120.
sled 2, 4-8, 10, 12, 15, 19, 21-22, 24-26, 30-32, 39-40, 50-51, 54, 62-63; 101, 105-6, 108, 111, 114, 116, 119-21, 137-38; 203-4, 206-8, 211, c212-13, 214-17, 221, 223-24; 301-2, 305, 307, 312-13, 316-18, 320, 323-25; 403-5, 409-16, 418-24, 428-36.
sleigh 3; 121, 135; 220; 407.
spring-runner sled 35.
three-kneed sleigh 225.

Comment:

flier: Metal runners--13. hand sled: Homemade--218; 311, 322; ⱡ405. Metal runners--29. Metal-clad wooden runners--218. hand sleigh: Homemade--202, ⱡ209. Wooden runners--201. sled: Bought--205; 312; 411. "Boughten"--30; 211, 217; 410. Homemade-- 4, ⱡ7-8, ⱡ10, ⱡ21-22, ⱡ24-26, ⱡ31; ⱡ206-8, ⱡ213-16, 221, ⱡ223-24; ⱡ301-2, ⱡ312, 320, ⱡ323-24; ⱡ403, ⱡ405, ⱡ409-10, 411. Metal runners--30; 203, 215; 312; 405, 411, 416, 431. Wooden runners--ⱡ7-8, ⱡ10, 12, ⱡ22, ⱡ24; ⱡ204, ⱡ206-8, 212, ⱡ213-14; ⱡ323, ⱡ325; ⱡ403, ⱡ409, 429, 431-32, 436. Metal-clad wooden runners--2, 4, 19, ⱡ21, ⱡ26, ⱡ31; 221, ⱡ223-24; ⱡ313, 320; ⱡ404,

ⱡ409, ⱡ412, 413, 416, 418, ⱡ419. sleigh: "Boughten"--220. Homemade--135; ⱡ407. Wooden runners--135. Metal-clad wooden runners--ⱡ407. spring-runner sled: Bought --35. three-kneed sleigh: Inf.'s was about 5' long and pulled by his dog--225.

c. Bobsled is the usual term for a vehicle consisting of two pairs of runners, one of which swivels for steering, supporting a long board or plank for several riders. The single response of tandem sled is from an Iowa informant whose maternal grandmother came from Massachusetts, where the form was found once during the New England survey. It also occurred twice in Maine.
bob 120-21, 151; 221. ~sled 6, 20, 23, 30, 32, 35, c36, 42, 54, 60-61, 64; 101, 106, 108, 111, 116-17, 119, 121-24, 127, 139, 145, 149, 152; 308, 316, 324; 405, 414, 416, 435. ~ sleigh 4, 51; 105, 118.
bobs 55. pair of ~ 118.
coaster ⱡ124, 125, 137; 307.
double sled 137.
sled 52; 308.
tandem sled 138.
toboggan 117, 136, 139.

Comment:

bob: Homemade--221. bobsled: Homemade-- 20. bobs: Homemade--ⱡ55. tandem sled: Pronounced /ˈtænmən ˌslɛd/--138. toboggan: Usu.: = bobsled--117.

d. A flat vehicle without runners but with one upturned end is always termed toboggan. Several additional words appeared as designating less common devices for sliding on snow. Terms in this group were not systematically collected.
barrel stave 202.
flat sled ⱡ220.
scoop shovel 211, ⱡⱡ214, 218.
scoot 23.
toboggan 2-3, 32; 102-3, 110, 114; c211, 218; 307, 318; 413; ⱡ414, 416, 428.

Comment:

flat sled: Made of two barrel staves-- 220. scoop shovel: Not a sled, but used to slide on--211, 218. Inf. found children using this in Jamestown--214. scoot: A bent barrel stave with a strap and heel block--23.

e. Horse-drawn vehicles for traversing snow are principally of two kinds, those with two sets of runners and those with one set. The former type, generally called bobsled or bobsleigh, is typically drawn by a team and used for any kind of freight. The latter type, generally called cutter or, less frequently, sleigh, consists of a box or compartment large enough for two or three passengers, supported on two runners, and drawn by a single horse. Two Type I northern Iowa speakers of Maine and New York ancestry respectively responded with pung, a relic New England term for a home-made sleigh often with solid wooden runners. One Type III Nebraska inf. with some New York background also reported the use of pung.

bob 120-21. ~sled 25, 32, 39, 45-47, 51-53, 57, 62-64, s65; 102-4, 106, 112-13, 119, 121, 124, *124, 125-26, 133, 136-37, 139, 144; *306, 307, 317-19, 324; sn413, 414-15, 420-22, sn424, 426, 428, 430, 432-34. ~ sleigh 59; 107, 109, 118.
cutter 44-46, 48, 52-53, 59-61, 63; 109, 118, 121; ˡ413, 414, sn415, †421, 422, 426, 428, 430, 433-34.
jumper 109.
pair of bobs 118.
pung 103, 116; 426.
sled 44, 46; 114, 151; 433.
sleigh 45-47, 51-52; 104, 106; 426, 428, 431, 433.
team sled 424.

Comment:

bobsled: For one horse--57. For one or two horses--46, 51. For two horses--39, 45, 52-53; 103-4, 133, 136. For one to four horses--47. bob sleigh: For two horses--59; 107, 109, 118. cutter: For one horse--44-46, 52-53, 59; 109, 118; 415, 428, 434. For one or two horses--60. "Fancy"--44. "One-seated shay"--414. = sleigh--433. jumper: Homemade--109. pair of bobs: For two horses--118. pung: For one horse--103, 116. Homemade--116. sled: For two horses--44, 46. sleigh: For one or two horses--47, 51. For two horses--45-46, 52; 104. Usu.; = bobsled--106. = cutter--426. "Sort of custom made"; more elegant than a 'sled' or 'bobsled'--433.

18.6 Current dictionaries as well as the New England Atlas do not distinguish clearly between two objects different in appearance and in function but often similar in designation. One is a rack with X-shaped ends for supporting a length of wood to be sawed into chunks for firewood; the other is a rack with ∧-shaped ends, customarily used with a like rack by a carpenter for supporting boards which he is planing or sawing. By different speakers both kinds of rack are called (saw)buck and (saw)horse, but not in the same proportion. Other terms also are used for both objects. The extent of this semantic overlap appears in H.B. Allen, "Semantic confusion: a report from the Atlas files," PADS No. 33 (1960), 3-13.

a. sawbuck (for firewood). NE 162. WG

25, 37, 59; F81.

Sawbuck, common in the originally Dutch- and German-speaking areas of New York and Pennsylvania, dominates the UM with a 61% frequency ranging from 72% in Minnesota to 40% in Nebraska. The more ambiguous sawhorse, widely used in the Atlantic states, is reported by one-third of all UM infs., with a range from 52% in North Dakota to 28% in Iowa and Nebraska. No clear distribution pattern of these two words emerges, although sawbuck seems slightly favored in the eastern part of the UM. But the minority term (wood)jack, carried west from the Alleghenies, also occurs several times in Midland speech territory; and rack, first reported in southeastern Ohio, has single occurrences in Iowa and Nebraska.

CL 65: Sawbuck has an over-all frequency of 62%, ranging from 74% in Minnesota to 49% in North Dakota; sawhorse has an over-all frequency of 40% with a range from 50% in North Dakota to 30% in Minnesota. The mail data correspond almost precisely to the field data. Jack occurs nine times in Midland territory.

billy goat 43.
buck 130; sncr427. wood ~ 135; :?304, 421.
bucksaw 32, 58.
horse 38.
jack 416-17. saw ~ 218; 405, 417. wood ~ 322; 416.
rack 403. saw ~ 147.
sawbuck 3, s4, ˡ*5, 7, :!sn8, :9, 10, :12, 13-16, 18-23, 26, :27, 28-30, sn†31, 33-35, :36, 37, 39-43, 45-48, :49, 51-53, †54, 55-58, 60-61, ˡ62, 63; 101, s103, 105-9, 111, s112, 114, s115, 117, 119-22, †123, 124-26, 128-29, 132-34, 136-38, s139, 140-43, s144, 146, 148-50, 152; 206-8, 210-13, ˡ214, 216-17, *219, 220, 222, 225; 301-3, ˡ305, 306-7, 309, 311, :312, 314, ?317, 320, 323, 325, :sn326, 328; 404, 408, 413-14, 418-20, 422, s423, 425, 428, ?431, *432, 433-35. s?436.
sawhorse 1-2, 5-6, 11, 17, 24-25, †31, 35, 43, c44, 50, 54, 60, 62, 64; 101, 103-4, 113, 116, 118, 123, 127, 131, 134, 140, 144-45, 151; 201-2, 204-5, 207-9, 214, 219, 221, 223-24; 308, 310, 316, cr317, 318-19, 324, 327; 401-2, 406-7, 409-10, :411, 412, 415, 424, 426, ?427, 429.
trestle 224.
wood horse, wooden ~ 65.
no response 59; 102, 110; 203, ?215, 226; 313, 321; 430, ?437.

Comment:

bucksaw: Inf. says this is the saw used

with the sawbuck--307. sawbuck: "Not much wood bucked up here now"--54. Inf. has heard this term applied to the saw--308. Inf. offered this term but corrected himself by saying that the sawbuck is the saw--317. Inf. offered this term but said that she actually does not know this object--431. sawhorse: Usu.--224. no response: Inf. never saw one--315. Referent not found here in the treeless plains area--321.

b. sawhorse (used by carpenters). NE 162. WG 25, 49, 59; F81.

Sawhorse, with 75% of the responses, and horse, with 15%, for a total of 90%, designate the carpenter's bench throughout most of the UM. Their Northern orientation, however, appears in the nonoccurrence of horse in Nebraska and its 2.6% frequency in South Dakota, and in the 42% frequency of sawhorse in Nebraska and 76% frequency in Iowa. The chief competing term is sawbuck, with 24% frequency in Nebraska. Trestle appears sporadically in Iowa, North Dakota, and Nebraska for the total of 3.5%; and (saw) bench, reported most heavily on the southern Atlantic coast and in southern West Virginia, turns up with four instances in Iowa and one in Nebraska.

CL 66: Since the mailed checklist offered only sawhorse and trestle for this item, sawhorse dominates the responses. Bench was twice written in; so was sawtable.

bench 44; 405; saw ~ 204, 207; 322; 405.
bucksaw jack *417.
carpenter horse 19; ~'s horse 1, 35; 310. ~'s sawhorse 202.
horse 6, 9, 13-14, 16, 18, 21-22, 34-35, 38, 49, 57-58; 122, 127, 129-30, 136, ¹141, 147-48, 150; 208, 212, 217, 222.
jack 143.
rack 207.
sawbuck 17, :25, 48; 135, 140; :sn401, sn402, 409, 415, 429-31, 434.
sawhorse 2-5, 7-8, 10-12, 15, s¹19, 20, s23, 24, 26-30, :?32, 33-34, 37, 39-45, *46, 47-48, 50-56, c59, 60-61, 63-64; 101-2, 104-21, 123-26, 128, :131, 132-34, 137-42, 145-46, 149, 151; 205-11, 213-16, 218-23, 225-26; 301-15, *316, 317-20, 323-28; 403-4, 407-8, 411, 413-14, 416, 418-23, 425-28, ¹431, *432, 433, 436-37.
sawing horse 36.
stanchion 103.
trestle ¹2-3; 129, 138, 146, 152; 224; 404, 435.
truss 420.
wooden horse 321.
no response ?31, 62, 65; 144; ?201, 203; :406, ?410, 412, 424.

Comment:

horse: "It's not a 'sawhorse'"--9. Inf. says this is the term used by carpenters --141. trestle: Inf. heard this term used by a carpenter--2. Inf. says it is taller than a 'sawhorse,' about 6' tall--404. Pronounced with /ʌ/, not /ɛ/--138; 224. no response: Husband says this is a 'horse'; she disagrees, but has no alternative--201.

19.1 strop. NE 156.

For the strip of leather used in sharpening a razor the usual designation is a variant of strap, although both the variants and the term hone refer also to a similarly used wooden bar covered with leather or an abrasive. Distribution varies significantly only with age and class. Strap /æ/ is favored by older inf.'s (I 52%, II 42%, III 38%), as is the infrequent strope /o/ (I 4%, II 1%, III 0). Strop /ɑ, ɒ, ɔ/ is favored by younger speakers (I 45%, II 62%, III 69%).

Reflecting the change from one variant to another is the functional contrast revealed by four infs. all of whom use strap as the noun but, for the verb, three of whom use strop and one of whom uses strope.

hone 13-14, 48, 59; 139; 307; 423.
razor strap /æ/ 16, 35, c61; 117, 127; 208; 305, 317-18; 429, 432, 434-36.
razor strop 32, 45, 52-53.
strap 4-6, ?8, 9, 13, 15-17, 24, 26, ?31, 34, 36, 38-41, 43, †46, 48-49, 56, 60, 63-65; 101, 105-6, 109, 113-15, 118, 123-24, 129, 131-35, 137-38, 143, :144, 145-46, 150-51; 201-2, 204-5, 207, 209-11, 216, !217, 220; 302-3, 306-7, †309, 310, †312, 316, 322-25, 327-28; 405, 407, 410-11, 415, 417, 420-24, 427, 433.
strop 1-3, 7, cr8, 10-12, 14, 18, 20-23, 25, 27-30, cr31, 32-33, 37, †39, 40, 42, †43, 44, *46, 47, s¹48, 50-51, 55, 57-58, s59, †60, 62-63; 102-4, 107-8, 110-12, 116, 119-22, 125-26, c127, 128, 130, *131, *134, 136, ¹139, 140-42, 147-49, 152; 203, 206, 212-15, 218-19, 221-23, 225-26; 301, 304, 308, →309, 312-16, 319-21, 326; 401-4, 406, 408-9, 412-14, 416, 418-19, 425-26, 428, 430-31, 433, 437.
strope 19, ?54; →124; 224; *302, 311.

Comment:

hone: Inf.'s usual term--59. Inf. says a hone is an abrasive bar with a handle--423. strap: Verb is 'strop'--137. Verb is 'strope'--*417. "They strop it on a strap" --216. "You hone it on a strap." "I don't know which it is"--63. strope: Inf. has used one for years but is unsure of its

name--54. "They call it 'strope' nowadays"
--124.

19.3a seesaw. NE 577. WG 16, 25, 47,
48, 59; F13, F79.

The recreational apparatus consisting
essentially of a balanced plank upon
which children may ride alternately up
and down is known as a teeter-totter by
four out of five UM infs. (Mn. 75%, Ia.
83%, N.D. 77%, S.D. 92%, Nb. 84%). This
Hudson Valley and New Jersey term dominates not only both the New England
equivalents teeter with its seven instances, four of which are in Minnesota,
and teeter board, preserved only in Minnesota, Iowa, and North Dakota, but also
the more literary and urban seesaw, reported from an evenly distributed 15% of
the infs., more than half of whom are in
Type I. Extension of teeter board into
the New England settlements along the
Ohio River may account for its greater UM
incidence in the Midland speech area of
Iowa.

CL 99: Distribution of the principal
terms among 1,045 respondents is closely
correlated with that reported by fieldworkers, even to the greater incidence of
teeter board in southern Iowa and the decline of all minor variants in the three
western states. Teetering-horse, not reported in the East, was checked by three
Minnesotans and one northern Iowan. This
term may be a hybrid derived from teetering board and the Midland ridy horse (not
recorded, however, in the UM); but probably significant is the fact that three
of the respondents had parents born in
Germany and one had all grandparents born
in Germany; the German term for rocking-
horse is Schaukelpferd. Local Massachusetts tilt appeared twice (Mn. and Ia.);
so did Plymouth Colony tinter board (Ia.
and Nb.).

  seesaw !3, 6, 17, 20, †24, 30, 32, 39,
41, 45, *45, 48, 51, 58, s59, ¹61; 106,
113, 115, 123, 126, 130; 202, 206, 209,
214, 222; 323, 327-28; 414, 417, 422,
424, 428.
  teeter 13, 29, †39, 56, 65; 221; 314;
420.
  teeter board 40, 47, 62, 65; 122, ¹131,
135, 139, 142, 144, 147; 218, !220.
  teetering board 132.
  teeter pole 25.
  teeter-totter !1, 2, !4, 5, 7-16, 18,
21-24, 26-28, 30, :31, 33-34, !35, 36-38,
42, f43, s44, 45-46, 48-51, !52, 53-55,
57-58, 60-61, 63-64; 101-5, 107-14, 116-
21, 123-31, 133-34, 136-38, 140-41, 143,
145-46, 148-49, c150, 151-52; 201, 203-5,

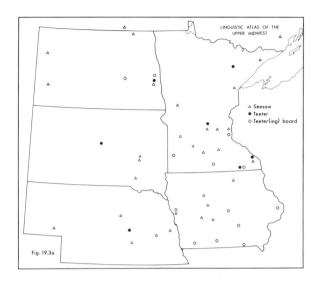

Fig. 19.3a

!207, 208, c210, !211-12, 213, !215-16,
217, !219, 221-26; 301-5, *306, 307-13,
315-22, !324, 325-26; 401, !402, 403-6,
:407, 408-9, :s410, 411-13, c†414, 415-
16, 418-19, 421, 423, 425-27, c428, 429-
37.
  teeting totter !44.
  no response 19.

Comment:

  seesaw: Term "used as a kid"; response
obtained by mail--24. teeter board: Verb
is seesaw--47. teeter-totter: Response
obtained by mail--24. Usu.--51; 113.
"More common here than 'seesaw'"--58, 61.
teeting totter: Pronounced [ˈtit?n̩ˌtɑɹɚ]
--44.

19.3b flying jenny.

  This item, not included in the eastern
worksheets, refers to a kind of homemade
merry-go-round consisting usually of a
plank or pole mounted so as to rotate
about its central axis when children push
it and jump on. Since the object itself
is increasingly rare, its designations
are often unknown. Merry-go-round, the
most common, appears in all UM states;
whirligig, with 18 occurrences, appears
largely in Northern speech territory;
flying Dutchman survives with 4 instances,
3 of which are in South Dakota; flying
jenny appears twice. In South Dakota 2
infs. report use of the device in winter,
either with sleds attached to the pole
ends or with the children wearing skates
as they push on the ice.

  circle teeter 35.
  flying Dutchman 150; sn305, :!309, 314.
  flying jenny sn37; *306.
  merry-go-round 13-15, 17-19, 38; 112,

119-20, 124-25; 202-4, 206, 208, 211,
c219, 223; 311-12, :s315, 318-20, 323,
325; 401, 404-5, 410, 412, 414, 417, 420,
430, 436.

swing board ?427.

whirligig sn29, 31, *37; 101, 103, s114;
sn201, :207, :209, :sn210, sn†212, :sn218,
220, sn221, 225; s¹310; *412, :419.

no response 1-12, 16, 20-28, 30, 32-34,
36, 39-65; 102, 104-11, 113-18, 121-23,
126-49, 151, ?152; 205, ?213-16, 217, 222,
?224, 226; 301-4, 307-8, 313, 316-17, 321,
?322, 324, 326, ?327-28; 402-3, :407, 408-
9, 411, 413, 415-16, ?418, 421-26, 428-29,
431-35, ?437.

Comment:

merry-go-round: A plank on a stump--19.
Made of an axle and one buggy wheel--223.
whirligig: One rotating plank--31. Used
only in the winter, with sleds attached
to pole ends--220. Common on ice--221.

19.4 coal hod. NE 148. WG 16, 25, 59,
50; F82.

Although now no longer found in urban
or even most rural situations, the hand-
carried container for coal is still so
well remembered that most infs. have a
name for it. The four common eastern
terms, bucket, hod, pail, and scuttle,
survive throughout the UM, with a distribution partly reflecting eastern origins.
(Coal) scuttle, general in New York
state, New Jersey, eastern Pennsylvania,
and the Ohio Western Reserve, dominates
each UM state except Iowa, and is used
by all five Canadian informants. (Coal)
hod, the regular term in New England, was
carried west to secondary settlements in
Ohio and West Virginia and appears as the
second most common UM term, actually being the most common in Iowa. It is absent,
however, from most of northern Minnesota
and from southern Nebraska. (Coal) pail,
a minority form correlating with Northern
pail (for milk or water), apparently was
tending to replace the older special terms
at the time when coal stoves became obsolete, as its incidence is higher in the
western, more recently settled, states.
(Coal) bucket, a Pennsylvania and Midland
word, is more common in the Midland speech
territory of Iowa and Nebraska, but its
frequency in Minnesota, in contrast with
only three occurrences in the related Wisconsin survey, attests further northern
extension of Midland features.
Two North Dakota infs. use the variant
skittle, also reported once in Wisconsin.
The mixing of two or more equivalent
terms in the same community more than
once yielded family diversity, several

infs. reporting the interchangeable use
of the two terms, the mother's and the
father's.

CL 27: The mail survey does not closely
correspond with the field data. Of the
1,060 respondents only 14% reported older
hod and 19% scuttle, while the two newer
generic terms pail and bucket, were
checked by 45% and 41% respectively.

bucket 5, 38; 128, 130, 134, 136; †209;
¹314. coal ~ 4, ¹6, 8, ¹12, 13, 16-17,
20, *26, ¹†36, 41, 44, 48, 56-57, ¹61,
63; 108, 112-15, *117, 126-27, 129, 135,
140, 142-43, 145-46, 148-50; →203, 207;
302, 304, 308-9, 313, 315, 319, 322; 404,
:410, 419, 421-22, 427,429-31, 433-34,
436-37.

coal shuttle 52; 306.
hod 6, 15, 65; †121, 122, ¹127, *134;

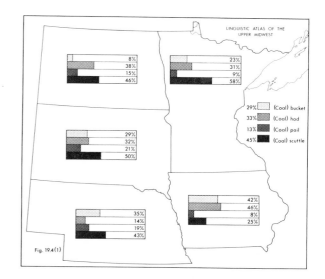

Fig. 19.4(1)

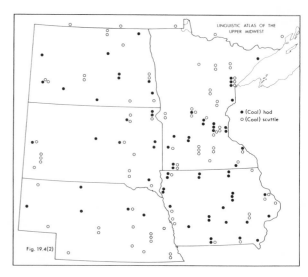

Fig. 19.4(2)

224

218-19, 225; ¹312; †405, 409. coal ~ 17-
18, 27, 29-33, 39-40, 42, 44-46, ¹47, 54,
60-61; 101-6, 109-10, ¹111, 116-18, 120,
130, :131, 132, †133, 141, 144-46, 148,
151-52; 208, 210-11, 214-15, 218, 222-23;
306-9, 314, 316-17, 319, 324; 403, ¹404,
¹408, 412-13, 416.
    pail 13. coal ~ 7, 19, 26, ¹42, 43,
¹47, 60; 102, 104, 108, ¹109, 133; 203,
206, 213, 224; 303, 305, 307, ¹313, 318,
321, ¹323, 328; 402, 406, 408, !411, †414,
415-17.
    scuttle 1-2, †5, 13-15, 23, 34, 64; 119,
†120, 123-24, ¹129; 204, 216-17, 221, 224,
¹225; 306, 311-12; ¹404. coal ~ 3, ¹8, 9-
12, 15-16, 18, 21-22, 24-29, :35, 36-37,
s40, †42, 45, †46, 47, 49-53, 55, 58-59,
*60, ¹61, 62; 101, 107, ¹109, 111, ¹113,
121, 125, 137-38, :139, *145, 147; 201-2,
205, 212, 214, 220, 226; 301, ¹302, 305,
308, 310, *316, 320, 322-23, 325-27;
c401, †405, 407, 414, †416, *417, 418-20,
423-26, 428-29, 432, 434-35.
    skittle †209. coal ~ ¹215.

Comment:

    coal scuttle: Used by inf.'s parents
(from N.Y.)--42. Usu.--26. "The right name
for it, I guess"--434. hod: Term used by
inf.'s father (from Wi.)--121. Inf. calls
it a 'coal bucket' but says, "It should
be 'hod'"--127. "The correct name for it"
--225. Inf. says this is common here--312.
coal hod: Used in inf.'s family--27. Used
by inf.'s grandfather--133. Usu.--29; 130.
Thinks she got this term from hardware
catalogs--42. scuttle: Used by inf.'s
mother (from Wi.)--120.

19.6 wheelbarrow. NE 163.

    Although primarily sought for its pro-
nunciation, the term wheelbarrow also
yielded eight widely-scattered equivalents, six of which humorously reflect
the one-time common employment of Irish
immigrant labor in railroad and building
construction.

    barrow 51.
    garden truck 62.
    Irish baby buggy 50. ~ baby carriage
!61. ~ buggy !323.
    Irishman's buggy 138; !208.
    Paddy's car !51.
    slop cart 48.
    wheelbarrow All other infs. except 313,
who did not respond.

19.7 whetstone (for sharpening a scythe).
NE 159. WG 40, 47, 60; F83.

    Dominant in the UM is the Northern and
Midland whetstone with a frequency of 82%,

but scythestone, also Northern and Midland, exhibits a scattered overall 12%
frequency, greatest in Iowa (20%). Recessive is the South Midland whetrock, reported in Iowa and southwestern South Dakota, and as a remembered and heard form
in Iowa and Nebraska. Both scythestone
and whetrock are used chiefly by old-
fashioned infs., not at all by any in
Type III. One Nebraska speaker of German
parentage responded with a German loanword Wetzstein /vɛtštaɪn/ as usual for
her. A semantic extension appeared in the
sporadic use of hone, specifically indicated as a scythe-sharpener; and a distinction appeared in the description of
a scythestone as being coarser than a
whetstone.

    brimstone 38.
    emery stone 208.
    file 307, *318, 319.
    hone 14, 19; 216, 221; 303, 324;
    pocket stone 50.
    scythestone 1, 6, 13, 21, 24, 30, 36,
61; 101, ¹105, 107, 112, 117, 119, 124-
25, 128, 135, 146; 206, 225; 306; 404-5,
427, 429.
    sharpening stone 120.
    sickle hone 35.
    soap stone 60.
    stone 13; 425.
    Wetzstein 415.
    whetrock 108, 132, 135, †145, 151; 320;
¹401.
    whetstone 2, :3, 4-5, 7-8, *9, 10-12,
15-17, c18, :s20, :22, 23, 25, sn26, 27-
29, 31-34, 37, 39-46, :47, 48-65; 102-6,
108-9, 111, 113-19, 121-23, 126-27, 129-
31, 133-34, 136-49, :s150, 152; sn201,
202-4, :205, ¹206, 207, 209, :210-11,
212-14, :215, 216-26; 301, :302, 304-5,
*306, 308-14, 316-18, 321-23, 325, 327-
28; 401, :402, 403, 407-10, :411, 412-14,
s415, 416, *417, 418-20, s421, 422-24,
s425, 426, s427, 428-37.
    no response 110; 315, 326; 406.

Comment:

    scythestone: Coarser than a 'hone' or
'whetstone'--119. sickle stone: Used on a
scythe [ɪsaɪˤ]--35. Wetzstein: Pronounced
[ɪvɛtˌʃtaɪn]--415. whetrock: Learned by
inf. while working in Ca. shipyards--108.
Term used by inf.'s father (from Ia.)--
145. whetstone: Offered by inf.'s son--*9.
Water is used on it--57.

20.3b kerosene. WG 14, 31, 33, 34, 36,
43, 44, 60; F84.

    Although Northern kerosene consistently
dominates the UM, with an average frequency of 90% despite a low of 62% in Nebras-

ka, Pennsylvania's coal oil long was a strong competitor throughout the area. In the three northern states, however, its present incidence is almost entirely in terms of overheard or distantly recalled occurrence. As the map shows, it is actually alive only in southern Iowa and Nebraska. Its range is: Mn. 12%, Ia. 22%, N.D. 4%, S.D. 4%, Nb. 49%; average for UM 20%. Western Pennsylvania's lamp oil did not survive the migration; one Minnesota inf. recalled it as formerly used in the era of kerosene lamps.

CL: Checklist data correspond remarkably, with a 90% frequency for kerosene and 20% for coal oil. Iowa reported 20% coal oil and Nebraska 50%.

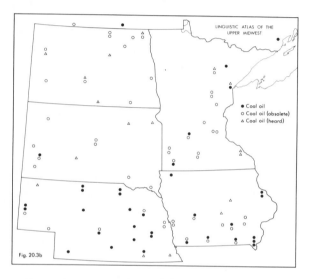

LINGUISTIC ATLAS OF THE UPPER MIDWEST

● Coal oil
○ Coal oil (obsolete)
△ Coal oil (heard)

Fig. 20.3b

coal oil 3, ¹11, †12, →13, !¹15, 16, †21, ¹†22, †23, †29, †33, †37, *43, †45-47, †52-53, ¹54-55, †59, 60; 101, ¹117, 119, 121, †124-25, 126, †127, ¹133, †134, 135, †136-37, †142, 143-44, †145, 146, †147, 148-50, †152; †201, 202, †204-5, ¹†206, ¹207, †208, ¹†209, !¹210, ¹211, ¹†213-14, ¹216, †217, ¹220, †221, ¹223, ¹†224; †301, ¹306, ¹308, †310, 311, ¹†312, ¹313, †314, ¹†315, †320, †323, †325; ¹401, c403, 404, c405, 406, 409-10, ¹†411, 412-13, sn†415, 416, †418, 419-20, 422, 424-25, †427-28, 429-30, 432, ¹433-34, †436, 437.
  fuel oil 318.
  kerosene ¹3, 7, 10-19, 21-26, 28-31, 33, 35-38, 41, c42, 43, c44, 45-47, 49-50, 52-55, 59, c60; 101-6, 108-11, 113-17, 119-29, *130, 131-41, →142, 144-50, 152; 201, 203-11, 213-19, 221-26; 301-7, 308-9, →310, ¹311, 312-19, →320, 321-27, c328; 401-3, ¹404, 406-8, 411-12, ¹413, 414-15, †416, 417, →418, 421, 423, 426-28, 430-

31, 433-36. ~ oil 27; 107; 212, 220; †302, 307.
  lamp oil †41.
  naphtha †12.
  no response 1-2, 4-6, 8-9, 20, 32, 34, 39-40, 48, 51, 56-58, 61-65; 112, 118, 151.

Comment:

  coal oil: "In the woods they used to call it 'coal oil' at times, or 'naphtha' some"--12. "When I was a boy"--21. Used by inf. when younger--37; 308; 428. "I used to call it 'coal oil'"--147; 427. "Some old-timers used to call it 'coal oil'"--22. "Some of those Yankees would say 'coal oil'"--23. "An awful lot said 'coal oil'"--207. Inf. heard this used by people who moved here from Nebraska--224. Used by inf.'s mother (from N.Y.)--29. Used by inf.'s mother (from Nb.)--325. "A lot of people today say 'coal oil'"--11. Inf. knows the term but says that it is not used here--54. Inf. calls it a dealer's term--55. Inf.'s usual term--412. kerosene: Inf. occasionally hears this here--3. kerosene oil: "The right thing" --220. Inf. says that it is higher grade than fuel oil--318.

22.2 vest.

Vest is the universal term for the sleeveless garment worn by a man under a coat; only two infs. offered waistcoat as an alternative.

  vest 1-44, !45, 46-65; 101-9, c110, 111-52; 201-26; 301-15, *316, 317-26, c327, 328; 401-14, 416-28, :429, 430-37.
  waistcoat 15, *39.
  no response 415.

22.3 trousers.

Pants and trousers are common in the UM, nearly half of the Infs. admitting use of both terms. The UM average is 85% for pants and 55% for trousers, with no appreciable regional variation. Where a distinction is made, trousers is viewed as more formal or, four times, as more recent. Only five instances of the innovation slacks occurred. Older breeches feebly survives in South Dakota and Nebraska. For seven infs. the ordinarily worn garment is jeans, particularized by three with the trade term, now almost generic, Levis.

  breeches ¹129; !¹403, 420.
  jeans 144; →312; 404, 424.
  Levis →312, 320; 404.
  overalls †312, 320.
  pant 223

pantaloons 113.

pants ¹1, 3-9, cr10, 11-18, ¹†19, !†21, cr22, 23-24, !25, 26-27, 29-32, 34-41, ?42, !43-46, 47-48, 50-52, 54-57, 59-62, cr64, 65; 101-3, 105-9, c110, 112-19, 122-25, 127-33, 135-46, 148, 150-52; 201, †202, 203-10, !211, 212-13, ¹214, 215-16, cr217-18, 219-22, 224-26; 301-9, ¹310, 311-15, *316, 317, !318, 320-25, !326, 328; 401-9, 411-13, 416-18, c419, 421, c422, 423-25, !426, †427, 428-30, 433-34, 436-37.

slacks 10, 33; →124; →301; 428.

trousers 1, c2, †3, ¹6, cr?7, 8, ?10, 14-15, 17-21, ?22, 23, 26, ¹27, 28, †29, 31, 33-34, 37-38, 40, cr42, !44, 48-50, 53, 57-58, 60-61, ¹62, 63, ?64; 101, 104, 106-7, 109, 111-12, ¹114, 117-21, 123, s¹124, 126-27, ¹129, 130-31, 133-34, 136, 139, 144-45, 147-50; 201, →202, 203, 205-6, 208, 210-11, →212, 213-14, 216, →217; ?218, 219, 221, 223-26; 301, 305, 307-8, 310, 313-14, 318-19, 324, →326; 402, 406, 410, 413-15, 420-21, 423-28, 430-33, 435-36.

no response 327.

Comment:

jeans: Made of cotton; others are made of wool--144. Originally a girl's term--312. Levis: Only one brand of jeans--320. overalls: They come to the waist; the others are 'bib overalls'--312. They come to the waist--320. pant: Usual form--223. pantaloons: Used in clothing stores--113. pants: "Used in olden days"--19. Older than 'trousers'--139, 145. "In this country they say 'pants'"--44. "Our expression here"--64. Working apparel--213; 313; 424, 436. Pants are a part of a suit; trousers are separate--413, 421, 428. Term used by inf.'s husband--324. Usu.--7-8, 10, 22, 26, 31, 50; 101, 107, 109, 112, 127; 206, 216-17, 219, 225-26; 314, 326; 425, 430, 433. slacks: Slacks are worn alone; trousers are a part of a suit--33. Slacks are looser than pants or trousers--428. trousers: Used "in the old country"--3. "In the early days 'trousers' was common"--23. "Today they're 'trousers'"--21. "Now they call it 'trousers'"--48. Used in "high-toned" situations--34. More formal than 'pants'--61. 425-26. 'Trousers' is more formal than 'breeches'--420. "More respectable name" --136. "More English"--308. "More correct"--430. "Your dress-up ones"--150. For dress--313; 424. Trousers are a part of a suit--208. Usu.--106, 131; 224. Inf. was instructed as a child not to say 'pants'--126.

22.4 I have brought your coat. NE 638.

Primarily intended to elicit forms of bring (See Volume 2), this item also produced 7 instances of fetched, widely distributed as were the 5 instances reported in New England. Two infs. consider fetched old-fashioned.

BROUGHT c1, 2-13, c15-18, 19-20, c21, 22-24, c25, 26-28, c29, 30, c31, f32, 33-34, c35, 36, c39-40, 41, c42, f43, 44-45, c46-47, 48-49, c50, 51-55, s56, 57-60, c61, 62-65; 101-32, c133, 134-52; 201-2, c203, 204-6, cvr207, 208-10, c211-12, 213, c214, 215-18, c219, 222-24, c225, 226; 301-5, *306, 307-15, 317-21, c322, 323-26, 328; 401-2, c403, 404, cvr406, 407-13, cvr414, 415-18, c419, 420-28, 430-33, s434, 435-37.

fetched 32, †40; c132, s†145; c204, ¹208; c425.

no response 4, 14, 37; 220-21; 316, 327; 405, 429.

23.4 umbrella. NE 367.

Umbrella, a pronunciation item, has a uniform 96% distribution but is accompanied by an overlapping 25% use of parasol, even to designate the device for protection against rain. In this sense parasol seems Midland-oriented: Mn. 17%, Ia. 38%, N.D. 3.8%, S.D. 43%, Nb. 22%. Semi-humorous bumbershoot, found in NE, survives in the use of six infs., five of them in the eastern UM.

bumbershoot !57-58, !62; 128, 145; 216.

parasol 7, 36, †40, 43-44, †46, 47, ¹48, 51, 57-59, 61, 64; 101-4, 107, 109, 112, 114-17, 129-30, 132-33, 136-37, 139, 145-46; 216; 305-9, 311-12, 318-19, 322-23, 325; 401-2, 409-10, †417, 418-19, 429, 437.

rain stick 15.

sunshade 308.

umbrella 1-6, 8-39, c40, cr41, 42-55, c56, 57-60, c61, 62-65; 101-6, 108-13, †114-15, 116-19, c120, 121-44, *145, 146-52; 201-24, c225, 226; 301-10, c311, 312-21, 323-28; †401, 403-7, c408, 410-28, 430-37.

Comment:

bumbershoot: The local term--57-58. parasol: Older than umbrella--116, 136, 139. For use in the sun--47, 57, 61; 109; 308-9; 418-19. For use in sun or rain--51; 139. For use in rain--58. = umbrella --101-2, 104, 117; 305-6, 312, 319, 323; 437. "It's fancy"--309. umbrella: Pronounced [ˈbrɛlə]--57. Usu.--323. Larger than a parasol--36; 103, 116, 130, 137; 311, 325.

23.5 bedspread. NE 341.

For the top covering on a bed the term bedspread and its simplex spread have a near monopoly in the UM. Older counterpane and the less frequent variant counterpin survive weakly for a total frequency of 4.8% with no occurrences in northern Minnesota, North Dakota, or Nebraska. Almost obsolete in the UM is the eastern coverlet or coverlid, reportedly in use by only three informants in Iowa. Both counterpane and coverlid are recalled by some infs. as old-fashioned words no longer in use.

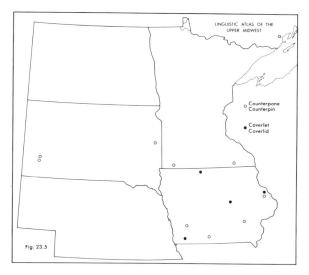

LINGUISTIC ATLAS OF THE
UPPER MIDWEST

○ Counterpane
Counterpin

● Coverlet
Coverlid

Fig. 23.5

bedspread 1-2, ¹3, 4-5, :7, cr8, 11-22, 24-25, 27, cr28, 29, 32-34,·37-40, 42-45, cr46, 47-48, 51-53, 57-64; 101-18, 126, 130-31, 133, 135-40, 143, s144, 145-50, 152; 201-3, 208-9, :210, 211-13, 216, cr219, 220, 222, 226; 302-5, *306, 307-10, :311, ¹312, 313-19, 323, 325, ¹326, 328; 402-3, 407-8, 410, 413-16, 419-25, 427-31, 433-36.

counterpane 3, ¹33, s†40, 61, 65; ¹†123, s¹127, †*130, 144, 152; †201, ¹214, †217; s!†309, 312, 317, !326. ~pin 120, 151. coverlet †48; 103, 118-19, ¹†122; †314. ~lid 142. ~ spread ?135.

spread 6, ?8, 9-10, 18, 23, 26, ?28, 30-32, 34-36, 41, ?46, 47, 49-50, 54-57, 64-65; 118, 120-25, 127-28, 132, 134, 141, 146, 151; 204-7, 214-15, 217-18, ?219, 221, 223-25; 301, 318, 320-22, 324-25, 327; 401, 404-6, 409, 411-12, 417-18, 426, 432, 437.

no response 129.

Comment:

bedspread: The more common local term--312. counterpane: Term used by inf.'s mother-in-law (from Me.)--33. Term used by inf.'s mother (from N.Y.)--309. Older than 'spread'--65. "Mostly they call them 'counterpane'"--214. coverlet: Formerly used in Missouri--314.

23.6 quilt or comforter. NE 342. WG 12, 13, 47, 48, 61; F89.

The multidimensional referential meanings of these terms, clustered about the central meaning, a secondary bed covering, have recently been confused by inconsistent commercial terminology. Department stores advertise "quilts" that turn out to be thick wool-filled tied coverings. A detailed study of this complexity appears in H. B. Allen, "Semantic confusion: a report from the Atlas files," PADS No. 33, 3-13 (1960).

Only the tied and filled covering was asked about in NE, but in the UM the tied and quilted varities were generally distinguished. Some infs., however, did not specify either "tied" or "sewn."

As terms, comfort and comforter retain their eastern distribution contrast. Comfort is sharply confined to the Midland territory in Iowa and eastern Nebraska; Northern comforter dominates elsewhere. Comfortable, common in Connecticut and the Hudson Valley, survives with only four infs. in Iowa and western South Dakota.

a. Unspecified as tied or quilted.
   comfort 128, 141, 147.
   comforter 6, 14-16, !44, c51, 64-65; 117, 140.
   eiderdown 6.
   featherbed 34.
   quilt 13-14, 39-40, 44, c51, 64-65; 117, 128, 140-41, 147, 151.

Comment:

comfort: Filled with cotton, wool, or down--147. comforter: Filled with cotton --16. Filled with cotton or wool--117, 140. Heavier than a quilt--117. Lighter than a quilt--44. = quilt--51, 64. eiderdown: "We used to call it an 'eiderdown' in the woods"--6. quilt: Filled with duck feathers--13. Filled with wool or cotton --117.

b. Sewn or quilted

For the sewn covering, whether made with many pieces or not, whether patterned or not, the generic term in the UM is quilt, with an over-all frequency of 95%. But in the Northern states of Minnesota and North Dakota ambiguity of reference has led to 35% and 32% frequency of comforter as well, with obvious overlapping. This ambiguity often is occasioned by uncertainty whether a quilt should be primarily identified as sewn or as filled with cotton batting instead of with wool batting. Some infs. use epithets such as "crazy" and "pieced" for clarity.

comfort 138, 148; 418, 435, †437.
comforter 1-3, 7, r9, 20, ¹21, 24, 26-27, 29, sn33, sn34, 37-38, †*43, 50, 53, 62-63; 129; 204, 208, 212, 216, 221-24; 302, 305, ¹312, 315; 404, 411-12, 417, 421. quilted ~ 108; 431.
corner rusher ¹†301.
coverlet *218.
puff 131. down ~ 33.
quilt sn1, 2-3, 5-6, ¹7, 8, :9, 10-12, 18, ¹20, 21-24, 26-29, 31-33, 35-38, 41-43, 45-46, 48-50, 53-56, 58, c59, 62-63; 101-16, 118-27, 129-39, 142-46, 149-50, 152; 201-4, c205, ?206, 207, 210, 212-13, c214, 215, c216, 217-19, 221-26; 301-9, c310, 311-14, 316-28; 401-3, c404, 405-16, 418-36, ¹437. crazy ~ 15, 34, 57. light ~ 209. patch ~ 25. piece ~ 64; 211. pieced ~ 407, 415. quilted ~ 4; 203; 318, 321. stitched ~ 4.
soogan 320; ¹†404.
no response 13-14, 16-17, 19, 30, 39-40, 44, 47, 60-61, 64-65; 117, 128, 140-41, 147, 151; 220.

Comment:

comfort: = quilt--138, 148; 418, 435, 437. Lined with cotton--437. comforter: = quilt--9, 20, 27, 37-38, 50, 62-63; 204, 212, 216, 221-24; 302, 305, 312; 404, 411-12. An old-fashioned word for 'quilt', but still heard--21. The cover is one piece of cloth; a 'quilt' is patchwork--24, 26, *27. Heavier than a quilt--24, 26, 29, 33. Lighter than a quilt--421. Lined with cotton--20, 62-63; 129; 305; 421. Lined with cotton or down--26. Lined with cotton or feathers--212. Lined with cotton or wool--37. Lined with wool--7. Lined with wool or down--1, 3. Lined with wool, down, or cotton--2. No lining--*43, 53. "Sewed"--7. A thin quilted pad next to the mattress--34. corner rusher: A stitched soogan with batting jammed into the corners--301. coverlet: A thin quilt --*218. puff: Lined with down--131. quilt: Lined with cotton--3, 10, 26, 36, 41, 48; 122, 127, 135-36, 142, 144, 150, 152; 318, 322-23, 328; 414, 419, 421, 424, 426, 430-32, 436. Lined with cotton or wool--5, 22-23, 28, 32-33, 42, 46; 123, 125, 131; 203; 225-26; 304, 310-11, 321; 408, 410, 429. No lining--6, 12, 35, 43, 53; 129. Lighter than a comforter--11, 24, 26, 31, 36, 45, 48-49, 54; 134, 145-46; 215; 324, 327-28; 401-3, 424, 426, 429, 431, 433-34. Heavier than a comforter--55; 421. "Some are sewed"--21. "Sewed"--35. soogan: Stuffed with cotton; inf. says soogans are still used in sheep camps--

320. Cowpuncher's name for any quilt--404.

c. Tied

The tied covering, conspicuous with yarn knots or tufts, is a 'comfort', 'comforter', or 'comfortable' to 76% of all infs., with comforter dominating all states but South Dakota, where competing ambiguous quilt has a 66% frequency. Quilt is least frequent in Iowa (16%) where it contrasts with both comfort and comforter.

Restricted to cattle country, including the Hereford area in the Nebraska sandhills, soogan persists in its sense of a comforter, wool-filled, for use in a cowpuncher's bed roll. Although twice described as filled with cotton, the soogan to former cattleman infs. had to be wool-filled, since when the soogan was wet only wool would dry out without wadding up in lumps.

CL 30: For the tied covering, the distribution pattern is essentially like that revealed by the field data. Comfort prevails in southern Iowa with 56%; quilt has 50% frequency in the Dakotas. Comfort and comforter together have a frequency of 75%.

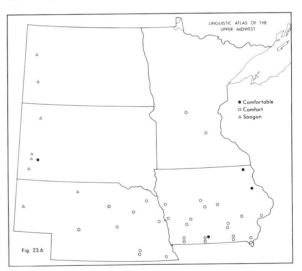

Fig. 23.6

LINGUISTIC ATLAS OF THE UPPER MIDWEST

● Comfortable
○ Comfort
△ Soogan

comfort 28, 35, ¹49; 115, ¹116, 122, 124, 127, 132, 135-36, 138, 142-43, c144, 145-46, 148, 150-51; *408, †410-11, 413, 416, 418, 420, 427, 432-33, 435, †437.
comfortable 107, 119, 144; *311.
comforter 1-2, sn4, 7-8, r9, 10-11, 17, 19-20, ¹21, 22-23, s†?25, 27, 29, †30, 31, sn33, 36-38, 41-42, 45-50, 54-55, r56, 58-59, *60, 61, 63; 101-5, 108, †110, 111, 113-14, 116, 118-21, 123-26, 130, †131, 133-34, 137, 139, 149, 152; 201, 204-6, 208, 210, ¹211, 212-18, ¹220, 221-

24, :225; 301, s†309, †310, ¹312, 313-15,
317, 324, ¹325, †326, 327-28; 401-2, c403,
404-5, †409, 411-12, 414, 417, 421-24,
426, 428-29, ¹430, 431-32, 434. wool ~
208. down ~ 319. tied ~ 3.
    coverlet ¹47.
    down puff 33.
    featherbed 305, 317.
    feather tick 307-8.
    quilt 4-5, ¹7, :9, 11-12, 17, 19, ¹20,
21-23, c25, 27, 30, 33-34, 37-38, 47, 50,
52, 60-61, 63; 105-6, 109-10, 112, 138;
202-4, 207, 211-12, c216, 219-26; 303-4,
309, 312-14, 318, 320-23, 326, ¬326, 328;
c404, 406-7, 410-12, 415, 418-19, 421,
425, 428, 430, 435-36, ¹437. feather ~
*306, 307. hand-tied ~ 111. heavy ~ 209;
408-9. knot ~ 407. knotted ~ 41. tied ~
18; 203; 310, 318, 321; 406. tufted ~ 29.
    soogan ¹†210, †214, ¹†301, 311, ¹†312;
¹†404, s†409.
    no response 6, 13-16, 24, 26, 32, 39-40,
43-44, 51, 53, 57, 62, 64-65; 117, 128-29,
140-41, 147; 302, 316.

Comment:

    comfort: Infrequent here--49. Lined with
cotton--35; 135, 144, 146, 150; 427, 437.
Lined with wool--122, 142. Lined with wool
or cotton--28; 124, 127, 136. Heavier
than a quilt--122, 124, 142, 145; 433. =
quilt--138; 418, 435, 437. Used by inf.'s
grandmother--410-11. comfortable: Lined
with cotton--144. comforter: Lined with
cotton--63; 111, 116; 315, 328; 414, 421,
423. Lined with down--4. Lined with wool
--7, 17, 36; 314; 431. Lined with wool or
down--1, 58; 426. Lined with wool, down,
or cotton--2. Lined with wool or cotton--
10-11, 20, 23, 37, 49, 59-61; 124, 152;
206, 213; 402, 430. Lined with feathers
or batting--212. Heavier than a quilt--
22, 29, 31, 33, 41-42, 45, 48; 124-25,
130, 134, 152; 215; 324, 327-28; 401-3,
414, 424, 426, 429, 434. Lighter than a
quilt--8, 55; 421. = quilt--19, *60; 138.
"That's an old name for 'quilt,' ain't
it?"--25. "That word's gotten away from
us"--409. Used by inf.'s paternal grandmother (from Oh.)--30. Used by inf.'s
grandmother--110. Old-fashioned word for
'quilt', but still heard here--21. Inf.
says this is a newer word than 'quilt'--
19. quilt: Lined with cotton--17, 25, 63;
207; 318, 322; 408, 419, 421, 437. Lined
with wool--12. Lined with cotton or wool
--4-5, 19, 22-23, 30, 33, 37, 52, 60-61;
203, 226; 304, 321; 410, 430. Lighter
than a comforter--11, 17. = comforter--
9, 27, 37-38, 47, 50, 61, 63; 204, 212,
216, 221-24; 313; 404, 411-12. "Some
'quilts' are quilted with knots of yarn"
--21. "The real name is 'quilt', but some
women call it a 'comforter'"--220. Inf.'s

usual term, but he would call it a 'comforter' to distinguish it from a sewn
'quilt'--225. Inf.'s usual term, but she
says, "It really is a 'comforter'"--326.
hand-tied quilt: Lined with cotton--111.
knotted quilt: Lined with wool--41. soogan: Cowpuncher's term--210, 214; 301,
311-12; 404. Lined with wool--311.

23.7 pallet (bed on the floor). WG 40,
61; F88.

    Not a distinct item in the NE work-
sheets, pallet was added to the NC and UM
lists as a possible indication of South
Midland influence. Although most infs.
have no name for a temporary bed on the
floor, the 35 infs. using pallet exhibit
a clear South Midland distribution that
at one time was strong enough to spread
slightly into western Nebraska. Competing
shakedown, though with only 20 occurrences, has a suggestively Northern distribution. Both terms are usually considered old-fashioned if known at all. Less
frequent bunk (on the floor), sometimes
like shakedown applied to a straw tick,
is not found in North Dakota or most of
Minnesota.

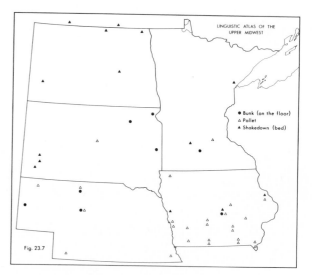

Fig. 23.7

    bed on the floor 53, 59, 61; 308, 328;
410, 424, 432.
    bunk 133; 306-7; 404, 409, 412. ~ on
the floor 51; 317.
    field bed *46.
    floorbed 407.
    flop 404.
    pallet 22, 35, s¹46, s65; 101, ¹110,
¹115, 118, 120, 124-25, 130-31, 133, 135,
:136, 137, 142, 144-48, 150-51; †215;
314; 401, cvr403, *412, ¹413-14, 429,
¹433, 434.

shake ⌐115.
shakedown 15, s37, 45; ⌐116, sn119,
*123, s⌐137, ⌐*141; 201, c202, 204, 207,
sn†212, 214, ⌐†215, 218; ⌐301, :311,
sn320, :326. ~ bed 132. straw tick 56.
straw tick 56.
trundle 54. ~ bed *45.
no response 1-14, 16-21, 23-26, ?27, 28-
34, 36, 38-41, ?42, 43-44, 47-50, 52, 55,
57-58, 60, 62-64; 102-9, 111-14, 117,
121-22, 126-29, 134, 138-40, 143, 149,
152; 203, 205-6, 208-9, :210, 211, 213,
216, ?217, ?219-20, 221-26; 302-5, 309,
:310, ?312, 313, 315-16, 318-19, 321-22,
?323, 324-25, 327; 402, 405-6, 408, 411,
415-23, 425-28, 430-31, 435-37.

Comment:

   field bed: For several people--*46. pallet: Inf. heard a lady from Ottumwa use
this term--110. Knows term from reading--
120. Used by inf.'s parents (from Vt.)--
215. A Missouri term--413. shakedown: Used
occ.--119. "We don't use 'shakedown'"--
*141.

23.8 It goes clear across. WG 61; F87.

   A. sought this in the context "He threw
it . . . the creek (the street, the room,
etc.)." Other fieldworkers occ. used other contexts, as appears from such responses as clear up there and clean back,
here included to show similar adverbial
use of clear and clean.
   Clear across, common on the Atlantic
coast, remains the dominant expression
in the UM, with an over-all frequency of
90%. Minnesota is not included in the
percentages, as this item was added after
the near-completion of fieldwork there.
Clean across, found by Kurath in eastern
Virginia and eastern North Carolina, turns
up at least once in each UM state. Plum
across, reportedly SM, was given by informants in SM speech territory in the UM,
with two additional instances in North Dakota. Way across, with apheresis of away,
is an infrequent variant in Iowa and the
Dakotas.

   all across 426. all the way across 38;
111, 126.
   clean across cvr25; 146-47; 203, 207,
sn208, sn212, 216; *306, 311, ⌐313, sn315;
†409, 427.
   clean up the hill c301. clean up there
15.
   clear across 30-31, :snc35, :36; 101-
10, 112-17, 119, 121-25, *126, 127-28,
130-32, c133, 134-35, 137-39, 141-42,
s143, c*145, *147, 148-50, 152; 201-2,
204-5, sn206, 209-10, sn211-12, 213-15,
:sn217, 219, ⌐221, 222-24, 226; c301,
302-4, c306, 307, 309-13, :314, 316-17,

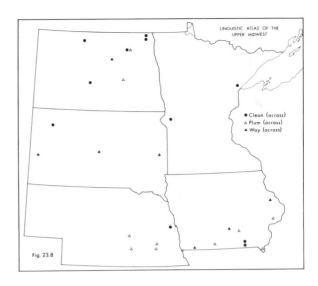

319-20, :sn321, c322, 323-28; 401-12,
sn413, 414-16, 418-26, 428-33, s434, 435-
37.
   clear back c220.
   clear over 305, 308.
   clear through c221.
   clear to the corner c417.
   plum across 136, 140, 144, †*145, 149;
⌐211, sn212, 218; 421, cvr423, c425, 426.
   plum away ⌐313.
   straight across 415.
   way across 120, †129, 134, 143; 211;
310, 315, 318.
   no response 1-14, 16-24, 26-29, 32-34,
37, 39-65; 118, 151.

Comment:

   plum away: Inf. says this is the common
expression here--313. way across: Inf.'s
usual expression--221.

24.2a meadow (low-lying grassland). NE
28, 29. WG 61; F90, F91.

   For grassland along a watercourse the
more general term in the UM is meadow,
with this distribution: Mn. 94%, Ia. 44%,
N.D. 66%, S.D. 45%, and Nb. 83%. Competing
with it are common eastern flat(s), Midland bottomland, South Midland bottom(s),
hay land, and swale. Bottomland, which
appeared only three times in Wisconsin
and once in Minnesota, is common in the
Midland area of southern Iowa and extends
into Nebraska and the Dakotas. Bottom(s),
missing in both Wisconsin and Minnesota,
appears in southern Iowa also, with some
extension westward. Flat(s), so far as
the Atlas records indicate, survives only
in the western panel, although other tes-
timony indicates its use in Minnesota as

well. The city-owned Mississippi river front area adjacent to the University of Minnesota campus is known as the 'river flats.' Hay land, reported only three times in Wisconsin, seems to be gaining in use, with seven occurrences in Minnesota and several more in the western panel. Swale, when offered as the equivalent of meadow, may have undergone a semantic shift in Nebraska, where it is not typically applied to low, marshy ground.

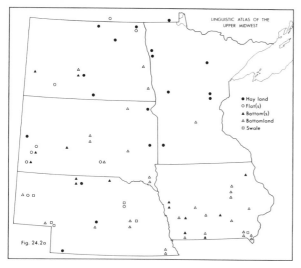

Fig. 24.2a

bottom 108, 122-23, 142, 151; 312-13; c405. ~ land 30; 107, 116-18, 126, 134, sn136, 137, 140, s141, 143-49; 209, 216-17, sn220, 226; 314-15, 321, 324-25, 328; 403, 405, s415, 419-21, 434-36. hay ~ c404. river ~ 131; 214; c305. second ~ 126; *145.
 bottoms 217; 320.
 flat 311-12.
 flats 202, 208, c215; c320; 409. hay ~ 321; c†404, 414.
 grassland 418.
 grazing land 209.
 hayfield 310, 322-23.
 hay land 1, 7, 9, 12, 20, 23-24, 47; 204, 207, 212, 217, 223; 308, c309, 319; 404, 418, 437.
 hay slough 219.
 lake bed 322.
 lowland 29; 118.
 meadow 2-3, c4, 5-6, 8, 10, 14-18, :sn19, :20, c21, 22-23, 25-29, c31, 32-34, 36, :38, 39-45, c46, 47-50, 52-61, c62-63, 64, sn65; 101-2, 104-5, c106, c109, 111-12, s113, 114-15, 119-20, 129, :?130, 131-32, sn133, 137-38, 150, 152; 202, †203, 205-6, 210, 213, 215-16, c217, 218, 221-23, 225, :226; 301, †309, 312-13, 326, 328; 401-2, c404, 405-8, 411-12, cvr414, 416-19, 421-26, 428-29, s430,

cvr414, 416-19, 421-26, 428-29, s430, 431, 433, 435, 437. hay ~ 11, 24, c29, 30, 36-37, 51; 201, 210-11, ¹219; 302, c322, 323, 325; c405, 408, c409, c417, 429. low ~ 224. ~ land :sn35, 51; 403, 410, 432.
 park 311.
 pasture 139, 150; 416, 433. ~ land 209; 319.
 peat land 29.
 pocket 320.
 prairie ¹7.
 swale ¹54; s142, 146; c409, 413, 420, 436.
 no response 13; 103, 110, 121, 124-25, 128, 135; 303-4, 306-7, 316-18, 327; 427.
Comment:

  bottom land: Usu. here--419. second bottom: Lowland not susceptible to flooding --126, *145. hayfield: Usu.--323. hay land: Usu.--223. meadow: Used infrequently by inf.--29; 120. "A Wisconsin word"--105. Rare here--433. hay meadow: A Missouri term--219. park: An open grassy place in the hills--311. pocket: Low grassland in hills or on the prairie--320.

24.2b to meadow cows (put them out to pasture).

  This item, added to the worksheets after half of Minnesota had been covered, did not turn out to be productive. Eastern meadow as a verb appeared only once, in Iowa. The universal expression is pasture.

  to graze 121; 320.
  to meadow 131.
  to pasture 29-30, 36; s111, 112, 119, 121-22, s124, 125, ¹126, 127, ¹130, 136; 201, 204-7, sn208, 211-13, 215-17, 219-20, c221, 222-25; 301-2, 304-5, *306, 309, 313-14, 319, 323-24; 401-3, 407, c409, 425, †428, 429-30, 433.

24.3 swamp. NE 30.

  This item was typically sought with such a question as "What do you call a low area, often with standing water, too wet for cultivation?" Because such an area may be with or without trees or shrubs, may or may not have a small pool of water within it, and may or may not be wet permanently instead of only during a wet season the responses vary considerably and do not necessarily always have precisely the same kind of referent. Even the same referent may be identified with contrasting terms by two infs. in the same community.
  Eastern swamp dominates the eastern panel and Nebraska but is less common in

North Dakota. Although some infs. consider a swamp to be characterized by trees or shrubs, others insist that it lacks them.

Eastern marsh, generally understood to name a treeless area, is still considered otherwise by a few speakers. The term is more widely used in Minnesota than elsewhere.

Eastern bog survives, particularly in South Dakota and Nebraska.

With 58%, slough nearly ties with swamp's 60% average for the entire UM. Slough exhibits strong regional contrast as a term indicating a feature characteristic of the treeless prairies. All North Dakota speakers use it and so do three-fourths of the South Dakotans.

Muskeg, designating a particular type of swamp, is used only in the area where such swamps occur, i.e., northern Minnesota.

Pot hole, like muskeg not reported in New England, seems, in the sense of a small depression with standing water, to be limited to North Dakota and its eastern fringe. Drainage of such haunts of wetland life may soon render the term archaic.

CL 130: Although the mail response gave slough a 65% frequency in the UM, the distribution was fairly even, with North Dakota having only 67% and South Dakota 65%. Swale was checked by 4%, widely scattered; so was draw. The basic pattern for swamp and marsh was not greatly different.

bayou c320.
bog 6, 10, 14, 17, 20, 22, 25, 33, 45-46, 55; 109, 117, 140; 225; 305, 307, c314, 320; 403-4, 406, 409, ¹420, 425-26. ~ hole 220. peat ~ 13, 17.

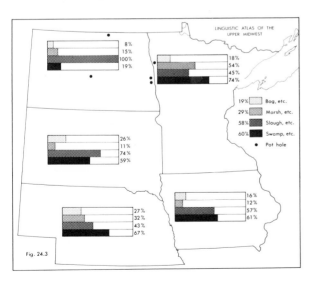

Fig. 24.3

boggy 40; 117, 141; 306; c414. ~ ground 101, 108. ~ land ¹7, 46; 132, c144; 222; 401, 434. ~ place ¹312, 314, 317, 326; 429.
bottoms 61; 150.
hummock land 28.
lake bed 315, 323.
lagoon 436.
lea ¹7.
loblolly 311.
lowland 44, 57.
low spot 47.
marsh 2-3, 5, 7-12, 15-18, 21-24, c¹25, 26, c29, 30, 32, 34, 37-38, 42, 44, 50, 52, sn54, 56, 58, s64, 65; 101, 117-18, ¹127, s146, 147, :150; 212, 218, 221-22; 305, s309, 310; 403-4, 411-12, ¹420, 421, sn422, 424-26, s433. ~ land 33, c45, 53; 431. meadow ~ 111.
marshy land 402. ~ place ¹312, 326; 429.
muskeg 4-5. ~ swamp 18.
peat bog 13, 17. ~ land 62.
pond 430.
pot hole ¹7, 8; 204, 217, 220-21.
seep 410.
slough sn2, 4, 7-8, :9, c16, 19-21, c25, 26-28, 34, 41-45, c46, 47-48, 50, 52-53, c59, 60, c61, 62; sn101, 102-4, 106, 109, 111-15, sn116, 117, 119, 124-25, 127-28, 133, 135-38, s¹139, 140, 143, 148-49, 152; 201, c202, 203-4, c205, 206-7, c208, 209-25, :sn226; 301-7, 313-19, 321-25, 328; ¹401, :¹403, 406-7, ¹408, †409-10, 412, ¹413, sn414, 419-21, sn422-23, 424-25, 427-28, 435, 437. ~ hole 436. ~ land 134. hay ~ 211. meadow ~ c44.
sloughy ground 325.
spring hole 17.
swale c61; †204; 302.
swamp 1-4, 6-7, 10-18, 21-22, c23, 24, 28, c29, 30-31, 33-35, c36, 37-40, 43-45, 49-50, 54-56, 59-60, c61, 63-65; 105, 107, 113-14, 116-18, 120-25, c126, 127-31, 134-37, 139, 142, 144-46, 150-51; 207, 217, c220, 221, c222, ¹226; 301-2, 306, c311, 312, 316, 318, 321, 323, 326, 328; 401, 404-5, 408, 413-14, sn415, 416, 418, c421, 422, sn423, 424-26, 428-29, 431, 433, 435. ~ land c35, 51, 57; 147; 307-9, 313; *432. muskeg ~ 18.
swampy 307. ~ area 319. ~ land 19; 403, 417. ~ place 409, 419.
no response 110; 327.

Comment:

bog: Wet and spongy ground--40; 109; 425. Wet and spongy ground without trees --10. Not as wet as a swamp--33. "If it was a 'bog', it wouldn't hold you up"--6. "You get mired in a bog"--225. Wet and spongy ground with trees--20. Wet and spongy ground with hummocks--404. Where cranberries grow--22; 426. Near trees-- 55. No trees--320. Uses only occ.--14.

boggy ground: Low ground that can be cultivated in dry years--108. boggy land: Wet and spongy ground with or without trees--144. Wet and spongy ground--222. boggy place: Wet and spongy ground--317. lake bed: Usu. here; = swamp--323. Filled with water during the spring and summer --315. lagoon: A temporary body of water in a field--436. lea: Heard used by itinerant workers--7. loblolly: A place where a cow can get mired--311. marsh: Wet and spongy ground--10, 26, 37, 50; 212; 424. Wet and spongy ground without trees--65. Where cranberries grow--21. On the prairie --44. Grassy, with scattered trees--5. A wet grassy area along a lake--15-17. "Where there is water and it's soupy all the time"--117. Standing water--101, 150; 222; 421-22. Standing water and trees-- 425. No trees--2, 23, 29, 42, 56; 118. With trees--38, 52. With or without trees --3. Uncommon here--24; 433. "An old fellow's term"--25. marsh land: Usu. here-- 45. Not usu. here--53; 431. meadow marsh: Might be a western word--111. muskeg: "More wet than a swamp is"--4. Bushes but no trees--5. pot hole: A low wet and spongy place that has been burned over by a prairie fire--7. Low ground without drainage where water stands temporarily-- 8; 217, 221. Low ground where water seeps to the surface--220. slough: "A wet place like a marsh"--2. Wet and spongy ground-- 4, 7, 43, 50, 62; 138, 148, 152; 301, 316-18, 323; 435. A temporary wet place that occ. dries up--8; 322. Wet and spongy ground without trees--321. Not as wet as a bog--109. Not as wet as a swamp--321. Standing water--9, 19-21, 26, 28, 34, 41-42; 114; 208, 211, 215, 218, 222-23, 225; 302; 407, 410, 412, 424. Standing water most of the time--44; 101-2, 112, 117, 127, 137, 149; 206; 303, 315; 427-28. This is the water in the center of a bog --25. A low place with a stream--408, 421-22. Standing water without trees--103, 111, 113; 224; 419. Standing water with or without trees--104; 212; 324. slough here refers to a small channel on one side of an island in the Missouri River-- 314. Without trees--47; 109, 116, 137; 414. With or without trees--53, 60. Rare here; inf. thinks it is a southern term-- 401. Not common here; inf. says is so called because it grows slough grass--413. Usu. here--53; 207; 313. Usu.--328. swamp: = marsh--11-12, 33; 221; 421, 426. Larger than a marsh--54. Smaller than a marsh --422. = slough--60; 114; 328; 423. Larger than a slough--43; 301. Smaller than a slough--220. Wet and spongy ground--7-8; 113; 301, 309. Wet and spongy ground with trees--10, 23, 56. Wet and spongy ground without trees--130, 133-34, 136.

Wet and spongy ground with or without trees--28. Wetter than a marsh--37; 118. Not so wet as a marsh--56. Standing water--61; 114, 137; 222; 312; 421-22, 435. Standing water without trees--123, 125, 129, 142; 207; 425. Standing water with trees--116, 124, 128, 145. Standing water with or without trees--117, 131; 408, 424, 428. Without trees--31, 33-34, 36, 38, 49, 55, 65; 126, 151; 326; 413, 418, 429. With trees--2-4, 30, 40, 44; 311. With or without trees--21-22, 24, 29, 59-60; 122; 328. The most common term here--12. swampy land: Wet and spongy land--35; 147. Standing water--19. With trees--51. = marsh--147. swampy place: "Nicer than to say 'slough'"--409.

24.4 coulee.

The range of possible physical characteristics of a small depression with a usually dry watercourse accounts in part for the variety of UM terms, but geographical distribution restrictions account for some.

Draw, the most common, has a general frequency of only 37%, with a strong preponderance in Midland territory, thus: Mn. 4.3%, Ia. 46%, N.D. 8%, S.D. 55%, Nb. 84%. Its distribution contrasts fairly sharply with that of two other eastern terms, ravine and run, and of three western terms, coulee, gulch, and canyon.

Ravine, which dominates Minnesota, clearly has a Northern area frequency: Mn. 61%, Ia. 2.2%, N.D. 20%, S.D. 27%, Nb. 16%.

Dry run, an obvious derivative of the North Midland run in the sense of 'stream,' marks the northeast segment of Iowa and the adjoining southeast segment of Minnesota.

Coulee, an American borrowing from American French, occurs in two distinct areas. In southeastern Minnesota it denotes a small gently sloping valley leading into either the Mississippi River or an immediate tributary. In North Dakota and extreme northwestern Minnesota it typically denotes a shallower depression, dry except during wet weather or spring thaws, that may extend for miles across the prairie.

Gulch, referring to a small valley with rather steep slopes, does occur once each in Minnesota and Iowa, but seems more appropriate to the topography of the western fringe, where most of the instances appear.

Canyon, also referring to a steep-sided valley, has moved east from the Spanish-speaking southwest so far as to be a normal word for local features in western

Nebraska and the Black Hills of South Dakota.

The single occurrence of buffalo wallow in South Dakota echoes an earlier day when buffalo roamed the open prairie and, by rolling over in a wet spot or muddy place, so deepened the depression that it persisted until plows cut through the tough buffalo grass.

CL 129: Mail responses correspond fairly well to the field data. Draw, though found in every state, is strongest in Midland territory (Mn. 55%, Ia. 79%, N.D. 35%, S.D. 89%, Nb. 89%). Coulee dominates North Dakota with 80% and occurs in Minnesota with 28% frequency. Ravine is stronger in Minnesota than elsewhere. In this sense swale, which occurred only 12 times during fieldwork, was reported by 98 respondents (11%), nearly all of whom were likewise in Minnesota, Iowa, and Nebraska. Seep, recorded only once in Iowa, was checked by 39 (5%) widely separated checklist respondents.

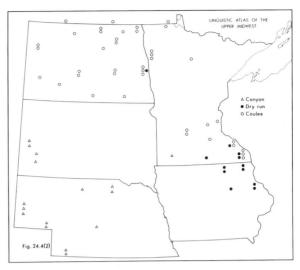

Fig. 24.4(2)

115-17, sn119, 122, 126, 128, 130-31, s132-33, 134, c135, s137, 138, 142, s146, 147, 149; 214, 222; 301-2, 304, sn309, 310-13, c314, 315, :c321, 326, ¹328; 401-4, :405, 406, sn407, s408, 409-12, c413, 417-19, 421-24, 426, 429-30, sn431, *432, 435, c436, 437. brush ~ c214.

  dry course 308.
  dry ditch 147.
  glen 45.
  gulch 46; 124; c309, 310-12, 315, 326; 409, 418.
  gully 5, 13, 21, 37, c¹47; 114, 118, 122, 125-26, 140, 151; 202, 222; 309-10; 408, 421, 428, 431. ~ wash 144.
  hollow c16, 54.
  pocket 418.
  ravine 5, 8, 10, c16, 19, 21, 26-27, 31-34, 39-43, 45-47, 50, †51, c52, 53, 60-62, f63, 64-65; 118; 201-2, 206, ¹207, 219, 221; 305, 314, 316, 318, 323, 328; 403-5, 410, 428.
  rivulet 319.
  run ¹51. bloody ~ 150. dry ~ 55, 57-58, 62; 105-8, 116, 119-20; 221.
  seep 135.
  slough 317.
  spillway 143.
  swale 53; 123, *145; 220; 403.
  vale 45.
  valley 44, 47, 50, c51, c59; 117, 127, 129, 145.
  wash 409. dry ~ 410. gully ~ 144.
  washout 414.
  no response 2-3, 6, 11-12, 14, 17-18, 22-25, 28-30, :35, 36, 38, 49; 103, 110, 113, 136, 139, 152; ?226; 306-7, 320, 324-25, 327; 415-16, 425, 433-34.

Comment:

  bayou: A ravine with a stream--211.
  canyon: Deeper than a draw or gulch--309-

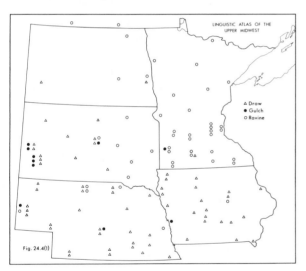

Fig. 24.4(1)

  bayou 211.
  bottom lands 47.
  buffalo wallow 322.
  canyon c59; 309-11, 326; 404, c405, 406, 409-11, c417, 418, cvr429, 436-37.
  coulee 1, sn4, sn7, 8, sn9, 10, s¹†19, s¹20, ¹27, ¹33, 34, *39, ¹44-45, 48, ¹52, c54, 55-56, sn57-58, ¹61-62, f63, :201, 202, c203, 204, c205, 206-24, s225; ¹309.
cedar ~ 209.
  creek 301, 303, 316, 323; 420. dry ~ 57; 225; 303-4, 323.
  cut 53.
  dale 7, 45.
  ditch 15; 121, 140-41, 148; 411, 427, 435.
  draw 19, 53; 101-2, 104, 109, 111-12,

11. Deeper than a draw or ravine--405. Deeper than a draw--429. Steeper sides than a draw--437. coulee: Has water in the spring or in wet weather--1; 205. "A coulee is a small stream that dries up in the summer"--7. A narrow ravine (c8' wide) without constantly running water--10. A small valley that might have water--57; 208. Has a small standing body of water--8. A dry depression along a level prairie; may extend for miles--219-20. Larger than a ravine--*39. = ravine--45. Deeper than a ravine--206. Larger than a dry run--55. A depression full of rocks and trees leading into a dry run--55. Inf. uses term only occ., but hears it quite often among local French Canadians--9. Uses term in North Dakota; here he says 'ravine'--34. Has not seen any coulees; says they are found in the Dakotas--44. Inf. says this term used in the Dakotas--52. Heard by inf. in North Dakota--¹33. Heard by inf. in Montana--19; 309. "Out in Montana they call them 'coulees'"--¹62. Heard by inf. near Red Wing--¹20. creek: Running water part of the time--301, 303, 316. Inf.'s term for the depression itself--323. draw: Deeper than a coulee--214. Larger than a gully--310. Common term here--328. gulch: Deeper than a draw--309-11. Steeper sides and shorter than a draw--312. Larger than a draw--315. Steeper sides than a draw--326. Deeper than a canyon--418. hollow: Usu.--54. pocket: The shallow slope leading into a canyon--418. ravine: Has water in it--21. Deeper than a gully--118. A depression without an outlet--201. Usu.--221. = draw--404. spillway: A soil conservation term--143. swale: Smaller than a coulee--220. The floor of a draw--403. vale: A small valley; = dale and glen--45. valley: Not common here--117. dry wash: = draw: shallow--410.

24.5 creek (small freshwater stream). NE 41. WG 13, 32, 40, 49, 61; F18, F83.

Although when asked, "What do you call a small stream, one smaller than a river?" some infs. insisted that they had no term except river, the common designation in the UM is creek. It shows no significant regional unbalance. Three terms competing with it, however, do have regional distribution. Brook and stream occur in almost precisely the same area, that is, most of Minnesota, eastern North Dakota, and southeastern Nebraska. They differ in two respects. Although their proportion is nearly identical among I and II speakers, brook has 50% frequency with Type III whereas stream has only 6%. Second, stream has a slightly greater oc-

currence in the Midland areas of Iowa and southeastern Nebraska. Fork, with an overall frequency of 2.4% but found only in Iowa, South Dakota, and Nebraska, clearly has Midland correlation. The two districts in Iowa reporting branch (with 20% frequency) may reflect its spread from Atlantic southern and upper Potomac regions. North Midland run lingers with only three infs.

The incidence of generic stream is reflected in the related occurrence of these terms in place names. Asked to name streams in the vicinity, Minnesota infs. identified 79 with creek, 29 with river, 13 with brook, besides Hammon Shoot, North Branch, and Whisky Ditch as single examples. Brook does not, however, appear in recorded Iowa stream names, which have the following totals: creek 42, river 22, spring 4, branch and fork 3, run 2 (Bloody R. and Trout R.), in addition to the singletons Rafferty's Slough and The Outlet. Less variety appeared in the western panel. In North Dakota 21 streams have creek in their proper names and 12 have river. In South Dakota 55 have creek and 15 have river. In Nebraska 66 streams were recorded with proper names including creek, 9 with river, 7 with branch, 2 with run, besides Fremont Slough. In no state does the term stream itself enter into a reported proper name combination.

   branch 107-8, 119-20, †135, 142-43, 145, 147, 149, 151; ¹404.
   brook 2, 6-7, 9, 11, 18, 21-24, 28, 33-34, 36, 38, 40, *41, 45-46, 48-49, 52-53, 56-58, ¹59, 62, 65; 106, 110, ¹111, 119, 130, 132, c150; 218, 220; 422, 424-26.
   brooklet 2.

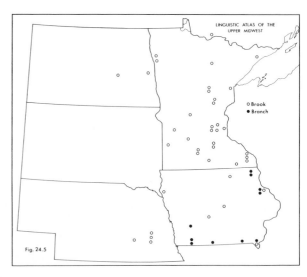

Fig. 24.5

creek c1, 2-5, sn6, 7-9, c10, 11-22,
c23, 24, c25, crc26, 27-30, c31, 32-35,
:36, cr37, c38, cr39, 40-41, c42-43, 44-
45, c46, 47, c48, 49, c50-51, 52, c53,
54-57, c58, 59, c60, 61-62, c63, 64, c65;
101-6, c107, 108-14, cr115, 116-49, c150,
151, c152; 201-5, c206, 207-12, c213,
214-17, c218, 219, c220, 221, c222, 223-
25; 301-4, 306-9, cr310, c311-13, 314-18,
c319, 320-21, c322, 323-28; c401-3, 404-
8, c409, 410-13, c414, 415-16, c417-18,
419-22, c423-24, 425-28, c429, 430, s431,
432-37.
  ditch 15; 136, 145.
  fork 122; 312, c320; 404, 428.
  freshet 44, 62.
  river 13-18, 32, 43-45, 51, 53, 56,
c59, 60-61, 65; 118, 135, 151; 301, 306-
8, 316-19, 322, 325; 418.
  rivulet 23, ?55, 58; 119, :144; 204;
305.
  run 57; 139; 224. ~way 201.
  shoot c57.
  spring 44. ~ branch 119. ~ creek 430.
~ stream 434.
  stream 3, 6, 10, c11, 12-15, 19-20,
c23, 25-26, 32, 37, 40, 44, 49, c56, 63;
107-8, 114, 116, 120-21, 139, 152; 212;
222, 226; 421, 424-25, 431-32, 435.

Comment:

  branch: Any tributary--107-8, 120.
Smaller than a creek--119, 142, 151.
Heard used by neighbors originally from
Virginia--404. brook: = creek--7, 11, 23-
24, *41, 48, 55, 59. Smaller than a
branch--119, 143. Larger than a creek--9,
21, 28; 201. Smaller than a creek--2, 22,
33; 106, 132; 218; 425-26. Larger than a
stream--424. Smaller than a stream--6, 49.
Spring fed--33, 65; 119. "It has rocks;
a creek doesn't"--2; 130; 422. "It has
trout in it"--34, 38, 40. It always has
water; a creek doesn't--52. Faster than
a creek--62. More rambling than a creek--
150. A book word for the inf.--150. Inf.
says not the usual word here--53. Usu.--
24. creek: Smaller than a river--25, 30,
43, 45, 51, 60-61; 106, 114, 124, 145,
151; 225; 306, 308, 316, 318-19. Usu.--
45, 55-56. ditch: Smaller than a creek--
145. fork: = creek--122. A branch of a
river--312. rivulet: Smaller than a brook
or creek--23. Larger than a creek--55.
Smaller than a creek--144; 204. run:
Smaller than a stream--139. It has water
in the spring; a 'creek' is permanent--
224. runway: Spring fed; smaller than a
creek--201. stream: = creek--207. Smaller than a branch--121. Larger than a
creek--10, 12, 37; 121, 222; 424. Smaller than a creek--3, 25, 32, 49, 63; 107,
114, 152; 435. Smaller than a river--6.
Especially in 'trout stream'--6, 10, 20.

"More non-committal than 'creek'"--421.
A "poetic" word--29.

24.8 butte. NE 38.

  This item was typically queried as
"What do you call an elevation of land,
not so high as a mountain, usually having
a flat top?" But variation in the question may have caused the eliciting of
hill, knoll, cliff, and bluff as well as
the likely butte. Iowa fieldworkers apparently asked "What is a butte?" and
hence recorded this term out of its geographical context.
  Butte, taken from American French, is
otherwise recorded generally as a name
for a known topographical feature. This
eroded elevation is peculiarly characteristic of the semiarid western portions
of Nebraska and the Dakotas. The term
butte is sometimes identified with bluff
and twice in Nebraska with the southwestern Spanish equivalent mesa, a form more
common in neighboring Colorado.

  bluff 25, 49, 55; 121; 217; 305; 406,
425.
  butte 37; 101, 105, 108, [1]109, 111,
116, s120, 122, s124, 125, 131, 141, 145,
[1]152; 202-7, 210-19, 221-24, s225, 226;
301-4, 306, 309-15, 320-21, 323-26, 328;
401-5, 407, c409, s410, 411-16, 418-23,
s?425, 426-28, s429, 430-31, 433, 435-37.
  cliff 118, 151.
  hill 1-2, c3, 4-5, 7-8, c10, 11-12, 14-
15, c16, 17, 19-28, 31, 33-34, 37, 41-47,
49-54, c59, 60-61, 63; 151; 201, 204-7,
209, 211-13, c214, 218-19; 307-8, c319,
323.
  knoll 44, 51, [1]54; 151; 205.
  mesa →[1]409, 425.
  mound 51.
  rise 9.
  no response 6, 13, 18, 29, 30, 32, 35-
36, 38-40, 48, 56-59, 62, 64-65; 102-4,
106-7, 110, 112-15, 117, 119, 123, 126-
30, 132-40, 142-44, 146-50; 208, 220;
317-18, ?322, 327; 408, 417, 424, 432,
434.

25.1 wharf. NE 183.

  For a wooden platform extending into a
river or lake the most widely used UM
term is dock. Competing with it, but not
always with a referent similar in size
or purpose, are landing, pier, and wharf.
Distribution patterns seem inconsistent:
dock has lowest frequency in North Dakota, landing in Iowa, pier in North Dakota, and wharf in South Dakota. A number
of infs. in the western panel of states
pointed out that the referent was unfa-

miliar to them in their particular region, so that any term used was a book word only. Development of water recreation areas on new man-made lakes is changing the situation.

dock 1-9, c10, 11-24, 26, *27, 28, 30-34, :35, 37-40, 43-48, 50-51, :52, c53, 56-59, 61, 63-65; 101-2, 104-6, 108-9, 111-14, 117, 119-21, 123-25, 127-33, 137-38, 141, 143-46, 149-50, 152; 204-7, 211,

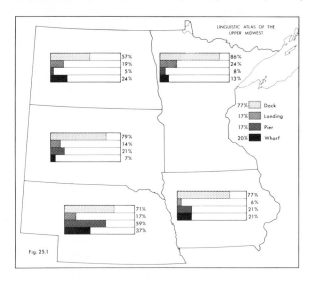

Fig. 25.1

213, 218-19, 221-22, 225-26; 306-8, 315-19, 321, 323, 328; 414, 416, :418, 420-21, ¹422, 424-29, 431, *432, 433-35, 437. loading ~ 121.

float 120.

landing c13, 22-25, 28, 34, 36-37, 39, :44, 49, 54-55; 120-21; 210, c212, 220; c314, :325; 409, c411, 434. boat ~ 119; 216; 430. ~ platform 38.

levee 39, 58.

pier c6, 33, 37, 42, 60; 102-3, 110, 118, s119, 121, 126, 134, 137, 149, 151; 203; 305, 316, 319; 413, 419, 420, sn421, 422-23, 425-26, 433, 435.

quay 7.

terminal 58; 120.

wharf 3, 11, ¹17, 46, 51, 54, 57, 59, 61, ?62; 101, 119-20, 122, 136-37, 140, 142, *145, s147, 148, s152; 201-2, 208, 217, 221; 328; 411, c413, sn414, ¹422, sn424, 425-28, 433.

no response 29, ?41; 107, 115-16, 135, 139; 209, 214-15, 223-24; 301-4, 309-13, 320, 322, 324, 326-27; 401-8, ?410, 412, 415, 417, 436.

Comment:

dock: Small--33, 57; 226; 328; 426, 428. For small boats--328. For large ships --152; 421, 427. On lakes or rivers--225-26. "At summer resorts"--426. "No use for

them here"--431. Not an active term for inf.--430, 433-34. Usu.--3. Usu. here--37, 51. float: For small boats--120. landing: For large boats--22. For small boats --214. = dock--24, 34. Fancy dock with seats, etc.--28. The common term here--39. "We don't have them"--409. landing platform: For steamers--38. pier: Term is used here for the breakwater--6. Larger than a dock--11, 51, 57, 61; 101; 221; 428. For large boats--51, 57; 152; 414, 424-25. Smaller than a dock--427. Synonymous with pier--414. "At the oceanside" --414. Heard used by an "out-of-town woman"--17. Inf. says this is a book word--411.

25.2a cement road. NE 43.

A rural or intercity highway paved with concrete, that is, with a hardened mixture of cement and of sand and gravel aggregate, is variously named in the UM. More than one-third of the infs., especially in Northern speech territory, call it "the pavement," a term perhaps increasing in use (I 33%, II 39%, III 56%). Paved road or highway is the term of one-fourth of the infs., with a Midland orientation. Paving is also distinctly Midland, with high frequency in Nebraska and Iowa and no occurrences in Minnesota. The descriptive concrete road or highway has a unique distribution, with high frequency in Minnesota and Nebraska and with probable increasing vitality (I 21%, II 24%, III 37%). Cement road or highway, however, seems to be waning (I 15%, II 10%, III 0). The single instance of hard road in eastern Iowa reflects its popularity in Illinois. Slab, also found only in Iowa, likewise is probably an Illinois import.

CL 89: Of 1,045 mail responses 85% offer pavement as the usual term in all UM states. Cement road, with 15.5%, is next. Paving, most frequent in Iowa and Nebraska, is next with 8%. Iowa and Nebraska report 22 choices of hard road and 12 of slab. Others less frequently checked are surface road, concrete road, concrete pavement, pike, paved road, and hard surface road. Of the two respondents accepting pike one, a Minnesotan of Danish ancestry, had lived for 10 years in Iowa, and the other, an Iowan, had both father and grandparents born in Pennsylvania, where pike is common.

big road 151.

cement 6, 35, 39-40, 59, 61-62; 119; 216; *306, 308, 317; 420, 428, c430. ~ highway 14; 214; 431. ~ pavement 225; 429. ~ road 16, 21, 44; 118, 151-52; 401.

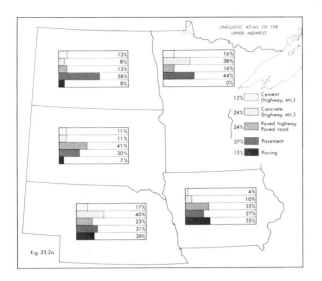

Fig. 25.2a

concrete 18-19, :36, 38, 40, r56, 57-60, c61; 101, 120, 150; 224; 421, 423-24, 426, 433-35. ~ highway 2, 33, 37, 43; 312, 315; 422, 427, 431. ~ pavement 436. ~ paving 146. ~ road 3, 13, 15-17, 22, 27, 48, 51; 105; 218; 322; 409, 411, 425, 436.

hard road 141. ~ surface 202. ~ surfaced road 321; 426.

hardtop 328.

highway 18, 32, 39, 53, c56, 57, 59, 61; 120-21, 123, 130-31, 136, 142, 144; 317-19.

paved highway 10, 24; 103, 113, 123, 127, 138; 306, 310, 314, 323; 404, 431.

paved road 4, 14, 23, 25, c29, 31, 33, 64-65; 105, 112, 114, 116, 122, 126-27, 130, 132, 137, 139, 144, 150; 203, 207, 220; 305, 307, 309, 321, 324-26; 401, 405, 411, 415, 425, 428.

pavement 7, :8, 9, 11-12, 17, 20, 22, 26, 28, 30, 32, 34, 41-47, 49-50, 52-53, c54, 55, 60, 63; 104, 110, 114, s115, 117, 124-25, 128, 135-36, 138, 140, 142-43, 145; 204-6, 208-10, sn212, 215, 217, 221-24, 226; 302-4, 311, 313, 316, 318-19; 402, 406, c409, 411, 417-18, sn424, 426, cvr427, 429, ¹435, 437.

paving 102, c103, 106-9, 111, 116, 126, 129, 131, 133-34, 147-49; 211, 219; 301, 320; 401, 407-8, 412-14, 419-20, *432.

slab 117, 149. ~ highway ¹435.

surface road 416.

no response 1, 5; 201, ?213; 327; 403, :410.

25.2b blacktop road. NE 43.

For a highway having some kind of bituminous surface the most common UM designation is blacktop (road). Its otherwise fairly even distribution is marked by

competing tarvia in Minnesota and the near absence of competition in Iowa.

Tarvia, originally a trademark, is the form used by one-fourth of the infs. in both Minnesota and South Dakota. A colloquial variant, tarvy, was reported by four infs. in Minnesota and one each in the Dakotas.

Oil(ed) road, though not unknown in Minnesota and Iowa, is most popular in South Dakota and Nebraska. This term apparently sometimes refers also to a rolled road surface compounded of heavy oil and clay or earth.

Mat and oil mat, not hitherto recorded, are familiar in eastern and southern Nebraska, where the sense appears to be an extension of mat designating a concrete slab or the base of such a slab.

Tar road and tarred road turned up in southern Minnesota and on both sides of the Minnesota-Dakota border.

Eastern macadam(ized road) is a book term to most UM residents, only five of whom reported actually using it; Eastern asphalt for a highway is equally moribund in the UM, with only six occurrences.

CL 90: Blacktop was checked as the usual name by 86% of the mail respondents, oil(ed) road by 18% (mostly in S.D. with 27% and Nb. with 37%, and tarvia 7% (mostly in Mn. with 22% and S.D. with 7%). Pavement, which only three field infs. had reported, was checked by 47 mail respondents (5%) scattered throughout the UM.

asphalt 202, 204, 224; 305-6; 426. ~ paving 129. ~ road 3, 62; 209; 418. ~ surfacing c3.

bitulithic street 150.

bituminous road 117.

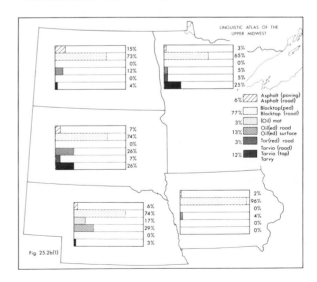

Fig. 25.2b(1)

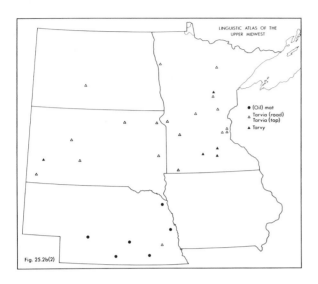

Fig. 25.2b(2)

black surface road 45.

blacktop 102, 5-6, 9-10, ¹11, 12, 14, 20, ¹22, 23-25, ¹*26, 27-31, 33-34, c35, 37, 40, 42-47, s¹48, 53-54, 56-58, 60-61, 64, s¹65; 101-6, 108-17, 119-28, 130-50, 152; 201, 203-8, 210-13, ¹214, 215, 218-19, 221-23, ¹224, 225-26; 301-3, ¹304, *306, 307-8, s309, 310, 312, sn313, 314-15, 317-18, 320-22, 324-26, 328; 401-2, 404, 406-9, :410, 411-14, 416, 420-22, 425-28, 430-31, 433-35, 437. ~ road 13, 17. blacktopped road 323.

hard surface road 220. hard surfaced road 321.

hardtop 38.

highway 317-19.

macadam 58; ?431. ~ road 51. macadamized road 44, 62.

mat *419, 431. oil ~ c408, 419, 422, 428, *432.

oil ¹411.

oil road 32; 104; ¹312, 316, 321; sn407, c408, 409, 412, 417, 436. oiled ~ 19, 43; 107; 209, 216; 302-4, 310, †313, ¹325; 405-6, 423, 429.

oil surface 308. oiled ~ 223.

paved road c214.

pavement sn424, 426, ¹436.

paving 419.

surfaced road 309.

tar 307; ¹407. ~ road 7. ~ top 305. tarred road 4, 63.

tarvia 8, ¹10, 11, c22, 24, 26-27, 37, 39-40, 61; 217; 308, ¹312, 313, 319-20; 426. ~ road 41; 302. ~ top *306.

tarvy 21, 48, 50, sn52; ¹224; 311.

no response 14-16, 36, 49, 55, 59; 118, 151; 327; 403, 415.

Comment:

blacktop: Usu.--24; 223. The most com-

mon local term--313. macadam: "Is it 'macadam'?"--431. oil road: Usu.--407. paving: Usu.--419. pavement: Inf. says this term used by farmers--436. tarvy: "That's only a trade name"--21.

25.3 byway. NE 44.

Rural roads that are not through high- ways have many designations in the UM, depending in large part upon their pur- pose and location. Of the 41 recorded terms, 26 do not appear in the New Eng- land Atlas. The most common, side road, is evenly distributed, with an average frequency of 55%, but the others are not. Second, with 27 infs. and a frequency of 55%, is dirt road. Actually both the re- ferent and this term are common in the area, but since the term refers rather to the composition than to the function or location of the road, fieldworkers were inconsistent in recording it.

Country road, with 25 instances, seems slightly Midland oriented (Mn. 9%, Ia. 15%, N.D. 8%, S.D. 4%, Nb. 22%), but fieldworker variation may be involved. Such variation affects the picture with county road, with a frequency of 16 times or 8%. Because county roads, like state highways, are found throughout the UM, A rarely recorded the term itself, and other fieldworkers recorded it only sporadically.

The 15 occurrences of byway and byroad are more obviously Midland oriented (Mn. 6%, Ia. 15%, N.D. 4%, S.D. 0, and Nb. 6%). Eastern bypath, however, seems not to have been carried west in this sense.

Next most common, trail, is clearly western (see chart). Trail, reminiscent of immigrant wagon trains and the open range, survives in the Great Plains, where there are still, even for automobiles, roads that meander over the prairies, across the coulees, and around the buttes without meekly following surveyor-drawn section lines. Trail's frequency is: Mn. 2%, Ia. 0, N.D. 23%, S.D. 41%, Nb. 11%.

Also clearly regional are cart road and cartway, both found in New England but in the UM peculiar to Minnesota, where they refer to a relatively shorter and narrow- er road than the country highway. In Min- nesota State Statutes of 1960, chapter 160, section 8, a town board is authorized to establish a cartway, which is then de- fined as a road two rods wide and not more than one-half mile long. The usual rural highway width is four rods.

Also limited to Minnesota, except for one instance just across the North Dako- ta border, is the specialized tote road. Reported in Maine as the designation of a temporary road used to transport equipment and supplies to a lumber camp, this term was carried west by loggers into Michigan and Wisconsin and ultimately into Minnesota, where it persists in the secondary forested areas still having logging operations. (For its relation to other tote expressions, see 71.4 and chart.)

back road 37, 48, sn49, 57, s58; 106; 309; 426.
branch road 118; 310; 403, ¹413.
byroad ¹28, 45-46, 55; 113, 115, 132-33,

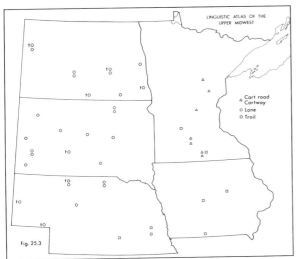

Fig. 25.3

135, 139, 151; ¹324; 429, 431. byway 54; 143; 204.
cart road 23, 51, 63. cartway 21, 29, 53, 62.
country road 1, 10-11, 40, 47, 58; 111, 120-21, 129, 134, 143-44, 146; 214, 224; 319; 402, 406, 409, 416-17, 425, *432, 435. ~ trail 406.
county road 17, 37, 42-43, 60; 222, 226; 305, 317; s415, 420, 422-23, 428, ¹431, 434.
crossroad 45; 421.
cutoff 35.
dead-end road 31; 436.
dirt road 16, 32, 48, 53; 117, 122-23, 125-26, c127, *130, 131, 134, 136, 140-42, 145-46, 148-49; 214; 424.
farm road 38. farmer's ~ 308.
feeder road 223; 308; 422.
fork 312.
grass road 307.
gravel road 15, 17, 39-40, 43, 48, 53, 59. graveled ~ 63; 305; 424.
jackrabbit highway †204.
lane ¹28, 62; 118, 128, 150; 423, sn424, 426.
mud road !130.
prairie road 47; 201; 301, 307, †313. ~ trail †313.

road 18, !52.
rural branch 312. ~ highway 316. ~ road 431.
secondary highway 425. ~ road 17.
section line 316; 421. ~ line road 59. ~ road 305.
side gravel 318.
side road 1-5, 8-9, 12-15, sn17, *19, 20-23, 25-27, ¹28, 33-34, 37, 39-41, sn42, 43-48, 50, s56, 57, s58, 60-62, sn64,s¹65; 101-5, s106, 107-10, 112, 114-16, 119-20, s121, 124, 137-38, 147, 150, 152; 202-3, 205-7, 209-13, 215-16, ¹218, 221, s222, 223-25; 302-4, *306, 308-11, 313, 315, 318, 320, 323-26, 328; 401, 405-7, c408, 410-11, 413-14, 419-20, 424, 425-27, 430-34, 437.
state road 434.
tote road 1, 14, c16, 33, 37; 207.
town road 7, 43. township 24, 29-30, 41, 57; 208, 219, 224-25; 307, 322.
trail ?6, 44; †209, 210, 216-17, †218, 219-20, †223, 224, sn†225; 301-2, c305, 306, sn309, ?310, 311-12, 314, 316, 320-21; †403, 412, †436. ~ road 404-5, †409. country ~ 406. prairie ~ †313.
trunk road 57.
no response 36; 327; 418.

Comment:

back road: Inferior, "sort of short cut"--426. byroad: A small, private road --115. cart road: Legally designated road 2 rods wide; regular road is 4 rods wide--23. cartway: 2 rods wide--21. To one farm--53, 62. lane: Narrow and private--150. To single farm house from road--423, s424, 426. section line: If the road coincides with the section line, as here--316, 421. trail: Private road, as across a pasture--224, 301. Non-vehicular road--6 ("Gunflint Trail isn't named right"); 310, 315, 321 ("tracks across the prairie"). Usu. here in the Sand Hills--412. Term dying out--312; 405. prairie ~: Ungraded road across the prairie--¹313.

25.5 He threw a stone at the dog. NE 35.

In a context requiring the meaning to be that of a missile thrown by hand, informants with Northern speech characteristics generally prefer stone, and those with Midland speech generally prefer rock. For the former a stone is smaller than a rock; for the latter the reverse is true. A few equate the two terms.
Of Midland incidence, with three occurrences, are variants of Irish dornick.
In the same context, according to the independent investigation of a Minnesota graduate student, Rex Beach, canorry, of unknown origin, appears in Stillwater,

Minnesota, where it was used by 14 out of 17 people over 30 years old, by 9 out of 12 between 20 and 30, and by 3 out of 8 under 20. But apparently canorry is not known to the two female field infs. in Washington County, where Stillwater is located.

Pebble(stone), although apparently designating an object smaller than a stone, still was employed in this context six times in Iowa and Nebraska. This Midland orientation does not correlate with its appearance six times in central Massachusetts in the NE Atlas study.

In the stoneless and boulderless dissected till plains of eastern Nebraska the urge to throw at a dog would have to be satisfied with a clod of earth, as recorded by four infs. there. "Rocks? Here?" one exclaimed to the fieldworker.

CL 101: The Midland-Northern contrast is sharper in the mailed data, which have rock as only 31% and stone as 80% in Minnesota, but rock with 77% and stone with 34% in southern Iowa. The total number of respondents, 1,047, have 63% stone and 51% rock.

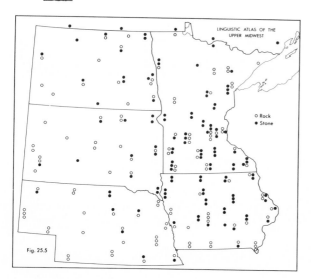

chunk ¹*130.
clod 416, 421, 423, 427.
donnicker 320. dornick s†145. dornicky sn†311.
pebble 119, 121; 401, 413, 419. ~stone †120.
rock 4, 6, 9, 11-16, 19-21, 33-35, 37, 39-41, 43-44, c45, c46, 47, c51, 53-54, †55, 58, c60-61, 62-63; ?104, 106-7, 113, 119-20, 122-23, 125, 128-30, 135, 139-40, 142-46, 148-52; 205-6, 210-12, 214-15, 217, 219, 221-22, 224-25; 301-3, 305-6, 309-12, c314, 315-16, 318, 320-22, 328; 401, 403-4, 407-12, 414, 416-18, 420,

422, 424-31, 433-34, 436-37.
stone 1-3, 5, 7-8, 10, 14, c16, 17-18, 21-33, †34, 36, 38, 40, 42-46, c47, 48-53, 55-58, c59, 60, c61, 62-65; 101-3, cr104, 105-19, 121, 124, 126-27, 131-34, 136-38, c139, 141, 147, :s150; 201-4, 207-9, 213, 216, 218-21, 223, 226; 304, 306-8, 313, 317, 319, 323-27; 402, 405-6, 413, 415, 421, 432, 435.

Comment:

rock: Larger--14, 17, 32, 44, 46, 51, 61-62; 139. Requires blasting--18. Rough fragment of a larger piece--58. Too big to lift--59. "Actually, 'clod' is much more common"--427. stone: Smaller--40, 43, 45, 47, 52-53, 58-60, 63. Larger--119. Might be larger--106. Round--58. = rock-- 21; 107, 113. "A 'stone' house, but a 'rock' in the middle of the road"--120.

26.1 I ran across him. NE 422.

Included in the worksheets because of the range of variants used with run (for which see Vol. 3), this item elicited also some lexical equivalents for the whole expression run across. Most infs. also use meet, which for some is the only term recorded (especially by Iowa fieldworkers). Others use see, apparently in the sense of a chance encounter. Without regional or type significance, these other terms are not listed here.

bump into ¹12, 14, 37, 57; 201, 222.
chance upon 18.
happen across *306.
meet up with c226.
happen to meet 318-19.
happen to see 316.

26.4 Call to a dog to attack another dog.

Often arousing amusement, this query typically elicited the common sic 'im. The southern Iowa and Nebraska distribution of the infrequent take 'im suggests a Midland leaning in contrast with the distribution of the variants with get, which may be Northern.

catch 'im 35. get after 'im 120. get 'im 38; 311, 326; 404. go and get 'im 10, 13; 224. go get 'im 12, 14, 33, 60; 126; 323, 328; 417, 430.
hunt 'im up 120.
sic 139, 147, 151.
sic 'im !1, 2, !3, 4-12, 14-19, !20, 21, ¹22, 23-26, !27, 28-32, 34-41, !42, 43, !44, 45, !46, 47, !48, 49-50, r51, 52-55, s¹56, 57-58, !59, !60, 61-63, !64, 65; 101-10, 112-19, 121-24, 127-34, 136-46, 148-50, !152; !201-204, 205, ¹206,

207-8, !209-10, 211-19, !220, 221-22,
!223-24, 225, !226; 301-9, !310, 311-13,
315-26; 401-2, !403, ¹404, 405-6, !407,
408-16, !417, 418-29, s430, 431, s432,
433-37.
  take 'im 122, 125, 135, 145; 204; 302;
429, *432.
  no response 111; 314, 327.

26.5 Call to summon dog.

In the UM a dog is summoned usually by
either Here! or an expression with Come!
As the chart reveals, the former is
clearly Midland oriented and the specific
Come here! has a contrasting Northern
dominance, although both are found
throughout the area.

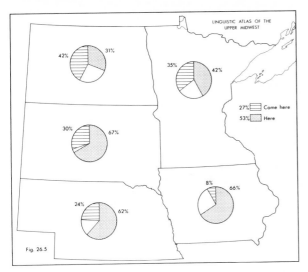

Fig. 26.5

  come (+ name) 23, 28, 35, 40, 43, 55,
57, 59, 64; 105, 126, 148; 203, 210, 223;
415, 422-23, 425. ~ here (+ name) 1-3, 7,
19, 24, 27, 29, 32-33, 36, 39, 43-45, 48,
51-53, 55-56, 58, 65; 125, 129, 142, 148;
204, 206-7, 209, 211, 214, 217, 219, 222,
!225, 226; 302, 305, 307-8, 311, 314-15,
320; 401-2, 407-8, 419, 424, 429-30, 433.
~ on (+ name) 4, 10, 20, 26; 103, 106,
128, 144; c218, 220; 309. ~ on here 19.
~ over here 220.
  here (+ name) 1, 3, 5, 8-10, 16-18,
21-22, 30-31, 36-38, 40-42, !46, 49-50,
54, 57, 60, !61, !63; 101-4, 108, 110-17,
119, 121-24, 130-31, 133, 136-37, 139-41,
143, 145-47, 149-50, 152; 201, 205, 208,
215-16, 218, 221, 224; *301, 303-4, *306,
308, 310-13, 318-19, 321-22, !323, 324-
26, 328; 403-6, 409-14, 416-18, 420-21,
425-28, 431, 434-36.
  hie (+ name) 6; 109; 433.
  oh (+ name) 120.
  (call by name) 13-16, 25, 34, 48, 50,

57, 62; 212; 316-17; 432.
  (snap fingers) 47, 62.
  (make a sucking noise) 54; 213.
  (whistle) 1, 5, 8, 12, 17, 20, 25-26,
29-30, 33-34, 37, 41, 44-53, 57-62; 107-
8, 117, 120, 127, 130, 132, 134-35, 138;
202-4, 212-13, 215-16, 224; 302, 305,
312, 316, 328; 409, 417-18, !419, 431,
437.
  no response 11; 118, 151; 327.

26.6 mongrel. NE 212.

For a dog of uncertain antecedents and
of little value two fairly evenly distributed terms compete in the UM. Mongrel,
with 58% frequency, may have slight Midland orientation: Mn. 65%, Ia. 59%, N.D.
35%, S.D. 61%, Nb. 59%. It is also more
favored by cultivated speakers: I 51%,
II 63%, III 74%. These slight imbalances
contrast with the use of cur and the older cur dog, which with an overall frequency of 43% occur as follows: Mn. 34%,
Ia. 53%, N.D. 50%, S.D. 32%, Nb. 50%.
Cur may be less favored by Type III
speakers: I 44%, II 44%, III 31%, but
evidence is insufficient.
  The 13 scattered responses of scrub and
scrub dog reveal no special pattern unless it is a slight Northern leaning
(Mn. 7%, Ia. 4%, N.D. 12%, S.D. 7%, Nb.
6%), but a sharply regional form is fice,
found almost exclusively in Iowa (24%)
and twice in Nebraska (6%) but not elsewhere. This word, sometimes appearing as
ficet /faɪst/, is to be correlated with
its derivative ficety (feisty). See 56.4,
57.3, and 57.4.

  alley dog 20; 431. bad ~ 7. common ~
133, 139; 209.
  bum 25.
  coolie !48.
  cross 13.
  crossbreed 120; 307.
  cur 6, ¹7, 8, 11, 15, 21-22, 26, 30,
:1†31, 33, 35, 39-40, *43, 45, !46, s48,
52-53, *60,; 103, sn107, 108, 117-18,
sn119, 120-22, 125-27, *130, 136, sn139,
140-41, 144-49, :150, 152; 204, 207,
212, 215-18, 221, cr222, 223; 301, 303,
309, 311-12, s313, 314, 320, :321, 323,
¹326; 401-2, :¹403, c404, 405-6, 408-14,
420, s424, 429, 433, 435, 437. ~ dog
10, 24-25; 124, 132; 211, sn220, 225;
410.
  curbstone setter 38; 110.
  duke's mixture 432.
  fice(t) sn112-13, sn115, 125, 130,
sn132-33, 145-46, sn147-48, 150; 426, 437.
  half-blood 113.
  Heinz !102.
  hound !32; ?222; 303, 315; 416. ~ dog

416.
  loafer 19.
  mix breed 16.
  mixed (dog) 56. ~ breed 305. mixture
305.
  mogul 138.
  mongrel 1-3, 6, 9-10, c11, 12, 14, 16,
18, 23, 27-28, 30, 33-34, 37-38, 40, *41,
!42, 43-47, s!48, 49-51, 54-55, 57-63,
65; 101-3, 105-6, s107, 109-17, 119-21,
123-24, 126, 128-31, 137, 142, 148-49,
151-52; 201-2, 205-6, 208, 210, 213-14,
226; 302, 304, 306, 308, 310-11, 313,
316-20, 324, c325, 326-28; 401-2, c404,
410, 413, 418-28, 431, 433-34, 436.
  mutt 5, 29; 202, 226; 410.
  no-account (hound) 213; 322. no-good
(dog) 134-35; 216.
  pooch 12-13.
  pot-licker 147.
  scrub (dog) 17, 20, !43, !63; 134, 143;
211, 219, 224; 306, 325; 430, 434.
  stray 57; 209.
  tramp (dog) 10, 35; 220; 309.
  worthless hound 203.
  no response :4, 36, 64; 104; :?407,
415, :417.

27.1 bull. NE 190. WG 19, 62; F94.

Although all UM infs. know the word
bull, some use it with reluctance, some
men avoid its use in the presence of
women, and many men (44%) and a somewhat
higher proportion of women (49%) admit
the at least occasional use of equivalent
terms that generally function as euphemisms. The great variety of terms in NE
(42) is not quite matched by the total
in the UM, however (27).
The more frequent variants in the UM
also occur in NE; only two, and a possible third, reflect exclusively Midland
and South Midland origin.
As in NE, the most common variant is
gentleman cow, with 38 instances (18%)
widely distributed in the UM. Sire, also
found in NE, has a clear Northern orientation in the UM: Mn. 17%, Ia. 8%, N.D. 27%,
S.D. 19%, Nb. 3%. Also clearly Northern
is NE critter, the 14 occurrences of
which (7%) are distributed thus: Mn. 7%,
Ia. 2%, N.D. 15%, S.D. 12%, Nb. 5%. NE
animal and male animal appear 29 times
(14%) rather evenly distributed.
Midland and South Midland male cow is
used by three Iowa infs., two with a
Pennsylvania parent and one with a Kentucky parent. South Midland ox survives
with seven infs., five of whom deem the
term old-fashioned. Eastern Virginia
steer is unaccountably reported in this
sense by two Minnesotans, one of British
parentage and the other of Icelandic par-

entage.
Ferdinand, perhaps not a term to survive, derives from the story Ferdinand
the Bull, popular not long before fieldwork took place.

  animal ¹20, 25; †119, †133, *145, ¹152;
†223; 302, 304, ¹305, 307, ¹†323, 324,
414, 431, †437. he ~ 48. male ~ 17, 25;
†113, †*116; †207, †214; 316-17; 420,
434.
  bovine !¹†35; ?†103.
  boy cow 423.
  bull 1-34, c35, 36-41, 43, :44, 45-47,
49-54, c55, 57-65; 101-5, 107-33, 135-43,
s144, 145-52; 201-10, !211, 212-24, c225,
226; 301-13, c314, 315-23, !324, 325-26,
328; 401-13, cvr414, 416-18, c419, 420-
28, c429, c430, 431, *432, 433-36, c437.
  calf's father !29.
  Chauncey †42.
  critter †1, †29; †117; c*203, †210,
†215, 224; 302, c313, c322; !†401, †411.
  country gentleman !57.
  duke 54; !317.
  Ferdinand !57; 119, 127; c†305, !319.
  gentleman bull !¹126. ~ cow 8, †10,
¹!†21, ¹†22, ¹34, ¹†37, 64; †102, †104,
†108, 109, †111, †116, †118, ¹121, 127,
134, †139, 140; †205, !¹†208, †212, ¹†213,
c!†214, 217; 308, !¹†309, !†313, 316,
!317, ¹325, !†328; !†401, †406, 416,
¹†417, 428, 431. ~ ox †101; †418.
  he animal 48. ~ cow †104.
  head of the herd 317.
  herd bull 61-62. ~ sire ¹30.
  Johnny cow †223.
  male ¹†220; ¹†311; †405, 414, †429,
¹†436. ~ cow 105, 109, 132. ~ critter
421. ~ steer †407.
  master of the barnyard 317.
  mister 131. ~ of the herd ¹7.
  ox 106, †114, †137, †138, †*145; †407,
*432.
  papa cow 414.
  sire 3-4, ¹8, 19, ¹24, 41-43, 53, 62;
122, 128, 144, 149; 203-4, 211, †216,
217, †*218, 221, †223; 302, ¹305, 306,
319, 322; †406, 413.
  steer 44, 47.
  stock animal 57; 107; c!¹†312. ~ critter 316.
  top ox ¹135.
  no response 327; 415.

Comment:

  critter: Usu. here--64. Ferdinand:
Jocular, not euphemistic--305. gentleman
cow: Jocular, not euphemistic--121. male
critter: Seldom used by inf.--421. sire:
Usu.--19. Inf. says this is a "technical"
term--62. = registered bull; not a
euphemism--41; 306.

27.3 _yoke_ (of oxen). NE 189.

Included primarily because of its relevance to plural forms, this item revealed several variants for the principal term, _yoke_. Although the use of oxen as draft animals was so unfamiliar to one-fifth of the UM infs. that they had no word for two oxen yoked for plowing, the remainder, proportionately most in Type I, recalled _yoke_, _team_, _span_, _pair_, and _brace_.

Most common, _yoke_ was reported by 62% of all responding infs. with no conspicuous regional patterns. _Team_, favored by 28%, has a distribution inconsistent with normal UM regional variations: Mn. 47%, Ia. 14%, N.D. 22%, S.D. 21%, Nb. 38%. _Pair_, the response of 13%, is also spread inconsistently: Mn. 10%, Ia. 11%, N.D. 22%, S.D. 13%, Nb. 14%. Four of the 7 instances of _span_ are in Minnesota.

brace *318.
pair c9, 11, 16, c20, c30, 41; c107, 109, 132, 147, f150; 204, 209, 215-16, 221; †304, 306, 319, 325; 421, c426, 428, 431.
span 7, 34, 45, 53; 139; c202; 323.
team 1-3, 5, c7, 15-16, 18-19, c20, ᴵ21, ?22, c25, 27, 31, 33, 35, c36, 42, 44, c48, 49-50, 55; 107, 118, 120-21, 139; c202, 203, ?207, c208, 217, ?220, 224; 303, c314, 316, 318, c327; †401, c403, c405, 417, 421, 424, 427-29, c430, ?432, 433, 434. ox ~ 104; 422, ᴵ434.
yoke sn1, 4, 7, 10, 12, 17-18, cvr19, c21, cr22, c23, 24, c25, c26, ?28, 29, c30, 32, 37, 39-40, ?43, 44, cvr46, 47, 51-54, c56, 57-63, 65; 101, 103-5, 108, c112, 113-14, 116, 118-19, 122, c124, 125-26, c129, 130, *134, 135, 137, 142-43, 145-46, 148, 151-52; c201, c202, 205-6, cr207, 208, 210, 212-14, 216, 218, cr220, 223, c225, 226; c301, †302, c305, 307-8, c309, c312, 313, †315, 316-17, 319-20, c322, 324, 328; 407, c409, 413-16, 418, 420, †422, 423, 425-27, cr432, 434.
no response 6, 8, 13-14, 38, 64; 102, 106, 110-11, 115, 117, 123, 127-28, 131, 133, 136, 138, 140-41, 144, 149; 211, ?219, 222; 310-11, 321, ?326; 402, 404, 406, 408, ?410, 411-12, 419, 436-37.

Comments:

pair: Inf. considers this wrong--21.
span: Harnessed, not yoked--7.

27.4(1) _calf_. NE 192.

In the UM the generic term for the young of cattle is _calf_. Four singleton variants appeared, _one_, _yearling_, insisted upon by a Minnesota woman not a farmwife and apparently unfamiliar with the usual specific meaning of the word.

The young male is generally called _bull calf_, although 16 widely distributed infs., all but 2 of them women, use the probably euphemistic _steer_ or _steer calf_.

The young female is usually known as _heifer_, with some scattered use of the redundant _heifer calf_. One Iowa farmer applied _heiferet_ to a young cow that had produced its first calf.

calf 1-2, 4, 6-14, c15, 16-18, c19, 20-24, 26-34, c35, 36-40, 42-43, c45, 46-47, 49-55, 57-65; 101, 104, 106, 108, 110-11, 116, 118-19, 121, 123-27, 129, 131-32, 134-35, 137, 139-41, 145-46, 148-52; 201, c202, 203-19, 221-26; 301, 304-10, 312-26, 328; 401-12, c413, cvr414, 415-18, 420-21, 423, c424, 425-37. critter ~ †117.
sucking ~ 56.
little wobblie 326.
yearling 26.

27.4(2) _male calf_.

bull 129-30, 151; 312, 318. ~ calf sᴵ3, 5-6, :7, 8, 10, 19, 22-25, *26, 27, 29-30, 33, 37, 41-42, 44, 49-50, 54-55, 62, 65; 102, 104-5, 107-9, 112-15, 117-28, 131, 133, 137-38, 143-49; 201-4, sn205, 206-12, 214, †215, 216-19, sn220, 221, :sn222, 223, 225; 301-2, s304, 306-7, 309, s310, 311, 313, 316, 320, ᴵ321, 325; 401, 403-4, 406, 409-12, s414, 416-18, 420-22, 424, 427-29, 431, 434, 436-37.
male calf 20-21, :c35; c419.
steer 4, 57; 213, 226; 305, 317, 321, 324. ~ calf 42; 103, 139, 151; 217; 301; 413, 432.
yearling bull 409.
young bull 31; 101, 116, 150; 302, 317, 322; 407.

27.4(3) female calf.

heifer 1-8, 19-28, 30-31, 33-34, 36, 41, 43, 45, 48-50, 54-58, 65; 101-9, 112-23, 125, 128-31, 133-34, 136-39, 143-46, 148-52; 201-19, c220, 221-22, 225-26; 301, 303-5, 309-10, c311, 312-13, 315, 317-18, 321, 323-25, 328; 401-4, 406-7, 409-12, 414, 416-19, 421-22, 424-25, 428-30, 433, 436-37. ~ calf 10, *26, 42, 44, 50, 62; 120, 124, 126-27, 147; 223; 301-2, 305-7, 316, 320, 322; 413, 420, 427, 431, *432, 434.
heiferet 108. mother calf 317.

Comment:

heifer: Older than a 'calf'--56, 58; 425. Until she has had one calf--301. Until she has had two calves--108. heifer calf: Less than a year old--301. heiferet: Between her first and second calves--108. no response to 27.4: 142; 327.

27.5 The cow is going to calve. NE 193.

The act of giving birth to a calf is indicated by three main groups of terms in the UM: those with calf or calve as a verb, those with come, and those with fresh or freshen. Come in fresh and come fresh incorporate the principal elements of the second and third groups.

With an average frequency of 40% calf/calve is the most common expression, distributed thus: Mn. 36%, Ia. 21%, N.D. 44%, S.D. 59%, Nb. 37%. The older form with /v/ occurs more often than that with /f/, with a ratio of five to three throughout the UM although /f/ is slightly more common in the Dakotas.

Next most frequent is freshen, with a frequency of 29%, as follows: Mn. 25%, Ia. 49%, N.D. 28%, S.D. 15%, Nb. 20%. Its suggestion of Midland orientation in the eastern strip, Minnesota and Iowa, slightly offsets the Northern bias of calf/calve. Come fresh, however, with an overall average of only 10%, is perhaps favored by more Northern than Midland speakers: Mn. 9%, Ia. 4%, N.D. 20%, S.D. 7%, Nb. 11%.

Come in has the clearest regional pattern: Mn. 20%, Ia. 8%, N.D. 24%, S.D. 4%, Nb. 6%. It is not reported in southern Iowa, and in Minnesota it is limited, with one exception, to the oldest settled portions. A semantic shift probably owing to foreign language background was reported by a Jamestown, N.D. inf.: A local doctor was telephoned at midnight by an excited Russian German farmer living fifteen miles out in the country. The farmer exclaimed, "My wife she's in a bad way. She's coming in." The doctor replied sympathetically that he would look after her, and went back to bed to await the farmer's arrival. At four o'clock in the morning the phone rang again. "Doctor, where are you? Why you not here?" The physician said, "But you said your wife was coming in." "She did already," was the response; "we got a baby and we need you right away."

Relic spring a calf likewise seems Northern, with a cluster of occurrences in se. Minnesota. Infs. elsewhere have a Northern background.

Have a calf, rare in the eastern panel and absent in North Dakota, appears in South Dakota and Nebraska.

Infrequent are calf out, come due, crop or get (a calf), in fold, be a springer, throw (a calf), and be with calf.

CL: Mail returns from 1,025 infs. support the Northern orientation of come in with 31 in Minnesota and only 8 in Nebraska.

Other principal terms appear with similar correlation. So does have a calf, which is common in only South Dakota and Nebraska, but the 5 instances of spring are also in those two states and not in Minnesota.

be fresh sn11, 23, 27, 60; 101, 103, 113, 118, 138-39, 142, 144, ¹150, 151; 215-16, 219, c225; 310, 319, sn328; 413, 417-18, 434-35. become ~ 23, 42, come ~ cvr4, 26, 28, s¹33, 37, 40, 53, 55; 109,

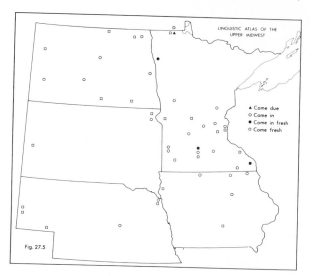

Fig. 27.5

▲ Come due
○ Come in
● Come in fresh
□ Come fresh

LINGUISTIC ATLAS OF THE UPPER MIDWEST

134; 204, 206, 209, 223-24; 307, 310, ¹312; 408-9, †410, 411, 436. come in ~ 7, 51, 58.

calf 1, 8-9, c13, 15-17, 47, 60-61; ¹120, 129, 131, 149; 201-2, 204-5, 209, 217-18; 303, ¹304, 305, 312, 316, 321, 325, 328; 403, 406, 412, 422. ~ out 302.

calve 3, 6, 11-13, :21, 23, 29-30, s¹33, 34, 43-45, 50; 102, s106, 108, 122-24; 126, 130, 132-33, 135, 141, 143, 148, 152; 207, 213, 216, 222; 301, 311, 313-15, 320, 322, 326; ¹401, 402, 409-10, 414, 416, 423, 428, 436-37.

come due 4. ~ in 1, 20, 24, sn30, 31, 39, 43, !46, 47, 49, 52, 59, 65; 103, 105, 107, 116; 208, 211, 214, 217, ¹218, 220; s¹301, ¹304, 308, ¹312; 407, ¹†416, 420.

drop 319. ~ a calf *41, *60; 224; 314, 324; 401, 419, 429.

freshen 2, ¹3, 5, 10, 14, 18-19, 22-23, 25, sn30, ¹41, 43-44, 53-54, 63-64; 104-5, s106, 107-9, 112, 114-15, 117, 119, ¹120, 122, 124-26, :127, 128, 136-37, 139, 145-49; ¹201, 203, 205, 208, 210, ¹213, 221, 225-26; 301, 306, ¹312, 313, 317, ¹323; 409, s421, 425-27, 429, 431, 437.

get a calf 415.

have a calf 35-36, 41; 101, 118, 121; 302, 307, !309, 318, 323; 405, 407, 411, 417, 421, 424, 430, 432.

(be) in calf 2.
(be) in fold 32.
spring 24, 48, 56, 62; 108; 202; 301-2;
[1]409.
(be) a springer 48; 125; 412.
throw a calf 57.
(be) with calf [1]20.
no response ?38; 110-11, 140; 212; 327;
404, 433.

Comment:

be fresh: Usu.--216. Said of milch
cows only--417. calf out: Inf. says this
is common here--302. calve: Usu.--44.
come fresh: Inf.'s more usu. term--53.
Said only of milch cows--411. come in:
Inf.'s more usu. term--47. drop a calf:
Common here--429. freshen: Said only of
milch cows--301, 312-13; 437.

27.8 stallion. NE 197.

Two expressions, stallion and stud, or
sometimes stud horse, occur throughout
the UM to designate the male horse used
for breeding. Because this item was added
in the second year of the project only 8
infs. were queried in Minnesota, but the
distribution of the variants there and
especially in the other states suggests
the Midland orientation of stud (horse)
and the Northern orientation of stallion.
Many infs. use both terms, with a selection according to the audience. Both terms
are considered by some infs. as taboo
forms, but no common euphemisms have
developed. Big horse, appearing once, and
sire are apparently euphemistic. A Type I
spinster housewife in Iowa preserves the
old distinction between horse and mare.

horse 144. big ~ [†]223.
sire 207; 302; 409.

stallion 29-31, 35-36; 101, 104-17,
119-25, 127-30, c131, 132-33, c137, 138-
43, 145-50, 152; c201, 202-26; 301-2,
[1]303, 304-7, 309-10, c312, 313, 315-19,
321, 323-26, 328; 401, 403-5, 408-9, 411-
14, 416, 418, s419, 420-22, 424-35, 437.
stud 30, 38; 102, 113, 118, *134, 135,
142, 147-48, 151-52; s[1]210, sn216, 218,
[1]220; 301-3, *306, 308-11, c312, 314,
320, 323; 401, [1]403, 404-6, 409-12, c414,
416-19, 421, 423, 428-30, 436-37. ~
horse [1]35; 103, 108, 119; 214, [†]217, 223-
24; [1]317, 322; :402, 407, 416, 428, 433.
no response 1-28, 32-34, 37, 39-65; 126,
136, 327; 415.

Comment:

big horse: Women's term--223. stallion:
Taboo--137; [†]223. "Delicate" word--416.
Used in front of, or by, women--302, 309;
404, 416. Usu.--412. Inf. says this is
the most common term--421, 433. stud:
Men's term--210; 310; 419. "Slang"--416.
Usu. stud horse: Taboo--[†]223.

28.1b spook, to shy, said of a horse.

Shy is the usual UM verb for the leap-
ing or jerking action of a startled
horse. In the cattle country along the
western fringe appears the equivalent
spook, used both transitively as in "He
spooked my horse," and intransitively as
in "My horse spooked." Some infs. added
the descriptive adjective spooky in the
sense of "skittish" or "easily startled."
Sashay, a single Iowa response, may be a
nonce metaphor.

become frightened 319.
bolt 18; 135. buck 317-18.
rear 22, 34, 49; ~ back 433; ~ up 433.
sashay 142. scare 313.

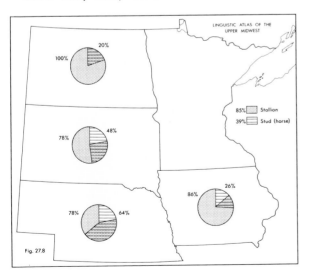

Fig. 27.8

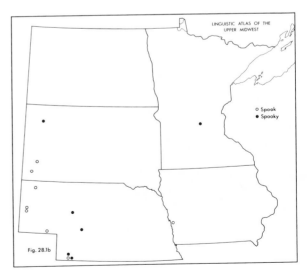

Fig. 28.1b

shy :1, 3, 6, s¹7, 8-9, 11, 18, s19-20,
21, s22, s24, 25, :26, 27-31, 33, 35, 37-
38, 41-42, sn49, 50, 54-55, 57; 101-9,
111-17, 119-20, 122-26, s127, 128-34,
136-40, 142-43, 145-46, 148-50, 152; 201-
7, sn208-209, 210, :211, sn212, 213-20,
222-26; 301-3, s304, 305, 309-15, 317,
320-26, s328; 401, 403-4, c405, 406-7,
¹*408, 409, 412-24, s425, 426-27, 429-31,
s432, s433, 434-37.

   spook 125; ¹302, 312, 320; 401, 409-10,
!436, 437.

   no response 2, 4-5, 10, 12-17, 23, 32,
36, 38-40, 43-48, 51-53, 56, 58-65; 110,
118, 121, 141, 144, 147, 151; 221; 306-8,
316, 327; 402, 411.

Comment:

   shy: Pronounced /ˈʃɔɪ/--149. Said of a
'spooky' horse--30; 412, 418, 429. "A
scairt /ˈskɛrt/ horse would 'shy'--124.
"A bronc is 'spooky'"--301. spook: "A
'spooky' horse is one that's been scared
at some time, or 'spooked'"--437.

28.3 horseshoes (the game). NE 199.

   A once common outdoor game in which two
or four players compete in attempting to
toss a horseshoe over or close to an em-
bedded stake is generally known as horseshoe or horseshoes. Players "play" or
"pitch" horseshoes. The earlier form of
the game, which employed a metal ring or
"quoit" as the object to be thrown, is
called quoits.

   The contrast between horseshoe and
horseshoes is both regional and social.
The singular horseshoe is favored by Type
I (57%) and less so by Type II (49%) and
still less by Type III (37%). It is also
favored by Midland speakers and less so
by Northern: Mn. 31%, Ia. 65%, N.D. 50%,
S.D. 67%, Nb. 62%.

   Although a few older infs. still apply
the term quoits and its variant quates to
the game using a metal ring, a larger
number have retained the term but shifted
the referent to the game with horseshoes.
This term clearly has a Northern orientation: Mn. 14%, Ia. 6%, N.D. 3%, S.D. 1%,
Nb. 0. The quates form, however, did not
survive the western population drive into
the Dakotas, for it is found only in the
first settled areas of Minnesota. Except
perhaps in Canada, both forms are probably obsolescent as designations for the
horseshoe game: Type I 18%, II 7%, and
III 0.

   barnyard golf !¹21, !54-55; 148.
   horseshoe 1, 4-5, 9-10, 12, 14, 17, 20,
¹21, 22, 29-31, 35, 37, 43, c47, 48, 50;
101-2, 104, 106, 109, 112-14, 116, 122-
24, 126-31, 133-38, 140, 142-50; 201,

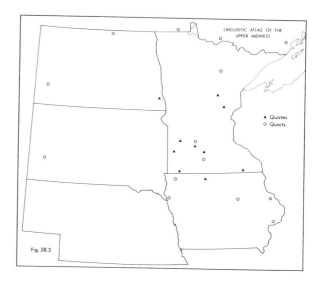

Fig. 28.3

△ Quates
○ Quoits

203, 205, 208-10, 212, 217, 220, 223-24,
226; 301-3, 305-9, 314, 316-22, 324-25;
401, 403-9, 412, 416-18, 421, 423, 425,
427, 429-32, 434, 436-37.
   horseshoes 7-8, 13, 15-16, 18-19, 24-
28, 33-34, 36, 38, 40-42, 44, c45, !46,
49, 54-60, 62-65; 105, c107, 108, 110-11,
115, 117-21, 125, 132, 139, 141, 151-52;
202, 204, 206, 211, 213, 215-16, →218,
219, 221-22, →¹225; 304, 307, 310, 312-
13, 315, 323, 326, 328; 402, 410-11, 413-
15, 419-20, 422, 424, 426, 428, 433, 435.
   quates ¹6, 21, 23, :?39, 42, 45-46, 51,
s¹52, 61, ¹62, c65; 103, †122; !†218,
225; ¹†312; †418, s¹424.
   quoits 1-3, 11, ¹†29, ¹33, ?*39, 44,
¹47, 53; 101, †109, 111, 116, 120, 141;
†202, 204, ¹210, 214; 311; ¹420, c†428.
   no response 327.

Comment:

   quates: Missile not a horseshoe; it is
round--45, 51, 61. Missile not a horseshoe, but is shaped like a horseshoe--225.
Pronounced /kwets/, but inf. says it is
spelled 'quoits'--46. "The men call it
'quates'"--424. quoits: Missile not a
horseshoe; it is round--111, 141. Missile
not a horseshoe, but is shaped like a
horseshoe--53; 101; 202. Heard by inf. in
Oh.--33. Rare here--47; 420. "Old country
term"--202.

28.5 ram. NE 200. WG 62, 49. F95.

   As in New England and the Middle Atlantic states the dominant term for the male
sheep is ram, with buck, also quite widely
distributed, a strong second. The relative
frequency is 67% to 45%. In addition 7
scattered instances of buck sheep occur.

The one example of sheep buck, from a retired Winona, Mn., farmer whose father
was born in Austria, surely is influenced
by the German Schafbock, as were the examples cited by Kurath in the German-
speaking area in Pennsylvania.

   Although one eastern Iowa inf. of South
Midland background described buck as an
old-fashioned taboo term, no others expressed any such feeling. It was reported
in use by about the same proportion of men
as of women. The only contrast in use of
buck and ram seems to be the rural/urban
division, as buck and buck sheep are much
more common among rural infs.

   buck 10, ¹12, 14, 19, 23-26, ¹30, 35,
41, 43-44, :s49, 50-54, 57, 59-62, ¹63;
101, 104-5, 107-9, 112-15, 117, 119, *123,
126-27, 132-35, 137-38, 142-43, 145-49,
151, ¹152; 204, ¹207, 208, 211, 213, 215-
18, 223-25; 301-17, ¹312, 313, 316-24,
:328; 401, ¹403, 404-5, 407, 415, 418,
420, 424, 427-29, 434, 436. ~ ram c323.
~ sheep 23, 34, ¹36, !46, 48, 64; 308;
*417, ¹435.
   ram 1-2, sn3, 4-8, !9, 11-12, 15-18,
20-24, 27-29, ¹30, 31, s32, 33-34, 36-43,
45-47, 51-55, ?58, 61-63, 65; 101-3, 106,
108, 111, 116, 118, 120-22, 124-26, :127,
128-29, :130, 131-32, 136-37, 139-41,
144, *145, 149-52; 201-3, 205-8, 210, 212,
214, 217-22, 224, 226; 301, 307-11, ¹312,
314, *318, 323, 325-26; †401, 402-3, ¹404,
406, 408-14, 416, :417, 418-28, 430-31,
*432, 433, 435-37.
   sheep 13. ~ buck 56.
   no response 110; :?209; 315, 327.

Comment:
   buck: Taboo--†137. Usu.--41, 43, 52, 54;
218; 301; 427. Claimed as usu., but inf.
used 'buck ram' in conversation--323. Inf.
says used by sheepmen--312. Inf. says
used by farmers--51, 53; 149. Pronounced
/ˈbɔk/--415. buck sheep: Usu.--23. ram:
Inf. says used by sheepmen--149.

28.6a   ewe.   NE 201.

   Intended primarily as a phonological
item and hence treated elsewhere, the
designation ewe for a female sheep has
the probably erroneous synonym doe reported in the use of three Minnesota infs.,
all in Type I. Two were housewives in
Duluth and Marine and one was a western
Minnesota highway worker. [Note: For
28.6b see Addenda.]

29.1   boar.   NE 206.

   The male of swine is commonly designated with the term boar in the UM, with
a variant boar pig chiefly in Minnesota

and North Dakota. The element pig appears
in several other compounds as well, all
of which are characteristically found in
Northern speech areas. Conversely, compounds with hog, the most common of
which is male hog, are characteristically
found in Midland speech areas. The pig
terms have a frequency of nearly 15% in
Minnesota but only 4% in Iowa; the hog
terms have a frequency of nearly 35% in
Iowa but only 7% in Minnesota. Each type
is represented twice in Canada.

   Nearly all the synonyms for boar seem
to have originated as euphemisms. Several
infs. frankly admitted that boar implies
male sexuality more strongly than is
desirable in conversation with women. They
and others add that such expressions as
male hog, male pig, and gentleman pig
are primarily women's terms.

   Although not deliberately sought, terms
for the castrated male were volunteered
by several infs.: barrow--53; 120, 124,
134, 149, 151; shoat--c61; and stag--135;
220.

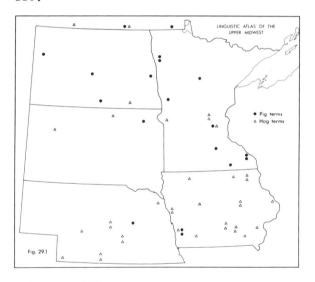

barrow 105.
   boar 1-2, sn3, 4-13, 15, 17-31, 34, :36,
37, 39-47, 49-55, 57-63, 65; 101-9, 111-
33, 135, s136, 137-52; 203-8, :209, 210-
22, c224, 225, :226; 301-3, 305-6, 308-21,
323-25, 327-28; 401-5, 407-9, :410, 411-
19, c420, 421-37. ~ hog 322. ~ pig c1, 7,
19, c35, 48, 56-57, 64; 125; 202, 210,
217, 223; 307. blue ~ 1.
   bull pig ·124.
   gentleman hog !¹125; 103. ~ pig 8; ¹416.
   he pig 8.
   hog 32-33; 108, 121, 134; 201.
   male hog s¹†1, 25, ¹30, :35; 105, †109,
†114, 116, †117, 124, 132, †133, :?136,
137, 151; c¹224; ¹302, 305, ¹318, ¹†323;
†407, 413-14, †418, 420, ¹423, 430-31,

437. ~ pig †10; 124; ¹216, ¹220, 221.
  papa hog 423.
  sire ¹217.
  stag 132.
  stock hog ¹30; 107, †109.
  top hog ¹135.
  no response 14, 16, 38; 110; 304, ?326;
:406.

Comment:

  barrow: Inf.'s term for a young male--
105. boar: Not used by women; disliked by
women--7, 8; †101, †114, 116, †133; 205,
212, 214; †309, †312; †436. "Some women
say 'male pig'"--8. Vulgarism; taboo
word--109, 137; *301, 310. "I just don't
like the word, but I'd rather say 'boar'
than 'sow'"--310. boar pig: Usu.--19.
stag: Inf.'s term for an old male--132.

29.2 hog. NE 206.

Despite the technical distinction between pig and hog based upon age and the
arbitrary weight of 120 pounds, most infs.
employ either one term or the other as a
generic. In this comprehensive sense, as
in such a context as "He raises ____,"
hog is widespread throughout the UM, with
no marked regional pattern. Pig, less
frequent but also widespread and perhaps
with a slight Northern orientation, is
more likely to be used by infs. without
a farm background.
For the female swine a usual distinction
is that gilt denotes a young female that
has not yet produced a litter, sow one
that has.

(1) generic or undescribed

  hog 1-5, ¹6, 9-12, 15, 19-24, c25, 26,
28-29, 31-32, 34, c35, 36-37, c40, 41-42,
c44, 45, 47, 49-50, c53, 54, c55, 57, 60,
64-65; 101, 106-7, 110, 118, 125, 131,
137-38, 140-41, 152; 201-7, 209-13, c214,
215-17, ¹218, 219-21, c224, c225, 226;
301-2, 305-6, 308, c309, 310-11, c312,
313, 315-17, c320, 321-26, 328; c401-2,
c403-4, 405-8, c409, 410-12, cvr413,
c414, 416-21, c423-24, 425-28, c429,
cvr430, 431-33, c434, 435, c436, 437.
  pig 13-14, c16, 17, 25-26, 32-33, 53,
57, !63; 106, 117-18, 121, 125, 132, 134,
145-46; 204-5, 207-9, 211, 215, 218, 220,
222-23; 315; 408, c409, 416, 422, c426,
c427.
  schwein 415.
  swine 308; cvr413, 425.
  no response 304.

Comment:

  hog: Usu.--209; 408, 425. "You feed
'pigs' but sell 'hogs'"--47.

(2) female hog

  gilt 53; 105, 108, 112, 117, 122-23,
125-26, 128, 132-33, 135-36, 142, :143,
145-49.
  sow 6, 13-18, 43-47, 51-53, 59-60, c61,
62-64; 101-17, 119-36, 138-46, c147, 148-
49; 306-8. ~ pig 56; 107, 143.

Comment:

  gilt: Inf.'s term for a young sow--105,
108, 112, 126, 132, 149. An unbred 'sow'--
133. sow pig: A young sow--107.

(3) adult hog

  hog 7, c8, 18, 27, c30, 33, 38-39, c43,
46, 48, c51, c52, 56, 58, c59, c61-62,
63; 102-3, 112, 115-16, 119, 139, 150-51;
c222, 223; 303, 314, 318-19, 327; 422.
  pig 6.

(4) young hog

  pig c15, 18-19, 24, 27, 30, 39-40, 43,
45-48, 50-52, 56, 58-60, c61, 62; 101-5,
107-9, 111-16, 119, 127, 129, 134, 138-
39, 147, 149, 151; 313; 403, 409, 421,
424, 436. baby ~ cr426. feeding ~ 105.
little ~ 403. young ~ 208.
  piglet *39; ?426.
  shoat 25, 51; 101, 103-5, sn106, 107-9,
111-16, 118-19, 121, 129, 132, sn134,
138-41, 148, 151; 208; 303, 306; 421,
424.

Comment:

  feeding pig: A half-grown hog--105.
shoat: A half-grown hog--101, 103-5, 107-
9, 111-15, 119, 129, 132, 134, 138; 421,
424. Pronounced /ˈʃɛɾts/--303. young pig:
Usu.--208.

29.6 castrate. NE 210.

Although for the act of castrating an
animal the term castrate is itself the
most common and the neutral expression
found in the UM, several other words also
appear, some with reference to certain
animals only and others as euphemisms.
The incidence of the more frequently used
terms is: alter 11%, castrate 81%, cut
37%, nut 5%, and trim (up) 7%. Only two
terms exhibit possible regional variation.
Trim is stronger in Iowa and Nebraska and
hence may be Midland. Alter is strongest
in eastern and southern Iowa and southern
Minnesota and hence may also be Midland
oriented. Two terms, spay and circumcise,
are obvious errors, probably resulting
from confusion. Some urban and female
infs. evinced unfamiliarity with any term.
  alter 6, c21, 57, 59, c61, ¹62; c107,
108, *116, 118-19, 125, 129, 134, 136,
139, s†142, 149, 151; c201, c216; 312,

†324; †424, 434.
  caponize c10, c34.
  casterize 24, 27; 417.
  castrate 1, 3-4, *5, 6-7, c8, 9-10, c11,
14-15, 19, 22-23, c25, ¹29, 30, 33-35,
37, :39-41, 42-54, c55, 56-58, 62-63, *64,
!65; 101-2, ?!103, 104-6, 109, 111-13,
115-28, 132-13, *134, 135-38, 140-49,
:?150, 151, :s152; 202-6, 208-11, c212,
213-15, 217-18, c221, 222-24, c225; 301-
3, 305-7, 309-10, c312, 313-19, ?320,
321, 323, *324, 325; c401, c403, 404,
407-8, 411-14, 416, 418-24, s425, 426-29,
431, *432, 435-37.
  change 104, 119.
  circumcise 308.
  cut 1, ¹7, :8, 12-13, 17-18, 23, 25,
27, c29, 30, 41, 43-46, 50-51, 54, 57;
101, 105, 108-9, 112, 114-15, *116, 117,
125, 130, 132, 138-42, 147-49; 202, 207-
8, 214, 218, c220, 224, ¹225; 301-2, 304,
309, 311-12, s¹313, 314, s¹315, 320-23,
*325; 404-5, 407, ¹†408, 409, 411, †414,
417-18, 420, s¹423, 424, ¹431, 434-35,
†436, 437.
  de-nut ¹134; ¹302.
  de-sex 424.
  fix :152; 206.
  make the sign of the eleven 121.
  neuter 131.
  nut ¹1, 6, ¹23, 35; 108, 111, 120, 141;
221-22; ¹302, 309, s¹315; 416, ¹429.
  operate 224; 317.
  pinch →128.
  spay 13, 47.
  sterilize :?32.
  take care of 416.
  tend to 139.
  tong 54.
  trim †30, :60; 113, c114, 115, 128,
132-33; 223; s¹301, *325; 420-21, 430. ~
up 120.
  no response :2, 16, 20, 26, 28, 31, 36,
38; 110; ?219, 226; ?326, 327-28; 402,
406, :410, 415, 433.
Comment:
  alter: Said of bull-calves--107, *116.
Said of colts, never of bulls--119. A
farmer's term--62. Used by inf.'s father
--424. Used in the presence of women--
125. "More polite" than 'cut'"; "the nice
name"--312; 434. caponize: Said of roost-
ers--10, 34. casterize: Not used in the
presence of women--27. castrate: Said of
bull-calves--323. Said of cats--47. Said
of horses--128, 132; 323. A farmer's
term--34, 57. Pronounced /kæstɨneɪt/--121.
cut: Said of bull-calves--105, 112, *116,
132. Said of dogs--23. Said of hogs--23,
30, 50, 54; 105, 112, *116, 117, 132;
304, 323. Said of horses--112. A man's
term--27, 41; 108; 218. Usu. local term
--312; 435. Usu.--309, 320. change: Said

of bulls, rams, and hogs--119. de-nut:
Inf. has heard this from other than farm-
ers--34. fix: Said of cats--152. make the
sign of the eleven: Inf. reports her
use of this in the presence of children--
121. nut: Said of cats and dogs--108.
Said of hogs--1, 6; 120; 429. A farmer's
term--221. operate: Used in the presence
of women--224. spay: Said of dogs--13,
47. take care of: "Delicate"--416. tong:
Said of lambs; so called because of the
tool used--54. trim: Said of bull-calves
--132. Said of hogs--128, 132-33. Used
by inf.'s father--30. Usu. local term--
223. trim up: Said of bulls--120.

29.7 bawl (of a calf being weaned).   NE
195. WG 19, 30, 62; F16.

  For the noise made by a hungry calf
during the weaning period the most common
UM word is bawl, with a general frequency
of 59%. Although in the East this term is
sharply Midland, it has spread widely in
the UM, where it competes on even terms
with bellow/beller in Minnesota and North
Dakota. Its distribution is Mn. 41%, Ia.
75%, N.D. 38%, S.D. 74%, Nb. 77%. On the
contrary, bellow and beller, of New England origin, exhibit a slight Northern
orientation: Mn. 41%, Ia. 20% (almost
entirely in the northern half), N.D. 38%,
S.D. 30%, Nb. 26%. Only 2 of the 10 instances of bellow appear in Midland
speech territory, but beller has pushed
into the Midland area of Nebraska.
  The relationship between the next two
terms, blat and bleat, is controversial.
Dictionary etymologists disagree as to
whether blat is an independent imitative
creation, a variant of bleat, or a back-
formation from the Spenserian creation
of blattant, Modern English blatant. This
last is certainly suspect, at least as
the source of the folk-word applied to
calves. The Supplement to the Oxford English Dictionary labels blat "U.S.," but
the word is omitted from the Dictionary
of Americanisms. Whether related or not,
blat and bleat occur in the same region,
the latter less frequently and less widespread. A Northern orientation is indicated by the presense of only two instances
of bleat in the southern half of Iowa
and none in southern Nebraska. Neither
occurs in eastern Iowa.
  Baa, offered as the use of five speakers not one of whom has a rural background, may result from confusion with
the name for a sheep's call.

CL 69: Checklist returns show a stronger
domination by bawl, but the same Northern
and Midland orientation for both bellow

and bawl. Blat again appears Northern, with 34 instances in Minnesota and only 23 in Iowa, none of which are in the southern third. Blare, a New England equivalent not reported by fieldworkers, seems to be the term used by 14 respondents, 8 in Minnesota, 2 in northern Iowa, and 2 in South Dakota. A Northern bias is evident.

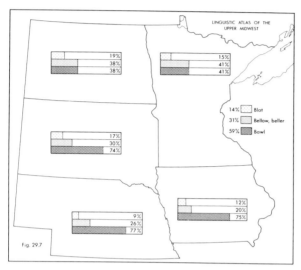

baa 12; 219; 309; 425.
bawl 1-3, 7-8, :sn10, 11-12, 18, 22, 24-25, 28, !30, :36, 37, 40, 43, 45, ?46, 50-51, c54, 59, 62; 101, 105-8, 111, cr112, 114, 116-20, 123-24, 126-27, c128, 129-32, 135-39, 141, 143-52; !202, 205-6, 208-9, !210, 211, !215, :216, 223; 301-3, 306-8, 310-14, 318, !320, 322, *324, 325, 328; 402-6, 408-9, 411-14, 420-24, c425, 426-27, 429-32, 434-37.
beller 4, 25-26, 39, 41, 43, 47-49, 52-54, 56, 58, ?60, 61, 63-64; 102, 104, 106, ?112, 115, 121-22, 133-34, 140; 201, 203, ¹205, 207-8, 212-13, ¹216, 221, 224, 226; 302, 304, *306, 307, 317, 321, !323; ¹404, 407, 412, 416, !417-18, 419, 421, 428, c430.
bellow 6, 19-21, 55, 57, 65; 142; 217; 430.
blat ?10, 13, 15-16, 23, 27, 31, 44, 50, 59; 103, 109, 113, 122, 125, 151; 204, 214, !218, 220, 225; 306, 312, 314, 316; 401, ¹404, 409-10.
bleat 14, !33, ?42; 222; ¹401, 413.
call 142.
cry 17, 36.
howl 17.
mew 35.
no response 5, 9, 29, 32, 34, 38; 110; 305, 315, 319, ?326, 327; 415, 433.
Comment:

beller: Pronounced /bæ|ɚ/--41; 140.
bleat: "Probably the right name, but we say 'blat'"--401.

30.1a low (during feeding time). NE 194. WG 19, 38, 49, 62; F29, F96.

Although for the noise made by a cow during feeding time the Midland bawl has spread widely into the UM Northern speech area, both bawl and the Northern-oriented bellow and beller are less favored by younger speakers than is the Northern and North Midland moo. Mew, a minor variant of moo, has four occurrences in Minnesota, three in North Dakota, and one each in Nebraska, South Dakota, and Manitoba.

Low, surviving either as a relic carried west from the South Atlantic coast, a relic of British usage, or a literary term, occurs three times in Iowa, twice in Nebraska, and twice in Minnesota. Loo, a minor form in Northern New England and New York state, remains in the speech of an eastern South Dakota Type I inf., three of whose grandparents came from New York.

CL 68: Although three-fourths of the 1,017 checklist returns report the use of moo without conspicuous regional differences, the Northern and Midland orientations of the minor variants are retained. No use of mew appears.

	Mn.	Ia.	N.D.	S.D.	Nb.	Ave.
bawl	1%	6%	4%	6%	5%	4%
bellow,-er	26%	15%	27%	24%	17%	21%
low	6%	6%	8%	9%	8%	7%

bawl 2, 15, 25, c37, 43, c50, 59; 113, 117-18, 124-28, 133, 135, 141-47, 151; 201-2, 204, 206-8, 213, 218, 220-21; 301-4, 309, 311-13, 318, 320, 324; 401, 403-

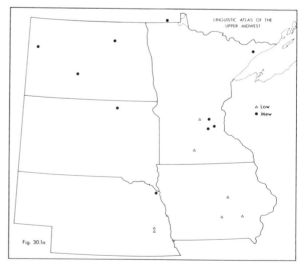

6, s410, 411-12, 414, 429, 434, 437.

  beller 16, 19, 41, 43, c44, 52, 56, 60, 64; 117, 134, 138, *145, 148, ¹149; 209, 216, 221, 223; 302, 306-7, 317; 402, 412, 414, 416, 418.

  bellow 31, 55; 103, 107, 124, 149; 211, 215, 222; 317; 411.

  holler 417.

  loo 316.

  low ¹2, *30, 53, †54; 118, 134, 152; 424-25.

  mew 1, 6, 32, 35, 38; 209, 212, 216; 305; 407, s?415.

  moo 2-5, 7-14, 17-18, 20-24, 26-27, sn28, 29, :30, 33-34, 36-37, 39-40, s¹41, 42, ¹43, c44, 45, c46, 47-51, 53, sn54, s¹56, 57-58, ¹59, 60-62, c63, 64-65; 101-6, 108-9, 111-12, s113, 114-17, 119-23, s¹124, 126, :127, 128-32, 136-41, 147, 149-52; 203, 205, 208, 210, 214, 217, 219, 222, 224-26; 302, *306, 308, 310, 314-15, 319, 321-26, 328; 401-2, 406, 408-11, 413-14, *417, 418, 420, 422-23, 426-28, 430-31, 433, 435-37.

  no response 110; 327; 419, 421, 432.

Comment:

151; 401, 406, 411, 437. beller: Pronounced [bæ^lɚ]--41. "A lot of them say 'beller'"--149. "A bull bellers, but a cow moos"--44. Louder than a moo--60; 402. Louder than a low--118. bellow: Louder than a moo--222; 411. holler: "All I ever knew"--417. moo: Usu.--53. Inf. says she learned this word from her school reader--*306.

30.2 whinny. NE 198. WG 21, 42-43, 47-48, 62-63; F40, F97.

For the noise made by a horse during feeding time four principal terms occur in varying proportions throughout the UM, all of them brought from the Atlantic coast.

Neigh, widespread in the east but not reported in WG, seems to have a slight Midland orientation in the UM. [See Fig. 30.2(1).] The minor variant /naɪ/ (apparently never written as nigh), which in England still exists in Yorkshire and Durham and persists in the speech of 7 users scattered in all New England states but Vermont, continues in the UM to have curious viability. But although 5 of the 12 Wisconsin infs. reporting neigh actually say /naɪ/, only 3 UM infs. do, one each in Iowa, South Dakota, and Nebraska. The occasionally met opinion that neigh is more literary and less rural is not supported by the data, which reveal that only 30 of the 77 occurrences are in urban or semi-urban communities and that only a slightly higher percentage of Type II

speakers use it .

Whinny, the most common term, co-exists with its old-fashioned variant, whinner. Greater frequency of the former in Minnesota than in Iowa reflects its Northern and North Midland background in the east.

Whinner, the popularity of which drops from 39% for Type I to 20% for Type II and to only 6% for Type III, is clearly losing ground to whinny and perhaps neigh. It likewise is Northern in orientation, as the data indicate: Mn. 28%, Ia. 21%, N.D. 46%, S.D. 41%, Nb. 17%.

Nicker, on the contrary, with its origin in the Virginia Piedmont, is Midland oriented. Only one Minnesotan uses it, and then as an alternative form; 16 Iowans, 31%, use it.

Several unusual equivalents apparently are phonetic variations of the common terms. Whinter is used by two Iowa and Nebraska infs., both with Midland ancestry. Whinker is the term of an inf. in se. Iowa. Snicker is used by a Minnesota Iron Range inf. and by another in southwestern Nebraska. A southeastern Iowa inf. whose grandmother was born in Virginia offers the solitary example of whinker, a variant found along the south Atlantic coast. Snicker, not reported in the east, is used by two infs., one on the Minnesota Iron Range and the other in southwestern Nebraska. Three widely scattered infs. have whine, pronounced /hwin/ by the one in Nebraska.

CL 79: Replies from 1,012 respondents generally support the field materials, although with a lower frequency of neigh.

	Mn.	Ia.	N.D.	S.D.	Nb.	Ave.
neigh	17%	13%	18%	18%	12%	14%
nicker	9%	31%	17%	23%	33%	23%
whinner	27%	13%	29%	20%	9%	19%
whinny	57%	59%	45%	60%	67%	58%

The rare Maine and Plymouth, Ma., whicker, not found by any fieldworker, was written in by two respondents in Iowa, one with Maine parents and the other with New York and Connecticut background. Four respondents volunteered whine.

  bray 24; :135; 209; 435.

  neigh 2-4, 7-8, 11, ¹12, 13-14, 16-18, ¹19, 29, 32-33, ¹34, 36, 38, 42, 44, 46-47, 51, 54-55, 58, 60, !61; 112, 116-17, 120-21, 124, 126, 128-29, ?130, 133-34, 136-38, 141, 144, *145, 146-50, 152; 202, 211, 214, 218, 225; 301, 308-10, 314-15, 317, 326; 402-3, 411, 414, ?418-19, 420-21, 424-26, 428, 430-31, 433, 436-37.

  nicker *46; *116, 119, 122, 125, 128, 131-32, 135-36, 142-43, *145, 146, 148-49, 151; 214; 311-12, ¹313-14, *318; 404, ¹411, :412, ¹413, 432.

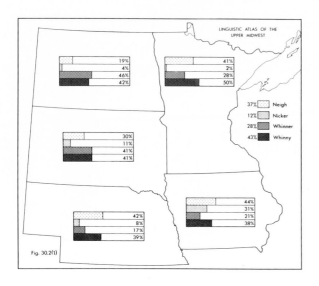

Fig. 30.2(1)

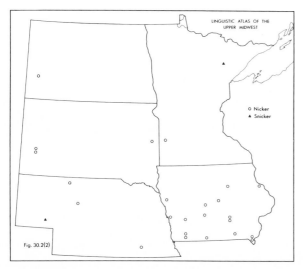

○ Nicker
▲ Snicker

Fig. 30.2(2)

snicker 14; 417.
snort 51.
squeal 59; 317.
whine 9; 321; 407.
whinker 147.
whinner 1, 8, 13, 21-22, 25, 27, 32, 39, cr40, 41, 49-50, 52, 56, !61, 63, 65; 101, 104, 106-7, 112-15, ¹132, 138-40; 201, 203-4, 206-8, 212, 214, 216, 220, 224-25; 302-5, 307, 311, †312, 316, 321-23, 325; ¹404, 405, 409, 421-22, 429, 437.
whinny 5-6, 10, 15-16, 18, 20, 23, 26, 28-31, 34, 37, ?40, 42-48, 51, 53-54, r57, 58-60, 62, 64; 102-3, 105, 108-12, s116, 117-19, 124-27, ?130, 137, 144-45, ¹150, 151-52; 205, 210, 213-15, 217, 219, 221-23, 226; 301, 306, 309, 312-13, 317-20, 324, 328; 401, ¹402, ¹403, 406, 408, 410, ¹411, 413, ¹†414, 416, cr418-19,

420, 423, 428, 434, 436.
  whinter *123; ¹411.
  no response :35; 327; 415.

Comment:

neigh: Heard infrequently--12. = whinner--130. = whinny--32; 137. Louder than a whinny--29. "Technical and literary"--309. Pronounced /naɪ/--51; 138, 424. nicker: Inf. says that here this is more common than 'whinny'--119. Not as loud as a whinner--214; 311. Not as loud as a whinny--312. snort: Pronounced /snɔɚnt/--51. whine: Pronounced [hwiˇin]--407. whinker: "We usually called it [hwɪŋkɚ]--147. whinner: The "right term"--40. Usu.--8; 214; 437. When lonesome or hungry--325. whinny: Usu.--42; 436. More common than 'neigh'--47; 301, 309. "Most of them say [ɪʰwɪniˇ], but [ɪʰwɪnoˇ] is right"--44. Pronounced [ɪʰwɨnɔə]--317. 'Nicker' is more common; 'whinny' is a call to other horses--119.

30.3 setting hen.   NE 214. WG 32, 33, 49, 63.

A hen about to lay a clutch of eggs and desirous of hatching them is said by some infs. to be "broody"; a hen actually on the nest is then a setting hen or a "cluck (hen)." Other infs., however, use the terms interchangeably or ambiguously, as is true of less frequent variants such as brooder, brood hen, and brooding hen.
By far the most common term is setting hen, with an overall average of 85%. Only Minnesota, with an overlapping frequency of 40% for cluck (hen) has an appreciably lower occurrence of setting hen (68%). Widely scattered, with no discernible geographical pattern, are the six instances of the equivalent setter, and the six of sitting hen. None of the latter come from an actual chicken-raiser.
Cluck, with the less common variants cluck hen, clucking hen, and clucky hen, is clearly more widespread in Northern speech territory. Its high frequency in Minnesota contrasts with only 6% in Iowa; the 27% frequency in North Dakota contrasts with a 3% frequency in Nebraska. This distribution denies an origin in Pennsylvania German kluck, as is suggested by Kurath in WG. Furthermore, only two of the infs. using cluck are of German background, besides one for cluck hen and one for clucking hen. The variant clook, not found in New England, is offered once in Minnesota by an inf. of German parentage, however; and also once in Nebraska by an inf. of Scottish background.
Broody and broody hen are widely scattered, although with no instances in

254

South Dakota.

Sour hen, the form used by a Swedish inf. in n. Minnesota, and reported by a North Dakota inf. as heard in the community, is a direct translation from Swedish.

brooder 51. ~ hen 420.
brood hen 224; [1]302. ~ing hen [1]137.
broody 149; 423. ~ hen ?[1]33, 41, 46, c64; 103, 109, 115; 206, 211, 218, 223;

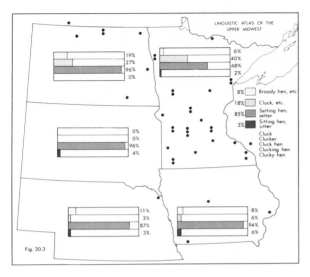

Fig. 30.3

[1]413, 418, 420, 425.
clook 48; 407.
cluck 5, 7, 19-20, 22, 26-28, 30, !34, 41-42, 44-45, 47, !53, 54, 58, 60, c61; 204-5, 208, [1]210-11, 224; [1]306, [1]317-18; †428. ~er [1]3, 8; 220. ~ hen 5, 7, 41, 43, 56; 140, 143; 203. ~ing hen 7, 15-16; :35; 201. ~y hen 115.
hatcher [1]2. hatching hen [1]3; 138; 201.
laying hen 107; 417.
mother hen 219.
setter 29, 50, [1]57; 225; 309; 430, 432.
setting biddy [1]62.
setting hen 1-4, 6, 9-14, cr17, 18, 21, 23-24, c25, [1]28, 30-31, :32, 33, 36, cr37, 38-40, 42, 44-47, 49-50, 52, 54-55, 57, 59-63, 65; 101-2, 104-9, 111-25, 127-42, 144-52; 201-2, 204-13, !214, 215, c216, 217-24, 226; 301-5, *306, 307-14, [1]315, 316-26, 328; 401-6, 408-16, 418-21, s[1]422, 423-24, 426-29, 431, 433-37.
sitter 122.
sitting hen ?17, 37; 126, 151; 315; 422.
sour hen 4; [1]203.
no response 110; 327.

Comment:

cluck: "Common here"--42. Used by local Scandinavian people--210. cluck hen: Pronounced /ɪklɑk ~/--56. hatching hen: Inf. says this is "better" than ʹsetting

hen'--201. setting hen: Usu.--420. sitting hen: Inf. admits this is hypercorrect--37. sour hen: A translation from Swedish --4. Used by inf.'s daughter-in-law, of German background--203.

30.4 chicken coop. NE 111, 112.

Although fieldworkers were inconsistent in recording the complex semantic distinctions underlying the various names for poultry shelters, three broad categories of such structures appear in the records. One category is that of a shelter for chicks, or for a hen with her chicks; a second includes shed-like buildings high enough for a man to stand in and usually having roosts and nests; the third comprises larger, barn-like buildings for a large number of chickens. The smallest shelter is usually A-shaped and about 3' high. The two other kinds have either slanting or hipped roofs, and often have south-facing windows.

The small shelter is typically known as a coop, chicken coop, or hen coop, although about one-half of the infs. using these terms reflect the view of the Devils Lake, N.D. inf. who remarked, "A coop is a coop regardless of size." Except for this broader application of coop to large as well as to small structures, the names for the former usually include the term house, as chicken house and hen house.

The common forms with coop and house were brought west from the Atlantic coast, but two New England terms, hen roost, and, for the enclosure, hen yard, are not in the UM findings. Chicken roost, a rare variant clustering in southern Connecticut, Rhode Island, and eastern Long Island, survives in the speech of one southern Minnesota inf. of New York and New Jersey parentage. NE hennery also survives in this same inf.'s speech as well as in that of two other Minnesotans. UM terms not reported in New England are "A" coop, chicken barn, chicken shed, chicken stable, and, for the enclosure, hen run.

One Iowa Type I inf. preserves the unusual Maine meaning for coop as crate for transporting poultry. Brooder (house), a term for a shelter for newly hatched chicks, also survives, principally in the eastern part of the UM.

No major regional patterns emerge.

"A" coop 312.
brooder 117, 145. ~ house 34, 47-48; 105, 113, 116, 122, 132-33, 138-39, 147; 220; 317.
chicken barn 425.
chicken house 4, 6, 10, 19, c25, 30,

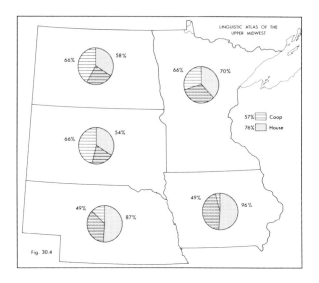

LINGUISTIC ATLAS OF THE
UPPER MIDWEST

57% ▥ Coop
76% ▨ House

Fig. 30.4

chicken coop: Small, A-shaped, 2 1/2'
to 3' high, for one hen, for chicks, or
for both--23-24, 26, 29, 65; 105, 107,
114, 116, 118, 121, 123, 139, 144, 150;
204; 418, 433. ("For a single family").
Not big enough to walk in--321. Smaller
than a 'hen house'--401. More common term
than 'hen house'--315. = hen coop--322.
Small and straight-walled--412. High
enough to walk in--5; 221, 226; 310, 312-
13, 326; 405, 419. 5' to 7' high--9; 218.
8' high--1. Of various sizes--20, 27, 36;
209-11, 212 ("A coop is a coop regardless
of size") = hen house--20-21, 64 ("Some
call it a hen house"); 215, 222; 313.
"Low building with many southern windows
--219. Sloping roof with a glass front--1.
"For many birds"--39-40. With doors and
windows--35. With slant roof and roosts--
435. Usu. local term--51. For transporting
chicks; made of laths--132. chicken house:
= chicken stable--106. Large--65; 102,
149-50; 314; 412. Large, 12' to 20' x 16'
to 60' with slant (shed) roof--108, 114,
149. Bigger and better made than a coop--
49. For more than one--32, 45, 47, 60,
63; 417-18, 420, 422, 433-34. Large enough
to walk in--402, 405-6, 411, 429, 436.
With shed or gable roof--107; 413-14,
421, 427, 430-31. With gable roof--328.
"Small barn with roosts and nests"--140.
Large or small--19, 33; 407. With south-
facing windows in front--124; 431, 433,
437. "More frequent term here than 'coop'
"--314. chicken shed: "Rough"--13. coop:
= the enclosure--2. For little chicks--6;
108, 120; 403. For small chicks and hen
--103. Small--14; 409. A-shaped--30-31;
436. Either A-shaped or large enough to
walk in--7. High enough to walk in--314.
Large with slant roof--111. 10' wide,
20' to 100' long, and 6' high--12. "Old
and rickety"--409. feeding coop: For
chicks only--118. hen coop = hen house--
28; 104. hen house = chicken house--224;
410. Larger than a chicken house--226;
322. Older term than 'chicken house'--40.
About 4' high--38. 5' or 6' high with
hip roof--25. ("Some hen houses are for
old and chicken houses for young"). 7' to
8' high with slant roof or, occasionally,
a gable roof, and of various lengths--8,
10, 21; 148; 207-8, 216-17, 222; 309;
410, 415. 8' or 9' high--224. 10' or 12'
high--4; 132. Large--24, 57; 105. ("With
a pointed roof"); 409. Large enough to
walk in--31; 325; 401, 403. Low frame
building with a gable roof--101, 142.
With a slant roof--103, 109, 115, 133,
147; 423, 428. With either a peaked or a
flat roof--146. "Not so high as a garage"
--26. Small or large--22 ("Wide variety
around here"). 29, 35; 201, 210; 408.
For grown chickens--7. For many chickens

32-33, 42, c45, c47, 48-50, 52, c54, 55,
60-61, ¹62, 63, 65; 102, 106-8, 114-15,
117, 119-21, 123-24, 128-29, 136, 138-
40, 143, 149-50; 205, c211, 215, 222,
224; 304, 308-9, ¹314, 321, 325; 401-2,
405-6, c407, 410-14, 417-18, 420-22, 424,
426-27, c429, 430-31, 433-34, 436-37.
hen ~ c2, 4, 7-8, 10, c14, 20-22, 24-26,
28-29, c31, :35, 37-38, †40, 46, 41, 53,
55, 57-59, →60, 62, ¹64; 101, 103-5, 109,
112-13, 115-18, 122, 125-28, 130-37, 141-
42, 144-48, 151-52; 201-2, 204, 207-8,
210, 214-15, †216, 217, 222, 224, 226;
303, 305, *306, 308-9, ¹312, 313, ¹315,
316, c317, 318, 322, ¹323, 325; 403-4,
408-10, 415, 421, 423, 425, 428-29, 432.
poultry ~ 52; →211; 319.
   chicken roost 61.
   chicken run ¹202.
   chicken shed 13.
   chicken stable 106, †143.
   coop 6, 14, 30, c31, c44, 49, 57; 103,
116, 118, 120, 137, 145, 151; 221; ¹306,
314, 320, 323; 403-4, 409, 436. chicken
~ 1, 5, 7, 9-10, 12-13, 15-16, c17, 18,
20-21, 23-24, 26-27, 29, 34-36, c39, 40-
41, 43-44, 50-51, 58, 64-65; 105-8, 111,
114, 118-19, 121, 123-24, 132-33, 139,
144, 150, 152; c203, 204, 206, 208-10,
212-13, 216-20, 223, 225-26; 302, 304,
¹305, 307, 310-13, cr315, 319, 321-26;
401, c405, 407-8, 412, ¹414, c415, 416-19,
¹420, 430, 433, 435. feeding ~ 118. hen ~
11, 28, †33, 56; 104, ¹112; ?315, c322;
402, c417.
   hennery 21, 44, →61.
   no response 3; 110; 301, 327.

Comment:

   brooder house: For clucks--34. For
small chicks--48; 113, 116, 122, 132, 139.
Smaller than a 'chicken house'--138.

--46, 53, 59. "For layers"--117. Has
roosts and nests--122, 126. Windows on
two sides--137. Windows in front--410.
Faces south--133, 147; 423. Modern and
clean--401. hennery: Used by "commercial
poultry-raisers"--21.

30.5 wishbone. NE 215. WG 47, 63; F98.

The fused clavicle or furcula of a
fowl, broken apart by two persons to see
which gets the longer part and hence his
"wish," is known generally in the UM by
the spreading Northern term wishbone. All
infs. except two in southern Iowa are familiar with this term. But in southern
Iowa and once in southeastern South Dakota the South Midland pully bone survives. Good luck bone, used in eastern
South Dakota by an inf. of Vermont and
Massachusetts parentage, may reflect the
New Hampshire and Massachusetts variant,
lucky bone.

CL 54: Wishbone almost exclusively
dominates the checklist responses. Pully
bone is the term of 29 respondents, 16
of whom live in Iowa and 11 of whom live
in Nebraska. Only one of the 29, in extreme Iowa, with parents from Vermont
and Maine, has a clear non-Midland background. Nearly all the others have at
least one parent or grandparent from
Indiana, Virginia, Illinois, or Kentucky.
New England lucky bone was checked by
three Iowa respondents, one in North Dakota, and one in South Dakota. Two of
these have New Hampshire or Vermont background; one, Wisconsin; and the others
have foreign-born parents. Breakbone, not
found on the Atlantic coast, was checked
by 6 respondents, 2 in southern Minnesota,
2 in Iowa, and one each in South Dakota
and Nebraska.

good luck bone 317.
pulling bone cr†150.
pully bone ¹130, †131, 132, 135, 145-
67, ?†150; 325; ¹429.
wishbone 1-41, !42, 43, r44, 45, !46,
47-65; 101-31, 133-34, 136-44, *145,
146-52; 201-9, !210, 211-19, !220, 221-
26; 301-5, *306, 307-13, !314, 315-23,
!324, 325-26, 328; 401-37.
no response 327.

Comment:

pulling bone: Used by inf.'s father--
150. pully bone: Used by inf. as a child
--131.

30.6 harslet. NE 209. WG 20, 21, 23,
38, 49, 64; F43, F103.

For the edible internal organs of a

pig or calf the key word, harslet, apparently has not been carried west from
coastal New England. No instances occurred in the UM. Indeed, the rarity
of farm butchering has led to almost
complete loss of any synonyms. Pluck, a
New England and North Midland term, is
actually used by a Duluth inf., and is
remembered as old-fashioned by three
other Minnesota infs. Lights and liver
and lights, deriving probably from western Maryland and western North Carolina,
has some scattered occurrences, mostly
in North Dakota. The southern chittlins,
with the fuller variant chitterlings, for
the intestines of a pig, is used by the
two Negro infs. in Minnesota and Iowa and,
perhaps because it is also found in
Yorkshire, England, is known to the Ft.
Frances, Ont. inf., whose paternal grandfather was of Scotch ancestry. Although
most infs. vouchsafed ignorance of any
names for what they did not consider
edible, some volunteered what they
thought to be roughly equivalent, such as
giblets (of a fowl), entrails, falls, innards, sweetbread, and tripe. The few instances are scattered, with no discernible
correlations.

chitterlings ¹37; 130; 323. chittlins
¹2, 35, s?†40; :130, sn132.
entrails ?47; 317.
falls 146.
giblets 118, ?130, 151; *306, 316, 318-
19.
innards !45.
intestines 44-45.
lights 35; 132, 139. liver and ~ 23,
s†31; 137; 204, 207-8, †210, sn212, 214,
sn218.
pluck 15, s?†44, ¹†48, s¹†65.
sweetbreads 14; 141.
tripe 39.
viscera 121.
vittles ?305.
wrinkles 130.
no response 1, 3-7, ?8, 9-13, 16-20,
?21, 22, 24-26, ?27, ?28, :29, 30, 32-34,
36, 38, ?41, ?42, 43, 46, 49-64; 101-17,
119-20, 122-29, 131, 133-36, 138, 140,
142-45, 147-49, ?150, ?152; 201, ?202,
203, 205-6, 209, 211, 213, 215-17, ?219,
220-26; 301-4, 307-11, ?312, 313-15, 320-
22, 324-28; 401-36, ?437.

Comment:

chitterlings: Heard used by Negroes in
St. Paul--37. Inf. learned this while
working in a packing house--323. chit-
lins: Inf.'s term for entrails used as
casing for sausage--132. giblets: Refers
to entrails of fowl--118, 130, 151; *306,
316, 318-19. viscera: Inf. learned this
while working in a packing house--121.

30.7 feeding time. NE 217.

Essentially rural, this item usually appeared in such late afternoon contexts as "Guess I'd better be gettin' home. It's about chore time." Chore time is the most common UM expression, with a general average of 78% and a slight Midland preponderance, as is shown by the increase from Minnesota's 60% to Iowa's 92%, and from 80% in the Dakotas to 87% in Nebraska. Less frequent milking time, with an overall average of 16%, is clearly Northern oriented, for Minnesota's 25% contrasts with Iowa's 1%; and the 19% frequency in the Dakotas contrasts with Nebraska's 8%. Feeding time, also with Northern orientation, has a 10% general average, with 16% in Minnesota and 6% in Iowa, and with 12% in the Dakotas and none in Nebraska.

CL 61: Milking time, not specified on the checklist, was not volunteered by any of the 1,040 respondents, but close correlation with the field data appears in the percentages for the two other terms:

	Mn.	Ia.	N.D.	S.D.	Nb.	Ave.
chore t.	74%	91%	73%	96%	88%	73%
feeding t.	18%	8%	19%	14%	11%	14%

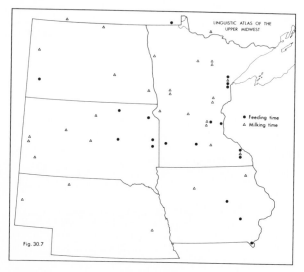

Fig. 30.7

chores 43, 48; 117, 120.
chore time 5, 7, 9-10, 20-22, s25, 26, sn27, 29-30, 34, 36-37, 40-42, 44-47, 50-51, r52, 53-54, 57-65; 101-9, 111-12, 114-19, 121-22, *123, 124-29, 131, 133-41, 143-46, 148-49, 151-52; !202, 203-6, 208, 210-13, 215-18, sn219, sn220, 221-22, 224-25; 301-4, *306, 311-14, 317-18, 320-23, 325, 328; 401, 403-18, 420-24, 426-31, s432, 433-36. chores ~ 4, 19, *43; 223; 319. choring ~ 132, 147.

cow time 223.
eating time 16.
feeding time 1, s13, 15, 17-18, c32, 39, 46, 51, 56, 58; 118, 150, 152; 214; 305, 308, 316-17, 319.
milking time 2, 8, ?9, 10-12, 16, 19-20, 23-25, 28, 32-33, 49, 57; 108, 113, s150; 201, 204, 210, 219, *225; 302, 304, 309-10, 315, 326; ¹402, 404, 409, 425.
quitting time 122, 127, 142.
supper time 14.
time for chores cr9, 28; 226; 419.
time to do chores 26, 55; 207, 211; 402, 417. ~ ~ ~ my chores 37. ~ ~ ~ the chores 3, 6, 23, 31, 49, 57; 209; 324; 412.
time to milk !207, 220; 437.
time to pail the cows 25.
no response 35, 38; 110, 130; 307, 327.

Comment:

chores time: Usu.--19. time for chores: Usu.--9.

31.1 and 2. Calls to cows. NE 218-19. WG 14, 20, 21, 26, 30, 63, 64; F99, F100.

Because calls to animals are unaffected by literate influences, their distribution affords good evidence for basic regional patterns. The eastern sharp division between Northern come boss and Midland sook cow is not as rigidly maintained in the UM, however, since the boss forms have clearly invaded the Midland speech areas of central Iowa and Nebraska. Only the three southern tiers of Iowa counties report consistent retention of sook and sook cow.

As with slop-pail (see 14.3), mingling of the westward population streams has produced hybrid forms. The accompanying map reveals that Midland soo and sook have been retained by some speakers in the face of the invasion, so that soo boss and sook boss occur within and around the pure Midland sook cow region of southern and southeastern Iowa. The analogous possibility, come cow, apparently did not develop, as no instances appear.

Most of the minor variants recorded in the Atlantic states did not survive the westward migration. West Virginia woo somehow was acquired in southeastern Nebraska by a farmer of Czech ancestry. Both infs. in Rolla, North Dakota, next to the Canadian border, use hi hi hi, not recorded by Kurath.

Calls to cows are usually repeated. Like children, cows seem not to respond to a single summons, even when hungry. Some infs. stress the first element in sook cow and come boss, some the second. No regional differences appear. In co boss the stress is perhaps more common on the second part. In the rare <u>here</u> <u>bossy</u> the first word is stressed.

Some infs. volunteered that they send a dog after cows instead of calling them: 43, 45-47, 51, 60, 62-63; 101; 220. Neither method is used in the western cattle country.

CL 70: Returns from 1,004 respondents closely support the field data, with <u>co boss</u> and <u>come boss</u> having an 85% to 90% frequency everywhere but in southern Iowa. There they have a frequency of 40% in contrast with 92% in the northern half of the state. The <u>sook</u> forms occur with 5% of northern Iowa speakers but with 59% of those in southern Iowa.

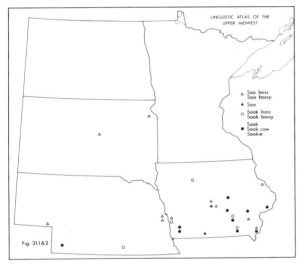

LINGUISTIC ATLAS OF THE UPPER MIDWEST

△ Soo boss
  Soo bossy
▲ Soo
○ Sook boss
  Sook bossy
● Sook
  Sook cow
  Sookie

Fig. 31.1 & 2

ap, ap, ap ¹6.
boss 118.
bossy *5, 24.
co boss 1, 8, 29, 33, ¹36, 47, 50, 54, c56, 57, 63; 109, 111, 116-18, *122, 126, 131; 202, 205, 208, 218, 223; ¹301, 306, 315-16, 319, 327-28; 427, 432. ~ bossy 2-3.
come boss 4, 7, 10-11, 15-16, 18-19, 22, 25, 28, 30-32, 39, 41-43, !44, 46, !48, :49, 51, !52, 53, 55-56, 61, !62, 64-65; 104-8, 112, 114-15, 122-24, 127, 133, 138-39; 203, 210, !211, 221-22, 224-25; 303, 307, 317-18, !321, 322-24, *325; ¹401, 404-6, 408-9, 412-14, 418, 420-21, ¹422, 423, 429-30, 434, ¹437. ~ bossy 12-13, 20, !21, 23, 26, 34, s¹36, ¹37, 45, 47, 59-60; 119, 140, 151; 206, 209, 212, !214, 215-16; 305; 407, †415, 433.
come (+ name) 40.
here boss 57; 315; 428. ~ bossy 102; 305; 416, ¹419, 426.
hey 57, 59.
hi 204-5, ~ boss 302.
huh boss 417.

soo 129, 145. ~ boss 119, 124, 128, 148; ¹†217; 308; 427-28, 436. ~ bossy 129, 152; 314.
sook sn†118, 132, 134, 140, 143, 147. ~ boss 113, 125, 146; *432. ~ bossy 135. ~ cow 136, 142, 149; 429.
sookie 137.
woo 435.
wooie ¹414.
call by name 14, 48, 58; 135, †150.
inarticulate call made by patting open mouth with hands 201.
no response 9, 17, ?27, 35, ?38; 101-2, 110, 120-21, 130, 141, 144; :207, ?213, ?219, 220, ?226; 304, 309, ?310-11, 312-13, 320, ?326; 402-3, 410-11, 424-25, 432.

Comment:

<u>come boss</u>: "Some people have a regular yodel"--7. "We just pound on a bucket"--51. High pitched voice--105. Usu. went after cows with a saddle horse--214. <u>sook</u>: Used by inf.'s mother from N.C.--118. Very high falsetto--132. no response: No calls for cows here in cattle country--312. No calls here, but "We honk the horn to get 'em to come to cake [of pressed cottonseed]"--320.

31.3 Calls to cows during milking. NE 220. WG 18-19, 24, 26, 64; F101.

To quiet cows during milking the most common call in the eastern states, <u>so</u>, often followed by <u>boss</u> or <u>bossy</u>, is also dominant in the UM. The minor variant <u>ho</u>, also sometimes followed by <u>boss</u> or <u>bossy</u>, is not recorded in WG but has scattered occurrences in Minnesota, with a few instances in the eastern parts of the Dakotas and Nebraska. Its seven occurrences in Wisconsin as well might suggest a Northern orientation. Rare New England <u>hoist</u> is preserved in southeastern Minnesota by a Type I inf. of New York state background.

CL 71: As with the field data, <u>so</u> dominates the responses. <u>Hoist</u>, however, is checked by 61 respondents: Mn. 6, Ia. 19, N.D. 2, S.D. 14, Nb. 20. This Midland weighting could reflect origination in southern New Jersey rather than in New England. (See <u>WG</u>.) Several respondents volunteered that its meaning is especially "move over," "lift that leg," rather than simply "stand still." The 30 ho variants, significant because they are all added to the checklist by the respondents, seem to have a Northern distribution: Mn. 10, Ia. 1, N.D. 3, S.D. 11, Nb. 5. Midland <u>saw</u>, not found during fieldwork, is the usage of one North Dakota respondent of Pennsylvania background and of one South Dakotan of Norwegian parentage.

call by name 4.
co boss 8; 201, sn[1]207.
(curse) 34, 43, 52; [1]403.
here bossy 140; 305; 421.
ho ?51, ?63; 143, 148; 323. ~ boss !11, 49, 57; 224. ~ bossy *5, 19, 37, 43, 64; 305; 415, 425. ~ there 224.
hoist/ haɪst/ 65.
hold still 34.
keep still !206; 417.
nice bossy 49.
so 53; 128, 135, 142, 146, s150; 202, 205, 221; 320, 327; 404. ~ boss [1]7, 14-16, 18, [1]21, 22, 24-25, 28-30, 32, 40-42, 44-45, !46, :47, 48, 50, 52-55, s56, 61-62, [1]63, 65; 101-2, 104-9, 111, 113-17, 119, 122, *123, 124-25, 130-32, 136-38, 145, 149; 202-5, 208, 210, !211, 213, 217-18, 220, 222; 301-3, 307, 310, *311, [1]312, 316-18, 321-22, 324-25, [1]326; 401, 403, 406-12, 414, 418, 420, 422, 424, 428-29, 431-32, 434, 436-37. ~ bossy !1, 2-3, [1]8, 10, 12, 23, 26, :†31, 59-60, 62; 112, 118, 129, 133, 139-40, 151; [1]206, 209-10, 212, 214-16, *219, :†223, 225; *306, 308-9, 314, 317; 411, 413, 427. ~ cow 416. ~ (+ name) 147; 416, 424.
stand still :?39, 56; 224; 417, !423, 430. ~ ~ damn you !62. ~ ~ you darn fool 219.
stay still 17.
steady boss 18; 148.
there now 223.
whoa *134.
no response 6, 9, 13, ?20, ?27, ?33, 35-36, ?38, 58; 103, 110, 120-21, 126-27, 141, 144, ?152; ?226; 304, 313, 315, 319, 328; 402, 405, 419, 426, 433, 435.

Comment:

so boss: "That's something I never did --talk to a cow"--7. "Some of it isn't printable"--45. so bossy: Heard frequently here--8. Used by inf.'s mother (from Ire.)--31.

31.4 Calls to calves. NE 218-19. WG 30, 64; F102.

Although most infs. are unfamiliar with any calls to cattle and some of the others do not distinguish between calls to cows and calls to calves, the usage of the remaining infs. reflects in general the major division in the eastern states but at the same time does not precisely support the assertion in the WG that "none of the local calls of the Atlantic seaboard have survived west of the Alleghenies."
The Northern generics co boss(y) and come boss(y) are, with two exceptions, limited to the UM Northern speech area, with the come forms more common in Minnesota. Come calf(y), however, though scattered in all the states, is most common in Nebraska and is found twice in southern Iowa, where it may be a merging of Northern come boss and Midland sook calf. The Midland sook terms dominate southern Iowa, are frequent in Nebraska, and are reported as the normal expressions of the Manitoba and Saskatchewan infs. Two instances of sooky appear in Minnesota, another in Manitoba. The variant sic calf occurs three times, twice along the southern edge of the UM in Iowa and Nebraska and once in western South Dakota.

Cussy, a minor variant found in eastern South Carolina, apparently survives in southern Nebraska, where it has been acquired by an inf. of Swedish parentage; a possibly related kissy is the term of a North Dakota inf. both of whose parents came from The Netherlands.

Kibby, which may be a variant of the cubby known in the Norfolk area of Virginia, also is the term of an inf. of Swedish parentage in northwestern North Dakota.

Homminick, a likely phonetic shift from the Pennsylvania German hommilie, is locally known to but not used by a northern South Dakota inf. living near the Missouri River.

CL 73: Support of the regional allegiance of sook and sook calf comes from the mail responses. Only 30% of the 110 informants in northern Iowa use these terms; 75% of the 110 respondents in the southern part of the state use them. The come terms are Northern in orientation:

	Mn.	Ia.	N.D.	S.D.	Nb.	Ave.
sook, etc.	14%	53%	17%	21%	47%	32%
come, etc.	58%	38%	58%	51%	38%	48%

bossy 204; 327.
calf 8; 205. ~y *5, :12, 15; 107, 114; 303; 408, 413, 418, 424.
co bossy 126; 218. ~ bossy 50; 109; 208; *306, 316.
come boss 30-31, 53; 412. ~ ~y 19, 44, 61, 64-65; 116, 132; 211; →[1]303, 317, 323.
come calf 125, 128; 401, 420, 432. ~ ~y 4, 21, 41, [1]53, ?55; 105, 115, 128, 148; 206, 215-16, 221; 301, →[1]303, 317, *325; 401, 407, 422-23. come on calfy !48.
come on sooky 1.
coo [1]7.
cussy 430.
here calf 416.
homminick [1]303.
kibby 203.
kissy 223.

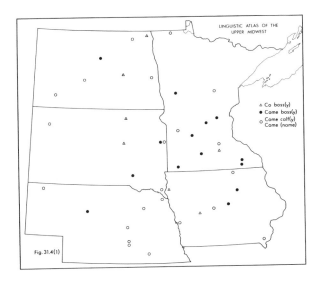

Fig. 31.4(1)

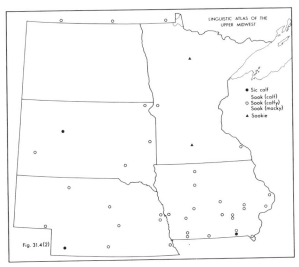

Fig. 31.4(2)

sic calf 147; *302; 429.
sook 1, s?12; 127; 201-2; 307. ~ calf
25, †31, ⊥50, 56; 104, 113, 124, 133,
*134, 137-39, 142-43, 145-46, 149; *311,
318, ⊥320; !404, ⊥406, 414, 421, 427,
436. ~ ~y 135-36, 151; 322; 428, 431, 434.
sook macky macky 140.
sooky 10, 52.
[ts·ts·ts] 39; †215.
[ts] calf 321.
woo ?435.
call by name 13-14, e.g., come Nellie--
415, come Tissy--48.
no response 2-3, 6, 9, 11, 16-18, 20,
22-24, 26-29, 32-38, 40, ?42, 43, 45-47,
49, 51, 54, 57-60, 62-63; 101-3, 106,
108, 110-12, 117-23, 129-31, 141, 144,
?150, ?152; ?207, 209, ?210, :212, ?213,
214, 217, ?218, 220, 222, 225, ?226; 304-

5, 308-10, ?312, 313-15, 319, 324, ?326,
328; 402-3, 405, ?409-10, 411, 417, 419,
425-26, 433, ?437.

Comment:

sook calf: Heard by inf.'s mother (from
Ire.)--31. Heard frequently here--50.
woo: Pronounced [wu:], "I imagine"--435.

31.5 Calls to draft oxen (or horses) to
direct them left or right.

No significant regional patterns appear
in the data for directional calls to
draft animals, typically haw to the left
and gee to the right. But the decline in
the use of such animals is reflected in
the uncertainty of 26 scattered infs. as
to which word means right and which means
left, and is even more sharply indicated
in the complete semantic reversal accepted by the 4 infs. who insist that gee is
equivalent to "Go left" and by the 6 reported as believing that haw means "Go
right."
Six scattered infs. in Northern speech
territory have the variant hee and two
have yee. A French-Canadian inf. in
northern Minnesota recalls his use of
the old calls scudahee and scudahay in
directing mules.

a. to the left
gee 1, 50; 107; 220.
haw 2, 4, *5, 6, c7, 8, 12, 15-18, 21,
23-30, :⊥31, †33, 40-43, c44, 45-48, 51-
53, c54, 55-56, 59-62, c63; 101, 105,
109, 113-14, 117-19, 122-31, 133-36, 138-
49, 151-52; c201-2, 204, †205, 206, 208,
†209, !210, 212, 216, 218, 221, 223-25;
303, r305, 306, 309, 311, 314, 316, 318,
c320, 323-24, 328; †401, 403-5, 407,
409, 413, ⊥414, 416-18, 420-22, 424-30,
432-35.
hee †20, 57; 101.
scudahee c7.

b. to the right
gee 2, 4, *5, 6, c7-8, 12, 15-18, 21,
23, :24, 25-30, :⊥31, †33, 40-48, 51-53,
c54, 55-56, 59-62, c63; 101, 105, 109,
113-14, 117-19, 122-31, 133-36, 138-49,
151-52; c201-2, 204, †205, 206, 208,
†209, !210, 212, 216, 218, 221, 223-24,
c225; 303, 305-6, 309, 311, 314, 316,
318, c320, 323-24, 328; †401, 403-5,
407, 409, 413, ⊥414, 416, 418, 420-22,
424-30, 432-35.
haw 1, †20, 50, 57; 107; 220.
scudahay c7.
yee 417.

c. directions confused or not known
gee 3, c⊥10, 13, 19, ⊥32, 37, 39, 65;
213-14, †215, 222; 301-2, 307-8, 317,
322, †325; 401, †423, 431.

haw 3, c¹10, 13, 19, ¹32, ¹†35, 37, 39,
†49, 65; 203, 213-14, †215, †217, 222;
301-2, 307-8, 317, 322, †325; 410, †423,
431.

hee †49; 203, †217.

yee c308.

no response 9, 11, 14, 22, 34, 36, ?38,
58, 64; 102-4, 106, 108, 110-12, 115-16,
120-21, 132, 137, ?150; ?207, 211, ?219,
?226; 304, 310, ?312, 313, 315, 319, 321,
?326, 327; 402, 406, 408, 411-12, 415,
419, 436, ?437.

Comment:

gee: Pronounced /gi/--*43. Inf. says
/gi͡ʔ/ is easier than /ǰi/--55. Pronounced
/ǰi/--432. haw: "Ox-drivers actually said
[ˌwə^ʰχ·ɔᵛ]"--23. gee and haw: Used by
inf.ʼs father--205, 209; 423. hee and
haw: Used by inf.ʼs father--20, 49.

31.6 Calls to horses in the pasture.
NE 222.

In the eastern part of the UM many infs.
reflect the decline of the use of horses
on the farm in their unawareness of any
calls to horses. In the west, where
horses are still raised, the great extent
of the grazing area led several infs. to
remark that they didn't call horses: "We
go 'n' get 'em."

Infs. who do or did call horses are
most likely to call them by name, especially in the northern UM: Mn. 80%,
Ia. 6%, N.D. 50%, S.D. 47%, Nb. 30%, or
45% overall. A fairly common nonverbal
call is the whistle, used by 19% of the
infs., evenly distributed except for
only 10% in North Dakota.

Come, followed by boy, jack, pony, or
a name, has a similar average, 20%, but
with a more uneven distribution·that has
apparently at least two correlations.
One is that it occurs in northern Iowa,
the first settled portion of Minnesota,
North Dakota, and the extended area
around the New York state settlement in
Nebraska--all of them Northern speech
oriented regions. The second is the non-
use of any kind of call in the western
fringe of the UM and, indeed, in much of
South Dakota.

Three probably related calls are kope,
kwope, and kup /kup/. The first two are
surely Midland, for they occur only in
Iowa (27%) and Nebraska (25%). Kup, however, may be Northern, since 3 of the 4
instances are in Northern speech territory in Minnesota and Iowa, and it was
found 4 times in Wisconsin (but kope
and kwope not at all).

CL 75: Although some differences exist,
the mail returns largely support the

field data. The call by name is most common (60% of 886 respondents) with a
manifest Northern influence: 71% in Minnesota compared with only 34% of 106
respondents in southern Iowa. Although
kope and kwope are checked by respondents
in the north, the preponderance is still
Midland: Minnesota with 16%, northern
Iowa with 19%, but southern Iowa with 54%.

co boy 142; 306-7.

coby 143.

come 221. ~ boy 50; 203, 205, 208, 223;
422, 437. ~ horsie ¹7; 216. ~ jack 140.
~ pony 140; 420. ~ (+ name) 40, 44, 56;
105, 107-8, 112, 115-17, 141; 206; 317;
413-14, 423-24, 432. ~ on (+ name) 224.

coo ?152.

here (+ name) 101-2.

hey 204.

horsie *5.

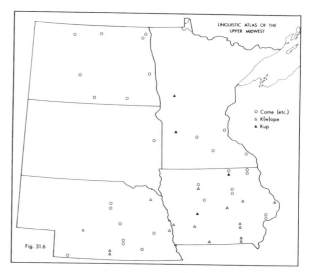

Fig. 31.6

kope 113, 118, 132, 136, 151; 407, 418,
427, †428, 430.

kope (+ name) 125, 139; 431.

kup 19, 41; 106, 126.

kwope ¹124, 135, 145-47.

wup *134.

call by name 2-4, *5, ¹6, 8, 10, 12-17,
21-26, ?27, 29-30, 32, 37, 41-43, 45-48,
50-53, 58-61, 63-64; 109, 150; 205, 207-
12, 214-15, 225; 302, 308, †313, 316,
321-23, 325; 401, 417, 421-22, 428-29.
(whinnering noise) 201.

whistle 21, 29, 37, 49-50, 52, 54, 61,
65; 107, 124, 127-28, 137-38, †139, 148-
49; 202, 218; *311, ¹312, 316, 318, 322,
¹326; 404, 416, 422, 428.

no response 1, 9, 11, 18, 20, 28, 31,
33-36, 38-39, 55, 57, 62; 103-4, 110-11,
114, 119-23, 128, 130-31, 133, 144; ?213,
217, ?219, 220, 222, ?226; 301, 303-5,
309-10, 314-15, 319-20, 324, 327-28;

402-3, 405-6, 408-12, 415, 419, 425-26, 433-36.

Comment:

come jack: Used for calling mules--140.
kope: Used by inf.'s father (from Wi.)--428.

31.7 Calls to horses to urge them on.
NE 223. WG 19, 43, 49, 65, 66; F107.

Various eastern local inciting calls to horses are not reported in the UM; different forms of get up, described in WG as "current in all three of the major areas," dominate all five states. Analysis of the field data, with the confirmation provided by the checklist returns, rather clearly indicates two regional correlations of the get up call that are not recognized by Kurath.

As the chart indicates, there is a consistent, though slight, increase in the frequency of get up along the dimension from north to south; there is a correspondingly consistent, though also slight, increase in the frequency of giddap along the dimension from south to north. Although both forms are thus found throughout the UM, Northern speakers slightly favor giddap and Midland speakers slightly favor get up.

The less frequent variants with an intrusive vowel, giddiup and giddiap, even more clearly have regional orientation. As chart 2 reveals, they are Northern.

Clucking as a speed-up signal also has a slight Northern orientation.

CL 74: Returns from 1,035 mail respondents remarkably support the inference that get up and giddap have some regional differentiation.

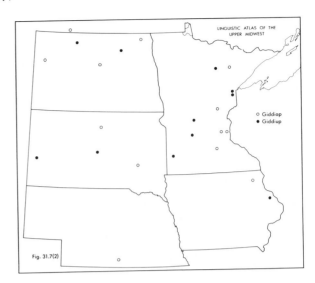

Fig. 31.7(2)

	Mn.	Ia.	N.D.	S.D.	Nb.	Ave.
get up	35%	49%	30%	42%	49%	42%
giddap	53%	43%	53%	48%	44%	48%

Although with neither sets of data are the differences great, the correlation appears more than coincidental, especially when the checklist returns for Iowa split for the northern and southern halves of the state. In northern Iowa 40% of 131 respondents use get up and 50% use giddap. In the southern half the ratio is reversed, with 59% of 116 respondents using get up and only 34% using giddap. In Minnesota, also, 14% of the respondents use giddiup, but in southern Iowa only 3%; in North Dakota 22%, but in Nebraska only 7%.

come on 13; [1]414.
get along 118; 222.
get up 3, 6, 8, 10-11, 13, 15-16, 19, 22-23, 25-27, 29, 31, 35-36, ?39, 41-42, 44-45, !46, 49, 52, 54, 57, 59-62; 104, 107, 115, 117, 122-24, 126-27, 129-33, 135-37, 139, 141, 145-47, 149-52; 203, 206, 212, 214-18, 221; 301, 305, 308-10, 313, 317, 321-22, 324, 327; 402, 405-7, 409, 411-13, 416-18, 420-21, 423, 427, 433-36.
giddap 1-2, 4, *5, 7, 9, 12, c14, 16, 20-21, 30, 32-34, 37, cr39, 50-51, 53, c55, 56, 58, 62-65; 101-3, 105-6, 109-14, 116, 118-20, 125, 128, 134, 138, 140, 142-44, 148-49; 202, 204-5, 207, 210, 213, 219-20, 222-26; 302, 306-7, 311-12, 314, 316, 318-19, [1]320, 323, 325-26; 401, 403-4, 408, 410, 415, 419, 422, 424-26, 428-30, 432-33, 435, 437.
giddiap 13, 24, 37, 40, 48; 108; 201, 208-9, 211; 304, 328; 431.
giddiup 11, 17-18, 28, 43, 47; 121; 203, 212; 310, 315.
go 47.

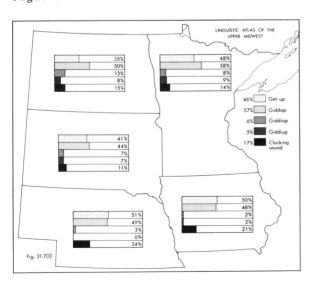

LINGUISTIC ATLAS OF THE UPPER MIDWEST

46% Get up
57% Giddap
6% Giddiop
5% Giddiup
17% Clucking sound

Fig. 31.7(1)

hi there 404.
[ˈhʌbʌp] ¹†312.
[s::] 320.
(clucking sound) 17, 23, 25, 32, 37, 42,
53, 56, 58; 113, 117-18, 124-25, 128,
132, 139, 149-51; 202, 205, 208, 222; 312-
13, 323; 404, 413, †414, 416-18, 424,
426-28.
(sucking sound) 117.
(whistle) 25; 423.
no response 38; 303.

Comment:

giddap: Usu.--62. Inf. says farmers
use this--320. [ˈhʌbʌp]: Inf. heard this
used by a Tennesseean about 1905--312.
[s::]: Inf. says this is used by ranchers, "grade-skinners," and Indians;
Indians also use [ʃ:]--320.

32.1 Calls to horses to stop them. NE
224. WG 16, 66; F108.

As a call to stop a horse whoa, which
WG describes as "rare outside the New
England settlements," apparently had
vitality not predictable from the eastern
atlas data, for it is the most common
form in all the UM: Mn. 55%, Ia. 73%,
N.D. 69%, S.D. 63%, Nb. 58%. The un-
aspirated woa, found throughout the east,
is less popular in the UM: Mn. 17%, Ia.
17%, N.D. 27%, S.D. 11%, Nb. 25%.
"Beyond the mountains," WG reports,
"it seems that only woa! and NE whoa!
survive." The accompanying chart, however, reveals not only that ho does
survive in the UM but also suggests that
its persistence here may be due to two
different migration influences. In the
east it occurs in the Atlantic coastal
areas south from Chesapeake Bay; in the
UM it occurs in the South Midland and
Midland territory of Iowa and Nebraska.
In the east it occurs also in western
Connecticut; in the UM it occurs in northeastern Iowa, and the older parts of Minnesota and Iowa, as well as in the Canadian strip along the U.S. boundary.
An Omaha housewife, in addition, remembers as an old-fashioned call the form
haw, which in the east is reported only
from eastern Virginia.

back 54. ~ up 13.
haw †428.
ho 4, 13, 15, 18-20, 31, 43, 47, 50-51,
55, 60, ?63, 65; 105-6, 117-18, 150, 152;
¹216, 224; 302, 305, 308, 318-19, 323,
327; 407, 415, 417, 423-24, 432, ¹436.
whoa !3, *5, 7, r9, 10-11, 17, 21, 23-
30, 32-33, 36-37, 39-42, 44-46, 49, 52-
53, 56, 59, 61-62, cr63, 64; 101-4, 107-
16, 118-28, 130-31, 133-34, 138-42, 144-
46, 151; 203-5, 207, 209-11, 213-15,

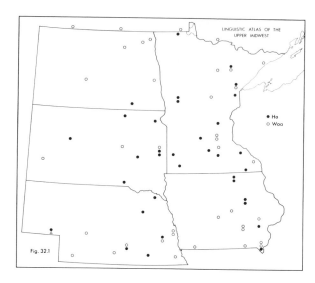

Fig. 32.1

LINGUISTIC ATLAS OF THE
UPPER MIDWEST

● Ho
○ Woa

217-20, 222-23, 225-26; 301, 304, 306-7,
309-10, 312-15, 320-22, 324-26, 328; 401-
6, 408-9, 411-14, 416, 419-21, 426, 431,
433, 437. ~ back 58.
whoop 8.
woa 1-2, 6, 12, 14, 16, 22, 34-35, 48,
57; 129, 132, 135-37, 143, 147-49; 201-2,
!206, 208, 212, 216, 221; 311, 316-17;
418, 422, 425, 427-30, 434, 436. ~ back
16.
no response 38; 303; 410.

Comment:

ho: Inf. reports having had an Eastern
hand who said [ˈhu]; the horses paid no
attention to him--436.

32.2 Calls to pigs at feeding time. NE
226. WG 20, 22, 26, 35, 37, 41, 43-44,
64; F24, F104.

Perhaps unlike human beings, pigs seem
to respond favorably to dialect diversity. A great variety of calls to pigs
at feeding time exists in the eastern
states, and, although some of them have
not been carried west, new variations appear in the UM. Most common are the repeated pig and the repeated piggy. In WG
Kurath did not differentiate these, but,
as with chick and chickie, the simple
form pig without the hypocoristic ending
apparently has greater acceptance among
Northern speakers. Nearly one-half of
the Minnesota infs. use it; yet it occurs
with only three speakers in the southern
two-thirds of Iowa. The contrast between
the frequency in North Dakota and that in
Nebraska is even greater, 76% and 18%.
This difference cuts across fieldworker
boundaries and is too great to be attributed to chance. Pig is often [pyg].
Next most common is the pooie set of

variants, including pooig. Occurring in the east in New Jersey and around Wheeling, West Virginia, the pooie terms clearly belong in the Midland speech stream, with an UM distribution ranging from a solitary occurrence in North Dakota to eight occurrences in Nebraska.

Eastern New England chook lives in two UM responses, one in Minnesota and one in South Dakota. Hooie has been brought west from Delaware and the lower Susquehanna Valley to be a still viable call in southern Iowa, southeastern South Dakota, and Nebraska. Wooie, a south Midland call found in Virginia and North Carolina, has a solitary echo in the South Midland speech area of southeastern Iowa and another in northwestern Nebraska in the speech of a woman whose father, though born in Minnesota, had enlisted in the Confederate army. Piggoop, also a North Carolina word, apparently has no UM survivors.

UM calls not found in New England nor treated in WG are sooie, ka-prig and prig, cooie, pigooie, and oink. Sooie, with the variants soo and sooig, is clearly Midland in origin, with an UM distribution as follows: Mn. 4%, Ia. 20%, N.D. 5%, S.D. 28%, Nb. 21%, average 14%. The rare ka-prig and prig are quite likely phonetic modifications of come pig and pig. Pigooie, a singleton, might be a blend of pig and another call. Onomatopoetic oink may be suspect as a bona fide call, as it is offered only by two southern Minnesota nonfarmers, one a lawyer and the other a retired banker.

All the calls ending in -ooie or -ooig occur in two versions, sometimes used by the same speaker. One version is short, and it is used in rapid staccato sequence. The other version, typically with unusually high pitch or even a falsetto, greatly prolongs either one or both of the two syllables.

CL 76: Responses from 968 respondents reveal that, as with the field data, the four most common calls are pig, piggy, pooie, and sooie.

	Mn.	Ia.	N.D.	S.D.	Nb.	Ave.
pig	45%	17%	56%	38%	28%	35%
piggy	31%	34%	25%	23%	35%	31%
pooie	6%	5%	6%	20%	19%	11%
sooie	8%	19%	12%	14%	20%	15%

These data confirm the putative Northern bias of pig and the Midland orientation of sooie. Chook was checked by 10 respondents, 8 of whom live in Minnesota, northern Iowa, or North Dakota. Another nonfarmer Minnesotan reported oink (7). Hooie has 9 instances in southern Iowa and two in North Dakota (9, 24). Kong,

kong, not found during fieldwork, occurs in Minnesota (67, 76, 87) and in South Dakota (26, 82). A write-in, spelled in various ways but apparently representing a call like [huːiːgi] whooeegy, is apparently Midland in orientation: Iowa (17-18, 25, 46, 74, 77, 84), South Dakota (33), and Nebraska (33, 92). Four other rare write-ins are wahoo (Ia. 90), pigga (N.D. 17, S.D. 35 and 66), perg (N.D. 23), and booch, booch (S.D. 63).

butch !42.
chook, chook 51; [1]309.
come pig, pig 29, 34, 49; 101, 105; 225. ~ piggy, piggy 22, 40, 44; 407.
cooie, cooie ?*47.
here pig, pig 24.
hoaie, hoaie [1]41-42, [1]53; 416.

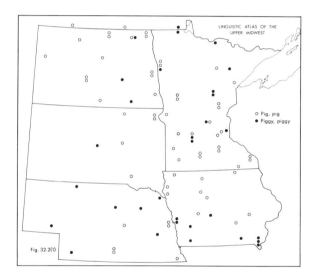

Fig. 32.2(1)

○ Pig, pig
● Piggy, piggy

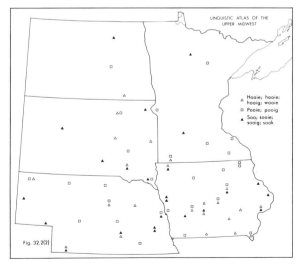

Fig. 32.2(2)

△ Hooie; hooie; hooig; wooie
□ Pooie; pooig
▲ Soo; sooie; sooig; sook

hooie, hooie !61; 101, 117, 127-28,
131, 133, 136, 138, 145; 224; 306, 316,
318, 322; 414, 423.
　hooie pig !429. ~ piggy 147.
　hooig 140; ¹312.
　ka-prig 317.
　oink 58, 62.
　pig, pig ¹3, ¹6-7, 8, 11, 15, 19-20,
23, 25, 37, 41, 43, *46, !48, 52-53, 56-
57, 59, 65; 104, 109, 111, 113-14, 126,
135, 137; 201-6, :!207, 208, 210-11, 216-
17, 220, !221, 223, 225; 305, 307-8, ¹309,
316, 323; ¹408, 420, 427-28, 430-31, 435.
　piggy, piggy 1, 4, *5, 9, 14, 21, 29,
45; 124-25, 129, 142, 146, 148-51; 206,
*219, 224; 315; 403, 413, 415, 417, 424,
429, ¹434.
　pigooie 115.
　poke 140.
　pooie, pooie 12, 54, 60, 64; 106-8,
112, 116, 124, 132, 143, 148; ¹223; *306,
328; 404, 406, ¹408, †412, †416, 418,
421, 427, 432.
　pooig 26, 50; 126; 218; ¹319, *325;
401, 413, 42.
　prig, prig 30; 317.
　sooie, sooie 10; 102, 118-19, 1̈22, 130,
139, 141, 151; †217, :¹226; 302, 308,
!321, 325; 409, ¹410, 422, 425-26, 428,
¹433.
　sooig, sooig 323.
　sook, sook !45; 118, 123; 212.
　sook-a-pig ¹61.
　sookie ¹411.
　soo pig 436-37.
　so, so ¹225.
　wooie, wooie 149; 401.
　clucking noise 1, 29.
　sucking noise 32.
　whistle 416.
　no response 2, 13, 16-18, ?27, 28, 31,
?33, 35-36, ?38, 39, 51, ?55, 63; 103,
110, 120-21, 134, 144, ?152; ?209, ?213-
14, :?!215, 222; 301, 303-4, 310, ?311,
313-14, 320, 326-27; 402, ?405, 419.

Comment:

　pooie: Used by inf.'s neighbor; an
Iowa call--223. sooie: Formerly used by
inf.'s husband--217. sooig: Inf. says
this is used to drive pigs away--323.

32.3　Calls to sheep from the pasture.
WG 16, 30, 42, 49, 65; F105.

　Because sheep-raising is not common on
UM farms and because in the western sheep
country the animals are not summoned by
calls, only 27 infs. could report their
use of a call to sheep. Most infs. seemed
unaware that such calls exist. New England
and New York state co-day or kuday
/ˌkə'de/ and co-dack or kudack /ˌkə'dæk/

turn up 4 times in Northern speech territory and once in the speech of a Nebraska farmer of presumable New York parentage. The 5 instances of New England co-nan
and co-nanny are similarly scattered, two
of them being in Canada. Midland sheep
and sheepy are the most common, exclusively dominating southern Iowa and extending
into southern Minnesota.

CL 77: Exactly one-half (50%) of the 712
mail respondents use or know sheepy (35%),
sheep (3%), or come sheep (12%), evenly
distributed except for low frequency in
extreme western South Dakota and western
Nebraska. Co-nan and co-nanny (10% of
the total) are clearly Northern with 16%
in Minnesota, 13% in northern Iowa, and
only 5% in southern Iowa. Only 14 respondents (2%) checked kuday/kudack,
which are sparsely distributed throughout
the UM.

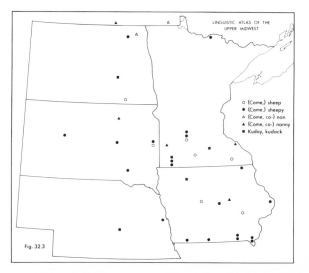

Fig. 32.3

　baa, baa 5, 10; 201, 215; 305.
　kudack 420.
　kuday 50, 59; ¹113; 218.
　lamby, lamby 137; 305. come ~ 60.
　nan, nan 1. co-~ 208.
　nanny, nanny *46; ¹206; ¹302. co-~
118. come ~ 54; 202. here ~ *306.
　pashay ¹147.
　sheep, sheep 45; 137; 318. come ~ 53,
64; 115; 224.
　sheepy, sheepy 5, *43, 60-61; 107, 132,
139, 143, 145-49; 206; 316; 427. come ~
44; 317, 322. here ~ 302.
　[ɚːː] *123.
　(whistle) 60.
　no response 2, ?3, 4, 6-9, 11-19, ?20,
21-32, ?33, 34-37, ?38, 39-40, ?41, ?42,
47-49, 51-52, ?55, 56-58, 62-63, ?65;
101-6, 108-12, 114, 116-17, 119-22, 124-
31, 133, 138, 140-42, 144, ?150, 151,

?152; ?203-4, 205, ?207, ?209-10, 211,
?212-14, 216, ?217, ?219, 220, ?221,
222-23, 225-26; 301, 303-4, 307-10,
?311, 313-15, 319-21, ?323, 324-28; 401-
4, ?405, 406-19, 421-26, 428-36, ?437.

Comment:

   come, nanny: "But they won't come"--
202. nanny, nanny: Inf. says this is
more common here than his own call--206.
Inf. has heard only one person ever call
sheep--312. pashay: "Heard one fellow
holler [ˌpəˈʃeᴸ ˌpəˈʃeᴸ] once"--147.
[ɚ::]: Used by inf. during a summer of
sheep-herding in Wyoming--*123.

32.4 Calls to chickens at feeding. NE
227. WG 21, 23-24, 44, 47, 65; F106.

   Although in WG Kurath describes chick
and chickie as found thoughout the east,
he does not indicate a distinction between
them that appeared in the initial field
returns in the North Central states and
that is rather clearly confirmed in the
UM. Although no sharp areal division can
be drawn, the simple chick (like pig;
see 32.2) has a significant Northern
orientation, and the hypocoristic chickie
is distinctly Midland in its weighting.
(See chart.)
   Biddy and come biddy, found in eastern
New England and along the Atlantic coast
from southern Delaware to Cape Charles,
is described in WG as not carried westward, but 3 southern Iowans use it, as
does one southern Minnesotan.
   Bee, in the east a typical Pennsylvania
German call, seems to be common among the
German Russians in southeastern North Dakota. A Rolette County, North Dakota,
farmer, of English parentage, demonstrated
his own call, a sustained high falsetto
[kɚ::t]. Other rare calls are chip, chookie, and cluck.

CL 78: Returns from 987 respondents support the Northern weighting of chick in
the eastern UM (northern Ia. 60%, southern Ia. 45%), but not in the west; they
do support the Midland weighting of chickie throughout the area (northern Iowa
40%, southern Iowa 55%).

	Mn.	Ia.	N.D.	S.D.	Nb.	Ave.
chick	72%	55%	69%	71%	66%	66%
chickie	26%	47%	28%	33%	38%	35%

Chuck (?[tʃʊk]) occurs 7 times in the
Northern speech zone (Mn. 1, 15, 35, 40,
50, 73; Ia. 1; N.D. 24). Cut occurs 5
times (Mn. 38, 48; S.D. 23; Nb. 89). Kip
is the form for two respondents (Mn. 48;
S.D. 55).
   Several write-in forms appear in the
·mailed returns. Most common is biddy

(Mn. 8, 40; Ia. 24, 93; N.D. 9, 48; S.D.
39, 66; Nb. 1, 18, 67), widely scattered.
Others are dippy (N.D. 44); tick (N.D.
55); tip (Mn. 15); tippy (Ia. 6 (2x); N.D.
17); tuck (S.D. 62); tup (N.D. 16);
tweet, tweet (Mn. 11; S.D. 33). One Iowa
woman wrote that she calls chickens with
"Come, little dee-dee."

   bee, bee 224.
   biddy, biddy 126, 138. come ~ 44; 144.
   chick, chick 2, ¹3, 5-7, 9-12, 14-17,
21-23, 25-26, !27, 28-31, 33-35, 37, 39,
41-43, 45-46, !48, 49-54, 56-57, 59-61,
65; 104, 106-7, 111, 113-14, 117-24, 127-
28, 131-32, 137, 139, 141, 148-50; 201-3,
205-8, 210-14, *216, c217, 218-19, !220,
221, 225, ¹226; 302, 305, *306, 307-10,
312, †314, 316-18, 321, 323, 327-28;
401-6, 408, 410, *412, 414, 418, 422-23,
427-28, 430, 432-33, 435-36. come ~ 36,

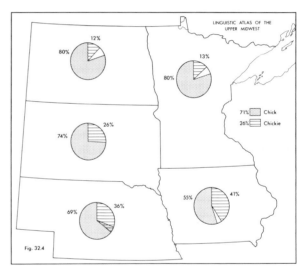

Fig. 32.4

55; 304, 319; 431, 437. here ~ 18, ¹22;
102; !313, 315, 326; 416, 426.
   chick, chick, chickie 145.
   chickie, chick, chick !152; 223; 420.
   chickie, chickie 1, 4, 24, 32, 40, 43,
?44, ?47, 64; 108-9, 112, 115-16, 125,
129, 133-36, 138, 142-43, 146-47, 151;
209, 215-16; 301, 311, 320, 322, 324-25;
407, 411, 413, 415, 417, 421, 424, 429,
434. come ~ :62; 105; 433. here ~ 14;
302; 409, 425.
   chip, chip 19.
   chookie, chookie 3.
   cluck, cluck 20; 101.
   cot, cot [kɚ::t] 204.
   tookie, tookie 140.
   no response 8, 13, ?38, 57, 63; 103,
110, 130; 222; 303; 419.

Comment:
   bee, bee: Inf. says this is common here
--224.

32.5 I want to <u>harness</u> the horses. NE 176.

As in the New England field responses, this item sometimes yielded terms for putting on a horse the arrangement of buckles and leather straps needed before being driven and sometimes terms for attaching a horse to a vehicle. For the former the usual term in the UM is <u>harness</u>, with the variant <u>harness up</u>. They are not differentiated by informant type or by area. New England <u>gear up</u> and <u>rig up</u> have not been carried west. For the second meaning <u>hitch (up)</u> occurs, with a single instance of <u>hook up</u>, both of which are found in New England.

dress †311.
harness 1-14, 16-17, 19-20, 22-24, c25, 26-31, c33, 34, 36-37, 39-42, 44-53, 55-58, 60-61, 63, 65; 101-8, 111-13, 115-19, 121-30, ?131, 133-49, 151-52; 201-2, c203, 204-10, c211, 212-15, 217-19, 221, c222, 223, 225-26; c301, 302-5, 307-13, c314, 315-17, 319-21, c322, 323-26, 328; 401-8, 410, 412-13, c414, 415-16, c417, 418, 420-28, 431-37. ~ up 21, 43, 54, 59, 64; 109, 114, 120, 132; 216, 220; 224; 318; 409, 411, 419, 429-30.
hitch 51; 319. ~ up 16, 18, 32, 45, 57, c62; 131, 150; 305-6, 317-18; 425.
hook up 118.
put on the gears 422.
put the harness on 15-16, 18, 35.
no response 38; 110; 327.

Comment:

hitch up: Attach to vehicle--317-18. hook up: Attach to vehicle--118. put on the gears: Put on ankle pads, knee pads, etc., as in harness racing or in training--422.

32.7 The horse on the left side of a team. NE 175. WG 14-15, 31, 46, 66; F109-10.

Like <u>gee</u> and <u>haw</u> (See 31.5), the historical terms for the right and the left horse of a team reveal not only uncertainty and ambiguity but also a complete reversal of meaning.
Three terms for the left-hand horse dominate the east coast, <u>nigh horse</u>, <u>near horse</u>, and <u>lead horse</u>, the first principally in eastern New England and around Delaware Bay, the second between the Connecticut River and the Potomac, and the third in southwestern Pennsylvania and the South Midland area along the Blue Ridge south of the Kanawha River.
Of these three, <u>lead horse</u> survives in the UM only in five scattered instances, including one in Ontario, besides the one

occurrence of <u>leader horse</u> in north central Minnesota. <u>Near horse</u> and <u>nigh horse</u> dominate the UM, <u>near</u> rather generally and <u>nigh</u> with marked Northern orientation. A few infs. in the Midland speech zone use the obvious <u>left horse</u> or <u>left-hand horse</u>. The guidance term <u>haw</u> has been carried into the expression <u>haw horse</u> in Iowa and Nebraska; and <u>guide horse</u>, <u>jerk-line horse</u>, and <u>wheel horse</u> occur with modified meanings. (For <u>jerk-line</u> see 32.8.)
As the comments reveal, however, some infs. are unsure whether <u>near</u> means right or left; and as many as 22% of the total number have switched referents and now use <u>off horse</u> to indicate the horse on left instead of on the right. Two other infs. use <u>gee horse</u> with the same meaning.

CL 63: Of 750 respondents marking their checklists exactly the same proportion use <u>near horse</u> and <u>nigh horse</u>, but with some regional contrast, <u>nigh</u> having Northern weighting and <u>near</u> Midland. Despite its chief Midland background <u>lead horse</u> has a slight Northern bias.

	Mn.	Ia.	N.D.	S.D.	Nb.	Ave.
nigh	48%	35%	39%	31%	23%	36%
near	26%	45%	21%	33%	48%	36%
lead	20%	15%	34%	20%	18%	20%

Two southern terms were volunteered as write-ins: <u>line horse</u> (Mn. 82; Ia. 34; N.D. 6, 26; S.D. 4, 35, 37; Nb. 32, 46) and <u>wheel horse</u> (Mn. 28; Ia. 40; N.D. 9, 12, 39; S.D. 3, 14, 16, 25, 32, 58, 69; Nb. 9, 56, 64). Eleven respondents wrote in <u>off horse</u> as their term to describe the horse on the left. Since 9 of them are in the Midland zone and since a similar contrast appears in the field data, this reversal of meaning does seem to be correlated with Midland speech.

gee horse 34; 125.
guide horse 431.
haw horse 149; 208; ?419, 427, 432, 437.
jerk-line horse 320.
lead horse 2, 20; 102; :226; 431. ~er horse 22.
left horse 7; 210, 224; 307; 417, 436. ~-hand horse 322; 401, 418.
near horse sn32, 33, 39, 44, cr46, 47-48, 63, 65; 101, ?108, s111, 113, ?115, 118, ?122, 124, 126, 132, 139, 146-47; :217, †223, *223, c225; 301, 311, ¹312, 323, ?325; 403, 405, 422, 429, *432, 434.
nigh horse :sn1, s3, ¹6, 8, 13, 15, c21, 23, s¹25, 27, ?29, 37, 40-41, 45, ?46, ¹47, :49, 51-54, 56, 59, 61-62; 104, :105, 107, ¹116, 119, 126, 138, 148, 152; 202, 204, 206-7, :¹210, 216, 220-22; ?309, 320; :sn407, 420.

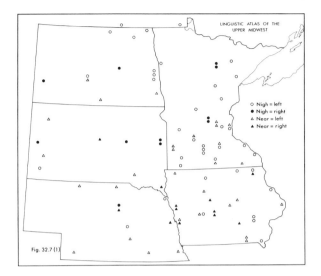

Fig. 32.7 (1)

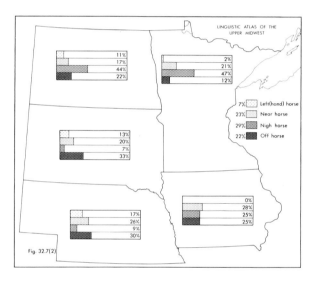

Fig. 32.7(2)

One of two horses in front of four others in a six-horse team--201, 203, 205, 209, 224. near horse: 'Off horse' is the one on the right--32, 44, 48; 124; 225; 422, *432, 434. Inf. not sure if the 'near horse' is on the right or left--108, 115, 122; 325. Term used by inf.'s father (from The Netherlands)--223. nigh horse: 'Off horse' is on the right--8, 40, 51, 53, 56, 59, 61; 105; 420. 'Far horse' is the one on the right--62. Inf. not sure whether the 'nigh horse' is on the right or left--29, 46; 309. ....Yankees said this....--47. Heard by inf. in N.D.--25. off horse: 'Gee horse' is on the right--149; 427. 'Lead horse' is on the right--42. 'Nigh horse' is on the right--11-12, 30; 214, 218; 316-18; 413. 'Near horse' is on the right--:123, 125, 128-29, 125, 128-29, 135; 314; 414, 427. Inf. not sure whether the 'off horse' is on the right or left--114, 122, 137, no response: Inf. has no term for the left horse but calls the one on the right the 'off horse'--201.

32.8 Lines for guiding horses. NE 177.

Added after most of Minnesota had been covered, this question about the term for the leather straps used in guiding horses revealed semantic niceties not recorded in current dictionaries. The source of the complexity is that such straps are used with saddle horses, with a single horse hitched to a vehicle, and also with a team hitched to a vehicle.

For some infs. the generic term is lines, and for others the generic is reins. Some use them as interchangeable generics. Some infs. distinguish between use with a saddle horse, for which their term is reins, and use with a hitched horse, for which the term is lines. Occasionally such an inf., however, will point out that for him reins also can be used with a single horse, but lines only with a team. In this varied use no marked patterning by either informant type or geographical area emerges in the UM.

Leathers, as an unspecified generic, occurs twice, from widely separated infs. A retired cattle rancher in western South Dakota uses the semantically distinct jerk-line, meaning a long single strap to guide the lead horse of a team.

a. in riding and driving, or unspecified leathers 36; 409.
lines 13, c17, 29; c111, 112-17, 119-20, 122, 124-26, 128-30, 132-33, *134, 135, :136, 137, 140, 142, 145-50, 152; 202-5, 208, c209, 212-13, 218, 221; sn304, 306-7, c322, s?¹326; 407, 412-15, 420, 423-24, 430, *432, 436.

off horse 11-12, 30, 42, 50; 109, ?114, ?122, :123, 125, 128-29, 135, ?137, ¹143, 145, 149; 214-15, 218, 223; 306, 314, 316-18, ?325; 404, 409, 413-14, 416, 424, 427, ¹430.
wheel horse ¹†326.
no response 4-5, 9-10, 14, 16-19, 24, 26, 28, 31, 35-36, ?38, 43, ?55, 57-58, 60, 64; 103, 106, 110, 112, 117, 120-21, 127, 130-31, 133-34, 136, 140-42, 144, ?150, 151; 201, 203, 205, 209, 211, ?212, ?213, ?219; 302-5, 308, 310, ?313, 315, 319, 321, 324, 327-28; 402, 406, :408, 410-11, ?412, 415, 421, 423, 425-26, 428, 433, 435.

Comment:

gee horse: 'Haw horse' is the one on the right--34. haw horse: 'Gee horse' is the one on the right--432. lead horse:

269

reins 35; 101-3, 110, c111, 112, 116,
119, 121-23, 127-38, *134, 141, 144, 150,
c152; 201, ¹202, →205, 207-8, 210-11,
219-20, 222; 302, 304-5, 308, 310, 315,
326; 409-10, 412, 416, 419, 422, 425-26,
431-33, 435-36.

b. in driving
    jerk-line 320.
    lines cr15, 30, 36; 104-9, 118, 138-39,
143; 206, 214-17, 222-25; 301-3, 309,
311-14, 316-18, 320-21, 325, 328; 401,
403-6, 408, 411, 417-18, 421, c429, 434,
437.
    reins c14, c?15, 31; ?†226; 319, 323-
24; 402.

c. in riding
    reins 30; 104-9, 118, 131, 138, sn139,
143; 206, c214, 215-17, 223-24; 301, 303,
*306, 309, 311-14, 316-18, c320, 321,
325, 328; 401, 403-6, 408, 411, 417-18,
421, c429, 434, 437.
    no response 1-12, 16, 18-28, 32-35, 37,
?38, 39-65; 151; 327; 427-28.

Comment:

    jerk-line: A line to the 'jerk-line
horse,' the left-hand horse of a lead
team--320. lines: Usu.--208. reins: Inf.
says this is the "correct" word, although
'lines' is the common usage--112. Inf.
thinks her father used this term--226.

33.1 A little way(s). NE 50. WG 29, 47,
66; F111.

    As a response to the question "How far
down the road is . . .?" the expression
a little way(s) easily dominates the UM,
with an average frequency of slightly
more than 90%. The Midland variant, a
little piece, survives feebly with a 6%
frequency in Iowa and 5% in Nebraska. For
various reasons the latter locution is
clearly dying out, despite its currency
in western Pennsylvania and northern
West Virginia, as well as in western
North Carolina. Two North Dakota infs.,
one with a Vermont background, have the
synonymous jaunt [dʒɒnt], which may, but
probably does not, reflect the single
occurrence of jaunt [dʒænt] reported by
LANE in eastern Massachusetts. Neutral
distance has a frequency of 10%.

CL 91: A 99% UM dominance by way(s) appears in the checklist returns of 1,045
respondents. For the Midland piece a
striking coincidental frequency of 6%
occurs for Iowa and 5% for Nebraska.

    few steps 31.
    little bit further 14. little further
on 120.
    little distance 106; 202, 207; 407.

close ~ 107. short ~ 15, 18, 31-32; 102-
3, 105, 107, 111-12, *116, 119, 126, 137,
150; r317; 401.
    little jaunt 215. jaunt 207.
    piece 37, c†46; 320. little ~ 45; 130,
:sn152; 309, ¹310, ¹326; ¹414, 428, 436.
short ~ 101.
    skip and a jump 311. spell 34. stone's
throw 121; 306. two whoops and a holler
113.
    way(s) 28, 34, 38-39, 48, 56; 121,
131; 213; 316, 318; c412, 432, 434-35.
little ~ 1-5, c6-7, 8-9, c10, 11, c13,
14-18, c19, r20, c21, 22-23, :25, 26-27,
29-33, 35-36, cr39, 41-47, 49-53, c54,
57-59, cr60, 61-64; 108-10, 113-18, c119,
s120, 122-29, 131-32, 134-36, 139-43,
145-46, s147, 148-50; 201, 203-5, c206,
208, c209, 210-12, 214, c216, 217-20,
223-24, c225, 226; 301, 303-6, 309-10,
312-15, 317, 321, c322, 323-25, cr326,
328; 402, c403, 404, c405, 406, cvr407,
c408, 409-11, 413-14, c415, 416, c417,
418-21, c422, 423, 425-29, c430, 431,
433, 437. short ~ 12, 24, ?39, 40, 55,
65; 104, 109, 133, 138, 144; 221-22;
307-8; 424.
    no response 151; 302, 319, 327.

Comment:

    piece: Used by inf. as a child--46.
spell: "That's a Southern expression"--
34.

33.2 a long way(s). NE 51.

    When the response to the question "How
far is it to . . .?" indicates considerable distance, the almost uniform UM expression uses either way or ways. Only
a scattered handful of infs. (18) use the
non-regional long distance or quite a
distance, and still fewer (6, only 3%)
report the declining Midland and South
Midland piece as either used or overheard locally. Cf. its somewhat greater
vitality in the corresponding expression treated in 33.1.

    long distance 14, 18, 30-31, 36; 111,
116, 130; 224; 311; 402. quite a distance 37; 105, 112, 120, 146; 317; 424.
    long haul 37.
    long jaunt 207. quite a jaunt 204.
    long piece 37. quite a piece *43; 101;
202; ¹404, ¹413.
    long stretch 62. quite a step ¹404.
    way(s) cr28, 34, 48, c51, 56; 412, 432,
434-35. long ~ 1-5, c6, 8-9, c10-11, 12,
c13, 14, c15, 16-17, 19-27, 29, 32-33,
c35, 36, 39, cr?40, 41-47, 49-55, 57-65;
s102, 106-15, 118, s119, 121-29, 131-32,
134-39, 141-45, 147-50, 152; c201, 203,
205-8, c209, 210-15, c216, 217-19, c220,
221-22, 224, 226; 301, 304-5, 307-8,

310, 312-13, 315-16, 318, 320, 322-26, c327, 328; 401, c403, 404, 406-7, 409, c410, 413, 415-23, 425-28, 431, 433, 436-37. long ~ off 130; cvr428. good long ~ 7. good ~ 38; c225. quite a ~ c7, c44, 53, c65; 102-4, 116-17, 133, 140, 149; 204, c213, c221, 223; c303, 309, 314, c321; c401, 414, c429, 430. way out c422.

no response 151; 302, 306, 319; 405, 408, 411.

33.3 You can find that anywhere(s). NE 709.

Two lexical variants, anyplace and any-where(s)--in some contexts somewhere(s)--appear in the UM in replies to "Where can you find . . . growing around here?" The where type is quite common except in South Dakota. Anyplace, in some accord with occasional belittling by textbooks, exhibits not only regional but also social variation. It is much stronger in the western half of the UM, and more likely to be used by less educated speakers than by educated speakers: 32% for both Type I and Type II but only 13% for Type III.

	Mn.	Ia.	N.D.	S.D.	Nb.	Ave.
anyplace	13%	22%	42%	62%	46%	31%
anywhere(s)	92%	91%	58%	29%	29%	76%

For the relative distribution of some-where and somewheres see Volume 2.

anyplace 22, 26, 31, 36-37, 57, 65; 106-7, 109, 121, 129, 136-37, 150, 152; 204, 206, 210, 213-14, 216-20, 223; 302, 305, 311-13, 318, 320, 323-26, 328; 401, 404-5, 407, 409, 414-15, 417, 420-22, 431-35, 437. 'most ~ c16; 144, 148; 306-7, 317.

anywhere(s) 1-5, c6, 7-12, c13, 14-15, 17-18, c19, 20, c21, 22-29, 33-34, 38-42, c43, 44-45, c46, 47-48, c49, 50, 52-55, s56, 57-58, 60-63, sn65; 101-3, c104-5, 106, c107, 108, 110-46, 149-50, s152; c201, 202-3, 205, 208-10, c211, 212-13, 215, f216, 221-22, sn223, 224, c225, 226; 301-2, cr304, 308, 310, 314-15, c320, 321-22, 326, :328; 402-4, 406, c407, 408, 410-13, cvr414, 416, 418-19, 421, 423, s424, 425-30, 432, sn433, s434-35, c436. ~ else c35. most ~ 32, c46, 51, 59; 147.

everywhere(s) 37, *43; c417. ~ else c225.

somewhere(s) c30, c35, c46; c207, c211, c216, c224; c309, c314, c323; c404. ~ else c209, c223.

no response 64; 151; 303, 316, 319, 327.

33.4 Nary a bit.

As a tag after such a statement as

"We'll not see any more trouble . . . ." the old-fashioned nary a bit still competes with such non-regional variants as at all and any more. Nary, developed as an autonomous form from the contradiction ne'er a, itself from never a, survives often, however, as a conscious archaism and as such is then used humorously. Several fieldworkers noted its use in other contexts as well. Most infs. were unfamiliar with nary and had no stereotyped tag in such a context.

33.4a We'll not see any more trouble, nary a bit.

any more 308, 318; 425, 427-28, 432-33, 435.
at all c13, 14, c15-16, 17, c18; 104-5, s106, 108, 118-19, c120, 121, c132-33, 139, s152.
nary a bit sn2, †7, sn20, †23, †31, 37, s?†43, 44, s†45, †46, s†48, 51, ¹†57, †60, 62-63, †65; ¹204, ¹†209, 215; 409.
no more 307.

33.4b other uses of nary

nary †10, †22, s!†28; ¹124, s†127, ¹149; 208, †211, ¹212, ¹220; 311, ¹†312, 404, ¹405, 409, 411. ~ a one 1, ¹3, 11, 42, †61; !†205, ¹216, 221; 429.
no response 4-6, 8, 12, 19, 21, 24-26, ?27, 29-30, 32-36, 38-41, 47, 49-50, 52-56, 58-59, 64; 101-3, 107, 109-17, 122-23, 125-26, 128-31, 134-38, 140-48, 150-51; 201-3, 206, ?207, 210, ?211, 213, ?217, 218, 222-26; 301-6, 309-10, 313-17, 319-21, ?322, 323-28; 401-3, !406, 407-8, ?410, 412-24, 430-31, 434, 436, ?437.

Comment:

nary: Used by inf.'s father (from I1.) --10. Used by inf.'s mother (from N.Y.)--22. Used by inf.'s mother--127. Used facetiously by inf.'s mother--411. Heard used facetiously--211. Used facetiously only by inf.--411. Inf. considers this Irish--212. Inf. considers this Southern--220. nary a bit: Used occ. by inf.--2, 20. Inf. has heard Iowans, he thinks, use this--23. Inf. considers this Scottish--44. Inf. has heard this used locally by Scottish people--204.

33.7 We cleared the land. NE 122.

For the action of removing trees and stumps from land in order to make it arable two terms compete in the UM. The more general clear is spread fairly uniformly over the five states. Grub, which is more likely to describe the removal of roots and stumps than of entire trees,

occurs principally in the originally
wooded areas now used for agriculture,
with an apparent Northern orientation in
southern Minnesota and northern Iowa. Because stump removal is not part of a logging operation, grub is not typical in
the forested regions of northern Minnesota.

Blast, reported once, refers to the
use of blasting powder to dislodge stumps.

	Mn.	Ia.	N.D.	S.D.	Nb.	Ave.
cleared	74%	78%	77%	100%	70%	75%
grubbed	47%	29%	46%	18%	27%	35%

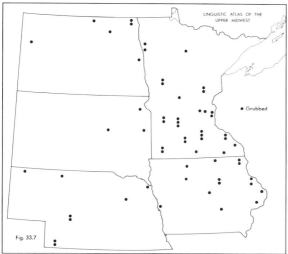

Fig. 33.7

blasted 48. ~ out 62.
brushed 34. ~ out 13.
cleaned up 56; †415.
cleared 1-6, 10-15, c16-17, 18, 21-26,
28-34, c37, 40, sn41, 42, †43, 44-47,
sn48, 51, c57, 58-62, sn64, 65; 101-3,
105-6, 108-9, 111, 115, 117-18, 120,
122-23, 126-31, 133-36, c137, 141-45,
147, 149, :s150, 152; 202, 204-6, 208,
213, 216, sn220, 221-22; 305-12, 316-20,
324-26; 402, 404, 408-11, 414, 420-21,
c422, 423-27, 430-33, 435. ~ off 61;
112, 114, 138, 146, 148; 434. ~ out c327.
~ up 39; 139; 220.
grubbed 7, 9-10, 19-20, 23, 36, 39-41,
44-45, †47, 48-49, c57, †58, c60, 63;
105, 116, 119, 121, 124, 135, 140; 204,
207, :212; 316; 401, 407, 418, 437. ~
out 24, 27, 32, 42-45, 50, 52-55, 61, 65;
104, 107-8, 113, 117, 132, 139; 208,
210, 220; 308, 317; 404, f413, 416, 419,
429.
logged 34. ~ off 202.
scrubbed off 202.
shrubbed 307.
stumped †61.
no response 8, 35, 38; 110, 125, 151;
201, 203, 209, ?211, 214-15, 217-19,

223-26; 301-4, 313-15, 321-23, 328; 403,
405-6, 412, 417, 428, 436.

Comment:

grubbed: Inf.'s usual term--41, 45.
"They 'grubbed' the land; afterwards it
was 'cleared' land"--124. stumped: Inf.
says this is used in the North--61.

33.8 Ditch along an upgraded road.

Not included in the eastern worksheets,
this item was added in the UM near the
end of the fieldwork in Minnesota because
of the significant appearance of borrow
pit and its congeners in the Colorado
survey. (See Marjorie Kimmerle and Patricia M. Gibby, "A word-list from Colorado," *Publication of the American Dialect Society*, No. 11 (April 1949), pp.
16-27; Marjorie Kimmerle, "The influence
of locale and human activity on some
words in Colorado," *American Speech*
25.161-67 (Oct. 1950).)
Most infs. in the four other states
use only the generic ditch to designate
the man-made depression for drainage
along a graded road. For some infs. in
the western sector of the UM, however,
especially in Nebraska but including also
the inf. in Estevan, Manitoba, the
equivalent term is borrow pit, with
several variants. The presence of borrow
pit in Iowa as a railroad term for an
excavation from which dirt has been removed or "borrowed" to build up a graded
right-of-way suggests that this sense
was extended to similarly caused excavation along a vehicle road. This explanation would then reject the etymology
suggested by the occurrence of the
variant barrow pit, with a possible reflection of the use of barrow in England
to mean a mound or small hill. One inf.
in North Dakota uses borrow itself as
the name perhaps through confusion with
burrow. Several infs. have the variant
bar pit or bar ditch, in which either
putative origin is quite obscured by the
phonetic modification of borrow or barrow.
Except for two occurrences in southeastern Nebraska, grader ditch ostensibly has
a South Midland orientation with its concentration in southeastern Iowa.
In Iowa gutter occurs twice in this
meaning.

	Ia.	N.D.	S.D.	Nb.	Ave.
ditch	74%	88%	95%	67%	79%
grader ~	16%	0%	0%	6%	7%
borrow, etc.	10%	12%	10%	20%	13%

CL 128: The 910 responding mail infs.
support quite closely the fieldwork data.
Grader ditch, with a 51% frequency in
southern Iowa and only 10% in northern

Iowa, again appears with Midland orientation, and borrow pit, with its variants, is most common in Nebraska. Gutter, however, is reported in all states.

	Mn.	Ia.	N.D.	S.D.	Nb.	Ave.
ditch	83%	67%	88%	70%	59%	71%
grader ~	12%	28%	11%	12%	28%	19%
borrow, etc.	2%	3%	6%	19%	26%	12%
gutter	8%	11%	6%	10%	9%	9%

bar ditch 321. ~ pit sn¹124, sn¹125, 140; ¹314; *417, 429, ¹436.
barrow pit 141-42; 320; 409.
borrow ['bɚo]218. ~ pit sn122, 123; 201, 214, 216, s222; 311; 404, 410, ¬411, sn430, ¬¹437.
ditch 29-31, 35-36; 101-8, 110-11, 113-17, 120-23, 125-33, 137, 139, 141-44, 148, 150, 152; 201-2, 204-7, 209-20, 222-26; 301-5, 307, 309-15, 321-26, 328; 401-8, 412-14, 417-20, 422-23, 426, 428, 430-31, 433-34. drainage ~ 416, 424-26, 434. grade ~ 224. grader ~ s¹124, 134, s¹136, 138, 145-49, sn150; 432-33. road ~ 112, 124, 152; 203, 208, 221, 224-25; 315-16, 405, 421, 427, 436-37.
gutter 109, 119.
no response 1-28, 32-34, 37-65; 118, 151; 306, 308, 317-19, 327; 415, 435.

Comment:

bar pit: Heard by inf. in Nb. with reference to a ditch along the rr.--314.
barrow pit: Along a rr.--140. borrow: Made by a road grader--218. borrow pit: Along a rr.--122. A gravel pit--201; 311. A place from which dirt is taken for fill, not necessarily along a road--216, 222; 430. Not necessarily along a road--404. "A construction term"--222.

34.1 second cutting (of hay, etc.)
NE 125. WG 16, 66, 67; F112.

Second crop and second cutting, in equal proportions, together dominate the UM as designations for a second growth of hay, clover, or alfalfa in one growing season. Reflecting its eastern occurrence in Maine and New Hampshire and especially in the Hudson Valley, second crop, as the accompanying graph indicates, reveals a decided Northern orientation. Second cutting, although also found in New York state and western Connecticut, has greater frequency south of Delaware Bay along the Atlantic Coast and hence in the Ohio valley; this distribution is reflected in its Midland orientation in the UM.
New England rowen and a variety of forms with after- (aftergrass, aftergrowth, aftermath) seem to have virtually disappeared from the rural vocabulary

as it was brought westward. Only one, aftergrass, appeared in the field interviews--that from an Iowan whose father came from Pennsylvania. Seed crop, not reported in LANE, is the usage of one South Dakota inf.

CL 62: Returns from 1,026 respondents confirm the Northern and Midland weighting of second crop and second cutting. Seed crop has scattered but fairly even distribution. Aftergrowth, a relic in northern Pennsylvania, is the term of two Nebraskans (3, 17), one whose paternal grandfather came from Pennsylvania and another with German ancestry. Aftermath, reported as scattered in southern New England, is the term of two Minnesotans (52, 61), one with Massachusetts and New Hampshire parents and the other with Vermont parents, and of two Nebraskans (5, 62), one of English parentage and the other with Canadian and New York state parents.

	Mn.	Ia.	N.D.	S.D.	Nb.	Ave.
second crop	67%	57%	54%	39%	18%	48%
~ cutting	41%	52%	54%	69%	92%	61%
seed crop	7%	5%	4%	12%	6%	7%

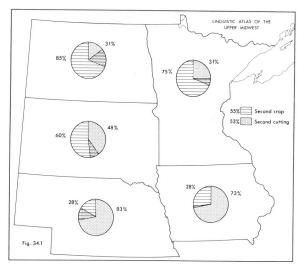

LINGUISTIC ATLAS OF THE UPPER MIDWEST

55% Second crop
53% Second cutting

Fig. 34.1

aftergrass 109.
second crop 1-6, c7, 8, 10-13, 16-24, c25, 26-28, 30-36, 39-41, 45, !46, 47, 49, 53-57, 61, 63, c64; 104-6, ?112, 116, 122, 126, 133, 135, 138-40, 142, s150, 152; 201-5, 207-15, 217-20, 222, 224-26; 302, 305-6, 310-15, 318-20, 322, 325-26; 401, 405, 407, 411-12, 414-15, 420, 424, 433. ~ cropping 37.
second cutting 6, 9, 20, 23, 29, 42-45, 47-48, 50-53, 58, 60-62, 65; 101-2, 107-9, 111, cr112, 113-15, 117-20, 122-25, 127-30, 132, 134, 136-37, 141-44, 146-49,

s150; 206, 208, 210, 216, 221-24; 301, c302, 303, 306, 308-9, ¹315, 316-17, 321, 323-24, 328; 403-6, 408-13, 416-23, 425-32, 434-37.

second growth 14-15, 17, 58-59; 207; 424, 434.

seed crop 312.

no response 38; 103, 110, 121, 131, 145, 151; 304, 307, 327; 402.

34.2 sheaf. NE 126. WG 49, 67; F113.

As the name for a tied bundle of cereal grain, as of wheat or oats, sheaf is widespread in New England and Pennsylvania, especially in urban and cultivated speech. In the UM it survives weakly in Minnesota and Iowa, though strongly in Canada. In the great wheat-growing regions of the UM bundle itself is the usual term. An occasional inf. would remark that sheaf is the correct name, if only because it is found in the hymn, "Bringing in the sheaves," but that "everyone" says "bundle." Bouquet appears once, cited as a slang creation of threshing crews.

	Mn.	Ia.	N.D.	S.D.	Nb.	Ave.
bundle	91%	86%	92%	96%	95%	91%
sheaf	14%	24%	8%	4%	14%	14%

CL 60: Close correlation with field data appears in the replies of 1,026 mail respondents, with bundle dominating the UM and sheaf weakest in the graingrowing regions. In addition, relic bind is the form checked by one Iowan (4) and by 2 North Dakotans (15, 32).

	Mn.	Ia.	N.D.	S.D.	Nb.	Ave.
bundle	79%	75%	82%	87%	83%	81%
sheaf	15%	26%	8%	10%	16%	16%

bouquet !206.
bundle 1, 4-15, 17, 19-28, ccr29, 30, c31, 32, c33, 34-37, 39, 41-44, c45, 46-55, s¹56, 57-65; 101-2, 104-6, c107, 108-9, 111-19, 121-28, s130, 132-38, 140-50; 203-13, 215-26; c301, 302-8, 310-21, c322, 323-26, 328; 401-26, 428-32, c434, 435-37.

sheaf 2-3, 6, 16, 18, †19, c?29, 40, c45, ¹46, c52, 56; †101, 103, 118, 120, :122, 129, *130, 131, ¹133, :136, 137, †138, 139, 149, 152; 201-2, ¹218, ¹225; †306, 309; 404, c413, 427, 429, *432.

no response 38; 110, 151; 214; 327.

Comment:

bouquet: Slang used by threshers--206.
bundle: Inf.'s more usual term--45; 404.
"But 'sheaf' is the right name"--225.
sheaf: "Same as a bundle, but done up by hand"--6. Inf. says this is an older word than 'bundle,' for the kind bound by hand--137. Inf. says he probably got 'sheaf' from the Bible; 'bundle' is his normal term--29. Biblical word--46. Used by inf.'s GF--101. "Never was used very much"--149. "The proper name, but we always said 'bundles'"--218.

34.4 shock (of corn, wheat, etc.) NE 126.

Like sheaf and bundle (see 34.2), shock as the name for a pile of such bundles or for an upright stack of cornstalks is rapidly becoming less common as modern harvesting machinery increasingly obviates the need for drying grain in the field after cutting. In the UM data shock dominates the five states, with the uniformly Canadian stook found once also in Rolette County, North Dakota, just south of the border.

A wide range appears in the number of bundles of wheat or oats piled in a shock. A small shock usually consists of 6 to 12 vertically stacked bundles, often with one or two in addition laid horizontally as caps. A long shock, more common when the grain is dry, may have from 14 to even 20 bundles. A round shock, used by some farmers, has from 4 to 10 bundles.

Stray terms reported--cock, pile, rick, and stack--probably are not bona fide, but are likely the result of confusion of meaning or of unfamiliarity with farm life.

CL 60: Shock likewise is the universal term reported by the mail respondents, with 8 indicating familiarity with stook, 2 in Minnesota, 3 in North Dakota, 1 in South Dakota, and 2 in Nebraska.

cock ¹12, 51.
pile 18.

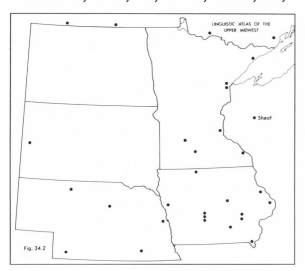

LINGUISTIC ATLAS OF THE UPPER MIDWEST

• Sheaf

Fig. 34.2

rick 122.

shock 4, *5, ¹6, 7-17, 19-21, cr22, c23, 24-28, c29, 30, c31, :?32, sn33, 34, :35, s36, 37, 39-43, c44, 45-51, c52, 53-55, 57, c58, 59-62, c63, 64-65; 101-9, 111-49, :s150, :152; 203-13, 215-16; 301-8, :309, 311-13, 315-18, 320-25, sn326, 328; 401-7, c408, 409-18, c419, 420-26, cvr427, 428-29, cvr430, 431, c432, 434-37.

stack ?22, :36, 40; 317; ?433.

stook 1-2, *3, ¹13, ¹46-47, 56; 201-2, 204; ¹*318.

no response 38; 110, 151; 214; 310, ?314, 319, 327.

Comment:

shock: Usu.--40. 4-12 bundles--101. 4-15 b.--409. 5-6 b.--58. 5-7 b.--205. 6 b.--21, 28, 34, 40, 47, 52, 61-63; 129; 217; 408. 6-7 b.--55; 407. 6-8 b.--42-43; 106, 118, 133; 212, 215; 316; 414-15, 424. 6-12 b.--429. 6-20 b.--316. 7 b.-- 12, ?27, 64-65; 114-15, 126-27, 137; 312. 7-9 b.--138. 7-10 b.--128. 7-12 b.--45; 108. 8 b.--25-26, 35, 54; 116; 203, 219, 222; 323. 8-10 b.--41, 46; 104, 113; 207, 209, 213; 301, 325. 8-11 b.--50. 8-12 b. --30; 107; 321; 436. 8-20 b.--405. 9 b.-- 24; 105, 112, 132; 224-25. 9-10 b.--401. 10 b.--48; 102, 124; 206, 211, 218. 10- 12 b.--20, 49; 147; 216, 220; 303; 402, 411-12. 10-14 b.--221. 10-15 b.--27. 10- 20 b.--223. 12 b.--4, 8, 29, 44; 139, 146; 311. 12-13 b.--56. 12-14 b.--210. 12-15 b.--322; *417. 12-16 b.--7. 14 b.-- 320. 14-16 b.--418. 15-20 b.--315. 18-20 b.--57. 20 b.--437. 25 b.--324. stack: Larger than a shock--317. 10-12 b.--36. Inf. doubtful about this; most wheat here is combined--433. stook: 6-7 b.--201. 9-12 b.--202. 10-12 b.--2. 12 b.--1. Inf. says his usual verb is 'stook up'--204. Heard in Otter Tail Co.--46. Canadian term--47. Heard used in Mont. by Canadian from Ont.--*318.

34.6 Two miles is the farthest he can go. NE 49.

Several expressions incorporating some variant of far occur in the given context. The most common is as far as, which seems to have a slight Northern orientation: Mn. 64%, Ia. 51%, N.D. 92%, S.D. 78%, Nb. 62%, ave. 65%.

Phrases with initial all--all the far, all the farther, all the farthest, all the furthest--are sometimes listed in usage handbooks as unacceptable but in the UM reveal no distinctive contrasts among the inf. levels: Type I 16%, Type II 17%, Type III 25%. They are evenly distributed except for their absence in

Nebraska: Mn. 21%, Ia. 22%, N.D. 19%, S.D. 22%, Nb. 0, Ave. 17%. Although both of the redundant forms fartherest and furtherest are recorded in LANE, only the former survives in the UM, with 4 infs. in Iowa and one in Nebraska.

all 224; 415-16, 421, 423, 425, 427-28, 431, 433, 435.
all the distance 51-52, 62.
all the far s¹48, 57, ¹58.
all the farther *9, sn27, ¹29, 32, sn34, sn37, 39, 42, 52, sn55, 57, 61; 111, s113, 117, 121, 127, 129, s132, 133-34, 136, 138, 147, 152; 212, s¹218, s¹221, ¹223; sn302, 303, *306, ¹313; ¹411, ¹420, 426.
all the fartherest ?137.
all the farthest 115, cr137, s150.
all the further ¹33, ¹47, 50, sn55, ¹62; 112, 114, 119, 140; sn208, ¹224; ¹323; s423, s430.
all the ways 62.
as far as 1-3, 5, 9, 11-12, c13, c15, 16-17, c18, 20-24, s25, 26, sn27, 28-30, 33-34, :2n35, :s36, 37-38, 43-47, 49, 51, 53, f54, 57, 60, 63-64; 102-3, 105-6, 108-10, 113, 116, 118, 120-22, 126, 128, 130-31, 135, 137, 139, 142-44, 146, 148- 49; 201, !202, 203, 205-19, :220, 221-24, 226; 301, sn302, 303, 306-15, 320-26, 328; 401-7, 409-12, s413, 414, c417, 419, s420-21, 422, s424, s428, 429, 432-33, 435-37.
the fartherest 123-25, 139, 145; c317.
the farthest s6, 7, *9, 10, 18, 20, 31, sn40, s56, 58; 101-2, 104, 107, 141; 204, 208, sn217; 304-5, 318-19.
the furthest 4, 13-14, 19, 41, ¹58; 106, 108; 201, ¹224, 225; 316.
the limit 62; f413, 420.
the most 433.
no farther than 65.
no response 8, 59; 151; 327; 408, 418, 434.

Comment:

all the farther: Inf. heard this among "farm folks"--221. all the further: "I patiently correct my children for saying this"--33.

35.5 Usual type of homemade bread. NE 281.

Some overlapping of responses occurs in this and the next two items because the same basic subject, bread, is queried from three different viewpoints. Further- more, because of some modification in the worksheets, these items do not cor- respond precisely with those in LANE. Analysis of the individual replies, how- ever, would make possible a number of comparisons.

Although even at the time of the UM fieldwork most infs., except some on farms or in rural communities, customarily bought commercial bread, a number still baked bread at home and most remembered the usual kind of bread baked at home when they were younger. Some of these admitted that from time to time they had to escape from the tasteless and insubstantial commercial variety by baking their own.

Typically, in the UM, homemade bread was made with white flour--in earlier days unbleached--yeast, salt, sugar, shortening (lard or butter), and water or, sometimes, milk. Loaves, usually somewhat larger than commercial loaves, were baked in large pans, 2, 3, or 4 to a pan--usually 3. Loaves were oblong, commonly 12" or 15" long and 4" or 5" wide, rounded on top, and weighing 1 or 1 1/2 pounds. Some infs. also made round loaves, although these appear to have been more common several decades ago. Such a loaf, one inf. said, was 18" in diameter.

The field data list this usual kind of bread made with white flour as simple bread, light bread, home-baked bread, homemade bread, potato bread (with "potato water" instead of plain water), salt-rising bread (leavened by a salted batter), sponge bread, white bread, wheat bread, yeast bread, and hop-yeast bread.

A few infs. insist that their usual homemade bread was not made with white flour. Kinds they report are corn bread, dark bread, graham bread, rye bread, and whole wheat bread.

No geographical pattern emerges.

bread 2-3, 6-7, 10-11, 16, 19, 21, 23, †27, 46, 48, 58; 102-4, 112-13, 115-16, 118, 129-31, 134, 137, 143, 150; 204-6, 208-9, c210, 211, 213-19, 223, 226; 302, c311, †312, 314, 320, 324-25, 328; 409, 416, 418, 421-22, 426, 433, 435.
  corn ~ c52.
  dark ~ 13, 16-17, 30, 42-43; c209; 316; †408, 431, †436.
  graham ~ 15, c63, 65.
  home-baked ~ 39, 64; 426, 434. homemade ~ 6, 34, 39; 101, 105-9, 111, 114, 119, 121, 132-33, 138, 140-41, 150; 425, 434.
  light ~ 17, 35; 124, *130, 135-36, 139, †145, 146-47, *148; 301, ¹303, c314, 316, c322; 401, 403, †411, 429, 432, 434.
  potato ~ 201.
  rye ~ 13, 18, 57; 425.
  salt-rising ~ 46, 59.
  sponge ~ 423.
  wheat ~ 17, 28, 31, 41, 45, 51, 56; 139; 207; 317; 415, 420, 427, 430, 434.
  white ~ 1, 4, †5, 8, 10, 14, 16, 20-22,

24-26, 28, †29, 30-33, 35-37, 40, 42-44, 47-50, c52, 53-55, 57, 60-62; 117, 120-23, 125-28, 142, 144-45, 148, †149, 152; 201-3, 206, 212-13, c219, 220-22, 224-26; 303-10, †312, 313, 318-21, 323, 326; 402, 404-7, †408, 410, 412-13, 417, 419-20, 424-25, 428, †437.
  whole wheat ~ 12, 15, 61.
  yeast ~ c213; 414, 423. hop-yeast ~ 46.
  no response 9, ?38; 110, 151; 315, 327.

Comment:

"All our homemade bread was potato bread"--201. "Only foreigners and Indians made round loaves"--214.

35.6 wheat bread (in loaves). NE 281. WG 20, 21, 39, 67; F30, F115.

For ordinary bread made with white flour, either homemade or commercial, slightly more than half of all UM infs. use the compound white bread, with initial or even stress. The apparent Northern bias of bread is almost certainly due to the fact that fieldworkers did not always record the simplex in their search for differentiated forms. Light bread reflects its South Midland origin by its occurrence in southern Iowa, Nebraska, and South Dakota. Wheat bread is a minor variant in each state except South Dakota, and yeast bread is the term of 5 infs., 3 of whom are in Nebraska.

	Mn.	Ia.	N.D.	S.D.	Nb.	Ave.
bread	29%	8%	62%	33%	19%	27%
light ~	3%	27%	0%	14%	16%	12%
wheat ~	8%	10%	4%	0%	14%	8%
white ~	77%	67%	50%	63%	57%	66%

CL 33: Except for the greater incidence of bread in Iowa and Nebraska, which indicates that the simplex is evenly distributed in the UM, the 1,054 checklist responses correlate quite closely with the field returns. Light bread similarly appears as South Midland with a 7% and 34% contrast between northern and southern Iowa. Yeast bread is the form checked by 9 scattered respondents.

	Mn.	Ia.	N.D.	S.D.	Nb.	Ave.
bread	34%	3%	41%	52%	48%	42%
light ~	3%	20%	1%	6%	16%	10%
wheat ~	7%	6%	2%	2%	4%	5%
white ~	66%	49%	66%	50%	52%	56%

  bread 2-3, 6-7, 9-11, c15, 16, 19, 21, 23, 27, 32, 40, 48, 58, 62, 64; 129, 131, 134, 143; 204-6, 208-9, c210, 211, 213-19, 223, 226; 302, c311, 312, 314-15, 320, 324-25, 328; 409, 416, 418, 421-22, 426, 433.
  light ~ 17, 35; 103, 106, 115, 118, 124, †125, *130, 132, 135-36, 139, †145, 146-47, *148, ¹†150; 301, ¹303, c314,

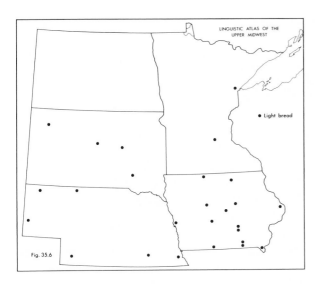

Fig. 35.6

316, c322; 401, 403, 411, 429, 432, 434.
sponge ~ 423.
wheat ~ 31-32, 41, 45, 56; 104, 107,
121, 132, 139; 207; 415, 420, 427, 430,
434.
white ~ 1, 4-5, 8, *9, 10, 12-16, 18,
20-22, 24-26, 28-31, 33-40, 42-44, 46-51,
c52, 53-55, 57, 59-63, 65; 101-2, 104-5,
108-14, 116-17, 120-23, 125-28, 130, 133,
137-38, 142, 144-45, 148-50, 152; 201-3,
206, 212-13, c219, 220-22, 224-26; 303-
10, 312-13, 317-21, 323, 326; 402, 404-8,
410, 412-13, 417, 419-21,424-25, 428,
430-31, 435-37.
yeast ~ 65; c213; 414, 422-23.
no response 119, 140-41, 151; 327.

Comment:

bread: Usu.--21, 48. sponge bread =
yeast bread--423. white bread: Usu.--420.
yeast bread: Inf.'s term for the white
bread she makes--65.

35.7 Other kinds of bread made with
flour. NE 287.

Since no systematic search was made
for names of specific types of rolls,
etc., the wide variety of terms found in
the field records is rather an indication
of the diversification of breadstuffs in
the UM than an index to any exact distribution patterns or a reflection of relative frequency. Fieldworkers differed in
their willingness to record a full variety; infs. differed in their recollection
of the bread types known to them.

Even so, several distinct correlations
appear. Infs. reporting (Boston) brown
bread, for instance, generally have
Northern speech background. Light bread
biscuits is the term of a Nebraskan
whose father was born in Kentucky. Sour-

dough biscuits is an old cowpunchers'
term on the open range of extreme western
UM. Squaw bread is a western term reminiscent of pioneer contacts with plains
Indians. Doughgods is also a western term
echoing the early days of range-riding
by cattlemen and cowpunchers. Lefse is
related to the Norwegian settlements and
limpa, a kind of rye bread, to the Swedish
migration. Scones, distinctly Scottish,
is found only in Canada and in the speech
of one Minnesotan whose father was born
in Canada.

In addition, a few terms were recorded
by fieldworkers despite their not quite
belonging to the general category of
kinds of bread. Coffee cake, actually
known throughout the UM, was specifically
reported by 21; 116; 210; and 433.
[juliˇkɑk], familiar in all regions settled by Scandinavians, was volunteered
only by 321. Kolachy, the name for a
kind of roll with a sweet filling, characteristic of Czech cooking, came from
43; *225; 321, 323; 435. The Minneapolis
Star, Sept. 23, 1959, reported: "Some
50,000 kolacky (Bohemian buns) are being
baked for distribution here [Montgomery,
Mn.] at the annual Kolacky Day celebration
Sunday." Kuchen, a kind of sweetened
bread with bits of candied fruit, sometimes baked in a round tin, reflects German settlement--20, 34, 51, 61; 304.
Pasties, a term introduced by Cornish
miners for ground beef rolled up in a
crust, was offered by Ontario 1 and, with
the specific Cousin Jack Pasties ["Cousin
Jack" is a nickname for a Cornishman],
by Minnesota *9. A Croatian inf., Minnesota 13, offered [pəˈti·tsə] as the
name of a roll filled with honey and
walnuts, rolled and baked, and
[ˌfoˈʊˇbəˈti·sə] as the name for Slovenian
bread dough. Minnesota inf. 13 volunteered
familiar apple tarts. A Nebraska inf.
(417) of Swedish parentage, said that a
kind of pudding is called [ˈœstɚ kɑkə],
and a North Dakotan (206) of Icelandic
parentage, reported that [ˈwiˇnɚˈtɛˋtə^],
an Icelandic term for a kind of prune
layer cake, is in common use in the
English of his community.

bannock c6.
biscuits 1, 4-5, 7-9, 11, 13-15, 17-18,
†19, c21, 22-24, 26-27, 29, 31-32, 34,
36, 39, 41-42, 44, 46-48, 51-53, 55-57,
59-61, 63, 65; 101, 103-5, 107-9, 115,
118, 120, 122-24, 127-28, 130-31, 133,
136, 138, 142-43, 145-47, 149; 206, 208,
211, 213, 216, 220, 223; 302-3, †312,
313, *318, 320-21, 324; 401, 403, 412,
414, 417, 420, 425-26, 428, 430, 434-35,
437. baking-powder ~ 1, †2, 3-6, 8-13,
15-16, 21, 23-24, c26, 27-28, 30-31, 33-

Fig. 35.7

LINGUISTIC ATLAS OF THE UPPER MIDWEST

○ Dough gods
● Drop biscuits

34, 36-37, 40, *41, 42, 49-50, 52, 54;
106, 108, 111, 115-16, 119, 121, 132,
139; 201, 203, 205, 208-9, 211-13, c214,
216-18, 221-23, *225, 226; 301-3, 310,
313, c314, 315, 319-21, 323-26; 401-2,
404-6, 410, 412, 416-17, →418, 420, 422,
429-31. bread ~ 37. buttermilk ~ 202;
401. cinnamon ~ 209. cloverleaf ~ 50.
drop ~ 429, 431. graham ~ 35. light ~
c135; *225; 405. light bread ~ 429. Parker House ~ 10. raised ~ 24, 27, 29, 31,
36, 50; 115; 204, 218; 409. saleratus ~
16, †40; 220. soda ~ ¹3, 10, 16, 21, 25,
29, †36, 37, 42, 49; 115, 118, 139, 143;
202, 204, 207, ¹208, 213, 218, 221, 223-
24; 301, c302, 313, 320, 322; †407, 416,
†418, 420-21, †422, 429. sour cream ~ 11.
sourdough ~ †302, 320; †409. sweet ~ *25.
sweet dough ~ 10. tea ~ 2, 49, 64; 106.
white dough ~ 57. yeast ~ 31.
  [bread] baking-powder bread 6; 119.
banana ~ 10, 28; 205, 219; 319. barley ~
48, 52; 305, 317. black ~ 140. Boston
brown ~ 422. bran ~ 44; 318. brown ~ 12,
27-30, 32, 44, 53; 109, 134, 137; 205,
225; 317; 424. buckwheat ~ 12. cabbage ~
425. caraway rye ~ 10. caraway seed ~ 25.
cinnamon ~ 49; 318; 431. coffee ~ 10, 16,
39; 209; 420, 431. cracked wheat ~ 32;
134; 308, 316, 318. currant ~ 3; 121.
dark ~ 13-14, 16-17, 30, 42-43; 117;
†224; 316; †408, 431, †436. date ~ 10.
farmer ~ ¹310. flat ~ 41; 216; †407.
French ~ 204. fried ~ 302, ¹313. ginger ~
202, 207. graham ~ 11, 15, 17, 25, 27-28,
30, 32, 37, 39-40, 42, 46-49, 53, 60, 62,
c63, 65; 104, 108-9, 114, 132, 134, 136-
37, 141, 143-46, 152; 203, 212, 218, 220-
23, 226; 305, 307, 317-19; 413, 415-16,
c417, 423, 430, 433-34, 436. gluten ~
222. half-thick ~ 4. hot ~ 37; †222. nut
~ 63; 202, 205, 219, 223; 305, 310; 402.

oatmeal ~ 20, 25, 33; 219; 305, 319;
415. orange ~ 219; 319. potato ~ 12, 22,
49; 140; 220-21, 223, 308, 326; 404-5,
407, 416, 427. prune ~ 305. quick ~ 54;
116; 203; 319; 431. raisin ~ 10, 12, 22,
29, 33, 63; 117, 121, 129, 141; 202,
214, 219, 223-24; 306; 402-3, 415, 419,
421. raisin rye ~ 319. rye ~ 11, 13, 17-
18, 22, 24, 27-28, 30, 32, 36-37, 39,
43-45, 48, 50-52, 55, 57-58, 60, 62;
101, 104, 117, 123, 128-29, 131, 134,
c135, 137-38, 148-49; 206-7, 212, 216,
220, 222-25; 305-8, 316-19, 321, 328;
402, 404, 407, 413, ¹414, 415-17, 419,
421-22, 425-27, 430, 435. saleratus ~
220. salt-raising ~ 101. salt-rising ~
42, 46, 59; 103, 113, 139; 422-23, 426,
434. sourdough ~ 57; 320. sour raisin ~
16. squaw ~ 313. swede ~ †418. sweet ~
14. thin ~ 4, 23; †418. wheat ~ 122; 419.
whole wheat ~ 12, 15, 17, 19-20, 22, 24,
26, 28, 32, 39-41, 44, 48, 50, 58-59,
61; 101, 112, 117, 123, 128, 130, 136,
141, 149; 221-22, 226; 305-6, 316, 319;
402, 404, 414, 416, 421-22, 426, *427,
430.
  buns 1-3, 12, 15-16, 19, 32, 37, 43,
47-48, 56, 61, 64-65; 101-2, 105, 118,
124, 127, 133, 137, 140; 201-3, 205, 208,
210-11, 214-15, 223; 301, 303, 316, *318;
416, 421, 426, 432. cinnamon ~ 14. cloverleaf ~ 210. three-day ~ 212.
  crescents 323.
  date loaf 319.
  doughboys 406.
  doughgods 6, 45; 214; 301, †302, c†311,
320; †401, 404, †405, ¹†412.
  early risers 220.
  fantans 402.
  gems 8; 317, 319, 323. graham ~ 405,
414.
  hardtack 17, 19.
  kugels †209.
  lefse 41; ¹210, 216; 319, 321.
  limpa 4; †407, †408, 430.
  muffins 5, 9-10, 16-17, 54; 113, 136;
206, 213, 226; 315, 317, 319, 323-24,
326; 414, *427.
pumpernickel 34, 62; 129, 140-41, 148;
319; 404.
  raisin loaf 1; 403.
  rolls 3, 6, 9, 11, 14, 17-18, 29, 33,
→46, 47, 61-65; 101, 104-6, 111, 114,
116, 120, 122-24, 127, 130, 137, 139,
142, 145-47, 150; 213, 215-18, 225-26;
301, 310, 313, 319, 321, 324, 326; 406,
408, 420, 424-26, 428, 431, 434, 436-37.
bread ~ 318. butter ~ 409. butterhorn ~
43. buttermilk ~ 28. caramel ~ 219. cinnamon ~ 1-2, 4, 10, 14, 20, c21, 22, *25,
26, 30-31, *41, 204, 206-11, 213, 215-17,
223; 301, 304, 318, 326; 403, 405, 409-10,
417-19, 436. cloverleaf ~ 20; 102, 121,
133; 326; 428, 431, 433. coffee ~ 118.

finger ~ 205; 325. dinner ~ 131. ice box
~ 28. jelly ~ 208. orange ~ 217. pan ~
20; 428. Parker House ~ 12, 22, 28; 102;
221; 304, 326; 401-2, *427, 428, 431.
raised ~ 149. sweet ~ 26; 102, 131; 205,
219, 224; 428. tea ~ 211, 219; 410, *427,
433. twisted ~ 407.
  rusks 105, 152.
  scones 28; 201-2, ¹205.
  [swiˇⁱtkiˇ] c323.
  [systɪkɑˇ] 203.
  no response ?38; 110, 125-26, 151; 309,
327; 411.

Comment:

  bannock: Baking-powder bread made in
a frying pan over an open fire in the
woods--6. dough gods: Biscuits dropped
in Mulligan stew--6. Fried--214; 301;
401, 404-5. = fried bread--302. = any
kind of biscuit--320. = baking-powder
biscuits; term used on ranches--311.
Heard used by old cowpunchers--412. drop
biscuits: Dough is more like a batter;
"Not a pretty looking biscuit"--429.
early risers: = baking powder biscuits--
220. farmer bread: Round loaf baked on
the bottom of the oven, not in a pan;
apparently common with Finnish people
here--310. half-thick bread: 1'-14" in
dia., 1/2" thick--4. hot breads = bis-
cuits--37. kugels: Bischits of sweet
dough and raisins; made by inf.'s mother
--209. Parker House bischits: Sweet-dough
biscuits--10. rusks: Round buns made with
sweetened dough; sometimes with raisins--
105. shingle: Inf. says this is Americans'
term for hardtack; flat bread fried on
both sides--19. squaw bread: = fried
bread--313. [ˈsystɪkɑˆ]: Danish bread,
rich with lard--203. [ˈswiˇⁱtkiˇ]: Sweet,
eggy dough fried in deep fat--323. tea
biscuits: = baking-powder biscuits--2.

36.1a corn bread (in large cakes). NE
286; WG 12, 14, 67; F116.

  For terms designating corn bread in
large cakes Kurath's observation in WG
is relevant to the UM situation. Although
recognizing that some regional forms have
great vitality, Kurath states that in
the Atlantic states corn bread "now predominates in the urbanized areas and is
widely used by the better educated in
most rural areas as well." Except in Minnesota corn bread is also the dominant
term in the UM but without complete dominance in urban areas, and it has been
widely adopted by the less educated as
well as by the well educated.
  Only one of the two main regional forms
of the Atlantic coast has retained
strength in the UM. Midland and Southern

corn pone, common in Pennsylvania, barely
survived the western migration; six instances occur in Midland speech area.
Northern johnny cake, however, is still
widely known in the entire Northern speech
area of the UM, although a number of infs.
acknowledge its old-fashioned status in
that it persists in the home but has given
way to corn bread in restaurants. It also
has lost ground among better educated
speakers: johnny cake Type I 47%, Type II
41%, Type III 29%; corn bread Type I 62%,
Type II 69%, Type III 71%.
  Corn cake occurs as the response of a
few widely scattered infs., as does cornmeal bread. Two infs., both of New York
state background, offer spoon bread, a
South Midland and Southern term for a
baked dish including cornmeal but eaten
with a spoon. One of them describes it as
"like a thick pancake of corn" and called
squaw bread by his father.
  UM distribution of the main terms follows:

	Mn.	Ia.	N.D.	S.D.	Nb.	Ave.
corn bread	38%	82%	52%	71%	97%	66%
johnny cake	67%	38%	46%	46%	5%	43%

CL 31: Returns from 1,053 respondents are
consistent with the field data. Only
three instances of corn pone appear.

	Mn.	Ia.	N.D.	S.D.	Nb.	Ave.
corn bread	43%	78%	47%	66%	94%	67%
johnny cake	69%	31%	60%	44%	19%	44%

  corn bread 6, 8, 13, 19-20, 32-33, 37-
40, ?41, 43-44, ¹46, ¹47, c51-52, 54-58,
¹59, 60-62, 64, ¹65; 101-2, 104-10, 112-
13, 118-23, 125-34, c135, 136-39, 141-43,
145-50, 152; 203-7, 210, 212, c213, 214-
16, 218, 220; 301-2, ?304, 305-7, 309,
¹310, c312, →313, 314-21, 323-26; 401-6,
408-17, c418, 419-34, 436-37.

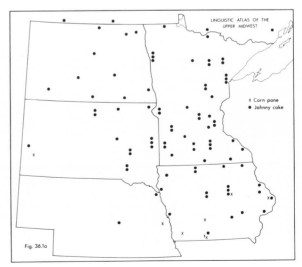

LINGUISTIC ATLAS OF THE
UPPER MIDWEST

x Corn pone
• Johnny cake

Fig. 36.1a

corn cake 1, 61; 146-47; 216; 308; 421, †432.
 corn pone 118, 130, s139, 142, †145; 311; 428.
 cornmeal bread 24, *25, 28; 209-10, 219, 221; 324; 407.
 johnny bread ?13, 16.
 johnny cake 2-5, ⌐6, !7, 8, *9, 10-12, cr13, 14-15, r16, 17, !21, 22-23, s⌐24, *25, 26-27, 29-31, ⌐32, †33, 34, 36, sn37, †39-40, cr41, 42, †43-44, 45-50, c51, †52, c53, 54, s56, 57, 59, †60, ⌐61, †62, 63, sn†64, 65; 102-5, 107, 111, 114-17, sn118, 119, 121, 124, ⌐126, ⌐128, c135, 138-40, 144; !201, 202, 204, 206, 208, 211, †214, 215, sn†216, 217, †218, 219, 223-25, †226; †301, 303, cr304, 305, 307, †309, 310, †313, 316-19, c322, 323, ⌐325, †326, 327-28; ⌐403, cvr407, ⌐413-14, †416, 420, †423.
 spoon bread 116; 413.
 squaw bread †413.
 no response 18, 35; 151; 222; 435.

Comment:

 corn cake: "The folks called it 'corn cake'"--432. johnny cake: Used by inf.'s mother--40. Used by inf.'s mother (from Wi.)--301. Used by inf. as a child--64; 416. Formerly used by inf.; she has adopted her husband's term, 'corn bread' --33. Formerly used by inf.; "Just lately I've been calling it 'corn bread'"--62. Inf. uses this at home, but not in restaurants--37. Inf. says this is the local term, not used in his family--24. squaw bread: Used by inf.'s father--413.

36.1b Other types of corn bread. NE 287.

 Although Boston brown bread, corn gems, and corn muffins all occur in New England, they and other minor variants are almost entirely restricted to Midland speech territory in the UM field records. This distribution probably reflects the relatively uncommon use of cornmeal in home baking in the northern areas.
 Puppies, with a solitary instance along the Mississippi in eastern Iowa, is clearly derived from southern hush puppy, the name of a deep-fried cornmeal cake. From the same inf. comes jolly boys, designating cakes made with both cornmeal and white flour.

 Boston brown bread 133.
 corn cake 434. ~ fingers 422. ~ flitters 132. ~ fritters 105. ~ gems 137. ~ sticks sn*130; 226; 407.
 corn muffins 1, †31; 104, 112, s128, 149; 204, 207, 212-13, 218; 309, 311, 320; 402, sn409, 411, 414, 420-22, 426, 429, 433, 436. cornmeal ~ 57; 115; 121;

203, 211, 215, 217; *301, 304, 328; 401.
 gems 102, 109-10, 115; *202.
 hoecake ⌐144.
 johnny cake 29.
 jolly boys 119.
 muffins 101-12, 105, 110, 117, 122, 124-25, 127, sn*130, 135, 141, 145-48, 150; 202, 222, 224; 310, 316; 405-7, 413, 424, 430.
 puppies 119.

Comment:

 corn cake: Muffins--434. gems: = corn muffins--115. Inf. says this is "a sissy word"--202. hoecake: Inf. doesn't know how this is made; she thinks the term is used by "darkies"--144. johnny cake: Also = muffins--29.

36.2 (homemade bread and) boughten bread. NE 285.
 With the expansion of commercial baking several terms develop to distinguish bread purchased in a store or bakery from bread baked at home. Those widespread in New England are also widespread in the UM. Most common, with even distribution throughout the UM, is baker's bread. Related is bakery bread, also evenly distributed except for its apparent lower frequency in Iowa and its nonoccurrence in Canada. Their social distribution, however, offers a clear contrast. Baker's bread declines from 60% for Type I through 51% for Type II to only 31% for Type III. Bakery bread, however, increases from only 19% for Type I through 33% for Type II to 50% for Type III. Almost as common as the latter is boughten bread, especially in Iowa, southern Minnesota, and the first settled portion of South Dakota. Other uses of boughten are reported as well. Less usual store bread is evenly distributed. Although only 3 infs. report the simplex bread, actually many remarked that ordinarily they would use it when there is no need to make a distinction.

	Mn.	Ia.	N.D.	S.D.	Nb.	Ave.
baker's bread	52%	57%	50%	57%	51%	54%
bakery bread	32%	12%	31%	29%	35%	27%
boughten bread	18%	37%	19%	29%	14%	24%

 baker bread 323. baker's ~ c1, 2-3, 6 8, c10, 13, 15-16, 21-24, 27, 30, 32-36, 39-40, 42, 44, !46, 48-52, !53, 54-55, 59; c101, 103-5, 107, 109, c110, 111, 114, 117, 119, 121-22, 124-26, 129-31, 133-34, 136, 140, 144, 146-49, 152; 201-5, 207-8, c211, c214, 216-18, c225; 301, 303-6, 308-9, 311-14, 317, ⌐*318, 321, :322, 324; c401, 402, c404, 406, c409, 412-13, 415-17, 420, 422-24, 428, 430-32, 434.

bakery bread :9, c11, 12, 14, 17-20, 25, 29, 37, *41, 45, 47, 57-58, 60-61, c62, 64-65; 108, 115, 123, 138-39, 145; 206, 210, 213, 219, 221-22, 224, 226; 302, 307, 315-16, 319-20, 325, 327; 403, 405, 408, 410-11, c418, 419, 421, 426-28, 433, 437.
bakeshop bread 31.
bought bread 14; 435. boughten ~ 4-5, c7, 24, 26, 28, c36, 41, 43, 50, 56, ¹58, 63; 102, 106, 112-17, 127-28, 132-35, c137, 142-43, 145, 150; 205, 212, 215, 220, 223; 302, 306-7, 310, !318, 319, c324, 328; 407, 411, 414, 429, 436.
bread 38; 120, 141.
factory bread 20.
store bread 14, ¹31, 37; 118, 131, *145; 209, 222; 320, 326; 425, 435. store-bought bread 425.
town bread 115.
no response 151.

Comment:

baker's bread: Inf.'s usual term--205.
boughten bread: Inf.'s usual term--411.

36.3a doughnut (made with sweetened, un-leavened dough). NE 284. WG 18, 21, 24-25, 47, 49, 69; F120.

Doughnut, the common East Coast term, also dominates the UM, with quite uniform distribution. Northern fried cake, common in upper New York state and northern Penn-sylvania, survives in the UM only in the first settled parts of the Northern speech area; several of the infs. declare it to be old-fashioned. Cake doughnut, a spe-cific used by those who employ the simplex for the raised variety (see 36.3b), is rare in Minnesota, Iowa, and South Dakota, nonexistent in North Dakota, but common in Nebraska. One southern Iowan remembered the rare North Carolina cookie. For the twisted variety a scattered half dozen retain the Dutch cruller that had spread from New York to the Philadelphia and Baltimore areas. Twister, a minor variant for this kind in Maine and New Hampshire, survives in two occurrences, one in a Maine-settled community. It was reported twice in Wisconsin.

	Mn.	Ia.	N.D.	S.D.	Nb.	Ave.
doughnut	82%	85%	92%	97%	89%	88%
cake doughnut	8%	6%	0%	11%	25%	10%
fried cake	29%	24%	8%	21%	22%	23%

CL 34: Data from 1,051 respondents support the field records, with further evidence for the decline of fried cake. One volun-teered that fry cake was the "old usage."

Only 10 scattered replies offer cruller: Mn. 36, 44, 52 "a richer fried cake in fancy shape"; Ia. 29, 57, 76, 88, 94; N.D. 15; Nb. 52. Pennsylvania German fat cake is the term of 2 Midland respondents, an Iowan of German parentage and a Ne-braskan of Swedish parentage: Ia. 56; Nb. 48.

	Mn.	Ia.	N.D.	S.D.	Nb.	Ave.
doughnut	88%	85%	94%	95%	94%	90%
cake doughnut	2%	2%	3%	5%	10%	4%
fried cake	15%	21%	7%	9%	12%	14%

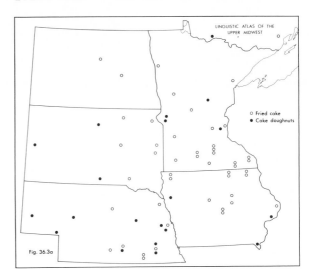

LINGUISTIC ATLAS OF THE UPPER MIDWEST

○ Fried cake
● Cake doughnuts

Fig. 36.3a

cookie †135.
crull 422.
cruller c47, *60; ¹112, 150; 202; †326.
dough god †12.
doughnut 1, 4-8, 10-26, 28-41, →42, 43-45, →46, 47, 49-50, c51, ¹52-53, 54-56, 59-61, ¹62, 63; 101-4, 106, s107, 108-10, 112-13, 115, ?116, 117-31, 133-38, sn139, 141-50, 152; 201, ¹202, 203-17, c219, 220-26; 301-22, 324, →325, 326-28; 401-2, !403, c404, 405-7, *408, 409-11, 413-14, 416-20, 423-26, 428-37. ~ twist 152.
baking powder ~ 320. cake ~ c2, 22, 25-26, 37; 111, 140, 150; 304, 310, 321; 411-12, 416-17, 423-24, 426, *427, 428. sweet ~ 134; 415. twisted ~ 44; 317.
fried cake ¹2, 3, †4, ¹6, ¹8, 9, †12, 15, 27, †32, 33, 39, †40, 42, †44-46, 48-50, 53, ¹54, 57-59, ¹60, †61, 62, †63, 64-65; 101-2, 105-8, †110, 114, †115, cr116, sn118, 132-33, †138, 139; †205, ¹†210, 211, ¹214, 218, †223; 305, †306, 308, 316-17, †318, 319, †324-25; †409, 413, ¹†414, †415, ¹418, †420, 423-24, 427, 430, ¹431, 432-33, ¹434.
fry cake ¹13, 19, c52; 323; 408, 430.
long John 152.
pretzel 16.
sinker 26, 37; *148, 149; 308.

twister †39; ¹†403.
no response 151; 421.

Comment:

cookie: No hole in the center--135.
crull: No hole in the center--422. cruller: Twisted--47, 60; 150; 326. Used by
inf.'s grandmother--326. dough god: Larger
than a 'doughnut'--12. doughnut: Usu.--
50. Usu. local term--202. fried cake:
Long or round--42. Twisted or round--52.
Twisted--39; 409. No hole in the center--
424. "A woods term; you seldom hear that"
--12. Used by inf.'s grandmother--318.
Used by inf.'s father--110. Used by inf.'s
father (from Pa.)--306. Used by inf.'s
mother (from Ont.)--203. Used by inf.'s
mother (from Nb.)--325. "We used to call
them 'fried cakes'"--415. "When I was a
kid"--420. Inf. considers this older than
'cake doughnut'--427. Inf. says this is
the "correct" or "proper" name--44; 211;
317. Inf. thinks it wrong to call this a
'doughnut'--323. pretzel: Twisted instead
of round--16. twister: Once used by inf.
--39.

36.3b doughnut (made with slightly sweetened and leavened dough).

Although for the doughnut made with
leavened dough about one-fifth of the UM
infs. retain the simple doughnut characteristic of western New England and the
Dutch settlement area of the Atlantic
coast, the majority distinguish this
variety by raised doughnut, with the
synonomous bread doughnut competing weakly in three states and on equal terms in
Nebraska. Fried cake also occurs, perhaps
ambiguously. Pennsylvania German fasnachs-
kuche probably has a single reflex in
the form ['fas‚nɑt] used by a Nebraskan
of Illinois and Ohio parentage. Grebble,
of unexplained origin, is the term used
by another Nebraskan, of German Russian
background. Pfannkuchen, reported by a
southern Minnesota of New York and New
Jersey parentage, here has a German dialect meaning; it originally referred to
pancakes.

bismarck 18; 219.
cruller ¹†28.
doughnut c2, 3, 9, 13-15, 17, 22, !27,
29, 39, 48, c51, ¹52, 53, 56-59, 64-65;
101, 105, 114, 127, 132, sn139, 140, 146,
150; 202; 303, 312, 323, 327; 407-8, 420-
22, 425, *427, 434. baked ~ 125. bread ~
†7, 25; 134, 150; 204; 409, 411-12, 414,
417, †428, 430-32. glazed ~ 437. light
bread ~ 152. light ~ 225. raised ~ c2,
4-6, 8, *9, 10-12, 14, 19-24, 26-28, 30-
38, *41, 42-47, 49-50, 60-61, :62, 63-64;
102-4, 106, 108, 110-11, 115-24, 128, 130-

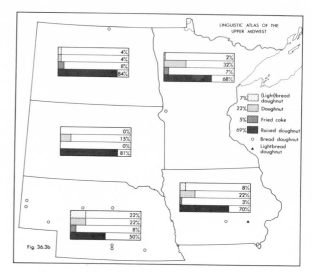

Fig. 36.3b

31, 133, 137-38, 141, 144-45, 148-49;
203-13, 215-16, 218-24, 226; 301-2, 304-7,
309-10, 313-17, *318, r319, 320-21, 324-
26, 328; 401-6, *408, 410, 413, †415, 416,
418, :419, 424, 426, 428-29, 433, *436.
white ~ 322. yeast ~ 318.
fas nat 433. ~ pretzel 433.
fried cake 15, c52, 55, 59; ¹109, 139;
¹217, 218;; 413, †420, 433, ¹434. light
dough ~ 214. raised ~ 139. sponge ~ 423.
grebble 425.
long John c225.
pfannkuchen 61.
sinker 309.
no response 1, 16, 54; 107,112-13, 126,
129, 135-36, 142-43, 146-47, 151; 201;
308, ?311; 435.

Comment:

bismarck: With jelly in the center--18;
219. bread doughnut: Used by inf.'s mother
(from Que.)--7. cruller: Twisted--28.
fas nat pretzel: Twisted--433. grebble:
Bread dough cut in squares about 4" by
4", slit lenthwise, pulled apart, and
deep fried. long John: Long and sugar
coated--225. pfannkuchen: With jelly in
the center--61.

36.4 griddle cakes (of wheat). NE 289.
WG 19-20, 22, 34-35, 46, 49, 69; F2,
F11, F21, F22, F121.

Although the WG describes the old expression griddle cakes as strong only in
eastern New England, with a marked decline in western New England and only
rare occurrence in upper New York, it
managed to survive the western migration
well enough to be the usual term for 12
Minnesotans and 3 North Dakotans. Elsewhere it is infrequent.

Pancakes, dominant everywhere on the

Atlantic coast except eastern New England, also dominates the UM. Nearly all infs. either have no other term or use it as an alternate. The older variant pan-i-cake or pannicake, recorded 3 times in Wisconsin fieldwork, has echoes in Minnesota and was overheard locally by an inf. in a Dutch community in North Dakota. This variant may be derived from Dutch pannekack.

Some regional variation appears with 2 of the remaining minor lexical variants, but more generally social differences mark their occurrence.

Flapjacks, widespread but decreasing in New England, where it is considered uncouth or amusing, is also declining in the UM, where it is reported by 13% of the Type I infs. and by 9% of the Type II but by none of Type III. Nor do these figures include the additional 19 infs. who consider the term archaic. It is sometimes characterized as relevant only to pancakes cooked outdoors, as on a camping trip. Less frequent slapjacks, also of New England origin, persists in the UM only with Type I speakers in Northern speech territory, where it is called old-fashioned.

Fritters, in the East limited to Maine, New Hampshire, and northeastern Massachusetts, appears in the UM in and around that part of east central Nebraska having a New York state orientation.

Hot cakes, according to the WG an expression peculiar to Philadelphia and the Delaware Bay area, has scattered occurrences in the UM, where it is more likely to be found on restaurant menus than in home speech.

Wheat cakes, with only 4 instances in all New England, still seems to exhibit Northern orientation in the UM, with 6 instances in Minnesota and only one each in the other states. It is distinctly preferred by better educated infs. (Type I, 1%; II, 7%; III 19%) and may also occur more often in hotel and restaurant use than in homes.

Flannel cakes, an old Pennsylvania term likely to have been carried by the Scotch-Irish down the Shenandoah Valley, is used by a Grand Marais, Minnesota, inf., whose mother came from Delaware, an Iowan whose mother came from North Carolina, and 2 Nebraskans with Midland backgrounds.

Batter cakes, a minor variant found south of the Potomac, occurs in the speech of an Iowa Negro whose father came from Virginia.

Some UM variants lack an east coast background. Doughgods, a western term cited by the *Dictionary of Americanisms* from a South Dakota newspaper article printed in 1899, is reported by 2 South Dakota infs. as an old cowpuncher's word. Fried cakes is reported in this sense by 3 widely scattered infs. Liver pads, a jocular metaphor hardly intended to flatter the cook, is an archaism found twice in Nebraska. Also vividly descriptive is the locution rawhide flapjacks used by a western Nebraska oldtimer. Sourdough pancakes is used by a northern Minnesota Type I inf. of part Indian parentage and with reservation background. Sweat pads is the graphic term of a western Nebraskan familiar with early pioneer days.

Incidental responses from some infs. yielded information about two kinds of cakes not made with wheat. Buckwheat cakes or pancakes is the form offered by infs. 120, 147, 150; 215; and 433. Corn cakes comes from infs. 401 and 409; cornmeal cakes, from 405; cornmeal pancakes, from †209 and 215. Both kinds of terms were recorded in New England but neither was systematically sought in the UM.

	Mn.	Ia.	N.D.	S.D.	Nb.	Ave.
pancakes	94%	100%	96%	89%	100%	96%
griddle cakes	18%	4%	12%	7%	3%	10%
flapjacks	12%	16%	0%	11%	5%	10%
wheat cakes	9%	2%	4%	4%	4%	5%
hot cakes	5%	2%	4%	4%	3%	3%
slapjacks	5%	0%	4%	11%	0%	3%

CL 122: Replies from 1,042 respondents largely confirm the field data, with some minor differences for less frequently reported items, particularly hot cakes, more favored by the respondents in the Dakotas, and griddle cakes, less often reported. Batter cakes turns up 3 times in Nebraska and once in southern Iowa and South Dakota.

	Mn.	Ia.	N.D.	S.D.	Nb.	Ave.
pancakes	95%	94%	93%	97%	97%	95%
griddle cakes	5%	4%	4%	4%	4%	5%
flapjacks	10%	6%	12%	10%	10%	9%
hot cakes	7%	6%	26%	16%	6%	12%

batter cakes 130.
cakes 221; →301, 316; 436.
dough gods †204, ¹†210.
flannel cakes 118; 402, 426. ~ pancakes 6.
flapjacks ¹2, ¹†3-5, ¹10-11, s†12, ¹15, 16, ¹21, !¹22, 23, ¹†33, ¹34, sn37, ¹39, ¹42, 44, *46, !54, ¹†55, 57, ¹58; †103, ¹109, 112-13, 117, 124, ¹127, 133-34, 140, 145; †202, ¹203, !†204, ¹†214, !¹220, †222, !¹223, †224; †301, 302, †309, ¹312-13, ?¹317, !*318, 320, ¹323-24, †326; ¹404, 405, †408-9, †412, †416, c422. rawhide ~ †409.
flitters ¹432.
flopjacks 8; ¹†216; †407.
fried cakes 1; ¹152; †221.
fritters 18; 413, 416, 424, 426, ¹432.
griddle cakes 1, ¹2-3, 6, ¹7, 11, 14,

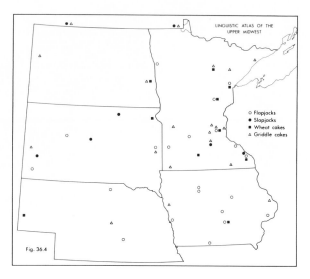

LINGUISTIC ATLAS OF THE UPPER MIDWEST

○ Flapjacks
● Slapjacks
■ Wheat cakes
△ Griddle cakes

Fig. 36.4

[1]20, [1]22, [1]28, [†]29, 33, 35, 37, 40, *41, 50, 61, [!][1]62, 65; 122, 139; 201, 210, [1]214, [1]217, 222, [1]225; 309, 319; 420, [†]437.

hot cakes [1]4, 14, →35, 50; 127; 210; 309; [1]404, 428.
liver pads [1]404, [†]429.
pancakes 1-4, c5, 6, c7, 8-11, 13-22, c23, 24-34, [†]35, 36-46, c47, 49-50, c51, 52, [†]53, 54-60, c61-62, 63-65; 101-50, 152; 201-5, c206, 207-12, c213, 214, 216-21, [†]222, 223-26; c301, 302-8, [†]309, 310, 312-13, 315-18, c319, c320, 321-28; 401-2, c403, 404-6, c407, 408-18, c419, 420-28, c429, 430-37.
pan-i-cakes *9, [1]47, [†]57, 64; [1]223.
potato pancakes 55; 209.
slapjacks 1, [1][†]26, [†]27, 48, !56; !201, [†]206; c311, c314, r[1]317; [†]429.
slopjacks 305.
sourdough pancakes 6, 11, 21; 215.
Swedish pancakes 4.
sweat pads [1]436.
wheat cakes 12, 17, 23, [1]34, c37, 53, 58; 134; 222; 308; 411.
no response 151.

Comment:

dough gods: Cowpunchers' term--210. flannel cakes: Raised with yeast--118. Thinner than 'pancakes'--426. Used by inf.'s husband--402. flapjacks: Lumberjacks' term--2-4, 10, 15, 21. Cowpunchers' term--214. Miners' term--309. Used by inf.'s grandfather--326. Used by inf.'s father (from Scot.)--5. Used by inf. as a child--103. "Men say 'flapjacks'"--127. Used by inf.'s children--203. Inf. says 'flapjacks' are cooked in a frying pan and 'pancakes' are cooked on a griddle--16. Sourdough--37. Larger than 'pancakes'--112. flopjacks: Inf. says this is a

"terrible" term; not "good English"--22. fried cakes: = pancakes--1. Used by inf. as a child--221. griddle cakes: Inf. is contemptuous of this term--62. Inf. considers this a restaurant term--40. Thinner than 'pancakes'--1. liver pads: a cowpunchers' term--404. pancake: Used by inf. in youth--222. pan-i-cake: Heard used by Norwegians--47. Used by inf. as a child--57. Common here--64; 223. rawhide flapjacks: Inf. says this kind is badly made, thin and tough--409. slapjacks: "That comes from the woods"--56. Lumberjacks' term--317. Used by inf. as a child--206. sourdough pancakes: = flapjacks--11. Swedish pancakes: Thinner than 'pancakes'--4. wheat cakes: Inf. says this is a restaurant term--23; 411.

36.6 cake of yeast. NE 290.

"What do you use to make bread dough rise?" is the typical question eliciting this item. Nearly all infs. responded simply "yeast" as the referent for the common commercial yeast cake. Only three times was it specified as a "cake" of "yeast" or of "east."

The "east" pronunciation is distinctly old-fashioned. Only 15 Type I infs. have it, and only 3 Type II. Furthermore, it occurs largely in the eastern half of the UM and rarely in the more recently settled western portion.

A few scattered infs. preserve various terms for the kinds of homemade liquid or sponge yeast used before the advent of the commercial cake variety. Some of these expressions indicate typical ingredients. Older names include: emptyings, old witch, sponge (starter), starter, self-starter, yeast starter, yeast foam, fresh yeast, hop yeast, jug yeast, liquid yeast, potato yeast, quick yeast, slop yeast, soft yeast, sponge yeast, and spook yeast.

Spook yeast, which the Wisconsin survey recorded three times, is the term of a Crow Wing, Minnesota, housewife who describes the variety as sweetened and salted potato water into which a cake of yeast has been put. Others in the community, she said, know the term. Apparently a similar variety an eastern Nebraskan of New York background picturesquely calls old witch.

New England emptins is preserved more formally as emptyings in the speech of a Marshall, Minnesota, housewife of Canadian and Michigan parentage.

Minor equivalents of yeast cake itself are compressed yeast, dry yeast, and hard yeast, and perhaps granulated yeast and baker's yeast (the bulk variety).

	Mn.	Ia.	N.D.	S.D.	Nb.	Ave.
yeast	92%	94%	88%	96%	97%	94%
east	12%	12%	12%	4%	5%	10%

CL 126: Although the 900 respondents checking the yeast item were not asked to distinguish between yeast and east, they likewise indicate the general occurrence of simple yeast as well as the existence of numerous variants, some of which had not been recorded during the fieldwork. Most widespread of these is dry yeast, with a possible slight Northern orientation; northern Iowa has 22% and southern Iowa 17%, and a similar weighting appears in the entire UM. Potato yeast and soft yeast persist as widely scattered terms for older kinds of yeast. Everlasting yeast, with no responses from Iowa and Nebraska, is clearly Northern (Mn. 5b, 38; N.D. 6, 9, 20, 21(2), 22, 28, 36, 37, 51; S.D. 6, 13, 18, 52, 63). Spook yeast appears three times (Ia. 20; N.D. 21, 49). Especially valid are responses voluntarily written in: baker's yeast (Mn. 15; N.D. 9; S.D. 24, 29, 55 "bakery yeast," 66); fresh yeast (Mn. 6, 12; S.D. 60); compressed yeast (Mn. 42; Ia. 52); holy water (Mn. 39; N.D. 8); buckwheat yeast (Mn. 81); cake yeast (N.D. 3); hop yeast (Ia. 76); moist yeast (Mn. 58).

	Mn.	Ia.	N.D.	S.D.	Nb.	Ave.
yeast	80%	79%	72%	72%	83%	78%
dry yeast	26%	20%	33%	33%	27%	27%
potato yeast	7%	8%	6%	7%	6%	7%
soft yeast	4%	6%	6%	9%	5%	6%

east 16, c21, r25, c35, 38, 52, c56; †125, †127, 129, 132, c136, 147, 149-50; 204, 207; 307; †411, c422, 427, ¹†433, ¹435. ~ cake ¹34; 220. ~ foam 220; 307. baker's ~ 149. dry ~ 6; ¹207; 307.

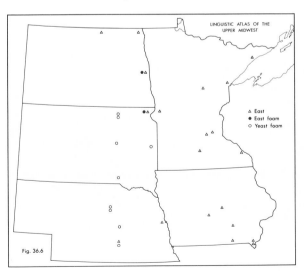

LINGUISTIC ATLAS OF THE UPPER MIDWEST

△ East
● East foam
○ Yeast foam

Fig. 36.6

emptyings c46.
old witch 413.
sponge 224. ~ starter 432.
starter s101, ¹103, 104-5, 115-16, 131-33, 145, 147; 217; 318; 416, c422, 423, 433. self-~ 102.
yeast 1-15, c16, 17-20, 22-24, 26-34, 36, c37, 39, c40, 41, c42, 43-45, c46, 47, c48, 49-50, c51, 53-54, c55, 56-58, c59, 60, !61, 62-65; 101-18, 120-28, 130-31, 133-38, 140-41, c142, 143-46, 148, crc150; 201-3, 205-6, 208-9, 211-19, 221-26; 301-6, 308-13, c314, 315-16, 318-19, c320, 321-24, 326-28; 401-12, c413, 414, 416-18, c419, 420-21, 424, 426, *427, 428-30, c431, 432-33, 435-37. ~ cake 210; 428. ~ foam 305-6, 316, 318, 323; 413-14, 420, 423. ~ starter 319. baker's ~ 416. compressed ~ 121; 306, 319; 414, *427, 428. dry ~ 13, 31; 139; 208, †209, †213, †217; 305-6, 308, 318-19, 325; 415-16, 420-21, 424-26, *427, 428, 431-32, 434. fresh ~ 428. granulated ~ 428. hard ~ 119, 139; 317. hop ~ 147; †214, 219; †324. jug ~ sn119, 137. liquid ~ 106, †150; 414. potato ~ !202; †422. powdered ~ 319. quick ~ 431. slop ~ 113. soft ~ 119, 139; 305, 317. sponge ~ 432. spook ~ sn22, sn40; s¹317, ¹†326.
no response 151-52.

Comment:

east: Used by inf.'s grandmother--411. Heard here years ago; "But I knew then it wasn't correct"--433. emptyings: Warm water, salt, and flour--46. old witch: Potatoes, yeast, and flour used as a starter--413. spook yeast: Potato water sweetened and salted with a cake of yeast in it; kept cold--22. Hops, potato water, and sugar--40. Self-perpetuating; kept alive with potato water--317. yeast: "I left the y off"--cr150.

36.7 yolk.

The inclusion of this item is primarily for the purpose of determining the distribution of the phonological variants yolk, yoke, and yelk, for which see Volume 2. The rare New England lexical equivalent yellow for the center of an egg survives in the speech of two UM infs., however, one an Iowan (147) with Iowa parents and the other a Nebraskan (434) with Canadian and New York parentage. All other infs. use one of the forms of yolk.

37.3 poached eggs. NE 295.

For eggs cooked by being dropped into boiling water or, sometimes, boiling milk the usual Atlantic coast epithet is

poached, with a fairly widespread equivalent dropped. Of these, only poached
is recorded in the speech of UM infs.
Since dropped eggs was reported only once
in the Wisconsin survey, and then in the
speech of a secondary infs., this term
apparently is obsolescent. Three perhaps
confused infs. offer coddled, scalloped,
and shirred as synonyms.

Poached itself occurs with 3 variants,
porched, pouched, and perched. Porched
and pouched, which in New England occur
as rare words in western Connecticut,
are the usage of 4 and of 3 UM infs.,
respectively. A lone North Dakotan housewife, a Type I speaker of foreign-language
background, has the unique perched.

    coddled ¹423.
    poached 1-5, c6, s7, 8-14, cr15, →16,
17-18, s19, 20-24, :sn25, 26-39, c40, 41-
42, c43, 44-47, s¹48, 49-58, 60-65; 101-
50, 152; 201-7, :208, 209-26; 301-6,
308-21, :322, 323-28; 401-17, c418, 419,
s420, 421, 423-29, 431-37.
    scalloped ?15.
    shirred s422.
    no reply 59; 151; 307; 430.

Comment:

    poached: Dropped, broken into boiling
water--1, 10-11, 20-24, 26, 30-31, 35-
39, 41-43, 45-47, 49-52, 54-55, 60-63;
123-25, 127-28, 136, 142, 144-45, 149;
201, 205, 207-9, 213, 217, 219-21; 311,
317, 320-21, 323-26; 403, 405, 407-12,
415, 418, 422, 424-28, 432, 437. Dropped,
broken into boiling water or milk--33;
212; 305; 404, 413, 416, 420. Broken into
a pan or dish which is placed in boiling
water--5, 32, 44, 47, 60, 65; 222; 326;
419. shirred: Inf. thinks they are
dropped, broken into boiling milk--422.

37.4b dried beef. NE 303.

    Beef dried and sometimes smoked for
preservation occurs in two main varieties,
with corresponding lexical designations.
Dried beef that is cut into thin slices
or chips is generally precisely that,
dried beef or, 4 times, dry beef, throughout the UM, but the frequent minor New
England variant, the Americanism chipped
beef or chip beef, has also been carried
west and is alive in the region. Since
this item is lacking in the North Central
worksheets and was added in the UM only
late in the Minnesota study, a Northern
orientation of chipped beef can be inferred only from its rarity in Iowa and
the declining frequency from North Dakota to Nebraska.
    Beef that has been cut into long strips
and dried in the open air is known by

the Americanisms jerked beef, jerky, or,
once, jerk. Because the process itself
is characteristic of pioneer life and
hence is old-fashioned, the terms themselves often are considered obsolescent.
Although remembered in New England as
early expressions, in the UM they survive
principally in South Dakota and Nebraska,
where some infs. associate them with
Indians. One South Dakotan also reports
the local use of a Sioux equivalent,
tado. A Nebraskan inf. says that one can
have jerked venison as well as jerked
beef. Smoked beef occurs only once, as
the term of a Type I Minnesota farmer of
New York State parentage.
    Bannock, insisted upon by a Type I
Nebraska housewife, seems to be an error.

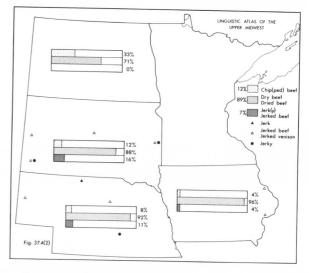

Fig. 37.4(2)

    bannock †401.
    chip beef 121.
    chipped beef sn30; ¹*130, 152; 201,
205, 207-8, 214-15, 218, 222; ¹304, 310,
¹312, 313, 326; c404, 406, ¹426, 433.
    dried beef 29-31, 35-36, 38, cvr47;
101-20, 122-28, 130-49; 201, 203-4, 209-
13, ¹215, 216-17, 219, 221, 223-26; 301-
4, 306, 308, 310-19, 322-25, 328; 401-3,
¹404, 405, 407-25, 427-32, 434-37.
    dry beef 129; 220; 305; 426.
    jerk 403.
    jerked beef 119, †*123, 141; †225;
†301, 309, †311, ¹312, 314, *318, 320;
†401, s¹403, 409, †411, snt412.
    jerky ¹125; ¹312, *318, 320; ¹†404,
†410, 422.
    smoked beef 29.
    tado 323.
    no response 1-28, 32-34, 37, 39-46,
48-65; 150-51; 202, ?206; 307, 321, 327.

Comment:

    chipped beef: Usu.--310. "Common here"

--426. dried beef: Inf. says this is commercial; she says "chipped beef"--215. Usu.--313. jerk: "The Sioux have that; they eat their 'jerk'"--403. jerked beef: Inf. says this is the name for the homemade kind--119; 411-12. "I've [ɛt] it with some Indians--hard as a rock"--225. Made by Indians--225; 312, 314; 401, 403. "I've eaten pounds of jerked beef. Father dried it on a pole 35 feet high above the flies. It got hard as flint. It was sliced thin and used in milk gravy."--409. jerky: Heard by informant in Co. and Az.--125. Made by Indians--312. Inf. says that 'jerky' or 'dried beef' is found further West, but not here--*318. Used by inf.'s uncle, a cowpuncher--410. tado: Inf. says this is a Sioux word, occasionally used here--323.

37.6a The meat is spoiled. NE 306.

As in the Atlantic states the common term in the UM to describe meat that has become "overripe" is SPOILED. (For grammatical variants see Volume 2.) Some infs., especially in Iowa, distinguish between "spoiled" meat, no longer fit to be eaten, and merely "tainted" meat, usable but probably calling for ketchup or meat sauce to smother the ripe flavor. One inf., a Minneapolis Negro of South Midland background, has the variant tainty. Rancid also appears as a synonym for tainted, as do stale and strong, both in Midland speech territory. Rotten, recorded 3 times in 3 different states, refers to meat so badly spoiled as to be quite unusable. That these variants do not appear in much of Minnesota and the western states may be a function of fieldworker A, who stressed the gram-

matical variations of SPOILED rather than the lexical differences for the item.

old 135.
rancid 14-16, 18, 31; 118, 127, 137; *318; 401.
rotten †16; 119; 306.
SPOILED 1-12, c13, 14-15, 17-24, c25, 26-29, s30, :31, 32-46, c47, 48, c49, 50, c51, 52-60, c61, 62-65; 101-2, 104-6, c107, 108-10, 112-21, 123, s124, 128-29, 131, 134, 136, 138-42, 144-49; 201-5, :sn206, 207-10, c211, 212-15, c216, 217-18, c219, 220-26; 301-8, :!309, 310-16, sn317, 318-26, c327, 328; :401, 402-4, c405, 406-37.
stale 124, 127, 133, ?136, 139, 143, 147; 307, 317.
strong 118, 127, :135; 307.
tainted 101-3, 108-11, 119, 122, 125, s¹126, 130, 132, 145, 147-49; 306, 316-17, 319. tainty 35.
no response 150-52.

37.6b The butter is rancid. NE 306.

Although with reference to butter this item was recorded by only two fieldworkers in New England and was included in the UM study only toward the end of the Minnesota phase, it is clear that the most common term both in New England and in the UM is rancid. Two unusual phonological variants turn up: ransom, once each in Iowa and the two Dakotas, and rancit, once in Nebraska. Neither was reported in LANE.

Butter that is conspicuously no longer fresh but still is usable is characterized by either strong or stale in each state studied. Probably with the same force two Iowa infs. and one Nebraskan use tainted, and seven scattered infs. use rank, with the variant ranky from a Type I Nebraska housewife.

Spoiled, used by 3 scattered infs. and stinking, used by one of the 3, are applied to butter so remote from freshness that it is no longer usuable.

Frowy, recorded once in the speech of a Type I northwestern Iowa inf. of Pennsylvania and Wisconsin parentage, is a solitary reflection of a New England minor variation recorded in LANE from 16 infs. Its range of meaning seems to include both that of rancid and that of spoiled.

frowy 101.
rancid 18, 29-31, sn36, 38; 102-8, 110-11, s114, 115-17, 119-24, s125, 126-31, 137, 140-41, 144-45, s146, 147-49; 201-3, 205-6, :207, 208, 210-15, s¹216, 217-24, 226; 301-2, 304-5, 308, c309, 310-21, 323-26, 328; 401-4, 406, 408-14, sn416, 418-28, 430-31, 433-34, 437.

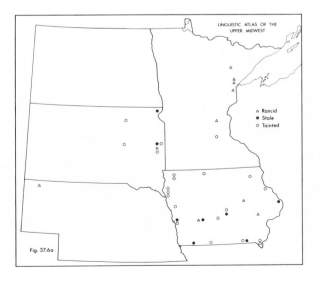

LINGUISTIC ATLAS OF THE UPPER MIDWEST

△ Rancid
● Stale
○ Tainted

Fig. 37.6a

rank 35; [1]139, *148; 322, 326; 405, 434.
  ranky 432.
  spoiled 36; 204; 306.
  stale 112, 122, 138, 147; 207, 224; 317, 319; 418, 429.
  stinking 306.
  strong 103, 109, 113, 115, 127, 132-36, 139, 143, *146, 148; 204, 209; *318, 326; 416, 418, 423, 427, 435-36.
  tainted 133, 142; 436.
  no response 1-17, 19-28, 32-34, 37, 39-65; 118, 150-52; 303, 307, 327; 407, 415, 417.

Comment:

  rancid: "Unusable"--427. strong: "Usable"--427.

37.7a head cheese. NE 305. WG 32.

Head cheese commonly names a food preparation composed of parts of the head, and sometimes of the feet, of swine, cut up fine, seasoned, boiled, and pressed. This Americanism (first in 1841 in the *Dictionary of Americanisms*) is common both on the east coast and in the UM. In the UM the stress is most frequently on the initial element, less frequently even, and only 3 or 4 times on the second syllable (infs. 7, 11, 305). One South Dakotan has the variant hedge cheese, also found in LANE.

Regional terms designating a somewhat similar preparation are the Americanisms scrapple (1855) and ponhaws (1869), both originating in the Pennsylvania German area. They refer typically to a food prepared from bits of meat, generally pork, seasoned with herbs, boiled with cornmeal, and sliced from a mold when cold. Ponhaws lives in the speech of a Nebraska housewife whose father came from Maryland; scrapple, much more vigorous, is scattered throughout the UM, but especially in southern Iowa and Nebraska. The variant Philadelphia scrapple is the expression used by two other Nebraskans.

A type III Minneapolis physician reports that his Swedish patients use silta, in an English context, for a product very much like head cheese. A Minnesota Type II Iron Range inf. of Croatian and Hungarian background has the term sultz for what others call head cheese.

A related food product, at least in the thinking of some infs., is known widely in Midland territory as souse. Sometimes the word refers only to pickled pigs' feet, but most infs. using it say that souse consists of meat scraps, pickled, and then molded in their own gelatin.

	Mn.	Ia.	N.D.	S.D.	Nb.	Ave.
head cheese	100%	98%	96%	93%	92%	97%
scrapple	3%	6%	8%	4%	31%	7%
souse	2%	2%	0%	11%	34%	9%

CL 38: Head cheese also dominates the mail returns of 1,038 respondents, with a full variant hog's head cheese, not reported in the field in the UM but found in New England. A much higher proportion of replies reveal familiarity with scrapple, but still with Midland orientation. Nineteen respondents check ponhaws (spelled panihoss on the checklist and respelled by two respondents (Mn. 8 and Ia. 3) as poonhuss). Souse also is checked by the respondents, but not with so great a proportion in South Dakota and Nebraska.

Several terms, apparently more or less equivalent in meaning, appear on the checklist returns as voluntary write-ins of the respondents. Most common is head-meat, with Midland orientation (Ia. 52, 62, 76; S.D. 61; Nb. 48, 65, 87). In Iowa's county 56 occurs hoghead chili. Minnesota's county 64, a German settlement, reports sultz (Cp. German Sulz). Iowa county 90 has jellied pork. Nebraska county 84 has head souse, 88 has choppel, and 92 has knip.

	Mn.	Ia.	N.D.	S.D.	Nb.	Ave.
head cheese	95%	80%	97%	94%	90%	90%
scrapple	12%	24%	20%	42%	50%	29%
souse	1%	7%	1%	5%	12%	5%

  head cheese 1-6, c7, 8-12, c13, 14-34, c35, 36-37, 39-51, c52, 53-54, c55, 56-65; 101-10, 112-19, 121-22, :123, 124-25, [1]126, 127-49; 201-8, 210-26; 301-5, [1]306, 307-11, 313, [1]314, 315-21, :322, 323-24, c325, 326, 328; 401-11, †412, 413, [1]414, 415-24, 426-29, 431-34, 436-37.

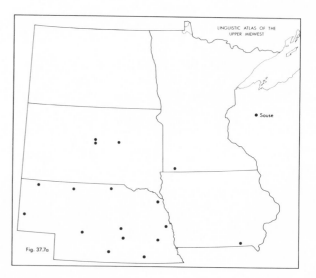
LINGUISTIC ATLAS OF THE UPPER MIDWEST

Souse

Fig. 37.7a

hedge cheese 312.
head sausage 209.
ponhaws 422.
Philadelphia scrapple 426, 428.
scrapple 24, *43; 110, 116, s136, 137,
¹147; 212, 217; †310, 320; c401, 402,
413, 422-24, 431-33, †436.
silta c34.
souse 61; s105, 147; ¹214; 314-16; 401,
404, *405, 408, :†409, 411, 419, 421-22,
426, 428, 431, 433.
sultz /zults/ 13.
no response 38; 111, 120, 150-52; 327;
430, 435.

Comment:

head cheese: Cooked, tied up, cooled,
sliced--16. "I never liked the name, so
I wouldn't eat it"--Head and scraps of
a hog, boiled off and seasoned, chopped,
and pressed into a loaf--413. Head,
tongue, liver, all boiled up, ground,
and molded in their own fat--414. =
souse; made from headmeat, in sour gela-
tin--426. Edible headmeat of hog, spiced,
cut up, put in stomach, recooked, turned
into a pan, and molded--428. scrapple:
mixed with cornmeal--24. Made from crack-
lings--116; the meat left in rendering
lard--218; 418, 421. = cracklings. Ground
pork and corn meal--402, 431. Scraps from
rendering mixed with mush, sliced, and
fried--413. souse: pickled pressed pork--
404. Meat scraps, pickled, and molded in
own gelatin--428. = sour head cheese--
431, 433. sultz: Legs and nose cut off,
boiled, seasoned with garlic, and put
out on plates to jell--51.

37.7b Kinds of sausage.

Because the question asking for various
kinds of sausage was not pushed by all
fieldworkers the data here are less than
comprehensive. The distribution of some
of the following terms may be greater
than is suggested by the number and location of responding infs.

blood palt. This is equated with blood
sausage by a southern Nebraska housewife.
See palt below. 413.
blood pudding. This kind of sausage containing so much blood that it is nearly
black is uniquely described by a North
Dakota Norwegian farmer who reports that
the Swedes make it in a pan and then
bake it. 104, 137, ¹138; 216; 404, ¹414.
blood sausage. This increasingly common
designation for blood pudding is familiar
throughout the UM. A North Dakota Norwegian farmer (216) says that the Norwegians
make it in a salt or sugar sack. 15-16,
36; 105, 109, *116, 117, s139, ¹147, 148-
49; 207, 209, 212, ¹215, 216, ¹219, 220,

223; 302, 304, 323, ¹328; ¹403, 404, 407,
*408, 421, 424, 427, 430-31.
blute. This word is supplied once as
a term for blood pudding. 208.
blutwurst. This German word for blood
pudding is occasionally used in English
context. 143; 415.
bologna. This familiar term is offered
by only a few infs.: 220-21; 323; 408,
417. The full term, bologna sausage, is
used by an eastern South Dakota farmer,
225.
Braunschweiger. This smoked liver
sausage is widely known, but only one
inf. named it: 17.
haggis. This is a Scotch dish consisting of the heart, liver, and lights boiled
together in the stomach of a sheep or
calf. Only one inf., a Manitoban, offers
it: 201.
liver cheese. Apparently the expression
is equivalent to liver sausage. ¹146,
147; ?†326.
liver sausage. The expression is widely
scattered in the UM, without regional
weighting. 14, 17; 101-2, 104-9, 120,
133, 138-39, s141; 207-10, 212, ¹215, 216,
218-20, 223-24; 328; *408, 414, 424-25,
432.
liverwurst. This German loanword for
liver sausage is fairly common, though
better known in German background areas,
such as in Nebraska. 117, 137, 149; 204-
5; 304, 324, 326; ¹403, 415, 425, 427,
430-31, 433-34.
meat rolls. The one inf. offering this
term says that they are made by rolling
the meat in sheets made from the stomach;
they are then cured and buried in an
oat bin. 407.
palt. The reporting inf., a northeastern Nebraskan of Swedish parentage,
describes palt as a kind of sausage made
with blood and flour. Cf. Swedish palt-
bröd, 'blood bread.' †408.
pepper sausage. 203.
Polish sausage. 212, 221.
rennerwurst. An Iowa farmer uses this
German word in English contexts. 117.
smoked sausage. 205; 436.
summer sausage. 221; 302, 311.

In addition, respondents to the checklist for 37.7a voluntarily wrote in
three terms without explanation: grits-
wurst, S.D. 60, 62; oatmeal sausage, S.D.
62; and scat, Nb. 6.

37.8 salt pork. NE 301. WG 12, 14, 32,
69-70; F122.

Although not used in the original Minnesota study, this question about meat
from the side or belly of swine yielded
some evidence of regional variation cor-

responding to Eastern patterns.

It is true that salt pork, the most common term, no longer sharply reflects its Northern origin, for its frequency in Nebraska is only slightly less than that in North Dakota. Sidemeat, however, with only one occurrence in North Dakota and another in South Dakota, but with ten occurrences in Nebraska, still is strongly Midland in character, as befits its dominance of Pennsylvania. Side pork, considered by Kurath in WG as a blend of Northern salt pork and Midland sidemeat, may reveal such a blending with a spread in northern Iowa and central Nebraska, areas where the two dialect streams have partly merged. There are also 3 scattered instances of side pork in South Dakota and 3 in the Red River valley.

Sowbelly, less common in the East, apparently experienced increasing frequency in the westward migration, with a subsequent decline. Its frequency drops from 27% for oldest infs. to 11% for middle-age infs. No Type III infs. have it. Seven of the 26 infs. using it already consider it old-fashioned and several others laughed when asked about it. A Type I western Nebraska "old-timer" offered the synonymous sow bosom, which Atwood also found in Texas.

Scattered infs., mostly in North Dakota, use bacon to designate salt pork; 4 others also use bacon but with the limiting salt or salted.

Salt back, not reported in the East, is the term of a western South Dakota cattleman of Ohio and Wisconsin parentage.

	Ia.	N.D.	S.D.	Nb.	Ave.
salt pork	75%	89%	77%	68%	77%
sidemeat	20%	4%	4%	38%	15%
side pork	16%	15%	12%	17%	15%
sowbelly	18%	31%	15%	14%	14%

CL 131: Checklist returns from 912 respondents vary greatly from those of the fieldwork, although Northern/Midland contrasts are maintained. In southern Iowa, for example, Midland sidemeat has 37% and in northern Iowa only 16%, while its hybrid counterpart side pork is stronger in northern Iowa (52%) than in southern Iowa (21%). But respondents, facing a number of printed terms, chose more widely than did field infs. from among their remembered names for the referent. They indicate greater use of side pork and sidemeat but less of sowbelly. South Midland middlins was volunteered by two respondents (Ia. 94 and Nb. 50), and the previously unreported fry pork by one (S.D. 66).

	Mn.	Ia.	N.D.	S.D.	Nb.	Ave.
salt pork	46%	32%	48%	41%	36%	40%
sidemeat	5%	25%	11%	18%	26%	18%
side pork	49%	38%	54%	46%	30%	42%
sowbelly	4%	25%	11%	18%	26%	18%

bacon 15; 114, 139; 206-7, 213, 216, 219, 223; 302; 432. salt ~ 132, 147; 432. salted ~ 133.

salt back 301.

salt pork 29-31, c35, 36, 38; 102, 106, 108-11, 113-17, 119-20, s121, 122-32, 135-36, 139-44, 146-49; 201-6, 208-10, 212-18, c219, 220, 222-26; 303-4, 308-10, 312-13, 315-19, 321-28; 401-2, 404-8, 411-13, 416, 418, sn421, 422, 424-30, ¹431,

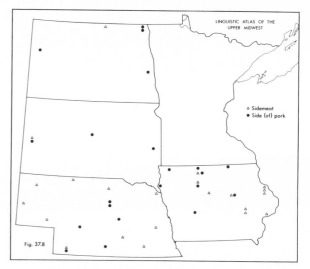

LINGUISTIC ATLAS OF THE UPPER MIDWEST

△ Sidemeat
● Side (of) pork

Fig. 37.8

433-34, 436. salted ~ 134; 302.

sidemeat 104, 112, 114, 118-21, 137-38, 141; 204; 309; 402-3, 406-7, 410, 417, 423-24, 429, *432.

side of pork 319.

side pork 101, 103, c104, 105, 110, 113, 118, 127; 207-8, 210, ¹220, 221; 310, 314; 413-14, 419-20, 431, 437.

sowbelly †103, sn104, s105, 108, 112, sn113, 115-16, ¹120, s121, 128, 133, 139; c†202, ¹203, !209, !214, 216, !217, 218, sn220, 224; 309, c311, ¹†312, ¹†313, s¹314, 315, †*318, 320, ¹328; 401, 406-7, 409, †412, s¹†418, 428, s429.

sow bosom 429.

no response 1-14, 16-28, 32-34, 37, 39-65; 107, 145, 150-52; 306, 327; 415, 435.

Comment:

bacon: = salt bacon--432. salt pork: Usu.--119. sidemeat: Fresh, not salted--133. side pork: Fresh, not salted--211. Fresh or salted--210. sowbelly: Fresh, not salted--36; 404. Used by inf.'s grandfather--103. Used infrequently be inf.; he says it is "vulgar"--216.

37.9 rind. NE 302.

For the tough outside skin on bacon
or salt pork the usual term is rind, in
the UM as in New England. (For phonological variants see Volume 2.) Ten scattered infs. say skin, also recorded in
LANE as a minor variant. Hide, not in
LANE, is the choice of 5 speakers, 3 in
Iowa and 2 in South Dakota. This item
was not queried in most of the Minnesota
field study.

hide 117, 141, 146; 303, 317.
rind 29-31, 36, 38; 101-12, 114-25,
127-40, 142-45, 147-49; 201-4, 206, 209-
11, 213-15, ¹216, 217-19, 221-26; 301-2,
304-20, 322-26; 328; 401-6, s407, 408-
14, 416-20, c421, 422-37.
skin 35; 112-13, 119; 205, 207, 212,
220; 317; 407.
no response 1-28, 32-34, 37, 39-65;
126, 150-52; 208; 321, 327; 415.

38.1 curdled milk. NE 298. WG 17, 25-26,
35-36, 38, 70; F124.

For milk that has become so sour as
to form curds most of the regional terms
on the Atlantic coast have been carried
into the UM but in varying degrees.
Eastern New England bonny-clabber does
not appear at all in the UM field records,
nor does western New England loppered
milk. The variant lobbered milk, however,
which was found in Rhode Island, Vermont,
and New York state, survives with 3 scattered infs.--two in Minnesota of Canadian
and of New York parentage and one in
South Dakota with New York parents. UM
variants probably due to confusion with
clabber milk are clobber milk (once in
Minnesota), clobbered milk (once each in
Minnesota and South Dakota), globber milk
(known once in Minnesota), and globbered
milk (twice in northern Iowa).
Southern clabber, described in the WG
as typically found south of Pennsylvania,
occurs with strength in the dominantly
Midland areas of southern Iowa and Nebraska. Clabber milk and clabbered milk,
which west of Pennsylvania had spread
north into the Western Reserve, retain
strength in basically Northern speech
territory in the UM. Although clabber itself occurs only once each in Minnesota
and North Dakota, clabbered milk has 13
instances in southern Minnesota and 4 in
North Dakota. They dominate Iowa and Nebraska. But that clabber terms may be
declining is suggested by the age distribution: Type I 52%, II 48%, and III 21%.

In the UM curdled milk, limited, according to the WG, to eastern Pennsylvania
and metropolitan New York, has extended
into much of the Northern speech area. It
is in the early settlements of southeastern Minnesota, the Twin Cities, and on
the Iron Range. It is common in eastern
North Dakota, in the extreme east and extreme west of South Dakota, and, scattered, in Nebraska. A variant curded milk
appears in northern Iowa.
Cruddled milk and crud, on the contrary,
do not in the UM reflect their importance
in western Pennsylvania. Two northwestern Minnesotans use cruddled milk and one
North Dakotan has overheard crud in his
community, Fargo. It does not appear in
the Iowa field responses. A suggestion has
been made that its decline is due to the
existence of a less pleasant sense of
cruddled and, especially, of crud.
Thick milk, probably from German Dicke-
milch or Pennsylvania German Dickemilich,
perhaps with Dutch or Scandinavian support in the UM, is the usage of sparsely
scattered infs. of widely varied parental
background. Scandinavian influence also
underlies the rare long milk and tet
milk proffered by a Swedish inf. in
northern Minnesota.
Blinky milk, apparently a South Midland
term although not listed in the WG, is
used by a western North Dakota Type I
inf. with the meaning "slightly sour, but
not yet curdled." Atwood reports that
the term is common in Texas and Oklahoma.
The North Dakotan's community was once
the railroad shipping point for cattle
driven north from the Texas Panhandle.
Many infs., principally in Minnesota,
profess to know no special term but use
sour milk without distinguishing between
ordinary sour milk and that with curds.
Some of these told the interviewer that
they were unaware that milk could become
so sour that curds would form in it.

CL 40: The 1,036 respondents checking
this item indicate a much higher frequency
of sour milk than that in the field records, though still with Northern orientation. Clabber and clabbered milk, however,
show a lower frequency, though retaining
their original Midland orientation. Curdled milk reveals a wide discrepancy, particularly in North Dakota. Thick milk is
widely scattered. Blinky milk is checked
by 9 respondents, 7 of whom are in Iowa
and one in Nebraska. New England bonny
clabber, not turned up in the field study,
is checked by 4 respondents (Mn. 52--of
New Hampshire and Massachusetts parentage, 58--of New York state parentage;
N.D. 58--with a Maine father; S.D. 33--
with a Kentucky father and an English

mother). <u>Cruddled milk</u> appears 5 times:
Ia. 77--with Missouri and California
parents, 86--with Missouri grandparents;
S.D. 20--with Scandinavian parents, 49--
with a Kansas father, 51--with Wisconsin
and South Dakota parents.

	Mn.	Ia.	N.D.	S.D.	Nb.	Ave.
clabbered m.	11%	20%	12%	26%	45%	22%
curdled m.	6%	3%	6%	4%	4%	5%
sour m.	83%	58%	78%	60%	47%	65%
thick m.	8%	2%	5%	4%	2%	4%

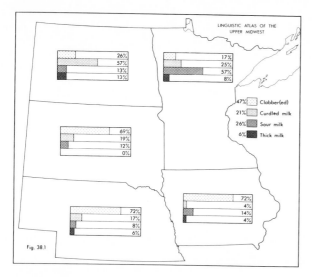

Fig. 38.1

blinky milk 214.
    clabber 22; :103, 110-11, 115, 117, 125,
127-28, 130-31, 135-36, 141-42, 146, 148;
214-15, 217; :s303, 314, 324; 401, 403,
*408, 409, 411-12, 414, 418, 423-24, 427,
430.
    clabber milk 28; 104, 133, 137, 140,
143; 212; 318, 323; 407, sn419, 428-29,
431-33.
    clabbered milk 10, 30, 33, s†39, 40,
42, c44, s†45, 46-47, 55, ¹59, †60, ¹62,
¹†63; 101-2, 108-9, 113, 116, †118, 119,
121, 124, 126, 132, 139, 145, 147, 149;
¹†210, 211, *216, 225; *301, 302, 305-6,
309, 312-13, 316, 320-22, 325, 327-28;
404-6, 413, ¹416, 417, ¹420, 421, ¹426,
434.
    clappered milk 44.
    clobber milk 21. clobbered ~ 31; 315.
    crud ¹222.
    cruddled milk 8, 25.
    curded milk 105.
    curdled milk 1, sn2, 5, 11-12, 23, 32,
35, 37-39, 57-59, 64-65; 138, 144; 202,
204-5, 207, *208, 213, 216, 218-19, 221-
23, 226; 301, 308, 310-11, 317; 407, 416,
419-20, 436-37.
    globber milk ¹34. globbered ~ 107, 114.
    lobbered milk 54, 61; s¹118; 316.
    long milk 4.

sour milk 2-4, 7, 9-10, 13-18, 20, 24,
26-27, 29, 33, 37, 41, 43-53, 59-63; 103,
106, 120-21, 123, 129, 134; 210, 216, 224;
304, 317, 326; 402, 410, 422, s425.
    tet milk 4.
    thick milk 36, 41, 45, 56, 59; 118,
122; 203, 214, 220; 415, c436.
    no response 6, 19; 150-52; 201, ?206,
209; 307, 319; 435.
Comment:

    clabbered milk: Used by inf.'s parents
(from N.Y. and N.C.)--118. "Cheese on
top and whey at the bottom"--305. "The
Germans here call it 'clabbered milk'"--
416. clappered milk: "That isn't said
much"--44. no response: Inf. says, "It
[the milk] cruddles," and calls the solids
'cruds'--307. Inf. calls the solids
'curds'--319.

38.2 cottage cheese. NE 299. WG 18,
21, 24, 71; F8, F125, F126.

    A conspicuous illustration of the stand-
ardizing effect of commercialization upon
the viability of regional terms is provided by the widespread acceptance of
cottage cheese as the designation for
drained milk curds. Identified by Kurath
in the WG as a trade name, this Americanism (1848 in DAm) not only is common in
the East but is so much more common in
the UM that it has left only as scattered
relics all but one of the regional terms
that once were much more widely known.
    Throughout the UM 9 out of 10 infs.
now use cottage cheese, some with the
acknowledgement that only recently have
they switched to it. Its strongest past
competition came from New England and
New York state Dutch cheese, which the
early settlers carried into all the UM
Northern speech areas. In the northern
section of Minnesota and in North Dakota,
however, the more numerous late 19th-
century European immigrants adopted the
already dynamic school and store expression cottage cheese. It is remarkable
that 32 of the 76 infs. familiar with
Dutch cheese declare that for them it
is old-fashioned; they no longer use it.
Some infs. admit that they retain it for
home use only [as I do--H.B.A.], having
learned that its use in markets and
restaurants makes for incomprehension.
    Two surviving regional terms appear
only in the Midland speech areas. Smearcase (anglicized from German Schmierkäse),
which already had spread from the Pennsylvania German area to Delaware, Maryland, and West Virginia, moved with the
westward migration into southern Iowa

and Nebraska, where more than one-third
of infs. knowing the term consider it
now old-fashioned in light of the rapid
encroachment of cottage cheese. Clabber
cheese, a South Midland and southern
Atlantic coastal term, is reflected in
the UM with a few instances along the
Des Moines River in southern Iowa and
near the Missouri River in southwestern
Iowa and southeastern Nebraska.
    One or two instances each also occur of
simple cheese (only in Minnesota), country cheese, cream cheese, curd, and curds
and whey (perhaps reflexes of the historic British curds still found in Maine
and New Hampshire), primost (a Norwegian
loanword for a cheese made by boiling
down the whey), Scotch cheese (perhaps
an unwitting transfer from Dutch cheese),
sour milk cheese (from eastern New England), and, only as overheard in a neighboring state, Schweitzer /swɑɪtsər/. Hudson valley pot cheese apparently does
not occur.

	Mn.	Ia.	N.D.	S.D.	Nb.	Ave.
clabber cheese	0%	8%	0%	0%	5%	3%
cottage cheese	89%	88%	80%	85%	97%	89%
Dutch cheese	15%	20%	36%	33%	16%	22%
smearcase	0%	12%	0%	4%	5%	4%

CL 39: Roughly the same proportional frequency appears in the usage of 1,036 respondents. The CL returns, however, extend the distribution of smearcase to
Minnesota and North Dakota, where nearly
all the users are second generation Germans or Russian Germans who are still
speakers of German. Apparently in the
Northern speech areas of the UM smearcase
has not spread into the non-German community as it earlier did in Pennsylvania.
Curds is offered by an Iowan (18) of
Maine and Canadian background, and crud,
a likely shortening of South Midland
crud cheese, is offered by a Nebraskan
(5) of Kansan and Iowan parentage.

    cheese 13, 16-18, ?39.
    clabber cheese 132, 135-36, 142; *417,
434.
    clabbered cheese ?44.
    cottage cheese 1-4, r5, 6-12, 14-15,
→16, 17-23, sn24, 26-28, ↓29, 30-35, 37-
38, cr39, 40-45, →46, 47-48, 50-51, c52,
53, c54, 55-58, f59, 60-64, ↓65; 101-6,
108-17, s→118, 119-31, 133-40, 143, 145-
49; 201-5, c208, 209-11, →212, 213-14,
216, ?217, →219, 220-24, 226; 302-3,
c305, 306, 308-10, →311-13, 314, →317,
318-19, →320, 321-22, :!323, 324-28; 401-
3, →404-6, 407-29, s430, 431-36, !437.
    country cheese 424.
    cream cheese 33; 127.
    curd :†220.
    curds and whey 14.

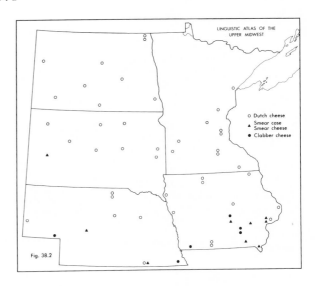

Fig. 38.2

Dutch cheese 16, †21-22, 24, :sn†27,
29, †31, 36, *37, 42, †45, 46, 48-49,
†50, 65; †101, 103-4, †105, 107, s108,
110, †113, †116-17, 118, 123, 139, 141,
144, *145; †205, :207, *208, c210, 211,
†212, ↓213, c215, cr217, 218, †219, †221,
223, 225; 301, :302, c304, 306, †310,
†312-13, ↓314, 315-17, 319-20, s↓323,
†324, †326-27; †401, †404, :405, 406,
↓408, †410, 411, †412, ↓413, c414, 416,
†419-20, †423, ↓427, 433.
    primost 41.
    Scotch cheese 59.
    smearcase †115, s↓118, †119, †124,
?130, 133, 137, †138, s140, 141, 146,
149; †301, 311; ↓413, †416, 418, †419,
↓420, ↓427, 433.
    smear cheese 140; ↓427.
    sour milk cheese :↓25, †31; 434.
    Schweitzer ↓314.
    no response 150-52; ?206; 307.

Comment:

    clabbered cheese: 'Cottage cheese' is
different--317. cottage cheese: Used because sold as such at the grocer's--110.
Cut coarser than 'smearcase'--149. "A
high-toned name"--317. Curds seasoned
with salt, spice, chives, etc.--428.
curd: Used by inf. as a boy--220. Dutch
cheese: Used by inf.'s mother (from
N.Y.)--27, (from Pa.)--105, (from Il.)--
324, (from Wi.)--410. Used by inf.'s
father (from R.I.)--31. Used by inf.'s
parents (from Pa. and Wi.)--101. Formerly used by inf.--50; 116-17; 221; 310.
An older term than 'cottage cheese'--306.
Inf. uses the term but considers it more
old-fashioned than 'cottage cheese'--414.
Usu.--46, 49; 104, 110. Inf. reports
this as the most common local term--223.
Inf. makes a lot of Dutch cheese--104.

primost: The whey boiled down--41. smearcase: Used by inf.'s mother--115, 138.
Inf. heard this from local Germans, with
final consonant sometimes /s/ and sometimes /z/--416. Inf. says this is used
by local Danes--420. Inf. uses this term
for cheese made at home--433. Used always
here about 50 years ago--119. Schweitzer:
Inf. heard this in Mo.--314.

38.3 sauce (sweet liquid poured over
pudding). NE 293.

For a variously flavored sweet liquid
served with pudding the nearly universal
UM word is sauce, as in the eastern
states. Dressing, sporadic in New England,
survives as a relic in the first settled
parts of the UM (6 Type I infs. and 2
Type II infs.) Dip, with only one New
England instance in Rhode Island and one
in Wisconsin, reveals a strong Midland
orientation by its concentration in
southern Iowa and Nebraska. An occasional
inf. restricts this word to mean only
sauce for ice cream. Related dope, of
Dutch origin, is an overheard term in
southeastern South Dakota. A minor New
England variant, pudding gravy, is used
by a secondary inf. in northeastern North
Dakota. Syrup, also found in LANE, occurs
narrowly in eastern South Dakota and
northern Iowa. Humorous equivalents goo,
goof, and goop appear once each. Hard
sauce, designating a soft but nonliquid
topping, as for fruitcake, is recorded
from 2 Iowa infs., but the term is actually well known throughout the UM. The
specific applesauce is in the records of
3 Minnesota infs.

	Mn.	Ia.	N.D.	S.D.	Nb.	Ave.
dip	3%	28%	4%	0%	10%	9%
dressing	3%	9%	4%	0%	3%	4%
sauce	89%	72%	92%	92%	90%	86%

CL 36: Except for greater incidence of
dressing in the five states, the returns
from 1,045 respondents match closely the
field data for the principal terms. In
addition dope occurs 11 times (6 in Ia.
and 5 in Nb.), and goop occurs twice in
Nebraska (61, 85). Topping, not in the
field records, is checked twice (Mn. 64,
S.D. 12).

	Mn.	Ia.	N.D.	S.D.	Nb.	Ave.
dip	2%	19%	0%	2%	9%	7%
dressing	13%	12%	13%	10%	16%	13%
sauce	89%	76%	90%	90%	85%	85%

  cream 139.
  dip 14, 22; 114, 124, 130, 133, 135-36,
s137-38, 139, 141, :142, 144-46, 148;
204; ¹⸸*311, †320; 406, †428, 429, 433.
  dope ¹†324.

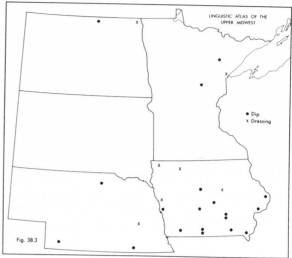

Fig. 38.3

dressing 17, 56; 101, 104, 111, 116;
207; ?306; 424.
  goo !221. goof 427. goop 416.
  pudding gravy *208.
  sauce 1-8, :*9, 10-15, 18, 20-22, sn23,
:24, ?:25, 26, :sn27, 28, :s29, :30, 32-
34, c35, *36, 37, 39, :†40, *41, 42-46,
c47, 48, sn49, sn50, 51, f52, 53-55,
r56, 57-65; 102, s104, 105-6, s107, 110,
112-13, 115-21, 123, :125, *126, 127-28,
130-31, 133-34, s136, 138, 140, 143-45,
148-49; 201-3, 205, sn207, 208-12, c214,
215-17, :218, 219-20, 222-26; 301, s302,
303-5, *306, 308-10, *311, 312-15, 320-
25, 327-28; 401-4, *405, 406, :sn407,
408-11, 413-14, c416, 417-23, sn424, 428,
431, 436-37. hard ~ 109, *122. pudding ~
31; 103; 213; 317, 319, 326; 426. sweet
~ 137. white ~ 315.
  syrup †16; 108, 117, 136, 145; 305,
c306, c316.
  no response 19, ?38; 129, 132, 147,
150-52; ?206; 307; 412, 415, 425, 430,
432, 434-35.
Comment:

  cream: A combination of cream and sugar
used over pudding. dip: Old word--139.
Used by inf.'s mother-in-law--311. Inf.
says a roundup cook would use this, too--
320. On ice cream--406. This term is from
her husband's mother; "We always call it
that"--14. Of sugar, flour, spice, and
salt--428. dope: Inf. says this is a
man's term--324. dressing: On pudding,
but 'sauce' on fruit cake--424. goop:
Inf.'s term for chocolate syrup only--416.
syrup: Used by inf.'s mother--16.

38.4 a bite (food eaten between meals).
NE 314. WG 14, 26, 32, 39, 71-72; F127.

  For food taken between regular meals

the generic lunch is found in both the East and the UM, with a semantic range from the most casual situation to the informal. In the UM it exhibits a slight Northern preponderance, perhaps because of the early decline of Northern bite. As a term for a light noon meal lunch is still common, but in the sense cited here its use in the UM is threatened, a circumstance revealed in the number of infs. who consider it old-fashioned if not already disused. The cause is not that eating between meals is going out of fashion; people have adopted another name for the practice.

With this meaning, three regional terms, bite, piece, and snack, broadly represent the Northern, Midland, and South Midland and Southern speech areas along the Atlantic coast. The extension of snack into megalopolis and even up the Hudson valley from New York city presaged its subsequent expansion into the Northern and Midland speech areas of the UM. It is true that a few infs. report it in New England, but apparently there as a older term, since several so specifically characterize it. But the western expansion of snack is not likely due simply to its being taken westward in the population shift. The use of snack in snack bar became familiar to members of the American armed forces during World War II; snack more recently has been disseminated nationally in advertising of various food products and equipment. The influence of the war and the recency of snack in Northern speech is suggested in the contrast between Wisconsin, with only two recorded occurrences (4%) in 1939, and Minnesota, with 29 occurrences (45%) in 1947-48. Further, 21 of the 96 UM infs. using snack say that it is an innovation they have recently adopted.

Bite, as in "Let's have a bite to eat" or "No, thanks, we had a bite before we left home," is common in New England and New York state but has barely survived in the eastern sector of the UM. No infs. in the Dakotas use it at all. Two of the 10 infs. consider it old-fashioned.

Piece, a Midland word common in Pennsylvania and found also in New York state, still shows some vitality in Iowa and Nebraska. Seven of the 22 infs. attesting it, however, call it an old expression no longer used. Piece probably suffers not only from the popularity of snack but also from the development of the taboo meaning of piece as an act of sexual intercourse.

Smack, an old term for a savory bit to eat, was recorded once in New England, along the Maine coast; but in LANE it

is questioned as probably being an error for snack. It appears four times in the UM, however, once in Ontario, once in eastern South Dakota, and twice in southeastern Nebraska.

Handout, rare in New England, is a singleton in the UM, the occurrence being in the eastern bulge of Iowa. Coffee and tea, in the sense of snack or lunch, appear once each. See also 62.8.

CL 37: The usage of 1,047 respondents conforms generally to the field returns, even to the indication of some Northern bias of lunch, especially in Iowa, where northern Iowa has 81% and southern Iowa only 53%.

	Mn.	Ia.	N.D.	S.D.	Nb.	Ave.
bite	3%	5%	6%	6%	9%	6%
lunch	88%	68%	91%	91%	76%	82%
piece	1%	21%	2%	3%	14%	9%
snack	19%	17%	14%	17%	27%	19%

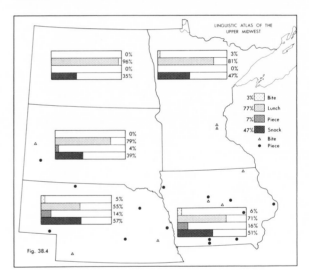

Fig. 38.4

bit 309.
bite sn36, 37, snↇ38; 107, 115, 132; ↇ222; 309; 426, c429.
coffee 30.
handout 139.
lunch 1-2, 4-7, 9-20, ↇ21, 23-27, 29-30, ↇ31, 34, 36-37, 41-45, cr46, 47-56, c57, 58, c!59, 60-62, c63, 65; 101-7, 109, 111-13, 115-20, 124-29, 132-34, 137-38, 140-43, 147-49; 201-2, c203, 204-5, 207-11, c212, 213-23, c224, 225-26; 301-8, 310-11, 313-18, ↇ320, 321-25, 327, ↇ328; 401-5, 407-8, 412-18, ↇ419, 420-23, cvr427, ↇ428, 429, 432-35, ↇ437.
piece ↇ103, 109, 114, 118, 137, 139, sn144, 145-46; ↇ215; 312, ↇ326; 403, ↇ406, ↇ411, ↀ414, 415, ↇ416, ↇ419, c422, 428, 436.
smack 3; 317; 422, 427.

snack 2, →¹5, 9-12, 14, 17-18, 20, →21, 22, 24-26, 28, ¹29, →31, 32-34, →35, 37-40, 42, !?46, 49, →¹51, 57-58, 62, 64; 101, 105-6, 108, 110-11, 114, 116, s117, sn120, 121-25, 127-28, 130-31, 133, 135-36, ¹139, 141, 146, 148-49; 202, 206, →¹207, 213, →214-15, 217-19, †220, 221; 304, →309-10, →¹311, →312, ¹314, 318-19, →320-21, 324, →326, →328; ¹†403, →404, →406, 409-10, →411, ¹413, 414, →419, 420-21, 423-26, 428-31, s432, 433, ¹434, 435-36, →437.

 tea 201.

 no response 8; 150-52.

Comment:

 bite: At night--37; 426. Less food than a 'lunch'--115. Used by inf. in youth--38; 222. Suggested by inf.'s daughter as her usual term and confirmed by inf.--36. lunch: Any time between meals--5; 323, 325; 413, 416, 435. Afternoon--9-10, 25; 221; 318, 324. At night--414, 428. Eaten sitting down--318. Inf. thinks this is a country expression--209. Usu.--11-12; 421. piece: More food than a 'lunch'--415. Used as a noun and a verb--118, 144. Used as a verb--414, 419, 422, 428, 436. Used by inf.'s mother (from Vt.) as a verb--215. Used by inf. in youth--306; 411, 416. "Older than 'lunch'"--137. smack: At night--317; 422, 427. snack: Any time between meals--33-34; 318; 423-24, 426, 435. At night--2, 5, 9-10, 24-25, 37, 42; 217-19, 221; 324; 420-21, 433. Eaten standing up--318. Less food than a lunch--20, 26, 34, 49; 215; 304; 423. Inf. heard this used by a German family--139. Inf. heard this used by people from Mo.--403. "Society calls it a 'snack'--220. Usu.--62. tea: In the afternoon--201.

38.7 I'm going to make some coffee. NE 310.

 Expressions for preparing coffee were usually obtained in such a context as "(I'm going to) make some coffee," although fieldworkers P and Wr ordinarily recorded only the verb and some infs. offered different contexts.

 The dominance of make is consistent with its status in New England. Four of 5 UM infs. use it in one context or another. But its UM dominance has been challenged by cook, a cognate translation from either the German or Scandinavian population. Not found in New England but reported directly 3 times in the Wisconsin survey, cook is recorded as the usage of 9 UM infs. of Swedish parentage, 4 of German, and 3 of Norwegian, altogether more than one-half the total of

28. The use of cook by the remaining 7 attests some acceptance by the general English-speaking community, although such acceptance does not appear to have occurred widely outside Minnesota.

 Brew, a minor variant in New England, remains minor in the UM, where a scattered few infs. in South Dakota and Nebraska use it. Four Minnesotans, in addition, report having heard others say it.

 Fix, listed only once in LANE, is, as the accompanying map shows, slightly more popular in the UM, where it is scattered in the northeast quadrant and in Nebraska but not in Iowa and most of South Dakota.

 Drip, a singleton in St. Paul, refers to the special process of preparing coffee by allowing hot water to drip through the grounds.

 Put on, not in New England, turns up once each in Minnesota and Nebraska.

 Heat, hot up, and warm up, though occ. recorded, refer to the act of reheating coffee rather than to making fresh coffee.

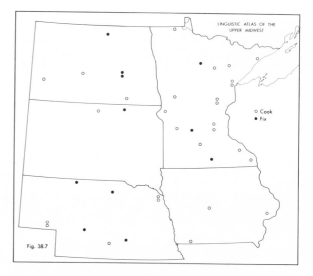

Fig. 38.7

 boil 13, 18, 35, †40, 48; 135; †221; 303, 314, 319; 421.
 brew ¹12, ¹17, ¹39; ¹128; 311, 320; →401, 422.
 cook 4, 6, ¹11, 12, 14, 16-17, 20, 23-24, c25, ¹26, 32, 34, ¹39-40, 41, ¹47, 51, 55, 58; 128, †137, 140, 143; c214, ¹215, 216, 224; ¹225; cr303; 407, *408, 417, 430, 436.
 drip 37.
 fix c10, *43, 62; 205, 218-19; 305; 403, 406, 419, 423.
 heat 48, 58.
 hot up 45.

make 1-3, 5, 7-9, c10, 11, [1]12, 13-16, 18-19, 21-22, 25-31, 33,[1]34, 36-39, *41, 42, 44-47, 49-50, 53-54, 56-57, 59-61, [1]62, 63-65; 101-25, 127-34, 136-49; 201, c202-3, 204, 206-12, c213-14, 215, 217, 220-23, *225, 226; c301, 302, 304-5, *306, 307-9, c310, 312-13, 315-18, 321-23, !324, 325-28; 401-5, 408-16, 418-19, 421, 424-29, 431-35, 437.

put on !52; 419.
warm up 43, 59.
no response 126, 150-52; 420.

Additional equivalent expressions recorded, not always sytematically, are these:

bring a spot of coffee (used by inf.'s wife, with reference to instant coffee)--409.

cook a pot of coffee--58.
fix a cup of coffee--219.
get a cup of coffee--328.
make a cup of coffee--26, 31, 44, 56, 63-64; 139; 310; 411, 413, 429.
make (you) a cup of tea--201.
make a little coffee--302.
make a pot of coffee--53; 112; 322; 401.
make tea--213.
put on some coffee--419.
put on the coffee--32.

For the omission of the determiner in make (cook, fix) coffee see Volume 2.

Comment:

boil: Used by inf.'s mother--40. cook: common here--11. Used by a Swedish friend--26. "Swedes and Germans say this" --40. Inf. says this is used by local Norwegians--47. Inf. says this is used by local Scandinavians--215. Inf. considers this the "proper" term--55. "I don't like to cook coffee every time I want it, so I keep it in a thermos bottle"--214. make: Used by inf.'s wife--12, 34, 62.

38.8 deep (apple) pie. NE 292. WG 20, 23.

Despite the lack of evidence for Minnesota, where this item was not sought, the data collected reveal a clear Northern and Midland contrast in the orientation of the two principal terms as well as the feeble survival of several Eastern regional minor variants.

For an apple pie with a thick upper crust and no bottom crust, steamed or baked in a pot or crock, the UM term with Midland orientation is (apple) cobbler and that with Northern orientation is deep apple pie, with its variants deep-dish apple pie and deep-dish pie. Cobbler,

recorded only twice in New England, apparently moved west with the Midland wave, for it is strongest in Iowa and Nebraska and less so in the Dakotas. The deep pie terms, found in southern New England, are consistently strongest in North Dakota and weakest in Iowa.

Apple pudding and apple dumpling are common New England terms which, however, only barely survive in the UM. Pudding occurs five times in northern Iowa and in six scattered communities elsewhere but not at all in the western fringe. Dumpling is the usage of 4 infs. in southern Iowa and of one North Dakotan of Vermont parentage.

Other expressions faintly echo eastern origins. One Nebraskan of New York parentage offers apple grunt, a localism in the Plymouth and Cape Cod area of Massachusetts. Apple John and apple Jonathan, restricted in LANE to Long Island Sound and secondary settlements in the Berkshires, is the usage of one North Dakotan of European parentage and of a South Dakotan whose mother came from New York state. Bird's-nest pudding, with 4 instances in New Hampshire not far from the New York state boundary, is the term used by a Des Moines, Iowa, inf. both of whose parents came from New York. Dutch apple pie, not found in New England, seems Midland-based, with one instance in southern Iowa and 3 in Nebraska. The lone occurrence of one-crust pie in the speech of a northern Iowan with Maine parents perhaps reflects its 3 occurrences in New England, one in Connecticut and 2 in the Upper Connecticut valley.

Some terms offered by infs. apparently refer to dishes similar to but not the same as deep apple pie. A combination of sliced apple and bread crumbs, or, sometimes, oatmeal, baked in a pan, is known variously as apple Betty, brown Betty, apple crisp, and apple crust. Apple Betty, reported in LANE from Rhode Island and Maine, is used by one UM inf., a Nebraskan whose mother came from Ohio. Brown Betty, scattered in southern New England, is used also by one UM inf., a Nebraskan with New York state parents. Apple crisp, not found in New England, appears in south central Iowa and apple crust is the term of a supplementary inf. in central Nebraska. Cobblet, not described by the inf., is from a Minneapolis Type I Negro of southern parentage. Rolypoly is offered by an Iowan as the name for a dish with both upper and lower crust and containing cherries, not apples. For the similar dessert with apples she uses cobbler.

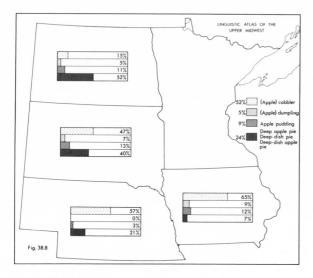

Fig. 38.8

apple Betty 423. ~ cobbler :31; 118, 124, 127, 142, 148; 218; 304, sn317, 321; 404, 412, 414, 422, 428, 434, 436. ~ crisp 134. ~ crust *418. ~ dumpling 135, 142-43; 215. ~ grunt c413. ~ John 210. ~ Jonathan 327. ~ pudding 104, 113-14, 116-17, 149; *207, 224; 316-17; 420.

bird's-nest pudding 116.
brown Betty 413.
cobbler 36; 101-2, 105-6, ¹108, 109-11, 115, 119, ¹120, 121-22, 125, 128-30, 132-33, s¹136, 137-39, 145, *146, 149; 221, 223; :315, 319-20, 326; 401, 403, 406-7, *408, 409, 411, 416, 425, 429.
cobblet 35.
deep apple pie s29; 118, 144; 201-2, 211, 217, 219, 222; 319, 326; 426, 433.
deep-dish apple pie 205, 208, 213-14, 226; *301, 328; 402, †410, 424, 428, *437.
deep-dish pie *30; :123, ¹131; 204; ¹*306, 310, 318; f432.
dumpling 108; 316, 322.
Dutch apple pie 136; 426, 431, 435. ~ pie 431.
one-crust pie 103.
roly-poly 115.
no response 1-28, 32-34, 37, ?38, 39-65; 107, 112, 126, 140-41, 147, 150-52; ?203, 206, ?209, ?212, ?216, 220, 225; ?302, 303, 305, 307-9, ?311, 312-13, ?314, 323-25; 405, 415, 417, 419, 421, 427, 430.

Comment:

cobbler: Baking powder crust--36. Fruit with dough wrapped around it, sewn with string, and steamed--105. = roly-poly, but with peaches or apples. "Peach cobbler is like an apple dumpling but it's made with peaches"--142. Baked with crust on bottom and served upside down--223.

Crust is like cake dough--315. Wrapped like a dumpling--317. Not so thick [as deep apple pie]--326. "Like an upside down cake" but made with pie dough. deep dish apple pie: Mother's term--410. Crust of crumbs or caramelized butter and sugar, etc.--428. Wife's term--436. deep dish pie: Could be with berries or pieplant, too--204. dumpling: Piecrust folded over apples--316. Apples wrapped in dough--317.

39.4 Sit down! Invitation to be seated at table. NE 318.

As in New England, the invitation to be seated for a meal is marked in the UM by a wide variety of expressions in at least three dimensions. One dimension is the contrast between inviting those in one room to move to another for the meal and inviting those already present to sit down. A second dimension ranges from whether the invitation is for guests who are strangers to whether it is for members of the immediate family. A third dimension, which partly overlaps the second, is that between the very formal, as found in "Dinner is served" and the extremely informal, as in "Stick your feet under the table and grab the biscuits." Some locutions are obviously at one extreme or the other, but others, such as "Dinner's ready," occur in both formal and informal situations and with guests as well as with the immediate family. No infs., however, indicated a situation in which the meal is announced formally by a servant.

Since fieldworkers differed in the extent to which they sought varied expressions for different contexts, the responses are not so consistently comprehensive as to allow inferences about regional patterns. Sit down, with its variants, is the most common formula throughout the UM. Sit up, however, is found only in Midland speech territory. The analogous set down and set up reveal social and educational correlation, with 15 of the 21 instances provided by Type I infs., 6 by Type II, and none by Type III. Be seated and its variants may have Northern orientation, as only a few of its occurrences are in the typical Midland area. The single example of Sit ye down is from a Canadian whose father had Scottish ancestry.

Most of the expressions listed below are self-indicative of the situation and of the degree of formality. The supplementary comment provides additional information about the relevance for family or for guests.

be seated 3, 12, 24, 26-27, 39-40; 101-4, 111-12, 116; 201, 210, 215, 217-18, 220; 310, 312, 319; sn433, 434-35. let's ~ 219; 326; 409, 436. now ~ 65. please ~ 24, 31, 37; 113; 426. if you'll please ~ 428. won't you ~? 221. you can ~ now 433.

come and eat 62-63. ~ and get it 9, !51, 58, !61; !¹214; 313, 315, 325, 328; 420, 428. ~ get your feet underneath the table 57. ~ in and have dinner 112. ~ and have dinner 125. will you please ~ now? 20. ~ on 426. ~ on, folks 20. ~ on in to dinner 43. ~ to dinner 2, 45, 53, 59, 62. please ~ to dinner 415. ~ to supper 426. ~ to the table 410, 424.

dinner's ready 5, 32, 44, 46-47, 51, 53, 58, 60, 63; 308, 317; 413-16, 420-23, 427-28, 430. supper's ready 44, 47. dinner's served 46, 49, 61; 413, 428, 431.

draw up 144. ~ a chair 55. ~ your chairs to the table please 48.

eating's bringing ¹47. let's eat 57.

find your place 65.

get up to the table 101. let's get to the table 37.

grab your places 38.

have a chair 319. will you ~ chair? 318. ~ meal 56. ~ seat 427. ~ seat there 316.

hunt up your hole 311.

move up to the table 19. pull up a chair ¹58. put on the feedbag 37. seat yourself for dinner 317.

set down 13, c15, 64; 115, c133, 135, 147; 225; 314, !320; 429. let's all ~ down 425. please ~ down 17. you ~ down c327. come in and ~ down c51. come on in and ~ down 35. ~ in 205. ~ up !52; 124; 305. ~ right up 109.

shall we all sit 20. will you all ~ 42. just ~ anyplace 402. ~ down 1, 7-11, c14, 18, 20, 23, 25, 28-29, 34, 36-38, 41, 48-50, s54, 56-57; 102, 104, 106, 108, 110, 112-14, 117-23, 126-32, 134, 136-42, 145-46, 148-49; 207, 212, 221-23; 310, 312, 315, 318, 321, 325-26; 401, 403, 406, 418. ~ ye down c201. let's ~ down 31; 208; 404, 411, 417, 437. let's all ~ down 436. please ~ down 17. please come and ~ down 2; 203. come and ~ down 4, 32. shall we ~ down? 33. ~ down and eat 306. ~ down and grab 408. ~ down here 22. won't you ~ down here? 208. ~ down to the table 213. please ~ here 21. you ~ here 21; 213. will you ~ here 10. come and ~ here 209. ~ in 202. ~ over 432. you may ~ over here 324. ~ up 45; 105; 324. well, folks, ~ up 422. let's ~ up 301. ~ up now 313. ~ up to the table 143. ~ up and eat 107. if you folks will ~ up, we'll have some dinner 430.

soup's on 37, !60, !62; 315; 416. stick your feet under the table and grab the biscuits 218.

take a chair 56; 311. ~ your places 319. will you ~ your places? 202.

no response 6, 16, 30; 150-52; 204, 206, 211, 216, 224, ?226; 302-4, 307, 309, 322.

Comment:

be seated: Formal or said to guests--101-3; 310, 312, 319. please be seated: Formal or said to guests--31, 37; 426. come and eat: Informal--62. come and get it: Said to family--325; 420. come on: Said to family--426. come on folks: Said to family--20. come to dinner: Said to family--20. please come to dinner: Said to guests--415. will you please come now?: Formal--20. come to supper: Said to family--426. dinner's ready: Formal or said to guests--420, 423. Informal or said to family--317; 413, 415, 422-23, 430. dinner's served: Formal or said to guests--49; 413. eating's bringing: Inf. says this is Scottish--47. find your places: Inf. says this is more formal than 'now be seated'--65. let's get to the table: Informal--37. have a chair: Said to guests--319. will you have a chair?: Said to guests--318. seat yourself for dinner: Said to guests--317. sit down: Informal or said to family--37, 49; 221; 310, 318, 325-26. Said to guests--108, 110. sit ye down: Said in conversation to fieldworker--201. let's sit down: Informal--31. please come and sit down: Formal--2. sit down to the table: Informal--213. you sit here: Said to guests--21; 213. will you sit here: Formal--10. you may sit over here: Said to guests--324. sit in: Said to family--202. sit up: Said to family--324. if you folks will sit up we'll have some dinner: Said to guests--430. well, folks, sit up: Said to guests--422. take your places: Said to family--319. will you take your places: Formal--202.

39.6 Help yourself to potatoes. NE 319.

The expression sought is the invitation of the host or person at the head of the table for everyone to help himself to potatoes or whatever else is being passed from hand to hand. Because fieldworkers A and M treated this as a phonological item, however, expressions with terms other than help yourself were recorded in only part of the UM.

Most of these other expressions incorporate have either in the imperative Have some or in the polite *Will you have some?*

do you care for 317.

have a 317. ~ some 53, *60; 101, 110, 126, 133, 137; 428. ~ some more 107-8; 422, 427. ~ some of this 45. you ~ some of this 56. will you ~ some? 59. won't you ~ some more? 423, 431. won't you please ~ some? 47. would you ~ more? 414.

help yourself 1-24, :!25, 26-45, !46, 48-55, 57-58, 60-64, ¹65; 102-6, 108-9, 111-25, 127-32, 134-36, 138-49; 202, c203, 204-26; 301-10, c311, 312-13, 315-19, c320, 321-26, 328; 401-3, 405-12, 417-19, 424-25, 429, 432-37. ~ to 421. ~ to the 413, 416, 420. ~ to more 430. ~ to some 415, 423. please ~ to 426.

pitch in 317; 404.

serve yourself 201.

take a helping 314. ~ some 127. ~ some more 107.

would you try this? 51.

no response 150-52; 327.

Comment:

help yourself: "Down South they say, 'What can I help you to?'"--6. Inf. says this is common, "But I wouldn't say that. We passed everything"--65.

39.7 I don't care for any (when declining food). NE 320.

In declining food proffered at the table most UM infs., like those in New England, use an expression that negates the word care. A greater degree of politeness appears when the expression is preceded by thank you or no thank you and when wouldn't is used rather than don't.

A few infs., but in smaller proportion than in New England, use wish instead of care. It is felt to be less blunt than care, and both are considered less blunt than the infrequent want.

No regional differences appear, unless it can be inferred that the simple no thank you has Northern orientation, and that I wouldn't care for any has Midland orientation.

Some infs. volunteer also their response when they are rejecting an additional serving. I've had plenty, with some variation, is the typical expression, made politer when prefaced by no thank you.

I don't care for any 2, 5-6, 8-10, 20, 22-24, 26, 28, 31, 33-34, 37-38, c39, 40-41, 43, 48-50, 52, s54, s56, 61, 64; 101-4, 106-7, 109-11, 115, 117-23, 125-26, 129-30, 133-40, 142, 147-48, s149; 202-6, 210-11, 213, 215, 217-18, 222, 224, 226; 301-4, 307, :310, 319, 321, 323-26, 328; 401, 403, 411-12, 415, 418, 424-26, 428, 432-33, 435-37. no thank you, I don't ~ for any 58; 423. thanks, I don't ~ for any 53. I don't believe I ~ for any 57; 314. I don't ~ for any more 32, 65; 105, 108, 114; 214; 306. I don't ~ for any of that 429. I don't ~ for it 1, 3, 7, 11-12, 21, 27, 42, 45; 143, 146; 207-9, 212, 216, 219-20, 225; 315; 402, 405-7, 419. no thanks, I don't ~ for it 404. I just don't ~ for it 320. I don't ~ for more 116. I don't ~ for none 132. I don't ~ for some 112; 203; 408. I don't ~ for this 30; 322. I wouldn't ~ for any sn118, 124, 127, 145; 313; 410, 434. I wouldn't ~ for more 141. I wouldn't ~ for that 417. I don't believe I'd ~ for that 221.

I don't choose ¹16. no thanks, I don't eat it 311. I don't feel hungry 32. I'm not hungry 52.

I don't think I'll have any 4. I don't think I want any 36. I don't want any more 305.

I don't wish any 144. I don't ~ for any 9, 34; 106, 145; 223; 409. I don't believe I ~ for any 57. I don't ~ any more 113, 128. I don't ~ for any more 55. I don't ~ it 201. I don't ~ for it 25.

I've had enough 47. I've had plenty 131; 317-18. I have plenty 316. no thanks, I've had plenty 416. no thank you, I have plenty 427. thanks, I had plenty 430. thank you, I've had plenty 414. thank you, I have a great plenty 413.

no thanks c51, 59, 63; 309. no thanks please 422. no thank you 14-15, 17-18, c39, 43-44, 46, !47, 51, 60-62; 119; 308, 312; 431. thank you 56.

no response 13, 19; 150-52; 327.

Comment:

no thank you: "I wouldn't say I didn't care for it"--312.

40.1 warmed over food. NE 313.

Although food that is reheated to be served at a later meal, as on the following day, is designated as warmed up or warmed over in nearly equal proportion in both New England and the UM, the distribution of warmed up in the UM is heavier in the Northern area and that of warmed over is heavier in the Midland area. No marked variation by social types appears.

A minor variant with heat is used by a few speakers, much less frequently than in New England. Only 2 infs., both Type I, use het as the preterit or participle of heat.

A few infs. volunteered leftover as an equivalent, although it does not directly refer to reheating: 44, 47, 52, ¹53, 60.

Others offered the noun leftovers: 48, 52; 122, 140-41; 308, 317, *318, 319. Neither of these was systematically recorded.

CL 32: Northern and Midland weighting of warmed up and warmed over is indicated also in the usage of 1,048 respondents.

	Mn.	Ia.	N.D.	S.D.	Nb.	Ave.
warmed up	62%	49%	62%	61%	63%	59%
warmed over	35%	52%	39%	39%	45%	42%

cooked over 57.
heated over 52; 121. ~ up 18; 120; 423, 426.
het over 135. ~ up c311.
leftovers 140-41; 308, 317, *318, 319.
reheated 14, 58; 421.
warmed over 3, 8-12, 14, 16, 22, 27, 30, 32-34, 42, ⌐43, 44, 48, 51, 54, 56, *60, 61-62, 64-65; 102, 104, 106-12,

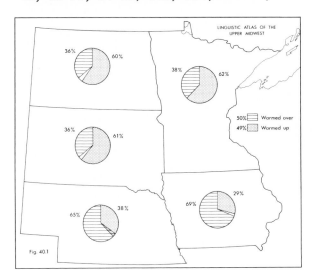

Fig. 40.1

LINGUISTIC ATLAS OF THE UPPER MIDWEST

50% Warmed over
49% Warmed up

:s⌐117, 118-20, 122-33, 136-38, 142-43, 145-49; 201, 203, 207, 212-13, 215, 222, 224-25; 301, 303, 305, 307, :309, c311, 312, ⌐313, 319, 321, 327; 402-3, 406, 408-10, 412-14, 418-22, !423, 426, 429-36, s437. ~ up 1-2, 4-7, 13, 15, 17, 19-21, 23-26, 28-29, 31-32, :s35, 36-41, 43, 45, !46, 47-50, 53, c55, 57, 59, *60, 63, c65; 101, 103, 105, 108, 113-17, 133-34, 139, 144, *146; 202, 204-5, 208-9, !210, 211, 214, 216-19, sn220, 221, 223, †226; 302, 304, 306, 310, 313-18, 320, 322-26, 328; 401, 404-5, 407, 409, 411, 415-16, !417, 424-25, 427-28, 433.
no response 150-52; 206.

Comment:

heated up: Food is 'heated up' for a person late for a meal but 'warmed over' from an earlier meal--426. warmed over: Inf. says 'warmed over' rolls or bis-

cuits, but 'warmed up' potatoes and other vegetables--409. Inf. says 'warmed over' for all food but a roast, which is 'heated up'--423. warmed up: Used by inf.'s mother (from Mich.)--226.

40.3 mush. NE 288. WG 17, 24; F2, F13.

For the peculiarly American pudding or porridge made of cornmeal the two terms hasty pudding and Indian pudding became common in New England and mush became general in the Midland and the South, with some extension, according to the WG, into the secondary New England settlement area and into the Hudson valley.

In the UM mush, sometimes corn mush or cornmeal mush, so much more extended its influence that it quite dominates all five states. A number of infs. volunteer the expression fried mush to designate how leftover mush is utilized.

Kurath's description of hasty pudding as rare west of the Hudson is apt for the UM, where two of the five occurrences are actually the recalled usage of parents with eastern background. Indian pudding appears once, in the conversation of a southwestern Minnesota housewife whose father was born in Quebec and whose mother came from Michigan. Two Canadian infs. use (cornmeal) porridge; two infs. use gruel, a New England minor variant; and one inf. has graham mush, apparently a term for mush made with graham meal rather than with cornmeal.

In the southern part of the Midland speech area, that is, in southern Iowa and Nebraska, many infs. supply hominy or lye hominy as the name of a similar dish made from kernels of corn from which the bran and germ have been removed by being soaked in a lye bath.

gruel 145; 319.
hasty pudding †103, 141; sn†317, †324; 420.
hominy 115, 117, 124, 136, 147-49; 403, 413-14, 416, 420, 423-28, 430-35. lye ~ 132, 138-39, *146.
Indian pudding c46.
mush 2-4, c5, 6, 8-12, 14, c20, 21-23, c23, 24-26, !27, 28-39, c40, 41-42, ?⌐43, 44-45, 47, 49-51, 54, c55, 56, c57, 59, 61-62, 64-65; 101-11, 113-22, 124-37, 139, 141-46; 203-7, *208, 209-10, c211, 212-17, c218-19, 220-21, c222, 223-26; 301-2, !303, 304, 306-7, c309-10, 311-12, c313-15, 316-18, c320, 321, c322-26, 328; 401-2, cvr403-4, 405-8, 410-13, c414, 416-18, c419, 420, c422, 423-25, 427, c428, 429, sn430, 431, c432, 433-37. corn ~ 15-16, 52, 60; 112, 123, 138, 147-48; 421. cornmeal ~ 13-16, c46, 53, 63; 149; 305, 308, c319; 426. graham ~ 418.

porridge 1, 18; 202; 426. cornmeal ~
201.
no response 7, 17, ?19, 48, 58; 140,
150-52; 327; 409, 415.
Comment:

hasty pudding: Used by inf.'s mother
(from Ma.)--317, (from Il.)--324. mush:
Sunday night supper, with milk; left
over for breakfast, fried, eaten with
butter and/or syrup--103. Served with
cream or milk and sugar--105, 107-8, 127.
Never heard of mush--58. corn mush: Usually for supper--147. fried mush: "Fried
the next morning"--105, 124, 127, 143,
147; 306, 317-19; 404, 416, 425. fried
cornmeal mush--308. graham mush: A Swedish
dish--418. hominy: The main course--117,
147. Dessert--*146.

40.4 homegrown vegetables. NE 253.

For vegetables grown at home for family
consumption the simple term vegetables,
with occasional more specific garden vegetables and homegrown vegetables is common
in New England along with less frequent
but widely distributed garden sauce,
garden stuff, and garden truck. The situation is similar in the UM, except that
vegetables is even more common and that
some distribution differences appear with
the minor variants.
In the UM vegetables, as the simple
form or in a phrase, is actually used by
nearly all infs., some of whom have it
as an alternate expression. Only a handful did not offer it at all: Mn. 3, Ia.
2, N.D. 3, S.D. 3, and Nb. 4.
Of the minor variants garden stuff has
greater vitality, with several occurrences
in all states but Iowa, where there is
only one. (Garden) truck is still active
in the western fringe, and (garden) sauce
or sass is the choice of 3 infs., one in
Iowa and 2 in the western fringe. Neither
sauce nor truck is known to younger infs.

garden stuff 7, c25, c33, 50, 56; 130;
215, 218, 223; 304, :313, ¹323-24, 325,
¹326; c405, sn408, 411, 417, 420, 422,
c430.
sass !127; ¹414. garden ~ sn✝65; ¹103;
✝133; 311; 410.
truck 320; 409. garden ~ 15, s✝31; 130;
c214; 302; 401, 436.
vegetables 1-2, c3-4, 5-12, c13, 14, 16,
c17, 18, c19, 20-28, 30-32, c35, 36-40,
c41, 42-49, 51-55, 57-65; 101-6, 108,
c109, 110-19, 121-37, 139, 142-49; 201-5,
c206, 207-13, 216-17, 219-26; 301-3, 305-
7, 309-10, 312-19, 321-26, c327; 401-8,
410-21, 423-29, c430, 431-35, 437. garden
~ 34, s56; 107; 328. green ~ 139. home-

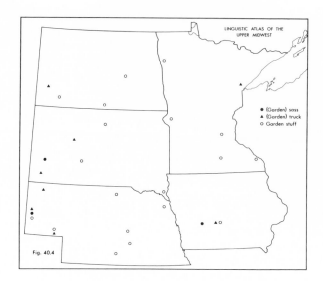

Fig. 40.4

grown vegetables 34; 120, 140, s141; 308.
no response 29; 150-52.

Comment:

garden sass: Used by inf.'s grandmother
(from Oh.)--65. Inf. thinks she has
heard this used by a family that moved
here from Ky.--103. Used by inf.'s grand-
father--133. Inf. says she would say
this to her mother and aunt (from Wi.)--
410. garden stuff: Inf. says this is the
usual local term--223.

40.5 vegetable garden (for home use).
NE 121.

As in New England, garden and vegetable
garden are the most common terms for a
small plot of ground where vegetables are
grown for home consumption. But in the
UM vegetable garden exhibits a sharp
Northern distribution pattern in northern
Iowa, Minnesota, and North Dakota, although it does not occur in the more recently settled Northern speech portions--
northern Minnesota and western North Dakota. For speakers who use vegetable
garden the simplex garden often denotes
a plot for flowers. Conversely, for many
speakers who use simple garden for vegetables the plot for flowers must be
especially marked by the descriptive
flower.
Rare variants, having no regional patterns except that the truck forms are in
Midland speech territory, include terms
with patch, plot, and spot.
CL 51: Returns from 1,052 respondents
correspond with fieldwork records, garden
being common in all states and vegetable
garden having an identical 18% over-all

frequency in both sets of data. <u>Vegetable garden</u> has a frequency in Minnesota of 26% and in southern Iowa of only 13%, and its Northern bias is suggested also by a 23% frequency in North Dakota and only 9% in South Dakota; but discrepancy appears with a 26% return in Nebraska. A higher incidence of <u>garden patch</u> marks the checklists, where it was checked by 84 respondents, or 8%.

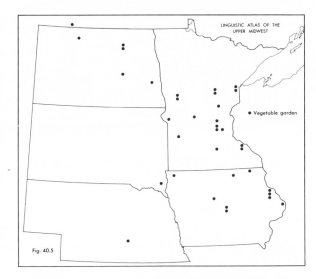

Fig. 40.5

LINGUISTIC ATLAS OF THE UPPER MIDWEST

• Vegetable garden

garden c1, 2-12, c13, 14, c15-16, c17, 18, 20, 22-25, 27, 30, 32-33, c35, 36, 38-41, 43-49, c50, 51-53, 56-62, c63, 64-65; 101, 103-4, 108, c109, 110-13, 115-18, 122-31, 134-38, 140-49; 201-2, 204-12, 214-18, c219, 220-21, 223-26; 301-7, 309-19, 321, c322, 323-26, c327, 328; 401-4, 406-37.
  garden patch 308.
  garden plot 308.
  garden spot c405.
  kitchen garden 28, 37; 116.
  truck garden 320.
  truck patch ¹*134, 136.
  vegetable garden 17-22, 24, 26, 28, 31, 33-34, 37, 42, 49, 54-55; 102, 105-7, 114, 119-21, 132-33, 139; 201, 203, 212-13, 218, 222; 324; c422.
  no response 29; 150-52.

Comment:
  garden: Usu.--116; 218. Inf. says the other kind is a 'flower garden'--2, 5-6, 11, 18, 24, 36, 38, 46-48, 53, 60-61, 63, 65; 205, 218, 223, 226; 401, 411, 413-16, 420-28, 432-35. Inf. says the other kind is a 'flower garden' or 'flower bed'--224. Inf. says the other kind is a 'flower garden' or 'flower border'--431. Inf. says the other kind is a 'flower bed'--225; 430. Contains vegetables and/or flowers--3, 10-11, 33; 225; 302, 327-28.

kitchen garden: Inf. says that 'garden' by itself suggests flowers--28. A newer term than 'garden'; inf. says she learned it from magazines--116. truck patch: Inf. says this is where one grows tomatoes, corn, and other vegetables that need more space--136. vegetable garden: Usu.--20. "But it has flowers, too"--21. Inf. says that a 'garden' might have either flowers or vegetables--33. Inf. says the other kind is a 'flower garden'--222.

40.6 <u>genuine maple syrup</u>. NE 308.

Intended to elicit the pronunciation of <u>genuine</u> and <u>syrup</u>, this item revealed also that for a number of infs. two terms other than <u>genuine</u> would normally be used in this context. From them <u>genuine</u> was obtained in other situations (see Volume 2).

Only in decidedly Northern speech territory is <u>genuine</u> more than a rarity. In all states but Minnesota it is less frequent than <u>pure</u>, and even <u>real</u> has scattered instances throughout the UM.

	Mn.	Ia.	N.D.	S.D.	Nb.	Ave.
genuine m.s.	38%	23%	16%	9%	8%	22%
pure m.s.	35%	21%	54%	60%	54%	42%
real m.s.	8%	13%	8%	9%	5%	8%

  genuine 6, 19, s20, 24, 26-28, 33, 34, 39-41, 48-50, 54, c55, 56, 62-65; 102, 105-6, 112, 119-21, 132, 141, 148-49; 206, s220, 221, c222; 302-3; 402-3, 433.
  pure 1-5, 8, 11-12, 20-23, 29-30, 32, 37-38, 58; 101, 103, 107, 110-11, 113-14, 116, 138, 147; 201-2, 205, 207, 209-13, c214, 215-20, 223-24, 226; 301-2, 309-10, 312-13, 315, 320-24, 326, 328; 401-6, c409, 410-12, 417-19, 423, 426, 429, 434-37.
  real 7, 16, 31, 33, 36; 104, 108, 115-16, 133, 137; 208, 211; 306, 326; 415, 422.

41.5 <u>What's that?</u> (when failing to hear an utterance). NE 594.

An oral indication that the listener had not heard or understood the speaker occurred typically in the restricted social context of the interview, so that the replies do not represent the full social range with respect either to class variation or to personal variation caused by adjustment to the temper of an occasion. Furthermore, except for a few scattered instances, only fieldworkers A and M recorded the interjectional queries that include the colloquial nasals <u>Hm?</u> and <u>Huh?</u>

Only one of the interjectional queries is clearly regional, the Canadian <u>Ey?</u>, which an American immigration officer described to fieldworker as useful in determining whether a person seeking to enter the United States is American or Canadian.

Hanh? is used by the two infs. in Minnesota with a French-speaking background.

Of the syntactic queries only How?, with Northern distribution mostly in Minnesota, and How's that?, with Midland distribution, indicate regional correlation. No such correlation appears with the varieties of the What? and Beg your pardon? queries.

All interjectional and syntactic queries, including the Pardon? variations, are characterized by the rising pitch pattern from pitch level 2 to pitch level 3, that is, from normal to high.

A few infs. indicate the need for repetition by a statement that they had not heard or understood or by a request such as Please repeat.

Come again? c9. I'm sorry c48.
I beg your pardon? c45; c201, c219. Beg your pardon? c34; c310. Beg pardon? c23, 53, 60-61; 127, 131; c214; c310; 408, 425, c435. Pardon? c3; c145; c202; 319, 324; 409, c419, 420, c423, c433. Pardon me? 18, ¹62; c413, c424.
I didn't get that c39. I didn't get what you said 103. I didn't just get that 146. I didn't quite get that c32. I don't get your drift c311.
I didn't hear you 43, 51, c53; 110-11. I didn't hear what you said c53. Please, I didn't hear what you said 48.
I didn't understand 51; 139. I don't understand 61; 317.
How? c10, c16, c25, c32, c36, c43, c52, c56, c65; 118, s133; c208, c209; c417, 421. How's that? c15, c21, 44; 106, 124, 132, 135, 138, 147-49; c216; c301, c311; c421, c427. How's that again? c311.
Repeat what you said 46. Please repeat that 32. Please repeat c434.
Say it over again c46. Sir? 37; c142; 425, 435. Speak it again? 59.
What did you say? 6, 28, 40, 58; 105, 112, 114, 119-21, 137, 139; 305, 307, 315, 316, c325; c430. What the hell did you say? 57. What say? c118. What? c1, c5, c11, 28, c38, *43, c!45, c47, c59; 102, 109, 113, 122-23, 128-30, s133, 134, 136, 141, c142, 143, c144; c210, c226; c301, c302, c306, 315-16, 318; c401, 409, c415, c416, 422, 426-27, c430, c432, c433. What is it? c327; c428. What was it? c401. What was that? c14, 15, 63; 101, 115; c203, c211; c320. What is that? 42. What's that? c13, 18, 26, 50, 62; 104, 108, 116, 126; c210; c308, c312; c412, c418. What's this? c49.

Which? c427. The which? c17.
eh? [ʔə‵ 'ɛ̃ɡ̊] 220. [ɛh] !319.
ey? [ɛ^ə^ʔ] 201.
hah? [hæɛ] c25, c59.
hanh? [hæ̃] c7, c21, c36; 432.
hey? [hẽʔ] c15.
hm? [mm?] c1, c11, c17, c24, c27, c33; c202, c²15-16; c301, c303, c309, c311, c314, c320; c406, c414, c427, c429.
huh? [ʌ̃ʌ̃ʔ] c314; [hʌ̃ʔ] c16, c43, !45, 54, c59;°c416, c423, c427.
no response 2, 4, 8, 12, 19-20, 22, 29-31, 35, 41, 64; 107,117, 125, 140, 150-52; 204-7, 212-13, 217-18, 221-25; 304, 313, 321-23, 326, 328; 402-5, 407, 410-11, 431, 436-37.

Comment:

hanh?: Said to husband--432.

42.1 Seed (of a cherry). NE 269.

In the UM three terms dominate the responses to "What do you call the hard kernel of a cherry?" -- pit, seed, and stone. Only the first and third of these were found in any frequency in New England, where pit is more frequent in the southwest and stone elsewhere. Seed occurred three times in the Upper Connecticut valley and once in the Berkshires.

Pit not only correspondingly dominates all the UM but appears to be gaining in popularity, since the proportion increases from 69% in Type I, through 83% in Type II, to 94% in Type III.

Stone, a UM minority form clearly Northern with two-thirds of its occurrences in Minnesota (though with five in the South Midland region of Iowa), seems conversely to be on the wane. Its 22% frequency among old-fashioned speakers contrasts with a frequency of only 12% among the middle-aged. Yet four of the Type III infs., 27%, use this term.

Seed apparently has been introduced by Midland and South Midland speakers into the UM, where its limitation to the three southwestern states unquestionably reflects its origin. Only one instance of seed appeared in the Wisconsin survey.

	Mn.	Ia.	N.D.	S.D.	Nb.	Ave.
pit	71%	82%	85%	74%	78%	77%
seed	5%	27%	4%	30%	22%	16%
stone	37%	10%	19%	4%	5%	18%

CL 45: The 1,054 mail respondents are in fairly close agreement with the field infs., both in proportion and in distribution of the various forms.

	Mn.	Ia.	N.D.	S.D.	Nb.	Ave.
pit	65%	64%	74%	80%	80%	71%
seed	12%	34%	15%	19%	24%	21%
stone	31%	7%	17%	6%	4%	13%

heart 57.
kernel *48; 310.
pit 2-5, 8-10, ¹11, 12, 14, 18, 20-23, 26-34, 37-38, ¹39, 40-47, 49-51, 53-56, 58-62, 65; 101-17, 119-28, 130-33, 137-39, 141-45, 149; 201-5, 208-11, cr212, 213-15, 217-19, 221-26; 301-4, 308-9, 311-20, ¹321, 323, ¹324-25, 326-28; 401-10, 413-14, 416, 418-20, 422-26, 428-29, 431-36.
seed 11, ¹21, 24, 35; 113, 118, 127, 129, 134-36, 138, 142, 145-46, 148-49; 220; 302, 305-6, 316, 321-22, 324-25; ¹403, 411-12, ¹413, 417, ¹418, 421, 427, 430, 435, 437.
stone 1, 6-7, ¹12, 13-17, 19, 25, ¹29, 30, 32, 34, 36-37, 39, 48, 52-53, r57, 58, ¹59, ¹60, 61, c63, 64; 138, 140, 143, 146-47; 206-7, ?212, 216, 222, 224, ¹225; 309, ¹325; ¹413, 415, 426, †428.
no response 150-52; 307.

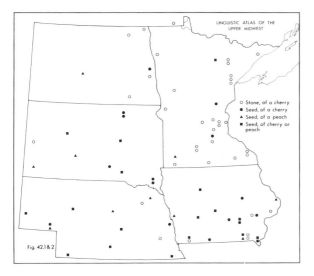

LINGUISTIC ATLAS OF THE UPPER MIDWEST

○ Stone, of a cherry
● Seed, of a cherry
▲ Seed, of a peach
■ Seed, of cherry or peach

Fig. 42.1 & 2

42.2 <u>stone</u> (of a peach).   NE 268.

For the hard kernel of a peach the UM has the same terms as for that in a cherry (see 42.1). They also appear in essentially the same distribution patterns, although not in the same proportions.

<u>Pit</u>, which in New England is more frequent in the southwest, is quite evenly spread throughout the UM, being favored by one-third to one-half of all speakers of all types.

<u>Stone</u>, in contrast with its use for the center of a cherry, is a majority form in Minnesota, Iowa, and Minnesota, and nearly that in South Dakota and Nebraska.

<u>Seed</u>, which in New England was found only twice in Maine and once in northern Vermont, again sharply reflects its Midland and South Midland origin by its frequency in southern Iowa, Nebraska, and

southern South Dakota. It is the usage of only one northern Minnesota informant, whose father came from Maine. One instance occurred in the Wisconsin survey.

CL 46: The distribution proportions found in the forms used by 1,053 respondents generally support those revealed in the fieldwork, although <u>pit</u> has a slightly higher over-all frequency. The background of <u>seed</u> is sharply suggested by its 58% frequency in southern Iowa in contrast with only 9% in northern Iowa.

	Mn.	Ia.	N.D.	S.D.	Nb.	Ave.
pit	48%	34%	39%	56%	46%	44%
seed	7%	32%	10%	10%	29%	19%
stone	49%	40%	58%	45%	35%	44%

nut 220.
pit 14, 22, 27-29, :30, 37, 41-42, 49-50, c51, 52, 54, 56, 63, 65; 101, 103, ?105, 106, 112-16, 122-23, 125, 127-28, ?131, 134, 144, 149; 203, 207, 212, 214-15, 217, 219, 221, 223-25; 302-3, 306, 308, 312, c313, 314, 317-18, 320-21, 325-27; 401, 403, 405-7, 410, 412-13, 416, 418, 429, 431-34, 436.
seed 11, 59; 113, 124, 127, 129, 135-36, 139, 142, 146-49; 216; 302, 313, 316, 320, c322, 324; 408, 411-12, 414, 421, 430, 435-37.
stone 1-10, 12, 14-21, 23, !24, 25-26, :30, 31-36, 38-40, 43-48, ?52, 53, 55, s56, 57-62, ¹63, 64, ¹65; 102, 104, cr105, 107-11, 117-21, 126, †127, s128, 130, 132-33, *134, 136-38, s139, 140-41, 143, 145, 148; 201-2, 204-9, !210, 211, 213, 215, 218, 222, ¹225, 226; 301, 303-5, 309-10, :311, 312, 315, 319, 323, 328; 402, 404, 409, 415, 417-20, 422-28, ¹429.
no response 13; 150-52; 307.

Comment:

<u>pit</u>: Usu.--312; 418. <u>seed</u>: Usu.--436. <u>stone</u>: Usu.--59.

42.3 <u>clingstone (peach)</u>.   NE 267.   WG 43, 47, 72; F128.

For the peach whose pit is hard to separate from the flesh the UM generally has either <u>clingstone peach</u> or <u>cling peach</u>. Both occur in New England, the former dominantly, and, with an increased frequency of <u>cling peach</u>, in the North Midland and West Midland speech areas.

<u>Clingstone</u> likewise dominates the UM, but <u>cling</u> is widespread as a minority variant, with slightly greater frequency in the Midland areas of Iowa and Nebraska.

Both <u>clingstone</u> and <u>cling</u> also seem by most speakers to be used substantively as the full designation, especially in informal context. The plural <u>clings</u> is actually the recorded response of Iowa infs. 122, 146, and 147. Its non-appearance elsewhere, like that of clingstone as a noun, may be due simply to fieldworker practice in recording the singular.

Only one inf., in Duluth, preserved the New England distinction of color; but apparently the distinction became reversed in transmission, since his term is "yellow cling," and New Englanders typically applied "white" to the clingstone and "yellow" to the freestone variety. Obviously derivative forms clinger and clingingstone appear once each in Minnesota and Nebraska. Other single instances, clinchstone, from a northern Minnesota French-Canadian farmer, and closestone, from a southern Minnesota farmer of Ohio parentage, may be nonceforms.

A rather large number of infs. had no distinctive terms at all; a few were even unaware of the two kinds of peach.

	Mn.	Ia.	N.D.	S.D.	Nb.	Ave.
cling (p.)	16%	29%	33%	11%	44%	27%
clingstone (p.)	74%	71%	63%	89%	53%	69%

CL 47: The 930 mail responses give a greater weight to clingstone and less weight to cling than is found in the field data. In addition, there are (curiously enough, nearly all in Northern speech territory) 36 occurrences of Virginia Piedmont plum peach and two occurrences (S.D. 26.2 and Nb. 49.1) of South Atlantic coast press peach.

	Mn.	Ia.	N.D.	S.D.	Nb.	Ave.
cling (p.)	16%	11%	19%	13%	6%	12%
clingstone (p.)	78%	89%	69%	80%	93%	84%
plum (p.)	6%	1%	10%	7%	1%	4%

clinchstone (peach) :7.
cling (peach) 10, 14, 16, c35, 37, *50; 103, 106, 108, 122, 125, 130-31, 135-36, 142, 145-47; 204-5, *207, 215-16, 219, 223, :224; 310, 316; 401, 404, 408, 411, 414, 418, 422, 424, s425, 426, 428-29, 431-32, 435-36. yellow ~ 17.
clinger c414.
clinging (peach) 49.
clingingstone (peach) *9.
clingstone (peach) s1, 2-3, 5-6, sn8, 10-11, st12, 15, 18, 20-23, sn24, 27-29, 31, 33-34, s39, 40, 42, *43, 44-47, s48, 51, 54-55, 60-61, c63, 64-65; 102, 104-5, 109-11, 113, 115-21, 123-24, 126-28, :129, 132-34, 137-41, 143-44, 148-49; 201-3, sn¹208, 209-14, 217-18, 220-21, 225-26; 301, 304-6, 308-9, 311, 314, 317-18, 320-21, 324-25, :326, 327-28; 402-3, :405, 406, 409-10, 412-13, st415, 416-17, 419-20, 423, 426-27, 430, 433-34.
closestone [kḷozstoun] peach 59.
Colorado (peach) 318.
Michigan (peach) 17.

no response 4, 13, 19, ?25, :26, 30, 32, 36, ?38, ?41, 52-53, 56-58, 62; 101, 107, 112, 114, 150-52; ?206, ?222; 302-3, 307, ?312, 313, 315, 319, ?322, ?323; :?407, 421, ?437.

Comment:

clingstone: Used by inf.'s mother (from Mi.)--12.

42.4 freestone (peach) NE 267. WG 47, 72; F129.

For the peach whose pit is easily separated from the flesh the UM term is freestone or freestone peach, common also in New England and the Midland area of the eastern United States.

One Nebraskan has the Virginia Piedmont soft peach and one Minnesotan on the Iron Range has the rare free peach that was recorded twice in the Connecticut valley of New England. Two Minnesotans and two South Dakotans offer Elberta, actually the name of a bred variety of freestone peach. The variety of synonyms found in the South and South Midland areas did not survive the westward migration even in the southeast section of Iowa.

Elberta (peach) 14, 63; 306, 318.
free peach 14.
freestone (peach) 1-7, :8, sn9, 10, sn11, 12, 15-18, 20-22, sn23, 26-35, 37, 39-40, 42-49, *50, 51, :s¹52, 54-56, 58, 60-61, s63; 101-3, cr104, 105, 108-11, 113, 115-28, :129, 130-39, s140, 141-49; 201-4, *208, 210-17, 219, 221, 223, 225-26; 301, 304-5, 308-11, c314, 316-17, 319-21, 324-28; 401-4, *405, 406, *408, 409-14, †415, 416-20, 422-34, s435, 436.
loose-stone (peach) 59.
non-cling peach ?104.
non-clingstone 318.
soft peach 312.
no response 13, 19, 24, ?25, 36, ?38, ?41, 53, 57, 62, 64-65; 106-7, 112, 114, 150-52; ?205-6, 207, ?209, ?218, ?220, ?222, :?224; 302-3, 307, 313, ?322-23; ?407, 421, ?437.

Comment:

Elberta: Inf. says this is "the brand name"--63.

42.6 shell (hard case of a walnut or hickory nut). NE 277.

As in New England, the common UM term is shell. Shuck, which in LANE occurs 24 times, all but two west of the Connecticut River, is preserved by only one UM inf., a South Dakotan of Pennsylvania and Ontario parentage. Although the

minor variant hull turned up only twice
in New England, there are five instances
in the UM, where its distribution with
three examples in southeastern Nebraska
indicates an immediate origin in the
Midland migration.

CL 49: Shell dominates the 1,021 mail
replies, but hull is a widespread minor
equivalent, especially in Nebraska with
32 of the 95 instances. A scattered few
report shuck. Confusion with the next
item (see 42.7) may have led 39 respondents to mark husk as their term.

	Mn.	Ia.	N.D.	S.D.	Nb.	Ave.
hull	7%	8%	9%	7%	15%	9%
husk	6%	1%	7%	4%	3%	4%
shell	89%	90%	83%	90%	82%	87%

hull 136; 322; 425, *432, 435.
peeling ?432.
shell 1-65; 101-29, :130, 131-35, :136,
137-49; 201-26; 301-2, 305-21, 323-28;
401-20, 422-24, 426-31, 433-34, 436-37.
shuck 306.
no response 150-52; 303-4; 421.

42.7 hull (the green outer covering of a
walnut or hickory nut). NE 277.

Although this item was recorded in New
England only when incidentally preferred,
the 23 instances of burr, largely in
Northeastern Massachusetts, southern
New Hampshire, and the southern tip of
Maine, and the 28 instances of shuck,
almost entirely in western Connecticut,
suggest a pattern relevant to the UM.

Typically, eastern New England burr
turns up only once in the UM, but southwestern New England shuck survives in the
older Northern settlement areas of Minnesota, Iowa, and South Dakota (see map).

Husk, which appeared seven times in
southern New Hampshire mostly west of
the burr area, is proportionately much
more frequent in the UM, where its orientation is clearly Northern.

Hull, a three-time rarity in eastern
New England, appears on the contrary as
the majority term in the UM, where its
primary concentration in southern Iowa
and Nebraska is that of Midland features.

Eight scattered infs. use shell for
both the inner and the outer coverings
(cf. 42.6), but two others (425 and 435)
reverse the usual meanings by using shell
for the outer and hull for the inner.

	Mn.	Ia.	N.D.	S.D.	Nb.	Ave.
hull	14%	69%	0%	20%	62%	41%
husk	54%	10%	71%	27%	23%	30%
shell	8%	8%	14%	0%	12%	8%
shuck	14%	12%	14%	20%	4%	12%

CL 48: Although the checks for three

of the terms correlate fairly well with
the fieldwork findings, those for shell
do not. Since 1,000 respondents marked
some term in this item and many of them
were presumably unfamiliar with nut-
trees and hence likely to confuse this
item with related CL 49 (see 42.6),
these figures are suspect.

bark c56.
burr 320.
hide 50.

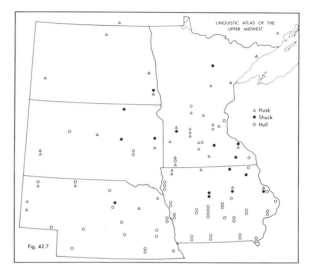

Fig. 42.7

hull :?17, c27, 39, s?46, ?47, 51, 58,
60, :s?63; 107, 109-11, 118, 121-49;
302, :s323, s324-25, 327, *328; 401, 403,
406, 414, 419-20, 422, 424, 426-29, 432-
34, 436.
husk 3, 6, 17, 21, 28-29, 33-34, 37,
*41, 43-45, *46, 51, 53, 55, 59, 61-62;
101-3, 116, 119; 202, 204, 214, *221,
226; c311, 312, 314, 319; 402, 404, 408-
9, 411, 416, s431.
outer cover s48.
outside shell 36.
pod 308.
shell 10, 57; 104, 106, 112-13; 215;
425, *432, 435.
shuck 12, 42, 49, 54, 64; 105, 108, 114-
15, 117, 120; 225; 306, 316-17; 413.
no response 1-2, 4, ?5, 7-9, 11, 13-16,
18-20, 22-26, 30, ?31, 32, ?35, ?38, 40,
52, 65; 150-52; 201, 203, ?205, 206-7,
?208, 209-12, ?213, 216, ?217-19, 220,
222-24; 301, 303-5, 307, ?309, 310, 313,
315, 318, 321-22, ?326; ?405, ?407, 410,
412, 415, 417-18, 421, 423, 430, ?437.

Comment:

husk: Used for hazelnuts, the only kind
found locally--6. Used for butternuts--34.

shell: "You husk the walnut shells in the corn grinder"--104. shuck: On hazelnuts--12.

42.8 peanuts.

This item was added shortly before the completion of the Minnesota fieldwork in order to help determine the South Midland influence in the UM. Peanuts is the universal term, except for the following. South Midland goobers does appear four times ([1]130, [1]144, 148; 320), but only twice as the customary word. A Minneapolis black inf. (35) uses googleberries as a jocular synonym.

In eastern South Dakota and northeastern Nebraska the query yielded also the volunteered information (from 203, 211, 218, and 305) that locally sunflower seeds are known as "Russian peanuts" because of their popularity with Russo-Germans in the area.

43.5 green onions. NE 258.

A variety of responses resulted from the query, "What do you call those slender onions eaten raw at the table?" Not all responses have the same referent.

In the entire UM the most common term is green onions, with no clear regional pattern. Winter onions, the leading minor variant, is not reported in LANE and, with its higher frequency in Nebraska and South Dakota, may have a Midland orientation despite its not being noted regularly by the Iowa fieldworkers. Young onions occurs infrequently in four states and more frequently in South Dakota. Sporadic instances of equivalent early onions, garden onions, grass onions, new onions, and table onions also turn up.

Infs. also offered terms for other varieties of onion or of related plants, apparently because of some similarity to green onions. The former group includes multipliers, with the synonymous potato onions, and seed onions, with the synonymous set onions. Multipliers are used like ordinary green onions but differ in that they propagate by the development of extra bulbs from a planted central bulb, hence the rough analogy with potatoes. The latter group includes chives, leeks, scallions and its variant scullions, and shallots. No patterns of distribution are noticeable except that scallions/scullions is not found in the South Dakota and Nebraska records.

	Mn.	Ia.	N.D.	S.D.	Nb.	Ave.
green ~	66%	77%	78%	65%	58%	69%
scallions	5%	7%	4%	0%	0%	4%
spring ~	2%	5%	0%	0%	8%	3%
winter ~	2%	2%	9%	27%	22%	10%
young ~	7%	5%	9%	19%	8%	8%

CL 50: Like the field infs., the 1,030 mail respondents consistently use green onions as the major term and young onions as a widespread minor variant. Otherwise the two sets of data manifest some lack of agreement. Winter onions, missing from the checklist, was nevertheless written in by 19 persons in the five states. Only 12 checked scallions, but a surprising 19% of all respondents use multipliers. Eight offered shallots, five potato onions, in addition to isolated instances of onion sets, set onions, table onions, and wild onions.

	Mn.	Ia.	N.D.	S.D.	Nb.	Ave.
green ~	75%	80%	79%	70%	85%	81%
multipliers	20%	7%	23%	22%	13%	19%
young ~	12%	11%	9%	9%	7%	10%

Bermuda onions ?307.
chives 57; 319.
early onions 112.
garden onions 328.
grass onions 4.
green onions 1-3, 5-6, [1]*8, 10-18, 20-22, 24, 26, 28, s29, 30-31, ?32, 33-34, 37, 40-42, :?43, 44-47, 49-50, 52-53, 55, 57, ?60, 61, 64, sn65; 101-2, 104-6, 108-11, 113-21, 123-25, *126, 127, 131-34, 136-38, 143, 145, 147-48; 202-5, 210, :211, 213, 215, c216, 217-20, :221, 222-23, sn224, 226; [1]302, 303, 306, 309-13, 318-23, 325-28; 401-2, c404, 405-6, :sn407, 410-12, s415, 416, 418-19, 421, 423-26, 428-29, s433, *436, 437.
leeks 18.
multipliers 46, 48; 208, 225; [1]314.
multiply onions 305.
new onions 40, 60; 128.
onions ?32, 63; 144, 149; 430.
potato onions 208.
scallions s39, 43.
scullions 27, 44; 103, 141; 212; [1]414.
seed onions 202, 208; 317.
set onions [1]9, 17, 44, r48, 54, c56; 139.
shallots r44; 111.
spring onions 62; 130, 139; 413, 422, 431.
table onions 36, →38, 58.
winter onions 4; 137; 201, 225; 304-5, 313-15, 322-23; 401, 403, 408, [1]413, 414, 417, 420, 423, 432.
young onions c19, 23, 25, c35, 122;

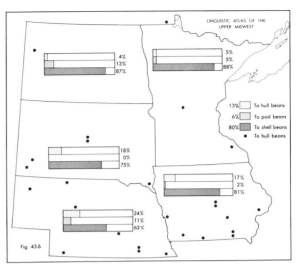

LINGUISTIC ATLAS OF THE
UPPER MIDWEST

13% To hull beans
6% To pod beans
80% To shell beans
• To hull beans

4%
13%
87%

5%
5%
88%

18%
0%
75%

17%
2%
81%

24%
11%
62%

Fig. 43.6

¹312, 317,

9, 135,
308,

[ə]--
en

43.
WG

As
state
remov
shell
as dec
vives i
in Iowa   .quency
test its   . Dakota at-

Pod, n_____ in WG but by LANE reported tw____ in Vermont, has gained proportionately in its westward extension,
with instances in all states but South
Dakota.

Shuck, found only four times in New
England, is not much stronger in the UM.

Thresh, in the form /θræʃ/, offered by
several infs., usually refers to the process of removing the pods by machinery
but some use it also for the housewife's
kitchen task.

Clean, husk, snap, and string also occur once or twice.

CL 41: Most of the 1,028 respondents use
shell and, as in the field returns, the
most frequent minor variant is Midland
hull, with pod and shuck widely scattered.

	Mn.	Ia.	N.D.	S.D.	Nb.	Ave.
shell	83%	69%	89%	77%	72%	77%
hull	15%	25%	9%	14%	25%	19%
pod	2%	6%	3%	8%	10%	6%
shuck	5%	5%	5%	5%	1%	4%

Hull has only 15% frequency in Northern
Iowa but 32% in southern Iowa.

clean 56.
fix 58.
hull 1, 27, 55; 124, 132-33, 135, 140,
142, 145, *146, 147; 209; 312, 314-15,
320, 325; 402, c403, 412, 422, 429, 432-
33, 435, 437.
husk 20, ¹34.
pod ¹34, 37, ¹*41, 50, 60; 101; 207,
218, 223; 404, 408, 420-21.

shell 2-3, c4, 5-26, 28-36, *37, 39-49,
51, s52, c53, 54, 57-61, 63, 65; ¹101,
102-6, 108-13, 115-23, 126-30, 133-34,
136-41, 143-44, *145, 146, 148-49; 202-4,
c205, *207, 208, :210, 211-18, c219, 220,
222, 224-26; 301-7, 309-11, 313, 317-19,
321-24, 326-28; 401, 404, *405, 406-7,
410-11, *412, 413-14, 416-19, 423-28, 430-
31, 434, 436.
shuck 10, ¹57, 62, 64; 107, 114, 117,
128; 221; 308, ¹326; 409.
snap 131.
string 130; 434.
take [them] out of the pods 415.
thresh c31, 60, 63; 217; 301, *316;
*405.
no response ?38; 125, 150-52; 201, ?206.

Comment:

pod: You 'pod' peas but 'thresh' beans
--60. "We 'shuck' beans but 'shell' peas
--117. shuck: Husband's term--326. thresh:
In the kitchen--c31. If by machinery--
217. On a farm, for many beans, but
'shell' in the kitchen--301. Beans are
'threshed' but not in the kitchen--405.

43.7 lima beans. NE 259. WG 39, 73.

For the bean (Phaseolus limensis) the
large, yellowish, flat seeds of which
are removed from the pod to be eaten,
the widespread UM designation is lima
bean. Perhaps because in the UM there has
been commercial distribution of cans of
the smaller Southern variety (Phaseolus
lunatus) known in the South as butter
bean, some confusion and ambiguity appear
in infs.' responses. The confusion is
complicated by the application of butter
beans to the dried form of the large
limas (the green stage being known as

lima beans), to a quite different variety also called wax beans, and, once, to a variety described as having edible black seeds.

Despite the confusion, the actual incidence of butter beans in southern Iowa clearly suggests the spread of a South Midland term.

Several Minnesotans and one Iowan use baby beans for the smaller variety. Singletons otherwise unattested are case beans (but compare caseknife beans found as a minor variant in New England), pencil pod beans, and shell beans.

Canadian infs. respond with broad beans for a similar but unrelated plant (*Vicia faba*), for which horse beans, used by a native of Duluth, may be an American equivalent.

	Mn.	Ia.	N.D.	S.D.	Nb.	Ave.
butter beans	10%	50%	0%	24%	30%	24%
lima beans	90%	85%	92%	96%	76%	88%

CL 42: From 1,025 respondents the replies rather closely confirm the field returns, except for butter beans in Iowa.

	Mn.	Ia.	N.D.	S.D.	Nb.	Ave.
butter beans	10%	26%	6%	16%	32%	19%
lima beans	92%	81%	95%	88%	83%	87%

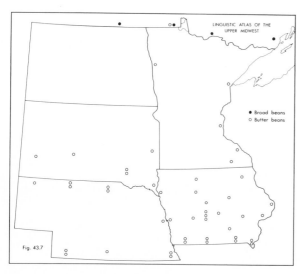

LINGUISTIC ATLAS OF THE UPPER MIDWEST

● Broad beans
○ Butter beans

Fig. 43.7

baby beans 10, 33, 37; 105. baby limas 143.

broad beans 1-3; 202.

butter ~ 1, s?5, sn9, 16, †31, 39, ¹40, s¹48, ¹54, 55, 64; 104, 108, 111, 113, 115, 117, 124, 127-30, 133, 136-37, 139-40, 142-49; 312-13, 319, ¹†320, 322-23, 325; 401, 403-6, ¹†410, ¹419, ¹424, 427, 429, 431, 434-35, 437.

case ~ 109.

horse ~ 16; ¹223.

lima ~ 1-6, sn7, 9-16, s17, 18, 20-23, :24, :s25, 26, s27, 28-30, :31, 32-38, 40, :41, 42-45, c46, 47-49, s50, 51, 53-56, s57, 58, !59, 60-65; 101-3, 105-6, 108-12, 114-27, 130-33, 135-39, 141-44, →145, 146, 148-49; 201, 203-5, 207-15, :216, 217-24, *225, 226; 301-2, 304-6, 308-21, 323-28; 402, 404, 406, s407, 408-26, sn427, 428, 430-31, 433, 436.

low bush ~ 17.

navy ~ 56-58; 134, 140, 145, 147; 432.

pencil pod ~ 18.

shell ~ 39, *46.

no response 8, 19, 52; 107, 150-52; ?206; 303, 307.

Comment:

baby beans: Green--1. Different from 'lima beans' in that each bean has its husk to be removed--2. Larger than 'lima beans'--3. butter beans: Inf. knows the word but not the referent--5, 54. Inf. says they are not 'lima beans' but are small, black beans the pods of which are also eaten--7. Used by inf.'s parents (from R.I. and Ire.)--31. Used by inf.'s mother (from Wi.)--410. Inf. heard this from a local woman (from In.)--40. "Many people call them 'butter beans'"--424. Larger than 'lima beans'--9; 142; 406. Smaller than 'lima beans'--1, 55, 64; 139; 323. Green--312. White--1; 146, 148. Yellow--9; 117, 124, 128, 147; 406. = lima beans--108, 117, 124, 127, 130, 136, 143-45, 149; 431. = wax beans--10, 50; 212. = "shelled green beans"--22. = string beans--28, 39. horse beans: Red --16. Inf. says this is a translation of Danish *paarde boonen*--223. lima beans: Green--9; 406. Green or white--20. White --1, 65; 312. White or speckled--136. Yellow--126, 135. Yellow or speckled-- 149. Pronounced [ˈlæmə]--Inf. hears this in grocery stores; her normal form is 'butter beans'--325. = butter beans--108, 136, 145. navy beans: Smaller than 'lima beans' --56. Large, flat, and yellow--134.

43.8 string beans. WG 31, 38, 47, 73; F40, F133.

In the UM beans that are eaten along with the pod are generally called by one of three terms carried west from fairly well marked source-areas in the Atlantic states. (This item was not sought in New England.)

String beans, found in Northern and North Midland territory north of the Potomac, has become the majority form in all the UM except Minnesota. In that state, where this item was added to the worksheets after the first summer of the survey, the expected incidence of string beans apparently has been reduced by the adoption of butter beans by some infs. unfamiliar with the original application of the latter to small lima beans (see 43.7).

Green beans, a West Midland form, has spread throughout the UM, perhaps with the help of the commercial preference for it as lacking the pejorative implications of "string" in string beans.

Snap beans, principally a South Midland expression found south of the Potomac, is minor in the UM, with its background reflected in the five occurrences in Iowa.

The specific variety known as wax beans, characterized by having yellowish, waxy pods, is identified as such by a scattered handful of infs.

The existence of several equivalent terms in the same area occasionally leads to arbitrary particularization. An example is provided by the North Dakota inf. (224) who classifies green beans as having short pods, butter beans as having long round pods, and string beans as having strings.

	Mn.	Ia.	N.D.	S.D.	Nb.	Ave.
green beans	32%	50%	50%	36%	44%	44%
snap ~	5%	10%	4%	7%	8%	8%
string ~	26%	60%	58%	68%	58%	57%

butter beans 2-3, 10, 22, 28, 50, 65; 204, 212, 224.
French-cut ~ 38.
green ~ 13-15, 17, 30, 36; 102, 105, 109-11, 114, 116, 120, 123, 127-32, 134-36, 138-39, 142, 145-47; 202-3, 205-6, 208-9, 211, 213, 217, c220, 222, c223, 224; 303-5, 308, 310, ¹312, 314, 316, 318, 322, 325; 401, 403, 406, 408, 410, 412, ¹413, 414-15, c419, 423-25, 428, 432, 435, 437.
green string ~ 16.
Kentucky wonder ~ 13.
low bush ~ 17.
shell ~ 215.
snap ~ c29; ¹104, 108, sn118, 137, †139, 141, 144; ¹214, c225; 301, 324; 409, ¹412, 413, ¹414, 434.
string ~ 13, 30-31, 35; 101-4, 106-8, 112-13, 116-19, 121-22, 124-27, 133, 137-41, 143, 146, 148-49; 203-4, 207-8, 210-12, 214-16, 218-19, 221, 224, 226; 302, 306-9, 311-15, 317-21, 323, 326-28; 401-2, 404-7, †410, 411, ¹413, 417-18, 420-22, 426-31, 433, 436.
wax ~ 13-15; 102, 106, 111, 138; 201, 204-5, 208-9, 211, 219; 312; 414, 428.
yellow ~ 314. yellow wax ~ 18.
no response 1, 4-9, 11, 18-21, 23-27, 32-34, 37, 39-49, 51-64; 115, 150-52; 416.

Comment:

butter beans: "The ripe string beans, with yellow pods"--50. "Green bean like beans is in the strings"--409. string beans: = green beans--30. "There are two kinds: wax beans and green beans"--211; 314. "But at the store it's 'green beans'--401. "They don't string any more"--Inf. says this term is going out of use because the strings now are bred out of the beans--428. wax beans: Yellow--18; 138; 203, 205, 208, 219. = yellow string beans. "Two kinds: one green and the other yellow"--201.

43.9 greens. WG 39, 72.

Added to the worksheets after the first year's fieldwork in order to determine whether Southern salat (for salad) had reached the UM, this item yielded only greens in response to the question, "What do you call the tops or stems of vegetables that you cook and eat, like beets or turnips or spinach?" Many infs. disclaimed knowledge of any term, saying that nothing like that was in their diet.

greens 15, 18, 29-31, 35-36, 38; 101-25, *126, 127-29, 131-49; 201-3, 205, 207-9, 211-19, 221-23, 225-26; 301-9, 311-13, 315-16, 318-19, 322-26, 328; 401-8, 410-14, 416-34, s435, 436-37.
no response 1-14, 16-17, 19-28, 32-34, 37, 39-65; 130, 150-52; 204, 206, 210, 220, 224; 310, 314, 317, 320-21, 327; 409, 415.

Comment:

greens: = tops of beets--103. "pigfeed"--417.

44.1 husks. NE 263. WG 40, 46, 47, 73; F30, F40, F134.

For the leaf-like covering on an ear of corn husks dominates the entire UM, as is consistent with its eastern origin in both the Northern and the North Midland areas. But Southern and South Midland shucks, recorded only half a dozen times in New England, is well represented in Iowa and Nebraska, in each of which state those who use only shucks are matched in number by those who use both terms. No significant variation appears, however, among the three types. In the Wisconsin survey shucks occurred three times.

	Mn.	Ia.	N.D.	S.D.	Nb.	Ave.
husks	91%	84%	92%	86%	64%	84%
shucks	6%	29%	12%	14%	61%	23%

CL 52: Choices reported by 1,025 re-

spondents corroborate the field returns. The South Midland background of shucks is conspicuous in the contrast between its 15% frequency in northern Iowa and its 54% frequency in the southern portion.

	Mn.	Ia.	N.D.	S.D.	Nb.	Ave.
husks	95%	70%	93%	88%	60%	79%
shucks	6%	33%	7%	14%	60%	25%

husks s1, 2-4, 6-8, 10-11, :s12, 13-28, c29, 30-36, 38, c39, 40-44, c45, 46-48, 50-56, 58-60, c61, 62-63, cr64, 65; 101-3, cr104, 105-8, 110-12, 115-19, 121-

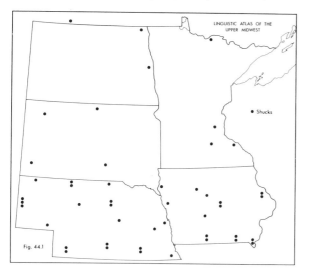

LINGUISTIC ATLAS OF THE UPPER MIDWEST

• Shucks

Fig. 44.1

32, 134-42, c143, 144-46, 149; 201-6, 208, 210-26; 302, 304-19, 322-28; 402, 404, 406-9, ¹413, 414-17, cr418, 419-22, 424-28, c430, 434, 436.

leaves 12; 209.

shucks 5, 37, ¹*46, 49, ¹51, r57, ?64; ?104, ¹105, c109, 113-14, 120, *122, 131, c132-33, ¹139, ¹143, 144-49; 201, 207, c220; 301, ¹302, 303, ¹312, 320-21; 401, 403-5, 409-13, cvr414, ?418, 420, 424, 428-33, 435-37.

no response ?9; 150-52; 423.

Comment:

husks: 'Husk' is a collective noun for inf.; she has no distinctive plural form--33. shucks: Inf. calls them 'shucks' on field corn and 'husks' on sweet corn--131.

44.2 sweet corn. NE 261. WG 48, 73; F41, F135.

Among the various UM designations for kinds of corn served on the cob at the table several regional preferences appear.

Sweet corn, which in New England shares popularity with green corn, has spread widely in the UM, where it is dominant

everywhere but in southern Iowa and Nebraska. Green corn occurs in the same areas, but with declining frequency, apparently having given ground to sweet corn in the western migration. (The Wisconsin survey reported eleven instances, or 22%.)

Second to sweet corn is the Midland and South Midland roasting ears (for connoisseurs either [ˈrostn̩ ɪrz] or [ˈrosn̩ ɪrz]), with its provenience strongly implied in its dominance in southern Iowa and Nebraska. Some infs. apply this term also to field corn, often particularized as young field corn, which can be served in this way while the kernels are still milky.

Corn on the cob, a rare three-timer in New England, is equally rare in all the UM except South Dakota and Nebraska. In the latter it is used by one-third of all the infs., and apparently is gaining in popularity.

Ear corn and the nonce-variant corn on the ear are limited to Nebraska and, with one example each, to southwestern Minnesota and western Iowa, close to the Nebraska border.

Table corn may be Canadian, as its two instances are in Manitoba and Saskatchewan.

Sugar corn, reported six times in western New England, survives weakly with one Minnesotan inf., whose father came from Maine.

Squaw corn, designating another variety having variegated kernels, mostly purplish, and cultivated especially by Indians, is used also in Manitoba and recalled by one northern Iowan housewife of Maine parentage.

Bantam corn also names a distinct variety, adapted for a northern climate and often more fully designated yellow bantam. The term was recorded only in Minnesota.

	Mn.	Ia.	N.D.	S.D.	Nb.	Ave.
~ on the cob	11%	2%	4%	21%	39%	14%
green ~	9%	4%	2%	7%	6%	7%
roasting ears	0%	41%	8%	21%	39%	21%
sweet ~	81%	92%	81%	82%	42%	77%

CL 53: Although the general distribution is similar in the 1,049 mail responses, they reveal a greater spread of roasting ears into southern Minnesota and North Dakota and a lower proportion of sweet corn throughout the UM. Sugar corn was written in as a volunteered response by a Nebraskan (65.2) whose paternal grandfather came from New Hampshire.

	Mn.	Ia.	N.D.	S.D.	Nb.	Ave.
~ on the cob	13%	4%	25%	18%	13%	13%
green ~	8%	2%	5%	2%	2%	4%
roasting ears	26%	71%	41%	76%	83%	59%
sweet ~	70%	49%	56%	38%	37%	51%

bantam corn 3, 18, 32.

corn on the cob 13-14, 31, 37-38, 54, 61; 121; 222; 301, 305, 312, 326-28; 402, 406, 408, 410, 413-14, 420-21, 425-26,

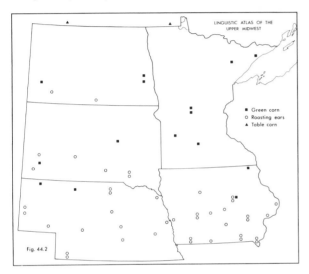

Fig. 44.2

428-31.

corn on the ear 414.

ear corn 61; 127; 413, 416, 427.

field ~ 13, 16; 117, 124, 126-27, 134, 136, 145; 215; 319. young ~ ~ 57; 319.

green ~ 6, 13, 27-28, 42, 51; 107, 118; 214, 220, :222; 316, 326; 401, 404.

roasting ears ¹40; ¹109, †110, 113, 117, sn118, 124, 126-28, 132, 134, 137-39, 141-43, 145-49; †209, 215, 223; 311, †312, 313, 320-21, c322, 323, ¹325; 405-7, 409, 411, 414, 417-18, 420, 422, 424, 427, 429, 437.

squaw corn †103; 202.

sugar ~ 40.

sweet ~ 2, 4-5, 7-11, 15-26, 29-30, 32-36, 39-41, 43-53, sn54, 55-60, 62-65; 101-20, 122-31, 133-36, 139-40, *141, 142-49; 202-7, :208, sn209, 210-11, :sn212, 213, sn215, 216-17, c218, 219, 221, 224, c225, 226; 301, c302, 303-4, c305, 306-11, 314-20, 324-28; 402-3, 405, sn410, 412, 415, 419-20, 430-36.

table ~ 1; 201.

no response 12; 150-52; 423.

Comment:

corn on the cob: "I never say 'roasting ears'"--402. roasting ears: May be field corn, too--117, 124, 126-28, 134, 146-49; 215; 420. Used by inf.'s neighbor (from In.)--40. Usu.--311; 405. Pronounced

['rozŋ ɪrz]; = field corn. Especially said at the table--320. squaw corn: Inf. used to raise this kind, said by him to be partly purple, and not as sweet as 'sweet corn' but with a good flavor. She often ground it for corn meal--103. sweet corn: Inf. says this is the most common local term--51. Inf. calls field corn 'horse'corn--120. Never serves field corn at the table--144. young field corn: "Eaten by farm families"--319.

44.3 <u>tassel</u> (top of corn stalk). NE 262.

For the inflorescence at the top of a corn stalk the eastern minor variants <u>bloom</u> and <u>blossom</u> barely survive in the UM, with one Canadian occurrence of <u>bloom</u> and two Minnesota instances of <u>blossom</u>.

Eastern <u>tassel</u> has come to dominate all the UM. An occasional inf. is unclear as to the meaning of the term; two infs. (2 and 5) specifically use it to designate the silk on an ear of corn.

bloom 2.

blossom 15, 19.

tassel 1, 3, sn4, 6-9, c10, 11, 13-26, :s27, 28-35, 37-43, c44, 45, *46, 47-57, s58, 59, cr60, 61-65; 101-49; 201-26; 301-11, ?312, 313-18, 320-26, 328; 401-4, 407-22, 424-37.

no response 12, ?36; 150-52; 319, 327; 405-6, 423.

Comment:

tassel: "If there's no tassel, then you get nubbins--25. We de-tassel corn--51. "It's pronounced /tɑsl̩/ but you de-tassel /dɪtæsl̩/ it." Inf.'s wife has /tæsl̩/ --117.

44.4 <u>silk</u> (on the ear of corn).

The silk on the mature ear of corn is so designated throughout the UM. Three infs. in Minnesota and one each in South Dakota and Nebraska confuse it with the tassel. (See 44.3.) The single use of <u>awn</u> by a machinist may result from unfamiliarity with farm terms. The single instance of <u>feather</u> in Manitoba, however, may represent a Canadianism, since the inf. reports the word as locally common. Hair and <u>whiskers</u> seem to be noncemetaphors.

Male infs. often volunteered that cornsilk provided their first juvenile introduction to smoking--"out behind the barn."

awn 309.

feather ¹202.

hair 214.

silk sn!1, 2-4, s⊥5, 6, c7, 8-11, 14-16, s⊥17, 18-46, r47, 48-57, c58, 59-60, c61, 62-65; 101-49; 201, ⊥202, 203-19, c220, 221-26; 301-8, ⊥309, 310-13, :314, 315-21, c322, 323-28; 401-22, 424-36, :437.

    tassel 5, 12-13; 204; ?312.
    whiskers 108; 309.
    no response 150-52; 423.

Comment:

    feather: "Common here"--202. hair: Usu.--214. silk: Inf. calls this a "Downeast" term--202. Pronounced /sɪlz/--36. Pronounced /sɪlt/--208.

44.5 muskmelon. NE 265.

Whatever distinction botanists make between muskmelons and cantaloupes is obviously unfamiliar to UM infs., some of whom consider the two as identical, and others of whom consider them different, but, as the comments below indicate, with no agreement upon what makes them different. Where a speaker uses both terms as synonyms, he may consider cantaloupe as more "proper."

Although in New England cantaloupe, as an expanding minority term, was reported as chiefly urban, in the UM its distribution coincides with the larger Midland/Northern contrast, since it has a decided Midland orientation with frequency in Iowa and Nebraska. Two North Dakotans and one Iowan consider it an innovation, a view supported by the 27% frequency with Type I, 40% with Type II, and 53% with Type III.

Muskmelon and mushmelon easily dominate the UM. Both are sometimes considered old-fashioned, but it is the latter that reveals a decline in popularity as well as a negative correlation with education. Mushmelon drops from 32% frequency among Type I infs. to only 22% among Type II, with only a single occurrence among the younger, college-educated, infs. Muskmelon, on the contrary, actually has a slightly higher incidence among the middleaged than among the older infs., Type I.

Twice sugar melon appears as a synonym for muskmelon, as does French melon in a French bilingual community in Minnesota, but honeydew melon, once offered, names a quite different variety, characterized by its smooth, pale-green rind in contrast to the rough gray rind of the other melons.

	Mn.	Ia.	N.D.	S.D.	Nb.	Ave.
cantaloupe	22%	55%	19%	33%	42%	34%
mushmelon	18%	37%	27%	33%	17%	26%
muskmelon	79%	65%	69%	67%	75%	72%

cantaloupe ⊥7, 14-15, 18, 28, 32, !35, 37, 39, ⊥45, 46-47, 51, ⊥52-53, 54-55, 61, ⊥62; 101, 106, 109-11, 114, 116, 118-23, 125, 127, 130-31, 136-37, 140-44, →145, 147, 149; 204, →205, →210, 213, 224; 304-5, 309, 312, 314, ⊥315, 318-19, 321, c326; 402, 408, 411-12, c413, s†415, 416, 422, 424, 426-28, 430-31, 433, 435.
  French melon 7.
  honeydew melon 416.
  mushmelon 11-12, 15, 19, 25, 32, c34, →37, ⊥40, ⊥47, 48, 51, 57, 64; 101, 105, 108-9, 114, 128-30, 135, 138, 140, 143-44, *145, 146-49; 203-4, 207, cr208, 209, 220, 223; 302-3, 305, 307-8, 311, *316, 317, ⊥319, 322; 407, ⊥410, c416, 421-22, c427, 430, ⊥433, ⊥435.
  muskmelon 1-2, c3, 4-6, sn7, 8-10, 13-14, 16-18, 20-24, 26-28, c29, 30-31, 33, 36-40, *41, 42-45, †46, ⊥47, 49-50, 52-63, 65; 102-7, 109, 111-13, 115-22, *123, 124-28, 132-34, 136-37, 139, 145, 149; 201-2, †205, 206, ?208, sn210, 211-19, c222, 224-26; 301, 304, 306, 309-10, 312-15, 318-21, 323-26, 328; 401, c402, 403-6, 408-11, c413, 414, s†415, 416-20, 425, 427-29, 431-34, ⊥435, 436-37.
  sugar melon 56; 415.
  no response 150-52; 327; 423.

Comment:

    cantaloupe: "The proper word" for a 'muskmelon'--55. "The most common term locally"--120. Different from a 'mushmelon' or 'muskmelon'--14, 28, 54; 109, 111, 116, 119, 122, 125, 127, 143, 147; 224; 309, 312, 321, 326; 408, 416, 422, 430. = mushmelon or muskmelon--45, 55; 101, 106, 114, 137; 204, 213; 314; 411, 427, 431. French melon: Inf. says this is the term used by French people; = muskmelon--7. honeydew melon: White skin and green meat--416. mushmelon: Used by inf. in youth--37. Used by inf.'s daughter--40. Usu.--51. "An older word than 'cantaloupe'"--140. Larger than a 'cantaloupe'--109, 147. Has a softer center than a 'cantaloupe'--143. A 'mushmelon' is round; a 'cantaloupe' is oblong --422. Pronounced [ˈmʌsˌmɛlən]--15. Pronounced [ˈmʌsˌmɛlən]--130, 144; 422. muskmelon: "The most common term locally" --47. Larger than a 'cantaloupe'--109, 116, 122, 125, 127; 312; 408, 416. Smaller than a 'cantaloupe'--111. A 'muskmelon' is green; a 'cantaloupe' is yellow or orange--111; 321; 413. A 'muskmelon' is oblong; a 'cantaloupe' is round--224; 309. A 'muskmelon' is smooth; a 'cantaloupe' is rough--224; 326; 428. Pronounced [ˈmʌˈʃkˌmɛlɪn]--109. Pronounced [ˈmʌstˌmɛlən]--60.

44.7 <u>toadstool</u>. NE 280.

For any of several poisonous varieties of fungus similar to mushrooms the UM almost unanimously uses <u>toadstool</u>, as is true also on the Atlantic coast. <u>Frogstool</u>, found once in northern Vermont, also is a oncer in the UM, where a southern Minnesotan of Welsh background is familiar with the term. <u>Stool</u> alone, rare in New England, is used by the same Duluth inf. who also uses <u>toad pod</u>. An Iowan businessman of Pennsylvania extraction uses <u>hell's angel</u> as the name for an extra large <u>toadstool</u>.

frogstool 52.
hell's angel 119.
stool 17. ~ pod 17.
toadstool 1-3, :sn4, 5, c6, 7, c8, 9-10, c11, 12-18, 20-26, !27, 28-30, :31, 32-34, :35, 36-40, 42, *43, c44, ct45, 46-51, 53-58, !59, 60, c61, 62-63, c64, 65; 101-49; 201-24, c225, 226; 301-4, 306, 308-15, *316, 317-24, c325, 326-28; 401-6, :407, 408-14, 416-22, 424-29, s430, 431-37.
no response 19, 41, 52; 150-52; 305, 307; 415, 423.

Comment:

<u>toadstool</u>: Term not very familiar, and it is not associated with the poisonous characteristic--32. "Useless"--44. "Smells bad"--57.

44.8 rust (on wheat)

This item, asking for terms for various fungus diseases of the stem, leaves, and kernel of the wheat plant, was included in the UM worksheets to elicit folk equivalents for technical words. Only the technical terms appear to be used, however, with varying definitions among farmers and with little or no distinction among urban residents. These varying interpretations are revealed in the comments below.

No geographical or social differentiation occurs.

black rust 4, 7-9, 19, 21, 25-26, 28, 33, 41-43, 46-47, 50-54, 50-52; 101, 104-5, 107, 109, 113-15, 117, 119, 122, 124, 128, 132, *134, 140, 145, 148-49; 201, 203, 205-8, 210, 212, 216-17, 221-25, ¹226; 301, 305-8, 316, 318, :321, 322, 325; 401, 411, 413-14, 417-18, 420-22, 427, 429, 431, *432, 436. black stem ~ 218; 434.
blight 17, 44, 62; 139.
brown rust 113. dry ~ 20. leaf ~ 37, 54; 142, 149; 210, 216, 221. orange ~ 418.
red ~ 4, 8-9, 19, 21, 25-26, 28, 33,

41, 46-47, 50-51, 53-54, 60-61; 101, 104-5, 107, 109, 114-15, 117, 122-24, 132, *134, 140, 145; 202-5, 207-8, 210-13, 216-18, 221, 223-25, ¹226; 301, 305-8, 316, 318, 320-22; 401, 411, 413, 417, 420-22, 427, 429-31, *432, 434-37.
rust 1-2, 10, 16-18, 22, 24, 34, :44, 45, 47, 51-53, c59, 60-63; 102-6, 108, 110, 112, 114, 116, 119, 121, 123, 125-26, 128-30, 132-33, *134, 135-38, 141-42, 145-47; 215, 219, 222; 305-6, 316-19, 325; 403, 409-10, 413-16, 420-21, 424, 426-28, 430-31, *432, s433, 435.
smut 16, 25; 204, 213; 305, 320, 324; 418. ~ black 16.
stem rust 29, 37, 41, 43, 50, 54; 142-43; 202, 206, 209, 216, 221-22; 421, 425.
yellow ~ 7.
no response 3, 5-6, 11-15, 23, ?27, 30-32, 35-36, 38-40, 48-49, 55-58, 64-65; 111, 118, 120, 127, 131, 144, 150-52; 214, 220; 302-4, 309-15, 323, 326-28; ?402, 404-6, ?407-8, 412, 419, 423.

Comment:

<u>black rust</u>: On kernel--201. Both 'black rust' and 'red rust' on kernel--117. On kernel; 'red rust' on stem--4; 318. On kernel; 'red rust' on kernel or stem--301. On kernel; 'red rust' on stem or leaf --401. = stem rust--221. On stem--26. Both 'black rust' and 'red rust' on stem --19, 26; 207, 216; 316; *432. On stem; 'red rust' on kernel--53. On stem; 'red rust on leaf--8; 203, 208, 210, 223-25; 322; 421, 436. On stem; 'red rust' on stem or leaf--124. On stem; 'red rust' on kernel or stem--212. On stem; 'smut' on kernel--418. On stem; 'yellow rust' on leaf--7. On kernel or stem--149. On kernel or stem; 'red rust' on stem only-- 25, 41. On leaf or stem--50. More serious than 'orange rust'--418. More serious than 'red rust'--4, 8, 19, 25-26, 46-47; 105, 107, 122; 210, 216-17, 225; 305-6, 316; 413, 417,420, 427, *432, 436. More serious than 'yellow rust'--7. <u>black stem rust</u>: More serious than 'red rust'--218; 434. <u>dry rust</u>: Red; on stem--20. <u>red rust</u>: More common than 'black rust'--51. = leaf rust--210, 221. On leaf--218. On stem--437. On stem; = smut--320. On stem; 'smut' on kernel--204, 218. <u>rust</u>: Brown; on kernel or stem--24. Red--414. <u>smut</u>: Brown; on kernel--25. <u>stem rust</u>: Red--37; 143, 147. More serious than 'leaf rust'-- 142.

44.9 <u>squash</u>.

This item was added to the worksheets during the second year of the study in order to ascertain whether the southern folk word <u>simlin</u> appears in the UM. Its

only occurrence is, however, in the derogatory personal epithet, simlin head,
used by a northeastern North Dakota inf.
who, unaware of the original meaning of
simlin, uses squash for the vegetable.
All other UM infs. likewise use squash,
sometimes with indications of particular
varieties such as acorn squash (105),
banana ~ (124), buttercup ~ (105), butter-
nut ~ (136), crookneck ~ (108, 124, 146-
47, 149), crooked neck ~ (103, 112),
gooseneck ~ (113), hubbard ~ (103, 105,
108, 113-14, 117, 124, 126-27, 136, 146-
47, 149; 308, 317), summer ~ (103, 118,
136, 144; c317), vegetable ~ (112).

45.7 screech owl. NE 230. WG 43, 46,
73; F136.

Although the inf. was first asked for
his designation of an owl with a harsh
cry, names of other varieties found locally were also recorded. As with wasps and
hornets (see 47.3) and with lima beans
(see 43.7), popular names and scientific
classifications do not necessarily correspond. The same name may serve for different varieties, and several names may
designate a single variety. Some infs.
know more than one term but are uncertain
how to distinguish them. For four infs.
of non-rural background all varieties
are known simply as owls.

All the varieties named by infs. are
found in the UM, but with uneven distribution. The barn owl is rare in western
sparsely inhabited sections, the burrowing owl is more common in prairie regions,
and the snowy owl only infrequently is
seen as far south as Iowa and Nebraska.

As on the Atlantic coast screech owl is
the most common UM term for the small
harsh-sounding owl (Otus asio), although
some instances of this term may refer to
the barn owl (Tyto alba). Midland squeech
owl survives feebly in the speech of
three southeastern Iowans and of one South
Dakotan of Ohio parentage. Scooch owl,
not previously recorded but perhaps related to Maryland scrooch owl, is used
by a southeast Iowa farmer with a Kentucky and Tennessee background. Cat owl
is the equivalent designation used by a
North Dakota farmer close to the Canadian
border, and a Duluth librarian insists
that night hawk is also a synonym.

With three exceptions the term barn owl
itself, together with the variant barnyard owl, is largely reported in Midland
speech territory, principally Iowa, as
is the infrequent equivalent monkey-faced
owl.

Horned owl, with the variants horn owl

and great horned owl, also refers to a
specific variety (Bubo virgianus). This
term is likewise found chiefly in the
Midland area, nearly half of the occurrences being in Iowa.

Burrowing owl is the "dictionary name"
for a small owl that lives in a hole in
the ground dug by itself or by such an
animal as a prairie dog. This term occurs only once in the UM, in western
North Dakota. More likely western terms
for this variety (Spetyta canicularia)
are prairie owl and prairie dog owl in

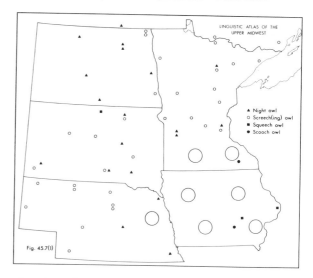

Fig. 45.7(1)

South Dakota and Nebraska and ground owl
in the eastern sector of the Dakota.

A not infrequent Canadian visitor in
the UM is the snowy owl (Nyctea scandi-
aca). One Duluth inf. calls it that, but
four scattered infs. know it as snow owl
and two Dakotans use arctic owl. Four
scattered infs. call it white owl. A related variety of arctic owl, the gray owl
(Scotiaptyx nebulosa), a very large bird
with grayish plumage, is reported under
that name in the Dakotas.

One Des Moines inf. uses the term mouse
owl, apparently as a synonym for the
short-eared owl (Asio flanneus).

The most common term throughout the UM,
hoot owl, or, rare, hooting owl, differs
from the preceding names in that it refers not to a specific variety but rather
to any of several varieties distinguished
by hooting instead of screeching. Even
more imprecise, since owls generally are
nocturnal, is the infrequent designation
night owl, which seems to have a Northern
orientation with the highest proportion
in the Dakotas. Two of the three Nebraska
infs. using it have New York state parent-

age.
Big-eyed chick, heard in western Nebraska, is probably not a local term.

	Mn.	Ia.	N.D.	S.D.	Nb.	Ave.
barn ~	3%	32%	4%	8%	11%	13%
hoot ~	77%	88%	50%	75%	55%	72%
night ~	8%	0%	33%	21%	8%	11%
screech ~	41%	72%	13%	25%	44%	44%

arctic owl 202; 306.
barn ~ 18, 29; 103, 108, 115, 123, 126, 128, 131, 133-34, 136, 141-43, 149-50;

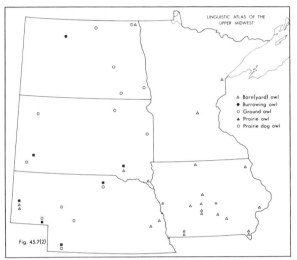

LINGUISTIC ATLAS OF THE UPPER MIDWEST

△ Barn(yard) owl
● Burrowing owl
○ Ground owl
▲ Prairie owl
□ Prairie dog owl

Fig. 45.7(2)

208; 323, 325; 410-11, 424, 428. barnyard ~ :130.
big-eyed chick ¹437.
burrowing owl *203.
cat ~ 206.
gray ~ 205, 220; 307.
great horned ~ 17, 45; 201; 306; 409.
ground ~ 205, 218, 224-25; 306, 317; 406.
hoot ~ 1-2, 4-6, 8-10, 12, 14, 16-17, 20-25, 27, 29-35, 37-40, ?*41, 42-43, c44, 46-53, 55, 57-58, 60-62; 101-2, 105-20, c121, 122-25, 127-29, 131-38, 140-45, 147-50; 201, 203-4, 210-11, 214-17, 221-22, 226; 301-2, 308, 311-13, *316, 317-18, c319, 320-21, 323-26, 328; 401, 403-4, 406, 408-9, 411, 413, 416, 418-19, 421, 423-24, 427-28, 430, 432-33, 435. hooting ~ 56, 59; 315.
horn owl 146-47; 224. horned ~ 105, 107, 116, 124, 134, 143, 145; 202; 311, 320, 325; 404-5, 419, 429.
monkey-faced ~ *328; 413, 422, 429.
mouse ~ 129.
night hawk 18.
night owl 11, 36, ?*41, 64; 202-3, 212-13, 216, 220, 222-23; 305, 316, 321-22, 326; 407, 420, 434.
owl 15; :402, 415, 425,

prairie dog owl 301, 320; 412, 418, 429, 437. prairie ~ 312, 322; 405, 409, 417, !436.
screech ~ 2, sn3, 5-7, s11, 12-13, *19, 21, 26, 28, 30, 37, 45, *46, 47-49, ¹50, 54-55, 57-59, 63, s¹64, 65; 101-13, 115-16, 118-22, 124-27, 130, 132-33, 137, 140, 143-49; 207-8, 225; 302, 306, 314, 320-21, ¹325, 328; 401, 403-4, 406, 410, 413-14, 416, 418, 424, 427-29, *432, 434.
screeching ~ 23. scootch ~ 135. squeech ~ 138-39; 303.
snow ~ 101, ¹103; 224; 422. snowy ~ 18.
white ~ 13; 103; 307; 424.
no response 151-52; 209, 219; ?304, 309-10, 327; 426.

Comment:

barn owl: Doesn't know any distinction between this and a 'hoot owl'--123. big-eyed chick: Inf. says this is used by local Mexicans--437. gray owl: Larger than a 'ground owl'--205. ground owl: Smaller than a 'screech owl'--225. hoot owl: Larger than a 'barn owl'--134, 142, 149. Big with a four- to five-foot wing spread--124. = horned owl--320. = night owl--42. Smaller than a 'night owl'--216. Larger than a 'mouse owl'--129. = screech owl--47-50. Different from a 'screech owl' --2, 5-6, 12, 21, 30, 37, *46, 56; 122, 325. Larger than a 'screech owl'--113, 124-25, 135, 143, 145, 147-49; 401, 424, 427, 432. Smaller than a 'screech owl'-- 30. = screeching owl--23. "Lives in badger holes"--216. A timber owl--113. "Size of a small chicken"--129. monkey-faced owl: "Lives in burrows"--*328. mouse owl: "Size of a jaybird"--129. night hawk: = screech owl; not the same as 'night owl' --18. night owl: Larger than a 'hoot owl' --216. More common term than 'screech owl' --64. "Hoots to beat the cars in the morning"--212. "It hoots at night"--323. "Lives in prairie dog holes"--312. = hoot owl--321, 326; 420. screech owl: "I can hear 'em a-hooin' [ə-'hut'n] at night"-- 314. "Goes 'hoo-hoo'"--*432. snow owl: = white owl--103.

45.8 dragonfly. WG 12, 14, 26, 30, 33-34, 42, 45-46; F5a, F15, F141.

Although not included in the New England worksheets, this item was investigated in the Middle and South Atlantic areas, with findings relevant to those in the UM.
Responses ordinarily were sought in the context, "What do you call the large four-winged insect that you might see hovering over a pond or marshy place?" This question often, though not systematically, was accompanied by a showing of a drawing of the insect as a clue to its identifi-

cation. Further discussion sometimes clar-
ified what was wanted. Fieldworkers generally felt that the responses were re-
liable, but Max D. Smith has expressed
doubt as a result of a survey of Kansas
college students, who were asked to check
lexical items listed beneath two pictures,
one of the dragonfly (*Odonata anisoptera*)
and one of the praying mantis (*Mantis
religiosa*). The students exhibited maximal
confusion, compounded by such volunteered
equivalents for dragonfly as damsel fly,
butterfly, grasshopper, katydid, walking-
stick, beetle, and helicopter. Despite
some recognized ambiguities in the Comment below, it may in turn be doubted
whether this study seriously jeopardizes
the Atlas findings. See Max D. Smith,
"The Dragonfly: Linguistic Atlas Under-
differentiation," *American Speech* (February, 1968).51-57.

Literary and urban dragonfly, widespread
on the Atlantic coast, is also found
throughout the UM, where it is used by
about one-third of all infs., with the
lowest frequency in North Dakota. In that
state only five infs. use it, three of
whom are of foreign language background
and four of whom are Type I. The fifth,
in Type II, recently adopted the term to
replace her earlier darning needle.

Colloquial darning needle, regularly
used in the North and in New England,
with expansion south to Philadelphia,
reflects that distribution by its dominance of Minnesota, northern Iowa, and
eastern North Dakota. The variant devil's
darning needle, minor in the North but
with a strong southern expansion as far
as southern West Virginia, reflects that
particular distribution by its UM occurrence as a minor term in Midland speech
territory, especially southern Iowa. The
probably hybrid devil's needle, devil fly,
and devil's fly also turn up as singletons. The interesting variant sewing
needle, with one instance of simple sewer,
is found in Minnesota. Unexplained Spanish needle appears in Nebraska.

Most Midland equivalents include snake
as the first component. Most common is
snakefeeder, the Iowa and Nebraska incidence of which correlates closely with
its eastern popularity in central and
western Pennsylvania and the upper Ohio
valley. Snake doctor, found in eastern
Pennsylvania and the Virginia Piedmont,
has likewise been carried west to retain
some feeble vitality in Midland territory.
Snake eater and the curious snake charmer
are also Midland but rare.

Spindle, in the east apparently restricted to New Jersey, is the term used
by one southern Minnesotan of Ohio parent-

age and by one North Dakotan of New York
parentage.

An unsolved problem is raised by the
frequency and distribution of mosquito
hawk, which, although an instance was
found by McDavid in upper New York, has
its eastern range principally from Chesapeake Bay southward into Delmarva, the
Virginia Tidewater, and the Carolina Piedmont as far as Georgia. Gordon Wood's
postal investigation (*Vocabulary Change:
A Study of Variation in Regional Words in
Eight of the Southern States*, Southern
Illinois University Press, 1970) reveals
mosquito hawk as "mid-Southern" with
greatest frequency in Georgia and Arkansas but with no expansion into Oklahoma.
E. B. Atwood (*The Regional Vocabulary of
Texas*, University of Texas Press, 1962)
reports it in Louisiana and the eastern
half of Texas, especially along the Gulf
coast. In the UM, however, mosquito hawk,
with the twice-occurring mosquito catcher,
is found almost exclusively in Minnesota
north of the two lower tiers of counties
and in eastern North Dakota, that is, in
territory having a minimal degree of
Midland and no Southern penetration.
Further study in the North Central states
may provide a bridge between the occurrence in New York state and the stronger
incidence in the UM.

airplane ¹306.
beetle 306.
darning needle 1-2, ¹3, 5, 10, s¹11, 20,
26, 28, 31, †33, 35, 37, 49-50, †51, 55,
¹†60; 102-4, 110, 114, 118, 134; 201-2,
205, :207, 212, :219, :221, 222, †226;
*303, 309, ¹314, 326-27, *328; 420.
devil's ~ ~ †45, !†46, !†61; 101, ¹103,
c105, ¹109, 111, s115-16, 120, 122, *134,
s¹136, s137, 139, 141, :144, 150; 204,

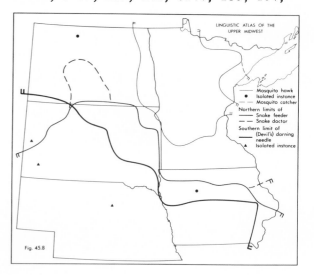

Fig. 45.8

210, 215, 221, ¹225; ¹310; †312; †410,
413, 428. devil's needle 7.
  devil fly s¹309. devil's ~ 310.
  doctor fly ¹121.
  dragon fly 2-3, 13-14, 29, 33-34, s?44,
45, →46, 47, 51, 53-54, 60-61; 103, 108,
113, 118, 121, *123, 129, 131, 136-37,
*141, 149; 206, ¹207, 214, sn223, 224,
226; 301-2, ¹305, *306, 308-9, 311-12,
¹314, 315, *318, 320, 323, 325, 328; 406,
409-11, 417, 419, 421, 424-26, 429-30,
sn431, 433.
  humming bird 431.
  mosquito catcher 15, 18.
  mosquito hawk 1, 8, 11, sn13, 21-24,
†26, :30, 33, 42, 45; 113, ¹125; 203,
208, 220, 225.
  needle 208; 316.
  sewer 12.
  sewing needle 14, 16-18, †34, 38, 43;
211.
  snake charmer 401. ~ doctor s¹118, 119,
:130, *138, 149; 216; *311, 314, ~ eater
*141; ¹302; 412, 433. ~ feeder 109, 113,
115, *116, 117, 123-25, 127-28, s¹131,
132-35, 137-38, 140, 142-43, 145-47, 150;
302-3, 306, *318, 322, sn†324, †325; 402-
6, ¹407, :408, †411, 414, 416, 418-19,
422, 427, 429, s431, s434, 437. ~ fly
:321.
  Spanish needle 420.
  spindle 59; 218.
  no response 4, 6, 9, 19, 25, ?27, 32,
36, 39-40, :41, 48, 52, 56-58, 62-65;
106-7, 112, 126, 148, 151-52; ?209, 213,
217; ?304, 307, 313, 317, 319; 415, 423,
432, 435, ?436.

Comment:

  darning needle: Usu.--2. The large
variety--8. A "book name"--46. Bigger than
a 'snake feeder'--135. Larger than a
'dragonfly'--309. Used when a child--51;
226. "It'll sew up a kid's mouth if he
says naughty words"--31. "It would sew
up my mouth if I lied"--53. devil fly =
darning needle--45. devil's darning needle: "If I didn't wear my bonnet, it
would sew my ears shut"--46. "It'll sew
your ears together;" used when a child--
61. An insect that doesn't fly; not the
same as a snake feeder--115. Doesn't
have any wings or as large a body as a
dragonfly--137. = walkingstick--141.
Inf.'s term for a kind of prickly grass,
not for an insect--317. Inf.'s name for
a kind of seed, not an insect--33. The
smaller variety, but this is usu. called
'snake feeder,' too--150. dragonfly: For
this inf. this term apparently means an
ichneumon fly--429. mosquito hawk: Small
variety, not the big--8, 53. Different
from a dragonfly--53. "When we were kids,
we always called them 'mosquito hawks'--

26. Smaller than a darning needle--1. A
bird, not an insect; = nighthawk--218.
sewing needle: Used when a child--34.
snake eater: Two boys, not infs., added
that this term is common here among
young boys--302. snake feeder: "Any more,
I call them 'dragonflies'"--325. Usu.--
406. Used when a child--411.

45.9 crawfish.

  Although information is absent from
the eastern and from the North Central
records, as well as from most of those
made in Minnesota, enough evidence appears in the UM to reveal that three of
the four terms for the fresh-water crus-
tacean are distributed according to the
general Northern-Midland pattern.
  Crab occurs in northern Iowa and in
the eastern Dakotas. The three out of
four responses in Minnesota are supported by supplementary evidence from University of Minnesota students who are
state residents. Crab is for them the
common term.
  In Midland territory the regional name
is crawdad or its hypocoristic equivalent crawdaddy. The latter is limited
to Iowa.
  The fourth term, crawfish, appears in
both the Northern and the Midland areas
as a variant which may be declining in
popularity. Its use is greater among the
old-fashioned speakers. Its historical
original, the literary crayfish that
provides the primary dictionary entry,
was not reported at all in the UM.
  No terms were elicited in the arid
western sections of the Dakotas, where
the referent itself is not found and is
not known to the infs.

	Ia.	N.D.	S.D.	Nb.	Ave.
crab	21%	58%	41%	7%	26%
crawdad(dy)	49%	0	23%	73%	46%
crawfish	47%	42%	23%	24%	35%

  crab c29, 30, :31; 102-9, 119, 126;
201-2, *203, 204, 218, 222, 224; 306-8,
316, 318-19, s325; 407-8, †418, ¹*432.
  crawdad 35; 111, 113-14, 121, *122,
125, 127-28, 130-31, 133, c137, 138,
140, 144, 149; 320, 323, s¹324; 402,
404-6, →409, 410-11, 413-14, 416, 419,
421, s423, 424-26, sn427, 428-29, 433,
435, :437.
  crawdaddy 101, 103, 123-24, 134, *145,
150; 328.
  crawfish 105, 109-10, 112-16, 120, 122,
129, 132, 135, ¹136, 137-38, 141-43, 145-
48; 206, 208, 220-21, 225; c311, 322,
:325; †409, *417, 418, 420, 422, 427,
429-30, ¹433.

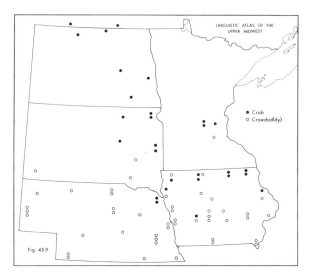

LINGUISTIC ATLAS OF THE
UPPER MIDWEST

● Crab
○ Crawdad(dy)

Fig. 45.9

no response 1-28, 32-34, 36-65; 117-
18, 139, 151-52; ?205, 207, ?209, ?210,
?211, 212-14, :215, 216, ?217, ?219,
?223, 226; 301-3, ?304, 305, 309-10,
?312, 313-15, 317, 321, 326-27.

Comment:

crawdad: Inf. alternated -/dæb/ with
-/dæd/--428. crawfish: Inf. responded
with plural crawfishes--132. Common
here--325.

46.1a varmints.

Asked for their word for small living
things considered unpleasant or undesirable, most infs. respond with varmints
or a phonetic variant. Although a large
proportion of infs., both urban and rural
and particularly in Type III, apparently
lack a generic term, one fieldworker recorded in Minnesota and Nebraska the
words pests and rodents, the former a
generic and the second restricted to rats
and mice.

A scattered half dozen have varmits,
with loss of nasal /n/ before /t/; an
equal number in North Dakota, besides one
in Iowa, use the original vermin or varmin without the excrescent /t/ and the
analogical /s/ plural. A few older infs.
of Scandinavian or German parentage retain /w/ for the initial consonant.

For the greater number of infs. using
varmints or one of its variants, the collective meaning is that of predatory or
destructive animals in general, ranging
from mice and rats to wolves and coyotes.
About two dozen, scattered widely
throughout the five states, extend the
generic sense to include insects. For
nearly as many, however, also widely
scattered, the meaning is limited to insects. A handful have only the metaphor-

ical application to people looked upon
as disreputable. The meaning 'worms,'
entertained by two infs. and conjectured
by two others, may simply be suggested
by the form of the word rather than actually accepted in use. No geographical
or social patterns correlate with the
semantic differences.

pests 45, 57-58, 63; 307.
rodents 40, 43, s45, 46-47, 51-53,
61-63; 305, 308, 319.
varmints s¹3, 7, sn8, s¹9, 10-12, 14,
sn20, ¹23, 24, 29-30, ¹†33, 34-35, sn37,
39, †40, ¹43, 44, 46, ¹51, s54, 55, 57-
58, 60, c61, 62, †65; 101-2, 105-6, s107,
108-11, 113, 115-16, 119, 122-30, ¹131,
132, s†133, ¹134, 135-37, 139, 141-50;
210, 213-14, ¹215, 217-18, ¹219, 220,
:sn221, 222-23; 301, sn302, ¹304, 306,
311, ¹313, ¹315, s317, 318, 320, ¹321,
c322, 324, ¹326; 401, 403-4, 406, ¹408,
409, ¹410, 412, ¹414, †416, 418, 420,
†422, 424, 428-32, ¹435, 437. varmits 27;
122; s208; 413, 423, 427. vermints 117;
203-4, 211-12, !216, c224. warmints ¹19,
48; 421, 434.
vermin 1-2, 45, 53; 120. varmin s¹63;
s118. wermin s?41.
no response 4-6, 13, 15-18, 21-22,
:?25, 26, 28, 31-32, 36, 38, 42, 49-50,
56, 59, 64; 103-4, 114, 121, 138, 140,
151-52; 201-2, ?205, 206-7, ?209, 225-26;
303, 309-10, 312, 314, 316, 323, ?325,
327-28; 402, 405, 411, 415, 417, 419,
425-26, 433, 437.

Comment:

rodents: Any destructive animals--47.
varmin: Insects--63. Worms--?118. varmints: Destructive animals--8-10, 12,
23-24, 30, 35, 37, 39-40, 44, 55, 57,
60-62; 101-3, 105, 107-8, 110, 113, 115,
122-26, 128-29, 131, 135-37, 139-42,
145-50; 210, 213, 220-23; 301, 311, 315,
320, 322, 326; 401, 403-4, 409, 414, 416,
420, 422, 428-29, 431-32, 435. Insects--
3, 7, 11, 65; 106, 127; 215, 219; 321;
430. = rodents--46. Worms--7; 127. Generic term for pests--20, 33; 109, 116,
120, 130, 132-34; 214, 217-18; 302, 304,
312, 324; 406, 408, 418, 437. Disreputable people--34, 55; 130, 144; 315; 409.
Used by inf.'s grandfather--133. varmits:
Destructive animals--112; 413, 423, 427.
Snakes--27. vermin: Destructive animals--
2, 45. Insects--1-2. = rodents--53.
vermints: Destructive animals--117. In-
sects--203, 211-13, 216. Generic term for
pests--204, 224. Disreputable people--
216. warmints: Destructive animals--48;
421, 434. wermin: Worms--?41.

46.1b skunk. WG 15, 48, 74; F137.

For the black and white beautiful but

320

occasionally bad-smelling animal *(Mephit-is mephitis)* the universal designation in the UM is <u>skunk</u>. A smaller Midland and Southern arboreal variety *(Spilogale pu-torius)* is often distinguished by the term <u>polecat</u> or, rarely, by <u>spotted skunk</u> in recognition of its having inter-rupted white stripes instead of the skunk's continuous V-shaped stripe. Re-portedly, however, <u>polecat</u> may be a femi-nine euphemism for <u>skunk</u> (see 220), and for some speakers the two terms seem interchangeable for either genus.

Except for two late interviews, infor-mation from Minnesota is lacking.

The not infrequent ambiguity resulting from the co-occurrence of <u>skunk</u> and <u>polecat</u> is compounded by the existence of <u>civet cat</u> in the same Midland speech area and occasionally in the Northern zone as well. With one exception, current com-mercial dictionaries as well as the *DAm* fail to associate this name of an Asian and African mammal with any North Ameri-can animal except the Mexican and south-western U.S. ring-tailed cacomistle. The Merriam-Webster *Third International,* however, is in accord with the UM evi-dence that the term is a common regional designation for varieties of the pole-cat or spotted skunk. The curiously high frequency of the term in Nebraska hints at its possible spread from the south-west. Wood did not find it in the South; Atwood found <u>civet cat</u> known to 6% of his infs. in <u>Texas</u> and <u>civvy cat</u> known to 2.2%. Its use in the <u>UM</u> is sometimes marked with uncertainty, but most infs. who know and use the term apparently do differentiate it from <u>skunk</u> as referring to a smaller and spotted animal and thus equate it with <u>polecat</u>.

Four infs. (314, 316, 420, 432), how-ever, claim that the three terms refer to three different animals differing in size and in marking, the skunk being the largest and having the V-shaped white stripe, the polecat being intermediate with interrupted stripes or spots, and the civet cat smallest and also spotted. And an older Nebraskan Type I inf. (407) describes the civet cat as solid gray in color, with legs longer than those of a skunk, and thinner in the body. Clearly the history, semantics, and distribution of <u>civet cat</u> in the U.S. call for more widespread and intensive investigation.

	Ia.	N.D.	S.D.	Nb.	Ave.
civet cat	14%	0	33%	62%	27%
polecat	14%	4%	22%	21%	15%
skunk	98%	100%	100%	100%	99%

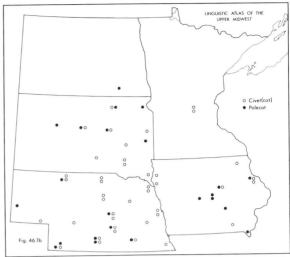

Fig. 46.1b   LINGUISTIC ATLAS OF THE UPPER MIDWEST
○ Civet(cat)
● Polecat

civet 404, 424. ~ cat 29-30; 108-9, 111, 118-20, 146; ¹302, 306, 314, *316, 317, 321-23, 325, 328; 403, c405, 406-8, 413-14, †415, 416, 419-23, 427-28, 430-32, 434, ¹435, 436-37.

polecat sn118, sn119, 130, 132-33, 135, 150; ¹216-17, ¹220, ¹222, 224; 302, 306, 308, ¹†312, 314, *316, ¹318, 319; 404, 411, ¹413, 420, 422, 429-31, *432, ¹433, ¹435, 437.

skunk 13, 15-18, 29-31, 35, !36, 38; 101-34, 136-41, c142, 143-49, c150; 201-2, c203, 204-17, !218, 219, c220, 222-24, c225, 226; c301, 302-8, c309, 310-21, c322, 323-26; c401, 402-4, c405, !406, 407-37. spotted ~ 404.

striped kitty 121; !318.
37, 39-65; 151-52; 221; 327.

Comment:

civet: Smaller than a skunk--404, 424. = <u>spotted</u> skunk--404. civet cat: Smaller than a skunk--29; 109, 120; 316-17, 321, 328; 403, 413, 419, 421-22, 427, 432, 434, 437. Smaller than a skunk and spot-ted--30; 323, 325; 405-6, 408. Spotted--306, 322. Striped; a skunk isn't--108, 146. Has two stripes on its back and many on its sides; a skunk has only two back stripes--436. Smaller than a skunk; solid color--420. Taller and thinner than a skunk--407. It can climb; a skunk cannot--29; 413. = <u>skunk</u>--415, 430, 435. Inf. says civet cats appeared in this locality c. 1920--322. Pronounced [sɪvɪk]--29, 120. Pronounced [sɪfɪk]--109. polecat: Spotted--132. Solid color--133. It has wider stripes than a skunk--316. It has stripes around its body; a skunk has stripes the length of its body--430. Smaller and less vicious than a skunk--224. = <u>skunk</u>--119; 302; 404, 413, 420, 422, 432, 437. Larger than a civet cat--432. = civet cat--119; 302. skunk: Inf.'s usual term--308. Inf. responded with 'skunk' for the plural--120. Larger than both a polecat and a civet cat--432. "Society women call them 'polecats'"--220.

46.2a ground squirrel. WG 15, 48, 74; F138.

For the Atlantic states Kurath describes a relatively simple pattern of distribution of two terms, the expanding Northern chipmunk and the declining Midland ground squirrel, both of which refer to the same animal, a small striped woodland terrestrial rodent, *Tamia striatus*. In the UM the situation is more complex. Although chipmunk (not actually sought by fieldworkers) continues unambiguously to designate the members of the *Tamia* genus where they occur -- in Iowa, Minnesota, and the Black Hills of South Dakota, ground squirrel here refers rather to any one or all of three closely related subgroups of a quite different genus, *Citellus*, and competes, often ambiguously, with 24 other terms, including the more popular gopher.

Because not all infs. reveal clear awareness of the characteristics of the three species, the distribution of the 25 competing terms reflects only in part the actual range of the animals themselves. Some infs. use two or more of the terms as generics or exhibit vagueness as to their exact reference. Most, however, make clear distinctions and provide evidence for grouping the terms as in the numbered sections below.

Ground squirrel itself is applied to each of the species but, except for several instances in eastern North Dakota and northern South Dakota, its distribution is restricted significantly in accord with its origin as an eastern expression. In the eastern United States the term contrasts with chipmunk; in the UM, though of course with its different meaning from that in the east, it contrasts with Northern-oriented gopher. Squirrel and its combinations dominate Iowa and Nebraska; gopher and its combinations dominate Minnesota and the Dakotas.

Grinnie, another Midland (western Pennsylvania and upper Ohio valley) name for the chipmunk, also has been carried westward with the same general transference of meaning. It occurs three times in Iowa. Of the various generic synonyms grinnie and unexplained squinny, apparently localized in Polk County, Iowa, are the only ones for which a fieldworker did not elicit a description permitting assignment to one of the three numbered sections. Gray squirrel, also eastern, likewise appears with a semantic shift in Nebraska and southeastern South Dakota, where, however, it clearly designates the gray gopher.

Many infs., chiefly rural, provide adequate identifying characteristics for the animals they name, but even these do not always agree upon the same name/referent relationship.

The most common subvariety or species is the thirteen-striped ground squirrel or Minnesota gopher, from which the state of Minnesota and the state university athletic teams derive their nicknames. It is found throughout the UM, except in the Arrowhead district of Minnesota north of Lake Superior. This animal (*Citellus tridecemlineatus* Mitchell) is brown with thirteen alternating stripes that do not extend upon its face as do those on the chipmunk. Its appearance leads to such epithets as found in streaked (/strikɪd/ or /strikt/) gopher and striped gopher, streaked and striped squirrel, and, once in Nebraska, striped picket pin. Picket pin derives from the characteristic posture of alertness when the animal is erect by its burrow.

Richardson's ground squirrel (*Citellus richardsonii* Sabine) is not known ordinarily by that designation but rather is usually known by flickertail, a word that provides the nickname of North Dakota as the Flickertail State. A dry-prairie rodent, it is common in North Dakota except west of the Missouri River, in the western edge area of Minnesota and Iowa, and in eastern South Dakota and eastern Nebraska. It lacks stripes and is dusty gray with a cinnamon buff on the hairs. The common name describes its habit of rapidly flicking its tail. It is called also simply gopher by those for whom it is the familiar representative of the genus, but there are also the minor descriptive variants field gopher, ground gopher, prairie gopher, and yellow gopher. One inf.'s confusion may appear in his use of mound gopher, for the animal he describes does not ordinarily make mounds, which are characteristic rather of the so-called true gopher, the pocket gopher. A northwestern Minnesota farmer uses graphic bobtail for presumably the same animal, although he likewise says that it makes a mound and yet is not a pocket gopher.

Franklin's ground squirrel (*Citellus franklinii* Sabine), found in most of the UM except the Arrowhead triangle of northeastern Minnesota and the western thirds of South Dakota and Nebraska, is usually descriptively called gray gopher. It is large and dark gray, long-tailed,

somewhat resembling the gray tree squirrel. A few infs. call it simply gopher,
a widespread number of others, mostly
in Midland speech territory, call it
ground squirrel or, with complete semantic leap, gray squirrel. A North Dakotan
curiously terms it flickertail with the
comment that this word and gray gopher
refer to the same animal, which he says
is larger than the striped gopher. Bushy
tail is a single response, also in North
Dakota.

See also Gary N. Underwood, "Midwestern terms for the ground squirrel,"
Western Folklore 29:3 (1970), 167-74.

	Mn.	Ia.	N.D.	S.D.	Nb.	Ave.
flickertail	5%	0	45%	0	0	7%
gopher	80%	24%	72%	48%	19%	50%
gray gopher	18%	4%	20%	10%	0	10%
striped gopher	40%	14%	60%	19%	3%	26%
ground squirrel	8%	78%	20%	24%	86%	44%

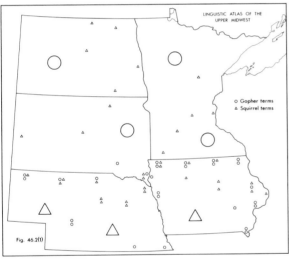

Fig. 46.2(1)

bobtail [1]7.
bushy tail 221.
flickertail 4, 8, 26; [1]113; 202, sn203,
204, 206, 208, 211, 213-14, 221, 224-25.
gopher 5-7, 9-10, c11, 12, 14, 17-18,
*19, 20, 22-28, 31-38, 40, 42, c44, 46,
c47, 48, c49, 50-55, 57-62, *63, 65; c101,
102-4, 109, 122-23, 140-41, 149-50, 152;
202-3, 205, 209-13, 215, 217-20, 222-26;
303-4, 308, 310, 312-13, 321, 323, 325,
328; 401-2, [1]403, 404, 418-19, 433, 435.
field ~ 10. grass ~ 202. gray ~ 22, 27,
30, 41, 43, 45-46, 53, 59-61; 105-6; 204,
208, 210, 218, 225; 303, 317. ground ~
62; 201, 207. mound ~ 25. pocket ~ 21;
212. prairie ~ 44, 47; 201, 219. squirre⁻
~ 25. streaked ~ 56, 64-65; 107-8; 223;
405. striped ~ 1, 4, 7-8, 10, *19, 20,
22, 25-27, 29-30, 41-43, 45, 47-48, 50,

53, 59-61; 104-8, 117, 121; 201-4, 206-10,
213, 218, 220-21, 223, 225; 301-2, 311,
320; c405. yellow ~ 27.
grinnie *122, 135-36.
picket pin 422. striped ~ ~ 409.
squinny [1]116, 128, 130-31.
ground squirrel 21, 30, 39, 45, 60;
c101, 102-3, 105, 110, 112, 114-15,
*116, [1]117, 118-19, 121-27, 129-35, 137-
40, *141, 142-43, 145-50; 204, 206, 211,
221, 224; 306, 309, 314, [1]318, 324-25;
401, 403-4, 406-9, 411-18, 420-22, 425-
37. gray ~ 322-23, 325; 413, 423. prairie ~ 44; *116, 147, streaked ~ *116;
322. striped ground ~ 424. striped ~
113, 117. Minnesota striped ~ 404.
no response 2-3, 13, 15-16; 111, 120,
144, 151; 216; 305, 307, 315-16, 319,
326-27; 410.

Comment:

flickertail: Heard by inf. in Mn. and
Dakotas--113. ground squirrel: Usu.--325.
Inf. says this is the usual local term--
403. squinny: Heard by inf. in Wy.--116.

The Meanings

(1) ground squirrel (generic or
undescribed):

flickertail sn203, 214.
gopher 7, 9-10, 14, 17-18, 20, 22-23,
25-27, 31-32, 34, 40, 42, c44, 46, c47,
48, c49, 51, 53, 57-62, *63, 65; c101,
102-4, 109, 122-23, 140-41, 149-50, 152;
202-3, 210, 218, 225; 304, 308, 328; 401,
433, 435. ground ~ 62. prairie ~ 44, 47.
grinnie *122, 135-36.
ground squirrel 39; c101, 102-3, 105,
110, 112, 114-15, *116, 118-19, 121-27,
129-35, 137-40, *141, 142-50; 306, 314,
[1]318; 404, 412, 414-15, 422, 425-27, 429,
431, 433-35. prairie ~ 44; *116, 147.
picket pin 422.
squinny [1]116, 128, 130-31.

(2) striped ground squirrel or thirteen-
lined ground squirrel:

gopher 6, c11, 12, 28, 35, 37-38, 50,
52, 54, 55; 209, 212, 215, 220, 224, 226;
313, 321, 323, 325; 402, [1]403, 404, 419.
grass ~ 202. pocket ~ 21; 212. streaked ~
56, 64-65; 107-8; 405. striped ~ 1, 4,
7-8, 10, *19, 20, 22, 25-27, 29-30, 41-
43, 45, 47-48, 50, 53, 59-61; 104-8, 117,
121; 201-4, 206-10, 213, 218, 220-21,
225; 301-2, 311-12, 320; 405.
ground squirrel 60; [1]117; 204; 309,
325; 401, 403, 406, 408, 411, 417, 430,
432, 436. streaked ~ *116; 322. striped
ground ~ 429. striped ~ 113, 117. Minnesota striped ~ 404.
striped picket pin 409.

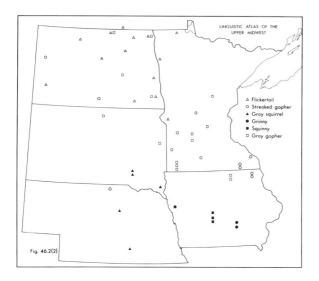

Fig. 46.2(2)

(3) flickertail or Richardson's
ground squirrel:

bobtail ¹7.
flickertail 4, 8, 26; 202, 206, 208,
211, 213, 221, 224-25.
gopher 24, 33, 36; 205, 211, 213, 219,
222-23. field ~ 10. ground ~ 201. mound
~ 25. prairie ~ 201, 219. yellow ~ 27.
ground squirrel 324; 407, 416, 428,
437.

(4) Franklin's ground squirrel or
gray gopher:

bushy tail 221.
flickertail 204.
gopher 5, *19; 217; 303, 310; 418.
gray ~ 22, 27, 30, 41, 43, 45-46, 53,
59-61; 105-6; 204, 208, 210, 218, 225;
303, 317. ground ~ 207. squirrel ~ 25.
ground squirrel 21, 30, 45; 206, 211,
221, 224; 409, 413, 418, 420-21. gray ~
322-23, *325; 413, 423.

46.3 ˙woodpecker.   WG 74.

Not included in the Minnesota survey,
this item was added later to ascertain
whether South Midland peckerwood had
penetrated into southeastern Iowa. No
instances were found, but infs. did provide names for local varieties known to
them. As with other fauna and flora few
infs., however, revealed more than a
foggy notion of the several varieties
actually observable in their neighborhoods.

The usual response to the query about
birds that drill holes in trees to obtain insects for food is redheaded woodpecker, although a widely distributed
minority offer simply woodpecker with
the admission that they know only the
redheaded kind. For this bird (*Mela-*

nerpes erythrocephalus) redhead alone is
a frequent shortening of the longer
phrase, and red-shafted woodpecker and
redtop turn up as singletons.

The flicker (*Colaptes aureatus luteus*),
found throughout the UM though only rarely in the western arid regions, is usually so called. It is once described
as red shaft flicker and four times as
flickertail, two occurrences of which
are noteworthy as offered by North Dakota infs. who know the same word as a
synonym for Richardson's ground squirrel.
(See 46.2.) A not uncommon equivalent in
the UM is yellowhammer. Two infs. use
high hole and high holder. Brown woodpecker, proffered by two Iowans, almost
surely refers to this bird as well.

Only a few infs. identify the downy
woodpecker (*Dryobates pubescens median-
us*) and the rarer hairy woodpecker (*Dryobates villosus septentrionalis*), once
with the comment that they are the same
except for size.

The red-bellied woodpecker (*Centurus
carolinus*) is known to only two Iowa
infs., one of whom calls it redbelly and
the other of whom uncertainly thinks it
might be called redbreasted woodpecker.

A Type III North Dakota inf. names the
pileated woodpecker (*Ceophoeus pileatus
abiecticola*), which is rather rare in
his region.

Four names occur only as single instances not readily assigned to any of
the varieties listed above: blackhead,
greenhead, striped woodpecker (the down-
y?), and yellow-shafted woodpecker.

blackhead 129.
brown woodpecker 117, *145. downy ~
116, *117, 122(as pl. downies), 123,
131, 152; 226; *306, *328; 404, c409.
flicker *117, *122, 123, 126-27, 137-
38, 144, 148-49; 221, 226; 306, 309,
323, 326, *328; 404, 406, 410-11, 419.
red shaft ~ 409.
flickertail 108; 202, 208; 325.
greenhead 109.
hairy woodpecker 131; 409.
high-hole 306. high-holder 105.
pileated woodpecker 222.
red-belly 131.
red-breasted woodpecker ?412.
redhead 112-13, 122(as pl. ~s), 125-26,
134, 144, 146-47(pl.), 148; 205; 308-9
(pl.), 317, 320(pl.); 408(pl.), 409.
red-headed woodpecker 29-30, 38; 105-8,
114-17, 123-24, 128, 133, 135, 137-38,
143, 145, 150, 152; 202, 213-14, 222,
224, 226; 302, 306, 312-16, 318, 321-26,
328; 401, 403, 405-6, 410-11, 414, 418-
19, 423, 427, 429, 431, 433, ¹434, 435.
redhead ~ 129-30, 132; 208; 309.
red-shafted ~ 204. redtop ~ 204.

sapsucker 125, 135, 147, 149; 311; 404.
striped woodpecker 320.
woodpecker 31, 35-36, 38; 101-13, 116-21, 126-33, 137-41, 146-47, 149-50, 152; 201, 206-7, 209-12, 214, 216-20; 305-8, 316-19; 402, 407, 413-17, 420-28, 430-35.
yellowhammer 30; 107, 113, 116, 122, 125, 127-28, 134-35, 147; 202, 214, 221, 225; 311, 320, *328; *417, 418, 422.
yellow-shafted woodpecker 404.
no response 1-28, 32-34, 37, 39-65; 136, 151; ?203, 215, 223; 301, 303-4, 310, 327; 412, ?436, 437.

Comment:

flicker: "Kind of a halfbreed wood-pecker"--309. hairy woodpecker: "Hairy and downy woodpeckers are the same except for size; both are black and white"--131. redbelly: "Looks like a flicker except for red splotches under the wings. It has a solid gray breast"--131. wood-pecker: Redheaded--31, 36, 38; 139, 149; 407, 422, 430. yellowhammer: = flicker--221. "Yellow under the wings and breast but speckledy otherwise"--127. no response: "No trees here to peck on"--223.

46.4 bullfrog. NE 231.

Eastern folk words for the bullfrog seem not to have emigrated to the UM. Most infs. offer bullfrog and a number, lacking that specialized awareness, use simply frog as a generic. Bull toad, croaker, greenhead, and water frog appear once each, all in the Midland speech area. Leap frog, in Iowa, is dubious.
In the arid North Dakota Badlands the inf. remarked, "The bullfrogs here are twelve years old before they learn how to swim."

bullfrog 1-8, c9, 10-31, 33-40, !41, 42-45, r46, 47-54, 56-65; 101-8, s109, 110-28, 130-35, 137-40, 142-50; 152; 202-8, 210, 212-13, c214, 215, :218, 219-22, 224-26; 302, 305-8, 312-14, 316-26, 328; c401, 402-6, 408-11, 413-14, †415, 416-24, 426-33, ¹434, 435, 437.
bull toad 121.
croaker 134; ¹204.
frog 13-14, 16, c24, 32, 45, 51; 111, 117, 126, 141, 148-49; 209, ?211, 216-17, 223; 301-4, 309-10, c323; 412-13, 415, 417, c423-24, 425-26, c429, 430-31, 434-36.
greenhead 413.
leap frog ?129.
water frog 434.
no response 55; 136, 151; 201; 311, 315, 327; ?407.

46.5 spring frog. NE 231.

Infs. were asked to name the small

tree frog (*Hyla crucifer*) to be heard making shrill peeping sounds in bushes near lakes or marshes in the spring of the year. Field records reveal general unawareness of any special term other than frog itself. Five Minnesota infs. and three Nebraskans classify it accurately as tree frog; five other Minnesotans call it tree toad. Three infs. in the same states have spring frog. One South Dakotan offers both peeping frog and peep toad, and another suggests inappropriate croaker. One North Dakotan of English parentage offers cricket frog, actually the name of a different species of tree frog (*Acris gryllus*) characterized by chirping rather than by peeping. Eastern spring peeper seems not to have been carried west of Michigan.
Other names offered probably refer to other species: grass frog, green frog, leap frog, and nightingale.

cricket frog 204.
croaker 320.
frog c9, 15, 17-18, 29-30, 32-33, 36, 39-41, c46, 47, 52, c53, 60, 62-63; 101-10, 112-15, c116, 117-25, 127-42, c143, 144-50; 201, 203, 209, 212-13, 215, 218, 221, 224; 311, 326; 407-8, 416, 427-28, 432-33. grass ~ 50, 61; 405. green ~ 1, 13, 22, 35. leap ~ 48, 58; ¹107. leopard ~ 51.
nightingale 202.
peeping frog 306.
peep toad 306.
spring frog :sn10, sn56; 424.
toad 325.
tree frog 13-14, 43-44, 51; 428, 431, 434.
tree toad 44-45, 53, 57, 59; *306.
no response 2, ?3, 4-7, ?8, 11-12, 16, 19-21, 23-24, ?25, 26-28, 31, 34, 37-38, 42, 49, 54-55, 64-65; 111, 126, 151, ?152; ?205, 206-9, ?210-11, 214, ?216, 217, ?219-20, 222, ?223, 225-26; 301-5, 307-8, ?309, 310, 312-14, ?315, 316-19, 321-25, 327-28; 401-4, 406, 409-15, 417-23, 425-26, 429-30, 435-37.

Comment:

tree frog: "Small and delicate"--13. "Foretells rain"--51.

46.6 toad. NE 232.

The common garden toad is known simply as toad throughout the UM. Eastern and Midland hoptoad barely survives with three scattered examples. Southern and South Midland toad-frog is retained by one Iowan of Tennessee and Kentucky parentage. Wart-frog likewise persists in the speech of one Iowan, and warty-toad in the speech of five infs., three of whom are in Iowa. Surely horned toad, however, and probably horny-toad refer to a quite different animal, a kind of lizard.

    frog 209.
    hop-toad 31; 126; 320.
    horned toad 421.
    horny-toad 214.
    toad 1-8, c9, 10-27, 29-34, c35, 36-48, !49, 50-51, s52, 53-54, c55, 56-65; 101-13, 115-24, 126-34, 136-41, 143-50, 152; :sn201, 202-8, 210-26; 301-4, c306, 307-15, c316, 317-26, 328; 401-2, c403, 404-14, 416-20, 422-37.
    toad-frog 135.
    tree toad 15; 413.
    wart-frog 142.
    warty-toad c42; 114, c115, 138; 401.
    no response 28; 125, 151; 305, 327; 415.

Comment:

    Toad: "A toad in the cellar will keep insects away"--56. "Gives warts"--62. Inf. considers frogs and toads identical--216. Inf. thinks toads are "rained down"--324. Inf. says a toad is a "real big frog"--425.

46.7a earthworm. NE 236. WG 14, 23, 26, 37; F24, F28, F35, F139, F140.

Although fishworm is common in central Massachusetts, the Connecticut valley, and eastern New York and Pennsylvania, it is remarkable that, along with distinctly minor localisms, it well-nigh disappeared from Northern speech in its western migration. Angleworm, dominant in New England and New York, so increased its dominance that it became the distinctively Northern form in the UM.

The widespread use of fishworm in West Virginia and southern Ohio, however, was sufficiently influential in the western movement of Midland and South Midland speech to make it the clear Midland marker in the UM.

The contrast is even more remarkable because, as a fisherman's term, fishworm could reasonably be predicted in northern Minnesota. Thousands of Iowa fishermen, all fishing with what they know as fishworms, fish there every summer. But they still buy their bait at roadside stands with signs definitively marked ANGLEWORMS or, occasionally in perhaps partial capitulation to the visitors, simply WORMS.

Dew worm, not reported in New England or along the Atlantic coast, is considered an innovation by two of the three Duluth infs. using it, and it appears once also in Saskatchewan, where the

inf. did not distinguish night crawlers (Cp. 46.7b.) Garden worm, from the same inf., may be a Canadianism. Grub worm probably was originally an error on the part of the female inf. Sucker, in southeastern Nebraska, is unexplained in this sense.

Literary earthworm appears as a relatively infrequent variant in all five states.

	Mn.	Ia.	N.D.	S.D.	Nb.	Ave.
angleworm	94%	61%	88%	92%	54%	78%
earthworm	6%	4%	4%	11%	8%	6%
fish(ing) worm	9%	51%	0	11%	54%	27%
worm	5%	12%	0	4%	8%	6%

CL 82: The general pattern of the major variants found in the field records appears likewise in the data from 1,045 mail respondents. Dew worm, however, here turns up not only in Minnesota near the Canadian border (5b.2, 7.1) but also six times in Iowa in both Northern and Midland speech territory (53.2, 54.2, 64.2, 65.2, 67.1, 76.5). Red worm, thought by Kurath as not having crossed the Hudson River, is the form checked by one Minnesotan whose father was born in Connecticut (78.2), by a Nebraskan with Ohio and New York state grandparents (57.1), and by another Nebraskan with Canadian grandparents (61.2).

	Mn.	Ia.	N.D.	S.D.	Nb.	Ave.
angleworm	96%	35%	95%	91%	33%	67%
earthworm	6%	7%	8%	11%	16%	10%
fishworm	5%	68%	6%	17%	74%	37%

The situation is more accurately revealed by a breakdown of the Iowa returns: the northern third has 59% angleworm and the southern two-thirds only 6%; the northern third has 46% fishworm and the southern two-thirds has 91%.

    angleworm 2, ¹3, 4-7, *8, :9, 10-28, c29, 30-41, ¹42, 43-51, 53-58, c59, 60-62, c63, 64-65; 101-6, c107, 108-11, 113-23, →124, 126, 129-30, 133, ¹137, 141, 143, 148-49, ¹150; 201, 203-5, 207-11, 213-22, :223, 224-26; 301-10, 312-13, c314, 315-26; c401-2, 403-4, 406, 408-9, 411, 413, 416, 419-24, 426-28, 434.
    bait 14, 18.
    dew worm s→15, sn→16, 17; 202.
    earthworm 18, 34, 42, 51, s⊥58; 122, 144; 206; 306, ¹312, ¹315, *316, 319; 425, 428, 431.
    fishworm 1, ?2, 3, 52, c55, 62; ¹107, 111-12, 117, 119, 121, 124-25, 127-28, 131-33, 135, :136, 137-40, 142, 145-49, 152; ¹202, ¹215; 306, c311, 314; ¹403, 405-6, 410, 412-15, 417-18, 423, 428-34, s435, 436, 437.

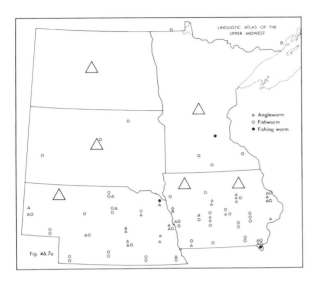

LINGUISTIC ATLAS OF THE
UPPER MIDWEST

△ Angleworm
○ Fishworm
● Fishing worm

Fig. 46.7a

fishing worm 34, ¹58; 150; 407.
garden worm 202.
ground worm 140.
grub worm 212.
sucker 435.
worm 8, 14-15, 17; 123, 125, 129, 134, 136, 141; 328; 426, 433, 435.
no response 151; 327.

Comment:

angl_eworm: "Brought in by Marquis de Mores" (See community note in Vol. 1)-- 214. "I guess 'fish worms' are really 'angleworms'"--423. fishworm: "Some children call them 'fish worms'"--403.

46.7b night crawler. NE 236. WG 75.

Erroneously identified in the WG as applied to a "mature earthworm," the term night crawler actually refers to a particular variety known for its large size and its practice of coming out of its burrow at night.

Most infs., especially non-anglers, do not recognize this as a special variety, sometimes commenting that no such worm is found locally. Nearly all of those who do distinguish it use night crawler. Night creeper and night worm are singletons recorded in central Minnesota, and one Minnesota inf. commented that his son had acquired in Minneapolis the equivalent night prowler, a form recorded only once in New England, in upper Vermont. In two Minnesota and Iowa Mississippi river communities dew worm is found.

dew worm 55; 140-41.
earthworm *316.
night crawler 6, 17, →24, 33-34, c35, 38, 42, *46, 51, 53, 55, 57, c!61, 62; 101-8, 110-17, 119-25, 127-34, 137-38,

142-43, 146-50, 152; c225; *316, 318, 321, 325-26; c402, 404, 409-10, 416, 426, 428, 433. ~ creeper 37. ~ worm 44.
no response 1-5, 7-16, 18-23, 25-29, 36, 39-41, 43, 45, 47-50, 52, 54, 56, 58-60, 63-65; 109, 118, 126, 135-36, 139, 144-45; 201-24, 226; 301-15, 317, 319-20, 322-24, 327-28; 401, 403, 405-8, 411-15, 417-25, 427, 429-32, 434-37.

Comment:

dew worm: "Wider and bigger;" = night crawler--140. night crawler: Bigger than an angleworm--42, 61-62; 321, 326; 426, 428, 433. Bigger and they come out at night--6, 44. "Just an angleworm that's had better feed"--404. "Found under boards"--46. A different variety or different "specie"--53, 61. "Both angleworms and night crawlers are earthworms"--51. Knows term from seeing it on a sign in Mo.--410.

46.8 rattlesnake.

The purpose of this UM addition to the worksheets was to ascertain the incidence of massassauga as the name of a small variety of rattlesnake (Sistrurus catenus). Only one inf., in southeastern North Dakota, is familiar with the term, although he comments that he had heard it also in Watonwan, in southern Minnesota.

Rattlesnake itself, however, appears as the generic throughout the UM, often with the comment that the reptile has been exterminated locally. Colloquial rattler also occurs, several times with epithets indicating particular varieties. Sidewinder also names such a variety, but one indigenous to the Southwest and not in the UM. Buzzer and rattlebug seem to be individualisms.

buzzer 320.
massasauga 225.
rattlebug 320.
rattler 17, 30, 39, c*43, 47-48, c51, c55, c60, c61, 64; 111, 121, 123, 125, 131, 137; 210, 221; 302-4, 309, 313, 315, 321, 323, 326; 406, 410-11, 418, 426, 437. diamond ~ 416. diamond-back ~ c405. ground ~ 140. prairie ~ ¹48, c65; 120, 141, 149; 312; 404, 409. swamp ~ c51. timber ~ 311.
rattlesnake 25, 29, c30, 32, 38, 40, 43-47, 49, c51, 52-54, 56-58, c59, 62-63; 101-17, 119, 122, 124, 126, 128-30, 132-36, 138-39, 142-48, 150, 152; 209-10, 212, 214-17, 223-24; 301, 305, 309-10, 314-15, 317, 322; 401-3, c405, 408, c410, 411, 413-28, c429, 430-36.
sidewinder 401.
no response 1-16, 18-24, 26-28, 31, 33-37, 41-42, 50; 118, 127, 151; 201-8,

211, 213, 218, ?219, 220, 222, 226; 302,
306-8, 316, 318-19, 324-25, 327-28; 407,
412.

46.9a turtle.

Except for unexplained blinding turtle
and snakeneck, both from the same Nebraska inf., few folk equivalents for
turtle appear in the UM. Both infs. in
Norfolk, Nb., do agree upon land turtle.
Two others in the Nebraska sandhill region use sand turtle, and one of them
also has water turtle and the better-
known snapping turtle and soft shell
turtle. These last two refer respectively to the predatory _Chelydra serpentina_
with its powerful jaws and to any member of the soft-backed family _Triony-_
chidae, but the other terms are not
readily assigned to particular varieties.
Most UM infs. know only the generic turtle or the phrase mud turtle, which designates any of several common freshwater
varieties.

blinding turtle 404. land ~ 413-14.
mossback 404.
mud turtle 29, 35; 103, 108, 111, 116,
140; 202, 212, 218, 220-23, 225-26; 301,
309, 311-13, 315-17, 319-20, 322-23, 328;
403, 407-8, 416, 435. sand ~ 405, 413.
snakeneck 404.
snapping turtle 103; 413-14. softshell
~ 413.
turtle 30-31, 36, 38; 101-2, 104-7,
109-15, 117-39, 141-50, 152; 201, 203-
11, 213-16, 219, 224; 304, s305, 306-8,
310, 318-19, 321, 325-26; 401-2, 405-6,
409-14, 417-37. water ~ 413.
no response 1-28, 32-34, 37, 39-65;
151; 217; 302-3, 314, 327; 415.

46.9b terrapin.

For most UM infs. terrapin is not a
meaningful word. Only in Iowa and Nebraska, Midland speech territory, is
there any recognition, and then it is,
with two exceptions, used to refer to
a dry land tortoise. (Dry)land turtle
is probably equivalent; so are fanci-
ful prairie schooner and sand terrapin
and yellow terrapin, all in Nebraska.

dry land turtle 137.
land turtle 120.
prairie schooner 429.
terrapin s102, s119, ¹120, s121, ¹130,
141, 145, s?149; ¹429. sand ~ 403. yellow ~ 404.
no response 1-65; 101, 103-18, 122-29,
131-36, 138-40, 142-44, 146-48, 150-52;
201-26; 301-28; 401-2, 405-28, 430-37.
Comment:

terrapin: Seen in a zoo--102. A salt-

water turtle--119, 130. Inf. knows the
term only through reading--120. Inf.
says it's a fish--121.

47.2 firefly. NE 238. WG 17, 33; F142.

Asked their word for the flying insect
that makes little flashes of light, UM
infs. rather evenly divide their responses between older firefly and the Americanism lightning bug.
The distribution, however, is less
even. Literary and New England firefly
is more strongly favored by Type II
speakers than by older and less educated
Type I, though not by the small sample
of college graduates. An occasional inf.
even remarks that firefly is newer and
that lightning bug is old-fashioned.
Regional distribution is also uneven.
Despite the dominance of lightning bug
in neighboring Wisconsin (68%) and in
New York state, this term is weighted
less heavily than firefly in the Northern speech area of the UM. It is, however, the most frequently used designation in the Midland speech zone,
though without a sharp isoglossic contrast. A possible factor is that the
insect itself is less common in the
northern part of the UM, so that the
book word is likely to be better known.
Less explicable is the spread of the
hybrid firebug. According to WG, its
eastern range is in Pennsylvania between the Susquehanna and the Allegheny
rivers and hence is distinctly North
Midland. Wood reports it in the South,
too, particularly in Mississippi, and
Atwood finds it in Texas. Yet--and its
16% frequency in Wisconsin is predictive
--in the UM its correlation is clearly
Northern. Only two examples appear in
Midland speech territory, one from an
eastern Nebraska inf. of Ohio parentage and one from a western South Dakotan whose father was likewise born in
Ohio.
Light bug and lighting bug are rare
variants, the second of which seems to
be rather a name for the glowworm.
June bug, generally accepted as the
name of a kind of beetle, is firmly accepted by several infs. as their term
for a firefly. This confusion--if that
is what it is--appears in all the UM
states except Iowa. (But see the checklist returns below.) Wood finds it occasionally in the South as well.
Box elder bug is clearly an error despite the inf.'s claim that it is his
usual expression for a firefly.

CL 83: From 1,043 respondents come data
confirming the generalizations from the
field interviews. Firefly dominates the
Northern area and lightning bug the Mid-

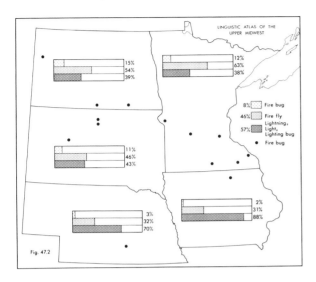

Fig. 47.2

land area. Firebug is likewise consistently Northern in its weighting. The
infrequent but widespread instances of
June bug are attested by the fact that
this is a write-in term, volunteered by
the respondents.

	Mn.	Ia.	N.D.	S.D.	Nb.	Ave.
firebug	10%	4%	14%	10%	4%	8%
firefly	59%	26%	67%	55%	37%	46%
June bug	1%	2%	2%	5%	4%	3%
lightning bug	45%	81%	30%	48%	78%	59%

box elder bug 404.
firebug 15-16, 26, 38, 43, 56, 62, 64;
106; 203, 209, 223-24; 302-4; 423.
firefly 1-2, 5-9, →10, ¹11, 14, 16-20,
22-24, 28-30, c31, 32-34, 36, 40, !41,
*43, 44-45, c46, 47-48, c49, 53-55, 61,
63, 65; 102, 106, 108, ¹110, 112, 115-16,
s117, 120-22, 126-27, 131, 133-34, ¹137,
150, 152; :201, 202, 205-6, 208, 210-11,
213, 216-19, 222, 226; 301, 308-10, →312,
313, c314, 315, 318, 323, 326-28; 402,
404, 406, 409-10, 412-13, 418, 422, 430-
31, 436.
glowworm 410, ¹425.
June bug 5; ¹225; ¹305, 306, 321; 405.
light bug 207. lighting ~ 13; 425.
lightning bug !3, :4, 10, !11-12, 13-
14, 17-18, 21-22, †23, 25, 27, 30, ¹33,
c35, 37, 39, 42, 50-52, 57-60; 101-5,
107, 109-11, 113-14, 116-32, 135-50,
152; 204, sn210, 212, 214-15, 220-21,
sn222, ¹223, !225; 305-7, 311, †312,
*316, 317-20, 322, 324-25; 401, 403-4,
406-8, 411, ¹413, 414-17, 419-21, 424,
426-30, 432-34, c435, 437.
no response 151.

Comment:

firefly: "One of those real swell
persnickety names"--11. None found here,
hence a book word for her--313. Inf.

considers this and 'glowworm' as names
for the same insect--410. June bug:
Usu.--5. Usual local term--225; 405.
lighting bug: Inf. distinguishes this
from 'lightning bug,' the latter naming
something with a "hard shell" (perhaps
hence = glowworm)--13. "Some people call
'em 'glowworms'"--425. lightning bug:
Usu.--22; 150, 152; 406. "If I was telling the kid I'd say 'lightning bugs' and
then I'd go on to say they were also
called 'fireflies'"--117. Used by inf.
as a child--23. "Older than 'firefly'"--
120.

47.3 and 4   wasp, hornet.   NE 239,
240-41.

Although wasp and hornet were sought
separately both in the eastern investigation and in UM fieldwork, the extraordinary semantic complexity and general
ambiguity in the responses makes it impossible to treat them separately here
except on an entirely superficial lexical basis. Accordingly, the replies for
both items have been combined, with full
notes from the sometimes puzzling and
contradictory comments.
To the zoologist the situation, though
complex, is not confused. Wasp for him
is a generic for any flying insect having a long slender body and a narrow
waist and belonging to the Vespidae,
Sphecidae, or related families. The
Sphecidae comprise those wasps known as
mud daubers because of the practice of
making a nest of mud cells. The Vespidae
consist of those wasps, usually called
hornets, that characteristically make a
nest of a paper-like substance resulting from their chewing up vegetable
fibers. Paper wasps or hornets identified by a black body and bright yellow
markings are specifically known as yellow jackets.
To UM infs. in general, however, most
of whom apparently have had only fleet-
ing and perhaps unhappy experiences with
these stinging insects, the physical
features, habits, and habitat that provide the zoologist with a basis for ca-
tegorization merge and intermix with a
result that reflects the lack of precision often found in popular attempts
to describe wild fauna and flora. This
mix appears in the comments below.
No regional pattern exists for the
three principal terms except that yellow
jacket is rare in most of the Dakotas.
The next terms, mud dauber and its rare
variants dirt dauber, mud mason, and
mud wasp, clearly have Midland correlation, with a range largely limited to
southern and eastern Nebraska.

hornet 2-3, c4, 5-6, s7, 8-12, 14-16, s17, 18, 20-24, s25, 26-28, ¹29, 30-35, 37-40, 42-43, c44, 45-48, :49, 50-51, sn52, 53-59, c60, 61-65; 101-5, sn106, 107-9, 111-14, sn115, 116-25, 127-39, s140, 141-49, sn150, 152; 202-5, ¹206, s207, 208, 210, sn212, 213-14, 217-26; 301, s302, ¹305, 306, 308-12, 314-15, ¹318, 320, 325-26, 328; 401-3, 405, 409-11, 413, ¹414, c415, sn417, 419-24, sn426, 427-29, 431, *432, 433-37. black ~ 13, 23, 50, 55. yellow ~ 13, 50.

mud dauber 113, 124-25, 133, 137, 142, 146-47, 149; 314, 328; 429, *432, ¹433, 434-35. dirt ~ 428.

mud mason 424.

wasp 1-16, 18, c19, 20, c21, 22-24, crc25, 26-27, s28, 29-43, c44-45, 46-47, c48, 49, s50, c52, 53-62, c63, 64-65; 101-38, 140-50, 152; 201-3, 206-9, 211-12, ¹214, 215-21, c222, 223-24, 226; 301-2, 304, 306-8, 310, 312-16, c317, 318-27; 401-21, c422, 423-37. black ~ 1; 406, 413, 417-18. blue ~ 404. hornet ~ 1. mud ~ 314. yellow ~ 1.

yellow jacket 3, 10-11, 14, 17-18, 22-23, 29, 33, 35, 37-39, 43, c44, 45, s¹48, c51, 53-62; 105, 113, 116-19, 121-22, 124, 128-29, 131, 134-35, 137-39, s140, 147, 150; 204, 208, 210, 213, 221, 225, ¹226; 306, 309, 311, ¹312, sn320; 401, 404, ¹405, 409, 413, ¹414, ¹418, 420, 422, ¹425, 427-28, 431, 433, 435. ~ jack c51. black jacket 4.

no response 151; 303.

Comment:

black jacket: Black, yellow stripes, small nest--4. black wasp: Black; mud nest--418. dirt dauber: Black, mud nest--428. hornet: Nest of mud--27; 114, 132, 139, 149, 152; 301, 328. Nest of paper--2, 22, 28, 30, 108, 125, 137-38. Nest in ground--37; 206, 208, 218, 220, 417. Nest on buildings or trees--2, 27, 30-31, 38, 44; 132, 137-38, 143, 149, 152; 202-3, 210, 213-14, 219-20, 223-25; 309, 311; 401-2. Nest larger than wasp's --134; 222. Nest smaller than wasp's--4, 65. Nest round, colony--10-11, 20, 26, 33, 35, 38; 104-5, 108, 113, 116, 128, 132, 137-38; 147; 207, 213, 217, 220, 225; 309-10, 314-15; 320; 402. Black-- 13, 35, 49-50, 54, 56; 104, 113, 124, 141, 147; 202, 204, 210, 218-19, 225; 311, 314; 401-2, 405, 409, 419. Brown-- 24, 35, 121; 223; 315, 328; 427-28. Blue-black--20. Yellow--10, 13, 23, 33- 34, 50; 105, 114, 123, 129, 146, 148; 203, 207, 217; 309, 311, 325; 435. Dark--21, 26, 31, 65; 106, 139; 320. 403. Yellow and black--2, 6, 11, 22, 27-28, 30, 37; 102, 117; 222, 306, 312; 422. Gray--4; 107-8, 116, 124. Yellow

stripes--4, 15; 145; 214; 424. Green-- 220; 436. Stinger in tail--4, 10-11, 20-21, 28, 35; 214, 218, 221-22, 225; 309, 314-15, 325. Stinger not in tail-- 22; 204, 207, 217, 223. Larger than wasp --2, 4, 21, 23, 42, 44, 56, 65; 124-25, 137, 147, 149; 219; 306; 405. Smaller than wasp--15, 26, 30, 34, 39, 58; 105, 109, 111, 123, 128, 131, 138, 142, 148, 150; 301, 310, 320. Same size as wasp-- 122, 203, 220. Larger than bee--11, 31, 34, 52; 103, 107-8, 142, 146, 207, 217- 19; 309. Smaller than bee--22, 35; 213, 314. Larger than yellow jacket--210, 311. Slim and long--10, 16, 34; 121; 214; 405. Fat and round--32-33, 39, 48, 51, 56, 62-63; 116, 135, 143, 145-46; 203; 401-2, 427. Small--148. Half inch long--6. Inch long--20. Similar to bee-- 53, 58; 103, 117, 135, 142; 225. = wasp --3, 20, 24, 50, 55, 60; 103, 121, 152; 203, 206, 214, 218, 223; 309, 312; 413, 426, 432. = yellow jacket--11, 23, 33, 61; 309. Generic term--50, 55. hornet wasp: "Nests on log close to ground. Blackish body, round stripes, and larg- er, with a stinger 'about a foot long.'" --1. mud dauber: Nest of mud--113, 124, 125, 137, 142, 146, 149; 328; 429, 433- 35. Nest on buildings--147, 149; 314. Yellow and black--113. Black and brown-- 137. Brown--328. Black--429. No sting- er--137. Has a stinger--434. Same as a 'wasp'--124; 432, 434. = hornet--328; 432. Larger than a 'wasp'--149. Larger than a 'hornet'--147. mud mason: Similar to wasp! Nest of mud.--424. wasp: Nest of mud--8, 30, 34; 101, 105, 109-10, 114-15, 122, 126-27, 133-34, 138, 150; 152; 211; 301, 321-33, 325, 328; 401, 405-6, 408, 416-17, 422-23, 427-28, 434, 436-37. Made of paper--21; 108, 137, 142-43; 208; 313, 320; 403, 410-12, 418, 429. Nest in ground--4, 19; 149; 206, 218, 224; 307. Nest on buildings and trees--1, 12, 29-30, 41, 43, 45, 52; 62-63; 127, 143, 149-50, 152; 201-3, 208-9, 212, 214, 219, 223; 309-10, 314- 15, 322, 328; 401-3, 405-6, 408, 410-12, 417, 419, 436. Nest smaller than hor- net's--134, 142; 315. Nest larger than hornet's--2. Nest round, colony--7, 9, 12, 27, 34, 37, 42, 65; 101, 106, 110, 113-14; 212, 217, 221; 302, 309-10, 313. Black--1, 3, 7, 30, 33; 101-2, 109-10, 116-17, 122, 124, 127, 138; 201, 212, 218; 315, 322, 325; 422, 426, 428. Brown--24, 26, 34; 115, 121, 127, 132- 33, 138, 147-48; 219, 223; 306, 314, 319, 321, 324, 328; 402, 407-8, 416, 427, 437. Blue--25. Yellow--21, 36, 56, 63, 65; 108, 113, 123, 141; 203, 207, 215, 217, 224; 309, 320, 323-24; 409-11, 419, 429, 436. Dark gray--124. Yellow

and black--6, 12, 38, 54; 107; 208; 301,
312-13, 316, 318; 401, 403, 406, 412,
417, 430. Yellow and green--49; 212.
Yellow and gray--19. 41. Brown and yel-
low--105; 302. Gray--2, 8-9, 42; 104,
137; 209, 218. Yellow stripes--15, 64;
114; 202, 214; 310; 414, 418. Dark--29,
111-12; 424, 435. Stinger in tail--1, 7,
12, 21, 30, 42, 65; 114, 116; 214, 218,
221, 224; 302, 309-10, 315, 323, 325;
402-3, 405-7, 410-12, 429, 436-37.
Stinger not in tail--9, 34, 38; 207,
215, 217, 220, 223; 321. Larger than
hornet--15, 26, 30, 34, 39, 58; 105,
109, 111, 123, 128, 131, 138, 142, 148,
150; 301, 310, 320. Smaller than hornet--
2, 4, 21, 23, 32, 42, 44, 56, 65; 124-25,
137, 147, 149; 219; 306; 405. Same size
as hornet--122; 203, 220. Smaller than
yellow jacket--4, 10. Larger than bee--
7, 9, 36, 41, 53, 65; 103, 126-27; 207,
212, 217-19; 304, 309, 321, 323; 407,
419, 436. Smaller than bee--8, 12, 42,
64; 106; 201, 215. Inch long--108, 111,
148; 315; 408, 410, 417, 426. Slim and
long--7, 26, 29, 32-34, 36, 39, 43, 48,
63; 101-2, 105, 108, 110, 113, 115-17,
121, 124-27, 129, 135, 137-38, 142-43,
145, 147, 150; 214, 216; 306, 313, 324;
402, 419, 424. = hornet--3, 20, 24, 35,
50, 55, 60; 103, 121, 152; 203, 206,
214, 218, 223; 309, 312, 326; 413, 426,
432. = yellow jacket--39, 45, 54, 58-59;
405, 409, 431. yellow jacket: Nest of
mud--311. Nest of paper--427. Nest in
trees--17, 43, 44. Nest in ground--56;
128, 138; 311; 422. Yellow--2, 35; 122,
129; 210; 427. Yellow and black--54;
306; 422. Yellow markings--29; 137.
Stinger in tail--35; 221. Smaller than
wasp--43, 56; 116. Smaller than hornet--
128, 138. Larger than wasp--44, 139.
Same size as hornet--122. = wasp--3, 37-
39, 45, 58-59, 62; 113; 208; 309, 312,
320; 401, 405, 409, 414, 418, 420, 431.
Is a hornet--10-11, 22-23, 33, 61; 117;
210, 225; 309; 428, 435. yellow wasp:
Nest large, cone-shaped--1.

47.5 <u>minnows</u>. NE 234. WG 23.

Any of various kinds of small fish
used as bait are generally known as
<u>minnows</u> or <u>minnies</u> in the UM. (For phon-
etic variations of the final syllable
in <u>minnows</u> see Vol. 2.) <u>Minnows</u> is common and widespread. The minor form <u>min-
nies</u> is more popular among Midland speakers and with older infs. than with younger. Its decline is shown by remarks that
it is a childhood term, since replaced
by <u>minnows</u>. Rare <u>minners</u> also is Midland in the UM.

<u>Shiners</u> is used as a second word by

some infs., who thus refer to minnows
having silvery light-reflecting scales.
It seems to have Northern speech orientation.

<u>Chubs</u>, reported from three infs., may
refer to the young of such fish as the
black bass when used as bait.

	Mn.	Ia.	N.D.	S.D.	Nb.	Ave.
minnies	8%	24%	15%	21%	16%	16%
minnows	92%	82%	89%	86%	89%	88%

chubs 130, 140; 307.
minners 132, c136.
minnies 6, †21, †23, 25, †33, 35, ¹47,
59, 62; 109, c113, 115, 128-29, *134,
c139, †141, 143, 146, 148-49, ¹150, †152;
207, 212, 215, 220; 301, 306, 311, †316,
c320, 327; :407, *410, 416-17, 429, 433,
s¹435.
minnows 1-4, 7-24, 26-33, c34, 36-58,
60-61, ¹62, 63-65; 101-8, 110-12, 114,
116-28, 130-31, 133-34, 136-38, c139,
141-45, 147-50; 201-6, 208-11, cr212,
213-14, 216-19, 221-26; cr301, 302-5,
307-10, →312, 313-16, c317, 318, c319,
321-26, 328; c401-2, 403-6, 408-14,
418-24, c425, 426-28, cr429, 430-31,
*432, 433-37. white ~ 13.
shiners 10, 13, sn33, 37, 48, 56-58;
130, s140; 222.
suckers 13. sucker minnows 13.
no response 5; 151.

Comment:

<u>chubs</u>: Larger than minnows--130, 140.
<u>minnies</u>: Used by inf. in childhood--21,
23, 33; 141; 415. "We called 'em 'minnies' although we knew they were 'minnows'"--433. Husband's term--410. "I
always call them 'minnies' but they're
called 'minnows' by some people"--62.
<u>shiners</u>: Better bait than minnows--10.
Larger than minnows--56. Flatter than
minnows--57. Usu.--222. "Silvery minnows"--58. "They shine in water"--58.

47.6 <u>spider web</u>. NE 242.

Fieldworkers attempted to prevent some
of the semantic ambiguity appearing in
the New England investigation of <u>spider
web</u> by considering it as two items, one
with an indoor referent and one with an
outdoor referent. But the overlapping
of other criterions for lexical distinction makes desirable a unified treatment
here.

The indoor/outdoor distinction, though
ignored in current dictionaries, appears
in the responses of 88 of the 206 infs.
(46%), but not with semantic consistency.
Although 68 identify the spider web as
found indoors and the cobweb outdoors,
17 use <u>spider web</u> with either indoor or
outdoor reference but <u>cobweb</u> with only

indoor reference, and two reverse that distinction. One lone inf. thinks that the spider web is found outdoors and the cobweb indoors.

As the comment below suggests, considerable semantic variation turns up in the use of these words. It is true that 42 (20%) of the infs. are limited to one or the other of the two terms in their active vocabularies, 23 for spider web and 19 for cobweb, and that 29 more, who use both terms, hold them to be synonymous. But for 135 infs. they have different meanings. Twenty-three, for example, differentiate a spider web as being patterned, whereas a cobweb is only a single strand; and seven more add that a cobweb may be patterned or single. Eight insist that a cobweb is just a spider web covered with dust. Other less common distinctions appear in the subsequent comment. Particularly striking is the belief of 31 infs. that cobwebs are not made by spiders. These semantic differences do not seem to be correlated with clear regional and type differences.

Unusual variants include boo chaser, cob, mosquito web, spider('s) nest, and spider net. Iowa mare's tail and Indian smoke, and probably dangler as well, refer to the single strands floating in the air during the fall months.

For a more detailed analysis of the same data see Gary N. Underwood, "Cobweb and spider web," *Word Watching*, 45, no. 4, 4-6 (April 1970).

boo chaser 128.
cob c51, 60.
cobweb 2-6, 8-18, s19, 20-22, :23, 24, c25, 26, 29-31, s¹32, 33, sn34, 36-37, 39-40, sn41, 42-44, c45, 46-51, ?52, 53-59, c60, c†61, 62-65; 101-17, 119-28, 130-33, 135-39, 141, 145-50, 152; 201-11, sn212, 213-14, :216, 217-19, s220, sn†221, 222-23, 225-26; 301-15, 317-26, 328; 401-7, 409-14, 416-21, c422, 423, 426-29, c430, 431, 433, 435-36, :437.
cob c51, 60.
    dangler 148.
    dust web 122; 224. heat ~ 121.
    Indian smoke 103.
    mare's tail 115.
    mosquito web c25.
    spider nest 19. ~ net 19. spider's nest ¹42.
    spider web 2-6, 8-12, 15-16, 18, 20-23, 26-37, 39-41, 43-51, ?52, 53-55, s56, 57-61, ¹63, 64-65; 101-21, 124-25, 127-29, 131-45, 147-50, 152; 202-4, 206, *208, 209-15, 217-26; 301-6, 308, 311-26; 401-2, c403, 405-9, 411-35, :437. spider's web 1, c7, 38, ¹62; 126; 216-17; 310.
    web 11, c25, 37-38, 42, c45; 122; 201,

225; 307, 316; c403, c409, 425, 436.
    no response 151; 327.

Comment:
    cobweb: A web with adherent dust--2, 25; 117; 213; 302, 314; 403, 422. Heavier and thicker than a 'spider web'--21. Smaller in design than a 'spider web'--34, 39; 124. Looser in design than a 'spider web'--61. Tangled old spider webs--45. "Many webs in one place"--51. "A messy mass"--433. Inf.'s term if the spider is gone; called a spider web when the spider is on the web--202. A patterned web; a 'spider web' is a single strand--430. Either a web or a strand--123, 125, 127, 131, 147, 149; 412. A strand only--10, 20, 26, 44, 47, 52-53, 55, 65; 106, 145; 203; 312, 320; 413, 419-20, 428, 431. A strand with adherent dust--40; 117; 414, 423. Found in a barn; 'cobweb' "is too bad a word to use for a web in the house"--50. Not made by a spider or an insect; an accumulation of dust or lint--3-4, 12, 22, 29, 31, 33-34, 42, 60; 137, 152; 218, 225-26; 301, 310, 315, 324; 401, 405, 417-18, 427, 429. "They just come"--46. "Just gathered from the air"--325. "Made by stove smoke --401. Made by "kind of a fly"--413. Indian smoke: Inf. says they float around in the fall and signal six weeks of Indian summer--103. mare's tail: A strand that floats around--115. mosquito web: Same as a spider web--25. web: A single strand--201. = cobweb--403. = spider web--409.

a. The indoor web.

	Mn.	Ia.	N.D.	S.D.	Nb.	Ave.
cobweb	82%	91%	84%	96%	70%	85%
spider web	58%	20%	16%	48%	79%	46%

CL 85: Returns from 1,036 respondents do not markedly change the picture presented by field data, although the correlation is not always close. The checklist returns do not provide semantic information other than the indoor/outdoor distinction, however. Spider's web is more frequent, with 48 instances.

	Mn.	Ia.	N.D.	S.D.	Nb.	Ave.
cobweb	75%	75%	64%	79%	86%	76%
spider web	31%	30%	39%	35%	31%	32%

cobweb 3-6, 8-14, 17-18, s19, 21, :23, 24, c25, 26, 29-31, 33-34, 36-37, 39-40, sn41, 49-50, 54-55, 58, 62-65; 101-16, 119-28, 130-33, 135-36, 138-39, 141, 145-50, 152; 201-11, sn212, 213-14, :216, 217-19, s220, sn†221, 223, 225-26; 301-15, 317-26, 328; 401-7, 409-13, 417-20, 422-23, 426, c430, 431, 433, :437.
    dust web *122; 224. heat ~ 121.
    spider nest 19. ~ net 19.

spider web 5, 8, 11-12, 20-21, 23, 26-
29, 31, 33-37, 39, 41, 50, 53, 55, 58,
63-64; 107, 124, 140-41, 143-44, 147,
149-50; 202-3, *208, 212, 215, 220-21;
302-3, 311-16, 319-21, 324-25; 401-2,
405, 407-9, 411-13, 415-20, 422-25, 428-
32, 434, 436. spider's ~ 38.
  web 11, 37-38, 42; 201; c403, c409,
425, 430.

b. The outdoor web.

	Mn.	Ia.	N.D.	S.D.	Nb.	Ave.
cobweb	35%	15%	36%	12%	24%	25%
spider web	62%	97%	88%	89%	85%	84%

CL 84: A somewhat higher proportion of
the 1,040 checklist respondents uses
cobweb for both indoor and outdoor reference than is true of the field infs.,
and the proportion similarly using spider web is somewhat lower. The latter
should be taken along with spider's web,
which has a much greater frequency than
in the field data, where it appeared
only once.

	Mn.	Ia.	N.D.	S.D.	Nb.	Ave.
cobweb	45%	41%	47%	45%	30%	41%
spider web	59%	65%	52%	65%	71%	63%
spider's web	8%	10%	15%	6%	14%	10%

  cobweb 5, 9, 13-14, 17, 21, 24, 37, 48,
53, 58, 62-63; 130, 141, 146-47, 150,
152; 201-5, 207-8, 210, sn212, sn†221;
309, 313, 328; 404, 410, 416, 420, 422-
23, c430, 431, 433.
  Indian smoke 103.
  mare's tail 115.
  spider web 3, 5-6, 10-12, 18, 20-21,
23, 25, 27-32, 34-35, 37, 49-50, 55,
58, 64; 101-14, 116, 119-21, 124-25,
127-28, 131-33, 135, 137-41, 144-45,
147-50, 152; 202-4, 206, *208, 209-15,
218-21, 223-26; 301-6, 308, 311-15, 317-
26; 401-2, c403, 411-12, 415, 417-20,
422-26, 428-34, :437. spider's ~ 126;
216-17; 310.
  web 37-38, 42; 122; 226; 307, 316; 425.

47.8 clump (of trees).

For a number of trees growing close
together and surrounded by open country,
an evenly distributed two-thirds of the
UM infs. use grove. A second word, used
by almost one-third, is clump, the higher incidence of which in Iowa suggests
possible Midland influence. A few infs.
who use both terms offer as a distinction that a clump is natural and small
and that a grove is planted and larger.

Thicket, with one exception limited
to western South Dakota and Nebraska,
exhibits a semantic shift because of
its having been applied in arid country
to small trees as well as to shrubbery.

Tree claim, originally a quasi-legal
designation, has its origin in the Timber Culture Act of Congress in 1873.
Under the provisions of that act, title
to 160 acres of public prairie land was
transferred to anyone who planted 40
acres of trees on the land and then kept
them growing for ten years.
Shelter belt developed during the dust
bowl period of the 1930's, when drouth
following excessive cultivation of arid
prairie land led to such annual dust
storms that federal funds were appropri-
ated to enable farmers to plant trees
as a preventive against wind erosion.
Bluff is a Canadianism that has reached
into North Dakota. The meaning, clump of
trees on the open prairie, is an extension of the sense, trees growing on or
along the eroded steep bank of a prairie
stream. Margaret Stobie describes it
thus: "A shift in the meaning of bluff
from 'steep bank' or the top of such a
bank to 'a grove of trees' evidently
occurred in the Red River settlements
in the 1860's. The transfer is clear in
files of The Nor'-Western, the first
British newspaper of the region." ("A
bluff is a grove of trees," English
Language Notes, 5, 49-51 (Sept. 1967).)
In this sense bluff is now common in
Saskatchewan, Manitoba, and Alberta.
Although Wood (1970) reports bluff as
referring to a growth of trees in the
South, the referent is still clearly
trees on a steep river bank. This development, then, is not identical and
is quite independent of that in Canada.
Copse and stand, infrequent synonyms
of grove, barely survive in the UM.
Hedge in this sense occurs once.
Bunch turns up several times, especially in Nebraska, as a non-technical
term used by those unfamiliar with one
of the specific names. So do cluster,
group, body, and patch.

	Mn.	Ia.	N.D.	S.D.	Nb.	Ave.
bunch	2%	2%	0	4%	12%	4%
clump	30%	51%	28%	15%	24%	32%
grove	68%	63%	60%	61%	61%	63%
thicket	0	0	4%	15%	9%	4%

  bluff c201, c202, 204.
  body 132.
  bunch 43; 138; 317; 407, 413, 424, 430.
  clump 1, 3, 10, sn12, s†19, 27, sn28,
29-31, 33, s37, *41, 43, 50, c54, 55,
63; 101, 103-5, 107-8, 113-16, 119-20,
122, 125-30, sn133, 141, 143, 145, 149-
50; †203, :†206, 210, 213, sn215, 217-
18, 222-23, s225; :f†309, 310-11, 313-
14; 401-3, 409, s420, 426-27, *432, 437.
  cluster 62; 108, 127; 429.
  copse 51; 309.

group 134; 215; 317.

grove 2, sn3, c4, 7-10, sn11, 13-15, c16, 17-18, s20, 21-26, 34, s35, 36-38, 42, 44-46, c47, 49, 51-53, 59-61; 101-3, 106, 109-15, 117, 120-21, 123-24, 131, 133-34, 136-37, 139-42, 144, 146-49, 152; 201, 203, 205, 207-11, sn212, 214, 216, 219, 221, c224, 226; 301, ¹303, 304-7, 312-13, 315, 318-21, c322, 323-24, c325, 328; 401, 403-6, 408, 410-11, 414, sn416, 418-19, 422-23, 425-26, 431, 433-35.

hedge 317.

patch 19; 302.

shelter belt *316, 319.

stand 37.

thicket 225; 311-12, 320, 326; c412, 419, 436.

tree claim 8; 308, 316.

no response 5-6, 32, 39-40, 48, 56-58, 64-65; 118, 135, 151; 220; 327; 415, 417, 421, 428.

Comment:

clump: A natural growth; a 'grove' is planted--101, 103. More used of bushes--108. Smaller than a 'grove'--10; 113-15, 126; 426. Natural--24. grove: Thicker than a 'copse'--51. Either a natural growth or planted--117, 146. Larger than a 'clump'--113-15, 120, 125, 133; 426. Larger than a 'thicket'--312; 419. Larger than a 'group'--134. An acre or so--134. Half acre or more--139. Planted--101, 103. Planted around a farmyard as a windbreak--106, 110, 147. group: If five or six trees--134. thicket: Of brush--311. Of chokecherry bushes--320.

48.1 sycamore.

Because the sycamore is not native to the UM., this item was unproductive. Few infs. were able to identify the tree or provide any name for it. The item was not sought after the first year of fieldwork.

48.3 poison ivy.

Any of various low shrubs or vines having three-lobed leaves and a highly irritant sap is known as poison ivy throughout the UM. Some infs. use poison oak to distinguish the shrub from the vine, although the reverse distinction also appears. Fieldworkers in Iowa apparently did not consistently record this variant. The equivalent poison vine, reported by Wood (1970) in Tennessee, Louisiana, and Arkansas, and by Atwood in Texas, exhibits South Midland orientation with its only occurrences in southeast Iowa. Poison ivory, a form produced by folk etymology and also found by Wood and Atwood, is used by

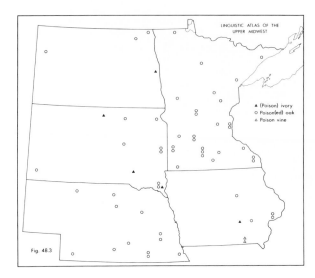

Fig. 48.3

four older speakers in the Dakotas and by one in Iowa. It seems to be declining.

	Mn.	Ia.	N.D.	S.D.	Nb.	Ave.
poison ivory	0	2%	4%	11%	0	2%
~ ivy	100%	96%	96%	93%	100%	98%
~ oak	40%	8%	12%	29%	32%	21%

poison ivory 220; 303, 322, *325. ivory 135.

poison ivy 1-4, c5, 6-14, 16-18, *19, 20-28, c29, 30-45, c46, 47-63, 65; 101-34, 136-42, 144-46, s147, 148-50, 152; 201-2, c203, 204-9, !210, 211-19, 221-26; 301-2, 304-21, 323-28; 401-37. poisoned ivy 15, 64. ivy 136, 143.

poison oak 4, 6, 10, ¹14, 20, 22-23, ¹24, *27, 28, 32, ¹37, 39-40, 42, 44-45, c46, 47, 50-53, 55, 57-58, c61, 62; 117, 140-41, 152; 206-7, 209; 306, 308, ¹312, *316, 318-20, 324-25; 404, 406, 413, 416, 423-24, 426, 430, 432-34, 437. poisoned oak 15.

poison vine 146-47.

no response 151.

Comment:

poison ivy: Has five leaves--50. A vine; 'poison oak' is a bush--434. poison oak: Inf. knows name only--*27, 28. Worse than 'poison ivy'--4; 209. Different from 'poison ivy'--6, 10, 55; 207; 404, 426, 433, 437. Has five leaves--20; 406. Has three leaves--50. Has leaves like an oak--22-23; 320. Has red leaves--324. A vine; 'poison ivy' is a low bush--432.

48.8a sugar maple. NE 247. WG 22, 31, 49, 75; F17, F143.

In New England and along the Atlantic coast the tree that is the source of maple sugar is generally known as sugar maple, with hard maple more common in western New England and in the New England settlement areas in Pennsylvania and New York state. The western range of the tree itself *(Acer saccharum)* extends to western Minnesota and central Iowa. In this eastern part of the UM hard maple dominates, with sugar maple a rather poor runner-up that also, however, occurs as a remembered term in Nebraska and South Dakota.

South Midland sugar tree turns up once in central Iowa. Eastern New England rock maple is offered twice in Iowa by infs. of Massachusetts and Ohio parentage. A scattered few other infs. use simple maple, sap tree, scarlet maple, sweet maple, and white maple. This last probably refers to the red maple *(Acer rubrum)*, which has a whitish bark. Several infs. evince unfamiliarity with the distinction, as they think maple sugar sap comes from the soft maple, a quite different tree *(Acer saccharinum)*.

	Mn.	Ia.
hard maple	60%	71%
maple (tree)	18%	4%
soft maple	2%	8%
sugar maple	32%	16%

CL 87: Nine hundred six respondents, even where the sugar maple does not grow, encircled their word for it on the checklist. With them the relationship between hard maple and sugar maple is preserved in maple-growing regions but is sharply reversed elsewhere. Six scattered respondents use rock maple.

hard maple 1, 3, 6, 12, 15, 17, 21-24, 27, 31, 33, 39, 42-46, 48-53, 56, 59, 61-62, 65; 101-3, 105-8, 110-11, 113-20, 122-24, 126-28, 130, 132-33, 135, 139-45, 148-49; 207-8, 220, 225-26; [1]311; [1]424, 427, 434.
maple 11, 32, 37; 112; 426. ~ tree 13, 16-18, 35, 57; 150.
rock maple 122, 152.
sap tree c214.
scarlet maple [1]29.
soft maple 39, ?63; 109, 121, 138, 140; 306.
sugar maple 2, 18, 26, 28-30, 34, 40-41, 43, 47, 55-56, 58, 60-61; 104, 125, 129, 131, 134, 136-37, [1]141, 146-47; 202, 221; 311, 320, 325, [1]326, 328; 401, ?402, 406, †413, [1]414, 416, 420, 426, 428, 430, [1]*432, 433.
sugar tree 118. maple ~ ~ [1]431.
sweet maple 134.
white maple 20, 43.
wild maple 135.
no response 4-5, 7, ?8, 9-10, 14, 19, 25, 36, ?38, 54, 64; 151; 201, ?203, 204-6, 209-13, 215-17, ?218, 219, 222-

24; 301-5, 307-10, 312-19, 321-24, 327; 403-5, 407-12, 415, 417-19, 421-23, 425, 429, 435-37.

Comment:

hard maple: Here used only for wood--6. Learned from relatives from near Burlington, Ia.--427. Learned from relatives from N.Y.--434. maple sugar tree: Learned on a trip to Pa.--431. sap tree: Seen in Mn.--214. scarlet maple: Because of color of leaves in fall--29. soft maple: Not tapped. sugar maple: Only a book word for inf.--26.

48.8b Place where sap is gathered. NE 247. WG 18, 36, 76; F144.

Only the two most common eastern terms, maple grove and sugar bush, have survived in the UM, and then only in the two states where sugar maples grow, Minnesota and Iowa. Maple grove, from southern New England and North Midland, is more frequent in Iowa (73%) than in Minnesota (51%). Sugar bush, an upstate New York and northern Pennsylvania expression, is distinctly Northern in distribution, with 43% in Minnesota and only four instances in northern Iowa. North Midland sugar camp appears once in Iowa, as does a new hybrid, maple camp. Sugar farm is a questioned term in southern Iowa. Orchard, also in Iowa, is reminiscent of South Midland and western New England sugar orchard. Maple bluff, once in Manitoba, is a Canadianism (see 47.8).

CL 88: Maple grove likewise is the favored form for 732 mail respondents, who check it even in non-maple-growing areas. The Dutch-derived Hudson valley sap bush, not observed during fieldwork, is checked by five scattered respondents. Eighteen more check sugar orchard, but since more than half of them do not live near maple trees, their replies may be uncertain.

	Mn.	Ia.	N.D.	S.D.	Nb.	Ave.
maple grove	54%	46%	44%	50%	55%	50%
sugar maple grove	14%	15%	20%	19%	18%	17%
sugar bush	22%	8%	10%	7%	5%	11%
sugar camp	9%	25%	16%	10%	15%	15%
sugar grove	5%	10%	8%	15%	10%	9%
sugar orchard	2%	1%	6%	4%	2%	2%

grove 15, 18, 35; :128, 129, :134, 136, :143, 144, 147. maple ~ 2-3, 17, c23, 31, :32, 37, 39, 43-44, →45, 47, s[1]48, 51-52, ?53, 58-59, [1]60, ?63; c107, 108-9, 112, 114, 120, 127, :131, 138, 140, 146, 148-49; 221; 426-27, 431. rock ~ ~ 152. sugar ~ ~ 137.

maple bluff 202.
maple camp 139.
orchard ¹125.
sugar bush 11-12, 15, 21-23, 29-30, 40, †45, :?46, 48, 54-56, 61-62, c65; 105, 116-17, :122; 225; †413, 434.
sugar camp 119.
sugar farm ?145.
no response 1, 4-10, 13-14, 16, 19-20, ?24, 25-28, 33-34, 36, ?38, :?41, 42, 49-50, 57, 64; 101-4, 106, 110-11, 113, 115, 118, 121, 123-24, 126, 130, 132-33, 135, 141-42, ?150, 151; 201, ?203, 204-17, ?218, 219-20, 222-24, 226; 301-28; 401-12, 414-25, 428-30, 432-33, 435-37.

Comment:

maple grove: "It's not proper. You never see many trees together"--52. Learned from relatives from near Burlington, Ia.--427. Learned on a trip to Pa.--431. orchard: Heard in Mn.--125. sugar bush: None here; inf. doesn't know where he learned the term--54. Used by inf.'s parents (from e. Ia.)--413. Learned from relatives from N.Y.--434.

49.1 I must ask my husband. NE 374.

Social rather than regional differentiation marks the various terms that can be used by a wife in the foregoing context. Universal in the UM is my husband, which most wives seem to use on all occasions, although some seem to reserve it for more formal situations, as in speaking to a stranger. Quite casual and probably intimate is the otherwise equivalent my hubby, found three times in Minnesota and once in Iowa.

Less formal than my husband is the mister, which is characteristically small-town and rural in distribution and perhaps Northern, since it was not recorded in Midland speech territory. Some infs. report familiarity with the expression but deny using it themselves.

Likewise informal and non-urban, and also perhaps not always existing in contrast with a more formal term, is my old man or the old man. It seems to be rather old-fashioned, as it is more likely to be the response of a Type I inf. than of a Type II inf., and it is reported as heard by infs. who do not themselves use it. Similar expressions, even less common and perhaps only jocular, are the boss and the manager, both of them obviously long antedating the Women's Liberation Movement.

A husband who is also a parent may be referred to informally as Daddy or Dad, chiefly in Iowa. One instance of Father

occurs in Iowa as the term used in talking to the children of the family.

Two wives of physicians report that they refer to their husbands as the doctor or Doctor.

Use of the given name sometimes occurs in conversation with persons on a first-name basis with the family. More formal is the use of the last name prefixed by Mr. One inf. reports dourly that his wife, with whom he was not on the best of terms, refers to him bluntly by only his last name.

the boss !46; 128; 208.
Dad *8, 14, 46, 64; 124-25, 130, 145, 147, 149. Daddy 14; 117, 142.
Doctor 426. the doctor 9.
Father 134.
my hubby 6, 18, 55; 121.
my husband 1, c2-3, 4-5, 7, *8, c10, 11-15, c16, 17-18, *19, 20-21, c22, 23-24, ?25, 26-27, c28, 30, 32, c33, 34, c36, 37, 39-40, *41, c42, 44, ¹46, 47-48, c49, 50-51, 53-55, 57-58, c59, 60-62, c63, c65; 101-18, *122, 123, *126, 127-28, 131-32, 134, 136-41, 143-45, *146, 148, 150, c152; 201-2, c203, 204-10, c211-12, 213, c214, 215-19, 22-26; *301, ¹302, 303-8, c310, 311-13, c313, 315, *316, c317, 318-22, c324-28; c401-3, 404, *405, 406, *408, 410-11, *412, 413, c414, 415-16, c417, 418, 420-22, c423, 424-27, c428, 430-31, 433-35. the ~ 43; c201, ¹210.
my man ¹14, s¹26, ¹29; 129, 141. my old ~ 13; !316. the ~ ~ c!5, ¹6, ¹18, 29; 128, 147; !209, ¹210-11; ¹302; ¹406. the man of the house 416.
the manager 203.
mister 56; c401. the ~ ¹17, s¹26, ¹32, ¹39, 40, 45, ¹47, 49, 52, s†57, s58; 144; ¹211; ¹302, sn313, 322; ¹406, ¹421, 423, ¹427, 432. Mister (+ name) 11; 405.
(first name) 34; 117, 124, 145. (last name only) 220.
no response 31, 35, 38; 114, 119-20, 133, 151; 309, 314, 323; 407, 409, 419, 429, 436-37.

Comment:

The doctor: Used by inf.'s wife--9. Father: to the children--134. my hubby: Informal; 'my husband' "to a stranger"--55. my husband: "Once in a while when I'm nice"--145. Usu.--313. the husband: "There's the husband," said by inf. as he was heard entering the kitchen from outdoors--201. (first name): To a friend --34. Usu.--145.

49.2 I must ask my wife. NE 375.

Although, as in New England, the UM husband's reference to his spouse is

typically my wife among all three inf.
types, some infs. alternate it with
(the) missis or, occasionally, my/the
old lady as a less formal term used
with friends and acquaintances. But a-
bout one-half of the infs. offering
missis or old lady do not also offer
the neutral or more formal term. A wife
with children is by some referred to
familiarly with Ma, Mama, Mom, or Mother
as proper names. Also informal, even
jocular, are the infrequently reported
better half, boss, calamity, old hag,
and squaw. Only one inf., of Type II,
reports referring to his wife as Mrs.
_____, although the nature of the
fieldworker's question may have prevented elicitation of this particular
response. It is conspicuous that only
one of the college graduates acknowl-
edges regular use of any of the informal or humorous designations. There seems
to be no regional pattern unless it is
that the frequency of the informal terms
is less in the three western states.

  my better half 6. the ~ ~ ¹31; 136.
  the boss !46; 122; ¹211; 408.
  Calamity !402.
  Ma 117, 142. Mama 9.
  missis 56; 323; 432. my ~ c5; *325.
the ~ s¹4, 10, ¹12, 17, ¹18, 22, !26,
sn27, ¹31-32, !¹33, 39-40, c41, 42,
45-46, ¹47, 48-49, c52, 54, c56, s58,
*64; 101, 105, 107, 113-14, 119, 122,
125, 128, 130, 135, 140-41, 144, 146-
47, c148-49; ¹201, c*203, ¹210-11,
*213, 215-16, c220, ¹223, c224, ¹226;
301, 313, c322-23; sn405, ¹406, 408,
423, c427.
  Mom ¹403. my little ~ c409.
  Mother 117, 142.
  Mrs. + (last name) 120.
  the old hag 209.
  my old lady ¹201; *316. the ~ ~ c3,
13; 141; ¹211, c225; ¹321; !402, !¹403,
!423.
  squaw !127.
  my wife 2, 4, *5, 6, c7, 10-11, c12-
13, 14, c15, 16-18, c19, 20, c21, c23,
24, c25, 27-28, c29, 30, ¹31, 32-34,
c35, 37, c38, 40-41, *43, c44, 47, c50-
51, 53, c54, 55-61, c62-63, 65; 102,
104-10, c111, 112, 115-18, c119, 120,
123-24, 126, 130-32, 134, 136-39, 141-
43, *145, 146-48, 150, 152; 201, c202,
*203, c204, 205-6, 209-10, ¹211, *213,
214-17, c218, 219, 221-26; c302, 303,
305-8, 310, c311-13, *316, 317-21, *324,
326; 401, ¹403, c404, 405-6, c407, 408,
c409, 410-11, c412, 413-15, c416, 418,
c419, 420, c421, 422, 424-26, 428, c429,
430-31, 433, c434, 435, c436-37. the ~
1, 8, 40, 46, 57; 101; c*203, 207-8,
c315, c320; cvr416.

my woman ¹42; 129, c135, 141. the ~
14, ¹39, 43; 105, 136, 144. the little
~ 209. my old ~ 13. the ~ ~ !¹2; 103,
!144; !209.
  no response 36; 121, 133, 151; 212;
304, 309, 314, 327-28; 417.

Comment:

  missis : "Is your missis light or dark?"
--5. the missis: Inf. considers this
common, esp. among Norwegians--4. Inf.
"boils" when her husband occ. says this--
10. Usu.--27, 54. Mrs. + name: Usu.--120.
the old lady: "If she's particularly
trying"--423. the old woman: Inf. claims
always to say this; his wife doesn't
mind--103. squaw: Said teasingly by
inf.'s husband--127. my wife: Usu.--27;
215. my woman: "Scandinavians use this"
--42.

49.3 widow. NE 389.

Throughout the UM as in New England
widow is common. Also widespread in New
England, except in the southwest corner
and in the western fringe, is the popular compound widow woman, with initial
stress. In the UM, however, widow woman
shows a clear Midland distribution pattern, perhaps because as an old-fashioned
term its decline may have been more rapid in the Northern population segment.
Widow lady, apparently considered more
polite, appeared four times in New England and survives with three widely
separated instances in the UM. Several
infs. volunteer also the specific grass
widow for a woman whose former husband
is alive and sod widow for one whose
husband has died. Both are informal.

CL 94: Confirmatory data come from 1,051
respondents with respect to the widespread use of widow and the Midland orientation of widow woman (20% in southern Iowa and 10% in the northern third),
but indicate a somewhat greater vitality
for widow lady.

	Mn.	Ia.	N.D.	S.D.	Nb.	Ave.
widow	90%	80%	93%	89%	91%	88%
~ lady	4%	9%	4%	5%	4%	5%
~ woman	8%	15%	6%	11%	10%	10%

  grass widow 14, 16-18, 31; 119; 201.
  sod widow 31; 119.
  widow 1-20, s21, 22, c23, 24-41, c42,
43-50, c51, 52-55, 57-65; 101-8, 110-31,
133-47, 149-50, 152; 202-13, 215-18,
220-24, c225; 301-26, 328; 402-4, c405,
406-12, 414-37.
  widow lady 132, s152; c219; ¹310;
cvr406.
  widow woman sn30, †40, 56; 109, 132,
148; sn209; 302, sn309, ¹310, c311,
cvr317, sn320, c322; 401, sn405, 406,

¹408, 412, c413, 417, snc429, 437.
  no response 115; 214; 327.

Comment:

  grass widow: A woman who has been deserted by her husband--16. A divorcee--
119. widow lady: "Sort of a joking way
of talking"--152. Inf. says this is
usual here--406.

49.5 Term of address for father. NE 371.

  An UM child, either young or older,
typically addresses his father with dad
or papa. Some infs. consider the former
to be more recent and the latter to be
both older and more appropriately used
by younger children.

  Daddy occurs as a minor variant, usually as a more intimate alternate. Although instances are too few to warrant
a firm conclusion, daddy may have Northern orientation in view of its greater
frequency in Minnesota and North Dakota
and the fact that two of the three Nebraska infs. have Northern family background.
Pa and paw, both informal, exhibit
some distributional contrast. Pa dominates Minnesota and is favored in the
Dakotas. Paw /pɔ/, on the contrary,
is clearly Midland. Kurath found only
one instance, as [pɒ], in southeastern
New England. In the UM its range is
chiefly Iowa and Nebraska, where its
greater frequency among Type I speakers
suggests that it is being considered as
old-fashioned.

  Although fieldworkers did not find
South Midland pappy, one Nebraskan of
Pennsylvania parentage uses the shorter
pap, and two other infs. have heard it.
Informal pop appears in Iowa; and two
infs., one in Minnesota and one in South

Dakota, use Czech tata and hypocoristic
tatinek.

  Considered more formal by some infs.,
but apparently the sole term once used
by others, is father. Two Iowa infs. report calling their fathers by the given
name.

  Rarely discernible in the limited data
are the well-known influences of the
emotional timbre of a situation -- play-
ful, matter-of-fact, affectionate, angry, etc. -- upon the choice of the term
of address. Within the speech of one
person the shift from daddy to dad to
father can readily occur as the mood of
a conversation changes, but such a
change in register calls for a different
kind of survey.

	Mn.	Ia.	N.D.	S.D.	Nb.	Ave.
dad	48%	45%	54%	57%	63%	52%
daddy	9%	2%	9%	3%	8%	7%
father	17%	18%	8%	4%	11%	13%
pa	31%	14%	9%	8%	3%	16%
papa	41%	31%	54%	43%	46%	42%
paw	0	18%	4%	4%	19%	9%

CL 92: The 1,055 mail checks of "familiar term for father" show a much greater weighting of dad than in the field
returns, but the relative frequencies
in the various states remain remarkably
consistent. Papa correspondingly declines. Daddy, however, is consistent
in having an even more suggestive Northern orientation. Only a few use father.
Paw occurs infrequently in all states,
but not as often as pop. Pap is checked
twice in Iowa and three times in Nebraska.

	Mn.	Ia.	N.D.	S.D.	Nb.	Ave.
dad	71%	60%	66%	72%	80%	70%
daddy	22%	15%	34%	24%	22%	22%
father	3%	2%	1%	2%	2%	2%
pa	22%	23%	29%	24%	12%	21%
papa	11%	15%	13%	15%	18%	15%
paw	3%	7%	4%	3%	0	4%

  dad 1-2, c5, 8, c9, c10, 13, 15, c17,
18, c24, 27, 30, 35, c36, ¹37, c38, 39,
c47, 48-49, c50, c→51, c52, 53-54, c55,
c57, 58, 60, c61, c63; 101, 104, 106,
110, 112, 119-23, →¹124, 125, 127-28,
130-32, 135, 138, 145, 147-48, 150, 152;
c201, 202, →203, 204-5, →207, c208, 210,
214, →217, 219, 221, 225-26; ¹301, 303-
8, 311, 315-16, 318, →¹319, 320-22, →324,
326, →328; →403, 404, c405, 406, c408,
409, c→411, c412, c414, 416, c419, c420,
cvr423, c425, 426-28, c429, 430-31, c432,
433, 435, c437.
  daddy 5, 26, 32, ¹37, →43, 44, 59;
121, →¹140; 206, 211, 224; c¹317, 326;
403, 411, 413.
  father c3, c6, c10, 21, 23, c33, →43,
49, 56, 59, c61; 101, 108, 110, 113-14,

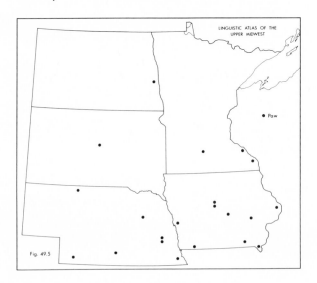

LINGUISTIC ATLAS OF THE
UPPER MIDWEST

• Paw

Fig. 49.5

129, 140, 142, 145; c204, 216; c317;
cvr413, c414, 415, 424.
 first name 103, 150.
 pa 8, 10-12, 14, 18-19, 29, 34, 41,
43, 46, 48, c58, c61, 62, 64-65; 105,
107, 109, 116-18, *134; 218, 223, 225;
324, 327; 413.
 pap ¹44; ¹139; c414.
 papa 4, 7, c9, 10, c13, c16, 17-22,
25-26, 28, 30-31, 33, 35, c*39, 40, 42,
r45, 47, 53, 59, 62; 102, 111, →116,
117, 120, *122, 126-27, 131, 134, 136,
141, 144-45, 149, 152; 203, 205, 207,
209-13, 215, 217, 220, 222, 224, 226;
301, c302, 304-6, 309-10, 312-13, 319,
325, 328; 401-3, 406-8, 410, 413, c414,
417-18, 421-22, 428, 430, 433, 436.
 paw ¹37, 51, c54, 57; 114, c115, 124,
c133, 137, 139, 143, 146, 149; !221;
314; 403, 416, 424-25, 429-30, 434.
 pop 122, 130, 150; 214.
 tata 43; 323. tatinek 323.
 no response 151.

Comment:

 Dad: Used when older--13, 53-54; 127,
131, 145; 205, 221; 305-6, 326, 406.
Used as a child--204. Used for stepfath-
er--210. Used by inf.'s daughter--324.
daddy: Used when older--26; 413. Used
as a child--5; 326, 411. Used by inf.'s
son--43. father: Used when older--33;
145. Used when younger--110. Usu.--49.
Inf.'s father objected to more familiar
terms--23. "Now that he's gone"--424.
first name: Usu.--150. pa: Used as a
child--8, 29, 41, 54, 64; 203, 225-26;
403, 413, 429. paw: Used as a child--
116. papa: Used when older--134. Used
as a child--9-10, 17, 26, 30-31, 33,
35, 53, 59; 117, 120, 127, 131, 145,
149, 152; 205, 211, 217; *305, 306, 325;
406, 417, 428, 433. Used by inf.'s child-
ren--116. tata: Czech--43; 323. tatinek:
Czech; used as a child--323.

49.6 Term of address for mother. NE 372.

 The general observation made for father (see 49.5) applies as well to the
terms of address to one's mother. Mother
and mama are the two almost equally widespread designations, the former sometimes exclusively and sometimes as an
adult formal alternative, the latter
usually informal and sometimes described
as used mostly during childhood.
 Ma and maw are also widespread but
less frequent forms. Although its range
is more extensive than that of paw, maw
likewise is more favored in Iowa, with
a 20% frequency in contrast with only
9% in Minnesota. Both ma and maw seem
now to be old-fashioned, since they are
used by 20% and 22% of the Type I speak-

ers respectively, but by only 10% of the
Type II speakers.
 Several times characterized as recent
or as used by children today, mom /mɑm/
is reported in use by only 13% of Type
I speakers but by 20% of Type II. Hypocoristic or childish mommy occurs only
three times. Rare are mam, mammy, maminka (Czech), mum, and mummy.

	Mn.	Ia.	N.D.	S.D.	Nb.	Ave.
ma	25%	17%	16%	10%	8%	17%
mama	42%	29%	64%	43%	58%	45%
maw	9%	20%	16%	14%	6%	16%
mom	8%	14%	12%	7%	42%	16%
mother	58%	43%	28%	50%	53%	48%

CL 93: The broad picture presented by
returns from 1,048 respondents is only
somewhat similar to that from field
records. The frequency of mom is twice
as great on the checklists, and maw is
much less common.

	Mn.	Ia.	N.D.	S.D.	Nb.	Ave.
ma	37%	31%	40%	32%	16%	31%
mama	29%	24%	32%	30%	32%	29%
maw	6%	9%	4%	3%	3%	5%
mom	39%	34%	51%	48%	61%	46%
mother	13%	22%	5%	16%	14%	15%

 first name 103.
 ma 8, c11, 12, 14, 27, 29, 34, c38,
43, 46, 48, 55, c58, c¹61, 62, 64-65;
101, 105, 107, 116-18, *134, 150; 218,
223, 225; 304, 324, 327; 401, 403, 416.
maw !35, 39, 41, 51, 54, c57; 114, c115,
124, c133, 137, 139, 141, 143, 146, 149;
202, 207, 221, 224; 308, 310, 314, 316;
420, 423.
 mam ¹44, 52. mammy ¹317.
 maminka 323.
 mama 2, 4-5, 7, 9, 13, 15, c16, 17-19,
21-22, 25-26, 28, 30-31, 37, 39-40, 42-
43, 45, 47, 50, 53, 62-63; 102, →¹116,
117, 120, *122, 123, 125-26, 128, 131,
134, 136, 141, 144-45, 149; 203, 205,
208-13, 215, 217, 219-22, 224, 226; 301,
c302, 304-6, 309-10, 312-13, 318-19,
325, 328; 402-4, 408, 411, 413-14, c416,
417-18, 421-22, 424, c425, 428, 430-31,
433-34, 436-37.
 mom ?1, 2, 6, →13, →¹33, ¹44, 57, 60;
112, 121, 127, 130, 135, 147, 152; →203,
208, 214; 310, ¹319, 321; 403, 405-6,
409-10, →411, 416, c→417, 419, 423, 425,
427, 429, 432, c→436. mommy 32; 109; 425.
 mother 1, 3, 8, 10, 12, c13, c→14,
c15-16, 17-18, 20-21, c23, 24-26, 30,
32-33, c37, c44-45, 46, c47-48, 49-50,
c51, 53, 56, 58-59, c60, 61-63; 101,
104, 106, 108, 110-11, 113-14, 119-20,
122-23, 125, 129, 131-32, 135, 138, 140,
142, 145, 148; 202, 204, 207-8, 216,
→217, 226; 303, 305, 307-8, 311, 315-20;
c322, 324, 326; 403-4, 406, 408-9, →411,
412, 415, 420, c424, c426-27, 428, 430,

c432, 433, 435-36, →437.
  mum 201, 204. mummy →20.
  no response 36; 151; 206; 407.

Comment:

  Ma: Used when younger--8, 12; 403.
Maw: Used when younger--202; 310; 423.
Usu.--316. Maminka: Czech--323. Mama:
Used when younger--25-26, 30, 37; 117,
120, 131, 149; 217; 310, 318; 403-4,
406, 433. Mother: Used when older--26,
58; 120; 208; 318-19; 403, 406, 411.
Usu.--135. Mum: Inf.'s mother objected
to his saying this--204.

50.1 grandfather. NE 381.

  As a term of address in the UM grandfather, though found in all five states
and among all three inf. types, is not
so general as is the less formal and
often more affectionate grandpa. Third
in frequency is familiar granddad, held
by two infs. to be a newer term, along
with the affectionate granddaddy reported twice in Minnesota. Gramp and grampy,
like the preceding brought from the east
coast, are sporadic hypocoristic forms.
Grandpapa, grandpap, and formal grandsire appear once each, the last as a
reference term in conversation with the
fieldworker. No clear distribution pattern emerges from the data, although
the isolated grandpap, as could be expected, is found in Midland territory.
  A recent non-English background is
reflected in the persistence of a term
from the native language of the grandfather, used despite the user's inability to speak the language, thus: /ˈɑvi/
Icelandic, /ˈgɛdə/ Czech, and pepère
French. The South Dakotan who said that
her own childhood expression was the
French bon papa /ˈbɑn ˌpɑpə/ did not
know how she acquired it.

  /ˈɑvi/ 47.
  bon papa 326.
  dan 102.
  /ˈgɛdə/ 43.
  gramp ¹28, !44, 51-52, ¹55; 110, 152;
→204, ¹214; 318. grampy 40.
  granddad 1, 3, ¹8, 12, 27, ¹55, c57,
61-62; 101, 115, 119, c138, →144; c208;
¹301, 308-9, c315, 318, 320; 410-11,
→412, 423, 425, 427. granddaddy !¹7, 32.
  grandfather c6, 13, 18, 20, ¹23, 24,
29, c31, 32, 35, 39, c40, 43-48, 50,
c51-52, 53, c54, 56, 58-59, c60, 61, 63;
118, 132, 134, 136, 140-42, 144-46, 148-
50; 305, 307-8, 314, *316, 317; 410,
413-14, c416, 421, 424-25, c426, 427,
cvr431, 432-35.
  grandpa 1-2, ¹5, 6, ¹7-8, 9-10, ¹11,
14-20, ¹23, 24, ¹25, 26, ¹28, 33-34,
37-40, 42-43, 45-51, 53-54, 56, 58, 60,

62-65; 103-6, c107, 110-11, 114, 116-18,
120, *122, 123-28, c133, 135, 137, 139,
141, 143, 147, 150; 201-2, 204-5, ¹207,
208-11, 215, ¹216, 217-21, ¹222, 224-26;
?301, 302-3, 306, 308, ¹312, 313-14,
317, 319, ¹324, 325, 328; c401, 402,
404, 408-9, †410, 413, c414, 415-17,
¹418, 419-20, 422, 424, 426, 428, 430-
31, 435-36.
  grandpap c429.
  grandpapa c59.
  grandsire c137.
  pepère 9; 208.
  no response 4, 21-22, 30, 36, 41; 108-
9, 112-13, 121, 129-31, 151; 203, 206,
212-13, 223; 304, ?310, 311, 321-23,
327; 405-7, 437.

Comment:

  /ˈɑvi/: Icelandic--47. dan: Not a name,
but a childhood word that "stuck"--102.
/ˈgɛdə/: Czech--43. Gramp: Used by inf.'s
grandchildren--214. Granddad: Used by
inf.'s grandchildren--301. Term of reference, not address--425. Granddaddy:
Used occ. by inf.'s grandchildren--7.
Grandfather: Term of reference, not ad-
dress--6, 35; 136; 307; 413-14, 416,
425, 431-32, 435. "Never called him anything else"--29. "Any other form is
disrespectful"--134. Grandpa: Used by
inf.'s grandchildren--7; 324; 418. Term
of reference, not address--319; 414,
420.

50.2 grandmother. NE 382, 383.

  Terms for one's grandmother are much
like those for a grandfather. (See
50.1.) The more dignified grandmother
exists as the sole expression for some
infs., a formal alternate to a familiar
term for others, and only a reference
word, rather than a vocative, for a few.
It is more favored in the eastern half
of the UM than in the western, where in
North Dakota its frequency drops to a
single instance.
  The widespread common term is grandma.
Rare examples occur of dammy (probably
a preserved 'baby-talk' word), gram,
grammy, granny, and mammy. The native
language of a grandmother may be inferred from the appearance of /ˈɑmi/
Icelandic, /bəˈbɪtʃkə/ Czech, and grandmère and ma mère French. But a South Dakotan's childhood use of French bon mama
/ˌbɑn ˈmɑmə/ she could not explain.

  /ˈɑmi/ 47.
  /ˌbəˈbɪtʃkə/ 43; 112.
  bon mama 326.
  dammy 326.
  gram →144, 152; ¹214. grammy 40; ¹403.
  grandma 1-2, ¹5, 6-7, ¹8, 9-10, 14,

c15, c16, 17-20, ¹23, 24, ¹25, 26-27, ¹28, 30, 32-34, 37-43, r45, 46, c47, 49-50, c51, c52, 53-54, ¹55, 56-65; 101, 103-8, 110-12, 114, 116-20, 123-28, 131, c133, 135, 137-39, 141, 143, 147, →149, 150; 201, c203, 204-5, 209-10, c211, 213, !215, ¹†216, 217-19, 221, ¹†222, 224, 226; 302, 304, 306, 308, ¹312, 313-15, 317-19, 324-25, 328; 401-2, ¹403, 404, c406, 408, c409, 410-13, 415-19, 422, c423, 424-26, ¹427, 428-31, 436-37.

grandmama 13, 40.
grandmère ¹†208.
grandmother 3, 6, 12-13, 18, 20, ¹23, 24, 29, c31, 32, c35, 39, c40, 43-48, 50, c51, 53, c54, 56, rc57, 58-63; 117-18, 122, 134, 136, 140, 142, 144-46, 148-50, c152; 202; 301, 303, 305-8, 316-17, 320, c327; 410, cvr413, 414, c416, ¹420, 421, 424-27, cvr431, 432-35.

granny 3, ¹8, ¹28, 44, 48; ¹207; 311.
ma mère 9.
mammy 102.
no response 4, 11, 21-22, 36; 109, 113, 115, 121, 129-30, 132, 151; 206, 212, 220, 223, 225; ?309-10, 321-23; 405, 407.

Comment:

gram: "Shows disrespect"--144. Used by inf.'s grandchildren--214. grandma: Said to one's own grandmother--8. grandmother: Term of reference, not of address--6, 35; 117; 301, 307; 413, 416, 431. granny: Used of someone else's grandmother--8. "She was a genuine /dʒɛnjuwaɪn/ old Pennsylvany Dutch granny"--311.

50.5 baby carriage. WG 77; F147.

Although New England and New York state baby carriage is spread throughout the UM and is even becoming socially preferred by some Midland speakers, its Northern origin is suggested by the greater frequency in Minnesota and North Dakota. But before the recent favoring of carriage, western Pennsylvania baby buggy had reached far into Northern speech territory, even to the extent of dominating Minnesota and being used by one-half of the infs. in North Dakota. A number of infs. acknowledge using both terms, sometimes one and sometimes the other.

Baby cab, according to Kurath not found east of southeastern Ohio and southern West Virginia, survived the Midland migration westward, but its low vitality outside Iowa hints at a current decline. Baby cart, not reported by Kurath but found four times by

Cassidy in Wisconsin, exists in the UM with three scattered instances. Go-cart is perhaps an inf.'s error.

Pram is a distinct Canadianism, although the full word perambulator is found south of the border as well, where its use may be accompanied by a feeling that an infant wheeled in a perambulator is superior to one pushed around in a buggy.

	Mn.	Ia.	N.D.	S.D.	Nb.	Ave.
baby) buggy	69%	72%	50%	71%	78%	69%
~) cab	0	12%	0	7%	3%	4%
~) carriage	46%	39%	65%	36%	22%	38%

CL 120: Lists from 1,052 respondents reveal a higher frequency of baby buggy and a lower frequency of carriage than in the field data, but still with a clear indication of a Northern provenience for the latter. Cab is Midland and dying. One instance of baby wagon was written in by a North Dakotan.

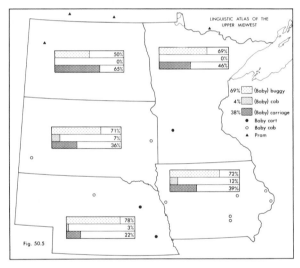

Fig. 50.5

	Mn.	Ia.	N.D.	S.D.	Nb.	Ave.
baby) buggy	85%	80%	74%	86%	95%	85%
~) cab	2%	13%	1%	6%	2%	5%
~) carriage	25%	15%	42%	20%	17%	22%

baby buggy ¹2, 4, 6, 8-13, 17, *19, cr21, 22-23, 25-26, →¹29, 30-32, 35-39, 41-42, *43, 44-45, †46, ¹47, c48, c50, 51, 53-54, 56-59, c61, 63-64; 102-4, s105, 106, 108-17, 119, 121, 124, 126-28, 130-31, 134, †136, 137-39, 141-42, 145-50, 152; 201, †203, ¹204, 205, 209-10, c211, 212-13, →¹215, 217, !219, 220, s221, 223-25, ¹226; 301-2, ¹303, 304-5, 307-9, †312, 313, cr314, 315, 319-20, cr321, 323-25, 327-28; 402-3, ¹404, 405-11, ¹413, 414-19, 422-23, 425-30, 432-37. buggy 13-16, 18, 34; c133, 144; *306, 316-19.

baby cab 118, †134, 135-36, 139; ¹323,

326; 413. cab 118, 121, 122; 318.

baby carriage 1-3, 5, 7, 11, 20, ?21, 24, 27-29, ¹30, 32-33, →35, 37-40, 43-44, *46, 47, 49, 52, 55, 57, 60-62, 65; 101-2, 107, 111, 117, 120, 122-25, ¹127, 129, 140, 143, →150, ¹152; 202, →203, 204, 206, 208, →209, →210, 213-16, 218, 220-22, ¹223, 226; 302-3, 305, 310-11, →312, ?314, 319, ?321, 322, 324; 401, ¹403, 404, 412, 420-21, 426-27, 431. carriage 59; 207; 308.

baby cart →41; 416, 424. go-cart !221; 430.

baby pram ¹2. pram →¹201, 202, →¹210.
perambulator 1, →3, 61; 144; 214, →219; 317, !→320; ¹404.

no response 132, 151.

Comment:

baby buggy: Usu.--11, 37; 111, 150; 210; 426-27. Inf. says this term is re-placing 'baby carriage'--44. Most com-mon locally--43. "But now they call it a pram"--213. Older than 'baby carriage' --319. "More natural than 'baby car-riage'"--427. baby carriage: "If you're buying them in a store, you'd ask for a baby carriage"--117. Inf.'s wife had the first one in the community--7. The newer name--46. Thinks her childhood term, though, was 'baby buggy'--226. Less used than 'baby buggy'--426. go-cart = baby carriage.

50.6 midwife.

Despite present-day recourse to hos-pitalization for childbirth, most UM infs. retain a name for a practically trained woman called upon regularly to assist during delivery in the home. The universal term is the book word midwife. Except for oversitting lady, one Minnesota inf.'s translation from Icelandic, all of the sparsely found equivalents occur chiefly outside the Northern speech area. South Midland grandma, granny, and granny woman (re-ported by Wood as frequent in Georgia and Tennessee) appear as obsolescent terms. Doctor woman has one user, in Nebraska; and nurse, midnurse, prac-tical nurse are also oncers. Some older infs. were reluctant to discuss this item with the fieldworker.

doctor woman 417.
grandma ✝121; sn✝429.
granny 132; ✝212. ~ woman ¹✝303, s¹✝325; sn✝429, sn✝436.
midwife 1-6, s8, s*19, 20-24, :25, 26-43, :44, 45-47, ✝48, 49-51, s52, 53-58, :s59, 60-63, *64, 65; 101-6, 108-13, 115-16, ✝117, 118-26, s✝127, 128-29, :130, 131, 133, 136-39, s140, 141-48, 150, 152; 201, *202, 203-17,

:218, 219-24, :s225, 226; 301-2, 304-5, 307-9, ✝310, 311-15, *316, 317-21, :!323, 324-26, 328; 401-3, *405, 406, :407, 408-9, :¹410, 411-14, 416-33, s434, s435, 437.

nurse →305. midnurse *116. practical nurse 127. wet nurse 308.

oversitting lady 47.

no response 7; 107, 114, 134-35, 149, 151; 306, ?322, 327; 404, 415.

Comment:

doctor woman: Used for a midwife, not a woman doctor--417. grandma: Inf.'s mother was a midwife; she was called by this term--121. granny: Used by inf.'s mother (from Ks.)--212. midwife: Inf. was once a midwife, but she objects to using the term; "You was just forced into [using] it"--403. Pronounced [mɛd~]--413. oversitting lady: Trans-lation from Icelandic--47. no response: Unmentionable topic for inf.--134, 149.

50.7 The boy resembles his father. NE 393.

Resembles and looks like are the two almost equally occurring expressions to indicate filial resemblance in features rather than in personality. Although found throughout the UM, the former clearly reveals slight Midland weight-ing and the latter clearly has slight Northern weighting. Takes after, much less frequent, may also be principally Northern. It is less popular in the west. Is the spit and image of, taken by many to be spitting image of, turns up almost as often and may also be Nor-thern oriented. Favors is uncommon. Some scattered infs. like the old metaphoric-al chip off the old block. One Minneso-tan of German extraction offers the slang is a dead ringer for.

	Mn.	Ia.	N.D.	S.D.	Nb.	Ave.
looks like	63%	43%	81%	79%	43%	59%
resembles	45%	65%	50%	46%	67%	55%
takes after	18%	12%	12%	7%	3%	12%

CL 98: The same relative distribution of resembles and its equivalents is found in the data from 1,049 respond-ents as in the field records, although with a greater frequency of takes after and favors and with the addition of 15 widely dispersed instances of features (Mn. 4; Ia. 3; N.D. 3; S.D. 1; Nb. 3).

	Mn.	Ia.	N.D.	S.D.	Nb.	Ave.
favors	6%	11%	8%	11%	25%	12%
looks like	49%	50%	45%	54%	49%	50%
resembles	54%	43%	54%	42%	40%	46%
takes after	24%	21%	23%	24%	25%	23%

favors 43, 54; ¹109, 130, 132; 217; 401.

is a chip off the old block 17, 53, 57; 119; 306, 311, 320; 405.

is a dead ringer for 51.

is the image of 61; 106, 133, s140, 148; 225; 312; 403. is the very image of 324. is the perfect image of 101. is the spitting image of 9, s¹22, 31, s35, 37, s¹39, 40, s51, 53, s56, 57, s¹58, !61; 144; 201, 203, ¹205, s¹226; 309-10, !¹324, ¹*328; 406, 410, ¹412.

is like 145. is the likeness of 418.

is the picture of 22, 60; 106; 323. is the very picture of 224. is the perfect picture of 401.

looks like 1, 3-6, 8-11, 13-15, c16, 17-18, 20, ¹21, :22, 25-34, 36, 39-40, 46-47, 49-50, 53-54, 59-60, 63-65; 104-6, 108, 118, 120-23, 125, 128, 131, 133-34, 136-38, 141, 144, 146-47, 149; 201-3, 207-16, 218-23, 225-26; 302-9, 312-13, 315, *316, 317-19, 321-22, 324-28; 403-7, 410-11, 413-14, 416-17, 421-22, sn426, 431, 437.

resembles 1, 5, 12, s¹14, 21, 24, 28, 30, 32, c33, 35-43, 45-47, 52, c53, 55-59, 65; 101-3, 105, 107-20, 122-23, 126-31, 135, 139-40, 143, 145, 148, 152; 203-5, 207, 210-14, 217, 219, 224, 226; 301-2, 304, 308-9, 311, 314, 320, 323-27; 402-4, 406, 408-10, 412, 415, 419-20, 423-30, 432-37.

takes after 2, 7, 14, 17, *19, 23, 33, 38, 43-45, ¹47, 48, s¹58, 62; 119, 124, 136, 142, sn149, 150; 206, c220, 224; 310, 314; 409. takes back after 7.

no response 151.

Comment:

is a chip off the old block: In manner rather than appearance--53, 57. is the spitting image of: Learned through reading--9. "Those dumb Swedes over in Albert Lea [Mn.] might not know any better than to say something like that" --51. looks like: Usu.--33. Used more commonly here than 'resembles' but she uses it only when she is being "careful"--426. takes after: In manner rather than appearance--33; 136, 149. Usu.-- 409.

51.1 She *raised* three children. NE 395.

Most UM infs. "raise" children, about one in five "brings up" children, and a very few, with a high school education, "rear" them.

Raised is the common form for all inf. types in the UM, slightly less so in the two northern states. *Brought up*, the minor variant, is also used by all three types, but with a rather definite Northern orientation. No South Dakota inf.

Fig. 51.1

uses it. The choice of *reared* by five male and six female infs. may reflect an old school usage dictum that *reared* refers to people and *raised* to animals. In conversation one older Nebraskan farmer used *grow*.

	Mn.	Ia.	N.D.	S.D.	Nb.	Ave.
brought up	46%	14%	15%	0	14%	22%
raised (up)	60%	82%	85%	93%	94%	78%
reared	6%	6%	0	7%	5%	5%

CL 95: Choices of 1,049 respondents confirm fairly well the field data, even the Northern and Midland bias of *brought up* and *raised*, respectively. South Dakota, however, now has *brought up*. Old-fashioned *fetched up* is a write-in response in Iowa (96.1) and in North Dakota (37.5).

	Mn.	Ia.	N.D.	S.D.	Nb.	Ave.
brought up	44%	28%	45%	29%	25%	34%
raised	60%	70%	60%	74%	76%	68%
reared	11%	13%	10%	15%	15%	13%

brought up c1, 3, 13-14, c15, c17, 18, c21, 25-26, :27, c33, 36-39, c40, 41, 43-44, 48, 51-52, 57, c58, 59-61, 63, 65; 104-5, s114, 115, 126, 132, 135, 149; 207-8, c211, 226; 408, 411, 420, ¹421, 426, 433.

grew c422.

raised c1-2, 3-8, c9, c10, 11, c12-13, 15-16, 19-20, c21, 22-24, c25, 28-34, c35, 36, 40, *41, ¹44, 45, c46-47, 49, c50, 53-54, c55, 56, 58, 60, 62, 64; 101-3, 106-13, 116-19, s¹120, 121-25, 127-31, 133-34, 136-44, 146-50, 152; 201-2, c203-4, 205-6, c209, 210, 212, c213, 214-15, c216, 217, c218-19, 220-22, c223-24, 225-26; 301-4, 306-8, c309, 310, c311, 313-22, c323, 324-26, c327, 328; c402-4, 405, ¹406, 407-8, c409-10, 412, 414-16, c417-18, 419, 421, c422-23,

sn424, 425-28, c429, 430-32, c434, 435, c436-37. ~ up c401, c413, c432.
    reared 42, 57, 60-61; 108, 145, 147; 305, c312; 406, 424.
    no response 151.

Comment:

    brought up: Usu.--33; 426. Inf. says this is "not right;" 'raised' is "best" --60. grew: "She was born and raised and grew a family here"--432. raised: Inf. doubts he uses this; he would say, "We had six kiddies"--120. "The Welcome Traveler program uses 'raised' a good bit"--136. "My nephew insists that I must say 'reared'"--424.

51.4 illegitimate child.

    Most UM terms for a child born out of wedlock suggest earlier social attitudes than those now prevailing. Nearly one-half (47%) of the infs. use the direct bastard at least occasionally, although not without awareness that to some persons it is a vulgarism. It seems to have a very slight Midland orientation. An almost equal number (46%), apparently in the belief that an expression that calumniates the helpless child is itself neutral, use illegitimate child. It seems to have a slight Northern orientation and to be more favored by high school graduates than is bastard.
    For reasons not adduced by this investigation the variety of terms is greater and more colorful in Midland speech territory. South Midland catch colt and woods colt are found in southern Iowa and, along with brush colt, are known to infs. elsewhere. Other lively but rare Midland euphemisms are baby born with burnt feet, child bred in the ditch, early variety, goose egg, maverick, mistake, and quickie. For four scattered infs. brat has this meaning. Other unusual equivalents are chance child, child born out of wedlock, common-law child, illegal child, illegit (perhaps medical jargon), love child, and outlaw baby. Use of the picturesque expressions is evenly divided between I and II infs. None is recorded from a college graduate.

    baby born with burnt feet 121.
    bastard !1, ¹3, 6-9, ¹11, 12-13, c16, 22-24, sn25, !27, !¹31, !35, 37-38, :41, 42, 45, 47, !50, 54, s¹55, !57, ¹58; 101-2, 104, ¹105, s107, 108, s¹109, 113, s114, 115, 118-19, ¹120, 124-25, 128-30, s132, 133, 135, 137, 139-41, 143, 145-46, 148, :150, ¹152; !204, !206, 208, ¹210, ¹214, s215, 216, ¹217, 218, sn220, 221-22, ¹223, !225; 301-2, :308-9, 311-

14, 316, 320, :323; !403, 404, s:n407, 411-12, ¹416, *417, !418, 419-26, 429, :430, *432, 433-35, 437. ~ child 34.
    brat ¹5, 22; 103, ¹105, 152; 219.
    brush colt ¹126.
    catch colt s¹†47, ¹50, !¹*64; 101, s¹105, 119, ¹124, 125, s145, :¹202; s:!n303, ¹†304, ¹†311, ¹314, s320, :¹321, 322, ¹323, ¹*328; ¹401, ¹403-4, sn405, 406, 412, 418, ¹420, 429, 437.
    chance child ¹204.
    child born out of wedlock 1, 17; 147, 149; 305; 421. child of an unwed mother :414. child without wedlock 418.
    child bred in the ditch 410.
    common-law child :40.
    early variety 138.
    fatherless child 5; 427.
    goose egg 115.
    illegit 34. ~ child 17.
    illegitimate child 2-4, 7, :8, 10-11, 13, 18, 20-21, 23, 26, 28, 31-33, 35-39, 42, sf44, 46, *48, 49-51, 53, c54, 56, 58-59, c60, 61, :c62, 63-65; 106, s107, 110-12, 117, 120-24, 134, 136, 149; 201, *202, 203, 205, !206, 208, 210-12, !213, 214-17, 219, 221, 223, 226; 301-2, 304, 308-10, 312-14, 317-19, 324-28; 401-2, :405, ¹406, 410, 412, 416, 419, 423-24, c425, 426, 429, 431, 437.
    illegal child :142.
    love child 120.
    maverick 320.
    mistake 302.
    outlaw baby c35.
    sooner kid s¹113, sn137, sn139.
    quickie ¹436. a little ~ c409.
    woods colt ¹*64; 137, *146, s147; ¹†312.
    no response 14-15, 19, :?30, 43; 116, 127, 131, 144; :?207, 209, 224; 306-7, 315; :?408, :413, 415, 428.

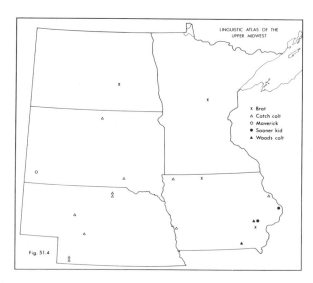

Fig. 51.4

X Brat
△ Catch colt
O Maverick
● Sooner kid
▲ Woods colt

LINGUISTIC ATLAS OF THE UPPER MIDWEST

Comment:

bastard: Inf. considers this word
coarse or vulgar--1, 3, 7, 23, 25, 31,
41-42, 50, 54-55, 58; 125, 137; 210,
216, 221, 223; 308, 312; 423-24. "It
doesn't taste well"--3. "A tough name"
--7. "A horrible expression"--31. "That
sounds too bad"--50. "Never spoke of
that way"--125. "A cruel term"--312. "I
don't think children deserve the name"--
423. "A dirty word; I never use it"--
424. "Never [used this] until just now"
--426. Inf. spelled the word--22; 425.
Inf. whispered the word--38. Inf.
wouldn't say it--214; 324. Inf. wouldn't
use this, but says her husband would--
215. A book word for inf.; she has no
term except a circumlocution--150. A
colorless word for inf.; he uses it at
any time--24. "You ask me the damndest
questions!"--57. "If he were a horse,
he'd be a 'fence colt'"--148. bastard
child: "Not ordinarily used"--34. brat:
Said she wouldn't use this herself--5.
catch colt: Inf. heard this used by a
New England lady in Marshall, Mn.--47.
Inf. uses the term with reference to
horses--124; 412, 418, 437. Used facetiously and rarely--420. child born
out of wedlock: Usu.--1. illegit: Inf.
says this is M.D. jargon--34. illegitimate child: Usu.--37, 42; 312; 405,
426. Pronounced with initial [1]=-206,
211. Pronounced [mə'dʒɪdɨɾi ~]--317.
sooner kid: A child born "too soon"--
137. Inf. says this is used by children,
especially boys--139. woods colt: Inf.
heard this "from Southerners"--312.

52.1 relatives NE 388.

Although several expressions are used
in the UM to refer collectively to members of one's family, including uncles
and aunts and cousins, no regional contrasts appear among them.

Relatives, the choice of two-thirds
of the infs., is somewhat more favored
by Type II speakers (76%) and by Type
III (75%) than by the older and less
well-educated speakers in Type I (56%).
Its doublets relation and relations contrariwise seem more homespun or old-
fashioned as the choice of 37% of Type
I infs. and of only 18% of those in
Type II.

A likely regional contrast is indicated between the collective relation and
the plural relations. Both forms are
found as minor variants in New England
and both occur in Wisconsin, where the
plural outnumbers the collective 9 to
7, but in the UM it seems that the collective form is dying out among North-

ern speakers. Its distribution is clearly Midland, only in Iowa and Nebraska,
except for two instances in Minnesota --
one from an inf. of Midland parentage
and one from an inf. of German background.

More than one-third of the infs. use
simple folks, but sometimes only to refer to parents in contrast with other
terms to include persons more distantly
related. Infrequent terms are people
and family itself. Older kinfolks and
kinsmen persist but not in the speech
of college graduates.

	Mn.	Ia.	N.D.	S.D.	Nb.	Ave.
folks	35%	29%	35%	46%	46%	37%
kinfolks,						
~smen	5%	10%	0	14%	3%	7%
people	5%	8%	12%	0	3%	5%
relation	3%	27%	0	0	18%	12%
relations	22%	10%	35%	21%	11%	18%
relatives	63%	61%	77%	71%	67%	66%

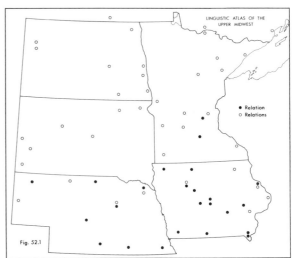

Fig. 52.1

CL 96: As in the field materials, two-
thirds of the 1,057 respondents use relatives, with relation and relations together in second place. The collective
form occurs throughout the UM but still
with slight Midland weighting. Folks is
somewhat less popular, however, as is
kinfolks. In addition, 9 scattered respondents use simple kin and 10 use
home folks.

	Mn.	Ia.	N.D.	S.D.	Nb.	Ave.
folks	13%	13%	17%	21%	26%	18%
kinfolks	2%	4%	4%	3%	3%	3%
people	2%	2%	1%	3%	5%	3%
relation	19%	26%	18%	27%	25%	23%
relations	14%	10%	17%	10%	11%	12%

connection 201.
family 36, 58; 111; 203, 205; 309.
folks c7, c11-12, 23-24, sn28, c29,
c31, 34, 36-37, sn41, c42, c46, c50-52,

c54, r57, c58, c61, c63, sn64; 102, 105,
107-8, 112, 117, 122, 125-26, 130-31,
136, 142-43, 147; 202, c203, 211, c215,
c217, sn220-21, c225-26; 301, ¹302, 303-
4, 309-10, c312, 320, 322, 324-25, c236-
27, 328; 401-2, c403, 404-6, 408, 410-
12, c417, 418-19, c428-29, c436-37.
  kin 45; 137; 217; 318, ¹319; c419.
~folk :30. ~folks 37, s¹65; 101, 118,
121, sn132; 311, 314. kinsmen c312.
  people cr9, 53, c62; c116, c137, 141,
147; 215, 218, 220; c413.
  relation 35, 48; 101, 104, 113, c114,
119, 129, 132-33, 135, 137, 142, 144,
149-50; c402, c405, 414, 418, 430, 432,
434. relations 2-3, 5-6, ?9, 14-15, c21,
25, 29, 36, 41, 44, ¹47, 56, 59; 108,
112, 120, 140, 152; 202, 208, c209, 210,
219-20, 222, 224, 226; 302, 306-7, 309,
311, 314, 320; 404, 408-9, c413. blood
relations 305. half-ass relations 404.
shirt-tail relations 25.
  relatives 1, 4, 8, 10, 13-14, 16-20,
22-24, 26, :27, 28-30, c31, 32-33, 37,
c38, 39-41, c42, 43-44, !46, 47, 49,
52-53, 55, 58, 60, c63, 64-65; 102-4,
106, 109-10, 114-16, 118, 120-28, 131,
133-34, c136, 137-40, 145-46, 148, 152;
201, 203-6, c207, 210-16, 219, 221-26;
302, 304-5, 308, 310-11, 313-14, c315,
316-26; 401-2, 404, 406, 408, 410-16,
c420, 421-22, c423, 424-28, 430-31,
433, 435.
  no response 151.

Comment:

  folks: Refers to parents only--24, 31,
41, 64; 131; 217, 225-26; 401. Refers to
immediate family only--29, 36-37, 42,
57; 125; 203, 221; 320, 325-26; 403-4,
410. kinfolks: Inf. says his father
said, "They're a-kin to me"--132. relations: Usu.--210. relatives: Usu.--
430.

52.8 jackleg preacher.

  This item was added to the UM worksheets to ascertain the spread of Southern and South Midland jackleg preacher.
It was not very productive. The foregoing term itself was recorded from only
one inf., a Minneapolis Negro of South
Midland parentage (35), who recalls its
use when he was younger. One Iowan (115)
remembered that her parents had earlier
used it of those "fly-by-nights."
  Equivalent horse 'n' buggy preacher
is the expression of one Iowan (140) and
tramp preacher of another (118). A Manitoban offers the synonymous stump
preacher, which might be a Canadianism.
It is not in the DAm and is not reported
by Wood nor Atwood.
  Some infs. respond with terms for a

traveling minister who preaches in several scattered small churches on a regular schedule: circuit preacher (124;
317) and circuit rider (116-17, 119,
122, 137, 146; 413, ¹420, 422, 425-26,
428, 432).

53.4 postman.

  This item was substituted for New
England selectman, unfamiliar in the UM,
in order to get information about
stressed and unstressed -man in a compound. But three different lexical responses also appeared. Most common is
mailman, with perhaps somewhat greater
weighting in Northern speech territory.
For about one-fourth of the infs. using
the next most frequent term, carrier
(and letter carrier or mail carrier),
the sense is restricted to that found
only in rural mail service. Others use
it of urban service as well. It may have
slight Midland weighting. Third most
frequent, with lowest proportion in the
Dakotas, is postman, which seems to retain vitality despite its lacking rein-
forcement from the verb post (instead
of mail), which is not American.

	Mn.	Ia.	N.D.	S.D.	Nb.	Ave.
carrier,etc.	29%	32%	19%	59%	51%	37%
mailman	80%	64%	81%	56%	49%	67%
postman	23%	20%	8%	15%	27%	20%

  carrier 304, c315, 328; 404, 412, 416,
c*425. letter ~ 34; 425. mail ~ 6, 13,
*19, 29-30, 35, 39, 41, 45, 51-52, 56-
62; 105-6, 116, 122, 124-25, 129, 131,
135-36, 140, 142, 146-48, 150; 201, 207,
216-17, 223; 303, 308, 311-16, 318, 320-
24; 403, 405, 407-8, 415, 417-18, 420,
424, 427, 429, 432-34, 437.
  mailman 1, 3-5, ¹6, c7, 8-10, 20-28,
31-40, ¹42, 43, 47-48, c49, 50-51, sn52,
53-58, c60, 61, 63-65; 101-4, 107-9,
111, 113-15, 117, 119-23, 126-28, 132-
34, 136, 138-39, 141, 143, 145, 149-50,
152; 202-6, 208-13, 215, 217-21, cr222,
224-26; 301-2, 305-7, 309-10, 314, ¹315,
316-19, 324-25, 328; c401, 406-8, 410,
414, 416, 419, 421-23, 425, 427, 430-31,
433, 435-36.
  postman 2, c11, 26, !¹29, 32-34, 40,
42-46, 55, c59, 61; 104, ¹106, 110-12,
sn116, 127, 130, 137, 144, 152; 201,
214, ?222; 312, 316, 319, 326; 402-4,
409, 411, 413, 417, 426, 428, 431.
  no response 118, 151; 327.

Comment:

  carrier: Rural--304, 328. mail carrier: Rural--39, 45, 56-57, 59-61; 105,
116; 203, 217; 303, 312, 316, 320-21;
403, 405, 417, 427, 437. In town--324.
Inf. says this is the general, official

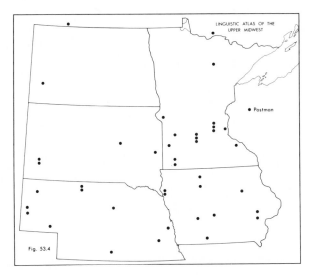

Fig. 53.4

term--433. "Usu. in the community"--51, 61. Usu.--52. mailman: Inf. heard this in Wi.--6. Rural--436. In town--328. Usu.--152; 431. postman: In town--45; 116; 312; 403, 417. Usu.--26, 61.

53.6 Negro. NE 452A and B.

Sought before the civil rights movement had crested and before Black became almost overnight the favored neutral if not ameliorative term, about 1950 this item elicited a variety of neutral and emotion-freighted responses that provide an implicitly poignant social commentary for that period.

It must be noted that a quarter of a century ago there actually was not a large Negro population in the UM. Outside such urban centers as the Twin Cities, Omaha, Sioux City, and Des Moines there were usually no more than a few permanent Negro families in a smaller city or town. In most smaller towns and widespread rural areas there were no Negroes at all. Attitudes underlying the replies often, then, reflect unfamiliarity coupled with bias derived from popular reading and social inheritance. A number of infs. were clearly uneasy in proffering their non-neutral terms to the fieldworkers.

Of all the expressions found in the UM to refer to a member of the Negro race, perhaps only Negro itself can be said to be usually devoid of some negative, patronizing, superior, or even contemptuous attitude on the part of the speaker, although for many infs. the several phrases with colored do seem to have a neutral signification. Both Negro and colored terms occur throughout the UM, the former more frequently.

Most commonly reported of all the terms and yet almost always recognized as so objectionable that it could not be used in conversation with a Negro is the word nigger. A few infs. who admit its use do so with some reluctance and a feeling of compunction. The variant nigra /nɪgrə/, in the South held generally to be politely neutral, occurs with perhaps the same feeling in the speech of five infs.

Except perhaps in black man and black people, the word black also appears only in expressions that are offensive to the point of being both demeaning and vulgar. They are listed below.

Equally demeaning are coon, jig, jigaboo, shine, skunk, and smoke. Although they perhaps sometimes occur with what the speaker would consider jocular intent, they are never funny to a Black.

Of the various terms recorded the only one which--while still suggesting the invidious presence of social distance--may be considered as also connoting some affection and friendly acceptance is darky. It is found in all five states.

African 29, 58; 142.
black bastard 12. ~ boy 201. ~ crow 113. ~ man 114, 136; 309. ~ people 56. ~ son of a bitch 124, 147. ~ trash 133.
burrhead ¹320.
color folks 423.
colored 131, 148-49; 307, 319. ~ boy c35; 303, ¹313; 409, 419. ~ folks 121; 306. ~ gentleman 418. ~ man 8, 12-13, 22-24, 27, 34, 36, 49; 110, 122, 128, 132, 140, 142; 207, 210, 213, 219; 328; 419, 422, 424, 429-30. ~ people 15, 21, c35, 40, 43; 104, 112, 115, 138, ¹152; 209, 212, c220, 223-25; 413, 426, 433. ~ person 5, 11, 31, 37-38, 50, 58; 102, 123; 204; 301, 310, 312, sn313, 315; c405, 406, 410, 428, 435.
coon 17, ¹†33, 34, 47, c50; 102, c107, 133, 138; c202, 205, 210, ¹213; 405, 408, 414, c416, sn418, 419, 428, †429, ¹431, ¹433-34.
darky 4, ¹11, 17, c19, ¹20, !25, 28, 30, 32, †33, !41, 44, 47-48, 55, 57, 59, 65; 106-7, sn108, 116, 118, †119, s121, 122, 132, 135, 137, 139, 143-44, 146, 149; 205, 211, c214, 218, 223-24; 309, sn313, !318, 320, 322, 324; 405, 415, 417, 419, 431-32, ¹433, 436.
jig 125. ~aboo *131.
Negro 1-12, 14, 17-18, 20, c21, 22-23, 25-26, 28-34, 36-42, *43, 44-49, 51-55, 57-65; 101-15, c116, 118-34, 136-47, 150, 152; 201, c202, 203-13, c214, 215, 217-19, 221-24, c225, 226; 301-2, 304-5, 308-9, 311-20, c321, 322, 324-26, 328; 401-6, 408-16, 418-31, *432, 433-37.

nigger 1-2, ¹3, ¹5, 6-9, ¹10, 13-15,
18, *19, ¹20, 21, 23, 26-27, 29-30, c31,
37-40, !45, 47, c50, c51, 52, !53, 56-
57, ¹58, 60-63, ¹64; 101-5, 107-9, ¹110-
11, 112, 114-15, ¹122, 123, 125, ¹126,
128, c129, 131-33, †135, 136, 138, 143,
145, s146, 147-49, ¹150, ?152; c201-2,
203, c204, ¹208, 210, 213, !215, c216,
217-18, c220, ¹221, c222, 225, ¹226;
301-10, ¹313, c314, ¹315, 316-20, c!321,
c322-23, †325, 328; 401, 403-5, c407,
408, ¹409, 413, 415-17, sn418, 419-22,
¹423, 424-25, ¹426, 427, 430, ¹431,
432-35, 437. Jamaican ~ c312.
   nigra c16, 24; c311, *316; *432.
   shine 125; ¹315; 419.
   skunk 108.
   smoke 419.
   no response 151; 327.

Comment:

   African: Not used in presence of Ne-
groes--29. Neutral--142. black crow: De-
rogatory--113. black man: Derogatory--
114, 136. black son of a bitch: Used
when mad at one--147. black trash: De-
rogatory--133. colored: Neutral--131.
colored folks: Polite--306. colored
man: Inf. would use this when talking
to a Negro--8, 12, 23, 27; 210, 213;
328. Neutral--110, 132, 142. Patroniz-
ing--422. "More honorable" than 'nigger'--430. colored people: Neutral--112,
115, 138; 212; 413, 433. colored person:
Inf. would use this when talking to a
Negro--50. Neutral--123; 428. Sentiment-
al--435. coon: Derogatory--47; 102, 107,
133, 138; 414, 419, 431, 433-34. Not used
in presence of Negroes--34. "It doesn't
sound quite nice"--431. darky: Deroga-
tory--32, 47; 107; 419. Not used in presence of Negroes--65. Neutral--4, 132,
144, 146; 415, 432-33. Polite--108.
Either neutral or polite--137. Inf.
Used as a child--33. Negro: Usu.--2,
34, 37; 222, 224; 408, 418. Inf. would
use this when talking to a Negro--26,
29, 34, 38, 65. Inf. says this should
not be used because Negroes don't like
it--43. Guarded usage--416. "Sounds kind
of rough"--424. "More honorable" than
'nigger'--430. nigger: Usu.--26; 101,
108. Formerly usu.--45. Common here--
215, 218. "Up here you'd call them 'niggers'"--6. "Ordinarily people say 'nigger' more than 'Negro'"--23. Not used
locally--64. Neutral--1; 101, 109, 132;
432. Inf. might use this jokingly--152.
Inf. usually eschews this word--21; 217.
Inf. says she wouldn't use this, but her
black cocker spaniel is named "Nigger"--
10. Inf. objects to this word--5; 122;
221; 313; 426, 431. Derogatory--5, 38-
40, 45, 47, 52, 57, 60; 102-3, 107, 110-

12, 114-15, 123, 126, 133, 136, 138,
143, 145-46, 148; 305-8, 316-19; 413,
415, 419-27, 431, 433-35. Not used in
presence of Negroes--9, 27, 29; 225;
301; 437. "They don't like to be called
'niggers'"--7. "Not proper"--8. "I don't
have much time for niggers"--62. "Derogatory term not used much anymore"--
149. "Any goddam nigger you ever saw"--
314. "It doesn't sound quite nice"--431.
Either neutral or derogatory--105.
shine: Heard in the Navy--315. Deroga-
tory--419. skunk: Derogatory--108.
smoke: Derogatory--419.

53.7 a rustic (neutral and derogatory
terms). NE 450.

For centuries the simple delights of
the countryside have held a romantic
appeal for the city dweller--from the
Roman poet Horace extolling the virtues
of his Sabine farm to the pastoral tradition in English poetry and the modern
urbanite with his summer cabin in the
woods. But the situation has always
been ambivalent. That appeal was balanced by the disdain felt by city people, with their physical and social and
cultural amenities, for what they considered the crude and narrowly restricted existence of their bucolic cousins.
   This disdain, reflected in the UM in
a proliferation of pejorative epithets
for rural residents, only recently has
undergone sharp erosion as automobile
highways, electric service, radio and
television, indoor plumbing, consolid-
ated schools, and other influential de-
velopments have obliterated many of the
historical contrasts between town and
country life. Some of the terms elicited two decades ago were already obsolescent and today are even obsolete.
But their remembered variety and vitality are colorful evidence of how sharp
was the social cleavage. Indeed, not all
the terms are yet disused. (For the full
picture in the UM see Harold B. Allen,
"Pejorative terms for midwest farmers,"
American Speech 33 (1958).260-265.)
   As of the period of fieldwork the most
common term in the UM is hayseed, which,
though found in all five states, seems
to exhibit slight Northern preference.
Simple farmer and phrases including
farmer occur next most frequently, although quite often only in a neutral
sense. Still familiar hick, alone or in
phrases, is offered by one-fourth of the
infs. in all states but Iowa. Rube,
clodhopper, and country jake are also
old terms found in all states but less
frequently.
   Rather clear regional variation marks

the concentration of Midland backwoods-man and its analogues in Iowa, of Mid-land and South Midland hillbilly in Iowa and Nebraska, and of Northern hayshaker in Minnesota. Eastern yokel is a victim of time and the western migration, for it barely survives in Minnesota and Iowa and no farther.

A number of terms have even more restricted distribution correlating with settlement patterns or ecological characteristics. Honyock in the sense "uncouth farmer of foreign origin" is found in the eastern part of Nebraska, with its substantial Bohemian (Czech) population base. A curious contrast occurs in the presence of honyocker, only rarely honyock, in the western portion of the Dakotas, where the still vividly recalled pejorative meaning is "damned homesteader." Used by a cattleman to a despised farmer whose plow had broken the plains and whose fences had cut off the open range, this term was a fighting word during the homesteading era. With the same meaning but perhaps with less attached opprobrium, sodbuster and soddy are also remembered western designations. Soddy, incidentally, also had the meaning "a sod house," not sought in the survey.

In the cutover timberland of northern Minnesota appear cedar savage and jack-pine farmer as derogatory epithets along with colorful rabbit choker.

In southwestern South Dakota a retired cattle rancher still uses tie hacks and woodticks as mildly contemptuous terms for homesteaders who about 1913 and 1914 settled in the foothills south of the Black Hills, where they cut the small timber and sold it for railroad ties.

Bushman is limited to Ontario; bush-whacker, however, though likewise found in Canada--in Manitoba--also turns up in southern Iowa. There, since the region lacks the bush terrain of Canada, the term may reflect its earlier pejorative use to designate a guerilla fighter for the Confederate cause during the Civil War. Another likely Canadianism is habitant, reported by a Manitoba inf. as an expression, not usually depreciatory, for a French Canadian settler in the backwoods.

Homesteaders in the Nebraska sandhill country are known as sandhillers or Kin-caiders, the latter an early common name derived from M. P. Kincaid, father of the homestead law modification by which homesteaders in that semi-arid region could prove up for 640 acres instead of the usual 160 acres.

Several additional terms of limited

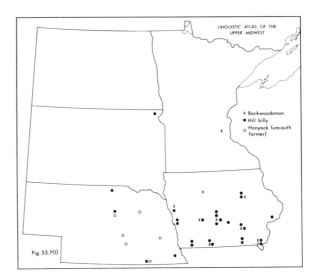

Fig. 53.7(1)

use appear in the detailed list below.

	Mn.	Ia.	N.D.	S.D.	Nb.	Ave.
clodhopper country)	2%	12%	16%	4%	17%	9%
jake big, etc.)	11%	22%	12%	0	11%	12%
farmer	41%	35%	16%	19%	14%	35%
hayseed	44%	25%	64%	38%	50%	42%
hick	25%	8%	24%	23%	36%	22%
hillbilly	0	43%	0	4%	11%	13%
rube	13%	8%	12%	4%	8%	9%

apple knocker 141.
backwoodsman 37; 113, 117, 122, 127, 130, 136, 145, 148, sn149. backwoods people 413. backwoodsy (adj.) 26; c121. backwooder 118.
barn folks 20.
boob 42.
bronco buster 201.
bushman 3. bushwhacker 1; 129, 145.
cattleman 403.
cedar savage 12.
clod buster 101; †208.
clodhopper !¹2, 55; 102, 113, s114, 119, s132, 133, 138-39; sn209, sn212, †214-15, 216, sn218; †313, 322, ¹†324, †325; †409, s413, 414-15, ¹416, s¹420, 421, s422, 428, 430-31.
corn husker 44.
country boy 424. ~ bum 3. ~ bumpkin ¹2, 37; :!55; ¹111; ¹†310. ~ cousin !219; 319. ~ farmer 113. ~ folk 65; 111; 207. ~ gook †8; 201. ~ guy 429. ~ hay-seed 64. ~ hick sn209, †226; 318; †401, †411, !417. ~ hunk ¹†29. ~ ike †323. ~ jack !56; 141. ~ jake !22, 23, !25, 37, 42, 60, !61; 102-5, 109, ¹111, 116, 119-20, 133, 152; 210, 213, 217; †311, †313-14, †328; †401, 403, 406, ¹410, ¹†412, c422, 434. ~ jay 431. ~ jig 139; 304-5. ~ jigger !25. ~ kid 436. ~ man 27; 207. ~ people 4; 215; 317. ~ punk ¹†29. ~

pumpkin 12. ~ rube 23.
  cowman 403.
  dummy 124, 140.
  farmer 3-5, 7, 10-14, 16-17, 22-25,
27-28, 31, †33, 34, †36, 37-38, 41-42,
50, 54, 63; 101, 104-9, 114-16, 119,
121, 132-33, 137-39; 201-5, 207, 209-13,
215-18, 220, 222-24; 309, 317-19, †323;
402-3, 408, 425-26. big ~ 37, 50. dumb
~ 306. lazy ~ c306.
  farm folks 49.
  goof 102.
  greenhorn 221; 418.
  habitant /₁ɑbiˈtã/ 1.
  hayseed ¹2, s3, 5, 8-9, !10, 14, s†19,
20-21, !22, 24, †26-27, 28, 30, s32, 33-
34, †36, c39, 40, :!41, !43, f!44,
!45, !48, :s49, 50, c51, !52, 53, s¹56,
57, †59, !60, 63, 65; 101, 105-6, 110,
s112, 115, 117, 119, †124, !129, 132-33,
138-39, sn147, !152; 201, ¹†202, 203,
s¹204, 205, sn207, 208, !209, 211, sn212,
†214, 215, ¹216, †217, 218, sn219,
sn†220, 221-24, ¹†225-26; 301-2, !†303,
304-5, 307, ¹†312, *316, !317, 318, !319,
¹321, 322, †323, ¹†324, †325, †328; †402,
†405, 406, !†407, 408, †411, ¹†412, 413,
s414, 415-16, 420-21, s422, 423-25, 427-
28, ¹429, 430, c432, 433-36, ¹437.
  hay shaker s¹5, ¹10, !22, 35, 47, 50,
53, 57, 60; 105; sn212; ¹†310, !†407,
s431.
  hick 5, 11, 14, 18, 28, 30, sn31, 34,
!43, r46, 47, 49-50, 54, s¹57, c58, !62;
116, 137, sn147; s¹204, sn207, sn212,
215, sn218, 221; 301-2, 309, 315, 319,
¹†324, :¹†325, †328; 406, :!†407, 408,
†409, 410, ¹†412, s413, 414, 420-24,
s427, 428, s431, 435, 437. big ~ 150.
~ farmer 219; 428.
  hillbilly 116-17, ¹122, 123-25, ¹126,
127-31, 134-36, 140, 142-45, *146, 148-
49; 307; 405, 413, 433-34. hilly billy
147.
  honyock †214, 215, 224; †301, †314;
414-15, sn421, 422, 425, 433. honyocker
¹†210; †302, 304, †311, c312, †313-14,
c320, s¹†326.
  jackfish farmer 220.
  jackpine farmer 23, 37.
  jackpine savage 1, †4, *5, !†10, sn21,
!22, sn31, 37; ¹125.
  jake 110.
  jayhawk 31. jayhawker 418.
  kincaider c†404.
  landsucker †313.
  lumberjack 1.
  mossback 11, 15-16; 106, ¹125; ¹†202,
216; s¹413, s¹420, s427.
  mountaineer 134.
  nester c320.
  oaf 102.
  old bachelor c17.
  old cowhand 201.

  people from the sticks 40, 60. guy ~
~ ~ 54. ~ ~ ~ 24; 122; 205; 314.
  poor whites 118.
  puddlejumper 413.
  rabbit choker 37.
  rancher 210, 214; 403.
  river rat 405.
  rube 3, 21, 33, !45, 47, 54, !61; 103,
120-21, 137; ¹216, 218, sn220, 222;
301, †328; !†407, †411, 423, s427, 433,
435, ¹437.
  reuben 21.
  rustic ¹†202.
  sandhiller 413.
  shotgun farmer 37.
  sluefoot 113.
  sodbuster 201, †203, s¹204, †208,
sn212, 224, ¹†225; †314; †406.
  soddy †311, ¹†312, †314.
  stubble jumper !62.
  tie hack c320.
  white trash 128.
  woodsman 1.
  wood tick c320.
  yahoo 140; sn413, 414, s¹420.
  yokel 2, 9, 33, 38, !62; 103, 108;
¹†312; †411.
  no response 6; 151; 206; 308, 327;
419.

Comment:

  appleknocker: Derogatory--141. backwoodsman: Derogatory--113, 117. Neu-
tral--127, 148-49. cattleman: Neutral--
403. clodhopper: Inf. says in his school
days these terms usually started a
fight--55. Derogatory--113, 119, 133,
138. Cattlemen's term for homesteaders--
313. country farmer: Derogatory, perhaps
jocular--113. ~ folk: Neutral--65; 111;
207. ~ hick: Derogatory--318. ~ jack:
Derogatory--141. ~ jake: Derogatory--
105, 109, 119, 133; 403, 434. ~ man:
Neutral--27. ~ people: Neutral--317. ~
rube: Derogatory--23. cowman: Neutral--
403. farmer: Neutral--22-25, 27, 41-42,
50, 54; 104-5, 107, 109, 115-16, 119,
137-39; 213, 217, 220, 224; 318; 403,
425-26. Derogatory--5, 7, 11-12; 108,
121, 133; 201-5, 207, 211-12, 216, 218.
big ~: Derogatory--50. farm folks: Neu-
tral--49. habitant: Used especially with
reference to a backwoodsman who had moved
there from French-speaking Canada.--1.
hayseed: Derogatory--41, 50, 65; 105,
110, 115, 119, 133, 138, 147; 424-25,
432-35. Jocular--317. Usu.--9, 45. "I've
been called all of those"--49. Inf. says
this word is going out of use since the
farmer has more money than town people--
52. hayshaker: Derogatory--50; 105.
Inf. says this is used with reference
to berry growers--10. hick: Derogatory--
50, 54; 147. Usu.--47. hick farmer:

350

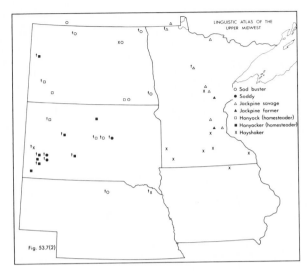

LINGUISTIC ATLAS OF THE
UPPER MIDWEST

○ Sod buster
● Soddy
△ Jackpine savage
▲ Jackpine farmer
□ Honyock (homesteader)
■ Honyocker (homesteader)
X Hayshaker

Fig. 53.7(2)

Inf.'s term for a man who farms "on the side" and lives in town--428. hillbilly: Derogatory--117, 127, 144, 148-49; 433-34. Neutral--140, *146. hilly billy: De-rogatory--147. honyock: Cattlemen's term for farmers--214-15; 301, 314. Inf.'s term for a stupid farmer--224. A for-eigner--422, 425. Inf thinks the term is German--422. honyocker: Cattlemen's term for farmers--210; 302, 313-14, 320. Inf.'s term for any farmer--304. "Nobody but a 'honyocker' would build a shed open on the north"--312. jack-fish farmer: "They live on fish from the [Red] river here"--220. jackpine farmer: Inf.'s term for someone from northern Mn.--23, 37. jackpine savage: Inf.'s term for someone from northern Mn.--37. Heard by inf. in Mn.--125. jake: Derogatory--110. landsucker: Catt-lemen's term for farmers--313. mossback: Heard by inf. in the South--125. nester: Cattlemen's term for a farmer--320. old bachelor: A hermit--17. guy from the sticks: Derogatory--54. rabbit choker: Inf.'s term for someone from northern Mn.--37. rancher: Neutral--214; 403. river rat: Derogatory for dweller on bottomland along the Niobrara River--405. rube: Derogatory--54; 433. shot-gun farmer: Inf.'s term for someone from northern Mn.--37. sluefoot: Derogatory--113. sodbuster: Cattlemen's term for farmers--314. soddy: Cattlemen's term for farmers--314.

CL 97: Data from 938 respondents (near-ly 100 preferring not to check this i-tem, sometimes with such a comment as "These words don't apply to our people here") diversify further the variegated picture constructed from the field re-cords. Twenty-five of the terms found

in field interviews appear also on the checklist returns, either as encircled selections or as volunteered write-ins. Sixteen additional write-ins are words not reported in field interviews.

In marked consistency with the field data, most commonly checked is hayseed, with farmer and hick terms, then coun-try jake and clodhopper as next most frequent.

Hillbilly appeared less often, how-ever, since it was not printed as such on the checklist. As a write-in it was volunteered by 11 scattered respondents. An accidental comment upon the use of checklists is provided by the fact that, however, the ghost phrase jackpine hill-billy was encircled three times. On the first version of the checklist this ex-pression appeared because of the inad-vertent omission of savage after jack-pine, so that jackpine and hillbilly were brought together as if they con-stituted a single expression. When the error was found, both hillbilly and jackpine savage were dropped from the list of suggested terms.

	Mn.	Ia.	N.D.	S.D.	Nb.	Ave.
clodhopper	10%	11%	10%	9%	13%	11%
country gentleman	14%	12%	18%	10%	6%	11%
country jake	4%	23%	4%	16%	13%	13%
backwoodsman	3%	4%	4%	2%	4%	3%
hayseed	52%	49%	57%	51%	54%	52%
farmer	7%	5%	4%	7%	4%	5%
hick	15%	10%	13%	20%	28%	16%
countryman	10%	5%	15%	10%	5%	8%

Specific instances of write-in terms recovered from the mail survey and not found in the field records are distrib-uted as follows:

	Mn.	Ia.	N.D.	S.D.	Nb.	Tot.
barnyard savage		1				1
brush hog		1				1
~ yankee	2					2
cowboy					1	1
farm boy			1			1
hillbilly	2	3	3	3	2	13
hoosier		1				1
John farmer	1					1
mountain boomer		1				1
oldtimer				1		1
pumpkin husker		1		1		2
railsplitter	1	2		1		4
shacker		1				1
timber rat		1				1

56.3 strong. NE 460.

This item appeared in reply to such a

query as "You'd say that a man who has unusual physical strength, who can lift heavy things easily, is pretty what?"

Some regional variation appears in the responses, but its significance may be questioned unless the variation occurs in replies recorded by the same fieldworker, as with husky and stout.

Strong, the common term, is used by seven or eight out of ten infs., with a slightly higher proportion in Nebraska. Husky, next most frequent in the UM, exhibits a very slight Northern bias in the eastern half but a significant one in the west. In contrast, stout is significantly Midland, with higher frequency in Iowa and Nebraska.

A number of other equivalents, some phrasal, also appear, ranging in acceptance from powerful, with an overall 13% frequency, to the single instances of made out of iron, brawny, and salty.

Although, unlike in NE (map 458), the UM fieldworkers did not seek terms for 'obese,' several infs. did volunteer that stout has this either as the only or as an alternate meaning.

	Mn.	Ia.	N.D.	S.D.	Nb.	Ave.
husky	40%	36%	42%	33%	11%	33%
muscular	14%	2%	19%	26%	11%	13%
powerful	12%	0	8%	11%	11%	8%
stout	17%	31%	8%	18%	24%	21%

able *210. able-bodied 52; 317. athletic 130. a big fella c59. brawny 131, 134; 310. has endurance 61. hard 45. hardy 12. healthy 17-18, 59.

husky 1, 3-6, 8, sn10, sn12, 14, 16, s18, sn19, 20, 25-26, 28, 30-31, sn36, 37, st39, ¹40, 41, sn42, s43, 45-47, 53, s56, 60; 103, c107, 108-10, s119, 123-25, 130-31, 136, 140, s141, 142, 144-45, 148, 152; sn201-2, 203, sn204, 213, 216-17, 221-24; 301-2, 309, 311, 313, sn320, s322, 323-24, 326; 404, sn412, 420, s421, 437.

made out of iron c405.

muscular 2, 8, 11, 20, 22, 24, 37; 127; 208, 214, 219, 223, 226; 301, 304, 308, 310, 313, 320, 328; 406, 409, 418. muscleful c19. well-muscled 12. pretty well-muscled 405.

powerful 9, 12, 20-21, 23, 33, 44, 56; 207, 215; 309-10, 312; 410-11, 410, 427.

robust 7, 18, 24, 32; 130; 225; 421. rugged 36; 125-26; 213-14; 301-2. salty 409. stalwart :42. stocky 9.

stout 2, 15-16, ¹29, 33, 35, 37, st39, 49, s50, st54, 59, 62, 64-65; 105, 114, c117, 122, †126, 127, s131, 134, 136, 139-41, 143, 146-50, s152; ¹210, 212; 303, 305, ¹312, 320, 323; 401, 403-4, 406-7, sn418, 424, 429, 434. ~-built 225. ~er than a bull c314.

strong 3, 7-8, 10-11, c13, 16-17, 21-

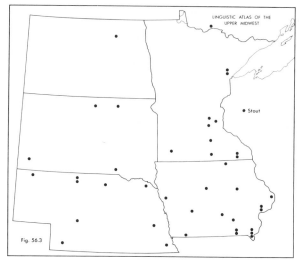

Fig. 56.3

24, 27, 29-30, 32, 34, 36, 38-41, 43, c44, 46-54, c55, s56, 57-59, 61-64; 101-2, 104-9, 111-13, 115-16, 118-23, 127-29, 132-33, 135-38, 140, 145-47, 149, c150, 152; 201-3, 215, 218-20, 222-24; 302, 304-8, 310-13, 315-19, 321-23, 325-26, 328; 401-3, 406-19, s421, 422-23, 425-26, c427, 428-33, 435-37. ~ as a horse 33. ~ enough 15.

sturdy 2; 106, 122. tough 12, 43, 45; c405. wiry 201.

no response 151; 327.

Comment:

husky: Usu.--47. powerful: Usu.--20. stout: = 'fat,' not 'strong'--10, 22, 44, 58; 131. = either 'fat' or 'strong' --117, 147-49. Inf. says this formerly meant 'strong' but now means 'fat'-- 126. Used by inf.'s father (from Can.) --54. Usu.--64. strong: Usu.--20; 418.

56.4 quite lively. NE 461.

A person with unusual vigor and vitality is described in many ways in the UM, although the possible variety may not be fully indicated in view of the variation in fieldworkers' practice in seeking for synonymous expressions.

Some infs. apply certain terms only to young people, with the additional meaning of 'agile' and 'quick-moving.' Some apply terms only to older people, with the implication that the physical or mental quality is greater than is to be expected for a person's age.

More likely to be applied to young people, for example, are full of life and lively, full of pep and peppy, and vivacious. More likely to be used of older people are active, agile, pert and right pert and exclusively and above all, spry. At least in the recorded instances full of piss and vinegar refers only to men.

No marked regional preferences appear except that feisty or ficety is characteristically only South Midland (see also 57.3 and 57.4), and that all U.S. examples of agile are in Midland territory. The single Canadian example occurs as /ˈeɪˌdʒaɪl/. No instances occur of the older eastern variant peart /pɪrt/ for pert /pɚt/.

CL 104 (1,049 respondents); 105 (1,035 respondents): The checklist divided this item by age groups, 104 for terms describing older people and 105 for terms describing young people. There are no significant deviations from the situation revealed by the field data.

Older

	Mn.	Ia.	N.D.	S.D.	Nb.	Ave.
active	52%	57%	57%	62%	61%	57%
peppy	8%	6%	15%	10%	12%	10%
spry	65%	59%	66%	67%	70%	65%
pert	0	3%	0	2%	6%	2%

Younger

	Mn.	Ia.	N.D.	S.D.	Nb.	Ave.
active	54%	40%	54%	50%	50%	49%
peppy	39%	49%	45%	50%	49%	46%
pert	2%	4%	3%	3%	10%	4%
quick	18%	21%	22%	15%	20%	19%

Terms are grouped thus: Y = for young people; O = for older people; E = for either, or undesignated.

able (E) 16; 319.
active (Y) 18; 102-3, 106, 122, 130, 136, 139, 147; 422. (O) 37, 45, 52, 58; 109, 119, 121, 127, 134-5, 143, 145; c206, 208, 211, 213; 303, 312, 317; 411, sn417, 426, 433. (E) 5, sn11, 15, 17, 19, 27, 29, 42, 49-51, 55; 104-5, 107, 110-11, 117, 124-26, 142, 146, 150, 152; 201, 203, 207, 216, 219, 225; 301, 304-5, 309, c314, 315, sn316, 318, 321; 401, 403, 407, ¹413, 414, 416, 432, 435-36.
agile (O) 150; 406, 411, 422. (E) 2; 314; 431.
alert (E) 36; 421.
ambitious (Y) 34; 127, 134. (O) 64. (E) 29; 144; 305-6, 317; 406.
got ambition (O) 135.
antsy (E) 131.
ball of fire (E) 409.
busy (E) 308.
chipper (E) 131; 425.
does a lot for her age (O) 308.
energetic (Y) 34. (O) 130; 402. (E) 40, 57; 126.
feisty (E) *132, †133.
fit (E) 210.
flip (E) !44.
foxy (O) 328.

frisky (Y) 133. (O) 4. (E) 36; 304, ¹313.
full of fun (E) 22; 221; 302.
full of ginger (E) 21; 218.
has lot of git (E) 4; 204.
go-getter 324.
has a lot of gumption (E) 224.
hale and hearty (E) 309.
healthy (E) 48.
hustler (Y) 132.
jolly (Y) 303. (E) 22; 412.
full of life (Y) 112; 206; 313, 323. (O) 9; 410. (E) 3, 31, 41, 49; 211; 417.
has lots of life (E) 12.
limber (O) ¹7. (E) 430.
a live bird (O) 25.
a live wire (Y) 33, c65. (E) 19, 41.
lively (Y) 4, 19, :41; sn109, 112-13, 115, 137, 140, sn149; 201; 310, 313, 324; 420. (O) 25, 28, 32, 58; 129, c147, 152; 217; 408, 433. (E) 1-3, c6, 10, sn11, 12, 14, 35, 37-38, 43, s48, 56-57; 102, 130; 205, 209, 212-16, 221-22; 304, 309, 312, 325; 405, 412, 414, 428-29.
nimble (Y) 108. (O) 317.
pep (E) 328.
pep of the party (E) 219.
full of pep (Y) 8, :30, 64; 114, 120-21; 208; 323; 402. (O) 9. (E) 5, 11, 22, 31, 38, 48, 57; 202, 209, 211, 214, 220; 301; 412, 419, 435.
has lot(s) of pep (Y) 326. (O) 25. (E) 140; 226; 311, 320; 408.
has plenty of pep (E) 37.
has lots of pepper (E) 12.
peppy (Y) 26, 50, 58, 65; 101, 107, 116, 119, 138, 141, 143, 145; 203, sn222; 312, sn326; 406, 410, 415, 424, 426-27, s430, 433, 437. (O) 44, sn55; 128, 147; 218. (E) 2, 10-11, 13, 21, 28, sn33, s42, 45, 51, 54; 122, 131, 148; 204-5, sn207, 210-12, 215-17, 223, sn224; 309, †310, 328; 401, sn431.
perky (O) 222.
pert (O) s¹8; 115; 210. (E) 118; s¹408.
right pert (O) sn326; sn426. (E) sn311.
full of piss and vinegar (Y) 323. (E) 120; 204, 208, 218; 404, ¹419, 437.
pretty well preserved (O) !46.
quick (Y) 145; 322. (E) 36; 146.
rugged (O) 45.
smart (Y) 322. (E) 118.
has lots of snap (O) 25.
snappy (O) 132. (E) 1.
full of spirit(s) (Y) 137. (E) 326.
sprightly (O) 123, 131.
spry (O) 1, sn2, 4-6, sn7, s¹8, 10, 18, sn20, 22, 24, sn26, sn28, 31, 33-34, 37, 39-40, sn41-42, 45, !47, 50, 52-54, sn55, sn58, 59-63, 65; 101-4, 106, sn107, ¹110, 112-17, 119, 121-22, 124-28, 130, s¹131, s132, 133, c135, 136-40, sn141, 142, 145-49; 201-4, 206, 209, 214-15, sn216, 218, c220, sn221-

22, 223, sn224, 225, sn226; 303, 306-7, 310, 313, 319, sn320, 322-26, *328; sn401-2, 404-6, 411, sn412, 413, sn414, 415, ¹416, sn419, 420-21, sn422, 423-24, 426-28, 433, !436. (E) sn3, sn11, 13-14, sn16, 21, 23, 29, sn35, 43-44, c!46, ¹51, 57, sn64; s105, 108, 111, 118, s120, 144; sn210, 212; s301, 302; s403, 407, c408, sn429, s430, sn431, 434.

  spunky (O) 134.
  has lots of steam (E) 20.
  supple (Y) 125. (O) 406.
  up and a-coming (O) 25.
  vigorous (O) 30. (E) 7; 120; 315.
  full of (has lots of) vim (Y) 132. (E) 139; 408.
  full of (has lots of) vim and vigor (Y) 437. (E) 20, 26, 37; 328.
  full of (has lots of) vim, vigor, and vitality (E) 304; 404.
  full of vitality (E) 219.
  vivacious (Y) 28, 33; 123; 411. (E) 10; 310; 410.
  wiry (O) 136. (E) 40.
  a good worker (E) 307.
  full of (has lots of) zip (O) 115. (E) 226.
  no response 151; 327; 418.

56.5 I'm afraid. NE 475.

Although both afraid and SCARED are common in the eastern U.S., the distribution in the UM rather strongly suggests some Northern bias for afraid. More Northern speakers are likely to use both words, with perhaps a slight semantic difference. More Midland area speakers are likely to use only one word, SCARED, for the whole semantic range. In general, when differentiation exists it seems to be based on the reference of afraid to a state of apprehension of some duration, and of SCARED to a temporarily induced reaction to a thing or event. Some also consider SCARED somewhat less dignified. It is usual in such phrases as SCARED to death.

SCARED occurs in two forms, scared and scairt, for the distribution of which see Volume 2.

Frightened, apparently disregarded by Iowa fieldworkers, is a less common equivalent held by some to indicate a weaker reaction or feeling than does either afraid or SCARED. Type II infs. are more likely to use it than are Type I.

Much less frequent as normal terms are fearful, leery, nervous, scary (of a person), shy, terrified, and timid.

	Mn.	Ia.	N.D.	S.D.	Nb.	Ave.
afraid	77%	24%	73%	54%	44%	55%
frightened	11%	2%	19%	21%	39%	16%
SCARED	71%	88%	85%	82%	84%	81%

  afeared ¹51.
  afraid 2, 8, 10, 12, c13, 14, c15, 18, 21-23, 25, 29-32, 37-41, 43, 46-47, 49-54, c55, 58-62, c63, 65; 102, s107, 109-10, 118, 126, 131, c135, 139-40, 150, 152; sn201, 203-8, 210-13, 218, c219-20, 221-22, 224-26; 301, 303, 309-10, c314, c318, 319-20, c322, 323-27; 401, 404, c405, 406, c410, 411-12, c414, 415, 418-19, 421-22, 426, 436-37. 'fraid 16-17; c116, c139; 305.
  fearful 38, 62; 216; c312; 409, 412.
  frightened c3, c11, 20, 33-34, 42, 65; 123; 202-3, c211, 215, 226; 305, 307, c312, 317, c319, 324; cvr403, 406, 410-11, c413, 416, 420, 427-28, 430-33, 435.
  leery 12; 204, 207.
  nervous 15; 207.
  scared 1, 4, c5, 6-9, c11, 12, 14, c15, c16, c19, 20, c21, :22, s23, 24, c25, 26-31, 33-34, c35, 36-37, 39, 42-43, c44, 45-48, sn49, 50, 52, 56-58, c64; 101-4, c105, 106-17, 119-22, c124, 125, 127-30, c132, 133-34, 136-38, 140-43, 145-46, 148-49; 201-2, 204, :208, c209, 210, 212-18, c219-20, 222, c223, 224-25; c303, c304, 305-8, sn310, :311, c312, !314, 315-16, c317, 318-21, 325-26, c327; 402, cvr403, c407, 408-9, †410, 411-12, c414, sn415, 416, c417, 418-21, 424, 426-28, c429, c430, 431-37. ~ stiff ¹29. ~ to death 10; 144; 205; 313, 328; c422, c425, 431. a-~ 123.
  scary c306.
  shy 404. terrified c201. timid 34; 317.
  no response 147, 151; 423.

Comment:

  afeared: Inf. says some people in Mankato who moved there from the Ozarks say this--51. afraid: Usu.--37, 62. "I was afraid it might be poison"--34. fearful: "More correct" than 'afraid'--62. "I'm fearful of being illiterate"--312. frightened: Stronger than 'scared'--420, 422, 428, 432, 435. Stronger than 'scairt'--416, 427, 430. Weaker than 'scared'--20, 33. scared: Usu.--47. Used by inf. in youth--410. Stronger than 'afraid'--110. Inf. deliberately avoids this word--226. "Us kids used to be so doggone scared"--25. "They were more scared than hurt"--29. "I was scairt to death"--305. "The horses was scairt [by a train]"--317. Inf. says a 'scary' movie 'scares' one but does not make him 'afraid'--426. scary: "Some people get scary"--306. shy: About going out in the dark--404. timid: Said of children--34.

56.8 stingy. NE 484.

Although this item was not sought in Minnesota, it is clear that the variety of picturesque folk terms found in the eastern states is poorly represented in the relatively few equivalents of stingy brought to the UM. This circumstance is perhaps due less to the decline of selfishness than to the possibility that selfishness has lost its colorful appeal to the imagination. Stingy is still a common word.

Almost as common as stingy is tight, which may appear in time-honored comparisons such as tight as bark on the tree. Close, next most likely to occur, seems to be rather old-fashioned. Near, cheap, chintzy, greedy, penurious, saving, scotch and scotchy, and selfish are additional replies, some offered by only one person.

A few of the infs. volunteered terms for persons having the quality, such as miser, skinflint, and tightwad. They are included in the list below.

	Ia.	N.D.	S.D.	Nb.	Ave.
close	14%	12%	25%	11%	14%
miser(ly)	8%	12%	18%	8%	12%
stingy	69%	88%	71%	54%	68%
tight	65%	62%	50%	62%	59%

cheap 104. chintzy s¹131.
close 114, 125, 128-29, 138, *146; 201, ¹214, 224; 302, ¹312, 313, 316, 320, 323-24, 327; *405, 406, s412, ¹435. ~-fisted 126; 419. ~ in his dealings 429. very ~ 226.
mean 118; 306. greedy 306.
miser 35, 38; 129; 318; 408. ~ly 29; 103, 111, 140; 202, 214, 226; 306, 318-20, 328; 412, 419.
near 119. a little ~ ¹202. quite ~ 152. very ~ →¹144.
penurious 426.
pinchpenny 408.
very saving 136.
scotch 31; 126; 223; 324. ~y 115. selfish 319. skinflint 118; 326; 406.
stingy 29, 31, 36; 102-3, 106-7, 109, 111-13, 115, 117, 119-24, 126-28, 132-37, 139, 141-44, 146-47, 149-50, 152; sn203, 205-6, !207, 208-10, !211, 212-26; 301-2, 305-6, 308-14, 318-19, sn320, 321, 324-25, 327; *328; 401, 404, *405, 406-13, 415, c417, 418, 421, 425-26, 428, 430, 434. ~ as the bark on a tree 317.
tight 38; 101-2, 104-6, 108-10, 112-13, 116-17, 120-22, 124-26, 128, 130-32, 134, 136, 138, 141-43, 145-48, 152;

Fig. 56.8

201-5, 207-9, 211, 213, 215-16, 221, 223-24; 301-2, 304, 307-10, 315-16, 320, 322-23, 326; 401-6, 410, sn412, 414, 416-18, 420, 422-24, 427, 431-33, 435, 437. so ~ he squeaks 313. ~ as bark on a tree 212. ~er than the bark on a hickory tree 30. ~er than the bark on a tree 419.
tightwad 35; 118, 121, 140, 148, 150; 220; 303, 315, 325, 328; 406, 409, 429, 434, 436.
no response 1-28, 32-34, 37-65; 151.

Comment:

miser: "He don't turn loose nothing"--35. "They are a miser"--129. penurious: Inf. says this is the common term in her family--426. stingy: Inf. says a 'stingy' person is 'tight,' but a 'tight' person is not necessarily 'stingy'--120. tightwad: One who is "foolishly 'tight'"--314.

57.1 queer.

The NE investigation treated this word as a verb, as in He queered himself with me. In the UM it was taken primarily as an adjective, to be considered both for its meaning and for its synonyms.

Of queer in the sense of "homosexual," Wentworth and Flexner (*Dictionary of American Slang*, 1960) state unequivocally, "Common since c1925, and now so common that the standard use is avoided." Only a handful of UM infs., however, admit this meaning, as either adjective or noun. For more than one-fourth, especially in Minnesota and North Dakota, queer means "mentally unbalanced" or "deranged." But the majority throughout the UM understand it in the milder sense "strange," "odd," "unconventional." The semantic range follows:

homosexual 34, 37; 108, 125; 211,
→¹312, 315; 423, 433.

mentally unbalanced or deranged 1, 4,
6, ¹7, 8, 11, ¹12, 13, 16, 19-21, 23-24,
¹26, 37, 42, 44-46, 51, 53-55, 57-59,
62; 121, 128, 138, 142-43; 205, 209-10,
215, 217-19, 221, 223, 225-26; 302, 306,
¹308, 317, 319; 403, 405, 420-21, 423,
429, 435.

strange or odd from a conventional
viewpoint 2-3, 5, 9-10, ¹12, 14, 17-18,
22-26, !27, 28-36, 38-41, 43, 45-50, 52,
54-56, 60-65; 101-17, 119-27, 129-37,
139-41, 144-49, sn150, 152; 201-5, !206,
207-8, 211-14, 216, 220, 222-26; 301,
303-4, sn305, 306, sn307, 309-16, sn318-
19, 320-26, 328; 401-4, 407-19, 421-22,
424-29, 431-37.

no response 15; 118, 151; 327; 406,
430.

Comment:

Inf. hesitates to use 'queer' to mean
"strange" after learning from her son
in the army that it also means "homosexual"--211. "I'd call you 'queer' for
gathering all this junk"--311.

Synonyms of queer, in the various
meanings, range from formal "harmlessly
psychopathic" to slang "loopy" and colorful "misty in the peak." No pronounced
correlations with area or with inf. type
appear.

abnormal 319.
addled 47.
balmy 34.
batty 308.
crazy 16.
different 145; 319; 426-27. ~, but
not crazy 22. ~ from an ordinary mortal
214. ~ from the ordinary in any way 149.
~ than other people 105.
dumb 306.
eccentric 14, 38, 62; 121, 141.
feeble-minded 306.
foolish 14; 307.
funny 7, 17, 36, 43; 307; 429. ~ ideas
or ways of doing things 325.
harmlessly psychopathic 58.
little bit lacking 427. something
lacking upstairs 44.
loony 34, 52.
misty in the peak 34.
notionable 204.
not all there 19; 317; 405, 423. not
all together 51. not (very) bright 203,
225. not conforming to ordinary standards of behavior 426. not like other
folks 148. not normal 7, 59, 65. not
quite goofy 37. not quite balanced 317.
odd 2, 4, 10-11, 32, 38, 44-45, 47,
61, 63, 65; 139, 148-49; 202, 205, 207,
209, 220; 316, 318-19, 328; 410, 413,
421-22, 425-26, 428.

off 64; 205, 210; 305, 308, 317; 401,
421, 424. ~ mentally 426. mentally ~
21, 58. a little ~ 138, 142; 217. a
little ~ in the upper story 420. ~ the
unbeaten path 428.
on the borderline 226.
out of the ordinary 22, 65; 203; 425,
432.
a little bit out of balance 1.
out of line with the average human
being 224.
partly cracked 19.
peculiar 216; 319, 324.
screwy 13.
silly 56.
simple 16; 223.
strange 18.
they haven't got all their marbles 37.
tetched 210; 435. touched 47, 62; 301,
319. touched in the head 420.
unusual 436.

57.2 obstinate. NE 471.

Although some of the more picturesque
folk terms to describe an obstinate person did not survive the western migration, he still can be characterized in
many ways in the UM, some rather conventional and some obviously restricted
to quite informal contexts.

Of the terms recorded, simple stubborn is most widespread, the usual expression of four out of five infs.
throughout the region. One in three,
more in Iowa than in Minnesota, report
the use of bull-headed.

The head interestingly serves as the
focus in several expressions, either
in comparison with a characteristically stubborn animal as in bull-headed
and, favored in North Dakota, pig-headed; or with reference to its physical
characteristics as in bone-headed, hard-
headed, headstrong, stiff-headed, strong-
headed, and, perhaps, the oncer stumble-
headed.

Next in frequency to bull-headed is
set, occasionally in the phrase set in
his ways, and twice with the older variant sot. [See Vol. 2.] Ornery persists
in all three inf. groups.

Of the other terms, listed below, the
most curious is otsny, offered in Winona,
Minnesota, by a Type III speaker of Polish descent. He said that it was common
in Winona and that he had heard it also
from Poles in Chicago. His belief that
it is not Polish has been confirmed as
has his statement that it is known and
used locally. One conjecture is that
the word is simply an incorrect version
of the pig latin for "snotty." The correct one, of course, would be notsy or
notsay. Another conjecture is that,
since Polish lacks the [ʌ] vowel, otsny

[atsni] is rather derived from an attempt by a Polish speaker to reproduce a pig latin form of "nuts." In a personal communication of January 29, 1951, Professor Frederick G. Cassidy rejects the pig latin origin as romantically implausible and proposes as more likely an attempt by a foreign speaker [in this case Polish?] to reproduce a rapid and perhaps slurred pronunciation of obstinate. The problem is unresolved.

[For the pronunciation of contrary see the volume on pronunciation.]

	Mn.	Ia.	N.D.	S.D.	Nb.	Ave.
bull-headed	25%	51%	27%	37%	28%	34%
contrary	8%	16%	19%	11%	8%	11%
obstinate	18%	8%	19%	11%	6%	13%
ornery	9%	6%	12%	4%	3%	7%
set	12%	18%	19%	11%	2%	16%

CL 106: Among 1,051 respondents the two most favored terms, as in the field data, are stubborn and bull-headed, but with headstrong in third place, perhaps because it was suggested on the checklist. Pig-headed, though infrequent, is consistently more likely in Minnesota and North Dakota. Owly, not found in the fieldwork in this sense, is accepted by 49 respondents. A tentative Northern bias of ornery is confirmed.

	Mn.	Ia.	N.D.	S.D.	Nb.	Ave.
bull-headed	28%	39%	43%	43%	48%	42%
contrary	11%	20%	13%	14%	23%	16%
headstrong	20%	20%	16%	20%	29%	22%
ornery	21%	9%	24%	21%	13%	17%
set	12%	11%	16%	16%	15%	14%
stubborn	60%	50%	65%	56%	59%	57%

  arbitrary 38.
  balky 102.
  bone-headed cvr314.
  bull-headed 1, 5, 8, !21, 22, 25, :26, 27, ¹28, !29, 30, 35, 37, c38, 40, †45, 49, 57; 101, 104, c105, s106-7, 108-9, 112, s113, 114, 117, 119-25, 127, 135, ¹137, 138-45, s146-7, sn149, s152; 201, 203, ¹205, sn208, †209, 210, ¹214, s¹216, 218, 220, !224, s226; :s!301, 302-3, 309-11, s†312, s¹313, 315, 320, !321, 323, s324, 326, s328; 405-6, sn!407, 408-9, !411, 412, s418, 419, 422, ¹435, 437.
  contrary 16-17, 20, 27, 40; 101, 103, 105, 115, 129, 132, 135, 145; 201, 206-7, 214-15; 302, 316, c325; 405.
  egotistical 119.
  firm 428. ~ as the rock of ages 317.
  hard-headed 125, 130, 132; 305; 403-4.
  has a chip on his shoulder 131.
  has a one-track mind 419.
  headstrong 36; 138, 145, 150; 224.
  independent 64.
  muley 110. mulish 102, s113, 131, 137, s139.

  obstinate 2, 14, :28, 30, 33, 37-38, 42, 49, 54-55, 57; 102, 131, 142, 150; 215, 219, 221-23; 312, 317, 326; 418-19.
  obstiferous †311.
  ornery c18, 30, c38, 40, 49, 64; 107, 111, 115; 201, 203, 225; 325; 407.
  otsny 58.
  persistent 11, 26.
  pig-headed ¹48, s56; *116, 118, ¹126, 129, s146; 201, c202, 204-5, sn208, ¹211, ¹214, sn217, 218, 222; s¹313, s322.
  positive 214.
  set :11, 29, 42; 116, 122, 128; 210, :217; 313, 326; 410, 429, 435-36. ~ in his mind 15. ~ in his ways 44, 48, 61; 108, 117, 133, 136, 146-47; 209, 224, 226; 327; 403, 406, 410, 420, 437.
  sot ¹†403. ~ in his ways 54.
  stiff-headed 223.
  strong-headed 140.
  stubborn 1, !3, 4, 6-10, 12-15, 17-19, 21-25, 28, 30-34, 37-39, !41, 43, 45, !46, 47, 50-53, c54, 55-59, c60, 61-63, *64, 65; 102-4, *105, 106-7, sn108, 109-11, 113, 116-17, 119, 121-24, 126-28, 130-31, 133-34, 136-39, 142-44, 146, 148-49, 152; !201, c202, 203-6, 210, ¹211, 212, :sn213, 214, 216-19, !220, 221-24, 226; 301-4, s!305, 306-7, 309-13, 315, 318-21, s324, 326-28; 401-2, 404-6, !407, 408, 410, 413-18, 420-21, 423-29, 431-37. damn ~ 208, 218. ~ as a mule !129; 411. ~ as an ox 120. (~ Dutchman 419.)
  stumble-headed *45.
  ugly 105.
  no response 151; 308; 430.

Comment:

  otsny: Inf. says this is not Polish; it is common locally--58. obstinate: "In better taste" than 'bull-headed'--38. "Stronger than 'stubborn'"--312. Usu.--54. stiff-headed: Inf. says this is a translation of Dutch steif kopf--223. stubborn: Inf. would use this to describe animals, but not people--119. Inf. says this usage would depend on the "society we are in"--149.

57.3 touchy. NE 470.

A person who is easily offended is describable by a variety of terms in the UM, although, as with 57.2, the variety is less than that in the eastern states. As infs. sometimes say, and as context sometimes reveals, the terms are only broadly synonymous.
Some, like sensitive and persnickety, represent a range from the formal to the informal; others, like feisty and thin-skinned, represent a different

kind of variation. Feistiness seems to imply active behavior, while a thin-skinned person may react by withdrawal.

Throughout the UM the most common epithet is touchy, offered widely by all types of infs. Only one, a Minnesotan, has tetchy, etymologically a different word although often erroneously held to be a phonetic variant of touchy.

Sensitive, next most frequent, clearly has Northern orientation with more than twice as many instances in Minnesota and North Dakota as in Iowa and Nebraska. The several other terms listed below are rare and scattered and, except for owly, feisty (ficety), and possibly thin-skinned, seem not to yield any regional correlation. The four instances of owly are in Minnesota and North Dakota; it not only does not appear in Midland speech territory but it also is lacking in NE. Feisty, found only in Iowa coincidentally with feist (fice) (see 26.6), is a clear South Midland term so restricted to speech that few of its users are sure of its spelling. Only one of the 14 occurrences of thin-skinned is in indisputable Midland territory.

Besides using descriptive adjectives, three infs. described an easily offended person in these ways: "He has to be handled with gloves"--328; "He's got a hot temper"--16; and "He wears his heart on his sleeve"--119.

	Mn.	Ia.	N.D.	S.D.	Nb.	Ave.
feisty	0	10%	0	0	0	
hot-headed	9%	8%	0	11%	0	6%
sensitive	35%	14%	48%	33%	19%	28%
thin-skinned	9%	6%	12%	4%	3%	7%
touchy	76%	74%	92%	59%	75%	76%

chicken-hearted 107. crabby 15. cranky 322; 413, 422. edgy s431.

easily hurt 53; 217; 325. ~ miffed 137. ~ offended 59; 147. ~ touched 116. easy miffed 429.

feisty s¹114, 122, 125, 130, sn132, sn139.

finicky 320; 428. funny 414. fussy 6, 8; 431. grouchy 428.

hot-headed 6, 35, 56, 64; 112, 127, 130, 140; 303, 306-7. hot-tempered 5.

nervous 19, 25; 140. ouchy 404.

owly sn37; 212-13, sn222.

peppery 10. persnickety ¹†133. pouty 143.

quick-tempered 58, 62; 307; 425.

sensitive 2, 10-11, 18, 20-21, 29, 32-33, 40, 44-46, 52-53, 55, 57, 60-63, 65; 103, 120, 128, 148-49, 152; 201, *203, 205-6, 208, 211, 215, 217-18, 221, 224, 226; 301-2, 309-10, 313, 315, 319, 326-27; 401-2, 404, 406, 410, 417, 426. over-~ 131. super-~ 11. too ~ c22.

sissy 108. sore-headed 102. sour 13. sulky 416.

thin-skinned 33-34, 37-38, 54-55; 101, 108, 110; 202, 216-17; 317; 409.

timid 135.

tetchy 13.

touchy 1-4, c5, 8, sn9-10, 12, 14-15, 17-20, :21, 22-23, :24, 25, :s26, :sn27, 28, :30, 31-32, 34-36, sn38, 39-41, :s42, c43, 44-49, c50, c51, 53, s¹54, sn55, 56-59, 62-63, s¹64-65; 101-3, s104, 105-6, s108, 109, s111, 113-19, 121-27, 129-31, s132, 133-38, s139, 141-43, ¹144, 145-49, s150, 152; 201, c202, 203-5, 207, sn208, 209-13, !215, sn216-17, 218-19, sn220-21, 222-23, sn224, 225, s226; :301, 302, s303, 304, 308-14, :s315, c316, s318, 320-21, s322, 323, s324, :326, sn327; sn401, s402, :s403, 404, s405, 406-8, 410-12, 415, s416, :sn417, sn418, :s419, 420-21, 423-29, 432-35, sn436, s437.

ugly 316.

no response 151; 214; 305; 430.

Comment:

easily offended: More formal than 'touchy'--59. feisty: A "feisty" person is someone who is too big for his breeches; a small man who is a trouble-maker is also called a 'feist'--122. A "cocky" person--125. A person who bristles easily--130. A person with his nose in other people's affairs--132. persnickety: Used by inf.'s MGF (from Ky.)--133. tetchy: Also means "a bit queer"--13. touchy: More common than 'sensitive'--45; 309. "Less refined than 'sensitive'--149. Usu.--202, 205; 417, 428. Also said of horses--401.

57.4 He got (became) angry. NE 472.
For describing a person who has lost

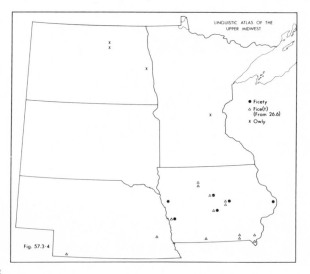

Fig. 57.3-4

his temper four out of five UM infs. ordinarily use mad, although some admit doing so with a sense of guilt derived from a school-delivered injunction that this word can mean only "insane." About one-third prefer angry on all occasions or use it in a context considered more formal. The degree of schooling presumably is a factor, as the frequency of angry increases from Type I to Type II.

With both of these terms there is a range of meaning from "irritation" to "fury." Some of the infs. use one or the other as a blanket designation for the whole range; others will indicate part of the range with other expressions more or less synonymous. Several such expressions found in NE, mostly folk terms, did not persist in the UM, but a number remain. Since not all field-workers sought for equivalents after obtaining one response, some terms listed below are probably more widely used than may be inferred from the two or three recorded instances.

Sore, by some held to be slang, is the most frequently reported minor synonym. Hot, either alone or in such phrases as hot under the collar, is next. Both occur in all five states. Related is het up, not used by younger and better educated infs.

Ugly, perhaps more widely received in the meaning "quarrelsome," is nevertheless accepted as a synonym of angry in the UM, certainly more extensively than the four scattered occurrences imply.

Owly, treated in 57.3 as having a milder denotation, seems to have the "angry" meaning for one Minnesotan; and this sense may be supported by the metaphorical extension illustrated by the following from the *Minneapolis Star*, June 3, 1958: "The weather, getting gradually owlier the past few days, broke loose today...Thunderstorms passed over the Twin Cities during the night, and a lightning strike or two was reported during the morning."

Most of the remaining infrequently recorded terms listed below are actually widely known, but a few are unusual either as words or as bearers of the meaning "angry." Rammy and ringy seem unattested elsewhere, although the latter might conceivably have had an earlier relationship with ring-tail, a hobo word defined in Wentworth and Flexner's *Dictionary of American Slang* (1960) as "A grouchy person." Off sorts most likely is a misinterpretation of out of sorts.

Several infs. volunteered equivalent expressions involving verbs:
  blew off 29.
  blew up 408, 410.
  blowed his top [1]404.
  flew in a fit 31.
  flew off the handle 43, 46, 51, 57; 117.
  pissed off [1]404.
  went off half-cocked 29.

	Mn.	Ia.	N.D.	S.D.	Nb.	Ave.
angry	34%	25%	50%	29%	28%	32%
mad	71%	92%	81%	93%	86%	83%
riled (up)	5%	4%	8%	4%	0	4%
sore	7%	6%	38%	7%	17%	12%

CL 107: Returns from 1,040 respondents modify the picture drawn from field data. Angry, as a standard literary word, was not included in the checklist, and mad percentages are very much like those in the field records. Owly, however, has a much higher frequency, enough so as to suggest a Northern orientation, especially in light of the 13% in northern Iowa contrasting with only 4% in southern Iowa. Ugly likewise appears with some Northern bias, again supported by a 7% frequency in northern Iowa and only a 4% frequency in the southern part of the state. Riled (up), contrariwise, is checked by more Midland speakers, with a 13% frequency in northern Iowa and 21% in the southern half. Wrathy, not recorded in fieldwork, is used by 56 respondents. Write-in terms volunteered by the respondents are: burned up -- Mn. 5a; steamed up -- Mn. 13; hot-headed -- Mn. 13; quick-tempered --Ia. 18; boiling --Ia. 17; hot and bothered -- Ia. 11; hot around the collar -- S.D. 55; hot under the collar -- Nb. 38, 61.

	Mn.	Ia.	N.D.	S.D.	Nb.	Ave.
het (up)	7%	8%	5%	7%	10%	8%
hot	5%	3%	7%	7%	9%	6%
mad	67%	74%	71%	74%	81%	73%
owly	23%	9%	26%	25%	4%	16%
riled (up)	12%	17%	12%	13%	22%	15%
ugly	9%	6%	11%	8%	6%	8%

  angry 1-2, 8, 10, 14, 17-18, 22, 28, 31, :33, 34, 37, 39-41, c44, 46, 55, sn56, 57, 61; 104, 106, 111, 120-23, 126, 131, 144-45, 150, 152; 201-3, 205, 208-9, 211-12, 214, 216, :217, 219, 224; 305, 309-10, 312, *316, 319, 321, 324; 403, c404, 406, 409-11, 417, 424, 428, 437.
  burned up 33; 411. burnt up 37.
  feisty sn115, sn139.
  fiery c29.
  finicky 311.
  furious 410.
  grouchy 114.
  hateful 132.

het up s↑40, 54; 409, 422.
pretty hostile 429.
hot 29, ¹42, 43; 125; 208, 222; 410.
red ~ 133. ~ and bothered :33. ~ around
the collar 404. ~ in the collar 225. ~
under the collar 24; 214; 328; 410, 412.
huffy 26 /hʌfi/; 217.
irritated c44; 101.
mad 3, :4, 5-6, c7, 9-10, 12-15, c16,
c17, s19, c20, 21-25, 27, 30, 32, sn33,
35, 37-40, 42-43, ¹44, 45-50, c51, 52-
55, 57-60, ¹61, 62-63, sn64, 65; 101-6,
c107, 108-20, 122-39, 142-43, 145-50,
152; 201, 203, 205-10, sn¹211, c212,
213, 215-16, 218-22, c223, 224-26; 301,
c302, 303-16, ¹319, 321-27; 401-3, 405-
7, 410-11, 413-23, 425-27, 429, 431-37.
~ as a hopping toad 317. awful ~ 36;
!318. fiery ~ 310. real ~ cvr414. right
~ 409. pretty ~ c320.
on his high horse 36.
out of humor 421.
out of sorts 421. off sorts 422.
owly 8.
piqued /pɪgd/ 14.
peeved 105, 122, 130, 147; 308.
put out 116.
rammy 408.
red-headed 141.
riled 14; 118. ~ up 11, 58; 105; 205,
221; s301, 310.
ringy /rɪŋi/ 214.
ruffled 58.
sore 13, 18, ¹34, 64; 121, 141, 147;
201-4, sn211, 212, sn217, 218, c220,
224; sn311, 313; 404, 412, 419, 421,
433, 435.
spunky 139.
stirred up 54.
ugly c8, 36; sn311; 404.
wrought up 18; 410.
no response 140, 151; 430.

Comment:

angry: More polite than 'mad'--39.
Inf. would use 'angry' rather than 'mad'
--120. "A city word"--209. finicky =
angry--311. mad: Usu.--22, 46; 224; 324.
Inf. admits to its use, but says it
shouldn't be used--55. Said more of animals; "not correct"--58. "Not correct,
though; in Webster's it means 'crazy'"--
63. Inf. thinks it incorrect--313; 406.
Inf. calls it a children's term--211.
"They've got their back up"--103. ringy:
"He got ringy over what was said"--214.
sore: Usu.--224. vicious: Stronger than
'mad'--16.

57.5 keep calm.

Not included in the original NE worksheets, this item has been sought in
later regional surveys. In the UM four
terms have almost equal over-all use in

admonitions to reduce excessive emotional reaction. Most common is calm, occurring in ~ down, ~ yourself, and keep ~,
with a total frequency of 47%. Next is
quiet, found in keep ~, be ~, and, as a
verb, ~ down, with a total frequency of
37%. Cool, appearing in ~ down, ~ off,
and principally keep ~, has a total frequency of 33%.
No prominent regional pattern appears
with these terms, unless it be the
slight Midland weighting of quiet. But
the quiet terms do have much higher acceptance among old-fashioned speakers,
with 54% response by Type I infs., 23%
by Type II, and only 13% by Type III.
Conversely, the calm terms are less
favored by older speakers, only 32% of
Type I, but 60% of Type II, and 69% of
Type III.
Several minor phrasal equivalents are
listed below, some with much wider use
than the few instances intimate. Fieldworkers did not always search for other
variants once a single response was obtained. Three of these reflect an earlier period: Don't unhitch here, gentle
down, and hold your horses; one, from
a Type II inf., the automotive age:
Don't blow a gasket.

	Mn.	Ia.	N.D.	S.D.	Nb.	Ave.
calm down	16%	22%	12%	19%	11%	21%
keep calm	41%	20%	23%	26%	20%	28%
keep cool	25%	20%	50%	33%	26%	28%
keep quiet	34%	40%	19%	33%	39%	32%

calm down 2, 4, s5, ¹7, 9-10, 22, 29,
33-34, 54-55; 101, 106-8, 110, 119, 121,
130, 137, 144-45; 207, 214, 219; 305-7,
326, 328; 406, 410, 412, 437. ~ yourself 20, 50; 126-27; 320-21; 404. be
~ s58; 426.
cool down 130, 142, 148; 224; 319. ~
off 21, 24-25, 37; 114, 128, 141; 222.
don't blow a gasket 38.
don't fly off the handle 20.
don't unhitch here 409.
ease off 422.
forget about it 147.
gentle down 409.
go slow 122.
hold on 36; 143. ~ ~ a little 129.
hold your horses 24. ~ your temper 4;
204; 418.
hush 11.
keep calm c1, r8, s13, 17-18, s20, 26,
28, 31-32, 38, c39, 40, 43, r44, 45-47,
¹51, 52, c53, 55, 57, *60, 61-65; 102-3,
118, 123, 127, 131, 134-35, 150, 152;
205, 211-13, 215, 226; 302, 310, 312-13,
315, 318-19; 401, 403, 421, 427-28, 433,
435.
keep cool 1, !2, 3, 6-7, 12-13, 15,
24, 30, 32, 41, 48, 53, 57-58; 102-3,

107, 112-13, 120, 122, 125, 140, 149;
202-4, 210, 214-18, 220-21, 223, 225;
302-3, 309, 319, 321-22, 324-26; 402,
¹404, 410, 415-16, 420, 424-25, 428,
431.

keep quiet 3, 5, 7, 9-12, 16, 19, 23,
25, 31, 35-36, 48-49, 51-52, 56-57, 59,
63; 101, 104-5, 109, 111, 114-16, 127,
129, 132-35, 137-39, 143, s145, 146,
152; 207, 209, 212, 224-25; 403-5, sn308,
314, 317, 320, 323, 325, 327; 409, 412,
414, 417, 419, 422-23, 427, 432, 434.

keep still 11, 27, 40, 42, 56; 136;
201, 209; 305; 407.

keep your head 208. ~ your shirt on
¹3, 12, 21, 37; 108, 111; 203, 216, 218,
222, 225; 301, ¹325, 326; 409, 411, 429,
433. ~ your temper 63; 208; 408. ~ your
temper down 405.

quiet down 29, 34, 65; 117, 124, 140;
206; 308, 316-17. ~en down 308; 436.
be ~ 136.

settle down 128. simmer ~ 125.

take it easy 23, 29, 57; 101, 111,
119, 123.

no response 14; 151; 311; 413, 430.

Comment:

calm down: "Better" than 'keep quiet'
--9. Usu.--55. keep calm: "Intellect-
uals say this"--51. keep your shirt on:
Used by inf.'s son--3.

57.6 tired. NE 479-82.

Although fieldworkers attempted to
elicit and hence distinguish mild and
strong terms, a practical difficulty
arose. A perhaps typically weak word
such as tired could appear very strong
if used with atypical stress, pitch,
and length. On the other hand, presumably a strong term such as bushed could
be used hyperbolically to describe a
person only slightly tired.

Of the terms recorded for this item
perhaps only three, tired, fatigue(d),
and the rather literary weary, can be
considered as fairly neutral. The bulk
seem usually to imply a somewhat accentuated state of weariness even up to the
point of near exhaustion.

A greater degree is sometimes shown
by all or out. A person "all used up"
may be more tired than one who is only
"used up." A person who is only "tuckered" may be less tired than one who is
"tuckered out." One who is "all tuckered out" is presumably about as tired
as one can be! But this interpretation
is countered by the colloquial tendency
to add a redundant out as a kind of
sense completive rather than as an in-

tensifier.

Expectedly, tired is universal. All
in is used by one-half of all infs.
Some terms like bushed, poohed, pooped,
and tuckered are more likely in very
informal speech. Poohed is more recent;
tuckered is more old-fashioned. From
South Dakota sources other than the
field data, it appears that a recent
and still current full form of too
pooped to pop has the addendum and too
numb to come. No clear distribution
pattern emerges. One inf. insisted upon
the form fatigue as adjectival without
the -d.

Twice, equivalent sentences were recorded: He's overdone himself--317; and
My pants are dragging--57.

	Mn.	Ia.	N.D.	S.D.	Nb.	Ave.
all in	54%	55%	77%	32%	33%	50%
bushed	14%	4%	12%	18%	3%	10%
done (etc.)	11%	8%	8%	0	3%	7%
exhausted	8%	14%	12%	8%	11%	10%
fagged (out)	15%	10%	8%	11%	19%	13%
petered (out)	12%	6%	15%	4%	11%	10%
played out	15%	2%	19%	25%	17%	14%
poohed (out)	11%	10%	8%	25%	19%	14%
tired (out)	91%	100%	92%	82%	89%	92%
tuckered (out)	17%	6%	12%	7%	11%	11%
weary	8%	8%	15%	11%	8%	9%

CL 108, 109: The 1,049 responses to
these two items on the checklists do
not differentiate in strength of meaning.

Since some of the returns from South
Dakota were accidentally destroyed, complete totals for that state do not exist. In general the checklist data are
consistent with those of the field
study.

	Mn.	Ia.	N.D.	S.D.	Nb.	Ave.
all in	71%	72%	69%	76%	74%	72%
done up	12%	16%	14%		22%	
done out	3%	4%	3%		1%	
fagged out	14%	15%	18%	17%	23%	17%
give out	7%	30%	16%		15%	
killed	1%	1%	5%		1%	
petered (out)	60%	36%	50%		54%	
tuckered (out)	13%	19%	18%	14%	14%	16%
used up	25%	21%	30%		15%	

Many respondents felt impelled to
write in their own terms when the checklist did not represent their own use.
Most of these appear also in the field
data: beat out (Mn. 54.5; N.D. 43.1;
Nb. 19.1, 33.1); bushed (Mn. 45.2, 68.3;
Nb. 19.2); dead (Ia. 17.3, 90.4; S.D.
48.3); done for (Mn. 85.1); down and
out (S.D. 22.1); exhausted (S.D. 30.2);
fatigued (S.D. 30.2); gone (Ia. 18.1;

S.D. 48.4, 66.1); poohed out (Ia. 16.3, 30.2 ["modern term"], 41.3, 63.4); pooped (Mn. 35.2; S.D. 25.2, 55.1; Nb. 19.2); tired out (Mn. 5a.11, 35.6; N.D. 37.4; S.D. 11.2, 33.2; Nb. 35.2, 39.3); dead tired (Ia. 55.1); weary (S.D. 30.2).
The write-ins not elicited also during field work are: all through (Mn. 54.5); hunkishnee /ˈhʌŋkɪʃɪˌni/ (Nb. 5.1); out of soap (S.D. 3.1); pooked out (Ia. 74.1; S.D. 25.2, 55.1; Nb. 19.2); worn out (Ia. 23.2, 72.1; S.D. 56.2; Nb. 31.2). [For worn out see Vol. 2.] Neither pooked nor hunkishnee apparently have been attested elsewhere; they call for further study.

all got !¹20.
all huffed 409.
all used up 314.
all in 2, 4-5, 8, 11-13, 17, 20, 22, 24-26, 29-30, 36-41, *43, 45, 50-51, 53-54, 56-57, 59-62; 102, 104-6, 108-9, 111-13, 117, 119, 122-24, 126, 128, 130, 133, 135, 138, 140, 143-45, 149-50; 201-3, 205-6, !207, 208-9, !210, 212, !215, 216, 218-25; 301-3, 305, 309, 313, 316, 323, 325; 402, ¹403, sn405, ¹406, s407, 411-12, 420, 426-27, 432-33, 435, 437. just ~ ~ 47. pretty near ~ ~ 15. ~ ~ but my shoelaces 131. ~ ~ but my shoe-strings 401. ~ ~ but the shoestrings 26; 141.
almost in 44.
at the end of (my) rope 319.
beat out 103, 121.
bushed 29, →¹30, →¹33, 34, 38, !44, !53, 57, !61, !64, 65; 102, 105; 202, 214, 221; 310-11, 320, !321, 327; 426.
dead 12; 115.
dished up 57.
done 19. all ~ 48. ~ for 29; 116, 121; 409. ~ in ¹28, 47; 131; 214. ~ out 201. ~ up 23, 33, sn55; †115, 149.
down and out ¹215.
down at the heels 328.
exhausted 3, 18, 34, 49, 58; 117, 119, 121-22, 127, 147, 150; 205, 212, 225; !304, 305; 402, 410-11, 413.
fagged s¹3; 122; 314; 404. ~ out 4, 8, sn21, 26, 38, 40, 58; s108, 114, 126, 128, s139, 143; 222; 311, !321; 403, sn405, 412, sn417, 425, 429. all ~ out 31, 45, 57; 211.
(too) far gone 119.
fatigue c136. ~d 317.
flattened 409.
give out 135; 404.
knocked up !¹1.
like a rag 326.
petered 126. ~ out s¹3, 6, 8, 23, 41, 43-44, 50, !53; s108, 143, 152; sn203, 216-17, →224; 328; s402, 407, 409, s411, 421, 437.

played out 1, !2, 10, 12, 14, 17, 23, 27, 37, 56; 116; 201-3, 205, 215, 218, 220; 302, 306, 313-14, 322, !323; 409, 414, 418, 424, 427, 434. all ~ ~ 48; 209; 307.
poohed ¹10; 101, 110, !131; 222; 310, ¹312, 314, 328; →402, 404, →408, 417, →437. all ~ 54. just ~ 42. ~ out 9, c11, 61; 125, ¹145; →¹211, ¹217; 301, ¹326, 327; *412, s431, 433. all ~ out 47, 57; →115; 226; 309, 320.
pooped →¹30, 50; 208; 308-9, 315, →¹326; 404, →408, →¹436. ~ out 5, !¹7, 24, 43, 58; !204, 224; 320, 322-23; c423. all ~ out 101; 303. too ~ to pop *328.
just spent 42.
sunk *412.
tired 1-5, c7, c10, 11-12, c13-14, 15, c16, 18-19, 22-28, 30-31, 33-36, 38, 41, 48-49, 51, 55-58, 60-61, 64; 101-5, 107-9, c110, 111-20, 123-27, 129-31, 133-43, 145-49; *202, 203-8, 210-13, c214-15, 216, 218-19, 221, 223-26; 301-4, 308-15, 317-20, 322-24, 326-27; 401-8, 410-14, 416-18, c419, 420-23, 425, 427, c428, 429, c432, 433-37. awful ~ 132. damn ~ 105. dead ~ 21, 46; 110, 112, 115, 150; 426. dog ~ 42. ~ as a dog *60. plenty ~ 54. pretty ~ 43. sure ~ 325. ~ out 6, 9, 17, 29, 44, 51, 63, 65; 106, 113, 120-22, 128, 144, 152; 217, 220; 328; 410. all ~ out 32, 39, c40, 52-53, 55, 59, 62; 209.
tuckered out 9, sn21, 28, 36-37, 44, s46, sn55; 118, 124, sn139; s?210, 216, s220, →224; sn320; ¹403, 412, sn417, cvr423. all ~ ~ 56, 60, 62-63; 223; 309. plum ~ ~ 421.
washed out 131.
weary 18, 20, 28, 40, 42; c101, 106, 145; 213, c217, 218-19; 319, 324, 326; 406, 418, 426. wearied 107.
whipped 103; s415.
woofed 10, 37.
no response 151; 430.

Comment:

all got: Used by inf.'s neighbor of German ancestry--20. all in: Used by inf.'s husband--406. bushed: Used by inf.'s daughter--33. = frustrated, not 'tired'--312. exhausted: Usu.--49. fatigue: "I'd be very 'fatigue'"--136. knocked up: Heard occ.; this British use sometimes raises laughter because of ambiguity--1. petered out: Said of supplies; not synonymous with 'tired'--45. poohed out: Usu.--9. pooped: "An old football expression"--50. Used by inf.'s daughter--326. pooped out: Usu.--5. = "breaking wind"--!→418. tired: Usu.--4.

58.1 She <u>got</u> <u>sick</u>. NE 492.

To indicate the onset of illness <u>get</u> <u>sick</u> is usual for nearly one-half of the <u>UM</u> infs. In NE its irregular occurrence amounted to only 13% of the total; in the UM its frequency is 45% throughout, and as high as 61% in S.D.

Actually, expressions with <u>take</u> outnumber the <u>get sick</u> responses, but themselves are differentiated by the contrast between active and passive forms. Those in the passive, e.g., "She was taken sick," are less popular in the western half of the UM than is the simple active "She took sick."

Apparently gaining in acceptance, except in North Dakota and Nebraska, are expressions with <u>become</u>: Type I, 6%; II, 15%; III, 25%.

<u>Ill</u>, as a minor variant of <u>sick</u> when it is a complement of <u>become</u> or <u>take</u>, but never with <u>get</u>, seems to reveal Northern preference, with 12% in Minnesota and North Dakota, but only 2% in Iowa and 3% in Nebraska. <u>Ill</u> is favored equally by Types I and II, and is offered once by a college graduate. To some users it connotes fastidiousness on the part of the speaker.

Sporadic examples also appear of be ill/stricken/ailing, <u>come down with</u> [an illness], <u>come sick</u>, <u>fall ill/sick</u>, <u>get all sicked up</u>.

	Mn.	Ia.	N.D.	S.D.	Nb.	Ave.
become sick	15%	10%	4%	14%	8%	11%
get ~	52%	26%	38%	61%	53%	45%
take ~	20%	36%	42%	18%	33%	29%
be taken ~	31%	38%	23%	21%	14%	28%

CL 110: The 1,031 respondents even more strongly favor <u>get sick</u> and also are evenly divided between the active and passive of <u>take sick</u>. Forms with <u>ill</u> were not listed but two write-in examples of <u>become sick</u> occur.

	Mn.	Ia.	N.D.	S.D.	Nb.	Ave.
get sick	77%	66%	75%	75%	78%	74%
take ~	11%	26%	14%	11%	15%	16%
be taken ~	15%	14%	17%	19%	12%	15%

became ailing 19. ~ ill 8, 10, 14, 18, 33; 101; c213; 304; 406. ~ sick 5, 8, ?9, 20, 22, 58; 102, 116, 119, 131; ?310, 319, 323-24; 410, 435.
came down with it 32. come (pret.) sick 409.
fell ill 33. ~ sick 428.
got sick 2, 4, cr9, ¹10, 12-14, c15-16, 18, ¹20, c21, 23, 25-26, f27, 29, 31-32, 34-40, 42-43, s48, 50-51, 53-54, sn55, 56, 58, 63-64; 110, 118, *122, 123, 126, 128-30, ?137, 139-41, 143, 145, s150; c203, 204, 206, 208, c209, 211, 213, 218, c220, 222; 302-4, 306-7,

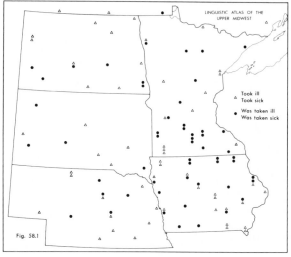

Fig. 58.1

309, 311, c312, 315, 318-20, 322-23, 325-26, 328; 401-2, 405, 407, 409-12, 416, 419, 421-22, cvr423, 424, 426, 433-34, 436-37. got all sicked up 409.
took ill 57; 201; 314. ~ sick c3, 5, 7, ¹10, 16-17, sn19, 24, ¹26, 30, *41, 57, 59-61; 101-2, 109, 112, 115, 117, 121, 124, 132-35, 138-39, 146-49, s150; c202, 205, 207, 209-10, 212, 216, 221, 223-24; cr310, 321, 323, 327; 403-4, 408, 414, 417, 421, 423, 425, 427, 431-32, ¹435. taken (pret.) sick 429.
was ill 317. ~ sick :27. ~ stricken 45.
was taken ill 1; 107; 214. ~ ~ sick 6, 8, 10-11, 22, 28, 41, c44, 45-49, 51-53, 55, 62, 65; 103-6, 108, 111, 113-14, 118-20, 122, 125, 127, 136, cr137, 142, 144; 215, 217, 219, 225-26; 301, 305, s308, 312-13, 316, 324; 406, 413, 415, 418, 420.
no response 151-52; 430.

Comment:

became ill: Usu.--10. got sick: Usu.--51; 410. "She got deathly sick"--16. took sick: Usu.--5. "I had been taking sick"--44. be taken sick: Usu.--53.

58.2 He <u>caught</u> <u>a</u> <u>cold</u>. NE 499.

To indicate that one has been victimized by mankind's persistent and still incurable malady, the common cold, UM infs. typically use one of three terms: <u>catch</u>, <u>get</u>, and <u>take</u>. Catch and take select either <u>cold</u> or <u>a cold</u> as a complement; <u>get</u> is restricted to <u>a cold</u> because of the quite different meaning signaled by <u>get cold</u>.

Four out of five UM infs., evenly distributed in the region, use <u>catch</u>, ordinarily recorded as the preterit <u>caught</u>. A regional bias appears with the presence or absence of the article, however. Twice as many Midland speakers tend to omit it, in contrast with those in Minnesota and North Dakota.

The less popular take phrases seem to find greater acceptance among Midland infs., who, in contrast with the situation of catch and the article, also slightly prefer take a cold to take cold.

Get a cold, a less common variant, is clearly Northern, with occurrences only in Minnesota and the northern strip of South Dakota. That it also is declining is suggested by its 8% frequency among Type I infs., a single instance recorded from a Type II inf., and only two instances from Type III infs. These data contrast with those in New England, where get is used by 144 infs., one-third of the total, with the heaviest concentrations, 82 infs., in New Hampshire and Maine.

A few scattered infs., mostly Type II, also have come down with a cold.

	Mn.	Ia.	N.D.	S.D.	Nb.	Ave.
catch cold	45%	70%	58%	50%	50%	54%
catch a cold	45%	20%	35%	32%	17%	31%
get a cold	14%	0	0	7%	0	5%
take cold	17%	22%	12%	11%	31%	19%
take a cold	5%	8%	0	4%	6%	5%

CL 111: From 1,050 respondents the returns support not only the dominance of catch, again with four out of five, but also the Midland tendency to favor catch cold without the article. Take cold likewise has a Midland orientation. Get a cold, however, is reported by mail from all five states rather than only the Northern two.

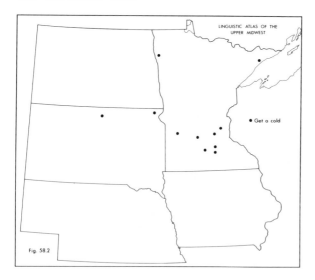

LINGUISTIC ATLAS OF THE UPPER MIDWEST

• Get a cold

Fig. 58.2

	Mn.	Ia.	N.D.	S.D.	Nb.	Ave.
catch cold	49%	56%	43%	54%	52%	52%
catch a cold	44%	30%	63%	34%	31%	39%
get a cold	8%	6%	7%	11%	12%	9%
take cold	12%	29%	9%	25%	29%	22%

came down with a cold 33; 121; 312-13. come down (pret.) with a cold 105, 113; 216.

caught a cold 1, 4, 8-11, 13-14, 16-18, 20, 24, 35, 37, 43, 47, 53, 63; s105, 108, 112, 115, 122, 126, 128-29, 138, 143, 145; 201, 203, 206, 209, 211, 216, 218, 221, 223; 309, 312-13, 315, 319-20, 324-26; 407, 409, 415, 419, 429, 436.

caught cold 2, 5, c11, 12, 15, 21, 23, 26, :27, 29-31, 33-34, 38-40, c42, 44, 52, c55, 56-59, 61, *64, 65; 101, 103-4, 106, 109-11, 114, 116-17, 120, *123, 124-25, 131, 133-35, 140-41, 144, 147-50; 202, 204-5, 207-8, 212-13, 215, 217, 219, 222, 224-26; 301-2, cr304, 306, 310-11, 314, 316-17, f318, 321-23, 327-28; 401-2, 405, 408, 410-12, 414, 416-18, 425-26, 428, 433-35, 437. catched cold 19; 220.

got a cold 6-7, 34, 36, 41, 43, 48, 50-51; 303, 307.

took a cold 3, 17, 28; 107, 119, 139, 146; 305; 404, 421. took cold 22, 25, 32, 45-46, 49, 51, 54, 57, 60, 62; 102, 106, 116, 118, 123, 127, 130, 132, 136-37, 142; 210, cr214, 222; ?304, 307-8; 401, 403, 406, 413, 420, 422-24, 427, 431-32.

no response 151-52; 430.

59.1 boil. NE 512.

In the UM the universal term for a painful inflammatory swelling of the skin—one that "comes to a head"—is boil. This item was considered as phonological by fieldworker A, who often sought it in the context, "What kind of sore did Job suffer from?" Other fieldworkers, however, also elicited carbuncle, designating typically a somewhat different, more painful and many-headed, inflammation. Two Iowans thus report older bile as used or heard, and another recalled having once heard the archaic bealing, found only once in New England. One South Dakotan uses both boil and fester.

boil (common).
bile [1]116, 135.
bealing [1]†137.
fester 308.

Comment:

carbuncle: "More than one head"--413, 423, 428. = boil--414, 421.

59.2 pus. NE 513.

As in New England, two words are widely found in the UM for the viscid fluid discharge from a boil or other open sore. A third, corruption, a rare archaism even in New England, survives in the UM only as a term recalled by one inf. as used by her Indiana-born mother.

Matter, although familiar to nearly one-half of the UM infs., seems nevertheless to be on the decline. Its greatest frequency is with the oldest and less educated Type I speakers, while conversely pus (which is also the term used by nurses and physicians) is more likely to occur with younger infs., Types II and III. Matter, furthermore, is less frequent in Midland territory, South Dakota and Iowa.

	Mn.	Ia.	N.D.	S.D.	Nb.	Ave.
matter	59%	26%	54%	39%	50%	46%
pus	54%	86%	65%	68%	67%	67%

core 44, 61-62; 317. corruption †403.
matter 1, :3, 4-5, ¹11, 12-19, ?21, 24-27, 31-33, ¹34, 35-37, 41, ¹42, 43, 45, 47-48, 50-53, 55-56, 58-59, 62-64; 104-5, 107, 110, 115, 118, †*122, 134-35, 138, 141, 143, †145, 146, 149, ¹†150; 203-4, 207, ¹208, 209, 211-12, 215, 217-18, 220, 222-25; 302-3, s¹305, s306, 307-8, †309, 311, ¹312, 316-19, 321-22, †325; †401, 403, †404, 405, 407, †410, 412-16, 418-21, ¹†423, 425, 429, 431-34.
pus 2, 6-11, →13, 14, 17-18, 20, cr21, 22-23, 28-30, 33-34, 37-40, 42, *43, 44, 46-47, 49, 51, 54, 57, 59-62, 65; 101-3, 105-6, 108-33, 136-40, 142-45, 147-48, 150; 201-3, 205-6, 208, 210-16, ¹218, 219, 221, ¹222, 224, 226; 301-2, 304-6, 309-10, 312-15, 319-20, 323-28; 401-2, ¹403, →404, 405-6, 408-12, s415, 417, 419, 421-24, 426-28, 432-33, 435-37.
no response 151-52; 430.

Comment:

corruption: Used by inf.'s mother (from In.)--403. matter: "Most people would say 'matter'"--11. Inf. would use this if it discharges by itself--37. Usu.--51; 215. pus: "A doctor would call it 'pus'"--143. Usu.--47; 212, 224.

59.4 proud flesh. NE 515.

For a granulated overgrowth of scar tissue the widespread though little used term in the UM, as in New England, is proud flesh. Of the few rare synonyms only one seems to have been carried west from New England.
Wild flesh, which also was reported once in the Wisconsin survey, is used

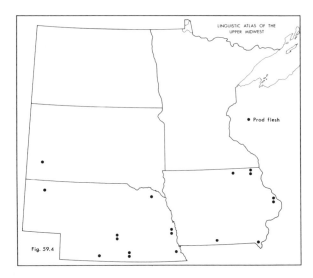

Fig. 59.4

by two infs. of German-speaking parentage, one in Minnesota and one in South Dakota. It is probably derived from the medical German wildes Fleisch, with the same meaning.

Dead flesh is a oncer in South Dakota, as is false flesh in North Dakota. Also in North Dakota is the curious overgrowth fresh, used by a Type I speaker of German-speaking ancestry. The form fresh may be due to a mishearing or a phonetic slip on the part of this inf., or it may be related to the similarly caused expression not infrequently found in the New England proud fresh.

Plowed flesh is another phonetic variant, but here with /r/ originally heard as /l/, sufficiently different so as to yield a new lexical item that semantically might be held to be not too inappropriate. In New England it was reported with 17 widely scattered occurrences, all but one from Type I speakers. As three of the four instances in the UM are also from Type I speakers, the form clearly is old-fashioned and probably nonstandard.

Prod flesh, also a phonetic variant, has a different origin. Weakening of the glide in the diphthong of proud produced a form which, since proud semantically does not seem to accord with flesh, apparently gained its own lexical independence although prod is even less semantically congruous. It is found only in Midland speech territory.

Scar tissue is offered once in Minnesota.

dead flesh 306.
false ~ 215.
overgrowth fresh 209.
plowed flesh 105; 307-8, 317.

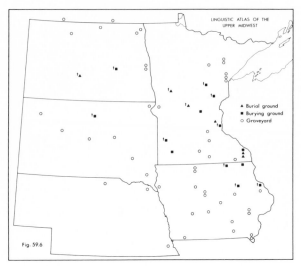

Fig. 59.6

prod ~ 105, 107-8, ¹110, 119, 121, 144, 150; 320; 402, 407, 420-21, 427-28, 431-33, 434.

proud ~ s1, 2, :3, 5-6, :7, 8-10, c11, 12-23, :24, 25-26, sn:27, 28, †29, 30-35, 37-38, s39, 40, 42, *43, 44-47, 49-57, 59-65; 101-4, 106, ¹107, 108-9, ¹110, 111-18, 120, 122-37, 139-43, 145-49; :201, 202-8, 210-14, ¹215, 216-23, 225-26; 301-5, 307, 309-13, :314, 315-16, 318, 321-28; 401, 403-6, 408-19, 422-24, 429, 433, 436-37.

prouded ~ ?138.

scar tissue 58.

wild flesh 48; †224.

Comment:

prod ~ 105, 107-8, ¹110, 119, 121,

false flesh: = proud flesh--¹215. proud ~: Inf. uncertain as to whether 'plowed flesh' or 'prod flesh' is correct, but insists that it is not 'proud' --105. Inf. has heard 'proud flesh' but considers that 'prod flesh' is correct--107. Inf. has heard rural people say both 'prod' and 'proud;' he is not sure which is right. wild ~: said of wire cuts on horses' legs--224.

59.6 cemetery. NE 525-26.

Although some settlers maintained the already disappearing custom of having a family interment plot on a farm, the infrequency and the archaic character of the Northern expressions burial ground and burying ground in the UM attest the fact that today it is historical only. These terms are reported as old-fashioned in northeastern Iowa and the southern half of Minnesota, areas of the earliest Northern settlement.

For some infs. burial ground and burying ground designate a similar plot adjoining a church and used for members of the congregation, or within or near a village or town and used for members of the community. The usual term, however, is graveyard, still widespread in the UM except in the most recently settled areas of the western sector and northern Minnesota, but now generally looked upon as old-fashioned. In the speech of most UM infs. the only, or the only active, designation is cemetery, which they apply alike to a small family plot and the huge burial areas in large cities.

Two old New England terms occur feebly. Churchyard is known to southern Minnesota infs. and God's acre is used by another.

One southern Minnesotan humorously volunteered the jocular marble orchard.

burial ground ¹7, †19, †27, 37, 57-58; †217. burying ~ ¹6, †21, †23, c25, 29, †40, !†46, 56, c59; †105, 107, †116, †119; †218; ¹†304; ?401.

cemetery 1-14, c15, c16, 17-24, 26-28, c29, 30-34, !35, c36, 37-39, c40, 41-53, c54, c55, 57-61, ¹62, 63-64, c65; 101-12, →113, 114-35, →136, 137-42, →143, 144-50; 202, c*204, →205, 206-8, →209, c210, 211-19, 222-26; 303-6, 308-12, c313, 314, 317-23, →324, 325-26, →327, !328; cr401, 402-4, 406, 408-11, →412, 413-29, 431-36, →437.

God's acre 51.

churchyard c18, †45.

graveyard ¹1, †2, ¹4, †5, ¹10, †11, 12-17, ¹18, †22-23, 25, s¹†26, ¹†28, †31, †33, 35, †37, †39-40, !†41-42, †43, †45, ¹†47, 48, 53, †61, 62, †64, 65; 103-4, 110, 113-15, †116, ¹117, 118, 121, †124, †126, 127, †129, 130, 132, †133, 136-38, 143, †144, 146, †147, 148-49; 201-3, c204, †205, 206, 208, †209, †210-16, †219, 220-21, †222-24; 301-2, 307, †310, c315, 316, 324, †325-27, sn328; †403, 405, †406, 407, †411-12, ¹416, †418, †429, 434, †437.

marble orchard !→61.

no response 151-52; 430.

Comment:

burial ground: Older 'cemetery'--57. Used by inf.'s mother (from Mn.)--217. burying ground: "Only of Indian cemeteries"--21. "Them's the words I use"--25. Older than 'cemetery,' but still used--107. cemetery: "The right word"--7. Usu.--17; 121. Inf. says "up-to-date people" use this--35. God's acre: Said seriously--51. graveyard: Used by inf. as a child--5, 37, 64; 126. Inf. objects

to this--10. Rural term--18. A small one
next to a rural church--33; 328. Still
heard occ.--43. Older than 'cemetery,'
but still used--53; 103, 110, 113, 115,
137, 149. Newer than 'cemetery'--138.
Unkept in contrast to a 'cemetery,'
which is cared for--202. "I was corrected in the sixth grade for using this"--
325.

59.7 casket. NE 524.

Coffin and casket occur in about the
same proportions throughout the UM, with
a relationship like that described in
the NE Atlas except that coffin is more
frequently considered old-fashioned.
Some infs. use both terms interchangeably. Others apply coffin only to the
older container, locally made, plain
and typically hexagonal or, as one inf.
said, "fiddle-shaped," and use casket
for the rectangular container, commer-
cially manufactured and often ostenta-
tiously ornate inside and out. Others
would now apply casket as a socially
more acceptable word to both the old-
fashioned and the modern objects. And
still others retain coffin under all
conditions.
With recollection of pioneer days one
Minnesotan and one Nebraskan, each Type
I, offer simply rough box.

	Mn.	Ia.	N.D.	S.D.	Nb.	Ave.
casket	55%	76%	58%	63%	58%	62%
coffin	62%	61%	54%	48%	50%	57%

casket 4-5, ¹7, →8, 10-11, 14, 18,
21-26, 28, →29-30, 31-37, →39-40, 42,
46-48, 51-52, ¹54, 55, 57-58, c61, 64;
101, 104-8, ¹109, 110-15, 117, 119-21,
123-25, sn→126, 127, 129, 131-34, 136-
41, →144, 145-46, ¹147, 148-49; 201-3,
→207, ¹208, →209, 211, →212, 213, →214-
15, →217, c219, sn224, 225-26; 301, 303-
4, 306-8, →312, 313, 316-19, 321, 323,
325-26, →328; →401, 402, 404-6, →407,
→412, 413-15, 417, 420-21, 423, 426,
428-29, 433-34, →437.
coffin 1-3, ¹4, †5, 6-10, †11, 12-13,
15-20, †21-24, ¹26, 27, ¹†28, 29, †30,
31, †32, 33-34, 37-38, †39-40, 41, 43,
c44, 45, c†46, †47, 48-50, †51-52, 53-
54, †55, 56-60, †61, 62-63, †64, 65;
102-10, 112, †115, 116, ¹117, †119-20,
122, 124, 126-28, †129, 130, 132, †133,
134-36, †137, 141-44, *145, †146, 147-
50; †202, sn†203, 204-6, †207, 208,
†209, c210, †211-13, 214-17, c218, c220,
221-23, †224-25; 302, 305, 307, 309-11,
†312-13, 314-15, 317, †318, 319-20,
†321, 322, 324, †325-26, †328; †401,
403, ¹†404, †405, †407, 408-11, †412,
414, 416, 418-19, ¹420, 422-25, 427,

†428-29, 431-32, 435-36, †437.
rough box 16; †303.
no response 118, 151-52; 327; 430.

Comment:

casket: More dignified than 'coffin'--
112. "Young people call it 'casket'"--
147. Inf. says this is heard more often
--319. Usu.--423. coffin: "The best
word"--7. Inf. says this is heard most
often--8. Formerly used by inf.--32,
40; 428. Older than 'casket' but still
used--34, 37, 54, 58; 106-7, 110, 141,
147; 414. Usu.--104. "Has an ugly sound"
--423. Shaped like a fiddle box; a 'casket' is rectangular--10, 21, 51; 148;
225. Home-made, as for indigent Indians
--10. The box enclosing the 'casket'--
33. Inf. is not sure that 'coffin' and
'casket' are synonymous--107.

60.3 rheumatism. NE 506.

Rheumatism is the well-nigh universal
term in the UM.
Two old-fashioned forms have been carried from the east coast. Rheumatiz survives with 15 scattered infs., but only
four of them--one in Minnesota and three
in Iowa--still use it. All are older
infs. Twelve, including some of the preceding, recall the variant rheumatics,
but only one, from whom it was recorded
in conversation, still has it as an active term. Rheumatics does not appear
in Minnesota or North Dakota.
Since the completion of the fieldwork,
rheumatism has begun to be replaced by
arthritis.

rheumatics !¹†202, !¹†210, †215,
¹†216, †217, ¹†218; c322, ¹†325; †405-
6, ¹†408, †412.
rheumatism (common)
rheumatiz !†23, 60, ¹†33, ¹†37, †40;
113, 135, 146; ¹†210, ¹†216, ¹†218,
†223; 317, ¹†325; 432.
no response 430.

Comment:

rheumatics: "Heard from old lady here"
--202. "Frequently heard at one time"--
215. "I've been bothered with lots of
rheumatics"--322. rheumatiz: "I heard
it from my landlady in Aitkin [Mn.]
years ago"--33. Her grandfather's term
--325.

60.5 jaundice. NE 511.

Asked their term for the illness during which the skin turns yellow, nine
out of ten UM infs. respond with either
the full yellow jaundice or, more likely, simply jaundice. The single word

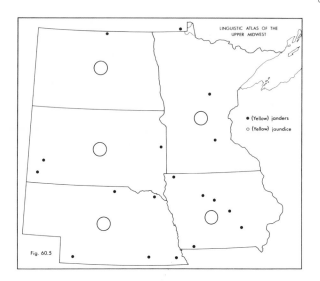

Fig. 60.5

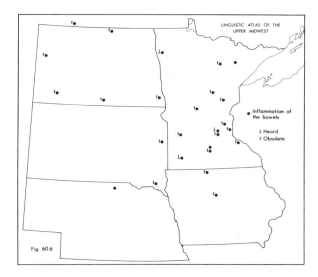

Fig. 60.6

designation seems to be winning out.

Eighteen Type I infs. retain the disappearing expression (yellow) janders, which for all but one has the /æ/ vowel as in /dʒændɚz/, a form distinctive enough for a few infs. to consider it a different word. [For the phonetic variations of this entry see the volume on pronunciation.]

One inf. uses the name of a related disease, yellow fever, and another confuses the names of two different diseases with his term yellow glanders.

	Mn.	Ia.	N.D.	S.D.	Nb.	Ave.
(yellow) janders	5%	12%	4%	11%	14%	9%
(yellow) jaundice	92%	89%	96%	86%	86%	90%

janders 1; 114, 135, †139, 143; :?204; :?309, 317. yellow ~ 21, 35; 101, 113, 132, cr204; :311, 320, †*328; 405, :407, 429, 432, 434.

jaundice 2-3, !5, 6-10, 13-16, 18-20, 23-24, 28-30, 32-34, 36, 39-40, 42, 44-45, !46, c47, :49, 51, 53-54, :!†55, 56-57, 61-62, 65; 102-3, 105-8, 110, 115-17, 119-31, 133-34, 136, 139-41, 144-49; 202, 206-7, 210-11, 213-15, 217, 221-23, :sn224, 226; 301, 306, cr309, 310, 312, 314-15, 326-28; :?403, 404, 409-11, 413, 422-24, 426-27, 431, 435. yellow ~ 4, 11-12, 14, 17, 22, 25-27, !¹†29, 31, 37-38, 41, 43, 45, 47-48, 50, 52, 57-58, 60, 63-64; 104, 109, 111-12, 137-38, 142, 150; 201, 203, 205, 208, !209, 212, 216, 218-19, :220, 225; 302-5, 307-8, 313, 318-19, 321-23, c324, 325; 401-2, cr403, 406, :408, 412, 414, 416-21, 425, 428, 433, 436-37.

yellow fever 59. ~ glanders 316.

no response 118, 151-52; 415, 430.

60.6 appendicitis. NE 509.

Appendicitis is the universal term in the UM. The older expression inflammation of the bowels, which appeared only four times in NE and each time was characterized as old-fashioned, retained some vitality as it moved westward. Twenty-four Type I and Type II infs., nearly all in Northern speech territory, recall it as once used, but for only two of them is it still an active form.

See also the volume on pronunciation.

appendicitis 1-20, c21, 22-34, !→35, 36, c37, 38-65; 101-17, 119-50; 201-13, c214, 215-26; 301-26, 328; 401-17, 419-29, 431-37.

inflammation of the bowels ¹7, †11, 13, †22-23, †27, ¹34, †35-36, †40, †42, 51, †52, †54, ¹59; †103, †114; †201, †204, †210, †215, †223, †225; †317, †325; 405, s407.

stomach trouble †55. summer complaint 437.

no response 118, 151-52; 327; 418, 430.

Comment:

appendicitis: "The Germans say 'taking them out' as if 'they' were in bunches" --47. inflammation of the bowels: Heard from patients over 70--34. Used by inf.'s parents (from Can.)--54.

60.7 vomit. NE 504.

The unpleasantness of the act of vomiting has led to the use of various jocular and euphemistic expressions which in the speech of many infs. regularly or at appropriate times replace older spew and puke and vomit itself because these are looked upon as crude and vulgar.

Usually considered neutral, throw up is the term most likely to be employed by UM infs. if the act must be referred to. It is found in all parts of the five states.

Puke is a close second, but it is often reported as a heard form or as one used more common in earlier days. Most infs. who admit to its current use comment upon its crudity and control also vomit or other terms to be used in formal contexts. The contrast typically appeared in the free conversation of a Minnesota inf., a physician (#9), who while speaking professionally used vomit and while telling an anecdote used puke. Only one inf., a Minnesota Type I farmer, professes puke as his usual expression. Several infs. remark that puke is not only a crudity but also that it is a boys' or men's word. Two infs. volunteer that puke is also a noun, one referring it to the meaning "an obnoxious person" and the other recalling it as an old nickname for a native of Missouri.

Historic spew, oldest of all the expressions and recorded from 112 of the 431 infs. in New England, clearly suffers from a rapid decline as a viable term. Only four UM infs. use it, and three of them are in Type I.

Vomit, widespread and by some held to be "polite" and the correct technical word, is likewise repugnant to a number of infs., who prefer throw up.

Heave, widespread though less common, seems to be considered jocular rather than crude.

Erp, obviously onomatopoetic, is most informal and more likely to be found in the speech of a child or of a woman.

Euphemistic phrases range from the fairly literal lose one's lunch to the almost whimsical toss (or woof) one's cookies (or biscuits).

No regional distribution appears in the UM data unless possibly erp may be Midland. Its occurrence is chiefly in Iowa and Nebraska.

bring it up 201.
erp 50; 101, !123, *131; ¹310; 401, →*412, ¹419, 431, 433, ¹436.
feed the fishes 108; !319; 424.
gurgitate !*122.
heave 4, 6, 8, !¹10, ¹20, !22, !¹31, 47, 58; 102, 108, 127, 130, 138-39, 143; *203, *215, !216, 222, →223; 309, ¹310, !313, !321, 323; ¹431, 437. ~ up !¹23, 25, !41; 111, *148; !209, 214, !218; 302, 312, 320; sn407, 408, 412, 420. ~ 'er up 308. ~ up to beat hell c311. ~ Jonah !317; ¹404, ¹429.
holler New York 214.

hoof up 214.
lose one's breakfast (lunch, dinner, supper) c33, 37; 111; 222; 316; 409-11, 417, 426. ~ one's guts 108.
nauseate 419. (be, become) ~d 26; 317, 319.
park one's cookies 125.
puke ¹1, ¹5, s¹6, 7-8, c9, !†12, 13, 18, !21, sn25, !26-27, 29-30, 34-35, !†36, 37, 42, !47, 50, !54, !55, !57; 102-3, 105, 107-8, !113, 115, 117, 119-20, 122, 124-26, s¹127, †128, 129-30, 133, 135, 139, *145, s146, 148-49, !¹150; 201, 203, !204, ¹205, !206-8, ¹210, †212, ¹213, †214, !215, ¹217, !219-20, 221-22, !†224, !225, ¹†226; †301, 302, 309, 312, !314, 315, !316, !320-21, !¹324, ¹325; !403, 404, sn!407, 408-9, †411, !413, 414, 416, !417, 418, ¹419, 421-22, !423, 425, 427, ¹429, s431, 433. ~ all over !¹313.
regurgitate 14; 131.
retch 314.
(be) seasick 308.
spew 218. ~ it out 59. ~ up 133; 420.
spit up 406.
throw one's oats !127. ~ up 1-4, ¹5, 6-8, ¹10, 14, 16-18, 20-21, !22, 23-24, 29-31, c32, 33-34, 36-37, c38, 40-42, 44, !46, 47-48, 50, 53, †54, 57-59, 62, 64-65; 101, 103-7, 109-10, 112, 114-16, 119, *122, 123-25, 128, 130-38, 142-43, 145-50; ¹202, 204-5, 208-10, c211, 212-13, 215-19, 223-24, ¹†226; 301-4, 306-10, c311, †312, 313-16, 318, 320, 323, 325-27, !328; 401-2, c403, 404-9, †410-11, 412-13, 415-17, 419-21, c422, 425-27, 429, 431-37. ~ it up c11; 322, 324; c418. ~ up one's dinner 327. ~ ~ ~ guts 12. ~ ~ ~ heels 431. ~ ~ ~ shoe soles 321. ~ ~ ~ victuals 139.
toss the biscuits 47. ~ one's cookies 37; ¹312; !423.
unload ¹404.
vomit 1-3, 5-6, 8, c9, 10, 12-25, 27-28, !29, 30-45, !46, 47, 49, !50, 51-55, c56, 57-65; 101-6, 108-17, 119-35, !136, 137-44, †145, 146-50; 201-26; 301-7, 309-11, →312, 313-28; 401-14, 416-19, 421, 423-29, 431-37.
woof one's cookies ¹436.
no response 118, 151-52; 430.

Comment:

erp: Jocular--50; 101. heave: Crude--4, 8; 310; 431. Jocular--108. Refers only to drunks--20. The final stages of vomiting--309. ~ up: "Vulgar term"--408. lose his guts: Jocular--108. nauseate: "He nauseates" (i.e., "vomits")--419. puke: Crude--1, 7-8, 37; 119, 125, 127, 129, 139, 146, 149; 205, 208, 210, 212, 215, 219, 221; 408-9, 413-14, 416, 418,

421-23, 425, 427, 433. "A pretty word"--47. "God, how I hate that word"--50. "A vulgar word"--54. "The crudest word I know. The only word I knew it by as a boy"--55. "Hideous"--*122. "Not very refined sounding"--150. "Very vulgar term"--222. "Nasty expression"--315. "That word makes me ill"--411. Men's term--25; 220. Boys' term--21, 27, 37; 221. Slang--18; 115. Jocular--102, 108, 120; 312, 316. Usu.--29. Inf. says a dog would 'puke'--126, 149; 206. "I'd almost forgotten this"--226. [as a noun] "That's a Missourian"--314. "An obnoxious person"--431. ~ all over: "Of an old drunk"--313. regurgitate: Act not completed--131. spew up: Of a baby--406. throw up: Crude--427, 435. Polite--8, 23, 62; 308. Usu.--42, 47, 64; 150; 327; 402. Used by inf.'s mother (from Can.)--54. ~ up one's heels: Jocular--431. toss one's cookies: Inf.'s daughter learned this at the Univ. of Iowa--312. "Got this from my boys in the service"--423. vomit: Crude--*426, 434. Polite--8, 24, 29, 40; 433. Usu.--2. unload: Especially heard on Saturday nights--404. woof one's cookies: Commonly heard here--436.

61.5 He is courting her. NE 404-5.

The question typically used by the fieldworker in eliciting this item was "If you see a young man regularly taking out the same girl, and he seems to be rather serious about her, what do you say he is doing?" The replies, although they always represent the point of view that the male is the active participant, vary greatly along two intersecting dimensions, of time and formality.

A complex of change, social and technological, had already greatly affected courtship patterns even in rural areas by the time of this survey, but older terms, often the same as those found in New England, survive, sometimes as recognized relics, in the speech of UM Type I and Type II infs. LANE attempts to distinguish terms with the meaning "woo" from those indicating simply "spend a good deal of time with," but such an attempt does not seem to be feasible with UM responses, which accordingly are treated as a single set.

With a number of varied responses and variations in the degree to which the fieldworker pushed for synonyms, the data are probably too incomplete to provide a picture of regional patterns, if indeed any exist in the UM. Some minor terms, nevertheless, are clearly associated with regional or local customs.

Courting her, the oldest of all the terms (first recorded in Lyly's *Euphues* in 1580) and the most common in New England, dominates the total UM because of its persistence among Type I infs. But of the infs. who do offer courting her, more than one-fourth stipulate that it is old-fashioned, and even then it is most frequent only in Minnesota, North Dakota, and Nebraska. Its over-all frequency declines from 60% for Type I through 45% for Type II to 38% for Type III.

Actually, the most frequent current expression revealed in the UM is going (steady) with her. Although only 36% of the Type I speakers have it, 60% of Type II do, and all but two of the college graduates (88%) likewise use it.

Two once common east coast terms occur in the UM but are declining. Keeping company with her is less often heard in the western tier of the UM states, and the Americanism sparking (1787), which one-half of the infs. consider archaic, is not even found in the records of interviews in the Dakotas.

A few other minor New England phrases very weakly survive, sometimes in isolated responses, such as attentive to her, beauing her, calling on her, chasing her (only once in New England), running around with her, stuck on her, and waiting on her.

But the tendency to reduce the number of variants, noticed in the treatment of a number of entries in this volume, is not manifest here. If anything, the many ways of considering courtship and its relation to local mores have yielded an even greater selection of equivalents in the UM than in New England. That some of them admittedly occur only as singletons does not necessarily signify that they are unique to the inf., for some are recognizably familiar even though they were not picked up in many interviews.

Rare but of unusual interest are metaphors reflecting local customs and views. In the North Dakota Badlands a Type I widow of cattle-ranching background has riding herd on her and building her a smoke, the latter with clear allusion to the Indian system of communicating with smoke-signals. An old South Dakota hotel-keeper with pioneer memories offers playing a big stack to her, but this reference to the game of poker he attributes to "backwoodsmen" from the nearby Black Hills. A Fargo, North Dakota, Type I inf., the oldest one interviewed in the UM, proffers leading her up to the snorting pole, as if the sought-after young lady were a wild filly to be tethered. Other more or less colorful expressions listed below are: has a case on her, has a crush on her, crashing her, giving her the rush (and rushing her), seeing his sweetie, selling her a bill of goods, shining up to her, sitting on her, squiring her around, stepping out with her, and thick with her.

Although the replies were sought by a question calling for a description of male behavior, a few infs. volunteered two related expressions describing the behavior of the couple. Both are actually common in the UM: They are going together (39, !45; 121, 136) and They are going steady (437).

	Mn.	Ia.	N.D.	S.D.	Nb.	Ave.
courting	54%	38%	77%	36%	61%	52%
going (steady)	w.40%	62%	50%	64%	28%	48%
keeping company	w. 15%	10%	9%	7%	8%	11%
sparking	6%	17%	0	0	6%	7%

CL 112: The discrepancy between the field data and the returns from 1,045 mail respondents is unusual, a fact that may in part be attributed to the circumstances that their average age is younger than that of the infs. and that the survey was made just as a change in the terminology was under way.

The checklists give both going (steady) with and keeping company a higher proportion and courting a much lower proportion than did the field records. Sparking, although here reported also from the Dakotas, is a poor fourth in the standing. Eight respondents check talking to (Mn. 5a.10, 63.4; Ia. 49.1, 78.1, 84.2; N.D. 1.2; Nb. 33.1, 57.3); three, walking out with (Ia. 32.1; N.D. 2.2, 43.1); and two, sitting up to (Ia. 32.1; Nb. 43.1). One each wrote in dating (Nb. 4.2) and paying attention to (Mn. 52.2).

	Mn.	Ia.	N.D.	S.D.	Nb.	Ave.
courting	11%	7%	14%	13%	9%	10%
going (steady)	w.67%	74%	75%	90%	91%	79%
keeping company	w. 36%	29%	34%	28%	29%	31%
sparking	6%	4%	3%	1%	3%	4%

has a heavy crush on her 202.
has a case on her 101.
[All the following expressions are complementary after a form of be]:
attendant upon her ¹†111.
attentive to her 120.
beauing her †325.
building her a smoke 214.

buzzing her →¹25.
calling on her 210, 224.
chasing her *19.
courting her sn†2, !3, 4-5, ¹6, 7-8, 10-14, !!15, 17, †19, †21, 22, :sn†23, †25, !†27, 28, s†29, 30-32, †33, !35, †36-37, 38, †40, *41, :s†42, *43, 44-46, †50, r51, !52, 53-54, †55, 56, 60-63, 65; 102, 104-7, 113, s115, ¹116, 119, †126, 129, 133, 137, 139-40, 142-43, †144-45, 147, 149; 201-4, †205, :206, 207-10, †211, 212-16, †217, 218-20, 222-23, 225, ¹†226; 305, 307, 311, †313, 318-20, 323-24, †325, 326; 401, †402, 404-5, †406, 409-15, 417, †418, 420-22, ¹†423, 426-28, 431, 433-36.
a-~ ~ 135. a-~ ~ quite heavy 132. trying to court her 317.
crashing her ¹8.
dating her →36, 50, →55; →213, →219; 302; →401, →406, 433. ~ ~ steady *→4.
falling for her 305.
giving her the rush †33.
going out with her 1, 9, 58; 148; 224; s415.
going steady with her 2-3, ¹5, 18, 20, 21, 24, →33, 34, 37, 53, 58; 110, 117, 121, 124, 126, 128, 130-31, 133-34, 150; 202-3, 210; 302-3, 309, 315, 318, 320, 323, 326-28; →402, 411, 416, 419, 437.
going to lead her up to the snorting pole 220.
going to see his sweetie 13.
going with her 6, 14, c16, 22-23, 26, 29, 39, !46, →47, 49-50, 53, 57, 59, 61; 101-6, 108, 111-12, 115-16, 119, 122-23, 125, 127, 136, s137-38, 146; 201, 205, 208, †211, 213, 218-19, 221-23, 226; 301-2, 304, 309-10, 312-14, 321, →325; ¹403, 424-25, c429, 432-33, s¹435, c437.
~ ~ ~ steady 109.
her beau 309.
her steady *48.
keeping company with her 1, ¹5, 10, 18, 22, ¹†25, 32, 34, 37, 46, 54, 64; 109, †110, c113, 141-42, 150; 210, 219, 223; †302, 314, 326; 401-3.
in love with her 306. making love to her 59, 61.
paying attention to her 11.
playing up a big stack to her ¹312.
riding herd on her 214.
running around with her 29, 57.
rushing her →7, †12; 108-9; 404, 408, 424, 435. ~ ~ right 316.
selling her a bill of goods 62.
serious 308.
setting out 47.
shining up to her †51.
sitting on her 320.
sparking her s¹2, 13, 16, †20, 47, †50, 54; 104-5, 115, †124, 133, 139, 142-43, †145, 147; †212, †214, †217; ¹†312, †325; 407, †418, 423.

squiring her †37. ~ ~ around 425.
stepping out with her 47; 208.
stuck on her 113.
sweet on her 12; 116; 307, †313.
pretty ~ ~ ~ 437.
taking her out 14, 26, 28.
thick with her 138. getting pretty ~
~ ~ 322.
waiting on her ¹*27; 144.
no response 114, 118, 151-52; 430.

Comment:

courting her: Usu.--7; 435. "I used
to hate that word"--11. dating her:
Supplied by daughter--4. "That's what
I hear most now"--55. going with her:
Inf. says this is most common locally--
433. setting out: Inf. says this would
be said of a widower--47. sparking her:
Used by inf.'s father (from Can.)--50.

61.6 She turned him down. NE 406,
407A-B.

Although the age-old tradition of the
male as the hunter and the female as the
hunted persists in the responses for
61.5 courting, it is also traditional
for the female to have the prerogative
of accepting or rejecting the male. As
the following replies show, the popular
terms for the rejection of a suitor--
usually with the implication of ending
an engagement or long courtship--range
from fairly neutral expressions to jocular expressions reflecting perhaps
even mildly sadistic pleasure, rather
than sympathy, over the male's unhappy
plight.

As in New England, many infs. freely
offer more than one term, a circumstance
suggesting the frequency of the situation and the variety of attitudes that
any one individual can hold toward the
persons affected. Although the frequency
figures below hint sometimes at a Midland or Northern orientation, they cannot be considered exhaustive; no clear
regional patterns emerge. A few terms,
however, are evidently experiencing
change in status, either becoming more
widely used or dying out.

Most common in the UM is turned him
down, the response of nearly one-half
of all the infs., with widespread jilted him next. But about one-fourth of
the infs. offer gave him the mitten,
which is the most frequently occurring
of a number of phrases with give, all
of them jocularly referring to something symbolically undesirable given by
the female to the male.

But gave him the mitten not only was
not carried solidly into the newest settlements but it seems to be less popu-

lar with younger speakers (I 34%, II 16%,
III 6%), whereas gave him the air and
gave him the gate are, if anything,
gaining in acceptance (respectively,
I 7%, II 21%, III 31%; and I 4%, II 24%,
III 31%).

The full list of responses appears
below.

	Mn.	Ia.	N.D.	S.D.	Nb.	Ave.
gave him						
the air	14%	6%	23%	18%	19%	15%
~ ~ ~ bounce	5%	6%	0	7%	6%	5%
~ ~ ~ cold						
shoulder	8%	4%	4%	0	0	5%
~ ~ ~ gate	9%	16%	12%	18%	22%	15%
~ ~ ~ mitten	21%	35%	20%	11%	25%	24%
jilted him	29%	43%	38%	54%	30%	37%
threw him						
over	6%	4%	19%	7%	14%	9%
turned him						
down	56%	33%	46%	43%	44%	45%

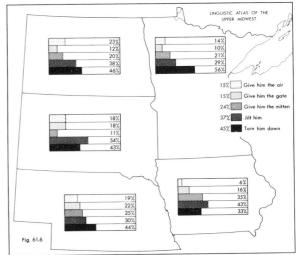

Fig. 61.6

CL 113: As with the preceding entry,
there is some discrepancy between the
field data and the information from
1,035 checklists. With both groups
turned him down is most common, and
jilted and gave him the mitten (or the
cold shoulder or the air) are next in
popularity. But the proportions in the
two groups differ.

In addition to one checking of kick
him (S.D. 61.1), scattered respondents
voluntarily wrote in the following
equivalents: call it quits (Mn. 4.3;
Nb. 12.1), ditched him (Mn. 65.1),
gave him his walking papers (S.D. 54.1),
gave him the brush-off (S.D. 35.3), gave
him the gate (N.D. 33.1), gave him the
go-by (S.D. 2.6; Nb. 37.1, 44.1, 53.1,
67.3), gave him the lemon (S.D. 10.2),
gave him the sack (Mn. 80.2; Ia. 37.1,
90.4; N.D. 9.3, 33.1), gave him up (Mn.
4.3; Nb. 12.2), put the skids under him

(S.D. 1.4), and quit him (Ia. 23.2, 49.2, 56.2; S.D. 14.2; Nb. 21.2). It would appear now that quit him is a Midland expression.

	Mn.	Ia.	N.D.	S.D.	Nb.	Ave.
gave him the air	13%	7%	15%	12%	14%	12%
~ ~ ~ bounce	3%	2%	4%	3%	2%	3%
~ ~ ~ cold shoulder	10%	9%	23%	16%	17%	14%
~ ~ ~ mitten	8%	23%	5%	8%	17%	13%
jilted him	14%	14%	14%	13%	14%	14%
threw him over	3%	2%	5%	1%	5%	3%
turned him down	67%	60%	71%	72%	69%	66%

bounced him *122.
broke their engagement 123. broke off 144. broke it off 131.
bumped him 42.
canned him !63; ¹†117; 220.
ditched him 30; :?130; 209, 224; !305, 307, 326.
dropped him 417, 426, 435. ~ ~ like a hot potato 43.
fired him 129, 135.
fooled him 56.
gave him the air 5, 8-9, 12, 28, sn33, 58, !60, 61; 102, 109, 150; !208, ¹211, 212-13, 221-22, 225; 302, 304, 309, 312, 320, :¹323; 405-6, 412, 419, 421, 425, ¹433, 437.
~ ~ the bounce !¹3, 10-11, 36; 137, 146, 148; 301; 405, ¹406, 418. ~ ~ ~ ~ stone 303.
~ ~ the brush 111; *203. ~ ~ the brush-off 37; 111; !201, 208; *328.
~ ~ the bum's rush 24.
~ ~ the butt 304.
~ ~ the cold shoulder 1, 3, 16, 22, 37; 105, 113, 138; !207; 425.
~ ~ the door 30; 320.
~ ~ the g.b. 61; 139.
~ ~ the gate !2, 9, :11, 21, 26, 38; 105, 108, 121, 125, 128, 137, *145, 149; !205, 210, 221; 301, 310, 325-26, *328; 406, 412, 416, 426, 428, 435-37.
~ ~ the go around 321. ~ ~ ~ go-by 6, 11, 44; 102, *122, 124; 214, 218; 312.
~ ~ the highball 204.
~ ~ the icy mitt 120.
~ ~ the mitten 21, 23, s29, !31, †33, !41, 42, !46, †47, !52, 54, !†55, !59-60, !62, 63-64, sn†65; 101, ¹103, 104, s106, 113, 115-16, *122, s¹†124, †125, s†126, 129, 132-33, 135, 137, 139-40, 142-43, 145-46, †147; 202, 204, sn215, 216-17, :220, 223; 317, 323, 325; ¹403, *405, s407, †409, ¹413, 417, sn418, 423-24, 427, 429, 431, ¹†433, 434.
~ ~ the run around 119. ~ ~ ~ runs 204.
~ ~ the sack 14, :24; 214; ¹314.
~ ~ the shovel !¹7.

~ ~ the slip !52; 322.
~ ~ up 4.
~ ~ his walking papers 2, 20, 36; 133; ¹211, 219, !224; !311, 315; 405.
handed him a lemon 212.
jilted him 3, 6, sn11, 16, 21, 28-29, 32, 34-35, 37, 39-40, 46, 53-54, *60, 61, 63; 101, 103, 105-9, 117, 119, ¹120, 121-22, 124-28, 130-31, 136, ¹144, 148-49; *203, 210, 213, 215-18, 223, 225-26; 302, 304, 310, 312-17, 319, 321, 323, !324, 326-27; 401-3, 408-9, 411-12, ¹413, 418, 422, 428, 431.
let him down 3, 42.
overthrew him 427.
passed him up 51.
quit him 65; 117, 143; 221, 223; 302, 307, 313, 325; 407, 432.
refused him 7, 38, 63; 112; 305-6, 316; 413-14, 422.
rejected him 12; 319.
sacked him 14.
said no 437.
side-tracked him 114.
stood him up 111, 119.
threw him 314. ~ ~ aside 209. ~ ~ over :1, 10, 12, ¹20, 53; 122, 149; 206, sn211, 217-18; 301; 404, 406, 409, 437.
~ ~ overboard 209.
turned a cold shoulder 203.
turned him down !2, 5, sn7, 8-10, 12-15, 17-20, 22, 24-25, !27, 29, 31, 37-39, 41, 43-44, !45, 47, 49-50, c51, 55-56, !60, 61; 102-4, 106, 109-12, 121, 126-27, 134, 140, 148, 150; 202-4, !205, 207-8, !210, 214-16, 219, 222, ¹226; 303, 305, 308-12, 314, 317-20, 322, 328; 402-4, 406-8, 410-11, 414-15, 419-21, 429, 431, 433. ~ ~ over 141.
went back on him 107, 128.
wouldn't have him 403.
no response 48, 57; 118, 151-52; 430.

Comment:

gave him the air: "That's slangy"--33. gave him the g.b.: Inf. says 'g.b.' stands for 'grand bounce'--61. Inf. does not know what 'g.b.' stands for, perhaps 'go-by'--139. gave him the mitten: Inf. says this is an old rural expression--103. "What was said when I was a kid"--147. jilted him: Inf. says that a girl is 'jilted' if she is left at the church--*43. Inf. says this is a lurid newspaper expression--120.

61.7 shivaree. NE 409.

As Alva Davis and Raven McDavid demonstrated ("Shivaree: An example of Cultural Diffusion," American Speech 24(1949).249-55.) the normal progression westward of terms for an informal noisy wedding celebration was effectively blocked by the appeal of Louisianan and Canadian French *charivari*, usually as shivaree with final stress. But a scattered one-fourth of the UM infs. have further Anglicized it by shifting the stress to the initial syllable. One inf., a Nebraska postal clerk, insists upon the full French form.

New England serenade is still favored by three Type I Minnesotans, each with New England or New York state ancestry. Midland belling, with the variant bell ringing, is retained by two Type I Iowans of Midland background, and jamboree, a rare New England term, is a oncer from a Duluth Type I speaker.

Although Davis and Mcdavid describe the custom in some detail, its rather rapid disappearance and the existence of some local variations make desirable a rather full use of inf. statements, either as summary descriptions of specific features or as individual comments.

belling †139.
bell ringing c132.
charivari 2, ¹28; 425.
jamboree 16.
serenade 11, 32, 65.
shivaree 1, ¹2, 3-10, 12-24, c25, 26-31, 33-34, !†35, 36-64, c65; 101-17, 119-21, 123-50; 201-6, !207, 208-13, c214, 216-18, !219, 220-26; 301-12, c313, 314-21, c322, 323-28; 401-2, c403, 404-15, cvr416, 417-29, 431-37.
no response 118, 122, 151-52; 430.

General description:

A shivaree is typically provided by friends of the couple, especially those of the same age group--1-5, 8-24, 26-30, 41, 50, 54, 57-58, 64-65; 149-50; 203, 205-10, 212, 214, 216-20, 222, 224-26; 304, 312, 314, 316, 322-23, 325, 327-28; 403, 406, 408, 410, 412-13, 416-17, 420-21, 429, 433-37.

Sometimes, however, a shivaree is unfriendly or may become so if the couple shows resentment or refuses to provide treats--22, 26-28, 58, 65; 216, 225; 409, 411, 412, 417, 437.

An essential feature is noise made in a number of ways, such as ringing bells; beating on pans or circular saws or anything else handy; blowing whistles and horns; firing shotguns; shooting off firecrackers; and just plain yelling--4, 7, 20, 25, 29; 101-50; 208, 211, 224, 226; 307, 310, 314, 316, 323, 326-28; 401-2, 405, 407, 409-11, 413-18, 420-35.

Treats sought by the shivaree crowd vary according to local customs and the age of the celebrants, ranging from candy for children to coffee and cake for women and cigars and liquor, usually

beer, for the men; sometimes provision for a treat comes in the form of money which then is to be used to buy, for example, a keg of beer elsewhere--1-3, 5, 8-10, 20-21, 23-24, 26-29, 35, 41, 50, 57-58; 101-17, 123-27, 131-35, 145, 148-50; 203-10, 212, 214, 217-19, 223-26; 304, 312, 314, 316, 321; 401-3, 405-7, 411, 416-18, 420-23, 426-27, 431, 433-35, 437.

Children sometimes participate--3, 5, 9, 12; 205, 217.

The occasion may be used for the giving of wedding presents to the couple--5; 203; 325-26.

In recent years the shivaree may be followed by a noisy automobile parade, often headed by the couple's car to which cans or other banging objects have been attached--26; 204, 211, 315-16, 323, 325, 328; 403-5, 419, 429.

The custom is largely rural--12, 33, 58; 218, 221; 326; 402.

The shivaree may be followed by a dance or, more commonly in some areas, is replaced by a dance in a rented hall--4, 7, 29; 215; 301-3, 316, 322, 324-36, 328; 407, 412, 418, 421, 437.

Although once popular in the community, the custom is now rarely observed or has quite disappeared--3, 7, 11, 20, 22-23, 30, 42, 55, 58; 123, 150; 201-2, 210-11, 213, 216-17, 219-20; 303, 309-12; 405, 408-10, 436.

Individual Comment:

"Usually friendly, especially when an old maid or an old bachelor gets married."--1.

"The local custom is to have a surprise party without the racket."--7.

"Sometimes the hat is passed for the dance. On one occasion $110 was raised."--8.

"I had that [a serenade] in 1897, but it's not much found any more."--11.

"Last week a couple had to ride in a wheelbarrow down the main street."--26.

"Mean ones sometimes threw stones at 'em."--27.

Inf. says a 'shivaree' is done by friends but may be a rough affair, while a 'serenade' is "high-toned."--65.

"It was a disgrace not to have a shivaree in an earlier day."--105.

"You rub resin on a barrel and pound saw blades."--109.

"They steal the bride."--112.

"They blow on wagon spindles."--113.

"They used to drag sticks of cordwood down the siding to make noise."--117.

"It's a disgrace not to have one."--119.

"You shakedown the groom and kidnap

him for a while, if·possible."--128.

A shivaree is not necessarily on the first night; it could be at any time during that week or the next.--131.

The crowd appointed a leader who kept the crowd from getting too destructive and dealt with the bridegroom.--142-43.

"We just had a little martial band came and played a few pieces."--146.

The crowd appointed a captain who had absolute control. Soon the bridegroom would call for the captain and ask what was wanted. If the bridegroom fired the first shot, the shivaree-ers would have to treat the newlyweds. But the captain appointed someone to slip ahead and shoot first.--147.

Often preceded by tricks, like putting a pig in the house or rice in the bed.--201.

Sometimes it became a housewarming.--204.

"It used to be unfriendly and cause trouble."--206.

"Friends paint up their car. A shivaree occurs on their return from a trip."--304.

Inf. hasn't heard of one for "Christ, how many years!"--311.

Serenade, with a guitar.--314.

A following dance is no longer observed.--321.

"I been to three shivarees in one night."--322.

"Used to be a noisy night celebration but now it's mostly in the day, with cans on cars and the like."--323.

"The couple provides a free wedding dance and the crowd throws money into a pot as a present."--328.

The dance no longer follows.--403.

"Now usually followed by speeding charges."--404 [local chief of police].

"Tipped over the Chic Sale."--409.

"The Russo-Germans have a three-day celebration, with a feast and a dance. A couple might spend as much as $2,000, but they expect to get it back when men pin bills on the dress of the bride or bridesmaid they're dancing with."--410-11.

"Crowd tries to get the couple out for embarrassment or they'll disable their car."--411.

"One man was thrown in the river and his bride kidnapped."--412.

"Embarrassing tricks."--423.

"Really a welcome from the townspeople."--426.

"A surprise visit on the return from the honeymoon."--433-35.

Friends persuade the groom to wheel the bride around the town square; then the groom treats the crowd at a local

show.--435.

"Might throw 'em in a water tank.... The Catholics have a dance."--437.

61.8 I'll _spank_ _you_. NE 397.

Since the LANE entry is for the noun _whipping_, a direct comparison with UM related verbal expressions is not possible, but it is clear that the rich and colorful variety of terms in New England for threatening a naughty child is not reflected in the meager use of what variety remains in the UM.

Spank is common in the UM, with the variants _give_ _you_ _a_ _spank_ _you_ and _give_ _you_ _a_ _spanking_. _Whip_, a poor second, with no occurrences at all in North Dakota, seems to have become old-fashioned by the time of final settlement in northern Minnesota and the western part of South Dakota and Nebraska.

Only two other expressions occur more than once: _lick_ _you_ (or _give_ _you_ _a_ _lick-_ _ing_) seems Northern with its sparse six examples in Minnesota and the Dakotas; _paddle_ _you_, also with six, likewise is not reported in Iowa.

Relics of earlier disciplinary behavior appear in the single occurrences of _blister_ _you_, _burn_ _you_ _with_ _a_ _board_, _give_ _you_ _what_ _for_, _give_ _you_ _what_ _Johnny_ _gave_ _the_ _drum_, _lather_ _you_, _shake_ _the_ _shoes_ _off_ _from_ _you_, _tan_ _your_ _jacket_, _thrash_ _you_, and _whale_ _the_ _daylights_ _out_ _of_ _you_. And a high school teacher offers academic _punish_ _you_.

blister you 417.
burn you with a board 101.
give you what for 33. ~ ~ what Johnny gave the drum 44.
lather you 29.
lick you †40, c51; 220; 316. give you a licking 4; 307.
paddle you 54; 218; 313, 325; 401, 404.
punish you 319.
shake the shoes off from you 402.
spank you 5-6, 8-9, 11-12, 15, 17-18, *19, 20-21, 23-29, 31-35, 37-44, !45, !46, 47-54, 56-64; 101-6, 109-17, 121, 123-24, 126-32, 133-37, 139-43, *145, 146-49, sn150; 201-11, 214-17, 219-22, 223, 225-26; 301, 303-5, 309-15, 318, 320-26, 328; 401, 403-5, :406, 407-13, 415-16, 418-19, 421-28, 431-37. give you a ~ ~ 2. give you a (good) spanking 36, 59; 107, 120, 138; 307; 420. take and spank you ¹21; s106, sn150; s¹222, 224.
tan your jacket 308.
thrash you 122.
whale the daylights out of you 37.
whip you 3, 19, 22, †35, 40, 65; 125,

143-45; 302, 306, 319; 407, 416. give
you a whipping 36.·

no response 1, 7, 10, 13-14, 16, 30,
55; 108, 118-19, 151-52; 212-13; 317,
327; 414, 429-30.

61.9 Attendants at a wedding.

a. best man.

For the male attendant upon the bridegroom the common term in the UM is best
man, for which more than two-thirds of
the UM infs. have stress on man, most
of the remainder on best, and six equally on the two words. Groomsman is rare--
twice each in Iowa and South Dakota. One
Iowan accepted the suggestion of archaic
waiter but normally uses best man.

A curious semantic shift occurs in
Iowa, where five infs. offer bridegroom
itself, apparently distinguishing between this and groom. Bride's groom,
once in North Dakota, is also curious;
it may be an error.

best man 29-31, 35-36, 38; 101-8, 110-
11, 113-17, 119-31, s132, 133-38, s139,
140-50; 201-11, 212-23, :224, 225-26;
301-16, s317, 318-21, s322, 323-24, 326-
28; 401-6, 408-29, 431-33, 435-37.
bridegroom 101, 109, 112, 139, 148.
bride's groom 212.
groomsman 106, 111; 317, 325.
waiter s135.
no response 1-28, 32, 37, 39-65; 118,
151-52; :?407, 430, 434.

Comment:

bridegroom: Inf. says 'bridegroom'
and 'best man' are synonymous; she always uses 'bridegroom' for the groom's
attendant and is hardly familiar with
'best man'--139.

b. bridesmaid.

For the female attendant upon the
bride the widespread designation is
bridesmaid. Maid of honor, without recognized difference of meaning, is found
within the same areas as a minor variant.

bridesmaid 29-31, 35-36, 38; 101-17,
119-49, s150; 201-15, 218-19, 221-26;
301-2, †304, 305-10, 312-28; 402-4,
406, 408-10, 412-29, 431-32, 434-37.
maid of honor 103, 106, 116; →215,
216-17; 305, 310-11, 326, 328; 401,
411, 425-26, 433, 435.
no response 1-28, 32, 37, 39-65; 118,
151-52; 220; 303; :?407, 430.

62.2 the whole crowd. (depreciative)
NE 415.

Most UM infs. apparently lack such
picturesque terms for depreciating a
group of people as were reported in NE.

Three-fourths of the Type II and Type
III infs. and more than one-half of
those in Type I simply use the common
gang; about one-half use crowd; and a-
bout one-fourth use bunch, not necessarily exclusively.

In the three western states shebang
and caboodle are much stronger than in
Minnesota and Iowa, although the full
expression kit and caboodle is strongest in Minnesota.

Offered as slightly pejorative, at
least in the sense of indiscriminate-
ness, are these sparsely occurring
terms: big and little business, community, country, countryside, creation,
outfit, kit and posse, mob, neighborhood, raft, shooting match, and works.
Perhaps neutral are clique, congregation, and town.

	Mn.	Ia.	N.D.	S.D.	Nb.	Ave.
bunch	24%	27%	40%	26%	23%	28%
caboodle	5%	9%	21%	17%	18%	16%
crowd	21%	32%	44%	43%	56%	48%
gang	62%	77%	60%	51%	70%	66%
shebang	13%	3%	40%	27%	27%	22%

bunch ¹2, 5, 7, 13, 22, 24-25, 38-41,
46, 49, 54, 63, 65; 101, c105, 106, 114,
117, 124, 132, 144, 148; 201, 203, 205,
209-10, 212-13, 217, 219, 222; 305, 307,
311, 315, c317, 320; 406-7, 409, 411,
417, 419, 424, 435.
business, big and little 59.
caboodle s†1, ¹2, ¹†5, s¹7, sn10, 11,
¹†12, c20, ¹21, sn22, s¹†25, 26, ¹*27,
¹†28, ¹41, !46, ¹48, s¹49, !¹56, 57;
104, s113, 119, ¹†120, 132, s133; sn204,
sn¹206, s†210, 212, 214-15, 221, sn†223;
s¹302, s304, !305, †309, †314, sn320,
¹322; ¹404, 407-9, 419, s420-21, s427,
429, 437.
clique 14; 328.
community 12; 216, 218; 303.
congregation 6.
country 221; 306; 429. ~side 8; 215.
creation 317.
crowd 2-3, 7, 10-11, 21, 27-28, 30,
32-34, 37-38, 42-48, 52-53, 55-56, s57,
59, 61-62, 64, s65; 103-5, 108, 110,
113, s114, 121, 141, 147-49; 202, 204,
210-11, 214, 217-18, 220, 222, 224-25;
307-9, 312, 314-15, 319-20, 326; 403,
405-6, 408-9, 411-13, s414, 418-19,
421, c422, 425-28, 432, 434, 436. damn
~ 316.
family 17.
gang 2-3, 5, s¹7, 8-10, ¹11, 12, c13,
21, 23-26, 28, 30, →¹33, c35, 36-38,
41, 43-46, 48-51, 54, s57, 58-64; 101-7,
109-12, 115-17, 119-21, 127, s133, 134,

136-39, 144, *145, 148, 150; 201-2, 205, 207, 209, 213-15, 219-20, sn221, 222, s223, 224-26; 301-4, 309-11, sn312, 320-21, 323, ?325, 326, 328; 401, 403-4, ¹405, 406, 408-9, 412, s413, 414, c416, 417, 419-26, s427, 428, 431, 433, 435-37.

group 17-18; 319.

kit and caboodle ¹2, †12, 14, sn†29, !32, 33, s37, s¹39, †40, sn!42, 47, 51, ¹53, †54, 55, ¹59, st60, s¹61, 62; 115, sn†124; sn208, ¹209, 215, 218; sn310, s311-12, †326; ¹*405, 406, s413, 428, s431.

kit and posse 214.

mob ¹57; 105, 108, 113, 119, 122-31, 134-36, 138, 140, 142-43, 146-47, 149; 404, 410, s431, s433.

neighborhood 1, 4, 6, 8, 19, 22, 29, 31, 34, 59; 204, 208, 212, 216, 221, 223-24, 226; c301, 302, 313-14, 322, 324-25; 402-3, 411, 417.

outfit 13, 15-18, 31, 40, 55; 222; 404, 409.

raft 409.

shebang ¹2, 4, ¹†5, sn22, 23, s24, ¹†28, s29, sn30-31; 102; 201, sn204, 205, 208, 210, s211, 212, ¹214, sn215-16, ¹217, 218, s223, 224; s¹302, s304, sn309-10, s312, ¹313, 314, 318, 320, 322, ¹324; sn401, s402, ¹404, ¹*405, 406-7, ¹408, 410, 412, s413, 419, 429, s433.

shooting match 14; s413, s420-21, s427.

town 6, 12; 211, 215; 310.

works 414, 429.

no response 118, 151-52; 327; 415, 430.

Comment:

caboodle: Inf. would use with reference to stock but not to people--206.
kit and caboodle: Used by inf.'s mother (from Mi.)--12. Used by inf.'s father (from Can.)--54. Formerly used by inf.--29. "Inanimate things"--312. shebang: An affair--2. Things, not people--29; 211; 312. An old house--36. Usu.--31.

62.3 a dance. NE 410.

The common UM name for an informal dance is simply dance, but several more descriptive minor equivalents brighten the lexical picture, though without significant regional patterning.

Shindig, along with the single nonce-variants shindik, shinadig, shinding, and the New England shindy, is a term used by four out of ten UM infs., especially in North Dakota and Nebraska. Hoedown, held to be old-fashioned and disused, survived longer in the newer settlements, as it is strongest in the

Dakotas and Nebraska. Although two infs. consider hop an innovation, others call it old-fashioned too. It likewise retains greater vitality in the western states.

Ball, offered by some infs., mostly in Minnesota, admittedly refers to a more pretentious affair than a kitchen or a country dance. Prom, a recent term for a school dance, appears twice. Barn dance, on the contrary, is an old term that survives to name the informal party in a barn, sometimes, though not necessarily, when a new barn is completed.

Square dance, actually common, is usually ignored by infs. because of the feeling that it denotes a kind of dancing rather than the social function. Old frolic is a oncer in Iowa.

Colorful kitchen sweat, twice in South Dakota and Nebraska, names specifically a progressive dance, one with a change in location from one house to another. Other lively colloquialisms, recorded once each, are hog wrestle, housewarming, jamboree (also in LANE), jig, jump, merry-go-round, rag, rat race, shakedown, snake wrestle, toe-crusher, and womb-shaking.

ball 12, 18, 20-21, 33-34, †35, 37, †39, 46, 61, 65; 126, s127, 141; 201, 215, 224; 309, 324.

dance 1-7, c8, 9-14, 16-21, c22, 24-26, 28-39, c40, 41-43, c44, 45, c46, 47-50, c51, 52-56, c57, 58, c59, c60, 61, 63-65; 101-13, 115, c116, 117, 119-27, 129-40, 142-50; 201-14, c215, 216, c217, 218-26; c301, 302, c303, 304, 306-18, 320, c321-22, 323-26, 328; c401, 402-6, c407, 408, c409, 410-12, 417-19, 422, 425-26, 429, 432-33, 436-37. barn ~ 10, 12, 29, 37, 55; 150; 201, 207, 213; c313; 416, †421. country ~ 17. square ~ 13-17; 424.

dancing party 62; 225; 305, 319.

frolic 132; ¹218.

hoedown 3, 6, *8, 22, st†42, 45, 50, !¹56; 104, 107, 114-15, 119, s132, 133, s¹139, 140, 149, ¹150; 204, sn†207, sn208, !210, ¹218, !†225; sn†312, ¹†325; ¹413, 416, 421-22, 427, †429.

hog wrestle 221.

hop 2, 18, 23, 26, 33, 41, †42; 108, 113; 203, 211, 216, 219; ¹301, 303-4, 310, †312, ¹313, 315, 320, 323, †324, →325; 402, 404, 406, sn407, →410, ¹411, 412, †417, ¹419, 425, †429, †433, 436-37.

housewarming 7.

jamboree *64.

jig †42.

jump →35.

kitchen sweat †301; 422.

merry-go-round †41.
prom 18; 203.
rag 418.
rat race ¹406.
shakedown 202.
shindig ¹1, 2, ¹3, →*4, 5-6, ¹8, 10, ¹11, †12, 17-18, s¹20, !21, 23-24, :25, sn26, 27, ¹29, †31, 34, sn†35, 37-38, s†42, †43, 45, s†48, 49, 51, 54-55, 57, c58, 65; 101-4, 108, 114, 116, 119, 121, 132-33, ¹137, 138, s140, 141, †145, 149; 201, ¹202, 203-5, sn†207, 208, 213-15, sn!216, 217-18, !219, 221, :222; 309-10, !311, †312, ¹313, 320-21, 323, †324, ¹325; !401, 403-8, ¹411, 412-13, ¹†414, 418, ¹419, 420, †421, 423, 427-28, †429, sn431, 435-36. shinadig 219. shindik 209. shinding 211. shindy c58.
snake wrestle 404.
toe-crusher 221.
womb-shaking 409.
no response 118, 128, 151-52; 327; 415, 430, 434.

Comment:

ball: Formal--12, 20-21, 33-34, 37; 126; 201; 324. "More of an affair"--46. "A thing of state"--61. "If you wanted to be fancy"--127. "A little better class dance, and private"--309. hoedown: Informal--225. Informal country dance--3. A square dance--6, 42; 204, 208; 312. "Where a bunch of people make fools of themselves with old-fashioned dances"--22. A Bohemian dance; "They have them right around here. That's where they really roll them on the floor"--50. hop: Informal--33; 211; 402. Old-time dance--26. Usu.--315. housewarming: Usually a dance--7. kitchen sweat: A progressive house-to-house dance--422. merry-go-round: A country dance--41. prom: A high school senior dance--203. shindig: Informal--2, 45; 202, 204-5, 210, 213, 219; 309, 324; 431. Informal country dance--3, 5. A rural term--21; 150. = barn dance--6; 215. A rowdy barn dance--12. "That's a rough-house affair"--1. Inf. says this is an Irish expression for a drunken brawl, like a barn dance--34. "A kind of rough dance"--65. = dance--6; 215. "Peppier than a dance"--65. Not necessarily a dance; any party--42, 57; 211. = dance; humorous--38; 401. A man's term--201. Slang--222. Used to dance in moccasins in the bush--202. Might include card-playing, too--212.

62.4 He played hooky. WG 23, 35, 44, 79; F157-58.

Although not sought in northern New England, this item appeared in the southern New England and Atlantic coast surveys and hence provides some background for the UM situation.

For a student's willful absence from school none of the expressions Kurath considers regional or local has been reported in the UM. But the three dominant terms occurring with varying frequency along the east coast do persist in the westward expansion.

Played hooky, common from western New England to North Carolina, is the majority form in the UM, with a Midland weighting revealed in the much higher frequency in Iowa and Nebraska. Skipped school, common in New York state and northern Pennsylvania but less so in West Virginia and Virginia, reflects that distribution in its Northern bias in the UM, where it is strong in Minnesota and the Dakotas but occurs only weakly in Iowa and Nebraska. One instance of a variant with class appears in eastern Nebraska, and plain skipped is the expression of an auxiliary inf. in Minnesota. No evidence suggests a trend toward or away from either played hooky or skipped school.

The third expression, played truant, seems to be declining. Not only is it less frequent in the three western states but it is also less frequent among Type II speakers than among Type I (7% to 13%), despite the feeling of a North Dakota Type I housewife that it is an innovation. Three Minnesotans offer the variant was truant and one Iowan has was a truant.

Several singletons appear in the UM: sneaked, shirked, was a-piking, was a-shirking out, was bumming from school, and was on the lam. Ratting, known from other sources to have been used in St. Paul schools more than a generation ago, did not turn up during the fieldwork.

	Mn.	Ia.	N.D.	S.D.	Nb.	Ave.
played hooky	54%	92%	69%	64%	97%	74%
~ truant	17%	10%	8%	4%	6%	10%
skipped sch.	51%	14%	46%	43%	3%	30%

CL 114: Played hooky likewise is dominant among 1,040 respondents, and likewise has Midland orientation. Checks of skipped school also confirm the field data with evidence of Northern orientation, especially when it is combined with the evidence for the variant skipped class, which the mail replies show in surprising strength. In addition, three Minnesotans (43.1, 49.1, 60.3) and one South Dakotan (23.1) have ran out of school, one Iowan (6.5) has skipped off from school, and three Iowans (62.1, 78.1, and 96.2) and one Nebraskan (33.1) have slipped off from school.

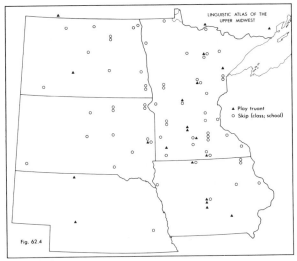

Fig. 62.4

LINGUISTIC ATLAS OF THE UPPER MIDWEST

▲ Play truant
○ Skip (class; school)

played hooky 1-3, 6, 8-10, 12, 14, 16, 23, 26, 29, !30, 31-35, ¹36, 37-40, 43, 46-47, s48, 52-55, 57-58, ¹59, 60, 64-65; 101-6, 108-17, 119, 121-28, 130-35, 137-50; 202-5, 207-10, sn212, 213-14, 216, †217, 218, 220-21, 223, 225-26; 301-4, 309-14, 317, 320-21, 323-26, 328; 401-6, :407, 408-14, 416, :417, 418-25, 427-28, 431-37.

played truant 2-3, 11, 15, 22, 27, 44-45, 51, 59, 63; 103, 128-29, 131, 136; 201, →217; 319; 403, 418.

skipped *48. ~ class 426. ~ school 4, :5, 7, 10-12, →13, 17-22, 24-25, 28, 32, 34, 40-42, 46, 49-50, c51, 53, 55, s56, 57, 61-63; 103, 107-8, 111, 117, 120, 128; 203, 205-6, 208, 211-13, 215, 219, 222, 224-25; 304-8, 315-16, 318-19, →320, 322, 327.

sneaked 428.
shirked 139.
was a-piking 132.
was a-shirking out 132.
was bumming from school 13.
was on the lam 34.
was truant 18, 36, 39. was a truant 122.
no response 118, 151-52; 415, 429-30.

62.8 kaffeeklatch.

This item calls for the designation of an informal daytime party, usually for women and usually with coffee. It was not present in the eastern dialect surveys. In the UM the replies disclose the fairly widespread occurrence of three separate groups of expressions, one with coffee, one composed of recent loanwords including kaffee-, and one with tea.

With coffee the customary word is party for infs. in all five states, al-

though coffee chat, ~ club, ~ fest, and ~ hour turn up, and, as a recent development on the analogy of tea, coffee has come to signify for some infs. the party itself, especially in Nebraska. A few infs., professing no term for the function, report simply saying such things as "Come over for coffee" (211, 213), "Come over for a cup of coffee" (424), or "Let's have coffee" (401).

The kaffee- (sometimes coffee) forms are all immediately derived from the first language of UM immigrants, particularly from Germany but also from The Netherlands, Norway, and Sweden. They are used in an English language context and often have been adopted by others in the community. They characterize especially the most recent German settlement areas of Nebraska and Minnesota. The forms with klatch /a/ and those with klutch /ʌ/ are phonetic variants but are treated separately here because several infs. insist upon their distinctiveness. Kaffe(e)-kalas is from colloquial Swedish, kaffe(e)-klat and kaffe(e)-lag are from Norwegian, and kaffee-klets is from Dutch.

Tea or, less often, tea party not only denotes the use of a different beverage but also connotes a somewhat more formal and, as one inf. puts it, "more genteel" affair. The term, and perhaps the function it names, is expectedly Canadian but it occurs elsewhere and with presumably a Midland orientation.

Occasionally the coffee or kaffee terms refer to a men's gathering, but the typical reference is to women, a fact supported by such male-oriented disparaging equivalents as gab fest or gab party, old ladies' gathering, old bag get-together, gossip party, and hen party. Additional expressions are listed below.

Two male infs. volunteer names for a woman who regularly goes to coffee parties. "She's a gadder," reports one Minnesotan (51); she's an "old klutcher," reports another (57).

Notable is the fact that although the social custom of informal coffee parties is observed throughout the UM, in residential areas of urban centers as well as in smaller communities, many infs. say that they have never heard any name for such a party; and in communities where the kaffee- forms are found some infs. insist that they have never heard them.

	Mn.	Ia.	N.D.	S.D.	Nb.	Ave.
coffee etc.	34%	15%	57%	43%	48%	37%
kaffee etc.	40%	21%	0	10%	30%	24%
tea etc.	18%	33%	17%	10%	17%	20%

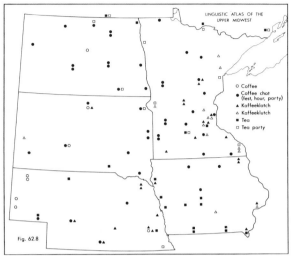

Fig. 62.8

breakfast 426.
brunch 414, 426.
club 125, 136, 142-43. ~ meeting 306.
coffee c304; 402, ¹410, 411, 414, 426.
afternoon ~ 409. ~ chat 21. ~ club c102,
120. ~ fest 20. ~ hour 416. ~ party 4,
c10, 12, 19-20, 24, c30, 39, *41, 42-43,
!46, 47-48, 63, 65; 104, c106; 203, 205,
210, 212, c213, 216, c217, 218, !219,
221, *224, 226; 303, 308, 313, 317, 319,
¹324, c325, :326, →328; 418, 431, 436.
gab fest 17; 411, 428. ~ party 320.
gathering 307. old ladies' ~ 15. social ~ 305.
get-together 214; 414. informal ~ 14.
old bag ~ 38.
hen party 5, 33, 54, !63; 125, 131,
146; c216, !218; 302, !308, 323; 404,
409, 437. hen's party 117.
kaffeeklatch ¹11, *21, 22, *27, 28,
s¹33, 34, 38-39, c51, s¹53, 55, s!¹56,
¹59, 60; 107-8, 111, †129, 140, *148;
¹*207, ¹223, 304; 407-8, †415, 418, 422,
425-26, 428, s¹431, 433. kaffeeklets
¹223. kaffeeklutch 14, sn15, ¹16, 26,
→31, sn35, 37, 40, !48, 57-58; s103,
134, 141; †209; c310. kaffe(e)-kalas 39.
kaffe(e)-klat 407. kaffe(e)-lag ¹19.
klutch party !48.
party 29; 206; 305-6, 308, 316.
tea 35, 45; 110, 123-24, 127-28, 130,
144-47, 150; 202, †215; ?309, 323; 404,
c417, 426. ~ party 3, 5, 7, 18, :25, 45,
!56; 202, 204, 224; 308, †328; 435. afternoon ~ 2, c3, †31; 208.
no response 1, 6, 8-9, 13, 32, 36, 44,
49-50, 52, 61-62, 64; 101, 105, 109,
112-14, 116, 118-19, 121, 126, 132-33,
137-39, 149, 151-52; 201, ?222, ?225;
301, 312, 314-15, 321-22, 327; 403,
?405, 406, 412-13, 419-21, 423, 429-30,
432, 434.

Comment:
   club: Organized--142. coffee: Informal but planned--411. Inf. says this is
common here--410. coffee party: Heard
in town, not in the country--324. An
invitation affair; same as 'afternoon
tea'--213. hen party: Men's term--302.
kaffeeklatch: Heard in Pembina, N.D.--
207. Heard in Dutch communities nearby--
223. Used in English if talking to Swedish women--418. Used by older people and
Swedes--431. "Middle-aged ladies gossip-
ing over coffee in a living room"--433.
kaffeeklutch: Used by inf.'s aunt--16.
"Commonly here means men out for coffee
in the morning"--37. kaffe(e)-lag: Wife
says this Norwegian term is occasionally used here--19. tea: Inf. says it is
called a 'coffee' in the morning and a
'tea' in the afternoon; 'kaffeeklatch'
and 'brunch' are going out of style and
are being replaced by 'breakfast' and
'coffee'--426. tea party: Used even
though coffee is served instead of tea--
204; 308, 328, 435.

63.3 railroad station. NE 544.

   The query, "Where do you go to take
a train?" elicited from nearly all UM
infs. the simple depot. The equivalent
railroad station and railway station
are used by about one-sixth of the infs.,
but since there is considerable overlap
and since a person using both terms usually favors depot in unguarded conversation, only 6.3% actually use the station forms exclusively.
   No significant regional patterns appear except that the station terms are
less frequent in Nebraska and South Dakota. Socially, however, a number of
infs. manifest an attitude that correlates with the fact that only 4% of the
Type I speakers use station exclusively, 7% of Type II, and 25% of the college graduates. The corresponding combined frequencies for those who use
station exclusively and for those who
use it only occasionally are Type I,
13%, Type II, 18%, and Type III, 31%.
   This prestigiousness is supported by
the inf. (119) who admits to depot and
yet calls it "improper" and by the inf.
(42) who, after offering depot, quickly adds station with the comment,
"That's the right word."
   Of the two station compounds that
with railroad occurs twice in Minnesota
and once each in Nebraska and Saskatchewan; that with railway occurs once
each in Minnesota and Iowa.
   For a more detailed UM study see
Harold B. Allen, "No epitaphs for Depot," American Speech 34(1959).233-34.

	Mn.	Ia.	N.D.	S.D.	Nb.	Ave.
depot	94%	92%	85%	97%	95%	93%
station	15%	22%	23%	14%	8%	17%

depot ¹1, 2-20, ¹21, 22-27, cr28, 29-34, c35, 36, c37, 38-41, ?42, 43-56, 58-65; 101-6, c107, 108-17, 119, 121-27, 129-30, 132, 134-50; 201, 203-6, 209-13, 215-16, c217, 218-26; 301-3, c304, 305-7, c308, 309-13, c314, 315-17, c318, 319-25, 327-28; 401-9, †410, 411-16, c417, 418, c419, 420-25, 427-29, 431-37.

station 1, ¹3, ¹11, 14, ?28, 33, crc42, 47, 53, 57, ¹61; 104, 110, 119-20, 123, 125-26, 128, 130-31; 207-8, 214, 217, ¹218, 224; 308-9, 319, 326; 403, 426. railroad ~ 44, 46; 202; →410. railway ~ 21; 133.

no response 118, 151-52; 430.

Comment:

depot: The most common term locally--1, 3, 44, 46-47. Usu.--33; 224. Inf. uses this but considers it improper--119. Inf. says 'Northwestern depot,' but 'Milwaukee station'--110.

63.8a boulevard.

No national or standard term exists in the United States for the strip of grass between a sidewalk and the street. The several names elicited by this item, original with the UM Atlas, reveal clear distribution patterns, but no information is available for correlating them with distribution in the eastern part of the nation.

Boulevard, the most frequent term, conspicuously characterizes the Northern speech area of the UM, including the Canadian strip along the border. Indeed, except for single instances of curb and terrace in Minnesota, the only deviation from the solid monopoly of boulevard is the subarea characterized by berm.

Unique here in this sense, berm is concentrated in Grand Forks, N.D., with decreasing frequency eastward toward Crookston, Mn., and northwestward to Devils Lake and Rolla, N.D. It appeared in a Grand Forks city ordinance as early as 1910. Supplementary verification that the trading zone of Grand Forks is the focal area for berm, with a suggestion that even here boulevard may be replacing it, appears in a survey made in 1955 of students at Mayville State College, N.D. In a group with homes in northwestern Minnesota and northeastern North Dakota the only students using berm outside Grand Forks county were from Traill county, immediately south of Grand Forks, and from Walsh and Pem-

bina counties, immediately north of Grand Forks. But in each of these counties students also use boulevard.

The Midland speech territory of the UM is unusually divided into rather clearly defined subareas by the distribution of three principal equivalents of boulevard. Parking, the most common, dominates with its use in the Midland area of Iowa and South Dakota and in extreme eastern and extreme western Nebraska. Central and west central Nebraska, however, is marked by the use of curb, which appears also in northern Iowa. A third term, terrace, has scattered instances in northern Iowa and in the southern tier of counties in Nebraska.

Minor variants, all but one of which are in Midland speech territory, are: grass strip, lawn, tree lawn, park, parking space, parking strip, and parkway.

	Mn.	Ia.	N.D.	S.D.	Nb.	Ave.
berm	2%	0	14%	0	0	---
boulevard	92%	10%	86%	33%	0	50%
curb	2%	5%	0	0	29%	6%
(tree) lawn	2%	8%	0	0	4%	3%
parking	0	60%	5%	48%	46%	28%
terrace	2%	13%	0	0	21%	7%

CL 119: Nine hundred sixty-six respondents provide secondary data that somewhat expand the areas of occurrence of the various forms and hence make difficult the drawing of isoglosses but nevertheless generally confirm the broad patterns established by the field records. Boulevard again is dominant in Minnesota and the Dakotas but it turns up also in Iowa and Nebraska. Berm again is primarily in northwestern Minnesota and northeastern North Dakota but it turns up also in the checklists of three respondents in northern Iowa and of one in South Dakota. The table below reveals the distribution of the main variants. In addition the checklists report sparse appearance of the following terms volunteered as write-ins: buffer strip (N.D. 40.2), curb lawn (S.D. 22.1), curbing (Ia. 12.1, 36.1), lawn (S.D. 2.3), park line (S.D. 60.1), parking place (Nb. 39.3), strip (Ia. 57.3; N.D. 10.1), and terrace (Mn. 12.2). A correspondent in Eagle Grove, in north central Iowa, reports the local use of tree bourn.

	Mn.	Ia.	N.D.	S.D.	Nb.	Ave.
berm	2%	1%	8%	1%	0	2%
boulevard	81%	13%	66%	31%	15%	41%
~ strip	2%	2%	3%	2%	2%	2%
parking	2%	56%	5%	28%	36%	27%
~ strip	3%	7%	2%	10%	11%	7%

	Mn.	Ia.	N.D.	S.D.	Nb.	Ave.
parkway	2%	10%	6%	15%	12%	9%
curb	0	2%	1%	1%	2%	1%
~ strip	3%	5%	8%	15%	25%	10%
sidewalk plot	4%	3%	6%	4%	6%	5%

berm 8; :204, 205, 212, ¹*221.
boulevard 1-5, 7, 9-11, 13-14, c→16, 17-21, 23-24, :¹25, 26-28, 30-39, c40, 42, *43, 44-50, c51, 52-54, c55, s¹56, 57-63, 65; 107-8, 140-41; 201-3, 206-7, 209-11, ¹212, 213, 216-22, 224, :225, 226; 303, c304, ?305, 307-8, 317-19.
curb 12; 105-6; 403-4, ¹405, 406, 412, 414, 417, c419, 436.
grass strip 117.
lawn 135, 143, 145; 415. tree ~ c40.
park ?147; ?311, 314. ~way 116, 120; 309; 419, 437.
parking 103, 109-11, 113-14, 122-31, 134, 136-37, 142, 144, *145, 146, ?147, 148; ¹210, 221; *301, 311-13, c314, 315, 320, s323-24, 325-26, 328; c401, 402, 408-11, 422, 424-28, 434. ~ space 426.
~ strip 311.
terrace 29; 101-2, 117, *132, 133; 405, †410, 416, :429, 431, 433-34.
no response 6, 15, 22, ?41, 64; 104, 112, 115, 118-19, 121, 138-39, 149-52; ?208, ?214-15, :?223; 302, 306, 310, 316, 321, ?322, ?327, ?407, 413, ?418, 420-21, 423, 430, 432, 435.

Comment:

berm: Inf.'s wife heard this in northern Ia.--221. boulevard: Inf.'s term for a grass strip in the middle of the street but not one between the sidewalk and street--22, c43; 416, 420. Inf. says this is also used in Winnipeg--1. Also a much-traveled street, probably quite wide--108. curb: Inf. would say, "He planted a tree in the 'curb'"--12; 403-4, 417. Inf.'s term for both the grass and the cement--406. Inf. calls the cement the 'curbing'--12. park: Inf. insists upon this--314. terrace: Fw. asked five residents other than infs. in Rock Rapids; all replied with terrace--102. If there is a high curbing, the grass strip would be a 'terrace'--117. tree lawn: Inf. says this is used in Benton Harbor, Mi.--40.

63.8b sidewalk.

Added to the worksheets after the Minnesota fieldwork was complete, this item was intended to ascertain the possible spread of the eastern Pennsylvania pavement. All UM responses, however, offered only sidewalk for the paved footway beside a street.

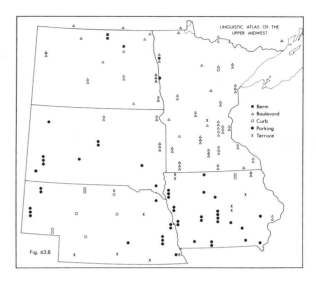

Fig. 63.8

LINGUISTIC ATLAS OF THE UPPER MIDWEST

■ Berm
□ Boulevard
△ Curb
● Parking
x Terrace

63.9 county seat. NE 348.

In the UM the administrative unit between the local community and the state is uniformly the county, and the community in which the county offices are located is without exception known as the county seat. One inf. in western Nebraska (435) redundantly identified it as county seat town.

64.1 streetcar. NE 184.

For a public conveyance running on rails in a city street the well-nigh universal UM term is streetcar. Fewer than one in ten infs. offer any other expression, usually trolley or trolley car, and only five scattered infs. have only such a variant. Two Duluth infs. recall mule car.

motor car 139.
mule car 15-16.
streetcar 1-2, c3, 4-21, c22, 23-26, 28-50, c51-53, 54-61, c62, 63-65; 101-17, 119-38, sn139, 140-50; 201-5, 207-14, 216, 218-26; 301-8, cr309, 311-13, c314, 316-26, 328; 401-18, 421-29, 431-37.
tramway ?309.
trolley ¹34, 58; 101, 127, →145, 148, †150; *230, 217, ¹221, c225; 310; ¹404, c419, 437. ~ car 14, †19, 37, s¹48, 53; 117, †124; 206, 215; 308; 420.
no response 27; 118, 151-52; 315, 327; 430.

Comment:

motor car: Larger than a streetcar; in Dubuque--1; 139. trolley: "Out East they say 'trolley'"--34.

Fig. 64.3

64.3 Civil War. NE 351.

Between the fieldwork for LANE and that for the LAUM the Second World War and the Korean War intervened. This, and the fact that another generation had been added to those that followed the war of 1861-65, contributed heavily to the decline of such partisan designations of that war as were known to the New England infs.

In the UM nearly all speakers use simply Civil War. A few, largely in Type I and in Iowa and Nebraska, offer The Rebellion, War of the Rebellion, War of '61, War Between the States, and War of the States, but only four of these do not also use Civil War.

Civil War 1-26, 28-30, c31, :32, 33-37, 39-45, c46-47, 48-53, c54, 55-65; 101-2, 104-6, 108-17, 119-44, 146-50; 203-5, 207-13, c214-15, 216-24, c225, 226; 301-6, 308-13, c314, 316-26, 328; s401, 402-6, 408-12, cvr413, 414, c416, 417, 419-21, c422, 423-29, 431, s432, 433-35, 437.
s401, 402-6, 408-12, cvr413, 414, c416, 417, 419-21, c422, 423-29, 431, s432, 433-35, 437.
The Rebellion *122; 418, *432. War of the Rebellion 18, †23, 37; 101, 103, 107, 119.
War between the States 103, ¹125, 130. War of the States 122-23.
War of '61 401.
no response 27, 38; 118, 151-52; 201-2, 206; 307, 315, 327; :407, 415, 430, 436.

Comment:

War of the Rebellion: "When I was a boy, it was always 'the War of the Rebellion'"--23.

64.7a New York State. NE 11.

This item is primarily phonological, but it has variants that are regionally patterned.

Although about three-fifths of the UM infs. do not distinguish by name the city and the state, nearly all the remainder do. More than one-third, most of them in Northern speech territory, say New York State. Some in southern Minnesota and a few scattered elsewhere retain York State, but acknowledge it as old-fashioned if not obsolete. State of New York also occurs but not in the older portions of the UM.

	Mn.	Ia.	N.D.	S.D.	Nb.	Ave.
New York	57%	85%	15%	44%	62%	58%
~ ~ State	41%	13%	73%	44%	29%	37%
State of N.Y.	2%	0	15%	4%	6%	4%
York State	5%	2%	0	7%	3%	4%

New York 3, 6, 11-19, 21-23, 29-30, 32, 35, 39-40, c42, 43, 45-46, c47, 51-53, 56-58, 60, c62, 63-64, c65; 101-7, 109, 111, 113, c115, 116-17, c119, 121-22, 124-28, 130-43, 145-50; 207, 209, 212, 226; 305-6, 308-10, c312, 316-19, 321, 324; 403-4, c405, 409-11, 413-16, 418, c419, 422-24, 427, 431-35.
New York State 1-2, 4-5, 7-9, 20, 24, 26, c27, 28, :29, 31, c33, 34, c37, 38, †40, *41, 42, 48-49, c50, 54-55, 61; 108, 110, 112, 120, 123, 144; 201-5, 210-11, 213, c214, 215, 217-24, c225, ¹226; 301-4, 314-15, 320, 322-23, 325, c326, 328; 401-2, 406, 408, †410, ¹412, c420, 421, 425-26, 428, s431, 437.
State of New York 10; 206-8, 216; 313; 417, 429.
York State c15, †40, 44, †45-46, ¹†54, c59, †62; c114, s¹139; †*218; c311, c327; ¹403, †409, ¹†411, c420, †426.
no response 25, 36; 118, 129, 151-52; 307; 407, 430, 436.

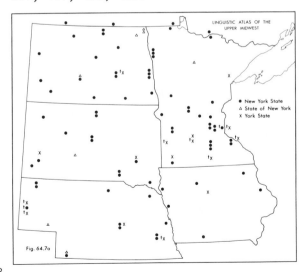

Fig. 64.7a

Comment:

New York State: Used by inf.'s mother
(from Mn.)--40. Used by inf.'s mother
(from Wi.)--410. York State: Used by
inf.'s parents (from N.Y.)--62; 409.
Used by inf.'s mother (from Mn.)--40.
Used by inf.'s mother (from N.Y.)--426.
Used by inf. in youth--46. Usu.--420.

66.7 devil. NE 532-33.

As a serious term devil is the nearly
universal UM designation for the supreme
evil spirit, with Satan as an alternate
fairly frequent among Midland speakers,
esp. in Iowa and Nebraska.

Both terms may also be used jocularly
or in such a context as "You be good or
the ----- will get you," said to a
child. But generally UM infs. use any
or several of a great variety of other
terms in such situations. These terms
are of two kinds, those referring to the
devil and those clearly referring to
some other imagined being. Some infs.,
however, use expressions in the first
group unaware of any reference to the
devil.

Besides devil and Satan, the first
group includes as its popular equivalent the old Nick, recorded frequently
in the three western states, and other
well-known if not widely used euphemisms:
the bad man (perhaps favored in Midland),
the old Harry (perhaps with Northern
orientation), and the old Scratch (almost surely Midland). Minor equivalents,
some found only once, are: Beelzebub,
the black man, the cuss, the demon himself, the deuce, the dickens, the evil
one, the guy with the pitchfork, his
nibs, the hook and driver, Lucifer, the
old boy himself, the old fellow himself,
the old man, the old man below, the old
mischief, the old rip, the old saint,
the red man, and the spirit.

[Dictionaries vary with respect to
capitalizing old, as in old Scratch.
Consistently, all old forms here are
lower case o.]

A number of infs. volunteered idiomatic uses of some of these, esp. "full
of the dickens" (30, 41), "full of the
old Harry" (30; 211, 225; 325), and
"full of the old Nick" (11, 30, 33; 150;
211, 214, 217-18, 225; 325; 403, 409-12,
418, 429).

The second group of expressions is almost exclusively restricted to speech
with a child. Most are etymologically
related. Commonest is boogieman (two-
thirds of the instances with /u/ and
one-third with /ʊ/, unsystematically
distributed). One variant, bogyman, oc-

curs only three times, all in Minnesota.
Another booger man (also with both /u/
and /ʊ/) is a minor form clearly with
Midland distribution. One inf. has heard
bugaboo in this connection; another offers goblin.

CL 115: From 959 respondents the checks
are not in close conformity with the
field data. The bad man is commonest.
Boogie man is used by one-third of the
respondents, with an apparent Northern
orientation. (Northern Iowa has 25% and
southern Iowa only 14%.) Booger man
(spelled bugger on the checklist) is
again clearly Midland. The old Nick,
the old Harry, and the old Scratch also
occur.

	Mn.	Ia.	N.D.	S.D.	Nb.	Ave.
bad man	43%	43%	39%	43%	38%	42%
boogie man	37%	20%	52%	37%	30%	33%
bugger man	10%	17%	9%	15%	25%	15%
old Harry	5%	8%	7%	4%	8%	6%
old Nick	11%	16%	10%	15%	15%	14%
old Scratch	4%	6%	2%	2%	3%	4%

All the following terms are normally
preceded by the, except his nibs and
the proper names Beelzebub, Lucifer,
and Satan.

bad man 8, [1]10, †22, 23, [1]31, [1]42,
64, [1]65; 109, 113, 133, 136-39; [1]211,
223-24; s[1]320; [1]403, 407, [1]410, s412,
417, sn419, 423, 429.
  Beelzebub 314; †428.
  black man ![1]3; 139; s[1]320.
  bogy man [1]†33, 41, 45.
  boody man †25.
  booger man 50, 60; sn103, 133, [1]150;
[1]213, 215, [1]225; 301, [1]302, [1]314, 315,
321, [1]†324, [1]325; [1]403, 408, *412,
sn414, 416, 422, sn431, 437. boogers
139. boogie man [1]1, [1]*4, [1]9, [1]11, 12,
14, 17-18, [1]21, 23-24, 26, :28, [1]29-31,
32, 34, c37, 38-39, 43, !44, 46-49, 51-
53, 57-58, 61-62, !63; 102, 104-5,
sn108, 111-12, 116, 119, 132; ![1]201,
203-4, ![1]205, [1]206, †209, 211-12, [1]214,
216, *218, 219, !†221, 222; 303, [1]304,
309-10, [1]312, 313, s[1]320, 323, 326;
[1]403, 404, 406, [1]410, 411, 413, 418,
sn419, sn421, sn425, 427, sn428. boogies
!†202.
  bugaboo [1]210.
  cuss 421.
  demon himself 319.
  deuce 420.
  devil 1-5, c6, 7-10, c11, 12-14, 16-
18, !19, 20-24, c25, 26, c27, 28-31,
:s32, 33-34, c35, 36, c37, 38-42, !43-
44, 45, !46, *48, 49-50, !51, 52-53,
!54, 55-56, 58-65; 101-17, 119-22, 124-
33, 135-38, s139, 140-50; 202-3, c204,
205, !306, 207-13, c214, 215-19, c220,

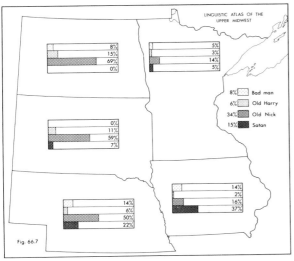

Fig. 66.7

LINGUISTIC ATLAS OF THE
UPPER MIDWEST

8% Bad man
6% Old Harry
34% Old Nick
15% Satan

221-26; 301-10, c311, 312-19, c320,
321-26, 328; 401-2, !403, c404, 405-7,
409-11, c412, 413-35, 437. old ~ 15;
201.

dickens ¹30; 208; 411, 414.
evil one 55; 106; 317, 319.
goblin 17; 119-20.
guy with the pitchfork 318.
hook and driver 57.
Lucifer 7, 58.
(his) nibs 62.
old boy himself 431.
old fellow himself 215.
old Harry ¹30, !31, !44; ¹126, 131,
s137, s147; 211-12, 215, 225; 320, :324,
325; 407, 419.
old man !54; 306. ~ ~ below 418.
old mischief 204.
old Nick 2-3, 10-12, 21-22, ¹30, 33,
47, s55; 101, 106, 123, 125, 127, 131,
135, 146, s147, ¹148, s149, ¹150; 201-
3, ¹205, 207, 210-12, ¹213, 214-19,
221-23, 225-26; 301-2, 304, 308, !309,
310-15, 320-21, 325-26, 328; 402-3,
406, 408-12, ¹416, 418-19, s422, 423,
427-30, sn431, 433, 437.
old Rip 115.
old saint 308.
old Scratch 46; 125-26, 132; 322;
†423, 431.
red man 8.
Satan 18, 48, 56; 101, 106, 117, 122-
24, 126-27, 129-31, 134-35, 142-43,
145, 147-48; *306, 319; 413-14, 423,
425, 427-28, 430, 432.
spirit c15.
spook 60; 208.
no response 118, 151-52; 327; 436.

Comment:

bad man: Formerly used by inf.--22.
Said to children--23, 64; 417. Inf.
disapproves of this--31, 65. Beelzebub:

Used by inf. as a child--428. boody
man: Used by inf.'s mother (from Ire.)--
25. booger man: Said to children--225;
414. Someone who isn't nice--431. Inf.
disapproves of this--324; 403. boogey
man: Said to children--1, 23-24, 38, 50;
309; 413, 425. More freq. than 'bad
man'--23. Inf. never associates this
with 'devil'--26. Not 'devil'--18; 103,
105, 108; 219. = devil--427. "We thought
that was some guy that come out of the
sewer"--34. devil: "That word a person
don't like to use"--415. goblin: Said
to children--119. hook and driver: Inf.
considers this an Irishism--57. old
Nick: Inf. does not consider this a
reference to the devil--422. old
Scratch: Used by inf.'s mother (from
Oh.)--423.

67.1 spook. NE 533.

Asked what people might expect to see
in a haunted house, most infs. said,
"a ghost," or "ghosts." Ghost apparently is ordinarily a neutral word, although for the skeptical it may be humorous. Spirit, used by a scattered one-
sixth of all UM infs., seems to be used
and understood in all seriousness.
Spook, however, very slightly more frequent in the two eastern states, generally connotes depreciation and disbelief,
and it rarely appears without a humorous overtone.
Eastern haunt and pokey spot have
nearly vanished, with only three instances of the former and one of the
latter, as have apparition, banshee,
demon, goblin, specter, evil spirit,
and wraith. The two examples of witch
may result from a misunderstood query.

	Mn.	Ia.	N.D.	S.D.	Nb.	Ave.
ghost	92%	94%	85%	93%	89%	91%
spirit	18%	18%	15%	11%	17%	17%
spook	58%	45%	42%	39%	36%	47%

apparition 126.
banshee c†25; 115.
demon 305.
ghost 1-10, !11, 12-23, c25, 26-30,
!31, 32-40, 42, r44-45, 47-55, 57-59,
61-65; 101-3, 105-17, 119-26, 128-43,
145-50; 201-2, c203-4, 205-6, 208-14,
216-17, 219-22, 224-26; 301-2, 304,
306-28; 401-14, 416-19, 421, 423-31,
s432, 433-35, 437.
goblin 53; 111, 115-16, 120-21.
haunt †37, 54; 101.
pokey spot s132.
specter 131.
spirit 2, 6, 8, 18, ¹21, 24, 26, c27,
38, 42, c52, 55, 62; 103, 108, 112,
121, 123, 127, 137, 149; 202, 205, 219,
223; 304, ?309, 314, 318; 402, 406,

410-11, 417, 420, ¹437. evil ~ 147.
  spook !2, sn3, !4-5, c7, 9, !10, 11,
¹12, 17, !20, 22-23, !24, sn26, 28-30,
!31, 32-33, :↑34, 37, 39-42, *43, 45,
!46, 48, 50-51, sn55, 56-58, 60, 63,
c64; 101-2, 104-8, 110, 113-14, 117,
124, 131-33, 137-39, 143-44, 148, 150;
203, !¹205, c!207, 208, 210, !212, 213,
215, 217-18, !220, 221, 223; 302-3,
305-6, sn309, 310, 312, !313, 320, !324,
326, 328; 403, c405, 406, :409, 410,
412, c414, 415, 419, 422, 429, 433,
437.
  witch 104; 305.
  wraith 309.
  no response 118, 151-52; 436.

Comment:

  ghost: Humorous--22, 31, 50; 411.
Serious--26. Both humorous and serious--
34. Usu.--33; 437. spirit: "I seen spirits in a Spiritualist church in Chicago"--27. Serious--41; 437. spook:
Humorous--2-3, 7, 9, 20, 22-23, 26, 28,
31; 208; 312, 320, 326; 406, 409-10,
429, 437. Serious; in "witchery"--50.
"A mild term"--55. "Scary"--58. Formerly used by inf.--34. Usu.--433.

67.5 certainly! (strong affirmation).
NE 590.

  To manifest strong or enthusiastic
approval or assent UM speakers resort
to a variety of formal and informal expressions in addition to using heavy
stress on common yes, yes sir, yeah,
and OK. These latter are treated in
67.6.

  No clear regional or social patterns
appear in the replies. Most formal are
the full statements, not usually recorded by the fieldworkers, such as I
agree and I should say so. Perhaps somewhat formal also are certainly, surely,
absolutely, and definitely. Informal and
most common is sure, either alone or in
phrases such as Sure thing and That's
for sure. Most of the remainder, listed below, are even more informal. Certain correlations may be determined,
such as that the you bet forms are used
by more than twice as many male infs.
as female infs., and that sure tends to
be avoided by Type III infs., only two
of whom admit this flat adverb during
the interview. (Two others carefully
use surely; the remainder have a variety
of terms.) Right! and Correct! do not
appear in the responses and apparently
have gained currency since the fieldwork.

  absolutely c42; 102, 127, 130; c431.
  certainly 14, 17-18, c37, 62; s105,

111, 114, 119, 121, 125, 131, 137, 139;
307, 318; s424, 435.
  definitely 58; 111.
  I agree 147, 149. I say c434. I say
so 415. I should say c428. I should say
so 40.
  of course 5, c13, 16; 103-6, 112-13,
c119, 139; 213. course c15-16.
  positively 58; 140.
  sure c4, 5-10, 12, c13, c16, c19-20,
26, c27, 28, c31-32, 36, c37, 41, c45-
47, 48, c51, c53, 56, c57-60, c62-63;
101, 104-5, c107, 108, 110-13, 115,
117, 119-20, 128-29, 132, c133, 138,
141, 143, 145, 148-49; c202, 204-5,
c206, 207-8, 210, 213, c215, 217-18,
c219, 223-24, c225, 226; 301-2, c303,
304, 307, c310, 313, c317, 324; c403,
c414, c417, c419, 420, c422-23, c428,
c431, c437. ~ mike 5. ~ thing 120; 208.
it ~ is 319. oh, ~ 1, c22, c24. oh yes,
~ c65. positive ~ 140. that's for ~
c50; c326; c414. to be ~ 435. why, ~
c63; 102; 421. surely 18, c57; 111, 124,
136, 144, 146; 420, 426.
  that's it c422. ~ so 39.
  absolutely right 126. damn ~ *145.
just ~ 56. that's ~ c43-44, 54; 109;
208; c416, 425, 427-28, c431, c433,
435. you're just ~ 222.
  yes indeed 114, 116, 139, s150. ~
sirree c22. absolutely ~ 138. certainly
~ 432. gosh ~ 102. indeed ~ c201. law-
sy ~ c401. mercy sakes ~ c22. oh ~ c27,
28, c29-30, c34, c57; c211; c414, c428,
c430, 436. oh God ~ 412. oh my ~ c414.
  yep 36, c44, c61; c225; 421.
  you bet 2, sn!3, 7-8, 10, 12, c13,
c19, c23, 34, 41, 49, 54, 58; 106, 117,
135, 148; 205, 207, c216, 219, 222, 224;
302, 304, c309, ¹313, 321; c407, 411,
418, c422, 429, c437. ~ ~cha c4, 9, *64;
122-23, 132, 134, c136, 142; c203, 208,
216; 321; c409, 410. ~ ~ your boots 208.
~ ~ your life c19, c25; 322-23. yes, ~ ~
c202. betcha my life 214.
  no response 11, 21, 33, 35, 38; 118,
151-52; 211-12, 220; 305-6, 308, 311-12,
314-16, 320, 325, 327-28; 402, 404, 406,
408, 413.

67.6 yes. NE 588.

  Most of the indications of simple affirmation, normal or stressed, were recorded during the conversation of the
interview, except in the records of H
and P, who noted few conversational
forms. Some infs., consequently, are
represented by one or two forms, others
by quite a variety. The resulting field
data can be suggestive rather than comprehensive; hence, no statistical summary is offered here.

Standard <u>yes</u> is recorded for 7 out of 10 UM infs., more frequently in Northern speech territory, Minnesota and North Dakota, than in Midland territory (a fact that may be due to fieldworker differences). The vowel ranges from [æ] to [ɛ] and from [æə] to [ɛə], with no obvious regional significance.

Also very common are <u>yeah</u> and <u>ya</u>. Even one speaker may manifest most of the varieties of <u>yeah</u>, with the vowel within the range indicated by [ɛə-æə-ɑe-ɜe-æ]. These variations occur throughout the UM, but the form itself is most frequently reported in Minnesota and Nebraska. <u>Ya</u> has two varieties found in all five states, one typified by [jɪ'ɑ] and the other by [jɑ]. It is perhaps noteworthy that 40% of the infs. who have <u>ya</u> in their speech have at least one parent born in Germany, Holland, or Scandinavia.

<u>Yep</u>, usually emphatic, occurs widely with these vowel variations [ɛ-e-ʌ] and, once, [ɑ]. Its frequency among Type I speakers is twice that among Type II's; no Type III speaker has it.

<u>Ay-a</u> ['ejɑ], found in western New England as a rare old form, is preserved in the speech of a South Dakota Type I speaker whose parents were born in Vermont and Massachusetts.

Although in Iowa a polite form, either <u>yes sir</u> or <u>yes ma'am</u>, was generally recorded whether typically used by the inf. or not, its sporadic appearance elsewhere and the overt attitudes of infs. attest the decline of such forms in ordinary conversation.

ach c415. ~ yes c415.
ay-a 317.
thee [ð̥i] 14.
ya c4, c6, c20, c22, c30-31, c44, c47, c52-53, c59, c63-64; c105, 114-15, 134, 142-43, 148; c203, c206, 209, c210-11, 216, c217-18, c220, c221-23, c225; c302, c310, c320-21, c324-25, c328; c401-2, c407, c409, c413, c415, c417-19, c421, c423, 427, c428, c433, c435-36.
yep c1, c8, c19, 36, c44, c59, c61; c218, c224-25; c301; 421, c429, c431, c432.
yeah c11-12, c15-17, c20, 22, c23, c25, 27-28, c31-33, c35, 36, c38, 41, c42, c44-47, c50-51, c54, c59-60, 62, c63; 107-8, 120, 127, 130, c133, 135, 138, 145-47, c150, c152; c202, c204, c206, 208, c220, c222-23, c225; c309, c312, c314, c322, c327; c401, c403, c404-5, c407, c412, c414, c416-17, c420, c422-23, 424, 426, c427-30, 433, c434, 435, c436-37.
yes c1-4, c7-8, c12-13, 14, c15-16, 17, c18-19, c21, 23, 24, 26-28, c29,

c30-33, c35, 36, c37, c39-40, c42-47, 48, c49-51, c53-57, c59-61, 62, c63, 64, c65; 101-4, 106, 108-13, 115, c116, 119-20, 125, 129, 131-32, 136-37, 141, 144, c152; c201-3, c205, c206-7, c209, 210, c211-16, 217, c218-24, 226; c303, 304, c309-14, c317, c320-23, c325-27; c401-2, cvr406, c407-8, c410, c413-14, c417-18, c421, 422, c424, 425, c426, c428-32, c434-35, 436, c437.
yes, ma'am c44; 101, 104, 116, 121, 139; 305-8, 316-19; c414, 421-22, 425. yes'm c44, c61; 121; 308. yes, my lady c44.
yes, sir 5, c6, c13, c15, 31, c35-36, c42, 44, 48, c50, 55, 58, c59, 64; 102, 105, 111-15, c119, 121-22, s124, 128-29, 132-33, 137-39, 145; c202, c218, c220, c222; 305-8, c314, 316-19, c320, c327; c404-5, c409, c414, 420-22, c424, 425, 432, c434, 435. yes siree 22.
no response 9-10; 117-18, 123, 126, 140, 149, 151; 315; 411.

Comment:

[ð̥i]: Finnish--14. yes: Usu.--33. yes, sir: Emphatic--5, 42, 55, 64; 405. Said to interviewer--31. Usu.--48. Polite--58; 425. Inf. says the use of 'sir' or 'ma'am' is "old-fashioned"-- 150. Not much used here now--435. Inf. doesn't "'sir' or 'ma'am' anybody"-- 103. Would never say "sir" or "ma'am"-- 10, 24, 39; 426.

67.7 <u>How are you?</u> (to an intimate friend). NE 424.

For an UM inf. a greeting to a close friend is likely to be older <u>How are you?</u>, common <u>Hello!</u>, or more recent <u>Hi!</u> The complete picture cannot be presented, however, as several of the fieldworkers sought only <u>How are you?</u>, for its stress and pitch patterns, and ignored other informal greeting terms, such as <u>Hello!</u> and <u>Hi!</u>

Stress in <u>How are you?</u> is typically on <u>are</u>, with reduced stress on <u>you</u>, unless the greeting is followed by such a word as <u>today</u>, in which case How may have secondary stress and the final phrase the primary stress. But when <u>How are you?</u> is a response to a similar greeting, it is usually preceded by <u>Fine</u>, <u>Great</u>, or the like, and then the stress is normally on <u>you</u>.

Several infs. specifically characterize <u>Hello!</u> as old-fashioned; even more point out that the usual current greeting is simply <u>Hi!</u>, so recent that it is not found in <u>LANE</u>.

<u>Howdy</u>, found twice in New England (Connecticut, as old-fashioned, and upper New Hampshire), is a minor UM vari-

ant limited to the western states. (See the accompanying map.) For other variations see the list below.

   good afternoon 207.
   hello 1, c2, →¹3, 4, 6, 10, 12-13, c15, 21-22, 27, 29, 31, 33, 36, †38, 39, 41-42; 148; 201, 205-6, 209-10, 213-15, 217, c218, 219-20, 222-23; 301, †303-4, 307, 310, c312, †313, 324, †325; 403, c418, 429. ~ there c59, 61; 322; 402. ~ there, neighbor 19.
   hi 4, 8, c9, 10, →13, 14, 17, 20, →21, 24, 26, 30, →31, 33, →35, 37, →38, 42, →46, 47, 49, 62; 127, 149; 201, c202-3, 205, 208, c209, !210, c211, 215-16, 221-23, c226; 301-3, →304, 310, c312, →313, 314-15, c→320, 323, →324-25, c326-28; 401-2, 404, c405, 406, c408-9, 410, c412, →417, 429, c436. ~ there 212; 321; 410-11, 429, c437. ~ ya 1.
   hidy do c303.
   how are you? 4, 6-8, 10, 16-18, 21, 24-25, 27-28, 32, 34, 36, 39-40, 43-45, !46, c47, 48-50, c52, 53-58, 60, 62-64; 101-2, 104-17, 119-26, 128-31, c132, 133-34, 136-47, 150; 219-20, 222, 225; 306-9, 311, 316, 318-19; c409, 413-17, 420-21, 423, 425-28, 430-35, c437. ~ ~ ~ anyway? c23. ~ ~ ~ doing? 315. ~ ~ ~ feeling? 16, 51. how you coming? 309. how you feeling? 135.
   how do c59. howdy 204; c312, 320, ¹323; c419, 422. howdy do †35.
   how do you do? 1, †3, c11, 14-15, 65; 127, 140, 148-49; 307; 424.
   how is everybody? 305. how's everything? c15. how's it getting along? 57.
   no response 5; 103, 118, 151-52; 317; 407.

Comment:

   good afternoon: Inf. says he usually gives a time-of-day salutation--207. hello: To an older person--205. hi: To children--21, 33. Usu.--10, 24; 215; 310. how do you do: Inf. says this but admits it is old-fashioned--3.

68.1 How do you do? (to a stranger). NE 425.

   In the UM, as in New England, the usual formal greeting to a stranger, as during an introduction, is How do you do?
   A contracted variation, Howdy do?, occurs 15 times, mostly in Iowa and South Dakota, and How do? occurs three times in Minnesota. All infs. using them are old-fashioned Type I speakers not inclined to formality.
   A fairly common equivalent greeting is (I'm) glad to meet you, which is favored by Type I speakers twice as

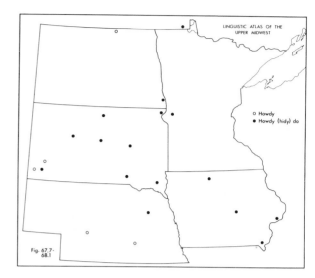

heavily as by those in Type II.
   Illogical (I'm) glad to know you is acknowledged equally by a scattered few Type I and II infs., mostly in Minnesota.

   hello 147; 216, ?221, 226; 304, 323. ~ there 404, 409.
   how are you? 8, 29; 320; 404, 408, 416, 420-21, s423, ?425, 426-27, 429-31, 434. well, ~ ~ ~ 422.
   how do? c23, 32, c59. howdy do? 1, c25; 104, 133, 140, 148; 225; c302, 307, 314, 316, 320, 322, 324; 415.
   how do you do? 2-7, 9-11, 13-22, 26, !27, 28, 30-31, 33-34, c36, 38-43, 45, 48-51, 53-56, 58, 60-62, s¹63, 64-65; 101-3, 105-8, 110-17, 119-21, 123-24, 126-29, 131-32, 134-39, 141, 144-46, 149-50; 201-3, c204, 205-13, c214, 215-19, 221-23, c224, 226; 304-5, *306, 309-10, 313, 315, 317, 319, 321, 323, 325-26; 401-3, 406, 410-11, 413-14, 417-19, 424, 428, 435, 437.
   (I'm) glad to know you 24, 47, 51, c57; 121, 318.
   (I'm) glad to meet you 12-13, 44, !46, 48, 52; 120, 122, 125, 142-43; 220; 308. glad to meet you, I'm sure 62. very glad to meet you 8.
   pleased to meet you 15, 32, 37, 45, 63; 103, 119, 128, 130; 305, 317.
   no response 35; 109, 118, 151-52; 301, ?303, 311-12, 327-28; 405, 407, 412, 432-33, 436.

Comment:

   glad to meet you: "But they say this is wrong"--46. glad to meet you, I'm sure: To a man--62. how do you do: "You say this if you're not particularly glad to meet them"--46. To a woman--62. "Generally to a lady; it's more formal"--125. Said upon being introduced; her greeting is 'hello'--226.

68.2 <u>Come again</u> (to a visitor upon departing). NE 428.

As in New England, the most frequent parting expression to a visitor is <u>Come again</u>, spread quite evenly but with a possible slight Northern bias.

<u>Call again</u>, a variant sparsely occurring in New England (eastern Ma. 7, R.I. 1, Cn. 1, N.H. 3, Vt. 1) survives with six instances in Minnesota, besides one each in Nebraska and South Dakota.

One-third of the UM infs. use <u>Come back</u>, either alone or in any of various expressions, the most common of which is <u>Come back again</u>. The strong Midland orientation of <u>Come back</u>, a form favored by older speakers, and, almost equally strong, of <u>Come back again</u>, favored by younger speakers, reflects the absence of these forms from the New England records.

<u>Come and see us</u> is a rare variant in Minnesota and North Dakota.

	Mn.	Ia.	N.D.	S.D.	Nb.	Ave.
come again	80%	61%	69%	64%	57%	68%
~ back	2%	12%	8%	8%	11%	7%
~ ~ again	14%	31%	23%	24%	30%	23%

call again 1, 14, 43, 48, 56, 59; 314; 429.

come again 2, 4-8, 11-13, 16, 18, :19, 21, 24-29, c30, 33-36, 39-46, 48-52, 54-58, 60-61, 63-65; 101, 103, 105-8, 110-11, 113, 115-16, 119-25, 129-30, 132, 134, 136, 140-42, 144-45; 201-3, 206-8, 210-15, 217-18, 220, 223, 225-26; 301, 303-6, 308-9, 311, crc313, 319, 324-27; 403, 406-7, 409-10, 412-13, 415, !417, 418, 420, 422, 424-26, 430, 434-37. ~ ~ sometime 53; 427. ~ ~ soon 17, 62; 137; 328. ~ ~ won't you? 131. please ~ ~ 47; 317.

come back [1]40, [1]46; 107, 109, 112, 146; 316; c402, 405, c409. ~ ~ and see us 203. ~ ~ anytime 102; 204. ~ ~ sometime sn35; 322; 401. ~ ~ soon 110.

come back again 9, c14, 15, 22-23, 31, 37-38; 104, 114, 117, 126-28, 133, 135, 138-39, 143, 147-50; 205, 216, !219, 221-22; 302, 310, ?313, 318, 320, 323; 408, 411, 419, 421, 423, 432-33. do ~ ~ ~ 428, 431. ~ ~ ~ sometime 209; 321; 404. be sure and ~ ~ ~ soon 32. come back real soon again 414.

come and see us 225. ~ ~ ~ ~ again 10, 20; 224. come see us again 416.

hurry back [1]431.

no response 3; 118, 151-52; 307, 312, 315.

Fig. 68.2

68.3a <u>Merry Christmas!</u> NE 430.

As in New England, nearly all UM infs. have the greeting <u>Merry Christmas!</u> Three in South Dakota and Nebraska say <u>Happy Christmas!</u>, a phrase that also appears twice in New England. One Minnesotan with a Kentucky parent, and one Iowan, have South Midland <u>Christmas gift!</u>, and three other infs. recall having heard it. The Minnesotan's son uses <u>Merry Christmas! Christmas greetings!</u> is an Iowa singleton.

Christmas gift 35; s[1]113, [1]†129, 135, [1]139; [1]†403.

Christmas greetings 147.

Happy Christmas 307, 317; 427.

Merry Christmas 1-5, !7, 8-10, 12-31, 33-34, →[1]35, 36-38, 41-47, 49-55, 59-61; 101-17, 119-50; 201-26; 301-6, 308-16, 318-27; 401-26, 428-35, 437.

no response 6, 11, 32, 39-40, 48, 56-58, 62-65; 118, 151-52; 328; 436.

68.5 Money is <u>scarce</u>.

Not sought in NE, this item calls for terms describing hard times. "Money is scarce," say most UM infs., with their lowest frequency in Nebraska and South Dakota. "Money is tight," say a great many infs., with their highest frequency in Nebraska and the Dakotas. The Midland orientation of <u>tight</u> appears stronger in terms of infs. who use this term exclusively. The frequency rises from 5% in Minnesota to 8% in Iowa (all in the southern portion), and from 3% in North Dakota and 6% in South Dakota to 30% in Nebraska.

<u>Short</u>, <u>close</u>, and <u>hard to get</u> are scattered variants.

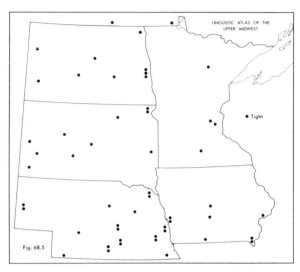

Fig. 68.5

	Mn.	Ia.	N.D.	S.D.	Nb.	Ave.
scarce	97%	92%	92%	92%	67%	88%
tight	8%	16%	38%	35%	51%	25%

close 307; ¹403.

hard to get 306.

scarce 2-11, s12, 13-65; 101-17, 119-23, 126-30, 132-40, 142-50; 201-10, 212-13, 215-26; 301-5, 308-10, 312, 314, 316-28; 401-2, :sn403, 404-6, 409, :s?410, 411-18, 421, 423-24, s427, s¹428, 429-31, s432, 433-37.

short 12; :125; 432.

tight 1, 12, 32, 37, 53; 124-25, 128, 131, sn141, 145, *148, 149; 202, 208-9, 211, 214, 216, 219-22; 302, 306-9, 311, 313, 315, 319-20, ¹323; 407-10, c413, 416, 419-23, 425-28, cvr430, 431, 436-37.

no response 118, 151-52.

69.2   coast lying down.   NE 576.   WG 18, 20, 25, 80; F7, F9, F162.

In the UM the act of a boy's throwing himself face down as he starts to coast downhill on a sled is known by a variety of regional expressions, most of which reflect a similar variety in the New England and Middle Atlantic states.

Belly-flop, common in western New England, dominates the Northern speech territory of the UM. Belly-bump, found in coastal and northern New England, is offered only by infs. in Minnesota and Dubuque, Iowa. Belly-gut, found from western Connecticut to the Great Lakes, survives with two infs. in Minnesota and one each in northeastern Iowa and in North Dakota.

Belly-buster, which spread west from Virginia, West Virginia, and southern Ohio, is the expression used by one-half of the Iowa and South Dakota speak-

ers and by three-fourths of those in Nebraska.

One rare variant, belly-bust, is scattered; another, belly-booster, is only in Iowa.

Although of the many east coast terms only two others, belly-bunt and belly-wopper, appear in the field records, several new variants appear in the UM. Belly-bunt is recorded only as attributed to the local Irish in Winona, Minnesota; belly-wopper, found in the lower Hudson Valley and in Maryland, turns up twice in Iowa (once as whopper) and once in Nebraska. Not recorded in the east are bellity-bumper, belly-butting, belly-coaster, belly-down, belly fashion, belly first, belly slam, belly slide, slamming, and the girls' term, boy fashion. Belly-bumper was volunteered by the inf.'s niece, a 50-year resident of Jackson County, Minnesota.

A rather surprising number of infs. disclaim knowledge of any term at all. Women especially declare that they are unfamiliar with any descriptive expression, perhaps because when they were children the belly- terms were considered too vulgar for their ears. Some infs., however, have another reason, the lack of opportunity for coasting. Four prairie dwellers sadly told the fieldworker that there are no hills where they live.

Some infs. remark that belly-flop means only, or sometimes also, a flat dive into water (43, 45, 57; 106; 203, 211, 222, 224; 315); others say the same thing about belly-buster (416, 419, 425, 437).

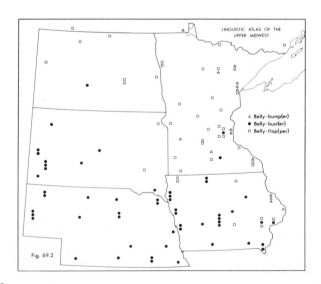

Fig. 69.2

△ Belly-bump(er)
● Belly-bust(er)
□ Belly-flop(per)

	Mn.	Ia.	N.D.	S.D.	Nb.	Ave.
belly-						
bump(er)	20%	10%	0	0	0	10%
~ buster	4%	47%	6%	50%	77%	35%
~ flop(per)	47%	17%	44%	10%	0	27%
~ gut	4%	3%	6%	0	0	3%

CL 116: As with many items having a number of variants, the returns from the 816 checklist respondents generally confirm the field data but broaden the areas of distribution. Belly-flop dominates the Northern sector but now has greater frequency elsewhere than the fieldwork indicates. Belly-buster likewise dominates the Midland sector but now has greater frequency in the Northern area. Belly-bump is checked by 65 scattered respondents, nearly half of whom are in the three western states where field records do not record it at all. Belly down, rare in the fieldwork, is reported by 83 widely spread respondents. The Northern/Midland orientation of these five most frequently checked terms is highlighted by the breakdown within Iowa:

	No. Iowa		So. Iowa	
belly-bump(er)	14	13%	2	2%
~ buster	36	32%	74	71%
~ down	14	13%	6	6%
~ flop	38	34%	17	16%

Belly-bunt, according to the checklists, is fairly evenly distributed within the five states. Belly-booster expectedly is checked by respondents in Iowa (30.2, 37.3, 71.1, 80.2, 84.3) and Nebraska (5.3, 67.1). Belly-gut is sparsely scattered throughout the UM (Mn. 18.2, 76.1; Ia. 30.1, 76.2; N.D. 27.1; S.D. 6.1; Nb. 79.1). Belly grinder, found around Wheeling, West Virginia, apparently has some UM life despite its absence from the field data, since it is checked in Minnesota (69.1), Iowa (6.4), N.D. (33.1), and Nebraska (33.1). Belly-kachug, not in the field data but possibly related to the belly-kachunk reported in LANE as a New London, Connecticut, expression, is checked by two Midland respondents, one in Iowa (57.2) of Illinois and English parentage and one in Nebraska (16.1) of Swedish parentage.

Besides the above-mentioned terms, the respondents voluntarily wrote in several expressions, presumably their natural ones: coast lying down--N.D. 17.1; S.D. 37.2; Nb. 23.1. belly-coaster--Nb. 32.1. belly-slide--Mn. 39.1; Ia. 76.5; S.D. 39.1; Nb. 12.2, 48.2, 80.2. belly-w(h)opper--Ia. 90.4, 95.2; N.D. 23.1; S.D. 13.2; Nb. 28.1, 39.2. belly-womper (from eastern Pa.)--Nb. 1.5.

Two respondents also wrote in the lugubrious note, "No hills."

	Mn.	Ia.	N.D.	S.D.	Nb.	Ave.
belly-						
bump(er)	13%	7%	7%	6%	4%	8%
~ bunt	3%	3%	4%	2%	4%	3%
~ buster	12%	51%	21%	46%	73%	41%
~ down	9%	9%	11%	15%	9%	10%
~ flop(per)	66%	26%	60%	28%	7%	37%

bellity bumper *139.
belly booster 116, 129, 141.
belly bump 1, sn†2, 12, c15, 16-17, 39-40, 42, 51, :?59; 119-21; :sc!†221; ¹302. ~ bumper 56. ~ bumps 13.
belly bunt ¹58.
belly bust :sn37; c150; !301; 413. ~ buster 50; 103-4, 109-11, 122, *123, 124-25, 127-28, 131-32, 138, 144, 146, 148; ¹213, c217; ¹302, 309, c310, !311, c312, 313, c315, c!320, 325, c326; 401-2, !404, 406, c407, 408-11, c412, 414, 422, 426, s427, 428, c429, 431-33, 435.
belly butting c215.
belly coaster *326.
belly down 145. (coast) ~ ~ 25.
belly fashion 62; c202, :sn205, 219.
belly first 321; c419.
belly flop sn3, 5, 8, sn9, !10, c11, 14, 18, 20, 22, 24, *26, !27, c30-31, 34, :36, 38, *43, !44, 47, c53, 54, 57-58, 61, :?63; 101-2, 106, 134, 140, c152; 201, *203, !204, ¹208, 210, c218, *219, 220; ¹302, 308, ¹315, ¹323, *328; s427. ~ flopper 137.
belly gut 21, !55; 108; c212.
belly slam 33, 35. ~ slammer 33.
belly slide 115. ~ sliding ?53; 420, 427.
belly whopper 111.
belly wopper *131; →408.
boy fashion 219.
coast(ing) 112, 114; 305, 316; 416, 423, 430-31. ~ laying down 32; 307. ~ lying down 64-65.
head first 1.
on your belly 6, c29, 48, 57. on your stomach 209.
slamming *145.
slide 105, 133; 318. ~ down c13. ~ down the hill 16; 306. ~ on your stomach 45.
no response 4, 7, 19, 23, ?28, :!41, 46, ?49, 52, 60; 107, 113, 117-18, 126, 135-36, 142-43, 147, 149, 151; 206, ?207, 211, 214, ?216, 222-23, ?224-26; 303-4, 314, 317, 319, 322, 324, ?327; ?403, 405, 415, ?417, 418, 421, 424-25, 434, ?436, 437.

Comment:

belly bump: Esp. refers to coasting over a bump or hillock--2. belly bunt:

Inf. says this is used by the Irish--58.
belly buster: Inf. says his mother told
him never to say this in the presence
of girls--312. Term for diving into
water, but not for coasting--416, 419,
sn425, 437. belly coaster: Inf. says he
used this as a boy when he lived near
Madison, Wi.--*326. [Ed: It was not recorded in the Wisconsin survey, however.] belly flop: Term for diving into
water, but not for coasting--45; 210,
222, 224. belly slam: For inf. this is
the verb and 'belly slammer' the noun--
33. belly wopper: Inf. says local boys
now use this term--408. slamming: Volunteered by inf.'s 19-year old son--145.

69.3 somersault. NE 578.

For the action of making a complete
vertical turn by placing one's hands
and head on the ground and then kicking
oneself over, there are two common related terms, somersault and somerset.
The obsolescence of the latter, already
manifest in the New England survey, is
thrice reaffirmed in the UM.

One indication of somerset's decline
is the fact that its frequency sharply
decreases from Type I (25%) to Type II
(10%) to Type III (6%) while that of
somersault increases from Type I (76%)
to Type II (91%) to Type III (100%).

Another indicator is the large number
of infs. who voluntarily remark that
somerset is old-fashioned or that it is
a word they had used in their childhood.
It may be, however, that, like the names
of children's games, somerset itself has
a persistence value among children, who
later in life will replace it by somersault as the "grown-up" word.

A possible third indicator is that apparently the term was growing less popular even by the time of the western
settlement, for somerset has a lower incidence in the Dakotas and Nebraska.

Although both forms occur in New England, the distribution in the UM suggests
a Midland preference for somerset, as
its frequency, though declining in relation to somersault, is still higher
in Iowa and Nebraska than in Northern
speech territory.

Two phonetic variants occur, somersaw
and somersit, both in Minnesota.

Handspring, offered by five Minnesotans
who insist upon this meaning for the
word, usually refers to a different kind
of vertical turn, in which the head does
not touch the ground. Headspring, once
in Iowa, may be a nonce-formation. Flip-
flop, usually limited to the backward
somersault, seems to three Nebraskans

to refer to the front variety as well.

	Mn.	Ia.	N.D.	S.D.	Nb.	Ave.
somersault	85%	70%	96%	89%	92%	84%
somerset	18%	28%	4%	11%	14%	17%

flip-flop 414, 435, 437.
handspring 13, 44-45, 59, 61.
headspring 108.
somersault 1-4, 6-14, 16-24, 26, :27,
28-31, 33-34, 36-47, 49-52, 55-58, 60-
64; 101-3, 105-6, sn108, 110-15, ?116,
117, 119-24, 126-28, 130-31, 133-34,
136, cr?138, 140-41, 143-45, 147, 149-
50; 201-16, →217, 219-23, c224, 225-26;
301-3, 305-7, 309-10, 313-28; 401-11,
413-26, c427, 428-31, *432, 433, 435-36.
somersaw 53.
somerset 5, 16, †23, 25, 30, 32, 35,
†40, †45-47, 48, 50-51, 54, 59; 104,
107, 109, cr116, ⊥122, ⊥*123, 125, 127,
†128, 129, 132, †135, 137-39, 142, †145,
146, 148; †208, †215, †217, 218, †222;
308, 311-12, ⊥313, †325; †401, †411,
412, †418-10, 431-32, 434, 437. somersit
15.
no response 118, 151-52; 304.

Comment:

headspring: Usu.--108. somersault:
Usu.--435. somerset: Used by inf. in
youth--208; 419. "We used to call it
'somerset'"--23. "When I was a kid, it
was 'somerset'"--45. "We said 'somerset'
as kids. 'Somersault' was an affectation"--222. Usu.--50-51. "I guess the
other ['somersault'] 's correct"--325.
Inf. says you would turn a 'somerset'
but if you had turned it, it would be
a 'somersault'--127.

70.7 stamp the floor. NE 583.

Since for the meaning "strike the
floor forcibly with one's foot" dictionaries record stomp, an originally phonetic variant of stamp, as a distinct
lexical entry and since some infs. consider these variants as separate words,
this item is treated here rather than
in the volume on pronunciation. Stamp
has the vowel /æ/; stomp has /ɑ/, /ɒ/,
or /ɔ/. There is one instance with /ʌ/,
here considered as stump.

In such a context as "She was so mad
that she stamped her foot" stomp is preferred by nearly three-fourths of the
Type I infs., two-thirds of Type II,
but only one-half of Type III. Conversely stamp seems to connote a somewhat
higher degree of schooling with the increase in frequency from Type I to Type
III.

Regional contrast also exists. Stamp
clearly has Northern orientation; stomp

has its greatest frequency in Iowa, Nebraska, and South Dakota.

Some speakers use both forms but differentiate them as does one Iowan (123),
who says, "You stamp your feet when
you're stompin'" or as do one North Dakotan (215) and two South Dakotans (324-
25), who say that a child "stamps" its
feet but a horse "stomps."

	Mn.	Ia.	N.D.	S.D.	Nb.	Ave.
stamp	42%	18%	52%	31%	22%	32%
stomp	61%	84%	42%	77%	78%	70%

stamp 1-4, 7-9, 13-14, 17, 21-22, 25-
26, 29-30, 33-34, :sn36, 43-44, 46-48,
53, 58, 62; 101, 103, 111-12, 120, 123,
127, 131, 149; :201, 202-6, 208, 211,
215, ?216, 217-18, 221, 223; ¹302, 304,
309-10, 319, 324-26, 328; 407, 415-16,
419, 423, 426, 428, 430.

stomp 5-6, 10-12, ¹13, 15-16, 18-20,
23-24, 27, c28, 31-32, 35, 37-38, c39,
40-42, *43, 45, ¹47, 49-52, 54, c55,
56-57, 59-61, 63-65; 102, 104-10, ¹111,
113-17, 119, 121-26, 128-30, 132-33,
*134, 135, :136, 137-48, 150, 152; 209-
10, 212-15, cr216, 219-20, 222, 224-26;
:301, 302-3, 305, 308, 311-18, ¹319,
320-25, :!327; 401-6, 408-10, cr411,
412-14, 417-18, 420-22, 424-25, 427,
429, 431-37.

stump c57.

no response 118, 151; 207; 306-7.

70.8 The baby <u>crawls</u> on all fours.
NE 582.

Although this item was added to the
UM worksheets only after the Minnesota
survey was virtually completed, evidence from the other states strongly
supports the inference, based upon the
dominance of <u>creep</u> in New England, that
<u>creep</u> is primarily Northern and <u>crawl</u>
is primarily Midland. <u>Creep</u> dominates
northern Iowa and the northern counties
of Nebraska. <u>Crawl</u> is almost exclusively
in southern Iowa and most of Nebraska,
with scattered occurrences in the Dakotas.

	Mn.	Ia.	N.D.	S.D.	Nb.	Ave.
crawl		52%	31%	36%	78%	
creep		62%	69%	68%	38%	

crawl 35, 38; 102, 104, ¹105, 110,
?115, ?119, 120-21, 124-28, 130-32,
134-36, 138, 140, 142-43, 145-50; 201,
203, 206-7, cr212, ¹215, 216, 220-22;
301, 307, 309-11, 314, 319, 321-22,
328; 402, 407-12, 414-19, 421-22, 424-
30, c431, 432-37.

creep 29-31, 36; 101-3, 105-14, cr115,
116-17, cr119, 122-23, 126, †127, 128-
29, 133, 137, 139, 141-42, 144-46, 152;
†201, 202, 204-5, 208-11, ?212, 213-15,

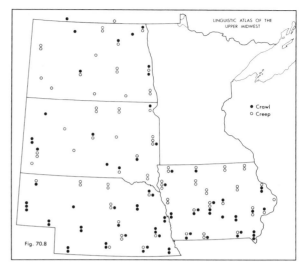

LINGUISTIC ATLAS OF THE
UPPER MIDWEST

● Crawl
○ Creep

Fig. 70.8

217-19, 221, 223-26; 302-6, 308, 312-13,
315-20, 323-27; 401, 403-6, c408, 413-14,
420, 422-23, ¹425, 426, 431-32.

no response 1-28, 32-34, 37, 39-65;
118, 151.

Comment:

<u>crawl</u>: Inf. says this is heard more
commonly than 'creep'--128. <u>creep</u>: Inf.
says this is heard more commonly than
'crawl'--102; 422. "Some say 'crawl,'
but 'creep' is right"--105. Term used
by inf.'s mother (from Ont.)--201. Inf.
says babies 'creep' on their stomachs
before they 'crawl' on their hands and
knees--142.

71.1 May I <u>take</u> you home? NE 402.

"After a dance or other social affair
how might a young man ask a girl for the
privilege of escorting her to her home?"
To this question most UM infs. replied
with either of two expressions, almost
evenly distributed among the five
states: "May I see you home?" and "May
I take you home?" <u>See</u> may have a slight
Midland orientation, and <u>take</u> a Northern.

Although these two are evenly distributed also among Type I and Type II infs.,
the preponderance of <u>take</u> over <u>see</u> among
Type III infs. suggests the increasing
acceptance of <u>take</u> and the decline of
<u>see</u>.

<u>Walk you home</u> occurs sparsely and then
mostly in Midland territory. Southern
<u>carry</u> is used by a Minnesotan whose
father was born in Alabama but it does
not appear in the south Midland area of
southeastern Iowa. Other occasional expressions appear below, including the
quite formal <u>escort you home</u>.

	Mn.	Ia.	N.D.	S.D.	Nb.	Ave.
see	47%	66%	54%	54%	49%	54%
take	61%	50%	58%	50%	51%	55%

accompany you home 32.
carry you home c35.
escort you home 14, cr39; 316-17, 319.
give you a lift 119; 409.
see you home :2, 3, 6, 10-12, 15-16, 18, 22-23, 27, 31-32, 36-37, 41-42, 45, †46, !47, 51, 54-55, 57, 59, 61-65; 101, 103-9, 111, 113-15, 117, 119, 122-25, 128-29, 133-38, 142-43, 146-49, 152; 201-4, 208, 210-11, 214, †215, 217-18, 220-21, 223-24; 301-3, 306, 308, ¹310, 311-13, 315, 317, 322, 324, cr325, 327-28; †401, 405, 408-10, 412-13, 417, †419, 420, 422, 424-25, †426, 428-29, 432, ?433, 434-35, 437.
show you the way home †34.
take you home :!1, 4-5, 7-10, 13-14, 16-21, 23-25, cr28, 30, 33-34, 36-38, 40, 43-44, →46, 48-50, 52-53, 56-58, 60, 63; 102, 104, 106, 110, 112-13, 115-16, 120-21, 124, 126-28, 130-32, 139-41, 143-46, 150; 201, 205-7, 209, →211, 212-13, 216, 219-22, 225-26; 302, 304-5, 307, 309-10, 314-15, 318-21, 323, ?325, 326; 402-4, 406-7, 411, 414-18, 421, 423-24, 426-27, 429, cr433, 437.
walk home with you ?28, ?39.
walk you home 26; →211; →¹301, ¹326; →402, †406, 431.
no response 29; 118, 151; 430, 436.

Comment:

see you home: Usu.--26; 128. "A lost art"--47. "Have the pleasure of seeing you home" was the inf.'s first response, but she admitted that it would be pretty formal--2. take you home: Usu.--18; 429.

71.4 I lugged that heavy suitcase down to the station. NE 165.

For nearly two-thirds of the UM infs. lug is the customary term for carrying an object heavy enough to require extra effort. Distribution, however, is uneven, with a clear Northern bias shown by the weighting in Minnesota and North Dakota.

About one-third of the infs., particularly in Midland speech territory, apparently have no special connotative term but use simple carry.

Two minor equivalents are found in all the five states except South Dakota -- pack and tote. Pack does not appear in LANE, but 22 instances of tote are reported in New England, where it was said to be related to the tote in tote road. (See also 18.1 and 25.3.) The scattered distribution there, however, throws some doubt upon this as the only interpreta-

tion, since instances appear in other areas than those where logging occurred (Cn. 5, R.I. 1, Ma. 6, Vt. 4, southern N.H. 1, Me. 5). In the UM a plausible inference might be that the tote in Minnesota and North Dakota has that derivation but that the tote in Iowa and Nebraska has a South Midland source. Yet any such inference is suspect until further research into the relation of the Northern tote and the Southern tote.
Carted, dragged, and walked are also reported.

	Mn.	Ia.	N.D.	S.D.	Nb.	Ave.
carry	22%	60%	19%	37%	47%	37%
lug	75%	50%	92%	67%	61%	65%
pack	3%	6%	8%	0	8%	5%
tote	5%	4%	12%	0	6%	5%

CL 117: Checklists from 1,031 respondents support the Northern preference for lug, especially in the data for Iowa, with 75% for the northern half and 54% for the southern half. The written replies are proportionately much greater for pack, which they conspicuously demonstrate to be dominantly Midland. In northern Iowa the percentage is 16%; in southern Iowa it is 35%. Tote, with 47 instances, is evenly distributed. Carry has a lower frequency than in the field materials, perhaps because it appeared on the checklist as the term to be defined and consequently selecting it was almost tantamount to writing it in. Hike appears sporadically: Mn. 2.2, 81.1; Ia. 18.4; N.D. 6.1, 23.1; Nb. 65.2. Cart appears once: Mn. 87.2.

carried 3, 6, 14, c15-16, 17-18, 28, 32, c→35, 48-49, 54, 63; 103-4, 108, 111, 114, 116-17, 119-20, 122-31, 133-34, 136, 139, 141-45, 148-49; 207, 217, 219, 221, 226; 301, 304-6, 313-14, 316, 318-19, 326; c401, 402-3, 413-15, 421-23, 427-28, 430-35.
carted *9.
dragged 57; 307; 427.
lugged 1-2, s¹3, 4, ¹5, ¹7, 8-10, sn11, c13, 15, 17-18, s19, 20-24, s25, 26, :sn27, s¹28, 29-34, 36-43, s¹44, 45, !46, 47-48, 50, 52, !53, sn54, 55, s¹56, sn57, 58, 60-64, ¹65; 101-2, s104, 105-7, 109, s110, ¹111, 112-13, 115, 117, 119, s120, 121, s¹124, 127, s132, 137-38, 140, *148, 149-50, 152; 201, c202, 203-5, !206, 207-10, !211, 212-16, :217, 219, :sn220, 221-24; :s301, 302-4, 306, 308-13, :s314, 315, 320-21, s322, :323, !324, 325, :s¹326, !327, 328; 402, ¹403, 404-6, :s407, 408-12, 416, !¹417, 418-20, ¹421, sn423, 424, c425, 428-29, s431, 433, 435-37.
packed ¹3, 12, 51; s103, c135, 146-47;

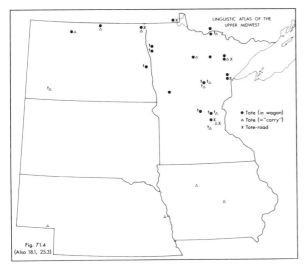

Fig. 71.4
(Also 18.1, 25.3)

218, 225; ¹302; 417-18, 422.

toted ¹3, ¹†5, c10, 14, ¹†21, †22,
s¹26, †31, ¹34, †35, 37, !¹54; 113, 132,
¹152; sn203, 205, 208, †215, s¹222,
¹223; ¹403, ¹421, sn427, snc436.

walked 56.

no response 59; 118, 151; 317; 426.

Comment:

dragged: Usu.--57. toted: "You could
say this years ago"--22. Used by inf.'s
father (from R.I.)--31. Used by inf.'s
sister-in-law (from Mt.)--223. Used fa-
cetiously--421. Inf. says this is a
Southern term--34, 54; 222.

71.6 Go bring me a knife. NE 153.

In the UM, as in New England, two
other words can replace bring in the
preceding sample request. Bring itself,
used almost equally among all three
inf. types, is twice as frequent in
Iowa as in Minnesota, but this seeming
Midland bias is not reflected in the
three western states. Get, slightly
more common than bring, likewise is
found equally among all three types but
is twice as frequent in Minnesota as in
Iowa, and this Northern bias is not reflected in the western half.

Scattered fetch, the minor variant,
clearly is on the way to obsolescence.
A few Type I infs. use it (two of them
Canadian), fewer in Type II, and none
in Type III. A third of them consider
it old-fashioned. This characterization
parallels its description by infs. who
give the term elsewhere. (See 22.4.)

	Mn.	Ia.	N.D.	S.D.	Nb.	Ave.
bring	32%	66%	46%	46%	30%	43%
fetch	8%	10%	0	11%	5%	7%
get	68%	36%	66%	54%	67%	58%

bring 2, 8, 10, 13, 20, 30, 32, c35,
?37, 44, →46, 48-49, 51, 53-54, 56, 60,
62; 101-4, 107-8, 110-11, 114-17, 120-
22, *123, 124-27, 130-33, 136, 138, 141,
145, 147-49; 201-2, 204-6, c208, 209,
215-17, 221, 226; 304-5, 307-8, 313, 316-
21, 324; c403, 404-6, 409, 413-14, 420-
21, 426, 431, 433. and ~ 16, 52, 59, 62;
144, 152; 323.

fetch 1, ¹2, cr3, ¹†7, 16, 31, †46,
47, 62; †124, 125, †127, 132, 140, ¹144,
146, sn147, †148-49; 311, sn320, sn327;
c422, 423. and ~ 63.

get ?3, 4, 6-7, 9, 11-12, 19, 21-28,
33-34, 36, cr37, 38-40, 42, 44, 47, c50,
54, 57-58, 61, 64-65; 105-6, 109-10,
112-13, 119, 123, 128-29, 131, 134-35,
137, 139, 142-43, s145, 150; 202-3, 205,
209-14, 218-19, 222, c223, 225; 301-3,
306, 309-10, c312, 314-15, 320, 322,
325-28; 401-2, c405, 412, 416-18, c419,
423-25, 427, 429-30, 432, 434-37. and ~
5, c14, 15, 17-18, 29, 41, 43-45, 47-48,
c51, 55; 207, 220, 224; 407-8, 410-11,
415, 428.

no response 118, 151.

Comment:

fetch: "I should say 'fetch,' I guess,
but I don't"--2. Formerly used by inf.--
46. Used by inf.'s father (from Iowa)--
127. "Old-timers say this"--148. Used by
inf.'s grandfather (from Va.); also
still heard in certain local families--
149. "Not very good English"--423.

71.7 goal in children's games. NE 585.

For the place to be reached safely in
any of various children's games the usual UM term is goal. The standard spelling, however, conceals two pronunciations /goI/ and /guI/, gool, the second of which
is coexistent with the first in Northern
speech territory: northern Iowa, Minnesota, northeastern South Dakota, and
North Dakota. It is not recorded elsewhere in the UM.

As with greasy and greazy (20.2) and
stamp and stomp (70.4), this situation
raises the popular but perhaps not linguistic question of when a word is a
word. For some Northern-oriented infs.
goal and gool are simply adults' and
children's variants, respectively. For
others they have different referents,
the first used in a description of football, hockey, or basketball, and only
the second used in a description of
children's games. Some using the latter,
indeed, expressed surprise that goal
and gool are related and can be considered forms of the same word. A still
different contrast is that of a Type I
Minnesota housewife who has goal for

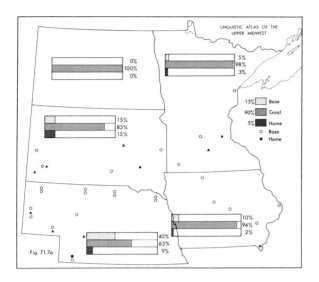

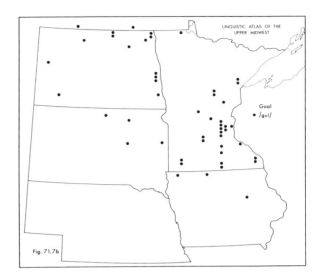

the place to get to in games and gool as the place to hide.

Two generally equivalent terms also occur, base and home. Base, only two instances of which appear in LANE and two in the Wisconsin survey, is clearly Midland, with acceptance greatest in Nebraska, Iowa, and South Dakota. Home, found four times in New England and twice in Wisconsin, turns up twice in Minnesota and once in extreme southeastern Iowa, but it has greater vitality in South Dakota and Nebraska.

base 18, 43, 60; 104, 115, 132, 139, 152; s306, 310, 318, 321, 326; 401-9, 411-12, 417, 437. home ~ 429.

goal /gol/ 1-3, 5-14, 17-20, 22, 24, :25, 26, 28, 30, 33, c34, 37, s¹38, 39-47, 49, 51-58, 61-62, 64-65; 101-16, 119-31, 133-38, 140-43, 145-50; 202-3, 207, ?208, 209, 211, 213-19, ?221, 223-26; 302, 304-5, 307-9, 311-15, 318-19, sn320, s322, 323-25, 327-28; 402-3, sn404, 412-14, 416, 420-28, ¹429, 430-31, *432, 433-35.

gool /gul/ 4, 15-16, 21-23, s¹26, :27, :29, 31-37, 39, ¹40, ¹42-43, *43, snr44, 48, 50, 54, sn57, 58-60, 62, !63; 101, 117; 201, sn203, :204, 205-7, cr208, 210, 212, 215, 220, cr221, 222, 225; 303, 306, ¹308, 316-17; ¹433. prison ~ /gul/ c103.

home 38, 51; 150; 316, 320, 326, 328; 410, 419, 436.

no response 118, 144, 151; 301; 415, 418.

Comment:

goal: /gol/ in ball games--22, 37, 62; 425. /gol/ is the place to get to in games; /gul/ is the place to hide--39. "Which is it?"--225. Inf. switched from

/gul/ to /gol/ after growing up--33-34, 54.

72.6 I want to get rid of him. NE 569.

Most UM infs., like those in New England, use get rid of to express the notion of becoming free of what is troublesome or unwanted. Shet, a phonetic variant of shut, is sparsely recorded in Midland speech territory and once in Minnesota. Shut itself does not occur. Other minor variants are ditch in Nebraska and be free of in South Dakota.

be free of 318.
ditch 409, 426.
get rid of 1-6, c7, 8-12, c13, 14-15, 17-18, 20-46, c47, *48, 49-55, s56, c57, 58, c59, 60-65; 101-13, c114, 115-17, 119, 121-50, 152; 201-26; 301-13, :314, 315-17, 319-26; 401-4, c405, 406-14, 416-20, c422, 423-29, c430, 431-37. ~ ~ on 19.
get shet of 37; ¹*122, ¹128, 132, †133, ¹148; 420.
no response 16; 118, 120, 151; 327-28; 415, 421.

Comment:

ditch: Jocular--426. get shet of: Used by inf.'s grandfather--133. Heard frequently in the community--148. Used facetiously--420.

72.8 rubber band.

Not sought in any of the eastern surveys, this item was added to the UM worksheets upon the discovery of the local incidence of rubber binder.

For the narrow circular band of rubber used to hold together cards, envelopes, and the like, most infs. use rubber band. Older elastic band is used by four of the five Canadian infs. and persists with four Minnesotans and one North Dakotan. Elastic, elastic rubber, and rubber elastic are rare variants, all in Northern territory except for one instance of elastic in Nebraska. Rubber ring is a central Minnesota singleton, probably a nonce-form.

Rubber binder seems to have the Twin Cities of Minneapolis and St. Paul as its focal area. The only occurrence outside southern Minnesota is in the speech of a Type II North Dakota housewife whose parents had lived in Minnesota, northwest of the Twin Cities. As with berm in Grand Forks (see 63.8), the origin and spread of rubber binder require intensive investigation. That it is not, however, as recent as two infs. believe, is indicated in a statement from Professor Carroll E. Reed (in a personal communication) that when in 1906 his mother, then 23, moved from Minneapolis to the Pacific Northwest she used rubber binder (and continued to use it despite the amused reaction of people who thought that she had invented the expression). One St. Paulite has simple binder.

	Mn.	Ia.	N.D.	S.D.	Nb.	Ave.
elastic (band)	14%	0	15%	7%	3%	8%
rubber	5%	0	0	4%	8%	3%
~ band	83%	100%	96%	93%	97%	93%
~ binder	17%	0	4%	0	0	6%

CL 118: Checklist returns strongly confirm the field data. Rubber band is universal. Rubber binder is sharply focused in the Twin Cities trading area, with 37 instances in the lower three-fourths of the state, two instances in Iowa, and one each in the other states: Mn. 4.1, 15.1, 17.2, 22.2, 26.1, 32.1, 34.3-4, 35.1, 38.1, 41.1, 41.3, 42.1, 44.2, 46.1-3, 47.1, 53.1-2, 54.1-5, 55.2-3, 55.7, 55.9, 55.11-12, 56.1-2, 62.1-2, 79.3, 83.2; Ia. 45.1, 52.3; N.D. 29.2; S.D. 12.2; Nb. 65.2. Of the five examples outside Minnesota three were checked by respondents who had once lived in Minnesota, and the mother of the fourth had moved to Nebraska from Wisconsin, close to Minnesota.

Elastic band is checked by 42 respondents scattered throughout the five states, mostly in the southwest quadrant: Mn. 3.3, 4.3, 5a.10, 10.1, 80.3; Ia. 42.3, 55.2, 69.1, 86.1; N.D. 3.3, 6.5, 9.3, 18.2, 43.3, 53.3; S.D. 5.2, 7.2, 30.4, 32.2, 33.2, 47.1, 49.2, 51.4, 52.1, 65.2-3.

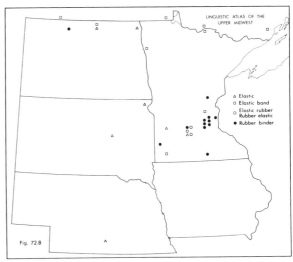

Fig. 72.8

band 16; 123, 125, 129, 134, 143; 426.
elastic †35, 42, 45; 205, 208, ¹219; 307, 316; 430. ~ band 1-3, c5, 8, 31, 60; 201, 204. ~ rubber 44.
rubber ¹→38, 44-45, 56; 316; 413, 424, 432. ~ elastic 43, 45.
rubber band :4, c5, 6-7, 9-12, c13, 14-15, 17-18, c19, 20-30, →31, 32-34, 37, 40-43, s44, 45-55, s56, 57-58, r59, 60-61, 63-65; 101-17, 119-22, 124, 126-28, 130-33, 135-42, 144-50, 152; 201-2, †203, 204-26; 301-6, 308-15, 317-28; 401-23, 425-37.
rubber binder ¹22, →24, †26, 33-34, →35, c36, 37-39, *43, s¹46, 47, s¹56, ¹58, 62; 203. binder 36.
rubber ring 44.
no response 118, 151.

Comment:

elastic band: Usu.--31. rubber: "Girls in the office generally just say, 'Give me a "rubber"'"--38. Usu.--31. rubber band: Usu.--33. rubber binder: "Not so common, but I've heard it"--22. Inf. says this is common here--26. "Some people don't know what that is, so you say 'rubber band'"--34. Inf. says this is used by girls in offices--58.

72.9 address a letter.

Nearly all UM infs. 'address' a letter. Only five retain older back. Its non-Northern origin is suggested by its five instances in Iowa and the one in Minnesota from an inf. with southern Ohio and Alabama parentage.

address 29-31, 35-36, 38; 101-17, c119, 120-31, 133-50, 152; 201-17, 219-26; 301-4, 306-27; 401-37.
back 35; 113, 130, 132, 136; ¹†433.

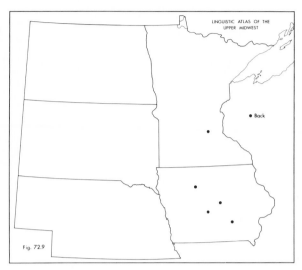

LINGUISTIC ATLAS OF THE UPPER MIDWEST

• Back

Fig. 72.9

no response 1-28, 32-34, 37, 39; 118, 151; 218; 305, 328.

73.2 Who taught you that? NE 666.

Two terms, taught and LEARNED, are found in the context of the same question. Other contexts appear in conversation: "They learn him to go after it"--25; "Who taught you such a trick?"--43; "My wife learnt her to cook"--51; "I tried to learn him"--112; "Who learnt you them naughty words?"--209; "You could learn them 'gee' and 'haw' in no time"--314; "That learnt me a whole lot"--322. And the participle appears in "She [a dog] was taught to be a baby"--204. (For the preterit forms of LEARNED see Vol. 2.)

The somewhat higher frequency of LEARNED in Iowa accords with Atwood's finding a higher frequency outside New England. The UM proportion, however, is much lower than the one-half to three-fourths found in the eastern United States, a fact presumably owing to school insistence that the only correct word is taught. Although nearly one-third of the uneducated use learn in the sense of 'teach,' only a handful of Type II do, and none in Type III.

LEARNED c13, 17, 19, !¹21, c25, 35, †40, 44, 48, c51; 101, 104, c105, c112, c113, 114, c132, 135, 138, 140, 142, 146-47; 209, 212, 220, 224; cvr305, 306, c314, c322; 407, 429-30, 432, 434.

taught 1-3, :4, 5-6, c7, 8-12, 14-17, c18, c20, 21-24, 26, :27, 28, c29, c30, 31-34, 36-43, cr?44, 45-46, c47, 49-50, c51, 52-60, c61, 62-65; 102-3, 106, c107, 108-11, 115-17, 119-31, 133-34, 136-37, 139, 141, f142, 143-45, 148-50, 152; 201-3, c204, 205-8, 210, c211, 213-

19, cr?220, 221-23, 225-26; 301-5, c306, 307-13, 315-21, 323-26, c327, 328; c401, 402-6, 408-16, c417, 418-28, cvr431, 433, 435-36, :437.

no response 118, 151.

73.3 children's nickname for one who "tattles." NE 587.

As in New England, the common, usually derisive term for one who "tattles" is tattle-tale. Tell-tale survives with two Minnesota and Iowa infs. Several minor New England variants do not occur in the UM, but several new ones do appear as rare forms: bawl baby, blabbermouth (but both blabber and blabmouth are in LANE), little liar, snitch baby and snitcher (but snitch is reported once in LANE from New Brunswick), squawker, stooge, stoolpigeon, tillytale, and whispering bird. The only inferable regional significance lies in the four snitch forms in the Twin Cities and the four instances of squealer in Midland territory (although it is a minor variant in New England).

bawl baby 26.
blabber mouth 404.
little liar 316.
snitch 35. ~ baby 34, 37. ~er 37; 101.
squawker 429.
squealer 111, 120; 411, 437.
stooge →219.
stoolpigeon 425.
tale bearer 219.
tattle 319. ~r 23, 46; 102; !207; 302, 323; 424, 434. ~tale 1-7, !8, 9-18, !19, 20-22, 24-30, !31, 32-34, 36-45, s¹46, 47-51, !52, 53-54, !55, 56-58, :59, 60-65; 101-11, 113-17, 119-27, 129-34, 136-39, 141-46, s147, 148-50, 152; 201, !202, 203-6, 208-18, †219, !220, 221-23, !224, 225-26; 301-5, s306, 307-22, 324-26; 401-6, !407, 408-16, !417, 418-22, !423, 425-26, !427, 428-29, !430, 431-35, 437. ~taler :?135.
telltale 45; 111.
tillytale 121.
whispering bird ¹25.
no response 112, 118, 128, 140, 151; 327-28; 436.

73.4 pick flowers. NE 252.

In the context "Will you pick some flowers for a bouquet?" the usual UM term is pick. Variants found in New England also occur, but weakly. Gather is used by 19 infs., mostly in Midland territory, but 10 of them also use pick. Cut is offered by 13, mostly in Iowa, but only five have this as their only term. Its meaning is probably restricted to picking with the aid of shears or

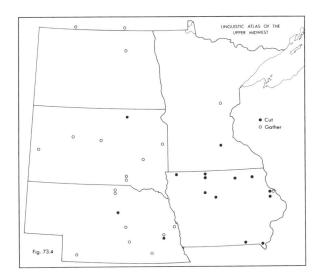

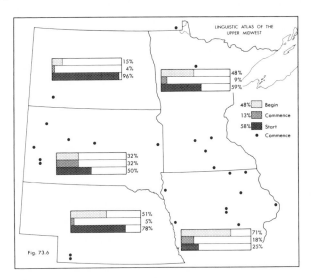

a knife. <u>Pluck</u>, not found in southwestern New England, has scattered appearance, as does <u>pull</u> in Iowa and Nebraska. The comment below reveals certain semantic descriptions.

cut 48; 101, 103-4, 106, 108, 113-14, 119, 121, 147, 149; 305; 414, 425, s432.
gather 23, ꟾ57; 119; 201-2, 213; 302, 310, c314, 317, 322-23, c327; 405-6, 420, 422, 424, 428-29, 432.
get 15, 18; 149.
pick 1, 3-14, 16-43, ꟾ44, 45-65; 101-13, 115-17, 119-27, 129-46, 148, 150, 152; 203-13, 215-26; 301-9, 311-13, 315-21, 324-28; 401-4, 406-13, ꟾ414, 415-19, 421, 423-24, 426-31, 433-37.
pluck ꟾ40, 44; 101, 130; 317.
pull 132, 149; 420, 429.
no response 2; 118, 128, 151; 214.

Comment:

<u>cut</u>: 'Cut' garden flowers but 'pick' or 'pluck' wildflowers--101, 106, 108. 'Cut' large flowers but 'pick' small ones--104, 111. pick: "They say 'pick' quite a bit, but I think 'pluck' is the best one"--44. pluck: "You 'pluck' chickens"--45. <u>pull</u>: Usu.--429.

73.6 He <u>began</u> to talk. NE 635.

In the context of the key sentence UM infs. use the preterit of one of these three verbs: <u>begin</u>, <u>commence</u>, and <u>start</u>. Started, the minority form in New England, has become the majority form in the UM, a fact accentuated by its highest frequency among the youngest group, Type III. BEGAN (for variants see Vol. 2), has likewise gained in acceptance. <u>Commenced</u>, on the contrary, seems to be losing ground.

A regional bias is suggested by the higher incidence of BEGAN forms in Iowa and Nebraska and of <u>start</u> in Minnesota and North Dakota, although <u>start</u> is also widespread in Nebraska.

BEGAN 4, 7-8, 11-12, 14, 18, 22-24, 29, ?30, 32-33, c37, 39-40, 42, 46, 48-51, 54-55, c56, 57-58, 61, f62, 63-65; c103, 104, c105, 106, 108, 111-13, 115, c116, 121-23, 125-27, 129-31, c132, 134, 136-38, c139, 140-49, s150; 206, 214-15, 217; 312, c315, 318-19, 321, 325-26; 401-2, c403, 405, 408-10, cvr413, c414, s418, 419-21, 424, cvr427, 428, 433-35.
commenced 1, c10, ꟾ13, c35, 44, cvr51, 63; c105, c107, c109, c116, ꟾ122, 124, c132-33, c135, c139, s150; c215; c301, 302, c309, cvr311, 312, cvr314, c317; cvr429, 437.
started 2, c3, 5-6, 9-10, 13, 15-18, c19, 20-21, 24-29, cr30, 31, 34, 38, 41, 43-45, 47, 50-53, 55, 58-60, 64; 101-2, c107, 108, 110-11, 114-15, 117, 119-20, s121, 150, s152; 201, c202, 203-6, c207, 208, c209, 210, c211-14, 215-16, 218-20, c221, 222-24, c225, 226; 302-4, 310, 313, 320, c322, 323-24, 326, 328; 403-4, 406-12, c414, 415, c416-17, 418-19, c422, 423-27, cvr428, cvr430, 431-32, c434, 436-37.
no response 36; 118, 128, 151; 305-8, 316, 327.

74.3b The road was <u>slippery</u>.

Because this item was added after the beginning of the UM survey there are only five instances for Minnesota, all of the term <u>slippery</u>. This hint of Northern orientation is supported by the exclusive use of <u>slippery</u> by North Dakota infs., with some decrease in its fre-

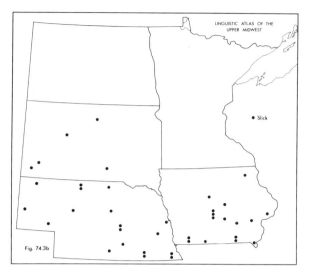

LINGUISTIC ATLAS OF THE
UPPER MIDWEST

• Slick

Fig. 74.3b

quency in South Dakota and still more
in Nebraska. Slick, on the other hand,
clearly has Midland bias despite its
spread into Northern speech territory.
Where the two terms conflict, some speakers assign them to different meanings,
such as slippery for a blacktop road
and slick for ice (403), or slippery
for either a wet road or an icy road
but slick for only an icy road (303),
or slick for a sled runner but slippery
for a road (401).

slick	Mn.	Ia.	N.D.	S.D.	Nb.	Ave.
slick		34%	0	19%	50%	
slippery		79%	100%	89%	64%	

CL 125: Strong confirmation of the
Northern-Midland contrast of slippery
and slick is provided by 918 checklist
respondents, especially in the Iowa
breakdown. Slippery has a 91% response
in northern Iowa and 61% in southern
Iowa; slick has 22% in northern and 48%
in southern. Two write-in instances of
greasy occur, one in northern Minnesota
from a respondent of Polish parentage
(12.2) and one in northeastern Iowa from
a respondent of Illinois parentage (23.1).

	Mn.	Ia.	N.D.	S.D.	Nb.	Ave.
slick	7%	34%	13%	31%	51%	30%
slippery	99%	78%	95%	85%	72%	84%

  icy 307, 316.
  skiddy 120.
  slick 108, 115, ¹128, 129-32, 134,
136, 140, 142-43, 145-47, 150, 152; 302,
304, 320-21, 326; c401, ¹402, 403-4,
c405, 410, 412, c414, 417, 420-21, c423,
424, 427, 431-35.
  slippery 29-31, 38; 101-6, 108-17,
119, 121-23, 125-28, 130-33, 135, 137-
38, 141, 144, 148-50, 152; 201-3, 205-
26; 301-13, 315-19, ¹320, 322-25, ¹326,

327-28; 401-3, 406-11, 413, 415-16, 418-
19, 421-23, 425-26, 428, !430, 436-37.
  no response 1-28, 32-37, 39-65; 107,
118, 124, 139, 151; 204; 314; 429.

76.1 Hole in a road.

  For a hole or depression in a street
or road a frequent UM term is chuckhole,
used by a majority of the infs. in Midland speech areas -- Iowa, South Dakota,
and Nebraska. Minnesota was not investigated. Chuckhole competes with the
simple generic hole, used by a majority
in the two Dakotas but much less frequent in Midland territory. A minor variant, pothole, is strong in North Dakota
but not elsewhere in the four states for
which data are available.
  Where these terms conflict, special
secondary meanings may develop. Thus a
chuckhole may be considered smaller than
a hole (224), it becomes a "pothole"
when filled with water during a rain
(203), it is found on a dirt or gravel
road but not on a paved road (418, 422,
424), or it may be found only in a road
in winter.
  Likewise a pothole may be larger than
a hole by extending across a road (216)
or it may be only in a field or pasture
and not in a road at all (324).
  Infrequent are blowout, blowup, chop
hole, ditchout, frost boil, mud hole,
pitch hole, rut, sink hole, thank you
ma'am, and washout.
  Volunteered also were the terms washboard (306; 420) or washboard road (224),
to describe a road with successive rip-
ples or small transverse ridges, and
heaves, to describe a road, particularly
of concrete, with undulations caused
usually by settling or by frost action.

	Mn.	Ia.	N.D.	S.D.	Nb.	Ave.
chuckhole		80%	42%	56%	86%	
hole		10%	66%	56%	25%	
pothole		2%	35%	7%	3%	

CL 133: The 913 respondents even more
decidedly identify chuckhole or chughole as the dominant UM form, with a
very slight Midland preference. North
Dakotans again are revealed as less
likely to use anything but the generic
hole rather than chuckhole but they also appear, along with Minnesotans, as
users of pothole, which definitely is
not Midland. One Minnesotan (54.5) and
one South Dakotan (12.3) volunteer
frost boil and a Nebraskan (74.2) offers a nonce-use of knot hole. Two --
a Minnesotan (37.2) and an Iowan (17.3)
-- wrote in washboard. "Potholes are
out on the prairie--usually springs,"
writes a southwest Minnesotan (50.3).

	Mn.	Ia.	N.D.	S.D.	Nb.	Ave.
chuckhole	80%	86%	70%	86%	90%	84%
chug hole	2%	5%	4%	2%	5%	4%
hole	11%	12%	24%	18%	14%	15%
pothole	20%	1%	20%	9%	0	15%

blowout 302. blowup 428.

chop hole 219.

chuck 101, †131, 148-49; 428. ~ hole 29-30, ⊥31; 101, s102, 103-4, s105-6, 107-13, ⊥114, 115, 117, 119-22, s⊥123, 124-30, 132-35, s137, 138-42, 145-47, 150, s⊥152; †202, snc203, 204, 209, sn214, s⊥215, 218, :225, s226; 303-4, 307-8, sn309, 310, ⊥312, sn313, 314, :315, 316, 320-21, s322, 325, s⊥326, 328; 401-2, :sn403, 404, sn405, 406-13, s414, 416, ⊥417, sn418-19, 420-24, 426, s427-28, 429-31, s432, 433-34, sn436, 437.

chug hole s136, 143; 418, 435. chunk hole 307.

ditchout 137.

frost boil 220.

gulch 317.

hole 30-31, 35-36, 38; 105-6, 131-32, 150; 201-6, 209-10, ?211, 212, 214-18, 223-24, 226; 301-4, 309, 311-14, 318, 323-27; 401, 405, 417-19, 424, 427, 434, 436. mud ~ 139. pitch ~ 116; 208.

pothole 123; sn202-3, 204, 207, sn210, cr211, sn213, 216-17; 309, 319; 425.

rut 121, 141; 420, 432.

sink hole 220.

thank you ma'am ⊥214; 311, 322.

washout 414.

no response 1-28, 32-34, 37, 39-65; 118, 144, 151; 305; 415.

Comment:

blowout: A hole in a dirt or gravel road--302. blowup: Caused at joints in pavement by freezing--428. chuck: "The road is full of 'chucks'"--101. "Not used since pioneer days. It's a break in a corduroy bush road"--202. chuckhole: In mud, but not pavement--418, 422, 424. Esp. "on rutty road; a pretty good-sized hole."--325. Usu. on a winter road--223. A foot across; a 'hole' is always larger--224. Smaller than a 'hole'--224. Chughole: Inf. says this is the "correct" form--418. hole: Usu.--150. pitch hole: Both inf. and his wife say this is common here--208. pothole: Inf. says this is a 'chuckhole' with water in it--203. Larger than a 'hole,' extending all across a road--216. In any road, esp. paved--425. 'Potholes' are not in a road, but are in fields or pastures--224; 324. rut: a hole, not a furrow--420.

76.2a Askew or diagonal. NE 547.

Except in the final stage this item

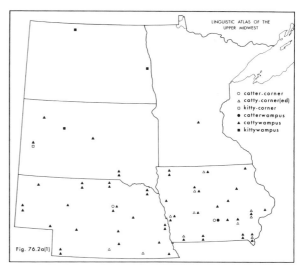

Fig. 76.2a(1)

LINGUISTIC ATLAS OF THE UPPER MIDWEST

○ catter-corner
△ catty-corner(ed)
□ kitty-corner
● catterwampus
▲ cattywampus
■ kittywampus

was not sought in Minnesota. Since fieldworkers varied considerably in their interpretation of its meaning, the data from the four other states are not easily classified. The central meaning usually sought is "diagonal" or "diagonally," as with reference to what extends or moves at an angle other than a right angle across any surface. Related is the meaning "not at the normal angle, that is, not at a right angle," as with reference to anything out of line, out, of plumb, or askew. An easy semantic shift is to the sense "disordered" or "irregular."

Comments of both infs. and fieldworkers sometimes indicate the specific meaning intended, but usually the reply is recorded without such indication. Fieldworker A shifted emphasis from the "irregular" meaning in North Dakota to the "diagonal" meaning in South Dakota, a fact perhaps accounting for the dominance of North Dakota by every which way and the appearance of cater-corner and its variants only in Iowa and Nebraska despite its known occurrence in New England. Two variants having /e/ rather than /æ/, with three instances in Iowa and Nebraska, may be only idiosyncratic spelling pronunciations, but they nevertheless parallel a similar singleton in lower Connecticut. Catering, also with /e/, appears once in the speech of an Iowa inf. both of whose parents were born in New York, and it likewise parallels three New England instances in New Hampshire, Vermont, and eastern Connecticut.

Despite the variety of fieldworker approaches and the uncertainty of the precise semantic assignment, the absence of cattywampus in New England and its high

frequency in Iowa, Nebraska, and southwestern South Dakota strongly identify
it as Midland. (For the use of this term
see also 76.2b, CL 134.)

Several unusual minor equivalents are
listed below.

antigodlin 101, 145; ¹405, ¹434. antigoglin 403.

askew 122.

cater/kætɚ/-corner 131; c413. ~/ketɚ/-
cornered 126.

catering 116.

catterwampus 131.

catty-angling †125. ~-corner 103, 124,
127, 142, 149; 431, 433. ~-cornered 113,
s133, 136-37, 152. ~-cross 421.

cattywampus sn30; 101-3, s104, 108,
s111, sn112, 113, s114-15, 117, 122,
s123, sn124, 125, 127-28, s¹129-30, 132,
s133, 134-35, 138, 140, 143-47, sn148,
150; 301, sn309, ¹*310, c311, 314, ¹315,
320, ¹321, 322-23; 401, 403, !404, 405-
7, !408, s†409, !410, 411, sn412, 413-
14, 416, 418, s420, 421, sn423, 426-29,
435-37.

cockeyed 128.

cornerways with the world 114.

crooked 110, 129. ~ with the world
104.

erratic 128.

every way 147.

every which way s31; 106, 120, s121;
203, 205, 208, 211, sn213, 215, 217-18,
¹219, 222-23; 326; 413, 424, c425, 431.

goglin across 322.

kitty-corner 310. ~wampus *203, ¹218,
sn221; 302, ¹304.

out of plum 111.

screwgied 108.

sidegoglin 407.

skiwobbily 115.

skweegy 109.

skygoglin 413, 429.

this way and that way c31; 201-2, 205,
207, 215, 224; c321; s?430.

whee-whaw s?¹145.

no response 1-29, 32-65; 105, 107,
118-19, 139, 141, 151; 204, 206, 209-10,
212, 214, 216, ?220, 225-26; 303, 305-8,
312-13, 316-19, 324-25, ?327, 328; 402,
415, 417, 419, 422.

Comment:

antigodlin: Twisted around--405.
Crooked--434. catercorner: "The house
is catercorner through the block"--413.
catty-angling: Used by inf.'s father
(from Ga.)--125. catty-corner: Diagonal-
ly--124; 431, 433. catty-cross: Diagonal-
ly--421. cattywampus: A lot of noise;
perhaps a riot--103. "All right. Hunky-
dory"--309. Diagonally--30; 320, 322-23;
412-14, 416, 418, 423, 426-29, 437.
Crooked--130, 148; 401, 407-9, 411, 436.

LINGUISTIC ATLAS OF THE
UPPER MIDWEST

● Everywhich way
△ This way and that way

Fig. 76.2a(2)

Aimlessly--421. In a mess--301. Twisted
around--405. Of a building out of line
with the lot--117. Set at an angle--122.
Of a building which is not square; "leaning from age"--147. Askew--150; 314;
406, 412, 436. = catty-corner--221. "He
lives cattywampus across the street"--
437. "He pointed cattywampus across the
street"--311. "It went cattywampus a-
cross the yard"--429. Like a short cut--
323. "Cattywampus of the bed," i.e., diagonally across it--403. Out of plumb--
404. Of a crooked mirror or picture--
406-8, 411. Of crooked driving--408.
every which way: Meandering--222. "My
hair is blowing every which way"--326.
No pattern--413. Irregular--431. goglin
across: Winding--322. kitty-corner: Di-
agonally--310. kittywampus: Diagonally--
302. skygoglin: "I cut it skygoglin,"
i.e., on the bias--429. this way and
that way: Irregular--430.

76.2b   sashaying.

More than one-half of the UM infs.
queried (not including most of those in
Mn.) use sashaying to describe the action of a woman who enters a room with
self-conscious body movements intended
to attract attention. The notion of deliberately exaggerated motion seems to
attach also to such minor equivalents
as flirting along, strutting, and swaggering.

The pronounced hip-swaying characteristic of the preceding sense suggests
another meaning, that of uncertain or
uneven movement. For some infs. this is
the dominant meaning of sashaying, and
it apparently is central in such variants as going cattywampus (cp. 76.2a),
going squeegy, meandering, moseying,

seesawing, shimmying, staggering, swaying, weaving, wheewhawing, wiggling, wabbling, and zigzagging. Zigzagging is offered by about one-third of the infs.

No clear regional pattern emerges with these terms except that going cattywampus is limited to Midland speech territory. A temporal pattern is suggested, however, by the remarks of several infs. that sashaying is an old-fashioned term no longer heard and by the fact that, while two-thirds of the Type I infs. use it, only one-half of those in Type II do.

CL 134: Except for the data for sashaying, returns from 793 respondents do not closely correspond to those from field interviews, a difference ascribable to the fact that, although the checklist clue is simply the phrase "going from side to side," the field-workers usually sought a reply by suggesting a social situation.

Nearly two-thirds of the respondents check sashaying, but nearly all the others, especially in Midland areas, check going cattywampus, apparently often in a sense more appropriate to others, especially in Midland areas, check going cattywampus, apparently often in a sense more appropriate to that treated in 76.2a. Many voluntarily wrote in swaying, weaving, and zigzagging, as follows:

	Mn.	Ia.	N.D.	S.D.	Nb.	Ave.
cattywampus	13%	37%	19%	26%	48%	31%
sashaying	69%	63%	59%	61%	60%	63%
weaving	2%	1%	2%	4%		2%
zigzagging	4%	4%	2%	5%	1%	3%

In addition, a number of minor variants occur, all of which are voluntary write-ins except antigodling, antigogling, and slabbing. The first two of these are clearly Midland.

In the checklists the minor variants are checked or written in as follows: antigodling: Mn. 60.3; Ia. 92.2, 94.1; S.D. 16.2; Nb. 19.2, 34.2, 47.4, 84.1, 87.2. antigogling: Ia. 98.1; S.D. 25.1, 33.6, 45.3; Nb. 57.3, 82.2, 93.3. careening: S.D. 55.1. dodging in and out: S.D. 12.2. rocking: S.D. 49.1. seesawing: Mn. 60.2; N.D. 20.1, 22.2, 30.1; S.D. 42.1, 69.1; Nb. 24.2. shimmying: N.D. 24.3. sidestepping: S.D. 38.3. sideswaying: N.D. 43.3. sigsagging: N.D. 3.3 [respondent with Norwegian background]. skidding: 50.3. slabbing: Mn. 26.4, 71.2; N.D. 6.1, 28.3, 43.1. staggering: Mn. 29.1; Ia. 11.2, 49.2; N.D. 23.3, 31.2; S.D. 22.1; Nb. 43.1. swerving: N.D. 23.1; S.D. 12.1. swinging: S.D. 62.2. wobbling: Mn. 56.2, 85.1; Ia. 23.1, 47.1, 51.2; N.D. 46.2;

S.D. 3.2, 49.1; Nb. 8.1, 61.1. wandering: N.D. 6.4. wigwagging: Mn. 33.2.

A few checklist respondents added comments as well. For sashaying there were written the following: "I use [sic] to call this 'sideways'"--Mn. 71.4; "Little use"--N.D. 50.2; "Drunk"--S.D. 21.2; "In square dancing only"--Nb. 51.1. For cattywampus there are these remarks: "Same as 'cattycorner'"--Nb. 40.3; "More particularly used to denote going diagonally cross-country"--Nb. 48.1; "Diagonally"--Nb. 51.1; "Should be 'caddywampus'"--Ia. 40.3.

bustling in 319.
flirting along 432.
going cattywampus s108, 119, 132; 418.
going squeegy 109.
meandering 416.
moseying 306; 431.
reeling 103.
sashaying 31, 35; s104, s107, sn116, 117, 121-22, sn123-24, 125, 130-31, s133, 135-36, s137, 139-40, 142, 145-46, s148; 201-4, !205, 207-8, 210, 212, sn213, 214-17, s†220, 221-22, 225; 301-4, †309, 310-11, !†312, !313, !315, 320-22, :323, s324, 326; 401-2, †403, 404-6, 408, sn409, 410-14, 418-19, sn422, 423, 426-27, 429, sn431, s435, 436-37.
seesawing 206.
shimmying 308.
staggering 149.
strutting 29, 38; 210-11, 217, 223, ?224; 317-18; 416, 420, 423, 425, 427-28, 433.
swaggering 29.
swaying 307.
weaving 101, 104, 106, 138, 150; 210, 224; 317-19; 402, 432.
whee-whawing 127. wiggling 317. wobbling 101, 111, 113; 317.
zigzagging 29, 35; 101, 108, 110-12, 119, 121, 139, 152; 204, 209-10, 214-17, 222-24, 226; :303, 304, 312, 314-15, 319, 321, 323-25; 413-14, 417, sn421, 422-23, 426-27, cvr428, 430-31, sn433, 435. zigging and zagging 212. going zig-zag 105.
no response 1-28, 32-34, 36-37, 39-65; 102, 114-15, 118, 120, 126, 128-29, 134, 141, 143-44, 147, 151; 206-7, ?218-19; 305, 316, 327-28; 407, 415, 424.

Comment:

going cattywampus: Unsteady on one's feet--119. sashaying: Strutting or walking with a flourish--31; 131; 202, 216, 222; 301, 303, 309-10, 313, 326; 401, 408, 410-12, 418-19, 427, 429, 436-37. "Putting on airs"--207. "Going around with airs a little bit"--304. Showing off "with mincing steps"--402. Swaggering--201, 222; 302, 312; 403, 431. Cavorting--35. "Smart-alecky"--414. Moving erratically--116. Staggering--117. Wobbling--136. Moving to the side--124. Sidestepping--125, 130, 142. Going in a crooked or circuitous route--320. Swerving around obstacles--323; 419. Weaving; "sashaying all over the road"--423. Merely moving or going--146; 311. 'Sashay' is synonymous with 'shy': a horse 'sashays' or 'shies'--142. Prancing or jumping around; "The horse would sashay a-about"--409. "Don't hear this much any more"--148. "That word ain't been used for many years"--220. whee-whawing: Staggering--127.

76.3a marbles.

Although data are largely missing from Minnesota, it is clear that marbles is the generic name for any of several children's games as well as for the small balls of clay, glass, steel, or other material with which the games are played. Many infs. have neither other term nor terms for particular varieties of marbles. For the game itself one inf. in Iowa uses the singular marble.

Migs and mibs are two widely known equivalents. Migs, with variants megs, mickies, and miggles, may have a Midland orientation although it extends into North Dakota. Mibs, with variants mibbles and possibly nibs, may have a Northern orientation. A 1954 radio series reporting UM findings produced letters from scattered eastern Minnesota listeners who affirmed mibs as their childhood term, although one resident of Owatonna, in southeastern Minnesota, recalled also that migs was used there between 1907 and 1920.

Some of the general and specific names found in the UM are also recorded in Kelsie B. Harder, "The Vocabulary of Marble Playing," *Publication of the American Dialect Society*, No. 23 (1955), pp. 3-33, but Harder does not have the following: bumpers, cornelians, dibs, mibbles, mickies, miggies, mossies, nibs, taw marbles, or two-lickers. None of these occurs with such frequency as to warrant an inference about distribution, except that dibs is found only in Canada.

agates 108. aggies 119, 137.
bummer marble 119.
commies 108-9, 148.
chinas 120.
cornelians 101, 108.
dibs →¹201, 202.
flints 148.
glassies 108, 119.
marbles 29-31, 35; 101-3, 105-17, 119,
122-38, 142-46, 148-50, 152; 201, 203-8, 210-11, 216-17, 220, 223-26; 302-8, 311, 313-14, 316-19, 322-26; 401, 403, 407, 413-17, 420-24, 426-37.
  megs 315; 411.
  mibs 35, 38; 111, *117, *123, 124, 128; 301, 309, :sn310; 418. mibbles 222.
  mickies *209.
  migs 111, 125, 130, ?143; sn204, 213, 218-19, 222; 312, 320, *328; 402, 406, sn407, 408-10, 412, c419, †422, 425, s428. miggies ⁱ†215. miggles 404.
  mossies 109. nibs 119.
  taws 121, 125, 145, 150. taw marbles 434.
  two-lickers 121.
  no response 1-28, 32-34, 36-37, 39-65; 104, 118, 139-41, 147, 151; ?212, 214, 221; 321, ?327; 405.

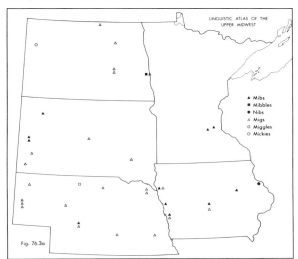

Fig. 76.3a

Comment:
  bummer: Large marble--119. marbles: "Children that played marble [sic]"--136. taw: A heavy marble--125. A large shooting marble--150. two-lickers: Small marbles--121.

76.3b starting line in marbles.

In some marble games the players toss, throw, shoot, or "lag" the taw marble from a line scratched in the ground. In the UM (data are not available from Minnesota) three sets of terms usually appear: lag(ging) line, taw or toe line, and starting line. Except that the variant toe seems to be limited to Northern speech territory, the distribution of the taw and lag expressions is not typical. Responses including taw appear throughout Iowa and also in southeastern Nebraska and the Black Hills of South Dakota. In Iowa, on the other hand, the lag forms appear only four times, twice in Dubuque, along the Mississippi, and twice in the extreme west, along the Missouri, but they are common in Nebraska and extend into South Dakota and eastern North Dakota.

That toe line results from folk etymology is supported by a South Dakotan's remark that it is so called because "You had to get your toes up there." The variant tawl, with excrescent /l/, is reported by Harder (see 76.3a) as being Southern.

Starting line is scattered and not common. Dead line, doubtful marble line, mark, scratch, shooting line, and throw line appear once each.

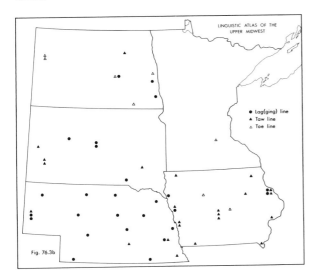

Fig. 76.3b

CL 136: Returns from 740 respondents confirm the evidence in the field data that lag (line) is strong in Nebraska and South Dakota but that taw (line) is strong in Iowa. Indeed, the checklist shows additionally a Midland leaning in Iowa, with a 48% frequency in the southern half in contrast with a 19% return in the northern. Starting line, provided as a choice on the checklist, was encircled by more than one-half the respondents, with probably Northern dominance. No instances of toe line were written in.

	Mn.	Ia.	N.D.	S.D.	Nb.	Ave.
lag(ging) line	16%	14%	20%	29%	44%	26%
starting ~	77%	56%	73%	62%	42%	61%
taw (~)	8%	32%	7%	13%	11%	15%

dead line 320.
lag line 111, 119, 123; *218, sn222; :323; 402, 404, :406, 408, 410-12, 414, 416, :†418, 419-20, 425, 428, 433, 437. lagging ~ 111, 120; :!225; 302, 314-15.

marble line ?322.
mark 220.
scratch 119.
shooting line 202.
starting line 38; 147; 211, ¹†215; ?316; 407, ¹413, 421, s431.
taw 101, 108, 116, 119, :122, 124-25, 129-30, 141, s152; 309, s310, 312, *328; 409. ~ line 120, 128, 143, 150; 213; s301, 311; 422, 425, sn434.
throw line ¹427.
toe line 35; 113, 132; *209, 210, 218, 220, :224; ¹304.
no response 1-29, ?30, :?31, 32-34, 36-37, 39-65; 102-7, 109-10, 112, 114-15, 117-18, 121, 126-27, 131, 133-40, 142, 144-46, 148-49, 151; 201, ?203, 204-6, ?207-8, ?212, 214, ?216-17, 219, 221, 223, 226; ?303, 305-8, ?313, 317-19, 321, ?324-25, :326, ?327; 401, ?403, 405, 415, 417, 423-24, 426, ?429, 430, 432, 435-36.

Comment:

marble line: Inf. may have improvised this term during the interview--322. scratch: "Start from 'taw' or 'scratch,' which is the 'lag line'"--119. taw: Starting line or a heavy marble--125. tawl: "Here the boys lag for 'tawls'"--404. toe line: "Because you had to get your toes up there"--220. no response: "Country boys didn't play much marbles" --430.

76.4 goose pimples.

A slight bristling of the hairs of the skin because of cold or fear is known as goose pimples to four out of five UM infs. (This item was not generally sought in Minnesota.) Most of the other infs., spread throughout the four states investigated, use goose flesh.

The variant goose bumps appears only in Iowa, with one Nebraskan reporting it as a heard term; it may have Midland orientation. Duck bumps seems to be a facetious synonym used by persons who otherwise say goose pimples or goose flesh. Also rare are chicken skin, goose hide, and goose skin.

	Ia.	N.D.	S.D.	Nb.	Ave.
goose flesh	29%	21%	19%	19%	23%
~ pimples	80%	75%	85%	89%	82%

CL 135: Returns from 906 respondents correspond closely to the field data for the two main terms. In addition, the checking of goose bumps offers a further hint that it is Midland oriented: Mn. 54.5, 64.2; Ia. 70.3; S.D. 11.3, 22.2, 25.1, 47.1, 48.1; Nb. 23.1, 33.1, 35.1, 39.2, 44.1, 56.2, 57.3, 65.2, 90.2. For 13 of these 18 respondents goose bumps

is only an alternate form.

Duck bumps likewise is usually only
an alternate form. It is checked by the
following: Mn. 26.3; Ia. 90.2; N.D.
30.2, 32.1, 50.3; S.D. 25.1, 58.2; Nb.
6.1, 44.1, 56.5; for all of whom except
two (S.D. 58.2 and Nb. 44.1) it occurs
along with either goose flesh or goose
pimples.

	Mn.	Ia.	N.D.	S.D.	Nb.	Ave.
goose flesh	15%	27%	27%	19%	29%	24%
~ pimples	91%	82%	84%	89%	82%	85%

chicken flesh ¹212.
chicken skin 223.
duck bumps *221; 414.
goose bumps 120, 131, 133; ¹403.
goose flesh 29, 31; 102-4, 112, 116,
119-20, *122, 125, 132, 134, 137, 146-
47; !202, 213-15, 219; 309, s311, 314,
320, 323-24; 402, 412, 419, c422, 426,
432-33.
goose hide 417.
goose pimples ¹29, 30-31, s35, 36, 38;
101, 104-11, 113-17, 119, 121-22, 124,
126-30, 133, 134-45, 148-50, 152; 201,
204-5, :sn207, 208-9, !210, 211-12, 216-
17, *218, :sn220, 221-24, 226; 301-8,
310, 313-15, *316, 317-19, 321, 323,
325-28; 401-6, :407, 408-11, 413-16,
418-21, 423-31, 433-37.
goose skin 206.
no response 1-28, 32-34, 37, 39-65;
118, 123, 151; 203, 225; 312, 322.

Comment:

duck bumps: Used facetiously--414.
goose pimples: Inf. says this is the
most common term here--31; 133. Usu.--
419.

76.5   cowboy.

This item was added for the fieldwork
in South Dakota and Nebraska in order
to elicit vocabulary of the cattle
country. Western North Dakota infs.,
already interviewed, were asked by mail
to report their choices.

A ranch employee who works with cattle
is still widely identified by cowboy or,
less often, by cowpuncher and in Nebraska by cowpoke. All three terms reflect
the days of the open range, when such
employees were specialists in riding the
range, rounding up cattle and branding
calves, and breaking horses. Several
infs. consider these terms already old-
fashioned or report them as used in pejorative or derisive contexts with
special reference to easterners who affect what they think is western dress.

The more diversified employee on a
modern mechanized ranch is increasingly
likely to be called by cowhand or ranchhand. In the Nebraska sandhill country
are also found hay-waddy and cow-waddy,
and the newer hayhand. In the sandhills
ranchers raise hay as a crop for feed for
their cattle.

One southwest Nebraskan recalls older
buckeroo, reminiscent of the days of the
northbound cattle drives but now obsolete.

Bronc(o) buster specifically refers
to a specialist in breaking wild range
horses. He may or may not be also a cowpuncher or ranchhand.

bronc(o) buster †414, 416.
buckeroo †429.
dude rancher →418.
cowboy 214-15; †302, 310, c311-12,
313, 326, 328; c401, 402, c403-4, 406-
7, †409-10, c411, 412, †413, cvr414,
416-20, sn421, c422, 423-28, c†429,
430-31, 433-34, 436-37. armchair ~ c404.
monkey ward ~ c311. pool hall ~ c404.
cowhand 214; 310, 313; 402, 405-6,
409, 412, 420, 427, 431, 433-35.
cowpoke c404, 406, 419.
cowpuncher †302, c309, c311-12, 313,
c320, s¹326; 401, 406, 409, †413-14,
418-19.
cow-waddy †413.
hayhand →409. hay-waddy 401, c404,
¹405, †409, 412.
herder 419.
hired hand 302, 313; 406, 434. hired
man 435.
horse wrangler †410, 413.
ranchhand 204, 215; 301-2, 309, s¹326;
403, c404, 408, →410, cvr414, 416, 421,
423, 425, 428, 430-31, *432.
no response 1-65; 101-52; 201-3, 216-
26; 303-8, 314-19, 321-25, 327; 415.

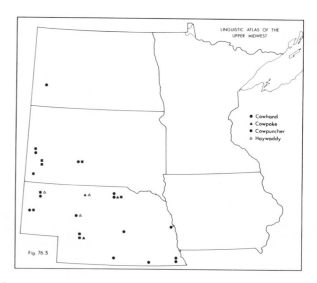

Fig. 76.5

Comment:

cowboy: A "cowboy" only rides the range; a "ranchhand" does all kinds of work--215; 421, 427. A rodeo performer--414. armchair ~: An easterner affecting western dress--404. monkey ward ~: An easterner seeking a job as a cowpuncher and dressed in fancy western clothes bought at Montgomery Ward--311. hay-waddy: A sandhill term; "He rides a mowing machine with his spurs on"--401. horse wrangler: A horse rancher or a horse-trader on a cattle ranch--413.

76.6 lasso.

In UM cattle country several terms appear for the long rope that, noosed at one end, is used in roping horses or cattle. Comments from infs. (see below) indicate some variation in the local frequency of these terms.

Most commonly reported is lariat, with redundant lariat rope. Two western Nebraskans consider its use more recent than that of the second widely spread term, lasso. [For this word see also the volume on pronunciation.] Rope itself is used by some infs., as is more descriptive throw rope. Catch rope is limited to North Dakota, and one instance of saddle rope appears in South Dakota. An inf. in the Nebraska sandhill country, familiar with the speech of the region, insists that local ranchhands also use twine in this sense.

A Scottsbluff, Nb., Type I inf. recalls the earlier use of Spanish reata, pronounced /reʃə/, with a full expression rawhide reata to designate a lariat made of leather rather than a rope.

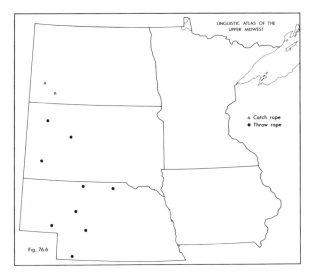

LINGUISTIC ATLAS OF THE
UPPER MIDWEST

△ Catch rope
● Throw rope

Fig. 76.6

lariat 310, c311, 312-13, 320, 326, 328; 402-4, 408-9, ¬410-11, 412-14, 418-21, 423, 426-28, ¹429, 431, 434-37. ~ rope 204, 215; 313; c409, c417, c424.
lasso 204, 215; 302; 401, 405-9, †410, 414-16, 418, 422, 424-25, 429-30, 432-33, 435.
reata †409. rawhide ~ †409.
rope 215; 309, 312-13, c320; 411-12, 414. catch ~ 214-15. saddle ~ 320. throw ~ 301-2, 312; 403-5, 412, 417-18, 437.
twine ¹404.
no response 1-65; 101-52; 201-3, 205-13, 216-26; 303-8, 314-19, 321-25, 327.

Comment:

lariat: Usu.--409. A dude ranch term--411. Now infreq.--412. ~ rope: "A special hard-twist rope"--409. "They had lariat ropes on their saddles"--417. lasso: Inf. uses this term as a verb but not as the name of the rope--313. "This word came in later. It was never used much here"--409. rope: Inf. doesn't think 'rope' was used much--409. saddle ~: "Cowpunchers always called 'em 'saddle ropes'"--320.

ADDENDA

a.

28.6b bellwether.

Not found in earlier regional worksheets and added in the UM after the near completion of the Minnesota fieldwork, this item yielded only a possible distribution pattern. The male sheep that leads a flock, usually with a bell on his neck, is known by historical bellwether in all five states. Bell sheep, perhaps an Americanism, is found principally in Iowa and Nebraska, with one instance in Saskatchewan. Leader may be Midland, as its Iowa spread is only in the southern segment, but it occurs also in the Dakotas. It is favored by older speakers. Lead sheep is rare; the parallel lead goat appears once in Nebraska. As the inf. comments (see below), judas has a specialized meaning. One South Dakota inf. reports that a female sheep used as flock leader is the bell ewe. But most infs. know too little about sheep to be familiar with any term.

bell ewe :320.
bell sheep 105, 113-14, 122, 124-25, 133, 137, 139, 145-46; 202, 204, 213; 308; 404, 414, 418, ¹420, 422, 426, 428.
bellwether s29, :¹30; 108, 111, 115-16, 119-20, *123, 125-26, 128-29, :131,

s132, 141-42, 149, :s152; 214, 221-23; 301-2, :309, *318, 325; 409, :410, 413.

    judas 130.

    leader ?136, :143, 147; 208, 215, 218, 224-25; 303, 306, 314; 401, 419, ¹*432.

    lead goat 425.

    lead sheep ?130; c414.

    no response 1-28, :31, 32-65; 101-4, 106-7, 109-10, 112, 117-18, 121, 127, 134-35, 138, 140, 144, 148, 150-51; 201, 203, ?205, 206-7, ?209, :?210, ?211, 212, 216-17, ?219, 220, 226; 304-5, 307, 310-13, 315-17, 319, 321-24, 326-28; 402-3, 405-6, :?407, 408, 411-12, 415-16, 421, 423-24, 427, ?429, 430-31, 433-37.

Comment:

    bellwether: Term probably learned from reading--30; 325. judas: Inf. says this is the goat or sheep that leads the flock into a slaughter house--130. lead goat: Inf. says this is used in packing houses--425.

b.

    Fieldworkers customarily supplemented their systematically collected responses by noting during an interview various unsolicited language matters presumably having some interest for a student of American English. Additional notes of this kind were made later from the wire or tape recordings. Among the lexical gleanings from these notes are these items not listed in the following general index.

    Definitions are usually those provided or suggested by an informant. Numerical references are to the field informants.

admire. Like; be pleased. "She admired to smell a skunk"--314.

agin. Against. 105, 107, 113, 132, 133, 139; "It's agin the law"--204; "right agin my ear"--314; "no charge agin her" --404, "agin the wind"--405, "insure agin a flood"--427, "It was right agin the stove"--429.

bell horse. In a string or cavy, the most amenable horse, belled, and used to guide the cavy when on the move. 320.

binder dump. The row of bundles dropped by the binder. Also: dump row. 417.

bitch lamp. = grease light. 429.

bow window. A curving bay window. 3.

buckberry. The buffaloberry. 410.

bug chaser. *Pejorative*. A ranger of the U.S. Forestry Service. 311.

bundlism. *Jocular*. An ailment of temporary harvest hands who grow tired of pitching bundles. 202.

carry, *sb*. The group of strayed calves

to be kept until they are transferred to another "wagon," one returning to the home outfit or home range. 311.

cavy /kævɪ/. The herd of horses with a roundup wagon, composed of the "strings" belonging to the cowpunchers. 320.

circle leader. The cowpuncher chosen by the wagon boss to head the four, six, or eight cowpunchers sent out to round up the cattle on the range. 320.

CY in a sack. A kind of sweet pudding. *A cowhands' term derived from the locally famous CY ranch.* Also: sonofabitch in a sack. 301.

day herd. The cattle rounded up each day, including the calves to be branded. 320.

deerberry. The North Dakota buffaloberry. 402.

dummy. A glass nest egg. 404.

dump row. = binder dump. 417.

funning. A joke. "We said it just as a funning."--422.

grease light. An improvised lamp consisting of a saucer or cup filled with oil or liquid grease, with a twisted rag serving as a wick. Also: slut and bitchlamp. 429.

hard sauce with a stick in it. A sauce containing hard liquor, usually whiskey. 120.

haywire, *sb*. A stomach upset. 15.

hot roll. A cowpuncher's bedroll. 320.

larrup. Any kind of syrup. 309.

latigo /lætɪgo/. A strap attaching the cinch to the saddle. 214.

little John. A baby calf of either sex. 320.

livery. A team and buggy. "He got a livery."--327.

maiden lettuce. Wilted lettuce, esp. shredded lettuce with a hot, sharp, bacon-flavored sauce. 433.

marbles. Testicles cut off by castration. 404.

mare's egg. A puff ball. 311.

monkey stove. A stove, such as was formerly used in railway depots, having a long slender top section and a bulging round base. 35.

mushrat. A muskrat. 31.

necking, *sb*. A pillow or equivalent, even a round can, as used by a cowpuncher when sleeping outdoors. 312.

nighthawk. A horse wrangler on night duty. 320.

pea soup. A French-Canadian. 212.

pistol. The last cowpuncher to catch his horse in the morning. 320.

rawhide, *vb*. To send out several cowpunchers on their own, to eat with sheepherders or by themselves, in order to discover the mavericks.

Hence: rawhiding, *sb*. This practice developed after the fencing-in of the range and the obsolescence of the roundup. 320.

right, *av*. Very. 105.

run a whizzer. To "pull a fast one;" to trick. 322.

sandblow. In a region with sandy sub-soil, an open space from which grass and topsoil have been removed and the sand exposed to wind erosion. 404.

schnitzel. To cut (green beans). "to schnitzel beans"--42. Also: schitzel. 424.

set afoot. To compel to walk. *Used in a cowhand's description of having been forced to walk instead of ride a horse.* "I got set afoot."--320.

slab, *vb*. To drag over (the ground) a heavy structure of wood slabs, in order to break clods. 322.

slut lamp. = grease light. *403 *(used by inf.'s brother.)*

sonofabitch in a sack. A sweet pudding. *A cowhands' term*. 301.

spook. A gambler on the downgrade; a tinhorn gambler. 312.

spooner. A dish for holding spoons. 120.

stack butt. The bottom layer of a hay-stack, used in this area to cover

sandblows. 404.

string. Two or more horses owned by one cowpuncher. 320.

team. Lead team: the front team in a series of teams hauling one or several wagons. Wheel team: the team in the rear. String team: any team, possibly one or one of several teams, between the lead team and the wheel team. Broncoes were put into a string team. Each team had its own pair of double-trees, attached by a ring to a chain running from the lead team back to the wagon.

tooth doctor. A dentist. 322.

tother. The other. "this, that, and tother"--31.

tumbling bar, ~ rod. On a horse-driven threshing machine, a bar transmitting power from the machine to the sepa-rator. 301.

turn. To pour. "to turn a cup of tea"--401.

vinegar jug. A disagreeable person. "She was a vinegar jug."--29.

warmed-upper. A warmed-up meal. 409.

warwhoop, *vb*. To emit war cries. "The Indians was warwhoopin' up here"--209.

zinc. A kitchen sink. 120, 138; 212.

Index

Index

A number in this lexical index refers to the item as found in the field worksheets and as sequentially ordered in the presentation in this volume. Thus the reference 63.8a for *boulevard* is a direction to the descriptive treatment under 63.8a and not to a page number. Item numbers appear at the top of the page in the lexical section of this volume.

Terms listed here may be from the field responses or from the mail returns.

Usually an attributive + noun combination with a specialized meaning, such as *country cousin* or *milk house*, is entered under the first element regardless of its being formally written as a compound or not. But to facilitate reference a few such terms are entered under both elements. When the second element is the key term in the worksheets the combination may, however, be listed under that element only; e.g., *barrel hoop* appears under *hoop*.

A verb is listed in the base form unless the item typically offers an inflected form, e.g., *glassies*, *lulling down*, and *sparking her*.

The symbol ~ is equivalent to ditto marks. The parentheses ( ) denote an optional form. Thus the entry *clearing (away)*, ~ *off*, ~ *up* is to be read as *clearing*, *clearing away*, *clearing off*, and *clearing up*. An italicized note in square brackets [ ] is an editorial example, a synonym, or a comment.

413

415

~s, 17.7a;
three-horse ~
17.7a,b; two-
horse ~ 17.7b
evening 3.5,6;
late ~ 3.6
every (which)
way 76.2a
evil one 66.7;
~ spirit 67.1
ewe 28.6a;
bell ~ 28.6b
exhausted 57.6
extra room 8.8

F

fading out 6.3
fagged (out),
all ~ out
57.6
fairing 5.3
fall ill, ~
sick 58.1
falling 6.3; ~
for her 61.5
falls [hars-
let] 30.6
false flesh
59.4
family 52.1,
62.2
fantans 35.7
farm 12.8
farmer, big ~,
country ~,
dumb ~, hick
~, jackfish
~, jackpine
~, lazy ~,
shotgun ~
53.7
farmyard 12.7
farthest 34.6
See v. 2.
fasnat (pret-
zel) 36.3b
fat cake 36.3a
father 49.1,5
fatherless
child 51.4
fatigue 57.6
faucet 15.5a,
b; barrel ~,
wood(en) ~
15.5b
favor (v.)
50.7
fearful 56.5
feather 44.4
featherbed
23.6a,b
feathertick
23.6b
feeble-minded
57.1
feed house
11.6
feeding floor
12.5; ~
ground 12.7;

~ time 30.7
feed the
fishes 60.7
Ferdinand 27.1
fester 59.1
fetch 18.1,
22.4, 71.6
fetch up 51.1
fice(t) 26.6;
~ty 57.3,4,
56.4
field 13.1; ~
bed 23.7; ~
corn 44.2
fiery 57.4
fight (v.)
75.6 See
v. 2.
file (n.) 19.7
file the floor
9.4b
fills 17.5
film 6.5b
find your
place 39.4
finicky 57.3,4
fire (v.) 61.6
fireboard 7.3
firebug 47.2
firedogs 7.2
firefly 47.2
fire ledge 7.3
fire shelf 7.3
firesticks 6.8
firm (as the
rock of ages)
57.2
fist (pl.)
55.6 See
v. 2.
fit (n.) 56.4
fit (v.) 22.5
See v. 2.
fix 29.6,
38.7, 43.6
flake ice 6.5b
flapjacks,
rawhide ~
36.4
flat(s) (n.),
hay ~s 24.2a
flatboat 18.4
flattened 57.6
flicker 46.3;
~tail 46.2a,
2a(1),2a(3),
2a(4), 46.3.
red shaft ~
46.3
flier 18.5a,b
flints 76.3a
flip 56.4
flip-flop 69.3
flirting along
76.2b
flitters 36.4
float 25.1
floor bed 23.7
flop 23.7
flopjacks 36.4
flower bowl, ~
jar, ~ pot, ~

urn 14.7
flue 6.7
fly in a fit,
~ off the
handle 57.4
flying Dutch-
man, ~ jenny
19.3b
folk, country
~, farm ~
53.7
folks 52.1;
barn ~ 53.7
fool him 61.6
foolish 57.1
for ["We named
the child
him"] 26.2;
~ ["wait
you"] 72.3
See v. 2.
forget about
it 57.5
fork 24.5,
25.3; ~s 17.5
fortnight 3.8
foxy 56.4
free of 72.6
free(stone)
[peach] 42.4
freeze 6.5a
See v. 2.
freeze 6.4,5a;
~ a little
ice, ~ a
scale of ice,
~ (a scum of)
ice, ~ over,
~ up 6.5a.
start to ~
6.5a
French harp
15.8a,b
French melon
44.5
fresh(er)
(adj.) 27.5;
~ yeast 36.6.
become ~ 27.5
freshening up
6.2
freshet 24.5
fried-čake
36.3a,b,4;
raised ~,
sponge ~
36.3b
frier 14.4
frightened
56.5; become
~ 28.1b
frisky 56.4
fritters 36.4;
corn ~ 36.1b
frog 46.4,5,6;
bull ~ 46.4;
cricket ~,
grass ~,
green ~ 46.5;
leap ~ 46.4,
5; leopard ~,
peeping ~,

spring ~
46.5; toad-~
46.6; tree ~
46.5; wart-~
46.6; water ~
46.4
frogstool 44.7
frolic 62.3
from ["He fell
___ a horse"]
28.1a See v.
2. ~ the
sticks 53.7
front room
6.6a
frost, black
~, white ~
6.4; white
~ed 6.5a
frostboil 76.1
frowy 37.6b
fruitcellar
8.8
fruit jar 14.7
fry cake 36.3a
fry(ing) pan
14.4
full of fun, ~
of ginger, ~
of life, ~ of
pep, ~ of piss
and vinegar,
~ of spirit
(s), ~ of vim
(and vigor),
~ of (vim,
vigor, and)
vitality, ~
of zip 56.4
funnel 15.6
funny 57.1,3
furious 57.4
further [dis-
tance] 33.1
See v. 2.
fuss around
9.1
fussy 57.3

G

gab fest 62.8
gad (stick),
ox ~ 15.7
gallery 9.6
gang 62.2
garbage can, ~
container
14.3
garden
(patch), ~
plot, ~ spot
40.5; ~ sass,
~ stuff 40.4.
kitchen ~,
truck ~,
vegetable ~
40.5
garret 8.5
gather (v.)
73.4

gathering
(n.), old
ladies' ~,
social ~ 62.8
gee! 31.5a,b,c
gee horse 32.7
gems 35.7,
36.1b; corn ~
36.1b; graham
~ 35.7
gentle down
57.5
gentleman cow
27.1
get 71.6,
73.4; ~ a
calf 27.5;
~ (a) cold
58.2; ~ a
little breeze
6.2; ~ all
sicked up
58.1; ~ bet-
ter 5.3; ~
calm 6.3; ~
fierce, ~
harder, ~
higher 6.2; ~
lower, ~ mild-
er 6.3; ~
pretty thick
with 61.5; ~
rid of 72.6
See v.2; ~
rougher 6.2;
~ sick 58.1;
~ stronger, ~
up 6.2; ~ up
to the table
39.4; ~ wind-
y, ~ worse
6.2
get (after)
'em! 26.4; ~
along! 31.7;
~ up! 6.2,
31.7. go ('n')
~ 'em! 26.4
ghost 67.1
giblets 30.6
giddap!, gid-
diap!, gid-
diup! 31.7
gilt 29.2a
gingerbread
35.7
give 73.5 See
v. 2.
give her the
rush 61.5
give him the
air (etc.)
61.6
give it a
smattering
9.1
give out 57.6
give you a
lift 71.1
give you what
for, ~ you
what Johnny

gave the drum
61.8
glad to know
you, ~ to
meet you 68.1
glass 14.7; ~
egg 13.7b
glassies 76.3a
glen 24.4
globber(ed)
milk 38.1
glowworm 47.2
go 20.6d See
v. 2.
go! 31.7
goad (stick),
ox ~, goard
stick 15.7
goal, prison ~
71.7
goblin 66.7,
67.1
go cart 50.5
go-devil 18.4
God's acre
59.6
go-getter 56.4
goglin across
76.2a
going (down)
6.3
going catty-
wampus, ~
squeegee, ~
zig-zag 76.2b
going out with
her, ~ steady
with her, ~
to see his
sweetie, ~
with her
steady 61.5
goo 38.3
goobers 42.8
Good afternoon
67.7
good luck bone
30.5
Good morning
3.4
good worker
56.4
goof 38.3,
53.7
goofy 57.1
googleberries
42.8
go over (the
room) 9.1
goop 38.3
goose bumps
76.4; ~ egg
51.4; ~ flesh,
~ hide, ~
pimples, ~
skin 76.4
gopher 46.2a,
2a(1),(2),(3),
(4); field ~
46.2a,2a(3);
grass ~
46.2a,2a(2);

418

422

10.4; hay ~
12.1; hog ~
12.5,5(3);
implement ~
11.4; machine
~ 10.4; milk
~ 12.4; oil
~, out ~ 10.4;
pig ~ 12.5,
5(3); pump ~
10.4; stock ~
12.4; storm ~
10.4; straw ~
12.4,5; tool
~ 10.4; wood
~ 8.6, 10.4;
work ~ 10.4
sheep 28.5,6a,
32.3; bell ~
28.6b; buck ~
28.5; lead ~
28.6b; nannie
~ 28.6a
sheepy,
sheepy! 32.2
sheet (of) ice
6.5b
shelf, cap ~,
clock ~, fire
~, mantle ~
7.3
shell 42.6,7,
43.6; ~ beans
43.7,8; ~ ice
6.5b. outside
~ 42.7
shelter 12.5,
5(3); ~ belt
47.8
shet 72.6
shillelagh
15.7
shimmying
76.2b
shin breaker
18.5a,b
shindig 62.3
shine (n.)
53.6
shiners 47.5
shine up to
her 61.5
shingle 35.7
shiplap 9.9
shirk, a-~ing
out 62.4
shirred 37.3
shit-house 10.5
shivaree 61.7
shoat 29.1,2c
shock 34.4;
hay ~ 12.3
shoot 24.5
shooting line
76.3b; ~
match 62.2
shop, tool ~,
work~ 10.4
short 68.5
shower, elec-
tric ~, thun-
der~ 5.4

show you the
way home 71.1
shrink 21.8
See v. 2.
shrubbed 33.7
shuck 42.6,7,
43.6; ~s 44.1
shut 9.7
shy 28.1b,
56.5
sic ('em)!
26.4; ~ calf
31.4
sick 58.1
sick at (etc.)
the stomach
61.1 See v. 2.
sidegoglin
76.2a
side gravel
25.3
side meat, ~
(of) pork
37.8
sidestepping
76.2b
sideswaying
76.2b
side-track him
61.6
sidewalk 63.8b
sidewinder
46.8
siding, clap-
board ~,
drop(-leaf)
~, groove ~,
house ~,
(ship)lap ~,
weather ~ 9.9
sigsagging
76.2b
silk 44.4
silly 57.1
silta 37.7a
simmer down
57.5
simple, a lit-
tle bit ~
57.1
singletree
17.6,7c
sinker 36.3a,b
Sir? 41.5
sire 27.1,8,
29.1; herd ~
27.1
sissy 57.3
sit 39.5 See
v. 2; ~ down
(etc.) 39.4
sitter, sit-
ting hen 30.3
sitting on her
61.5
sitting room
6.6a
skewer 14.4
skiddy 74.3b
skiff(ing) of
ice 6.5b
skigoglin

76.2a
skillet 14.4
skim (v.) 6.5a
skim of ice
6.5b
skin 37.9
skinflint 56.8
skip (class),
~ school 62.4
skittle 14.4,
19,4; coal ~
19.4
skiwobbly
76.2a
skunk 46.1b,
53.6; spotted
~ 46.1b
slab 25.2a; ~
fence 13.4
slabbing 76.2b
slackening
(up) 6.3
slacks 22.3
slam 69.2
slapjacks 36.4
slat fence
13.2
sled 18,4,
18.5a,b,c,e;
coaster ~
18.5a,b; corn
~ 18.4; doub-
le ~ 18.5a,c;
flat ~ 18.5a,
d; ground ~
18.5a; hand ~
18.5a,b; hay
~ 18.4; long
~, mud ~,
sliding ~
18.5a; spring-
runner ~
18.5a,b;
stone ~ 18.4;
tandem ~
18.5a,c; team
~ 18.5a,e;
water ~ 18.4;
winter ~
18.5a
sledge 18.4
sleeping room
8.2
sleigh 18.4,
5a,b,e; hand
~, three-
kneed ~·
18.5a,b; wa-
ter ~ 18.4
slick (adj.)
74.3b
slick up 9.1
slide (down),
~ on your
stomach, ~
down the hill
69.2
slip 18.4
slippery 74.3b
slop can 14.3
slopjacks 36.4
slop jar 14.3

slough 24.3,4;
~y ground, ~
land 24.3.
hay ~ 24.2a,
3; meadow ~
24.3
slowing down
6.3
sluefoot 53.7
smack 38.4
smart 56.4
smearcase 38.2
smoke 53.6
smoked beef
37.4b; ~ sau-
sage 37.7b
smokehouse 8.6
smut (black)
44.8
snack 38.4
snake charmer,
~ doctor, ~
eater, ~
feeder, ~ fly
45.8
snake fence,
13.4,4(2); ~
and rider
fence 13.4b,
4(1)
snakesneck
46.9a
snake wrestle
62.3
snap 43.6
snappy 56.4
sneak (v.)
62.4
snicker 30.2
snitch (baby),
~er 73.3
snort 30.2
so! 31.3,
32.2; ~ boss-
(y)!, ~ cow!
31.3
social 62.8
sodbuster,
soddy 53.7
sofa 8.1,1(2),
1(3),1(4),
1(5),1(6)
soft peach
42.4
somersault,
somersaw,
somerset 69.3
soo!, ~
(boss)(y)!
31.1,2; ~ pig
32.2
soogan 23.6a,b
sooie, sooie!,
sooig, sooig!
32.2; sook!
31.1,2,4,
32.2; ~-a-pig!
32.2; ~ boss-
(y)! 31.1,2;
~ calf(y)!
31.4; ~ cow!
31.1,2; ~

macky macky!
31.4; ~y!
31.1,2,4,
32.2
sooner kid
51.4
sore 57.4; ~-
headed 57.3
sot (in his
ways) 57.4
soup's on 39.4
sour 57.3; ~
hen 30.3; ~
milk 38.1
souse 37.7a
sow 29.2a; ~
belly, ~ bos-
om 37.8
span (n.) 27.3
See v. 2.
spank (v.),
take and ~
you 61.8 See
v. 2.
spanking (n.)
61.8
spare room
8.2,8
sparking her
61.5
spay 29.6
spectre 67.1
spend 57.6
spew, ~ up
60.7
spicket
15.5a,b
spider 14.4; ~
nest 47.6,6a;
~'s nest 47.6
spigot 15.5b
spiketooth
18.3a,b
spillway 24.4
spindle 45.8
spirit 66.7,
67.1
spit up 60.7
split rail
fence 13.4
spoil (v.)
37.6a See
v. 2.
spoiled
37.6a,b
sponge 36.6
spook 28.1b,
66.7, 67.1
spoon, bread
~, mixing ~,
tea~, tin ~,
wooden ~ 14.6
spout 15.5b;
(eave) ~ing,
rain ~(ing),
drain ~s,
eave(s) ~s,
roof ~s, wa-
ter ~s 10.3
spread, cover
~ 23.5
spreader 17.7a

sprightly 56.4
sprigot 15.5b
spring 24.5,
27.5; ~er
27.5; ~ peep-
er 46.5;
~tooth 18.3a,
c
sprocket 15.5b
spry 56.4
spunky 56.4,
57.4
squall 5.4
squash, acorn
~, banana ~,
buttercup ~,
crookneck ~,
gooseneck ~,
hubbard ~,
summer ~,
vegetable ~
44.9
squaw 49.2; ~
corn 44.2
squawker 73.3
squeal 30.2;
~er 73.3
squeegy 76.2a
squinny
46.2a(1)
squiring her
61.5
squirrel 46.2a;
gray ~ 46.2a,
2a(4); ground
~ 46.2a,2a(1),
(2),(3),(4);
Minnesota
striped ~
46.2a,2a(2);
prairie ~
46.2a,2a(1);
streaked ~,
striped
(ground) ~
46.2a,2a(2)
stable 12.4;
chicken ~
30.4; cow ~
11.4; hog ~
12.5; horse ~
11.4; pig ~
12.5
stack 12.2,3,
34.4; round ~
12.2; small ~
12.3
stag 29.1,1a
staggering
76.2b
stake and rid-
er(ed) fence
13.4,4(2)
stake fence
13.2
stale 37.6a,b
stall 12.5,
5(2)
stallion 27.8
stalwart 56.3
stamp (v.)
70.7

424